W9-BNK-081

Dictionary of
Medical Terms

Specialist dictionaries

Dictionary of Accounting	978 0 7136 8286 1
Dictionary of Agriculture	978 0 7136 7778 2
Dictionary of Aviation	978 0 7136 8734 7
Dictionary of Banking and Finance	978 0 7136 7739 3
Dictionary of Business	978 0 7136 7918 2
Dictionary of Computing	978 0 7475 6622 9
Dictionary of Economics	978 0 7136 8203 8
Dictionary of Environment and Ecology	978 0 7475 7201 5
Dictionary of Food Science and Nutrition	978 0 7136 7784 3
Dictionary of Human Resources and Personnel Management	978 0 7136 8142 0
Dictionary of ICT	978 0 7475 6990 9
Dictionary of Information and Library Management	978 0 7136 7591 7
Dictionary of Law	978 0 7136 8318 9
Dictionary of Leisure, Travel and Tourism	978 0 7136 8545 9
Dictionary of Marketing	978 0 7475 6621 2
Dictionary of Media Studies	978 0 7136 7593 1
Dictionary of Nursing	978 0 7136 8286 8
Dictionary of Politics and Government	978 0 7475 7220 6
Dictionary of Publishing and Printing	978 0 7136 7589 4
Dictionary of Science and Technology	978 0 7475 6620 5
Dictionary of Sport and Exercise Science	978 0 7136 7785 0

Easier English™ titles

Easier English Basic Dictionary	978 0 7475 6644 1
Easier English Basic Synonyms	978 0 7475 6979 4
Easier English Intermediate Dictionary	978 0 7475 6989 3
Easier English Student Dictionary	978 0 7475 6624 3

Check Your English Vocabulary workbooks

Academic English	978 0 7136 8285 4
Banking and Finance	978 0 7136 8250 2
Business and Administration	978 0 7136 7916 8
Computers and Information Technology	978 0 7136 7917 5
Human Resources	978 0 7475 6997 8
IELTS	978 0 7136 7604 4
Law	978 0 7136 7592 4
Living in the UK	978 0 7136 7914 4
Medicine	978 0 7136 7590 0
PET	978 0 7475 6627 4
Phrasal Verbs and Idioms	978 0 7136 7805 5
TOEFL®	978 0 7136 8414 8
TOEIC®	978 0 7136 7508 5

Visit our website for full details of all our books: **www.acblack.com**

Dictionary of
Medical Terms

fourth edition

A & C Black • London

www.acblack.com

While every effort has been made to be as accurate as possible, the author, advisers, editors and publishers of this book cannot be held liable for any errors and omissions, or actions that may be taken as a consequence of using it.

First published in Great Britain in 1987
as *English Medical Dictionary*

Second edition published 1993
Third edition published 2000
Fourth edition published 2004
Reprinted 2005, 2007, 2009

A & C Black Publishers Ltd
36 Soho Square, London W1D 3QY

© P. H. Collin 1987, 1993, 2000
© Bloomsbury Publishing Plc 2004
© A & C Black Publishers Ltd 2005

All rights reserved. No part of this publication may be reproducedin any form or by any means without the permission of the publishers

A CIP record for this book is available from the British Library

ISBN-13: 978-1-4081-2551-9

Text Production and Proofreading
Heather Bateman, Ruth Hillmore, Daisy Jackson, Sarah Lusznat, Katy McAdam, Charlotte Regan

This book is produced using paper that is made from wood grown in managed, sustainable forests. It is natural, renewable and recyclable. The logging and manufacturing processes conform to the environmental regulations of the country of origin.

Text computer typeset by A & C Black
Printed in Spain by Graphycems

Preface

This dictionary provides the user with the basic vocabulary currently being used in a wide range of healthcare situations. The areas covered include the technical language used in diagnosis, patient care, surgery, pathology, general practice, pharmacy, dentistry and other specialisations, as well as anatomical and physiological terms. Informal, everyday and sometimes euphemistic terms commonly used by people in discussing their condition with healthcare professionals are also included, as are common words used in reading or writing reports, articles or guidelines.

The dictionary is designed for anyone who needs to check the meaning or pronunciation of medical terms, but especially for those working in health-related areas who may not be healthcare professionals or for whom English is an additional language. Each headword is explained in clear, straightforward English. Pronunciations, uncommon plurals and uncommon verb forms are provided. Illustrations of some basic anatomical terms are also included.

Very many people have helped or advised on the compilation and checking of the dictionary in its various editions. In particular, thanks are due to Dr Judith Harvey for her helpful comments and advice on this fourth edition and to Dr Marie Condon for some revisions and clarification. Also to Lesley Bennun, Lesley Brown and Margaret Baker who copy-edited the text and Dinah Jackson who revised the pronunciations.

Pronunciation Guide

The following symbols have been used to show the pronunciation of the main words in the dictionary.

Stress is indicated by a main stress mark (') and a secondary stress mark (,). Note that these are only guides, as the stress of the word changes according to its position in the sentence.

Vowels		*Consonants*	
æ	back	b	buck
ɑː	harm	d	dead
ɒ	stop	ð	other
aɪ	type	dʒ	jump
aʊ	how	f	fare
aɪə	hire	g	gold
aʊə	**hour**	h	head
ɔː	course	j	yellow
ɔɪ	annoy	k	cab
e	head	l	leave
eə	**fair**	m	mix
eɪ	make	n	nil
eʊ	go	ŋ	sing
ɜː	word	p	print
iː	keep	r	rest
i	happy	s	save
ə	about	ʃ	shop
ɪ	fit	t	take
ɪə	near	tʃ	change
u	annual	θ	theft
uː	pool	v	value
ʊ	book	w	work
ʊə	**tour**	x	loch
ʌ	shut	ʒ	measure
		z	zone

A

A /eɪ/ *noun* a human blood type of the ABO system, containing the A antigen (NOTE: Someone with type A can donate to people of the same group or of the AB group, and can receive blood from people with type A or type O.)

AA *abbr* Alcoholics Anonymous

A & E /ˌeɪ ənd 'iː/, **A & E department** /ˌeɪ ənd 'iː dɪˌpɑːtmənt/ *noun* same as **accident and emergency department**

A & E medicine /ˌeɪ ənd 'iː ˌmed(ə)sɪn/ *noun* the medical procedures used in A & E departments

AB /ˌeɪ 'biː/ *noun* a human blood type of the ABO system, containing the A and B antigens (NOTE: Someone with type AB can donate to people of the same group and receive blood from people with type O, A, AB or B.)

ab- /æb/ *prefix* away from

ABC /ˌeɪ biː 'siː/ *noun* the basic initial checks of a casualty's condition. Full form **airway, breathing and circulation**

abdomen /'æbdəmən/ *noun* a space inside the body below the diaphragm, above the pelvis and in front of the spine, containing the stomach, intestines, liver and other vital organs ○ *pain in the abdomen* (NOTE: For other terms referring to the abdomen, see words beginning with **coeli-, coelio-**.)

    COMMENT: The abdomen is divided for medical purposes into nine regions: at the top, the right and left hypochondriac regions with the epigastrium between them; in the centre, the right and left lumbar regions with the umbilical between them; and at the bottom, the right and left iliac regions with the hypogastrium between them.

abdomin- /æbdɒmɪn/ *prefix* same as **abdomino-** (*used before vowels*)

abdominal /æb'dɒmɪn(ə)l/ *adjective* located in the abdomen, or relating to the abdomen

abdominal aorta /æbˌdɒmɪn(ə)l eɪ'ɔːtə/ *noun* the part of the aorta which lies between the diaphragm and the point where the aorta divides into the iliac arteries. See illustration at KIDNEY in Supplement

abdominal cavity /æbˌdɒmɪn(ə)l 'kævɪti/ *noun* the space in the body below the chest

abdominal distension /æbˌdɒmɪn(ə)l dɪs'tenʃ(ə)n/ *noun* a condition in which the abdomen is stretched because of gas or fluid

abdominal pain /æb'dɒmɪn(ə)l peɪn/ *noun* pain in the abdomen caused by indigestion or more serious disorders

abdominal viscera /æbˌdɒmɪn(ə)l 'vɪsərə/ *plural noun* the organs which are contained in the abdomen, e.g. the stomach, liver and intestines

abdominal wall /æb'dɒmɪn(ə)l wɔːl/ *noun* muscular tissue which surrounds the abdomen

abdomino- /æbdɒmɪnəʊ/ *prefix* referring to the abdomen

abdominopelvic /æbˌdɒmɪnəʊ'pelvɪk/ *adjective* referring to the abdomen and pelvis

abdominoperineal /æbˌdɒmɪnəʊperɪ'niːəl/ *adjective* referring to the abdomen and perineum

abdominoperineal excision /æbˌdɒmɪnəʊperɪˌniːəl ɪk'sɪʒ(ə)n/ *noun* a surgical operation that involves cutting out tissue in both the abdomen and the perineum

abdominoposterior /æbˌdɒmɪnəʊpɒ'stɪəriə/ *adjective* referring to a position of a fetus in the uterus, where the fetus's abdomen is facing the mother's back

abdominoscopy /æbˌdɒmɪ'nɒskəpi/ *noun* an internal examination of the abdomen, usually with an endoscope

abdominothoracic /æbˌdɒmɪnəʊθɔː'ræsɪk/ *adjective* referring to the abdomen and thorax

abduce /æb'djuːs/ *verb* same as **abduct**

abducens nerve /æb'djuːs(ə)nz ˌnɜːv/ *noun* the sixth cranial nerve, which controls the muscle which makes the eyeball turn outwards

abducent /æb'djuːs(ə)nt/ *adjective* referring to a muscle which brings parts of the body away from each other or moves them away from the central line of the body or a limb. Compare **adducent**

abducent nerve /æb'djuːsənt ˌnɜːv/ *noun* same as **abducens nerve**

abduct /æb'dʌkt/ *verb* (*of a muscle*) to pull a leg or arm in a direction which is away from the centre line of the body, or to pull a toe or finger away from the central line of a leg or arm. Compare **adduct**

abduction /æb'dʌkʃən/ *noun* the movement of a part of the body away from the centre line of the body or away from a neighbouring part. Opposite **adduction**. See illustration at **ANATOMICAL TERMS** in Supplement

'Mary was nursed in a position of not more than 90° upright with her legs in abduction.' [*British Journal of Nursing*]

abductor /æb'dʌktə/, **abductor muscle** /æb 'dʌktə ˌmʌs(ə)l/ *noun* a muscle which pulls a part of the body away from the centre line of the body or away from a neighbouring part. Opposite **adductor**

aberrant /æ'berənt/ *adjective* not usual or expected

aberration /ˌæbə'reɪʃ(ə)n/ *noun* an action or growth which is not usual or expected

ablation /æ'bleɪʃ(ə)n/ *noun* the removal of an organ or of a part of the body by surgery

abnormal /æb'nɔːm(ə)l/ *adjective* not usual ○ *abnormal behaviour* ○ *an abnormal movement*

'…the synovium produces an excess of synovial fluid, which is abnormal and becomes thickened. This causes pain, swelling and immobility of the affected joint.' [*Nursing Times*]

abnormality /ˌæbnɔː'mælɪti/ *noun* a form or condition which is not usual (NOTE: For other terms referring to abnormality, see words beginning with **terat-, terato-**.)

'Even children with the milder forms of sickle-cell disease have an increased frequency of pneumococcal infection. The reason for this susceptibility is a profound abnormality of the immune system in children with SCD.' [*Lancet*]

abocclusion /ˌæbɒ'kluːʒ(ə)n/ *noun* a condition in which the teeth in the top and bottom jaws do not touch

aboral /æb'ɔːrəl/ *adjective* situated away from or opposite the mouth

abort /ə'bɔːt/ *verb* to eject an embryo or fetus, or to cause an embryo or fetus to be ejected, and so end a pregnancy before the fetus is fully developed

abortifacient /ə,bɔːtɪ'feɪʃ(ə)nt/ *noun* a drug or instrument which provokes an abortion

abortion /ə'bɔːʃ(ə)n/ *noun* a situation where a fetus leaves the uterus before it is fully developed, especially during the first 28 weeks of pregnancy, or a procedure which causes this to happen □ **to have an abortion** to have an operation to make a fetus leave the uterus during the first period of pregnancy

COMMENT: In the UK, an abortion can be carried out legally if two doctors agree that the mother's life is in danger, that she risks grave permanent injury to the physical or mental health of herself or her children, or that the fetus is likely to be born with severe disabilities.

abortionist /ə'bɔːʃ(ə)nɪst/ *noun* a person who helps a woman abort, usually a person who performs an illegal abortion

abortion pill /ə'bɔːʃ(ə)n pɪl/ *noun* a drug that causes an abortion to occur very early in pregnancy

abortion trauma syndrome /ə,bɔːʃ(ə)n 'trɔːmə ,sɪndrəʊm/ *noun* a set of symptoms sometimes experienced in the period after an abortion including guilt, anxiety, depression, low self-esteem, eating and sleeping disorders and suicidal thoughts

abortive /ə'bɔːtɪv/ *adjective* not successful ○ *an abortive attempt*

abortive poliomyelitis /ə,bɔːtɪv ,pəʊliəʊ maɪə'laɪtɪs/ *noun* a mild form of polio which only affects the throat and intestines

abortus /ə'bɔːtəs/ *noun* a fetus which is expelled during an abortion or miscarriage

abortus fever /ə'bɔːtəs ,fiːvə/ *noun* same as **brucellosis**

ABO system /ˌeɪ biː 'əʊ ,sɪstəm/ *noun* a system of classifying blood groups. ◊ **blood group**

abrasion /ə'breɪʒ(ə)n/ *noun* a condition in which the surface of the skin has been rubbed off by a rough surface and bleeds

COMMENT: As the intact skin is an efficient barrier to bacteria, even minor abrasions can allow infection to enter the body and thus should be cleaned and treated with an antiseptic.

abreact /ˌæbri'ækt/ *verb* to release unconscious psychological tension by talking about or regularly remembering the events that caused it

abreaction /ˌæbri'ækʃən/ *noun* the treatment of a person with a neurosis by making him or her think again about past bad experiences

abruptio placentae /ə,brʌptiəʊ plə'sentiː/ *noun* an occasion when the placenta suddenly comes away from the uterus earlier than it should, often causing shock and bleeding

abscess /'æbses/ *noun* a painful swollen area where pus forms ○ *She had an abscess under a tooth.* ○ *The doctor decided to lance the abscess.* (NOTE: The formation of an abscess is often accompanied by a high temperature. The plural is **abscesses**.)

COMMENT: An acute abscess can be dealt with by opening and draining when it has reached the stage where sufficient pus has been formed. A chronic abscess is usually treated with drugs.

absolute alcohol /ˌæbsəluːt 'ælkəhɒl/ *noun* alcohol which contains no water

absorb /əb'zɔːb/ *verb* to take up or soak up something, especially a liquid, into a solid ○ *Cotton wads are used to absorb the discharge from the wound.*

absorbable suture /əb,zɔː'bəb(ə)l 'suːtʃə/ *noun* a suture which will eventually be absorbed into the body, and does not need to be removed

absorbent cotton /əb,zɔːbənt ˈkɒt(ə)n/ *noun* a soft white material used as a dressing to put on wounds

absorption /əbˈzɔːpʃən/ *noun* **1.** the process by which a liquid is taken into a solid **2.** the process of taking into the body substances such as proteins or fats which have been digested from food and enter the bloodstream from the stomach and intestines □ **absorption rate** the rate at which a liquid is absorbed by a solid

abstainer /əbˈsteɪnə/ *noun* a person who does not drink alcohol

abstinence /ˈæbstɪnəns/ *noun* a deliberate act of not doing something over a period of time, especially not eating or drinking ○ *abstinence from alcohol*

abulia /əˈbuːliə/ *noun* a lack of willpower

abuse *noun* /əˈbjuːs/ **1.** the act of using something wrongly ○ *the abuse of a privilege* **2.** the illegal use of a drug or overuse of alcohol ○ *substance abuse* **3.** same as **child abuse 4.** bad treatment of a person ○ *physical abuse* ○ *sexual abuse* ■ *verb* /əˈbjuːz/ **1.** to use something wrongly ○ *Heroin and cocaine are drugs which are commonly abused.* □ **to abuse one's authority** to use one's powers in an illegal or harmful way **2.** to treat someone badly ○ *sexually abused children* ○ *He had physically abused his wife and child.*

a.c. *adverb* (*used on prescriptions*) before food. Full form **ante cibum**

acanthosis /ə,kænˈθəʊsɪs/ *noun* a disease of the prickle cell layer of the skin, where warts appear on the skin or inside the mouth

acapnia /eɪˈkæpniə/ *noun* the condition of not having enough carbon dioxide in the blood and tissues

acariasis /,ækəˈraɪəsɪs/ *noun* the presence of mites or ticks on the skin

acaricide /əˈkærɪsaɪd/ *noun* a substance which kills mites or ticks

acarophobia /,ækərəˈfəʊbiə/ *noun* an unusual fear of mites or ticks

acatalasia /eɪ,kætəˈleɪziə/ *noun* an inherited condition which results in a lack of catalase in all tissue

accessory /əkˈsesəri/ *noun* something which helps something else to happen or operate, but may not be very important in itself ■ *adjective* helping something else to happen or operate

accessory nerve /əkˈsesəri ,nɜːv/ *noun* the eleventh cranial nerve which supplies the muscles in the neck and shoulders

accessory organ /ək,sesəri ˈɔːgən/ *noun* an organ which has a function which is controlled by another organ

accident /ˈæksɪd(ə)nt/ *noun* **1.** an unpleasant event which happens suddenly and harms someone's health ○ *She had an accident in the kitchen and had to go to hospital.* ○ *Three people were killed in the accident on the motorway.* **2.** chance, or something which happens by chance ○ *I met her by accident at the bus stop.*

accidental injury /,æksɪdent(ə)l ˈɪndʒəri/ *noun* an injury that happens to someone in an accident

accident and emergency department /,æksɪd(ə)nt ənd ɪˈmɜːdʒənsi dɪ,pɑːtmənt/ *noun* the part of a hospital which deals with people who need urgent treatment because they have had accidents or are in sudden serious pain. Abbr **A & E**

accident form /ˈæksɪd(ə)nt fɔːm/, **accident report form** /,æksɪd(ə)nt rɪˈpɔːt fɔːm/ *noun* a form to be filled in with details of an accident

accident prevention /,æksɪd(ə)nt prɪˈvenʃən/ *noun* the work of taking action or changing procedures to prevent accidents from happening

accident ward /ˈæksɪd(ə)nt wɔːd/ *noun* a ward for urgent accident victims. Also called **casualty ward**

accommodation /ə,kɒməˈdeɪʃ(ə)n/, **accommodation reflex** /ə,kɒməˈdeɪʃ(ə)n ,riːfleks/ *noun* (*of the lens of the eye*) the ability to focus on objects at different distances, using the ciliary muscle

accommodative squint /ə,kɒmədeɪtɪv ˈskwɪnt/ *noun* a squint when the eye is trying to focus on an object which is very close

accouchement /əˈkuːʃmɒŋ/ *noun* the time when a woman is being looked after because her baby is being born, or has just been born

accretion /əˈkriːʃ(ə)n/ *noun* a gradual increase in size, as through growth or external addition ○ *an accretion of calcium around the joint*

ACE /eɪs/ *noun* an enzyme that increases blood pressure

acebutolol /,æsɪˈbjuːtəlɒl/ *noun* a drug which reduces both the heart rate and how strongly the heart muscles contract, used in the treatment of high blood pressure and irregular heart rhythms

ACE inhibitor /ˈeɪs ɪn,hɪbɪtə/ *noun* same as **angiotensin-converting enzyme inhibitor**

acephalus /eɪˈsefələs/ *noun* a fetus born without a head

acetabuloplasty /,æsɪˈtæbjʊləʊ,plæsti/ *noun* a surgical operation to repair or rebuild the acetabulum

acetabulum /,æsɪˈtæbjʊləm/ *noun* the part of the pelvic bone, shaped like a cup, into which the head of the femur fits to form the hip joint. Also called **cotyloid cavity** (NOTE: The plural is **acetabula**.)

acetaminophen /ə,siːtə'mɪnəfən/ *noun US* same as **paracetamol**

acetazolamide /ə,siːtə'zɒləmaɪd/ *noun* a drug which helps a person to produce more urine, used in the treatment of oedema, glaucoma and epilepsy

acetonaemia /ə,siːtəʊ'niːmiə/ same as **ketonaemia**

acetone /'æsɪtəʊn/ *noun* a colourless volatile substance formed in the body after vomiting or during diabetes. ◊ **ketone**

acetonuria /ə,siːtəʊ'njuːriə/ *noun* the presence of acetone in the urine, shown by the fact that the urine gives off a sweet smell

acetylcholine /,æsɪtaɪl'kəʊliːn/ *noun* a substance released from nerve endings, which allows nerve impulses to move from one nerve to another or from a nerve to the organ it controls

COMMENT: Acetylcholine receptors are of two types, muscarinic, found in parasympathetic post-ganglionic nerve junctions, and nicotinic, found at neuromuscular junctions and in autonomic ganglia. Acetylcholine acts on both types of receptors, but other drugs act on one or the other.

acetylcoenzyme A /,æsɪtaɪlkəʊ,enzaɪm 'eɪ/ *noun* a compound produced in the metabolism of carbohydrates, fatty acids and amino acids

acetylsalicylic acid /,æsɪtaɪl,sæləsɪlɪk 'æsɪd/ *noun* ♦ **aspirin**

achalasia /,ækə'leɪziə/ *noun* the condition of being unable to relax the muscles

ache /eɪk/ *noun* a pain which goes on for a time, but is not very severe ○ *He complained of various aches and pains.* ■ *verb* to have a pain in part of the body ○ *His tooth ached so much he went to the dentist.*

Achilles tendon /ə,kɪliːz 'tendən/ *noun* a tendon at the back of the ankle which connects the calf muscles to the heel and which acts to pull up the heel when the calf muscle is contracted

achillorrhaphy /,ækɪ'lɔːrəfi/ *noun* a surgical operation to stitch a torn Achilles tendon

achillotomy /,ækɪ'lɒtəmi/ *noun* a surgical operation to divide the Achilles tendon

aching /'eɪkɪŋ/ *adjective* causing someone a continuous mild pain ○ *aching legs*

achlorhydria /,eɪklɔː'haɪdriə/ *noun* a condition in which the gastric juices do not contain hydrochloric acid, a symptom of stomach cancer or pernicious anaemia

acholia /eɪ'kəʊliə/ *noun* the absence or failure of the secretion of bile

acholuria /,eɪkɒ'luːriə/ *noun* the absence of bile colouring in the urine

acholuric jaundice /,eɪkəluːrɪk 'dʒɔːndɪs/ *noun* a disease where unusually round red blood cells form, leading to anaemia, an enlarged spleen and the formation of gallstones. Also called **hereditary spherocytosis**

achondroplasia /,eɪkɒndrə'pleɪziə/ *noun* an inherited condition in which the long bones in the arms and legs do not grow fully while the rest of the bones in the body grow as usual, resulting in dwarfism

achromatopsia /,eɪkrəʊmə'tɒpsiə/ *noun* a rare condition in which a person cannot see any colours, but only black, white and shades of grey

achy /'eɪki/ *adjective* feeling aches all over the body (*informal*)

aciclovir /eɪ'saɪkləʊviə/ *noun* a drug that is effective against herpesviruses. Also called **acyclovir**

acid /'æsɪd/ *noun* a chemical compound containing hydrogen, which reacts with an alkali to form a salt and water

acidaemia /,æsɪ'diːmiə/ *noun* a state in which the blood has too much acid in it. It is a feature of untreated severe diabetes.

acid–base balance /,æsɪd 'beɪs ,bæləns/ *noun* the balance between acid and base, i.e. the pH level, in plasma

acidity /ə'sɪdɪti/ *noun* **1.** the level of acid in a liquid ○ *The alkaline solution may help to reduce acidity.* **2.** same as **hyperacidity**

acidosis /,æsɪ'dəʊsɪs/ *noun* **1.** a condition when there are more acid waste products such as urea than usual in the blood because of a lack of alkali **2.** same as **acidity**

acidotic /,æsɪ'dɒtɪk/ *adjective* relating to acidosis

acid reflux /,æsɪd 'riːflʌks/ *noun* a condition caused by a faulty muscle in the oesophagus allowing the acid in the stomach to pass into the oesophagus

acid stomach /,æsɪd 'stʌmək/ *noun* same as **hyperacidity**

aciduria /,æsɪ'djʊəriə/ *noun* a condition in which there is a higher level of acidity of the urine than is desirable

acinus /'æsɪnəs/ *noun* **1.** a tiny sac which forms part of a gland **2.** part of a lobule in the lung (NOTE: The plural is **acini**.)

acne /'ækni/ *noun* an inflammation of the sebaceous glands during puberty which makes blackheads appear on the skin, usually on the face, neck and shoulders. These blackheads often then become infected. ○ *She is using a cream to clear up her acne.*

acne rosacea /,ækni rəʊ'zeɪʃə/ *noun* same as **rosacea**

acne vulgaris /,ækni vʊl'gɑːrɪs/ *noun* same as **acne**

acoustic /ə'kuːstɪk/ *adjective* relating to sound or hearing

acoustic nerve /ə'kuːstɪk nɜːv/ *noun* the eighth cranial nerve which governs hearing and balance

acoustic neurofibroma /ə,kuːstɪk ,njuərəʊfaɪ'brəʊmə/, **acoustic neuroma** /ə ,kuːstɪk njuə'rəʊmə/ *noun* a tumour in the sheath of the auditory nerve, causing deafness

acoustic trauma /ə,kuːstɪk 'trɔːmə/ *noun* physical damage caused by sound waves, e.g. hearing loss, disorientation, motion sickness or dizziness

acquired /ə'kwaɪəd/ *adjective* referring to a condition which is neither congenital nor hereditary and which a person develops after birth in reaction to his or her environment

acquired immunity /ə,kwaɪəd ɪ'mjuːnɪti/ *noun* an immunity which a body acquires from having caught a disease or from immunisation, not one which is congenital

acquired immunodeficiency syndrome /ə,kwaɪəd ,ɪmjʊnəʊdɪ'fɪʃ(ə)nsi ,sɪndrəʊm/, **acquired immune deficiency syndrome** /ə ,kwaɪəd ɪm,juːn dɪ'fɪʃ(ə)nsi ,sɪndrəʊm/ *noun* a viral infection which breaks down the body's immune system. Abbr **AIDS**

acrivastine /ə'krɪvə stiːn/ *noun* a drug which reduces the amount of histamine produced by the body. It is used in the treatment of rhinitis, urticaria and eczema.

acro- /ækrəʊ/ *prefix* referring to a point or tip

acrocephalia /,ækrəʊsə'feɪliə/ *noun* same as **oxycephaly**

acrocephaly /,ækrəʊ'sefəli/ *noun* same as **oxycephaly**

acrocyanosis /,ækrəʊsaɪə'nəʊsɪs/ *noun* a blue coloration of the extremities, i.e. the fingers, toes, ears and nose, which is due to poor circulation

acrodynia /,ækrəʊ'dɪniə/ *noun* a children's disease, caused by an allergy to mercury, where the child's hands, feet and face swell and become pink, and the child is also affected with fever and loss of appetite. Also called **erythroedema, pink disease**

acromegaly /,ækrəʊ'megəli/ *noun* a disease caused by excessive quantities of growth hormone produced by the pituitary gland, causing a slow enlargement of the hands, feet and jaws in adults

acromial /ə'krəʊmiəl/ *adjective* referring to the acromion

acromioclavicular /,ækrəʊmaɪəʊklə 'vɪkjʊlə/ *adjective* relating to the acromion and the clavicle

acromion /ə'krəʊmiən/ *noun* the pointed top of the scapula, which forms the tip of the shoulder

acronyx /'ækrɒnɪks, 'eɪkrɒnɪks/ *noun* a condition in which a nail grows into the flesh

acroparaesthesia /,ækrəʊpærɪs'θiːziə/ *noun* a condition in which the patient experiences sharp pains in the arms and numbness in the fingers after sleep

acrophobia /,ækrə'fəʊbiə/ *noun* a fear of heights

acrosclerosis /,ækrəʊsklə'rəʊsɪs/ *noun* sclerosis which affects the extremities

ACTH *abbr* adrenocorticotrophic hormone

actinomycin /,æktɪnəʊ'maɪsɪn/ *noun* an antibiotic used in the treatment of children with cancer

actinomycosis /,æktɪnəʊmaɪ'kəʊsɪs/ *noun* a fungal disease transmitted to humans from cattle, causing abscesses in the mouth and lungs (pulmonary actinomycosis) or in the ileum (intestinal actinomycosis)

action potential /'ækʃən pə,tenʃəl/ *noun* a temporary change in electrical potential which occurs between the inside and the outside of a nerve or muscle fibre when a nerve impulse is sent

active /'æktɪv/ *adjective* **1.** (*of a person*) lively and energetic ○ *Although she is over eighty she is still very active.* Opposite **passive 2.** (*of a disease*) having an effect on a patient ○ *experienced two years of active rheumatoid disease* Compare **dormant 3.** (*of a drug*) having medicinal effect

active immunity /,æktɪv ɪ'mjuːnɪti/ *noun* immunity which is acquired by catching and surviving an infectious disease or by vaccination with a weakened form of the disease, which makes the body form antibodies

active ingredient /,æktɪv ɪn'griːdiənt/ *noun* the main medicinal ingredient of an ointment or lotion, as opposed to the base

active movement /,æktɪv 'muːvmənt/ *noun* movement made by a person using his or her own willpower and muscles

active principle /,æktɪv 'prɪnsɪp(ə)l/ *noun* the main medicinal ingredient of a drug which makes it have the required effect on a person

activities of daily living /æk,tɪvɪtiz əv ,deɪli 'lɪvɪŋ/ *noun* a scale used by geriatricians and occupational therapists to assess the capacity of elderly or disabled people to live independently. Abbr **ADLs**

activity /æk'tɪvɪti/ *noun* **1.** what someone does ○ *difficulty with activities such as walking and dressing* **2.** the characteristic behaviour of a chemical ○ *The drug's activity only lasts a few hours.* □ **antibacterial activity** effective action against bacteria

act on /'ækt ɒn/, **act upon** /'ækt ə,pɒn/ *verb* **1.** to do something as the result of something which has been said ○ *He acted on his doctor's advice and gave up smoking.* **2.** to have an effect on someone or something ○ *The antibiotic acted quickly on the infection.*

act out /,ækt 'aʊt/ *verb* to express negative feelings by behaving in a socially unacceptable way

acuity /ə'kjuːɪti/ *noun* keenness of sight, hearing or intellect

acupressure /'ækjʊpreʃə/ *noun* a treatment which is based on the same principle as acupuncture in which, instead of needles, fingers are used on specific points on the body, called pressure points

acupuncture /'ækjʊpʌŋktʃə/ *noun* a treatment based on needles being inserted through the skin into nerve centres in order to relieve pain or treat a disorder

acupuncturist /'ækjʊˌpʌŋktʃərɪst/ *noun* a person who practises acupuncture

acute /ə'kjuːt/ *adjective* **1.** referring to a disease or condition which develops rapidly and can be dangerous ○ *an acute abscess* Opposite **chronic 2.** referring to pain which is sharp and intense (*informal*) ○ *He felt acute chest pains.*

acute abdomen /əˌkjuːt 'æbdəmən/ *noun* any serious condition of the abdomen which requires surgery

acute bed /ə'kjuːt bed/ *noun* a hospital bed reserved for people requiring immediate treatment

'…the survey shows a reduction in acute beds in the last six years. The bed losses forced one hospital to send acutely ill patients to hospitals up to sixteen miles away.' [*Nursing Times*]

acute care /ə'kjuːt keə/ *noun* medical or surgical treatment in a hospital, usually for a short period, for a patient with a sudden severe illness or injury

acute disseminated encephalomyelitis /əˌkjuːt dɪˌsemɪneɪtɪd enˌkefələʊmaɪə 'laɪtɪs/ *noun* an encephalomyelitis or myelitis believed to result from an autoimmune attack on the myelin of the central nervous system

acute glaucoma /əˌkjuːt glɔː'kəʊmə/ *noun* same as **angle-closure glaucoma**

acute hospital /ə'kjuːt ˌhɒspɪt(ə)l/ *noun* a hospital where people go for major surgery or intensive care of medical or surgical conditions

acutely /ə'kjuːtli/ *adverb* **1.** having or causing a suddenly developing medical condition ○ *acutely ill patients* ○ *acutely toxic chemicals* **2.** extremely (*informal*)

acute lymphocytic leukaemia /əˌkjuːt ˌlɪmfəsɪtɪk luː'kiːmiə/ *noun* a form of leukaemia that is the commonest cancer affecting children

acute nonlymphocytic leukaemia /ə ˌkjuːt ˌnɒnlɪmfəsɪtɪk luː'kiːmiə/ *noun* a form of leukaemia that affects adults and children and is usually treated with chemotherapy

acute pancreatitis /əˌkuːt ˌpæŋkriə'taɪtɪs/ *noun* inflammation after pancreatic enzymes have escaped into the pancreas, causing symptoms of acute abdominal pain

acute respiratory distress syndrome /ə ˌkjuːt rɪˌspɪrət(ə)ri dɪ'stres ˌsɪndrəʊm/ *noun* an infection of the lungs, often following injury, which prevents them functioning properly. Abbr **ARDS**

acute rheumatism *noun* same as **rheumatic fever**

acute rhinitis /əˌkjuːt raɪ'naɪtɪs/ *noun* a virus infection which causes inflammation of the mucous membrane in the nose and throat

acute suppurative arthritis /əˌkjuːt ˌsʌ pjʊrətɪv ɑːθ'raɪtɪs/ *noun* same as **pyarthrosis**

acute toxicity /əˌkjuːt tɒk'sɪsɪti/ *noun* a level of concentration of a toxic substance which makes people seriously ill or can cause death

acute yellow atrophy /əˌkjuːt ˌjeləʊ 'ætrəfi/ ♦ **yellow atrophy**

acyclovir /eɪ'saɪkləʊvɪə/ *noun* same as **aciclovir**

acystia /eɪ'sɪstiə/ *noun* a condition in which a baby is born without a bladder

AD *abbr* Alzheimer's disease

Adam's apple /ˌædəmz 'æp(ə)l/ *noun* a part of the thyroid cartilage which projects from the neck below the chin in a man. Also called **laryngeal prominence**

adapt /ə'dæpt/ *verb* **1.** to change one's ideas or behaviour to fit into a new situation ○ *She has adapted very well to her new job in the children's hospital.* **2.** to change something to make it more useful ○ *The brace has to be adapted to fit the patient.*

adaptation /ˌædæp'teɪʃ(ə)n/ *noun* **1.** a change which has been or can be made to something **2.** the act of changing something so that it fits a new situation **3.** the process by which sensory receptors become accustomed to a sensation which is repeated

ADD *abbr* attention deficit disorder

addicted /ə'dɪktɪd/ *adjective* physically or mentally dependent on a harmful substance □ **addicted to alcohol** *or* **drugs** needing to take alcohol or a harmful drug regularly

addictive /ə'dɪktɪv/ *adjective* referring to a drug which is habit-forming and which people can become addicted to

Addison's anaemia /ˌædɪs(ə)nz ə'niːmiə/ same as **pernicious anaemia** [Described 1849. After Thomas Addison (1793–1860), from Northumberland, founder of the science of endocrinology.]

Addison's disease /'ædɪs(ə)nz dɪˌziːz/ *noun* a disease of the adrenal glands, causing a change in skin colour to yellow and then to dark brown and resulting in general weakness, anaemia, low blood pressure and wasting away. Treatment is with corticosteroid injections. [Described 1849. After Thomas Addison (1793–1860), from Northumberland, founder of the science of endocrinology.]

adducent /ə'djuːs(ə)nt/ *adjective* referring to a muscle which brings parts of the body together or moves them towards the central line of the body or a limb. Compare **abducent**

adduct /ə'dʌkt/ *verb* (*of a muscle*) to pull a leg or arm towards the central line of the body, or to pull a toe or finger towards the central line of a leg or arm. Opposite **abduct**

adducted /ə'dʌktɪd/ *adjective* referring to a body part brought towards the middle of the body

adduction /ə'dʌkʃən/ *noun* the movement of a part of the body towards the midline or towards a neighbouring part. Compare **abduction**. See illustration at **ANATOMICAL TERMS** in Supplement

adductor /ə'dʌktə/, **adductor muscle** /ə'dʌktə ˌmʌs(ə)l/ *noun* a muscle which pulls a part of the body towards the central line of the body. Opposite **abductor**

aden- /ædɪn/ *prefix* same as **adeno-** (*used before vowels*)

adenectomy /ˌædɪ'nektəmi/ *noun* the surgical removal of a gland

adenine /'ædəniːn/ *noun* one of the four basic chemicals in DNA

adenitis /ˌædɪ'naɪtɪs/ *noun* inflammation of a gland or lymph node. ◊ **lymphadenitis**

adeno- /ædɪnəʊ/ *prefix* referring to glands

adenocarcinoma /ˌædɪnəʊkɑːsɪ'nəʊmə/ *noun* a malignant tumour of a gland

adenohypophysis /ˌædɪnəʊhaɪ'pɒfɪsɪs/ *noun* the front lobe of the pituitary gland which secretes most of the pituitary hormones

adenoid /'ædɪnɔɪd/ *adjective* like a gland

adenoidal /ˌædɪ'nɔɪd(ə)l/ *adjective* referring to the adenoids

adenoidal expression /ˌædɪnɔɪd(ə)l ɪk'spreʃ(ə)n/ *noun* a common symptom of a child suffering from adenoids, where his or her mouth is always open, the nose is narrow and the top teeth appear to project forward

adenoidal tissue /ˌædɪnɔɪd(ə)l 'tɪʃuː/ *noun* same as **adenoids**

adenoidectomy /ˌædɪnɔɪ'dektəmi/ *noun* the surgical removal of the adenoids

adenoidism /'ædɪnɔɪdɪz(ə)m/ *noun* the condition of a person with adenoids

adenoids /'ædɪnɔɪdz/ *plural noun* a mass of tissue at the back of the nose and throat that can restrict breathing if enlarged. Also called **pharyngeal tonsils**

adenoid vegetation /ˌædɪnɔɪd ˌvedʒə'teɪʃ(ə)n/ *noun* a condition in children where the adenoidal tissue is covered with growths and can block the nasal passages or the Eustachian tubes

adenolymphoma /ˌædɪnəʊlɪm'fəʊmə/ *noun* a benign tumour of the salivary glands

adenoma /ˌædɪ'nəʊmə/ *noun* a benign tumour of a gland

adenoma sebaceum /ˌædɪnəʊmə sə'beɪʃəm/ *noun* a skin condition of the face shown by raised red vascular bumps appearing in late childhood or early adolescence

adenomyoma /ˌædɪnəʊmaɪ'əʊmə/ *noun* a benign tumour made up of glands and muscle

adenopathy /ˌædɪ'nɒpəθi/ *noun* a disease of a gland

adenosclerosis /ˌædɪnəʊsklə'rəʊsɪs/ *noun* the hardening of a gland

adenosine /ə'denəʊsiːn/ *noun* a drug used to treat an irregular heartbeat

adenosine diphosphate /ə,denəʊsiːn daɪ 'fɒsfeɪt/ *noun* a chemical compound which provides energy for processes to take place within living cells, formed when adenosine triphosphate reacts with water. Abbr **ADP**

adenosine triphosphate /ə,denəʊsiːn traɪ'fɒsfeɪt/ *noun* a chemical which occurs in all cells, but mainly in muscle, where it forms the energy reserve. Abbr **ATP**

adenosis /ˌædɪ'nəʊsɪs/ *noun* any disease or disorder of the glands

adenovirus /'ædɪnəʊˌvaɪrəs/ *noun* a virus which produces upper respiratory infections and sore throats and can cause fatal pneumonia in infants

ADH *abbr* antidiuretic hormone

ADHD *noun* full form **attention deficit hyperactivity disorder**. ◗ **hyperactivity**

adhesion /əd'hiːʒ(ə)n/ *noun* a stable connection between two parts in the body, either in a healing process or between parts which are not usually connected

adhesive dressing /əd,hiːsɪv 'dresɪŋ/ *noun* a dressing with a sticky substance on the back so that it can stick to the skin

adhesive strapping /əd,hiːsɪv 'stræpɪŋ/ *noun* overlapping strips of adhesive plaster used to protect a lesion

adipo- /ædɪpəʊ/ *prefix* referring to fat

adipose /'ædɪpəʊs/ *adjective* containing fat, or made of fat

COMMENT: Fibrous tissue is replaced by adipose tissue when more food is eaten than is necessary.

adipose degeneration /ˌædɪpəʊs dɪ ,dʒenə'reɪʃ(ə)n/ *noun* an accumulation of fat in the cells of an organ such as the heart or liver, which makes the organ less able to perform its proper function. Also called **fatty degeneration**

adipose tissue /ˌædɪpəʊs 'tɪʃuː/ *noun* a tissue where the cells contain fat

adiposis /ˌædɪ'pəʊsɪs/ *noun* a state where too much fat is accumulated in the body

adiposis dolorosa /ædɪ,pəʊsɪs ˌdɒlə 'rəʊsə/ *noun* a disease of middle-aged women in which painful lumps of fatty substance form in the body. Also called **Dercum's disease**

adiposogenitalis /ædɪ,pəʊsəʊ,dʒenɪ'teɪlɪs/ *noun* same as **Fröhlich's syndrome**

adiposuria /ə'dɪpəʊ'juːriə/ *noun* the presence of fat in the urine

adiposus /ˌædɪˈpəʊsəs/ ♦ **panniculus adiposus**

aditus /ˈædɪtəs/ *noun* an opening or entrance to a passage

adjustment /əˈdʒʌstmənt/ *noun* a specific directional high-speed movement of a joint performed by a chiropractor

adjuvant /ˈædʒʊvənt/ *adjective* referring to treatment by drugs or radiation therapy after surgery for cancer ■ *noun* a substance added to a drug to enhance the effect of the main ingredient

adjuvant therapy /ˈædʒʊvənt ˌθerəpi/ *noun* therapy using drugs or radiation after cancer surgery

ADLs *abbr* activities of daily living

administer /ədˈmɪnɪstə/ *verb* to give someone medicine or a treatment □ **to administer orally** to give a medicine by mouth

admission /ədˈmɪʃ(ə)n/ *noun* the act of being registered as a hospital patient

admit /ədˈmɪt/ *verb* to register a patient in a hospital ○ *He was admitted to hospital this morning.*

'80% of elderly patients admitted to geriatric units are on medication' [*Nursing Times*]

'...ten patients were admitted to the ICU before operation, the main indications being the need for evaluation of patients with a history of severe heart disease' [*Southern Medical Journal*]

adnexa /ædˈneksə/ *plural noun* structures attached to an organ

adolescence /ˌædəˈles(ə)ns/ *noun* the period of life when a child is developing into an adult

adolescent /ˌædəˈles(ə)nt/ *noun* a person who is at the stage of life when he or she is developing into an adult ■ *adjective* developing into an adult, or occurring at that stage of life ○ *adolescent boys and girls* ○ *adolescent fantasies*

adopt /əˈdɒpt/ *verb* **1.** to decide to use a particular plan or idea or way of doing something ○ *The hospital has adopted a new policy on visiting.* **2.** to become the legal parent of a child who was born to other parents

adoptive /əˈdɒptɪv/ *adjective* **1.** taking over the role of something else **2.** referring to people who have adopted a child or a child that has been adopted ○ *adoptive parents*

adoptive immunotherapy /əˌdɒptɪv ɪmjʊnəˈθerəpi/ *noun* a treatment for cancer in which the patient's own white blood cells are used to attack cancer cells

COMMENT: This technique can halt the growth of cancer cells in the body but it can have distressing toxic side-effects.

ADP *abbr* adenosine diphosphate

adrenal /əˈdriːn(ə)l/ *adjective* situated near the kidney ■ *noun* same as **adrenal gland**

adrenal body /əˈdriːn(ə)l ˌbɒdi/ *noun* same as **adrenal gland**

adrenal cortex /əˌdriːn(ə)l ˈkɔːteks/ *noun* the firm outside layer of an adrenal gland, which secretes a series of hormones affecting the metabolism of carbohydrates and water

adrenalectomy /əˌdriːnəˈlektəmi/ *noun* the surgical removal of one of the adrenal glands

adrenal gland /əˈdriːn(ə)l glænd/ *noun* one of two endocrine glands at the top of the kidneys which secrete cortisone, adrenaline and other hormones. Also called **adrenal body, adrenal**. See illustration at KIDNEY in Supplement

adrenaline /əˈdrenəlɪn/ *noun* a hormone secreted by the medulla of the adrenal glands which has an effect similar to stimulation of the sympathetic nervous system (NOTE: The US term is **epinephrine**.)

COMMENT: Adrenaline is produced when a person experiences surprise, shock, fear or excitement and it speeds up the heartbeat and raises blood pressure. It is administered as an emergency treatment of acute anaphylaxis and in cardiopulmonary resuscitation.

adrenal medulla /əˌdriːn(ə)l meˈdʌlə/ *noun* the inner part of the adrenal gland which secretes adrenaline and noradrenaline. Also called **suprarenal medulla**

adrenergic /ˌædrəˈnɜːdʒɪk/ *adjective* referring to a neurone or receptor which is stimulated by adrenaline. ◊ **beta blocker**

adrenergic receptor /ˌædrənɜːdʒɪk rɪˈseptə/ *noun* same as **adrenoceptor**

COMMENT: Three types of adrenergic receptor act in different ways when stimulated by adrenaline. Alpha receptors constrict the bronchi, beta 1 receptors speed up the heartbeat and beta 2 receptors dilate the bronchi.

adrenoceptor /əˌdrenəʊˈseptə/ *noun* a cell or neurone which is stimulated by adrenaline. Also called **adrenoreceptor, adrenergic receptor**

adrenocortical /əˌdriːnəʊˈkɔːtɪk(ə)l/ *adjective* relating to the cortex of the adrenal glands

adrenocorticotrophic hormone /əˌdriːnəʊˌkɔːtəkəʊtrɒfɪk ˈhɔːməʊn/ *noun* a hormone secreted by the pituitary gland, which makes the cortex of the adrenal glands produce corticosteroids. Abbr **ACTH**. Also called **corticotrophin**

adrenogenital syndrome /əˌdriːnəʊˈdʒenɪt(ə)l ˌsɪndrəʊm/ *noun* a condition caused by overproduction of male sex hormones, where boys show rapid sexual development and females develop male characteristics

adrenoleukodystrophy /əˌdriːnəʊˌluːkəʊˈdɪstrəfi/ *noun* an inherited disorder of the adrenal glands in boys

adrenolytic /ədriːnəʊˈlɪtɪk/ *adjective* acting against the secretion of adrenaline

adrenoreceptor /əˌdrenəʊrɪˈseptə/ *noun* same as **adrenoceptor**

adsorbent /æd'sɔːbənt/ *adjective* being capable of adsorption

adsorption /æd'sɔːpʃ(ə)n/ *noun* the attachment of one substance to another, often the bonding of a liquid with a gas or vapour which touches its surface

adult /'ædʌlt, ə'dʌlt/ *adjective* grown-up ○ *Adolescents reach the adult stage about the age of eighteen or twenty.* ■ *noun* someone who is no longer a child

adult coeliac disease /,ædʌlt 'siːliæk dɪ,ziːz/ *noun* a condition in adults where the villi in the intestine become smaller and so reduce the surface which can absorb nutrients

adult dentition /,ædʌlt den'tɪʃ(ə)n/ *noun* the 32 teeth which an adult has

adulteration /ə,dʌltə'reɪʃ(ə)n/ *noun* the act of making something less pure by adding another substance

adult-onset diabetes /,ædʌlt ,ɒnset ,daɪə'biːtiːz/ *noun* a form of diabetes mellitus that develops slowly in older people as the body becomes less able to use insulin effectively

adult respiratory distress syndrome /,ædʌlt rɪ,spɪrət(ə)ri dɪ'stres ,sɪndrəʊm/ *noun* a description of various lung infections which reduce the lungs' efficiency. Abbr **ARDS**

advanced trauma life support /əd,vɑːnst ,trɔːma 'laɪf sə,pɔːt/ *noun* the management of a trauma patient during the critical first hour after injury. Abbr **ATLS**

adventitia /,ædven'tɪʃə/ *noun* same as **tunica adventitia**

adventitious /,ædvən'tɪʃəs/ *adjective* on the outside or in an unusual place

adventitious bursa /,ædvɒntɪʃəs 'bɜːsə/ *noun* a bursa which develops as a result of continued pressure or rubbing

adverse /'ædvɜːs/ *adjective* harmful or unfavourable □ **the treatment had an adverse effect on his dermatitis** the treatment made the dermatitis worse

adverse occurrence /,ædvɜːs ə'kʌrəns/ *noun* a harmful event which occurs during treatment

adverse reaction /,ædvɜːs ri'ækʃən/ *noun* a situation where someone experiences harmful effects from the application of a drug

advocacy /'ædvəkəsi/ *noun* active support for something, especially in order to help people who would have difficulty in gaining attention without your help

adynamic ileus /eɪ,daɪnæmɪk 'ɪliəs/ *noun* same as **paralytic ileus**

aegophony /iː'gɒfəni/ *noun* a high sound of the voice heard through a stethoscope, where there is fluid in the pleural cavity

aer- /eə/ *prefix* same as **aero-** (*used before vowels*)

aeration /eə'reɪʃ(ə)n/ *noun* the adding of air or oxygen to a liquid

aero- /eərəʊ/ *prefix* referring to air

aeroba /eə'rəʊbə/, **aerobe** /'eərəʊb/ *noun* a tiny organism which needs oxygen to survive

aerobic /eə'rəʊbɪk/ *adjective* needing oxygen to live, or taking place in the presence of oxygen

aerobic respiration /eə,rəʊbɪk ,respə'reɪʃ(ə)n/ *noun* the process where the oxygen which is breathed in is used to conserve energy as ATP

aeroembolism /,eərəʊ'embəlɪz(ə)m/ *noun* same as **air embolism**

aerogenous /eə'rɒdʒənəs/ *adjective* referring to a bacterium which produces gas

aerophagia /,eərə'feɪdʒə/, **aerophagy** /eə'rɒfədʒi/ *noun* the habit of swallowing air when suffering from indigestion, so making the stomach pains worse

aerosol /'eərəsɒl/ *noun* tiny particles of a liquid such as a drug or disinfectant suspended in a gas under pressure in a container and used as a spray

aetiological agent /,iːtiəlɒdʒik(ə)l 'eɪdʒ(ə)nt/ *noun* an agent which causes a disease

aetiology /,iːti'ɒlədʒi/ *noun* **1.** the cause or origin of a disease **2.** the study of the causes and origins of diseases (NOTE: [all senses] The US spelling is **etiology**.)

'…a wide variety of organs or tissues may be infected by the Salmonella group of organisms, presenting symptoms which are not immediately recognised as being of Salmonella aetiology' [*Indian Journal of Medical Sciences*]

afebrile /eɪ'fiːbraɪl/ *adjective* with no fever

affect /ə'fekt/ *verb* to make something or someone change, especially to have a bad effect on something or someone ○ *Some organs are rapidly affected if the patient lacks oxygen for even a short time.* ■ *noun* same as **affection**

affection /ə'fekʃən/, **affect** /ə'fekt/ *noun* the general state of a person's emotions

'Depression has degrees of severity, ranging from sadness, through flatness of affection or feeling, to suicide and psychosis' [*British Journal of Nursing*]

affective /ə'fektɪv/ *adjective* relating to a person's moods or feelings

affective disorder /ə'fektɪv dɪs,ɔːdə/ *noun* a condition which changes someone's mood, making him or her depressed or excited

afferent /'æf(ə)rənt/ *adjective* conducting liquid or electrical impulses towards the inside. Opposite **efferent**

afferent nerve *noun* same as **sensory nerve**

afferent vessel /'æf(ə)rənt ,ves(ə)l/ *noun* a tube which brings lymph to a gland

affinity /ə'fɪnɪti/ *noun* an attraction between two substances

aflatoxin /,æflə'tɒksɪn/ *noun* a poison produced by some moulds in some crops such as peanuts

African trypanosomiasis /ˌæfrɪkən ˌtrɪpənəʊsəʊˈmaɪəsɪs/ *noun* same as **sleeping sickness**

afterbirth /ˈɑːftəbɜːθ/ *noun* the tissues, including the placenta and umbilical cord, which are present in the uterus during pregnancy and are expelled after the birth of a baby

aftercare /ˈɑːftəkeə/ *noun* **1.** the care of a person who has had an operation. Aftercare treatment involves changing dressings and helping people to look after themselves again. **2.** the care of a mother who has just given birth

after-effect /ˈɑːftər ɪˌfekt/ *noun* a change which appears only some time after the cause ○ *The operation had some unpleasant after-effects.*

after-image /ˈɑːftər ˌɪmɪdʒ/ *noun* an image of an object which remains in a person's sight after the object itself has gone

afterpains /ˈɑːftəpeɪnz/ *plural noun* regular pains in the uterus which are sometimes experienced after childbirth

afunctional /eɪ ˈfʌŋkʃən(ə)l/ *adjective* which does not function properly

agalactia /ˌeɪɡəˈlækʃə/ *noun* a condition in which a mother is unable to produce milk after childbirth

agammaglobulinaemia /eɪˌɡæməɡlɒbjʊlɪˈniːmiə/ *noun* a deficiency or absence of immunoglobulins in the blood, which results in a reduced ability to provide immune responses

agar /ˈeɪɡɑː/, **agar agar** /ˌeɪɡɑːr ˈeɪɡɑː/ *noun* a culture medium based on an extract of seaweed used for growing microorganisms in laboratories

age /eɪdʒ/ *noun* the number of years which a person has lived ○ *What's your age on your next birthday?* ○ *He was sixty years of age.* ○ *The size varies according to age.* ■ *verb* to grow old

age group /ˈeɪdʒ ɡruːp/ *noun* all the people of a particular age or within a particular set of ages ○ *the age group 20–25*

ageing /ˈeɪdʒɪŋ/, **aging** *noun* the fact of growing old

COMMENT: Changes take place in almost every part of the body as the person ages. Bones become more brittle and skin becomes less elastic. The most important changes affect the blood vessels which are less elastic, making thrombosis more likely. This also reduces the supply of blood to the brain, which in turn reduces the mental faculties.

ageing process /ˈeɪdʒɪŋ ˌprəʊses/ *noun* the physical changes which take place in a person as he or she grows older

agency /ˈeɪdʒənsi/ *noun* **1.** an organisation which carries out work on behalf of another organisation, e.g. one which recruits and employs nurses and supplies them to hospitals temporarily when full-time nursing staff are unavailable **2.** the act of causing something to happen ○ *The disease develops through the agency of bacteria present in the bloodstream.*

'The cost of employing agency nurses should be no higher than the equivalent full-time staff.' [*Nursing Times*]

'Growing numbers of nurses are choosing agency careers, which pay more and provide more flexible schedules than hospitals.' [*American Journal of Nursing*]

agenesis /eɪˈdʒenəsɪs/ *noun* the absence of an organ, resulting from a failure in embryonic development

agent /ˈeɪdʒənt/ *noun* **1.** a chemical substance which makes another substance react **2.** a substance or organism which causes a disease or condition **3.** a person who acts as a representative of another person or carries out some kinds of work on his or her behalf

agglutinate /əˈɡluːtɪneɪt/ *verb* to form into groups or clusters, or to cause things to form into groups or clusters

agglutination /əˌɡluːtɪˈneɪʃ(ə)n/ *noun* the act of coming together or sticking to one another to form a clump, as of bacteria cells in the presence of serum, or blood cells when blood of different types is mixed ◇ **agglutination test 1.** a test to identify bacteria **2.** a test to identify if a woman is pregnant

agglutinin /əˈɡluːtɪnɪn/ *noun* a factor in a serum which makes cells stick together in clumps

agglutinogen /ˌæɡluːˈtɪnədʒən/ *noun* a factor in red blood cells which reacts with a specific agglutinin in serum

aggravate /ˈæɡrəveɪt/ *verb* to make something worse ○ *Playing football only aggravates his knee injury.* ○ *The treatment seems to aggravate the disease.*

aggression /əˈɡreʃ(ə)n/ *noun* the state of feeling violently angry towards someone or something

aggressive /əˈɡresɪv/ *adjective* referring to treatment which involves frequent high doses of medication

aging /ˈeɪdʒɪŋ/ *noun* another spelling of **ageing**

agitated /ˈædʒɪteɪtɪd/ *adjective* moving about or twitching nervously because of worry or another psychological state ○ *The person became agitated and had to be given a sedative.*

agitation /ˌædʒɪˈteɪʃ(ə)n/ *noun* a state of being very nervous and anxious

aglossia /eɪˈɡlɒsiə/ *noun* the condition of not having a tongue from birth

agnosia /æɡˈnəʊziə/ *noun* a brain disorder in which a person fails to recognise places, people, tastes or smells which they used to know well

agonist /ˈæɡənɪst/ *noun* **1.** a muscle which causes part of the body to move and another muscle to relax when it contracts. Also called

prime mover 2. a substance which produces an observable physiological effect by acting through specific receptors. ◊ **antagonist**

agony /'ægəni/ *noun* a very severe physical or emotional pain ○ *He lay in agony on the floor.* ○ *She suffered the agony of waiting for weeks until her condition was diagnosed.*

agoraphobia /,æg(ə)rə'fəʊbiə/ *noun* a fear of being in open spaces. Compare **claustrophobia**

agoraphobic /,æg(ə)rə'fəʊbɪk/ *adjective* afraid of being in open spaces. Compare **claustrophobic**

agranulocytosis /ə,grænjʊləʊsaɪ'təʊsɪs/ *noun* a usually fatal disease where the number of granulocytes, a type of white blood cell, falls sharply because of a bone marrow condition

agraphia /eɪ'græfiə/ *noun* the condition of being unable to put ideas into writing

AHF *abbr* antihaemophilic factor

aid /eɪd/ *noun* **1.** help **2.** a machine, tool or drug which helps someone do something ○ *He uses a walking frame as an aid to exercising his legs.* ■ *verb* to help someone or something ○ *The procedure is designed to aid the repair of tissues after surgery.*

AID /,eɪ aɪ 'diː/ *noun* full form **artificial insemination by donor**. now called **DI**

AIDS /eɪdz/, **Aids** *noun* a viral infection which breaks down the body's immune system. Full form **acquired immunodeficiency syndrome, acquired immune deficiency syndrome**

COMMENT: AIDS is a disease caused by the human immunodeficiency virus (HIV). It is spread mostly by sexual intercourse and can affect anyone. It is also transmitted through infected blood and plasma transfusions, through using unsterilised needles for injections, and can be passed from a mother to a fetus. The disease takes a long time, usually years, to show symptoms, and many people with HIV are unaware that they are infected. It causes a breakdown of the body's immune system, making the patient susceptible to any infection and often results in the development of rare skin cancers. It is not curable.

AIDS dementia /,eɪdz dɪ'menʃə/ *noun* a form of mental degeneration resulting from infection with HIV

AIDS-related complex /,eɪdz rɪ,leɪtɪd 'kɒmpleks/, **AIDS-related condition** /,eɪdz rɪ ,leɪtɪd kən'dɪʃ(ə)n/ *noun* early symptoms shown by someone infected with the HIV virus, e.g. weight loss, fever and herpes zoster. Abbr **ARC**

AIH *abbr* artificial insemination by husband

ailment /'eɪlmənt/ *noun* an illness, though not generally a very serious one ○ *Chickenpox is one of the common childhood ailments.*

ailurophobia /,aɪlʊərə'fəʊbiə/ *noun* a fear of cats

air /eə/ *noun* a mixture of gases, mainly oxygen and nitrogen, which cannot be seen, but which exists all around us and which is breathed ○ *Open the window and let some fresh air into the room.* ○ *He breathed the polluted air into his lungs.*

air bed /'eə bed/ *noun* a mattress which is filled with air, used to prevent the formation of bedsores. ◊ **conduction**

airborne infection /,eəbɔːn ɪn'fekʃən/ *noun* an infection which is carried in the air

air conduction /'eə kən,dʌkʃən/ *noun* the process by which sounds pass from the outside to the inner ear through the auditory meatus

air embolism /eər 'embəlɪz(ə)m/ *noun* a blockage caused by bubbles of air, that stops the flow of blood in vessels

air hunger /'eə ,hʌŋgə/ *noun* a condition in which the patient needs air because of lack of oxygen in the tissues

air passage /'eə ,pæsɪdʒ/ *noun* any tube which takes air to the lungs, e.g. the nostrils, pharynx, larynx, trachea and bronchi

air sac /'eə sæk/ *noun* a small sac in the lungs which contains air. ◊ **alveolus**

airsick /'eəsɪk/ *adjective* feeling sick because of the movement of an aircraft

airsickness /'eəsɪknəs/ *noun* a queasy feeling, usually leading to vomiting, caused by the movement of an aircraft

airway /'eəweɪ/ *noun* a passage through which air passes, especially the trachea

airway clearing /'eəweɪ ,klɪərɪŋ/ *noun* making sure that the airways in a newborn baby or an unconscious person are free of any obstruction

airway obstruction /,eəweɪ əb'strʌkʃ(ə)n/ *noun* something which blocks the air passages

akathisia /,eɪkə'θɪsiə/ *noun* restlessness

akinesia /,eɪkɪ'niːziə/ *noun* a lack of voluntary movement, as in Parkinson's disease

akinetic /,eɪkɪ'netɪk/ *adjective* without movement

alacrima /eɪ'lækrɪmə/ *noun* same as **xerosis**

alactasia /,eɪlæk'teɪziə/ *noun* a condition in which there is a deficiency of lactase in the intestine, making the patient incapable of digesting lactose, the sugar in milk

alalia /eɪ'leɪliə/ *noun* a condition in which a person completely loses the ability to speak

alanine /'æləniːn/ *noun* an amino acid

alanine aminotransferase /,æləniːn ə ,miːnəʊ'trænsfəreɪz/ *noun* an enzyme which is found in the liver and can be monitored as an indicator of liver damage. Abbr **ALT**

alar cartilage /,eɪlə 'kɑːtɪlɪdʒ/ *noun* cartilage in the nose

alba /'ælbə/ ✦ **linea alba**

Albee's operation /'ɔːlbiːz ɒpə,reɪʃ(ə)n/ *noun* **1.** a surgical operation to fuse two or more vertebrae **2.** a surgical operation to fuse the femur to the pelvis [After Frederick Houdlett Albee (1876–1945), US surgeon]

albicans /'ælbɪkænz/ **♦ corpus albicans**

albinism /'ælbɪnɪz(ə)m/ *noun* a condition in which a person lacks the pigment melanin and so has pink skin and eyes and white hair. It is hereditary and cannot be treated. ◊ **vitiligo**

albino /æl'biːnəʊ/ *noun* a person who is deficient in melanin and has little or no pigmentation in the skin, hair or eyes

albuginea /,ælbjuː'dʒɪniə/ *noun* a layer of white tissue covering a part of the body

albuginea oculi /,ælbjʊdʒɪniə 'ɒkjʊlaɪ/ *noun* same as **sclera**

albuminometer /,ælbjʊmɪ'nɒmɪtə/ *noun* an instrument for measuring the level of albumin in the urine

albuminuria /,ælbjʊmɪ'njʊəriə/ *noun* a condition in which albumin is found in the urine, usually a sign of kidney disease, but also sometimes of heart failure

albumose /'ælbjʊməʊz/ *noun* an intermediate product in the digestion of protein

alcohol /'ælkəhɒl/ *noun* a pure colourless liquid which is formed by the action of yeast on sugar solutions and forms part of drinks such as wine and whisky

COMMENT: Alcohol is used medicinally to dry wounds or harden the skin. When drunk, alcohol is rapidly absorbed into the bloodstream. It is a source of energy, so any carbohydrates taken at the same time are not used by the body and are stored as fat. Alcohol is a depressant, not a stimulant, and affects the way the brain works.

alcohol abuse /'ælkəhɒl ə,bjuːs/ *noun* the excessive use of alcohol adversely affecting a person's health

alcohol addiction /'ælkəhɒl ə,dɪkʃən/ *noun* a condition in which a person is dependent on the use of alcohol

alcohol-fast /'ælkəhɒl fɑːst/ *adjective* referring to an organ stained for testing which is not discoloured by alcohol

alcoholic /,ælkə'hɒlɪk/ *adjective* 1. containing alcohol 2. caused by alcoholism ○ *alcoholic poisoning* ■ *noun* a person who is addicted to drinking alcohol and shows changes in behaviour and personality

alcoholic cardiomyopathy /,ælkəhɒlɪk ,kɑːdiəʊmaɪ'ɒpəθi/ *noun* a disease of the heart muscle arising as a result of long-term heavy alcohol consumption

alcoholic cirrhosis /,ælkəhɒlɪk sɪ'rəʊsɪs/ *noun* cirrhosis of the liver caused by alcoholism

alcoholic hepatitis /,ælkəhɒlɪk ,hepə'taɪtɪs/ *noun* inflammation of the liver as a result of long-term heavy alcohol consumption, often leading to cirrhosis

Alcoholics Anonymous /,ælkəhɒlɪks ə'nɒnɪməs/ *noun* an organisation of former alcoholics which helps people to overcome their dependence on alcohol by encouraging them to talk about their problems in group therapy. Abbr **AA**

alcoholicum /,ælkə'hɒlɪkəm/ **♦ delirium alcoholicum**

alcoholism /'ælkəhɒlɪz(ə)m/ *noun* excessive drinking of alcohol which becomes addictive

alcohol poisoning /'ælkəhɒl ,pɔɪz(ə)nɪŋ/ *noun* poisoning and disease caused by excessive drinking of alcohol

alcohol rub /'ælkəhɒl rʌb/ *noun* the act of rubbing a bedridden person with alcohol to help protect against bedsores and as a tonic

alcoholuria /,ælkəhɒ'ljʊəriə/ *noun* a condition in which alcohol is present in the urine (NOTE: The level of alcohol in the urine is used as a test for drivers who are suspected of driving while drunk.)

aldosterone /æl'dɒstərəʊn/ *noun* a hormone secreted by the cortex of the adrenal gland, which regulates the balance of sodium and potassium in the body and the amount of body fluid

aldosteronism /æl'dɒst(ə)rənɪz(ə)m/ *noun* a condition in which a person produces too much aldosterone, so that there is too much salt in the blood. This causes high blood pressure and the need to drink a lot of liquids.

alert /ə'lɜːt/ *adjective* referring to someone who takes an intelligent interest in his or her surroundings ○ *The patient is still alert, though in great pain.*

aleukaemic /,eɪluː'kiːmɪk/ *adjective* 1. referring to a state where leukaemia is not present 2. referring to a state where leucocytes are not normal

Alexander technique /,ælɪg'zɑːndə tek,niːk/ *noun* a method of improving the way a person stands and moves, by making them much more aware of how muscles behave

alexia /eɪ'leksiə/ *noun* a condition in which the patient cannot understand printed words. Also called **word blindness**

alfacalcidol /,ælfə'kælsɪdɒl/ *noun* a substance related to vitamin D, used by the body to maintain the right levels of calcium and phosphate, and also as a drug to help people who do not have enough vitamin D

algesimeter /,æld ʒɪ'sɪmɪtə/ *noun* an instrument to measure the sensitivity of the skin to pain

-algia /ældʒiə/ *suffix* a word ending that indicates a painful condition

algid /'ældʒɪd/ *adjective* referring to a stage in a disease that causes fever during which the body becomes cold

algophobia /,ælgəʊ'fəʊbiə/ *noun* an unusually intense fear of pain

alienation /ˌeɪliəˈneɪʃ(ə)n/ *noun* a psychological condition in which a person develops the feeling of not being part of the everyday world, and as a result often becomes hostile to other people

alignment /əˈlaɪnmənt/ *noun* the arrangement of something in a straight line, or in the correct position in relation to something else

alimentary /ˌælɪˈment(ə)ri/ *adjective* providing food, or relating to food or nutrition

alimentary canal /ˌælɪˌment(ə)ri kəˈnæl/ *noun* a tube in the body going from the mouth to the anus and including the throat, stomach and intestine, through which food passes and is digested

alimentary system /ˌælɪˈment(ə)ri ˌsɪstəm/ *noun* same as **digestive system**

alimentation /ˌælɪmenˈteɪʃ(ə)n/ *noun* the act of providing food or nourishment

aliquot /ˈælɪkwɒt/ *noun* a part of a larger thing, especially a sample of something which is taken to be examined

alive /əˈlaɪv/ *adjective* living, not dead ○ *The man was still alive, even though he had been in the sea for two days.* (NOTE: **Alive** cannot be used in front of a noun: *The person is alive* but *a living person.* Note also that **live** can be used in front of a noun: *The person was injected with live vaccine.*)

alkalaemia /ˌælkəˈliːmiə/ *noun* an excess of alkali in the blood

alkali /ˈælkəlaɪ/ *noun* one of many substances which neutralise acids and form salts (NOTE: The UK plural is **alkalis**, but the US plural is **alkalies**.)

alkaline /ˈælkəlaɪn/ *adjective* containing more alkali than acid

alkalinity /ˌælkəˈlɪnɪti/ *noun* the level of alkali in a body ○ *Hyperventilation causes fluctuating carbon dioxide levels in the blood, resulting in an increase of blood alkalinity.*

COMMENT: Alkalinity and acidity are measured according to the pH scale. pH7 is neutral, and pH8 and upwards are alkaline. Alkaline solutions are used to counteract the effects of acid poisoning and also of bee stings. If strong alkali, such as ammonia, is swallowed, the patient should drink water and an acid such as orange juice.

alkaloid /ˈælkəlɔɪd/ *noun* one of many poisonous substances found in plants and used as medicines, e.g. atropine, morphine or quinine

alkalosis /ˌælkəˈləʊsɪs/ *noun* a condition in which the alkali level in the body tissue is high, producing cramps

alkaptonuria /ˌælkæptəˈnjʊəriə/ *noun* a hereditary condition where dark pigment is present in the urine

allantoin /əˈlæntəʊɪn/ *noun* powder from the herb comfrey, used to treat skin disorders

allantois /əˈlæntəʊɪs/ *noun* one of the membranes in the embryo, shaped like a sac, which grows out of the embryonic hindgut

allele /əˈliːl/ *noun* one of two or more alternative forms of a gene, situated in the same area on each of a pair of chromosomes and each producing a different effect

allergen /ˈælədʒən/ *noun* a substance which produces hypersensitivity

COMMENT: Allergens are usually proteins and include foods, dust, hair of animals, as well as pollen from flowers. Allergic reaction to serum is known as **anaphylaxis**. Treatment of allergies depends on correctly identifying the allergen to which the patient is sensitive. This is done by patch tests in which drops of different allergens are placed on scratches in the skin. Food allergens discovered in this way can be avoided, but other allergens such as dust and pollen can hardly be avoided and have to be treated by a course of desensitising injections.

allergenic /ˌæləˈdʒenɪk/ *adjective* producing an allergic reaction ○ *the allergenic properties of fungal spores*

allergenic agent /ˌælədʒenɪk ˈeɪdʒənt/ *noun* a substance which produces an allergy

allergic /əˈlɜːdʒɪk/ *adjective* having an allergy to something ○ *She is allergic to cats.* ○ *I'm allergic to penicillin.*

allergic agent /əˈlɜːdʒɪk ˌeɪdʒənt/ *noun* a substance which produces an allergic reaction

allergic purpura /əˌlɜːdʒɪk ˈpɜːpjʊərə/ *noun* a form of the skin condition purpura, found most often in children

allergic reaction /əˌlɜːdʒɪk riˈækʃən/ *noun* an effect produced by a substance to which a person has an allergy, such as sneezing or a skin rash

allergic rhinitis /əˌlɜːdʒɪk raɪˈnaɪtɪs/ *noun* inflammation in the nose and eyes caused by an allergic reaction to plant pollen, mould spores, dust mites or animal hair. ◊ **hayfever**

allergist /ˈælədʒɪst/ *noun* a doctor who specialises in the treatment of allergies

allergy /ˈælədʒi/ *noun* an unusual sensitivity to some substances such as pollen or dust, which cause a physical reaction such as sneezing or a rash in someone who comes into contact with them ○ *She has an allergy to household dust.* ○ *He has a penicillin allergy.* (NOTE: You **have an allergy** or you **are allergic to** something.)

allergy bracelet /ˈælədʒi ˌbreɪslət/ *noun* ♦ **medical alert bracelet**

alleviate /əˈliːvieɪt/ *verb* to make pain or discomfort less severe ○ *The drug is effective in alleviating migraine headaches.*

allied health professional /ˌælaɪd ˈhelθ prəˌfeʃ(ə)n(ə)l/ *noun* a professional working in medicine who is not a doctor or nurse, e.g. a physiotherapist or paramedic

allo- /ˈæləʊ/ *prefix* different

allodynia /ˌæləˈdɪniə/ *noun* pain of the skin caused by something such as clothing which usually does not cause pain

allogeneic /ˌælədʒəˈneɪɪk/ *adjective* ((*of body tissues*)) genetically different and therefore incompatible when transplanted

allograft /ˈæləʊgrɑːft/ *noun* same as **homograft**

allopathy /əˈlɒpəθi/ *noun* the treatment of a condition using drugs which produce opposite symptoms to those of the condition. Compare **homeopathy**

allopurinol /ˌæləʊˈpjʊərɪnɒl/ *noun* a drug which helps to stop the body producing uric acid, used in the treatment of gout

all or none law /ˌɔːl ɔː ˈnʌn lɔː/ *noun* the rule that the heart muscle either contracts fully or does not contract at all

allylestrenol /ˌælaɪlˈestrənɒl/ *noun* a steroid used to encourage pregnancy

alopecia /ˌæləʊˈpiːʃə/ *noun* a condition in which hair is lost. Compare **hypotrichosis**

alopecia areata /æləʊˌpiːʃə ˌæriˈeɪtə/ *noun* a condition in which the hair falls out in patches

alpha /ˈælfə/ *noun* the first letter of the Greek alphabet

alpha-adrenoceptor antagonist /ˌælfə ə ˌdriːnəʊrɪˈseptə ænˌtæɡənɪst/, **alpha-adrenoceptor blocker** /ˈælfə əˌdriːnəʊrɪˈseptə ˌblɒkə/ *noun* a drug which can relax smooth muscle, used to treat urinary retention and hypertension. Also called **alpha blocker**

alpha cell /ˈælfə sel/ *noun* a type of cell found in the islets of Langerhans, in the pancreas, which produces glucagon, a hormone that raises the level of glucose in the blood. ◊ **beta cell**

alpha-fetoprotein /ˌælfə ˌfiːtəʊˈprəʊtiːn/ *noun* a protein produced by the liver of the human fetus, which accumulates in the amniotic fluid. A high or low concentration is tested for by amniocentesis in the antenatal diagnosis of spina bifida or Down's syndrome, respectively.

alpha rhythm /ˈælfə ˌrɪðəm/ *noun* the pattern of electrical activity in the brain of someone who is awake but relaxed or sleepy, registering on an electroencephalograph at 8–13 hertz

Alport's syndrome /ˈɔːlpɔːts ˌsɪndrəʊm/ *noun* a genetic disease of the kidneys which sometimes causes a person to lose his or her hearing and sight

alprostadil /ælˈprɒstədɪl/ *noun* a drug which makes blood vessels wider, used to treat impotence, prevent coagulation, and maintain babies with congenital heart conditions

ALS *abbr* **1.** amyotrophic lateral sclerosis **2.** antilymphocytic serum

ALT *abbr* alanine aminotransferase

alternative medicine /ɔːlˌtɜːnətɪv ˈmed(ə)sɪn/ *noun* the treatment of illness using therapies such as homoeopathy or naturopathy which are not considered part of conventional Western medicine. ◊ **complementary medicine**

altitude sickness /ˈæltɪtjuːd ˌsɪknəs/ *noun* a condition caused by reduced oxygen in the air above altitudes of 7000 to 8000 feet (3600 metres). Symptoms include headaches, breathlessness, fatigue, nausea and swelling of the face, hands and feet. Also called **high-altitude sickness, mountain sickness**

aluminium /ˌæləˈmɪniəm/ *noun* a metallic element extracted from the ore bauxite (NOTE: The US spelling is **aluminum**. The chemical symbol is **Al**.)

aluminium hydroxide /æləˌmɪniəm haɪˈdrɒksaɪd/ *noun* a chemical substance used as an antacid to treat indigestion. Formula: $Al(OH)_3$ or $Al_2O_3.3H_2O$.

alveolar /ˌælvɪˈəʊlə, ælˈviːələ/ *adjective* referring to the alveoli

alveolar bone /ˌælvɪˈəʊlə bəʊn/ *noun* part of the jawbone to which the teeth are attached

alveolar duct /ˌælvɪˈəʊlə dʌkt/ *noun* a duct in the lung which leads from the respiratory bronchioles to the alveoli. See illustration at LUNGS in Supplement

alveolar wall /ˌælvɪˈəʊlə wɔːl/ *noun* one of the walls which separate the alveoli in the lungs

alveolitis /ˌælviəˈlaɪtɪs/ *noun* inflammation of an alveolus in the lungs or the socket of a tooth

alveolus /ˌælvɪˈəʊləs, ælˈviːələs/ *noun* a small cavity, e.g. an air sac in the lungs or the socket into which a tooth fits. See illustration at LUNGS in Supplement (NOTE: The plural is **alveoli**.)

Alzheimer plaque /ˈæltshaɪmə plæk/ *noun* a disc-shaped plaque of amyloid found in the brain in people who have Alzheimer's disease

Alzheimer's disease /ˈæltshaɪməz dɪˌziːz/ *noun* a disease where a person experiences progressive dementia due to nerve cell loss in specific brain areas, resulting in loss of mental faculties including memory [Described 1906. After Alois Alzheimer (1864–1915), Bavarian physician.]

COMMENT: No single cause of Alzheimer's disease has been identified, although an early onset type occurs more frequently in some families, due to a mutation in a gene on chromosome 21. Risk factors include age, genes, head injury, lifestyle and environment.

amalgam /əˈmælgəm/ *noun* a mixture of metals, based on mercury and tin, used by dentists to fill holes in teeth

amaurosis /ˌæmɔːˈrəʊsɪs/ *noun* blindness caused by disease of the optic nerve

amaurosis fugax /ˌæmɔːˈrəʊsɪs ˈfjuːgæks/ *noun* temporary blindness in one eye, caused by problems of circulation

amaurotic familial idiocy /ˌæmɔːˈrɒtɪk fə ˌmɪliəl ˈɪdiəsi/, **amaurotic family idiocy** /ˌæmɔːˈrɒtɪk ˌfæm(ə)li ˈɪdiəsi/ *noun* same as **Tay-Sachs disease**

amb- /æmb/ *prefix* same as **ambi-** (*used before vowels*)

ambi- /æmbi/ *prefix* both

ambidextrous /ˌæmbɪˈdekstrəs/ *adjective* referring to a person who can use both hands equally well and who is not right- or left-handed

ambiguous genitalia /æmˌbɪgjuəs ˌdʒenɪ ˈteɪliə/ *noun* a congenital condition in which the outer genitals do not look typical of those of either sex

ambisexual /ˌæmbɪˈsekʃuəl/ *adjective, noun* same as **bisexual**

amblyopia /ˌæmbliˈəʊpiə/ *noun* a lack of normal vision without a structural cause. A common example is squint and other forms may be caused by the cyanide in tobacco smoke or by drinking methylated spirits.

amblyopic /ˌæmbliˈɒpɪk/ *adjective* affected by amblyopia

amblyoscope /ˈæmbliəʊskəʊp/ *noun* an instrument for measuring the angle of a squint and how effectively someone uses both their eyes together. Also called **orthoptoscope**

ambulance /ˈæmbjʊləns/ *noun* a van for taking sick or injured people to hospital ○ *The injured man was taken away in an ambulance.* ○ *The telephone number of the local ambulance service is in the phone book.* ◊ **St John Ambulance Association and Brigade**

ambulant /ˈæmbjələnt/ *adjective* able to walk

ambulation /ˌæmbjʊˈleɪʃ(ə)n/ *noun* walking □ **early ambulation is recommended** patients should try to get out of bed and walk about as soon as possible after the operation

ambulatory /ˌæmbjʊˈleɪt(ə)ri/ *adjective* referring to a patient who is not confined to bed but is able to walk

'…ambulatory patients with essential hypertension were evaluated and followed up at the hypertension clinic' [*British Medical Journal*]

ambulatory care /ˌæmbjʊˌleɪt(ə)ri ˈkeə/ *noun* treatment of a patient which does not involve staying in hospital during the night

ambulatory fever /ˌæmbjʊˈleɪt(ə)ri ˌfiːvə/ *noun* a mild fever where the patient can walk about and can therefore act as a carrier, e.g. during the early stages of typhoid fever

ameba /əˈmiːbə/ *noun US* same as **amoeba**

amelia /əˈmiːliə/ *noun* the absence of a limb from birth, or a condition in which a limb is short from birth

amelioration /əˌmiːliəˈreɪʃ(ə)n/ *noun* the process of getting better

ameloblastoma /ˌæmɪləʊblæˈstəʊmə/ *noun* a tumour in the jaw, usually in the lower jaw

amenorrhoea /ˌeɪmenəˈriːə/ *noun* the absence of one or more menstrual periods, usual during pregnancy and after the menopause

ametropia /ˌæmɪˈtrəʊpiə/ *noun* a condition in which the eye cannot focus light correctly onto the retina, as in astigmatism, hypermetropia and myopia. Compare **emmetropia**

amfetamine /æmˈfetəmiːn/ *noun* an addictive drug, similar to adrenaline, used to give a feeling of wellbeing and wakefulness. Also called **amphetamine**

amikacin /ˌæmɪˈkeɪsɪn/ *noun* a type of antibiotic used to treat infections caused by aerobic bacteria

amiloride /əˈmɪləraɪd/ *noun* a drug which helps to increase the production of urine and preserve the body's supply of potassium

amino acid /əˌmiːnəʊ ˈæsɪd/ *noun* a chemical compound which is broken down from proteins in the digestive system and then used by the body to form its own protein

COMMENT: Amino acids all contain carbon, hydrogen, nitrogen and oxygen, as well as other elements. Some amino acids are produced in the body itself, but others have to be absorbed from food. The eight essential amino acids are: isoleucine, leucine, lysine, methionine, phenylalanine, threonine, tryptophan and valine.

aminobutyric acid /əˌmiːnəʊbjʊtɪrɪk ˈæsɪd/ *noun* ◊ **gamma aminobutyric acid**

aminoglycoside /əˌmiːnəʊˈglaɪkəsaɪd/ *noun* a drug used to treat many Gram-negative and some Gram-positive bacterial infections (NOTE: Aminoglycosides include drugs with names ending in **-cin**: **gentamicin**.)

aminophylline /ˌæmɪˈnɒfɪliːn/ *noun* a drug that makes the bronchial tubes wider, used in the treatment of asthma

amiodarone /ˌæmiˈɒdərəʊn/ *noun* a drug that makes the blood vessels wider, used in the treatment of irregular heartbeat

amitosis /ˌæmɪˈtəʊsɪs/ *noun* the multiplication of a cell by splitting of the nucleus

amitriptyline /ˌæmɪˈtrɪptɪliːn/ *noun* a sedative drug used to treat depression and persistent pain

amlodipine /æmˈlɒdɪpiːn/ *noun* a drug that helps to control the movement of calcium ions through cell membranes. It is used to treat hypertension and angina.

ammonia /əˈməʊniə/ *noun* a gas with a strong smell, a compound of nitrogen and hydrogen, which is a usual product of human metabolism

ammonium /əˈməʊniəm/ *noun* an ion formed from ammonia

amnesia /æmˈniːziə/ *noun* loss of memory

amnia /ˈæmniə/ plural of **amnion**

amnihook /'æmnihʊk/ *noun* a hooked instrument used to induce labour by pulling on the amniotic sac

amnio /'æmniəʊ/ *noun* same as **amniocentesis** (*informal*)

amniocentesis /ˌæmniəʊsen'tiːsɪs/ *noun* a procedure which involves taking a test sample of the amniotic fluid during pregnancy using a hollow needle and syringe

COMMENT: Amniocentesis and amnioscopy, the examination and testing of the amniotic fluid, give information about possible congenital disorders in the fetus as well as the sex of the unborn baby.

amniography /ˌæmni'ɒgrəfi/ *noun* an X-ray of the womb

amnion /'æmniən/ *noun* the thin sac containing the amniotic fluid which covers an unborn baby in the uterus. Also called **amniotic sac**

amnioscope /'æmniəskəʊp/ *noun* an instrument used to examine a fetus through the cervical channel, before the amniotic sac is broken

amnioscopy /ˌæmni'ɒskəpi/ *noun* an examination of the amniotic fluid during pregnancy

amniotic /ˌæmni'ɒtɪk/ *adjective* relating to the amnion

amniotic cavity /ˌæmniɒtɪk 'kævɪti/ *noun* a space formed by the amnion, full of amniotic fluid

amniotic fluid /ˌæmniɒtɪk 'fluːɪd/ *noun* the fluid contained in the amnion which surrounds an unborn baby

amniotic sac /ˌæmniɒtɪk 'sæk/ *noun* same as **amnion**

amniotomy /ˌæmni'ɒtəmi/ *noun* a puncture of the amnion to help induce labour

amoeba /ə'miːbə/ *noun* a form of animal life, made up of a single cell (NOTE: The plural is **amoebae**.)

amoebiasis /ˌæmi'baɪəsɪs/ *noun* an infection caused by amoebae which can result in amoebic dysentery in the large intestine (intestinal amoebiasis) and sometimes affects the lungs (pulmonary amoebiasis)

amoebic /ə'miːbɪk/ *adjective* relating to or caused by amoebae

amoebic dysentery /əˌmiːbɪk 'dɪs(ə)ntri/ *noun* a form of dysentery mainly found in tropical areas that is caused by *Entamoeba histolytica* which enters the body through contaminated water or unwashed food

amoebicide /ə'miːbɪsaɪd/ *noun* a substance which kills amoebae

amorphous /ə'mɔːfəs/ *adjective* with no regular shape

amoxicillin /ə'mɒksɪsɪlɪn/ *noun* an antibiotic

Amoxil /ə'mɒksɪl/ a trade name for amoxicillin

amphetamine /æm'fetəmiːn/ *noun* same as **amfetamine**

amphetamine abuse /æm'fetəmiːn əˌbjuːs/ *noun* the repeated addictive use of amphetamines which in the end affects the mental faculties

amphiarthrosis /ˌæmfiɑː'θrəʊsɪs/ *noun* a joint which only has limited movement, e.g. one of the joints in the spine

amphotericin /ˌæmfəʊ'terɪsɪn/ *noun* an antifungal agent, used against *Candida*

ampicillin /ˌæmpɪ'sɪlɪn/ *noun* a type of penicillin, used as an antibiotic

ampoule /'æmpuːl/, **ampule** /'æmpjuːl/ *noun* a small glass container, closed at the neck, used to contain sterile drugs for use in injections

ampulla /æm'pʊlə/ *noun* a swelling of a canal or duct, shaped like a bottle (NOTE: The plural is **ampullae**.)

amputate /'æmpjʊteɪt/ *verb* to remove a limb or part of a limb in a surgical operation ○ *The patient's leg needs to be amputated below the knee.* ○ *After gangrene set in, surgeons had to amputate her toes.*

amputation /ˌæmpjʊ'teɪʃ(ə)n/ *noun* the surgical removal of a limb or part of a limb

amputee /ˌæmpjʊ'tiː/ *noun* someone who has had a limb or part of a limb removed in a surgical operation

amygdala /ə'mɪgdələ/ *noun* an almond-shaped body in the brain, at the end of the caudate nucleus of the thalamus. Also called **amygdaloid body**

amygdaloid body /ə'mɪgdələɪd ˌbɒdi/ *noun* same as **amygdala**

amyl- /æm(ə)l/ *prefix* referring to starch

amylase /'æmɪleɪz/ *noun* an enzyme which converts starch into maltose

amyl nitrate /ˌæm(ə)l 'naɪtreɪt/ *noun* a drug used to reduce blood pressure (NOTE: Amyl nitrate is also used as a recreational drug.)

amyloid /'æmɪlɔɪd/ *noun* a waxy protein that forms in some tissues during the development of various diseases, e.g. forming disc-shaped plaques in the brain in Alzheimer's disease

amyloid disease /'æmɪlɔɪd dɪˌziːz/ *noun* same as **amyloidosis**

amyloidosis /ˌæmɪlɔɪ'dəʊsɪs/ *noun* a disease of the kidneys and liver, where amyloid develops in the tissues. Also called **amyloid disease**

amyloid precursor protein /ˌæmɪlɔɪd pri'kɜːsə ˌprəʊtiːn/ *noun* a compound found in cell membranes from which beta amyloid is derived. A mutation of the gene causes early-onset Alzheimer's disease in a few families.

amylopsin /ˌæmɪ'lɒpsɪn/ *noun* an enzyme which converts starch into maltose

amylose /'æmɪləʊz/ *noun* a carbohydrate of starch

amyotonia /ˌeɪmaɪə'təʊniə/ *noun* a lack of muscle tone

amyotonia congenita /ˌeɪmaɪəˈtəʊniə kən
ˈdʒenɪtə/ *noun* a congenital disease of children in which the muscles lack tone. Also
called **floppy baby syndrome**

amyotrophia /eɪˌmaɪəˈtrəʊfiə/ *noun* a condition in which a muscle wastes away

amyotrophic lateral sclerosis /eɪ
ˌmaɪətrɒfɪk ˌlætər(ə)l skləˈrəʊsɪs/ *noun* a
motor neurone disease in which the limbs
twitch and the muscles gradually waste away.
Also called **Gehrig's disease**. Abbr **ALS**

amyotrophy /eɪˌmaɪˈɒtrəfi/ same as **amyotrophia**

an- /æn/ *prefix* same as **ana-** (*used before vowels*)

ana- /ænə/ *prefix* without or lacking

anabolic /ˌænəˈbɒlɪk/ *adjective* referring to a
substance which synthesises protein
'...insulin, secreted by the islets of Langerhans, is
the body's major anabolic hormone, regulating the
metabolism of all body fuels and substrates'
[*Nursing Times*]

anabolic steroid /ænəˌbɒlɪk ˈstɪərɔɪd/
noun a drug which encourages the synthesis of
new living tissue, especially muscle, from nutrients

anabolism /æˈnæbəlɪz(ə)m/ *noun* the process of building up complex chemical substances on the basis of simpler ones

anacrotism /əˈnækrətɪz(ə)m/ *noun* a second
stroke in the pulse

anaemia /əˈniːmiə/ *noun* a condition in
which the level of red blood cells is less than
usual or where the haemoglobin is less, making it more difficult for the blood to carry oxygen. The symptoms are tiredness and pale colour, especially pale lips, nails and the inside of
the eyelids. The condition can be fatal if not
treated. (NOTE: The US spelling is **anemia**.)

anaemic /əˈniːmɪk/ *adjective* having anaemia
(NOTE: The US spelling is **anemic**.)

anaerobe /ˈænərəʊb, ænˈeərəʊb/ *noun* a
microorganism which lives without oxygen,
e.g. the tetanus bacillus

anaerobic /ˌænəˈrəʊbɪk/ *adjective* **1.** not
needing oxygen for metabolism ○ *anaerobic
bacteria* **2.** without oxygen ○ *anaerobic conditions*

anaesthesia /ˌænəsˈθiːziə/ *noun* **1.** a state,
deliberately produced in a patient by a medical
procedure, in which he or she can feel no pain,
either in a part or in the whole of the body **2.** a
loss of feeling caused by damage to nerves
(NOTE: The US spelling is **anesthesia**.)

anaesthesiologist /ˌænəsθiːziˈɒlədʒɪst/
noun US a specialist in the study of anaesthetics

anaesthetic /ˌænəsˈθetɪk/ *adjective* inducing loss of feeling ■ *noun* a substance given to
someone to remove feeling, so that he or she
can undergo an operation without pain

'Spinal and epidural anaesthetics can also cause
gross vasodilation, leading to heat loss'
[*British Journal of Nursing*]

anaesthetic induction /ˌænəsˈθetɪk ɪn
ˈdʌkʃən/ *noun* a method of inducing anaesthesia in a patient

anaesthetic risk /ˌænəsθetɪk ˈrɪsk/ *noun*
the risk that an anaesthetic may cause serious
unwanted side effects

anaesthetise /əˈniːsθətaɪz/, **anaesthetize**
verb to produce a loss of feeling in a person or
in part of the person's body

anaesthetist /əˈniːsθətɪst/ *noun* a specialist
who administers anaesthetics

anal /ˈeɪn(ə)l/ *adjective* relating to the anus

anal canal /ˌeɪn(ə)l kəˈnæl/ *noun* a passage
leading from the rectum to the anus

analeptic /ˌænəˈleptɪk/ *noun* a drug used to
make someone regain consciousness or to
stimulate a patient

anal fissure /ˌeɪn(ə)l ˈfɪʃə/ *noun* a crack in
the mucous membrane of the wall of the anal
canal

anal fistula /ˌeɪn(ə)l ˈfɪstjʊlə/ *noun* a fistula
which develops between the rectum and the
outside of the body after an abscess near the
anus. Also called **fistula in ano**

analgesia /ˌæn(ə)lˈdʒiːziə/ *noun* a reduction
of the feeling of pain without loss of consciousness

analgesic /ˌæn(ə)lˈdʒiːzɪk/ *adjective* relating to analgesia ■ *noun* a painkilling drug
which produces analgesia and reduces pyrexia
COMMENT: There are two types of analgesic:
non-opioid such as paracetamol and aspirin
(acetylsalicylic acid), and opioid such as codeine phosphate. Opioid analgesics are used
for severe pain relief such as in terminal care,
as cough suppressants and to reduce gut motility in cases of diarrhoea. Analgesics are
commonly used as local anaesthetics, for example in dentistry.

anally /ˈeɪn(ə)li/ *adverb* through the anus ○
The patient is not able to pass faeces anally.

anal passage /ˌeɪn(ə)l ˈpæsɪdʒ/ *noun* same
as **anus**

anal sphincter /ˌeɪn(ə)l ˈsfɪŋktə/ *noun* a
strong ring of muscle which closes the anus

anal triangle /ˌeɪn(ə)l ˈtraɪæŋg(ə)l/ *noun*
the posterior part of the perineum. Also called
rectal triangle

analyse /ˈænəlaɪz/ *verb* to examine something in detail ○ *The laboratory is analysing
the blood samples.* ○ *When the food was analysed it was found to contain traces of bacteria.* (NOTE: The US spelling is **analyze**.)

analyser /ˈænəlaɪzə/ *noun* a machine which
analyses blood or tissue samples automatically
(NOTE: The US spelling is **analyzer**.)

analysis /əˈnæləsɪs/ *noun* an examination of
a substance to find out what it is made of
(NOTE: The plural is **analyses**.)

analyst /'ænəlɪst/ *noun* **1.** a person who examines samples of substances or tissue, to find out what they are made of **2.** same as **psychoanalyst**

anamnesis /ˌænæm'niːsɪs/ *noun* someone's medical history, especially given in their own words

anamnestic /ˌænæm'nestɪk/ *adjective* showing a secondary immunological response to an antigen some time after immunisation

anaphase /'ænəfeɪz/ *noun* a stage in cell division, after the metaphase and before the telophase

anaphylactic /ˌænəfɪ'læktɪk/ *adjective* relating to or caused by extreme sensitivity to a substance

anaphylactic shock /ˌænəfɪlæktɪk 'ʃɒk/ *noun* a sudden severe reaction, which can be fatal, to something such as an injected substance or a bee sting

anaphylaxis /ˌænəfɪ'læksɪs/ *noun* **1.** extreme sensitivity to a substance introduced into the body **2.** same as **anaphylactic shock**

anaplasia /ˌænə'pleɪsiə/ *noun* the loss of a cell's typical characteristics, caused by cancer

anaplastic /ˌænə'plæstɪk/ *adjective* referring to anaplasia

anaplastic neoplasm /ˌænəplæstɪk 'niːəʊplæz(ə)m/ *noun* a cancer where the cells are not similar to those of the tissue from which they come

anarthria /æn'ɑːθriə/ *noun* the loss of the ability to speak words properly

anasarca /ˌænə'sɑːkə/ *noun* the presence of fluid in the body tissues. ◊ **oedema**

anastomose /ə'næstəməʊz/ *verb* to join two blood vessels or tubular structures together

anastomosis /əˌnæstə'məʊsɪs/ *noun* a connection made between two blood vessels or tubular structures, either naturally or by surgery

anat. *abbr* **1.** anatomical **2.** anatomy

anatomical /ˌænə'tɒmɪk(ə)l/ *adjective* relating to the anatomy ○ *the anatomical features of a fetus*

anatomical position /ˌænətɒmɪk(ə)l pə'zɪʃ(ə)n/ *noun* in anatomy, the standard position of the body from which all directions and positions are derived. The body is assumed to be standing, with the feet together, the arms to the side, and the head, eyes and palms facing forward.

anatomy /ə'nætəmi/ *noun* **1.** the structure, especially the internal structure, of the body **2.** the branch of science that studies the structure of the bodies of humans, animals and plants ○ *They are studying anatomy.* □ **the anatomy of a bone** a description of the structure and shape of a bone

ancillary staff /æn'sɪləri stɑːf/ *noun* the staff in a hospital who are not administrators,

doctors or nurses, e.g. cleaners, porters, kitchen staff

ancillary worker /æn'sɪləri ˌwɜːkə/ *noun* someone who does a job for patients such cooking or cleaning which is supplementary to medical care

anconeus /æŋ'kəʊniəs/ *noun* a small triangular muscle at the back of the elbow

Ancylostoma /ˌænsɪlə'stəʊmə/ *noun* a parasitic worm in the intestine which holds onto the wall of the intestine with its teeth and lives on the blood and protein of the carrier

ancylostomiasis /ˌænsɪləʊstə'maɪəsɪs/ *noun* a disease of which the symptoms are weakness and anaemia, caused by a hookworm which lives on the blood of the carrier. In severe cases the person may die.

androgen /'ændrədʒən/ *noun* a male sex hormone, testosterone or androsterone, which increases the male characteristics of the body

androgenic /ˌændrə'dʒenɪk/ *adjective* producing male characteristics

androgynous /ˌæn'drɒdʒənəs/ *adjective* same as **hermaphrodite**

andrology /æn'drɒlədʒi/ *noun* the study of male sexual characteristics and subjects such as impotence, infertility and the male menopause

androsterone /æn'drɒstərəʊn/ *noun* one of the male sex hormones

anemia /ə'niːmiə/ *noun US* same as **anaemia**

anencephalous /ˌænen'kefələs/ *adjective* having no brain

anencephaly /ˌænen'kefəli/ *noun* the absence of a brain, which causes a fetus to die a few hours after birth

anergy /'ænədʒi/ *noun* **1.** a state of severe weakness and lack of energy **2.** lack of immunity

anesthesia, etc /ˌænəs'θiːʒə/ *US* same as **anaesthesia, etc**

aneurine /ə'njʊərɪn/ *noun* same as **Vitamin B₁**

aneurysm /'ænjərɪz(ə)m/ *noun* a swelling caused by the weakening of the wall of a blood vessel

COMMENT: Aneurysm usually occurs in the wall of the aorta, 'aortic aneurysm', and is often due to atherosclerosis, and sometimes to syphilis.

angi- /ændʒi/ *prefix* same as **angio-** (*used before vowels*)

angiectasis /ˌændʒi'ektəsɪs/ *noun* a swelling of the blood vessels

angiitis /ˌændʒi'aɪtɪs/ *noun* an inflammation of a blood vessel

angina /æn'dʒaɪnə/ *noun* a pain in the chest following exercise or eating, which is caused by an inadequate supply of blood to the heart muscles because of narrowing of the arteries.

It is commonly treated with nitrates or calcium channel blocker drugs.

anginal /æn'dʒaɪnəl/ *adjective* referring to angina ○ *He suffered anginal pains.*

angina pectoris /æn,dʒaɪnə 'pektərɪs/ *noun* same as **angina**

angio- /ændʒɪəʊ/ *prefix* referring to a blood vessel

angiocardiogram /,ændʒɪəʊ'kɑːdiəgræm/ *noun* a series of pictures resulting from angiocardiography

angiocardiography /,ændʒɪəʊkɑːdi'ɒgrəfi/ *noun* an X-ray examination of the cardiac system after injection with an opaque dye so that the organs show up clearly on the film

angiodysplasia /,ændʒɪəʊdɪs'pleɪziə/ *noun* a condition where the blood vessels in the colon dilate, resulting in loss of blood

angiogenesis /,ændʒɪəʊ'dʒenəsɪs/ *noun* the formation of new blood vessels, e.g. in an embryo or as a result of a tumour

angiogram /'ændʒɪəʊgræm/ *noun* an X-ray picture of blood vessels

angiography /,ændʒɪ'ɒgrəfi/ *noun* an X-ray examination of blood vessels after injection with an opaque dye so that they show up clearly on the film

angiology /,ændʒɪ'ɒlədʒi/ *noun* the branch of medicine which deals with blood vessels and the lymphatic system

angioma /,ændʒɪ'əʊmə/ *noun* a benign tumour formed of blood vessels, e.g. a naevus

angioneurotic oedema /,ændʒɪəʊnjʊˌrɒ↓tɪk ɪ'diːmə/ *noun* a sudden accumulation of liquid under the skin, similar to nettle rash

angiopathy /,ændʒɪ'ɒpəθi/ *noun* a disease of vessels such as blood and lymphatic vessels

angioplasty /'ændʒɪəʊˌplæsti/ *noun* plastic surgery to repair a blood vessel, e.g. a narrowed coronary artery

angiosarcoma /,ændʒɪəʊsɑː'kəʊmə/ *noun* a malignant tumour in a blood vessel

angioscope /'ændʒɪəʊskəʊp/ *noun* a long thin surgical instrument threaded into a patient's blood vessels to allow surgeons to observe and perform operations without making large incisions

angiospasm /'ændʒɪəʊspæz(ə)m/ *noun* a spasm which constricts blood vessels

angiotensin /'ændʒɪəʊtensɪn/ *noun* a polypeptide which affects blood pressure by causing vasoconstriction and increasing extracellular volume

COMMENT: The precursor protein, alpha-2-globulin is converted to angiotensin I, which is inactive. A converting enzyme changes angiotensin I into the active form, angiotensin II . Drugs which block the conversion to the active form, ACE inhibitors, are used in the treatment of hypertension and heart failure.

angiotensin-converting enzyme inhibitor /,ændʒɪəʊtensɪn kən,vɜːtɪŋ 'enzaɪm ɪn,hɪbɪtə/ *noun* a drug which inhibits the conversion of angiotensin I to angiotensin II, which constricts arteries, used in the treatment of hypertension and heart failure. Also called **ACE inhibitor** (NOTE: ACE inhibitors have names ending in **-pril**: captopril.)

COMMENT: Contraindications include use with diuretics, when hypotension can occur and should be avoided in patients with renovascular disease.

angle-closure glaucoma /,æŋgəl ,kləʊʒə glɔː'kəʊmə/ *noun* an unusually high pressure of fluid inside the eyeball caused by pressure of the iris against the lens, trapping the aqueous humour. Also called **acute glaucoma**

angular stomatitis /,æŋgjʊlə ,stəʊmə'taɪtɪs/ *noun* a condition of the lips, mouth and cheeks characterised by cracks and fissures and caused by a bacterial infection

angular vein /'æŋgjʊlə veɪn/ *noun* a vein which continues the facial vein at the side of the nose

anhedonia /,ænhɪ'dəʊniə/ *noun* a psychological condition in which a person is unable to enjoy all the experiences that most people enjoy

anhidrosis /,ænhɪ'drəʊsɪs/ *noun* a condition in which sweating by the body is reduced or stops completely

anhidrotic /,ænhɪ'drɒtɪk/ *adjective* referring to a drug which reduces sweating

anhydraemia /,ænhaɪ'driːmiə/ *noun* a lack of sufficient fluid in the body

anhydrous /æn'haɪdrəs/ *adjective* referring to compounds or crystals that contain no water

anhydrous alcohol /,ænhaɪdrəs 'ælkəhɒl/ *noun* same as **absolute alcohol**

anidrosis /,ænɪ'drəʊsɪs/ *noun* same as **anhidrosis**

aniridia /,ænɪ'rɪdiə/ *noun* a congenital absence of the iris

anisocytosis /,ænaɪsəʊsaɪ'təʊsɪs/ *noun* a variation in size of red blood cells

anisomelia /,ænaɪsəʊ'miːliə/ *noun* a difference in length of the legs

anisometropia /,ænaɪsəʊmə'trəʊpiə/ *noun* a state where the refraction in the two eyes is different

ankle /'æŋkəl/ *noun* the part of the body where the foot is connected to the leg □ **he twisted his ankle**, **he sprained his ankle** he hurt it by stretching it or bending it

anklebone /'æŋkəlˌbəʊn/ *noun* same as **talus**

ankle jerk /'æŋkəl dʒɜːk/ *noun* a sudden jerk as a reflex action of the foot when the back of the ankle is tapped

ankle joint /'æŋkəl dʒɔɪnt/ *noun* a joint which connects the bones of the lower leg (the tibia and fibula) to the talus

ankyloblepharon /ˌæŋkɪləʊˈblefərɒn/ *noun* a state where the edges of the eyelids are stuck together

ankylose /ˈæŋkɪləʊz/ *verb* to fuse together, or to cause bones to fuse together

ankylosing spondylitis /ˌæŋkɪləʊzɪŋ spɒndɪˈlaɪtɪs/ *noun* a condition occurring more frequently in young men, in which the vertebrae and sacroiliac joints are inflamed and become stiff

ankylosis /ˌæŋkɪˈləʊsɪs/ *noun* a condition in which the bones of a joint fuse together

Ankylostoma /ˌæŋkɪlˈstəʊmə/ *noun* same as **Ancylostoma**

ankylostomiasis /ˌæŋkɪləʊstəˈmaɪəsɪs/ *noun* same as **ancylostomiasis**

ANLL *abbr* acute nonlymphocytic leukaemia

annular /ˈænjʊlə/ *adjective* shaped like a ring

annulus /ˈænjʊləs/ *noun* a structure shaped like a ring

ano- /ænəʊ/ *prefix* referring to the anus

anococcygeal /ˌænəkɒksɪˈdʒiːəl/ *adjective* referring to both the anus and coccyx

anodyne /ˈænədaɪn/ *noun* a drug which reduces pain, e.g. aspirin or codeine ■ *adjective* referring to drugs that bring relief from pain or discomfort

anomalous /əˈnɒmələs/ *adjective* different from what is usual

anomalous pulmonary venous drainage /əˌnɒmələs ˌpʌlmən(ə)ri ˈviːnəs ˌdreɪnɪdʒ/ *noun* a condition in which oxygenated blood from the lungs drains into the right atrium instead of the left

anomaly /əˈnɒməli/ *noun* something which is different from the usual

anomie /ˈænəmi/ *noun* a psychological condition in which a person develops the feeling of not being part of the everyday world, and behaves as though they do not have any supporting social or moral framework

anonychia /ˌænəˈnɪkiə/ *noun* a congenital absence of one or more nails

anopheles /əˈnɒfəliːz/ *noun* a mosquito which carries the malaria parasite

anoplasty /ˈeɪnəʊplæsti/ *noun* surgery to repair the anus, as in treating haemorrhoids

anorchism /ænˈɔːkɪz(ə)m/ *noun* a congenital absence of testicles

anorectal /ˌeɪnəʊˈrekt(ə)l/ *adjective* referring to both the anus and rectum

anorectic /ˌænəˈrektɪk/ *noun* a medicine that suppresses the appetite ■ *adjective* relating to life-threatening loss of appetite

anorexia /ˌænəˈreksiə/ *noun* loss of appetite

anorexia nervosa /ænəˌreksiə nɜːˈvəʊsə/ *noun* a psychological condition, usually found in girls and young women, in which a person refuses to eat because of a fear of becoming fat

anorexic /ˌænəˈreksɪk/ *adjective* 1. referring to anorexia 2. having anorexia ○ *The school has developed a programme of counselling for anorexic students.*

anosmia /ænˈɒzmiə/ *noun* the lack of the sense of smell

anovulant /ænˈɒvjələnt/ *noun* a drug that prevents ovulation, e.g. a birth-control pill

anovular /ænˈɒvjʊlə/ *adjective* without an ovum

anovular bleeding /ænˌɒvjʊlə ˈbliːdɪŋ/ *noun* bleeding from the uterus when ovulation has not taken place

anovulation /ænˌɒvjʊˈleɪʃ(ə)n/ *noun* a condition in which a women does not ovulate and is therefore infertile

anoxaemia /ˌænɒkˈsiːmiə/ *noun* a reduction of the amount of oxygen in the blood

anoxia /ænˈɒksiə/ *noun* a lack of oxygen in body tissue

anoxic /ænˈɒksɪk/ *adjective* referring to anoxia or lacking oxygen

anserina /ˌænsəˈraɪnə/ ♦ **cutis anserina**

antacid /æntˈæsɪd/ *adjective* preventing too much acid forming in the stomach or altering the amount of acid in the stomach ■ *noun* a substance that stops too much acid forming in the stomach, used in the treatment of gastrointestinal conditions such as ulcers, e.g. calcium carbonate or magnesium trisilicate

antagonism /ænˈtægənɪz(ə)m/ *noun* 1. the opposing force that usually exists between pairs of muscles 2. the interaction between two or more chemical substances in the body that reduces the effect that each substance has individually

antagonist /ænˈtægənɪst/ *adjective* 1. referring to a muscle which opposes another muscle in a movement 2. referring to a substance which opposes another substance ■ *noun* a substance which acts through specific receptors to block the action of another substance, but which has no observable physiological effect itself ○ *Atropine is a cholinergic antagonist and blocks the effects of acetylcholine.*

ante- /ænti/ *prefix* before

ante cibum /ˌænti ˈtʃɪbəm, ˌænti ˈsiːbəm/ *adverb* full form of **a.c.**

anteflexion /ˌæntiˈflekʃən/ *noun* the curving forward of an organ, e.g. the usual curvature of the uterus

antegrade amnesia /ˌæntigreɪd æmˈniːziə/ *noun* a form of memory loss relating to the things that happen after a traumatic event

antemortem /ˌæntiˈmɔːtəm/ *noun* the period before death

antenatal /ˌæntiˈneɪt(ə)l/ *adjective* during the period between conception and childbirth

antenatal clinic /ˌæntiˈneɪt(ə)l ˌklɪnɪk/ *noun* a clinic where expectant mothers are taught how to look after babies, do exercises and have medical checkups. Also called **maternity clinic**

antenatal diagnosis /ˌæntiˌneɪt(ə)l ˌdaɪəg
'nəʊsɪs/ *noun* a medical examination of a
pregnant woman to see if the fetus is developing in the usual way. Also called **prenatal diagnosis**

antepartum /ˌæntiˈpɑːtəm/ *noun* the period
of three months before childbirth ■ *adjective*
referring to the three months before childbirth

antepartum haemorrhage /ˌæntipuːtəm
ˈhemərɪdʒ/ *noun* bleeding from the vagina before labour. Abbr **APH**

anterior /ænˈtɪəriə/ *adjective* in front. Opposite **posterior**

anterior aspect /ænˌtɪəriə ˈæspekt/ *noun* a
view of the front of the body, or of the front of
part of the body. See illustration at ANATOMICAL
TERMS in Supplement

anterior chamber /ænˌtɪəriə ˈtʃeɪmbə/
noun part of the aqueous chamber of the eye
which is in front of the iris

anterior fontanelle /ænˌtɪəriə fɒntəˈnel/
noun the cartilage at the top of the head where
the frontal bone joins the two parietals

anterior jugular /ænˌtɪəriə ˈdʒʌgjʊlə/ *noun*
a small jugular vein in the neck

anterior nares /ænˌtɪəriə ˈneəriːz/ *plural
noun* the two nostrils. Also called **external
nares**

anterior superior iliac spine /ænˌtɪəriə
sʊˌpɪəriə ˈɪliæk spaɪn/ *noun* a projection at
the front end of the iliac crest of the pelvis

anterior synechia /ænˌtɪəriə sɪˈnekiə/
noun a condition of the eye, where the iris
sticks to the cornea

anterograde amnesia /ˌæntərəʊɡreɪd æm
ˈniːziə/ *noun* a brain condition in which the
person cannot remember things which happened recently

anteversion /ˌæntiˈvɜːʃ(ə)n/ *noun* the tilting
forward of an organ, whether usual, as of the
uterus, or unusual

anthelmintic /ˌænθelˈmɪntɪk/ *noun* a substance which removes worms from the intestine ■ *adjective* removing worms from the intestine

anthracosis /ˌænθrəˈkəʊsɪs/ *noun* a lung
disease caused by breathing coal dust

anthrax /ˈænθræks/ *noun* a disease of cattle
and sheep which can be transmitted to humans

COMMENT: Caused by *Bacillus anthracis*, anthrax can be transmitted by touching infected
skin, meat or other parts of an animal, including bone meal used as a fertiliser. It causes
pustules on the skin or in the lungs, 'woolsorter's disease'.

anthrop- /ænθrəp/ *prefix* referring to human
beings

anthropometry /ˌænθrəˈpɒmətri/ *noun* the
study of human body measurements (NOTE:
The uses of anthropometry include the design of
ergonomic furniture and the examination and
comparison of populations.)

anti- /ænti/ *prefix* against

antiallergenic /ˌæntiæləˈdʒenɪk/ *adjective*
referring to something such as a cosmetic
which will not aggravate an allergy

antiarrhythmic /ˌæntieɪˈrɪðmɪk/ *adjective*
referring to a drug which corrects an irregular
heartbeat

antiasthmatic /ˌæntiæsˈmætɪk/ *adjective*
referring to a drug that is used to treat asthma

antibacterial /ˌæntibækˈtɪəriəl/ *adjective*
destroying bacteria

antibiogram /ˌæntiˈbaɪəɡræm/ *noun* a laboratory technique which establishes to what degree an organism is sensitive to an antibiotic

antibiotic /ˌæntibaɪˈɒtɪk/ *adjective* stopping
the spread of bacteria ■ *noun* a drug which is
developed from living substances and which
stops the spread of bacteria, e.g. penicillin ○
He was given a course of antibiotics. ○ *Antibiotics have no effect against viral diseases.*

COMMENT: Penicillin is one of the commonest
antibiotics, together with streptomycin, tetracycline, erythromycin and many others. Although antibiotics are widely and successfully
used, new forms of bacteria have developed
which are resistant to them.

antibody /ˈæntɪbɒdi/ *noun* a protein that is
stimulated by the body to produce foreign substances such as bacteria, as part of an immune
reaction ○ *Tests showed that he had antibodies
in his blood.*

antibody-negative /ˌæntɪbɒdi ˈneɡətɪv/
adjective showing none of a particular antibody in the blood ○ *The donor tested antibody-negative.*

antibody-positive /ˌæntɪbɒdi ˈpɒzɪtɪv/ *adjective* showing the presence of particular antibodies in the blood ○ *The patient is HIV antibody-positive.*

anti-cancer drug /ˌænti ˈkænsə drʌg/ *noun*
a drug which can control or destroy cancer
cells

anticholinergic /ˌæntikəʊliˈnɜːdʒɪk/ *adjective* blocking nerve impulses which are part of
the stress response ■ *noun* one of a group of
drugs which are used to control stress

anticholinesterase /ˌæntikəʊlɪnˈestəreɪz/
noun a substance which blocks nerve impulses
by reducing the activity of the enzyme
cholinesterase

anticoagulant /ˌæntikəʊˈæɡjʊlənt/ *adjective* slowing or stopping the clotting of blood ■
noun a drug which slows down or stops the
clotting of blood, used to prevent the formation of a thrombus (NOTE: Anticoagulants have
names ending in **-parin**: **heparin**.)

anticonvulsant /ˌæntikənˈvʌls(ə)nt/ *adjective* acting to control convulsions ■ *noun* a
drug used to control convulsions, as in the
treatment of epilepsy, e.g. carbamazepine

anti-D /ˌænti ˈdi/, **anti-D gamma-globulin**
/ˌænti ˌdiː ˌgæmə ˈɡlɒbjʊlɪn/ *noun* Rh D im-

munoglobulin, used to treat pregnant women who develop antibodies when the mother is Rh-negative and the fetus is Rh-positive

antidepressant /ˌæntidɪ'pres(ə)nt/ *adjective* acting to relieve depression ◼ *noun* a drug used to relieve depression by stimulating the mood of a depressed person. Examples are tricyclic antidepressants, selective serotonin reuptake inhibitors and monoamine oxidase inhibitors.

antidiabetic /ˌæntidaɪə'betɪk/ *noun* a drug used in the treatment of diabetes ◼ *adjective* referring to an antidiabetic drug

antidiarrhoeal /ˌæntidaɪə'riːəl/ *noun* a drug used in the treatment of diarrhoea ◼ *adjective* referring to an antidiarrhoeal drug (NOTE: [all senses] The US spelling is **antidiarrheal**.)

anti-D immunoglobulin /ˌænti ˌdiː ɪmjʊnəʊ'glɒbjʊlɪn/ *noun* immunoglobulin administered to Rh-negative mothers after the birth of an Rh-positive baby, to prevent haemolytic disease of the newborn in the next pregnancy

antidiuretic /ˌæntidaɪjʊ'retɪk/ *noun* a substance which stops the production of excessive amounts of urine ○ *hormones which have an antidiuretic effect on the kidneys* ◼ *adjective* preventing the excessive production of urine

antidiuretic hormone /ˌæntidaɪjʊˌretɪk 'hɔːməʊn/ *noun* a hormone secreted by the posterior lobe of the pituitary gland which acts on the kidneys to regulate the quantity of salt in body fluids and the amount of urine excreted by the kidneys. Also called **vasopressin**

antidote /'æntɪdəʊt/ *noun* a substance which counteracts the effect of a poison ○ *There is no satisfactory antidote to cyanide.*

antiembolic /ˌæntiem'bɒlɪk/ *adjective* preventing embolism

antiemetic /ˌænti'metɪk/ *noun* a drug which prevents vomiting ◼ *adjective* acting to prevent vomiting

antiepileptic drug /ˌæntiepɪ'leptɪk drʌg/ *noun* a drug used in the treatment of epilepsy and convulsions, e.g. carbamazepine

antifibrinolytic /ˌæntifaɪbrɪnə'lɪtɪk/ *adjective* acting to reduce fibrosis

antifungal /ˌænti'fʌŋgəl/ *adjective* referring to a substance which kills or controls fungal and yeast infections, e.g. candida and ringworm (NOTE: Antifungal drugs have names ending in **-conazole: fluconazole**.)

antigen /'æntɪdʒən/ *noun* a substance that stimulates the body to produce antibodies, e.g. a protein on the surface of a cell or microorganism

antigenic /ˌæntɪ'dʒenɪk/ *adjective* referring to a substance which stimulates the formation of antibodies

antihaemophilic factor /ˌæntihiːmə'fɪlɪk ˌfæktə/ *noun* factor VIII, used to encourage blood-clotting in haemophiliacs. Abbr **AHF**

antihelminthic /ˌæntihel'mɪnθɪk/ *noun* a drug used in the treatment of worm infections such as threadworm, hookworm or roundworm

antihistamine /ˌænti'hɪstəmiːn/ *noun* a drug used to control the effects of an allergy which releases histamine, or reduces gastric acid in the stomach for the treatment of gastric ulcers (NOTE: Antihistamines have names ending in **-tidine: loratidine** for allergies, **cimetidine** for gastric ulcers.)

anti-HIV antibody /ˌænti ˌeɪtʃ aɪ viː 'ænti bɒdi/ *noun* an antibody which attacks HIV

antihypertensive /ˌæntihaɪpə'tensɪv/ *adjective* acting to reduce blood pressure ◼ *noun* a drug used to reduce high blood pressure

anti-inflammatory /ˌænti ɪn'flæmət(ə)ri/ *adjective* referring to a drug which reduces inflammation

antilymphocytic serum /ˌæntilɪmfəʊ'sɪtɪk ˌsɪərəm/ *noun* a serum used to produce immunosuppression in people undergoing transplant operations. Abbr **ALS**

antimalarial /ˌæntimə'leəriəl/ *noun* a drug used to treat malaria and in malarial prophylaxis ◼ *adjective* treating or preventing malaria

antimetabolite /ˌæntimə'tæbəlaɪt/ *noun* a substance which can replace a cell metabolism, but which is not active

antimicrobial /ˌæntimaɪ'krəʊbiəl/ *adjective* acting against microorganisms that cause disease

antimigraine /ˌænti'maɪgreɪn/ *noun* a drug used in the treatment of migraine

antimitotic /ˌæntimaɪ'tɒtɪk/ *adjective* preventing the division of a cell by mitosis

antimuscarinic /ˌæntimʌskə'rɪnɪk/ *adjective* referring to a drug which blocks acetylcholine receptors found on smooth muscle in the gut and eye

antimycotic /ˌæntimaɪ'kɒtɪk/ *adjective* destroying fungi

antinauseant /ˌænti'nɔːziənt/ *adjective* referring to a drug which helps to suppress nausea

antioxidant /ˌænti'ɒksɪd(ə)nt/ *noun* a substance which makes oxygen less damaging, e.g. in the body or in foods or plastics ○ *antioxidant vitamins*

antiperistalsis /ˌæntiperɪ'stælsɪs/ *noun* a movement in the oesophagus or intestine which causes their contents to move in the opposite direction to usual peristalsis, so leading to vomiting

antiperspirant /ˌænti'pɜːspɪ(ə)rənt/ *noun* a substance which prevents sweating ◼ *adjective* preventing sweating

antipruritic /ˌæntiprʊˈrɪtɪk/ *noun* a substance which prevents itching ■ *adjective* preventing itching

antipsychotic /ˌæntɪsaɪˈkɒtɪk/ *noun* a neuroleptic or major tranquilliser drug which calms disturbed people without causing sedation or confusion by blocking dopamine receptors in the brain

COMMENT: Extrapyramidal side-effects can occur from the use of antipsychotics, including Parkinsonian symptoms and restlessness.

antipyretic /ˌæntipaɪˈretɪk/ *noun* a drug which helps to reduce a fever ■ *adjective* reducing fever

anti-Rh body /ˌænti ɑːr ˈeɪtʃ ˌbɒdi/ *noun* an antibody formed in a mother's blood in reaction to a Rhesus antigen in the blood of the fetus

antisepsis /ˌæntɪˈsepsɪs/ *noun* a procedure intended to prevent sepsis

antiseptic /ˌæntɪˈseptɪk/ *adjective* preventing harmful microorganisms from spreading ○ *She gargled with an antiseptic mouthwash.* ■ *noun* a substance which prevents germs growing or spreading ○ *The nurse painted the wound with antiseptic.*

antiserum /ˌæntiˈsɪərəm/ *noun* ♦ **serum** (NOTE: The plural is **antisera**.)

antisocial /ˌæntiˈsəʊʃ(ə)l/ *adjective* referring to behaviour which is harmful to other people

antispasmodic /ˌæntispæzˈmɒdɪk/ *noun* a drug used to prevent spasms

antitetanus serum /ˌænti ˈtetənəs ˌsɪərəm/ *noun* a serum which protects a patient against tetanus. Abbr **ATS**

antithrombin /ˌænti ˈθrɒmbɪn/ *noun* a substance present in the blood which prevents clotting

antitoxic serum /ˌænti ˈtɒksɪk ˌsɪərəm/ *noun* an immunising agent, formed of serum taken from an animal which has developed antibodies to a disease, used to protect a person from that disease

antitoxin /ˌæntiˈtɒksɪn/ *noun* an antibody produced by the body to counteract a poison in the body

antitragus /ˌæntiˈtreɪgəs/ *noun* a small projection on the outer ear opposite the tragus

antituberculous drug /ˌæntitjʊˈbɜːkjʊləs drʌg/ *noun* a drug used to treat tuberculosis, e.g. Isoniazid or rifampicin

antitussive /ˌæntiˈtʌsɪv/ *noun* a drug used to reduce coughing

antivenin /ˌæntiˈvenɪn/, **antivenom** /ˌænti ˈvenəm/, **antivenene** /ˌæntivəˈniːn/ *noun* a substance which helps the body to fight the effects of a particular venom from a snake or insect bite

antiviral /ˌæntiˈvaɪrəl/ *adjective* referring to a drug or treatment which stops or reduces the damage caused by a virus ■ *noun* same as **antiviral drug**

antiviral drug /ˌæntiˈvaɪrəl drʌg/ *noun* a drug which is effective against a virus (NOTE: Antiviral drugs have names ending in **-ciclovir**.)

antra /ˈæntrə/ plural of **antrum**

antral /ˈæntrəl/ *adjective* referring to an antrum

antral puncture /ˌæntrəl ˈpʌŋktʃə/ *noun* making a hole in the wall of the maxillary sinus to remove fluid

antrectomy /ænˈtrektəmi/ *noun* the surgical removal of an antrum in the stomach to prevent gastrin being formed

antroscopy /ænˈtrɒskəpi/ *noun* an examination of an antrum

antrostomy /ænˈtrɒstəmi/ *noun* a surgical operation to make an opening in the maxillary sinus to drain an antrum

antrum /ˈæntrəm/ *noun* any cavity inside the body, especially one in bone (NOTE: The plural is **antra**.)

anuria /ænˈjʊəriə/ *noun* a condition in which the patient does not make urine, either because of a deficiency in the kidneys or because the urinary tract is blocked

anus /ˈeɪnəs/ *noun* a short passage after the rectum at the end of the alimentary canal, leading outside the body between the buttocks and through which faeces are passed. See illustration at **DIGESTIVE SYSTEM** in Supplement, **UROGENITAL SYSTEM (MALE)** in Supplement (NOTE: For other terms referring to the anus, see **anal** and words beginning with **ano-**.)

anvil /ˈænvɪl/ *noun* same as **incus**

anxiety /æŋˈzaɪəti/ *noun* the state of being very worried and afraid

anxiety disorder /æŋˈzaɪəti dɪsˌɔːdə/ *noun* a mental disorder where someone is very worried and afraid, e.g. a phobia

anxiety neurosis /æŋˈzaɪəti njʊˌrəʊsɪs/ *noun* a neurotic condition where the patient is anxious and has morbid fears

anxiolytic /ˌæŋksiəˈlɪtɪk/ *noun* a drug used in the treatment of anxiety ■ *adjective* treating anxiety

anxious /ˈæŋkʃəs/ *adjective* **1.** very worried and afraid ○ *My sister is ill – I am anxious about her.* **2.** eager ○ *She was anxious to get home.* ○ *I was anxious to see the doctor.*

aorta /eɪˈɔːtə/ *noun* the main artery in the body, which sends blood containing oxygen from the heart to other blood vessels around the body. See illustration at **HEART** in Supplement

COMMENT: The aorta is about 45 centimetres long. It leaves the left ventricle, rises where the carotid arteries branch off, then goes downwards through the abdomen and divides into the two iliac arteries. The aorta is the blood vessel which carries all arterial blood from the heart.

aortic /eɪˈɔːtɪk/ *adjective* relating to the aorta

aortic aneurysm /eɪˌɔːtɪk ˈænjəˌrɪz(ə)m/ *noun* a serious aneurysm of the aorta, associated with atherosclerosis

aortic arch /eɪˈɔːtɪk ɑːtʃ/ *noun* a bend in the aorta which links the ascending aorta to the descending aorta

aortic hiatus /eɪˌɔːtɪk haɪˈeɪtəs/ *noun* an opening in the diaphragm through which the aorta passes

aortic incompetence /eɪˌɔːtɪk ˈɪnkɒmpɪt(ə)ns/ *noun* a condition in which the aortic valve does not close properly, causing regurgitation

aortic regurgitation /eɪˌɔːtɪk rɪˌɡɜːˈdʒɪteɪʃ(ə)n/ *noun* a backward flow of blood caused by a malfunctioning aortic valve

aortic sinuses /eɪˌɔːtɪk ˈsaɪnəsɪz/ *plural noun* swellings in the aorta from which the coronary arteries lead back into the heart itself

aortic stenosis /eɪˌɔːtɪk steˈnəʊsɪs/ *noun* a condition in which the aortic valve is narrow, caused by rheumatic fever

aortic valve /eɪˌɔːtɪk ˈvælv/ *noun* a valve with three flaps, situated at the opening into the aorta

aortitis /ˌeɪɔːˈtaɪtɪs/ *noun* inflammation of the aorta

aortography /ˌeɪɔːˈtɒɡrəfi/ *noun* an X-ray examination of the aorta after an opaque substance has been injected into it

a.p. *adverb* before a meal. Full form **ante prandium**

apathetic /ˌæpəˈθetɪk/ *adjective* referring to a person who takes no interest in anything

apathy /ˈæpəθi/ *noun* the condition of not being interested in anything, or of not wanting to do anything

aperient /əˈpɪəriənt/ *noun* a substance which causes a bowel movement, e.g. a laxative or purgative ■ *adjective* causing a bowel movement

aperistalsis /ˌeɪperɪˈstælsɪs/ *noun* a lack of the peristaltic movement in the bowel

Apert's syndrome /ˈæpɜːts ˌsɪndrəʊm/ *noun* a condition in which the skull grows tall and the lower part of the face is underdeveloped

aperture /ˈæpətʃə/ *noun* a hole

apex /ˈeɪpeks/ *noun* **1.** the top of the heart or lung **2.** the end of the root of a tooth

apex beat /ˈeɪpeks biːt/ *noun* a heartbeat which can be felt if the hand is placed on the heart

Apgar score /ˈæpɡɑː skɔː/ *noun* a method of judging the condition of a newborn baby in which the baby is given a maximum of two points on each of five criteria: colour of the skin, heartbeat, breathing, muscle tone and reaction to stimuli [Described 1952. After Virginia Apgar (1909–74), US anaesthesiologist.]

'…in this study, babies having an Apgar score of four or less had 100% mortality. The lower the Apgar score, the poorer the chance of survival' [*Indian Journal of Medical Sciences*]

APH *abbr* antepartum haemorrhage

aphagia /eɪˈfeɪdʒiə/ *noun* a condition in which a person is unable to swallow

aphakia /eɪˈfeɪkiə/ *noun* the absence of the crystalline lens in the eye

aphakic /eɪˈfeɪkɪk/ *adjective* referring to aphakia

aphasia /eɪˈfeɪziə/ *noun* a condition in which a person is unable to speak or write, or to understand speech or writing because of damage to the brain centres controlling speech

apheresis /ˌæfəˈriːsɪs/ *noun* the transfusion of blood, from which some components have been removed, back into a patient

aphonia /eɪˈfəʊniə/ *noun* a condition in which a person is unable to make sounds

aphrodisiac /ˌæfrəˈdɪziæk/ *noun* a substance which increases sexual urges ■ *adjective* increasing sexual desire

aphtha /ˈæfθə/ *noun* a small white ulcer which appears in groups in the mouth in people who have the fungal condition thrush (NOTE: The plural is **apthae**.)

aphthous stomatitis /ˌæfθəs ˌstəʊməˈtaɪtɪs/ *noun* canker sores which affect the mucous membrane in the mouth

aphthous ulcer /ˌæfθəs ˈʌlsə/ *noun* same as **mouth ulcer**

apical /ˈæpɪk(ə)l/ *adjective* situated at the top or tip of something

apical abscess /ˌæpɪk(ə)l ˈæbses/ *noun* an abscess in the socket around the root of a tooth

apicectomy /ˌæpɪˈsektəmi/ *noun* the surgical removal of the root of a tooth

aplasia /eɪˈpleɪziə/ *noun* a lack of growth of tissue

aplastic /eɪˈplæstɪk/ *adjective* unable to develop new cells or tissue

aplastic anaemia /eɪˌplæstɪk əˈniːmiə/ *noun* anaemia caused by the bone marrow failing to form red blood cells

apnea /æpˈniːə/ *noun US* same as **apnoea**

apneusis /æˈpnuːsɪs/ *noun* a breathing pattern caused by brain damage, in which each breath is held for a long time

apnoea /æpˈniːə/ *noun* the stopping of breathing (NOTE: The US spelling is **apnea**.)

apnoeic /æpˈniːɪk/ *adjective* where breathing has stopped (NOTE: The US spelling is **apneic**.)

apocrine /ˈæpəkraɪn/ *adjective* referring to apocrine glands

apocrine gland /ˈæpəkraɪn ɡlænd/ *noun* a gland producing body odour where parts of the gland's cells break off with the secretions, e.g. a sweat gland

apocrinitis /ˌæpəkrɪˈnaɪtɪs/ *noun* the formation of abscesses in the sweat glands

apolipoprotein E /ə,pɒlɪpəprəʊtiːn 'iː/ *noun* a compound found in three varieties which transport lipids within the cell and across cell membranes, the genes for two of which are linked with increased risk of Alzheimer's disease. Abbr **ApoE**

apomorphine /,æpəʊ'mɔːfiːn/ *noun* a substance that comes from morphine, used to make a person cough, sleep or be sick (NOTE: It is administered under the skin and is used to treat drug overdose, accidental poisoning and Parkinson's disease.)

aponeurosis /,æpəʊnjʊ'rəʊsɪs/ *noun* a band of tissue which attaches muscles to each other

apophyseal /æpə'fɪzɪəl/ *adjective* referring to apophysis

apophysis /ə'pɒfəsɪs/ *noun* a growth of bone, not at a joint

apophysitis /æpəfɪ'saɪtɪs/ *noun* inflammation of an apophysis

apoplexy /'æpəpleksi/ *noun* same as **cerebrovascular accident** (*dated*)

apoptosis /ə'pɒptəsɪs/ *noun* a form of cell death that is necessary both to make room for new cells and to remove cells whose DNA has been damaged and which may become cancerous

APP *abbr* amyloid precursor protein

apparatus /,æpə'reɪtəs/ *noun* equipment used in a laboratory or hospital ○ *The hospital has installed new apparatus in the physiotherapy department.* ○ *The blood sample was tested in a special piece of apparatus.* (NOTE: No plural: use *a piece of apparatus*; *some new apparatus*.)

appendage /ə'pendɪdʒ/ *noun* a part of the body or piece of tissue which hangs down from another part

appendectomy /,æpən'dektəmi/ *noun US* same as **appendicectomy**

appendiceal /,æpən'dɪsɪəl/ *adjective* relating to the appendix ○ *There is a risk of appendiceal infection.*

appendiceal colic /,æpəndɪsɪəl 'kɒlɪk/ *noun* colic caused by an inflamed appendix

appendicectomy /ə,pendɪ'sektəmi/ *noun* the surgical removal of an appendix

appendicitis /ə,pendɪ'saɪtɪs/ *noun* inflammation of the vermiform appendix

COMMENT: Appendicitis takes several forms. In **acute appendicitis** there is a sudden attack of severe pain in the right lower part of the abdomen, accompanied by a fever. Acute appendicitis usually requires urgent surgery. In **chronic appendicitis**, the appendix is slightly inflamed, giving a dull pain or a feeling of indigestion over a period of time (a 'grumbling appendix').

appendicular /,æpən'dɪkjʊlə/ *adjective* **1.** referring to body parts which are associated with the arms and legs **2.** relating to the appendix

appendicular skeleton /æpən'dɪkjʊlə ,skelɪt(ə)n/ *noun* part of the skeleton, formed of the pelvic girdle, pectoral girdle and the bones of the arms and legs. Compare **axial skeleton**

appendix /ə'pendɪks/ *noun* **1.** a small tube attached to the caecum which serves no function but can become infected, causing appendicitis. Also called **vermiform appendix**. See illustration at DIGESTIVE SYSTEM in Supplement **2.** any small tube or sac hanging from an organ

apperception /,æpə'sep(ə)n/ *noun* the conscious recognition of a stimulus

appetite /'æpɪtaɪt/ *noun* the feeling of wanting food □ **good appetite** interest in eating food □ **loss of appetite** becoming uninterested in eating food

applanation tonometry /æplə,neɪʃ(ə)n tə 'nɒmətri/ *noun* the measuring of the thickness of the cornea

appliance /ə'plaɪəns/ *noun* a piece of apparatus used on the body ○ *He was wearing a surgical appliance to support his neck.*

application /,æplɪ'keɪʃ(ə)n/ *noun* **1.** the process of putting a medication or bandage on a body part ○ *Two applications of the lotion should be made each day.* **2.** the process of asking officially for something, usually in writing ○ *If you are applying for the job, you must fill in an application form.*

applicator /'æplɪkeɪtə/ *noun* an instrument for applying a substance

appointment /ə'pɔɪntmənt/ *noun* an arrangement to see someone at a particular time ○ *I have an appointment with the doctor* or *to see the doctor on Tuesday.*

apposition /,æpə'zɪʃ(ə)n/ *noun* **1.** the relative positioning of two things **2.** cell growth in which layers of new material are deposited on existing ones

appraisal /ə'preɪz(ə)l/ *noun* a judgment or opinion on something or somebody, especially one which decides how effective or useful they are

apprehension /,æprɪ'henʃən/ *noun* a feeling of anxiety or fear that something bad or unpleasant will happen

approach /ə'prəʊtʃ/ *noun* **1.** a way of dealing with a problem ○ *The authority has adopted a radical approach to the problem of patient waiting lists.* **2.** a method used by a surgeon when carrying out an operation

approve /ə'pruːv/ *verb* □ **to approve of something** to think that something is good ○ *I don't approve of patients staying in bed.* ○ *The Medical Council does not approve of this new treatment.*

apraxia /eɪ'præksɪə/ *noun* a condition in which someone is unable to make proper movements

apyrexia /ˌeɪpaɪ'reksiə/ *noun* the absence of fever

apyrexial /ˌeɪpaɪ'reksiəl/ *adjective* no longer having any fever

aqua /'ækwə/ *noun* water

aqueduct /'ækwɪdʌkt/ *noun* a tube which carries fluid from one part of the body to another

aqueduct of Sylvius /ˌækwɪdʌkt əv 'sɪlviəs/ *noun* same as **cerebral aqueduct**

aqueous /'eɪkwiəs, 'ækwiəs/ *adjective* referring to a solution made with water ■ *noun* a fluid in the eye between the lens and the cornea

aqueous humour /ˌeɪkwiəs 'hjuːmə/ *noun* same as **aqueous**. see illustration at EYE in Supplement

AR *abbr* attributable risk

arachidonic acid /əˌrækɪdɒnɪk 'æsɪd/ *noun* an essential fatty acid

arachnidism /ə'ræknɪdɪz(ə)m/ *noun* poisoning by the bite of a spider

arachnodactyly /əˌræknəʊ'dæktɪli/ *noun* a congenital condition in which the fingers and toes are long and thin

arachnoid /ə'ræknɔɪd/ *noun* the middle of the three membranes covering the brain. ◊ **dura mater**

arachnoiditis /əˌræknɔɪ'daɪtɪs/ *noun* inflammation of the arachnoid

arachnoid mater /ə'ræknɔɪd ˌmeɪtə/, **arachnoid membrane** /ə'ræknɔɪd ˌmembreɪn/ *noun* same as **arachnoid**

arachnoid villi /əˌræknɔɪd 'vɪlaɪ/ *plural noun* villi in the arachnoid which absorb cerebrospinal fluid

arborisation /ˌɑːbəraɪ'zeɪʃ(ə)n/, **arborization** *noun* the branching ends of some nerve fibres, of a motor nerve in muscle fibre or of venules, capillaries and arterioles

arbor vitae /ˌɑːbə 'vaɪtiː/ *noun* the structure of the cerebellum or of the uterus which looks like a tree

arbovirus /'ɑːbəʊˌvaɪrəs/ *noun* a virus transmitted by blood-sucking insects

arc /ɑːk/ *noun* 1. a nerve pathway 2. part of a curved structure in the body

ARC *abbr* AIDS-related complex *or* AIDS-related condition

arc eye /'ɑːk aɪ/ *noun* temporary painful blindness caused by ultraviolet rays, especially in arc welding

arch /ɑːtʃ/ *noun* a curved part of the body, especially under the foot

arch- /ɑːtʃ/ *prefix* chief, most important

arcuate /'ɑːkjuət/ *adjective* arched

arcuate artery /'ɑːkjuət ˌɑːtəri/ *noun* a curved artery in the foot or kidney

arcuate ligaments /'ɑːkjuət ˌɑːtəri/ *plural noun* three ligaments forming a fibrous arch to which the diaphragm is attached

arcus /'ɑːkəs/ *noun* an arch

arcus senilis /ˌɑːkəs sə'naɪlɪs/ *noun* an opaque circle around the cornea of the eye which can develop in old age

ARDS /ɑːdz/ *abbr* adult respiratory distress syndrome

areata /ˌæri'eɪtə/ *noun* ♦ **alopecia areata**

areola /ə'riːələ/ *noun* 1. the coloured part round a nipple 2. in the eye, the part of the iris closest to the pupil

areolar tissue /ə'riːələ ˌtɪʃuː/ *noun* a type of connective tissue

arginine /'ɑːdʒɪniːn/ *noun* an amino acid which helps the liver form urea

argon laser /'ɑːgɒn ˌleɪzə/ *noun* a laser used in sealing blood vessels and destroying specific lesions

Argyll Robertson pupil /ɑːˌgaɪl 'rɒbətsən ˌpjuːp(ə)l/ *noun* a condition of the eye, in which the lens is able to focus but the pupil does not react to light. It is a symptom of tertiary syphilis or of locomotor ataxia.

ariboflavinosis /eɪˌraɪbəʊfleɪvɪ'nəʊsɪs/ *noun* a condition caused by not having enough vitamin B_2. The symptoms are very oily skin and hair and small cuts in the mouth.

arm /ɑːm/ *noun* the part of the body from the shoulder to the hand, formed of the upper arm, the elbow and the forearm ○ *She broke her arm skiing.* ○ *Lift your arms up above your head.* (NOTE: For other terms referring to the arm see words beginning with **brachi-, brachio-**.)

arm bones /'ɑːm bəʊnz/ *plural noun* the humerus, the ulna and the radius

armpit /'ɑːmpɪt/ *noun* the hollow under the shoulder, between the upper arm and the body, where the upper arm joins the shoulder, containing several important blood vessels, lymph nodes and sweat glands. Also called **axilla**

arm sling /'ɑːm slɪŋ/ *noun* a support for an injured arm that prevents it from moving by tying it against the chest

Arnold-Chiari malformation /ˌɑːnəld ki 'eəri mælfɔːˌmeɪʃ(ə)n/ *noun* a congenital condition in which the base of the skull is malformed, allowing part of the cerebellum into the spinal canal [Described 1894. After Julius A. Arnold (1835–1915), Professor of Pathological Anatomy at Heidelberg, Germany, and Hans von Chiari (1851–1916), Professor of Pathological Anatomy at Strasbourg and later at Prague, Czech Republic.]

aromatherapist /əˌrəʊmə'θerəpɪst/ *noun* a person specialising in aromatherapy

aromatherapy /əˌrəʊmə'θerəpi/ *noun* treatment to relieve tension and promote wellbeing in which fragrant oils and creams containing plant extracts are massaged into the skin

arousal /ə'raʊz(ə)l/ *noun* 1. feelings and physical signs of sexual desire 2. the act of waking up from sleep, unconsciousness or a drowsy state

arrector pili /əˌrektə ˈpaɪlaɪ ˌmʌs(ə)l/ *noun* a small muscle which contracts and makes the hair on the skin stand up when someone is cold or afraid

arrest /əˈrest/ *noun* the stopping of a bodily function. ◊ **cardiac arrest**

arrhythmia /əˈrɪðmiə/ *noun* a variation in the rhythm of the heartbeat

'Cardiovascular effects may include atrial arrhythmias but at 30°C there is the possibility of spontaneous ventricular fibrillation' [*British Journal of Nursing*]

arrhythmic /əˈrɪðmɪk/ *adjective* (*of a heartbeat or breathing*) rhythmically irregular. ◊ **antiarrhythmic**

arsenic /ˈɑːsnɪk/ *noun* a chemical element which forms poisonous compounds such as arsenic trioxide and which was formerly used in some medicines (NOTE: The chemical symbol is **As**.)

ART *abbr* assisted reproductive technology

artefact /ˈɑːtɪfækt/ *noun* something which is made or introduced artificially

arter- /ɑːtə/ *prefix* same as **arterio-** (*used before vowels*)

arterial /ɑːˈtɪəriəl/ *adjective* relating to arteries □ **arterial supply to the brain** the supply of blood to the brain by the internal carotid arteries and the vertebral arteries

arterial bleeding /ɑːˌtɪəriəl ˈbliːdɪŋ/ *noun* bleeding from an artery

arterial block /ɑːˈtɪəriəl blɒk/ *noun* the blocking of an artery by a blood clot

arterial blood /ɑːˈtɪəriəl blʌd/ *noun* same as **oxygenated blood**

arterial haemorrhage /ɑːˌtɪəriəl ˈhem(ə)rɪdʒ/ *noun* a haemorrhage of bright red blood from an artery

arteriectomy /ɑːˌtɪəriˈektəmi/ *noun* the surgical removal of an artery or part of an artery

arterio- /ɑːtɪəriəʊ/ *prefix* referring to arteries

arteriogram /ɑːˈtɪəriəʊgræm/ *noun* an X-ray photograph of an artery, taken after injection with an opaque dye

arteriography /ɑːˌtɪəriˈɒgrəfi/ *noun* the work of taking X-ray photographs of arteries after injection with an opaque dye

arteriole /ɑːˈtɪəriəʊl/ *noun* a very small artery

arteriopathy /ɑːˌtɪəriˈɒpəθi/ *noun* a disease of an artery

arterioplasty /ɑːˈtɪəriəʊplæsti/ *noun* plastic surgery to make good a damaged or blocked artery

arteriorrhaphy /ɑːˌtɪəriˈɔːrəfi/ *noun* the act of stitching an artery

arteriosclerosis /ɑːˌtɪəriəʊskləˈrəʊsɪs/ *noun* the arterial disease atherosclerosis (*dated*)

arteriosus /ɑːˌtɪəriˈəʊsəs/ *noun* ♦ **ductus arteriosus**

arteriotomy /ɑːˌtɪəriˈɒtəmi/ *noun* a puncture made in the wall of an artery

arteriovenous /ɑːˌtɪəriəʊˈviːnəs/ *adjective* referring to both an artery and a vein

arteritis /ˌɑːtəˈraɪtɪs/ *noun* inflammation of the walls of an artery

artery /ˈɑːtəri/ *noun* a blood vessel taking blood from the heart to the tissues of the body

COMMENT: In most arteries the blood has been oxygenated in the lungs and is bright red in colour. In the pulmonary artery, the blood is deoxygenated and so is darker. The arterial system begins with the aorta which leaves the heart and from which all the arteries branch.

arthr- /ɑːθr/ *prefix* same as **arthro-** (*used before vowels*)

arthralgia /ɑːˈθrældʒə/ *noun* pain in a joint

arthrectomy /ɑːˈθrektəmi/ *noun* the surgical removal of a joint

arthritic /ɑːˈθrɪtɪk/ *adjective* affected by or relating to arthritis ○ *She has an arthritic hip.* ■ *noun* a person suffering from arthritis

arthritis /ɑːˈθraɪtɪs/ *noun* a painful inflammation of a joint. ◊ **osteoarthritis, rheumatoid arthritis, reactive arthritis**

arthro- /ɑːθrəʊ/ *prefix* referring to a joint

arthroclasia /ˌɑːθrəʊˈkleɪʒə/ *noun* removal of ankylosis in a joint

arthrodesis /ˌɑːθrəʊˈdiːsɪs/ *noun* a surgical operation in which a joint is fused in position, so preventing pain from movement

arthrodynia /ˌɑːθrəʊˈdɪniə/ *noun* pain in a joint

arthrogram /ˈɑːθrəʊgræm/ *noun* an X-ray of the inside of a damaged joint

arthrography /ɑːˈθrɒgrəfi/ *noun* X-ray photography of a joint

arthrogryposis /ˌɑːθrəʊgrɪˈpəʊsɪs/ *noun* a group of disorders in which movement becomes progressively restricted

arthropathy /ɑːˈθrɒpəθi/ *noun* a disease in a joint

arthroplasty /ˈɑːθrəʊplæsti/ *noun* a surgical operation to repair or replace a joint

arthroscope /ˈɑːθrəʊskəʊp/ *noun* an instrument which is inserted into the cavity of a joint to inspect it

arthroscopy /ɑːˈθrɒskəpi/ *noun* a procedure to examine the inside of a joint by means of an arthroscope

arthrosis /ɑːˈθrəʊsɪs/ *noun* the degeneration of a joint

arthrotomy /ɑːˈθrɒtəmi/ *noun* a procedure that involves cutting into a joint to drain pus

articular /ɑːˈtɪkjʊlə/ *adjective* referring to joints

articular cartilage /ɑːˌtɪkjʊlə ˈkɑːtəlɪdʒ/ *noun* a layer of cartilage at the end of a bone where it forms a joint with another bone. See illustration at **BONE STRUCTURE** in Supplement, **SYNOVIAL JOINT** in Supplement

articular facet /ɑː,tɪkjʊlə 'fæsɪt/ *noun* the point at which a rib articulates with the spine

articular process /ɑː,tɪkjʊlə 'prəʊses/ *noun* a piece of bone which sticks out of the neural arch in a vertebra and links with the next vertebra

articulate /ɑː'tɪkjʊleɪt/ *verb* to be linked with another bone in a joint

articulating bone /ɑː'tɪkjʊleɪtɪŋ bəʊn/ *noun* a bone which forms a joint

articulating process /ɑː'tɪkjʊleɪtɪŋ ,prəʊses/ *noun* same as **articular process**

articulation /ɑː,tɪkjʊ'leɪʃ(ə)n/ *noun* a joint or series of joints

artificial /,ɑːtɪ'fɪʃ(ə)l/ *adjective* **1.** made by humans and not a natural part of the body ○ *artificial cartilage* ○ *artificial kidney* ○ *artificial leg* **2.** happening not as a natural process but through action by a doctor or another person or a machine ○ *artificial feeding*

artificial insemination /,ɑːtɪfɪʃ(ə)l ɪn ,semɪ'neɪʃ(ə)n/ *noun* the introduction of semen into a woman's uterus by artificial means

artificial insemination by donor /,ɑːtɪ↓ fɪʃ(ə)l ɪnsemɪ,neɪʃ(ə)n baɪ 'dəʊnə/ *noun* same as **donor insemination**. Abbr **AID**

artificial insemination by husband /,ɑːtɪfɪʃ(ə)l ɪnsemɪ,neɪʃ(ə)n baɪ 'hʌzbənd/ *noun* artificial insemination using the semen of the husband. Abbr **AIH**

artificial lung /,ɑːtɪfɪʃ(ə)l 'lʌŋ/ *noun* a machine through which a person's deoxygenated blood is passed to absorb oxygen to take back to the bloodstream

artificial pneumothorax /,ɑːtɪfɪʃ(ə)l ,njuːməʊ'θɔːræks/ *noun* a former method of treating tuberculosis, in which air was introduced between the layers of the pleura to make the lung collapse

artificial respiration /,ɑːtɪfɪʃ(ə)l ,respɪ'reɪ↓ ɪʃ(ə)n/ *noun* a way of reviving someone who has stopped breathing, e.g. mouth-to-mouth resuscitation

artificial rupture of membranes /,ɑːtɪ fɪʃ(ə)l ,rʌptʃər əv 'membreɪnz/ *noun* the breaking of the amniotic sac with an amni-hook, so releasing the amniotic fluid

artificial ventilation /,ɑːtɪfɪʃ(ə)l ,ventɪ 'leɪʃ(ə)n/ *noun* breathing which is assisted or controlled by a machine

arytenoid /,ærɪ'tiːnɔɪd/ *adjective* located at the back of the larynx

arytenoid cartilage /ærɪ'tiːnɔɪd ,kɑːtɪlɪdʒ/ *noun* a small cartilage at the back of the larynx

arytenoidectomy /,ærɪ,tiːnɔɪd'ektəmi/ *noun* an operation to remove the arytenoid cartilage

asbestosis /,æsbe'stəʊsɪs/ *noun* a disease of the lungs caused by inhaling asbestos dust

COMMENT: Asbestos was formerly widely used in cement and cladding and other types of fire-proof construction materials. It is now recognised that asbestos dust can cause many lung diseases, leading in some cases to forms of cancer.

ascariasis /,æskə'raɪəsɪs/ *noun* a disease of the intestine and sometimes the lungs, caused by infestation with *Ascaris lumbricoides*

Ascaris lumbricoides /,æskərɪs lʌmbrɪ 'kɔɪdiːz/ *noun* a type of large roundworm which is a parasite in the human intestine

ascending /ə'sendɪŋ/ *adjective* going upwards

ascending aorta /ə,sendɪŋ eɪ'ɔːtə/ *noun* the first section of the aorta as it leaves the heart and turns upwards. Compare **descending aorta**

ascending colon /ə,sendɪŋ 'kəʊlɒn/ *noun* the first part of the colon which goes up the right side of the body from the caecum. Compare **descending colon**. See illustration at **DIGESTIVE SYSTEM** in Supplement

Aschoff nodules /'æʃɒf ,nɒdjuːlz/, **Aschoff's nodules** /'æʃɒfs ,nɒdjuːlz/ *plural noun* nodules which are formed mainly in or near the heart in rheumatic fever

ascites /ə'saɪtiːz/ *noun* an unusual accumulation of fluid from the blood in the peritoneal cavity, occurring in heart and kidney failure or as a result of malignancy

ascorbic acid /ə,skɔːbɪk 'æsɪd/ *noun* same as **Vitamin C**

COMMENT: Ascorbic acid is found in fresh fruit, especially oranges and lemons and in vegetables. Lack of Vitamin C can cause anaemia and scurvy.

ASD *abbr* autistic spectrum disorders

-ase /eɪz, eɪs/ *suffix* enzyme

asepsis /eɪ'sepsɪs/ *noun* the absence of microorganisms which cause infection, usually achieved by sterilisation

aseptic /eɪ'septɪk/ *adjective* sterilised, or involving sterilisation, and therefore without infection

aseptic surgery /eɪ,septɪk 'sɜːdʒəri/ *noun* surgery using sterilised equipment, rather than relying on antiseptic drugs to kill harmful microorganisms. Compare **antiseptic**

aseptic technique /eɪ,septɪk tek'niːks/ *noun* a method of doing something using sterilised equipment

asexual /eɪ'sekʃʊəl/ *adjective* not sexual, not involving sexual intercourse

asexual reproduction /eɪ,sekʃʊəl ,riːprə 'dʌkʃ(ə)n/ *noun* reproduction of a cell by cloning

Asian flu /,eɪʒ(ə)n 'fluː/ *noun* ♦ **flu**

-asis /əsɪs/ ♦ **-iasis**

asleep /ə'sliːp/ *adjective* sleeping ○ *The patient is asleep and must not be disturbed.* (NOTE: **Asleep** cannot be used in front of a noun:

the patient is asleep but a sleeping patient.) □
she fell asleep she began to sleep □ fast asleep
sleeping deeply

asparagine /ə'spærədʒiːn/ *noun* an amino
acid

aspartame /ə'spɑːteɪm/ *noun* a protein produced from aspartic acid, used to make substances sweeter

aspartate aminotransferase /ə,spɑːteɪt ə
,miːnəʊ'trænsfəreɪz/ *noun* an enzyme found
in heart muscle, liver cells, skeletal muscle
cells and some other tissues. It is used in the
diagnosis of liver disease and heart attacks.

aspartic acid /ə,spɑːtɪk 'æsɪd/ *noun* an
amino acid

aspect /'æspekt/ *noun* a direction from
which the body is viewed, e.g. the view from
above is the 'superior aspect'

Asperger's syndrome /'æspɜːdʒəz ,sɪn
drəʊm/ *noun* a developmental disorder characterised by difficulty in social interaction and
a restricted range of interests, more common
in boys than girls [Described 1944. After Hans
Asperger (1906–80), Austrian psychiatrist.]

aspergillosis /,æspɜːdʒɪ'ləʊsɪs/ *noun* infection of the lungs with the fungus *Aspergil-
lus*

aspermia /eɪ'spɜːmiə/ *noun* the absence of
sperm in semen

asphyxia /æs'fɪksiə/ *noun* a condition in
which someone is prevented from breathing,
e.g. by strangulation or breathing poisonous
gas, and therefore cannot take oxygen into the
bloodstream

asphyxia neonatorum /æs,fɪksiə ,niːəʊn↓
eɪ'tɔːrəm/ *noun* failure to breathe in a newborn baby

asphyxiate /æs'fɪksieɪt/ *verb* to prevent
someone from breathing, or be prevented from
breathing ○ *An unconscious patient may become asphyxiated or may asphyxiate if left lying on his back.* ◊ **suffocate**

asphyxiation /əs,fɪksi'eɪʃ(ə)n/ *noun* the
state of being prevented from breathing, or the
act of preventing someone from breathing. ◊
suffocation

aspirate /'æspɪreɪt/ *verb* **1.** to remove liquid
or gas by suction from a body cavity **2.** to inhale something, especially a liquid, into the
lungs

aspiration /,æspɪ'reɪʃ(ə)n/ *noun* **1.** the act of
removing fluid from a cavity in the body, often
using a hollow needle **2.** same as **vacuum suction**

aspiration pneumonia /,æspɪreɪʃ(ə)n
njuː'məʊniə/ *noun* a form of pneumonia in
which infected matter is inhaled from the
bronchi or oesophagus

aspirator /'æspɪreɪtə/ *noun* an instrument
used to suck fluid out of a cavity such as the
mouth or the site of an operation

aspirin /'æsprɪn/ *noun* a common pain-killing drug, or a tablet containing this drug. Also
called **acetylsalicylic acid**

assay /'æseɪ, ə'seɪ/ *noun* the testing of a substance. ◊ **bioassay, immunoassay**

assimilate /ə'sɪmɪ,leɪt/ *verb* to take into the
body's tissues substances which have been absorbed into the blood from digested food

assimilation /ə,sɪmɪ'leɪʃ(ə)n/ *noun* the action of assimilating food substances

assistance /ə'sɪst(ə)ns/ *noun* help

assistant /ə'sɪst(ə)nt/ *noun* a person who
helps someone, usually as a job

assisted conception /ə,sɪstɪd kən
'sepʃ(ə)n/, **assisted reproduction** /ə,sɪstɪd
,riːprə'dʌkʃ(ə)n/ *noun* the use of a technique
such as in vitro fertilisation to help someone to
become pregnant

assisted respiration /ə,sɪstɪd ,respə'reɪ↓
ɪʃ(ə)n/ *noun* the use of a machine to help
breathing

assisted suicide /ə,sɪstɪd 'suːɪsaɪd/ *noun*
the suicide of someone who is terminally ill
with the help of a doctor or friend at the re-
quest of the person who is dying

associate /ə'səʊsieɪt/ *verb* to be related to or
connected with something ○ *side effects which
may be associated with the drug* ○ *The condition is often associated with diabetes.*

associate nurse /ə,səʊsiət 'nɜːs/ *noun* a
nurse who assists a primary nurse by carrying
out agreed care for someone based on a plan
designed by a primary nurse

association area /ə,səʊsi'eɪʃ(ə)n ,eəriə/
noun an area of the cortex of the brain which is
concerned with relating stimuli coming from
different sources

association neuron /ə,səʊsi'eɪʃ(ə)n
,njʊərɒn/ *noun* a neuron which links an association area to the main parts of the cortex

association tract /ə,səʊsi'eɪʃ(ə)n trækt/
noun one of the tracts which link areas of the
cortex in the same cerebral hemisphere

asthenia /æs'θiːniə/ *noun* a condition in
which someone is weak and does not have any
strength

asthenic /æs'θenɪk/ *adjective* referring to a
general condition in which someone has no
strength and no interest in things

asthenopia /,æsθɪ'nəʊpiə/ *noun* same as
eyestrain

asthma /'æsmə/ *noun* a lung condition characterised by narrowing of the bronchial tubes,
in which the muscles go into spasm and the
person has difficulty breathing. ◊ **cardiac asthma**

asthmatic /æs'mætɪk/ *adjective* having the
lung disease asthma, or relating to asthma ○
He has an asthmatic attack every spring. □
acute asthmatic attack a sudden attack of
asthma ■ *noun* a person who has asthma

asthmatic bronchitis /æs,mætɪk brɒŋ 'kaɪtɪs/ *noun* asthma associated with bronchitis

asthmaticus /æs'mætɪkəs/ *adjective* ♦ **status asthmaticus**

astigmatic /,æstɪg'mætɪk/ *adjective* referring to astigmatism □ **he is astigmatic** he has astigmatism

astigmatism /ə'stɪgmətɪz(ə)m/ *noun* a condition in which the eye cannot focus vertical and horizontal lines simultaneously, leading to blurring of vision

astragalus /ə'strægələs/ *noun* an old name for the talus (anklebone)

astringent /ə'strɪndʒənt/ *noun* a substance which makes the skin tissues contract and harden ■ *adjective* referring to an astringent

astrocyte /'æstrəsaɪt/ *noun* a star-shaped cell of the connective tissue of the nervous system

astrocytoma /,æstrəsaɪ'təumə/ *noun* a type of brain tumour which develops slowly in the connective tissue of the nervous system

asymmetric /,æsɪ'metrɪk/ *adjective* shaped or arranged so that the two sides do not match or balance each other

asymmetry /æ'sɪmətri/ *noun* a state in which the two sides of the body or of an organ do not resemble each other

asymptomatic /,eɪsɪmptə'mætɪk/ *adjective* not showing any symptoms of disease

asynclitism /æ'sɪŋklɪtɪz(ə)m/ *noun* in childbirth, a situation in which the head of the baby enters the vagina at an angle

asynergia /,æsɪ'nɜːdʒə/, **asynergy** /æ'sɪnədʒi/ *noun* awkward movements and bad coordination, caused by a disorder of the cerebellum. Also called **dyssynergia**

asystole /eɪ'sɪstəli/ *noun* a state in which the heart has stopped beating

ataractic /,ætə'ræktɪk/ *noun* a drug which has a calming effect ■ *adjective* calming

ataraxia /,ætə'ræksiə/, **ataraxis** /,ætə'ræksɪs/ *noun* the state of being calm and not worrying

ataraxic /,ætə'ræksɪk/ *noun, adjective* same as **ataractic**

ataxia /ə'tæksiə/ *noun* a failure of the brain to control movements

ataxic /ə'tæksɪk/ *adjective* having ataxia, or relating to ataxia

ataxic gait /ə,tæksɪk 'geɪt/ *noun* a way of walking in which the person walks unsteadily due to a disorder of the nervous system

ataxy /ə'tæksi/ *noun* same as **ataxia**

atelectasis /,ætə'lektəsɪs/ *noun* the failure of a lung to expand properly

atenolol /ə'tenələl/ *noun* a drug used in controlling blood pressure and angina

ateriovenous malformation /ɑː,tɪəriəu ,viːnəs mælfɔː'meɪʃ(ə)n/ *noun* a condition in which the arteries and veins in the brain are not properly formed, leading to strokes or epilepsy. Abbr **AVM**

atherogenesis /,æθərəu'dʒenɪsɪs/ *noun* the formation of fatty deposits (**atheromas**) in arteries

atherogenic /,æθərəu'dʒenɪk/ *adjective* referring to something which may produce atheroma

atheroma /,æθə'rəumə/ *noun* thickening of the walls of an artery by deposits of a fatty substance such as cholesterol

atheromatous /,æθə'rɒmətəs/ *adjective* referring to atheroma

atherosclerosis /,æθərəusklə'rəusɪs/ *noun* a condition in which deposits of fats and minerals form on the walls of an artery, especially the aorta or one of the coronary or cerebral arteries, and prevent blood from flowing easily

atherosclerotic /,æθərəusklə'rɒtɪk/ *adjective* referring to atherosclerosis

atherosclerotic plaque /,æθərəusklərɒtɪk 'plæk/ *noun* a deposit on the walls of arteries

athetosis /,æθə'təusɪs/ *noun* repeated slow movements of the limbs, caused by a brain disorder such as cerebral palsy

athlete's foot /,æθliːts 'fut/ *noun* an infectious skin disorder between the toes, caused by a fungus. Also called **tinea pedis**

atlas /'ætləs/ *noun* the top vertebra in the spine, which supports the skull and pivots on the axis or second vertebra

atmospheric pressure /,ætməsferɪk 'preʃə/ *noun* the pressure of the air on the surface of the Earth

COMMENT: Disorders due to variations in atmospheric pressure include mountain sickness and caisson diseases.

atomic cocktail /ə,tɒmɪk 'kɒkteɪl/ *noun* a radioactive substance in liquid form, used to diagnose or treat cancer (*informal*)

atomiser /'ætəmaɪzə/ *noun* an instrument which sprays liquid in the form of very small drops like mist. Also called **nebuliser**

atonic /eɪ'tɒnɪk/ *adjective* referring to lack of muscle tone or tension

atony /'ætəni/ *noun* a lack of tone or tension in the muscles

atopen /'ætəpen/ *noun* an allergen which causes an atopy

atopic /eɪ'tɒpɪk/ *adjective* referring to conditions arising from an inherited tendency to react to specific allergens, as in hay fever, some skin conditions and asthma

atopic eczema /eɪ,tɒpɪk 'eksɪmə/, **atopic dermatitis** /eɪ,tɒpɪk dɜːmə'taɪtɪs/ *noun* a type of eczema often caused by a hereditary allergy

atopy /'ætəpi/ *noun* a hereditary allergic reaction

ATP *abbr* adenosine triphosphate

atracurium /ˌætrə'kjʊəriəm/ *noun* a drug used as a relaxant

atresia /ə'triːziə/ *noun* an unusual closing or absence of a tube in the body

atretic /ə'tretɪk/ *adjective* referring to atresia

atretic follicle /əˌtretɪk 'fɒlɪk(ə)l/ *noun* the scarred remains of an ovarian follicle

atri- /eɪtri/ *prefix* referring to an atrium

atria /'eɪtriə/ plural of **atrium**

atrial /'eɪtriəl/ *adjective* referring to one or both of the atria of the heart

atrial fibrillation /ˌeɪtriəl faɪbrɪ'leɪʃ(ə)n/ *noun* a rapid uncoordinated fluttering of the atria of the heart, which causes an irregular heartbeat

atrial septal defect /ˌeɪtriəl 'sept(ə)l ˌdiːfekt/ *noun* a congenital condition in which a hole in the wall between the two atria of the heart allows blood to flow through the heart and lungs. Compare **ventricular septal defect**

atrioventricular /ˌeɪtriəʊven'trɪkjʊlə/ *adjective* referring to the atria and ventricles

atrioventricular bundle /ˌeɪtriəʊven ˌtrɪkjʊlə 'bʌnd(ə)l/ *noun* a bundle of modified cardiac muscle which conducts impulses from the atrioventricular node to the septum and then divides to connect with the ventricles. Also called **AV bundle, bundle of His**

atrioventricular groove /ˌeɪtriəʊven ˌtrɪkjʊlə 'gruːv/ *noun* a groove round the outside of the heart, showing the division between the atria and ventricles

atrioventricular node /ætriəʊven'trɪkjʊlə nəʊd/ *noun* a mass of conducting tissue in the right atrium of the heart, which continues as the atrioventricular bundle and passes impulses from the atria to the ventricles. Also called **AV node**

at-risk /ət 'rɪsk/ *adjective* exposed to danger or harm of some kind ○ *at-risk children*

atrium /'eɪtriəm/ *noun* **1.** one of the two upper chambers in the heart. See illustration at **HEART** in Supplement **2.** a cavity in the ear behind the eardrum (NOTE: The plural is **atria**.)

　　COMMENT: The two atria in the heart both receive blood from veins. The right atrium receives venous blood from the superior and inferior venae cavae and the left atrium receives oxygenated blood from the pulmonary veins.

atrophic cirrhosis /æˌtrɒfɪk sɪ'rəʊsɪs/ *noun* advanced portal cirrhosis in which the liver has become considerably smaller and clumps of new cells are formed on the surface of the liver where fibrous tissue has replaced damaged liver cells. Also called **hobnail liver**

atrophic gastritis /æˌtrɒfɪk gæ'straɪtɪs/ *noun* inflammation of the stomach caused by being unable to produce enough acid to kill bacteria

atrophic vaginitis /æˌtrɒfɪk ˌvædʒɪ'naɪtɪs/ *noun* inflammation, thinning and shrinking of the tissues of the vagina caused by a lack of oestrogen

atrophy /'ætrəfi/ *noun* the wasting of an organ or part of the body ■ *verb* (*of an organ or part of the body*) to waste away

atropine /'ætrəpiːn/ *noun* an alkaloid substance derived from the poisonous plant belladonna and used, among other things, to enlarge the pupil of the eye, to reduce salivary and bronchial secretions during anaesthesia and as a muscarinic antagonist

ATS /ˌeɪ tiː 'es/ *abbr* antitetanus serum

attack /ə'tæk/ *noun* a sudden occurrence of an illness ○ *He had an attack of fever.* ○ *She had two attacks of laryngitis during the winter.*

attempted suicide /əˌtemptɪd 'suːɪsaɪd/ *noun* an unsuccessful attempt to kill oneself

attending physician /əˌtendɪŋ fɪ'zɪʃ(ə)n/ *noun* a doctor who is looking after a particular patient ○ *He was referred to the hypertension unit by his attending physician.*

attention deficit disorder /əˌtenʃən 'defɪsɪt dɪsˌɔːdə/ *noun* a condition in which a person is unable to concentrate, does things without considering their actions properly and has little confidence. It occurs mainly in children. Abbr **ADD**

attention deficit hyperactivity disorder /əˌtenʃən ˌdefɪsɪt ˌhaɪpəræk'tɪvɪti dɪs ˌɔːdə/ *noun* a condition in which a child has an inability to concentrate and shows disruptive behaviour. Abbr **ADHD**

attention deficit syndrome /əˌtenʃən 'defɪsɪt ˌsɪndrəʊm/ *noun* same as **attention deficit disorder**

attenuation /əˌtenjuˈeɪʃ(ə)n/ *noun* a reduction in the effect or strength of something such as a virus, either because of environmental conditions or as a result of a laboratory procedure

atticotomy /ˌætɪ'kɒtəmi/ *noun* the removal of the wall in the inner ear. Also called **cortical mastoidectomy**

attitude /'ætɪtjuːd/ *noun* **1.** an opinion or general feeling about something ○ *a positive attitude towards the operation* **2.** a way of standing or sitting

attributable risk /əˌtrɪbjʊtəb(ə)l 'rɪsk/ *noun* a measure of the excess risk of disease due to exposure to a particular risk. The excess risk of bacteriuria in oral contraceptive users attributable to the use of oral contraceptives is 1,566 per 100,000. Abbr **AR**

attrition /ə'trɪʃ(ə)n/ *noun* the condition of being worn away, as may be caused by friction ○ *Examination showed attrition of two extensor tendons.*

atypical /eɪ'tɪpɪk(ə)l/ *adjective* not usual or expected ○ *an atypical renal cyst*

audi- /ɔːdi/ *prefix* same as **audio-** (*used before vowels*)

audible limits /ˌɔːdəb(ə)l 'lɪmɪts/ *plural noun* upper and lower limits of the sound frequencies which can be heard by humans

audio- /ɔːdiəʊ/ *prefix* referring to hearing or sound

audiogram /'ɔːdiəʊɡræm/ *noun* a graph drawn by an audiometer

audiologist /ˌɔːdi'ɒlədʒɪst/ *noun* a specialist who deals in the treatment of hearing disorders

audiology /ˌɔːdi'ɒlədʒi/ *noun* the scientific study of hearing, especially for diagnosing and treating hearing loss

audiometer /ˌɔːdi'ɒmɪtə/ *noun* an apparatus for testing hearing, especially for testing the range of sounds that the human ear can detect

audiometry /ˌɔːdi'ɒmətri/ *noun* the science of testing hearing

audit /'ɔːdɪt/ *noun* a check on figures, scientific data or procedures ○ *a medical audit regarding the outpatient appointment system*

audit cycle /'ɔːdɪt ˌsaɪk(ə)l/ *noun* the cycle in which medical topics are selected for review, observation and comparison with agreed standards and changes are decided on

auditory /'ɔːdɪt(ə)ri/ *adjective* relating to hearing

auditory acuity /ˌɔːdɪt(ə)ri ə'kjuːɪti/ *noun* the ability to hear sounds clearly

auditory canals /ˌɔːdɪt(ə)ri kə'nælz/ *plural noun* the external and internal passages of the ear

auditory nerve /'ɔːdɪt(ə)ri nɜːv/ *noun* the eighth cranial nerve which governs hearing and balance. See illustration at EAR in Supplement. Also called **vestibulocochlear nerve**

auditory ossicles /ˌɔːdɪt(ə)ri 'ɒsɪk(ə)lz/ *plural noun* the three little bones, the malleus, incus and stapes, in the middle ear

Auerbach's plexus /ˌaʊərbɑːks 'pleksəs/ *noun* a group of nerve fibres in the intestine wall [Described 1862. After Leopold Auerbach (1828–97), Professor of Neuropathology at Breslau, now in Poland.]

aura /'ɔːrə/ *noun* a warning sensation which is experienced before an attack of epilepsy, migraine or asthma

aural /'ɔːrəl/ *adjective* referring to the ear

aural polyp /ˌɔːrəl 'pɒlɪp/ *noun* a polyp in the middle ear

aural surgery /ˌɔːrəl 'sɜːdʒəri/ *noun* surgery on the ear

auricle /'ɔːrɪk(ə)l/ *noun* the tip of each atrium in the heart

auriculae /ɔː'rɪkjʊliː/ ♦ **concha auriculae**

auricular /ɔː'rɪkjʊlə/ *adjective* **1.** referring to the ear **2.** referring to an auricle

auricular vein /ɔː'rɪkjʊlə veɪn/ *noun* a vein which leads into the posterior facial vein

auriscope /'ɔːrɪskəʊp/ *noun* an instrument for examining the ear and eardrum. Also called **otoscope**

auscultation /ˌɔːskəl'teɪʃ(ə)n/ *noun* the act of listening to the sounds of the body using a stethoscope

auscultatory /ɔː'skʌltət(ə)ri/ *adjective* referring to auscultation

Australia antigen /ɒˈstreɪliə ˌæntɪdʒən/ *noun* an antigen produced on the surface of liver cells infected with the hepatitis B virus

autism /'ɔːtɪz(ə)m/ *noun* a condition developing in childhood, characterised by difficulty in social interaction, language and communication problems, learning difficulties and obsessional repetitive behaviour (NOTE: Autism is more common in boys than in girls.)

autistic /ɔː'tɪstɪk/ *adjective* affected by, or relating to, autism

autistic spectrum disorders /ɔːˌtɪstɪk ˌspektrəm dɪs'ɔːdəz/ *plural noun* autism in all its different forms and degrees of severity. Abbr **ASD**

auto- /ɔːtəʊ/ *prefix* self

autoantibody /ˌɔːtəʊ'æntɪbɒdi/ *noun* an antibody formed to attack antigens in the body's own cells

autoclavable /'ɔːtəʊˌkleɪvəb(ə)l/ *adjective* able to be sterilised in an autoclave ○ *Waste should be put into autoclavable plastic bags.*

autoclave /'ɔːtəʊkleɪv/ *noun* equipment for sterilising surgical instruments using heat under high pressure ■ *verb* to sterilise equipment using heat under high pressure ○ *Autoclaving is the best method of sterilisation.*

autogenous /ɔː'tɒdʒənəs/, **autogenic** /ˌɔːtəʊ'dʒenɪk/ *adjective* produced either in the person's body, or using tissue from the person's own body ○ *an autogenous vein graft*

autograft /'ɔːtəɡrɑːft/ *noun* a transplant made using parts of the person's own body

autoimmune /ˌɔːtəʊ'mjuːn/ *adjective* referring to an immune reaction in a person against antigens in their own cells

autoimmune disease /ˌɔːtəʊˌmjuːn dɪ'ziːz/ *noun* a disease in which the person's own cells are attacked by autoantibodies ○ *Rheumatoid arthritis is thought to be an autoimmune disease.*

autoimmunisation /ˌɔːtəʊˌɪmjʊnaɪ'zeɪʃ(ə)n/, **autoimmunization** *noun* the process leading to an immune reaction in a person to antigens produced in their own body

autoimmunity /ˌɔːtəʊ'mjuːnɪti/ *noun* a condition in which a person's own cells are attacked by autoantibodies

autoinfection /ˌɔːtəʊɪn'fekʃ(ə)n/ *noun* an infection by a microorganism already in the body, or infection of one part of the body by another part

autointoxication /ˌɔːtəʊɪntɒksɪˈkeɪʃ(ə)n/ *noun* the poisoning of the body by toxins produced in the body itself

autologous /ɔːˈtɒləgəs/ *adjective* referring to a graft or other material coming from the same source

autologous transfusion /ɔːˌtɒləgəs trænsˈfjuːʒ(ə)n/ *noun* a blood transfusion in which the blood is removed from the body for later transfusion after an operation. ◊ **transfusion**

autolysis /ɔːˈtɒləsɪs/ *noun* a situation in which cells destroy themselves with their own enzymes

automatic /ˌɔːtəˈmætɪk/ *adjective* **1.** done without conscious thought ○ *an automatic reaction* **2.** (*of a machine or process*) able to work by itself, without anyone giving instructions

automatism /ɔːˈtɒmətɪz(ə)m/ *noun* a state in which a person acts without consciously knowing that he or she is acting

COMMENT: Automatic acts can take place after concussion or epileptic fits. In law, automatism can be a defence to a criminal charge when the accused states that he or she acted without knowing what they were doing.

autonomic /ˌɔːtəˈnɒmɪk/ *adjective* governing itself independently

autonomic nervous system /ɔːtəˌnɒmɪk ˈnɜːvəs ˌsɪstəm/ *noun* the nervous system formed of ganglia linked to the spinal column. It regulates the automatic functioning of the main organs such as the heart and lungs and works when a person is asleep or even unconscious. ◊ **parasympathetic nervous system, sympathetic nervous system**

autonomy /ɔːˈtɒnəmi/ *noun* the state of being free to act as one wishes

autoplasty /ˈɔːtəʊplæsti/ *noun* the repair of someone's body using tissue taken from another part of their body

autopsy /ˈɔːtɒpsi/ *noun* the examination of a dead body by a pathologist to find out the cause of death ○ *The autopsy showed that he had been poisoned.* Also called **post mortem**

autosomal /ˌɔːtəʊˈsəʊm(ə)l/ *adjective* referring to an autosome

autosome /ˈɔːtəʊsəʊm/ *noun* a chromosome that is not a sex chromosome

autotransfusion /ˌɔːtəʊtrænsˈfjuːʒ(ə)n/ *noun* an infusion into a person of their own blood

auxiliary /ɔːgˈzɪliəri/ *adjective* providing help ○ *The hospital has an auxiliary power supply in case the electricity supply breaks down.* ■ *noun* an assistant

avascular /eɪˈvæskjʊlə/ *adjective* with no blood vessels, or with a deficient blood supply

avascular necrosis /əˌvæskjʊlə ne ˈkrəʊsɪs/ *noun* a condition in which tissue cells die because their supply of blood has been cut

AV bundle /ˌeɪ ˈviː ˈbʌnd(ə)l/ *noun* same as **atrioventricular bundle**

average /ˈæv(ə)rɪdʒ/ *noun* **1.** the usual amount, size, rate, etc. ○ *Her weight is above (the) average.* **2.** a value calculated by adding together several quantities and then dividing the total by the number of quantities ■ *adjective* **1.** usual ○ *Their son is of above average weight.* **2.** calculated by adding together several quantities and then dividing the total by the number of quantities ○ *The average age of the group is 25.*

aversion therapy /əˈvɜːʃ(ə)n ˌθerəpi/ *noun* a treatment by which someone is cured of a type of behaviour by making him or her develop a great dislike for it

avitaminosis /eɪˌvɪtəmɪˈnəʊsɪs/ *noun* a disorder caused by a lack of vitamins

AVM *abbr* arteriovenous malformation

AV node /ˌeɪ ˈviː nəʊd/ *noun* same as **atrioventricular node**

AVPU *noun* a method of rating if a person is conscious: A = alert; V = verbal, responding to verbal commands; P = pain, responding to pain; U = unconscious

avulse /əˈvʌls/ *verb* to tear tissue or a body part away by force

avulsion /əˈvʌlʃən/ *noun* an act of pulling away tissue or a body part by force

avulsion fracture /əˌvʌlʃ(ə)n ˈfræktʃə/ *noun* a fracture in which a tendon pulls away part of the bone to which it is attached

awake /əˈweɪk/ *adjective* not asleep ○ *He was still awake at 2 o'clock in the morning.* □ **wide awake** very awake

aware /əˈweə/ *adjective* **1.** conscious enough to know what is happening ○ *She is not aware of what is happening around her.* **2.** knowing about something ○ *The surgeon became aware of a problem with the heart-lung machine.*

awareness /əˈweənəs/ *noun* the fact of being aware, especially of a problem

'…doctors should use the increased public awareness of whooping cough during epidemics to encourage parents to vaccinate children' [*Health Visitor*]

axial /ˈæksiəl/ *adjective* referring to an axis

axial skeleton /ˌæksiəl ˈskelɪt(ə)n/ *noun* the bones that make up the vertebral column and the skull. Compare **appendicular skeleton**

axilla /ækˈsɪlə/ *noun* same as **armpit** (*technical*) (NOTE: The plural is **axillae**.)

axillary /ækˈsɪləri/ *adjective* referring to the armpit

axillary artery /ækˌsɪləri ˈɑːtəri/ *noun* an artery leading from the subclavian artery in the armpit

axillary nodes /ækˈsɪləri nəʊdz/ *plural noun* part of the lymphatic system in the arm

axillary temperature /ækˌsɪləri ˌtemprɪ ˈtʃə/ *noun* the temperature in the armpit

axis /'æksɪs/ *noun* **1.** an imaginary line through the centre of the body **2.** a central vessel which divides into other vessels **3.** the second vertebra on which the atlas sits (NOTE: The plural is **axes**.)

axodendrite /ˌæksəʊ'dendraɪt/ *noun* an appendage like a fibril on the axon of a nerve

axolemma /ˌæksə'lemə/ *noun* a membrane covering an axon

axon /'æksɒn/ *noun* a nerve fibre which sends impulses from one neurone to another, linking with the dendrites of the other neurone. See illustration at NEURONE in Supplement

axon covering /'æksɒn ˌkʌv(ə)rɪŋ/ *noun* the myelin sheath which covers a nerve

Ayurvedic medicine /ˌaɪəveɪdɪk 'med(ə)s(ə)n/ *noun* a traditional Hindu system of healing that reviews a person's state of health and lifestyle and recommends treatment based on herbal products, dietary control and spiritual practices

azathioprine /ˌeɪzə'θaɪəpriːn/ *noun* a drug which suppresses the immune response, used after transplant surgery to prevent rejection

-azepam /æzɪpæm/ *suffix* used in names of benzodiazepines ○ *diazepam*

azidothymidine /ˌeɪzɪdəʊ'θaɪmɪdiːn/ *noun* a drug used in the treatment of AIDS. Abbr **AZT**. Also called **zidovudine**

azo- /eɪzəʊ/ *prefix* containing a nitrogen group

azoospermia /ˌeɪzəʊə'spɜːmiə/ *noun* the absence of sperm

azotaemia /ˌeɪzəʊ'tiːmiə/ *noun* the presence of urea or other nitrogen compounds in the blood

azoturia /ˌeɪzəʊ'tjʊəriə/ *noun* the presence of urea or other nitrogen compounds in the urine, caused by kidney disease

AZT *abbr* azidothymidine

azygous /'æzɪgəs/ *adjective* single, not one of a pair

azygous vein /'æzɪgəs veɪn/ *noun* a vein which brings blood back into the vena cava from the abdomen

B

babesiosis /bəˌbiːziˈəʊsɪs/ *noun* a disease caused by infection of red blood cells by a protozoan introduced by a tick bite

Babinski reflex /bəˌbɪnski ˈriːfleks/, **Babinski's reflex** /bəˌbɪnskiz ˈriːfleks/ *noun* an unusual curling upwards of the big toe when a finger is lightly run across the sole of the foot, while the others turn down and spread out, a sign of hemiplegia and pyramidal tract disease. Compare **plantar reflex** [Described 1896. After Joseph François Felix Babinski (1857–1932), French-born son of Polish refugees. A pupil of Charcot, he was head of the Neurological clinic at Hôpital de la Pitié, 1890–1927.]

Babinski test /bəˈbɪnski test/ *noun* a test for a Babinski reflex

baby /ˈbeɪbi/ *noun* a very young child who is not yet old enough to talk or walk ○ *Babies start to walk when they are about 12 months old.* (NOTE: If you do not know the sex of a baby you can refer to the child as **it**: *The baby was sucking its thumb*)

baby blues /ˈbeɪbi bluːz/ *plural noun* same as **postnatal depression** (*informal*)

baby care /ˈbeɪbi keə/ *noun* the act of looking after babies

baby clinic /ˈbeɪbi ˌklɪnɪk/ *noun* a special clinic which deals with babies

bacillaemia /ˌbæsɪˈliːmiə/ *noun* an infection of the blood by bacilli

bacillary /bəˈsɪləri/ *adjective* referring to bacilli

bacillary dysentery /bəˌsɪləri ˈdɪs(ə)ntri/ *noun* dysentery caused by the bacillus *Shigella* in contaminated food

bacille Calmette-Guérin /bæˌsiːl ˌkælmet ˈgæræn/ *noun* full form of **BCG** [After A. Calmette (1863–1933) and C. Guérin (1872–1961), French bacteriologists.]

bacilluria /ˌbæsɪˈljʊəriə/ *noun* the presence of bacilli in the urine

bacillus /bəˈsɪləs/ *noun* a bacterium shaped like a rod (NOTE: The plural is **bacilli**.)

back /bæk/ *noun* **1.** the part of the body from the neck downwards to the waist, which is made up of the spine and the bones attached to it (NOTE: For other terms referring to the back, see **dorsal** and words beginning with **dorsi-**, **dorso-**.) **2.** the other side from the front ○ *She has a swelling on the back of her hand.* ◊ **dorsum**

backache /ˈbækeɪk/ *noun* pain in the back, often without a specific cause

COMMENT: Backache can result from bad posture or muscle strain, but it can also be caused by rheumatism (lumbago), fevers such as typhoid fever and osteoarthritis. Pains in the back can also be referred pains from gallstones or kidney disease.

backbone /ˈbækbəʊn/ *noun* a series of bones, the vertebrae, linked together to form a flexible column running from the pelvis to the skull. Also called **rachis, spine**

background carboxyhaemoglobin level /ˌbækgraʊnd kɑːˌbɒksi hiːməˈgləʊbɪn ˌlev(ə)l/ *noun* the level of carboxyhaemoglobin in the blood of a person who is not exposed to high levels of carbon monoxide

back muscles /ˈbæk ˌmʌs(ə)lz/ *plural noun* the strong muscles in the back which help hold the body upright

back pain /ˈbæk peɪn/ *noun* pain in the back, especially long-lasting or severe pain

backside /ˈbæksaɪd/ *noun* someone's buttocks (*informal*)

back strain /ˈbæk streɪn/ *noun* a condition in which the muscles or ligaments in the back have been strained

baclofen /ˈbækləʊfen/ *noun* a drug that relaxes skeletal muscles which are in spasm, either because of injury or as a result of multiple sclerosis

bacteraemia /ˌbæktəˈriːmiə/ *noun* the fact of having bacteria in the blood. Bacteraemia is not necessarily a serious condition. Compare **septicaemia**. ◊ **blood poisoning**

bacteria /bækˈtɪəriə/ *plural of* **bacterium**

bacterial /bækˈtɪəriəl/ *adjective* relating to bacteria or caused by bacteria ○ *Children with sickle-cell anaemia are susceptible to bacterial infection.*

bacterial plaque /bækˈtɪəriəl ˌplæk/ *noun* a hard smooth bacterial deposit on teeth

bacterial pneumonia /bæk,tɪərɪəl njuː'məʊnɪə/ noun a form of pneumonia caused by pneumococcus. ◊ **bronchopneumonia**

bacterial strain /bæk,tɪərɪəl 'streɪn/ noun a group of bacteria which are different from others of the same general type

bactericidal /bæktɪərɪ'saɪd(ə)l/ adjective referring to a substance which destroys bacteria

bactericide /bæk'tɪərɪsaɪd/ noun a substance which destroys bacteria

bacteriological /bæktɪərɪə'lɒdʒɪk(ə)l/ adjective referring to bacteriology

bacteriologist /bæk,tɪəri'ɒlədʒɪst/ noun a doctor who specialises in the study of bacteria

bacteriology /bæk,tɪəri'ɒlədʒi/ noun the scientific study of bacteria

bacteriolysin /bæk,tɪəri'ɒlɪsɪn/ noun a protein, usually an immunoglobulin, which destroys bacterial cells

bacteriolysis /bæk,tɪəri'ɒlɪsɪs/ noun the destruction of bacterial cells

bacteriolytic /bæk,tɪərɪə'lɪtɪk/ adjective referring to a substance which can destroy bacteria

bacteriophage /bæk'tɪərɪəfeɪdʒ/ noun a virus which affects bacteria

bacteriostasis /bæk,tɪəriəʊ'steɪsɪs/ noun the action of stopping bacteria from multiplying

bacteriostatic /bæk,tɪəriəʊ'stætɪk/ adjective referring to a substance which does not kill bacteria but stops them from multiplying

bacterium /bæk'tɪərɪəm/ noun a microscopic organism. Some types are permanently present in the gut and can break down food tissue, but many can cause disease. (NOTE: The plural is **bacteria**.)

COMMENT: Bacteria can be shaped like rods (bacilli), like balls (cocci) or have a spiral form (spirochaetes). Bacteria, especially bacilli and spirochaetes, can move and reproduce very rapidly.

bacteriuria /bæk,tɪəri'jʊərɪə/ noun a condition in which bacteria are present in the urine

Bactrim /'bæktrɪm/ a trade name for co-trimoxazole

bad breath /bæd 'breθ/ noun same as **halitosis** (informal)

Baghdad boil /bægdæd 'bɔɪl/, **Baghdad sore** /bægdæd 'sɔː/ noun a skin disease of tropical countries caused by the parasite Leishmania. Also called **Oriental sore**

bag of waters /bæg əv 'wɔːtəz/ noun part of the amnion which covers an unborn baby in the uterus and contains the amniotic fluid

BAHA abbr bone anchored hearing aid

Baker's cyst /beɪkəz 'sɪst/ noun a swelling filled with synovial fluid, at the back of the knee, caused by weakness of the joint membrane [Described 1877. After William Morrant Baker (1838–96), member of staff at St Bartholomew's Hospital, London, UK.]

baker's itch /beɪkəz 'ɪtʃ/, **baker's dermatitis** /'beɪkəz dɜːmə'taɪtɪs/ noun an irritation of the skin caused by handling yeast

BAL abbr British anti-lewisite

balance /'bæləns/ noun **1.** the act of staying upright, not falling □ **he stood on top of the fence and kept his balance** he did not fall off **2.** the proportions of substances in a mixture, e.g. in the diet ○ to maintain a healthy balance of vitamins in the diet

balanced diet /bælənst 'daɪət/ noun a diet which provides all the nutrients needed in the correct proportions

balance of mind /bæləns əv 'maɪnd/ noun someone's mental state □ **disturbed balance of mind** a state of mind when someone is for a time incapable of reasoned action, because of illness or depression

balanitis /bælə'naɪtɪs/ noun inflammation of the glans of the penis

balanoposthitis /bælənəʊpɒs'θaɪtɪs/ noun inflammation of the foreskin and the end of the penis

balantidiasis /bæləntɪ'daɪəsɪs/ noun an infestation of the large intestine by a parasite Balantidium coli, which causes ulceration of the wall of the intestine, leading to diarrhoea and finally dysentery

balanus /'bælənəs/ noun the round end of the penis. ◊ **glans**

bald /bɔːld/ adjective with no hair, especially on the head □ **he is going bald** or **he is becoming bald** he is beginning to lose his hair

baldness /'bɔːldnəs/ noun the state of not having any hair

COMMENT: Baldness in men is hereditary; it can also occur in both men and women as a reaction to an illness or to a drug.

Balkan frame /bɔːlkən 'freɪm/, **Balkan beam** /bɔːlkən 'biːm/ noun a frame fitted above a bed to which a leg in plaster can be attached. ◊ **Pearson bed**

ball /bɔːl/ noun **1.** the soft part of the hand below the thumb **2.** the soft part of the foot below the big toe

ball and cage valve /bɔːl ən 'keɪdʒ vælv/ noun an artificial heart valve, formed of a silicon ball which moves inside a metal cage to open and shut the valve

ball and socket joint /bɔːl ənd 'sɒkɪt dʒɔɪnt/ noun a joint where the round end of a long bone is attached to a cup-shaped hollow in another bone in such a way that the long bone can move in almost any direction. Compare **ginglymus**

balloon /bə'luːn/ noun a bag of light material inflated with air or a gas, used to unblock arteries

balloon angioplasty /bə,luːn ˌændʒiə'plæsti/ *noun* same as **percutaneous angioplasty**

balloon catheter /bə'luːn ˌkæθɪtə/ *noun* a tube that can be inserted into a blood vessel or other body part and then inflated, e.g. to widen a narrow artery

ballottement /bə'lɒtmənt/ *noun* a method of examining the body by tapping or moving a part, especially during pregnancy

balneotherapy /ˌbælniəʊ'θerəpi/ *noun* the treatment of diseases by bathing in hot water or water containing beneficial natural chemicals

balsam /'bɔːls(ə)m/ *noun* a mixture of resin and oil, used to rub on sore joints or to put in hot water and use as an inhalant. ◊ **friar's balsam**

ban /bæn/ *verb* to say that something is not permitted ○ *Smoking is banned throughout the building.* ○ *Use of this drug has been banned.*

bandage /'bændɪdʒ/ *noun* a piece of cloth which is wrapped around a wound or an injured limb ○ *His head was covered with bandages.* ■ *verb* to wrap a piece of cloth around a wound ○ *She bandaged his leg.* ○ *His arm is bandaged up.*

Bandl's ring /'bænd(ə)lz rɪŋ/ same as **retraction ring** [After Ludwig Bandl (1842–92), German obstetrician]

bank /bæŋk/ *noun* a place where blood or organs from donors can be stored until needed. ◊ **blood bank**

Bankart's operation /'bæŋkɑːts ɒpəˌreɪʃ(ə)n/ *noun* an operation to repair a recurrent dislocation of the shoulder [First performed 1923. After Arthur Sydney Blundell Bankart (1879–1951), first orthopaedic surgeon at the Middlesex Hospital, London, UK.]

Banti's syndrome /'bæntiz ˌsɪndrəʊm/, **Banti's disease** /'bæntiz dɪˌziːz/ *noun* same as **splenic anaemia** [Described 1882. After Guido Banti (1852–1925), Florentine pathologist and physician.]

Barbados leg /bɑːˌbeɪdɒs 'leg/ *noun* a form of elephantiasis, a large swelling of the leg due to a Filaria worm

barber's itch /ˌbɑːbəz 'ɪtʃ/, **barber's rash** /ˌbɑːbəz 'ræʃ/ *noun* same as **sycosis barbae**

barbital /'bɑːbɪtəl/ *noun US* same as **barbitone**

barbitone /'bɑːbitəʊn/ *noun* a type of barbiturate

barbiturate /bɑː'bɪtʃʊrət/ *noun* a sedative drug

barbiturate abuse /bɑː'bɪtʃʊrət əˌbjuːs/ *noun* repeated addictive use of barbiturates which in the end affects the brain

barbiturate dependence /bɑː'bɪtʃʊrət dɪˌpendəns/ *noun* being dependent on regularly taking barbiturate tablets

barbiturate poisoning /bɑː'bɪtʃʊrət ˌpɔɪz(ə)nɪŋ/ *noun* poisoning caused by an overdose of barbiturates

barbotage /ˌbɑːbə'tɑːʒ/ *noun* a method of spinal analgesia by which cerebrospinal fluid is withdrawn and then injected back

bare /beə/ *adjective* with no covering □ **bare area of the liver** a large triangular part of the liver not covered with peritoneum

bariatrics /ˌbæri'ætrɪks/ *noun* the medical treatment of obesity

barium /'beəriəm/ *noun* a chemical element, forming poisonous compounds, used as a contrast medium when taking X-ray photographs of soft tissue (NOTE: The chemical symbol is **Ba**.)

barium enema /ˌbeəriəm 'enɪmə/ *noun* a liquid solution containing barium sulphate which is put into the rectum to increase the contrast of an X-ray of the lower intestine

barium meal /ˌbeəriəm 'miːl/, **barium solution** /ˌbeəriəm sə'luːʃ(ə)n/ *noun* a liquid solution containing barium sulphate which someone drinks to increase the contrast of an X-ray of the alimentary tract

barium sulphate /ˌbeəriəm 'sʌlfeɪt/ *noun* a salt of barium not soluble in water and which shows as opaque in X-ray photographs

Barlow's disease /'bɑːləʊz dɪˌziːz/ *noun* scurvy in children, caused by a lack of vitamin C [Described 1882. After Sir Thomas Barlow (1845–1945), physician at various London hospitals and to Queen Victoria, King Edward VII and King George V.]

Barlow's sign /'bɑːləʊz saɪn/ *noun* a test for congenital dislocation of the hip, in which a sudden movement is felt and sometimes a sound is heard when the joint is manipulated

baroreceptor /ˌbærəʊrɪ'septə/ *noun* one of a group of nerves near the carotid artery and aortic arch, which senses changes in blood pressure

barotitis /ˌbærəʊ'taɪtɪs/ *noun* pain in the ear caused by differences in air pressure, e.g. during air travel

barotrauma /ˌbærəʊ'trɔːmə/ *noun* an injury caused by a sharp increase in pressure

Barr body /'bɑː ˌbɒdi/ *noun* a dense clump of chromatin found only in female cells, which can be used to identify the sex of a baby before birth [Described 1949. After Murray Llewellyn Barr (1908–95), head of the Department of Anatomy at the University of Western Ontario, Canada.]

Barre-Guillain syndrome /ˌbæreɪ 'giː jæn ˌsɪndrəʊm/ *noun* ♦ **Guillain-Barré syndrome**

barrel chest /ˌbærəl 'tʃest/ *noun* a chest formed like a barrel, caused by asthma or emphysema

barrier cream /'bæriə kriːm/ *noun* a cream put on the skin to prevent the skin coming into contact with irritating substances

barrier method /'bæriə ˌmeθəd/ *noun* a method of contraception in which the entry of sperm to the womb is blocked by a protective device such as a condom or diaphragm

barrier nursing /'bæriə ˌnɜːsɪŋ/ *noun* the nursing of someone who has an infectious disease. It involves keeping them away from other patients and making sure that faeces and soiled bedclothes do not carry the infection to other patients.

'…those affected by salmonella poisoning are being nursed in five isolation wards and about forty suspected sufferers are being barrier nursed in other wards' [*Nursing Times*]

bartholinitis /ˌbɑːθəlɪ'naɪtɪs/ *noun* inflammation of the Bartholin's glands

Bartholin's glands /'bɑːθəlɪnz glændz/ *plural noun* two glands at the side of the vagina and between it and the vulva, which secrete a lubricating substance. Also called **greater vestibular glands** [After Caspar Bartholin (1655–1748), Danish anatomist]

basal /'beɪs(ə)l/ *adjective* located at the bottom of something, or forming its base

basal cell /'beɪs(ə)l sel/ *noun* a cell from the stratum germinativum. ◊ **stratum**

basal cell carcinoma /ˌbeɪs(ə)l ˌsel ˌkɑːsɪ'nəʊmə/ *noun* same as **rodent ulcer**

basale /bə'seɪli/ *adjective* ◆ **stratum**

basal ganglia /ˌbeɪs(ə)l 'gæŋgliə/ *noun* masses of grey matter at the base of each cerebral hemisphere which receive impulses from the thalamus and influence the motor impulses from the frontal cortex

basalis /bə'seɪlɪs/ ◆ **decidua**

basal metabolic rate /ˌbeɪsɪk metə'bɒlɪk reɪt/ *noun* the amount of energy used by the body in exchanging oxygen and carbon dioxide when at rest. It was formerly used as a way of testing thyroid gland activity. Abbr **BMR**

basal metabolism /ˌbeɪs(ə)l mə'tæbə ˌlɪz(ə)m/ *noun* the minimum amount of energy needed to keep the body functioning and the temperature standard when at rest

basal narcosis /ˌbeɪs(ə)l nɑː'kəʊsɪs/ *noun* the administration a narcotic before a general anaesthetic

basal nuclei /ˌbeɪs(ə)l 'nuːkliaɪ/ *plural noun* masses of grey matter at the bottom of each cerebral hemisphere

base /beɪs/ *noun* **1.** the bottom part ○ *the base of the spine* □ **base of the brain** the bottom surface of the cerebrum **2.** the main ingredient of an ointment, as opposed to the active ingredient **3.** a substance which reacts with an acid to form a salt ■ *verb* to use something as a base □ **cream based on zinc oxide** cream which uses zinc oxide as a base

Basedow's disease /'bæzɪdəʊz dɪˌziːz/ *noun* a form of hyperthyroidism [Described 1840. After Carl Adolph Basedow (1799–1854), general practitioner in Mersburg, Germany.]

basement membrane /'beɪsmənt ˌmem breɪn/ *noun* a membrane at the base of an epithelium

basic /'beɪsɪk/ *adjective* **1.** very simple, from which everything else comes □ **basic structure of the skin** the two layers of skin, the inner dermis and the outer epidermis **2.** referring to a chemical substance which reacts with an acid to form a salt

basic salt /ˌbeɪsɪk 'sɔːlt/ *noun* a chemical compound formed when an acid reacts with a base

basilar /'bæzɪlə/ *adjective* referring to a base

basilar artery /ˌbæzɪlə 'ɑːtəri/ *noun* an artery which lies at the base of the brain

basilar membrane /ˌbæzɪlə 'membreɪn/ *noun* a membrane in the cochlea which transmits nerve impulses from sound vibrations to the auditory nerve

basilic /bə'sɪlɪk/ *adjective* important or prominent

basilic vein /bəˌzɪlɪk 'veɪn/ *noun* a large vein running along the inside of the arm

basin /'beɪs(ə)n/ *noun* a large bowl

basophil /'beɪsəfɪl/ *noun* a type of white blood cell which has granules in its cytoplasm and contains histamine and heparin

basophilia /ˌbeɪsə'fɪliə/ *noun* an increase in the number of basophils in the blood

basophilic granulocyte /ˌbeɪsəfɪlɪk 'grænjʊləsaɪt/ *noun* same as **basophil**

basophilic leucocyte /ˌbeɪsəfɪlɪk 'luːkəsaɪt/ *noun* same as **basophil**

Batchelor plaster /'bætʃələ ˌplɑːstə/ *noun* a plaster cast which keeps both legs apart [After J.S. Bachelor (b. 1905), British orthopaedic surgeon]

bathe /beɪð/ *verb* to wash a wound ○ *He bathed the grazed knee with boiled water.*

Batten's disease /'bæt(ə)nz dɪˌziːz/ *noun* a hereditary disease which affects the enzymes of the brain, causing cells in the brain and eye to die

battered baby syndrome /'bætəd ˌbeɪbi ˌsɪndrəʊm/, **battered child syndrome** /'bætəd 'tʃaɪld 'sɪndrəʊm/ *noun* a condition in which a baby or small child is frequently beaten, usually by one or both of its parents, sustaining injuries such as multiple fractures

battledore placenta /'bæt(ə)ldɔː pləˌsentə/ *noun* a placenta where the umbilical cord is attached at the edge and not at the centre

Bazin's disease /'beɪzɪnz dɪˌziːz/ *noun* same as **erythema induratum** [Described 1861. After Pierre Antoine Ernest Bazin (1807–78), dermatologist at Hôpital St Louis, Paris, France.]

He was an expert in parasitology associated with skin conditions.]

BC *abbr* bone conduction. ♦ **osteophony**

BCC *abbr* Breast Cancer Campaign

B cell /'biː sel/ *noun* same as **beta cell**

BCG /ˌbiː siː 'dʒiː ˌvæksiːn/, **BCG vaccine** *noun* a vaccine which immunises against tuberculosis. Full form **bacille Calmette-Guérin**

BCh *abbr* Bachelor of Surgery

BDA *abbr* British Dental Association

bearing down /ˌbeərɪŋ 'daʊn/ *noun* a stage in childbirth when the woman starts to push out the baby from the uterus

bearing-down pain /ˌbeərɪŋ 'daʊn peɪn/ *noun* pain felt in the uterus during the second stage of labour (NOTE: Bearing-down pain is also associated with uterine prolapse.)

beat joint /'biːt dʒɔɪnt/ *noun* an inflammation of a joint such as the elbow (beat elbow) or knee (beat knee) caused by frequent sharp blows or other pressure

Beck inventory of depression /ˌbek ˌɪnvənt(ə)ri əv dɪ'preʃ(ə)n/ *noun* one of the rating scales for depression, in which a series of 21 questions refers to attitudes frequently shown by people suffering from depression

beclomethasone /ˌbeklə'meθəsəʊn/ *noun* a steroid drug usually used in an inhaler to treat asthma or hay fever

becquerel /'bekərel/ *noun* an SI unit of measurement of radiation. Abbr **Bq** (NOTE: Now used in place of the **curie**.)

bed bath /'bed bɑːθ/ *noun* an act of washing the whole body of someone who is unable to get up to wash. Also called **blanket bath**

bed blocker /'bed ˌblɒkə/ *noun* a patient who does not need medical attention but continues to stay in hospital because suitable care is not available elsewhere

bed blocking /'bed ˌblɒkɪŋ/ *noun* the fact of people being kept in hospital because other forms of care are not available, which means that other people cannot be treated

bedbug /'bedbʌg/ *noun* a small insect which lives in dirty bedclothes and sucks blood

bed occupancy /'bed ˌɒkjʊpənsi/ *noun* the percentage of beds in a hospital which are occupied

bed occupancy rate /bed 'ɒkjʊpənsi ˌreɪt/ *noun* the number of beds occupied in a hospital shown as a percentage of all the beds in the hospital

bedpan /'bedpæn/ *noun* a dish into which someone can urinate or defecate without getting out of bed

bed rest /'bed rest/ *noun* a period of time spent in bed in order to rest and recover from an illness

bedridden /'bed.rɪd(ə)n/ *adjective* referring to someone who has been too ill to get out of bed over a long period of time

bedside manner /ˌbedsaɪd 'mænə/ *noun* the way in which a doctor behaves towards a patient, especially a patient who is in bed □ **a good bedside manner** the ability to make patients feel comforted and reassured

bedsore /'bedsɔː/ *noun* an inflamed patch of skin on a bony part of the body, which develops into an ulcer, caused by pressure of the part on the mattress after lying for some time in one position. Special beds such as air beds, ripple beds and water beds are used to try to prevent the formation of bedsores. Also called **pressure sore, decubitus ulcer**

bedtable /'bedteɪb(ə)l/ *noun* a specially designed table which can be used by a person sitting up in bed

bedwetting /'bedwetɪŋ/ *noun* same as **nocturnal enuresis** (NOTE: This term is used mainly about children.)

Beer's knife /'bɪəz naɪf/ *noun* a knife with a triangular blade, used in eye operations [After George Joseph Beer (1763–1821), German ophthalmologist]

behaviour /bɪ'heɪvjə/ *noun* a way of acting ○ *His behaviour was very aggressive.* (NOTE: The US spelling is **behavior**.)

behavioural /bɪ'heɪvjərəl/ *adjective* relating to behaviour (NOTE: The US spelling is **behavioral**.)

behavioural scientist /bɪˌheɪvjərəl 'saɪəntɪst/ *noun* a person who specialises in the study of behaviour

behaviourism /bɪ'heɪvjərɪz(ə)m/ *noun* a psychological theory proposing that only someone's behaviour should be studied to discover their psychological problems

behaviourist /bɪ'heɪvjərɪst/ *noun* a psychologist who follows behaviourism

behaviour therapy /bɪˌheɪvjə 'θerəpi/ *noun* a form of psychiatric treatment in which someone learns how to improve their condition

Behçet's syndrome /'beɪsets ˌsɪndrəʊm/ *noun* a chronic condition of the immune system with no known cause, experienced as a series of attacks of inflammation of small blood vessels accompanied by mouth ulcers and sometimes genital ulcers, skin lesions and inflamed eyes [Described 1937. After Halushi Behçet (1889–1948), Turkish dermatologist.]

behind /bɪ'haɪnd/ *noun* same as **buttock** (*informal*)

bejel /'bedʒəl/ *noun* a non-venereal form of syphilis which is endemic among children in some areas of the Middle East and elsewhere and is caused by a spirochaete strain of bacteria

belch /beltʃ/ *noun* the action of allowing air in the stomach to come up through the mouth ■ *verb* to allow air in the stomach to come up through the mouth

belching /'beltʃɪŋ/ *noun* the action of allowing air in the stomach to come up through the mouth. Also called **eructation**

belladonna /ˌbelə'dɒnə/ *noun* **1.** a poisonous plant with berries containing atropine. Also called **deadly nightshade 2.** a form of atropine extracted from the belladonna plant

belle indifférence /ˌbel æn'dɪferɑːns/ *noun* an excessively calm state in a person, in a situation which would usually produce a show of emotion

Bellocq's cannula /beˌlɒks 'kænjʊlə/, **Bellocq's sound** /beˌlɒks 'saʊnd/ *noun* an instrument used to control a nosebleed [After Jean Jacques Bellocq (1732–1807), French surgeon]

Bell's mania /ˌbelz 'meɪniə/ *noun* a form of acute mania with delirium [After Luther Vose Bell (1806–62), American physiologist]

Bell's palsy /ˌbelz 'pɔːlzi/ *noun* paralysis of the facial nerve on one side of the face, preventing one eye being closed. Also called **facial paralysis** [Described 1821. After Sir Charles Bell (1774–1842), Scottish surgeon. He ran anatomy schools, first in Edinburgh and then in London. Professor of Anatomy at the Royal Academy.]

belly /'beli/ *noun* **1.** same as **abdomen 2.** the fatter central part of a muscle

bellyache /'belieɪk/ *noun* a pain in the abdomen or stomach

belly button /'beli ˌbʌt(ə)n/ *noun* the navel (*informal*)

Bence Jones protein /ˌbens 'dʒəʊnz ˌprəʊtiːn/ *noun* a protein found in the urine of people who have myelomatosis, lymphoma, leukaemia and some other cancers [Described 1848. After Henry Bence Jones (1814–73), physician at St George's Hospital, London, UK.]

bends /bendz/ *plural noun* □ **the bends** ♦ **caisson disease**

Benedict's solution /'benɪdɪkts səˌluːʃ(ə)n/ *noun* a solution used to carry out Benedict's test

Benedict's test /'benɪdɪkts test/ *noun* a test to see if sugar is present in the urine [Described 1915. After Stanley Rossiter Benedict (1884–1936), physiological chemist at Cornell University, New York, USA.]

benign /bə'naɪn/ *adjective* generally harmless

benign growth /bə'naɪn grəʊθ/ *noun* same as **benign tumour**

benign pancreatic disease /bəˌnaɪn ˌpæŋkri'ætɪk dɪˌziːz/ *noun* chronic pancreatitis

benign prostatic hypertrophy /bɪˌnaɪn prɒˌstætɪk haɪ'pɜːtrəfi/ *noun* a nonmalignant enlargement of the prostate. Abbr **BPH**

benign tumour /bəˌnaɪn 'tjuːmə/ *noun* a tumour which will not grow again or spread to other parts of the body if it is removed surgically, but which can be fatal if not treated. Also called **benign growth**. Opposite **malignant tumour**

Bennett's fracture /ˌbenɪts 'fræktʃə/ *noun* a fracture of the first metacarpal, the bone between the thumb and the wrist [Described 1886. After Edward Halloran Bennett (1837–1907), Irish anatomist, later Professor of Surgery at Trinity College, Dublin, Ireland.]

bent /bent/ *adjective* □ **bent double** bent over completely so that the face is towards the ground ○ *He was bent double with pain.*

benzocaine /'benzəkeɪn/ *noun* a drug with anaesthetic properties used in some throat lozenges and skin creams

benzodiazepine /ˌbenzəʊdaɪ'æzəpiːn/ *noun* a drug which acts on receptors in the central nervous system to relieve symptoms of anxiety and insomnia, although prolonged use is to be avoided (NOTE: Benzodiazepines have names ending in **-azepam: diazepam.**)

benzoin /'benzəʊɪn/ *noun* a resin used to make friar's balsam

benzyl benzoate /ˌbenzɪl 'benzəʊeɪt/ *noun* a colourless oily liquid which occurs naturally in balsams, used in medicines and perfumes

benzylpenicillin /ˌbenzɪl peni'sɪlɪn/ *noun* an antibacterial drug used against streptococcal infections, meningococcal meningitis and other serious infections

bereavement /bɪ'riːvmənt/ *noun* the loss of someone, especially a close relative or friend, through death

beriberi /ˌberi'beri/ *noun* a disease of the nervous system caused by lack of vitamin B_1

COMMENT: Beriberi is prevalent in tropical countries where the diet is mainly formed of white rice, which is deficient in thiamine.

berylliosis /bəˌrɪli'əʊsɪs/ *noun* poisoning caused by breathing in particles of the poisonous chemical compound beryllium oxide

Besnier's prurigo /ˌbenieɪz prʊ'raɪgəʊ/ *noun* an itchy skin rash on the backs of the knees and the insides of the elbows [After Ernest Besnier (1831–1909), French dermatologist]

beta /'biːtə/ *noun* the second letter of the Greek alphabet

beta-adrenergic receptor /ˌbiːtə ˌædrə'nɜːdʒɪk/ *noun* one of two types of nerve endings that respond to adrenaline by speeding up the heart rate or dilating the bronchi

beta amyloid /ˌbiːtə 'æmɪlɔɪd/ *noun* a waxlike protein formed from amyloid precursor protein in nerve cells which aggregates in Alzheimer's disease to form plaques

beta blocker /'biːtə ˌblɒkə/ *noun* a drug which reduces the activity of the heart (NOTE: Beta blockers have names ending in **-olol: atenolol, propranolol hydrochloride.**)

beta cell /'biːtə sel/ *noun* a type of cell found in the islets of Langerhans, in the pancreas, which produces insulin. Also called **B cell**. ◊ **alpha cell**

Betadine /'biːtədiːn/ *noun* a trade name for a form of iodine

betamethasone /ˌbiːtəˈmeθəsəʊn/ *noun* a very strong corticosteroid drug

beta rhythm /'biːtə ˌrɪθəm/ *noun* a pattern of electrical waves in the brain of someone who is awake and active, registering on an electroencephalograph at 18–30 hertz

betaxolol /bɪˈtæksəlɒl/ *noun* a beta blocker drug used in the treatment of high blood pressure and glaucoma

bethanechol /beˈθænɪkɒl/ *noun* an agonist drug used to increase muscle tone after surgery

Betnovate /'betnəveɪt/ *noun* a trade name for an ointment containing betamethasone

bi- /baɪ/ *prefix* two or twice

bias /'baɪəs/ *noun* a systematic error in the design or conduct of a study which could explain the results

bicarbonate of soda /baɪˈkɑːbənət əv 'səʊdə/ *noun* same as **sodium bicarbonate**

bicellular /baɪˈseljʊlə/ *adjective* having two cells

biceps /'baɪseps/ *noun* any muscle formed of two parts joined to form one tendon, especially the muscles in the front of the upper arm (biceps brachii) and the back of the thigh (biceps femoris). ◊ **triceps** (NOTE: The plural is **biceps**.)

bicipital /baɪˈsɪpɪt(ə)l/ *adjective* **1.** referring to a biceps muscle **2.** with two parts

biconcave /baɪˈkɒŋkeɪv/ *adjective* referring to a lens which is concave on both sides

biconvex /baɪˈkɒnveks/ *adjective* referring to a lens which is convex on both sides

bicornuate /baɪˈkɔːnjuət/ *adjective* divided into two parts (NOTE: The word is sometimes applied to a malformation of the uterus.)

bicuspid /baɪˈkʌspɪd/ *adjective* with two points ■ *noun* a premolar tooth

bicuspid valve /ˌbaɪˈkʌspɪd ˌvælv/ *noun* same as **mitral valve**. see illustration at HEART in Supplement

b.i.d. *adverb* (*used on prescriptions*) twice daily. Full form **bis in die**

bifid /'baɪfɪd/ *adjective* in two parts

bifida /'bɪfɪdə/ ♦ **spina bifida**

bifocal /baɪˈfəʊk(ə)l/ *adjective* referring to lenses made with two sections which have different focal lengths, one for looking at things which are near, the other for looking at things which are far away

bifocal glasses /baɪˌfəʊk(ə)l 'glɑːsɪz/, **bifocal lenses** /baɪˈfəʊk(ə)l 'lenzɪz/, **bifocals** /baɪˈfəʊk(ə)lz/ *plural noun* spectacles with lenses which have two types of lens combined in the same piece of glass, the top part being used for seeing at a distance and the lower part for reading

bifurcate /'baɪfəkeɪt/ *adjective* separating or branching off into two parts ■ *verb* to split or branch off into two parts

bifurcation /ˌbaɪfəˈkeɪʃ(ə)n/ *noun* a place where something divides into two parts

bigeminy /baɪˈdʒemɪni/ *noun* same as **pulsus bigeminus**

big toe /bɪg 'təʊ/ *noun* the largest of the five toes, on the inside of the foot. Also called **great toe**

biguanide /baɪˈgwɑːnaɪd/ *noun* a drug which lowers blood sugar, used in the treatment of Type II diabetes

bilateral /baɪˈlæt(ə)rəl/ *adjective* affecting both sides

bilateral adrenalectomy /baɪˌlæt(ə)rəl əˌdriːnəˈlektəmi/ *noun* the surgical removal of both adrenal glands

bilateral pneumonia /baɪˌlæt(ə)rəl njuːˈməʊniə/ *noun* pneumonia affecting both lungs

bilateral vasectomy /baɪˌlæt(ə)rəl vəˈsektəmi/ *noun* a surgical operation to cut both vasa deferentia and so make a man sterile

bile /baɪl/ *noun* a thick bitter brownish yellow fluid produced by the liver, stored in the gall bladder and used to digest fatty substances and neutralise acids (NOTE: For other terms referring to bile, see words beginning with **chol-**.)

COMMENT: In jaundice, excess bile pigments flow into the blood and cause the skin to turn yellow.

bile acid /'baɪl ˌæsɪd/ *noun* an acid found in the bile, e.g. cholic acid

bile canal /'baɪl kəˌnæl/ *noun* a very small vessel leading from a hepatic cell to the bile duct

bile duct /'baɪl dʌkt/ *noun* a tube which links the cystic duct and the hepatic duct to the duodenum

bile pigment /'baɪl ˌpɪgmənt/ *noun* colouring matter in bile

bile salts /'baɪl sɔːlts/ *plural noun* sodium salts of bile acids

bilharzia /bɪlˈhɑːtsiə/ *noun* **1.** a fluke which enters the bloodstream and causes bilharziasis. Also called **Schistosoma 2.** same as **bilharziasis** (NOTE: Although strictly speaking, **bilharzia** is the name of the fluke, it is also generally used for the name of the disease: *bilharzia patients*; *six cases of bilharzia*.)

bilharziasis /ˌbɪlhɑːˈtsaɪəsɪs/ *noun* a tropical disease caused by flukes in the intestine or bladder. Also called **bilharzia, schistosomiasis**

COMMENT: The larvae of the fluke enter the skin through the feet and lodge in the walls of the intestine or bladder. They are passed out of the body in stools or urine and return to water, where they lodge and develop in the water snail, the secondary host, before going back into humans. Patients experience fever and anaemia.

bili- /'bɪli/ *prefix* referring to bile (NOTE: For other terms referring to bile, see words beginning with **chol-, chole-**.)

biliary /'bɪliəri/ *adjective* referring to bile

biliary colic /ˌbɪliəri 'kɒlɪk/ *noun* pain in the abdomen caused by gallstones in the bile duct or by inflammation of the gall bladder

biliary fistula /ˌbɪliəri 'fɪstjʊlə/ *noun* an opening which discharges bile on to the surface of the skin from the gall bladder, bile duct or liver

bilious /'bɪliəs/ *adjective* 1. referring to bile 2. referring to nausea (*informal*)

biliousness /'bɪliəsnəs/ *noun* a feeling of indigestion and nausea (*informal*)

bilirubin /ˌbɪli'ruːbɪn/ *noun* a red pigment in bile

bilirubinaemia /ˌbɪliruːbɪ'niːmiə/ *noun* an excess of bilirubin in the blood

biliuria /ˌbɪli'jʊəriə/ *noun* the presence of bile in the urine. Also called **choluria**

biliverdin /ˌbɪli'vɜːdɪn/ *noun* a green pigment in bile, produced by oxidation of bilirubin

Billings method /'bɪlɪŋz ˌmeθəd/ *noun* a method of birth control which uses the colour and consistency of the cervical mucus as guides to whether ovulation is taking place

Billroth's operations /'bɪlrɒθs ɒpəˌreɪʃ(ə)nz/ *plural noun* surgical operations in which the lower part of the stomach is removed and the part which is left is linked to the duodenum (Billroth I) or jejunum (Billroth II) [Described 1881. After Christian Albert Theodore Billroth (1829–94), Prussian surgeon.]

bilobate /baɪ'ləʊbeɪt/ *adjective* with two lobes

bimanual /baɪ'mænjuəl/ *adjective* done with two hands, or needing both hands to be done

binary /'baɪnəri/ *adjective* made of two parts

binary fission /ˌbaɪnəri 'fɪʃ(ə)n/ *noun* the process of splitting into two parts in some types of cell division

binaural /baɪn'ɔːrəl/ *adjective* using, or relating to, both ears

binder /'baɪndə/ *noun* a bandage which is wrapped round a limb to support it

Binet's test /'bɪneɪz test/ *noun* an intelligence test for children [Originally described 1905 but later modified at Stanford University, California, USA. After Alfred Binet (1857–1911), French psychologist and physiologist.]

binocular /bɪ'nɒkjʊlə/ *adjective* referring to the two eyes

binocular vision /bɪˌnɒkjʊlə 'vɪʒ(ə)n/ *noun* ability to see with both eyes at the same time, which gives a stereoscopic effect and allows a person to judge distances. Compare **monocular**

binovular /bɪ'nɒvjʊlə/ *adjective* referring to twins who develop from two different ova

bio- /baɪəʊ/ *prefix* referring to living organisms

bioactive /ˌbaɪəʊ'æktɪv/ *adjective* producing an effect in living tissue or in a living organism

bioassay /ˌbaɪəʊə'seɪ/ *noun* a test of the strength of a drug, hormone, vitamin or serum, by examining the effect it has on living animals or tissue

bioavailability /ˌbaɪəʊəveɪlə'bɪliti/ *noun* the extent to which a nutrient or medicine can be taken up by the body

biochemical /ˌbaɪəʊ'kemɪk(ə)l/ *adjective* referring to biochemistry

biochemistry /ˌbaɪəʊ'kemɪstri/ *noun* the chemistry of living tissues

biocide /'baɪəʊsaɪd/ *noun* a substance which kills living organisms

biocompatibility /ˌbaɪəʊkəmpætə'bɪliti/ *noun* the compatibility of a donated organ or artificial limb with the living tissue into which it has been introduced or with which it is brought into contact

biodegradable /ˌbaɪəʊdɪ'greɪdəb(ə)l/ *adjective* easily decomposed by organisms such as bacteria or by the effect of sunlight, the sea, etc.

bioengineering /ˌbaɪəʊendʒɪ'nɪərɪŋ/ *noun* same as **biomedical engineering**

bioethics /'baɪəʊˌeθɪks/ *noun* the study of the moral and ethical choices in medical research and treatment of patients, especially when advanced technology is available

biofeedback /ˌbaɪəʊ'fiːdbæk/ *noun* the control of the autonomic nervous system by someone's conscious thought, as he or she sees the results of tests or scans

biogenesis /ˌbaɪəʊ'dʒenəsɪs/ *noun* a theory that living organisms can only develop from other living organisms

biohazard /'baɪəʊˌhæzəd/ *noun* a danger to human beings or their environment, especially one from a poisonous or infectious agent

bioinstrumentation /ˌbaɪəʊɪnstrəmen'teɪʃ(ə)n/ *noun* instruments used to record and display information about the body's functions, or the use of such instruments

biological /ˌbaɪə'lɒdʒɪk(ə)l/ *adjective* referring to biology

biological clock /ˌbaɪəlɒdʒɪk(ə)l 'klɒk/ *noun* the rhythm of daily activities and bodily processes such as eating, defecating or sleeping, frequently controlled by hormones, which repeats every twenty-four hours. Also called **circadian rhythm**

biological parent /ˌbaɪə,lɒdʒɪk(ə)l 'peərəmt/ *noun* a parent who was physically involved in producing a child

biologist /baɪ'ɒlədʒɪst/ *noun* a scientist who specialises in biology

biology /baɪ'ɒlədʒi/ *noun* the study of living organisms

biomaterial /ˌbaɪəʊməˈtɪərɪəl/ *noun* a synthetic material which can be used as an implant in living tissue

biomedical engineering /ˌbaɪəʊmedɪk(ə)l,endʒɪˈnɪərɪŋ/ *noun* the application of engineering science such as robotics and hydraulics to medicine

biomedicine /ˈbaɪəʊˌmed(ə)s(ə)n/ *noun* **1.** the use of the principles of biology, biochemistry, physiology and other basic sciences to solve problems in clinical medicine **2.** the study of the body's ability to withstand unusual or extreme environments

biometry /baɪˈɒmətri/ *noun* the science which applies statistics to the study of living things □ **biometry of the eye** measurement of the eye by ultrasound □ **biometry of a fetus** the measurement of the key parameters of growth of a fetus by ultrasound

biomonitoring /ˈbaɪəʊˌmɒnɪt(ə)rɪŋ/ *noun* the measurement and tracking of a chemical substance in a living organism or biological material such as blood or urine, usually to check environmental pollution or chemical exposure

bionic ear /baɪˈɒnɪk ɪə/ *noun* a cochlear implant (*informal*)

bionics /baɪˈɒnɪks/ *noun* the process of applying knowledge of biological systems to mechanical and electronic devices

biopharmaceutical /ˌbaɪəʊfɑːməˈsuːtɪk(ə)l/ *noun* a drug produced by biotechnological methods

biophysical profile /ˌbaɪəʊfɪzɪk(ə)l ˈprəʊfaɪl/ *noun* a profile of a fetus, based on such things as its breathing movement and body movement

biopsy /ˈbaɪɒpsi/ *noun* the process of taking a small piece of living tissue for examination and diagnosis ○ *The biopsy of the tissue from the growth showed that it was benign.*

biorhythm /ˈbaɪəʊrɪð(ə)m/ *noun* a regular process of change which takes place within living organisms, e.g. sleeping, waking or the reproductive cycle (NOTE: Some people believe that biorhythms affect behaviour and mood.)

biosensor /ˈbaɪəʊˌsensə/ *noun* a device that uses a biological agent such as an enzyme or organelle to detect, measure or analyse chemicals (NOTE: Biosensors are increasingly used in tests to diagnose medical conditions such as blood pressure.)

biostatistics /ˌbaɪəʊstəˈtɪstɪks/ *plural noun* statistics used in medicine and the study of disease

biosurgery /ˈbaɪəʊˌsɜːdʒəri/ *noun* the use of living organisms in surgery and post-surgical treatment, especially the use of maggots or leeches to clean wounds

biotechnology /ˌbaɪəʊtekˈnɒlədʒi/ *noun* **1.** the use of biological processes in industrial production, e.g. in the production of drugs **2.** same as **genetic modification**

biotherapy /ˈbaɪəʊˌθerəpi/ *noun* the treatment of disease with substances produced through the activity of living organisms such as sera, vaccines or antibiotics

biotin /ˈbaɪətɪn/ *noun* a type of vitamin B found in egg yolks, liver and yeast

biparietal /ˌbaɪpəˈraɪət(ə)l/ *adjective* referring to the two parietal bones

biparous /ˈbɪpərəs/ *adjective* producing twins

bipennate /baɪˈpeneɪt/ *adjective* referring to a muscle with fibres which rise from either side of the tendon

bipolar /baɪˈpəʊlə/ *adjective* with two poles. See illustration at NEURONE in Supplement

bipolar disorder /ˌbaɪˌpəʊlə dɪsˈɔːdə/ *noun* a psychological condition in which someone moves between mania and depression and experiences delusion. Also called **manic-depressive illness, manic depression**

bipolar neurone /baɪˌpəʊlə ˈnjʊərəʊn/ *noun* a nerve cell with two processes, a dendrite and an axon, found in the retina. See illustration at NEURONE in Supplement. Compare **multipolar neurone, unipolar neurone**

birth /bɜːθ/ *noun* the act of being born □ **to give birth** to have a baby ○ *She gave birth to twins.*

birth canal /ˈbɜːθ kəˌnæl/ *noun* the uterus, vagina and vulva

birth control /ˈbɜːθ kənˌtrəʊl/ *noun* same as **contraception**

birth control pill /ˈbɜːθ kənˌtrəʊl pɪl/ *noun* same as **oral contraceptive**

birth defect /ˈbɜːθ ˌdiːfekt/ *noun* same as **congenital anomaly** (NOTE: The word 'defect' is now avoided.)

birthing /ˈbɜːθɪŋ/ *noun* the process of giving birth using natural childbirth methods ■ *adjective* designed to help in childbirth

birthing chair /ˈbɜːθɪŋ tʃeə/ *noun* a special chair in which a woman sits to give birth

birthing pool /ˈbɜːθɪŋ puːl/ *noun* a special large bath in which pregnant women can relax before and when giving birth

birthing room /ˈbɜːθɪŋ ruːm/ *noun* an area set up for childbirth in a hospital or other building to provide comfortable and homely surroundings

birth injury /ˈbɜːθ ˌɪndʒəri/ *noun* an injury which a baby experiences during a difficult birth, e.g. brain damage

birthmark /ˈbɜːθmɑːk/ *noun* an unusual coloured or raised area on the skin which someone has from birth. Also called **naevus**

birth mother /ˈbɜːθ ˌmʌðə/ *noun* the woman who gave birth to a child

birth parent /ˈbɜːθ ˌpeərənt/ *noun* one of the parents that physically produced a child

birth plan /bɜːθ plæn/ *noun* a list of a pregnant woman's wishes about how the birth of her baby should take place, e.g. whether she wants a natural birth and what pain relief she should be given

birth rate /'bɜːθ reɪt/ *noun* the number of births per year, shown per thousand of the population ○ *a birth rate of 15 per thousand* ○ *There has been a severe decline in the birth rate.*

birth trauma /'bɜːθ ˌtrɔːmə/ *noun* an injury caused to a baby during delivery

birth weight /'bɜːθ weɪt/ *noun* the weight of a baby at birth

bisacodyl /ˌbaɪsə'kəʊdɪl/ *noun* a laxative drug

bisexual /baɪ'sekʃuəl/ *noun* someone who has both male and female sexual partners ■ *adjective* referring to a person who is sexually attracted to both males and females. Compare **heterosexual, homosexual**

bisexuality /ˌbaɪsekʃu'ælɪti/ *noun* the state of being sexually attracted to both males and females

bis in die /ˌbɪs ɪn 'diːeɪ/ *adverb* full form of **b.i.d.**

bismuth /'bɪzməθ/ *noun* a chemical element (NOTE: The chemical symbol is **Bi.**)

bismuth salts /'bɪzməθ sɔːlts/ *plural noun* salts used to treat acid stomach and formerly used in the treatment of syphilis

bistoury /'bɪstəri/ *noun* a sharp thin surgical knife

bite /baɪt/ *verb* **1.** to cut into something with the teeth ○ *He bit a piece out of the apple.* □ **to bite on something** to hold onto something with the teeth ○ *The dentist told him to bite on the bite wing.* **2.** (*of an insect*) to puncture someone's skin ■ *noun* **1.** the action of biting or of being bitten **2.** a place or mark where someone has been bitten ○ *a dog bite* ○ *an insect bite*

bite wing /'baɪt wɪŋ/ *noun* a holder for dental X-ray film, which a person clenches between the teeth, so allowing an X-ray of both upper and lower teeth to be taken

Bitot's spots /ˌbiːtəʊz 'spɒts/ *plural noun* small white spots on the conjunctiva, caused by vitamin A deficiency [Described 1863. After Pierre A. Bitot (1822–88), French physician.]

bivalve /'baɪvælv/ *noun* an organ which has two valves ■ *adjective* referring to a bivalve organ

black eye /ˌblæk 'aɪ/ *noun* bruising and swelling of the tissues round an eye, usually caused by a blow

blackhead /'blækhed/ *noun* same as **comedo** (*informal*)

black heel /'blæk ˌhiːl/ *noun* a haemorrhage inside the heel, characterised by black spots

black out /ˌblæk 'aʊt/ *verb* to have sudden loss of consciousness ○ *I suddenly blacked out and I can't remember anything more*

blackout /'blækaʊt/ *noun* a sudden loss of consciousness (*informal*) ○ *She must have had a blackout while driving.* Also called **fainting fit**

black spots /ˌblæk 'spɒts/ *plural noun* □ **black spots in front of the eyes** moving black dots seen when looking at something, more noticeable when a person is tired or run-down, and more common in shortsighted people

blackwater fever /'blækwɔːtə ˌfiːvə/ *noun* a form of malaria where haemoglobin from red blood cells is released into plasma and makes the urine dark

bladder /'blædə/ *noun* any sac in the body, especially the sac where the urine collects before being passed out of the body ○ *He is suffering from bladder trouble.* ○ *She is taking antibiotics for a bladder infection.*

Blalock's operation /'bleɪlɒks ɒpəˌreɪʃ(ə)n/, **Blalock-Taussig operation** /ˌbleɪlɒk 'tɔːsɪg ɒpəˌreɪʃ(ə)n/ *noun* a surgical operation to connect the pulmonary artery to the subclavian artery, in order to increase blood flow to the lungs of someone who has tetralogy of Fallot

bland /blænd/ *adjective* referring to food which is not spicy, irritating or acid

bland diet /ˌblænd 'daɪət/ *noun* a diet in which someone eats mainly milk-based foods, boiled vegetables and white meat, as a treatment for peptic ulcers

blanket bath /'blæŋkɪt bɑːθ/ *noun* same as **bed bath**

blast /blɑːst/ *noun* **1.** a wave of air pressure from an explosion which can cause concussion **2.** an immature form of a cell before distinctive characteristics develop

-blast /blæst/ *suffix* referring to a very early stage in the development of a cell

blast injury /'blɑːst ˌɪndʒəri/ *noun* a severe injury to the chest following a blast

blasto- /blæstəʊ/ *prefix* referring to a germ cell

blastocoele /'blæstəʊsiːl/ *noun* a cavity filled with fluid in a morula (NOTE: The US spelling is **blastocele.**)

blastocyst /'blæstəʊsɪst/ *noun* an early stage in the development of an embryo

Blastomyces /ˌblæstəʊ'maɪsiːz/ *noun* a type of parasitic fungus which affects the skin

blastomycosis /ˌblæstəʊmaɪ'kəʊsɪs/ *noun* an infection caused by *Blastomyces*

blastula /'blæstjʊlə/ *noun* the first stage of the development of an embryo in animals

bleb /bleb/ *noun* a blister. Compare **bulla**

bled /bled/ ♦ **bleed**

bleed /bliːd/ verb to lose blood ○ His knee was bleeding. ○ He was bleeding from a cut on the head. (NOTE: **bleeding – bled**)

bleeder /'bliːdə/ noun **1.** a blood vessel which bleeds during surgery **2.** a person who has haemophilia (informal)

bleeding /'bliːdɪŋ/ noun an unusual loss of blood from the body through the skin, through an orifice or internally

COMMENT: Blood lost through bleeding from an artery is bright red and can rush out because it is under pressure. Blood from a vein is darker red and flows more slowly.

bleeding point /'bliːdɪŋ pɔɪnt/, **bleeding site** /'bliːdɪŋ saɪt/ noun a place in the body where bleeding is taking place

bleeding time /'bliːdɪŋ taɪm/ noun a test of the clotting ability of someone's blood, by timing the length of time it takes for the blood to congeal

blenno- /blenəʊ/ prefix referring to mucus

blennorrhagia /ˌblenəʊˈreɪdʒə/ noun **1.** the discharge of mucus **2.** gonorrhoea

blennorrhoea /ˌblenəˈriːə/ noun **1.** the discharge of watery mucus **2.** gonorrhoea

bleomycin /ˌbliːəʊˈmaɪsɪn/ noun an antibiotic used to treat forms of cancer such as Hodgkin's disease

blephar- /blefər/ prefix same as **blepharo-** (used before vowels)

blepharitis /ˌblefəˈraɪtɪs/ noun inflammation of the eyelid

blepharo- /blefərəʊ/ prefix referring to the eyelid

blepharoconjunctivitis /ˌblefərəʊkənˌdʒʌŋktɪˈvaɪtɪs/ noun inflammation of the conjunctiva of the eyelids

blepharon /'blefərɒn/ noun an eyelid

blepharospasm /'blefərəʊspæz(ə)m/ noun a sudden contraction of the eyelid, as when a tiny piece of dust gets in the eye

blepharotosis /ˌblefərəʊˈtəʊsɪs/ noun a condition in which the upper eyelid is half closed because of paralysis of the muscle or nerve

blind /blaɪnd/ adjective not able to see ■ plural noun □ **the blind** people who are blind. ◊ **visually impaired** ■ verb to make someone blind ○ He was blinded in the accident.

blind gut /ˌblaɪnd ˈɡʌt/ noun same as **caecum**

blind loop syndrome /blaɪnd ˈluːp ˌsɪndrəʊm/ noun a condition which occurs in cases of diverticulosis or of Crohn's disease, with steatorrhoea, abdominal pain and megaloblastic anaemia

blindness /'blaɪndnəs/ noun the fact of not being able to see

blind spot /'blaɪnd spɒt/ noun the point in the retina where the optic nerve joins it, which does not register light

blind study /ˌblaɪnd ˈstʌdi/ noun an investigation to test an intervention such as giving a drug, in which a person does not know if he or she has taken the active medicine or the placebo

blink /blɪŋk/ verb to close and open the eyelids rapidly several times or once ○ He blinked in the bright light.

blister /'blɪstə/ noun a swelling on the skin containing serum from the blood, caused by rubbing, burning or a disease such as chickenpox ■ verb to produce blisters

bloated /'bləʊtɪd/ adjective experiencing the uncomfortable sensation of a very full stomach

block /blɒk/ noun **1.** the stopping of a function **2.** something which obstructs **3.** a large piece of something ○ A block of wood fell on his foot. **4.** a period of time ○ The training is in two three-hour blocks. **5.** one of the different buildings forming a section of a hospital ○ The patient is in Block 2, Ward 7. ○ She is having treatment in the physiotherapy block. ■ verb to fill the space in something and stop other things passing through it ○ The artery was blocked by a clot. ○ He swallowed a piece of plastic which blocked his oesophagus.

blockage /'blɒkɪdʒ/ noun **1.** something which obstructs ○ There is a blockage in the rectum. **2.** the act of being obstructed ○ The blockage of the artery was caused by a blood clot.

blocker /'blɒkə/ noun a substance which blocks an action. ◊ **beta blocker**

blocking /'blɒkɪŋ/ noun a psychiatric disorder, in which someone suddenly stops one train of thought and switches to another

blood /blʌd/ noun a red liquid moved around the body by the pumping action of the heart (NOTE: For other terms referring to blood, see words beginning with **haem-, haemo-, haemato-**.) ◊ **blood chemistry** or **chemistry of the blood 1.** the substances which make up blood can be analysed in blood tests, the results of which are useful in diagnosing disease **2.** the record of changes which take place in blood during disease and treatment

COMMENT: Blood is formed of red and white cells, platelets and plasma. It circulates round the body, going from the heart and lungs along arteries, and returns to the heart through the veins. As it moves round the body it takes oxygen to the tissues and removes waste material which is cleaned out through the kidneys or exhaled through the lungs. It also carries hormones produced by glands to the various organs which need them. The body of an average adult contains about six litres or ten pints of blood.

blood bank /'blʌd bæŋk/ noun a section of a hospital or a special centre where blood given by donors is stored for use in transfusions

blood blister /'blʌd ˌblɪstə/ *noun* a swelling on the skin with blood inside, caused by nipping the flesh

blood-borne virus /ˌblʌd bɔːn 'vaɪrəs/ *noun* a virus carried by the blood

blood-brain barrier /ˌblʌd breɪn 'bæriə/ *noun* the process by which some substances, which in other parts of the body will diffuse from capillaries, are held back by the endothelium of cerebral capillaries, preventing them from coming into contact with the fluids round the brain

blood casts /'blʌd kɑːsts/ *plural noun* pieces of blood cells which are secreted by the kidneys in kidney disease

blood cell /'blʌd sel/ *noun* a red or a white cell in the blood

blood clot /'blʌd klɒt/ *noun* a soft mass of coagulated blood in a vein or an artery. Also called **thrombus**

blood clotting /'blʌd ˌklɒtɪŋ/ *noun* the process by which blood changes from being liquid to being semi-solid and so stops flowing

blood corpuscle /'blʌd ˌkɔːpʌs(ə)l/ *noun* ♦ **blood cell**

blood count /'blʌd kaʊnt/ *noun* a test to count the number and types of different blood cells in a sample of blood, in order to give an indication of the condition of the person's blood as a whole

blood culture /'blʌd ˌkʌltʃə/ *noun* a method of testing a sample of blood by placing it on a culture medium to see if foreign organisms in it grow

blood donor /'blʌd ˌdəʊnə/ *noun* a person who gives blood which is then used in transfusions to other people

blood dyscrasia /ˌblʌd dɪs'kreɪziə/ *noun* any unusual blood condition such as a low cell count or platelet count

blood formation /'blʌd fɔːˌmeɪʃ(ə)n/ *noun* same as **haemopoiesis**

blood-glucose level /ˌblʌd 'gluːkəʊz ˌlev(ə)l/ *noun* the amount of glucose present in the blood. The usual blood-glucose level is about 60–100 mg of glucose per 100 ml of blood.

blood group /'blʌd gruːp/ *noun* one of the different groups into which human blood is classified. Also called **blood type**

COMMENT: Blood is classified in various ways. The most common classifications are by the agglutinogens (factors A and B) in red blood cells and by the Rhesus factor. Blood can therefore have either factor (Group A and Group B) or both factors (Group AB) or neither (Group O) and each of these groups can be Rhesus negative or positive.

blood grouping /'blʌd ˌgruːpɪŋ/ *noun* the process of classifying people according to their blood groups

blood-letting /'blʌd ˌletɪŋ/ *noun* same as **phlebotomy**

blood loss /'blʌd lɒs/ *noun* loss of blood from the body by bleeding

blood picture /'blʌd ˌpɪktʃə/ *noun US* a full blood count

blood pigment /'blʌd ˌpɪgmənt/ *noun* same as **haemoglobin**

blood plasma /'blʌd ˌplæzmə/ *noun* a yellow watery liquid which makes up the main part of blood

blood platelet /'blʌd ˌpleɪtlət/ *noun* a small blood cell which releases thromboplastin and which multiplies rapidly after an injury, encouraging the coagulation of blood

blood poisoning /'blʌd ˌpɔɪz(ə)nɪŋ/ *noun* a condition in which bacteria are present in the blood and cause illness (*informal*) ◊ **septicaemia, bacteraemia, toxaemia**

blood pressure /'blʌd ˌpreʃə/ *noun* the pressure, measured in millimetres of mercury, at which the blood is pumped round the body by the heart □ **high blood pressure** *or* **raised blood pressure** a level of blood pressure which is higher than usual

'…raised blood pressure may account for as many as 70% of all strokes. The risk of stroke rises with both systolic and diastolic blood pressure in the normotensive and hypertensive ranges. Blood pressure control reduces the incidence of first stroke and aspirin appears to reduce the risk of stroke after TIAs' [*British Journal of Hospital Medicine*]

COMMENT: Blood pressure is measured using a sphygmomanometer. A rubber tube is wrapped round the patient's arm and inflated and two readings of blood pressure are taken: the systolic pressure, when the heart is contracting and so pumping out, and the diastolic pressure, which is always a lower figure, when the heart relaxes. Healthy adult values are considered to be 160/95, unless the patient is diabetic or has heart disease, when lower target values are set.

blood product /'blʌd ˌprɒdʌkt/ *noun* a substance such as plasma taken out of blood and used in the treatment of various medical conditions

blood relationship /ˌblʌd rɪ'leɪʃ(ə)nʃɪp/ *noun* a relationship between people who come from the same family and have the same parents, grandparents or ancestors, as opposed to a relationship by marriage

blood sample /'blʌd ˌsɑːmpəl/ *noun* a sample of blood, taken for testing

blood serum /'blʌd ˌsɪərəm/ *noun* ♦ **serum**

bloodshot /'blʌdʃɒt/ *adjective* referring to an eye with small specks of blood in it from a small damaged blood vessel

bloodstained /'blʌdsteɪnd/ *adjective* having blood in or on it ○ *He coughed up bloodstained sputum.*

bloodstream /'blʌdstriːm/ *noun* the blood flowing round the body ○ *Hormones are secreted by the glands into the bloodstream.*

blood sugar /ˌblʌd 'ʃʊgə/ noun glucose present in the blood

blood sugar level /ˌblʌd 'ʃʊgə ˌlev(ə)l/ noun the amount of glucose in the blood, which is higher after meals and in people with diabetes

blood test /'blʌd test/ noun a laboratory test of a blood sample to analyse its chemical composition ○ The patient will have to have a blood test.

blood transfusion /'blʌd trænsˌfjuːʒ(ə)n/ noun a procedure in which blood given by another person or taken from the patient at an earlier stage is transferred into the patient's vein

blood type /'blʌd taɪp/ noun same as **blood group**

blood typing /'blʌd ˌtaɪpɪŋ/ noun the analysis of blood for transfusion factors and blood group

blood urea /ˌblʌd jʊ'riːə/ noun urea present in the blood. A high level occurs following heart failure or kidney disease.

blood vessel /'blʌd ˌves(ə)l/ noun any tube which carries blood round the body, e.g. an artery, vein or capillary (NOTE: For other terms referring to blood vessels, see words beginning with angi-, angio-.)

blood volume /'blʌd ˌvɒljuːm/ noun the total amount of blood in the body

blotch /blɒtʃ/ noun a reddish patch on the skin

blot test /'blɒt test/ noun ♦ **Rorschach test**

blue baby /ˌbluː 'beɪbi/ noun a baby who has congenital cyanosis, born either with a congenital heart condition or with a collapsed lung, which prevents an adequate supply of oxygen reaching the tissues, giving the baby's skin a slight blue colour (informal)

blue disease /'bluː dɪ'ziːz/, **blueness** / 'bluːnəs/ noun ♦ **cyanosis**

blue litmus /ˌbluː 'lɪtməs/ noun treated paper which indicates the presence of acid by turning red

blurred vision /ˌblɜːd 'vɪʒ(ə)n/ noun a condition in which someone does not see objects clearly

blush /blʌʃ/ noun a rush of red colour to the skin of the face, caused by emotion ■ verb to go red in the face because of emotion

bm abbr bowel movement

BM abbr Bachelor of Medicine

BMA abbr British Medical Association

BMI abbr body mass index

BMJ abbr British Medical Journal

BMR abbr basal metabolic rate

BMR test /ˌbiː ˌem 'ɑː test/ noun a test of thyroid function

BNF abbr British National Formulary

bodily /'bɒdɪli/ adjective referring to the body ○ The main bodily functions are controlled by the sympathetic nervous system.

body /'bɒdi/ noun 1. the physical structure of a person, as opposed to the mind 2. the main part of a person's body, not including the head or arms and legs 3. a dead person ■ an amount of something ■ noun 1. the main part of something □ **body of sternum** the main central part of the breastbone □ **body of vertebra** the main part of a vertebra which supports the weight of the body □ **body of the stomach** main part of the stomach between the fundus and the pylorus. See illustration at STOMACH in Supplement 2. ♦ **foreign body**

body cavity /'bɒdi ˌkævɪti/ noun an opening in the body, e.g. the mouth, oesophagus, vagina, rectum or ear

body fat /'bɒdi fæt/ noun tissue where the cells contain fat which replaces the fibrous tissue when too much food is eaten

body fluid /'bɒdi ˌfluːɪd/ noun a liquid in the body, e.g. water, blood or semen

body image /ˌbɒdi 'ɪmɪdʒ/ noun the mental image which a person has of their own body. Also called **body schema**

body language /'bɒdi ˌlæŋgwɪdʒ/ noun the expression on your face, or the way you hold your body, interpreted by other people as unconsciously revealing your feelings

body mass index /ˌbɒdi 'mæs ˌɪndeks/ noun a figure obtained by dividing someone's weight in kilos by the square of his or her height in metres. 19–25 is considered usual. Abbr **BMI**

COMMENT: If a person is 1.70m (5ft 7in.) and weighs 82kg (180 lbs), his or her BMI is 28 and so above average.

body odour /ˌbɒdi 'əʊdə/ noun an unpleasant smell caused by perspiration

body scan /'bɒdi skæn/ noun an examination of the whole of the body using ultrasound or other scanning techniques

body schema /ˌbɒdi 'skiːmə/ noun same as **body image**

body substance isolation /'bɒdi ˌsʌbstəns aɪsə,leɪʃ(ə)n/ noun making sure that a trauma victim is kept isolated from the possibility of infection from moist body substances

body temperature /'bɒdi ˌtempri,tʃə/ noun the internal temperature of the human body, usually about 37°C

Boeck's disease /'beks dɪ,ziːz/, **Boeck's sarcoid** /'beks ,sɑːkɔɪd/ noun same as **sarcoidosis** [Described 1899. After Caesar Peter Moeller Boeck (1845–1913), Professor of Dermatology at Oslo, Norway.]

Bohn's nodules /ˌbɔːnz 'nɒdjuːlz/, **Bohn's epithelial pearls** plural noun tiny cysts found in the mouths of healthy infants`

boil /bɔɪl/ *noun* a tender raised mass of infected tissue and skin, usually caused by infection of a hair follicle by the bacterium *Staphylococcus aureus*. Also called **furuncle**

bolus /'bəʊləs/ *noun* **1.** a mass of food which has been chewed and is ready to be swallowed **2.** a mass of food passing along the intestine

bonding /'bɒndɪŋ/ *noun* the process by which a psychological link is formed between a baby and its mother ○ *In autistic children bonding is difficult.*

bone /bəʊn/ *noun* **1.** calcified connective tissue **2.** one of the calcified pieces of connective tissue which make the skeleton ○ *There are several small bones in the human ear.* See illustration at SYNOVIAL JOINT in Supplement ◊ **bone structure 1.** the system of jointed bones forming the body **2.** the arrangement of the various components of the bone

COMMENT: Bones are formed of a hard outer layer (compact bone) which is made up of a series of layers of tissue (Haversian systems) and a softer inner part (cancellous bone *or* spongy bone) which contains bone marrow.

bone-anchored hearing aid /,bəʊn ,æŋkəd 'hɪərɪŋ eɪd/ *noun* a hearing aid that is fitted surgically into the skull, usually behind the ear. Abbr **BAHA**

bone conduction /'bəʊn kən,dʌkʃ(ə)n/ *noun* same as **osteophony**

bone damage /'bəʊn ,dæmɪdʒ/ *noun* damage caused to a bone ○ *extensive bruising but no bone damage*

bone graft /'bəʊn grɑːft/ *noun* a piece of bone taken from one part of the body to repair a another bone

bone marrow /'bəʊn ,mærəʊ/ *noun* soft tissue in cancellous bone (NOTE: For other terms referring to bone marrow, see words beginning with **myel-, myelo-**.)

COMMENT: Two types of bone marrow are to be found: red bone marrow or myeloid tissue, which forms red blood cells and is found in cancellous bone in the vertebrae, the sternum and other flat bones. As a person gets older, fatty yellow bone marrow develops in the central cavity of long bones.

bone marrow transplant /,bəʊn 'mærəʊ ,trænsplɑːnt/ *noun* the transplant of marrow from a donor to a recipient

bone scan *noun* a scan which tracks a radioactive substance injected into the body to find areas where a bone is breaking down or repairing itself

Bonney's blue /,bɒnɪz 'bluː/ *noun* a blue dye used as a disinfectant [After William Francis Victor Bonney (1872–1953), British gynaecologist]

bony /'bəʊni/ *adjective* **1.** relating to bones, or made of bone **2.** referring to a part of the body where the structure of the bones underneath can be seen ○ *thin bony hands*

bony labyrinth /,bəʊni 'læbərɪnθ/ *noun* a hard part of the temporal bone surrounding the membranous labyrinth in the inner ear. Also called **osseous labyrinth**

booster /'buːstər ɪn,dʒekʃ(ə)n/, **booster injection** *noun* a repeat injection of vaccine given some time after the first injection to maintain the immunising effect

boracic acid /bə,ræsɪk 'æsɪd/ *noun* a soluble white powder used as a general disinfectant. Also called **boric acid**

borax /'bɔːræks/ *noun* a white powder used as a household cleaner and disinfectant

borborygmus /,bɔːbə'rɪgməs/ *noun* a rumbling noise in the abdomen, caused by gas in the intestine (NOTE: The plural is **borborygmi**.)

borderline /'bɔːdəlaɪn/ *adjective* **1.** not clearly belonging to either one of two categories ○ *a borderline case* **2.** referring to a medical condition likely to develop in someone unless an effort is made to prevent it **3.** characterised by emotional instability and self-destructive behaviour ○ *a borderline personality*

Bordetella /,bɔːdə'telə/ *noun* a bacterium of the family *Brucellaceae* (NOTE: *Bordetella pertussis* causes whooping cough.)

boric acid /,bɔːrɪk 'æsɪd/ *noun* same as **boracic acid**

born /bɔːn/ *verb* □ **to be born** to begin to live outside the mother's uterus

Bornholm disease /'bɔːnhəʊm dɪ,ziːz/ *noun* same as **epidemic pleurodynia**

bottle-fed /'bɒt(ə)l fed/ *adjective* referring to a baby which is fed from a bottle. Compare **breast-fed**

bottle feeding /,bɒt(ə)l 'fiːdɪŋ/ *noun* the act of giving a baby milk from a bottle, as opposed to breast feeding. Compare **breast feeding**

bottom /'bɒtəm/ *noun* **1.** the part of the body on which you sit. ◊ **buttock 2.** the anus (*informal*)

bottom shuffling /'bɒtəm ,ʃʌf(ə)lɪŋ/ *noun* the process by which a baby who cannot yet walk moves around by moving itself along on its hands and buttocks

botulinum toxin /,bɒtjʊ'laɪnəm ,tɒksɪn/ *noun* a poison produced by the bacterium *Clostridium botulinum* and used, in small doses, to treat muscular cramps and spasms

botulism /'bɒtjʊlɪz(ə)m/ *noun* a type of food poisoning, often fatal, caused by a toxin of *Clostridium botulinum* in badly canned or preserved food. Symptoms include paralysis of the muscles, vomiting and hallucinations.

bougie /'buːʒiː/ *noun* a thin tube which can be inserted into passages in the body such as the oesophagus or rectum, either to allow liquid to be introduced or to dilate the passage

bout /baʊt/ *noun* a sudden attack of a disease, especially one which recurs ○ *He is recovering from a bout of flu.* □ **bout of fever** a period when someone is feverish ○ *She has recurrent bouts of malarial fever.*

bovine spongiform encephalopathy /ˌbəʊvaɪn ˌspʌndʒɪfɔːm enˌkefəˈlɒpəθi/ *noun* a fatal brain disease of cattle. Abbr **BSE.** ◊ **Creutzfeldt-Jakob disease.** Also called **mad cow disease**

bowel /ˈbaʊəl/ *noun* the intestine, especially the large intestine (NOTE: **Bowel** is often used in the plural in everyday language.) □ **to open the bowels** to have a bowel movement

bowel movement /ˈbaʊəl ˌmuːvmənt/ *noun* **1.** an act of passing faeces out of the body through the anus ○ *The patient had a bowel movement this morning.* Also called **motion.** ◊ **defecation 2.** the amount of faeces passed through the anus

bowels /ˈbaʊəlz/ *plural noun* same as **bowel**

Bowen's disease /ˈbəʊɪnz dɪˌziːz/ *noun* a form of carcinoma, appearing as red plaques on the skin

bowl /bəʊl/ *noun* a wide shallow container used for holding liquids

bow-legged /ˌbəʊ ˈlegɪd/ *adjective* with bow legs

bow legs /bəʊ ˈlegz/ *noun* a state where the ankles touch and the knees are apart when a person is standing straight. Also called **genu varum**

Bowman's capsule /ˌbəʊmənz ˈkæpsjuːl/ *noun* the expanded end of a renal tubule, surrounding a glomerular tuft in the kidney, which filters plasma in order to reabsorb useful foodstuffs and eliminate waste. Also called **Malpighian glomerulus, glomerular capsule** [Described 1842. After Sir William Paget Bowman (1816–92), surgeon in Birmingham and later in London, who was a pioneer in work on the kidney and in ophthalmology.]

BP *abbr* **1.** blood pressure **2.** British Pharmacopoeia

BPH *abbr* benign prostatic hypertrophy

Bq *symbol* becquerel

brace /breɪs/ *noun* any type of splint or appliance worn for support, e.g. a metal support used on children's legs to make the bones straight or on teeth which are forming badly ○ *She wore a brace on her front teeth.*

bracelet /ˈbreɪslət/ *noun* ♦ **identity bracelet, medical alert bracelet**

brachi- /breɪki/ *prefix* same as **brachio-** (*used before vowels*)

brachial /ˈbreɪkiəl/ *adjective* referring to the arm, especially the upper arm

brachial artery /ˈbreɪkiəl ˌɑːtəri/ *noun* an artery running down the arm from the axillary artery to the elbow, where it divides into the radial and ulnar arteries

brachialis muscle /ˌbreɪkiˈeɪlɪs ˌmʌs(ə)l/ *noun* a muscle that causes the elbow to bend

brachial plexus /ˌbreɪkiəl ˈpleksəs/ *noun* a group of nerves at the armpit and base of the neck which lead to the nerves in the arms and hands. Injury to the brachial plexus at birth leads to Erb's palsy.

brachial pressure point /ˌbreɪkiəl ˈpreʃə pɔɪnt/ *noun* the point on the arm where pressure will stop bleeding from the brachial artery

brachial vein /ˈbreɪkiəl veɪn/ *noun* a vein accompanying the brachial artery, draining into the axillary vein

brachio- /breɪkiəʊ/ *prefix* referring to the arm

brachiocephalic artery /ˌbreɪkiəʊsəˌfælɪk ˈɑːtəri/ *noun* the largest branch of the arch of the aorta, which continues as the right common carotid and right subclavian arteries

brachiocephalic vein /ˌbreɪkiəʊsəˌfælɪk ˈveɪn/ *noun* one of a pair of large veins on opposite sides of the neck that join to form the superior vena cava. Also called **innominate vein**

brachium /ˈbreɪkiəm/ *noun* an arm, especially the upper arm between the elbow and the shoulder (NOTE: The plural is **brachia**.)

brachy- /bræki/ *prefix* short

brachycephaly /ˌbrækiˈsefəli/ *noun* a condition in which the skull is shorter than usual

brachytherapy /ˌbrækiˈθerəpi/ *noun* a radioactive treatment in which the radioactive material actually touches the tissue being treated

Bradford's frame /ˈbrædfədz freɪm/ *noun* a frame of metal and cloth, used to support a patient [After Edward Hickling Bradford (1848–1926), US orthopaedic surgeon]

brady- /brædɪ/ *prefix* slow

bradycardia /ˌbrædɪˈkɑːdiə/ *noun* a slow rate of heart contraction, shown by a slow pulse rate of less than 70 beats per minute

bradykinesia /ˌbrædɪkaɪˈniːziə/ *noun* a condition in which the someone walks slowly and makes slow movements because of disease

bradykinin /ˌbrædɪˈkaɪnɪn/ *noun* a chemical produced in the blood when tissues are injured, that plays a role in inflammation. ◊ **kinin**

bradypnoea /ˌbrædɪpˈniːə/ *noun* unusually slow breathing (NOTE: The US spelling is **bradypnea.**)

Braille /breɪl/ *noun* a system of writing using raised dots on the paper to indicate letters which a blind person can read by passing their fingers over the page ○ *The book has been published in Braille.* [Introduced 1829–30. After Louis Braille (1809–52), blind Frenchman and teacher of the blind; he introduced the system which had originally been proposed by Charles Barbier in 1820.]

brain /breɪn/ *noun* the part of the central nervous system situated inside the skull. Also called **encephalon.** See illustration at BRAIN in Supplement

COMMENT: The main part of the brain is the cerebrum, formed of two sections or hemispheres, which relate to thought and to sensations from either side of the body. At the back of the head and beneath the cerebrum is the cerebellum which coordinates muscle reaction and balance. Also in the brain are the hypothalamus which governs body temperature, hunger, thirst and sexual urges, and the tiny pituitary gland which is the most important endocrine gland in the body.

brain covering /'breɪn ˌkʌv(ə)rɪŋ/ *noun* ♦ meninges

brain damage /'breɪn ˌdæmɪdʒ/ *noun* damage caused to the brain as a result of oxygen and sugar deprivation, e.g. after a haemorrhage, accident, or though disease

brain-damaged /'breɪn ˌdæmɪdʒd/ *adjective* referring to someone who has experienced brain damage

brain death /'breɪn deθ/ *noun* a condition in which the nerves in the brain stem have died, and the person can be certified as dead, although the heart may not have stopped beating

brain haemorrhage /breɪn 'hem(ə)rɪdʒ/ *noun* same as **cerebral haemorrhage**

brain scan /'breɪn skæn/ *noun* an examination of the inside of the brain, made by passing X-rays through the head, using a scanner, and reconstituting the images on a computer monitor

brain scanner /'breɪn ˌskænə/ *noun* a machine which scans the interior of the body, used to examine the brain

brain stem /'breɪn stem/ *noun* the lower narrow part of the brain which connects the brain to the spinal cord

brain tumour /'breɪn tjuːmə/ *noun* a tumour which grows in the brain

COMMENT: Tumours may grow in any part of the brain. The symptoms of brain tumour are usually headaches and dizziness, and as the tumour grows it may affect the senses or mental faculties. Operations to remove brain tumours can be very successful.

brain wave /'breɪn stem/ *noun* a rhythmic wave of voltage produced by electrical activity in the brain tissue

bran /bræn/ *noun* the outside covering of the wheat seed, removed when making white flour, but an important source of roughage in the diet

branch /brɑːntʃ/ *noun* any part which grows out of a main part ■ *verb* to split out into smaller parts ○ *The radial artery branches from the brachial artery at the elbow.*

branchia /'bræŋkiə/ *noun* a breathing organ similar to the gill of a fish found in human embryos in the early stages of development (NOTE: The plural is **branchiae**.)

branchial /'bræŋkiəl/ *adjective* referring to the branchiae

branchial cyst /ˌbræŋkiəl 'sɪst/ *noun* a cyst on the side of the neck of an embryo

branchial pouch /ˌbræŋkiəl 'paʊtʃ/ *noun* a pouch on the side of the neck of an embryo

Braun's frame /ˌbraʊnz 'freɪm/, **Braun's splint** /ˌbraʊnz 'splɪnt/ *noun* a metal splint and frame to which pulleys are attached, used for holding up a fractured leg while the person is lying in bed [After Heinrich Friedrich Wilhelm Braun (1862–1934), German surgeon]

Braxton-Hicks contractions /ˌbrækstən 'hɪks kənˌtrækʃənz/ *plural noun* contractions of the uterus which occur throughout a pregnancy and become more frequent and stronger towards the end [After Dr Braxton-Hicks, 19th century British physician]

break /breɪk/ *noun* the point at which a bone has broken □ **clean break** a break in a bone which is not complicated and where the two parts will join again easily

breakbone fever /'breɪkbəʊn ˌfiːvə/ *noun* same as **dengue**

break down /ˌbreɪk 'daʊn/ *verb* 1. to experience a sudden physical or psychological illness (*informal*) ○ *After she lost her husband, her health broke down.* 2. to start to cry and become upset (*informal*) ○ *She broke down as she described the symptoms to the doctor.* 3. to split or cause to split into smaller chemical components, as in the digestion of food

breakdown /'breɪkdaʊn/ *noun* ♦ **nervous breakdown**

breakdown product /'breɪkdaʊn ˌprɒdʌkt/ *noun* a substance which is produced when a compound is broken down into its parts

breast /brest/ *noun* one of two glands in a woman which secrete milk. Also called **mamma** (NOTE: For other terms referring to breasts, see words beginning with **mamm-, mammo-, mast-, masto-**.)

breast augmentation /'brest ˌɔːgmenteɪʃ(ə)n/ *noun* a surgical procedure to increase the size of the breast for cosmetic purposes

breastbone /'brestbəʊn/ *noun* a bone which is in the centre of the front of the thorax and to which the ribs are connected. Also called **sternum**

breast cancer /'brest ˌkænsə/ *noun* a malignant tumour in a breast

breast-fed /'brest fed/ *adjective* referring to a baby which is fed from the mother's breasts ○ *She was breast-fed for the first two months.*

breast feeding /'brest ˌfiːdɪŋ/ *noun* feeding a baby from the mother's breasts as opposed to from a bottle. Compare **bottle feeding**

breast implant /'brest ˌɪmplɑːnt/ *noun* a sac containing silicone, implanted to improve the appearance of a breast

breast milk /'brest mɪlk/ *noun* the milk produced by a woman who has recently had a baby

breast palpation /'brest pæl,peɪʃ(ə)n/ noun feeling a breast to see if a lump is present which might indicate breast cancer

breast pump /'brest pʌmp/ noun an instrument for taking milk from a breast

breast reconstruction noun the construction of a new breast for a woman who has had a breast removed because of cancer

breast reduction /'brest rɪ,dʌkʃ(ə)n/ noun a reduction of the size of the breast for cosmetic purposes

breath /breθ/ noun air which goes in and out of the body when you breathe ○ *He ran so fast he was out of breath.* ○ *Stop for a moment to get your breath back.* ○ *She took a deep breath and dived into the water.* □ **to hold your breath** to stop breathing out, after having inhaled deeply

breathe /briːð/ verb to take air in and blow air out through the nose or mouth ○ *The patient has begun to breathe normally.* □ **to breathe in** to take air into your lungs □ **to breathe out** to let the air out of your lungs ○ *He breathed in the smoke from the fire and it made him cough.* ○ *The doctor told him to take a deep breath and breathe out slowly.*

COMMENT: Children breathe about 20 to 30 times per minute, men 16–18 per minute, and women slightly faster. The breathing rate increases if the person is taking exercise or has a fever. Some babies and young children hold their breath and go blue in the face, especially when crying or during a temper tantrum.

breath-holding attack /'breθ ,həʊldɪŋ ə ,tæk/ noun a period when a young child stops breathing, usually because he or she is angry

breathing /'briːðɪŋ/ noun same as **respiration** ○ *If breathing is difficult or has stopped, begin artificial ventilation immediately.* (NOTE: For other terms referring to breathing see words beginning with **pneum-, pneumo-, pneumat-, pneumato-.**)

breathing rate /'briːðɪŋ reɪt/ noun the number of times a person breathes in and out in a specific period

breathless /'breθləs/ adjective referring to someone who finds it difficult to breathe enough air ○ *After running upstairs she became breathless and had to sit down.*

breathlessness /'breθləsnəs/ noun difficulty in breathing enough air

'26 patients were selected from the outpatient department on grounds of disabling breathlessness present for at least five years' [*Lancet*]

breath sounds /'breθ saʊndz/ noun hollow sounds made by the lungs and heard through a stethoscope placed on a person's chest, used in diagnosis

breech /briːtʃ/ noun the buttocks, especially of a baby

breech birth /'briːtʃ ,bɜːθ/, **breech delivery** /'briːtʃ dɪ,lɪv(ə)ri/ noun a birth in which the baby's buttocks appear first rather than its head

breech presentation /briːtʃ ,prez(ə)n 'teɪʃ(ə)n/ noun a position of the baby in the uterus in which the buttocks will appear first during childbirth

breed /briːd/ verb to reproduce, or reproduce animals or plants ○ *The bacteria breed in dirty water.* ○ *Insanitary conditions help to breed disease.*

bregma /'bregmə/ noun the point at the top of the head where the soft gap between the bones of a baby's skull hardens

bretylium tosylate /brə,tɪliəm 'tɒsɪleɪt/ noun an agent used to block adrenergic transmitter release

bridge /brɪdʒ/ noun **1.** the top part of the nose where it joins the forehead **2.** an artificial tooth or set of teeth which is joined to natural teeth which hold it in place **3.** a part joining two or more other parts

Bright's disease /'braɪts dɪ,ziːz/ noun inflammation of the kidneys, characterised by albuminuria and high blood pressure. Also called **glomerulonephritis** [Described 1836. After Richard Bright (1789–1858), physician at Guy's Hospital, London, UK.]

bring up /,brɪŋ 'ʌp/ verb **1.** to look after and educate a child **2.** to cough up material such as mucus from the lungs or throat **3.** to vomit (*informal*)

British anti-lewisite /,brɪtɪʃ ,ænti'luːɪsaɪt/ noun an antidote for gases which cause blistering, also used to treat cases of poisoning such as mercury poisoning. Abbr **BAL**

British Dental Association /,brɪtɪʃ 'dent(ə)l əsəʊsi,eɪʃ(ə)n/ noun in the UK, a professional association of dentists. Abbr **BDA**

British Medical Association /,brɪtɪʃ 'medɪk(ə)l əsəʊsi,eɪʃ(ə)n/ noun in the UK, a professional association of doctors. Abbr **BMA**

British National Formulary /,brɪtɪʃ ,næʃ(ə)nəl 'fɔːmjʊləri/ noun a book listing key information on the prescribing, dispensing and administration of prescription drugs used in the UK. Abbr **BNF**

British Pharmacopoeia /,brɪtɪʃ ,fɑːməkə 'piːə/ noun a book listing drugs approved in the UK and their dosages. Abbr **BP**

COMMENT: Drugs listed in the British Pharmacopoeia have the letters BP written after them on labels.

brittle /'brɪt(ə)l/ adjective easily broken ○ *The people's bones become brittle as they get older.*

brittle bone disease /,brɪt(ə)l 'bəʊn dɪ ,ziːz/ noun **1.** same as **osteogenesis imperfecta 2.** same as **osteoporosis**

Broadbent's sign /'brɔːdbents saɪn/ noun a movement of someone's left side near the lower ribs at each beat of the heart, indicating adhesion between the diaphragm and pericardium in cases of pericarditis [After Sir William

Henry Broadbent (1835–1907), British physician]

broad ligament /ˌbrɔːd ˈlɪɡəmənt/ noun peritoneal folds supporting the uterus on each side

broad-spectrum antibiotic /ˌbrɔːd ˌspektrəm ˌæntibaɪˈɒtɪk/ noun an antibiotic used to control many types of microorganism

Broca's aphasia /ˌbrəʊkəz əˈfeɪziə/ noun a condition in which someone is unable to speak or write, as a result of damage to Broca's area

Broca's area /ˈbrəʊkəz ˌeəriə/ noun an area on the left side of the brain which governs the motor aspects of speaking [Described 1861. After Pierre Henri Paul Broca (1824–80), French surgeon and anthropologist. A pioneer of neurosurgery, he also invented various instruments, described muscular dystrophy before Duchenne, and recognised rickets as a nutritional disorder before Virchow.]

Brodie's abscess /ˌbrəʊdiz ˈæbses/ noun an abscess of a bone, caused by staphylococcal osteomyelitis [Described 1832. After Sir Benjamin Collins Brodie (1783–1862), British surgeon.]

bromhidrosis /ˌbrɒmhɪˈdrəʊsɪs/ noun a condition in which body sweat has an unpleasant smell

bromide /ˈbrəʊmaɪd/ noun a bromine salt (NOTE: Bromides are used as sedatives.)

bromine /ˈbrəʊmiːn/ noun a chemical element (NOTE: The chemical symbol is **Br**.)

bromism /ˈbrəʊmɪz(ə)m/ noun chronic ill health caused by excessive use of bromides

bromocriptine /ˌbrəʊməʊˈkrɪptiːn/ noun a drug which functions like dopamine, used to treat excessive lactation, breast pain, some forms of infertility, growth disorder and Parkinson's disease

bronch- /brɒŋk/, **bronchi-** /brɒŋki/ prefix same as **broncho-** (used before vowels)

bronchi /ˈbrɒŋkaɪ/ plural of **bronchus**

bronchial /ˈbrɒŋkiəl/ adjective referring to the bronchi

bronchial asthma /ˌbrɒŋkiəl ˈæsmə/ noun a type of asthma mainly caused by an allergen or by exertion

bronchial breath sounds /ˌbrɒŋkiəl ˈbreθ ˌsaʊndz/ plural noun distinctive breath sounds from the lungs which help diagnosis

bronchial pneumonia /ˌbrɒŋkiəl njuːˈməʊniə/ noun same as **bronchopneumonia**

bronchial tree /ˈbrɒŋkiəl triː/ noun a system of tubes (bronchi and bronchioles) which take the air from the trachea into the lungs

bronchiectasis /ˌbrɒŋkiˈektəsɪs/ noun a disorder of the bronchi which become wide, infected and filled with pus (NOTE: Bronchiectasis can lead to pneumonia.)

bronchio- /brɒŋkiəʊ/ prefix referring to the bronchioles

bronchiolar /ˌbrɒŋkiˈəʊlə/ adjective referring to the bronchioles

bronchiole /ˈbrɒŋkiəʊl/ noun a very small air tube in the lungs leading from a bronchus to the alveoli. See illustration at LUNGS in Supplement

bronchiolitis /ˌbrɒŋkiəʊˈlaɪtɪs/ noun inflammation of the bronchioles, usually in small children

bronchitic /brɒŋˈkɪtɪk/ adjective 1. referring to bronchitis 2. referring to a person who has bronchitis

bronchitis /brɒŋˈkaɪtɪs/ noun inflammation of the mucous membrane of the bronchi □ **acute bronchitis** an attack of bronchitis caused by a virus or by exposure to cold and wet

broncho- /brɒŋkəʊ/ prefix referring to the windpipe

bronchoconstrictor /ˌbrɒŋkəʊkənˈstrɪktə/ noun a drug which narrows the bronchi

bronchodilator /ˌbrɒŋkəʊdaɪˈleɪtə/ noun a drug which makes the bronchi wider, used in the treatment of asthma and allergy (NOTE: Bronchodilators usually have names ending in -**terol**; however, the most common bronchodilator is **salbutamol**.)

'19 children with mild to moderately severe perennial bronchial asthma were selected. These children gave a typical history of exercise-induced asthma and their symptoms were controlled with oral or aerosol bronchodilators' [Lancet]

bronchogram /ˈbrɒŋkəʊɡræm/ noun an X-ray picture of the bronchial tubes obtained by bronchography

bronchography /brɒŋˈkɒɡrəfi/ noun an X-ray examination of the lungs after an opaque substance has been put into the bronchi

bronchomediastinal trunk /ˌbrɒŋkəʊ miːdiəˌstaɪn(ə)l ˈtrʌŋk/ noun the set of lymph nodes draining part of the chest

bronchomycosis /ˌbrɒŋkəʊmaɪˈkəʊsɪs/ noun an infection of the bronchi by a fungus

bronchophony /brɒŋˈkɒfəni/ noun vibrations of the voice heard over the lungs, indicating solidification in the lungs

bronchopleural /ˌbrɒŋkəʊˈplʊərəl/ adjective referring to a bronchus and the pleura

bronchopneumonia /ˌbrɒŋkəʊnjuːˈməʊniə/ noun an infectious inflammation of the bronchioles, which may lead to general infection of the lungs

bronchopulmonary /ˌbrɒŋkəʊˈpʌlmən(ə)ri/ adjective referring to the bronchi and the lungs

bronchorrhoea /ˌbrɒŋkəʊˈriːə/ noun the secretion of mucus by the bronchi

bronchoscope /ˈbrɒŋkəʊskəʊp/ noun an instrument which is passed down the trachea into the lungs, which a doctor can use to inspect the inside passages of the lungs

bronchoscopy /brɒŋˈkɒskəpi/ *noun* an examination of a person's bronchi using a bronchoscope

bronchospasm /ˈbrɒŋkəʊspæz(ə)m/ *noun* a tightening of the bronchial muscles which causes the tubes to contract, as in asthma

bronchospirometer /ˌbrɒŋkəʊspaɪˈrɒmɪtə/ *noun* an instrument for measuring the volume of the lungs

bronchospirometry /ˌbrɒŋkəʊspaɪˈrɒmɪtri/ *noun* a procedure for measuring the volume of the lungs

bronchostenosis /ˌbrɒŋkəʊsteˈnəʊsɪs/ *noun* an unusual constriction of the bronchial tubes

bronchotracheal /ˌbrɒŋkəʊtrəˈkiːəl/ *adjective* referring to the bronchi and the trachea

bronchus /ˈbrɒŋkəs/ *noun* one of the two air passages leading from the trachea into the lungs, where they split into many bronchioles. See illustration at LUNGS in Supplement (NOTE: The plural is **bronchi**.)

bronze diabetes /ˌbrɒnz daɪəˈbiːtiːz/ *noun* same as **haemochromatosis**

Broviac catheter /ˈbrəʊviæk ˌkæθɪtə/ *noun* a type of thin catheter used to insert into a vein

brow /braʊ/ *noun* **1.** same as **forehead 2.** same as **eyebrow**

brown fat /braʊn ˈfæt/ *noun* dark-coloured body fat that can easily be converted to energy and helps to control body temperature

Brown-Séquard syndrome /ˌbraʊn ˈseɪkɑː ˌsɪndrəʊm/ *noun* a condition in which the spinal cord has been partly severed or compressed, with the result that the lower half of the body is paralysed on one side and loses feeling in the other side [Described 1851. After Charles Edouard Brown-Séquard (1817–94), French physiologist.]

Brucella /bruːˈselə/ *noun* a type of rod-shaped bacterium

brucellosis /ˌbruːsɪˈləʊsɪs/ *noun* a disease which can be caught from cattle or goats or from drinking infected milk, spread by a species of the bacterium *Brucella*. The symptoms include tiredness, arthritis, headache, sweating, irritability and swelling of the spleen. Also called **abortus fever, Malta fever, mountain fever, undulant fever**

Brufen /ˈbruːfən/ a trade name for ibuprofen

bruise /bruːz/ *noun* a dark painful area on the skin, where blood has escaped under the skin following a blow. ◊ **black eye** ■ *verb* to cause a bruise on part of the body ○ *She bruised her knee on the corner of the table.* □ **she bruises easily** even a soft blow will give her a bruise

bruised /bruːzd/ *adjective* painful after a blow or showing the marks of a bruise ○ *a badly bruised leg*

bruising /ˈbruːzɪŋ/ *noun* an area of bruises ○ *The baby has bruising on the back and legs.*

bruit /bruːt/ *noun* an unusual noise heard through a stethoscope

Brunner's glands /ˈbrʊnəz ˌglændz/ *plural noun* glands in the duodenum and jejunum [Described 1687. After Johann Konrad Brunner (1653–1727), Swiss anatomist at Heidelberg, then at Strasbourg.]

bruxism /ˈbrʌksɪz(ə)m/ *noun* the action of grinding the teeth, as a habit

BSE *abbr* bovine spongiform encephalopathy

bubo /ˈbjuːbəʊ/ *noun* a swelling of a lymph node in the groin or armpit

bubonic plague /bjuːˌbɒnɪk ˈpleɪg/ *noun* a usually fatal infectious disease caused by *Yersinia pestis* in the lymph system, transmitted to humans by fleas from rats

COMMENT: Bubonic plague was the Black Death of the Middle Ages. Its symptoms are fever, delirium, vomiting and swelling of the lymph nodes.

buccal /ˈbʌk(ə)l/ *adjective* referring to the cheek or mouth

buccal cavity /ˈbʌk(ə)l ˌkævɪti/ *noun* the mouth

buccal fat /ˈbʌk(ə)l fæt/ *noun* a pad of fat separating the buccinator muscle from the masseter

buccal smear /ˈbʌk(ə)l smɪə/ *noun* a gentle scraping of the inside of the cheek with a spatula to obtain cells for testing

buccinator /ˈbʌksɪneɪtə/ *noun* a cheek muscle which helps the jaw to move when chewing

Budd–Chiari syndrome /ˌbʌd kɪˈeəri ˌsɪndrəʊm/ *noun* a disease of the liver, where thrombosis has occurred in the hepatic veins [Described 1845. After George Budd (1808–82), Professor of Medicine at King's College Hospital, London; Hans von Chiari (1851–1916), Viennese pathologist who was Professor of Pathological Anatomy at Strasbourg and later at Prague.]

budesonide /bjuːˈdesənaɪd/ *noun* a corticosteroid drug taken by inhalation or in tablets, used in the treatment of hay fever and nasal polyps

Buerger's disease /ˈbɜːgəz dɪˌziːz/ *noun* same as **thromboangiitis obliterans** [Described 1908. After Leo Buerger (1879–1943), New York physician of Viennese origin.]

buffer /ˈbʌfə/ *noun* **1.** a substance that keeps a constant balance between acid and alkali **2.** a solution where the pH is not changed by adding acid or alkali ■ *verb* to prevent a solution from becoming acid

buffer action /ˈbʌfə ˌækʃən/ *noun* the balancing process between acid and alkali

buffered /ˈbʌfəd/ *adjective* prevented from becoming acid ○ *buffered aspirin*

bug /bʌg/ *noun* an infectious disease (*informal*) ○ *He caught a bug on holiday.* ○ *Half the staff have got a stomach bug.*

build /bɪld/ noun the general size and shape of a person's body ○ *He has a heavy build for his height.* ○ *The girl is of slight build.*

build up /ˌbɪld ˈʌp/ verb to form gradually by being added to, or to form something in this way (NOTE: **building – built**)

build-up /ˈbɪld ʌp/ noun a gradual process of being added to ○ *a build-up of fatty deposits on the walls of the arteries*

built /bɪlt/ adjective referring to the general size of a person's body ○ *a heavily built man* ○ *She's slightly built.*

bulb /bʌlb/ noun a round part at the end of an organ or bone □ **bulb of the penis** the round end of the penis. Also called **glans penis**

bulbar /ˈbʌlbə/ adjective 1. referring to a bulb 2. referring to the medulla oblongata

bulbar paralysis /ˌbʌlbə pəˈrælɪsɪs/, **bulbar palsy** /ˌbʌlbə ˈpɔːlzi/ noun a form of motor neurone disease which affects the muscles of the mouth, jaw and throat

bulbar poliomyelitis /ˌbʌlbə ˌpəʊliəʊmaɪə-ˈlaɪtɪs/ noun a type of polio affecting the brain stem, which makes it difficult for a person to swallow or breathe

bulbospongiosus muscle /ˌbʌlbəʊ-spʌndʒiˈəʊsəs ˌmʌsəl/ noun a muscle in the perineum behind the penis

bulbourethral gland /ˌbʌlbəʊjuˈriːθrəl ˌglænd/ noun one of two glands at the base of the penis which secrete into the urethra. ◊ **gland**

bulge /bʌldʒ/ verb to push out ○ *The wall of the abdomen becomes weak and part of the intestine bulges through.*

bulging /ˈbʌldʒɪŋ/ adjective sticking out ○ *bulging eyes*

bulimia /buˈlɪmiə/, **bulimia nervosa** /bu-ˌlɪmiə nəˈvəʊsə/ noun a psychological condition in which a person eats too much and is incapable of controlling his or her eating. The eating is followed by behaviour designed to prevent weight gain, e.g. vomiting, use of laxatives or excessive exercise.

bulimic /buˈlɪmɪk/ adjective 1. referring to bulimia 2. having bulimia ■ noun someone who has bulimia

bulla /ˈbʊlə/ noun a large blister (NOTE: The plural is **bullae**.)

bumetanide /bjuːˈmetənaɪd/ noun a drug which helps a patient to produce urine, used in the treatment of swelling caused by fluid accumulating in the tissues

bump /bʌmp/ noun a slightly swollen part on the skin, caused by something such as a blow or sting

bumper fracture /ˈbʌmpə ˌfræktʃə/ noun a fracture in the upper part of the tibia (NOTE: It has this name because it can be caused by a blow from the bumper of a car.)

bundle /ˈbʌnd(ə)l/ noun a group of nerves running in the same direction

bundle branch block /ˈbʌnd(ə)l brɑːntʃ ˌblɒk/ noun an unusual condition of the heart's conduction tissue

bundle of His /ˌbʌnd(ə)l əv ˈhɪs/ noun same as **atrioventricular bundle** [Described 1893. After Ludwig His (1863–1934), Professor of Anatomy successively at Leipzig, Basle, Göttingen and Berlin.]

bunion /ˈbʌnjən/ noun an inflammation and swelling of the big toe, caused by tight shoes which force the toe sideways so that a callus develops over the joint between the toe and the metatarsal

buphthalmos /bʌfˈθælməs/ noun a type of congenital glaucoma occurring in infants

bupivacaine /bjuːˈpɪvəkeɪn/ noun a powerful local anaesthetic, used in epidural anaesthesia

buprenorphine /bjuːˈprenəfiːn/ noun an opiate drug used in the relief of moderate to severe pain, and as an opioid substitute in treating drug addiction

Burkitt's tumour /ˌbɜːkɪts ˈtjuːmə/, **Burkitt's lymphoma** /ˌbɜːkɪts lɪmˈfəʊmə/ noun a malignant tumour, usually on the maxilla, found especially in children in Africa [Described 1957. After Denis Parsons Burkitt (1911–93), formerly Senior Surgeon, Kampala, Uganda; later a member of the Medical Research Council (UK).]

burn /bɜːn/ noun an injury to skin and tissue caused by light, heat, radiation, electricity or chemicals ■ verb to harm or destroy something by fire ○ *She burnt her hand on the hot frying pan.* ○ *Most of his hair or his skin was burnt off.* (NOTE: **burning – burnt** or **burned**)
COMMENT: The modern classification of burns is into two categories: deep and superficial. Burns were formerly classified as first, second or third degree and are still sometimes referred to in this way.

burning /ˈbɜːnɪŋ/ adjective referring to a feeling similar to that of being hurt by fire ○ *She had a burning pain or in her chest.*

burnout /ˈbɜːnaʊt/ noun a feeling of depression, fatigue and lack of energy caused by stress and being overworked ○ *He suffered a burnout and had to go on leave.*

burns unit /ˈbɜːnz ˌjuːnɪt/ noun a special department in a hospital which deals with burns

burp /bɜːp/ noun (informal) noun an act of allowing air in the stomach to come up through the mouth ■ verb to allow air in the stomach to come up through the mouth □ **to burp a baby** to pat a baby on the back until it burps

burr /bɜː/ noun a bit used with a drill to make holes in a bone such as the cranium or in a tooth

bursa /ˈbɜːsə/ noun a sac containing fluid, forming part of the usual structure of a joint such as the knee and elbow, where it protects against frequent pressure and rubbing (NOTE: The plural is **bursae**.)

bursitis /bɜːˈsaɪtɪs/ *noun* the inflammation of a bursa, especially in the shoulder

Buscopan /ˈbʌskəpæn/ a trade name for a form of hyoscine

butobarbitone /ˌbjuːtəʊˈbɑːbɪtəʊn/ *noun* a barbiturate drug used as a sedative and hypnotic

buttock /ˈbʌtək/ *noun* one of the two fleshy parts below the back, on which a person sits, made up mainly of the gluteal muscles. Also called **nates**

buttonhole surgery /ˈbʌt(ə)nhəʊl ˌsɜːdʒəri/ *noun* a surgical operation through a small hole in the body, using an endoscope

bypass /ˈbaɪpɑːs/ *noun* **1.** a surgical operation to redirect the blood, usually using a grafted blood vessel and usually performed when one of the person's own blood vessels is blocked **2.** a new route for the blood created by a bypass operation

byssinosis /ˌbɪsɪˈnəʊsɪs/ *noun* a lung disease which is a form of pneumoconiosis caused by inhaling cotton dust

C

c *symbol* centi-

C *symbol* Celsius

CABG *abbr* coronary artery bypass graft

cachet /'kæʃeɪ/ *noun* a quantity of a drug wrapped in paper, to be swallowed

cachexia /kæ'keksiə/ *noun* a state of ill health characterised by wasting and general weakness

cadaver /kə'dævə/ *noun* a dead body, especially one used for dissection

cadaveric /kə'dævərɪk/, **cadaverous** /kə 'dæv(ə)rəs/ *adjective* referring to a person who is thin or wasting away

caeca /'siːkə/ plural of **caecum**

caecal /'siːk(ə)l/ *adjective* referring to the caecum

caecosigmoidostomy /ˌsiːkəʊˌsɪgmɔɪ 'dɒstəmi/ *noun* an operation to open up a connection between the caecum and the sigmoid colon

caecostomy /siː'kɒstəmi/ *noun* a surgical operation to make an opening between the caecum and the abdominal wall to allow faeces to be passed without going through the rectum and anus

caecum /'siːkəm/ *noun* the wider part of the large intestine in the lower right-hand side of the abdomen at the point where the small intestine joins it and which has the appendix attached to it. See illustration at DIGESTIVE SYSTEM in Supplement. Also called **cecum** (NOTE: The plural is **caeca**.)

caesarean /sɪ'zeəriən/, **caesarean section** /sɪ'zeəriən ˌsekʃən/ *noun* a surgical operation to deliver a baby by cutting through the abdominal wall into the uterus. Compare **vaginal delivery** (NOTE: The US spelling is **cesarean**.)

COMMENT: A caesarean section is performed only when it appears that natural childbirth is impossible or might endanger mother or child, and only after the 28th week of gestation.

caesium /'siːziəm/ *noun* a radioactive element, used in treatment by radiation (NOTE: The chemical symbol is **Cs**.)

caesium-137 /ˌsiːziəm wʌn θriː 'sev(ə)n/ *noun* a radioactive substance used in radiology

café au lait spots /ˌkæfeɪ əʊ 'leɪ spɒts/ *plural noun* brown spots on the skin, which are an indication of von Recklinghausen's disease

caffeine /'kæfiːn/ *noun* an alkaloid found in coffee, tea and chocolate, which acts as a stimulant

COMMENT: Apart from acting as a stimulant, caffeine also helps in the production of urine. It can be addictive, and exists in both tea and coffee in about the same percentages as well as in chocolate and other drinks.

caisson disease /'keɪs(ə)n dɪˌziːz/ *noun* a condition in which a person experiences pains in the joints and stomach, and dizziness caused by nitrogen in the blood. Also called **the bends**, **compressed air sickness**, **decompression sickness**

COMMENT: The disease occurs in a person who has moved rapidly from high atmospheric pressure to a lower pressure area, such as a diver who has come back to the surface too quickly after a deep dive. The first symptoms, pains in the joints, are known as 'the bends'. The disease can be fatal.

calamine /'kæləmaɪn/, **calamine lotion** / 'kæləmaɪn ˌləʊʃ(ə)n/ *noun* a lotion, based on zinc oxide, which helps relieve skin irritation, caused e.g. by sunburn or chickenpox

calc- /kælk/ *prefix* same as **calci-** (used before vowels)

calcaemia /kæl'siːmiə/ *noun* a condition in which the blood contains an unusually large amount of calcium

calcaneal /kæl'keɪniəl/ *adjective* referring to the calcaneus

calcaneal tendon /kælˌkeɪniəl 'tendən/ *noun* the Achilles tendon, the tendon at the back of the ankle which connects the calf muscles to the heel and which acts to pull up the heel when the calf muscle is contracted

calcaneus /kæl'keɪniəs/, **calcaneum** /kæl 'keɪniəm/ *noun* the heel bone, situated underneath the talus. See illustration at FOOT in Supplement

calcareous degeneration /kælˌkeəriəs dɪ ˌdʒenə'reɪʃ(ə)n/ *noun* the formation of calcium on bones or at joints in old age

calci- /kælsɪ/ *prefix* referring to calcium

calcification /ˌkælsɪfɪˈkeɪʃ(ə)n/ *noun* a process of hardening caused by the formation of deposits of calcium salts

COMMENT: Calcification can be expected in the formation of bones, but can occur unusually in joints, muscles and organs, where it is known as calcinosis.

calcified /ˈkælsɪfaɪd/ *adjective* made hard ○ *Bone is calcified connective tissue.*

calcinosis /ˌkælsɪˈnəʊsɪs/ *noun* a medical condition where deposits of calcium salts form in joints, muscles and organs

calcitonin /ˌkælsɪˈtəʊnɪn/ *noun* a hormone produced by the thyroid gland, which is believed to regulate the level of calcium in the blood. Also called **thyrocalcitonin**

calcium /ˈkælsiəm/ *noun* a metallic chemical element which is a major component of bones and teeth and which is essential for various bodily processes such as blood clotting (NOTE: The chemical symbol is **Ca**.)

COMMENT: Calcium is an important element in a balanced diet. Milk, cheese, eggs and certain vegetables are its main sources. Calcium deficiency can be treated by injections of calcium salts.

calcium antagonist /ˈkælsiəm ænˌtæɡənɪst/ *noun* a drug which makes the arteries wider and slows the heart rate. It is used in the treatment of angina.

calcium channel blocker /ˈkælsiəm ˌtʃæn(ə)l ˌblɒkə/, **calcium blocker** /ˈkælsiəm ˌblɒkə/ *noun* a drug which affects the smooth muscle of the cardiovascular system, used in the treatment of angina and hypertension (NOTE: Calcium channel blockers have names ending in **-dipine: nifedipine**. Not to be used in heart failure as they reduce cardiac function further.)

calcium deficiency /ˈkælsiəm dɪˌfɪʃ(ə)nsi/ *noun* a lack of calcium in the bloodstream

calcium phosphate /ˌkælsiəm ˈfɒsfeɪt/ *noun* the main constituent of bones

calcium supplement /ˈkælsiəm ˌsʌplɪmənt/ *noun* the addition of calcium to the diet, or as injections, to improve the level of calcium in the bloodstream

calculosis /ˌkælkjʊˈləʊsɪs/ *noun* a condition in which calculi exist in an organ

calculus /ˈkælkjʊləs/ *noun* a hard mass like a little piece of stone, which forms inside the body. Also called **stone** (NOTE: The plural is **calculi**.)

COMMENT: Calculi are formed of cholesterol and various inorganic substances, and are commonly found in the bladder, the gall bladder (gallstones) and various parts of the kidney.

Caldwell–Luc operation /ˌkɔːldwel ˈluːk ɒpəˌreɪʃ(ə)n/ *noun* a surgical operation to drain the maxillary sinus by making an incision above the canine tooth [Described 1893. After George Walter Caldwell (1834–1918), US physician; Henri Luc (1855–1925), French laryngologist.]

calf /kɑːf/ *noun* a muscular fleshy part at the back of the lower leg, formed by the gastrocnemius muscles (NOTE: The plural is **calves**.)

caliber /ˈkælɪbə/ *noun US* same as **calibre**

calibrate /ˈkælɪbreɪt/ *verb* 1. to measure the inside diameter of a tube or passage 2. to measure the sizes of two parts of the body to be joined together in surgery 3. to adjust an instrument or piece of equipment against a known standard

calibrator /ˈkælɪbreɪtə/ *noun* 1. an instrument used to enlarge a tube or passage 2. an instrument for measuring the diameter of a tube or passage

calibre /ˈkælɪbə/ *noun* the interior diameter of a tube or of a blood vessel

caliectasis /ˌkeɪliˈektəsɪs/ *noun* swelling of the calyces

caliper /ˈkælɪpə/ *noun* 1. an instrument with two legs, used for measuring the width of the pelvic cavity 2. an instrument with two sharp points which are put into a fractured bone and weights attached to cause traction 3. a leg splint made of rods and straps and usually fastened to the lower leg to enable the hip bone rather than the foot to support the person's weight when walking

calliper /ˈkælɪpə/ *noun* same as **caliper 3**

callisthenic /ˌkælɪsˈθenɪk/ *adjective* relating to callisthenics

callisthenics /ˌkælɪsˈθenɪks/ *plural noun* energetic physical exercises for improving fitness and muscle tone, including push-ups, sit-ups and star jumps

callosity /kəˈlɒsɪti/ *noun* a hard patch on the skin, e.g. a corn, resulting from frequent pressure or rubbing. Also called **callus**

callosum /kəˈləʊs(ə)m/ ⸌ **corpus callosum**

callus /ˈkæləs/ *noun* 1. same as **callosity** 2. tissue which forms round a broken bone as it starts to mend, leading to consolidation ○ *Callus formation is more rapid in children and young adults than in elderly people.*

calm /kɑːm/ *adjective* quiet, not upset ○ *The patient was delirious but became calm after the injection.*

calomel /ˈkæləmel/ *noun* mercurous chloride, a poisonous substance used to treat pinworms in the intestine. Formula: Hg_2Cl_2.

calor /ˈkælə/ *noun* heat

caloric /kəˈlɒrɪk/ *adjective* referring to calories or to heat

caloric energy /kəˌlɒrɪk ˈenədʒi/ *noun* the amount of energy shown as a number of calories

caloric requirement /kəˌlɒrɪk rɪˈkwaɪəmənt/ *noun* the amount of energy shown in calories which a person needs each day

calorie /'kæləri/ *noun* **1.** a unit of measurement of heat or energy, equivalent to the amount of heat needed to raise the temperature of 1g of water by 1°C. Now called **joule 2.** also **Calorie** a unit of measurement of energy in food (*informal*) ○ *a low-calorie diet* Now called **joule** □ **to count calories** to be careful about how much you eat

calvaria /kæl'veəriə/, **calvarium** /kæl-'veəriəm/ *noun* the top part of the skull

calyx /'keɪlɪks/ *noun* a part of the body shaped like a cup especially the tube leading to a renal pyramid. See illustration at KIDNEY in Supplement (NOTE: The plural is **calyces**.)

COMMENT: The renal pelvis is formed of three major calyces, which themselves are formed of several smaller minor calyces.

CAM *abbr* complementary and alternative medicine

camphor /'kæmfə/ *noun* white crystals with a strong smell, made from a tropical tree, used to keep insects away or as a liniment

camphor oil /'kæmfə ɔɪl/, **camphorated oil** /'kæmfəreɪtɪd ɔɪl/ *noun* a mixture of 20% camphor and oil, used as a rub

Campylobacter /'kæmpɪləʊ,bæktə/ *noun* a bacterium which is a common cause of food poisoning in humans and of spontaneous abortion in farm animals

canal /kə'næl/ *noun* a tube along which something flows

canaliculitis /,kænəlɪkju'laɪtɪs/ *noun* inflammation of the tear duct canal

canaliculotomy /,kænəlɪkju'lɒtəmi/ *noun* a surgical operation to open up a little canal

canaliculus /,kænə'lɪkjʊləs/ *noun* a little canal, e.g. a canal leading to the Haversian systems in compact bone, or a canal leading to the lacrimal duct (NOTE: The plural is **canaliculi**.)

cancellous bone /'kænsələs ,bəʊn/ *noun* a light spongy bone tissue which forms the inner core of a bone and also the ends of long bones. See illustration at BONE STRUCTURE in Supplement

cancer /'kænsə/ *noun* a malignant growth or tumour which develops in tissue and destroys it, which can spread by metastasis to other parts of the body and which cannot be controlled by the body itself ○ *Cancer cells developed in the lymph.* ○ *She has been diagnosed as having lung cancer* or *as having cancer of the lung.* (NOTE: For other terms referring to cancer, see words beginning with **carcin-**.)

COMMENT: Cancers can be divided into cancers of the skin (**carcinomas**) or cancers of connective tissue such as bone or muscle (**sarcomas**). They have many causes. Many are curable by surgery, by chemotherapy or by radiation, especially if they are detected early.

cancerophobia /,kænsərəʊ'fəʊbiə/ *noun* a fear of cancer

cancerous /'kænsərəs/ *adjective* referring to cancer ○ *The X-ray revealed a cancerous growth in the breast.*

cancer phobia /'kænsə ,fəʊbiə/ *noun* same as **cancerophobia**

cancrum oris /,kæŋkrəm 'ɔːrɪs/ *noun* severe ulcers in the mouth, leading to gangrene. Also called **noma**

Candida /'kændɪdə/ *noun* a type of fungus which causes mycosis. Also called **Monilia**

'It is incorrect to say that oral candida is an infection. Candida is easily isolated from the mouths of up to 50% of healthy adults and is a normal commensal.' [*Nursing Times*]

Candida albicans /,kændɪdə 'ælbɪkænz/ *noun* one type of Candida which is usually present in the mouth and throat without causing any illness, but which can cause thrush

candidate /'kændɪdeɪt/ *noun* someone who could have an operation ○ *These types of patients may be candidates for embolisation.*

candidate vaccine /'kændɪdeɪt ,væksiːn/ *noun* a vaccine which is being tested for use in immunisation

candidiasis /,kændɪ'daɪəsɪs/, **candidosis** /,kændɪ'dəʊsɪs/ *noun* infection with a species of the fungus Candida

COMMENT: When the infection occurs in the vagina or mouth it is known as 'thrush'. Thrush in the mouth usually affects small children.

canicola fever /kə'nɪkələ ,fiːvə/ *noun* a form of leptospirosis, giving high fever and jaundice

canine /'keɪnaɪn/, **canine tooth** /'keɪnaɪn ,tuːθ/ *noun* a pointed tooth next to an incisor. See illustration at TEETH in Supplement

COMMENT: There are four canines in all, two in the upper jaw and two in the lower. Those in the upper jaw are referred to as the 'eyeteeth'.

canities /kə'nɪʃiiːz/ *noun* a loss of pigments, which makes the hair turn white

canker sore /'kæŋkə ,sɔː/ *noun* same as **mouth ulcer**

cannabis /'kænəbɪs/ *noun* a drug made from the dried leaves or flowers of the Indian hemp plant. Recreational use of cannabis is illegal and its use to relieve the pain associated with conditions such as multiple sclerosis is controversial. Also called **hashish**, **marijuana**

COMMENT: Cannabis has analgesic properties, and the possibility that it should be legalised for therapeutic use in conditions of chronic pain is being debated.

cannabis resin /,kænəbɪs 'rezɪn/ *noun* an addictive drug, a purified extract made from the flowers of the Indian hemp plant

cannula /'kænjʊlə/ *noun* a tube with a trocar or blunt needle inside, inserted into the body to introduce fluids

cannulate /'kænjʊleɪt/ *verb* to put a cannula into a vein or cavity to give drugs or to drain away fluid

canthal /'kænθəl/ *adjective* referring to the corner of the eye

cantholysis /kæn'θɒləsɪs/ *noun* same as **canthoplasty**

canthoplasty /'kænθəplæsti/ *noun* **1.** an operation to repair the canthus of the eye **2.** an operation to cut through the canthus to enlarge the groove in the eyelid

canthus /'kænθəs/ *noun* a corner of the eye

canula *noun* another spelling of **cannula**

canulate *verb* another spelling of **cannulate**

cap /kæp/ *noun* **1.** a covering which protects something **2.** an artificial hard covering for a damaged or broken tooth

CAPD *abbr* continuous ambulatory peritoneal dialysis

capeline bandage /'kæpəlaɪn ˌbændɪdʒ/ *noun* a bandage shaped like a cap, either for the head, or to cover a stump after amputation

capillary /kə'pɪləri/ *noun* **1.** a tiny blood vessel between the arterioles and the venules, which carries blood and nutrients into the tissues **2.** any tiny tube carrying a liquid in the body

capillary bleeding /kəˌpɪləri 'bliːdɪŋ/ *noun* bleeding where blood oozes out from small blood vessels

capita /'kæpɪtə/ plural of **caput**

capitate /'kæpɪteɪt/, **capitate bone** /'kæpɪteɪt ˌbəʊn/ *noun* the largest of the eight small carpal bones in the wrist. See illustration at HAND in Supplement

capitellum /ˌkæpɪ'teləm/ *noun* a rounded enlarged part at the end of a bone, especially this part of the upper arm bone, the humerus, that forms the elbow joint with one of the lower bones, the radius. Also called **capitulum of humerus** (NOTE: The plural is **capitella**.)

capitis /kə'paɪtɪs/ ♦ **corona capitis**

capitular /kə'pɪtjʊlə/ *adjective* describing the rounded end (**capitulum**) of a bone

capitulum /kə'pɪtjʊləm/ *noun* the rounded end of a bone which articulates with another bone, e.g. the distal end of the humerus (NOTE: The plural is **capitula**.)

capitulum of humerus /kəˌpɪtjʊləm əv 'hjuːmərəs/ *noun* same as **capitellum**

caplet /'kæplət/ *noun* a small oblong tablet with a covering that dissolves easily and which usually cannot be broken in two

caps. *abbr* capsule

capsular /'kæpsjʊlə/ *adjective* referring to a capsule

capsule /'kæpsjuːl/ *noun* **1.** a membrane round an organ or joint **2.** a small hollow digestible case filled with a drug that is taken by swallowing ○ *She swallowed three capsules of painkiller.* ○ *The doctor prescribed the drug in capsule form.*

capsulectomy /ˌkæpsjʊ'lektəmi/ *noun* the surgical removal of the capsule round a joint

capsulitis /ˌkæpsjʊ'laɪtɪs/ *noun* inflammation of a capsule

capsulotomy /ˌkæpsjʊ'lɒtəmi/ *noun* a surgical procedure involving cutting into the capsule around a body part, e.g. cutting into the lens of the eye during the removal of a cataract

captopril /'kæptəprɪl/ *noun* a drug which helps to prevent the arteries from being made narrower by an angiotensin. It is used to control high blood pressure.

caput /'kæpət/ *noun* **1.** the head **2.** the top of part of something (NOTE: [all senses] The plural is **capita**.)

carbamazepine /ˌkɑːbə'mæzəpiːn/ *noun* a drug which reduces pain and helps to prevent convulsions. It is used in the treatment of epilepsy, pain and bipolar disorder.

carbenoxolone /ˌkɑːbə'nɒksələʊn/ *noun* a liquorice agent, used to treat stomach ulcers

carbidopa /ˌkɑːbɪ'dəʊpə/ *noun* an inhibitor used to enable levodopa to enter the brain in larger quantities in the treatment of Parkinson's disease

carbimazole /kɑː'bɪməzəʊl/ *noun* a drug which helps to prevent the formation of thyroid hormones, used in the management of hyperthyroidism

carbohydrate /ˌkɑːbəʊ'haɪdreɪt/ *noun* **1.** a biological compound containing carbon, hydrogen and oxygen. Carbohydrates derive from sugar and are an important source of food and energy. **2.** food containing carbohydrates ○ *high carbohydrate drinks*

carbolic acid /kɑːˌbɒlɪk 'æsɪd/ *noun* same as **phenol**

carbon /'kɑːbən/ *noun* one of the common non-metallic elements, an essential component of living matter and organic chemical compounds (NOTE: The chemical symbol is **C**.)

carbon dioxide /ˌkɑːbən daɪ'ɒksaɪd/ *noun* a colourless gas produced by the body's metabolism as the tissues burn carbon, and breathed out by the lungs as waste (NOTE: The chemical symbol is CO_2.)

COMMENT: Carbon dioxide can be solidified at low temperatures and is known as 'dry ice' or 'carbon dioxide snow', being used to remove growths on the skin.

carbon dioxide snow /ˌkɑːbən daɪˌɒksaɪd 'snəʊ/ *noun* solid carbon dioxide, used in treating skin growths such as warts, or to preserve tissue samples

carbonic anhydrase /kɑːˌbɒnɪk æn'haɪdreɪz/ *noun* an enzyme which acts as a buffer and regulates the body's water balance, including gastric acid secretion and aqueous humour production

carbon monoxide /ˌkɑːbən mə'nɒksaɪd/ *noun* a poisonous gas found in fumes from car engines, from burning gas and cigarette smoke (NOTE: The chemical symbol is **CO**.)

COMMENT: Carbon monoxide is dangerous because it is easily absorbed into the blood and takes the place of the oxygen in the blood, combining with haemoglobin to form carboxyhaemoglobin, which has the effect of starving the tissues of oxygen. Carbon monoxide has no smell and people do not realise that they are being poisoned by it. They become unconscious, with a characteristic red colouring to the skin. Poisoning with car exhaust fumes is sometimes used as a method of suicide. The treatment for carbon monoxide poisoning is very rapid inhalation of fresh air together with carbon dioxide if this can be provided.

carbon monoxide poisoning /ˌkɑːbən məˈnɒksaɪd ˌpɔɪz(ə)nɪŋ/ *noun* poisoning caused by breathing carbon monoxide

carboxyhaemoglobin /kɑːˌbɒksihiːmə ˈɡləʊbɪn/ *noun* a compound of carbon monoxide and haemoglobin formed when a person breathes in carbon monoxide from tobacco smoke or car exhaust fumes

carboxyhaemoglobinaemia /kɑːˌbɒksi hiːməˌɡləʊbɪˈniːmiə/ *noun* the presence of carboxyhaemoglobin in the blood

carbuncle /ˈkɑːbʌŋkəl/ *noun* a localised staphylococcal infection, which goes deep into the tissue

carcin- /kɑːsɪn/ *prefix* same as **carcino-** (*used before vowels*)

carcino- /kɑːsɪnə/ *prefix* referring to carcinoma or cancer

carcinogen /kɑːˈsɪnədʒən/ *noun* a substance which produces a carcinoma or cancer

COMMENT: Carcinogens are found in pesticides such as DDT, in asbestos, tobacco, aromatic compounds such as benzene and radioactive substances.

carcinogenesis /ˌkɑːsɪnəˈdʒenəsɪs/ *noun* the process of forming a carcinoma in tissue

carcinogenic /ˌkɑːsɪnəˈdʒenɪk/ *adjective* causing a carcinoma or cancer

carcinoid /ˈkɑːsɪnɔɪd/ *noun* an intestinal tumour, especially in the appendix, which causes diarrhoea

carcinoid syndrome /ˈkɑːsɪnɔɪd ˌsɪndrəʊm/ *noun* a group of symptoms which are associated with a carcinoid tumour

carcinoid tumour /ˈkɑːsɪnɔɪd ˌtjuːmə/ same as **carcinoid**

carcinoma /ˌkɑːsɪˈnəʊmə/ *noun* a cancer of the epithelium or glands

carcinoma in situ /kɑːsɪˌnəʊmə ɪn ˈsɪtju/ *noun* the first stage in the development of a cancer, where the epithelial cells begin to change

carcinomatosis /ˌkɑːsɪnəʊməˈtəʊsɪs/ *noun* a carcinoma which has spread to many sites in the body

carcinomatous /ˌkɑːsɪˈnɒmətəs/ *adjective* referring to carcinoma

carcinosarcoma /ˌkɑːsɪnəʊsɑːˈkəʊmə/ *noun* a malignant tumour containing elements of both a carcinoma and a sarcoma

cardi- /kɑːdi/ *prefix* same as **cardio-** (*used before vowels*)

cardia /ˈkɑːdiə/ *noun* 1. an opening at the top of the stomach which joins it to the gullet 2. the heart

cardiac /ˈkɑːdiæk/ *adjective* 1. referring to the heart 2. referring to the cardia

cardiac achalasia /ˌkɑːdiæk ˌækəˈleɪziə/ *noun* a condition in which the patient is unable to relax the cardia, the muscle at the entrance to the stomach, with the result that food cannot enter the stomach. ◊ **cardiomyotomy**

cardiac arrest /ˌkɑːdiæk əˈrest/ *noun* a condition in which the heart muscle stops beating

cardiac asthma /ˌkɑːdiæk ˈæsmə/ *noun* difficulty in breathing caused by heart failure

cardiac catheter /ˌkɑːdiæk ˈkæθɪtə/ *noun* a catheter passed through a vein into the heart, to take blood samples, to record pressure or to examine the interior of the heart before surgery

cardiac catheterisation /ˌkɑːdiæk ˌkæθɪtəraɪˈzeɪʃ(ə)n/ *noun* a procedure which involves passing a catheter into the heart

cardiac cirrhosis /ˌkɑːdiæk sɪˈrəʊsɪs/ *noun* cirrhosis of the liver caused by heart disease

cardiac compression /ˌkɑːdiæk kəmˈpreʃ(ə)n/ *noun* the compression of the heart by fluid in the pericardium

cardiac conducting system /ˌkɑːdiæk kənˈdʌktɪŋ ˌsɪstəm/ *noun* the nerve system in the heart which links an atrium to a ventricle, so that the two beat at the same rate

cardiac cycle /ˌkɑːdiæk ˈsaɪk(ə)l/ *noun* the repeated beating of the heart, formed of the diastole and systole

cardiac decompression /ˌkɑːdiæk ˌdiːkəmˈpreʃ(ə)n/ *noun* the removal of a haematoma or constriction of the heart

cardiac failure /ˌkɑːdiæk ˈfeɪljə/ *noun* same as **heart failure**

cardiac glycoside /ˌkɑːdiæk ˈɡlaɪkəsaɪd/ *noun* a drug used in the treatment of tachycardia and atrial fibrillation, e.g. digoxin

cardiac impression /ˌkɑːdiæk ɪmˈpreʃ(ə)n/ *noun* 1. a concave area near the centre of the upper surface of the liver under the heart 2. a depression on the mediastinal part of the lungs where they touch the pericardium

cardiac index /ˌkɑːdiæk ˈɪndeks/ *noun* the cardiac output per square metre of body surface, usually between 3.1 and 3.8 l/min/m² (litres per minute per square metre)

cardiac infarction /ˌkɑːdiæk ɪnˈfɑːkʃən/ *noun* same as **myocardial infarction**

cardiac monitor /ˌkɑːdiæk ˈmɒnɪtə/ *noun* same as **electrocardiograph**

cardiac murmur /ˌkɑːdiæk ˈmɜːmə/ *noun* same as **heart murmur**

cardiac muscle /ˈkɑːdiæk ˌmʌs(ə)l/ *noun* a muscle in the heart which makes the heart beat

cardiac neurosis /ˌkɑːdiæk njuːˈrəʊsɪs/ *noun* same as **disordered action of the heart**

cardiac notch /ˌkɑːdiæk ˈnɒtʃ/ *noun* **1.** a point in the left lung, where the right inside wall is bent. See illustration at **LUNGS** in Supplement **2.** a notch at the point where the oesophagus joins the greater curvature of the stomach

cardiac orifice /ˌkɑːdiæk ˈɒrɪfɪs/ *noun* an opening where the oesophagus joins the stomach

cardiac output /ˌkɑːdiæk ˈaʊtpʊt/ *noun* the volume of blood expelled by each ventricle in a specific time, usually between 4.8 and 5.3l/min (litres per minute)

cardiac pacemaker /ˌkɑːdiæk ˈpeɪsↆmeɪkə/ *noun* an electronic device implanted on a patient's heart, or which a patient wears attached to the chest, which stimulates and regulates the heartbeat

cardiac patient /ˈkɑːdiæk ˌpeɪʃ(ə)nt/ *noun* a patient who has a heart disorder

cardiac reflex /ˌkɑːdiæk ˈriːfleks/ *noun* the reflex which controls the heartbeat automatically

cardiac surgery /ˌkɑːdiæk ˈsɜːdʒəri/ *noun* surgery to the heart

cardiac tamponade /ˌkɑːdiæk ˌtæmpəˈneɪd/ *noun* pressure on the heart when the pericardial cavity fills with blood. Also called **heart tamponade**

cardiac vein /ˈkɑːdiæk veɪn/ *noun* one of the veins which lead from the myocardium to the right atrium

cardinal /ˈkɑːdɪn(ə)l/ *adjective* most important

cardinal ligaments /ˌkɑːdɪn(ə)l ˈlɪɡəmənts/ *plural noun* ligaments forming a band of connective tissue that extends from the uterine cervix and vagina to the pelvic walls. Also called **Mackenrodt's ligaments**

cardio- /kɑːdiəʊ/ *prefix* referring to the heart

cardiogenic /ˌkɑːdiəˈdʒenɪk/ *adjective* resulting from activity or disease of the heart

cardiogram /ˈkɑːdiəɡræm/ *noun* a graph showing the heartbeat, produced by a cardiograph

cardiograph /ˈkɑːdiəɡrɑːf/ *noun* an instrument which records the heartbeat

cardiographer /ˌkɑːdiˈɒɡrəfə/ *noun* a technician who operates a cardiograph

cardiography /ˌkɑːdiˈɒɡrəfi/ *noun* the action of recording the heartbeat

cardiologist /ˌkɑːdiˈɒlədʒɪst/ *noun* a doctor who specialises in the study of the heart

cardiology /ˌkɑːdiˈɒlədʒi/ *noun* the study of the heart, its diseases and functions

cardiomegaly /ˌkɑːdiəʊˈmeɡəli/ *noun* an enlarged heart

cardiomyopathy /ˌkɑːdiəʊmaɪˈɒpəθi/ *noun* a disease of the heart muscle

cardiomyoplasty /ˌkɑːdiəʊˈmaɪəʊˌplæsti/ *noun* an operation to improve the functioning of the heart, by using the latissimus dorsi as a stimulant

cardiomyotomy /ˌkɑːdiəʊmaɪˈɒtəmi/ *noun* an operation to treat cardiac achalasia by splitting the ring of muscles where the oesophagus joins the stomach. Also called **Heller's operation**

cardiopathy /ˌkɑːdiˈɒpəθi/ *noun* any kind of heart disease

cardiophone /ˈkɑːdiəfəʊn/ *noun* a microphone attached to a patient to record sounds, usually used to record the heart of an unborn baby

cardioplegia /ˌkɑːdiəʊˈpliːdʒiə/ *noun* the stopping of a patient's heart, by chilling it or using drugs, so that heart surgery can be performed

cardiopulmonary /ˌkɑːdiəʊˈpʌlmən(ə)ri/ *adjective* relating to both the heart and the lungs

cardiopulmonary bypass /ˌkɑːdiəʊ ˌpʌlmən(ə)ri ˈbaɪpɑːs/ *noun* a machine or method for artificially circulating the patient's blood during open-heart surgery. The heart and lungs are cut off from the circulation and replaced by a pump.

cardiopulmonary resuscitation /ˌkɑːdiəʊˌpʌlmən(ə)ri rɪˌsʌsɪˈteɪʃ(ə)n/ *noun* an emergency technique to make a person's heart start beating again. It involves clearing the airways and then alternately pressing on the chest and breathing into the mouth. Abbr **CPR**

cardiopulmonary system /ˌkɑːdiəʊ ˈpʌlmən(ə)ri ˌsɪstəm/ *noun* the heart and lungs considered together as a functional unit

cardiorespiratory /ˌkɑːdiəʊrɪˈspɪrɪt(ə)ri/ *adjective* referring to both the heart and the respiratory system

cardioscope /ˈkɑːdiəskəʊp/ *noun* an instrument formed of a tube with a light at the end, used to inspect the inside of the heart

cardiospasm /ˈkɑːdiəʊspæz(ə)m/ *noun* same as **cardiac achalasia**

cardiothoracic /ˌkɑːdiəʊθɒˈræsɪk/ *adjective* referring to the heart and the chest region ○ *a cardiothoracic surgeon*

cardiotocography /ˌkɑːdiəʊtɒˈkɒɡrəfi/ *noun* the recording of the heartbeat of a fetus

cardiotomy /ˌkɑːdiˈɒtəmi/ *noun* an operation that involves cutting the wall of the heart

cardiotomy syndrome /ˌkɑːdiˈɒtəmi ˌsɪndrəʊm/ *noun* fluid in the membranes round the heart after cardiotomy

cardiotoxic /ˌkɑːdiəʊˈtɒksɪk/ *adjective* which is toxic to the heart

cardiovascular /ˌkɑːdiəʊˈvæskjʊlə/ *adjective* referring to the heart and the blood circulation system

cardiovascular disease /ˌkɑːdiəʊ ˈvæskjʊlə dɪˌziːz/ *noun* any disease which affects the circulatory system, e.g. hypertension

'…cardiovascular diseases remain the leading cause of death in the United States' [*Journal of the American Medical Association*]

cardiovascular system /ˌkɑːdiəʊ ˈvæskjʊlə ˌsɪstəm/ *noun* the system of organs and blood vessels by means of which the blood circulates round the body and which includes the heart, arteries and veins

cardioversion /ˌkɑːdiəʊˈvɜːʃ(ə)n/ *noun* a procedure to correct an irregular heartbeat by applying an electrical impulse to the chest wall. ◊ **defibrillation**

carditis /kɑːˈdaɪtɪs/ *noun* inflammation of the connective tissue of the heart

caregiver /ˈkeəˌgɪvə/ *noun* same as **carer**

care pathway /ˈkeə ˌpɑːθweɪ/ *noun* the entire process of diagnosis, treatment and care that a patient goes through

care plan /ˈkeə plæn/ *noun* a plan drawn up by the nursing staff for the treatment of an individual patient

'…all relevant sections of the nurses' care plan and nursing process had been left blank' [*Nursing Times*]

carer /ˈkeərə/, **caregiver** /ˈkeəˌgɪvə/ *noun* someone who looks after a sick or dependent person

'…most research has focused on those caring for older people or for adults with disability and chronic illness. Most studied are the carers of those who might otherwise have to stay in hospital for a long time' [*British Medical Journal*]

caries /ˈkeərɪz/ *noun* decay in a tooth or bone

carina /kəˈriːnə/ *noun* a structure shaped like the bottom of a boat, e.g. the cartilage at the point where the trachea branches into the bronchi

cariogenic /ˌkeəriəʊˈdʒenɪk/ *adjective* referring to a substance which causes caries

carminative /ˈkɑːmɪnətɪv/ *noun* a substance which relieves colic or indigestion ■ *adjective* relieving colic or indigestion

carneous mole /ˌkɑːniəs ˈməʊl/ *noun* matter in the uterus after the death of a fetus

carotenaemia /ˌkærətɪˈniːmiə/ *noun* an excessive amount of carotene in the blood, usually as a result of eating too many carrots or tomatoes, which gives the skin a yellow colour. Also called **xanthaemia**

carotene /ˈkærətiːn/ *noun* an orange or red pigment in carrots, egg yolk and some oils, which is converted by the liver into vitamin A

carotid /kəˈrɒtɪd/, **carotid artery** /kəˌrɒtɪd ˈɑːtəri/ *noun* either of the two large arteries in the neck which supply blood to the head

COMMENT: The common carotid artery is in the lower part of the neck and branches upwards into the external and internal carotids. The carotid body is situated at the point where the carotid divides.

carotid artery thrombosis /kəˌrɒtɪd ˌɑːtəri θrɒmˈbəʊsɪs/ *noun* the formation of a blood clot in the carotid artery

carotid body /kæˌrɒtɪd ˈbɒdi/ *noun* tissue in the carotid sinus which is concerned with cardiovascular reflexes

carotid pulse /kəˌrɒtɪd ˈpʌls/ *noun* a pulse felt in the carotid artery at the side of the neck

carotid sinus /kæˌrɒtɪd ˈsaɪnəs/ *noun* an expanded part attached to the carotid artery, which monitors blood pressure in the skull

carp- /kɑːp/ *prefix* same as **carpo-** (*used before vowels*)

carpal /ˈkɑːp(ə)l/ *adjective* referring to the wrist

carpal bones /ˈkɑːp(ə)l bəʊnz/, **carpals** /ˈkɑːp(ə)lz/ *plural noun* the eight bones which make up the carpus or wrist. See illustration at **HAND** in Supplement

carpal tunnel release /ˌkɑːp(ə)l ˈtʌn(ə)l rɪ ˌliːs/ *noun* an operation to relieve the compression of the median nerve

carpal tunnel syndrome /ˌkɑːp(ə)l ˈtʌn(ə)l ˌsɪndrəʊm/ *noun* a condition, usually affecting women, in which the fingers tingle and hurt at night. It is caused by compression of the median nerve.

carphology /kɑːˈfɒlədʒi/ *noun* the action of pulling at the bedclothes, a sign of delirium in typhoid and other fevers. Also called **floccitation**

carpi /ˈkɑːpi/ *plural of* **carpus**

carpo- /kɑːpəʊ/ *prefix* referring to the wrist

carpometacarpal joint /ˌkɑːpəʊmetə ˈkɑːp(ə)l ˈdʒɔɪnt/ *noun* one of the joints between the carpals and metacarpals. Also called **CM joint**

carpopedal spasm /ˌkɑːpəʊpiːd(ə)l ˈspæz(ə)m/ *noun* a spasm in the hands and feet caused by lack of calcium

carpus /ˈkɑːpəs/ *noun* the bones by which the lower arm is connected to the hand. Also called **wrist**. See illustration at **HAND** in Supplement (NOTE: The plural is **carpi**.)

COMMENT: The carpus is formed of eight small bones (the carpals): the capitate, hamate, lunate, pisiform, scaphoid, trapezium, trapezoid and triquetral.

carrier /ˈkæriə/ *noun* **1.** a person who carries bacteria of a disease in his or her body and who can transmit the disease to others without showing any signs of being infected with it ○ *Ten per cent of the population are believed to be unwitting carriers of the bacteria.* **2.** an insect which carries disease and infects humans **3.** a healthy person who carries a chromosome variation that gives rise to a hereditary disease such as haemophilia or Duchenne muscular dystrophy

carry /'kæri/ *verb* to have a disease and be capable of infecting others

cartilage /'kɑːtɪlɪdʒ/ *noun* thick connective tissue which lines and cushions the joints and which forms part of the structure of an organ. Cartilage in small children is the first stage in the formation of bones.

cartilaginous /ˌkɑːtɪ'lædʒɪnəs/ *adjective* made of cartilage

cartilaginous joint /ˌkɑːtɪ'lædʒɪnəs dʒɔɪnt/ *noun* **1.** **primary cartilaginous joint** same as **synchondrosis 2.** **secondary cartilaginous joint** same as **symphysis**

caruncle /kə'rʌŋkəl/ *noun* a small swelling

cascara /kæ'skɑːrə/, **cascara sagrada** /kæ ˌskɑːrə sə'grɑːdə/ *noun* a laxative made from the bark of a tropical tree

case /keɪs/ *noun* **1.** a single occurrence of a disease ○ *There were two hundred cases of cholera in the recent outbreak.* **2.** a person who has a disease or who is undergoing treatment ○ *The hospital is only admitting urgent cases.*

caseation /ˌkeɪsi'eɪʃ(ə)n/ *noun* the process by which dead tissue decays into a firm and dry mass. It is characteristic of tuberculosis.

case control study /keɪs kən'trəʊl ˌstʌdi/ *noun* an investigation in which a group of patients with a disease are compared with a group without the disease in order to study possible causes

case history /'keɪs ˌhɪst(ə)ri/ *noun* details of what has happened to a patient undergoing treatment

casein /'keɪsiɪn/ *noun* one of the proteins found in milk

caseinogen /ˌkeɪsi'ɪnədʒən/ *noun* the main protein in milk, from which casein is formed

Casey's model /'keɪsiz ˌmɒd(ə)l/ *noun* a model for the care of child patients, where the parents are involved in the treatment

cast /kɑːst/ *noun* a mass of material formed in a hollow organ or tube and excreted in fluid

castor oil /ˌkɑːstər 'ɔɪl/ *noun* a plant oil which acts as a laxative

castration /kæ'streɪʃ(ə)n/ *noun* the surgical removal of the sexual organs, usually the testicles, in males

casualty /'kæʒuəlti/ *noun* **1.** a person who has had an accident or who is suddenly ill ○ *The fire caused several casualties.* ○ *The casualties were taken by ambulance to the nearest hospital.* **2.** also **casualty department** same as **accident and emergency department** ○ *The accident victim was rushed to casualty.*

casualty ward /'kæʒuəlti wɔːd/ *noun* same as **accident ward**

CAT /kæt/ *noun* same as **computerised axial tomography**

cata- /kætə/ *prefix* downwards

catabolic /ˌkætə'bɒlɪk/ *adjective* referring to catabolism

catabolism /kə'tæbəlɪz(ə)m/ *noun* the process of breaking down complex chemicals into simple chemicals

catalase /'kætəleɪz/ *noun* an enzyme present in the blood and liver which catalyses the breakdown of hydrogen peroxide into water and oxygen

catalepsy /'kætəlepsi/ *noun* a condition often associated with schizophrenia, where a person becomes incapable of sensation, the body is rigid and he or she does not move for long periods

catalyse /'kætəlaɪz/ *verb* to act as a catalyst and help make a chemical reaction take place (NOTE: The US spelling is **catalyze**.)

catalysis /kə'tæləsɪs/ *noun* a process where a chemical reaction is helped by a substance (the catalyst) which does not change during the process

catalyst /'kætəlɪst/ *noun* a substance which produces or helps a chemical reaction without itself changing ○ *an enzyme which acts as a catalyst in the digestive process*

catalytic /ˌkætə'lɪtɪk/ *adjective* referring to catalysis

catalytic reaction /ˌkætəlɪtɪk ri'ækʃən/ *noun* a chemical reaction which is caused by a catalyst which does not change during the reaction

catamenia /ˌkætə'miːniə/ *noun* menstruation (*technical*)

cataplexy /'kætəpleksi/ *noun* a condition in which a person's muscles become suddenly rigid and he or she falls without losing consciousness, possibly caused by a shock

cataract /'kætərækt/ *noun* a condition in which the lens of the eye gradually becomes hard and opaque

COMMENT: Cataracts form most often in people after the age of 50. They are sometimes caused by a blow or an electric shock. Cataracts can easily and safely be removed by surgery.

cataract extraction /'kætərækt ɪkˌstrækʃ(ə)n/ *noun* the surgical removal of a cataract from the eye

cataractous lens /kætə'ræktəs lenz/ *noun* a lens on which a cataract has formed

catarrh /kə'tɑː/ *noun* inflammation of the mucous membranes in the nose and throat, creating an excessive amount of mucus

catarrhal /kə'tɑːrəl/ *adjective* referring to catarrh ○ *a catarrhal cough*

catatonia /ˌkætə'təʊniə/ *noun* a condition in which a psychiatric patient is either motionless or shows violent reactions to stimulation

catatonic /ˌkætə'tɒnɪk/ *adjective* referring to behaviour in which a person is either motionless or extremely violent

catatonic schizophrenia /ˌkætətɒnɪk ˌskɪtsəʊ'friːniə/ *noun* a type of schizophrenia where the patient is alternately apathetic or very active and disturbed

catching /'kætʃɪŋ/ *adjective* infectious (*informal*) ○ *Is the disease catching?*

catchment area /'kætʃmənt ,eəriə/ *noun* an area around a hospital which is served by that hospital

catecholamines /kætə'kɒləmi:nz/ *plural noun* the hormones adrenaline and noradrenaline which are released by the adrenal glands

category /'kætɪg(ə)ri/ *noun* a classification, the way in which things can be classified ○ *His condition is of a non-urgent category.*

catgut /'kætgʌt/ *noun* a thread made from part of the intestines of sheep, now usually artificially hardened, used to sew up cuts made during surgery

COMMENT: Catgut is slowly dissolved by fluids in the body after the wound has healed and therefore does not need to be removed. Ordinary catgut will dissolve in five to ten days; hardened catgut takes up to three or four weeks.

catharsis /kə'θɑ:sɪs/ *noun* purgation of the bowels

cathartic /kə'θɑ:tɪk/ *adjective* laxative or purgative

catheter /'kæθɪtə/ *noun* a tube passed into the body along one of the passages in the body

catheterisation /,kæθɪtəraɪ'zeɪʃ(ə)n/, **catheterization** *noun* the act of putting a catheter into a patient's body

'…high rates of disconnection of closed urine drainage systems, lack of hand washing and incorrect positioning of urine drainage bags have been highlighted in a new report on urethral catheterisation' [*Nursing Times*]

'…the technique used to treat aortic stenosis is similar to that for any cardiac catheterisation. A catheter introduced through the femoral vein is placed across the aortic valve and into the left ventricle.' [*Journal of the American Medical Association*]

catheterise /'kæθɪtəraɪz/, **catheterize** *verb* to insert a catheter into a patient

CAT scan /'kæt skæn/, **CT scan** /,si: 'ti: skæn/ *noun* same as **CT scan**

cat-scratch disease /'kæt skrætʃ dɪ,zi:z/, **cat-scratch fever** /'kæt skrætʃ ,fi:və/ *noun* an illness in which the patient has a fever and swollen lymph glands, thought to be caused by a bacterium transmitted to humans by the scratch of a cat. It may also result from scratching with other sharp points.

cauda equina /,kɔ:də ɪ'kwaɪnə/ *noun* a group of nerves which go from the spinal cord to the lumbar region and the coccyx

caudal /'kɔ:d(ə)l/ *adjective* (*in humans*) referring to the cauda equina

caudal anaesthetic /,kɔ:d(ə)l ,ænəs'θetɪk/ *noun* an anaesthetic, injected into the base of the spine to remove feeling in the lower part of the body. It is often used in childbirth.

caudal analgesia /,kɔ:d(ə)l ,æn(ə)l 'dʒi:ziə/ *noun* a method of pain relief that involves injecting an anaesthetic into the base of the spine to remove feeling in the lower part of the body

caudal block /'kɔ:d(ə)l blɒk/ *noun* a local analgesia of the cauda equina nerves in the lower spine

caudate /'kɔ:deɪt/ *adjective* like a tail

caudate lobe /'kɔ:deɪt ləʊb/ *noun* a lobe at the back of the liver, behind the right and left lobes. Also called **posterior lobe**

caul /kɔ:l/ *noun* **1.** a membrane which sometimes covers a baby's head at birth **2.** same as **omentum**

cauliflower ear /,kɒliflaʊər 'ɪə/ *noun* a permanently swollen ear, caused by blows in boxing

causalgia /kɔ:'zældʒə/ *noun* burning pain in a limb, caused by a damaged nerve

causal organism /,kɔ:z(ə)l 'ɔ:gənɪz(ə)m/ *noun* an organism that causes a particular disease

caustic /'kɔ:stɪk/ *noun* a chemical substance that destroys tissues that it touches ■ *adjective* corrosive and destructive

cauterisation /,kɔ:təraɪ'zeɪʃ(ə)n/, **cauterization** *noun* the act of cauterising ○ *The growth was removed by cauterisation.*

cauterise /'kɔ:təraɪz/, **cauterize** *verb* to use burning, radiation or laser beams to remove tissue or to stop bleeding

cautery /'kɔ:təri/ *noun* a surgical instrument used to cauterise a wound

cava /'keɪvə/ ♦ **vena cava**

cavernosum /,kævə'nəʊsəm/ ♦ **corpus cavernosum**

cavernous breathing sounds /,kævənəs 'bri:ðɪŋ ,saʊndz/ *plural noun* hollow sounds made by the lungs and heard through a stethoscope placed on a patient's chest, used in diagnosis

cavernous haemangioma /,kævənəs ,hi:mændʒɪ'əʊmə/ *noun* a tumour in connective tissue with wide spaces which contain blood

cavernous sinus /,kævənəs 'saɪnəs/ *noun* one of two cavities in the skull behind the eyes, which form part of the venous drainage system

cavitation /,kævɪ'teɪʃ(ə)n/ *noun* the forming of a cavity

cavity /'kævɪti/ *noun* a hole or space inside the body

cc *abbr* cubic centimetre

CCU *abbr* coronary care unit

CD4 /,si: di: 'fɔ:/ *noun* a compound consisting of a protein combined with a carbohydrate which is found in some cells and helps to protect the body against infection □ **CD4 count** a test used to monitor how many CD4 cells have been destroyed in people with HIV

CDH *abbr* congenital dislocation of the hip

cecum /'siːkəm/ *noun US* same as **caecum**

cefaclor /'sefəklɔː/ *noun* an antibacterial drug used to treat septicaemia

cefotaxime /ˌsefə'tæksiːm/ *noun* a synthetic cephalosporin used to treat bacterial infection by pseudomonads

-cele /siːl/ *suffix* referring to a swelling

celiac /'siːliæk/ *adjective US* same as **coeliac**

cell /sel/ *noun* a tiny unit of matter which is the base of all plant and animal tissue (NOTE: For other terms referring to cells, see words beginning with **cyt-, cyto-**.)

COMMENT: The cell is a unit which can reproduce itself. It is made up of a jelly-like substance (cytoplasm) which surrounds a nucleus and contains many other small structures which are different according to the type of cell. Cells reproduce by division (mitosis) and their process of feeding and removing waste products is metabolism. The division and reproduction of cells is the way the human body is formed.

cell body /'sel ˌbɒdi/ *noun* the part of a nerve cell which surrounds the nucleus and from which the axon and dendrites begin

cell division /'sel dɪˌvɪʒ(ə)n/ *noun* the way in which a cell reproduces itself. ♦ **mitosis, meiosis**

cell membrane /'sel ˌmembreɪn/ *noun* a membrane enclosing the cytoplasm of a cell. ◊ **columnar cell, target cell**

cellular /'seljʊlə/ *adjective* 1. referring to cells, or formed of cells 2. made of many similar parts connected together

cellular tissue /ˌseljʊlə 'tɪʃuː/ *noun* a form of connective tissue with large spaces

cellulite /'seljʊlaɪt/ *noun* lumpy deposits of subcutaneous fat, especially in the thighs and buttocks

cellulitis /ˌseljʊ'laɪtɪs/ *noun* a usually bacterial inflammation of connective tissue or of the subcutaneous tissue

cellulose /'seljʊləʊs/ *noun* a carbohydrate which makes up a large percentage of plant matter

COMMENT: Cellulose is not digestible and is passed through the digestive system as roughage.

Celsius /'selsiəs/ *noun* a metric scale of temperature on which 0° is the point at which water freezes and 100° is the point at which water boils under average atmospheric conditions. Also called **centigrade**. ◊ **Fahrenheit** (NOTE: It is usually written as a **C** after the degree sign: **52°C** (say: 'fifty-two degrees Celsius').) [Described 1742. After Anders Celsius (1701–44), Swedish astronomer and scientist.]

COMMENT: To convert Celsius temperatures to Fahrenheit, multiply by 1.8 and add 32. So 20°C is equal to 68°F. Celsius is used in many countries, though not in the US, where the Fahrenheit system is still preferred.

Celsius temperature /'selsiəs ˌtemprɪtʃə/ *noun* temperature as measured on the Celsius scale

CEMACH /'siːmæʃ/ *noun* a UK research project investigating the causes of infant deaths and stillbirths. Full form **Confidential Enquiry into Maternal and Child Health**

cement /sɪ'ment/ *noun* 1. an adhesive used in dentistry to attach a crown to the base of a tooth 2. same as **cementum**

cementum /sɪ'mentəm/ *noun* a layer of thick hard material which covers the roots of teeth

census /'sensəs/ *noun* a systematic count or survey

center /'sentə/ *noun US* same as **centre**

-centesis /senti:sɪs/ *suffix* puncture

centi- /senti/ *prefix* one hundredth (10^{-2}). Symbol **c**

centigrade /'sentɪɡreɪd/ *noun* same as **Celsius**

centile chart /'sentaɪl tʃɑːt/ *noun* a chart showing the number of babies who fall into each percentage category, as regards, e.g., birth weight

centilitre /'sentiliːtə/, **centiliter** *noun* a unit of measurement of liquid equal to one hundredth of a litre. Symbol **cl**

centimetre /'sentimiːtə/, **centimeter** *noun* a unit of measurement of length equal to one hundredth of a metre. Symbol **cm**

central /'sentrəl/ *adjective* referring to the centre

central canal /ˌsentrəl kə'næl/ *noun* a thin tube in the centre of the spinal cord containing cerebrospinal fluid

central line /'sentrəl laɪn/ *noun* a catheter inserted through the neck, used to monitor central venous pressure in conditions such as shock where fluid balance is severely upset

central nervous system /ˌsentrəl 'nɜːvəs ˌsɪstəm/ *noun* the brain and spinal cord which link together all the nerves

central sulcus /ˌsentrəl 'sʌlkəs/ *noun* one of the grooves which divide a cerebral hemisphere into lobes

central temperature /ˌsentrəl 'temprɪtʃə/ *noun* the temperature of the brain, thorax and abdomen, which is constant

central vein /ˌsentrəl 'veɪn/ *noun* a vein in the liver

central venous pressure /ˌsentrəl 'viːnəs ˌpreʃə/ *noun* blood pressure in the right atrium of the heart, which can be measured by means of a catheter

centre /'sentə/ *noun* 1. the middle point, or the main part of something ○ *The aim of the examination is to locate the centre of infection.* 2. a large building 3. the point where a group of nerves come together (NOTE: [all senses] The US spelling is **center**.)

centrifugal /ˌsentrɪˈfjuːɡ(ə)l, senˈtrɪfjʊɡ(ə)l/ *adjective* moving away from the centre

centrifugation /ˌsentrɪfjuːˈɡeɪʃ(ə)n/, **centrifuging** /ˈsentrɪfjuːdʒɪŋ/ *noun* the process of separating the components of a liquid in a centrifuge

centrifuge /ˈsentrɪfjuːdʒ/ *noun* a device to separate the components of a liquid by rapid spinning

centriole /ˈsentriəʊl/ *noun* a small structure found in the cytoplasm of a cell, which involved in forming the spindle during cell division

centripetal /ˌsentrɪˈpiːt(ə)l, senˈtrɪpɪt(ə)l/ *adjective* moving towards the centre

centromere /ˈsentrəmɪə/ *noun* a constricted part of a chromosome, seen as a cell divides

centrosome /ˈsentrəsəʊm/ *noun* the structure in the cytoplasm of a cell, near the nucleus, and containing the centrioles

centrum /ˈsentrəm/ *noun* the central part of an organ (NOTE: The plural is **centra**.)

cephal- /sefəl/ *prefix* same as **cephalo-** (*used before vowels*)

cephalalgia /ˌsefəˈlældʒə/ *noun* same as **headache**

cephalexin /ˌsefəˈleksɪn/ *noun* an antibiotic used to treat infections of the urinary system or respiratory tract

cephalhaematoma /ˌsefəlhiːməˈtəʊmə/ *noun* a swelling found mainly on the head of babies delivered with forceps

cephalic /səˈfælɪk/ *adjective* referring to the head

cephalic index /səˌfælɪk ˈɪndeks/ *noun* a measurement of the shape of the skull

cephalic presentation /səˌfælɪk ˌprez(ə)nˈteɪʃ(ə)n/ *noun* the usual position of a baby in the uterus, where the baby's head will appear first

cephalic version /səˌfælɪk ˈvɜːʃ(ə)n/ *noun* turning a wrongly positioned fetus round in the uterus, so that the head will appear first at birth

cephalo- /sefələʊ/ *prefix* referring to the head

cephalocele /ˈsefələʊsiːl/ *noun* a swelling caused by part of the brain passing through a weak point in the bones of the skull

cephalogram /ˈsefələʊɡræm/ *noun* an X-ray photograph of the bones of the skull

cephalometry /ˌsefəˈlɒmɪtri/ *noun* measurement of the head

cephalopelvic /ˌsefələʊˈpelvɪk/ *adjective* referring to the head of the fetus and the pelvis of the mother

cephalopelvic disproportion /ˌsefələʊ ˌpelvɪk ˌdɪsprəˈpɔːʃ(ə)n/ *noun* a condition in which the pelvic opening of the mother is not large enough for the head of the fetus

cephalosporin /ˌsefələʊˈspɔːrɪn/ *noun* a drug used in the treatment of bacterial infection

cephradine /ˈsefrədiːn/ *noun* an antibacterial drug used to treat sinusitis and urinary tract infections

cerclage /sɜːˈklɑːʒ/ *noun* the act of tying things together with a ring

cerea /ˈsɪəriə/ ♦ **flexibilitas cerea**

cerebellar /ˌserəˈbelə/ *adjective* referring to the cerebellum

cerebellar ataxia /ˌserəbelər əˈtæksiə/ *noun* a disorder where a person staggers and cannot speak clearly, due to a disease of the cerebellum

cerebellar cortex /ˌserəbelə ˈkɔːteks/ *noun* the outer covering of grey matter which covers the cerebellum

cerebellar gait /ˌserəbelə ˈɡeɪt/ *noun* a way of walking where a person staggers along, caused by a disease of the cerebellum

cerebellar peduncle /ˌserəbelə pɪˈdʌŋk(ə)l/ *noun* a band of nerve tissue connecting parts of the cerebellum

cerebellar syndrome /ˌserəbelə ˈsɪndrəʊm/ *noun* a disease affecting the cerebellum, the symptoms of which are lack of muscle coordination, spasms in the eyeball and impaired speech

cerebellum /ˌserəˈbeləm/ *noun* a section of the hindbrain, located at the back of the head beneath the back part of the cerebrum. See illustration at BRAIN in Supplement

COMMENT: The cerebellum is formed of two hemispheres with the vermis in the centre. Fibres go into or out of the cerebellum through the peduncles. The cerebellum is the part of the brain where voluntary movements are coordinated and is associated with the sense of balance.

cerebr- /serəbr/ *prefix* same as **cerebro-** (*used before vowels*)

cerebra /səˈriːbrə/ *plural of* **cerebrum**

cerebral /ˈserəbrəl/ *adjective* referring to the cerebrum or to the brain in general

cerebral aqueduct /ˌserəbrəl ˈækwɪdʌkt/ *noun* a canal connecting the third and fourth ventricles in the brain. Also called **aqueduct of Sylvius**

cerebral artery /ˌserəbrəl ˈɑːtəri/ *noun* one of the main arteries which take blood into the brain

cerebral cavity /ˌserəbrəl ˈkævɪti/ *noun* one of the four connected fluid-filled spaces in the brain

cerebral cortex /ˌserəbrəl ˈkɔːteks/ *noun* the outer layer of grey matter which covers the cerebrum

cerebral decompression /ˌserəbrəl ˌdiːkəmˈpreʃ(ə)n/ *noun* the removal of part of the skull to relieve pressure on the brain

cerebral dominance /ˌserəbrəl ˈdɒmɪnəns/ *noun* the usual condition where the centres for various functions are located in one cerebral hemisphere

cerebral haemorrhage /ˌserəbrəl ˈhem(ə)rɪdʒ/ *noun* bleeding inside the brain from a cerebral artery. Also called **brain haemorrhage**

cerebral hemisphere /ˌserəbrəl ˈhemɪsfɪə/ *noun* one of the two halves of the cerebrum

cerebral infarction /ˌserəbrəl ɪnˈfɑːkʃən/ *noun* the death of brain tissue as a result of reduction in the blood supply to the brain

cerebral ischaemia /ˌserəbrəl ɪˈskiːmiə/ *noun* failure in the blood supply to the brain

cerebral palsy /ˌserəbrəl ˈpɔːlzi/ *noun* a disorder mainly due to brain damage occurring before birth, or due to lack of oxygen during birth, associated with poor coordination of muscular movements, impaired speech, hearing and sight, and sometimes mental impairment (NOTE: Premature babies are at higher risk.)

cerebral peduncle /ˌserəbrəl pɪˈdʌŋk(ə)l/ *noun* a mass of nerve fibres connecting the cerebral hemispheres to the midbrain. See illustration at BRAIN in Supplement

cerebral thrombosis /ˌserəbrəl θrɒmˈbəʊsɪs/ *noun* same as **cerebrovascular accident**

cerebral vascular accident /ˌserəbrəl ˌvæskjʊlər ˈæksɪd(ə)nt/ *noun* same as **cerebrovascular accident**

cerebration /ˌserəˈbreɪʃ(ə)n/ *noun* brain activity

cerebro- /serəbrəʊ/ *prefix* referring to the cerebrum

cerebrospinal /ˌserəbrəʊˈspaɪn(ə)l/ *adjective* referring to the brain and the spinal cord

cerebrospinal fever /ˌserəbrəʊspaɪn(ə)l ˈfiːvə/ *noun* same as **meningococcal meningitis**

cerebrospinal fluid /ˌserəbrəʊspaɪn(ə)l ˈfluːɪd/ *noun* fluid which surrounds the brain and the spinal cord. Abbr **CSF**

COMMENT: CSF is found in the space between the arachnoid mater and pia mater of the brain, within the ventricles of the brain and in the central canal of the spinal cord. It consists mainly of water, with some sugar and sodium chloride. Its function is to cushion the brain and spinal cord and it is continually formed and absorbed to maintain the correct pressure.

cerebrospinal meningitis /ˌserəbrəʊ spaɪn(ə)l ˌmenɪnˈdʒaɪtɪs/ *noun* same as **meningococcal meningitis**

cerebrospinal tract /ˌserəbrəʊspaɪn(ə)l ˈtrækt/ *noun* one of the main motor pathways in the anterior and lateral white columns of the spinal cord

cerebrovascular /ˌserəbrəʊˈvæskjʊlə/ *adjective* referring to the blood vessels in the brain

cerebrovascular accident /ˌserəbrəʊ ˌvæskjʊlər ˈæksɪd(ə)nt/ *noun* a sudden blocking of or bleeding from a blood vessel in the brain resulting in temporary or permanent paralysis or death. Also called **stroke**

cerebrovascular disease /ˌserəbrəʊ ˌvæskjʊlə dɪˈziːz/ *noun* a disease of the blood vessels in the brain

cerebrum /səˈriːbrəm/ *noun* the largest part of the brain, formed of two sections, the cerebral hemispheres, which run along the length of the head. The cerebrum controls the main mental processes, including the memory. Also called **telencephalon**

certificate /səˈtɪfɪkət/ *noun* an official paper which states something

certify /ˈsɜːtɪfaɪ/ *verb* to make an official statement in writing about something ○ *He was certified dead on arrival at hospital.*

cerumen /səˈruːmen/ *noun* wax which forms inside the ear. Also called **earwax**

ceruminous gland /səˈruːmɪnəs ˌglænd/ *noun* a gland which secretes earwax. See illustration at EAR in Supplement

cervic- /sɜːvɪk/ *prefix* same as **cervico-** (*used before vowels*)

cervical /ˈsɜːvɪk(ə)l, səˈvaɪk(ə)l/ *adjective* **1.** referring to the neck **2.** referring to any part of the body which is shaped like a neck, especially the cervix of the uterus

cervical canal /ˌsɜːvɪk(ə)l kəˈnæl/ *noun* a tube running through the cervix, from the point where the uterus joins the vagina to the entrance of the uterine cavity. Also called **cervicouterine canal**

cervical cancer /ˌsɜːvɪk(ə)l ˈkænsə/ *noun* a cancer of the cervix of the uterus

cervical collar /ˌsɜːvɪk(ə)l ˈkɒlə/ *noun* a special strong orthopaedic collar to support the head of a person with neck injuries or a condition such as cervical spondylosis

cervical erosion /ˌsɜːvɪk(ə)l ɪˈrəʊʒ(ə)n/ *noun* a condition in which the epithelium of the mucous membrane lining the cervix uteri extends outside the cervix

cervical ganglion /ˌsɜːvɪk(ə)l ˈgæŋgliən/ *noun* one of the bundles of nerves in the neck

cervical incompetence /ˌsɜːvɪk(ə)l ˈɪnkɒmpɪt(ə)ns/ *noun* a dysfunction of the cervix of the uterus which is often the cause of spontaneous abortions and premature births and can be remedied by Shirodkar's operation

cervical intraepithelial neoplasia /ˌsɜːvɪk(ə)l ˌɪntrəepɪˌθiːliəl niːəʊˈpleɪʒə/ *noun* changes in the cells of the cervix which may lead to cervical cancer. Abbr **CIN**

cervical nerve /ˌsɜːvɪk(ə)l ˈnɜːv/ *noun* spinal nerve in the neck

cervical node /ˌsɜːvɪk(ə)l ˈnəʊd/ *noun* lymph node in the neck

cervical plexus /ˌsɜːvɪk(ə)l ˈpleksəs/ *noun* a group of nerves in front of the vertebrae in the neck, which lead to nerves supplying the skin and muscles of the neck, and also the phrenic nerve which controls the diaphragm

cervical rib /ˌsɜːvɪk(ə)l 'rɪb/ *noun* an extra rib sometimes found attached to the vertebrae above the other ribs and which may cause thoracic inlet syndrome

cervical smear /ˌsɜːvɪk(ə)l 'smɪə/ *noun* a test for cervical cancer, where cells taken from the mucus in the cervix of the uterus are examined

cervical spondylosis /ˌsɜːvɪk(ə)l spɒndɪ 'ləʊsɪs/ *noun* a degenerative change in the neck bones. ◊ **spondylosis**

cervical vertebrae /ˌsɜːvɪk(ə)l 'vɜːtɪbriː/ *plural noun* the seven bones which form the neck

cervicectomy /ˌsɜːvɪ'sektəmi/ *noun* the surgical removal of the cervix uteri

cervices /'sɜːvɪsiːz/ *plural of* **cervix**

cervicitis /ˌsɜːvɪ'saɪtɪs/ *noun* inflammation of the cervix uteri

cervico- /sɜːvɪkəʊ/ *prefix* **1.** referring to the neck **2.** referring to the cervix of the uterus

cervicography /ˌsɜːvɪ'kɒɡrəfi/ *noun* the act of photographing the cervix uteri, used as a method of screening for cervical cancer

cervicouterine canal /ˌsɜːvɪkəʊˌjuːtəraɪn kə'næl/ *noun* same as **cervical canal**

cervix /'sɜːvɪks/ *noun* **1.** any narrow neck of an organ **2.** the neck of the uterus, the narrow lower part of the uterus leading into the vagina. Also called **cervix uteri**

CESDI *noun* full form **Confidential Enquiry into Stillbirths and Deaths in Infancy.** ◈ **CEMACH**

cesium /'siːziəm/ *noun US* same as **caesium**

cestode /'sestəʊd/ *noun* a type of tapeworm

cetrimide /'setrɪmaɪd/ *noun* a mixture of ammonium compounds, used in disinfectants and antiseptics

CF *abbr* cystic fibrosis

CFT *abbr* complement fixation test

chafe /tʃeɪf/ *verb* to rub something, especially to rub against the skin ○ *The rough cloth of the collar chafed the girl's neck.*

chafing /'tʃeɪfɪŋ/ *noun* irritation of the skin due to rubbing ○ *She was experiencing chafing of the thighs.*

Chagas' disease /'tʃɑːɡəs dɪˌziːz/ *noun* a type of sleeping sickness found in South America, transmitted by insect bites which pass trypanosomes into the bloodstream. Children are mainly affected and if untreated the disease can cause fatal heart block in early adult life. [Described 1909. After Carlos Chagas (1879–1934), Brazilian scientist and physician.]

CHAI *abbr* Commission for Healthcare Audit and Improvement

chalasia /tʃə'leɪziə/ *noun* an excessive relaxation of the oesophageal muscles, which causes regurgitation

chalazion /kə'leɪziən/ *noun* same as **meibomian cyst**

challenge /'tʃælɪndʒ/ *verb* to expose someone to a substance to determine whether an allergy or other adverse reaction will occur ■ *noun* exposure of someone to a substance to determine whether an allergy or other adverse reaction will occur

chalone /'keɪləʊn, 'kæləʊn/ *noun* a hormone which stops a secretion, as opposed to those hormones which stimulate secretion

chamber /'tʃeɪmbə/ *noun* a hollow space (atrium or ventricle) in the heart where blood is collected

chancre /'ʃæŋkə/ *noun* a sore on the lip, penis or eyelid which is the first symptom of syphilis

chancroid /'ʃæŋkrɔɪd/ *noun* a venereal sore with a soft base, situated in the groin or on the genitals and caused by the bacterium *Haemophilus ducreyi*. Also called **soft chancre**

change of life /ˌtʃeɪndʒ əv 'laɪf/ *noun* same as **menopause** (*dated informal*)

chapped /tʃæpt/ *adjective* referring to skin which is cracked due to cold

characterise /'kærɪktəraɪz/, **characterize** *verb* to be a typical or special quality or feature of something or someone ○ *The disease is characterised by the development of lesions throughout the body.*

characteristic /ˌkærɪktə'rɪstɪk/ *noun* a quality which allows something to be recognised as different ○ *Cancer destroys the cell's characteristics.* ■ *adjective* being a typical or distinguishing quality ○ *symptoms characteristic of anaemia* ○ *The inflammation is characteristic of shingles.*

charcoal /'tʃɑːkəʊl/ *noun* a highly absorbent substance, formed when wood is burnt in the absence of oxygen, used to relieve diarrhoea or intestinal gas and in cases of poisoning

COMMENT: Charcoal tablets can be used to relieve diarrhoea or flatulence.

Charcot's joint /ˌʃɑːkəʊz 'dʒɔɪnt/ *noun* a joint which becomes deformed because the patient cannot feel pain in it when the nerves have been damaged by syphilis, diabetes or leprosy [Described 1868. After Jean-Martin Charcot (1825–93), French neurologist.]

Charcot's triad /ˌʃɑːkəʊz 'traɪæd/ *noun* three symptoms of multiple sclerosis: rapid eye movement, tremor and scanning speech

charleyhorse /'tʃɑːlihɔːs/ *noun US* a painful cramp in a leg or thigh (*informal*)

Charnley clamps /ˌtʃɑːnli 'klæmps/ *plural noun* metal clamps fixed to a rod through a bone to hold it tight

chart /tʃɑːt/ noun a record of information shown as a series of lines or points on graph paper ○ *a temperature chart*

charting /'tʃɑːtɪŋ/ noun the preparation and updating of a hospital patient's chart by nurses and doctors

ChB abbr bachelor of surgery

CHC abbr **1.** child health clinic **2.** community health council

CHD abbr coronary heart disease

check-up /'tʃek ʌp/ noun a general examination by a doctor or dentist ○ *She went for a check-up.* ○ *He had a heart check-up last week.*

cheek /tʃiːk/ noun **1.** one of two fleshy parts of the face on each side of the nose **2.** either side of the buttocks (*informal*)

cheekbone /'tʃiːkbəʊn/ noun an arch of bone in the face beneath the cheek which also forms the lower part of the eye socket

cheil- /kaɪl/ prefix same as **cheilo-** (*used before vowels*)

cheilitis /kaɪ'laɪtɪs/ noun inflammation of the lips

cheilo- /kaɪləʊ/ prefix referring to the lips

cheiloschisis /ˌkaɪləʊ'ʃaɪsɪs/ noun a double cleft upper lip

cheilosis /kaɪ'ləʊsɪs/ noun swelling and cracks on the lips and corners of the mouth caused by lack of vitamin B

cheiro- /keɪrəʊ/ prefix referring to the hand

cheiropompholyx /ˌkeɪrəʊ'pɒmfəlɪks/ noun a disorder of the skin in which tiny blisters appear on the palms of the hand

chelate /'kiːleɪt/ verb to treat someone with a chelating agent in order to remove a heavy metal such as lead from the bloodstream

chelating agent /'kiːleɪtɪŋ ˌeɪdʒənt/ noun a chemical compound which can combine with some metals, used as a treatment for metal poisoning

cheloid /'kiːlɔɪd/ noun same as **keloid**

chemical /'kemɪk(ə)l/ adjective referring to chemistry ■ noun a substance produced by a chemical process or formed of chemical elements

'The MRI body scanner is able to provide a chemical analysis of tissues without investigative surgery' [*Health Services Journal*]

chemical composition /ˌkemɪk(ə)l ˌkɒmpə'zɪʃ(ə)n/ noun the chemicals which make up a substance ○ *They analysed the blood samples to find out their chemical composition.*

chemical symbol /ˌkemɪk(ə)l 'sɪmbəl/ noun letters which represent a chemical substance ○ *Na is the symbol for sodium.*

chemist /'kemɪst/ noun a shop where you can buy medicine, toothpaste, soap and similar items ○ *Go to the chemist to get some cough*

medicine. ○ *The tablets are sold at all chemists.* ○ *There's a chemist on the corner.*

chemistry /'kemɪstri/ noun the study of substances, elements and compounds and their reactions with each other ◇ **blood chemistry** or **chemistry of the blood 1.** substances which make up blood, which can be analysed in blood tests, the results of which are useful in diagnosing disease **2.** a record of changes which take place in blood during disease and treatment

chemo /'kiːməʊ/ noun chemotherapy (*informal*)

chemo- /kiːməʊ/ prefix referring to chemistry

chemoreceptor /ˌkiːməʊrɪ'septə/ noun a cell which responds to the presence of a chemical compound by activating a nerve, e.g. a taste bud reacting to food or cells in the carotid body reacting to lowered oxygen and raised carbon dioxide in the blood

chemosis /kiː'məʊsɪs/ noun swelling of the conjunctiva

chemotaxis /ˌkiːməʊ'tæksɪs/ noun the movement of a cell when it is attracted to or repelled by a chemical substance

chemotherapeutic agent /ˌkiːməʊθerə'pjuːtɪk ˌeɪdʒənt/ noun a chemical substance used to treat a disease

chemotherapy /ˌkiːməʊ'θerəpi/ noun the use of drugs such as antibiotics, painkillers or antiseptic lotions to fight a disease, especially using toxic chemicals to destroy rapidly developing cancer cells

chest /tʃest/ noun **1.** the upper front part of the body between the neck and stomach. Also called **thorax 2.** same as **thorax** (NOTE: For other terms referring to the chest, see **pectoral** and words beginning with **steth-, thorac-, thoraco-**.)

chest cavity /'tʃest ˌkævɪti/ noun a space in the body containing the diaphragm, heart and lungs

chest examination /'tʃest ɪgˌzæmɪneɪʃ(ə)n/ noun an examination of someone's chest by percussion, stethoscope or X-ray

chest muscle /'tʃest ˌmʌs(ə)l/ noun same as **pectoral muscle**

chest pain /'tʃest peɪn/ noun pain in the chest which may be caused by heart disease

chesty /'tʃesti/ adjective having phlegm in the lungs, or having a tendency to chest complaints

Cheyne–Stokes respiration /ˌtʃeɪn 'stəʊks respɪˌreɪʃ(ə)n/, **Cheyne–Stokes breathing** /'briːðɪŋ/ noun irregular breathing, usually found in people who are unconscious, with short breaths gradually increasing to deep breaths, then reducing again, until breathing appears to stop

CHI abbr Commission for Health Improvement

chiasm /'kaɪæz(ə)m/, **chiasma** /kaɪ'æzmə/ *noun* ♦ optic chiasma

chickenpox /'tʃɪkɪn,pɒks/ *noun* an infectious disease of children, with fever and red spots which turn into itchy blisters. Also called **varicella**

COMMENT: Chickenpox is caused by a herpesvirus. In later life, shingles is usually a re-emergence of a dormant chickenpox virus and an adult with shingles can infect a child with chickenpox.

Chief Medical Officer /tʃiːf 'medɪk(ə)l ,ɒfɪsə/ *noun* in the UK, a government official responsible for all aspects of public health. Abbr **CMO**

Chief Nursing Officer /tʃiːf 'nɜːsɪŋ ,ɒfɪsə/ *noun* in the UK, an official appointed by the Department of Health to advise Government Ministers and provide leadership to nurses and midwives. Abbr **CNO**

chilblain /'tʃɪlbleɪn/ *noun* a condition in which the skin of the fingers, toes, nose or ears becomes red, swollen and itchy because of exposure to cold. Also called **erythema pernio**

child /tʃaɪld/ *noun* a young boy or girl. Child is the legal term for a person under 14 years of age. (NOTE: The plural is **children**. For other terms referring to children, see words beginning with **paed-**, **paedo-** or **ped-**, **pedo-**.)

child abuse /'tʃaɪld ə,bjuːs/ *noun* cruel treatment of a child by an adult, including physical and sexual harm

childbearing /'tʃaɪldbeərɪŋ/ *noun* the act of carrying and giving birth to a child

childbirth /'tʃaɪldbɜːθ/ *noun* the act of giving birth. Also called **parturition**

child care /'tʃaɪld keə/ *noun* the care of young children and study of their special needs

child health clinic /tʃaɪld 'helθ ,klɪnɪk/ *noun* a special clinic for checking the health and development of small children under school age. Abbr **CHC**

childhood illness /,tʃaɪldhʊd 'ɪlnəs/ *noun* an illness which mainly affects children and not adults

child-proof /'tʃaɪld pruːf/ *adjective* designed so that a child cannot use it ○ *child-proof containers* ○ *The pills are sold in bottles with child-proof lids or caps.*

child protection /,tʃaɪld prə'tekʃən/ *noun* the measures taken to avoid abuse, neglect or exploitation of any kind towards children

children /'tʃɪldrən/ plural of **child**

children's hospital /'tʃɪldrənz ,hɒspɪt(ə)l/ *noun* a hospital which specialises in treating children

chill /tʃɪl/ *noun* a short illness causing a feeling of being cold and shivering, usually the sign of the beginning of a fever, of flu or a cold

chin /tʃɪn/ *noun* the bottom part of the face, beneath the mouth

Chinese medicine /,tʃaɪniːz 'med(ə)sɪn/ *noun* a system of diagnosis, treatment and prevention of illness developed in China over many centuries. It uses herbs, minerals and animal products, exercise, massage and acupuncture.

Chinese restaurant syndrome /,tʃaɪniːz 'rest(ə)rɒnt ,sɪndrəʊm/ *noun* an allergic condition which gives people severe headaches after eating food flavoured with monosodium glutamate (*informal*)

chiro- /kaɪrəʊ/ *prefix* referring to the hand

chiropodist /kɪ'rɒpədɪst/ *noun* a person who specialises in treatment of minor disorders of the feet

chiropody /kɪ'rɒpədi/ *noun* the study and treatment of minor diseases and disorders of the feet

chiropractic /,kaɪrəʊ'præktɪk/ *noun* the treatment and prevention of disorders of the neuromusculoskeletal system by making adjustments primarily to the bones of the spine

chiropractor /'kaɪrəʊ,præktə/ *noun* a person who treats musculoskeletal disorders by making adjustments primarily to the bones of the spine

chiropracty /'kaɪrəʊ,prækti/ *noun* same as **chiropractic** (*informal*)

Chlamydia /klə'mɪdiə/ *noun* a bacterium that causes trachoma and urogenital diseases in humans and psittacosis in birds, which can be transmitted to humans. It is currently a major cause of sexually transmitted disease.

chlamydial /klə'mɪdiəl/ *adjective* referring to infections caused by *Chlamydia*

chloasma /kləʊ'æzmə/ *noun* the presence of brown spots on the skin from various causes

chlor- /klɔːr/ *prefix* same as **chloro-** (*used before vowels*)

chlorambucil /klɔː'æmbjʊsɪl/ *noun* a drug which is toxic to cells, used in cancer treatment

chloramphenicol /,klɔːræm'fenɪkɒl/ *noun* a powerful antibiotic which sometimes causes the collapse of blood cell production, so is used only for treating life-threatening diseases such as meningitis

chlordiazepoxide /,klɔːdaɪ,æzi'pɒksaɪd/ *noun* a yellow crystalline powder, used as a tranquilliser and treatment for alcoholism

chlorhexidine /klɔː'heksɪdiːn/ *noun* a disinfectant mouthwash

chloride /'klɔːraɪd/ *noun* a salt of hydrochloric acid

chlorination /,klɔːrɪ'neɪʃ(ə)n/ *noun* sterilisation by adding chlorine

COMMENT: Chlorination is used to kill bacteria in drinking water, in swimming pools and sewage farms, and has many industrial applications such as sterilisation in food processing.

chlorinator /'klɔːrɪneɪtə/ *noun* apparatus for adding chlorine to water

chlorine /'klɔːriːn/ *noun* a powerful greenish gas, used to sterilise water (NOTE: The chemical symbol is **Cl**.)

chlormethiazole /ˌklɔːme'θaɪəzəʊl/ *noun* a sedative used in the treatment of people with alcoholism

chloro- /klɔːrəʊ/ *prefix* referring to chlorine

chloroform /'klɒrəfɔːm/ *noun* a powerful drug formerly used as an anaesthetic

chloroma /klɔː'rəʊmə/ *noun* a bone tumour associated with acute leukaemia

chloroquine /'klɔːrəkwɪn/ *noun* a drug used to prevent and treat malaria, but to which resistance has developed in some parts of the world

chlorosis /klɔː'rəʊsɪs/ *noun* a type of severe anaemia due to iron deficiency, affecting mainly young girls

chlorothiazide /ˌklɔːrəʊ'θaɪəzaɪd/ *noun* a drug which helps the body to produce more urine, used in the treatment of high blood pressure, swelling and heart failure

chloroxylenol /ˌklɔːrəʊ'zaɪlənɒl/ *noun* a chemical used as an antimicrobial agent in skin creams and in disinfectants

chlorpheniramine /ˌklɔː'fen'aɪrəmiːn/, **chlorpheniramine maleate** /ˌklɔːfenaɪrəmiːn 'mælieɪt/ *noun* an antihistamine drug

chlorpromazine hydrochloride /klɔːˌprəʊməziːn ˌhaɪdrəʊ'klɔːraɪd/ *noun* a drug used to treat schizophrenia and other psychoses

chlorpropamide /klɔː'prəʊpəmaɪd/ *noun* a drug which lowers blood sugar, used in the treatment of diabetes

chlorthalidone /klɔː'θælɪdəʊn/ *noun* a diuretic

ChM *abbr* Master of Surgery

choana /'kəʊənə/ *noun* any opening shaped like a funnel, especially the one leading from the nasal cavity to the pharynx (NOTE: The plural is **choanae**.)

chocolate cyst /ˌtʃɒklət 'sɪst/ *noun* an ovarian cyst containing old brown blood

choke /tʃəʊk/ *verb* to stop breathing because the windpipe becomes blocked by a foreign body or by inhalation of water, or to stop someone breathing by blocking the windpipe □ **to choke on (something)** to take something into the windpipe instead of the gullet, so that the breathing is interrupted ○ *A piece of bread made him choke* or *He choked on a piece of bread.*

choking /'tʃəʊkɪŋ/ *noun* a condition in which someone is prevented from breathing. ◊ **asphyxia**

chol- /kɒl/ *prefix* same as **chole-** (*used before vowels*)

cholaemia /kə'liːmiə/ *noun* the presence of an unusual amount of bile in the blood

cholagogue /'kɒləgɒg/ *noun* a drug which encourages the production of bile

cholangiocarcinoma /kəˌlændʒiəʊˌkɑːsɪ'nəʊmə/ *noun* a rare cancer of the cells of the bile ducts

cholangiography /kəˌlændʒi'ɒgrəfi/ *noun* an X-ray examination of the bile ducts and gall bladder

cholangiolitis /kəˌlændʒiəʊ'laɪtɪs/ *noun* inflammation of the small bile ducts

cholangiopancreatography /kəˌlændʒiəʊˌpæŋkriə'tɒgrəfi/ *noun* an X-ray examination of the bile ducts and pancreas

cholangitis /ˌkəʊlæn'dʒaɪtɪs/ *noun* inflammation of the bile ducts

chole- /kɒli/ *prefix* referring to bile

cholecalciferol /ˌkɒlɪkæl'sɪfərɒl/ *noun* a form of vitamin D found naturally in fish-liver oils and egg yolks

cholecystectomy /ˌkɒlɪsɪ'stektəmi/ *noun* the surgical removal of the gall bladder

cholecystitis /ˌkɒlɪsɪ'staɪtɪs/ *noun* inflammation of the gall bladder

cholecystoduodenostomy /ˌkɒlɪsɪstəˌdjuːədɪ'nɒstəmi/ *noun* a surgical operation to join the gall bladder to the duodenum to allow bile to pass into the intestine when the main bile duct is blocked

cholecystogram /ˌkɒlɪ'sɪstəgræm/ *noun* an X-ray photograph of the gall bladder

cholecystography /ˌkɒlɪsɪ'stɒgrəfi/ *noun* an X-ray examination of the gall bladder

cholecystokinin /ˌkɒlɪsɪstəʊ'kaɪnɪn/ *noun* a hormone released by cells at the top of the small intestine. It stimulates the gall bladder, making it contract and release bile.

cholecystotomy /ˌkɒlɪsɪ'stɒtəmi/ *noun* a surgical operation to make a cut in the gall bladder, usually to remove gallstones

choledoch- /kəledək/ *prefix* referring to the common bile duct

choledocholithiasis /kəˌledəkəlɪ'θaɪəsɪs/ *noun* same as **cholelithiasis**

choledocholithotomy /kəˌledɪkəʊlɪ'θɒtəmi/ *noun* a surgical operation to remove a gallstone by cutting into the bile duct

choledochostomy /kəˌledə'kɒstəmi/ *noun* a surgical operation to make an opening in a bile duct

choledochotomy /kəledə'kɒtəmi/ *noun* a surgical operation to make a cut in the common bile duct to remove gallstones

cholelithiasis /ˌkɒlɪlɪ'θaɪəsɪs/ *noun* a condition in which gallstones form in the gall bladder or bile ducts. Also called **choledocholithiasis**

cholelithotomy /ˌkɒlɪlɪ'θɒtəmi/ *noun* the surgical removal of gallstones by cutting into the gall bladder

cholera /'kɒlərə/ *noun* a serious bacterial disease spread through food or water which has been infected by *Vibrio cholerae* ○ *A cholera epidemic broke out after the flood.*

COMMENT: The infected person experiences diarrhoea, cramp in the intestines and dehydration. The disease is often fatal and vaccination is only effective for a relatively short period.

choleresis /kəˈlɪərəsɪs/ *noun* the production of bile by the liver

choleretic /ˌkɒlɪˈretɪk/ *adjective* referring to a substance which increases the production and flow of bile

cholestasis /ˌkɒlɪˈsteɪsɪs/ *noun* a condition in which all bile does not pass into the intestine but some remains in the liver and causes jaundice

cholesteatoma /kə،lestiəˈtəʊmə/ *noun* a cyst containing some cholesterol found in the middle ear and also in the brain

cholesterol /kəˈlestərɒl/ *noun* a fatty substance found in fats and oils, also produced by the liver and forming an essential part of all cells

COMMENT: Cholesterol is found in brain cells, the adrenal glands, liver and bile acids. High levels of cholesterol in the blood are found in diabetes. Cholesterol is formed by the body, and high blood cholesterol levels are associated with diets rich in animal fat, such as butter and fat meat. Excess cholesterol can be deposited in the walls of arteries, causing atherosclerosis.

cholesterolaemia /kə،lestərəˈliːmiə/ *noun* a high level of cholesterol in the blood

cholesterosis /kə،lestəˈrəʊsɪs/ *noun* inflammation of the gall bladder with deposits of cholesterol

cholic acid /ˌkəʊlɪk ˈæsɪd/ *noun* one of the bile acids

choline /ˈkəʊliːn/ *noun* a compound involved in fat metabolism and the precursor for acetylcholine

cholinergic /ˌkəʊlɪˈnɜːdʒɪk/ *adjective* referring to a neurone or receptor which responds to acetylcholine

cholinesterase /ˌkəʊlɪˈnestəreɪz/ *noun* an enzyme which breaks down a choline ester

choluria /kəʊˈljʊəriə/ *noun* same as **biliuria**

chondr- /kɒndr/ *prefix* referring to cartilage

chondritis /kɒnˈdraɪtɪs/ *noun* inflammation of a cartilage

chondroblast /ˈkɒndrəʊblæst/ *noun* a cell from which cartilage develops in an embryo

chondrocalcinosis /ˌkɒndrəʊ،kælsɪˈnəʊsɪs/ *noun* a condition in which deposits of calcium phosphate are found in articular cartilage

chondrocyte /ˈkɒndrəʊsaɪt/ *noun* a mature cartilage cell

chondrodysplasia /ˌkɒndrəʊdɪsˈpleɪziə/ *noun* a hereditary disorder of cartilage which is linked to dwarfism

chondrodystrophy /ˌkɒndrəʊˈdɪstrəfi/ *noun* any disorder of cartilage

chondroma /kɒnˈdrəʊmə/ *noun* a tumour formed of cartilaginous tissue

chondromalacia /ˌkɒndrəʊməˈleɪʃə/ *noun* degeneration of the cartilage of a joint

chondrosarcoma /ˌkɒndrəʊsɑːˈkəʊmə/ *noun* a malignant, rapidly growing tumour involving cartilage cells

chorda /ˈkɔːdə/ *noun* a cord or tendon (NOTE: The plural is **chordae**.)

chordae tendineae /ˌkɔːdaɪ tenˈdɪniaɪ/ *plural noun* tiny fibrous ligaments in the heart which attach the edges of some of the valves to the walls of the ventricles

chordee /ˈkɔːdiː/ *noun* a painful condition where the erect penis is curved, a complication of gonorrhoea

chorditis /kɔːˈdaɪtɪs/ *noun* inflammation of the vocal cords

chordotomy /kɔːˈdɒtəmi/ *noun* a surgical operation to cut a cord such as a nerve pathway in the spinal cord in order to relieve intractable pain

chorea /kɔːˈriːə/ *noun* a sudden severe twitching, usually of the face and shoulders, which is a symptom of disease of the nervous system

chorion /ˈkɔːriən/ *noun* a membrane covering the fertilised ovum

chorionic /ˌkɔːriˈɒnɪk/ *adjective* referring to the chorion

chorionic gonadotrophin /kɔːri،ɒnɪk gəʊnədəʊˈtrəʊfɪn/ *noun* ♦ **human chorionic gonadotrophin**

chorionic villi /kɔːri،ɒnɪk ˈvɪlaɪ/ *plural noun* tiny finger-like folds in the chorion

chorionic villus sampling /kɔːri،ɒnɪk ˈvɪləs ˌsɑːmplɪŋ/ *noun* an antenatal screening test carried out by examining cells from the chorionic villi of the outer membrane surrounding an embryo, which have the same DNA as the fetus

choroid /ˈkɔːrɔɪd/ *noun* the middle layer of tissue which forms the eyeball, between the sclera and the retina. See illustration at EYE in Supplement

choroiditis /ˌkɔːrɔɪˈdaɪtɪs/ *noun* inflammation of the choroid in the eyeball

choroidocyclitis /kɔː،rɔɪdəʊsaɪˈklaɪtɪs/ *noun* inflammation of the choroids and ciliary body

choroid plexus /ˌkɔːrɔɪd ˈpleksəs/ *noun* part of the pia mater, a network of small blood vessels in the ventricles of the brain which produce cerebrospinal fluid. See illustration at EYE in Supplement

Christmas disease /ˈkrɪsməs dɪˌziːz/ *noun* same as **haemophilia B** [After Mr Christmas, the person in whom the disease was first studied in detail]

Christmas factor /ˈkrɪsməs ˌfæktə/ noun same as **Factor IX**

chrom- /krəʊm/ prefix same as **chromo-** (used before vowels)

-chromasia /krəmeɪziə/ suffix referring to colour

chromatid /ˈkrəʊmətɪd/ noun one of two parallel filaments making up a chromosome

chromatin /ˈkrəʊmətɪn/ noun a network which forms the nucleus of a cell and can be stained with basic dyes

chromatography /ˌkrəʊməˈtɒgrəfi/ noun a method of separating chemicals through a porous medium, used in analysing compounds and mixtures

chromatophore /krəʊˈmætəfɔː/ noun any pigment-bearing cell in the eyes, hair and skin

chromic acid /ˌkrəʊmɪk ˈæsɪd/ noun an unstable acid existing only in solution or in the form of a salt, sometimes used in the removal of warts

chromicised catgut /ˌkrəʊmɪsaɪzd ˈkætgʌt/ noun catgut which is hardened with chromium to make it slower to dissolve in the body

chromium /ˈkrəʊmiəm/ noun a metallic trace element (NOTE: The chemical symbol is Cr.)

chromo- /krəʊməʊ/ prefix referring to colour

chromosomal /ˌkrəʊməˈsəʊm(ə)l/ adjective referring to chromosomes

chromosomal aberration /ˌkrəʊmə-səʊm(ə)l ˌæbəˈreɪʃ(ə)n/ noun same as **chromosome aberration**

chromosome /ˈkrəʊməsəʊm/ noun a rod-shaped structure in the nucleus of a cell, formed of DNA, which carries the genes

COMMENT: Each human cell has 46 chromosomes, 23 inherited from each parent. The female has one pair of X chromosomes, and the male one pair of XY chromosomes, which are responsible for the sexual difference. Sperm from a male have either an X or a Y chromosome. If a Y chromosome sperm fertilises the female's ovum the child will be male.

chromosome aberration /ˈkrəʊməsəʊm ˌæbəreɪʃ(ə)n/ noun a change from the usual number or arrangement of chromosomes

chromosome mapping /ˈkrəʊməsəʊm ˌmæpɪŋ/ noun a procedure by which the position of genes on a chromosome is established

chronic /ˈkrɒnɪk/ adjective **1.** referring to a disease or condition which lasts for a long time ○ He has a chronic chest complaint. Opposite **acute 2.** referring to serious pain (informal)

chronic abscess /ˌkrɒnɪk ˈæbses/ noun an abscess which develops slowly over a period of time

chronic appendicitis /ˌkrɒnɪk əˌpendɪˈsaɪtɪs/ noun a condition in which the vermiform appendix is always slightly inflamed. ◊ **grumbling appendix**

chronic catarrhal rhinitis /ˌkrɒnɪk kəˌtɑːrəl raɪˈnaɪtɪs/ noun a persistent form of inflammation of the nose where excess mucus is secreted by the mucous membrane

chronic fatigue syndrome /ˌkrɒnɪk fə ˈtiːg ˌsɪndrəʊm/ noun same as **myalgic encephalomyelitis**

chronic glaucoma /ˌkrɒnɪk glɔːˈkəʊmə/ noun same as **open-angle glaucoma**

chronic granulomatous disease /ˌkrɒnɪk ˌgrænjʊˈləʊmətəs dɪˌziːz/ noun a type of inflammation where macrophages are converted into epithelial-like cells as a result of infection, as in tuberculosis or sarcoidosis

chronic obstructive airways disease /ˌkrɒnɪk əbˌstrʌktɪv ˈeəweɪz dɪˌziːz/ noun Abbr **COAD**. Now called **chronic obstructive pulmonary disease**

chronic obstructive pulmonary disease /ˌkrɒnɪk əbˌstrʌktɪv ˈpʌlmən(ə)ri dɪˌziːz/ noun any of a group of progressive respiratory disorders where someone experiences loss of lung function and shows little or no response to steroid or bronchodilator drug treatments, e.g. emphysema and chronic bronchitis. Abbr **COPD**

chronic pancreatitis /ˌkrɒnɪk pæŋkriə ˈtaɪtɪs/ noun a persistent inflammation occurring after repeated attacks of acute pancreatitis, where the gland becomes calcified

chronic periarthritis /ˌkrɒnɪk periːˈθraɪtɪs/ noun inflammation of tissues round the shoulder joint. Also called **scapulohumeral arthritis**

chronic pericarditis /ˌkrɒnɪk perikɑːˈdaɪtɪs/ noun a condition in which the pericardium becomes thickened and prevents the heart from functioning normally. Also called **constrictive pericarditis**

Chronic Sick and Disabled Persons Act 1970 /ˌkrɒnɪk ˌsɪk ən dɪsˌeɪb(ə)ld ˈpɜːs(ə)nz ækt/ noun an Act of Parliament in the UK which provides benefits such as alterations to their homes for people with long-term conditions

chronic toxicity /ˌkrɒnɪk tɒkˈsɪsɪti/ noun exposure to harmful levels of a toxic substance over a period of time

chrysotherapy /ˌkraɪsəʊˈθerəpi/ noun treatment which involves gold injections

Chvostek's sign /tʃəˈvɒsteks saɪn/ noun an indication of tetany, where a spasm is produced if the facial muscles are tapped

chyle /kaɪl/ noun a fluid in the lymph vessels in the intestine, which contains fat, especially after a meal

chylomicron /ˌkaɪləʊˈmaɪkrɒn/ noun a particle of chyle present in the blood

chyluria /kaɪˈljʊəriə/ noun the presence of chyle in the urine

chyme /kaɪm/ *noun* a semi-liquid mass of food and gastric juices, which passes from the stomach to the intestine

chymotrypsin /ˌkaɪməʊˈtrɪpsɪn/ *noun* an enzyme which digests protein

Ci *abbr* curie

cicatrise /ˈsɪkətraɪz/, **cicatrize** *verb* to heal and form a scar, or to cause a wound to heal and form a scar

cicatrix /ˈsɪkətrɪks/ *noun* same as **scar**

-ciclovir /sɪkləvɪə/ *suffix* used in the names of antiviral drugs

-cide /saɪd/ *suffix* referring to killing

cilia /ˈsɪliə/ plural of **cilium**

ciliary /ˈsiliəri/ *adjective* 1. referring to the eyelid or eyelashes 2. referring to cilia

ciliary body /ˈsɪliəri ˌbɒdi/ *noun* the part of the eye which connects the iris to the choroid. See illustration at EYE in Supplement

ciliary ganglion /ˌsɪliəri ˈgæŋgliən/ *noun* a parasympathetic ganglion in the orbit of the eye, supplying the intrinsic eye muscles

ciliary muscle /ˈsɪliəri ˌmʌs(ə)l/ *noun* a muscle which makes the lens of the eye change its shape to focus on objects at different distances. See illustration at EYE in Supplement

ciliary processes /ˌsɪliəri ˈprəʊsesɪz/ *plural noun* the ridges behind the iris to which the lens of the eye is attached

ciliated epithelium /ˌsɪlieɪtɪd epɪˈθiːliəm/ *noun* simple epithelium where the cells have tiny hairs or cilia

cilium /ˈsɪliəm/ *noun* 1. an eyelash 2. one of many tiny hair-like processes which line cells in passages in the body and by moving backwards and forwards drive particles or fluid along the passage (NOTE: The plural is **cilia**.)

-cillin /sɪlɪn/ *suffix* used in the names of penicillin drugs ○ *amoxycillin*

cimetidine /sɪˈmetɪdiːn/ *noun* a drug which reduces the production of stomach acid, used in peptic ulcer treatment

cimex /ˈsaɪmeks/ *noun* a bedbug or related insect which feeds on birds, humans and other mammals (NOTE: The plural is **cimices**.)

CIN *abbr* cervical intraepithelial neoplasia

-cin /sɪn/ *suffix* referring to aminoglycosides ○ *gentamicin*

cinematics /ˌsɪnɪˈmætɪks/ *noun* the science of movement, especially of body movements

cineplasty /ˈsɪnɪplæsti/ *noun* an amputation where the muscles of the stump of the amputated limb are used to operate an artificial limb

cineradiography /ˌsɪnireɪdiˈɒgrəfi/ *noun* the practice of taking a series of X-ray photographs for diagnosis, or to show how something moves or develops in the body

cinesiology /sɪˌniːsiˈɒlədʒi/ *noun* the study of muscle movements, particularly in relation to treatment

cingulectomy /ˌsɪŋgjʊˈlektəmi/ *noun* a surgical operation to remove the cingulum

cingulum /ˈsɪŋgjʊləm/ *noun* a long curved bundle of nerve fibres in the cerebrum (NOTE: The plural is **cingula**.)

cinnarizine /ˈsɪnərəziːn/ *noun* an antihistaminic used to treat Ménière's disease

ciprofloxacin /ˌsaɪprəʊˈflɒksəsɪn/ *noun* a powerful antibiotic used in eye drops to treat corneal ulcers and surface infections of the eye, and in the treatment of anthrax in humans

circadian /sɜːˈkeɪdiən/ *adjective* referring to a pattern which is repeated approximately every 24 hours

circadian rhythm /sɜːˌkeɪdiən ˈrɪð(ə)m/ *noun* same as **biological clock**

circle of Willis /ˌsɜːk(ə)l əv ˈwɪlɪs/ *noun* a circle of branching arteries at the base of the brain formed by the basilar artery, the anterior and posterior cerebral arteries, the anterior and posterior communicating arteries and the internal carotid arteries [Described 1664. After Thomas Willis (1621–75), English physician and anatomist.]

circular fold /ˈsɜːkjʊlə fəʊld/ *noun* a large transverse fold of mucous membrane in the small intestine

circulation /ˌsɜːkjʊˈleɪʃ(ə)n/ *noun* □ **circulation (of the blood)** movement of blood around the body from the heart through the arteries to the capillaries and back to the heart through the veins ○ *She has poor circulation in her legs.* ○ *Rub your hands to get the circulation going.*

COMMENT: Blood circulates around the body, carrying oxygen from the lungs and nutrients from the liver through the arteries and capillaries to the tissues. The capillaries exchange the oxygen for waste matter such as carbon dioxide which is taken back to the lungs to be expelled. At the same time the blood obtains more oxygen in the lungs to be taken to the tissues. The circulation pattern is as follows: blood returns through the veins to the right atrium of the heart. From there it is pumped through the right ventricle into the pulmonary artery, and then into the lungs. From the lungs it returns through the pulmonary veins to the left atrium of the heart and is pumped from there through the left ventricle into the aorta and from the aorta into the other arteries.

circulatory /ˌsɜːkjʊˈleɪt(ə)ri/ *adjective* referring to the circulation of the blood

circulatory system /ˌsɜːkjʊˈleɪt(ə)ri ˌsɪstəm/ *noun* a system of arteries and veins, together with the heart, which makes the blood circulate around the body

circum- /sɜːkəm/ *prefix* around

circumcise /ˈsɜːkəmsaɪz/ *verb* to remove the foreskin of the penis

circumcision /ˌsɜːkəmˈsɪʒ(ə)n/ *noun* the surgical removal of the foreskin of the penis

circumduction /ˌsɜːkəm'dʌkʃən/ *noun* the action of moving a limb so that the end of it makes a circular motion

circumflex /'sɜːkəmfleks/ *adjective* bent or curved

circumflex artery /'sɜːkəmfleks ˌɑːtəri/ *noun* a branch of the femoral artery in the upper thigh

circumflex nerve /'sɜːkəmfleks nɜːv/ *noun* a sensory and motor nerve in the upper arm

circumoral /ˌsɜːkəm'ɔːrəl/ *adjective* referring to rashes surrounding the lips

circumvallate papillae /sɜːkəmˌvæleɪt pə'pɪli/ *plural noun* large papillae at the base of the tongue, which have taste buds

cirrhosis /sə'rəʊsɪs/ *noun* a progressive disease of the liver, often associated with alcoholism, in which healthy cells are replaced by scar tissue □ **cirrhosis of the liver** hepatocirrhosis, a condition where some cells of the liver die and are replaced by hard fibrous tissue

COMMENT: Cirrhosis can have many causes: the commonest cause is alcoholism (alcoholic cirrhosis or Laennec's cirrhosis). It can also be caused by heart disease (cardiac cirrhosis), by viral hepatitis (postnecrotic cirrhosis), by autoimmune disease (primary biliary cirrhosis) or by obstruction or infection of the bile ducts (biliary cirrhosis).

cirrhotic /sɪ'rɒtɪk/ *adjective* referring to cirrhosis ○ *The patient had a cirrhotic liver.*

cirs- /sɜːs/ *prefix* referring to dilation

cirsoid /'sɜːsɔɪd/ *adjective* referring to a varicose vein which is dilated

cirsoid aneurysm /ˌsɜːsɔɪd 'ænjərɪz(ə)m/ *noun* a condition in which arteries become swollen and twisted

cisplatin /sɪs'pleɪtɪn/ *noun* a chemical substance which may help fight cancer by binding to DNA. It is used in the treatment of ovarian and testicular cancer.

cistern /'sɪstən/, **cisterna** /sɪ'stɜːnə/ *noun* a space containing fluid

cisterna magna /sɪˌstɜːnə 'mægnə/ *noun* a large space containing cerebrospinal fluid, situated underneath the cerebellum and behind the medulla oblongata

citric acid /ˌsɪtrɪk 'æsɪd/ *noun* an acid found in fruit such as oranges, lemons and grapefruit

citric acid cycle /ˌsɪtrɪk 'æsɪd ˌsaɪk(ə)l/ *noun* an important series of events concerning amino acid metabolism, which takes place in the mitochondria in the cell. Also called **Krebs cycle**

citrullinaemia /ˌsɪtrʊlɪ'niːmiə/ *noun* a deficiency of an enzyme which helps break down proteins

citrulline /'sɪtrʊliːn, 'sɪtrʊlaɪn/ *noun* an amino acid

CJD *abbr* Creutzfeldt-Jakob disease

cl *abbr* centilitre

clamp /klæmp/ *noun* a surgical instrument to hold something tightly, e.g. a blood vessel during an operation ■ *verb* to hold something tightly

clap /klæp/ *noun* same as **gonorrhoea** (*slang*)

classic /'klæsɪk/ *adjective* referring to a typically well-known symptom ○ *She showed classic heroin withdrawal symptoms: sweating, fever, sleeplessness and anxiety.*

classification /ˌklæsɪfɪ'keɪʃ(ə)n/ *noun* the work of putting references or components into order so as to be able to refer to them again and identify them easily ○ *the ABO classification of blood*

classify /'klæsɪfaɪ/ *verb* to put references or components into order so as to be able to refer to them again and identify them easily ○ *The medical records are classified under the surname of the patient.* ○ *Blood groups are classified according to the ABO system.*

claudication /ˌklɔːdɪ'keɪʃ(ə)n/ *noun* the fact of limping or being lame

COMMENT: At first, the person limps after having walked a short distance, then finds walking progressively more difficult and finally impossible. The condition improves after rest.

claustrophobia /ˌklɔːstrə'fəʊbiə/ *noun* a fear of enclosed spaces or crowded rooms. Compare **agoraphobia**

claustrophobic /ˌklɔːstrə'fəʊbɪk/ *adjective* afraid of being in enclosed spaces or crowded rooms. Compare **agoraphobic**

clavicle /'klævɪk(ə)l/ *noun* same as **collarbone**

clavicular /klə'vɪkjʊlə/ *adjective* referring to the clavicle

clavus /'kleɪvəs/ *noun* **1.** a corn on the foot **2.** severe pain in the head, like a nail being driven in

claw foot /ˌklɔː 'fʊt/ *noun* a deformed foot with the toes curved towards the instep and with a very high arch. Also called **pes cavus**

claw hand /ˌklɔː 'hænd/ *noun* a deformed hand with the fingers, especially the ring finger and little finger, bent towards the palm, caused by paralysis of the muscles

clean /kliːn/ *adjective* **1.** free from dirt, waste products or unwanted substances **2.** sterile or free from infection ○ *a clean dressing* ○ *a clean wound* **3.** not using recreational drugs

cleanliness /'klenlinəs/ *noun* the state of being clean ○ *The report praised the cleanliness of the hospital kitchen.*

clear /klɪə/ *adjective* **1.** easily understood ○ *The doctor made it clear that he wanted the patient to have a home help.* ○ *The words on the medicine bottle are not very clear.* **2.** not cloudy and easy to see through ○ *a clear glass bottle* ○ *The urine sample was clear.* **3.** □ **clear of** free from ○ *The area is now clear of infection.* ■ *verb* to take away a blockage ○ *The inhalant will clear your blocked nose.* ○ *He is on* *antibiotics to try to clear the congestion in his lungs.*

clear up /ˌklɪər ˈʌp/ *verb* to get better ○ *His infection should clear up within a few days.* ○ *I hope your cold clears up before the holiday.*

cleavage /ˈkliːvɪdʒ/ *noun* the repeated division of cells in an embryo

cleavage lines *plural noun* same as **Langer's lines**

cleft /kleft/ *noun* a small opening or hollow place in a surface or body part ■ *adjective* referring to a surface or body part which has separated into two or more sections

cleft foot /ˌkleft ˈfʊt/ *noun* same as **talipes**

cleft lip /ˌkleft ˈlɪp/ *noun* a congenital condition in which the upper lip fails to form in the usual way during fetal development. Also called **harelip**

cleft palate /ˌkleft ˈpælət/ *noun* a congenital condition in which the palate does not fuse during fetal development, causing a gap between the mouth and nasal cavity in severe cases

COMMENT: A cleft palate is usually associated with a cleft lip. Both can be successfully corrected by surgery.

cleido- /klaɪdəʊ/ *prefix* referring to the clavicle

cleidocranial dysostosis /ˌklaɪdəʊkreɪnɪəl ˌdɪsɒsˈtəʊsɪs/ *noun* a hereditary bone malformation, with protruding jaw, lack of collarbone and malformed teeth

clerking /ˈklɑːkɪŋ/ *noun* the practice of writing down the details of a person on admission to a hospital (*informal*)

client /ˈklaɪənt/ *noun* a person visited by a health visitor or social worker

climacteric /klaɪˈmæktərɪk/ *noun* **1.** same as **menopause 2.** a period of diminished sexual activity in a man who reaches middle age

climax /ˈklaɪmæks/ *noun* **1.** an orgasm **2.** the point where a disease is at its worst ■ *verb* to have an orgasm

clindamycin /ˌklɪndəˈmaɪsɪn/ *noun* a powerful antibiotic used to treat severe infections and acne

clinic /ˈklɪnɪk/ *noun* **1.** a small hospital or a department in a large hospital which deals only with out-patients or which specialises in the treatment of particular medical conditions ○ *He is being treated in a private clinic.* ○ *She was referred to an antenatal clinic.* **2.** a group of students under a doctor or surgeon who examine patients and discuss their treatment

clinical /ˈklɪnɪk(ə)l/ *adjective* **1.** referring to the physical assessment and treatment of patients by doctors, as opposed to a surgical operation, a laboratory test or experiment **2.** referring to instruction given to students at the bedside of patients as opposed to class instruction with no patient present **3.** referring to a clinic

'…we studied 69 patients who met the clinical and laboratory criteria of definite MS' [*Lancet*]

'…the allocation of students to clinical areas is for their educational needs and not for service requirements' [*Nursing Times*]

clinical audit /ˌklɪnɪk(ə)l ˈɔːdɪt/ *noun* an evaluation of the standard of clinical care

clinical care /ˌklɪnɪk(ə)l ˈkeə/ *noun* the care and treatment of patients in hospital wards or in doctors' surgeries

clinical effectiveness /ˌklɪnɪk(ə)l ɪˈfektɪvnəs/ *noun* the ability of a procedure or treatment to achieve the desired result

clinical governance /ˌklɪnɪk(ə)l ˈɡʌv(ə)nəns/ *noun* the responsibility given to doctors to coordinate audit, research, education, use of guidelines and risk management to develop a strategy to raise the quality of medical care

clinically /ˈklɪnɪkli/ *adverb* using information gathered from the treatment of patients in a hospital ward or in the doctor's surgery ○ *Smallpox is now clinically extinct.*

clinical medicine /ˌklɪnɪk(ə)l ˈmed(ə)s(ə)n/ *noun* the study and treatment of patients in a hospital ward or in the doctor's surgery, as opposed to in the operating theatre or laboratory

clinical nurse manager /ˌklɪnɪk(ə)l ˈnɜːs ˌmænɪdʒə/ *noun* the administrative manager of the clinical nursing staff of a hospital

clinical nurse specialist /ˌklɪnɪk(ə)l nɜːs ˈspeʃ(ə)lɪst/ *noun* a nurse who specialises in a particular branch of clinical care

clinical pathology /ˌklɪnɪk(ə)l pəˈθɒlədʒi/ *noun* the study of disease as applied to the treatment of patients

clinical psychologist /ˌklɪnɪk(ə)l saɪˈkɒlədʒɪst/ *noun* a psychologist who studies and treats sick patients in hospital

clinical thermometer /ˌklɪnɪk(ə)l θəˈmɒmɪtə/ *noun* a thermometer used in a hospital or by a doctor for measuring a person's body temperature

clinical trial /ˌklɪnɪk(ə)l ˈtraɪəl/ *noun* a trial carried out in a medical laboratory on a person or on tissue from a person

clinician /klɪˈnɪʃ(ə)n/ *noun* a doctor, usually not a surgeon, who has considerable experience in treating patients

clinodactyly /ˌklaɪnəʊˈdæktɪli/ *noun* permanent bending of a finger to one side

clip /klɪp/ *noun* a piece of metal with a spring, used to attach things together

clitoris /ˈklɪtərɪs/ *noun* a small erectile female sex organ, situated at the anterior angle of the vulva, which can be excited by sexual activity. See illustration at UROGENITAL SYSTEM (FEMALE) in Supplement

cloaca /kləʊˈeɪkə/ *noun* the end part of the hindgut in an embryo

clomipramine /ˌkləʊˈmɪprəmiːn/ *noun* a drug used to treat depression, phobias and obsessive-compulsive disorder

clonazepam /kləʊˈnæzɪpæm/ *noun* a drug used to treat epilepsy

clone /kləʊn/ *noun* a group of cells derived from a single cell by asexual reproduction and so identical to the first cell ■ *verb* to reproduce an individual organism by asexual means

clonic /ˈklɒnɪk/ *adjective* **1.** referring to clonus **2.** having spasmodic contractions

clonic spasms /ˌklɒnɪk ˈspæz(ə)mz/ *plural noun* spasms which recur regularly

clonidine /ˈklɒnɪdiːn/ *noun* a drug which relaxes and widens the arteries, used in the treatment of hypertension, migraine headaches and heart failure

cloning /ˈkləʊnɪŋ/ *noun* the reproduction of an individual organism by asexual means

clonorchiasis /ˌkləʊnəˈkaɪəsɪs/ *noun* a liver condition, common in the Far East, caused by the fluke *Clonorchis sinensis*

clonus /ˈkləʊnəs/ *noun* the rhythmic contraction and relaxation of a muscle, usually a sign of upper motor neurone lesions

close /kləʊz/ *verb* **1.** to become covered with new tissue as part of the healing process **2.** to fix together the sides of a wound after surgery to allow healing to take place

closed fracture /ˌkləʊzd ˈfræktʃə/ *noun* same as **simple fracture**

Clostridium /klɒˈstrɪdiəm/ *noun* a type of bacteria

COMMENT: Species of Clostridium cause botulism, tetanus and gas gangrene.

clot /klɒt/ *noun* a soft mass of coagulated blood in a vein or an artery ○ *The doctor diagnosed a blood clot in the brain.* ○ *Blood clots occur in thrombosis.* ■ *verb* to change from a liquid to a semi-solid state, or to cause a liquid to do this ○ *His blood does not clot easily.* (NOTE: **clotting – clotted**)

clotrimazole /klɒˈtrɪməzəʊl/ *noun* a drug used to treat yeast and fungal infections

clotting /ˈklɒtɪŋ/ *noun* the action of coagulating

clotting factors /ˌklɒtɪŋ ˈfæktəz/ *plural noun* substances in plasma, called Factor I, Factor II, and so on, which act one after the other to make the blood coagulate when a blood vessel is damaged

COMMENT: Deficiency in one or more of the clotting factors results in haemophilia.

clotting time /ˈklɒtɪŋ taɪm/ *noun* the time taken for blood to coagulate under usual conditions. Also called **coagulation time**

cloud /klaʊd/ *noun* the disturbed sediment in a liquid

cloudy /ˈklaʊdi/ *adjective* referring to liquid which is not transparent but which has an opaque substance in it

clubbing /ˈklʌbɪŋ/ *noun* a thickening of the ends of the fingers and toes, a sign of many different diseases

club foot /ˌklʌb ˈfʊt/ *noun* same as **talipes**

cluster /ˈklʌstə/ *noun* **1.** a group of small items which cling together **2.** a significant subset in a statistical sample, e.g. of numbers of people affected by a particular disease or condition

cluster headache /ˈklʌstə ˌhedeɪk/ *noun* a headache which occurs behind one eye for a short period

Clutton's joint /ˈklʌt(ə)nz ˌdʒɔɪnt/ *noun* a swollen knee joint occurring in congenital syphilis [Described 1886. After Henry Hugh Clutton (1850–1909), surgeon at St Thomas's Hospital, London, UK.]

cm *abbr* centimetre

CMHN *abbr* community mental health nurse

CM joint /ˌsiː ˈem dʒɔɪnt/ *plural noun* same as **carpometacarpal joint**

CMO *abbr* Chief Medical Officer

CMV *abbr* cytomegalovirus

C/N *abbr* charge nurse

CNS *abbr* central nervous system

COAD *abbr* chronic obstructive airways disease

coagulant /kəʊˈæɡjʊlənt/ *noun* a substance which can make blood clot

coagulase /kəʊˈæɡjʊleɪz/ *noun* an enzyme produced by a staphylococcal bacteria which makes blood plasma clot

coagulate /kəʊˈæɡjʊleɪt/ *verb* to change from liquid to semi-solid, or cause a liquid to do this ○ *His blood does not coagulate easily.* ◊ **clot**

COMMENT: Blood coagulates when fibrinogen, a protein in the blood, converts into fibrin under the influence of the enzyme thrombokinase.

coagulation /kəʊˌæɡjʊˈleɪʃ(ə)n/ *noun* the action of clotting

coagulation time /kəʊæɡjuˈleɪʃ(ə)n taɪm/ *noun* same as **clotting time**

coagulum /kəʊˈæɡjʊləm/ *noun* same as **blood clot** (NOTE: The plural is **coagula**.)

coalesce /ˌkəʊəˈles/ *verb* to combine, or to cause things to combine, into a single body or group

coalescence /ˌkəʊəˈles(ə)ns/ *noun* the process by which wound edges come together when healing

coarctation /ˌkəʊɑːkˈteɪʃ(ə)n/ *noun* the process of narrowing □ **coarctation of the aorta** congenital narrowing of the aorta, which results in high blood pressure in the upper part of the body and low blood pressure in the lower part

coarse tremor /ˌkɔːs ˈtremə/ *noun* severe trembling

coat /kəʊt/ *noun* a layer of material covering an organ or a cavity ■ *verb* to cover something with something else

coated tongue /ˌkəʊtɪd ˈtʌŋ/ *noun* same as **furred tongue**

coating /ˈkəʊtɪŋ/ *noun* a thin covering ○ *a pill with a sugar coating*

cobalt /ˈkəʊbɔːlt/ *noun* a metallic element (NOTE: The chemical symbol is **Co**.)

cobalt 60 /ˌkəʊbɔːlt/ *noun* a radioactive isotope which is used in radiotherapy to treat cancer

cocaine /kəˈkeɪn/ *noun* a narcotic drug not generally used in medicine because its use leads to addiction, but sometimes used as a surface anaesthetic

cocci /ˈkɒki/ plural of **coccus**

coccidioidomycosis /kɒkˌsɪdɪɔɪˌdəʊmaɪˈkəʊsɪs/ *noun* a lung disease, caused by inhaling spores of the fungus *Coccidioides immitis*

coccus /ˈkɒkəs/ *noun* a bacterium shaped like a ball (NOTE: The plural is **cocci**.)

COMMENT: Cocci grow together in groups: either in clusters (staphylococci) or in long chains (streptococci).

coccy- /ˈkɒksi/ *prefix* referring to the coccyx

coccydynia /ˌkɒksiˈdɪniə/ *noun* a sharp pain in the coccyx, usually caused by a blow. Also called **coccygodynia**

coccygeal vertebrae /kɒkˌsɪdʒɪəl ˈvɜːtɪbreɪ/ *plural noun* the fused bones in the coccyx

coccyges /kɒkˈsaɪdʒiːz/ plural of **coccyx**

coccygodynia /ˌkɒksigəʊˈdɪniə/ *noun* same as **coccydynia**

coccyx /ˈkɒksɪks/ *noun* the lowest bone in the backbone (NOTE: The plural is **coccyges**.)

COMMENT: The coccyx is a rudimentary tail made of four bones which have fused together into a bone in the shape of a triangle.

cochlea /ˈkɒkliə/ *noun* a spiral tube inside the inner ear, which is the essential organ of hearing. See illustration at EAR in Supplement (NOTE: The plural is **cochleae**.)

COMMENT: Sounds are transmitted as vibrations to the cochlea from the ossicles through the oval window. The lymph fluid in the cochlea passes the vibrations to the organ of Corti which in turn is connected to the auditory nerve.

cochlear /ˈkɒkliə/ *adjective* referring to the cochlea

cochlear duct /ˈkɒkliə dʌkt/ *noun* a spiral channel in the cochlea

cochlear implant /ˌkɒkliə ˈɪmplɑːnt/ *noun* a type of hearing aid for profound hearing loss

cochlear nerve /ˈkɒkliə nɜːv/ *noun* a division of the auditory nerve

Cochrane database /ˌkɒkrən ˈdeɪtəbeɪs/ *noun* a database of regular reviews carried out on research

code /kəʊd/ *noun* **1.** a system of numbers, letters or symbols used to represent language or information **2.** same as **genetic code** ■ *verb* **1.** to convert instructions or data into another form **2.** (*of a codon or gene*) to provide the genetic information which causes a specific amino acid to be produced ○ *Genes are sections of DNA that code for a specific protein sequence.*

codeine /ˈkəʊdiːn/, **codeine phosphate** /ˌkəʊdiːn ˈfɒsfeɪt/ *noun* a common painkilling drug that can also be used to suppress coughing and in the treatment of diarrhoea

code of conduct /ˌkəʊd əv ˈkɒndʌkt/ *noun* a set of general rules showing how a group of people such as doctors or nurses should work

cod liver oil /ˌkɒd lɪvər ˈɔɪl/ *noun* a fish oil which is rich in calories and vitamins A and D

-coele /siːl/ *suffix* referring to a hollow (NOTE: The US spelling is usually **-cele**.)

coeli- /siːli/ *prefix* same as **coelio-** (*used before vowels*) (NOTE: The US spelling is usually **celi-**.)

coeliac /ˈsiːliæk/ *adjective* referring to the abdomen

coeliac artery /ˌsiːliæk ˈɑːtəri/, **coeliac axis** /ˌsiːliæk ˈæksɪs/ *noun* the main artery in the abdomen leading from the abdominal aorta and dividing into the left gastric, hepatic and splenic arteries. Also called **coeliac trunk**

coeliac disease /ˌsiːliæk dɪˈziːz/ *noun* same as **gluten-induced enteropathy**

coeliac ganglion /ˌsiːliæk ˈgæŋgliən/ *noun* a ganglion on each side of the origins of the diaphragm, connected with the coeliac plexus

coeliac plexus /ˌsiːliæk ˈpleksəs/ *noun* a network of nerves in the abdomen, behind the stomach

coeliac trunk /ˌsiːliæk ˈtrʌŋk/ *noun* same as **coeliac artery**

coelio- /siːliəʊ/ *prefix* referring to a hollow, usually the abdomen (NOTE: The US spelling is usually **celio-**.)

coelioscopy /ˌsiːliˈɒskəpi/ *noun* an examination of the peritoneal cavity by inflating the abdomen with sterile air and passing an endoscope through the abdominal wall (NOTE: The plural is **coelioscopies**.)

coelom /ˈsiːləm/ *noun* a body cavity in an embryo, which divides to form the thorax and abdomen (NOTE: The plural is **coeloms** or **coelomata**.)

coffee ground vomit /ˈkɒfi graʊnd ˌvɒmɪt/ *noun* vomit containing dark pieces of blood, indicating that the person is bleeding from the stomach or upper intestine

cognition /kɒgˈnɪʃ(ə)n/ *noun* the mental action or process of gaining knowledge by using your mind or your senses, or knowledge gained in this way

cognitive /ˈkɒgnɪtɪv/ *adjective* referring to the mental processes of perception, memory, judgment and reasoning ○ *a cognitive impairment*

cognitive disorder /ˌkɒgnɪtɪv dɪsˈɔːdə/ *noun* impairment of any of the mental processes of perception, memory, judgment and reasoning

cognitive therapy /ˌkɒgnɪtɪv ˈθerəpi/ *noun* a treatment of psychiatric disorders such as anxiety or depression which encourages people to deal with their negative ways of thinking

cohort /ˈkəʊhɔːt/ *noun* a group of people sharing a particular characteristic such as age or gender who are studied in a scientific or medical investigation

cohort study /ˈkəʊhɔːt ˌstʌdi/ *noun* an investigation in which a group of people are classified according to their exposure to various risks and studied over a period of time to see if they develop a specific disease, in order to evaluate the links between risk and disease

coil /kɔɪl/ *noun* a device fitted into a woman's uterus as a contraceptive

coinfection /ˌkəʊɪnˈfekʃ(ə)n/ *noun* infection with two or more diseases or viruses at the same time

coital /ˈkəʊɪt(ə)l/ *adjective* referring to sexual intercourse

coitus /ˈkəʊɪtəs/, **coition** /kəʊˈɪʃ(ə)n/ *noun* same as **sexual intercourse**

coitus interruptus /ˌkəʊɪtəs ɪntəˈrʌptəs/ *noun* removal of the penis from the vagina before ejaculation, sometimes used as a method of contraception although it is not very efficient

cold /kəʊld/ *adjective* not warm or hot ■ *noun* an illness, with inflammation of the nasal passages, in which someone sneezes and coughs and has a blocked and running nose ○ *She had a heavy cold.* Also called **common cold, coryza**

COMMENT: A cold usually starts with a virus infection which causes inflammation of the mucous membrane in the nose and throat. Symptoms include running nose, cough and loss of taste and smell. Coronaviruses have been identified in people with colds, but there is no cure for a cold at present.

cold burn /ˈkəʊld bɜːn/ *noun* an injury to the skin caused by exposure to extreme cold or by touching a very cold surface

cold cautery /kəʊld ˈkɔːtəri/ *noun* the removal of a skin growth using carbon dioxide snow

cold compress /kəʊld ˈkɒmpres/ *noun* a wad of cloth soaked in cold water, used to relieve a headache or bruise

cold pack /ˈkəʊld pæk/ *noun* a cloth or a pad filled with gel or clay which is chilled and put on the body to reduce or increase the temperature

cold sore /ˈkəʊld sɔː/ *noun* a painful blister, usually on the lips or nose, caused by herpes simplex Type I

colectomy /kəˈlektəmi/ *noun* a surgical operation to remove the whole or part of the colon (NOTE: The plural is **colectomies**.)

colic /ˈkɒlɪk/ *noun* **1.** pain in any part of the intestinal tract. Also called **enteralgia, tormina 2.** crying and irritability in babies, especially from stomach pains

COMMENT: Although colic can refer to pain caused by indigestion, it can also be caused by stones in the gall bladder or kidney.

colicky /ˈkɒlɪki/ *adjective* referring to colic ○ *She had colicky pains in her abdomen.*

coliform bacterium /ˌkəʊlifɔːm bækˈtɪəriəm/ *plural noun* any bacterium which is similar to *Escherichia coli*

colistin /kɒˈlɪstɪn/ *noun* an antibiotic which is effective against a wide range of organisms and is used to treat gastrointestinal infections

colitis /kəˈlaɪtɪs/ *noun* inflammation of the colon. Also called **colonitis**

collagen /ˈkɒlədʒən/ *noun* a thick protein fibre forming bundles, which make up the connective tissue, bone and cartilage

collagen disease /ˈkɒlədʒən dɪˌziːz/ *noun* any disease of the connective tissue

COMMENT: Collagen diseases include rheumatic fever, rheumatoid arthritis, periarteritis nodosa, scleroderma and dermatomyositis.

collagenous /kəˈlædʒɪnəs/ *adjective* **1.** containing collagen **2.** referring to collagen disease

collapse /kəˈlæps/ *noun* **1.** a condition in which someone is extremely exhausted or semi-conscious ○ *She was found in a state of collapse.* **2.** a condition in which an organ becomes flat or loses air ○ *lung collapse* ■ *verb* **1.** to fall down in a semi-conscious state ○ *After running to catch his train he collapsed.* **2.** to become flat, or lose air

collapsed lung /kəˈlæpsd lʌŋ/ *noun* same as **pneumothorax**

collarbone /ˈkɒləbəʊn/ *noun* one of two long thin bones which join the shoulder blades to the breastbone. Also called **clavicle** (NOTE: Collarbone fracture is one of the most frequent fractures in the body.)

collateral /kəˈlæt(ə)rəl/ *adjective* secondary or less important

'…embolisation of the coeliac axis is an effective treatment for severe bleeding in the stomach or duodenum, localized by endoscopic examination. A good collateral blood supply makes occlusion of a single branch of the coeliac axis safe.' [*British Medical Journal*]

collateral circulation /kəˌlæt(ə)rəl ˌsɜːkjʊˈleɪʃ(ə)n/ *noun* an enlargement of some secondary blood vessels as a response when the main vessels become slowly blocked

collection chamber /kəˈlekʃən ˌtʃeɪmbə/ *noun* a section of the heart where blood collects before being pumped out

Colles' fracture /ˈkɒlɪs(ɪz) ˌfræktʃə/ *noun* a fracture of the lower end of the radius with displacement of the wrist backwards, usually when someone has stretched out a hand to try to break a fall [After Abraham Colles (1773–1843), Irish surgeon]

colliculus /kə'lɪkjʊləs/ *noun* one of four small projections (**superior colliculi** and **inferior colliculi**) in the midbrain. See illustration at BRAIN in Supplement (NOTE: The plural is **colliculi**.)

collodion /kə'ləʊdiən/ *noun* a liquid used for painting on a clean wound, where it dries to form a flexible covering

colloid /'kɒlɔɪd/ *noun* **1.** a mass of tiny particles of one substance dispersed in another substance **2.** the particles which are suspended in a colloid **3.** a thick jelly-like substance which stores hormones, produced in the thyroid gland ■ *adjective* relating to or resembling a colloid ○ *colloid acne*

collyrium /kə'lɪriəm/ *noun* a solution used to bathe the eyes (NOTE: The plural is **collyria**.)

colo- /kɒləʊ/ *prefix* referring to the colon

coloboma /ˌkɒləʊ'bəʊmə/ *noun* a condition in which part of the eye, especially part of the iris, is missing

colon /'kəʊlɒn/ *noun* the main part of the large intestine, running from the caecum at the end of the small intestine to the rectum

COMMENT: The colon is about 1.35 metres in length, and rises from the end of the small intestine up the right side of the body, then crosses beneath the stomach and drops down the left side of the body to end as the rectum. In the colon, water is extracted from the waste material which has passed through the small intestine, leaving only the faeces which are pushed forward by peristaltic movements and passed out of the body through the rectum.

colonic /kə'lɒnɪk/ *adjective* referring to the colon

colonic irrigation /kəˌlɒnɪk ɪrɪ'geɪʃ(ə)n/ *noun* the washing out of the contents of the large intestine using a tube inserted in the anus

colonitis /ˌkɒlə'naɪtɪs/ *noun* same as **colitis**

colonoscope /kə'lɒnəskəʊp/ *noun* a surgical instrument for examining the interior of the colon

colonoscopy /ˌkɒlə'nɒskəpi/ *noun* an examination of the inside of the colon, using a colonoscope passed through the rectum (NOTE: The plural is **colonoscopies**.)

colony /'kɒləni/ *noun* a group or culture of microorganisms

colorectal /ˌkəʊləʊ'rekt(ə)l/ *adjective* referring to both the colon and rectum

colostomy /kə'lɒstəmi/ *noun* a surgical operation to make an opening between the colon and the abdominal wall to allow faeces to be passed out without going through the rectum (NOTE: The plural is **colostomies**.)

COMMENT: A colostomy is carried out when the colon or rectum is blocked, or where part of the colon or rectum has had to be removed.

colostomy bag /kə'lɒstəmi bæg/ *noun* a bag attached to the opening made by a colostomy, to collect faeces as they are passed out of the body

colostrum /kə'lɒstrəm/ *noun* a fluid rich in antibodies and low in fat, secreted by the mother's breasts at the birth of a baby, before the true milk starts to flow

colour blindness /'kʌlə ˌblaɪndnəs/ *noun* a condition of being unable to tell the difference between specific colours

COMMENT: Colour blindness is a condition which almost never occurs in women. The commonest form is the inability to tell the difference between red and green. The Ishihara test is used to test for colour blindness.

colour index /'kʌlər ˌɪndeks/ *noun* the ratio between the amount of haemoglobin and the number of red blood cells in a specific amount of blood

colouring /'kʌlərɪŋ ˌmætə/, **colouring matter** *noun* a substance which colours an organ

colp- /kɒlp/ *prefix* same as **colpo-** (*used before vowels*)

colpitis /kɒl'paɪtɪs/ *noun* same as **vaginitis**

colpo- /kɒlpəʊ/ *prefix* referring to the vagina

colpocele /'kɒlpəsiːl/ *noun* same as **colpoptosis**

colpocystitis /ˌkɒlpəʊsɪ'staɪtɪs/ *noun* inflammation of both the vagina and the urinary bladder

colpocystopexy /ˌkɒlpə'sɪstəpeksi/ *noun* a surgical operation to lift and stitch the vagina and bladder to the abdominal wall (NOTE: The plural is **colpocystopexies**.)

colpohysterectomy /ˌkɒlpəʊhɪstə'rektəmi/ *noun* a surgical operation in which the womb is removed through the vagina (NOTE: The plural is **colpohysterectomies**.)

colpopexy /'kɒlpəpeksi/ *noun* a surgical operation to fix a prolapsed vagina to the abdominal wall (NOTE: The plural is **colpopexies**.)

colpoplasty /'kɒlpəplæsti/ *noun* a surgical operation to repair a damaged vagina (NOTE: The plural is **colpoplasties**.)

colpoptosis /ˌkɒlpə'təʊsɪs/ *noun* a prolapse of the walls of the vagina. Also called **colpocele** (NOTE: The plural is **colpoptoses**.)

colporrhaphy /kɒl'pɒrəfi/ *noun* a surgical operation to stitch a prolapsed vagina (NOTE: The plural is **colporrhaphies**.)

colposcope /'kɒlpəʊskəʊp/ *noun* a surgical instrument used to examine the inside of the vagina. Also called **vaginoscope**

colposcopy /kɒl'pɒskəpi/ *noun* an examination of the inside of the vagina (NOTE: The plural is **colposcopies**.)

colposuspension /ˌkɒlpəʊsə'spenʃən/ *noun* a surgical operation to strengthen the pelvic floor muscles to prevent incontinence

colpotomy /kɒl'pɒtəmi/ *noun* a surgical operation to make a cut in the vagina (NOTE: The plural is **colpotomies**.)

column /'kɒləm/ *noun* ♦ **vertebral column**

columnar /kə'lʌmnə/ *adjective* shaped like a column

columnar cell /kə'lʌmnə sel/ *noun* a type of epithelial cell shaped like a column

coma /'kəumə/ *noun* a state of unconsciousness from which a person cannot be awakened by external stimuli

COMMENT: A coma can have many causes: head injuries, diabetes, stroke or drug overdose. A coma is often fatal, but a patient may continue to live in a coma for a long time, even several months, before dying or regaining consciousness.

comatose /'kəumətəus/ *adjective* **1.** unconscious or in a coma **2.** like a coma

combined therapy /kəm,baɪnd 'θerəpi/ *noun* the use of two or more treatments at the same time

comedo /'kɒmɪdəu/ *noun* a small point of dark, hard matter in a sebaceous follicle, often found associated with acne on the skin of adolescents (NOTE: The plural is **comedones**.)

come down with /,kʌm 'daun wɪθ/ *verb* to catch a cold, flu or other minor illness (*informal*)

come out in /,kʌm 'aut ɪn/ *verb* to have something such as spots or a rash appear on the skin (*informal*)

come round /,kʌm 'raund/ *verb* to regain consciousness, e.g. after being knocked out

comfort /'kʌmfət/ *verb* to help make someone less anxious or unhappy, especially when something bad has just happened

comfortable /'kʌmf(ə)təb(ə)l/ *adjective* in a stable physical condition

comforter /'kʌmfətə/ *noun* **1.** someone who helps to make another person less anxious or unhappy **2.** a baby's dummy

commando operation /kə'mɑːndəu ,ɒpəreɪʃ(ə)n/, **commando procedure** /kə'mɑːndəu prə,siːdʒə/ *noun* a major operation to combat cancer of the face and neck. It involves the removal of facial features, which are later rebuilt.

commensal /kə'mens(ə)l/ *noun* an animal or plant which lives on another animal or plant but does not harm it in any way. Both may benefit from the association. ○ *Candida is a commensal in the mouths of 50% of healthy adults.* (NOTE: If a commensal causes harm, it is a **parasite**.) ■ *adjective* living on another animal or plant

comminuted fracture /,kɒmɪnjuːtɪd 'fræktʃə/ *noun* a fracture where the bone is broken in several places

Commission for Health Improvement in the UK, the independent inspection body for the National Health Service, with the role of helping to raise standards of patient care. It aims to identify where improvement is required and share good practice. Abbr **CHI**

commissure /'kɒmɪsjuə/ *noun* a structure which joins two similar tissues, e.g. a group of nerves which crosses from one part of the central nervous system to another. ◊ **corpus callosum, grey commissure, white commissure**

commit /kə'mɪt/ *verb* to arrange legally for someone to enter a mental health facility, perhaps without the person's consent

commitment /kə'mɪtmənt/ *noun* an act of legally making someone enter a mental health facility

Committee on Safety of Medicines /kə ,mɪti ɒn ,seɪfti əv 'med(ə)sɪnz/ *noun* the official body which advises the British Government on the safety and quality of medicines

commode /kə'məud/ *noun* a special chair with a removable basin used as a toilet by people with limited mobility

common /'kɒmən/ *adjective* **1.** frequently occurring **2.** shared □ **(in) common** belonging to more than one thing or person ○ *These viral diseases have several symptoms in common.*

common bile duct /,kɒmən 'baɪl dʌkt/ *noun* a duct leading to the duodenum, formed of the hepatic and cystic ducts

common carotid artery /,kɒmən kə'rɒtɪd ,ɑːtəri/ *noun* the main artery running up each side of the lower part of the neck. Also called **carotid**

common cold /,kɒmən 'kəuld/ *noun* same as **cold**

common hepatic duct /,kɒmən hɪ'pætɪk dʌkt/ *noun* a duct from the liver formed when the right and left hepatic ducts join

common iliac artery /,kɒmən 'ɪliæk ,ɑːtəri/ *noun* one of two arteries which branch from the aorta in the abdomen and in turn divide into the internal iliac artery, leading to the pelvis, and the external iliac artery, leading to the leg

common iliac vein /,kɒmən 'ɪliæk veɪn/ *noun* one of the veins draining the legs, pelvis and abdomen, which unite to form the inferior vena cava

common salt /,kɒmən 'sɔːlt/ *noun* a white powder used to make food, especially meat, fish and vegetables, taste better. Also called **sodium chloride**

COMMENT: Too much salt in the diet is to be avoided, as it is implicated in hypertension. Persistent diarrhoea or vomiting can lead to a dangerous loss of salt from the body.

common wart /,kɒmən 'wɔːt/ *noun* a wart which appears mainly on the hands

communicable disease /kə ,mjuːnɪkəb(ə)l dɪ'ziːz/ *noun* a disease which can be passed from one person to another or from an animal to a person. ◊ **contagious disease, infectious disease**

communicating artery /kə'mju:nɪkeɪtɪŋ ˌɑːtəri/ *noun* one of the arteries which connect the blood supply from each side of the brain, forming part of the circle of Willis

community /kə'mju:nɪti/ *noun* a group of people who live and work in a district ○ *The health services serve the local community.*

community care /kəˌmju:nɪti 'keə/ *noun* the providing of help to people such as those who are elderly or mentally ill in order to allow them to stay in their own homes, rather than requiring them to be cared for in hospitals or care homes

community health /kəˌmju:nɪti 'helθ/ *noun* the health of a local community, or provision of services for a local community

community health council /kəˌmju:nɪti 'helθ ˌkaʊnsəl/ *noun* a statutory body of interested people from outside the medical professions charged with putting forward the patients' point of view on local health issues. Abbr **CHC**

community hospital /kə'mju:nɪti ˌhɒspɪt(ə)l/ *noun* a hospital serving a local community

community medicine /kə'mju:nɪti 'med(ə)s(ə)n/ *noun* the study of medical practice which examines groups of people and the health of the community, including housing, pollution and other environmental factors

community mental health nurse /kəˌmju:nɪti ˌment(ə)l 'helθ ˌnɜːs/ *noun* a specialist nurse who works in a particular district visiting people in the area with mental health problems. Abbr **CMHN**

community midwife /kəˌmju:nɪti 'mɪdˌwaɪf/ *noun* a midwife who works in a community as part of a primary health care team

community nurse /kəˌmju:nɪti 'nɜːs/ *noun* a nurse who treats people in a local community

community psychiatric nurse /kəˌmju:nɪti ˌsaɪki'ætrɪk/ *noun* . Also called **community mental health nurse**. Abbr **CPN**

community services /kəˌmju:nɪti 'sɜːvɪsɪz/ *plural noun* nursing services which are available to the community

community trust /kəˌmju:nɪti 'trʌst/ *noun* an independent non-profit-making body set up to represent an area of public concern

compact bone /ˌkɒmpækt 'bəʊn/ *noun* a type of bone tissue which forms the hard outer layer of a bone. See illustration at **BONE STRUCTURE** in Supplement

compatibility /kəmˌpætɪ'bɪlɪti/ *noun* **1.** the ability of two drugs not to interfere with each other when administered together **2.** the ability of a body to accept organs, tissue or blood from another person and not to reject them

compatible /kəm'pætɪb(ə)l/ *adjective* able to function together without being rejected ○ *The surgeons are trying to find a compatible*

donor or *a donor with a compatible blood group.*

compensate /'kɒmpənseɪt/ *verb* **1.** to give someone an amount of money or something else to pay for loss or damage **2.** (*of an organ*) to make good the failure of an organ by making another organ, or the undamaged parts of the same organ, function at a higher level ○ *The heart has to beat more strongly to compensate for the narrowing of the arteries.* **3.** to emphasise a particular ability or personality characteristic in order to make the lack of another one seem less bad

compensation /ˌkɒmpən'seɪʃ(ə)n/ *noun* **1.** something which makes something else seem less bad or less serious **2.** an amount of money or something else given to pay for loss or damage ○ *The drugs caused him to develop breathing problems, so he thinks he's entitled to medical compensation.* **3.** the act of giving money to pay for loss or damage ○ *compensation for loss of a limb* **4.** a situation where the body helps to correct a problem in a particular organ by making another organ, or the undamaged parts of the same organ, function at a higher level **5.** behaviour that emphasises a particular ability or personality characteristic in order to make the lack of another one seem less bad

competence /'kɒmpɪt(ə)ns/ *noun* the ability to do something well, measured against a standard, especially ability which you get through experience or training ○ *encouraging the development of professional competence in the delivery of care to patients*

complaint /kəm'pleɪnt/ *noun* **1.** an expression of dissatisfaction about something or someone ○ *The hospital administrator wouldn't listen to the complaints of the consultants.* **2.** an illness ○ *a chest complaint* ○ *a nervous complaint*

complement *noun* /'kɒmplɪmənt/ a substance which forms part of blood plasma and is essential to the work of antibodies and antigens ■ *verb* /'kɒmplɪment/ to complete something by providing useful or pleasing qualities which it does not itself have

complementary /ˌkɒmplɪ'ment(ə)ri/ *adjective* **1.** combining with or adding to something else ○ *Ultrasound and CT provide complementary information.* **2.** used in or using complementary medicine ○ *complementary therapies* **3.** referring to genes which are necessary to each other and produce their effect only when they are present together

complementary medicine /ˌkɒmplɪment(ə)ri 'med(ə)sɪn/ *noun* alternative medicine in the forms which are now accepted by practitioners of conventional Western medicine, e.g. acupuncture and osteopathy

complement fixation test /ˌkɒmplɪˌment fɪk'seɪʃ(ə)n test/ *noun* a test to measure the amount of complement in antibodies and antigens. Abbr **CFT**

complete abortion /kəmˌpliːt əˈbɔːʃ(ə)n/ noun an abortion where the whole contents of the uterus are expelled

complete blood count /kəmˌpliːt ˈblʌd kaʊnt/ noun a test to find the exact numbers of each type of blood cell in a sample of blood. Abbr **CBC**

complex /ˈkɒmpleks/ noun **1.** (in psychiatry) a group of ideas which are based on the experience a person has had in the past and which influence the way he or she behaves **2.** a group of items, buildings or organs ○ He works in the new laboratory complex. **3.** a group of signs and symptoms due to a particular cause. ◊ **syndrome** ■ adjective complicated ○ A gastrointestinal fistula can cause many complex problems, including fluid depletion.

complexion /kəmˈplekʃən/ noun the general colour of the skin on the face ○ People with fair complexions burn easily in the sun.

compliance /kəmˈplaɪəns/ noun the agreement of a patient to co-operate with a treatment

complicated fracture /ˌkɒmplɪkeɪtɪd ˈfræktʃə/ noun a fracture with an associated injury of tissue, as when a bone has punctured an artery

complication /ˌkɒmplɪˈkeɪʃ(ə)n/ noun **1.** a condition in which two or more conditions exist in someone, whether or not they are connected ○ He was admitted to hospital suffering from pneumonia with complications. **2.** a situation in which someone develops a second condition which changes the course of treatment for the first ○ She appeared to be improving, but complications set in and she died in a few hours.

'…sickle cell chest syndrome is a common complication of sickle cell disease, presenting with chest pain, fever and leucocytosis' [British Medical Journal]

'…venous air embolism is a potentially fatal complication of percutaneous venous catheterization' [Southern Medical Journal]

compos mentis /ˌkɒmpɒs ˈmentɪs/ adjective not affected by a mental disorder (NOTE: The phrase is from Latin and means 'of sound mind'.)

compound /ˈkɒmpaʊnd/ noun a chemical substance made up of two or more components ■ adjective made up of two or more components

compound fracture /ˌkɒmpaʊnd ˈfræktʃə/ noun a fracture where the skin surface is damaged or where the broken bone penetrates the surface of the skin. Also called **open fracture**

compress noun /ˈkɒmpres/ a wad of cloth soaked in hot or cold liquid and applied to the skin to relieve pain or swelling, or to force pus out of an infected wound ■ verb /kəmˈpres/ to squeeze or press something

compressed air sickness /kəmˌprest ˈeə ˌsɪknəs/ noun same as **caisson disease**

compression /kəmˈpreʃ(ə)n/ noun **1.** the act of squeezing or pressing ○ The first-aider applied compression to the chest of the casualty. **2.** a serious condition in which the brain is compressed by blood or cerebrospinal fluid accumulating in it or by a fractured skull

compression stocking /kəmˌpreʃ(ə)n ˈstɒkɪŋ/ noun a strong elastic stocking worn to support a weak joint in the knee or to hold varicose veins tightly

compression syndrome /kəmˈpreʃ(ə)n ˌsɪndrəum/ noun pain in muscles after strenuous exercise

compulsion /kəmˈpʌlʃən/ noun **1.** an act of forcing someone to do something, or the fact of being forced to do something ○ You are under no compulsion to treat a violent patient. **2.** a strong psychological force which makes someone do something, often unwillingly ○ She felt a sudden compulsion to wash her hands again.

compulsive /kəmˈpʌlsɪv/ adjective referring to a feeling which cannot be stopped ○ She has a compulsive desire to steal.

compulsive eating /kəmˌpʌlsɪv ˈiːtɪŋ/ noun a psychological condition in which someone has a continual desire to eat. ◊ **bulimia**

compulsive–obsessive disorder /kəm ˌpʌlsɪv əbˈsesɪv dɪsˌɔːdə/ noun same as **obsessive–compulsive disorder**

compulsory admission /kəmˌpʌlsəri əd ˈmɪʃ(ə)n/ noun the process of admitting someone who is mentally ill to hospital for treatment whether or not they consent

computed tomography /kəmˌpjuːtɪd tə ˈmɒgrəfi/ noun same as **computerised axial tomography**. Abbr **CT**

computerised axial tomography /kəm ˌpjuːtəraɪzd ˌæksiəl təˈmɒgrəfi/ noun a system of examining the body in which a narrow X-ray beam, guided by a computer, photographs a thin section of the body or of an organ from several angles, using the computer to build up an image of the section. Abbr **CAT**. Also called **computed tomography**

-conazole /ˈkɒnəzəʊl/ suffix used in the names of antifungal drugs ○ fluconazole

concave /ˈkɒnkeɪv/ adjective curving towards the middle ○ a concave lens

conceive /kənˈsiːv/ verb **1.** (of a woman) to become pregnant with a child. ♦ **conception 2.** □ **to be conceived** (of a child) to come into existence through the fertilisation of an ovum ○ Our son was conceived during our holiday in Italy.

concentrate /ˈkɒnsəntreɪt/ noun a solution from which water has been removed ■ verb **1.**

to give full attention to something **2.** □ **to concentrate on** to examine something in particular **3.** to reduce a solution and increase its strength by evaporation

concept /'kɒnsept/ *noun* a thought or idea, or something which someone might be able to imagine

conception /kən'sepʃən/ *noun* the point at which a woman becomes pregnant and the development of a baby starts

COMMENT: Conception is usually taken to be either the moment when the sperm cell fertilises the ovum, or a few days later, when the fertilised ovum attaches itself to the wall of the uterus.

conceptual framework /kən,septʃuəl 'freɪmwɜːk/ *noun* the theoretical basis on which something is formed

conceptus /kən'septəs/ *noun* an embryo or fetus together with all the tissues that surround it during pregnancy (NOTE: The plural is **conceptuses.**)

concha /'kɒŋkə/ *noun* a part of the body shaped like a shell (NOTE: The plural is **conchae.**)

concha auriculae /,kɒŋkə ɔː'rɪkjʊliː/ *noun* the depressed part of the outer ear that leads to the inner ear

concordance /kən'kɔːd(ə)ns/ *noun* **1.** a state in which two or more things are in the correct or expected relationship to each other. For example, the atrioventricular concordance is the relationship between the atria and the ventricles in the heart. **2.** the fact of two related people sharing the same genetic characteristic ○ *the concordance of schizophrenia in identical twins* **3.** an agreement between a professional and a patient on a course of treatment, especially related to use of medicines

concretion /kən'kriːʃ(ə)n/ *noun* a mass of hard material which forms in the body, e.g. a gallstone or deposits on bone in arthritis

concussed /kən'kʌst/ *adjective* referring to someone who has been hit on the head and has lost and then regained consciousness ○ *He was walking around in a concussed state.*

concussion /kən'kʌʃ(ə)n/ *noun* **1.** the act of applying force to any part of the body **2.** loss of consciousness for a short period, caused by a blow to the head

concussive /kən'kʌsɪv/ *adjective* causing concussion

condensed /kən'denst/ *adjective* made compact or more dense

condition /kən'dɪʃ(ə)n/ *noun* **1.** the particular state of someone or something ○ *in poor condition* ○ *Her condition is getting worse.* ○ *The conditions in the hospital are very good.* **2.** a particular illness, injury or disorder ○ *He is being treated for a heart condition.*

conditioned reflex /kən,dɪʃ(ə)nd 'riːfleks/ *noun* an automatic reaction by a person to a

stimulus, or an expected reaction to a stimulus which comes from past experience

conditioned response /kən,dɪʃ(ə)nd rɪ 'spɒns/ *noun* a response to a stimulus as a result of associating it with an earlier stimulus

COMMENT: The classic example of a conditioned response is Pavlov's experiment with dogs in which they produced saliva, ready to eat their food, when a bell rang, because on previous occasions they had been fed when the bell was rung.

condom /'kɒndɒm/ *noun* a rubber sheath worn on the penis during intercourse as a contraceptive and also as a protection against sexually transmitted disease

conducting system /kən'dʌktɪŋ ,sɪstəm/ *noun* the nerve system in the heart which links an atrium to a ventricle, so that the two beat at the same rate

conduction /kən'dʌkʃən/ *noun* the process of passing heat, sound or nervous impulses from one part of the body to another

conduction fibre /kən'dʌkʃən ,faɪbə/ *noun* a fibre which transmits impulses, e.g. in the bundle of His

conductive /kən'dʌktɪv/ *adjective* referring to conduction

conductive deafness /kən,dʌktɪv 'defnəs/, **conductive hearing loss** /kən,dʌktɪv 'hɪərɪŋ lɒs/ *noun* deafness caused by inadequate conduction of sound into the inner ear

conductor /kən'dʌktə/ *noun* **1.** a substance or object which allows heat, electricity, light or sound to pass along it or through it **2.** a tube with a groove in it along which a knife is slid to cut open a sinus

condyle /'kɒndaɪl/ *noun* a rounded end of a bone which articulates with another

condyloid process /'kɒndɪlɔɪd ,prəʊses/ *noun* a projecting part at each end of the lower jaw which forms the head of the jaw, joining the jaw to the skull

condyloma /,kɒndɪ'ləʊmə/ *noun* a growth usually found on the vulva (NOTE: The plural is **condylomas** or **condylomata.**)

cone /kəʊn/ *noun* **1.** a shape with a circular base or top and a part that tapers to a point, or an object with this shape **2.** one of two types of cell in the retina of the eye which is sensitive to light, used especially in the perception of bright light and colour. ◊ **rod** ■ *verb* to show a rapid change for the worse in neurological condition due to herniation of the midbrain through the foramen magnum in the skull, caused by raised pressure inside the brain (NOTE: **cones – coning – coned**)

cone biopsy /'kəʊn baɪ,ɒpsi/ *noun* the removing of a cone of tissue from the cervix for examination

confabulation /kən,fæjʊ'leɪʃ(ə)n/ *noun* the act of making up plausible stories to cover up loss of memory

confidentiality /ˌkɒnfɪdenʃiˈælɪti/ *noun* an obligation not to reveal professional information about a person or organisation

confined /kənˈfaɪnd/ *adjective* kept in a place ○ *She was confined to bed with pneumonia.* ○ *Since his accident he has been confined to a wheelchair.*

confinement /kənˈfaɪnmənt/ *noun* the period when a woman giving birth stays in hospital, from the beginning of labour until some time after the birth of her baby. This period is very short nowadays.

confounding factor /kənˈfaʊndɪŋ ˌfæktə/ *noun* a factor which has an association with both a disease and a risk factor and thus complicates the nature of the relationship between them

confused /kənˈfjuːzd/ *adjective* unable to think clearly or act rationally ○ *Many severely confused patients do not respond to spoken communication.*

confusion /kənˈfjuːʒ(ə)n/ *noun* the state of being confused

congeal /kənˈdʒiːl/ *verb* (*of fat or blood*) to become solid

congenita /kənˈdʒenɪtə/ ♦ **amyotonia congenita**

congenital /kənˈdʒenɪt(ə)l/ *adjective* existing at or before birth

congenital aneurysm /kənˌdʒenɪt(ə)l ˈænjərɪz(ə)m/ *noun* a weakening of the arteries at the base of the brain, present at birth

congenital anomaly /kənˌdʒenɪt(ə)l ə ˈnɒməli/ *noun* a medical condition arising during development of the fetus and present at birth. Also called **congenital defect**

COMMENT: A congenital condition is not always inherited from a parent through the genes, as it may be due to factors such as a disease which the mother had during pregnancy, e.g. German measles, or a drug which she has taken.

congenital cataract /kənˌdʒenɪt(ə)l ˈkætərækt/ *noun* a cataract which is present at birth

congenital defect /kənˌdʒenɪt(ə)l ˈdiːfekt/ *noun* same as **congenital anomaly** (NOTE: The word 'defect' is now avoided.)

congenital dislocation of the hip /kənˌdʒenɪt(ə)l dɪsləˌkeɪʃ(ə)n əv ðə ˈhɪp/ *noun* a condition in which a person is born with weak ligaments in the hip, so that the femur does not stay in position in the pelvis

congenital heart disease /kənˌdʒenɪt(ə)l ˈhɑːt dɪˌziːz/, **congenital heart defect** /kənˌdʒenɪt(ə)l ˈhɑːt ˈdiːfekt/ *noun* a heart condition existing at birth

congenital hyperthyroidism *noun* a disease caused by a malfunction of the thyroid before birth or in early life

congenitally /kənˈdʒenɪtli/ *adverb* at or before birth ○ *The baby is congenitally incapable of absorbing gluten.*

congenital malformation /kənˌdʒenɪt(ə)l ˌmælfɔːˈmeɪʃ(ə)n/ *noun* a malformation which is present at birth, e.g. a cleft palate

congenital syphilis /kənˌdʒenɪt(ə)l ˈsɪfɪlɪs/ *noun* syphilis which is passed on from a mother to her unborn child

congenital toxoplasmosis /kənˌdʒenɪt(ə)l ˌtɒksəʊplæzˈməʊsɪs/ *noun* a condition in which a baby has been infected with toxoplasmosis by its mother while still in the uterus

congested /kənˈdʒestɪd/ *adjective* with blood or fluid inside □ **congested face** a red face, caused by blood rushing to the face

congestion /kənˈdʒestʃən/ *noun* an accumulation of blood in an organ. ◊ **nasal congestion**

congestive /kənˈdʒestɪv/ *adjective* referring to congestion

congestive heart failure /kənˌdʒestɪv ˈhɑːt ˌfeɪljə/ *noun* a condition in which the heart is unable to pump away the blood returning to it fast enough, causing congestion in the veins

coni /ˈkəʊni/ *plural of* **conus**

conisation /ˌkɒnaɪˈzeɪʃ(ə)n/, **conization** *noun* the surgical removal of a cone-shaped piece of tissue

conjoined twins /kənˌdʒɔɪnd ˈtwɪnz/ *plural noun* twins who are joined together at birth. Also called **Siamese twins**

COMMENT: Conjoined twins are always identical and can be joined at the head, chest or hip. In some cases they can be separated by surgery, but this is not possible if they share a single important organ such as the heart.

conjugate /ˈkɒndʒʊgət/, **conjugate diameter** /ˌkɒndʒʊgət daɪˈæmɪtə/ *noun* a measurement of space in a woman's pelvis, used to calculate if it is large enough for a child to be delivered

conjunctiva /ˌkɒndʒʌŋkˈtaɪvə/ *noun* a membrane which covers the front of the eyeball and the inside of the eyelids. See illustration at EYE in Supplement (NOTE: The plural is **conjunctivas** or **conjunctivae**.)

conjunctival /ˌkɒndʒʌŋkˈtaɪv(ə)l/ *adjective* referring to the conjunctiva

conjunctivitis /kənˌdʒʌŋktɪˈvaɪtɪs/ *noun* inflammation of the conjunctiva from a range of causes

connective tissue /kəˌnektɪv ˈtɪʃuː/ *noun* tissue which forms the main part of bones and cartilage, ligaments and tendons, in which a large proportion of fibrous material surrounds the tissue cells

Conn's syndrome /ˈkɒnz ˌsɪndrəʊm/ *noun* a condition in which excessive production of the hormone aldosterone causes fluid retention and high blood pressure

consanguinity /ˌkɒnsæŋˈgwɪnɪti/ *noun* a blood relationship between people

conscious /ˈkɒnʃəs/ *adjective* **1.** awake and aware of what is happening ○ *He became conscious in the recovery room two hours after the operation.* **2.** deliberate and intended ○ *a conscious choice*

-conscious /kɒnʃəs/ *suffix* giving importance to ○ *health-conscious* ○ *safety-conscious*

consciously /ˈkɒnʃəsli/ *adverb* in a deliberate and knowing way

consciousness /ˈkɒnʃəsnəs/ *noun* the state of being mentally alert and knowing what is happening □ **to lose consciousness** to become unconscious □ **to regain consciousness** to become conscious after being unconscious

consensus management /kənˈsensəs ˌmænɪdʒmənt/ *noun* a form of management which aims to get everyone to agree on what actions should be taken

consent /kənˈsent/ *noun* agreement to allow someone to do something ○ *The parents gave their consent for their son's heart to be used in the transplant operation.*

consent form /kənˈsent fɔːm/ *noun* a form which a patient signs to show that he or she agrees to have a particular operation

conservative /kənˈsɜːvətɪv/ *adjective* **1.** reluctant to accept new things **2.** (*of a treatment*) designed to help relieve symptoms or preserve health with a minimum of medical intervention or risk ○ *Symptoms usually resolve with conservative treatment.*

consolidation /kənˌsɒlɪˈdeɪʃ(ə)n/ *noun* **1.** a stage in mending a broken bone in which the callus formed at the break changes into bone **2.** a condition in which part of the lung becomes solid, e.g. in pneumonia

constipated /ˈkɒnstɪpeɪtɪd/ *adjective* unable to pass faeces often enough

constipation /ˌkɒnstɪˈpeɪʃ(ə)n/ *noun* difficulty in passing faeces

COMMENT: Constipated bowel movements are hard and may cause pain in the anus. Constipation may be caused by worry or by a diet which does not contain enough roughage or by lack of exercise, as well as by more serious diseases of the intestine.

constituent /kənˈstɪtjuənt/ *noun* a substance which forms part of something ○ *the chemical constituents of nerve cells*

constitution /ˌkɒnstɪˈtjuːʃ(ə)n/ *noun* the general health and strength of a person ○ *She has a strong constitution* or *a healthy constitution.* ○ *He has a weak constitution and is often ill.*

constitutional /ˌkɒnstɪˈtjuːʃ(ə)nəl/ *adjective* referring to a person's constitution ■ *noun* a short walk taken for health reasons

constitutionally /ˌkɒnstɪˈtjuːʃ(ə)n(ə)li/ *adverb* because of a person's constitution

constrict /kənˈstrɪkt/ *verb* **1.** to make a passage narrower ○ *a constricted bowel* **2.** to slow down or stop the flow of something such as blood

constriction /kənˈstrɪkʃən/ *noun* the process of becoming narrow, or the state of being narrow. ◊ **stenosis**

constrictive /kənˈstrɪktɪv/ *adjective* restricting

constrictive pericarditis /kənˌstrɪktɪv perikɑːˈdaɪtɪs/ *noun* same as **chronic pericarditis**

constrictor /kənˈstrɪktə/ *noun* a muscle which squeezes an organ or which makes an organ contract

consult /kənˈsʌlt/ *verb* to ask someone for his or her opinion ○ *He consulted an eye specialist.*

consultancy /kənˈsʌltənsi/ *noun* the post of consultant ○ *She was appointed to a consultancy at a London hospital.*

consultant /kənˈsʌltənt/ *noun* a doctor who is a senior specialist in a particular branch of medicine and who is consulted by GPs ○ *She was referred to a consultant at the orthopaedic hospital.*

consultation /ˌkɒnsəlˈteɪʃ(ə)n/ *noun* **1.** a discussion between two doctors about a case **2.** a meeting between a doctor and a patient, in which the doctor may examine the patient, discuss his or her condition and prescribe treatment

consulting room /kənˈsʌltɪŋ ruːm/ *noun* a room where a doctor sees his or her patients

consumption /kənˈsʌmpʃən/ *noun* **1.** the act of taking food or liquid into the body ○ *the patient's increased consumption of alcohol* **2.** a former name for pulmonary tuberculosis

contact /ˈkɒntækt/ *noun* **1.** an act of touching someone or something, or the state of touching □ **to have (physical) contact with someone** *or* **something** to actually touch someone or something □ **to be in** *or* **come into contact with someone** to be near to or touching someone ○ *The hospital is anxious to trace anyone who may have come into contact with the patient.* **2.** an act of getting in touch or communicating with someone **3.** a person who has been in contact with a person suffering from an infectious disease ○ *Now that Lassa fever has been diagnosed, the authorities are anxious to trace all contacts which the patient may have met.* ■ *verb* to meet or get in touch with someone

contact dermatitis /ˌkɒntækt ˌdɜːmə ˈtaɪtɪs/ *noun* inflammation of the skin caused by touch, e.g. by touching some types of plant, soap or chemical. Also called **irritant dermatitis**

contact lens /ˈkɒntækt lenz/ *noun* a tiny plastic lens which fits over the eyeball and is worn instead of spectacles to improve eyesight

contact tracing /'kɒntækt ˌtreɪsɪŋ/ *noun* the process of tracing people with whom someone with an infectious disease has been in contact

contagion /kən'teɪdʒən/ *noun* **1.** the process of spreading a disease by touching an infected person or objects which an infected person has touched **2.** a disease spread by touch ○ *The contagion spread through the whole school.*

contagious /kən'teɪdʒəs/ *adjective* able to be transmitted by touching an infected person or objects which an infected person has touched □ **contagious stage** the period when a disease such as chickenpox is contagious and can be transmitted to someone else

contagious disease /kən,teɪdʒəs dɪ'ziːz/ *noun* a disease which can be transmitted by touching an infected person or objects which an infected person has touched. ◊ **communicable disease, infectious disease**

containment /kən'teɪnmənt/ *noun* **1.** action taken to restrict the spread of something undesirable or dangerous such as a disease ○ *government policy of containment of the SARS virus* **2.** the eradication of a global disease such as smallpox by removing it region by region

contaminant /kən'tæmɪnənt/ *noun* a substance which contaminates something

contaminate /kən'tæmɪneɪt/ *verb* **1.** to make something impure by touching it or by adding something to it ○ *Supplies of drinking water were contaminated by refuse from the factories.* ○ *The whole group of tourists fell ill after eating contaminated food.* **2.** to spread infection to someone or something

contamination /kən,tæmɪ'neɪʃ(ə)n/ *noun* the action of contaminating something, or the state of being contaminated ○ *The contamination resulted from polluted water.*

continence /'kɒntɪnəns/ *noun* **1.** the ability to control the discharge of urine and faeces **2.** self-restraint

continent /'kɒntɪnənt/ *adjective* able to exercise control over the discharge of urine and faeces

continuing education /kən,tɪnjuɪŋ edjʊ'keɪʃ(ə)n/ *noun* regular courses or training designed to bring professional people up to date with the latest developments in their particular field

continuous ambulatory peritoneal dialysis /kən,tɪnjuəs ,æmbjʊlət(ə)ri perɪtə,niːəl daɪ'æləsɪs/ *noun* a method of dialysis of people while they are walking about. Abbr **CAPD**

continuous positive airways pressure /kən,tɪnjuəs ,pɒzɪtɪv 'eəweɪz ,preʃə/ *noun* a method used in intensive care which forces air into the lungs of someone with lung collapse. Abbr **CPAP**

contra- /kɒntrə/ *prefix* against, opposite, contrasting

contraception /,kɒntrə'sepʃən/ *noun* the prevention of pregnancy, e.g. by using devices such as a condom or an IUD, or drugs in the form of contraceptive pills or injections at regular intervals. Also called **birth control**

contraceptive /,kɒntrə'septɪv/ *adjective* preventing conception ○ *a contraceptive device* or *drug* ■ *noun* a drug or device which prevents pregnancy

contraceptive sheath /,kɒntrə'septɪv ʃiːθ/ *noun* same as **condom**

contraceptive sponge /,kɒntrə'septɪv spʌndʒ/ *noun* a piece of synthetic sponge impregnated with spermicide, which is inserted into the vagina before intercourse

contract /kən'trækt/ *verb* **1.** to become smaller and tighter, or make a muscle or part of the body smaller and tighter ○ *As the muscle contracts the limb moves.* ○ *The diaphragm acts to contract the chest.* **2.** to catch a disease ○ *He contracted Lassa fever.* **3.** to make a formal or legally binding agreement with someone to do something ○ *An outside firm is contracted to do the hospital cleaning.* ■ *noun* a formal or legally binding agreement

contractibility /'kɒntræktɪbɪlɪti/ *noun* the capacity to contract

contractile tissue /kən,træktaɪl 'tɪʃuː/ *noun* the tissue in muscle which makes the muscle contract

contraction /kən'trækʃən/ *noun* **1.** the act of making something smaller or of becoming smaller ○ *the contraction of dental services* **2.** a tightening movement which makes a muscle shorter, which makes the pupil of the eye smaller or which makes the skin wrinkle **3.** a movement of the muscles of the uterus occurring during childbirth ○ *Her contractions began at one o'clock.*

contracture /kən'træktʃə/ *noun* a permanent tightening of a muscle caused by fibrosis

contraindication /,kɒntrəɪndɪ'keɪʃ(ə)n/ *noun* something which suggests that someone should not be treated with a specific drug or not continue with a specific treatment because circumstances make that treatment unsuitable

contralateral /,kɒntrə'lætərəl/ *adjective* located on or affecting the opposite side of the body. Opposite **ipsilateral**

contrast medium /'kɒntrɑːst ,miːdiəm/ *noun* a radio-opaque dye, or sometimes gas, put into an organ or part of the body so that it will show clearly in an X-ray photograph ○ *In an MRI scan no contrast medium is required; in a CAT scan iodine-based contrast media are often required.*

contrecoup /'kɒntrəkuː/ *noun* an injury to one point of an organ such as the brain, caused by a blow received on an opposite point of the organ

control *verb* **1.** to have the ability or authority to direct someone or something ○ *Sometimes* *we need help to control people who think they have waited too long.* **2.** to limit or restrain something ○ *administered drugs to control the pain* ■ *noun* **1.** the ability or authority to control something ○ *After her stroke she had no control over her left arm.* ○ *The administrators are in control of the admissions policy.* **2.** a person or group whose test data are used as a comparison in a study **3.** a comparison in a study

control group /kən'trəʊl gruːp/ *noun* a group of people who are not being treated but whose test data are used as a comparison in a study

controlled drug /kən,trəʊld 'drʌg/ *noun* a drug which is not freely available, which is restricted by law and classified as A, B, or C and of which possession may be an offence. Also called **controlled substance**

controlled respiration /kən,trəʊld ,respə'reɪʃ(ə)n/ *noun* the control of a person's breathing by an anaesthetist during an operation, when regular breathing has stopped

controlled substance /kən,trəʊld 'sʌbstəns/ *noun* same as **controlled drug**

controlled trial /kən,trəʊld 'traɪəl/ *noun* a trial in which members of one group are treated with a test substance and those of another group are treated with a placebo as a control

controls assurance /kən'trəʊlz ə,ʃʊərəns/ *noun* a process designed to provide evidence that NHS organisations are doing their best to manage themselves both in order to meet their objectives and to protect patients, staff and the public against risks of all kinds

contused wound /kən,tjuːzd 'wuːnd/ *noun* a wound caused by a blow where the skin is bruised as well as torn and bleeding

contusion /kən'tjuːʒ(ə)n/ *noun* same as **bruise**

conus /'kəʊnəs/ *noun* a structure shaped like a cone (NOTE: The plural is **coni**.)

convalesce /,kɒnvə'les/ *verb* to get back to good health gradually after an illness or operation

convalescence /,kɒnvə'les(ə)ns/ *noun* a period of time when someone is convalescing

convalescent /,kɒnvə'les(ə)nt/ *adjective* referring to convalescence ■ *noun* someone who is convalescing

convalescent home /,kɒnvə'les(ə)nt həʊm/ *noun* a type of hospital where people can recover from illness or surgery

convergent strabismus /kən,vɜːdʒənt strə'bɪzməs/, **convergent squint** /kən,vɜːdʒənt 'skwɪnt/ *noun* a condition in which one or both of a person's eyes look towards the nose. Also called **cross eye**

conversion /kən'vɜːʃ(ə)n/ *noun* the process of changing one thing into another ○ *the conversion of nutrients into tissue*

convex /'kɒnveks/ *adjective* curving towards the outside ○ *a convex lens*

convoluted /'kɒnvəluːtɪd/ *adjective* folded and twisted

convoluted tubule /,kɒnvəluːtɪd 'tjuːbjuːl/ *noun* a coiled part of a nephron

convolution /,kɒnvə'luːʃ(ə)n/ *noun* a twisted shape ○ *the convolutions of the surface of the cerebrum*

convulse /kən'vʌls/ *verb* to shake violently and uncontrollably

convulsion /kən'vʌlʃən/ *noun* the rapid involuntary contracting and relaxing of the muscles in several parts of the body ○ *The child had convulsions.* ◊ **fit** (NOTE: Often used in the plural.)

COMMENT: Convulsions in children may be caused by brain disease such as meningitis but can also often be found at the beginning of a disease such as pneumonia which is marked by a sudden rise in body temperature. In adults, convulsions are usually associated with epilepsy.

convulsive /kən'vʌlsɪv/ *adjective* referring to convulsions ○ *He had a convulsive seizure.* ◊ **electroconvulsive therapy**

Cooley's anaemia /'kuːliz ə,niːmiə/ *noun* same as **thalassaemia** [Described 1927. After Thomas Benton Cooley (1871–1945), Professor of Paediatrics at Wayne College of Medicine, Detroit, USA.]

Coombs' test /'kuːmz test/ *noun* a test for antibodies in red blood cells, used as a test for erythroblastosis fetalis and other haemolytic syndromes [Described 1945. After Robin Royston Amos Coombs (1921–), Quick Professor of Biology, and Fellow of Corpus Christi College, Cambridge, UK.]

coordinate /kəʊ'ɔːdɪneɪt/ *verb* **1.** to make things work together ○ *He was unable to coordinate the movements of his arms and legs.* **2.** to organise a complex procedure

'…there are four recti muscles and two oblique muscles in each eye, which coordinate the movement of the eyes and enable them to work as a pair' [*Nursing Times*]

coordination /kəʊ,ɔːdɪ'neɪʃ(ə)n/ *noun* **1.** the combining of two or more things as an effective unit, or the way things combine effectively ○ *requires coordination between nursing staff and doctors* **2.** the ability to use two or more parts of the body at the same time to carry out a movement or task ○ *The patient showed lack of coordination between eyes and hands.*

'Alzheimer's disease is a progressive disorder which sees a gradual decline in intellectual functioning and deterioration of physical coordination' [*Nursing Times*]

COPD *abbr* chronic obstructive pulmonary disease

coping mechanism /'kəʊpɪŋ ,mekənɪz(ə)m/ *noun* a method of dealing with situations which cause psychological stress

copper /'kɒpə/ *noun* a metallic trace element (NOTE: The chemical symbol is **Cu**.)

copr- /kɒpr/ *prefix* faeces

coprolith /'kɒprəlɪθ/ *noun* a lump of hard faeces in the bowel

coproporphyrin /ˌkɒprəˈpɔːfərɪn/ *noun* porphyrin excreted by the liver

copulate /'kɒpjʊleɪt/ *verb* to have sexual intercourse

copulation /ˌkɒpjʊˈleɪʃ(ə)n/ *noun* same as **sexual intercourse**

cor /kɔː/ *noun* the heart

coraco-acromial /ˌkɒrəkəʊ əˈkrəʊmiəl/ *adjective* referring to the coracoid process and the acromion

coracobrachialis /ˌkɒrəkəʊbrækiˈeɪlɪs/ *noun* a muscle on the medial side of the upper arm, below the armpit

coracoid process /'kɒrəkɔɪd ˌprəʊses/ *noun* a projecting part on the shoulder blade

cord /kɔːd/ *noun* a long flexible structure in the body like a thread

cordectomy /kɔːˈdektəmi/ *noun* a surgical operation to remove a vocal cord (NOTE: The plural is **cordectomies**.)

cordon sanitaire /ˌkɔːdɒn ˌsænɪˈteə/ *noun* a restriction of movement to and from an area to control the spread of a disease

cordotomy /kɔːˈdɒtəmi/ *noun* another spelling of **chordotomy**

corectopia /ˌkɔːrekˈtəʊpiə/ *noun* ectopia of the pupil of the eye

corium /'kɔːriəm/ *noun* same as **dermis**

corn /kɔːn/ *noun* a hard painful lump of skin usually on a foot, where something such as a tight shoe has rubbed or pressed on the skin. Also called **heloma**

cornea /'kɔːniə/ *noun* a transparent part of the front of the eyeball. See illustration at EYE in Supplement (NOTE: The plural is **corneae**. For other terms referring to the cornea, see words beginning with **kerat-, kerato-**.)

corneal /'kɔːniəl/ *adjective* relating to a cornea

corneal abrasion /ˌkɔːniəl əˈbreɪʒ(ə)n/ *noun* a scratch on the cornea, caused by something sharp getting into the eye

corneal bank /'kɔːniəl bæŋk/ *noun* a place where eyes of dead donors can be kept ready for use in corneal grafts

corneal graft /ˌkɔːniəl ˈɡrɑːft/ *noun* 1. a surgical operation to graft corneal tissue from a donor or from a dead person to replace diseased tissue. Also called **corneal transplant, keratoplasty 2.** a piece of corneal tissue used in a graft

corneal reflex /ˌkɔːniəl ˈriːfleks/ *noun* a reflex from touching or hitting the cornea which makes the eyelid close

corneal transplant /'kɔːniəl ˌtrænsplɑːnt/ *noun* same as **corneal graft**

cornification /ˌkɔːnɪfɪˈkeɪʃ(ə)n/ *noun* same as **keratinisation**

cornu /'kɔːnjuː/ *noun* 1. a structure in the body which is shaped like a horn 2. each of the four processes of the thyroid cartilage (NOTE: The plural is **cornua**.)

corona /kəˈrəʊnə/ *noun* a structure in the body which is shaped like a crown

corona capitis /kəˌrəʊnə ˈkæpɪtɪs/ *noun* the crown of the head or top part of the skull

coronal /'kɒrən(ə)l, kəˈrəʊn(ə)l/ *adjective* 1. referring to a corona 2. referring to the crown of a tooth

coronal plane /ˌkɒrən(ə)l ˈpleɪn/ *noun* a plane at right angles to the median plane, dividing the body into dorsal and ventral halves. See illustration at ANATOMICAL TERMS in Supplement

coronal suture /ˌkɒrən(ə)l ˈsuːtʃə/ *noun* a horizontal joint across the top of the skull between the parietal and frontal bones

coronary /'kɒrən(ə)ri/ *noun* same as **coronary thrombosis** (*informal*) ■ *adjective* referring to any structure shaped like a crown, but especially to the arteries which supply blood to the heart muscles

coronary artery /'kɒrən(ə)ri ˌɑːtəri/ *noun* one of the two arteries which supply blood to the heart muscles

coronary artery bypass graft /ˌkɒrən(ə)ri ˌɑːtəri ˈbaɪpɑːs ɡrɑːft/, **coronary artery bypass** /ˌkɒrən(ə)ri ˈɑːtəri ˌbaɪpɑːs/ *noun* a surgical operation to treat angina by grafting pieces of vein around the diseased part of a coronary artery

coronary care unit /ˌkɒrən(ə)ri ˈkeə ˌjuːnɪt/ *noun* the section of a hospital caring for people who have heart disorders or who have had heart surgery. Abbr **CCU**

coronary circulation /ˌkɒrən(ə)ri ˌsɜːkjʊˈleɪʃ(ə)n/ *noun* blood circulation through the arteries and veins of the heart muscles

coronary heart disease /ˌkɒrən(ə)ri ˈhɑːt dɪˌziːz/ *noun* any disease affecting the coronary arteries, which can lead to strain on the heart or a heart attack. Abbr **CHD**

'…coronary heart disease (CHD) patients spend an average of 11.9 days in hospital. Among primary health care services, 1.5% of all GP consultations are due to CHD.' [*Health Services Journal*]

'…apart from death, coronary heart disease causes considerable morbidity in the form of heart attack, angina and a number of related diseases' [*Health Education Journal*]

coronary ligament /ˌkɒrən(ə)ri ˈlɪɡəmənt/ *noun* folds of peritoneum connecting the back of the liver to the diaphragm

coronary obstruction /ˌkɒrən(ə)ri əbˈstrʌkʃ(ə)n/, **coronary occlusion** /ˌkɒrən(ə)ri əˈkluːʒ(ə)n/ *noun* a thickening of the walls of the coronary arteries or a blood clot in the coronary arteries which prevents blood from reaching the heart muscles and leads to heart failure

coronary sinus /ˌkɒrən(ə)ri 'saɪnəs/ noun a vein which takes most of the venous blood from the heart muscles to the right atrium

coronary thrombosis /ˌkɒrən(ə)ri θrɒm 'bəʊsɪs/ noun a blood clot which blocks the coronary arteries, leading to a heart attack. Also called **coronary**

coronary vein /ˈkɒrən(ə)ri veɪn/ noun a vein that drains blood from the muscles of the heart

coronavirus /kəˈrəʊnəˌvaɪrəs/ noun a type of virus which has been identified in people who have the common cold

coroner /ˈkɒrənə/ noun a public official, either a doctor or a lawyer, who investigates sudden or violent deaths

COMMENT: Coroners investigate deaths which are caused by poison, violence, neglect or deprivation, deaths from unnatural causes, during the post-operative recovery period and when the doctor feels unable to give a reliable cause of death. They also investigate deaths of prisoners and deaths involving the police.

coronoid process /ˈkɒrənɔɪd ˌprəʊses/ noun 1. a projecting piece of bone on the ulna 2. a projecting piece on each side of the lower jaw

corpora plural of **corpus**

corpse /kɔːps/ noun the body of a dead person

cor pulmonale /ˌkɔː ˌpʌlməˈneɪli/ noun pulmonary heart disease in which the right ventricle is enlarged

corpus /ˈkɔːpəs/ noun any mass of tissue (NOTE: The plural is **corpora**.)

corpus albicans /ˌkɔːpəs ˈælbɪkænz/ noun scar tissue which replaces the corpus luteum in the ovary

corpus callosum /ˌkɔːpəs kəˈləʊsəm/ noun the thick band of nerve fibres that connects the two hemispheres of the brain and allows them to communicate. See illustration at BRAIN in Supplement (NOTE: The plural is **corpora callosa**.)

corpus cavernosum /ˌkɔːpəs ˌkævə ˈnəʊsəm/ noun a part of the erectile tissue in the penis and clitoris. See illustration at URO- GENITAL SYSTEM (MALE) in Supplement (NOTE: The plural is **corpora cavernosa**.)

corpuscle /ˈkɔːpʌs(ə)l/ noun 1. a small round mass 2. a cell in blood or lymph

corpus haemorrhagicum /ˌkɔːpəs ˌhemə ˈrædʒɪkəm/ noun a blood clot formed in an ovary where a Graafian follicle has ruptured (NOTE: The plural is **corpora haemorrhagica**.)

corpus luteum /ˌkɔːpəs ˈluːtiəm/ noun a body which forms in each ovary after a Graafian follicle has ruptured. The corpus luteum secretes the hormone progesterone to prepare

the uterus for implantation of the fertilised ovum. (NOTE: The plural is **corpora lutea**.)

corpus spongiosum /ˌkɔːpəs spʌnʒɪ 'əʊsəm/ noun the part of the penis round the urethra, forming the glans. See illustration at UROGENITAL SYSTEM (MALE) in Supplement (NOTE: The plural is **corpora spongiosa**.)

corpus striatum /ˌkɔːpəs ˌstraɪˈeɪtəm/ noun a mass of nervous tissue in each cerebral hemisphere (NOTE: The plural is **corpora striata**.)

corrective /kəˈrektɪv/ adjective intended to correct an irregularity or problem ○ corrective lenses ■ noun a drug which changes the harmful effect of another drug

Corrigan's pulse /ˌkɒrɪgənz ˈpʌls/ noun a condition occurring in the arterial pulse in the neck in which there is a visible rise in pressure followed by a sudden collapse, caused by aortic regurgitation. Also called **water-hammer pulse**

corrosive /kəˈrəʊsɪv/ adjective destroying tissue ■ noun a substance which destroys tissue, e.g. acid or alkali

corrugator muscle /ˈkɒrəgeɪtə ˌmʌs(ə)l/ noun one of the muscles which produce vertical wrinkles on the forehead when someone frowns

corset /ˈkɔːsɪt/ noun a piece of stiff clothing worn on the chest or over the trunk to support the body, e.g. after a back injury

cortex /ˈkɔːteks/ noun the outer layer of an organ, as opposed to the soft inner medulla (NOTE: The plural is **cortices** or **cortexes**.)

Corti /ˈkɔːti/ ⬥ organ of Corti

cortical /ˈkɔːtɪk(ə)l/ adjective referring to a cortex

cortical mastoidectomy /ˌkɔːtɪk(ə)l ˌmæstɔɪˈdektəmi/ noun same as **atticotomy**

cortices plural of **cortex**

corticospinal /ˌkɔːtɪkəʊˈspaɪn(ə)l/ adjective referring to both the cerebral cortex and the spinal cord

corticosteroid /ˌkɔːtɪkəʊˈstɪərɔɪd/ noun 1. any steroid hormone produced by the cortex of the adrenal glands 2. a drug which reduces inflammation, used in asthma, gastro-intestinal disease and in adrenocortical insufficiency

corticosterone /ˌkɔːtɪkəʊˈstɪərəʊn/ noun a hormone secreted by the cortex of the adrenal glands

corticotrophin /ˌkɔːtɪkəʊˈtrəʊfɪn/ noun same as **adrenocorticotrophic hormone** (NOTE: The US spelling is **corticotropin**.)

cortisol /ˈkɔːtɪsɒl/ noun same as **hydrocortisone**

cortisone /ˈkɔːtɪzəʊn/ noun a hormone secreted in small quantities by the adrenal cortex ○ The doctor gave her a cortisone injection in the ankle.

COMMENT: Synthetic cortisone was used in the treatment of rheumatoid arthritis, asthma and skin disorders, but it is now replaced by other drugs.

Corynebacterium /kəʊˌraɪnibæk'tɪəriəm/ noun a genus of bacteria which includes the bacterium which causes diphtheria

coryza /kə'raɪzə/ noun an illness, with inflammation of the nasal passages, in which someone sneezes and coughs and has a blocked and running nose (technical) Also called **cold, common cold**

cosmetic surgery /kɒzˌmetɪk 'sɜːdʒəri/ noun a surgical operation to improve a person's appearance

COMMENT: Whereas plastic surgery may be prescribed by a doctor to correct skin or bone conditions or the effect of burns or after a disfiguring operation, cosmetic surgery is carried out on the instructions of the patient to remove wrinkles, enlarge breasts or make some other perceived improvement.

cost- /kɒst/ prefix same as **costo-** (used before vowels)

costal /'kɒst(ə)l/ adjective referring to the ribs

costal cartilage /ˌkɒst(ə)l 'kɑːtəlɪdʒ/ noun cartilage which forms the end of each rib and either joins the rib to the breastbone or to the rib above

costal pleura /ˌkɒst(ə)l 'plʊərə/ noun a part of the pleura lining the walls of the chest

costive /'kɒstɪv/ adjective same as **constipated** ■ noun a drug which causes constipation

costo- /kɒstəʊ/ prefix referring to the ribs

costocervical trunk /ˌkɒstəʊsɜːvɪk(ə)l 'trʌŋk/ noun a large artery in the chest

costodiaphragmatic /ˌkɒstəʊdaɪəfræg'mætɪk/ adjective referring to both the ribs and the diaphragm

costovertebral joint /ˌkɒstəʊvɜːtɪbr(ə)l 'dʒɔɪnt/ noun a joint between the ribs and the vertebral column

cot death /'kɒt deθ/ noun ♦ **sudden infant death syndrome** (NOTE: The US term is **crib death**.)

co-trimoxazole /ˌkəʊ traɪ'mɒksəzəʊl/ noun a drug used to combat bacteria in the urinary tract

cottage hospital /ˌkɒtɪdʒ 'hɒspɪt(ə)l/ noun a small local hospital that admits patients under the care of a general practitioner

cotton bud /'kɒtən bʌd/ noun a little stick with some cotton wool usually at both ends, used for cleaning cavities

cotton wool /ˌkɒtən 'wʊl/ noun purified fibres from the cotton plant used to clean the skin or as padding ○ She dabbed the cut with cotton wool soaked in antiseptic. (NOTE: The US term is **absorbent cotton**.)

cotyledon /ˌkɒtɪ'liːd(ə)n/ noun one of the divisions of a placenta

cotyloid cavity /'kɒtɪlɔɪd ˌkæviti/ noun same as **acetabulum**

couch /kaʊtʃ/ noun a long bed on which a person lies when being examined by a doctor in a surgery

couching /'kaʊtʃɪŋ/ noun a surgical operation to displace the opaque lens of an eye as a treatment for cataracts

cough /kɒf/ noun a reflex action, caused by irritation in the throat, when the glottis is opened and air is sent out of the lungs suddenly □ **barking cough** a loud noisy dry cough □ **dry cough** a cough where no phlegm is produced □ **hacking cough** a continuous short dry cough ■ an infection that causes coughing ○ She has a bad cough and cannot make the speech. ■ verb to send air out of the lungs suddenly because the throat is irritated ○ The smoke made him cough. ○ She has a cold and keeps on coughing and sneezing.

coughing fit /'kɒfɪŋ fɪt/ noun a sudden attack of coughing

cough medicine /'kɒf ˌmed(ə)sɪn/, **cough linctus** /'kɒf ˌlɪŋktəs/, **cough mixture** noun a liquid taken to soothe the irritation which causes a cough

cough suppressant /'kɒf sə,presənt/ noun an opioid or sedative antihistamine drug such as pholcodine which suppresses the cough reflex

cough up /ˌkɒf 'ʌp/ verb to cough hard to expel a substance from the trachea ○ He coughed up phlegm. ○ She became worried when the girl started coughing up blood.

counselling /'kaʊnsəlɪŋ/ noun a method of treating especially psychiatric disorders in which a specialist talks with a person about his or her condition and how to deal with it

counsellor /'kaʊnsələ/ noun a person who advises and talks with someone about his or her problems

counteract /ˌkaʊntər'ækt/ verb to act against something or reduce the effect of something ○ The lotion should counteract the irritant effect of the spray on the skin.

counteraction /ˌkaʊntər'ækʃən/ noun the action of one drug which acts against another drug

counterextension /ˌkaʊntərɪk'stenʃən/ noun an orthopaedic treatment in which the upper part of a limb is kept fixed and traction is applied to the lower part of it

counterirritant /ˌkaʊntər'ɪrɪt(ə)nt/ noun a substance which alleviates the pain in an internal organ by irritating an area of skin whose sensory nerves are close to those of the organ in the spinal cord

counterirritation /ˌkaʊntərɪrɪ'teɪʃ(ə)n/ noun a skin irritant applied artificially to alleviate the pain in another part of the body

counterstain /'kaʊntəsteɪn/ noun a stain used to identify tissue samples, e.g. red dye used to identify Gram-negative bacteria after having first stained them with violet dye ■ verb to stain specimens with a counterstain

coupling /'kʌplɪŋ/ noun **1.** an act of joining together or linking two people, things or processes **2.** something which joins two things, especially a device for connecting two pieces of pipe, hose or tube

course /kɔːs/ noun **1.** a programme of study or training ○ went on a course to update his nursing skills **2.** a series of drugs to be taken, or a series of sessions of treatment ○ We'll put you on a course of antibiotics.

course of treatment /ˌkɔːs əv 'triːtmənt/ noun a series of applications of a treatment, e.g. a series of injections or physiotherapy

cover test /'kʌvə test/ noun a test for a squint in which an eye is covered and its movements are checked when the cover is taken off

Cowper's glands /'kuːpəz glændz/ plural noun two glands at the base of the penis which secrete into the urethra. Also called **bulbourethral glands** [Described 1700. After William Cowper (1666–1709), English surgeon.]

cowpox /'kaʊpɒks/ noun an infectious viral disease of cattle which can be transmitted to humans. It was used as a constituent of the first vaccines for smallpox.

cox- /kɒks/ prefix the hip joint

coxa /'kɒksə/ noun the hip joint (NOTE: The plural is **coxae**.)

coxalgia /kɒk'sældʒə/ noun pain in the hip joint

coxa vara /ˌkɒksə 'veərə/ noun an unusual development of the hip bone, making the legs bow

Coxsackie virus /kɒk'sæki ˌvaɪrəs/ noun one of a group of enteroviruses which enter the cells of the intestines and can cause diseases such as aseptic meningitis and Bornholm disease [After Coxsackie, New York, where the virus was first identified]

CPAP abbr continuous positive airways pressure

CPN abbr community psychiatric nurse

CPR abbr cardiopulmonary resuscitation

crab /kræb/, **crab louse** /'kræb laʊs/ noun a louse, *Phthirius pubis*, which infests the pubic region and other parts of the body with coarse hair. Also called **pubic louse**

crack /kræk/ noun a thin break ○ There's a crack in one of the bones in the skull. ■ verb to make a thin break in something, or become split ○ She cracked a bone in her leg. □

cracked lip a lip where the skin has split because of cold or dryness

cradle /'kreɪd(ə)l/ noun a metal frame put over a person in bed to keep the weight of the bedclothes off the body ■ verb to carry a child with one arm under the thigh and the other under the upper back

cradle cap /'kreɪd(ə)l kæp/ noun a yellow deposit on the scalp of babies, caused by seborrhoea

cramp /kræmp/ noun a painful involuntary spasm in the muscles, in which the muscle may stay contracted for some time

crani- /kreɪni/ prefix same as **cranio-** (used before vowels)

cranial /'kreɪniəl/ adjective referring to the skull

cranial bone /'kreɪniəl bəʊn/ noun one of the bones in the skull

cranial cavity /'kreɪniəl ˌkævɪti/ noun a space inside the bones of the cranium, in which the brain is situated

cranial nerve /'kreɪniəl nɜːv/ noun each of the nerves, twelve on each side, which are connected directly to the brain, governing mainly the structures of the head and neck

COMMENT: The cranial nerves are the olfactory, optic, loculomotor, trochlear, trigeminal, (ophthalmic, maxillary and mandibular), abducent, facial, auditory (vestibular and cochlear), glossopharyngeal, vagus, accessory and hypoglossal.

cranio- /kreɪniəʊ/ prefix the skull

craniometry /ˌkreɪni'ɒmɪtri/ noun the process of measuring skulls to find differences in size and shape

craniopharyngioma /ˌkreɪniəʊfəˌrɪndʒi'əʊmə/ noun a tumour in the brain originating in the hypophyseal duct (NOTE: The plural is **craniopharyngiomas** or **craniopharyngiomata**.)

craniostenosis /ˌkreɪniəʊste'nəʊsɪs/, **craniosynostosis** /ˌkreɪniəʊˌsɪnəʊ'stəʊsɪs/ noun the early closing of the bones in a baby's skull, so making the skull contract

craniotabes /ˌkreɪniəʊ'teɪbiːz/ noun thinness of the bones in the occipital region of a child's skull, caused by rickets, marasmus or syphilis

craniotomy /ˌkreɪni'ɒtəmi/ noun a surgical operation on the skull, especially one cutting away part of the skull (NOTE: The plural is **craniotomies**.)

cranium /'kreɪniəm/ noun same as **skull** (NOTE: The plural is **craniums** or **crania**.)

COMMENT: The cranium consists of the occipital bone, two parietal bones, two temporal bones and the frontal, ethmoid and sphenoid bones.

cream /kriːm/ noun a medicinal oily substance, used to rub on the skin

creatine /'kriːətiːn/ noun a compound of nitrogen found in the muscles, produced by protein metabolism and excreted as creatinine

creatine phosphate /ˌkriːətiːn 'fɒsfeɪt/ noun a store of energy-giving phosphate in muscles

creatinine /kri'ætəni:n/ *noun* a substance which is the form in which creatine is excreted

creatinine clearance /kri,ætəni:n 'kliərəns/ *noun* removal of creatinine from the blood by the kidneys

creatinuria /kri,ætɪ'njuəriə/ *noun* excess creatine in the urine

creatorrhoea /,kri:ətə'ri:ə/ *noun* the presence of undigested muscle fibre in the faeces, occurring in some pancreatic diseases

Credé's method /kre'deɪz ,meθəd/ *noun* **1.** a method of extracting a placenta by massaging the uterus through the abdomen **2.** the putting of silver nitrate solution into the eyes of a baby born to a mother who has gonorrhoea, in order to prevent gonococcal conjunctivitis [Described 1860. After Karl Sigmund Franz Credé (1819–92), German gynaecologist.]

creeping eruption /,kri:pɪŋ ɪ'rʌpʃən/ *noun* an itching skin complaint, caused by larvae of various parasites which creep under the skin

crepitation /,krepɪ'teɪʃ(ə)n/ *noun* an unusual soft crackling sound heard in the lungs through a stethoscope. Also called **rale**

crepitus /'krepɪtəs/ *noun* **1.** a harsh crackling sound heard through a stethoscope in a person with inflammation of the lungs **2.** a scratching sound made by a broken bone or rough joint

crest /krest/ *noun* a long raised part on a bone

crest of ilium /,krest əv 'ɪliəm/ *noun* same as **iliac crest**

cretinism /'kretɪnɪz(ə)m/ *noun* now called **congenital hyperthyroidism** (NOTE: This term is regarded as offensive.)

Creutzfeldt-Jakob disease /,krɔɪtsfelt 'jækɒb dɪ,zi:z/ *noun* a disease of the nervous system caused by a slow-acting prion which eventually affects the brain. It may be linked to BSE in cows. Abbr **CJD**. ◊ **variant CJD** [Described 1920 by H.G. Creutzfeldt (1885–1964); 1921 by A.M. Jakob (1884–1931), German psychiatrists]

cribriform /'krɪbrɪfɔ:m/ *adjective* having small holes like a sieve

cribriform plate /'krɪbrɪfɔ:m pleɪt/ *noun* the top part of the ethmoid bone which forms the roof of the nasal cavity and part of the roof of the eye sockets

crick /krɪk/ *noun* a painful stiffness in the neck or back (*informal*)

cricoid /'kraɪkɔɪd/ *adjective* relating to the lowest part of the cartilage of the larynx

cricoid cartilage /,kraɪkɔɪd 'kɑ:təlɪdʒ/ *noun* ring-shaped cartilage in the lower part of the larynx. See illustration at **LUNGS** in Supplement

cri-du-chat syndrome /,kri: dju: 'ʃɑ: ,sɪn drəum/ *noun* a congenital condition, caused by loss of part of chromosome 5, which is characterised in babies by a cry suggestive of that of a cat

Crigler-Najjar syndrome /,krɪglə 'nædʒɑ: ,sɪndrəum/ *noun* a genetically controlled condition in which bilirubin cannot be formed, leading to jaundice or even brain damage

criminal abortion /,krɪmɪn(ə)l ə'bɔ:ʃ(ə)n/ *noun* an abortion which is carried out illegally

crisis /'kraɪsɪs/ *noun* **1.** a situation or period of difficulty demanding action ○ *Is there a crisis in the health service?* **2.** a turning point in a disease, after which the person may start to become better or very much worse

COMMENT: Many diseases progress to a crisis and then the patient rapidly gets better. The opposite situation where the patient gets better very slowly is called lysis.

crista /'krɪstə/ *noun* **1.** a ridge, e.g. the border of a bone **2.** a fold in the inner membrane of a mitrochondrion (NOTE: The plural is **cristae**.)

crista galli /,krɪstə 'gælaɪ/ *noun* a projection from the ethmoid bone

criterion /kraɪ'tɪəriən/ *noun* an accepted standard used in making a decision or judgment about something (NOTE: The plural is **criteria**.)

critical /'krɪtɪk(ə)l/ *adjective* **1.** referring to a crisis **2.** extremely serious ○ *He was taken to hospital in a critical condition* **3.** which criticises ○ *The report was critical of the state of aftercare provision.*

critical list /'krɪtɪk(ə)l lɪst/ *noun* the list of patients in a hospital whose condition is medically life-threatening

CRNA *abbr* certified registered nurse anaesthetist

Crohn's disease /'krəunz dɪ,zi:z/ *noun* a persistent inflammatory disease, usually of the lower intestinal tract, characterised by thickening and scarring of the intestinal wall and obstruction [Described 1932. After Burrill Bernard Crohn (1884–1983), New York physician.]

COMMENT: No certain cause has been found for Crohn's disease, where only one section of the intestine becomes inflamed and can be blocked.

cromolyn sodium /,krəuməlɪn 'səudiəm/ *noun* a drug that helps to prevent the release of histamine and other substances which cause many of the symptoms of asthma and hay fever

cross-dresser *noun* someone who wears clothes usually worn by people of the opposite sex, e.g. a transvestite

cross-dressing /krɒs 'dresɪŋ/ *noun* the practice of wearing clothes usually worn by people of the opposite sex, e.g. by transvestites

cross eye /'krɒs aɪ/ *noun* same as **convergent strabismus** (*informal*)

cross-eyed /,krɒs 'aɪd/ *adjective* having convergent strabismus (*informal*)

cross-infection /krɒs ɪn'fekʃən/ *noun* an infection passed from one patient to another in hospital, either directly or from nurses, visitors or equipment

crossmatch /krɒs'mætʃ/ *verb* (*in transplant surgery*) to match a donor to a recipient as closely as possible to avoid tissue rejection. ◊ **blood group**

crossmatching /krɒs'mætʃɪŋ/ *noun* the process of matching a transplant donor to a recipient as closely as possible to avoid tissue rejection

cross-resistance /ˌkrɒs rɪ'zɪstəns/ *noun* the development by a disease agent of resistance to a number of similar drugs or chemicals of the same class

cross-section /'krɒs ˌsekʃən/ *noun* **1.** a small part of something, taken to be representative of the whole ○ *The team consulted a cross-section of hospital ancillary staff.* **2.** a sample cut across a specimen for examination under a microscope ○ *He examined a cross-section of the lung tissue.*

crotamiton /krə'tæmɪt(ə)n/ *noun* a chemical that kills mites, used to treat scabies

crotch /krɒtʃ/ *noun* the point where the legs meet the body, where the genitals are. Also called **crutch**

croup /kruːp/ *noun* acute infection of the upper respiratory passages which blocks the larynx, affecting children

COMMENT: The patient's larynx swells, and he or she breathes with difficulty and has a barking cough. Attacks usually occur at night. They can be fatal if the larynx becomes completely blocked.

crown /kraʊn/ *noun* **1.** the top part of a tooth above the level of the gums **2.** an artificial top attached to a tooth **3.** the top part of the head ■ *verb* to put an artificial crown on a tooth

crowning /'kraʊnɪŋ/ *noun* **1.** the act of putting an artificial crown on a tooth **2.** a stage in childbirth in which the top of the baby's head becomes visible

cruciate /'kruːʃiət/ *adjective* shaped like a cross

cruciate ligament /ˌkruːʃiət 'lɪgəmənt/ *noun* any ligament shaped like a cross, especially either of two ligaments behind the knee which prevent the knee from bending forwards

crude death rate /kruːd 'deθ reɪt/ *noun* the number of deaths in a year, divided by the total population

crura /'krʊərə/ *plural of* **crus**

crural /'krʊərəl/ *adjective* referring to the thigh, leg or shin

crura of the diaphragm /ˌkrʊərə əv ðə 'daɪəfræm/ *plural noun* the long muscle fibres joining the diaphragm to the lumbar vertebrae

crus /krʌs/ *noun* a long projecting part (NOTE: The plural is **crura**.)

crus cerebri /krʌs 'serɪbraɪ/ *noun* each of the nerve tracts between the cerebrum and the medulla oblongata (NOTE: The plural is **crura cerebri**.)

crush fracture /'krʌʃ ˌfræktʃə/ *noun* a fracture by compression of the bone

crush syndrome /'krʌʃ ˌsɪndrəʊm/ *noun* a condition in which a limb has been crushed, as in an accident, causing kidney failure and shock

crus of penis /ˌkrʌs əv 'piːnɪs/ *noun* a part of a corpus cavernosum attached to the pubic arch

crust /krʌst/ *noun* a dry layer of blood, pus or other secretion that forms over a cut or sore

crutch /krʌtʃ/ *noun* **1.** a strong support for someone with an injured leg, formed of a stick with a T-bar which fits under the armpit, especially formerly, or a holding bar and elbow clasp **2.** same as **crotch**

cry- /kraɪ/ *prefix* same as **cryo-** (*used before vowels*)

cryaesthesia /ˌkraɪiːs'θiːziə/ *noun* the fact of being sensitive to cold

cryo- /kraɪəʊ/ *prefix* cold

cryobank /'kraɪəʊbæŋk/ *noun* a place where biological material such as semen and body tissue can be stored at extremely low temperatures

cryoprecipitate /ˌkraɪəʊprɪ'sɪpɪtət/ *noun* a precipitate such as from blood plasma, which separates out on freezing and thawing

COMMENT: Cryoprecipitate from blood plasma contains Factor VIII and is used to treat haemophilia.

cryoprobe /'kraɪəʊprəʊb/ *noun* an instrument used in cryosurgery with a tip that is kept very cold to destroy tissue

cryosurgery /ˌkraɪəʊ'sɜːdʒəri/ *noun* surgery which uses extremely cold instruments to destroy tissue

cryotherapy /ˌkraɪəʊ'θerəpi/ *noun* treatment using extreme cold, as in removing a wart with dry ice

crypt /krɪpt/ *noun* a small cavity in the body

crypto- /krɪptəʊ/ *prefix* hidden

cryptocci /ˌkrɪptə'kɒki/ *plural of* **cryptococcus**

cryptococcal meningitis /ˌkrɪptəkɒk(ə)l menɪn'dʒaɪtɪs/ *noun* a form of meningitis that is a feature of cryptococcosis

cryptococcosis /ˌkrɪptəʊkə'kəʊsɪs/ *noun* an infection mainly affecting the brain or nervous system, caused by the fungus *Cryptococcus neoformans*. It occurs most often in people with HIV infection.

cryptococcus /ˌkrɪptə'kɒkəs/ *noun* one of several single-celled yeasts which exist in the soil and can cause disease (NOTE: The plural is **cryptococci**.)

cryptomenorrhoea /ˌkrɪptəʊmenəˈriːə/ noun the retention of menstrual flow, usually caused by an obstruction

cryptorchidism /krɪpˈtɔːkɪdɪz(ə)m/, **cryptorchism** /krɪpˈtɔːkɪz(ə)m/ noun a condition in a young male in which the testicles do not move down into the scrotum

cryptosporidia /ˌkrɪptəʊspəˈrɪdiə/ plural of **cryptosporidium**

cryptosporidiosis /ˌkrɪptəʊspəˌrɪdiˈəʊsɪs/ noun an infectious condition of humans and domestic animals, spread by an intestinal parasite *Cryptosporidium parvum*. Its symptoms are fever, diarrhoea and stomach cramps.

cryptosporidium /ˌkrɪptəʊspəˈrɪdiəm/ noun a parasite which contaminates drinking water supplies, causing intestinal infection (NOTE: The plural is **cryptosporidia**.)

crypts of Lieberkühn /ˌkrɪpts əv ˈliːbəkuːn/ plural noun tubular glands found in the mucous membrane of the small and large intestine, especially those between the bases of the villi in the small intestine. Also called **Lieberkühn's glands** [Described 1745. After Johann Nathaniel Lieberkühn (1711–56), Berlin anatomist and physician.]

crystal /ˈkrɪstəl/ noun a chemical formation of hard regular-shaped solids

crystalline /ˈkrɪstəlaɪn/ adjective clear like pure crystal

crystal violet /ˌkrɪst(ə)l ˈvaɪələt/ noun same as **gentian violet**

CSF abbr cerebrospinal fluid

CT abbr computed tomography

CT scan /ˌsiː ˈtiː skæn/ noun a computer picture of a slice of the body or an organ produced by a CT scanner. Also called **CAT scan**

CT scanner /ˌsiː ˈtiː ˌskænə/ noun a device which directs a narrow X-ray beam at a thin section of the body from various angles, using a computer to build up a complete picture of the cross-section. Also called **CAT scanner**

cubital /ˈkjuːbɪt(ə)l/ adjective referring to the ulna

cubital fossa /ˌkjuːbɪt(ə)l ˈfɒsə/ noun a depression in the front of the elbow joint

cubitus /ˈkjuːbɪtəs/ noun same as **ulna**

cuboid /ˈkjuːbɔɪd/, **cuboid bone** /ˈkjuːbɔɪd bəʊn/ noun one of the tarsal bones in the foot. See illustration at FOOT in Supplement

cuboidal cell /kjuːˈbɔɪd(ə)l sel/ noun a cube-shaped epithelial cell

cuff /kʌf/ noun 1. an inflatable ring put round the arm and inflated when blood pressure is being measured 2. an inflatable ring put round an endotracheal tube to close the passage

cuirass respirator /kwɪˌræs ˈrespɪreɪtə/ noun a type of artificial respirator which surrounds only the chest

culdoscope /ˈkʌldəʊskəʊp/ noun an instrument used to inspect the interior of a woman's pelvis, introduced through the vagina

culdoscopy /kʌlˈdɒskəpi/ noun an examination of the interior of a woman's pelvis using a culdoscope

culture /ˈkʌltʃə/ noun 1. the shared values and behaviour of a group 2. microorganisms or tissues grown in a culture medium in a laboratory ■ verb to grow microorganisms or tissues in a culture medium

culture medium /ˈkʌltʃə ˌmiːdiəm/ noun a substance in which a culture of microorganisms or tissue is grown in a laboratory, e.g. agar

cumulative /ˈkjuːmjʊlətɪv/ adjective growing by adding

cumulative action /ˌkjuːmjʊlətɪv ˈækʃən/ noun an effect of a drug which is given more often than it can be excreted and so accumulates in the tissues

cuneiform /ˈkjuːnɪfɔːm/, **cuneiform bone** /ˈkjuːnɪfɔːm bəʊn/ noun one of the three tarsal bones in the foot. See illustration at FOOT in Supplement

cupola /ˈkjuːpələ/ noun 1. a dome-shaped structure 2. a piece of cartilage in a semicircular canal which is moved by the fluid in the canal and connects with the vestibular nerve

curable /ˈkjuərəb(ə)l/ adjective able to be cured ○ *a curable form of cancer*

curare /kjʊˈrɑːri/ noun a drug derived from South American plants, antagonist to acetylcholine and used surgically to paralyse muscles during operations without causing unconsciousness (NOTE: Curare is the poison used to make poison arrows.)

curative /ˈkjuərətɪv/ adjective able to cure

cure /kjʊə/ noun a particular way of making someone well or of stopping an illness ○ *Scientists are trying to develop a cure for the common cold.* ■ verb to make someone healthy ○ *She was completely cured.* ○ *Can the doctors cure his bad circulation?*

curettage /kjʊəˈretɪdʒ/ noun the procedure of scraping the inside of a hollow organ, often the uterus, to remove a growth or tissue for examination. Also called **curettement**

curette /kjʊəˈret/ noun a surgical instrument like a long thin spoon, used for scraping the inside of an organ (NOTE: The US spelling is **curet**.) ■ verb to scrape an organ with a curette (NOTE: **curettes – curetting – curetted**. The US spelling is **curet**.)

curettement same as **curettage**

curie /ˈkjʊəri/ noun a former unit of measurement of radioactivity, replaced by the becquerel. Symbol Ci

Curling's ulcer /ˌkɜːlɪŋz ˈʌlsə/ noun an ulcer of the duodenum following severe injury to the body

curvature /'kɜːvətʃə/ *noun* the way in which something bends from a straight line ○ *greater* or *lesser curvature of the stomach*

curvature of the spine /ˌkɜːvətʃər əv ðə 'spaɪn/ *noun* an unusual bending of the spine forwards or sideways

cushingoid /'kʊʃɪŋɔɪd/ *adjective* showing symptoms of Cushing's disease

Cushing's disease /'kʊʃɪŋz dɪˌziːz/, **Cushing's syndrome** /'kʊʃɪŋz ˌsɪndrəʊm/ *noun* a condition in which the adrenal cortex produces too many corticosteroids [Described 1932. After Harvey Williams Cushing (1869–1939), surgeon, Boston, USA.]

> COMMENT: The syndrome is caused either by a tumour in the adrenal gland, by excessive stimulation of the adrenals by the basophil cells of the pituitary gland, or by a corticosteroid-secreting tumour. The syndrome causes swelling of the face and trunk, weakening of the muscles, raised blood pressure and retention of salt and water in the body.

cusp /kʌsp/ *noun* **1.** the pointed tip of a tooth **2.** a flap of membrane forming a valve in the heart

cuspid /'kʌspɪd/ *noun* same as **canine**

cut /kʌt/ *noun* **1.** a reduction in the number or amount of something **2.** a place where the skin has been penetrated by a sharp instrument ○ *She had a bad cut on her left leg.* ○ *The nurse will put a bandage on your cut.* ■ *verb* **1.** to make an opening in something using a knife, scissors or other sharp thing ○ *The surgeon cut the diseased tissue away with a scalpel.* ○ *She cut her finger on the broken glass.* **2.** to reduce the number or amount of something ○ *Accidents have been cut by 10%.* (NOTE: **cutting – cut**)

cut- *prefix* referring to the skin

cutaneous /kjuː'teɪniəs/ *adjective* referring to the skin

cutaneous leishmaniasis /kjuːˌteɪniəs liːʃmə'naɪəsɪs/ *noun* a form of skin disease caused by the tropical parasite *Leishmania.* Also called **Delhi boil**

cutdown /'kʌtdaʊn/ *noun* the procedure of cutting a vein to insert a cannula or administer an intravenous drug

cuticle /'kjuːtɪk(ə)l/ *noun* **1.** same as **epidermis 2.** a strip of epidermis attached at the base of a nail

cutis /'kjuːtɪs/ *noun* the skin

cutis anserina /ˌkjuːtɪs 'ænseraɪnə/ *noun* a reaction of the skin when someone is cold or frightened, the skin being raised into many little bumps by the action of the arrector pili muscles. Also called **goose bumps**

CVA *abbr* cerebrovascular accident

cyan- /saɪən/ *prefix* same as **cyano-** (*used before vowels*)

cyanide /'saɪənaɪd/ *noun* a poison which kills very rapidly when drunk or inhaled

cyano- /saɪənəʊ/ *prefix* blue

cyanocobalamin /ˌsaɪənəʊkəʊ'bæləmɪn/ same as **Vitamin B₁₂**

cyanosed /'saɪənəʊst/ *adjective* with blue skin ○ *The patient was cyanosed round the lips.*

cyanosis /ˌsaɪə'nəʊsɪs/ *noun* a condition characterised by a blue colour of the peripheral skin and mucous membranes, a symptom of lack of oxygen in the blood, e.g. in heart or lung disease

cyanotic /ˌsaɪə'nɒtɪk/ *adjective* referring to or having cyanosis

cyclandelate /sɪ'klændəleɪt/ *noun* a drug used to treat cerebrovascular disease

cycle /'saɪk(ə)l/ *noun* a series of events which recur regularly

cyclic /'sɪklɪk, 'saɪklɪk/ *adjective* **1.** occurring or repeated in cycles **2.** referring to organic compounds composed of a closed ring of atoms

cyclical /'sɪklɪk(ə)l/ *adjective* referring to cycles

cyclical vomiting /ˌsɪklɪk(ə)l 'vɒmɪtɪŋ/ *noun* repeated attacks of vomiting

-cycline /saɪklɪn/ *suffix* used in names of antibiotics ○ *tetracycline*

cyclitis /sɪ'klaɪtɪs/ *noun* inflammation of the ciliary body in the eye

cyclizine /'saɪklɪziːn/ *noun* an antihistamine drug that can be used to control nausea and vomiting

cyclo- /saɪkləʊ/ *prefix* cycles

cyclodialysis /ˌsaɪkləʊdaɪ'æləsɪs/ *noun* a surgical operation to connect the anterior chamber of the eye and the choroid, as a treatment of glaucoma

cyclopentolate /ˌsaɪkləʊ'pentəleɪt/ *noun* a drug used to paralyse the ciliary muscle

cyclophosphamide /ˌsaɪkləʊ'fɒsfəmaɪd/ *noun* a drug which suppresses immunity, used in the treatment of leukaemia, lymphoma, Hodgkin's disease and tumours

cycloplegia /ˌsaɪkləʊ'pliːdʒə/ *noun* paralysis of the ciliary muscle which makes it impossible for the eye to focus properly

cyclopropane /ˌsaɪkləʊ'prəʊpeɪn/ *noun* a flammable hydrocarbon gas used as a general anaesthetic and in organic synthesis

cyclothymia /ˌsaɪkləʊ'θaɪmiə/ *noun* a mild form of bipolar disorder in which the person experiences alternating depression and excitement

cyclotomy /saɪ'klɒtəmi/ *noun* a surgical operation to make a cut in the ciliary body (NOTE: The plural is **cyclotomies**.)

-cyclovir /saɪkləʊvɪə/ *suffix* used in the names of antiviral drugs

cyesis /saɪ'iːsɪs/ *noun* same as **pregnancy** (*technical*)

cylinder /'sɪlɪndə/ *noun* ♦ **oxygen cylinder**

cyst /sɪst/ *noun* an unusual growth in the body shaped like a pouch, containing liquid or semi-liquid substances

cyst- /sɪst/ *prefix* the bladder

cystadenoma /ˌsɪstədɪˈnəʊmə/ *noun* an adenoma in which fluid-filled cysts form (NOTE: The plural is **cystadonomas** or **cystadonomata**.)

cystalgia /sɪˈstældʒə/ *noun* pain in the urinary bladder

cystectomy /sɪˈstektəmi/ *noun* a surgical operation to remove all or part of the urinary bladder (NOTE: The plural is **cystectomies**.)

cystic /ˈsɪstɪk/ *adjective* **1.** referring to cysts **2.** referring to a bladder

cystic artery /ˌsɪstɪk ˈɑːtəri/ *noun* an artery leading from the hepatic artery to the gall bladder

cystic duct /ˈsɪstɪk dʌkt/ *noun* a duct which takes bile from the gall bladder to the common bile duct

cysticercosis /ˌsɪstɪsɜːˈkəʊsɪs/ *noun* a disease caused by infestation of tapeworm larvae from pork

cysticercus /ˌsɪstɪˈsɜːkəs/ *noun* the larva of a tapeworm of the genus *Taenia*, found in pork, which is enclosed in a cyst (NOTE: The plural is **cysticerci**.)

cystic fibrosis /ˌsɪstɪk faɪˈbrəʊsɪs/ *noun* a hereditary disease in which there is malfunction of the exocrine glands such as the pancreas, in particular those which secrete mucus, causing respiratory difficulties, male infertility and malabsorption of food from the gastrointestinal tract. Also called **fibrocystic disease, mucoviscidosis**

COMMENT: The thick mucous secretions cause blockage of ducts and many serious secondary effects in the intestines and lungs. Symptoms include loss of weight, abnormal faeces and bronchitis. If diagnosed early, cystic fibrosis can be controlled with vitamins, physiotherapy and pancreatic enzymes.

cystic vein /ˈsɪstɪk veɪn/ *noun* a vein which drains the gall bladder

cystine /ˈsɪstiːn/ *noun* an amino acid. It can cause stones to form in the urinary system of people who have a rare inherited metabolic disorder.

cystinosis /ˌsɪstɪˈnəʊsɪs/ *noun* a disorder affecting the absorption of amino acids, resulting in excessive amounts of cystine accumulating in the kidneys

cystinuria /ˌsɪstɪˈnjʊəriə/ *noun* cystine in the urine

cystitis /sɪˈstaɪtɪs/ *noun* inflammation of the urinary bladder, which makes someone pass water often and with a burning sensation

cystocele /ˈsɪstəsiːl/ *noun* a hernia of the urinary bladder into the vagina

cystogram /ˈsɪstəgræm/ *noun* an X-ray photograph of the urinary bladder

cystography /sɪˈstɒgrəfi/ *noun* an examination of the urinary bladder by X-rays after radio-opaque dye has been introduced

cystolithiasis /ˌsɪstəlɪˈθaɪəsɪs/ *noun* a condition in which stones are formed in the urinary bladder

cystometer /sɪˈstɒmɪtə/ *noun* an apparatus which measures the pressure in the bladder

cystometry /sɪˈstɒmɪtri/ *noun* measurement of the pressure in the bladder

cystopexy /sɪˈstɒpeksi/ *noun* a surgical operation to fix the bladder in a different position. Also called **vesicofixation** (NOTE: The plural is **cystopexies**.)

cystoplasty /ˈsɪstəˌplæsti/ *noun* a surgical operation on the bladder (NOTE: The plural is **cystoplasties**.)

cystoscope /ˈsɪstəskəʊp/ *noun* an instrument made of a long tube with a light at the end, used to inspect the inside of the bladder

cystoscopy /sɪˈstɒskəpi/ *noun* an examination of the bladder using a cystoscope (NOTE: The plural is **cystoscopies**.)

cystostomy /sɪˈstɒstəmi/, **cystotomy** /sɪˈstɒtəmi/ *noun* a surgical operation to make an opening between the bladder and the abdominal wall to allow urine to pass without going through the urethra. Also called **vesicostomy** (NOTE: The plurals are **cystostomies** and **cystotomies**.)

cystourethrography /ˌsɪstəʊˌjʊərɪˈθrɒgrəfi/ *noun* X-ray examination of the bladder and urethra

cystourethroscope /ˌsɪstəʊjʊˈriːθrəskəʊp/ *noun* an instrument used to inspect the bladder and urethra

cyt- /saɪt/ *prefix* same as **cyto-** (*used before vowels*)

cyto- /saɪtəʊ/ *prefix* cell

cytochemistry /ˌsaɪtəʊˈkemɪstri/ *noun* the study of the chemical activity of cells

cytodiagnosis /ˌsaɪtəʊdaɪəɡˈnəʊsɪs/ *noun* diagnosis after examination of cells

cytogenetics /ˌsaɪtəʊdʒəˈnetɪks/ *noun* a branch of genetics which studies the function of cells, especially chromosomes, in heredity

cytokine /ˈsaɪtəʊkaɪn/ *noun* a protein secreted by cells of the lymph system which is involved in controlling response to inflammation

cytokinesis /ˌsaɪtəʊkɪˈniːsɪs/ *noun* changes in the cytoplasm of a cell during division

cytological smear /ˌsaɪtəlɒdʒɪk(ə)l ˈsmɪə/ *noun* a sample of tissue taken for examination under a microscope

cytology /saɪˈtɒlədʒi/ *noun* the study of the structure and function of cells

cytolysis /saɪˈtɒləsɪs/ *noun* the breaking down of cells

cytomegalovirus /ˌsaɪtəʊˈmegələʊˌvaɪrəs/ *noun* one of the herpesviruses which can cause serious congenital disorders in a fetus if it infects the pregnant mother. Abbr **CMV**

cytometer /saɪ'tɒmɪtə/ *noun* an instrument attached to a microscope, used for measuring and counting the number of cells in a specimen

cytopenia /ˌsaɪtəʊ'piːniə/ *noun* a deficiency of cellular elements in blood or tissue

cytoplasm /'saɪtəʊplæz(ə)m/ *noun* a substance inside the cell membrane which surrounds the nucleus of a cell

cytoplasmic /ˌsaɪtəʊ'plæzmɪk/ *adjective* referring to the cytoplasm of a cell

cytosine /'saɪtəʊsiːn/ *noun* one of the four basic chemicals in DNA

cytosome /'saɪtəʊsəʊm/ *noun* the body of a cell, not including the nucleus

cytotoxic /ˌsaɪtəʊ'tɒksɪk/ *adjective* **1.** referring to a drug or agent which prevents cell division **2.** referring to cells in the immune system which destroy other cells

cytotoxic drug /ˌsaɪtəʊtɒksɪk 'drʌg/ *noun* a drug which reduces the reproduction of cells, used to treat cancer

cytotoxin /ˌsaɪtəʊ'tɒksɪn/ *noun* a substance which has a toxic effect on cells

D

d /diː/ *symbol* deci-

da *symbol* deca-

dab /dæb/ *verb* to touch something lightly ○ *He dabbed around the cut with a piece of cotton wool.*

da Costa's syndrome /dɑː ˈkɒstəz ˌsɪndrəʊm/ *noun* same as **disordered action of the heart** [Described 1871. After Jacob Mendes da Costa (1833–1900), Philadelphia surgeon, who described this condition in soldiers in the American Civil War.]

dacryo- /dækriəʊ/ *prefix* tears

dacryoadenitis /ˌdækriəʊædɪˈnaɪtɪs/ *noun* inflammation of the lacrimal gland

dacryocystitis /ˌdækriəʊsɪˈstaɪtɪs/ *noun* inflammation of the lacrimal sac when the tear duct, which drains into the nose, becomes blocked

dacryocystography /ˌdækriəʊsɪˈstɒɡrəfi/ *noun* contrast radiography to determine the site of an obstruction in the tear ducts

dacryocystorhinostomy /ˌdækriəʊˌsɪstəʊraɪˈnɒstəmi/ *noun* a surgical operation to bypass a blockage from the tear duct which takes tears into the nose. Abbr **DCR** (NOTE: The plural is **dacryocystorhinostomies**.)

dacryolith /ˈdækriəʊlɪθ/ *noun* a stone in the lacrimal sac

dacryoma /ˌdækriˈəʊmə/ *noun* a benign swelling in one of the tear ducts (NOTE: The plural is **dacryomas** or **dacryomata**.)

dactyl /ˈdæktɪl/ *noun* a finger or toe

dactyl- /dæktɪl/ *prefix* same as **dactylo-** (*used before vowels*)

dactylitis /ˌdæktɪˈlaɪtɪs/ *noun* inflammation of the fingers or toes, caused by bone infection or rheumatic disease

dactylo- /dæktɪləʊ/ *prefix* referring to the fingers or toes

dactylology /ˌdæktɪˈlɒlədʒi/ *noun* signs made with the fingers in place of words when talking to a person who is unable to hear, or when a person who is unable to hear or speak wants to communicate

dactylomegaly /ˌdæktɪləʊˈmeɡəli/ *noun* a condition in which a person has longer fingers than usual

DAH *abbr* disordered action of the heart

daily /ˈdeɪli/ *adverb* every day ○ *Take the medicine twice daily.*

Daltonism /ˈdɔːltənɪz(ə)m/ *noun* the commonest form of colour blindness, in which someone cannot see the difference between red and green. Also called **protanopia** [Described 1794. After John Dalton (1766–1844), English chemist and physician. Founder of the atomic theory, he himself was colour-blind.]

damage /ˈdæmɪdʒ/ *noun* harm done to things ○ *The disease caused damage to the brain cells.* ■ *verb* to harm something ○ *His hearing* or *his sense of balance was damaged in the accident.*

damp /dæmp/ *adjective* slightly wet ○ *You should put a damp compress on the bruise.*

D & C /diː ən/ *abbr* dilatation and curettage

dander /ˈdændə/ *noun* very small fragments that fall from the feathers, hair or skin of animals or people

dandruff /ˈdændrəf/ *noun* pieces of dead skin from the scalp which fall out when the hair is combed. Also called **pityriasis capitis, scurf**

D and V /ˌdiː ən ˈviː/ *abbr* diarrhoea and vomiting

Dandy-Walker syndrome /ˌdændi ˈwɔːkə ˌsɪndrəʊm/ *noun* a congenital condition in which there is no Magendie's foramen in the brain

danger /ˈdeɪndʒə/ *noun* the possibility of harm or death ○ *Unless the glaucoma is treated quickly, there's a danger that the patient will lose his eyesight* or *a danger of the patient losing his eyesight.* □ **out of danger** no longer likely to die

dangerous /ˈdeɪndʒərəs/ *adjective* causing harm or death

dangerous drug /ˌdeɪndʒərəs ˈdrʌɡ/ *noun* **1.** a drug which is harmful and is not available to the general public, e.g. morphine or heroin **2.** a poison which can only be sold to specific persons

dark adaptation /dɑːk ˌædæpˈteɪʃ(ə)n/ *noun* the reflex changes which enable the eye to continue to see in dim light. For example, the pupil becomes larger and the rods in the retina become more active than the cones.

darkening /ˈdɑːknɪŋ/ *noun* the act of becoming darker in colour ○ *Darkening of the tissue takes place after bruising.*

data /ˈdeɪtə/ *plural noun* information in words or figures about a particular subject, especially information which is available on computer (NOTE: In scientific usage, **data** is used with a plural verb: *The data are accurate.* In everyday language, **data** is often used with a singular verb: *The recent data supports our case.*)

data bank /ˈdeɪtə bæŋk/ *noun* a store of information in a computer ○ *The hospital keeps a data bank of information about possible kidney donors.*

database *noun* a structured collection of information in a computer that can be automatically retrieved and manipulated

Data Protection Act /ˌdeɪtə prəˈtekʃ(ə)n/ *noun* a parliamentary act intended to protect information about individuals that is held on computers. It ensures that all information is stored securely and allows people to have access to their entries.

daughter /ˈdɔːtə/ *noun* a female child of a parent ○ *They have two sons and one daughter.*

daughter cell /ˈdɔːtə sel/ *noun* any of the cells which develop by mitosis from a single parent cell

day blindness /ˈdeɪ ˌblaɪndnəs/ *noun* same as **hemeralopia**

day care /ˈdeɪ keə/ *noun* supervised recreation or medical care provided during the day for people who need special help, e.g. some elderly people or small children

day case /ˈdeɪ keɪs/ *noun* same as **day patient**

day case surgery /ˈdeɪ keɪs ˌsɜːdʒəri/ *noun* same as **day surgery**

day centre /ˈdeɪ ˌsentə/ *noun* a place providing day care

day hospital /ˈdeɪ ˌhɒspɪt(ə)l/ *noun* a hospital where people are treated during the day and go home in the evenings

day nursery /ˈdeɪ ˌnɜːs(ə)ri/ *noun* a place where small children can be looked after during the daytime while their parents or guardians are at work

day patient /ˈdeɪ ˌpeɪʃ(ə)nt/ *noun* a patient who is in hospital for treatment for a day and does not stay overnight. Also called **day case**

day patient care /ˈdeɪ peɪʃ(ə)nt keə/ *noun* care for patients who are resident in a hospital during the daytime only

day recovery ward /deɪ rɪˈkʌv(ə)ri wɔːd/ *noun* a ward where day patients who have had

minor operations can recover before going home

day surgery /ˈdeɪ ˌsɜːdʒəri/ *noun* a surgical operation which does not require the patient to stay overnight in hospital. Also called **day case surgery**

dazed /deɪzd/ *adjective* confused in the mind ○ *She was found walking about in a dazed condition.* ○ *He was dazed after the accident.*

dB *abbr* decibel

DCR *abbr* dacryocystorhinostomy

DDS *abbr US* doctor of dental surgery

DDT *abbr* dichlorodiphenyltrichloroethane

de- /diː/ *prefix* removal or loss

dead /ded/ *adjective* **1.** no longer alive ○ *My grandparents are both dead* ○ *The woman was rescued from the crash, but was certified dead on arrival at the hospital* **2.** not sensitive ○ *The nerve endings are dead.* ○ *His fingers went dead.*

deaden /ˈded(ə)n/ *verb* to make something such as pain or noise less strong ○ *The doctor gave him an injection to deaden the pain.*

dead fingers /ded ˈfɪŋgəz/ *noun* same as **Raynaud's disease**

deadly nightshade /ˌdedli ˈnaɪtʃeɪd/ *noun* same as **belladonna**

dead man's fingers /ˌded mænz ˈfɪŋgəz/ *noun* same as **Raynaud's disease**

dead space /ded speɪs/ *noun* a breath in the last part of the process of breathing in air which does not get further than the bronchial tubes

deaf /def/ *adjective* not able to hear in circumstances where most people would ○ *You have to speak slowly and clearly when you talk to Mr Jones because he's quite deaf.* ◊ **hearing-impaired** ■ *plural noun* □ **the deaf** people who are deaf

deaf and dumb /ˌdef ən ˈdʌm/ *noun* not able to hear or to speak (NOTE: This term is regarded as offensive.)

deafen /ˈdef(ə)n/ *verb* to make someone deaf for a time ○ *He was deafened by the explosion.*

deafness /ˈdefnəs/ *noun* the fact of being unable to hear in circumstances where most people would ◊ **partial deafness 1.** the condition of being able to hear some tones, but not all **2.** a general dulling of the whole range of hearing

COMMENT: Deafness has many degrees and many causes: old age, viruses, exposure to continuous loud noise or intermittent loud explosions, and diseases such as German measles.

deaminate /diːˈæmɪneɪt/ *verb* to remove an amino group from an amino acid, forming ammonia

deamination /diːˌæmɪˈneɪʃ(ə)n/ *noun* the process by which amino acids are broken down in the liver and urea is formed

COMMENT: After deamination, the ammonia which is formed is converted to urea by the liver, while the remaining carbon and hydrogen from the amino acid provide the body with heat and energy.

death /deθ/ *noun* the permanent end of all natural functions

death certificate /'deθ sə,tɪfɪkət/ *noun* an official document signed by a doctor stating that a person has died and giving details of the person and the cause of death

death rate /'deθ reɪt/ *noun* the number of deaths per year per thousand of population ○ *The death rate from cancer of the liver has remained stable.*

debilitate /dɪ'bɪlɪteɪt/ *verb* to make someone or something weak ○ *He was debilitated by a long illness.*

debilitating disease /dɪ,bɪlɪteɪtɪŋ dɪ'ziːz/ *noun* a disease which makes the person weak

debility /dɪ'bɪlɪti/ *noun* general weakness

debridement /dɪ'briːdmənt/ *noun* the removal of dirt or dead tissue from a wound to help healing

deca- /dekə/ *prefix* ten. Symbol **da**

Decadron /'dekədrɒn/ a trade name for dexamethasone

decalcification /diː,kælsɪfɪ'keɪʃ(ə)n/ *noun* the loss of calcium salts from teeth and bones

decannulation /diː,kænjʊ'leɪʃ(ə)n/ *noun* the removal of a tracheostomy tube

decapitation /dɪ,kæpɪ'teɪʃ(ə)n/ *noun* the act or process of cutting off the head of a person or animal

decapsulation /diː,kæpsjʊ'leɪʃ(ə)n/ *noun* a surgical operation to remove a capsule from an organ, especially from a kidney

decay /dɪ'keɪ/ *noun* **1.** the process by which tissues become rotten, caused by the action of microorganisms and oxygen **2.** damage caused to tissue or a tooth by the action of microorganisms, especially bacteria ■ *verb (of tissue)* to rot ○ *The surgeon removed decayed matter from the wound.*

deci- /desi/ *prefix* one tenth (10^{-1}) ○ *decigram* Symbol **d**

decibel /'desɪbel/ *noun* a unit of measurement of the loudness of sound, used to compare different levels of sound. Symbol **dB**

COMMENT: Normal conversation is at about 50dB. Very loud noise with a value of over 120dB, e.g. that of aircraft engines, can cause pain.

decidua /dɪ'sɪdjuə/ *noun* a membrane which lines the uterus after fertilisation (NOTE: The plural is **deciduas** or **deciduae**.)

COMMENT: The decidua is divided into several parts: the **decidua basalis**, where the embryo is attached, the **decidua capsularis**, which covers the embryo and the **decidua vera** which is the rest of the decidua not touching the embryo. It is expelled after the birth of the baby.

decidual /dɪ'sɪdjuəl/ *adjective* referring to the decidua

deciduoma /dɪ,sɪdju'əʊmə/ *noun* a mass of decidual tissue remaining in the uterus after birth (NOTE: The plural is **deciduomas** or **deciduomata**.)

deciduous /dɪ'sɪdjuəs/ *adjective* referring to teeth discarded at a later stage of development

deciduous dentition /dɪ,sɪdjuəs den 'tɪʃ(ə)n/ *noun* the set of twenty teeth which are gradually replaced by the permanent teeth as a child grows older

deciduous tooth /dɪ'sɪdjuəs tuːθ/ *noun* same as **primary tooth**

decilitre /'desɪliːtə/ *noun* a unit of measurement of liquid equal to one tenth of a litre. Symbol **dl** (NOTE: The US spelling is **deciliter**.)

decimetre /'desɪmiːtə/ *noun* a unit of measurement of length equal to one tenth of a metre. Symbol **dm** (NOTE: The US spelling is **decimeter**.)

decompensation /diː,kɒmpən'seɪʃ(ə)n/ *noun* a condition in which an organ such as the heart cannot cope with extra stress placed on it and so is unable to perform its function properly

decompose /,diːkəm'pəʊz/ *verb* to rot or become putrefied (NOTE: **decomposing – decomposed**)

decomposition /,diːkɒmpə'zɪʃ(ə)n/ *noun* the process where dead matter is rotted by the action of bacteria or fungi

decompression /,diːkəm'preʃ(ə)n/ *noun* **1.** reduction of pressure **2.** a controlled reduction of atmospheric pressure which occurs as a diver returns to the surface

decompression sickness /,diːkəm ,preʃ(ə)n 'sɪknəs/ *noun* same as **caisson disease**

decongest /,diːkən'dʒest/ *verb* to loosen or disperse mucus in the nasal passages, sinuses or bronchi

decongestant /,diːkən'dʒestənt/ *adjective* reducing congestion and swelling ■ *noun* a drug which reduces congestion and swelling, sometimes used to unblock the nasal passages

decontamination /,diːkəntæmɪ'neɪʃ(ə)n/ *noun* the removal of a contaminating substance such as radioactive material

decortication /diː,kɔːtɪ'keɪʃ(ə)n/ *noun* the surgical removal of the cortex of an organ □ **decortication of a lung** a surgical operation to remove part of the pleura which has been thickened or made stiff by chronic empyema

decrudescence /,diːkruː'des(ə)ns/ *noun* a reduction in the symptoms of a disease

decubitus /dɪ'kjuːbɪtəs/ *noun* the position of a person who is lying down

decubitus ulcer /dɪ,kjuːbɪtəs 'ʌlsə/ *noun* same as **bedsore**

decussation /,diːkʌ'seɪʃ(ə)n/ *noun* the crossing of nerve fibres in the central nervous system. Also called **chiasm**

deep /di:p/ *adjective* located, coming from or reaching relatively far inside the body. Opposite **superficial**

deep cervical vein /di:p 'sɜ:vɪk(ə)l veɪn/ *noun* a vein in the neck which drains into the vertebral vein

deep dermal burn /di:p 'dɜ:m(ə)l bɜ:n/ *noun* a burn which is so severe that a graft will be necessary to repair the skin damage. Also called **full thickness burn**

deep facial vein /di:p 'feɪʃ(ə)l veɪn/ *noun* a small vein which drains from the pterygoid process behind the cheek into the facial vein

deeply /'di:pli/ *adverb* so as to take in a large amount of air ○ *He was breathing deeply.*

deep plantar arch /di:p 'plæntər ɑ:tʃ/ *noun* a curved artery crossing the sole of the foot

deep vein /di:p 'veɪn/ *noun* a vein which is inside the body near a bone, as opposed to a superficial vein near the skin

deep-vein thrombosis /ˌdi:p veɪn θrɒm 'bəʊsɪs/ *noun* a condition arising when a thrombus formed in the deep veins of a leg or the pelvis travels to a lung where it may cause death. The condition may affect anyone who is inactive for long periods. Also called **phlebothrombosis**. Abbr **DVT**

defecate /'defəkeɪt/, **defaecate** *verb* to pass faeces out from the bowels through the anus (NOTE: **defecating – defecated**)

defecation /ˌdefə'keɪʃ(ə)n/, **defaecation** *noun* the act of passing out faeces from the bowels

defect /'di:fekt/ *noun* **1.** an unsatisfactory or imperfect feature of something **2.** a lack of something which is necessary

defective /dɪ'fektɪv/ *adjective* working badly or wrongly formed ○ *The surgeons operated to repair a defective heart valve.* ■ *noun* a person suffering from severe mental impairment (NOTE: The noun use is regarded as offensive.)

defence /dɪ'fens/ *noun* **1.** resistance against an attack of a disease **2.** behaviour of a person which is aimed at protecting him or her from harm (NOTE: The US spelling is **defense**.)

defence mechanism /dɪ'fens ˌmekənɪz(ə)m/ *noun* a subconscious reflex by which a person prevents himself or herself from showing emotion

defense /dɪ'fens/ *noun US* same as **defence**

defensive medicine /dɪˌfensɪv 'med(ə)s(ə)n/ *noun* extensive diagnostic testing before treatment to minimise the likelihood of a patient suing the doctor or hospital for negligence

deferent /'defərənt/ *adjective* **1.** going away from the centre **2.** referring to the vas deferens

defervescence /ˌdefə'ves(ə)ns/ *noun* a period during which a fever is subsiding

defibrillation /di:ˌfɪbrɪ'leɪʃ(ə)n/ *noun* a procedure to correct an irregular heartbeat by applying a large electrical impulse to the chest wall, especially in potentially life-threatening circumstances. Also called **cardioversion**

defibrillator /di:'fɪbrɪleɪtə/ *noun* an apparatus used to apply an electric impulse to the heart to make it beat regularly

defibrination /di:ˌfaɪbrɪ'neɪʃ(ə)n/ *noun* the removal of fibrin from a blood sample to prevent clotting

deficiency /dɪ'fɪʃ(ə)nsi/ *noun* a lack of something necessary

deficiency disease /dɪ'fɪʃ(ə)nsi dɪˌzi:z/ *noun* a disease caused by lack of an essential element in the diet such as vitamins or essential amino and fatty acids

deficient /dɪ'fɪʃ(ə)nt/ *adjective* not meeting the required standard □ **deficient in something** not containing the necessary amount of something ○ *His diet is deficient in calcium* or *he has a calcium-deficient diet.*

deficit /'defɪsɪt/ *noun* the amount by which something is less than it should be

defloration /ˌdi:flɔː'reɪʃ(ə)n/ *noun* the act of breaking the hymen of a virgin, usually at the first sexual intercourse

deflorescence /ˌdi:flɔː'res(ə)ns/ *noun* the disappearance of a rash

deformans /di:'fɔːmənz/ **♦ osteitis deformans**

deformation /ˌdi:fɔː'meɪʃ(ə)n/ *noun* the process of becoming deformed, or the state of being deformed ○ *The later stages of the disease are marked by bone deformation.*

deformed /dɪ'fɔːmd/ *adjective* not shaped or formed in the expected way

deformity /dɪ'fɔːmɪti/ *noun* an unusual shape of part of the body

degenerate /dɪ'dʒenəreɪt/ *verb* to change so as not to be able to function ○ *His health degenerated so much that he was incapable of looking after himself.*

degeneration /dɪˌdʒenə'reɪʃ(ə)n/ *noun* a change in the structure of a cell or organ so that it no longer works properly

degenerative disease /dɪˌdʒen(ə)rətɪv dɪ 'zi:z/, **degenerative disorder** /dɪ ˌdʒen(ə)rətɪv dɪs'ɔːdə/ *noun* a disease or disorder in which there is progressive loss of function of a part of the body, or in which a part of the body fails to repair itself

degenerative joint disease /dɪ ˌdʒen(ə)rətɪv 'dʒɔɪnt dɪˌzi:z/ *noun* same as **osteoarthritis**

deglutition /ˌdi:glu:'tɪʃ(ə)n/ *noun* the action of passing food or liquid, and sometimes also air, from the mouth into the oesophagus (*technical*) Also called **swallowing**

dehisced /dɪ'hɪst/ *adjective* referring to a wound which has split open after being closed

dehiscence /dɪ'hɪs(ə)ns/ *noun* the act of opening wide

dehydrate /ˌdiː'haɪ'dreɪt/ *verb* to lose water, or cause someone or something to lose water ○ *During strenuous exercise it's easy to become dehydrated.* (NOTE: **dehydrating – dehydrated**)

dehydration /ˌdiː'haɪ'dreɪʃ(ə)n/ *noun* loss of water

'...an estimated 60–70% of diarrhoeal deaths are caused by dehydration' [*Indian Journal of Medical Sciences*]

COMMENT: Water is more essential than food for a human being's survival. If someone drinks during the day less liquid than is passed out of the body in urine and sweat, he or she begins to dehydrate.

dehydrogenase /ˌdiː'haɪ'drɒdʒəneɪz/ *noun* an enzyme that transfers hydrogen between chemical compounds

déjà vu /ˌdeɪʒɑː 'vuː/ *noun* an illusion that a new situation is a previous one being repeated, usually caused by a disease of the brain

Déjerine-Klumpke's syndrome *noun* same as **Klumpke's paralysis**

deleterious /ˌdelɪ'tɪəriəs/ *adjective* damaging or harmful

Delhi boil /ˌdeli 'bɔɪl/ *noun* same as **cutaneous leishmaniasis**

delicate /'delɪkət/ *adjective* **1.** easily broken or harmed ○ *The bones of a baby's skull are very delicate.* ○ *The eye is covered by a delicate membrane.* **2.** easily falling ill ○ *His delicate state of health means that he is not able to work long hours.* **3.** requiring great care or sensitivity ○ *The surgeons carried out a delicate operation to join the severed nerves.*

delirious /dɪ'lɪriəs/ *adjective* affected by delirium. A person can become delirious because of shock, fear, drugs or fever.

delirium /dɪ'lɪriəm/ *noun* a mental state in which someone is confused, excited and restless and has hallucinations

delirium tremens /dɪˌlɪriəm 'triːmenz/, **delirium alcoholicum** /dɪˌlɪriəm ˌælkə'hɒlɪkəm/ *noun* a state of mental illness usually found in long-term alcoholics who attempt to give up alcohol consumption. It includes hallucinations about insects, trembling and excitement. Abbr **DTs**

delivery /dɪ'lɪv(ə)ri/ *noun* the birth of a child

delivery bed /dɪ'lɪv(ə)ri bed/ *noun* a special bed on which a mother lies to give birth

delivery room /dɪ'lɪv(ə)ri ruːm/ *noun* a room in a hospital specially equipped for women to give birth

delta /'deltə/ *noun* the fourth letter of the Greek alphabet

delta hepatitis /ˌdeltə ˌhepə'taɪtɪs/ *noun* a severe form of hepatitis caused by an RNA virus in conjunction with the hepatitis B virus. Also called **hepatitis delta**

delta virus /ˌdeltə 'vaɪrəs/ *noun* the RNA virus which causes delta hepatitis

delta wave /'deltə weɪv/ *noun* a slow brain wave which is produced in the front of the brain by adults in deep sleep, registering a frequency of 3.5 hertz

deltoid /'deltɔɪd/, **deltoid muscle** /'deltɔɪd ˌmʌs(ə)l/ *noun* a big triangular muscle covering the shoulder joint and attached to the humerus, which lifts the arm sideways

deltoid tuberosity /ˌdeltɔɪd ˌtjuːbə'rɒsɪti/ *noun* a raised part of the humerus to which the deltoid muscle is attached

delusion /dɪ'luːʒ(ə)n/ *noun* a false belief which a person holds which cannot be changed by reason ○ *He suffered from the delusion that he was wanted by the police.*

dementia /dɪ'menʃə/ *noun* the loss of mental ability and memory due to organic disease of the brain, causing disorientation and personality changes

'AIDS dementia is a major complication of HIV infection, occurring in 70–90% of patients' [*British Journal of Nursing*]

dementia of the Alzheimer's type /dɪ ˌmenʃə əv ði 'æltshaɪməz ˌtaɪp/ *noun* a form of mental degeneration probably due to Alzheimer's disease

dementia paralytica /dɪˌmenʃə ˌpærə'lɪtɪkə/ *noun* mental degeneration due to the tertiary stage of syphilis

dementia praecox /dɪˌmenʃə 'priːkɒks/ *noun* same as **schizophrenia** (*old*)

dementing /dɪ'mentɪŋ/ *adjective* referring to someone with dementia

demi- /demi/ *prefix* half

demographic forecast /ˌdeməgræfɪk 'fɔːkɑːst/ *noun* a forecast of the numbers of people of different ages and sexes in an area at some time in the future

demography /dɪ'mɒgrəfi/ *noun* the study of populations and environments or changes affecting populations

demulcent /dɪ'mʌlsənt/ *noun* a soothing substance which relieves irritation in the stomach

demyelinating /diː'maɪəlɪneɪtɪŋ/ *adjective* relating to the destruction of the myelin sheath round nerve fibres

demyelination /diːˌmaɪəlɪ'neɪʃ(ə)n/ *noun* the destruction of the myelin sheath round nerve fibres, caused, e.g. by injury to the head, or as the main result of multiple sclerosis

denatured alcohol /diːˌneɪtʃəd 'ælkəhɒl/ *noun* ethyl alcohol such as methylated spirit, rubbing alcohol or surgical spirit with an additive, usually methyl alcohol, to make it unpleasant to drink

dendrite /'dendraɪt/ *noun* a branched structure growing out from a nerve cell, which receives impulses from the nerve endings of other nerve cells at synapses. See illustration at NEURONE in Supplement. Also called **dendron**

dendritic /den'drɪtɪk/ *adjective* referring to a dendrite

dendritic ulcer /den,drɪtɪk 'ʌlsə/ *noun* a branching ulcer on the cornea, caused by a herpesvirus

dendron /'dendrɒn/ *noun* same as **dendrite**

denervation /,di:nə'veɪʃ(ə)n/ *noun* the stopping or cutting of the nerve supply to a part of the body

dengue /'deŋgi/ *noun* a tropical disease caused by an arbovirus transmitted by mosquitoes, characterised by high fever, pains in the joints, headache and rash. Also called **breakbone fever**

denial /dɪ'naɪəl/ *noun* a person's refusal to accept that he or she has a serious medical problem

Denis Browne splint /,denɪs braʊn 'splɪnt/ *noun* a metal splint used to correct a club foot [Described 1934. After Sir Denis John Wolko Browne (1892–1967), Australian orthopaedic and general surgeon working in Britain.]

dens /denz/ *noun* a tooth, or something shaped like a tooth

dent- /dent/ *prefix* referring to a tooth or teeth

dental /'dent(ə)l/ *adjective* referring to teeth or to the treatment of teeth ○ *dental caries* ○ *dental surgeon*

dental care /'dent(ə)l keə/ *noun* the examination and treatment of teeth

dental caries /,dent(ə)l 'keəriz/ *noun* the rotting of a tooth. Also called **dental decay**

dental cyst /,dent(ə)l 'sɪst/ *noun* a cyst near the root of a tooth

dental decay /,dent(ə)l dɪ'keɪ/ *noun* same as **dental caries**

dental floss /'dent(ə)l flɒs/ *noun* a soft thread which can be pulled between the teeth to help keep them clean

dental hygiene /,dent(ə)l 'haɪdʒiːn/ *noun* procedures to keep the teeth clean and healthy

dental impaction /,dent(ə)l ɪm'pækʃ(ə)n/ *noun* a condition in which a tooth is closely pressed against other teeth and cannot grow normally

dental plaque /,dent(ə)l 'plæk/ *noun* a hard smooth bacterial deposit on teeth, which is the probable cause of caries

dental plate /'dent(ə)l pleɪt/ *noun* a prosthesis made to the shape of the mouth, which holds artificial teeth

dental prosthesis /,dent(ə)l prɒs'θiːsɪs/ *noun* one or more false teeth

dental pulp /,dent(ə)l 'pʌlp/ *noun* soft tissue inside a tooth

dental surgeon /'dent(ə)l ,sɜːdʒən/ *noun* a person who is qualified to practise surgery on teeth

dental surgery /'dent(ə)l ,sɜːdʒəri/ *noun* 1. the office and operating room of a dentist 2. surgery carried out on teeth

dentine /'dentiːn/ *noun* a hard substance which surrounds the pulp of teeth, beneath the enamel (NOTE: The US spelling is **dentin**.)

dentist /'dentɪst/ *noun* a person who is qualified to look after teeth and gums

dentistry /'dentɪstri/ *noun* the profession of a dentist, or the branch of medicine dealing with teeth and gums

dentition /den'tɪʃ(ə)n/ *noun* the number, arrangement and special characteristics of all the teeth in a person's jaws

COMMENT: Children have incisors, canines and molars, which are replaced over a period of years by the permanent teeth: eight incisors, four canines, eight premolars and twelve molars, the last four molars being called the wisdom teeth.

dentoid /'dentɔɪd/ *adjective* shaped like a tooth

denture /'dentʃə/ *noun* a set of false teeth, fixed to a device which fits inside the mouth

deodorant /di'əʊd(ə)rənt/ *noun* a substance which hides or prevents unpleasant smells ■ *adjective* hiding or preventing odours

deontology /,di:ɒn'tɒlədʒi/ *noun* the ethics of duty and of what is morally right or wrong

deoxygenate /di:'ɒksɪdʒəneɪt/ *verb* to remove oxygen from something

deoxygenated blood /di:,ɒksɪdʒəneɪt 'blʌd/ *noun* blood from which most of the oxygen has been removed by the tissues. It is darker than arterial oxygenated blood. Also called **venous blood**. Compare **deoxygenated blood**

deoxyribonucleic acid /di:,ɒksɪ,raɪbəʊ nju:,kli:ɪk 'æsɪd/ *noun* full form of **DNA**

Department of Health /dɪ,pɑːtmənt əv 'helθ/ *noun* in the UK, the government department in charge of health services. Abbr **DH**

dependant /dɪ'pendənt/ *noun* a person who is looked after or supported by someone else ○ *He has to support a family of six children and several dependants.*

dependence /dɪ'pendəns/, **dependency** /dɪ'pendənsi/ *noun* the fact of needing the support of something or someone such as a carer, nurse or doctor, or of being addicted to a drug

dependent /dɪ'pendənt/ *adjective* 1. needing the support of someone or something 2. addicted to a drug 3. referring to a part of the body which is hanging down

dependent relative /dɪ,pendənt 'relətɪv/ *noun* a person who is looked after by another member of the family

depersonalisation /di:,pɜːs(ə)n(ə)laɪ 'zeɪʃ(ə)n/, **depersonalization** *noun* a psychiatric state in which someone does not believe he or she is real

depilation /ˌdepɪ'leɪʃ(ə)n/ *noun* the removal of hair

depilatory /dɪ'pɪlət(ə)ri/ *noun* a substance which removes hair ■ *adjective* removing hair

depletion /dɪ'pliːʃ(ə)n/ *noun* the act or process of something being reduced

Depo-Provera a trademark for a progesterone derivative used in birth control and the treatment of endometriosis which is administered by three-monthly injection

deposit /dɪ'pɒzɪt/ *noun* a substance which is attached to part of the body ○ *Some foods leave a hard deposit on teeth.* ○ *A deposit of fat forms on the walls of the arteries.* ■ *verb* to attach a substance to part of the body ○ *Fat is deposited on the walls of the arteries.*

depressant /dɪ'pres(ə)nt/ *noun* a drug which reduces the activity of part of the body, e.g. a tranquilliser

depressed /dɪ'prest/ *adjective* **1.** experiencing a mental condition that prevents someone from carrying out the normal activities of life in the usual way □ **clinically depressed** Same as **depressed 2.** feeling miserable and worried (*informal*) ○ *He was depressed after his exam results.* **3.** referring to something such as a metabolic rate which is below the usual level

depressed fracture /dɪˌprest 'fræktʃə/ *noun* a fracture of a flat bone such as those in the skull where part of the bone has been pushed down lower than the surrounding parts

depression /dɪ'preʃ(ə)n/ *noun* **1.** a mental condition that prevents someone from carrying out the normal activities of life in the usual way **2.** a hollow on the surface of a part of the body

depressive /dɪ'presɪv/ *adjective* relating to, causing, or experiencing mental depression ○ *He is in a depressive state.* ■ *noun* **1.** a substance which causes depression **2.** someone experiencing depression

depressor /dɪ'presə/ *noun* **1.** a muscle which pulls part of the body downwards **2.** a nerve which reduces the activity of an organ such as the heart and lowers blood pressure

deprivation /ˌdeprɪ'veɪʃ(ə)n/ *noun* **1.** the fact of not being able to have something that you need or want ○ *sleep deprivation* **2.** the lack of basic necessities of life

deradenitis /dɪˌrædɪ'naɪtɪs/ *noun* inflammation of the lymph nodes in the neck

Dercum's disease /'dɜːkəmz dɪˌziːz/ *noun* same as **adiposis dolorosa** [Described 1888. After François Xavier Dercum (1856–1931), Professor of Neurology at Jefferson Medical College, Philadelphia, USA.]

derealisation /diːˌrɪəlaɪ'zeɪʃ(ə)n/, **derealization** *noun* a psychological state in which someone feels the world around him or her is not real

derivative /dɪ'rɪvətɪv/ *noun* a substance which is derived from another substance

derm- /dɜːm/ *prefix* same as **derma-** (*used before vowels*)

-derm /dɜːm/ *suffix* skin

derma- /dɜːmə/ *prefix* skin

dermal /'dɜːm(ə)l/ *adjective* referring to the skin

dermatitis /ˌdɜːmə'taɪtɪs/ *noun* inflammation of the skin

'…various types of dermal reaction to nail varnish have been noted. Also contact dermatitis caused by cosmetics such as toothpaste, soap, shaving creams.' [*Indian Journal of Medical Sciences*]

dermatitis artefacta /ˌdɜːmətaɪtɪs ˌɑːtɪ'fæktə/ *noun* injuries caused by someone to their own skin

dermatitis herpetiformis /ˌdɜːmətaɪtɪs hə ˌpetɪ'fɔːmɪs/ *noun* a type of dermatitis where large itchy blisters form on the skin

dermato- /dɜːmətəʊ/ *prefix* referring to the skin

dermatochalasis /ˌdɜːmətəʊkə'læsɪs/ *noun* a condition where a fold of skin moves down over the eyelid, common in older people

dermatographia /ˌdɜːmətəʊ'græfiə/ *noun* same as **dermographia**

dermatological /ˌdɜːmətə'lɒdʒɪk(ə)l/ *adjective* referring to dermatology

dermatologist /ˌdɜːmə'tɒlədʒɪst/ *noun* a doctor who specialises in the study and treatment of the skin and its diseases

dermatology /ˌdɜːmə'tɒlədʒi/ *noun* the study and treatment of the skin and its diseases

dermatome /'dɜːmətəʊm/ *noun* **1.** a special knife used for cutting thin sections of skin for grafting **2.** an area of skin supplied by one spinal nerve

dermatomycosis /ˌdɜːmətəʊmaɪ'kəʊsɪs/ *noun* a skin infection caused by a fungus that is not a dermatophyte

dermatomyositis /ˌdɜːmətəʊmaɪəʊ'saɪtɪs/ *noun* a collagen disease with a wasting inflammation of the skin and muscles

dermatophyte /'dɜːmətəʊfaɪt/ *noun* a fungus belonging to one of three genera which affect the skin or hair, causing tinea

dermatophytosis /ˌdɜːmətəʊfaɪ'təʊsɪs/ *noun* a fungal infection of the skin caused by a *dermatophyte*

dermatoplasty /'dɜːmətəʊplæsti/ *noun* a skin graft, replacing damaged skin by skin taken from another part of the body or from a donor

dermatosis /ˌdɜːmə'təʊsɪs/ *noun* a disease of the skin

dermis /'dɜːmɪs/ *noun* a thick layer of living skin beneath the epidermis. Also called **corium**

dermo- /dɜːməʊ/ *prefix* same as **derma-**

dermographia /ˌdɜːməˈgræfiə/ *noun* a swelling on the skin produced by pressing with a blunt instrument, usually an allergic reaction. Also called **dermatographia**

dermoid /ˈdɜːmɔɪd/ *adjective* 1. referring to the skin 2. like skin

dermoid cyst /ˈdɜːmɔɪd sɪst/ *noun* a cyst found under the skin, usually in the midline, containing hair, sweat glands and sebaceous glands

Descemet's membrane /deʃəˈmets ˌmembreɪn/ *noun* one of the deep layers of the cornea [Described 1785. After Jean Descemet (1732–1810), French physician; Professor of Anatomy and Surgery in Paris.]

descending aorta /dɪˌsendɪŋ eɪˈɔːtə/ *noun* the second section of the aorta, which turns downwards. Compare **ascending aorta**

descending colon /dɪˌsendɪŋ ˈkəʊlɒn/ *noun* the third section of the colon which goes down the left side of the body. Compare **ascending colon**. See illustration at DIGESTIVE SYSTEM in Supplement

descending tract /dɪˌsendɪŋ ˈtrækt/ *noun* a set of nerves which takes impulses away from the head

desensitisation /diːˌsensɪtaɪˈzeɪʃ(ə)n/, **desensitization** *noun* 1. the act of making someone or something no longer sensitive to something such as an allergen 2. the treatment of an allergy by giving a person injections of small quantities of the substance to which he or she is allergic over a period of time until they become immune to it

desensitise /diːˈsensətaɪz/, **desensitize** *verb* 1. to deaden a nerve and remove sensitivity ○ *The patient was prescribed a course of desensitising injections.* 2. to treat someone suffering from an allergy by giving graduated injections of the substance to which he or she is allergic over a period of time until they become immune to it

designer drug /dɪˈzaɪnə drʌg/ *noun* a drug that has been modified to enhance its properties (*informal*)

desogestrel /ˌdesəˈdʒestrəl/ *noun* a hormone used an as oral contraceptive

desquamate /ˈdeskwəmeɪt/ *verb* (*of skin*) to peel off, or be removed in layers

desquamation /ˌdeskwəˈmeɪʃ(ə)n/ *noun* 1. the continual process of losing the outer layer of dead skin 2. peeling off of the epithelial part of a structure

detach /dɪˈtætʃ/ *verb* to separate one thing from another ○ *an operation to detach the cusps of the mitral valve*

detached retina /dɪˌtætʃt ˈretɪnə/ *noun* a condition in which the retina becomes partially separated from the eyeball, causing loss of vision. Also called **retinal detachment**

COMMENT: A detached retina can be caused by a blow to the eye, or simply is a condition

occurring in old age. If left untreated the eye will become blind. A detached retina can sometimes be attached to the choroid again using lasers.

detect /dɪˈtekt/ *verb* to sense or to notice, usually something which is very small or difficult to see ○ *an instrument to detect microscopic changes in cell structure* ○ *The nurses detected a slight improvement in the patient's condition.*

detection /dɪˈtekʃən/ *noun* the action of detecting something ○ *the detection of sounds by nerves in the ears* ○ *the detection of a cyst using an endoscope*

detergent /dɪˈtɜːdʒənt/ *noun* a cleaning substance which removes grease and bacteria

COMMENT: Most detergents are not allergenic but some biological detergents which contain enzymes to remove protein stains can cause dermatitis.

deteriorate /dɪˈtɪəriəreɪt/ *verb* to become worse ○ *The patient's condition deteriorated rapidly.*

deterioration /dɪˌtɪəriəˈreɪʃ(ə)n/ *noun* the fact of becoming worse ○ *The nurses were worried by the deterioration in the patient's reactions.*

determine /dɪˈtɜːmɪn/ *verb* to find out something by examining the evidence ○ *Health inspectors are trying to determine the cause of the outbreak of Salmonella poisoning.*

detox /diːˈtɒks/ *noun* same as **detoxication** (*informal*)

detoxication /diːˌtɒksɪˈkeɪʃ(ə)n/, **detoxification** /diːˌtɒksɪfɪˈkeɪʃ(ə)n/ *noun* the removal of toxic substances to make a poisonous substance harmless

detrition /dɪˈtrɪʃ(ə)n/ *noun* the fact of wearing away by rubbing or use

detritus /dɪˈtraɪtəs/ *noun* rubbish produced when something disintegrates

detrusor muscle /dɪˈtruːzə ˌmʌs(ə)l/ *noun* the muscular coat of the urinary bladder

Dettol /ˈdetɒl/ *noun* a trade name for a disinfectant containing chloroxylenol

detumescence /ˌdiːtjuːˈmes(ə)ns/ *noun* 1. (*of the penis or clitoris after an erection or orgasm*) the process of becoming limp 2. (*of a swelling*) the process of disappearing

deuteranopia /ˌdjuːtərəˈnəʊpiə/ *noun* a form of colour blindness in which someone cannot see green

develop /dɪˈveləp/ *verb* 1. to become larger and stronger, or more complex ○ *The embryo is developing normally.* ○ *A swelling developed under the armpit.* ○ *The sore throat developed into an attack of meningitis.* 2. to make something start to happen ○ *We're developing a new system for dealing with admission to A & E.* 3. to make something start to grow or become larger, stronger or more complex ○ *He does exercises to develop his muscles.* 4. to start to have an illness ○ *The baby* *may be developing a cold.* ○ *He developed complications and was rushed to hospital.*

'...rheumatoid arthritis is a chronic inflammatory disease which can affect many systems in the body, but mainly the joints. 70% of sufferers develop the condition in the metacarpophalangeal joints.' [*Nursing Times*]

development /dɪ'veləpmənt/ *noun* **1.** the process of growing, or of becoming larger and stronger, or more complex ○ *The development of the embryo takes place in the uterus.* **2.** something which happens and causes a change in a situation ○ *Report any developments to me at once.*

developmental /dɪˌveləp'ment(ə)l/ *adjective* referring to the development of an embryo

developmental delay /dɪˈveləpmənt(ə)l dɪˌleɪ/ *noun* the fact of being later than usual in developing, either physically or psychologically

deviance /'diːviəns/ *noun* sexual behaviour which is considered unusual

deviated nasal septum /ˌdiːvieɪtɪd ˌneɪz(ə)l 'septəm/, **deviated septum** /ˌdiːvieɪtɪd 'septəm/ *noun* an unusual position of the septum of the nose which may block the nose and cause nosebleeds

deviation /ˌdiːvi'eɪʃ(ə)n/ *noun* **1.** the fact of being different from what is usual or expected or something which is different from what is usual or expected **2.** an unusual position of a joint or of the eye, as in strabismus

Devic's disease /də'vɪks dɪˌziːz/ *noun* same as **neuromyelitis optica** [Described 1894. After Devic, a French physician who died in 1930.]

dexamethasone /ˌdeksə'meθəsəʊn/ *noun* a synthetic steroid drug that is used to treat inflammation and hormonal imbalances

Dexa scan *noun* a technique to assess changes in someone's bone density, as in osteoporosis or in Paget's disease. Full form **Dual Energy X-Ray Absorptiometry**

dextro- /dekstrəʊ/ *prefix* referring to the right, or the right side of the body

dextrocardia /ˌdekstrəʊ'kɑːdiə/ *noun* a congenital condition in which the apex of the heart is towards the right of the body instead of the left. Compare **laevocardia**

dextromoramide /ˌdekstrə'mɔːrəmaɪd/ *noun* an opioid drug used to reduce pain

dextrose /'dekstrəʊz/ *noun* same as **glucose**

DH *abbr* Department of Health

dhobie itch /ˌdəʊbi 'ɪtʃ/ *noun* same as **tinea cruris**

DI *abbr* donor insemination

di- /daɪ/ *prefix* two, double

dia- /daɪə/ *prefix* **1.** through or throughout **2.** across **3.** in different or opposite directions **4.** apart

diabetes /ˌdaɪə'biːtiːz/ *noun* **1.** one of a group of diseases which cause the body to pro-

duce large amounts of urine. ◊ **gestational diabetes 2.** same as **diabetes mellitus**

diabetes insipidus /ˌdaɪəˌbiːtiːz ɪn'sɪpɪdəs/ *noun* a rare disorder of the pituitary gland causing an inadequate amount of the hormone vasopressin, which controls urine production, to be produced, leading to excessive passing of urine and extreme thirst

diabetes mellitus /ˌdaɪəˌbiːtiːz 'melɪtəs/ *noun* a disease where the body cannot control sugar absorption because the pancreas does not secrete enough insulin

COMMENT: Diabetes mellitus has two forms: Type I may have a viral trigger caused by an infection which affects the cells in the pancreas which produce insulin; Type II is caused by a lower sensitivity to insulin, is common in older people, and is associated with obesity. Symptoms of diabetes mellitus are tiredness, unusual thirst, frequent passing of water and sweet-smelling urine. Blood and urine tests show high levels of sugar. Treatment for Type II diabetes involves keeping to a strict diet and reducing weight, and sometimes the use of oral hypoglycaemic drugs such as glibenclamide. Type II diabetes is treated with regular injections of insulin.

diabetic /ˌdaɪə'betɪk/ *adjective* **1.** referring to diabetes mellitus **2.** referring to food which contains few carbohydrates and sugar ○ *diabetic chocolate* ■ *noun* a person who has diabetes

diabetic cataract /ˌdaɪəbetɪk 'kætərækt/ *noun* a cataract which develops in people who have diabetes

diabetic coma /ˌdaɪəbetɪk 'kəʊmə/ *noun* a state of unconsciousness caused by untreated diabetes

diabetic diet /ˌdaɪəbetɪk 'daɪət/ *noun* a diet which is low in carbohydrates and sugar

diabetic retinopathy /ˌdaɪəbetɪk retɪ'nɒpəθi/ *noun* a disease of the retina, caused by diabetes

diabetogenic /ˌdaɪəbetə'dʒenɪk/ *adjective* which causes diabetes

diabetologist /ˌdaɪəbe'tɒlədʒɪst/ *noun* a doctor specialising in the treatment of diabetes mellitus

diaclasia /ˌdaɪə'kleɪziə/ *noun* a fracture made by a surgeon to repair an earlier fracture which has set badly, or to correct a deformity

diadochokinesis /daɪˌædəkəʊkaɪ'niːsɪs/ *noun* the natural ability to make muscles move limbs in opposite directions

diagnose /'daɪəgnəʊz/ *verb* to identify a condition or illness, by examining the person and noting symptoms ○ *The doctor diagnosed appendicitis.* ○ *The patient was diagnosed with rheumatism.*

diagnosis /ˌdaɪəg'nəʊsɪs/ *noun* the act of diagnosing a condition or illness ○ *The doctor's diagnosis was a viral infection, but the child's parents asked for a second opinion.* ○ *They* *found it difficult to make a diagnosis.* Compare **prognosis** (NOTE: The plural is **diagnoses**.)

diagnostic /ˌdaɪəgˈnɒstɪk/ *adjective* referring to diagnosis

diagnostic and treatment centre /ˌdaɪəgnɒstɪk ən ˈtriːtmənt ˌsentə/ *noun* a facility mainly for day surgery or short-term stay, where a range of planned operations such as joint replacements, hernia repair and cataract removal can be undertaken. Abbr **DTC**

diagnostic imaging /ˌdaɪəgnɒstɪk ˈɪmɪdʒɪŋ/ *noun* scanning for the purpose of diagnosis, e.g. of a pregnant woman to see if the fetus is healthy

diagnostic process /ˌdaɪəgˌnɒstɪk ˈprəʊsəs/ *noun* the series of steps taken in making a diagnosis

diagnostic radiographer *noun* ♦ **radiographer**

diagnostic test /ˌdaɪəgnɒstɪk ˈtest/ *noun* a test which helps a doctor diagnose an illness

dialysate /daɪˈælɪsət/ *noun* material which is subjected to dialysis

dialyse /ˈdaɪəlaɪz/ *verb* to treat someone using a kidney machine

dialyser /ˈdaɪəlaɪzə/ *noun* an apparatus which uses a membrane to separate solids from liquids, e.g. a kidney machine

dialysis /daɪˈæləsɪs/ *noun* **1.** a procedure in which a membrane is used as a filter to separate soluble waste substances from the blood **2.** same as **renal dialysis**

diapedesis /ˌdaɪəpɪˈdiːsɪs/ *noun* the movement of white blood cells through the walls of the capillaries into tissues in the development of inflammation

diaphoresis /ˌdaɪəfəˈriːsɪs/ *noun* excessive perspiration

diaphoretic /ˌdaɪəfəˈretɪk/ *noun* a drug which causes sweating ■ *adjective* causing sweating

diaphragm /ˈdaɪəfræm/ *noun* **1.** a thin layer of tissue stretched across an opening, especially the flexible sheet of muscle and fibre which separates the chest from the abdomen and moves to pull air into the lungs in respiration **2.** same as **vaginal diaphragm**

COMMENT: The diaphragm is a muscle which, in breathing, expands and contracts with the walls of the chest. The average rate of respiration is about 16 times a minute.

diaphragmatic /ˌdaɪəfrægˈmætɪk/ *adjective* referring to a diaphragm, or like a diaphragm

diaphragmatic hernia /ˌdaɪəfrægmætɪk ˈhɜːniə/ *noun* a condition in which a membrane and organ in the abdomen pass through an opening in the diaphragm into the chest

diaphragmatic pleura /ˌdaɪəfrægmætɪk ˈplʊərə/ *noun* part of the pleura which covers the diaphragm

diaphragmatic pleurisy /ˌdaɪəfrægmætɪk ˈplʊərɪsi/ *noun* inflammation of the pleura which covers the diaphragm

diaphyseal /ˌdaɪəˈfɪziəl/ *adjective* referring to a diaphysis

diaphysis /daɪˈæfəsɪs/ *noun* the long central part of a long bone. Also called **shaft**. See illustration at **BONE MARROW** in Supplement

diaphysitis /ˌdaɪəfəˈsaɪtɪs/ *noun* inflammation of the diaphysis, often associated with rheumatic disease

diarrhoea /ˌdaɪəˈriːə/ *noun* a condition in which someone frequently passes liquid faeces ○ *attack of diarrhoea* ○ *mild/severe diarrhoea* (NOTE: The US spelling is **diarrhea**.)

COMMENT: Diarrhoea can have many causes: types of food or allergy to food; contaminated or poisoned food; infectious diseases, such as dysentery; sometimes worry or other emotions.

diarrhoeal /ˌdaɪəˈriəl/ *adjective* referring to or caused by diarrhoea

diarthrosis /ˌdaɪɑːˈθrəʊsɪs/ *noun* same as **synovial joint**

diastase /ˈdaɪəsteɪz/ *noun* an enzyme which breaks down starch and converts it into sugar

diastasis /ˌdaɪəˈsteɪsɪs/ *noun* **1.** a condition in which a bone separates into parts **2.** dislocation of bones at an immovable joint

diastema /ˌdaɪəˈstiːmə/ *noun* **1.** an unusually wide space between adjacent teeth **2.** an unusual gap in any body part or organ

diastole /daɪˈæstəli/ *noun* the part of the process involved in each beat of the heart when its chambers expand and fill with blood. The period of diastole (usually 95 mmHg) lasts about 0.4 seconds in an average heart rate. Compare **systole**

diastolic /ˌdaɪəˈstɒlɪk/ *adjective* relating to the diastole

diastolic pressure /ˌdaɪəstɒlɪk ˈpreʃə/ *noun* blood pressure taken at the diastole (NOTE: Diastolic pressure is always lower than systolic.)

diathermy /ˌdaɪəˈθɜːmi/ *noun* the use of high-frequency electric current to produce heat in body tissue

COMMENT: The difference between medical and surgical uses of diathermy is in the size of the electrodes used. Two large electrodes will give a warming effect over a large area (**medical diathermy**); if one of the electrodes is small, the heat will be concentrated enough to coagulate tissue (**surgical diathermy**).

diathermy knife /ˌdaɪəˈθɜːmi naɪf/ *noun* a knife used in surgical diathermy

diathermy needle /daɪəˌθɜːmi ˈniːd(ə)l/ *noun* a needle used in surgical diathermy

diathermy snare /ˌdaɪəˈθɜːmi sneə/ *noun* a snare which is heated by electrodes and burns away tissue

diathesis /daɪˈæθəsɪs/ *noun* the general inherited constitution of a person in relation to their susceptibility to specific diseases or allergies

diazepam /daɪˈæzəpæm/ *noun* a tranquilliser used in the short term to treat anxiety and as a muscle relaxant. In the long term it is potentially addictive.

diazoxide /ˌdaɪəˈzɒksaɪd/ *noun* a drug used as a vasodilator, to reduce hypertension

DIC *abbr* disseminated intravascular coagulation

dicephalus /daɪˈsefələs/ *noun* a fetus with two heads

dichlorphenamide /ˌdaɪklɔːˈfenəmaɪd/ *noun* a drug used to treat glaucoma

dichromatism /ˌdaɪkrəʊˈmætɪz(ə)m/ *noun* colour blindness in which only two of the three primary colours can be seen. Compare **monochromatism, trichromatism**

diclofenac sodium /ˌdaɪkləʊfenæk ˈsəʊdiəm/ *noun* an anti-inflammatory drug used to treat rheumatic disease

dicrotic pulse /daɪˌkrɒtɪk ˈpʌls/, **dicrotic wave** /daɪˌkrɒtɪk ˈweɪv/ *noun* a pulse which occurs twice with each heartbeat

dicrotism /ˈdaɪkrətɪz(ə)m/ *noun* a condition in which the pulse occurs twice with each heartbeat

die /daɪ/ *verb* to stop living ○ *His father died last year.* ○ *She died in a car crash.* (NOTE: **dying – died**)

diencephalon /ˌdaɪenˈsefələn, ˌdaɪen ˈkefəlɒn/ *noun* the central part of the forebrain, formed of the thalamus, hypothalamus, pineal gland and third ventricle

diet /ˈdaɪət/ *noun* the amount and type of food eaten ○ *a balanced diet* ■ *verb* to reduce the quantity of food you eat, or to change the type of food you eat, in order to become thinner or healthier ○ *He is dieting to try to lose weight.*

dietary /ˈdaɪət(ə)ri/ *noun* a system of nutrition and energy ○ *The nutritionist supervised the dietaries for the patients.* ■ *adjective* referring to a diet

dietary fibre /ˈdaɪət(ə)ri ˌfaɪbə/ *noun* fibrous matter in food, which cannot be digested. Also called **roughage**

COMMENT: Dietary fibre is found in cereals, nuts, fruit and some green vegetables. There are two types of fibre in food: insoluble fibre, e.g. in bread and cereals, which is not digested, and soluble fibre, e.g. in vegetables and pulses. Foods with the highest proportion of fibre include wholemeal bread, beans and dried apricots. Fibre is thought to be necessary to help digestion and avoid developing constipation, obesity and appendicitis.

dietetic /ˌdaɪəˈtetɪk/ *adjective* referring to diets

dietetic principles /ˌdaɪətetɪk ˈprɪnsəp(ə)lz/ *noun* rules concerning the body's needs in food, vitamins or trace elements

dietetics /ˌdaɪəˈtetɪks/ *noun* the study of food, nutrition and health, especially when applied to people's food intake

dieting /ˈdaɪətɪŋ/ *noun* the act of attempting to reduce weight by reducing the amount of food eaten ○ *Eat sensibly and get plenty of exercise, then there should be no need for dieting.*

dietitian /ˌdaɪəˈtɪʃ(ə)n/ *noun* someone who specialises in the study of diet, especially someone in a hospital who supervises dietaries as part of the medical treatment of patients. ◊ **nutritionist**

Dietl's crisis /ˈdiːt(ə)lz ˌkraɪsɪs/ *noun* a painful blockage of the ureter, causing back pressure on the kidney which fills with urine and swells [After Joseph Dietl (1804–78), Polish physician]

diet sheet /ˈdaɪət ʃiːt/ *noun* a list of suggestions for quantities and types of food given to someone to follow

differential /ˌdɪfəˈrenʃəl/ *adjective* referring to a difference

differential blood count /ˌdɪfərenʃəl ˈblʌd ˌkaʊnt/, **differential white cell count** /ˌdɪfərenʃəl ˈwaɪt sel ˌkaʊnt/ *noun* a test that shows the amounts of different types of white blood cell in a blood sample

differential diagnosis /ˌdɪfəˌrenʃ(ə)l ˌdaɪəgˈnəʊsɪs/ *noun* the identification of one disease from a number of other similar diseases by comparing the range of symptoms of each

differentiation /ˌdɪfərenʃiˈeɪʃ(ə)n/ *noun* the development of specialised cells during the early embryo stage

diffuse *verb* /dɪˈfjuːz/ to spread through tissue, or cause something to spread ○ *Some substances easily diffuse through the walls of capillaries.* ■ *adjective* /dɪˈfjuːs/ referring to a disease which is widespread in the body, or which affects many organs or cells

diffusion /dɪˈfjuːʒ(ə)n/ *noun* **1.** the process of mixing a liquid with another liquid, or a gas with another gas **2.** the passing of a liquid or gas through a membrane

digest /daɪˈdʒest/ *verb* to break down food in the alimentary canal and convert it into components which are absorbed into the body

digestible /daɪˈdʒestɪb(ə)l/ *adjective* able to be digested ○ *Glucose is an easily digestible form of sugar.*

digestion /daɪˈdʒestʃ(ə)n/ *noun* the process by which food is broken down in the alimentary canal into components which can be absorbed by the body

digestive /daɪˈdʒestɪv/ *adjective* relating to digestion

digestive enzyme /daɪˌdʒestɪv ˈenzaɪm/ *noun* an enzyme which encourages digestion

digestive juice /daɪ'dʒestɪv juːs/ *noun* ♦ gastric juice, intestinal juice (*usually plural*)

digestive system /daɪ'dʒestɪv ˌsɪstəm/ *noun* the set of organs such as the stomach, liver and pancreas which are associated with the digestion of food. Also called **alimentary system**

digestive tract /daɪ'dʒestɪv trækt/ *noun* same as **alimentary canal**

digestive tube /daɪ'dʒestɪv tjuːb/ *adjective* US same as **alimentary canal**

digit /'dɪdʒɪt/ *noun* **1.** a finger or a toe **2.** a number

digital /'dɪdʒɪt(ə)l/ *adjective* **1.** referring to fingers or toes **2.** representing data or physical quantities in numerical form

digitalin /ˌdɪdʒɪ'teɪlɪn/, **digitalis** /ˌdɪdʒɪ'teɪlɪs/ *noun* a drug derived from foxglove leaves, used in small doses to treat heart conditions

digitalise /'dɪdʒɪtəlaɪz/, **digitalize** *verb* to treat someone who has heart failure with digoxin

digital palpation /ˌdɪdʒɪt(ə)l pæl'peɪʃ(ə)n/ *noun* an examination of part of the body by feeling it with the fingers

digital vein /'dɪdʒɪt(ə)l veɪn/ *noun* a vein draining the fingers or toes

digitoxin /ˌdɪdʒɪ'tɒksɪn/ *noun* an extract of foxglove leaves, used as a drug to stimulate the heart in cases of heart failure or irregular heartbeat

digoxin /daɪ'dʒɒksɪn/ *noun* an extract of foxglove leaves, which acts more rapidly than digitoxin when used as a heart stimulant

dihydrocodeine tartrate /daɪˌhaɪdrəʊ ˌkəʊdiːn 'tɑːtreɪt/ *noun* an analgesic used to treat severe pain

dilatation /ˌdaɪleɪ'teɪʃ(ə)n/, **dilation** /daɪ 'leɪʃ(ə)n/ *noun* **1.** the act of making a hollow space or a passage in the body bigger or wider ○ *dilatation of the cervix during labour* **2.** expansion of the pupil of the eye as a reaction to bad light or to drugs

dilatation and curettage /ˌdaɪleɪˌteɪʃ(ə)n ən kjʊə'retɪdʒ/ *noun* a surgical operation to scrape the interior of the uterus to obtain a tissue sample or to remove products of miscarriage. Abbr **D & C**

dilate /daɪ'leɪt, dɪ'leɪt/ *verb* to become wider or larger, or make something become wider or larger ○ *The veins in the left leg have become dilated.* ○ *The drug is used to dilate the pupil of the eye.*

dilator /daɪ'leɪtə/ *noun* **1.** an instrument used to widen the entrance to a cavity **2.** a drug used to make part of the body expand

dilator pupillae muscle /daɪˌleɪtə pjuː'pɪli ˌmʌs(ə)l/ *noun* a muscle in the iris which pulls the iris back and so makes the pupil expand

diltiazem hydrochloride /dɪlˌtaɪəzəm ˌhaɪdrə'klɔːraɪd/ *noun* a calcium channel blocker used to treat hypertension

diluent /'dɪljuənt/ *noun* a substance which is used to dilute a liquid, e.g. water

dilute /daɪ'luːt/ *adjective* with water added ■ *verb* to add water to a liquid to make it less concentrated ○ *Dilute the disinfectant in four parts of water.*

dilution /daɪ'luːʃ(ə)n/ *noun* **1.** the action of diluting **2.** a liquid which has been diluted

dimenhydrinate /ˌdaɪmen'haɪdrəneɪt/ *noun* an antihistamine drug that relieves travel sickness

dimetria /daɪ'miːtriə/ *noun* a condition in which a woman has a double uterus

dioptre /daɪ'ɒptə/ *noun* a unit of measurement of the refraction of a lens (NOTE: The US spelling is **diopter**.)

COMMENT: A one dioptre lens has a focal length of one metre; the greater the dioptre, the shorter the focal length.

dioxide /daɪ'ɒksaɪd/ ♦ **carbon dioxide**

dioxin /daɪ'ɒksɪn/ *noun* an extremely poisonous gas

DIP *abbr* distal interphalangeal joint

diphenoxalate /ˌdaɪfen'ɒksɪleɪt/ *noun* a drug related to pethidine that is used to treat diarrhoea, sometimes mixed with a little atropine in commercial preparations

diphtheria /dɪf'θɪəriə/ *noun* a serious infectious disease of children, caused by the bacillus *Corynebacterium diphtheriae*, characterised by fever and the formation of a fibrous growth like a membrane in the throat which restricts breathing

COMMENT: Symptoms of diphtheria are a sore throat, followed by a slight fever, rapid pulse and swelling of glands in the neck. The 'membrane' which forms can close the air passages, and the disease is often fatal, either because the patient is asphyxiated or because the heart becomes fatally weakened. The disease is also highly infectious, and all contacts of the patient must be tested. The Schick test is used to test if a person is immune or susceptible to diphtheria. In countries where infants are immunised the disease is rare.

diphtheroid /'dɪfθərɔɪd/ *adjective* referring to a bacterium similar to the diphtheria bacterium

-dipine /dɪpɪn/ *suffix* used in the names of calcium channel blockers ○ *nifedipine*

dipl- /dɪpl/ *prefix* same as **diplo-** (*used before vowels*)

diplacusis /ˌdɪplə'kjuːsɪs/ *noun* a disorder of the cochlea in which a person hears one sound as two sounds of different pitch

diplegia /daɪ'pliːdʒə/ *noun* paralysis of a similar part on both sides of the body, e.g. paralysis of both arms. Compare **hemiplegia**

diplegic /daɪ'pliːdʒɪk/ *adjective* referring to diplegia

diplo- /ˈdɪpləʊ/ *prefix* double

diplococcus /ˌdɪpləʊˈkɒkəs/ *noun* a bacterium which usually occurs in pairs as a result of incomplete cell division, e.g. a pneumococcus (NOTE: The plural is **diplococci**.)

diploe /ˈdɪpləʊiː/ *noun* a layer of spongy bone tissue filled with red bone marrow, between the inner and outer layers of the skull

diploid /ˈdɪplɔɪd/ *adjective* referring to a cell where there are two copies of each chromosome, except the sex chromosome. In humans the diploid number of chromosomes is 46.

diplopia /dɪˈpləʊpiə/ *noun* a condition in which someone sees single objects as double. Also called **double vision**

dipsomania /ˌdɪpsəʊˈmeɪniə/ *noun* an uncontrollable desire to drink alcohol

direct contact /dɪˌrekt ˈkɒntækt/ *noun* a situation where someone or something physically touches an infected person or object

directions /daɪˈrekʃənz/ *noun* □ **directions for use** (*on a bottle of medicine, etc.*) instructions showing how to use something and how much of it to use

director /daɪˈrektə/ *noun* an instrument used to limit the incision made with a surgical knife

dis- /dɪs/ *prefix* **1.** undoing or reversal **2.** removal from **3.** lacking or deprived of

disability /ˌdɪsəˈbɪlɪti/ *noun* a condition in which part of the body does not function in the usual way and makes some activities difficult or impossible. ◊ **learning disability**

'…disability – any restriction or lack (resulting from an impairment) of ability to perform an activity in the manner or within the range considered normal for a human being' [*WHO*]

disable /dɪsˈeɪb(ə)l/ *verb* to make someone unable to do some activity ○ *He was disabled by a lung disease.*

disabled /dɪsˈeɪb(ə)ld/ *noun* people suffering from a physical or mental condition which makes some activities difficult or impossible

Disabled Living Foundation /dɪsˌeɪb(ə)ld ˈlɪvɪŋ faʊnˌdeɪʃ(ə)n/ *noun* a charity which aims to help disabled people live independently

disablement /dɪsˈeɪb(ə)lmənt/ *noun* a condition which makes some activities difficult or impossible

disabling disease /dɪsˌeɪblɪŋ dɪˈziːz/ *noun* a disease which makes some activities difficult or impossible

disarticulation /ˌdɪsɑːtɪkjʊˈleɪʃ(ə)n/ *noun* the amputation of a limb at a joint, which does not involve dividing a bone

disc /dɪsk/ *noun* a flat round structure. ◊ **intervertebral disc**

discharge *noun* /ˈdɪstʃɑːdʒ/ **1.** the secretion of liquid from an opening **2.** the process of sending a patient away from a hospital because the treatment has ended ■ *verb* /dɪsˈtʃɑːdʒ/ **1.** to secrete liquid out of an opening ○ *The*

wound discharged a thin stream of pus. **2.** to send a patient away from hospital because the treatment has ended ○ *He was discharged from hospital last week.* □ **to discharge yourself** to decide to leave hospital and stop taking the treatment provided

discharge planning /ˈdɪstʃɑːdʒ ˌplænɪŋ/ *noun* the work of making a plan for when a patient leaves hospital to live at home

discharge rate /ˈdɪstʃɑːdʒ reɪt/ *noun* the number of patients with a particular type of disorder who are sent home from hospitals in a particular area (shown as the number per 10,000 of population)

discoloration /dɪsˌkʌləˈreɪʃ(ə)n/ *noun* a change in colour

discolour /dɪsˈkʌlə/ *verb* to change the colour of something ○ *His teeth were discoloured from smoking cigarettes.* (NOTE: The US spelling is **discolor**.)

COMMENT: Teeth can be discoloured in fluorosis. If the skin on the lips is discoloured it may indicate that the person has swallowed a poison.

discomfort /dɪsˈkʌmfət/ *noun* a feeling of mild pain ○ *You may experience some discomfort after the operation.*

discrete /dɪˈskriːt/ *adjective* separate, not joined together

discrete rash /dɪˌskriːt ˈræʃ/ *noun* a rash which is formed of many separate spots, which do not join together into one large red patch

disease /dɪˈziːz/ *noun* a condition that stops the body from functioning in the usual way ○ *an infectious disease* ○ *She is suffering from a very serious disease of the kidneys* or *from a serious kidney disease.* ○ *He is a specialist in occupational diseases.* (NOTE: The term **disease** is applied to all physical and mental reactions which make a person ill. Diseases with distinct characteristics have individual names. For other terms referring to disease, see words beginning with **path-**, **patho-**.)

diseased /dɪˈziːzd/ *adjective* affected by a disease ○ *The surgeon cut away the diseased tissue.*

disfigure /dɪsˈfɪɡə/ *verb* to change someone's appearance so as to make it less pleasant to look at ○ *Her legs were disfigured by scars.*

dish /dɪʃ/ *noun* a shallow open container

disinfect /ˌdɪsɪnˈfekt/ *verb* to make the surface of something or somewhere free from microorganisms ○ *She disinfected the skin with surgical spirit.* ○ *All the patient's clothes have to be disinfected.*

disinfectant /ˌdɪsɪnˈfektənt/ *noun* a substance used to kill microorganisms on the surface of something

disinfection /ˌdɪsɪnˈfekʃən/ *noun* the removal of microorganisms on the surface of something

COMMENT: The words **disinfect, disinfectant,** and **disinfection** are used for substances which destroy microorganisms on instruments, objects or the skin. Substances used to kill microorganisms inside infected people are **antibiotics.**

disinfest /ˌdɪsɪnˈfest/ verb to free a place, person or animal from insects or other pests

disinfestation /ˌdɪsɪnfeˈsteɪʃ(ə)n/ noun the removal of insects or other pests from a place, person or animal

dislocate /ˈdɪsləkeɪt/ verb to displace a bone from its usual position at a joint, or to become displaced ○ He fell and dislocated his elbow. ○ The shoulder joint dislocates easily.

dislocation /ˌdɪsləˈkeɪʃ(ə)n/ noun a condition in which a bone is displaced from its usual position at a joint. Also called **luxation**

dismember /dɪsˈmembə/ verb to cut off or pull off someone's arms or legs, often violently or in an accident

dismemberment /dɪsˈmembəmənt/ noun the state of being dismembered

disorder /dɪsˈɔːdə/ noun a condition in which part of the body is not functioning correctly ○ The doctor specialises in disorders of the kidneys or in kidney disorders.

disordered /dɪsˈɔːdəd/ adjective not functioning correctly

disordered action of the heart /dɪsˌɔːdəd ˈækʃən əv ðiː hɑːt/ noun a condition in which someone has palpitations, breathlessness and dizziness, caused by effort or worry. Also called **da Costa's syndrome, cardiac neurosis.** Abbr **DAH**

disorientated /dɪsˈɔːriənˌteɪtɪd/ adjective referring to someone who is confused and does not know where he or she is

disorientation /ˌdɪsɔːriənˈteɪʃ(ə)n/ noun a condition in which someone is confused and does not know where he or she is

dispensary /dɪsˈpensəri/ noun a place where drugs are prepared or mixed and given out according to a doctor's prescription, e.g. part of a chemist's shop or a department in a hospital

dispense /dɪsˈpens/ verb to supply medicine according to a prescription

dispenser /dɪsˈpensə/ noun someone who supplies medicine according to a prescription, especially in a hospital

dispensing optician /dɪsˈpensɪŋ ɒpˈtɪʃ(ə)n/ noun a person who fits and sells glasses but does not test eyes

dispensing practice /dɪsˈpensɪŋ ˌpræktɪs/ noun a doctor's practice which dispenses prescribed medicines to its patients

displace /dɪsˈpleɪs/ verb to put something out of its usual place

displaced intervertebral disc /dɪsˌpleɪsd ɪntəˌvɜːtɪbr(ə)l ˈdɪsk/ noun a disc which has moved slightly, so that the soft interior passes through the tougher exterior and causes pressure on a nerve

displacement /dɪsˈpleɪsmənt/ noun the fact of being moved out of the usual position ○ fracture of the radius together with displacement of the wrist

disposable /dɪsˈpəʊzəb(ə)l/ adjective designed to be thrown away after use ○ disposable syringes

disposition /ˌdɪspəˈzɪʃ(ə)n/ noun a person's general character or tendency to act in a particular way

disproportion /ˌdɪsprəˈpɔːʃ(ə)n/ noun a lack of proper relationships between two things

dissecans /ˈdɪsəkænz/ ♦ osteochondritis dissecans

dissect /daɪˈsekt/ verb to cut and separate tissues in a body to examine them

dissecting aneurysm /ˌdaɪsektɪŋ ˈænjəˌrɪz(ə)m/ noun an aneurysm which occurs when the inside wall of the aorta is torn and blood enters the membrane

dissection /daɪˈsekʃən/ noun the action of cutting and separating parts of a body or an organ as part of a surgical operation, an autopsy or a course of study

'…renal dissection usually takes from 40–60 minutes, while liver and pancreas dissections take from one to three hours. Cardiac dissection takes about 20 minutes and lung dissection takes 60 to 90 minutes.' [Nursing Times]

disseminated /dɪˈsemɪneɪtɪd/ adjective occurring in every part of an organ or in the whole body

disseminated intravascular coagulation /dɪˌsemɪneɪtɪd ɪntrəˌvæskʊlə kəʊˌæɡjʊˈleɪʃ(ə)n/ noun a disorder that causes extensive clot formation in the blood vessels, followed by severe bleeding. Abbr **DIC**

disseminated lupus erythematosus /dɪˌsemɪneɪtɪd ˌluːpəs ˌerɪθiːməˈtəʊsɪs/ noun an inflammatory disease where a skin rash is associated with widespread changes in the central nervous system, the cardiovascular system and many organs. Abbr **DLE**

disseminated sclerosis /dɪˌsemɪneɪtɪd skləˈrəʊsɪs/ noun same as **multiple sclerosis**

dissemination /dɪˌsemɪˈneɪʃ(ə)n/ noun the fact of being widespread throughout the body

dissociate /dɪˈsəʊsieɪt/ verb 1. to separate parts or functions 2. in psychiatry, to separate part of the conscious mind from the rest

dissociated anaesthesia /dɪˌsəʊsiˌeɪtɪd ˌænəsˈθiːziə/ noun a loss of sensitivity to heat, pain or cold

dissociation /dɪˌsəʊʃiˈeɪʃ(ə)n/ noun 1. the separation of parts or functions 2. (in psychiatry) a condition in which part of the consciousness becomes separated from the rest and becomes independent

dissociative disorder /dɪˈsəʊsɪətɪv dɪs
ˌɔːdə/ *noun* a type of hysteria in which someone shows psychological changes such as a
split personality or amnesia rather than physical ones

dissolve /dɪˈzɒlv/ *verb* to absorb or disperse
something in liquid ○ *The gut used in sutures
slowly dissolves in the body fluids.*

distal /ˈdɪst(ə)l/ *adjective* further away from
the centre of a body

distal convoluted tubule /ˌdɪst(ə)l
ˌkɒnvəluːtɪd ˈtjuːbjuːl/ *noun* a part of the
kidney filtering system before the collecting
ducts

Distalgesic /ˌdɪst(ə)lˈdʒiːzɪk/ a trade name
for the analgesic co-proxamol

distal interphalangeal joint /ˌdɪst(ə)l
ˌɪntəfəˈlændʒɪəl ˌdʒɔɪnt/ *noun* a joint nearest
the end of the finger or toe. Abbr **DIP**

distally /ˈdɪst(ə)li/ *adverb* placed further
away from the centre or point of attachment.
Opposite **proximally**. See illustration at **ANA-
TOMICAL TERMS** in Supplement

distal phalanges /ˌdɪst(ə)l fəˈlændʒiːz/
noun bones nearest the ends of the fingers and
toes

distended /dɪˈstendɪd/ *adjective* made larger
by gas such as air, by liquid such as urine, or
by a solid

distended bladder /dɪˌstendɪd ˈblædə/
noun a bladder which is full of urine

distension /dɪsˈtenʃən/ *noun* a condition in
which something is swollen ○ *Distension of
the veins in the abdomen is a sign of blocking
of the portal vein.*

distichiasis /ˌdɪstɪˈkaɪəsɪs/ *noun* the presence of extra eyelashes, sometimes growing on
the meibomian glands

distil /dɪˈstɪl/ *verb* to separate the component
parts of a liquid by boiling and collecting the
condensed vapour

distillation /ˌdɪstɪˈleɪʃ(ə)n/ *noun* the action
of distilling a liquid

distilled water /dɪˌstɪld ˈwɔːtə/ *noun* water
which has had impurities by distillation

distort /dɪˈstɔːt/ *verb* to twist something into
an unusual shape ○ *His lower limbs were distorted by the disease.*

distortion /dɪˈstɔːʃ(ə)n/ *noun* the act of
twisting part of the body out of its usual shape

distraction /dɪˈstrækʃən/ *noun* **1.** something
that takes a person's attention away from
something else **2.** a state where someone is
very emotionally and mentally troubled

distress /dɪˈstres/ *noun* unhappiness caused
by pain or worry ○ *mental distress*

district general hospital /ˌdɪstrɪkt
ˌdʒen(ə)rəl ˈhɒspɪt(ə)l/ *noun* a hospital
which serves the needs of the population of a
specific district

district nurse /ˌdɪstrɪkt ˈnɜːs/ *noun* a nurse
who visits and treats people in their homes

disturb /dɪˈstɜːb/ *verb* **1.** to interrupt what
someone is doing ○ *Her sleep was disturbed
by the other patients in the ward.* **2.** to upset or
worry someone

disturbed /dɪˈstɜːbd/ *adjective* affected by a
psychiatric disorder ○ *severely disturbed children*

disulfiram /daɪˈsʌlfɪræm/ *noun* a drug used
to treat alcoholism by causing severe nausea if
alcohol is consumed with it

dithranol /ˈdɪθrənɒl/ *noun* an anti-inflammatory drug used to treat dermatitis and psoriasis

diuresis /ˌdaɪjʊˈriːsɪs/ *noun* an increase in
the production of urine

diuretic /ˌdaɪjʊˈretɪk/ *adjective* causing
kidneys to produce more urine ■ *noun* a substance which makes the kidneys produce more
urine and, in the treatment of oedema and hypertension

diurnal /daɪˈɜːn(ə)l/ *adjective* **1.** happening in
the daytime **2.** happening every day

divarication /daɪˌværɪˈkeɪʃ(ə)n/ *noun* **1.**
separation into widely spread branches **2.** the
point at which a structure forks or divides

divergence /daɪˈvɜːdʒəns/ *noun* **1.** a condition in which one eye points directly at the object of interest but the other does not **2.** the
process of moving apart to follow different
courses **3.** the amount of difference between
two quantities, especially where the difference
is unexpected **4.** a deviation from a typical behaviour pattern or expressed wish

divergent strabismus /daɪˌvɜːdʒənt strə
ˈbɪzməs/, **divergent squint** /daɪˌvɜːdʒənt
ˈskwɪnt/ *noun* a condition in which a person's
eyes both look away from the nose. Opposite
convergent strabismus

diverticula /ˌdaɪvəˈtɪkjʊlə/ plural of **diverticulum**

diverticular disease /ˌdaɪvəˈtɪkjʊlə dɪ
ˌziːz/ *noun* a disease of the large intestine,
where the colon thickens and diverticula form
in the walls, causing pain in the lower abdomen

diverticulitis /ˌdaɪvətɪkjʊˈlaɪtɪs/ *noun* inflammation of diverticula formed in the wall of
the colon

diverticulosis /ˌdaɪvətɪkjʊˈləʊsɪs/ *noun* a
condition in which diverticula form in the intestine but are not inflamed. In the small intestine, this can lead to blind loop syndrome.

diverticulum /ˌdaɪvəˈtɪkjʊləm/ *noun* a little
sac or pouch which develops in the wall of the
intestine or another organ (NOTE: The plural is
diverticula.)

division /dɪˈvɪʒ(ə)n/ *noun* the action of cutting or splitting into parts

divulsor /dɪˈvʌlsə/ *noun* a surgical instrument used to expand a passage in the body

dizygotic /ˌdaɪzaɪˈɡɒtɪk/ *adjective* developed from two separately fertilised eggs

dizygotic twins /ˌdaɪzaɪɡɒtɪk ˈtwɪnz/ *plural noun* twins who are not identical and not always of the same sex because they come from two different ova fertilised at the same time. Also called **fraternal twins**

dizziness /ˈdɪzɪnəs/ *noun* the feeling that everything is going round because the sense of balance has been affected

dizzy /ˈdɪzi/ *adjective* feeling that everything is going round because the sense of balance has been affected ○ *The ear infection made her feel dizzy for some time afterwards.* ○ *He experiences dizzy spells.*

dl *abbr* decilitre

DLE *abbr* disseminated lupus erythematosus

dm *abbr* decimetre

DMD *abbr US* doctor of dental medicine

DNA /ˌdiː en ˈeɪ/ *noun* one of the nucleic acids, the basic genetic material present in the nucleus of each cel. Full form **deoxyribonucleic acid**

DNA fingerprint /ˌdiː en eɪ ˈfɪŋɡəprɪnt/ *noun* same as **genetic fingerprint**

DNA fingerprinting /ˌdiː en eɪ ˈfɪŋɡə ˌprɪntɪŋ/ *noun* same as **genetic fingerprinting**

DNR *abbr* do not resuscitate

DOA *abbr* dead on arrival

dobutamine /dəʊˈbjuːtəmiːn/ *noun* a drug used to stimulate the heart

doctor /ˈdɒktə/ *noun* **1.** a person who has trained in medicine and is qualified to examine people when they are ill to find out what is wrong with them and to prescribe a course of treatment **2.** a title given to a qualified person who is registered with the General Medical Council (NOTE: **Doctor** is shortened to **Dr** when written before a name.)

COMMENT: In the UK surgeons are traditionally not called 'Doctor', but are addressed as 'Mr', 'Mrs', etc. The title 'doctor' is also applied to persons who have a higher degree from a university in a non-medical subject. So 'Dr Jones' may have a degree in music, or in any other subject without a connection with medicine.

doctor-assisted suicide /ˌdɒktə əˌsɪstɪd ˈsuːɪsaɪd/ *noun* the suicide of someone with an incurable disease carried out with the help of a doctor (NOTE: Doctor-assisted suicide is illegal in most countries.)

Döderlein's bacillus /ˈdɜːdəlaɪnz bə ˌsɪlʌs/ *noun* a bacterium usually found in the vagina [After Albert Siegmund Gustav Döderlein (1860–1941), German obstetrician and gynaecologist]

dolicho- /ˈdɒlɪkəʊ/ *prefix* long

dolichocephalic /ˌdɒlɪkəʊseˈfælɪk/ *adjective* referring to a person with an unusually long skull

dolichocephaly /ˌdɒlɪkəʊˈsefəli/ *noun* a condition of a person who has a skull which is longer than usual, the measurement across the skull being less than 75% of the length of the head from front to back

dolor /ˈdɒlə/ *noun* pain

dolorimetry /ˌdɒləˈrɪmətri/ *noun* the measurement of pain

dolorosa /ˌdɒləˈrəʊsə/ ♦ **adiposis dolorosa**

domiciliary /ˌdɒmɪˈsɪliəri/ *adjective* at home or in the home

domiciliary care /ˌdɒmɪˈsɪliəri keə/ *noun* personal, domestic, or nursing care provided at home for people who need it

domiciliary midwife /ˌdɒmɪsɪliəri ˈmɪdwaɪf/ *noun* a nurse with special qualification in midwifery, who can assist in childbirth at home

domiciliary services /ˌdɒmɪˈsɪliəri ˌsɜːvɪsɪz/ *plural noun* nursing services which are available to people in their homes

domiciliary visit /ˌdɒmɪsɪliəri ˈvɪzɪt/ *noun* a visit to the patient's home

dominance /ˈdɒmɪnəns/ *noun* the characteristic of a gene form (**allele**) that leads to the trait which it controls being shown in any individual carrying it

dominant /ˈdɒmɪnənt/ *adjective* important or powerful ■ *noun* (*of an allele*) having the characteristic that leads to the trait which it controls being shown in any individual carrying it. Compare **recessive**

COMMENT: Since each physical trait is governed by two genes, if one is recessive and the other dominant, the resulting trait will be that of the dominant gene.

domino booking /ˈdɒmɪnəʊ ˌbʊkɪŋ/ *noun* an arrangement for the delivery of a baby, where the baby is delivered in hospital by a midwife and the mother and child return home soon afterwards

Donald-Fothergill operation /ˌdɒnəld ˈfɒðəɡɪl ɒpəˌreɪʃ(ə)n/ *noun* an operation to close the neck of the vagina

donate /dəʊˈneɪt/ *verb* to agree to give blood, tissue, organs, or reproductive material to be used to treat another person

donor /ˈdəʊnə/ *noun* a person who gives blood, tissue, organs or reproductive material to be used to treat another person

donor card /ˈdəʊnə kɑːd/ *noun* a card carried by people stating that they give permission for their organs to be transplanted into other people after they have died

donor insemination /ˌdəʊnə ɪnsemɪ ˈneɪʃ(ə)n/ *noun* artificial insemination using the sperm of an anonymous donor. Abbr **DI**

dopa /ˈdəʊpə/ *noun* a chemical related to adrenaline and dopamine. It occurs naturally in the body and in the form levodopa is used to treat Parkinson's disease.

dopamine /ˈdəʊpəmiːn/ *noun* a substance found in the medulla of the adrenal glands, which also acts as a neurotransmitter. Lack of dopamine is associated with Parkinson's disease.

dopaminergic /ˌdəʊpəmɪ'nɜːdʒɪk/ *adjective* referring to a neurone or receptor stimulated by dopamine

Doppler transducer /'dɒplə trænzˌdjuːsə/ *noun* a device to measure blood flow, commonly used to monitor fetal heart rate

Doppler ultrasound /ˌdɒplə 'ʌltrəsaʊnd/ *noun* the use of the Doppler effect in ultrasound to detect red blood cells

Doppler ultrasound flowmeter /ˌdɒplə ˌʌltrəsaʊnd 'fləʊmiːtə/ *noun* a device which measures the flow of blood and detects steady or irregular flow, allowing abnormalities or blockages to be detected

dormant /'dɔːmənt/ *adjective* inactive for a time ○ *The virus lies dormant in the body for several years.*

dorsa /'dɔːsə/ plural of **dorsum**

dorsal /'dɔːs(ə)l/ *adjective* **1.** referring to the back. Opposite **ventral 2.** referring to the back of the body

dorsal vertebrae /ˌdɔːs(ə)l 'vɜːtɪbreɪ/ *plural noun* the twelve vertebrae in the back between the cervical vertebrae and the lumbar vertebrae

dorsi- /dɔːsi/ *prefix* referring to the back

dorsiflexion /ˌdɔːsɪ'flekʃən/ *noun* flexion towards the back of part of the body, e.g. raising the foot at the ankle. Compare **plantar flexion**

dorso- /dɔːsəʊ/ *prefix* same as **dorsi-**

dorsoventral /ˌdɔːsəʊ'ventrəl/ *adjective* **1.** referring to both the front and the back of the body **2.** extending from the back of the body to the front

dorsum /'dɔːsəm/ *noun* the back of any part of the body (NOTE: The plural is **dorsa**.)

dosage /'dəʊsɪdʒ/ *noun* a measured quantity of a drug calculated to be necessary for someone ○ *a low dosage* ○ *The doctor decided to increase the dosage of antibiotics.* ○ *The dosage for children is half that for adults.*

dose /dəʊs/ *noun* **1.** a measured quantity of a drug or radiation which is to be given to someone at one time ○ *It is dangerous to exceed the prescribed dose.* **2.** a short period of experiencing a minor illness (*informal*) ○ *a dose of flu* **3.** an infection with a sexually transmitted disease (*informal*) ■ *verb* to provide someone with medication (*informal*) ○ *She has been dosing herself with laxatives.*

dosimeter /dəʊ'sɪmɪtə/ *noun* an instrument which measures the amount of X-rays or other radiation received

dosimetry /dəʊ'sɪmətri/ *noun* the act of measuring the amount of X-rays or radiation received, using a dosimeter

double-blind randomised controlled trial /ˌdʌb(ə)l blaɪnd ˌrændəmaɪzd kənˌtrəʊld 'traɪəl/ *noun* a trial used to test new treatments in which patients are randomly placed in either the treatment or the control group without either the patient or doctor knowing which group any particular patient is in

double blind study /ˌdʌb(ə)l 'blaɪnd ˌstʌdi/ *noun* an investigation to test an intervention in which neither the patient nor the doctor knows if the patient is receiving active medication or a placebo

double-jointed /ˌdʌb(ə)l 'dʒɔɪntɪd/ *adjective* able to bend joints to an unusual degree (*informal*)

double pneumonia /ˌdʌb(ə)l njuː'məʊniə/ *noun* same as **bilateral pneumonia**

double uterus /ˌdʌb(ə)l 'juːt(ə)rəs/ *noun* a condition in which the uterus is divided into two sections by a membrane. Also called **uterus didelphys.** ◊ **dimetria**

double vision /ˌdʌb(ə)l 'vɪʒ(ə)n/ *noun* same as **diplopia** (*informal*)

douche /duːʃ/ *noun* a liquid forced into the body to wash out a cavity, or a device used for washing out a cavity

Douglas bag /'dʌɡləs bæɡ/ *noun* a bag used for measuring the volume of air breathed out of the lungs

Douglas' pouch /'dʌɡləsɪz paʊtʃ/ *noun* the rectouterine peritoneal recess

down below /daʊn bɪ'ləʊ/ *adverb* used to refer politely to the genital area (*informal*)

Down's syndrome /'daʊnz ˌsɪndrəʊm/ *noun* a condition due to the existence of an extra copy of chromosome 21, in which a baby is born with slanting eyes, a wide face, speech difficulties and usually some degree of learning difficulty [Described 1866. After John Langdon Haydon Down (1828–96), British physician at Normansfield Hospital, Teddington, UK.]

downstairs /daʊn'steəz/ *adverb* used to refer politely to the genital area (*informal*)

down there /daʊn ðeə/ *adverb* used to refer politely to the genital area (*informal*)

doxepin /'dɒksɪpɪn/ *noun* a drug used as a sedative and antidepressant

doxycycline /ˌdɒksi'saɪkliːn/ *noun* a widely used antibiotic derived from tetracycline

doze /dəʊz/ *verb* to sleep lightly for a short time

dozy /'dəʊzi/ *adjective* sleepy ○ *These antihistamines can make you feel dozy.*

DPT *abbr* diphtheria, whooping cough, tetanus

DPT vaccine /ˌdiː piː 'tiː ˌvæksiːn/, **DPT immunisation** /ˌdiː piː 'tiː ɪmjʊnaɪˌzeɪʃ(ə)n/ *noun* a combined vaccine or immunisation against the three diseases, diphtheria, whooping cough and tetanus

Dr *abbr* doctor (NOTE: used when writing someone's name: *Dr Smith*)

drachm /dræm/ *noun* a measure used in pharmacy, equal to 3.8 g dry weight or 3.7 ml liquid measure

dracontiasis /ˌdrækɒnˈtaɪəsɪs/, **dracunculiasis** /drəˌkʌŋkjʊˈlaɪəsɪs/ *noun* a tropical disease caused by the guinea worm *Dracunculus medinensis* which enters the body from infected drinking water and forms blisters on the skin, frequently leading to secondary arthritis, fibrosis and cellulitis

Dracunculus /drəˈkʌŋkjʊləs/ *noun* a parasitic worm which enters the body and rises to the skin to form a blister. The infection frequently leads to secondary arthritis, fibrosis and cellulitis. Also called **guinea worm**

dragee /dræˈʒeɪ/ *noun* a sugar-coated tablet or pill

drain /dreɪn/ *noun* a tube to remove liquid from the body ■ *verb* to remove liquid from the body ○ *an operation to drain the sinus* ○ *They drained the pus from the abscess.*

drainage /ˈdreɪnɪdʒ/ *noun* the removal of liquid from the site of an operation or pus from an abscess by means of a tube or wick left in the body for a time

drape /dreɪp/ *noun* a thin material used to place over someone about to undergo surgery, leaving the operation site uncovered

draw /drɔː/ *verb* to drain a liquid such as blood, pus or water from a wound or incision

drawn /drɔːn/ *adjective* appearing tired and careworn, usually as a result of anxiety, grief or illness

draw-sheet /ˈdrɔː ʃiːt/ *noun* a sheet under a person in bed, folded so that it can be pulled out as it becomes soiled

drepanocyte /ˈdrepənəʊsaɪt/ *noun* same as **sickle cell**

drepanocytosis /ˌdrepənəʊsaɪˈtəʊsɪs/ *noun* same as **sickle-cell anaemia**

dress /dres/ *verb* **1.** to put on clothes, or put clothes on someone **2.** to clean a wound and put a covering over it ○ *Nurses dressed the wounds of the accident victims.*

dresser /ˈdresə/ *noun* someone who assists a surgeon during operations

dressing /ˈdresɪŋ/ *noun* a covering or bandage applied to a wound to protect it ○ *The patient's dressings need to be changed regularly.*

dribble /ˈdrɪb(ə)l/ *verb* to let liquid flow slowly out of an opening, especially saliva out of the mouth

dribbling /ˈdrɪblɪŋ/ *noun* **1.** the act of letting saliva flow out of the mouth **2.** same as **incontinence** (*informal*)

drill /drɪl/ *noun* a tool which rotates very rapidly to make a hole, especially a surgical instrument used in dentistry to remove caries ■ *verb* to make a hole with a drill ○ *A small hole is drilled in the skull.* ○ *The dentist drilled one of her molars.*

Drinker respirator /ˈdrɪŋkə ˌrespɪreɪtə/ *noun* a machine which encloses the whole of the body except the head, and in which air pressure is increased and decreased, so forcing the person to breathe in and out. Also called **iron lung**

drip /drɪp/ *noun* a system for introducing liquid slowly and continuously into the body, by which a bottle of liquid is held above a person and the fluid flows slowly down a tube into a needle in a vein or into the stomach ○ *After her operation, the patient was put on a drip.*

drip feed /ˈdrɪp fiːd/ *noun* a drip containing nutrients

drop /drɒp/ *noun* **1.** a small quantity of liquid **2.** a sudden reduction or fall in the quantity of something ○ *a drop in pressure* ■ *plural noun* **drops** liquid medicine for the eye, nose, or ear administered with a dropper ■ *verb* **1.** to fall or let something fall ○ *Pressure in the artery dropped suddenly.* **2.** to reduce suddenly

drop attack /ˈdrɒp əˌtæk/ *noun* a condition in which a person suddenly falls down, though he or she is not unconscious, caused by sudden weakness of the spine

droperidol /drɒˈperɪdɒl/ *noun* a drug used to keep someone in a calm state before an operation

drop foot /ˈdrɒp fʊt/ *noun* a condition, caused by a muscular disorder, in which the ankle is not strong and the foot hangs limp

droplet /ˈdrɒplət/ *noun* a very small quantity of liquid

droplet infection /ˈdrɒplət ɪnˌfekʃən/ *noun* an infection developed by inhaling droplets containing a virus, e.g. from a sneeze

drop off /ˌdrɒp ˈɒf/ *verb* (*informal*) **1.** to fall asleep **2.** to get less

dropper /ˈdrɒpə/ *noun* a small glass or plastic tube with a rubber bulb at one end, used to suck up and expel liquid in drops

dropsy /ˈdrɒpsi/ *noun* same as **oedema** (*dated*)

drop wrist /drɒp ˈrɪst/ *noun* a condition caused by a muscular disorder, in which the wrist is not strong and the hand hangs limp

drown /draʊn/ *verb* to die by inhaling liquid

drowning /ˈdraʊnɪŋ/ *noun* death as a result of inhaling liquid

drowsiness /ˈdraʊzinəs/ *noun* sleepiness ○ *The medicine is likely to cause drowsiness.*

drowsy /ˈdraʊzi/ *adjective* sleepy ○ *The injection will make you feel drowsy.*

drug /drʌg/ *noun* **1.** a natural or synthetic chemical substance which is used in medicine and affects the way in which organs or tissues function ○ *She was prescribed a course of pain-killing drugs.* ○ *The drug is being monitored for possible side-effects.* **2.** a substance taken by choice which produces a strong effect on a person's feelings and state of mind ○ *recreational drug* ○ *controlled drugs*

COMMENT: There are three classes of controlled drugs: **Class 'A' drugs** such as cocaine, heroin, crack and LSD; **Class 'B' drugs** such as amphetamines and codeine; and **Class 'C' drugs** such as cannabis and benzphetamine. The drugs are covered by five schedules under the Misuse of Drugs Regulations: **Schedule 1:** drugs which are not used medicinally, such as cannabis and LSD, for which possession and supply are prohibited. **Schedule 2:** drugs which can be used medicinally such as heroin, morphine, cocaine, and amphetamines: these are fully controlled as regards prescriptions by doctors, safe custody in pharmacies, registering of sales, etc. **Schedule 3:** barbiturates, which are controlled as regards prescriptions, but need not be kept in safe custody; **Schedule 4:** benzodiazepines, which are controlled as regards registers of purchasers; **Schedule 5:** other substances for which invoices showing purchasers; **Schedule 5:** other substances for which invoices showing purchase must be kept.

drug abuse /'drʌg ə,bjuːs/ *noun* ▸ **substance abuse**

drug abuser /'drʌg ə,bjuːzə/ *noun* a person who regularly uses drugs for non-medical purposes

drug addict /'drʌg ,ædɪkt/ *noun* a person who is physically and mentally dependent on taking a particular drug regularly ○ *a heroin addict* ○ *a morphine addict*

drug addiction /'drʌg ə,dɪkʃən/ *noun* the fact of being mentally and physically dependent on taking a particular drug regularly. Also called **drug dependence**

drug allergy /'drʌg ,æləʤi/ *noun* a reaction to a particular drug

drug dependence /'drʌg dɪ,pendəns/ *noun* same as **drug addiction**

drug-related /'drʌg rɪ,leɪtɪd/ *adjective* associated with the taking of drugs

drug tolerance /'drʌg ,tɒlərəns/ *noun* a condition in which a drug has been given to someone for so long that his or her body no longer reacts to it, and the dosage has to be increased

drunk /drʌŋk/ *adjective* intoxicated with too much alcohol

dry /draɪ/ *adjective* **1.** not wet ○ *The surface of the wound should be kept dry.* **2.** containing only a small amount of moisture ○ *She uses a cream to soften her dry skin.* (NOTE: **drier – driest**) ■ *verb* to remove moisture from something (NOTE: **dries – drying – dried**)

dry beriberi /,draɪ beri'beri/ *noun* beriberi associated with loss of feeling and paralysis

dry burn /,draɪ 'bɜːn/ *noun* an injury to the skin caused by touching a very hot dry surface

dry drowning /,draɪ 'draʊnɪŋ/ *noun* death in which someone's air passage has been constricted by being under water, though he or she does not inhale any water

dry-eye syndrome /draɪ 'aɪ ,sɪndrəʊm/ *noun* same as **xerosis**

dry gangrene /,draɪ 'gæŋgriːn/ *noun* a condition in which the blood supply to a limb has been cut off and the tissue becomes black

dry ice /,draɪ 'aɪs/ *noun* solid carbon dioxide

dryness /'draɪnəs/ *noun* the state of being dry ○ *dryness in the eyes, accompanied by rheumatoid arthritis* ○ *She complained of dryness in her mouth.*

dry out /,draɪ 'aʊt/ *verb* **1.** same as **dry 2. 2.** to treat someone for alcoholism, or undergo treatment for alcoholism (*informal*)

dry socket /draɪ 'sɒkɪt/ *noun* inflammation of the socket of a tooth which has just been removed

DTC *abbr* diagnostic and treatment centre

DTs *abbr* delirium tremens

Duchenne muscular dystrophy /duː,ʃen ,mʌskjʊlə 'dɪstrəfi/, **Duchenne's muscular dystrophy** /duː,ʃenz ,mʌskjʊlə 'dɪstrəfi/, **Duchenne** /duː'ʃen/ *noun* an inherited form of muscular dystrophy that weakens the muscles of the upper respiratory and pelvic areas. It usually affects boys and causes early death. [Described 1849. After Guillaume Benjamin Arnaud Duchenne (1806–75), French neurologist.]

Ducrey's bacillus /duː,kreɪz bə'sɪləs/ *noun* a type of bacterium found in the lungs, causing chancroid [Described 1889. After Augusto Ducrey (1860–1940), Professor of Dermatology in Pisa, then Rome, Italy.]

duct /dʌkt/ *noun* a tube which carries liquids, especially one which carries secretions

duct gland /'dʌkt glænd/ *noun* same as **exocrine gland**

ductless /'dʌktləs/ *adjective* without a duct

ductless gland /,dʌktləs 'glænd/ *noun* same as **endocrine gland**

ductule /'dʌktjuːl/ *noun* a very small duct

ductus /'dʌktəs/ *noun* same as **duct**

ductus arteriosus /,dʌktəs ɑː,tɪəri'əʊsəs/ *noun* in a fetus, the blood vessel connecting the left pulmonary artery to the aorta so that blood does not pass through the lungs

ductus deferens /,dʌktəs 'defərənz/ *noun* one of two tubes along which sperm pass from the epididymus to the seminal vesicles near the prostate gland. Also called **vas deferens**. See illustration at UROGENITAL SYSTEM (MALE) in Supplement

ductus venosus /,dʌktəs vɪ'nəʊsəs/ *noun* in a fetus, the blood vessel connecting the portal sinus to the inferior vena cava

dull /dʌl/ *adjective* referring to pain which is not strong but which is continuously present ○ *She complained of a dull throbbing pain in her head.* ○ *He felt a dull pain in the chest.* ■ *verb* to make a sensation or awareness of a sensation less sharp ○ *The treatment dulled the pain for a while.* ○ *The drug had dulled her senses.*

dumb /dʌm/ *adjective* not able to speak

dumbness /'dʌmnəs/ *noun* same as **mutism**

dumping syndrome /'dʌmpɪŋ ˌsɪndrəum/ *noun* same as **postgastrectomy syndrome**

duo- /djuːəu/ *prefix* two

duoden- /djuːəudiːn/ *prefix* referring to the duodenum

duodenal /ˌdjuːəu'diːn(ə)l/ *adjective* referring to the duodenum

duodenal papillae /djuːəuˌdiːn(ə)l pə'pɪliː/ *plural noun* small projecting parts in the duodenum where the bile duct and pancreatic duct open

duodenal ulcer /djuːəuˌdiːn(ə)l 'ʌlsə/ *noun* an ulcer in the duodenum

duodenoscope /ˌdjuːəu'diːnəuskəup/ *noun* an instrument used to examine the inside of the duodenum

duodenostomy /ˌdjuːəudɪ'nɒstəmi/ *noun* a permanent opening made between the duodenum and the abdominal wall

duodenum /ˌdjuːə'diːnəm/ *noun* the first part of the small intestine, going from the stomach to the jejunum. See illustration at **DIGESTIVE SYSTEM** in Supplement

COMMENT: The duodenum is the shortest part of the small intestine, about 250 mm long. It takes bile from the gall bladder and pancreatic juice from the pancreas and continues the digestive processes started in the mouth and stomach.

duplex imaging /ˌdjuːpleks 'ɪmɪdʒɪŋ/ *noun* a type of ultrasonic imaging where the speed of the flow of blood is measured

Dupuytren's contracture /duːˌpwiːtrənz kən'træktʃə/ *noun* a condition in which the palmar fascia becomes thicker, causing the fingers, usually the middle and fourth fingers, to bend forwards [Described 1831. After Baron Guillaume Dupuytren (1775–1835), French surgeon.]

dura /'djuərə/ *noun* same as **dura mater**

dural /'djuər(ə)l/ *adjective* referring to the dura mater

dura mater /ˌdjuərə 'meɪtə/ *noun* the thicker outer membrane of the three covering the brain. Also called **dura, pachymeninx**. ◊ **arachnoid**

duty /'djuːti/ *noun* the activities which a person has to do as part of their job ○ *What are the duties of a night sister?* (NOTE: The plural is **duties**.) □ **to be on duty** to be working ○ *She's on duty from 2 p.m. till 10 p.m.* □ **a duty of care** the requirement to treat a patient in an appropriate way, as part of the work of being a health professional

duty nurse /'djuːti nɜːs/ *noun* a nurse who is on duty

duty rota /'djuːti ˌrəutə/ *noun* a list of duties which have to be done and the names of the people who will do them

d.v.t., DVT *abbr* deep-vein thrombosis

dwarfism /'dwɔːfɪz(ə)m/ *noun* a condition in which the growth of a person has stopped, leaving him or her much smaller than average

COMMENT: Dwarfism may be caused by achondroplasia, where the long bones of the arms and legs do not develop fully but the trunk and head are of average size. Dwarfism can have other causes such as rickets or deficiency in the pituitary gland.

dynamic splint /daɪˌnæmɪk 'splɪnt/ *noun* a splint which uses springs to help the person move

dynamometer /ˌdaɪnə'mɒmɪtə/ *noun* an instrument for measuring the force of muscular contraction

-dynia /dɪniə/ *suffix* pain

dys- /dɪs/ *prefix* difficult or impaired

dysaesthesia /ˌdɪsiːs'θiːziə/ *noun* 1. the impairment of a sense, in particular the sense of touch 2. an unpleasant feeling of pain experienced when the skin is touched lightly

dysarthria /dɪs'ɑːθriə/, **dysarthrosis** /ˌdɪsɑː'θrəusɪs/ *noun* difficulty in speaking words clearly, caused by damage to the central nervous system

dysbarism /'dɪsbɑːrɪz(ə)m/ *noun* any disorder caused by differences between the atmospheric pressure outside the body and the pressure inside

dysbasia /dɪs'beɪziə/ *noun* difficulty in walking, especially when caused by a lesion to a nerve

dyschezia /dɪs'kiːziə/ *noun* difficulty in passing faeces

dyschondroplasia /ˌdɪskɒndrəu'pleɪziə/ *noun* a condition in which the long bones are shorter than usual

dyschromatopsia /ˌdɪskrəumə'tɒpsiə/ *noun* a condition where someone cannot distinguish colours

dyscoria /dɪs'kɔːriə/ *noun* 1. an unusually shaped pupil of the eye 2. an unusual reaction of the pupil

dyscrasia /dɪs'kreɪziə/ *noun* any unusual body condition (*dated*)

dysdiadochokinesia /ˌdɪsdaɪˌædəkəukaɪ'niːsiə/, **dysdiadochokinesis** /ˌdɪsdaɪˌædəkəukaɪ'niːsɪs/ *noun* the inability to carry out rapid movements, caused by a disorder or lesion of the cerebellum

dysenteric /ˌdɪsən'terɪk/ *adjective* referring to dysentery

dysentery /'dɪs(ə)ntri/ *noun* an infection and inflammation of the colon, causing bleeding and diarrhoea

COMMENT: Dysentery occurs mainly in tropical countries. The symptoms include diarrhoea, discharge of blood and pain in the intestines. There are two main types of dysentery: **bacillary dysentery**, caused by the bacterium *Shigella* in contaminated food, and **amoebic dysentery** or amoebiasis, caused by a parasitic amoeba *Entamoeba histolytica* spread through contaminated drinking water.

dysfunction /dɪs'fʌŋkʃən/ *noun* an unusual functioning of an organ

dysfunctional /dɪs'fʌŋkʃən(ə)l/ *adjective* **1.** not working properly **2.** unable to relate to other people emotionally or socially

dysfunctional uterine bleeding /dɪs ˌfʌŋkʃən(ə)l ˌjuːtəraɪn 'bliːdɪŋ/ *noun* bleeding in the uterus not caused by a menstrual period

dysgenesis /dɪs'dʒenəsɪs/ *noun* unusual development

dysgerminoma /dɪsˌdʒɜːmɪ'nəʊmə/ *noun* a malignant tumour of the ovary or testicle

dysgraphia /dɪs'ɡræfiə/ *noun* difficulty in writing caused by a brain lesion

dyskariosis /dɪsˌkæri'əʊsɪs/ *noun* the fact of becoming mature in an unusual way

dyskinesia /ˌdɪskaɪ'niːziə/ *noun* the inability to control voluntary movements

dyslalia /dɪs'leɪliə/ *noun* a disorder of speech, caused by an unusual development of the tongue

dyslexia /dɪs'leksiə/ *noun* a disorder of development, where a person is unable to read or write properly and confuses letters

dyslexic /dɪs'leksɪk/ *adjective* referring to dyslexia ■ *noun* a person suffering from dyslexia

dyslipidaemia /ˌdɪslɪpɪ'diːmiə/ *noun* an imbalance of lipids

dyslogia /dɪs'ləʊdʒə/ *noun* difficulty in putting ideas into words

dysmaturity /ˌdɪsmə'tʃʊərɪti/ *noun* a condition affecting newborn babies, shown by wrinkled skin, long fingernails and toenails and relatively little body fat

dysmenorrhoea /ˌdɪsmenə'riːə/ *noun* pain experienced at menstruation

dysostosis /ˌdɪsɒs'təʊsɪs/ *noun* unusual formation of bones

dyspareunia /ˌdɪspæ'ruːniə/ *noun* difficult or painful sexual intercourse in a woman

dyspepsia /dɪs'pepsiə/ *noun* a condition in which a person feels pains or discomfort in the stomach, caused by indigestion

dyspeptic /dɪs'peptɪk/ *adjective* referring to dyspepsia

dysphagia /dɪs'feɪdʒiə/ *noun* difficulty in swallowing

dysphasia /dɪs'feɪziə/ *noun* difficulty in speaking and putting words into the correct order

dysphemia /dɪs'fiːmiə/ *noun* same as **stammering**

dysphonia /dɪs'fəʊniə/ *noun* difficulty in speaking caused by impairment of the vocal cords, or by laryngitis

dysplasia /dɪs'pleɪziə/ *noun* an unusual development of tissue

dyspnoea /dɪsp'niːə/ *noun* difficulty or pain in breathing

dyspnoeic /dɪsp'niːɪk/ *adjective* difficult or painful when breathing

dyspraxia /dɪs'præksiə/ *noun* difficulty in carrying out coordinated movements

dysrhythmia /dɪs'rɪðmiə/ *noun* an unusual rhythm, either in speaking or in electrical impulses in the brain

dyssocial /dɪs'səʊʃ(ə)l/ *adjective* same as **antisocial**

dyssynergia /ˌdɪsɪ'nɜːdʒiə/ *noun* same as **asynergia**

dystaxia /dɪs'tæksiə/ *noun* an inability to coordinate the muscles

dystocia /dɪs'təʊsiə/ *noun* difficult childbirth

dystonia /dɪs'təʊniə/ *noun* disordered muscle tone, causing involuntary contractions which make the limbs deformed

dystrophia /dɪs'trəʊfiə/ *noun* the wasting of an organ, muscle or tissue due to lack of nutrients in that part of the body. Also called **dystrophy**

dystrophia adiposogenitalis /dɪsˌtrəʊfiə ædɪˌpəʊsəʊdʒenɪ'teɪlɪs/ *noun* same as **Fröhlich's syndrome**

dystrophia myotonica /dɪsˌtrəʊfiə ˌmaɪəʊ'tɒnɪkə/ *noun* same as **myotonic dystrophy**

dystrophy /'dɪstrəfi/ *noun* same as **dystrophia**

dysuria /dɪs'jʊəriə/ *noun* difficulty in passing urine

E

ear /ɪə/ *noun* an organ on the side of the head which is used for hearing (NOTE: For other terms referring to ears, see **auricular** and words beginning with **ot-, oto-**.)

COMMENT: The outer ear is shaped in such a way that it collects sound and channels it to the eardrum. Behind the eardrum, the three ossicles in the middle ear vibrate with sound and transmit the vibrations to the cochlea in the inner ear. From the cochlea, the vibrations are passed by the auditory nerve to the brain.

Ear, Nose & Throat /ɪə ˌnəʊz ən ˈθrəʊt/ *noun* the study of the ear, nose and throat. Abbr **ENT**. Also called **otorhinolarngology**

earache /ˈɪəreɪk/ *noun* pain in the ear. Also called **otalgia**

ear canal /ˈɪə kəˌnæl/ *noun* one of several passages in or connected to the ear, especially the external auditory meatus, the passage from the outer ear to the eardrum

eardrum /ˈɪədrʌm/ *noun* the membrane at the end of the external auditory meatus leading from the outer ear, which vibrates with sound and passes the vibrations on to the ossicles in the middle ear. Also called **myringa, tympanum** (NOTE: For other terms referring to the eardrum, see words beginning with **tympan-, tympano-**.)

early /ˈɜːli/ *adjective* **1.** happening at the beginning of a period of time □ **early diagnosis** diagnosis made at the onset of an illness □ **early treatment** treatment given almost as soon as the illness has started **2.** (*of a condition or illness*) in its first stage ○ *early synovitis* □ **during early pregnancy** within the first months of pregnancy ■ *adverb* at the beginning of a period of time ○ *The treatment is usually successful if the condition is diagnosed early.*

early onset pre-eclampsia /ˌɜːli ˌɒnset ˌpriː ɪˈklæmpsiə/ *noun* pre-eclampsia which appears earlier than the 37th week of the pregnancy

ear ossicle /ˈɪə ˌɒsɪk(ə)l/ *noun* ♦ **auditory ossicles**

earwax /ˈɪəwæks/ *noun* same as **cerumen**

ease /iːz/ *verb* to make pain or worry less ○ *She had an injection to ease the pain in her leg.*

○ *The surgeon tried to ease the patient's fears about the results of the scan.*

eating disorder /ˈiːtɪŋ dɪsˌɔːdə/ *noun* an illness that causes the usual pattern of eating to be disturbed, e.g. anorexia or bulimia

eating habits /ˈiːtɪŋ ˌhæbɪts/ *plural noun* the types and quantities of food regularly eaten by a person ○ *The dietitian advised her to change her eating habits.*

Ebola virus /ɪˈbəʊlə ˌvaɪrəs/ *noun* a highly contagious virus found in West Africa. Patients who are affected with it vomit, have bloody diarrhoea and blood seeps through their skin.

eburnation /ˌiːbəˈneɪʃ(ə)n/ *noun* the conversion of cartilage into a hard mass with a shiny surface like bone

ecbolic /ekˈbɒlɪk/ *noun* a substance which produces contraction of the uterus and so induces childbirth or abortion ■ *adjective* causing contraction of the uterus

ecchondroma /ˌekənˈdrəʊmə/ *noun* a benign tumour on the surface of cartilage or bone

ecchymosis /ˌekɪˈməʊsɪs/ *noun* a dark area on the skin made by blood which has escaped into the tissues after a blow. Also called **bruise, contusion**

eccrine /ˈekrɪn/ *adjective* referring to a gland, especially a sweat gland, which does not disintegrate and remains intact during secretion. Also called **merocrine**

eccyesis /ˌeksaɪˈiːsɪs/ *noun* same as **ectopic pregnancy**

ecdysis /ˈekdɪsɪs/ *noun* same as **desquamation**

ECG *abbr* electrocardiogram

echinococciasis /ɪˌkaɪnəʊkɒˈkaɪəsɪs/, **echinococcosis** /ɪˌkaɪnəʊkəˈkəʊsɪs/ *noun* a disorder caused by a tapeworm *Echinococcus granulosus* which forms hydatid cysts in the lungs, liver, kidneys or brain

Echinococcus granulosus /ɪˌkaɪnəʊkɒkəs ˌgrænjʊˈləʊsəs/ *noun* a type of tapeworm, usually found in animals, but sometimes transmitted to humans, causing hydatid cysts in the lungs, liver, kidneys or brain

echo- /ekəʊ/ *prefix* referring to sound

echocardiogram /ˌekəʊˈkɑːdiəgræm/ noun a record of heart movements made using ultrasound

echocardiography /ˌekəʊkɑːdiˈɒgrəfi/ noun the use of ultrasound to examine the heart

echoencephalography /ˌekəʊenˌkefəˈlɒgrəfi/ noun the use of ultrasound to examine the brain

echography /eˈkɒgrəfi/ noun same as ultra-sonography

echokinesis /ˌekəʊkaɪˈniːsɪs/ noun same as echopraxia

echolalia /ˌekəʊˈleɪliə/ noun the repetition of words spoken by another person

echopraxia /ˌekəʊˈpræksiə/ noun the meaningless imitation of another person's actions

echovirus /ˈekəʊˌvaɪrəs/ noun one of a group of viruses which can be isolated from the intestine and which can cause serious illnesses such as aseptic meningitis, gastroenteritis and respiratory infection in small children. Compare **reovirus**

eclabium /ɪˈkleɪbiəm/ noun the turning outwards of the lips. ◊ **eversion**

eclampsia /ɪˈklæmpsiə/ noun a serious condition of pregnant women at the end of pregnancy, caused by toxaemia, in which the woman has high blood pressure and may go into a coma. ◊ **pre-eclampsia**

ecmnesia /ekˈniːziə/ noun a condition in which someone is not able to remember recent events, while remembering clearly events which happened some time ago

E. coli /ˌiː ˈkəʊlaɪ/ noun same as **Escherichia coli**

economy class syndrome /ɪˈkɒnəmi klɑːs ˌsɪndrəʊm/ noun same as **deep-vein thrombosis** (*informal*)

écraseur /ˌeɪkrɑːˈzɜː/ noun a surgical instrument, usually with a wire loop, used to cut a part or a growth off at its base

ecstasy /ˈekstəsi/ noun 1. feeling of extreme happiness 2. a powerful stimulant and hallucinatory illegal drug (*informal*) Also called **methylenedioxymethamphetamine**

ECT abbr electroconvulsive therapy

ect- /ekt/ prefix same as **ecto-** (*used before vowels*)

ectasia /ekˈteɪziə/ noun the dilatation of a passage

ecthyma /ekˈθaɪmə/ noun a skin disorder that is a serious form of impetigo which penetrates deep under the skin and leaves scars

ecto- /ektəʊ/ prefix outside

ectoderm /ˈektəʊdɜːm/ noun the outer layer of an early embryo. Also called **embryonic ectoderm**

ectodermal /ˌektəʊˈdɜːm(ə)l/ adjective referring to the ectoderm

-ectomy /ektəmi/ suffix referring to the removal of a part by surgical operation

ectoparasite /ˌektəʊˈpærəsaɪt/ noun a parasite which lives on the skin. Compare **endoparasite**

ectopia /ekˈtəʊpiə/ noun a condition in which an organ or part of the body is not in its usual position

ectopic /ekˈtɒpɪk/ adjective not in the usual position. Opposite **entopic**

ectopic heartbeat /ekˌtɒpɪk ˈhɑːtbiːt/ noun an unusual extra beat of the heart which originates from a point other than the sinoatrial node. Also called **extrasystole, premature beat**

ectopic pacemaker /ekˌtɒpɪk ˈpeɪsmeɪkə/ noun an unusual focus of the heart muscle which takes the place of the sinoatrial node

ectopic pregnancy /ekˌtɒpɪk ˈpregnənsi/ noun a pregnancy where the fetus develops outside the uterus, often in one of the Fallopian tubes. Also called **extrauterine pregnancy, eccyesis**

ectro- /ektrəʊ/ prefix referring to a usually congenital absence or lack of something

ectrodactyly /ˌektrəʊˈdæktɪli/ noun a congenital absence of all or part of a finger

ectrogeny /ekˈtrɒdʒəni/ noun a congenital absence of a part at birth

ectromelia /ˌektrəʊˈmiːliə/ noun a congenital absence of one or more limbs

ectropion /ekˈtrəʊpiən/ noun a turning of the edge of an eyelid outwards. ◊ **eversion**

eczema /ˈeksɪmə/ noun a non-contagious inflammation of the skin, with an itchy rash and blisters

eczematous /ekˈsemətəs/ adjective referring to eczema

eczematous dermatitis /ekˌsemətəs ˌdɜːməˈtaɪtɪs/ noun an itchy inflammation or irritation of the skin due to an allergic reaction to a substance which a person has touched or absorbed

EDD abbr expected date of delivery

edema /ɪˈdiːmə/ noun US same as **oedema**

edentulous /ɪˈdentjʊləs/ adjective having lost all teeth

edible /ˈedɪb(ə)l/ adjective able to be eaten without causing harm

EDTA noun a colourless chemical that can bind to heavy metals to remove them from the bloodstream. Full form **ethylene diamine tetra-acetate**

Edwards' syndrome /ˈedwədz ˌsɪndrəʊm/ noun a severe genetic disorder that results in malformations of the brain, kidney, heart, hands and feet. It is caused by an extra copy of chromosome 18 and those people who have it usually die within six months.

EEG abbr electroencephalogram

EFA abbr essential fatty acid

effacement /ɪˈfeɪsmənt/ noun the thinning of the cervix before it dilates in childbirth

effect /ɪ'fekt/ *noun* a result of a drug, treatment, disease or action ○ *The antiseptic cream has had no effect on the rash.* ■ *verb* to make something happen (*formal*) ○ *They will have to effect a change in procedures.* ○ *In some circumstances these drugs can effect surprising cures.*

effective /ɪ'fektɪv/ *adjective* having an effect ○ *Embolisation is an effective treatment for severe haemoptysis.*

effective dose /ɪˌfektɪv 'dəʊs/ *noun* a size of dose which will produce the effect required

effector /ɪ'fektə/ *noun* a nerve ending in muscles or glands which is activated to produce contraction or secretion

efferens /'efərəns/ ♦ **vas efferens**

efferent /'efərənt/ *adjective* carrying something away from part of the body or from the centre. Opposite **afferent**

efferent duct /'efərənt dʌkt/ *noun* a duct which carries a secretion away from a gland

efferent nerve /'efərənt nɜːv/ *noun* same as **motor nerve**

efferent vessel /'efərənt ˌves(ə)l/ *noun* a vessel which drains lymph from a gland

effleurage /ˌeflɜː'rɑːʒ/ *noun* a form of massage where the skin is stroked in one direction to increase blood flow

effort syndrome /'efət ˌsɪndrəʊm/ *noun* same as **disordered action of the heart**

effusion /ɪ'fjuːʒ(ə)n/ *noun* **1.** a discharge of blood, fluid or pus into or out of an internal cavity **2.** fluid, blood or pus which is discharged

egg /eg/ *noun* **1.** a reproductive cell produced in the female body by an ovary, and which, if fertilised by the male sperm, becomes an embryo **2.** an egg with a hard shell, laid by a hen or other bird, which is used for food

egg cell /'eg sel/ *noun* an immature ovum or female cell

ego /'iːgəʊ, 'egəʊ/ *noun* (*in psychology*) the part of the mind which is consciously in contact with the outside world and is influenced by experiences of the world

Egyptian ophthalmia /ɪˌdʒɪpʃ(ə)n ɒf'θælmiə/ *noun* same as **trachoma**

EHO *abbr* Environmental Health Officer

EIA *abbr* exercise-induced asthma

eidetic imagery /aɪˌdetɪk 'ɪmɪdʒəri/ *noun* the recall of extremely clear pictures in the mind

Eisenmenger syndrome /'aɪzənmeŋə ˌsɪndrəʊm/ *noun* heart disease caused by a septal defect between the ventricles, with pulmonary hypertension [Described 1897. After Victor Eisenmenger (1864–1932), German physician.]

ejaculate /ɪ'dʒækjʊˌleɪt/ *verb* to send out semen from the penis

ejaculation /ɪˌdʒækjʊ'leɪʃ(ə)n/ *noun* the sending out of semen from the penis

ejaculatio praecox /ɪdʒækjʊˌleɪʃiəʊ 'priːkɒks/ *noun* a situation where a man ejaculates too early during sexual intercourse

ejaculatory /ɪ'dʒækjʊlətri/ *adjective* referring to ejaculation

ejaculatory duct /ɪ'dʒækjʊlətri dʌkt/ *noun* one of two ducts leading from the seminal vesicles through the prostate gland to the urethra. See illustration at **UROGENITAL SYSTEM (MALE)** in Supplement

eject /ɪ'dʒekt/ *verb* to send out something with force ○ *Blood is ejected from the ventricle during systole.*

ejection /ɪ'dʒekʃən/ *noun* the act of sending out something with force

EKG *abbr US* electrocardiogram

elastic /ɪ'læstɪk/ *adjective* which can be stretched and compressed and return to its former shape

elastic bandage /ɪˌlæstɪk 'bændɪdʒ/ *noun* a stretchy bandage used to support a weak joint or for the treatment of a varicose vein

elastic cartilage /ɪˌlæstɪk 'kɑːtəlɪdʒ/ *noun* flexible cartilage, e.g. in the ear and epiglottis

elastic fibre /ɪˌlæstɪk 'faɪbə/ *noun* fibre which can expand easily and is found in elastic cartilage, the skin and the walls of arteries and the lungs. Also called **yellow fibre**

elastic hose /ɪ'læstɪk həʊz/ *noun* same as **surgical hose**

elasticity /ˌɪlæ'stɪsɪti/ *noun* the ability to expand and be compressed and to return to the former shape

elastic tissue /ɪˌlæstɪk 'tɪʃuː/ *noun* connective tissue which contains elastic fibres, e.g. in the walls of arteries or of the alveoli in the lungs

elastin /ɪ'læstɪn/ *noun* a protein which occurs in elastic fibres

elation /ɪ'leɪʃ(ə)n/ *noun* the state of being happy, stimulated and excited

elbow /'elbəʊ/ *noun* a hinged joint where the upper arm bone (**humerus**) joins the forearm bones (**radius** and **ulna**)

elbow crutch /'elbəʊ krʌtʃ/ *noun* a crutch which surrounds the arms at the elbows and has a handle to hold lower down the shaft

elderly /'eldəli/ *adjective* older than 65 ○ *a home for elderly single women* ○ *She looks after her two elderly parents.* ■ *noun* □ **the elderly** people aged over 65

elective /ɪ'lektɪv/ *adjective* **1.** referring to a chemical substance which tends to combine with one substance rather others **2.** referring to surgery or treatment which someone can choose to have but is not urgently necessary to save their life

elective care /ɪˌlektɪv ˈkeə/ *noun* hospital care which is planned in advance, rather than a response to an emergency

Electra complex /ɪˈlektrə ˌkɒmpleks/ *noun* (*in psychology*) a condition in which a girl feels sexually attracted to her father and sees her mother as an obstacle

electric shock /ɪˌlektrɪk ˈʃɒk/ *noun* a sudden passage of electricity into the body, causing a nervous spasm or, in severe cases, death

electric shock treatment /ɪˌlektrɪk ˈʃɒk ˌtriːtmənt/ *noun* same as **electroconvulsive therapy** (*informal*)

electro- /ɪˈlektrəʊ/ *prefix* referring to electricity

electrocardiogram /ɪˌlektrəʊˈkɑːdiəgræm/ *noun* a chart which records the electrical impulses in the heart muscle. Abbr **ECG, EKG**

electrocardiograph /ɪˌlektrəʊˈkɑːdiəgrɑːf/ *noun* an apparatus for measuring and recording the electrical impulses of the muscles of the heart as it beats

electrocardiography /ɪˌlektrəʊkɑːdiˈɒgrəfi/ *noun* the process of recording the electrical impulses of the heart

electrocardiophonography /ɪˌlektrəʊ kɑːdiəʊfəˈnɒgrəfi/ *noun* the process of electrically recording the sounds of the heartbeats

electrocautery /ɪˌlektrəʊˈkɔːtəri/ *noun* same as **galvanocautery**

electrochemical /ɪˌlektrəʊˈkemɪk(ə)l/ *adjective* referring to electricity and chemicals and their interaction

electrocoagulation /ɪˌlektrəʊkəʊˌæɡjʊ ˈleɪʃ(ə)n/ *noun* the control of haemorrhage in surgery by passing a high-frequency electric current through divided blood vessels

electroconvulsive therapy /ɪˌlektrəʊkən ˌvʌlsɪv ˈθerəpi/ *noun* the treatment of severe depression and some mental disorders by giving someone who has been anaesthetised small electric shocks in the brain to make him or her have convulsions. Abbr **ECT**. Also called **electroplexy**

electrode /ɪˈlektrəʊd/ *noun* the conductor of an electrical apparatus which touches the body and carries an electric shock

electrodesiccation /ɪˌlektrəʊdesɪ ˈkeɪʃ(ə)n/ *noun* same as **fulguration**

electroencephalogram /ɪˌlektrəʊɪn ˈsefələgræm/ *noun* a chart on which the electrical impulses in the brain are recorded. Abbr **EEG**

electroencephalograph /ɪˌlektrəʊɪnˈsefələ grɑːf/ *noun* an apparatus which records the electrical impulses in the brain

electroencephalography /ɪˌlektrəʊɪnsefə ˈlɒgrəfi/ *noun* the process of recording the electrical impulses in the brain

electrolysis /ɪlekˈtrɒləsɪs/ *noun* the destruction of tissue such as unwanted hair by applying an electric current

electrolyte /ɪˈlektrəlaɪt/ *noun* a chemical solution which can conduct electricity

electrolyte mixture /ɪˈlektrəlaɪt ˌmɪkstʃə/ *noun* a pint (0.56 litres) of boiled water with a teaspoonful of sugar and a generous pinch of table salt used for the prevention of diarrhoea

electrolytic /ɪˌlektrəˈlɪtɪk/ *adjective* referring to electrolytes or to electrolysis

electromyogram /ɪˌlektrəˈmaɪəʊgræm/ *noun* a chart showing the electric currents in active muscles. Abbr **EMG**

electromyography /ɪˌlektrəʊmaɪˈɒgrəfi/ *noun* the study of electric currents in active muscles

electronic stethoscope /ˌelektrɒnɪk ˈsteθəskəʊp/ *noun* a stethoscope with an amplifier which makes sounds louder

electronystagmography /eˌlektrəʊ ˌnɪstæɡˈmɒgrəfi/ *noun* measuring of nystagmus

electrooculogram /ɪˌlektrəʊˈɒkjʊləgræm/ *noun* a record of the electric currents round the eye, induced by eye movements

electrooculography /ɪˌlektrəʊˌɒkjʊˈlɒ grəfi/ *noun* recording the electric currents round the eye, induced by eye movements, especially for use in remote control

electrophoresis /ɪˌlektrəʊfəˈriːsɪs/ *noun* the analysis of a substance by the movement of charged particles towards an electrode in a solution

electroplexy /ɪˈlektrəpleksi/ *noun* same as **electroconvulsive therapy**

electroretinogram /ɪˌkektrəʊˈretɪnəgræm/ *noun* the printed result of electroretinography. Abbr **ERG**

electroretinography /ɪˌlektrəʊretɪˈnɒ grəfi/ *noun* the process of recording electrical changes in the retina when stimulated by light

electrosurgery /ɪˌlektrəʊˈsɜːdʒəri/ *noun* an operation in which the surgeon uses an electrical current to cut or cauterise tissue

electrotherapy /ɪˌlektrəʊˈθerəpi/ *noun* the treatment of a disorder such as some forms of paralysis by using low-frequency electric current to try to revive the muscles

element /ˈelɪmənt/ *noun* a basic simple chemical substance which cannot be broken down into simpler substances. ◊ **trace element**

elephantiasis /ˌelɪfənˈtaɪəsɪs/ *noun* a condition in which parts of the body swell and the skin becomes hardened, frequently caused by infestation with various species of the parasitic worm *Filaria*

elevate /ˈelɪveɪt/ *verb* to raise something or to lift something up ○ *To control bleeding, apply pressure and elevate the part.*

elevation /ˌeləˈveɪʃ(ə)n/ *noun* a raised part

elevation sling /ˌelɪˈveɪʃ(ə)n slɪŋ/ *noun* a sling tied round the neck, used to hold an injured hand or arm in a high position to control bleeding

elevator /ˈelɪveɪtə/ *noun* **1.** a muscle which raises part of the body **2.** a surgical instrument used to lift part of a broken bone

eliminate /ɪˈlɪmɪneɪt/ *verb* to remove waste matter from the body ○ *The excess salts are eliminated through the kidneys.*

elimination /ɪˌlɪmɪˈneɪʃ(ə)n/ *noun* the removal of waste matter from the body

elimination diet /ɪˌlɪmɪˈneɪʃ(ə)n ˌdaɪət/ *noun* a structured diet where different foods are eliminated one at a time in order to see the effect on symptoms, used in conditions such as allergies and attention deficit hyperactivity disorder

ELISA /ɪˈlaɪzə/ *noun* a process in which an enzyme binds to an antibody or antigen and causes a colour change that shows the presence or amount of protein in a sample of biological material. Full form **enzyme-linked immunosorbent assay**

elixir /ɪˈlɪksə/ *noun* a sweet liquid which hides the unpleasant taste of a drug

elliptocytosis /ɪˌlɪptəʊsaɪˈtəʊsɪs/ *noun* a condition in which unusual oval-shaped red cells appear in the blood

emaciated /ɪˈmeɪʃieɪtɪd/ *adjective* very thin and extremely underweight

emaciation /ɪˌmeɪsiˈeɪʃ(ə)n/ *noun* **1.** the fact of being extremely thin and underweight **2.** the loss of body tissue

emaculation /ɪˌmækjʊˈleɪʃ(ə)n/ *noun* the removal of spots from the skin

emasculation /ɪˌmæskjʊˈleɪʃ(ə)n/ *noun* **1.** the removal of the penis **2.** the loss of male characteristics

embalm /ɪmˈbɑːm/ *verb* to preserve a dead body by using special antiseptic chemicals to prevent decay

embolectomy /ˌembəˈlektəmi/ *noun* a surgical operation to remove a blood clot

emboli /ˈembəli/ *plural of* **embolus**

embolisation /ˌembəlaɪˈzeɪʃ(ə)n/, **embolization** *noun* the use of emboli inserted down a catheter into a blood vessel to treat internal bleeding

'…once a bleeding site has been located, a catheter is manipulated as near as possible to it, so that embolization can be carried out. Many different materials are used as the embolus.' [*British Medical Journal*]

embolism /ˈembəlɪz(ə)m/ *noun* the blocking of an artery by a mass of material, usually a blood clot, preventing the flow of blood

embolus /ˈembələs/ *noun* **1.** a mass of material which blocks a blood vessel, e.g. a blood clot, air bubble or fat globule **2.** material inserted into a blood vessel down a catheter to treat internal bleeding (NOTE: The plural is **emboli**.)

embrocation /ˌembrəˈkeɪʃ(ə)n/ *noun* same as **liniment**

embryo /ˈembriəʊ/ *noun* an unborn baby during the first eight weeks after conception (NOTE: After eight weeks, the unborn baby is called a **fetus**.)

embryological /ˌembriəˈlɒdʒɪk(ə)l/ *adjective* referring to embryology

embryology /ˌembriˈɒlədʒi/ *noun* the study of the early stages of the development of an embryo

embryonic /ˌembriˈɒnɪk/ *adjective* **1.** referring to an embryo **2.** in an early stage of development

embryonic ectoderm /ˌembriɒnɪk ˈektəʊdɜːm/ *noun* ♦ **ectoderm**

embryonic membrane /ˌembriɒnɪk ˈmembreɪn/ *noun* one of the two layers around an embryo providing protection and food supply, i.e. the **amnion** and the **chorion**

embryonic mesoderm /ˌembriɒnɪk ˈmesəʊdɜːm/ *noun* ♦ **mesoderm**

emergency /ɪˈmɜːdʒənsi/ *noun* a situation where urgent immediate action has to be taken

emergency medical technician /ɪˌmɜːdʒənsi ˌmedɪk(ə)l tekˈnɪʃ(ə)n/ *noun* US a trained paramedic who gives care to victims at the scene of an accident or in an ambulance. Abbr **EMT**

emergency medicine /ɪˌmɜːdʒənsi ˈmed(ə)s(ə)n/ *noun* the treatment of patients whose condition is serious and requires urgent immediate action

emergency room /ɪˈmɜːdʒənsi ruːm/ *noun* US the part of a hospital where people who need urgent immediate treatment are dealt with

emergency ward /ɪˈmɜːdʒənsi wɔːd/ *noun* the part of a hospital where people who need urgent immediate treatment are dealt with

emesis /ˈeməsɪs/ *noun* same as **vomiting**

emetic /ɪˈmetɪk/ *noun* a substance which causes vomiting ■ *adjective* causing vomiting

EMG *abbr* electromyogram

eminence /ˈemɪnəns/ *noun* something which protrudes from a surface, e.g. a lump on a bone or swelling on the skin

emissary vein /ˈemɪsəri ˌveɪn/ *noun* a vein through the skull which connects the venous sinuses with the scalp veins

emission /ɪˈmɪʃ(ə)n/ *noun* a discharge or release of fluid

emmenagogue /ɪˈmenəgɒg/ *noun* a drug which will help increase menstrual flow

emmetropia /ˌemɪˈtrəʊpiə/ *noun* the correct focusing of light rays by the eye onto the retina giving normal vision. Compare **ametropia**

emollient /ɪˈmɒliənt/ *noun* a substance which soothes or smooths the skin, e.g. to prevent the development of eczema ■ *adjective* smoothening

emotion /ɪˈməʊʃ(ə)n/ *noun* a strong feeling

emotional disorder /ɪˌməʊʃ(ə)nəl dɪsˈɔːdə/ *noun* a disorder due to worry, stress, grief or other strong emotion

emotional immaturity /ɪˌməʊʃ(ə)nəl ɪməˈtʃʊəti/ *noun* lacking in emotional development

empathy /ˈempəθi/ *noun* the ability to understand the problems and feelings of another person

emphysema /ˌemfɪˈsiːmə/ *noun* a condition in which the walls of the alveoli of the lungs break down, reducing the surface available for gas exchange and resulting in a lower oxygen level in the blood and shortness of breath. It can be caused by smoking, living in a polluted environment, old age, asthma or whooping cough. ◊ **surgical emphysema**

empirical treatment /ɪmˌpɪrɪk(ə)l ˈtriːtmənt/ *noun* treatment which is based on symptoms and clinical experience rather than on a thorough knowledge of the cause of the disorder

empowerment /ɪmˈpaʊəmənt/ *noun* the act of giving someone authority and power to make decisions that will affect them

empyema /ˌempaɪˈiːmə/ *noun* the collection of pus in a cavity, especially in the pleural cavity. Also called **pyothorax**

EMS *abbr* Emergency Medical Services

EMT *abbr US* emergency medical technician

emulsion /ɪˈmʌlʃən/ *noun* a combination of liquids such as oil and water which do not usually mix

EN *abbr* enrolled nurse

EN(G) *abbr* enrolled nurse (general)

EN(M) *abbr* enrolled nurse (mental)

EN(MH) *abbr* enrolled nurse (mental handicap)

en- /en, ɪn/ *prefix* 1. in, into 2. to provide with 3. to cause to be 4. to put into or cover with 5. to go into

enalapril /eˈnæləprɪl/ *noun* a drug used for the short-term management of high blood pressure

enamel /ɪˈnæm(ə)l/ *noun* the hard white shiny outer covering of the crown of a tooth

enanthema /ˌenənˈθiːmə/ *noun* a rash on a mucous membrane, such as that of the mouth or vagina, produced by the action of toxic substances on small blood vessels

enarthrosis /ˌenɑːˈθrəʊsɪs/ *noun* a ball and socket joint, e.g. the hip joint

encapsulated /ɪnˈkæpsjʊleɪtɪd/ *adjective* enclosed in a capsule or in a sheath of tissue

encefalin /enˈkefəlɪn/ *noun* another spelling of **encephalin**

encephal- /enkefəl/ *prefix* same as **encephalo-** (used before vowels)

encephalin /enˈkefəlɪn/ *noun* a peptide produced in the brain which acts as a natural pain-

killer. ◊ **endorphin** (NOTE: The US spelling is **enkephalin**.)

encephalitis /enˌkefəˈlaɪtɪs, enˌsefəˈlaɪtɪs/ *noun* inflammation of the brain

COMMENT: Encephalitis is caused by any of several viruses (**viral encephalitis**) and is also associated with infectious viral diseases such as measles or mumps. The variant **St Louis encephalitis** is transmitted by mosquitoes.

encephalitis lethargica /ˌenkefəlaɪtɪs lɪˈθɑːdʒɪkə/ *noun* same as **lethargic encephalitis**

encephalo- /enkefələ/ *prefix* referring to the brain

encephalocele /enˈkefələʊsiːl/ *noun* a condition in which the brain protrudes through a congenital or traumatic gap in the skull bones

encephalogram /enˈkefələgræm/, **encephalograph** /enˈkefələgrɑːf/ *noun* an X-ray photograph of the ventricles and spaces of the brain taken after air has been injected into the cerebrospinal fluid by lumbar puncture

encephalography /enˌkefəˈlɒgrəfi/ *noun* an X-ray examination of the ventricles and spaces of the brain taken after air has been injected into the cerebrospinal fluid by lumbar puncture

COMMENT: The air takes the place of the cerebrospinal fluid and makes it easier to photograph the ventricles clearly. This technique has been superseded by CT and MRI.

encephaloid /enˈkefəlɔɪd/ *adjective* like brain tissue

encephaloma /enˌkefəˈləʊmə/ *noun* a tumour of the brain

encephalomalacia /enˌkefələʊməˈleɪʃiə/ *noun* softening of the brain

encephalomyelitis /enˌkefələʊmaɪəˈlaɪtɪs/ *noun* a group of diseases which cause inflammation of the brain and the spinal cord

encephalomyelopathy /enˌkefələʊmaɪəˈlɒpəθi/ *noun* any condition where the brain and spinal cord are diseased

encephalon /enˈkefəlɒn/ *noun* same as **brain** (NOTE: The plural is **encephala**.)

encephalopathy /enˌkefəˈlɒpəθi/ *noun* any disease of the brain

enchondroma /ˌenkɒnˈdrəʊmə/ *noun* a tumour formed of cartilage growing inside a bone

enchondromatosis /ˌenkɒndrɒməˈtəʊsɪs/ *noun* a condition in which a tumour formed of cartilage grows inside a bone

encopresis /ˌenkəʊˈpriːsɪs/ *noun* faecal incontinence not associated with a physical condition or disease

encounter group /ɪnˈkaʊntə gruːp/ *noun* a form of treatment of psychological disorders, where people meet and talk about their problems in a group

encysted /en'sɪstɪd/ *adjective* enclosed in a capsule like a cyst

end- /end/ *prefix* same as **endo-** (*used before vowels*)

endanger /ɪn'deɪndʒə/ *verb* to put someone or something at risk ○ *The operation may endanger the life of the patient.*

endarterectomy /ˌendɑːtə'rektəmi/ *noun* the surgical removal of the lining of a blocked artery. Also called **rebore**

endarteritis /ˌendɑːtə'raɪtɪs/ *noun* inflammation of the inner lining of an artery

endarteritis obliterans /ˌendɑːtˌraɪtɪs ə 'blɪtərənz/ *noun* a condition where inflammation in an artery is so severe that it blocks the artery

end artery /'end ˌɑːtəri/ *noun* the last section of an artery which does not divide into smaller arteries and does not join to other arteries

endaural /end'ɔːrəl/ *adjective* inside the ear

endemic /en'demɪk/ *adjective* referring to any disease which is very common in specific places ○ *This disease is endemic to Mediterranean countries.*

endemic haemoptysis /en,demɪk hiː 'mɒptəsɪs/ *noun* same as **paragonimiasis**

endemic syphilis /en,demɪk 'sɪfəlɪs/ *adjective* same as **bejel**

endemic typhus /en,demɪk 'taɪfəs/ *noun* fever transmitted by fleas from rats

endemiology /en,diːmi'ɒlədʒi/ *noun* the study of endemic diseases

end-expiratory /ˌend ɪk'spaɪrətri/ *noun* ♦ **positive end-expiratory pressure**

endo- /endəʊ/ *prefix* inside

endobronchial /endəʊ'brɒŋkiəl/ *adjective* inside the bronchi

endocardial /ˌendəʊ'kɑːdiəl/ *adjective* referring to the endocardium

endocardial pacemaker /ˌendəʊkɑːdiəl 'peɪsmeɪkə/ *noun* a pacemaker attached to the lining of the heart

endocarditis /ˌendəʊkɑːˈdaɪtɪs/ *noun* inflammation of the membrane lining of the heart

endocardium /ˌendəʊ'kɑːdiəm/ *noun* a membrane which lines the heart. See illustration at **HEART** in Supplement

endocervicitis /ˌendəʊsɜːvɪ'saɪtɪs/ *noun* inflammation of the membrane in the neck of the uterus

endocervix /ˌendəʊ'sɜːvɪks/ *noun* a membrane which lines the neck of the uterus

endochondral /ˌendəʊ'kɒndrəl/ *adjective* inside a cartilage

endocrine /'endəʊkraɪn/ *adjective* relating to the endocrine glands or the hormones they secrete

endocrine gland /'endəʊkraɪn glænd/ *noun* a gland without a duct which produces hormones which are introduced directly into the bloodstream, e.g. the pituitary gland, thyroid gland, the adrenal gland and the gonads. Also called **ductless gland**. Compare **exocrine gland**

endocrine system /'endəʊkraɪn ˌsɪstəm/ *noun* a system of related ductless glands

endocrinologist /ˌendəʊkrɪ'nɒlədʒɪst/ *noun* a doctor who specialises in the study of endocrinology

endocrinology /ˌendəʊkrɪ'nɒlədʒi/ *noun* the study of the endocrine system, its function and effects

endoderm /'endəʊdɜːm/ *noun* the inner of three layers surrounding an embryo. Also called **entoderm**

COMMENT: The endoderm gives rise to most of the epithelium of the respiratory system, the alimentary canal, some of the ductless glands the bladder and part of the urethra.

endodermal /ˌendəʊ'dɜːm(ə)l/ *adjective* referring to the endoderm. Also called **entodermal**

endodontia /ˌendəʊ'dɒnʃiə/ *noun* treatment of chronic toothache by removing the roots of a tooth

endogenous /en'dɒdʒənəs/ *adjective* developing or being caused by something inside an organism. Compare **exogenous**

endogenous depression /en,dɒdʒənəs dɪ'preʃ(ə)n/ *noun* depression caused by no obvious external factor

endogenous eczema /en,dɒdʒənəs 'ek sɪmə/ *noun* eczema which is caused by no obvious external factor

endolymph /'endəʊlɪmf/ *noun* a fluid inside the membranous labyrinth in the inner ear

endolymphatic duct /ˌendəʊlɪmfætɪk 'dʌkt/ *noun* a duct which carries the endolymph inside the membranous labyrinth

endolysin /en'dɒlɪsɪn/ *noun* a substance present in cells, which kills bacteria

endometria /ˌendəʊ'miːtriə/ plural of **endometrium**

endometrial /ˌendəʊ'miːtriəl/ *adjective* referring to the endometrium

endometrial laser ablation /ˌendəʊmiːtriəl 'leɪzə əb,leɪʃ(ə)n/ *noun* a gynaecological surgical procedure using a laser to treat fibroids or other causes of thickening of the lining of the uterus

endometriosis /ˌendəʊmiːtri'əʊsɪs/ *noun* a condition affecting women, in which tissue similar to the tissue of the uterus is found in other parts of the body

endometritis /ˌendəʊmɪ'traɪtɪs/ *noun* inflammation of the lining of the uterus

endometrium /ˌendəʊ'miːtriəm/ *noun* the mucous membrane lining the uterus, part of which is shed at each menstruation (NOTE: The plural is **endometria**.)

endomyocarditis /ˌendəʊmaɪəʊkɑːˈdaɪtɪs/ *noun* inflammation of the muscle and inner membrane of the heart

endomysium /ˌendəʊˈmɪsiəm/ *noun* connective tissue around and between muscle fibres

endoneurium /ˌendəʊˈnjʊəriəm/ *noun* fibrous tissue between the individual fibres in a nerve

endoparasite /ˌendəʊˈpærəsaɪt/ *noun* a parasite which lives inside its host, e.g. in the intestines. Compare **ectoparasite**

endophthalmitis /ˌendɒfθælˈmaɪtɪs/ *noun* inflammation of the interior of the eyeball

end organ /ˈend ˌɔːgən/ *noun* a nerve ending with encapsulated nerve filaments

endorphin /enˈdɔːfɪn/ *noun* a peptide produced by the brain which acts as a natural painkiller. ◊ **encephalin**

endoscope /ˈendəskəʊp/ *noun* an instrument used to examine the inside of the body, made of a thin tube which is passed into the body down a passage. The tube has a fibre optic light, and may have small surgical instruments attached.

endoscopic retrograde cholangiopancreatography /ˌendəʊskɒpɪk ˌretrəgreɪd kəˈlændʒiəʊpæŋkriəˈtɒgrəfi/ *noun* a method used to examine the pancreatic duct and bile duct for possible obstructions. Abbr **ERCP**

endoscopy /enˈdɒskəpi/ *noun* an examination of the inside of the body using an endoscope

endoskeleton /ˈendəʊˌskelɪt(ə)n/ *noun* the inner structure of bones and cartilage in an animal

endosteum /enˈdɒstiəm/ *noun* a membrane lining the bone marrow cavity inside a long bone

endothelial /ˌendəʊˈθiːliəl/ *adjective* referring to the endothelium

endothelioma /ˌendəʊθiːliˈəʊmə/ *noun* a malignant tumour originating inside the endothelium

endothelium /ˌendəʊˈθiːliəm/ *noun* a membrane of special cells which lines the heart, the lymph vessels, the blood vessels and various body cavities. Compare **epithelium, mesothelium**

endotoxin /ˌendəʊˈtɒksɪn/ *noun* a toxic substance released after the death of some bacterial cells

endotracheal /ˌendəʊˈtreɪkiəl/ *adjective* same as **intratracheal**

endotracheal tube /ˌendəʊˈtreɪkiəl tjuːb/ *noun* a tube passed down the trachea, through either the nose or mouth, in anaesthesia or to help a person breathe

end plate /ˈend pleɪt/ *noun* the end of a motor nerve, where it joins muscle fibre

end stage renal disease /ˌend steɪdʒ ˈriːn(ə)l dɪˌziːz/ *noun* the stage of kidney disease at which uraemia occurs and dialysis needs to start. Abbr **ESRD**

enema /ˈenɪmə/ *noun* a liquid substance put into the rectum to introduce a drug into the body, to wash out the colon before an operation or for diagnosis

enema bag /ˈenəmə bæg/ *noun* a bag containing the liquid for an enema, attached to a tube into the rectum

energy /ˈenədʒi/ *noun* the force or strength to carry out activities ○ *You need to eat certain types of food to give you energy.*

enervation /ˌenəˈveɪʃ(ə)n/ *noun* **1.** general nervous weakness **2.** a surgical operation to remove a nerve

engagement /ɪnˈgeɪdʒmənt/ *noun* (*in obstetrics*) the moment where part of the fetus, usually the head, enters the pelvis at the beginning of labour

engorged /ɪnˈgɔːdʒd/ *adjective* excessively filled with liquid, usually blood

engorgement /ɪnˈgɔːdʒmənt/ *noun* the excessive filling of a vessel, usually with blood

enkephalin /enˈkefəlɪn/ *noun* US same as **encephalin**

enophthalmos /ˌenɒfˈθælməs/ *noun* a condition in which the eyes are very deep in their sockets

enostosis /ˌenəˈstəʊsɪs/ *noun* a harmless growth inside a bone, usually in the skull or in a long bone

enrolled /ɪnˈrəʊld/ *adjective* registered on an official list

Enrolled Nurse /ɪnˌrəʊld ˈnɜːs/ *noun* ♦ **second-level nurse**

ensiform /ˈensifɔːm/ *adjective* shaped like a sword

ensiform cartilage /ˌensifɔːm ˈkɑːtəlɪdʒ/ *noun* same as **xiphoid process**

ENT *abbr* Ear, Nose & Throat

Entamoeba coli /ˌentəmiːbə ˈkəʊlaɪ/ *noun* a harmless intestinal parasite

Entamoeba gingivalis /ˌentəmiːbə ˌdʒɪndʒɪˈvælɪs/ *noun* an amoeba that lives in the gums and tonsils, and causes gingivitis

Entamoeba histolytica /ˌentəmiːbə ˌhɪstəˈlɪtɪkə/ *noun* an intestinal amoeba which causes amoebic dysentery

ENT department /ˌiː en ˈtiː dɪˌpɑːtmənt/ *noun* a department of otorhinolaryngology

ENT doctor /ˌiː en ˈtiː ˌdɒktə/ *noun* same as **otorhinolaryngologist**

enter- /entə/ *prefix* same as **entero-** (*used before vowels*)

enteral /ˈentərəl/ *adjective* **1.** referring to the intestine. Compare **parenteral 2.** referring to medication or food which is taken by mouth or through a nasogastric tube

enteral feeding /ˌentərəl 'fiːdɪŋ/ *noun* the feeding of a person by a nasogastric tube or by the infusion of liquid food directly into the intestine. Also called **enteral nutrition**

'Standard nasogastric tubes are usually sufficient for enteral feeding in critically ill patients' [*British Journal of Nursing*]

enteralgia /ˌentər'ældʒə/ *noun* same as **colic**

enterally /'entərəli/ *adverb* referring to a method of feeding a person by nasogastric tube or directly into the intestine

'All patients requiring nutrition are fed enterally, whether nasogastrically or directly into the small intestine' [*British Journal of Nursing*]

enteral nutrition /ˌentərəl njuː'trɪʃ(ə)n/ *noun* same as **enteral feeding**

enterectomy /ˌentər'ektəmi/ *noun* the surgical removal of part of the intestine

enteric /en'terɪk/ *adjective* referring to the intestine

enteric-coated /en,terɪk 'kəʊtɪd/ *adjective* referring to a capsule with a coating which prevents it from being digested and releasing the drug until it reaches the intestine

enteric fever /en,terɪk 'fiːvə/ *noun* US **1.** any one of three fevers (typhoid, paratyphoid A and paratyphoid B) **2.** any febrile disease of the intestines

enteritis /ˌentə'raɪtɪs/ *noun* inflammation of the mucous membrane of the intestine

entero- /entərəʊ/ *prefix* referring to the intestine

Enterobacteria /ˌentərəʊbæk'tɪəriə/ *noun* a family of Gram-negative bacteria, including Salmonella, Shigella, Escherichia and Klebsiella

enterobiasis /ˌentərəʊ'baɪəsɪs/ *noun* a common children's disease, caused by threadworms in the large intestine which cause itching round the anus. Also called **oxyuriasis**

Enterobius /ˌentə'rəʊbiəs/ *noun* a small thin nematode worm, one species of which, *Enterobius vermicularis*, infests the large intestine and causes itching round the anus. Also called **threadworm**, **pinworm**

enterocele /'entərəʊsiːl/, **enterocoele** /'enterəʊsiːl/ *noun* a hernia of the intestine

enterocentesis /ˌentərəʊsen'tiːsɪs/ *noun* surgical puncturing of the intestines where a hollow needle is pushed through the abdominal wall into the intestine to remove gas or fluid

enterococcus /ˌentərəʊ'kɒkəs/ *noun* a streptococcal bacterium that lives in the intestine (NOTE: The plural is **enterococci**.)

enterocoele /'enterəʊsiːl/ *noun* another spelling of **enterocele**

enterocolitis /ˌentərəʊkə'laɪtɪs/ *noun* inflammation of the colon and small intestine

enterogastrone /ˌentərəʊ'gæstrəʊn/ *noun* a hormone released in the duodenum, which controls secretions of the stomach

enterogenous /ˌentərəʊ'dʒiːnəs/ *adjective* originating in the intestine

enterolith /'entərəʊlɪθ/ *noun* a stone in the intestine

enteron /'entərɒn/ *noun* the whole intestinal tract

enteropathy /ˌentə'rɒpəθi/ *noun* any disorder of the intestine. ◊ **gluten-induced enteropathy**

enteropeptidase /ˌentərəʊ'peptɪdeɪz/ *noun* an enzyme produced by glands in the small intestine

enteroptosis /ˌentərɒp'təʊsɪs/ *noun* a condition in which the intestine is lower than usual in the abdominal cavity

enterorrhaphy /ˌentər'ɔːrəfi/ *noun* a surgical operation to stitch up a perforated intestine

enteroscope /'entərəskəʊp/ *noun* an instrument for inspecting the inside of the intestine

enterospasm /'entərəʊ,spæz(ə)m/ *noun* an irregular painful contraction of the intestine

enterostomy /ˌentə'rɒstəmi/ *noun* a surgical operation to make an opening between the small intestine and the abdominal wall

enterotomy /ˌentə'rɒtəmi/ *noun* a surgical incision in the intestine

enterotoxin /ˌentərəʊ'tɒksɪn/ *noun* a bacterial exotoxin which particularly affects the intestine

enterovirus /ˌentərəʊ'vaɪrəs/ *noun* a virus which prefers to live in the intestine. Enteroviruses include poliomyelitis virus, Coxsackie viruses and the echoviruses.

enterozoon /ˌentərəʊ'zəʊɒn/ *noun* a parasite which infests the intestine (NOTE: The plural is **enterozoa**.)

entoderm /'entəʊdɜːm/ *noun* same as **endoderm**

entodermal /ˌentəʊ'dɜːm(ə)l/ *adjective* same as **endodermal**

Entonox /'entənɒks/ *noun* a gas consisting of 50% oxygen and 50% nitrous oxide that is used as a painkiller during childbirth

entopic /ɪn'tɒpɪk/ *adjective* located or taking place in the usual position. Opposite **ectopic**

entropion /ɪn'trəʊpiən/ *noun* a turning of the edge of the eyelid towards the inside

enucleate /ɪ'njuːklieɪt/ *verb* to remove something completely

enucleation /ɪ,njuːkli'eɪʃ(ə)n/ *noun* **1.** the surgical removal of all of a tumour **2.** the surgical removal of the whole eyeball

enuresis /ˌenjʊ'riːsɪs/ *noun* the involuntary passing of urine

enuretic /ˌenjʊ'retɪk/ *adjective* referring to enuresis, or causing enuresis

envenomation /ɪn,venə'meɪʃ(ə)n/ *noun* the use of snake venom as part of a therapeutic treatment

environment /ɪn'vaɪrənmənt/ *noun* the conditions and influences under which an organism lives

environmental /ɪn,vaɪrən'ment(ə)l/ *adjective* referring to the environment

Environmental Health Officer /ɪn ,vaɪrənment(ə)l 'helθ ,ɒfɪsə/ *noun* an official of a local authority who examines the environment and tests for air pollution, bad sanitation, noise pollution and similar threats to public health. Abbr **EHO**

environmental temperature /ɪn,vaɪrən ment(ə)l 'temprɪtʃə/ *noun* the temperature of the air outside the body

enzymatic /,enzaɪ'mætɪk/ *adjective* referring to enzymes

enzyme /'enzaɪm/ *noun* a protein substance produced by living cells which aids a biochemical reaction in the body (NOTE: The names of enzymes mostly end with the suffix -**ase**.)

COMMENT: Many different enzymes exist in the body, working in the digestive system, in the metabolic processes and helping the synthesis of certain compounds.

enzyme-linked immunosorbent assay /,enzaɪm lɪŋkt ,ɪmjʊnəʊ,sɔːbənt 'æseɪ/ *noun* full form of **ELISA**

eonism /'iːənɪz(ə)m/ *noun* cross-dressing, when a male wears female dress

eosin /'iːəʊsɪn/ *noun* a red crystalline solid used as a biological staining dye

eosinopenia /,iːəʊsɪnə'piːniə/ *noun* a reduction in the number of eosinophils in the blood

eosinophil /,iːəʊ'sɪnəfɪl/ *noun* a type of cell that can be stained with eosin

eosinophilia /,iːəʊsɪnə'fɪliə/ *noun* an excess of eosinophils in the blood

eparterial /,epɑː'tɪəriəl/ *adjective* situated over or on an artery

ependyma /ɪ'pendɪmə/ *noun* a thin membrane which lines the ventricles of the brain and the central canal of the spinal cord

ependymal /ɪ'pendɪm(ə)l/ *adjective* referring to the ependyma

ependymal cell /ɪ'pendɪm(ə)l sel/ *noun* one of the cells which form the ependyma

ependymoma /ɪ,pendɪ'məʊmə/ *noun* a tumour in the brain originating in the ependyma

ephedrine /'efɪdriːn/ *noun* a drug that relieves asthma and blocked noses by causing the air passages to widen

ephidrosis /,efɪ'drəʊsɪs/ *noun* an unusual amount of sweat

epi- /epɪ/ *prefix* on or over

epiblepharon /,epɪ'blefərɒn/ *noun* an unusual fold of skin over the eyelid, which may press the eyelashes against the eyeball

epicanthus /,epɪ'kænθəs/, **epicanthic fold** / ,epɪkænθɪk 'fəʊld/ *noun* a large fold of skin

in the inner corner of the eye, common in babies and also found in adults of some groups such as the Chinese

epicardial /,epɪ'kɑːdiəl/ *adjective* referring to the epicardium

epicardial pacemaker /,epɪkɑːdiəl 'peɪs meɪkə/ *noun* a pacemaker attached to the surface of the ventricle

epicardium /,epɪ'kɑːdiəm/ *noun* the inner layer of the pericardium which lines the walls of the heart, outside the myocardium. See illustration at HEART in Supplement

epicondyle /,epɪ'kɒndaɪl/ *noun* a projecting part of the round end of a bone above the condyle

epicondylitis /,epɪkɒndɪ'laɪtɪs/ *noun* same as **tennis elbow**

epicranium /,epɪ'kreɪniəm/ *noun* the five layers of the scalp, the skin and hair on the head covering the skull

epicranius /,epɪ'kreɪniəs/ *noun* a scalp muscle

epicritic /,epɪ'krɪtɪk/ *adjective* referring to the nerves which govern the fine senses of touch and temperature

epidemic /,epɪ'demɪk/ *adjective* spreading quickly through a large part of the population ○ *The disease rapidly reached epidemic proportions.* ■ *noun* an outbreak of an infectious disease which spreads very quickly and affects a large number of people

epidemic pleurodynia /,epɪdemɪk ,plʊərə 'dɪniə/ *noun* a viral disease affecting the intestinal muscles, with symptoms like influenza, such as fever, headaches and pains in the chest. Also called **Bornholm disease**

epidemic typhus /,epɪdemɪk 'taɪfəs/ *noun* fever with headaches, mental disorder and a rash, caused by lice which come from other humans

epidemiological /,epɪ,diːmiə'lɒdʒɪk(ə)l/ *adjective* concerning epidemiology

epidemiologist /,epɪ,diːmi'ɒlədʒɪst/ *noun* a person who specialises in the study of diseases in groups of people

epidemiology /,epɪ,diːmi'ɒlədʒi/ *noun* the study of diseases in the community, in particular how they spread and how they can be controlled

epidermal /,epɪ'dɜːm(ə)l/ *adjective* referring to the epidermis

epidermis /,epɪ'dɜːmɪs/ *noun* the outer layer of the skin, including the dead skin on the surface. Also called **cuticle**

epidermoid cyst /,epɪdɜːmɔɪd 'sɪst/ *noun* same as **sebaceous cyst**

epidermolysis /,epɪdɜː'mɒləsɪs/ *noun* separation of the epidermis from the tissue underneath, usually forming a blister

epidermolysis bullosa /ˌepɪdɜːˌmɒləsɪs bʊˈləʊsə/ *noun* a group of disorders where blisters form on the skin

Epidermophyton /ˌepɪdɜːˈmɒfɪtən/ *noun* a fungus which grows on the skin and causes athlete's foot, among other disorders

epidermophytosis /ˌepɪˌdɜːməʊfaɪˈtəʊsɪs/ *noun* a fungus infection of the skin, e.g. athlete's foot

epididymal /ˌepɪˈdɪdɪm(ə)l/ *adjective* referring to the epididymis

epididymectomy /ˌepɪdɪdɪˈmektəmi/ *noun* the removal of the epididymis

epididymis /ˌepɪˈdɪdɪmɪs/ *noun* a long twisting thin tube at the back of the testis, which forms part of the efferent duct of the testis, and in which spermatozoa are stored before ejaculation. See illustration at UROGENITAL SYSTEM (MALE) in Supplement

epididymitis /ˌepɪdɪdɪˈmaɪtɪs/ *noun* inflammation of the epididymis

epididymo-orchitis /epɪˌdɪdɪməʊ ɔːˈkaɪtɪs/ *noun* inflammation of the epididymis and the testes

epidural /ˌepɪˈdjʊərəl/ *adjective* on the outside of the dura mater. Also called **extradural** ■ *noun* same as **epidural anaesthesia**

epidural anaesthesia /epɪˌdjʊərəl ˌænəsˈθiːziə/ *noun* a local anaesthesia in which anaesthetic is injected into the space between the vertebral canal and the dura mater

epidural block /ˌepɪdjʊərəl ˈblɒk/ *noun* analgesia produced by injecting an analgesic solution into the space between the vertebral canal and the dura mater

epidural space /ˌepɪdjʊərəl ˈspeɪs/ *noun* a space in the spinal cord between the vertebral canal and the dura mater

epigastric /ˌepɪˈɡæstrɪk/ *adjective* referring to the upper abdomen ○ *The patient complained of pains in the epigastric area.*

epigastrium /ˌepɪˈɡæstriəm/ *noun* the part of the upper abdomen between the ribcage and the navel. Also called **the pit of the stomach**

epigastrocele /ˌepɪˈɡæstrəʊsiːl/ *noun* a hernia in the upper abdomen

epiglottis /ˌepɪˈɡlɒtɪs/ *noun* a flap of cartilage at the root of the tongue which moves to block the windpipe when food is swallowed, so that the food does not go down the trachea

epiglottitis /ˌepɪɡlɒˈtaɪtɪs/ *noun* inflammation and swelling of the epiglottis

epilation /ˌepɪˈleɪʃ(ə)n/ *noun* the process of removing hair by destroying the hair follicles

epilepsy /ˈepɪlepsi/ *noun* a disorder of the nervous system in which there are convulsions and loss of consciousness due to a disordered discharge of cerebral neurones

COMMENT: The commonest form of epilepsy is major epilepsy or 'grand mal', where a person loses consciousness and falls to the ground with convulsions. A less severe form is minor epilepsy or 'petit mal', where attacks last only a few seconds, and the person appears simply to be hesitating or thinking deeply.

epileptic /ˌepɪˈleptɪk/ *adjective* having epilepsy, or relating to epilepsy ■ *noun* a person with epilepsy (NOTE: The word 'epileptic' to describe a person is now avoided.)

epileptic fit /ˌepɪleptɪk ˈfɪt/ *noun* an attack of convulsions, and sometimes unconsciousness, due to epilepsy

epileptiform /ˌepɪˈleptɪfɔːm/ *adjective* being similar to epilepsy

epileptogenic /ˌepɪˌleptəʊˈdʒenɪk/ *adjective* causing epilepsy

epiloia /ˌepɪˈlɔɪə/ *noun* a hereditary disease of the brain associated with learning disabilities, epilepsy and tumours on the kidney and heart. Also called **tuberose sclerosis**

epimenorrhagia /ˌepɪmenəˈreɪdʒə/ *noun* very heavy bleeding during menstruation occurring at very short intervals

epimenorrhoea /ˌepɪmenəˈriːə/ *noun* menstruation at shorter intervals than twenty-eight days

epimysium /ˌepɪˈmaɪsiəm/ *noun* a connective tissue binding striated muscle fibres

epinephrine /ˌepɪˈnefrɪn/ *noun* US same as **adrenaline**

epineurium /ˌepɪˈnjʊəriəm/ *noun* a sheath of connective tissue round a nerve

epiphenomenon /ˌepɪfəˈnɒmɪnən/ *noun* an unusual symptom which may not be caused by a disease

epiphora /eˈpɪfərə/ *noun* a condition in which the eye fills with tears either because the lacrimal duct is blocked or because excessive tears are being secreted

epiphyseal /ˌepɪˈfɪziəl/ *adjective* referring to an epiphysis

epiphyseal cartilage /epɪˌfɪziəl ˈkɑːtəlɪdʒ/ *noun* a type of cartilage in the bones of children and adolescents which expands and hardens as the bones grow to full size

epiphyseal line /epɪˈfɪziəl laɪn/ *noun* a plate of epiphyseal cartilage separating the epiphysis and the diaphysis of a long bone

epiphysis /eˈpɪfəsɪs/ *noun* the area of growth in a bone which is separated from the main part of the bone by cartilage until bone growth stops. See illustration at BONE STRUCTURE in Supplement. Compare **diaphysis, metaphysis**

epiphysis cerebri /eˌpɪfəsɪs səˈriːbri/ *noun* the pineal gland. See illustration at BONE STRUCTURE in Supplement

epiphysitis /ˌepɪfɪˈsaɪtɪs/ *noun* inflammation of an epiphysis

epiplo- /epɪpləʊ/ *prefix* referring to the omentum

epiplocele /eˈpɪpləʊsiːl/ *noun* a hernia containing part of the omentum

epiploic /ˌepɪˈpləʊɪk/ *adjective* referring to the omentum

epiploon /eˈpɪpləʊɒn/ *noun* same as **omentum**

episclera /ˈepɪsklɪərə/ *noun* the outer surface of the sclera of the eyeball

episcleritis /ˌepɪskləˈraɪtɪs/ *noun* inflammation of the outer surface of the sclera in the eyeball

episi- /əpɪziəʊ/, **episio-** /əpɪzi/ *prefix* referring to the vulva

episiorrhaphy /əˌpɪziˈɔːrəfi/ *noun* a procedure for stitching torn labia majora

episiotomy /əˌpɪziˈɒtəmi/ *noun* a surgical cut of the perineum near the vagina to prevent tearing during childbirth

episode /ˈepɪsəʊd/ *noun* a separate occurrence of an illness

episodic /ˌepɪˈsɒdɪk/ *adjective* happening in separate but related incidents, e.g. asthma which occurs in separate attacks

epispadias /ˌepɪˈspeɪdiəs/ *noun* a congenital condition where the urethra opens on the top of the penis and not at the end. Compare **hypospadias**

epispastic /ˌepɪˈspæstɪk/ *noun* same as **vesicant**

epistaxis /ˌepɪˈstæksɪs/ *noun* same as **nose-bleed**

epithalamus /ˌepɪˈθæləməs/ *noun* the part of the forebrain containing the pineal body

epithelial /ˌepɪˈθiːliəl/ *adjective* referring to the epithelium

epithelialisation /ˌepɪˌθiːliəlaɪˈzeɪʃ(ə)n/, **epithelialization** *noun* the growth of skin over a wound

epithelial layer /epɪˌθiːliəl ˈleɪə/ *noun* the epithelium

epithelial tissue /epɪˌθiːliəl ˈtɪʃuː/ *noun* epithelial cells arranged as a continuous sheet consisting of one or several layers

epithelioma /epɪθiːliˈəʊmə/ *noun* a tumour arising from epithelial cells

epithelium /ˌepɪˈθiːliəm/ *noun* the layer or layers of cells covering an organ, including the skin and the lining of all hollow cavities except blood vessels, lymphatics and serous cavities. Compare **endothelium, mesothelium**

COMMENT: Epithelium is classified according to the shape of the cells and the number of layers of cells which form it. The types of epithelium according to the number of layers are: **simple epithelium** (epithelium formed of a single layer of cells) and **stratified epithelium** (epithelium formed of several layers of cells). The main types of epithelial cells are: **columnar epithelium** (simple epithelium with long narrow cells, forming the lining of the intestines); **ciliated epithelium** (simple epithelium where the cells have little hairs, forming the lining of air passages); **cuboidal epithelium** (with cube-shaped cells, forming the lining of glands and intestines) and **squamous epi-**

thelium or **pavement epithelium** (with flat cells like scales, forming the lining of the pericardium, peritoneum and pleura).

epituberculosis /ˌepɪtjuˌbɜːkjʊˈləʊsɪs/ *noun* swelling of the lymph node in the thorax, due to tuberculosis

eponym /ˈepənɪm/ *noun* a procedure, disease or part of the body which is named after a person

COMMENT: An eponym can refer to a disease or condition such as Dupuytren's contracture, or Guillain–Barré syndrome, a part of the body such as circle of Willis, an organism such as Leishmania, a surgical procedure such as Trendelenburg's operation or an appliance such as Kirschner wire.

Epsom salts /ˌepsəm ˈsɔːlts/ *noun* same as **magnesium sulphate**

Epstein–Barr virus /ˌepstaɪn ˈbɑː ˌvaɪrəs/ *noun* a virus which probably causes glandular fever. Also called **EB virus** [Isolated and described 1964. After Michael Anthony Epstein (b. 1921), Bristol pathologist; Murray Llewellyn Barr (1908–95), Canadian anatomist and cytologist, head of the Department of Anatomy at the University of Western Ontario, Canada.]

epulis /ɪˈpjuːlɪs/ *noun* a small fibrous swelling on a gum

equi- /iːkwɪ, ekwɪ/ *prefix* equal

equilibrium /ˌiːkwɪˈlɪbriəm/ *noun* a state of balance

equinovarus /ɪˌkwaɪnəʊˈveərəs/ *noun* ♦ talipes

equipment /ɪˈkwɪpmənt/ *noun* apparatus or tools which are required to do something ○ *The centre urgently needs surgical equipment.* ○ *The surgeons complained about the out-of-date equipment in the hospital.* (NOTE: No plural: for one item say *a piece of equipment.*)

ER *abbr* **1.** *US* emergency room **2.** endoplasmic reticulum

eradicate /ɪˈrædɪkeɪt/ *verb* to remove something completely ○ *international action to eradicate tuberculosis*

eradication /ɪˌrædɪˈkeɪʃ(ə)n/ *noun* the act of removing something completely

Erb's palsy /ˌɜːbz ˈpɔːlzi/, **Erb's paralysis** /ˌɜːbz pəˈræləsɪs/ *noun* a condition in which an arm is paralysed because of birth injuries to the brachial plexus. ◊ **Bell's palsy**

ERCP *abbr* endoscopic retrograde cholangiopancreatography

erect /ɪˈrekt/ *adjective* stiff and straight

erectile /ɪˈrektaɪl/ *adjective* able to become erect

erectile dysfunction /ɪˌrektaɪl dɪsˈfʌŋkʃən/ *noun* a condition in which a man finds it difficult or impossible to have or maintain an erection during intercourse

erectile tissue /ɪˈrektaɪl ˌtɪʃuː/ *noun* vascular tissue which can become erect and stiff when engorged with blood, e.g. the corpus cavernosum in the penis

erection /ɪ'rekʃən/ *noun* a state where a body part such as the penis becomes swollen because of engorgement with blood

erector /ɪ'rektə/ *noun* a small muscle which raises a body part

erector spinae /ɪ,rektə 'spaɪniː/ *noun* a large muscle starting at the base of the spine, and dividing as it runs up the spine

erepsin /ɪ'repsɪn/ *noun* a mixture of enzymes produced by the glands in the intestine, used in the production of amino acids

erethism /'erəθɪz(ə)m/ *noun* unusual irritability

ERG *abbr* electroretinogram

ergograph /'ɜːgəʊɡrɑːf/ *noun* apparatus which records the work of one or several muscles

ergometrine maleate /,ɜːɡəʊmetriːn 'mæliʲeɪt/ *noun* a drug used to speed up the delivery of the placenta in childbirth and to control postnatal bleeding

ergonomics /,ɜːɡə'nɒmɪks/ *noun* the study of humans at work

ergot /'ɜːɡət/ *noun* a disease of rye caused by the fungus *Clariceps purpurea*

ergotamine /ɜː'ɡɒtəmiːn/ *noun* a drug that causes narrowing of blood vessels and alleviates migraine, derived from the ergot fungus

ergotism /'ɜːɡətɪz(ə)m/ *noun* poisoning caused by eating rye which has been contaminated with the ergot fungus

COMMENT: The symptoms of ergotism are muscle cramps and dry gangrene in the fingers and toes.

erogenous /ɪ'rɒdʒənəs/ *adjective* producing sexual excitement

erogenous zone /ɪ'rɒdʒənəs zəʊn/ *noun* a part of the body which, if stimulated, produces sexual arousal, e.g. the penis, clitoris or nipples

erosion /ɪ'rəʊʒ(ə)n/ *noun* the action of wearing away tissue or breaking down tissue

erotic /ɪ'rɒtɪk/ *adjective* relating to or arousing the feeling of sexual desire

ERPC *abbr* evacuation of retained products of conception

eructation /,iːrʌk'teɪʃ(ə)n/ *noun* same as **belching**

erupt /ɪ'rʌpt/ *verb* to break through the skin ○ *The permanent incisors erupt before the premolars.*

eruption /ɪ'rʌpʃən/ *noun* 1. something which breaks through the skin, e.g. a rash or pimple 2. the appearance of a new tooth in a gum

ery- /erɪ/ *prefix* same as **erythro-**

erysipelas /,erɪ'sɪpələs/ *noun* a contagious skin disease, where the skin on the face becomes hot, red and painful, caused by *Streptococcus pyogenes*

erysipeloid /,erɪ'sɪpəlɔɪd/ *noun* a bacterial skin infection caused by touching infected fish or meat

erythema /,erɪ'θiːmə/ *noun* redness on the skin, caused by hyperaemia of the blood vessels near the surface

erythema ab igne /,erɪθiːmə æb 'ɪɡneɪ/ *noun* a pattern of red lines on the skin caused by exposure to heat

erythema induratum /,erɪθiːmə ,ɪndjuˈreɪtəm/ *noun* a tubercular disease where ulcerating nodules appear on the legs of young women. Also called **Bazin's disease**

erythema multiforme /,erɪθiːmə 'mʌltiˌfɔːmi/ *noun* the sudden appearance of inflammatory red patches and sometimes blisters on the skin

erythema nodosum /,erɪθiːmə nəʊ'dəʊsəm/ *noun* an inflammatory disease where red swellings appear on the front of the legs

erythema pernio /,erɪθiːmə 'pɜːniəʊ/ *noun* same as **chilblain**

erythema serpens /,erɪθiːmə 'sɜːpens/ *noun* a bacterial skin infection caused by touching infected fish or meat

erythematosus /,erɪ,θiːmə'təʊsɪs/ ♦ **lupus**

erythematous /,erɪ'θiːmətəs/ *adjective* referring to erythema

erythr- /erɪθr/ *prefix* same as **erythro-** (*used before vowels*)

erythraemia /,erɪ'θriːmiə/ *noun* a blood disorder where the number of red blood cells increases sharply, together with an increase in the number of white cells, making the blood thicker and slower to flow. Also called **polycythaemia vera**

erythrasma /,erɪ'θræzmə/ *noun* a persistent bacterial skin infection occurring in a fold in the skin or where two skin surfaces touch, such as between the toes. It is caused by *Corynebacterium*.

erythro- /ɪrɪθrəʊ/ *prefix* red

erythroblast /ɪ'rɪθrəblæst/ *noun* a cell which forms an erythrocyte or red blood cell

erythroblastosis /ɪ,rɪθrəʊblæ'stəʊsɪs/ *noun* the presence of erythroblasts in the blood, usually found in haemolytic anaemia

COMMENT: Usually erythroblastosis occurs where the mother is rhesus negative and has developed rhesus positive antibodies, which are passed into the blood of a rhesus positive fetus.

erythroblastosis fetalis /ɪ,rɪθrəʊblæˌstəʊsɪs fiː'tɑːlɪs/ *noun* a blood disease affecting newborn babies, caused by a reaction between the rhesus factor of the mother and the fetus

erythrocyanosis /ɪ,rɪθrəsaɪə'nəʊsɪs/ *noun* red and purple patches on the skin of the thighs, often accompanied by chilblains and made worse by cold

erythrocyte /ɪ'rɪθrəsaɪt/ *noun* a mature red blood cell

'...anemia may be due to insufficient erythrocyte production, in which case the corrected reticulocyte count will be low, or it may be due to hemorrhage or hemolysis, in which cases there should be reticulocyte response' [*Southern Medical Journal*]

erythrocyte sedimentation rate /ɪ,rɪθrə saɪt sedɪmen'teɪʃ(ə)n reɪt/ *noun* a test that measures how fast erythrocytes settle in a sample of blood plasma, used to confirm whether various blood conditions are present. Abbr **ESR**

erythrocytosis /ɪ,rɪθrəsaɪ'təʊsɪs/ *noun* an increase in the number of red blood cells in the blood

erythroderma /ɪ,rɪθrə'dɜːmə/ *noun* a condition in which the skin becomes red and flakes off

erythroedema /ɪ,rɪθrɔɪ'diːmə/ *noun* same as **acrodynia**

erythrogenesis /ɪ,rɪθrə'dʒenəsɪs/, **erythropoiesis** /ɪ,rɪθrəpɔɪ'iːsɪs/ *noun* the formation of red blood cells in red bone marrow

erythromelalgia /ɪ,rɪθrəmel'ældʒə/ *noun* a painful swelling of blood vessels in the extremities

erythromycin /ɪ,rɪθrə'maɪsɪn/ *noun* a antibacterial drug suitable for people who are sensitive to penicillin

erythropenia /ɪrɪθrə'piːniə/ *noun* a condition in which a person has a low number of erythrocytes in their blood

erythroplasia /ɪ,rɪθrə'pleɪziə/ *noun* the formation of lesions on the mucous membrane

erythropoiesis /ɪ,rɪθrəpɔɪ'iːsɪs/ *noun* same as **erythrogenesis**

erythropoietin /ɪ,rɪθrə'pɔɪətɪn/ *noun* a hormone which regulates the production of red blood cells

COMMENT: Erythropoietin can now be produced by genetic techniques and is being used to increase the production of red blood cells in anaemia.

erythropsia /,erɪ'θrɒpsiə/ *noun* a condition in which someone sees things as if coloured red

Esbach's albuminometer /,esbɑːks ,æl bjuːmɪ'nɒmɪtə/ *noun* a glass for measuring albumin in urine, using Esbach's method

eschar /'eskɑː/ *noun* a dry scab, e.g. one forming on a burn

escharotic /,eskə'rɒtɪk/ *noun* a substance which produces an eschar

Escherichia /,eʃə'rɪkiə/ *noun* a bacterium commonly found in faeces

Escherichia coli /eʃə,rɪkiə 'kəʊlaɪ/ *noun* a Gram-negative bacterium associated with acute gastroenteritis. Also called **E. coli**

escort nurse /'eskɔːt ,nɜːs/ *noun* a nurse who goes with patients to the operating theatre and back again to the ward

Esmarch's bandage /'esmɑːks ,bændɪdʒ/ *noun* a rubber band wrapped round a limb as a tourniquet before a surgical operation and left in place during the operation so as to keep the site free of blood [Described 1869. After Johann Friedrich August von Esmarch (1823–1908), Professor of Surgery at Kiel, Germany.]

esophagus /iː'sɒfəgəs/ *noun* US spelling of **oesophagus**

esotropia /esə'trəʊpiə/ *noun* a type of squint, where the eyes both look towards the nose. Also called **convergent strabismus**

espundia /ɪ'spuːndiə/ ♦ **leishmaniasis**

ESR *abbr* erythrocyte sedimentation rate

ESRD *abbr* end-stage renal disease

essence /'es(ə)ns/ *noun* a concentrated oil from a plant, used in cosmetics, and sometimes as analgesics or antiseptics

essential /ɪ'senʃəl/ *adjective* **1.** extremely important ○ *It is essential to keep accurate records.* **2.** necessary for health ○ *essential nutrients* **3.** without obvious cause ○ *essential hypertension* Also called **idiopathic 4.** extracted from a plant ○ *essential oil*

essential amino acid /ɪ,senʃəl ə,miːnəʊ 'æsɪd/ *noun* an amino acid which is necessary for growth but which cannot be synthesised in the body and has to be obtained from the food supply

COMMENT: The essential amino acids are: isoleucine, leucine, lysine, methionine, phenylalanine, threonine, tryptophan and valine.

essential dysmenorrhoea /ɪ,senʃəl dɪs menə'riːə/ *noun* same as **primary dysmenorrhoea**

essential element /ɪ,senʃəl 'elɪmənt/ *noun* a chemical element which is necessary to the body's growth or function, e.g. carbon, oxygen, hydrogen and nitrogen

essential fatty acid /ɪ,senʃəl ,fæti 'æsɪd/ *noun* an unsaturated fatty acid which is necessary for growth and health. Abbr **EFA**

COMMENT: The essential fatty acids are linoleic acid, linolenic acid and arachidonic acid.

essential hyperkinesia /ɪ,senʃəl ,haɪpəkɪ 'niːziə/ *noun* a condition of children where their movements are excessive and repeated

essential hypertension /ɪ,senʃəl 'haɪpə ,tenʃən/ *noun* high blood pressure without any obvious cause

essential oil /ɪ,senʃəl 'ɔɪl/ *noun* a medicinal or fragrant oil distilled from some part of a plant

essential tremor /ɪ,senʃəl 'tremə/ *noun* an involuntary slow trembling movement of the hands often seen in elderly people

essential uterine haemorrhage /ɪ,senʃəl ,juːtəraɪn 'hem(ə)rɪdʒ/ *noun* heavy uterine bleeding for which there is no obvious cause

estrogen /'iːstrədʒən/ *noun* US same as **oestrogen**

ethambutol /ɪˈθæmbjʊtɒl/ *noun* a drug that is part of the treatment for bacterial infections such as tuberculosis

ethanol /ˈeθənɒl/ *noun* a colourless liquid, present in alcoholic drinks such as whisky, gin and vodka, and also used in medicines and as a disinfectant. Also called **ethyl alcohol**. ◊ **pure alcohol**

ethene /ˈiːθiːn/ *noun* same as **ethylene**

ether /ˈiːθə/ *noun* an anaesthetic substance, now rarely used

ethical /ˈeθɪk(ə)l/ *adjective* 1. concerning ethics 2. referring to a drug available on prescription only

ethical committee /ˈeθɪk(ə)l kəˌmɪti/ *noun* a group of specialists who monitor experiments involving human beings or who regulate the way in which members of the medical profession conduct themselves

ethinyloestradiol /ˌeθɪn(ə)lˌiːstrəˈdaɪɒl/ *noun* an artificial hormone related to oestrogen that is effective in small doses. It forms part of hormone replacement therapy.

ethmoid /eθˈmɔɪd/, **ethmoidal** /eθˈmɔɪd(ə)l/ *adjective* referring to the ethmoid bone or near to the ethmoid bone

ethmoidal sinuses /eθˌmɔɪd(ə)l ˈsaɪnəsɪz/ *plural noun* air cells inside the ethmoid bone

ethmoid bone /ˈeθmɔɪd bəʊn/ *noun* a bone which forms the top of the nasal cavity and part of the orbits

ethmoidectomy /ˌeθmɔɪˈdektəmi/ *noun* an operation to remove the lining between the sinuses

ethmoiditis /ˌeθmɔɪˈdaɪtɪs/ *noun* inflammation of the ethmoid bone or of the ethmoidal sinuses

ethnic /ˈeθnɪk/ *adjective* relating to a culturally or racially distinctive group of people

ethyl alcohol /ˌiːθaɪl ˈælkəhɒl/ *noun* same as **ethanol**

ethylene /ˈeθəliːn/ *noun* a gas used as an anaesthetic

ethylestrenol /ˌeθ(ə)lˈestrənɒl/ *noun* an anabolic steroid

etiology /ˌiːtiˈɒlədʒi/ *noun US* same as **aetiology**

eu- /juː/ *prefix* good, well

eubacteria /ˌjuːbækˈtɪəriə/ *noun* true bacteria with rigid cell walls

eucalyptol /ˌjuːkəˈlɪptəl/ *noun* a substance obtained from eucalyptus oil

eucalyptus /ˌjuːkəˈlɪptəs/ *noun* a genus of tree growing mainly in Australia, from which a strongly smelling oil is distilled

eucalyptus oil /ˌjuːkəˈlɪptəs ɔɪl/ *noun* an aromatic medicinal oil distilled from the leaves of various species of tree in the genus *Eucalyptus*

COMMENT: Eucalyptus oil is used in pharmaceutical products especially to relieve congestion in the respiratory passages.

eugenics /juːˈdʒenɪks/ *noun* the study of how to improve the human race by genetic selection

eunuch /ˈjuːnək/ *noun* a castrated male

eupepsia /juːˈpepsiə/ *noun* good digestion

euphoria /juːˈfɔːriə/ *noun* a feeling of extreme happiness

euplastic /juːˈplæstɪk/ *adjective* referring to tissue which heals well

Eustachian canal /juːˈsteɪʃ(ə)n kəˌnæl/ *noun* a passage through the porous bone forming the outside part of the Eustachian tube

Eustachian tube /juːˈsteɪʃ(ə)n tjuːb/ *noun* the tube which connects the pharynx to the middle ear. See illustration at **EAR** in Supplement [Described 1562, but actually named after Eustachio by Valsalva a century later. Bartolomeo Eustachio (1520–74), physician to the Pope and Professor of Anatomy in Rome.]

COMMENT: The Eustachian tubes balance the air pressure on each side of the eardrum. When a person swallows or yawns, air is allowed into the Eustachian tubes and equalises the pressure with the normal atmospheric pressure outside the body. The tubes can be blocked by an infection, as in a cold, or by pressure differences, as inside an aircraft, and if they are blocked, the hearing is impaired.

euthanasia /ˌjuːθəˈneɪziə/ *noun* the painless killing of an incurably ill person or someone in a permanent coma in order to end their distress. Also called **mercy killing** (NOTE: This practice is illegal in most countries.)

euthanise /ˈjuːθənaɪz/, **euthanize** *verb* to kill an incurably ill person or someone in a permanent coma

euthyroid /juːˈθaɪrɔɪd/ *noun* a condition where the thyroid is functioning normally

euthyroidism /juːˈθaɪrɔɪdɪz(ə)m/, **euthyroid state** /juːˈθaɪrɔɪd ˌsteɪt/ *noun* the fact of having a healthy thyroid gland

eutocia /juːˈtəʊsiə/ *noun* a standard childbirth

evacuant /ɪˈvækjuənt/ *noun* a medicine which makes a person have a bowel movement

evacuate /ɪˈvækjueɪt/ *verb* to discharge faeces from the bowel, or to have a bowel movement

evacuation /ɪˌvækjuˈeɪʃ(ə)n/ *noun* the act of removing the contents of something, especially discharging faeces from the bowel

evacuation of retained products of conception /ɪvækjuˌeɪʃ(ə)n əv rɪˌteɪnd ˌprɒdʌkts əv kənˈsepʃən/ *noun* a D & C operation performed after an abortion or miscarriage to ensure the uterus is left empty. Abbr **ERPC**

evacuator /ɪ'vækjueɪtə/ *noun* an instrument used to empty a cavity such as the bladder or bowel

evaluate /ɪ'væljueɪt/ *verb* 1. to examine and calculate the quantity or level of something ○ *The laboratory is still evaluating the results of the tests.* 2. to examine someone and calculate the treatment required
'…all patients were evaluated and followed up at the hypertension unit' [*British Medical Journal*]

evaluation /ɪ,væljuˈeɪʃ(ə)n/ *noun* the act of examining and calculating the quantity or level of something ○ *In further evaluation of these patients no side-effects of the treatment were noted.*
'…evaluation of fetal age and weight has proved to be of value in the clinical management of pregnancy, particularly in high-risk gestations' [*Southern Medical Journal*]

eventration /ˌiːvenˈtreɪʃ(ə)n/ *noun* the pushing of the intestine through the wall of the abdomen

eversion /ɪ'vɜːʃ(ə)n/ *noun* the act of turning towards the outside or turning inside out. See illustration at ANATOMICAL TERMS in Supplement □ **eversion of the cervix** a condition after laceration during childbirth, where the edges of the cervix sometimes turn outwards

evertor /ɪ'vɜːtə/ *noun* a muscle which makes a limb turn outwards

evidence-based /'evidəns beɪst/ *adjective* based on the results of well-designed trials of specific types of treatment for specific conditions ○ *evidence-based practice*

evidence-based medicine /'evid(ə)ns beɪst ˌmed(ə)sɪn/ *noun* medical practice where findings from research are used as the basis for decisions

evisceration /ɪ,vɪsəˈreɪʃ(ə)n/ *noun* 1. the surgical removal of the abdominal viscera. Also called **exenteration** 2. removal of the contents of an organ □ **evisceration of the eye** surgical removal of the contents of an eyeball

evolution /ˌiːvəˈluːʃ(ə)n/ *noun* a process of change in organisms which takes place over a very long period involving many generations

evulsion /ɪ'vʌlʃən/ *noun* the act of extracting something by force

Ewing's tumour /'juːɪŋz 'tjuːmə/, **Ewing's sarcoma** /ˌjuːɪŋz sɑːˈkəʊmə/ *noun* a malignant tumour in the marrow of a long bone [Described 1922. After James Ewing (1866–1943), Professor of Pathology at Cornell University, New York, USA.]

ex- /eks/ *prefix* same as **exo-** (*used before vowels*)

exacerbate /ɪɡ'zæsə,beɪt/ *verb* to make a condition more severe ○ *The cold damp weather will only exacerbate his chest condition.*

exacerbation /ɪɡ,zæsə'beɪʃ(ə)n/ *noun* 1. the fact of making a condition worse 2. a period when a condition becomes worse
'…patients were re-examined regularly or when they felt they might be having an exacerbation. Exacerbation rates were calculated from the number of exacerbations during the study' [*Lancet*]

examination /ɪɡ,zæmɪˈneɪʃ(ə)n/ *noun* 1. an act of looking at someone or something carefully ○ *From the examination of the X-ray photographs, it seems that the tumour has not spread.* 2. the act of looking at someone to find out what is wrong with him or her ○ *The surgeon carried out a medical examination before operating.* 3. a written or oral test to see if a student is progressing satisfactorily (NOTE: In this sense, often abbreviated to **exam**.)

examine /ɪɡ'zæmɪn/ *verb* 1. to look at or to investigate someone or something carefully ○ *The tissue samples were examined in the laboratory.* 2. to look at and test someone to find out what is wrong with him or her ○ *The doctor examined the patient's heart.*

exanthem /ɪɡ'zænθəm/ *noun* a skin rash found with infectious diseases like measles or chickenpox

exanthematous /ˌeksænˈθemətəs/ *adjective* referring to an exanthem or like an exanthem

exanthem subitum /ɪɡ,zænθəm 'sʊbɪtəm/ *noun* same as **roseola infantum**

excavator /'ekskəveɪtə/ *noun* a surgical instrument shaped like a spoon

excavatum /'ekskəveɪtəm/ **♦ pectus excavatum**

exception /ɪk'sepʃən/ *noun* 1. something that does not fit into or is excluded from a general rule or pattern 2. the act or condition of being excluded

excess /ɪk'ses/ *noun* too much of a substance ○ *The gland was producing an excess of hormones.* ○ *The body could not cope with an excess of blood sugar.* □ **in excess of** more than ○ *Short men who weigh in excess of 100 kilos are very overweight.*

excessive /ɪk'sesɪv/ *adjective* more than normal ○ *The patient was passing excessive quantities of urine.* ○ *The doctor noted an excessive amount of bile in the patient's blood.*

excessively /ɪk'sesɪvli/ *adverb* too much ○ *She has an excessively high blood pressure.* ○ *If the patient sweats excessively, it may be necessary to cool his body with cold compresses.*

exchange transfusion /ɪks,tʃeɪndʒ træns 'fjuːʒ(ə)n/ *noun* a method of treating leukaemia or erythroblastosis in newborn babies, where almost all the blood is removed from the body and replaced with healthy blood

excipient /ɪk'sɪpiənt/ *noun* a substance added to a drug so that it can be made into a pill

excise /ɪk'saɪz/ *verb* to cut something out

excision /ɪkˈsɪʒ(ə)n/ *noun* an operation by a surgeon to cut and remove part of the body such as a growth. Compare **incision**

excitation /ˌeksɪˈteɪʃ(ə)n/ *noun* the state of being mentally or physically aroused

excitatory /ɪkˈsaɪtətri/ *adjective* tending to excite

excite /ɪkˈsaɪt/ *verb* 1. to stimulate someone or something 2. to give an impulse to a nerve or muscle

excited /ɪkˈsaɪtɪd/ *adjective* 1. very lively and happy 2. aroused

excitement /ɪkˈsaɪtmənt/ *noun* 1. the act of being excited 2. the second stage of anaesthesia

excoriation /ɪkskɔːriˈeɪʃ(ə)n/ *noun* a raw skin surface or mucous membrane after rubbing or burning

excrement /ˈekskrɪmənt/ *noun* same as **faeces**

excrescence /ɪkˈskres(ə)ns/ *noun* a growth on the skin

excreta /ɪkˈskriːtə/ *plural noun* waste material from the body, especially faeces

excrete /ɪkˈskriːt/ *verb* to pass waste matter out of the body, especially to discharge faeces ○ *The urinary system separates waste liquids from the blood and excretes them as urine.*

excretion /ɪkˈskriːʃ(ə)n/ *noun* the act of passing waste matter, e.g. faeces, urine or sweat, out of the body

excruciating /ɪkˈskruːʃieɪtɪŋ/ *adjective* extremely painful ○ *He had excruciating pains in his head.*

exenteration /ekˌsentəˈreɪʃ(ə)n/ *noun* same as **evisceration**

exercise /ˈeksəsaɪz/ *noun* 1. physical or mental activity, especially the active use of the muscles as a way of keeping fit, correcting a deformity or strengthening a part ○ *Regular exercise is good for your heart.* ○ *He doesn't do* or *take enough exercise.* 2. a particular movement or action designed to use and strengthen the muscles ■ *verb* to take exercise, or exert part of the body in exercise ○ *He exercises twice a day to keep fit.*

exercise cycle /ˈeksəsaɪz ˌsaɪk(ə)l/ *noun* a type of cycle which is fixed to the floor, so that someone can pedal on it for exercise

exercise-induced asthma /ˌeksəsaɪz ɪn ˌdjuːst ˈæsmə/ *noun* asthma which is caused by exercise such as running or cycling. Abbr **EIA**

exertion /ɪgˈzɜːʃ(ə)n/ *noun* physical activity

exfoliation /eksˌfəʊliˈeɪʃ(ə)n/ *noun* the loss of layers of tissue such as sunburnt skin

exfoliative /eksˈfəʊlieɪtɪv/ *adjective* referring to exfoliation

exfoliative dermatitis /eksˌfəʊliətɪv ˌdɜːməˈtaɪtɪs/ *noun* a typical form of dermatitis where the skin becomes red and comes off in flakes

exhalation /ˌekshəˈleɪʃ(ə)n/ *noun* 1. the act of breathing out 2. air which is breathed out ▶ opposite **inhalation**

exhale /eksˈheɪl/ *verb* to breathe out. Opposite **inhale**

exhaust /ɪgˈzɔːst/ *verb* to tire someone out

exhaustion /ɪgˈzɔːstʃən/ *noun* extreme tiredness or fatigue

exhibitionism /ˌeksɪˈbɪʃ(ə)nɪz(ə)m/ *noun* a desire to show the genitals to a person of the opposite sex

exo- /eksəʊ/ *prefix* out of, outside

exocrine /ˈeksəkraɪn/ *adjective* □ **exocrine secretions of the pancreas** enzymes carried from the pancreas to the second part of the duodenum

exocrine gland /ˈeksəkraɪn glænd/ *noun* a gland with ducts which channel secretions to particular parts of the body such as the liver, the sweat glands, the pancreas and the salivary glands. Compare **endocrine gland**

exogenous /ekˈsɒdʒənəs/ *adjective* developing or caused by something outside the organism. Compare **endogenous**

exomphalos /ekˈsɒmfələs/ *noun* same as **umbilical hernia**

exophthalmic goitre /ˌeksɒfˈθælmɪk ˈgɔɪtə/ *noun* a form of hyperthyroidism, in which the neck swells and the eyes protrude. Also called **Graves' disease**

exophthalmos /ˌeksɒfˈθælməs/ *noun* protruding eyeballs

exoskeleton /ˈeksəʊˌskelɪt(ə)n/ *noun* the outer skeleton of some animals such as insects. Compare **endoskeleton**

exostosis /ˌeksəˈstəʊsɪs/ *noun* a benign growth on the surface of a bone

exotic /ɪgˈzɒtɪk/ *adjective* referring to a disease which occurs in a foreign country

exotoxin /ˌeksəʊˈtɒksɪn/ *noun* a poison, produced by bacteria, which affects parts of the body away from the place of infection, e.g. the toxins which cause botulism or tetanus

COMMENT: Diphtheria is caused by a bacillus. The exotoxin released causes the generalised symptoms of the disease such as fever and rapid pulse while the bacillus itself is responsible for the local symptoms in the upper throat.

exotropia /ˌeksəʊˈtrəʊpiə/ *noun* same as **divergent strabismus**

expectant mother /ɪkˌspektənt ˈmʌðə/ *noun* a pregnant woman

expected date of delivery /ɪkˌspektɪd ˌdeɪt əv dɪˈlɪv(ə)ri/ *noun* the day on which a doctor calculates that the birth of a baby will take place

expectorant /ɪkˈspekt(ə)rənt/ *noun* a drug which helps someone to cough up phlegm

expectorate /ɪkˈspektəreɪt/ verb to cough up phlegm or sputum from the respiratory passages

expectoration /ɪkˌspektəˈreɪʃ(ə)n/ noun the act of coughing up fluid or phlegm from the respiratory tract

expel /ɪkˈspel/ verb to send something out of the body ○ Air is expelled from the lungs when a person breathes out.

experiential learning /ɪkˌspɪərienʃəl ˈlɜːnɪŋ/ noun the process of learning from experience

experiment /ɪkˈsperɪmənt/ noun a scientific test conducted under set conditions ○ The scientists did some experiments to try the new drug on a small sample of people.

expert patient /ˌekspɜːt ˈpeɪʃ(ə)nt/ noun a patient with a long-term illness who has been taught how to manage his or her own medical care

expiration /ˌekspəˈreɪʃ(ə)n/ noun 1. the act of breathing out, or pushing air out of the lungs ○ Expiration takes place when the chest muscles relax and the lungs become smaller. Opposite **inspiration** 2. death 3. dying

expiratory /ekˈspɪrət(ə)ri/ adjective referring to the process of breathing out

expire /ɪkˈspaɪə/ verb 1. to breathe out 2. to die

explant /eksˈplɑːnt/ noun tissue taken from a body and grown in a culture in a laboratory ■ verb 1. to take tissue from a body and grow it in a culture in a laboratory 2. to remove an implant

explantation /ˌeksplɑːnˈteɪʃ(ə)n/ noun 1. the act of taking tissue from a body and growing it in a culture in a laboratory 2. the removal of an implant

exploration /ˌekspləˈreɪʃ(ə)n/ noun a procedure or surgical operation where the aim is to discover the cause of symptoms or the nature and extent of an illness

exploratory /ɪkˈsplɒrət(ə)ri/ adjective referring to an exploration

exploratory surgery /ɪkˌsplɒrət(ə)ri ˈsɜːdʒəri/ noun a surgical operation in which the aim is to discover the cause of a person's symptoms or the nature and extent of an illness

explore /ɪkˈsplɔː/ verb to examine a part of the body in order to make a diagnosis

expose /ɪkˈspəʊz/ verb 1. to show something which was hidden ○ The operation exposed a generalised cancer. ○ The report exposed a lack of medical care on the part of some of the hospital staff. 2. to place something or someone under the influence of something ○ He was exposed to the disease for two days. ○ She was exposed to a lethal dose of radiation.

exposure /ɪkˈspəʊʒə/ noun 1. the fact of being exposed to something ○ his exposure to radiation 2. the fact of being damp, cold and with

no protection from the weather ○ The survivors of the crash were all suffering from exposure after spending a night in the snow.

express /ɪkˈspres/ verb to squeeze liquid or air out of something, especially to squeeze out breast milk for a baby to feed on later

expression /ɪkˈspreʃ(ə)n/ noun 1. the look on a person's face which shows what he or she thinks and feels ○ His expression showed that he was annoyed. 2. the act of pushing something out of the body ○ the expression of the fetus and placenta during childbirth

exquisitely tender /ɪkˌskwɪzɪtli ˈtendə/ adjective producing a sharp localised pain or tenderness when touched

exsanguinate /ɪkˈsæŋgwɪneɪt/ verb to drain blood from the body

exsanguination /ɪkˌsæŋgwɪˈneɪʃ(ə)n/ noun the removal of blood from the body

exsufflation /ˌeksəˈfleɪʃ(ə)n/ noun an act of forcing breath out of the body

extend /ɪkˈstend/ verb to stretch out, or cause something to stretch out ○ The patient is unable to extend his arms fully.

extension /ɪkˈstenʃən/ noun 1. the stretching or straightening out of a joint 2. the stretching of a joint by traction

extensor /ɪkˈstensə/, **extensor muscle** /ɪk ˈstensə ˌmʌs(ə)l/ noun a muscle which makes a joint become straight. Compare **flexor**

exterior /ɪkˈstɪəriə/ noun the outside of something

exteriorisation /ɪkˌstɪəriəraɪˈzeɪʃ(ə)n/, **exteriorization** noun a surgical operation to bring an internal organ to the outside surface of the body

externa /ɪkˈstɜːnə/ ♦ otitis externa

external /ɪkˈstɜːn(ə)l/ adjective on the outside, especially outside the surface of the body. Opposite **internal** □ **the lotion is for external use only** it should only be used on the outside of the body

external auditory canal /ɪkˌstɜːn(ə)l ˈɔːdɪt(ə)ri kəˌnæl/, **external auditory meatus** /ɪkˌstɜːn(ə)l ˌɔːdɪt(ə)ri mɪˈeɪtəs/ noun a tube in the skull leading from the outer ear to the eardrum. See illustration at EARin Supplement

external cardiac massage /ɪkˌstɜːn(ə)l ˌkɑːdiæk ˈmæsɑːʒ/ noun a method of making someone's heart start beating again by rhythmic pressing on the breastbone

external ear /ɪkˌstɜːn(ə)l ˈɪə/ noun same as **outer ear**

external haemorrhoids /ɪkˌstɜːn(ə)l ˈhemərɔɪdz/ plural noun haemorrhoids in the skin just outside the anus

external iliac artery /ɪkˌstɜːn(ə)l ˈɪliæk ˌɑːtəri/ noun an artery which branches from the aorta in the abdomen and leads to the leg

external jugular /ˌɪkˌstɜːn(ə)l ˈdʒʌɡjʊlə/ noun the main jugular vein in the neck, leading from the temporal vein

externally /ɪkˈstɜːn(ə)li/ adverb on the outside of the body ○ *The ointment should only be used externally*

external nares plural noun same as **anterior nares**

external oblique /ɪkˌstɜːn(ə)l əˈbliːk/ noun an outer muscle covering the abdomen

external otitis /ɪkˌstɜːn(ə)l əˈtaɪtɪs/ noun same as **otitis externa**

external respiration /ɪkˌstɜːn(ə)l ˌrespɪˈreɪʃ(ə)n/ noun the part of respiration concerned with oxygen in the air being exchanged in the lungs for carbon dioxide from the blood

exteroceptor /ˈekstərəʊˈseptə/ noun a sensory nerve which is affected by stimuli from outside the body, e.g. in the eye or ear

extinction /ɪkˈstɪŋkʃən/ noun 1. the destruction or stopping of something 2. the lessening or stopping of a conditioned behavioural response through lack of reinforcement

extirpate /ˈekstɜːˌpeɪt/ verb to remove something by surgery

extirpation /ekstɜːˈpeɪʃ(ə)n/ noun the total removal of a structure, an organ or growth by surgery

extra- /ekstrə/ prefix outside

extracapsular /ˌekstrəˈkæpsjʊlə/ adjective outside a capsule

extracapsular fracture /ˌekstrəˌkæpsjʊlə ˈfræktʃə/ noun a fracture of the upper part of the femur, which does not involve the capsule round the hip joint

extracellular /ˌekstrəˈseljʊlə/ adjective outside cells

extracellular fluid /ˌekstrəseljʊlə ˈfluːɪd/ noun a fluid which surrounds cells

extract noun /ˈekstrækt/ a preparation made by removing water or alcohol from a substance, leaving only the essence □ **liver extract** concentrated essence of liver ■ verb /ɪkˈstrækt/ to take out something ○ *Adrenaline extracted from the animal's adrenal glands is used in the treatment of asthma.*

'...all the staff are RGNs, partly because they do venesection, partly because they work in plasmapheresis units which extract plasma and return red blood cells to the donor' [*Nursing Times*]

extraction /ɪkˈstrækʃən/ noun 1. the removal of part of the body, especially a tooth 2. in obstetrics, delivery, usually a breech presentation, which needs medical assistance

extradural /ˌekstrəˈdjʊərəl/ adjective same as **epidural**

extradural haematoma /ˌekstrəˌdjʊərəl hiːməˈtəʊmə/ noun a blood clot which forms in the head outside the dura mater, caused by a blow

extradural haemorrhage /ˌekstrəˌdjʊərəl ˈhem(ə)rɪdʒ/ noun a serious condition where

bleeding occurs between the dura mater and the skull

extraembryonic /ˌekstrəembriˈɒnɪk/ adjective referring to part of a fertilised ovum, such as the amnion, allantois and chorion which is not part of the embryo

extraembryonic membranes /ˌekstrə embriˌɒnɪk ˈmembreɪnz/ plural noun membranes which are not part of the embryo

extrapleural /ˌekstrəˈplʊərəl/ adjective outside the pleural cavity

extrapyramidal /ˌekstrəpɪˈræmɪd(ə)l/ adjective outside the pyramidal tracts

extrapyramidal system /ˌekstrəpɪ ˌræmɪd(ə)l ˈsɪstəm/ noun a motor system which carries motor nerves outside the pyramidal system

extrapyramidal tracts /ˌekstrəpɪ ˌræmɪd(ə)l ˈtrækts/ plural noun same as **extrapyramidal system**

extrasensory /ˌekstrəˈsensəri/ adjective involving perception by means other than the usual five senses

extrasystole /ˌekstrəˈsɪstəli/ noun same as **ectopic heartbeat**

extrauterine /ˌekstrəˈjuːtəraɪn/ adjective occurring or developing outside the uterus

extrauterine pregnancy /ˌekstrəjuːtəraɪn ˈpregnənsi/ noun same as **ectopic pregnancy**

extravasation /ekˌstrævəˈseɪʃ(ə)n/ noun a situation where a bodily fluid, such as blood or secretions, escapes into tissue

extraversion /ˌekstrəˈvɜːʃ(ə)n/ noun same as **extroversion**

extravert /ˈekstrəvɜːt/ noun same as **extrovert**

extremities /ɪkˈstremətiz/ plural noun the parts of the body at the ends of limbs, e.g. the fingers, toes, nose and ears

extremity /ɪkˈstremɪti/ noun 1. a limb 2. the part of a limb farthest away from the body, especially the hand or foot 3. a situation or state of great distress or danger 4. the greatest intensity of something

extrinsic /eksˈtrɪnsɪk/ adjective external, originating outside a structure

extrinsic allergic alveolitis /eksˌtrɪnsɪk ə ˌlɜːdʒɪk ˌælviəˈlaɪtɪs/ noun a condition in which the lungs are allergic to fungus and other allergens

extrinsic factor /eksˌtrɪnsɪk ˈfæktə/ noun a former term for vitamin B$_{12}$, which is necessary for the production of red blood cells

extrinsic ligament /eksˌtrɪnsɪk ˈlɪgəmənt/ noun a ligament between the bones in a joint which is separate from the joint capsule

extrinsic muscle /eksˌtrɪnsɪk ˈmʌs(ə)l/ noun a muscle which is some way away from the part of the body which it operates

extroversion /ekstrəˈvɜːʃ(ə)n/ noun 1. (in psychology) a condition in which a person is interested in people and things other than themselves **2.** a congenital turning of an organ inside out

extrovert /'ekstrəvɜːt/ *noun* a person who is interested in people and things in the external world

extroverted /'ekstrəʊ,vɜːtɪd/ *adjective* **1.** (*of a person*) interested in people and things other than oneself **2.** (*of an organ*) turned inside out

extubation /,ekstjuː'beɪʃ(ə)n/ *noun* the removal of a tube after intubation

exudate /'eksjudeɪt/ *noun* fluid which is deposited on the surface of tissue as the result of a condition or disease

exudation /,eksju'deɪʃ(ə)n/ *noun* the escape of material such as fluid or cells into tissue as a defence mechanism

eye /aɪ/ *noun* the part of the body with which a person sees (NOTE: For other terms referring to the eye, see **ocular**, **optic** and words beginning with **oculo-**, **ophth-**, **ophthalm-**, **ophthalmo-**.)

eyeball /'aɪbɔːl/ *noun* the round ball of tissue through which light passes, located in the eye socket and controlled by various muscles

COMMENT: Light rays enter the eye through the cornea, pass through the pupil and are refracted through the aqueous humour onto the lens, which then focuses the rays through the vitreous humour onto the retina at the back of the eyeball. Impulses from the retina pass along the optic nerve to the brain.

eye bank /'aɪ bæŋk/ *noun* a place where parts of eyes given by donors can be kept for use in grafts

eyebath /'aɪbɑːθ/ *noun* a small dish into which a solution can be put for bathing the eye

eyebrow /'aɪbraʊ/ *noun* an arch of skin with a line of hair above the eye

eye drops /'aɪ drɒps/ *plural noun* medicine in liquid form which is put into the eye in small amounts

eyeglasses /'aɪ,glɑːsɪz/ *plural noun* US glasses or spectacles for correcting vision

eyelash /'aɪlæʃ/ *noun* a small hair which grows out from the edge of the eyelid

eyelid /'aɪlɪd/ *noun* a piece of skin which covers the eye. Also called **blepharon, palpebra** (NOTE: For other terms referring to the eyelids, see words beginning with **blephar-, blepharo-**.)

eye ointment /'aɪ ,ɔɪntmənt/ *noun* an ointment in a special tube to be used in eye treatment

eyesight /'aɪsaɪt/ *noun* the ability to see ○ *He has got very good eyesight.* ○ *Failing eyesight is common in elderly people.*

eye socket /'aɪ ,sɒkɪt/ *noun* same as **orbit**

eye specialist /'aɪ ,speʃəlɪst/ *noun* same as **ophthalmologist**

eyestrain /'aɪstreɪn/ *noun* tiredness in the muscles of the eye with a headache, which may be caused by an activity such as reading in bad light or working on a computer screen. Also called **asthenopia**

eye surgeon /'aɪ ,sɜːdʒ(ə)n/ *noun* a surgeon who specialises in operations on eyes

eye test /'aɪ test/ *noun* an examination of the inside of an eye to see if it is working correctly, and if the person needs glasses

eyetooth /'aɪtuːθ/ *noun* a canine tooth, one of two pairs of pointed teeth next to the incisors (NOTE: The plural is **eyeteeth**.)

F

F *abbr* Fahrenheit

face /feɪs/ *noun* the front part of the head, where the eyes, nose and mouth are placed ■ *verb* to have your face towards or to look towards something ○ *Please face the screen.*

face delivery /'feɪs dɪˌlɪv(ə)ri/ *noun* a birth where the baby's face appears first

face lift /'feɪs lɪft/, **face-lifting operation** /'feɪs ˌlɪftɪŋ ɒpəˌreɪʃ(ə)n/ *noun* a surgical operation to remove wrinkles on the face and neck

face mask /'feɪs mɑːsk/ *noun* **1.** a rubber mask that fits over the nose and mouth and is used to administer an anaesthetic **2.** a piece of gauze which fits over the mouth and nose to prevent droplet infection

face presentation /'feɪs prez(ə)nˌteɪʃ(ə)n/ *noun* a position of a baby in the uterus where the face will appear first at birth

facet /'fæsɪt/ *noun* a flat surface on a bone

facet syndrome /'fæsɪt ˌsɪndrəʊm/ *noun* a condition in which a joint in the vertebrae becomes dislocated

facial /'feɪʃ(ə)l/ *adjective* relating to, or appearing on, the face ○ *The psychiatrist examined the patient's facial expression.*

facial artery /'feɪʃ(ə)l ˌɑːtəri/ *noun* an artery which branches off the external carotid into the face and mouth

facial bone /'feɪʃ(ə)l bəʊn/ *noun* one of the fourteen bones which form the face

COMMENT: The bones which make up the face are: two maxillae forming the upper jaw; two nasal bones forming the top part of the nose; two lacrimal bones on the inside of the orbit near the nose; two zygomatic or malar bones forming the sides of the cheeks; two palatine bones forming the back part of the top of the mouth; two nasal conchae or turbinate bones which form the sides of the nasal cavity; the mandible or lower jaw; and the vomer in the centre of the nasal septum.

facial nerve /'feɪʃ(ə)l nɜːv/ *noun* the seventh cranial nerve, which governs the muscles of the face, the taste buds on the front of the tongue and the salivary and lacrimal glands

facial paralysis /ˌfeɪʃ(ə)l pəˈræləsɪs/ *noun* same as **Bell's palsy**

facial vein /'feɪʃ(ə)l veɪn/ *noun* a vein which drains down the side of the face into the internal jugular vein

-facient /feɪʃənt/ *suffix* making or causing ○ *abortifacient*

facies /'feɪʃiːz/ *noun* someone's facial appearance, used as a guide to diagnosis

facilitation /fəˌsɪlɪ'teɪʃ(ə)n/ *noun* an act where several slight stimuli help a neurone to be activated

facilities /fə'sɪlɪtiz/ *plural noun* something such as equipment, accommodation, treatment or help that is provided for people who need them ○ *the provision of aftercare facilities*

factor /'fæktə/ *noun* **1.** something which has an influence or which makes something else take place **2.** a substance, variously numbered, e.g. Factor I, Factor II, in the plasma, which makes the blood coagulate when a blood vessel is injured

Factor II /ˌfæktə 'tuː/ same as **prothrombin**

Factor IX /ˌfæktə 'naɪn/ *noun* a protein in plasma which promotes the clotting of blood and is lacking in people with haemophilia B. Also called **Christmas factor**

Factor VIII /ˌfæktər 'eɪt/ *noun* a protein in plasma which promotes the clotting of blood and is lacking in people with haemophilia A

Factor XI /ˌfæktər ɪ'lev(ə)n/ *noun* a protein in plasma which promotes the clotting of blood and is lacking in people with haemophilia C

Factor XII /ˌfæktə 'twelv/ *noun* a protein in plasma which promotes the clotting of blood and is lacking in some people with haemophilia. Also called **Hageman factor**

faculty /'fæk(ə)lti/ *noun* the ability to do something

fade away /feɪd ə'weɪ/ *verb* to be in the process of dying (*informal*)

faecal /'fiːk(ə)l/ *adjective* referring to faeces

faecal impaction /ˌfiːk(ə)l ɪm'pækʃən/ *noun* a condition in which a hardened mass of faeces stays in the rectum

faecal incontinence /ˌfiːk(ə)l ɪnˈkɒntɪnəns/ noun an inability to control the bowel movements

faecalith /ˈfiːkəlɪθ/ noun same as **coprolith**

faecal matter /ˈfiːk(ə)l ˌmætə/ noun solid waste matter from the bowels

faeces /ˈfiːsiːz/ plural noun solid waste matter passed from the bowels through the anus. Also called **stools, bowel movement** (NOTE: For other terms referring to faeces, see words beginning with **sterco-**.)

Fahrenheit /ˈfærənhaɪt/, **Fahrenheit scale** /ˈfærənhaɪt skeɪl/ noun a scale of temperatures where the freezing and boiling points of water are 32° and 212° under standard atmospheric pressure (NOTE: Used in the US, but less common in the UK. Usually written as an **F** after the degree sign: **32°F** (say: 'thirty-two degrees Fahrenheit').)

COMMENT: To convert degrees Fahrenheit into degrees Celsius, subtract 32 and divide the remainder by 1.8.

fail /feɪl/ verb **1.** not to be successful in doing something ○ *The doctor failed to see the symptoms.* ○ *She has failed her pharmacy exams.* ○ *He failed his medical and was rejected by the police force.* **2.** to become weaker and less likely to recover

failing /ˈfeɪlɪŋ/ adjective weakening, or becoming closer to death

failure to thrive /ˌfeɪljə tə ˈθraɪv/ noun same as **marasmus**

faint /feɪnt/ verb to stop being conscious for a short time and, usually, fall down ■ noun a loss of consciousness for a short period, caused by a temporary reduction in the blood flow to the brain

fainting fit /ˈfeɪntɪŋ fɪt/, **fainting spell** /ˈfeɪntɪŋ spel/ noun same as **syncope** ○ *She often had fainting fits when she was dieting.*

Fairbanks' splint /ˈfeəbæŋks splɪnt/ noun a special splint used for correcting Erb's palsy

faith healing /ˈfeɪθ ˌhiːlɪŋ/ noun the treatment of pain or illness by a person who prays and may also lay his or her hands on the patient

falciform /ˈfælsɪfɔːm/ adjective in the shape of a sickle

falciform ligament /ˌfælsɪfɔːm ˈlɪgəmənt/ noun a piece of tissue which separates the two lobes of the liver and attaches it to the diaphragm

fall /fɔːl/ verb □ **to fall pregnant, to fall for a baby** to become pregnant

fall asleep /ˌfɔːl əˈsliːp/ verb to go to sleep

fallen arches /ˌfɔːlən ˈɑːtʃɪz/ plural noun a condition in which the arches in the sole of the foot are not high

fall ill /ˌfɔːl ˈɪl/ verb to get ill or to start to have an illness ○ *He fell ill while on holiday and had to be flown home.*

Fallopian tube /fəˈləʊpiən tjuːb/ noun one of two tubes which connect the ovaries to the uterus. See illustration at UROGENITAL SYSTEM (FEMALE) in Supplement. Also called **oviduct, salpinx** (NOTE: For other terms referring to Fallopian tubes, see words beginning with **salping-, salpingo-**.) [Described 1561. After Gabriele Fallopio (1523–63), Italian man of medicine. He was Professor of Surgery and Anatomy at Padua, where he was also Professor of Botany.]

COMMENT: Once a month, ova (unfertilised eggs) leave the ovaries and move down the Fallopian tubes to the uterus. At the point where the Fallopian tubes join the uterus, an ovum may be fertilised by a sperm cell. Sometimes fertilisation and development of the embryo take place in the Fallopian tube itself. This is called an ectopic pregnancy, and can be life-threatening if not detected early.

Fallot's tetralogy /ˌfæləʊz teˈtrælədʒi/ noun same as **tetralogy of Fallot** [Described 1888. After Etienne-Louis Arthur Fallot (1850–1911), Professor of Hygiene and Legal Medicine at Marseilles, France.]

false /fɔːls/ adjective not true or not real

false pains /ˌfɔːls ˈpeɪnz/ plural noun pains which appear to be labour pains but are not

false pregnancy /ˌfɔːls ˈpregnənsi/ noun a condition in which a woman believes wrongly that she is pregnant and displays symptoms and signs of pregnancy

false rib /ˌfɔːls ˈrɪb/ noun one of the bottom five ribs on each side which are not directly attached to the breastbone

false teeth /ˌfɔːls ˈtiːθ/ plural noun dentures, artificial teeth made of plastic, which fit in the mouth and take the place of teeth which have been extracted

false vocal cords /ˌfɔːls ˈvəʊk(ə)l ˌkɔːdz/ plural noun same as **vestibular folds**

falx /fælks/, **falx cerebri** /ˌfælks ˈserəbri/ noun a fold of the dura mater between the two hemispheres of the cerebrum

familial /fəˈmɪliəl/ adjective referring to a family

familial adenomatous polyposis /fəˌmɪliəl ˌædəˌnɒmətəs ˌpɒliˈpəʊsɪs/ noun a hereditary disorder where polyps develop in the small intestine. Abbr **FAP**

familial disorder /fəˌmɪliəl dɪsˈɔːdə/ noun a hereditary disorder which affects several members of the same family

family /ˈfæm(ə)li/ noun a group of people who are related to each other, especially mother, father and children

family doctor /ˌfæm(ə)li ˈdɒktə/ noun a general practitioner

family planning /ˌfæm(ə)li ˈplænɪŋ/ noun the use of contraception to control the number of children in a family

family planning clinic /ˌfæm(ə)li ˈplænɪŋ ˌklɪnɪk/ noun a clinic which gives advice on contraception

family therapy /ˌfæm(ə)li ˈθerəpi/ noun a type of psychotherapy where members of the family of a person with a disorder meet a therapist to discuss the condition and try to come to terms with it

famotidine /fə'mɒtɪdiːn/ *noun* a histamine which reduces the secretion of gastric acid and is used to treat ulcers

Fanconi syndrome /fæn'kəʊni ˌsɪndrəʊm/ *noun* a kidney disorder where amino acids are present in the urine [Described 1927. After Guido Fanconi (b.1892), Professor of Paediatrics at the University of Zurich, Switzerland.]

fantasise /'fæntəsaɪz/, **fantasize** *verb* to imagine that things have happened

fantasy /'fæntəsi/ *noun* a series of imaginary events which someone believes really took place

FAP *abbr* familial adenomatous polyposis

farcy /'fɑːsi/ *noun* a form of glanders which affects the lymph nodes

farinaceous /ˌfærɪ'neɪʃəs/ *adjective* referring to flour, or containing starch

farmer's lung /ˌfɑːməz 'lʌŋ/ *noun* a type of asthma caused by an allergy to rotting hay

FAS *abbr* fetal alcohol syndrome

fascia /'feɪʃə/ *noun* fibrous tissue covering a muscle or an organ (NOTE: The plural is **fasciae**.)

fascia lata /ˌfeɪʃə 'lætə/ *noun* a wide sheet of tissue covering the thigh muscles

fasciculation /fəˌsɪkjʊ'leɪʃ(ə)n/ *noun* small muscle movements which appear as trembling skin

fasciculus /fə'sɪkjʊləs/ *noun* a bundle of nerve fibres (NOTE: The plural is **fasciculi**.)

fasciitis /ˌfæʃi'aɪtɪs/ *noun* an inflammation of the connective tissue between muscles or around organs

fascioliasis /fəˌsiə'laɪəsɪs/ *noun* a disease caused by parasitic liver flukes

Fasciolopsis /ˌfæsiəʊ'lɒpsɪs/ *noun* a type of liver fluke, often found in the Far East, which is transmitted to humans through contaminated waterplants

fast /fɑːst/ *noun* a period of going without food, e.g. to lose weight or for religious reasons ■ *verb* to go without food ○ *The patient should fast from midnight of the night before an operation.*

fastigium /fæ'stɪdʒiəm/ *noun* the highest temperature during a bout of fever

fat /fæt/ *adjective* big and round in the body ○ *You ought to eat less – you're getting too fat.* (NOTE: **fatter – fattest**) ■ *noun* **1.** a white oily substance in the body, which stores energy and protects the body against cold **2.** a type of food which supplies protein and Vitamins A and D, especially that part of meat which is white, and solid substances like lard or butter produced from animals and used for cooking, or liquid substances like oil ○ *If you don't like the fat on the meat, cut it off.* ○ *Fry the eggs in some fat.*

(NOTE: **Fat** has no plural when it means the substance; the plural **fats** is used to mean different types of fat. For other terms referring to fats, see also **lipid** and words beginning with **steato-**.)

COMMENT: Fat is a necessary part of the diet because of the vitamins and energy-giving calories which it contains. Fat in the diet comes from either animal fats or vegetable fats. Animal fats such as butter, fat meat or cream, are saturated fatty acids. It is believed that the intake of unsaturated and polyunsaturated fats, mainly vegetable fats and oils, and fish oil, in the diet, rather than animal fats, helps keep down the level of cholesterol in the blood and so lessens the risk of atherosclerosis. A low-fat diet does not always help to reduce body weight.

fatal /'feɪt(ə)l/ *adjective* causing or resulting in death ○ *He had a fatal accident.* ○ *Cases of bee stings are rarely fatal.*

fatality /fə'tælɪti/ *noun* a death as the result of something other than natural causes ○ *There were three fatalities during the flooding.*

fatally /'feɪt(ə)li/ *adverb* in a way which causes death ○ *His heart was fatally weakened by the lung disease.*

father /'fɑːðə/ *noun* a biological or adoptive male parent

fatigue /fə'tiːg/ *noun* very great tiredness ■ *verb* to tire someone out ○ *He was fatigued by the hard work.*

fatigue fracture /fə'tiːg ˌfræktʃə/ *noun* ♦ **stress fracture**

fat-soluble /ˌfæt 'sɒljʊb(ə)l/ *adjective* able to dissolve in fat ○ *Vitamin D is fat-soluble.*

fatty /'fæti/ *adjective* containing fat

fatty acid /ˌfæti 'æsɪd/ *noun* an organic acid belonging to a group that occurs naturally as fats, oils and waxes. ◊ **essential fatty acid**

fatty degeneration /ˌfæti dɪˌdʒenə'reɪʃ(ə)n/ *noun* same as **adipose degeneration**

fauces /'fɔːsiːz/ *noun* an opening between the tonsils at the back of the throat, leading to the pharynx

favism /'feɪvɪz(ə)m/ *noun* a type of inherited anaemia caused by an allergy to beans

favus /'feɪvəs/ *noun* a highly contagious type of ringworm caused by a fungus which attacks the scalp

FDA *abbr* US Food and Drug Administration

fear /fɪə/ *noun* a state where a person is afraid of something ○ *fear of flying*

febricula /fe'brɪkjʊlə/ *noun* a low fever

febrifuge /'febrɪfjuːdʒ/ *noun* a drug which prevents or lowers a fever, e.g. aspirin ■ *adjective* preventing or lowering fever

febrile /'fiːbraɪl/ *adjective* referring to a fever, or caused by a fever

febrile convulsion /ˌfiːbraɪl kən'vʌlʃ(ə)n/ *noun* a convulsion in a child, lasting a short time, associated with a fever

febrile disease /'fiːbraɪl dɪˌziːz/ *noun* a disease which is accompanied by fever

fecal /'fiːk(ə)l/ *adjective US* same as **faecal**

fecundation /ˌfekən'deɪʃ(ə)n/ *noun* the act of bringing male and female reproductive matter together. Also called **fertilisation**

feeble /'fiːb(ə)l/ *adjective* very weak

feed /fiːd/ *verb* to give food to someone ○ *He has to be fed with a spoon.* ○ *The baby has reached the stage when she can feed herself.* (NOTE: **feeding – fed**)

feed back /ˌfiːd 'bæk/ *verb* to give information or comments on something that has been done ○ *The patients' responses were fed back to the students.*

feedback /'fiːdbæk/ *noun* **1.** information or comments about something which has been done ○ *The initial feedback from patients on the new service was encouraging.* **2.** the linking of the result of an action back to the action itself

feeding /'fiːdɪŋ/ *noun* the action of giving someone something to eat. ◊ **breast feeding, bottle feeding, intravenous feeding**

feeding cup /'fiːdɪŋ kʌp/ *noun* a special cup with a spout, used for feeding people who cannot feed themselves

feel /fiːl/ *verb* **1.** to touch someone or something, usually with your fingers ○ *The midwife felt the abdomen gently.* □ **to feel someone's pulse** to establish someone's pulse rate, usually by holding the inner wrist **2.** to give a sensation ○ *My skin feels hot and itchy.* **3.** to have a sensation ○ *When she got the results of her test, she felt relieved.* ○ *He felt ill after eating the fish.* **4.** to believe or think something ○ *The doctor feels the patient is well enough to be moved out of intensive care.* (NOTE: **feeling – felt**)

feeling /'fiːlɪŋ/ *noun* **1.** a sensation ○ *a prickling feeling* **2.** an emotional state or attitude to something

Fehling's solution /'feɪlɪŋz sə,luːʃ(ə)n/ *noun* a solution used in Fehling's test to detect sugar in urine [Described 1848. After Hermann Christian von Fehling (1812–85), Professor of Chemistry at Stuttgart, Germany.]

Fehling's test /'feɪlɪŋz test/ *noun* a test for the presence of aldehydes and sugars in a biological sample by means of Fehling's solution

felon /'felən/ *noun* same as **whitlow**

Felty's syndrome /'feltiːz ˌsɪndrəʊm/ *noun* a condition, associated with rheumatoid arthritis, in which the spleen is enlarged and the number of white blood cells increases [Described 1924. After Augustus Roi Felty (1895–1963), physician at Hartford Hospital, Connecticut, USA.]

female condom /ˌfiːmeɪl 'kɒndɒm/ *noun* a rubber sheath inserted into the vagina before intercourse, covering the walls of the vagina and the cervix

female sex hormone /ˌfiːmeɪl 'seks ˌhɔːməʊn/ *noun* same as **oestrogen**

feminisation /ˌfemɪnaɪ'zeɪʃ(ə)n/, **feminization** *noun* the development of female characteristics in a male

femora /'femərə/ plural of **femur**

femoral /'femərəl/ *adjective* referring to the femur or to the thigh

femoral artery /ˌfemərəl 'ɑːtəri/ *noun* a continuation of the external iliac artery, which runs down the front of the thigh and then crosses to the back of the thigh

femoral canal /ˌfemərəl kə'næl/ *noun* the inner tube of the sheath surrounding the femoral artery and vein

femoral head /ˌfemərəl 'hed/ *noun* the head of the femur, the rounded projecting end part of the thigh bone which joins the acetabulum at the hip

femoral hernia /ˌfemərəl 'hɜːniə/ *noun* a hernia of the bowel at the top of the thigh

femoral neck /ˌfemərəl 'nek/ *noun* the narrow part between the head and the diaphysis of the femur. Also called **neck of the femur**

femoral nerve /'femərəl nɜːv/ *noun* a nerve which governs the muscle at the front of the thigh

femoral pulse /ˌfemərəl 'pʌls/ *noun* a pulse taken in the groin

femoral triangle /ˌfemərəl 'traɪæŋgəl/ *noun* a slight hollow in the groin which contains the femoral vessels and nerve. Also called **Scarpa's triangle**

femoral vein /'femərəl veɪn/ *noun* a vein running up the upper leg, a continuation of the popliteal vein

femoris /'femərɪs/ *noun* ♦ **rectus femoris**

femur /'fiːmə/ *noun* the bone in the top part of the leg which joins the acetabulum at the hip and the tibia at the knee. Also called **thighbone**. See illustration at PELVIS in Supplement (NOTE: The plural is **femora**.)

-fen /fen/ *suffix* used in names of non-steroidal anti-inflammatory drugs ○ *ibuprofen*

fenestra /fə'nestrə/ *noun* a small opening in the ear

fenestra ovalis /fə,nestrə əʊ'vɑːlɪs/ *noun* same as **oval window**

fenestra rotunda /fə,nestrə rəʊ'tʌndə/ *noun* same as **round window**

fenestration /ˌfenə'streɪʃ(ə)n/ *noun* a surgical operation to relieve deafness by making a small opening in the inner ear

fenoprofen /ˌfenəʊ'prəʊfen/ *noun* a non-steroidal, anti-inflammatory drug that is used to manage the pain of arthritis

fentanyl /'fentənɪl/ *noun* a narcotic drug that is a powerful painkiller

fermentation /ˌfɜːmen'teɪʃ(ə)n/ *noun* a process where carbohydrates are broken down by enzymes from yeast and produce alcohol. Also called **zymosis**

ferric /'ferɪk/ *adjective* containing iron with a valency of three

ferritin /'ferɪtɪn/ *noun* a protein found in the liver that binds reversibly to iron and stores it for later use in making haemoglobin in red blood cells

ferrous /'ferəs/ *adjective* containing iron with a valency of two

ferrous sulphate /ˌferəs 'sʌlfeɪt/ *noun* a white or pale green iron salt that is used in the treatment of iron-deficient anaemia

ferrule /'feruːl/ *noun* a metal or rubber cap or ring that strengthens and protects the lower end of a crutch or walking stick ■ *verb* to fit a ferrule onto a crutch or walking stick

fertile /'fɜːtaɪl/ *adjective* able to produce children. Opposite **sterile**

fertilisation /ˌfɜːtɪlaɪ'zeɪʃ(ə)n/, **fertilization** *noun* the joining of an ovum and a sperm to form a zygote and so start the development of an embryo

fertilise /'fɜːtəlaɪz/, **fertilize** *verb* (*of a sperm*) to join with an ovum

fertility /fɜː'tɪlɪti/ *noun* the fact of being fertile. Opposite **sterility**

fertility drug /fɜː'tɪlɪti drʌg/ *noun* a drug that stimulates ovulation, given to women undergoing in vitro fertilisation

fertility rate /fɜː'tɪlɪti reɪt/ *noun* the number of births per year calculated per 1000 females aged between 15 and 44

FESS *abbr* functional endoscopic sinus surgery

fester /'festə/ *verb* (*of an infected wound*) to become inflamed and produce pus ○ *His legs were covered with festering sores.*

festination /ˌfestɪ'neɪʃ(ə)n/ *noun* a way of walking in which a person takes short steps, seen in people who have Parkinson's disease

fetal /'fiːt(ə)l/ *adjective* referring to a fetus

fetal alcohol syndrome /ˌfiːt(ə)l 'ælkəhɒl ˌsɪndrəʊm/ *noun* damage caused to the fetus by alcohol in the blood of the mother, which affects the growth of the embryo, including its facial and brain development. Abbr **FAS**

fetal distress /ˌfiːt(ə)l dɪ'stres/ *noun* a condition, e.g. a heart or respiratory problem, in which a fetus may not survive if the condition is not monitored and corrected

fetal dystocia /ˌfiːt(ə)l dɪs'təʊsiə/ *noun* a difficult childbirth caused by a malformation or malpresentation of the fetus

fetal heart /ˌfiːt(ə)l 'hɑːt/ *noun* the heart of the fetus

fetalis /fiː'tɑːlɪs/ ♦ **erythroblastosis fetalis**

fetal monitor /ˌfiːt(ə)l 'mɒnɪtə/ *noun* an electronic device which monitors the fetus in the uterus

fetal position /'fiːt(ə)l pəˌzɪʃ(ə)n/ *noun* a position where a person lies curled up on his or her side, like a fetus in the uterus

fetishism /'fetɪʃɪz(ə)m/, **fetichism** *noun* a psychological disorder in which someone gets sexual satisfaction from touching objects

fetishist /'fetɪʃɪst/, **fetichist** *noun* a person who has fetishism

feto- /fiːtəʊ/ *prefix* fetus

fetoprotein /ˌfiːtəʊ'prəʊtiːn/ *noun* ♦ **alpha-fetoprotein**

fetor /'fiːtə/ *noun* a bad smell

fetoscope /'fiːtəskəʊp/ *noun* a stethoscope used in fetoscopy

fetoscopy /fɪ'tɒskəpi/ *noun* an examination of a fetus inside the uterus, taking blood samples to diagnose blood disorders

fetus /'fiːtəs/ *noun* an unborn baby from two months after conception until birth, before which it is called an embryo

FEV *abbr* forced expiratory volume

fever /'fiːvə/ *noun* **1.** a rise in body temperature ○ *She is running a slight fever.* ○ *You must stay in bed until the fever has gone down.* **2.** a condition when the temperature of the body is higher than usual ▶ also called **pyrexia**

COMMENT: Average oral body temperature is about 98.6°F or 37°C and rectal temperature is about 99°F or 37.2°C. A fever often makes the patient feel cold, and is accompanied by pains in the joints. Most fevers are caused by infections. Infections which result in fever include cat-scratch fever, dengue, malaria, meningitis, psittacosis, Q fever, rheumatic fever, Rocky Mountain spotted fever, scarlet fever, septicaemia, typhoid fever, typhus and yellow fever.

fever blister /'fiːvə ˌblɪstə/ *noun* same as **fever sore**

feverfew /'fiːvəfjuː/ *noun* a herb, formerly used to reduce fevers, but now used to relieve migraine

feverish /'fiːvərɪʃ/ *adjective* with a fever ○ *He felt feverish and took an aspirin.* ○ *She is in bed with a feverish chill.*

fever sore /'fiːvə sɔː/ *noun* a cold sore or burning sore, usually on the lips

fiber /'faɪbə/ *noun* US same as **fibre**

fibr- /faɪbr/ *prefix* referring to fibres, fibrous (*used before vowels*)

-fibrate /faɪbreɪt/ *suffix* used in names of lipid-lowering drugs

fibre /'faɪbə/ *noun* **1.** a structure in the body shaped like a thread **2.** same as **dietary fibre**

fibre optics /ˌfaɪbər 'ɒptɪks/, **fibreoptics** *noun* the use of thin fibres which conduct light and images to examine internal organs

fibrescope /'faɪbəskəʊp/ *noun* a device made of bundles of optical fibres which is passed into the body, used for examining internal organs

fibril /'faɪbrɪl/ *noun* a very small fibre

fibrillate /'faɪbrɪleɪt/ *verb* to undergo rapid irregular uncontrolled contractions, or make the heart or muscles undergo this type of contraction

fibrillating /'faɪbrɪleɪtɪŋ/ *adjective* with fluttering of a muscle ○ *They applied a defibrillator to correct a fibrillating heartbeat.*

fibrillation /ˌfaɪbrɪ'leɪʃ(ə)n/ *noun* the fluttering of a muscle

'Cardiovascular effects may include atrial arrhythmias but at 30°C there is the possibility of spontaneous ventricular fibrillation' [*British Journal of Nursing*]

fibrin /'fɪbrɪn/ *noun* a protein produced by fibrinogen, which helps make blood coagulate

COMMENT: Removal of fibrin from a blood sample is called defibrination.

fibrin foam /'fɪbrɪn fəʊm/ *noun* a white material made artificially from fibrinogen, used to prevent bleeding

fibrinogen /fɪ'brɪnədʒən/ *noun* a substance in blood plasma which produces fibrin when activated by thrombin

fibrinolysin /ˌfɪbrɪ'nɒləsɪn/ *noun* an enzyme which digests fibrin. Also called **plasmin**

fibrinolysis /ˌfɪbrɪ'nɒləsɪs/ *noun* the removal of blood clots from the system by the action of fibrinolysin on fibrin. Also called **thrombolysis**

fibrinolytic /ˌfɪbrɪnə'lɪtɪk/ *adjective* referring to fibrinolysis ○ *fibrinolytic drugs* Also called **thrombolytic**

fibro- /faɪbrəʊ/ *prefix* referring to fibres

fibroadenoma /ˌfaɪbrəʊˌædɪ'nəʊmə/ *noun* a benign tumour formed of fibrous and glandular tissue

fibroblast /'faɪbrəʊblæst/ *noun* a long flat cell found in connective tissue, which develops into collagen

fibrocartilage /ˌfaɪbrəʊ'kɑːtɪlɪdʒ/ *noun* cartilage and fibrous tissue combined

COMMENT: Fibrocartilage is found in the discs of the spine. It is elastic like cartilage and pliable like fibre.

fibrochondritis /ˌfaɪbrəʊkɒn'draɪtɪs/ *noun* inflammation of the fibrocartilage

fibrocyst /'faɪbrəʊsɪst/ *noun* a benign tumour of fibrous tissue

fibrocystic /ˌfaɪbrəʊ'sɪstɪk/ *adjective* referring to a fibrocyst

fibrocystic disease /ˌfaɪbrəʊ'sɪstɪk dɪˌziːz/, **fibrocystic disease of the pancreas** /ˌfaɪbrəʊˌsɪstɪk dɪˌziːz əv ðə 'pæŋkriəs/ *noun* same as **cystic fibrosis**

fibrocyte /'faɪbrəʊsaɪt/ *noun* a cell which derives from a fibroblast and is found in connective tissue

fibroelastosis /ˌfaɪbrəʊˌiːlæ'stəʊsɪs/ *noun* a deformed growth of the elastic fibres, especially in the ventricles of the heart

fibroid /'faɪbrɔɪd/ *adjective* like fibre ■ *noun* same as **fibroid tumour**

fibroid degeneration /ˌfaɪbrɔɪd dɪˌdʒenə'reɪʃ(ə)n/ *noun* the change of healthy tissue to fibrous tissue, e.g. as in cirrhosis of the liver

fibroid tumour /ˌfaɪbrɔɪd 'tjuːmə/ *noun* a benign tumour in the muscle fibres of the uterus. Also called **uterine fibroid, fibromyoma**

fibroma /faɪ'brəʊmə/ *noun* a small benign tumour formed in connective tissue

fibromuscular /ˌfaɪbrəʊ'mʌskjʊlə/ *adjective* referring to fibrous tissue and muscular tissue

fibromyoma /ˌfaɪbrəʊmaɪ'əʊmə/ *noun* same as **fibroid tumour**

fibroplasia /ˌfaɪbrəʊ'pleɪziə/ *noun* ♦ **retrolental fibroplasia**

fibrosa /faɪ'brəʊsə/ ♦ **osteitis fibrosa cystica**

fibrosarcoma /ˌfaɪbrəʊsɑː'kəʊmə/ *noun* a malignant tumour of the connective tissue, most common in the legs

fibrosis /faɪ'brəʊsɪs/ *noun* the process of replacing damaged tissue by scar tissue

fibrositis /ˌfaɪbrə'saɪtɪs/ *noun* a painful inflammation of the fibrous tissue which surrounds muscles and joints, especially the muscles of the back

fibrous /'faɪbrəs/ *adjective* made of fibres, or like fibre

fibrous capsule /ˌfaɪbrəs 'kæpsjuːl/ *noun* fibrous tissue surrounding a kidney. Also called **renal capsule**

fibrous joint /'faɪbrəs dʒɔɪnt/ *noun* a joint where fibrous tissue holds two bones together so that they cannot move, as in the bones of the skull

fibrous pericardium /ˌfaɪbrəs ˌperɪ'kɑːdiəm/ *noun* the outer part of the pericardium which surrounds the heart, and is attached to the main blood vessels

fibrous tissue /ˌfaɪbrəs 'tɪʃuː/ *noun* strong white tissue which makes tendons and ligaments and also scar tissue

fibula /'fɪbjʊlə/ *noun* the thinner of the two bones in the lower leg between the knee and the ankle. Compare **tibia** (NOTE: The plural is **fibulae**.)

fibular /'fɪbjʊlə/ *adjective* referring to the fibula

field /fiːld/ *noun* an area of interest ○ *He specialises in the field of community medicine.* ○ *Don't see that specialist with your breathing problems – his field is obstetrics.*

field of vision /ˌfiːld əv 'vɪʒ(ə)n/ *noun* same as **visual field**

fight or flight reaction /ˌfaɪt ɔː 'flaɪt riˌækʃən/ *noun* the theory that an organism which is faced with a threat reacts either by preparing to fight or to escape

fil- /fɪl/ *prefix* referring to a thread

filament /'fɪləmənt/ *noun* a long thin structure like a thread

filamentous /ˌfɪləˈmentəs/ *adjective* like a thread

Filaria /fɪˈleəriə/ *noun* a thin parasitic worm which is found especially in the lymph system, and is passed to humans by mosquitoes (NOTE: The plural is **Filariae**.)

COMMENT: Infestation with Filariae in the lymph system causes elephantiasis.

filariasis /ˌfɪləˈraɪəsɪs/ *noun* a tropical disease caused by parasitic threadworms in the lymph system, transmitted by mosquito bites

filiform /ˈfɪlɪfɔːm/ *adjective* shaped like a thread

filiform papillae /ˌfɪlɪfɔːm pəˈpɪliː/ *plural noun* papillae on the tongue which are shaped like threads, and have no taste buds

filipuncture /ˈfɪlɪpʌŋktʃə/ *noun* the procedure of putting a wire into an aneurysm to cause blood clotting

fill /fɪl/ *verb* □ **to fill a tooth** to put metal into a hole in a tooth after it has been drilled

filling /ˈfɪlɪŋ/ *noun* **1.** a surgical operation carried out by a dentist to fill a hole in a tooth with amalgam **2.** amalgam, metallic mixture put into a hole in a tooth by a dentist

film /fɪlm/ *noun* a very thin layer of a substance covering a surface

filter /ˈfɪltə/ *noun* a piece of paper or cloth through which a liquid is passed to remove any solid substances in it ■ *verb* to pass a liquid through a membrane, piece of paper or cloth to remove solid substances ○ *Impurities are filtered from the blood by the kidneys.*

filtrate /ˈfɪltreɪt/ *noun* a substance which has passed through a filter

filtration /fɪlˈtreɪʃ(ə)n/ *noun* the action of passing a liquid through a filter

filum /ˈfaɪləm/ *noun* a structure which is shaped like a thread

filum terminale /ˌfaɪləm ˌtɜːmɪˈneɪli/ *noun* the thin end section of the pia mater in the spinal cord

FIM *abbr* functional independence measure

fimbria /ˈfɪmbriə/ *noun* a fringe, especially the fringe of hair-like processes at the end of a Fallopian tube near the ovaries (NOTE: The plural is **fimbriae**.)

final common pathway /ˌfaɪn(ə)l ˌkɒmən ˈpɑːθweɪ/ *noun* linked neurones which take all impulses from the central nervous system to a muscle

fine /faɪn/ *adjective* **1.** healthy ○ *He was ill last week, but he's feeling fine now.* **2.** referring to something such as hair or thread which is very thin ○ *There is a growth of fine hair on the back of her neck.* ○ *Fine sutures are used for delicate operations.*

finger /ˈfɪŋgə/ *noun* one of the five parts at the end of the hand, but usually not including the thumb (NOTE: The names of the fingers are: **lit-** **tle finger**, **third finger** or **ring finger**, **middle finger**, **forefinger** or **index finger**.)

COMMENT: Each finger is formed of three finger bones (the **phalanges**), but the thumb has only two.

fingernail /ˈfɪŋgəneɪl/ *noun* a hard thin growth covering the end of a finger ○ *ridged and damaged fingernails*

finger-nose test /ˌfɪŋgə ˈnəʊz test/ *noun* a test of coordination, where the person is asked to close their eyes, stretch out their arm and then touch their nose with their index finger

fingerprint /ˈfɪŋgəprɪnt/ *noun* a mark left by a finger when something is touched. ◊ **genetic fingerprint**

fingerstall /ˈfɪŋgəstɔːl/ *noun* a cover for an infected finger, attached to the hand with strings

fireman's lift /ˌfaɪəmənz ˈlɪft/ *noun* a way of carrying an injured person by putting their body over one shoulder

firm /fɜːm/ *noun* a group of doctors and consultants in a hospital, especially one to which a trainee doctor is attached during clinical studies (*informal*)

first aid /ˌfɜːst ˈeɪd/ *noun* help given by a non-medical person to someone who is suddenly ill or injured before full-scale medical treatment can be given ○ *She gave him first aid in the street until the ambulance arrived.*

first-aider /ˌfɜːst ˈeɪdə/ *noun* a person who gives first aid to someone who is suddenly ill or injured

first-aid kit /ˌfɜːst ˈeɪd ˌkɪt/ *noun* a box with bandages and dressings kept ready to be used in an emergency

first-aid post /ˌfɜːst ˈeɪd ˌpəʊst/, **first-aid station** /ˌfɜːst ˈeɪd ˌsteɪʃ(ə)n/ *noun* a place where injured people can be taken for immediate care

first-degree burn /ˌfɜːst dɪˌgriː ˈbɜːn/ *noun* a former classification of the severity of a burn, where the skin turns red

first-degree haemorrhoids /ˌfɜːst dɪˌgriː ˈhemərɔɪdz/ *plural noun* haemorrhoids which remain in the rectum

first-degree relative /ˌfɜːst dɪˌgriː ˈrelətɪv/ *noun* a relative with whom an individual shares 50% of their genes, e.g. a father, mother, sibling or child

first-ever stroke /ˌfɜːst ˌevə ˈstrəʊk/ *noun* a stroke which someone has for the first time in his or her life

first intention /fɜːst ɪnˈtenʃən/ *noun* the healing of a clean wound where the tissue forms again rapidly and no prominent scar is left

first-level nurse /ˌfɜːst ˌlev(ə)l ˈnɜːs/, **first-level Registered Nurse** /ˌfɜːst ˌlev(ə)l ˌredʒ ɪstəd ˈnɜːs/ *noun* a nurse who has passed qualifying examinations, is registered as such with the Nursing and Midwifery Council and can act in an independent decision-making role. Compare **second-level nurse**

fissile /ˈfɪsaɪl/ *adjective* able to split or be split

fission /ˈfɪʃ(ə)n/ *noun* the act of dividing into two or more parts

fissure /ˈfɪʃə/ *noun* a crack or groove in the skin, tissue or an organ □ **horizontal and oblique fissures** grooves between the lobes of the lungs. See illustration at LUNGS in Supplement

fist /fɪst/ *noun* a hand which is tightly closed

fistula /ˈfɪstjʊlə/ *noun* a passage or opening which has been made unusually between two organs, often near the rectum or anus

fistula in ano /ˌfɪstjʊlə ɪn ˈænəʊ/ *noun* same as **anal fistula**

fit /fɪt/ *adjective* strong and physically healthy ○ *She exercises every day to keep fit.* ○ *The doctors decided the patient was not fit for surgery.* (NOTE: **fitter – fittest**) □ **he isn't fit enough to work** he is still too ill to work ■ *noun* a sudden attack of a disorder, especially convulsions and epilepsy ○ *She had a fit of coughing.* ○ *He had an epileptic fit.* ○ *The baby had a series of fits.* ■ *verb* **1.** to attach an appliance correctly ○ *The surgeons fitted the artificial hand to the patient's arm* or *fitted the patient with an artificial hand.* **2.** to provide a piece of equipment for someone to wear ○ *She was fitted with temporary support.* **3.** to have convulsions ○ *The patient has fitted twice.* (NOTE: **fitting – fitted**. Note also: you fit someone **with** an appliance.)

fitness /ˈfɪtnəs/ *noun* the fact of being strong and healthy ○ *Being in the football team demands a high level of physical fitness.* ○ *He had to pass a fitness test to join the police force.*

fixated /fɪkˈseɪtɪd/ *adjective* referring to a person who has too close an attachment to another person, often to a parent

fixation /fɪkˈseɪʃ(ə)n/ *noun* a psychological disorder where a person does not develop beyond a particular stage

fixative /ˈfɪksətɪv/ *noun* a chemical used in the preparation of samples on slides

fixator /fɪkˈseɪtə/ *noun* a metal rod placed through a bone to keep a part of the body rigid

fixed oil /ˌfɪkst ˈɔɪl/ *noun* **1.** an oil which is liquid at 20°C **2.** liquid fats, especially those used as food

flab /flæb/ *noun* soft fat flesh (*informal*) ○ *He's doing exercises to try to fight the flab.*

flabby /ˈflæbi/ *adjective* with soft flesh ○ *She has got flabby from sitting at her desk all day.*

flaccid /ˈflæksɪd, ˈflæsɪd/ *adjective* soft or flabby

flaccidity /flækˈsɪdɪti, flæˈsɪdɪti/ *noun* the state of being flaccid

flagellate /ˈflædʒəlæt/ *noun* a type of parasitic protozoan which uses whip-like hairs to swim, e.g. *Leishmania*

flagellum /fləˈdʒeləm/ *noun* a tiny growth on a microorganism, shaped like a whip (NOTE: The plural is **flagella**.)

Flagyl /ˈflædʒaɪl/ a trade name for metronidazole

flail /fleɪl/ *verb* to thrash around with uncontrollable or violent movements, particularly of the arms

flail chest /ˈfleɪl tʃest/ *noun* a condition in which the chest is not stable, because several ribs have been broken

flake /fleɪk/ *noun* a thin piece of tissue ○ *Dandruff is formed of flakes of dead skin on the scalp.*

flake fracture /ˈfleɪk ˌfræktʃə/ *noun* a fracture where thin pieces of bone come off

flake off /ˌfleɪk ˈɒf/ *verb* to fall off as flakes

flap /flæp/ *noun* a flat piece attached to something, especially a piece of skin or tissue still attached to the body at one side and used in grafts

flare /fleə/ *noun* red colouring of the skin at an infected spot or in urticaria

flashback /ˈflæʃbæk/ *noun* a repeated and very vivid memory of a traumatic event

flash burn /ˈflæʃ bɜːn/ *noun* a burn caused when a body part is briefly exposed to a source of intense heat

flat foot /ˌflæt ˈfʊt/, **flat feet** /ˌflæt ˈfiːt/ *noun* a condition in which the soles of the feet lie flat on the ground instead of being arched as usual. Also called **pes planus**

flatline /ˈflætlaɪn/ *verb* to fail to show on a monitor any of the electrical currents associated with heart or brain activity ■ *noun* a monitor readout on an EEG or ECG indicating total cessation of brain or cardiac activity, respectively

flatulence /ˈflætjʊləns/ *noun* gas or air which collects in the stomach or intestines causing discomfort

COMMENT: Flatulence is generally caused by indigestion, but can be made worse if the person swallows air (**aerophagy**).

flatulent /ˈflætjʊlənt/ *adjective* having flatulence, or caused by flatulence

flatus /ˈfleɪtəs/ *noun* air and gas which collects in the intestines and is painful

flatworm /ˈflætwɜːm/ *noun* any of several types of parasitic worm with a flat body, e.g. a tapeworm. Compare **roundworm**

flea /fliː/ *noun* a tiny insect which sucks blood and is a parasite on animals and humans

COMMENT: Fleas can transmit disease, most especially bubonic plague which is transmitted by infected rat fleas.

flecainide /fleˈkeɪnaɪd/ *noun* a drug that helps to correct an irregular heartbeat

flesh /fleʃ/ *noun* tissue containing blood, forming the part of the body which is not skin, bone or organs

flesh wound /ˈfleʃ wuːnd/ *noun* a wound which only affects the fleshy part of the body ○ *She had a flesh wound in her leg.*

fleshy /ˈfleʃi/ *adjective* **1.** made of flesh **2.** fat

flex /fleks/ *verb* to bend something □ **to flex a joint** to use a muscle to make a joint bend

flexibilitas cerea /ˌfleksɪˌbɪlɪtəs ˈsɪəriə/ *noun* a condition in which, if someone's arms or legs are moved, they remain in that set position for some time

flexion /ˈflekʃən/ *noun* the act of bending a joint

Flexner's bacillus /ˌfleksnəz bəˈsɪləs/ *noun* a bacterium which causes bacillary dysentery

flexor /ˈfleksə/, **flexor muscle** /ˈfleksə ˌmʌs(ə)l/ *noun* a muscle which makes a joint bend. Compare **extensor**

flexure /ˈflekʃə/ *noun* **1.** a bend in an organ **2.** a fold in the skin

floaters /ˈfləʊtəz/ *plural noun* same as **muscae volitantes**

floating kidney /ˌfləʊtɪŋ ˈkɪdni/ *noun* same as **nephroptosis**

floating rib /ˌfləʊtɪŋ ˈrɪb/ *noun* one of the two lowest ribs on each side, which are not attached to the breastbone

floccillation /ˌflɒksɪˈleɪʃ(ə)n/ *noun* the action of constantly touching the bedclothes, a sign that someone is approaching death

floccitation /ˌflɒksɪˈteɪʃ(ə)n/ *noun* same as **carphology**

flooding /ˈflʌdɪŋ/ *noun* same as **menorrhagia**

floppy baby syndrome /ˌflɒpi ˈbeɪbi ˌsɪn drəʊm/ *noun* same as **amyotonia congenita**

flora /ˈflɔːrə/ *noun* bacteria which exist in a particular part of the body

florid /ˈflɒrɪd/ *adjective* with an unhealthily glowing pink or red complexion

floss /flɒs/ *noun* same as **dental floss** ■ *verb* to clean the teeth with dental floss

flow /fləʊ/ *noun* **1.** a movement of liquid or gas ○ *They used a tourniquet to try to stop the flow of blood.* **2.** the amount of liquid or gas which is moving ○ *The meter measures the flow of water through the pipe.*

flowmeter /ˈfləʊmiːtə/ *noun* a meter attached to a pipe, e.g. as in anaesthetic equipment, to measure the speed at which a liquid or gas moves in the pipe

flu /fluː/ *noun* **1.** same as **influenza 2.** a very bad cold (*informal*) (NOTE: Sometimes written '**flu** to show it is a short form of **influenza**.)

flucloxacillin /fluːˈklɒksəsɪlɪn/ *noun* a drug related to penicillin and effective against streptococcal infections and pneumonia

fluconazole /fluːˈkɒnəzəʊl/ *noun* a drug used to treat fungal infections such as candidiasis

fluctuation /ˌflʌktʃuˈeɪʃ(ə)n/ *noun* the feeling of movement of liquid inside part of the body or inside a cyst when pressed with the fingers

fluid /ˈfluːɪd/ *noun* **1.** a liquid **2.** any gas, liquid or powder which flows

fluid balance /ˈfluːɪd ˌbæləns/ *noun* the maintenance of the balance of fluids in the body during dialysis or other treatment

fluke /fluːk/ *noun* a parasitic flatworm which settles inside the liver, in the bloodstream and in other parts of the body

flunitrazepam /ˌfluːnaɪˈtræzɪpæm/ *noun* a tranquilliser that, because of its association with 'date rape' cases, is a controlled drug in the UK

fluorescence /fluəˈres(ə)ns/ *noun* the sending out of light from a substance which is receiving radiation

fluorescent /fluəˈres(ə)nt/ *adjective* referring to a substance which sends out light

fluoridate /ˈflɔːrɪdeɪt/ *verb* to add fluoride to a substance, usually to drinking water, in order to help prevent tooth decay

fluoride /ˈfluəraɪd/ *noun* a chemical compound of fluorine and sodium, potassium or tin ○ *fluoride toothpaste*

COMMENT: Fluoride will reduce decay in teeth and is often added to drinking water or to toothpaste. Some people object to fluoridation and it is thought that too high a concentration, such as that achieved by highly fluoridated water and the use of a highly fluoridated toothpaste, may discolour the teeth of children.

fluorine /ˈfluəriːn/ *noun* a chemical element found in bones and teeth (NOTE: The chemical symbol is **F**.)

fluoroscope /ˈfluərəskəʊp/ *noun* an apparatus which projects an X-ray image of a part of the body onto a screen, so that the part of the body can be examined as it moves

fluoroscopy /fluəˈrɒskəpi/ *noun* an examination of the body using X-rays projected onto a screen

fluorosis /flɔːˈrəʊsɪs/ *noun* a condition caused by excessive fluoride in drinking water

COMMENT: At a low level, fluorosis causes discoloration of the teeth, and as the level of fluoride rises, ligaments can become calcified.

fluoxetine /fluːˈɒksətiːn/ *noun* a drug that increases serotonin in the brain and is used to treat anxiety and depression

flush /flʌʃ/ *noun* a red colour in the skin ■ *verb* **1.** to wash a wound with liquid **2.** (*of person*) to turn red

flushed /flʌʃt/ *adjective* with red skin, e.g. due to heat, emotion or overeating ○ *Her face was flushed and she was breathing heavily.*

flutter /ˈflʌtə/, **fluttering** /ˈflʌtərɪŋ/ *noun* a rapid movement, especially of the atria of the heart, which is not controlled by impulses from the sinoatrial node

flux /flʌks/ *noun* an excessive production of liquid from the body

focal /'fəʊk(ə)l/ *adjective* referring to a focus

focal distance /,fəʊk(ə)l 'dɪstəns/, **focal length** /,fəʊk(ə)l 'leŋθ/ *noun* the distance between the lens of the eye and the point behind the lens where light is focused

focal epilepsy /,fəʊk(ə)l 'epɪlepsi/ *noun* epilepsy arising from a localised area of the brain

focal myopathy /,fəʊk(ə)l maɪ'ɒpəθi/ *noun* destruction of muscle tissue caused by a substance injected in an intramuscular injection

focus /'fəʊkəs/ *noun* 1. the point where light rays converge through a lens 2. the centre of an infection (NOTE: The plural is **foci**.) ■ *verb* 1. to adjust a lens until an image is clear and sharp 2. to see clearly ○ *He has difficulty in focusing on the object.*

focus group /'fəʊkəs gruːp/ *noun* a discussion group of lay people brought together under professional guidance to discuss issues such as care

foetal /'fiːt(ə)l/ *adjective* another spelling of **fetal** (NOTE: The spelling **foetal** is common in general use in British English, but the spelling **fetal** is the accepted international spelling for technical use.)

foetor /'fiːtə/ *noun* another spelling of **fetor**

foetoscope /'fiːtəskəʊp/ *noun* another spelling of **fetoscope**

foetoscopy /fɪ'tɒskəpi/ *noun* another spelling of **fetoscopy**

foetus /'fiːtəs/ *noun* another spelling of **fetus** (NOTE: The spelling **foetus** is common in general use in British English, but the spelling **fetus** is the accepted international spelling for technical use.)

folacin /'fəʊləsɪn/ *noun* same as **folic acid**

fold /fəʊld/ *noun* a part of the body which is bent so that it lies on top of another part

folic acid /,fəʊlɪk 'æsɪd/ *noun* a vitamin in the Vitamin B complex found in milk, liver, yeast and green vegetables such as spinach, which is essential for creating new blood cells

COMMENT: Lack of folic acid can cause anaemia and neural tube disorders in the developing fetus. It can also be caused by alcoholism.

folie à deux /,fɒli æ 'dɜː/ *noun* a rare condition where a psychological disorder is communicated between two people who live together

follicle /'fɒlɪk(ə)l/ *noun* a tiny hole or sac in the body

COMMENT: An ovarian follicle goes through several stages in its development. The first stage is called a primordial follicle, which then develops into a primary follicle and becomes a mature follicle by the sixth day of the period. This follicle secretes oestrogen until the ovum has developed to the point when it can break out, leaving the corpus luteum behind.

follicle-stimulating hormone /,fɒlɪk(ə)l ,stɪmjʊleɪtɪŋ 'hɔːməʊn/ *noun* a hormone produced by the pituitary gland which stimulates ova in the ovaries and sperm in the testes. Abbr **FSH**

follicular /fə'lɪkjʊlə/, **folliculate** /fə'lɪkjʊlət/ *adjective* referring to follicles

follicular tumour /fə,lɪkjʊlə 'tjuːmə/ *noun* a tumour in a follicle

folliculin /fə'lɪkjʊlɪn/ *noun* an oestrone, a type of oestrogen ○ *She is undergoing folliculin treatment.*

folliculitis /fə,lɪkjʊ'laɪtɪs/ *noun* inflammation of the hair follicles, especially where hair has been shaved

follow /'fɒləʊ/, **follow up** /,fɒləʊ 'ʌp/ *verb* to check on someone who has been examined before in order to assess the progress of a disease or the results of treatment

follow-up /'fɒləʊ ʌp/ *noun* a check on someone who has been examined before

'…length of follow-ups varied from three to 108 months. Thirteen patients were followed for less than one year, but the remainder were seen regularly for periods from one to nine years' [*New Zealand Medical Journal*]

fomentation /,fəʊmen'teɪʃ(ə)n/ *noun* same as **poultice**

fomites /'fəʊmɪtiːz/ *plural noun* objects touched by someone with a communicable disease which can then be the means of passing on the disease to others

fontanelle /,fɒntə'nel/, **fontanel** *noun* the soft cartilage between the bony sections of a baby's skull

COMMENT: The fontanelles gradually harden over a period of months and by the age of 18 months the bones of the baby's skull are usually solid.

food allergen /'fuːd ,ælədʒen/ *noun* a substance in food which produces an allergy

food allergy /'fuːd 'ælədʒi/ *noun* an allergy to a specific food such as nuts, which causes a severe reaction that may lead to life-threatening anaphylactic shock

food canal /'fuːd kə,næl/ *noun* the passage from the mouth to the rectum through which food passes and is digested

food intolerance /'fuːd ɪn'tɒlərəns/ *noun* an adverse reaction to some foods such as oranges, eggs, tomatoes and strawberries

food poisoning /'fuːd ,pɔɪz(ə)nɪŋ/ *noun* an illness caused by eating food which is contaminated with bacteria

foot /fʊt/ *noun* the end part of the leg on which a person stands

COMMENT: The foot is formed of 26 bones: 14 phalanges in the toes, five metatarsals in the main part of the foot and seven tarsals in the heel.

footpump /'fʊtpʌmp/ *noun* a device to reduce the risk of post-operative deep-vein thrombosis by mechanical use of leg muscles

foramen /fə'reɪmən/ *noun* a natural opening inside the body, e.g. the opening in a bone through which veins or nerves pass (NOTE: The plural is **foramina**.)

foramen magnum /fə,reɪmən 'mægnəm/ *noun* the hole at the bottom of the skull where the brain is joined to the spinal cord

foramen ovale /fə,reɪmən əʊ'vɑːleɪ/ *noun* an opening between the two parts of the heart in a fetus

COMMENT: The foramen ovale usually closes at birth, but if it stays open the blood from the veins can mix with the blood going to the arteries, causing cyanosis.

foramina /fə'reɪmɪnə/ plural of **foramen**

forced expiratory volume /,fɔːst ek'spɪrət(ə)ri ,vɒljuːm/ *noun* the maximum amount of air that can be expelled in a given time. Abbr **FEV**

force-feed /,fɔːs 'fiːd/ *verb* to make someone swallow food against their will, e.g. by using a tube to put it directly down their throat

forceps /'fɔːseps/ *noun* a surgical instrument with handles like a pair of scissors, made in different sizes and with differently shaped ends, used for holding and pulling

forceps delivery /'fɔːseps dɪ,lɪv(ə)ri/ *noun* childbirth where the doctor uses forceps to help the baby out of the mother's uterus

fore- /fɔː/ *prefix* in front

forearm /'fɔːrɑːm/ *noun* the lower part of the arm from the elbow to the wrist

forearm bones /'fɔːrɑːm bəʊnz/ *plural noun* the ulna and the radius

forebrain /'fɔːbreɪn/ *noun* the front part of the brain in an embryo

forefinger /'fɔːfɪŋgə/ *noun* the first finger on the hand, next to the thumb

foregut /'fɔːgʌt/ *noun* the front part of the gut in an embryo

forehead /'fɔːhed/ *noun* the part of the face above the eyes

foreign /'fɒrɪn/ *adjective* **1.** not belonging to your own country ○ *foreign visitors* ○ *a foreign language* **2.** referring to something that is found where it does not naturally belong, especially something found in the human body that comes from a source outside the body ○ *a foreign object* ○ *foreign matter*

foreign body /,fɒrɪn 'bɒdi/ *noun* a piece of material which is not part of the surrounding tissue and should not be there, e.g. sand in a cut, dust in the eye or a pin which has been swallowed ○ *The X-ray showed the presence of a foreign body.* □ **swallowed foreign bodies** something which should not have been swallowed, e.g. a pin, coin or button

foremilk /'fɔːmɪlk/ *noun* the relatively low-fat milk with a high sugar content that is produced by a woman at the beginning of a breast feed

forensic /fə'rensɪk/ *adjective* relating to the use of science in solving criminal investigations or settling legal cases

forensic medicine /fə,rensɪk 'med(ə)sɪn/ *noun* the branch of medical science concerned with finding solutions to crimes against people and which involves procedures such as conducting autopsies on murdered people or taking blood samples from clothes

foreskin /'fɔːskɪn/ *noun* the skin covering the top of the penis, which can be removed by circumcision. Also called **prepuce**

forewaters /'fɔːwɔːtəz/ *plural noun* fluid which comes out of the vagina at the beginning of childbirth when the amnion bursts

forgetful /fə'getf(ə)l/ *adjective* referring to someone who often forgets things ○ *She became very forgetful, and had to be looked after by her sister.*

forgetfulness /fə'getf(ə)lnəs/ *noun* a condition in which someone often forgets things ○ *Increasing forgetfulness is a sign of old age.*

form /fɔːm/ *noun* **1.** shape **2.** a piece of paper with blank spaces which you have to write in ○ *You have to fill in a form when you are admitted to hospital.* **3.** a state or condition ○ *in good form* □ **he's in good form today** he is very amusing, he is doing things well ■ *verb* to make or to be the main part of something ○ *Calcium is one the elements which form bones* or *bones are mainly formed of calcium.* ○ *An ulcer formed in his duodenum.* ○ *In diphtheria a membrane forms across the larynx.*

formaldehyde /fɔː'mældɪhaɪd/ *noun* a gas with an unpleasant smell that is a strong disinfectant. When dissolved in water to make **formalin**, it is also used to preserve medical specimens.

formalin /'fɔːməlɪn/ *noun* a solution of formaldehyde in water, used to preserve medical specimens

formation /fɔː'meɪʃ(ə)n/ *noun* the action of forming something ○ *Drinking milk helps the formation of bones.*

formication /,fɔːmɪ'keɪʃ(ə)n/ *noun* an itching feeling where the skin feels as if it were covered with insects

formula /'fɔːmjʊlə/ *noun* **1.** a way of indicating a chemical compound using letters and numbers, e.g. H_2SO_4 **2.** instructions on how to prepare a drug **3.** *US* powdered milk for babies (NOTE: The plural is **formulas** or **formulae**.)

formulary /'fɔːmjʊləri/ *noun* a book that lists medicines together with their formulae

fornix /'fɔːnɪks/ *noun* an arch (NOTE: The plural is **fornices**.) □ **fornix of the vagina** space between the cervix of the uterus and the vagina

fornix cerebri /,fɔːnɪks 'serɪbraɪ/ *noun* a section of white matter in the brain between the hippocampus and the hypothalamus. See illustration at BRAIN in Supplement

fortification figures /ˌfɔːtɪfɪ'keɪʃ(ə)n ˌfɪgəz/ *plural noun* patterns of coloured light, seen as part of the aura before a migraine attack occurs

foscarnet /fɒs'kɑːnət/ *noun* an antiviral drug administered by intravenous injection that is effective against herpesviruses that are resistant to acyclovir. It is especially used for people with AIDS.

fossa /'fɒsə/ *noun* a shallow hollow in a bone or the skin

foster children /'fɒstə ˌtʃɪldrən/ *plural noun* children brought up by people who are not their own parents

foster parent /'fɒstə ˌpeərənt/ *noun* a woman or man who brings up a child born to other parents

Fothergill's operation /'fɒðəgɪlz ɒpəˌreɪʃ(ə)n/ *noun* a surgical operation to correct prolapse of the uterus [After W. E. Fothergill (1865–1926), British gynaecologist.]

foundation hospital /faʊnˌdeɪʃ(ə)n 'hɒspɪt(ə)l/ *noun* in the UK, a proposed type of hospital that would be independent of its Local Health Authority in financial matters

fourchette /fʊə'ʃet/ *noun* a fold of skin at the back of the vulva

fovea /'fəʊviə/, **fovea centralis** /ˌfəʊviə sen 'trɑːlɪs/ *noun* a depression in the retina which is the point where the eye sees most clearly. See illustration at EYE in Supplement

FP10 /ˌef piː 'ten/ *noun* in the UK, an NHS prescription from a GP

fracture /'fræktʃə/ *verb* 1. (*of bone*) to break ○ *The tibia fractured in two places.* 2. to break a bone ○ *He fractured his wrist.* ■ *noun* a break in a bone ○ *rib fracture* or *fracture of a rib*

fractured /'fræktʃəd/ *adjective* broken ○ *He had a fractured skull.* ○ *She went to hospital to have her fractured leg reset.*

fragile /'frædʒaɪl/ *adjective* easily broken ○ *Elderly people's bones are more fragile than those of adolescents.*

fragile-X syndrome /ˌfrædʒaɪl 'eks ˌsɪn drəʊm/ *noun* a hereditary condition in which part of an X chromosome is constricted, causing mental impairment

fragilitas /frə'dʒɪlɪtəs/ *noun* fragility or brittleness

fragilitas ossium /frəˌdʒɪlɪtəs 'ɒsiəm/ *noun* a hereditary condition where the bones are brittle and break easily, similar to osteogenesis imperfecta

frail /freɪl/ *adjective* weak, easily broken ○ *Grandfather is getting frail, and we have to look after him all the time.* ○ *The baby's bones are still very frail.*

framboesia /fræm'biːziə/ *noun* same as **yaws**

frame /freɪm/ *noun* 1. the particular size and shape of someone's body 2. a solid support for something. ◊ **walking frame, Zimmer frame**

framework /'freɪmwɜːk/ *noun* the main bones which make up the structure of part of the body

framycetin /fræ'maɪsətɪn/ *noun* an antibiotic

fraternal twins /frəˌtɜːn(ə)l 'twɪnz/ *plural noun* same as **dizygotic twins**

freckle /'frek(ə)l/ *noun* a harmless small brownish patch on the skin that becomes more noticeable after exposure to the sun. Freckles are often found in people with fair hair. Also called **lentigo** ■ *verb* to mark something, or become marked with freckles

freckled /'frek(ə)ld/ *adjective* with brown spots on the skin

freeze /friːz/ *verb* to anaesthetise part of the body (*informal*) ○ *They froze my big toe to remove the nail.*

freeze dry /ˌfriːz 'draɪ/ *verb* to freeze something rapidly then dry it in a vacuum

freeze drying /'friːz ˌdraɪɪŋ/ *noun* a method of preserving food or tissue specimens by freezing rapidly and drying in a vacuum

Freiberg's disease /'fraɪbɜːgz dɪˌziːz/ *noun* osteochondritis of the head of the second metatarsus [Described 1914. After Albert Henry Freiberg (1869–1940), US surgeon.]

Frei test /'fraɪ test/ *noun* a test for the venereal disease lymphogranuloma inguinale [Described 1925. After Wilhelm Siegmund Frei (1885–1943), Professor of Dermatology at Berlin, Germany. He settled in New York, USA.]

fremitus /'fremɪtəs/ *noun* vibrations or trembling in part of someone's body, felt by the doctor's hand or heard through a stethoscope

French letter /ˌfrentʃ 'letə/ *noun* ♦ **condom** (*informal*)

frenectomy /frə'nektəmi/ *noun* an operation to remove a frenum

Frenkel's exercises /'frenkəlz ˌeksəsaɪzɪz/ *plural noun* exercises for people who have locomotor ataxia, to teach coordination of the muscles and limbs

frenotomy /frə'nɒtəmi/ *noun* an operation to split a frenum

frenum /'friːnəm/, **frenulum** /'frenjʊləm/ *noun* a fold of mucous membrane under the tongue or by the clitoris

frequency /'friːkwənsi/ *noun* 1. the number of times something takes place in a given time ○ *the frequency of micturition* 2. the rate of vibration in oscillations

fresh air /ˌfreʃ 'eə/ *noun* open air ○ *They came out of the hospital into the fresh air.*

fresh frozen plasma /ˌfreʃ ˌfrəʊz(ə)n 'plæzmə/ *noun* plasma made from freshly donated blood, and kept frozen

fretful /'fretf(ə)l/ *adjective* referring to a baby that cries, cannot sleep or seems unhappy

Freudian /'frɔɪdiən/ *adjective* understandable in terms of Freud's theories, especially with regard to human sexuality ■ *noun* someone who is influenced by or follows Freud's theories or methods of psychoanalysis

friable /'fraɪəb(ə)l/ *adjective* easily broken up into small pieces

friar's balsam /ˌfraɪəz 'bɔːlsəm/ *noun* a mixture of various plant oils, including benzoin and balsam, which can be inhaled as a vapour to relieve bronchitis or congestion

friction /'frɪkʃən/ *noun* the rubbing together of two surfaces

friction fremitus /ˌfrɪkʃən 'fremɪtəs/ *noun* a scratching sensation felt when the hand is placed on the chest of someone who has pericarditis

friction murmur /ˌfrɪkʃən 'mɜːmə/ *noun* the sound of two serous membranes rubbing together, heard with a stethoscope in someone who has pericarditis or pleurisy

Friedländer's bacillus /'friːdlendəz bə ˌsɪləs/ *noun* the bacterium *Klebsiella pneumoniae* which can cause pneumonia [Described 1882. After Carl Friedländer (1847–87), pathologist at the Friedrichshain Hospital, Berlin, Germany.]

Friedman's test /'friːdmənz test/ *noun* a test for pregnancy [After Maurice H. Friedman (b. 1903), US physician.]

Friedreich's ataxia /ˌfriːdraɪks ə'tæksiə/ *noun* an inherited nervous disease which affects the spinal cord and is associated with club foot, an unsteady walk and speech difficulties. Also called **dystrophia adiposogenitalis** [Described 1863. After Nicholaus Friedreich (1825–82), Professor of Pathological Anatomy at Würzburg, later Professor of Pathology and Therapy at Heidelberg, Germany.]

frigidity /frɪ'dʒɪdɪti/ *noun* the fact of being unable to experience orgasm, sexual pleasure or sexual desire

fringe medicine /'frɪnʒ ˌmed(ə)sɪn/ *noun* types of medical practice which are not usually taught in medical schools, e.g. homeopathy or acupuncture (*informal*)

frog plaster /'frɒg ˌplɑːstə/ *noun* a plaster cast made to keep the legs in an open position after an operation to correct a dislocated hip

Fröhlich's syndrome /'frɜːlɪks ˌsɪndrəʊm/ *noun* a condition in which someone becomes obese and the genital system does not develop, caused by an adenoma of the pituitary gland [Described 1901. After Alfred Fröhlich (1871–1953), Professor of Pharmacology at the University of Vienna, Austria.]

frontal /'frʌnt(ə)l/ *adjective* referring to the forehead or to the front of the head. Opposite **occipital**

frontal bone /'frʌnt(ə)l bəʊn/ *noun* a bone forming the front of the upper part of the skull behind the forehead

frontal lobe /'frʌnt(ə)l ləʊb/ *noun* the front lobe of each cerebral hemisphere

frontal lobotomy /ˌfrʌnt(ə)l ləʊ'bɒtəmi/ *noun* formerly, a surgical operation on the brain to treat mental illness by removing part of the frontal lobe

frontal sinus /ˌfrʌnt(ə)l 'saɪnəs/ *noun* one of two sinuses in the front of the face above the eyes and near the nose

front passage /frʌnt 'pæsɪdʒ/ (*informal*) **1.** same as **urethra 2.** same as **vagina**

frostbite /'frɒstbaɪt/ *noun* an injury caused by very severe cold which freezes tissue

frostbitten /'frɒstbɪt(ə)n/ *adjective* having frostbite

COMMENT: In very cold conditions, the outside tissue of the fingers, toes, ears and nose can freeze, becoming white and numb. Thawing of frostbitten tissue can be very painful and must be done very slowly. Severe cases of frostbite may require amputation because the tissue has died and gangrene has set in.

frozen shoulder /ˌfrəʊz(ə)n 'ʃəʊldə/ *noun* stiffness and pain in the shoulder, caused by inflammation of the membranes of the shoulder joint after injury or a period of immobility, when deposits may form in the tendons

frozen watchfulness /ˌfrəʊz(ə)n 'wɒtʃfəlnəs/ *noun* an expression of petrified fear on a child's face, especially in children who have been abused

fructose /'frʌktəʊs/ *noun* fruit sugar found in honey and some fruit, which together with glucose forms sucrose

fructosuria /ˌfrʌktəʊ'sjʊəriə/ *noun* the presence of fructose in the urine

frusemide /'fruːsəmaɪd/ *noun* same as **furosemide**

FSH *abbr* follicle-stimulating hormone

fugax /'fjuːgæks/ ♦ **amaurosis fugax**

-fuge /fjuːdʒ/ *suffix* driving away

fugue /fjuːg/ *noun* a condition in which someone loses his or her memory and leaves home

fulguration /ˌfʌlgə'reɪʃ(ə)n/ *noun* the removal of a growth such as a wart by burning with an electric needle. Also called **electrodesiccation**

full term /ˌfʊl 'tɜːm/ *noun* a complete pregnancy of forty weeks ○ *She has had several pregnancies but none has reached full term.*

full thickness burn /fʊl 'θɪknəs bɜːn/ *noun* same as **deep dermal burn**

fulminant /'fʊlmɪnənt/, **fulminating** /'fʊlmɪˌneɪtɪŋ/ *adjective* referring to a dangerous disease which develops very rapidly

'…the major manifestations of pneumococcal infection in sickle-cell disease are septicaemia, meningitis and pneumonia. The illness is frequently fulminant' [*The Lancet*]

fumes /fjuːmz/ *plural noun* gas or smoke

fumigate /ˈfjuːmɪgeɪt/ *verb* to kill insects in an area by using gas or smoke

fumigation /ˌfjuːmɪˈgeɪʃ(ə)n/ *noun* the process of killing insects in an area with gas or smoke

function /ˈfʌŋkʃən/ *noun* the particular work done by an organ ○ *What is the function of the pancreas?* ○ *The function of an ovary is to form ova.* ■ *verb* to work in a particular way ○ *The heart and lungs were functioning normally.* ○ *His kidneys suddenly stopped functioning.*

'...insulin's primary metabolic function is to transport glucose into muscle and fat cells, so that it can be used for energy' [*Nursing '87*]

'...the AIDS virus attacks a person's immune system and damages the ability to fight other disease. Without a functioning immune system to ward off other germs, the patient becomes vulnerable to becoming infected'
[*Journal of American Medical Association*]

functional /ˈfʌŋkʃən(ə)l/ *adjective* referring to a disorder or illness which does not have a physical cause and may have a psychological cause, as opposed to an organic disorder

functional endoscopic sinus surgery /ˌfʌŋkʃən(ə)l ˌendəskɒpɪk ˈsaɪnəs ˌsɜːdʒəri/ *noun* the removal of soft tissue in the sinuses using an endoscope. Abbr **FESS**

functional enuresis /ˌfʌŋkʃən(ə)l ˌenjʊˈriːsɪs/ *noun* bedwetting which has a psychological cause

functional independence measure /ˌfʌŋkʃən(ə)l ˌɪndɪˈpendəns ˌmeʒə/ *noun* a measure of disability. Abbr **FIM**

fundus /ˈfʌndəs/ *noun* **1.** the bottom of a hollow organ such as the uterus **2.** the top section of the stomach, above the body of the stomach

fungal /ˈfʌŋgəl/ *adjective* relating to, or caused by, fungi ○ *a fungal skin infection*

fungate /ˈfʌŋgeɪt/ *verb* (*of some skin cancers*) to increase rapidly at a late stage of tumour formation

fungicide /ˈfʌŋgɪsaɪd/ *noun* a substance used to kill fungi

fungiform papillae /ˌfʌŋgɪfɔːm pəˈpɪliː/ *noun* rounded papillae on the tip and sides of the tongue, which have taste buds

fungoid /ˈfʌŋgɔɪd/ *adjective* like a fungus

fungus /ˈfʌŋgəs/ *noun* an organism such as yeast or mould, some of which cause disease (NOTE: The plural is **fungi**. For other terms referring to fungi, see words beginning with **myc-**, **myco-**.)

COMMENT: Some fungi can become parasites of man, and cause diseases such as thrush.

Other fungi, such as yeast, react with sugar to form alcohol. Some antibiotics, such as penicillin, are derived from fungi.

fungus disease /ˈfʌŋgəs dɪˌziːz/ *noun* a disease caused by a fungus

fungus poisoning /ˈfʌŋgəs ˌpɔɪz(ə)nɪŋ/ *noun* poisoning by eating a poisonous fungus

funiculitis /fjuːnɪkjʊˈlaɪtɪs/ *noun* inflammation of the spermatic cord

funiculus /fjuːˈnɪkjʊləs/ *noun* one of the three parts of the white matter in the spinal cord ○ *The three parts are called the lateral, anterior and posterior funiculus.*

funis /ˈfjuːnɪs/ *noun* an umbilical cord

funnel chest /ˌfʌn(ə)l ˈtʃest/ *noun* same as **pectus excavatum**

funny bone /ˈfʌni bəʊn/ *noun* same as **olecranon** (*informal*)

funny turn /ˈfʌni tɜːn/ *noun* a dizzy spell (*informal*)

furfuraceous /ˌfɜːfjəˈreɪʃəs/ *adjective* referring to skin which is scaly

Furley stretcher /ˈfɜːli ˌstretʃə/ *noun* a stretcher made of a folding frame with a canvas bed, with carrying poles at each side and small feet underneath

furor /ˈfjʊərɔː/ *noun* an attack of wild violence, especially in someone who is mentally unwell

furosemide a drug which causes an increase in urine production, used to relieve water retention in the body. Also called **frusemide**

furred tongue /fɜːd ˈtʌŋ/ *noun* a condition when the papillae of the tongue are covered with a whitish coating. Also called **coated tongue**

furuncle /ˈfjʊərʌŋkəl/ *noun* same as **boil**

furunculosis /fjʊəˌrʌŋkjʊˈləʊsɪs/ *noun* a condition in which several boils appear at the same time

fuse /fjuːz/ *verb* to join together to form a single structure, or to join two or more things together ○ *The bones of the joint fused.*

fusidic acid /fjuːˌsɪdɪk ˈæsɪd/ *noun* an antibiotic used to prevent protein synthesis

fusiform /ˈfjuːzɪfɔːm/ *adjective* referring to muscles which are shaped like a spindle, with a wider middle section which becomes narrower at each end

fusion /ˈfjuːʒ(ə)n/ *noun* the act of joining, especially a surgical operation to relieve pain in the joint by joining the bones at the joint permanently so that they cannot move

Fybogel /ˈfaɪbəʊdʒel/ a trade name for ispaghula

G

g *abbr* gram

GABA /'gæbə/ *abbr* gamma aminobutyric acid

gag /gæg/ *noun* an instrument placed between the teeth to stop the mouth from closing ■ *verb* to experience a reaction similar to that of vomiting ○ *Every time the doctor tries to examine her throat, she gags.* ○ *He started gagging on the endotracheal tube.*

gain /geɪn/ *noun* an act of adding or increasing something ○ *The baby showed a gain in weight of 25g* or *showed a weight gain of 25g.* ■ *verb* to obtain something, or to increase ○ *to gain in weight* or *to gain weight*

gait /geɪt/ *noun* a way of walking

galact- /gəlækt/ *prefix* same as **galacto-** (*used before vowels*)

galactagogue /gə'læktəgɒg/ *noun* a substance which stimulates the production of milk

galacto- /gəlæktəʊ/ *prefix* referring to milk

galactocele /gə'læktəsiːl/ *noun* a breast tumour which contains milk

galactorrhoea /gəˌlæktə'rɪə/ *noun* the excessive production of milk

galactosaemia /gəˌlæktə'siːmiə/ *noun* a congenital condition where the liver is incapable of converting galactose into glucose, with the result that a baby's development may be affected (NOTE: The treatment is to remove galactose from the diet.)

galactose /gə'læktəʊs/ *noun* a sugar which forms part of milk, and is converted into glucose by the liver

galea /'geɪliə/ *noun* **1.** any part of the body shaped like a helmet, especially the loose band of tissue in the scalp (NOTE: The plural is **galeae**.) **2.** a type of bandage wrapped round the head

gall /gɔːl/ *noun* same as **bile**

gall bladder /'gɔːl ˌblædə/ *noun* a sac situated underneath the liver, in which bile produced by the liver is stored. See illustration at **DIGESTIVE SYSTEM** in Supplement

COMMENT: Bile is stored in the gall bladder until required by the stomach. If fatty food is present in the stomach, bile moves from the gall bladder along the bile duct to the stomach. Since the liver also secretes bile directly into the duodenum, the gall bladder is not an essential organ and can be removed by surgery.

Gallie's operation /'gæliz ɒpəˌreɪʃ(ə)n/ *noun* a surgical operation where tissues from the thigh are used to hold a hernia in place [Described 1921. After William Edward Gallie (1882–1959), Professor of Surgery at the University of Toronto, Canada.]

gallipot /'gælipɒt/ *noun* a little container for ointment

gallium /'gæliəm/ *noun* a metallic element a radioisotope of which is used to detect tumours or other tissue disorders (NOTE: The chemical symbol is **Ga**.)

gallop rhythm /'gæləp ˌrɪð(ə)m/ *noun* the rhythm of heart sounds, three to each cycle, when someone is experiencing tachycardia

gallstone /'gɔːlstəʊn/ *noun* a small stone formed from insoluble deposits from bile in the gall bladder. ◊ **calculus**

COMMENT: Gallstones can be harmless, but some cause pain and inflammation and a serious condition can develop if a gallstone blocks the bile duct. Sudden pain going from the right side of the stomach towards the back indicates that a gallstone is passing through the bile duct.

galvanism /'gælvənɪz(ə)m/ *noun* a treatment using low voltage electricity

galvanocautery /ˌgælvənəʊ'kɔːtəri/ *noun* the removal of diseased tissue using an electrically heated needle or loop of wire. Also called **electrocautery**

gamete /'gæmiːt/ *noun* a sex cell, either a spermatozoon or an ovum

gamete intrafallopian transfer /ˌgæmiːt ɪntrəfəˌləʊpiən 'trænsfɜː/ *noun* a technique to combine eggs and sperm outside the body and then insert them into the Fallopian tubes. Abbr **GIFT**

gametocide /gə'miːtəʊsaɪd/ *noun* a drug which kills gametocytes

gametocyte /gə'miːtəʊsaɪt/ *noun* a cell which is developing into a gamete

gametogenesis /gəˌmiːtəʊ'dʒenəsɪs/ *noun* the process by which a gamete is formed

gamgee tissue /ˈgæmdʒiː ˌtɪʃuː/ noun a surgical dressing, formed of a layer of cotton wool between two pieces of gauze

gamma /ˈgæmə/ noun the third letter of the Greek alphabet

gamma aminobutyric acid /ˌgæmə ə ˌmiːnəʊbjuːˌtɪrɪk ˈæsɪd/ noun an amino acid neurotransmitter. Abbr **GABA**

gamma camera /ˈgæmə ˌkæm(ə)rə/ noun a camera for taking photographs of parts of the body into which radioactive isotopes have been introduced

gamma globulin /ˌgæmə ˈglɒbjʊlɪn/ noun a protein found in plasma, forming antibodies as protection against infection

COMMENT: Gamma globulin injections are sometimes useful as a rapid source of protection against a wide range of diseases.

gamma ray /ˈgæmə reɪ/ noun a ray which is shorter than an X-ray and is given off by radioactive substances

gangli- /ˈgæŋgli/ prefix referring to ganglia

ganglion /ˈgæŋgliən/ noun **1.** a mass of nerve cell bodies and synapses usually covered in connective tissue, found along the peripheral nerves with the exception of the basal ganglia **2.** a cyst of a tendon sheath or joint capsule, usually at the wrist, which results in a painless swelling containing fluid (NOTE: [all senses] The plural is **ganglia**.)

ganglionectomy /ˌgæŋgliəˈnektəmi/ noun the surgical removal of a ganglion

ganglionic /ˌgæŋgliˈɒnɪk/ adjective referring to a ganglion. ◊ **postganglionic**

gangrene /ˈgæŋgriːn/ noun a condition in which tissues die and decay, as a result of bacterial action, because the blood supply has been lost through injury or disease of the artery ○ After she had frostbite, gangrene set in and her toes had to be amputated.

gangrenous /ˈgæŋgrɪnəs/ adjective referring to, or affected by, gangrene

Ganser state /ˈgænsə ˌsteɪt/ noun same as **pseudodementia** [After Sigbert Joseph Maria Ganser (1853–1931), psychiatrist at Dresden and Munich, Germany]

gargle /ˈgɑːg(ə)l/ noun a mildly antiseptic solution used to clean the mouth ■ verb to put some antiseptic liquid solution to the back of the mouth and then breathe out air through it

gargoylism /ˈgɑːgɔɪlɪz(ə)m/ noun a congenital condition of the metabolism which causes polysaccharides and fat cells to accumulate in the body, resulting in mental impairment, swollen liver and coarse features. Also called **Hurler's syndrome**

gas /gæs/ noun **1.** a substance such as nitrogen, carbon dioxide or air, which is neither solid nor fluid at ordinary temperatures and can expand infinitely (NOTE: The plural **gases** is used only when referring to different types of gas.) **2.** gas which accumulates in the stomach or alimentary canal and causes pain

gas and air analgesia /ˌgæs ənd 'eə æn(ə)l,dʒiːziə/ noun a form of analgesia used when giving birth, in which a mixture of air and gas is given

gas chromatography /ˌgæs ˌkrəʊmə'tɒgrəfi/ noun a method of separating chemicals by passing them through a gas, used in analysing compounds and mixtures

gas exchange /ˈgæs ɪks,tʃeɪndʒ/ noun the process by which oxygen in the air is exchanged in the lungs for waste carbon dioxide carried by the blood

gas gangrene /gæs ˈgæŋgriːn/ noun a complication of severe wounds in which the bacterium *Clostridium welchii* breeds in the wound and then spreads to healthy tissue which is rapidly decomposed with the formation of gas

gash /gæʃ/ noun a long deep cut made accidentally by something sharp ○ She had to have three stitches in the gash in her thigh. ■ verb to make a long deep cut in something accidentally ○ She gashed her hand on the broken glass.

gasp /gɑːsp/ noun a short breath taken with difficulty ○ His breath came in short gasps. ■ verb to breathe with difficulty taking quick breaths ○ She was gasping for breath.

gas pain /ˈgæs peɪn/ noun a pain caused by excessive formation of gas in the stomach or intestine. ◊ **flatus**

gas poisoning /ˈgæs ˌpɔɪz(ə)nɪŋ/ noun poisoning by breathing in carbon monoxide or other toxic gas

Gasserian ganglion /gəˌsɪəriən ˈgæŋgliən/ noun same as **trigeminal ganglion** [After Johann Laurentius Gasser (1723–65), Professor of Anatomy in Vienna, Austria. He left no writings, and the ganglion was given his name by Anton Hirsch, one of his students, in his thesis of 1765.]

gastr- /gæstr/ prefix same as **gastro-** (used before vowels)

gastralgia /gæˈstrældʒə/ noun pain in the stomach

gastrectomy /gæˈstrektəmi/ noun the surgical removal of the stomach

gastric /ˈgæstrɪk/ adjective referring to the stomach

gastric acid /ˌgæstrɪk ˈæsɪd/ noun hydrochloric acid secreted into the stomach by acid-forming cells

gastric artery /ˌgæstrɪk ˈɑːtəri/ noun an artery leading from the coeliac trunk to the stomach

gastric flu /ˌgæstrɪk ˈfluː/ noun any mild stomach disorder (informal)

gastric juice /ˈgæstrɪk dʒuːs/ noun the mixture of hydrochloric acid, pepsin, intrinsic factor and mucus secreted by the cells of the lining membrane of the stomach to help the digestion of food (NOTE: Often used in the plural.)

gastric lavage /ˌgæstrɪk 'lævɪdʒ/ *noun* a lavage of the stomach, usually to remove a poisonous substance which has been absorbed. Also called **stomach washout**

gastric pit /ˌgæstrɪk 'pɪt/ *noun* a deep hollow in the mucous membrane forming the walls of the stomach

gastric ulcer /ˌgæstrɪk 'ʌlsə/ *noun* an ulcer in the stomach. Abbr **GU**

gastric vein /ˌgæstrɪk 'veɪn/ *noun* a vein which follows the gastric artery

gastrin /'gæstrɪn/ *noun* a hormone which is released into the bloodstream from cells in the lower end of the stomach, stimulated by the presence of protein, and which in turn stimulates the flow of acid from the upper part of the stomach

gastrinoma /ˌgæstrɪ'nəʊmə/ *noun* a tumour of the islet cells, leading to excessive gastric acid

gastritis /gæ'straɪtɪs/ *noun* inflammation of the stomach

gastro- /gæstrəʊ/ *prefix* referring to the stomach

gastrocele /'gæstrəʊsiːl/ *noun* a condition in which part of the stomach wall becomes weak and bulges out. Also called **stomach hernia**

gastrocnemius /ˌgæstrɒk'niːmiəs/ *noun* a large calf muscle

gastrocolic /ˌgæstrəʊ'kɒlɪk/ *adjective* referring to the stomach and colon

gastrocolic reflex /ˌgæstrəʊkɒlɪk 'riːfleks/ *noun* a sudden peristalsis of the colon produced when food is taken into an empty stomach

gastroduodenal /ˌgæstrəʊˌdjuːəʊ'diːn(ə)l/ *adjective* referring to the stomach and duodenum

gastroduodenal artery /ˌgæstrəʊdˌjuːəʊdiːn(ə)l 'ɑːtəri/ *noun* an artery leading from the gastric artery towards the pancreas

gastroduodenoscopy /ˌgæstrəʊˌdjuːəʊdɪ'nɒskəpi/ *noun* an examination of the stomach and duodenum

gastroduodenostomy /ˌgæstrəʊˌdjuːəʊdɪ'nɒstəmi/ *noun* a surgical operation to join the duodenum to the stomach so as to bypass a blockage in the pylorus

gastroenteritis /ˌgæstrəʊentə'raɪtɪs/ *noun* inflammation of the membrane lining the intestines and the stomach, caused by a viral infection and resulting in diarrhoea and vomiting

gastroenterologist /ˌgæstrəʊentə'rɒlədʒɪst/ *noun* a doctor who specialises in the digestive system and its disorders

gastroenterology /ˌgæstrəʊentə'rɒlədʒi/ *noun* the study of the digestive system and its disorders

gastroenterostomy /ˌgæstrəʊentə'rɒstəmi/ *noun* a surgical operation to join the small intestine directly to the stomach so as to bypass a peptic ulcer

gastroepiploic /ˌgæstrəʊepɪ'plɔɪk/ *adjective* referring to the stomach and greater omentum

gastroepiploic artery /ˌgæstrəʊepɪˌplɔɪk 'ɑːtəri/ *noun* an artery linking the gastroduodenal artery to the splenic artery

Gastrografin /ˌgæstrəʊ'græfɪn/ a trade name for an enema used in bowel X-rays

gastroileac reflex /ˌgæstrəʊˌɪliæk 'riːfleks/ *noun* automatic relaxation of the ileocaecal valve when food is present in the stomach

gastrointestinal /ˌgæstrəʊɪn'testɪn(ə)l/ *adjective* referring to the stomach and intestine ○ *gastrointestinal bleeding.* Abbr **GI**

gastrojejunostomy /ˌgæstrəʊdʒɪdʒuː'nɒstəmi/ *noun* a surgical operation to join the jejunum to the stomach

gastrolith /'gæstrəʊlɪθ/ *noun* a calculus in the stomach

gastrology /gæ'strɒlədʒi/ *noun* the study of the stomach and diseases of the stomach

gastro-oesophageal reflux /ˌgæstrəʊ ɪ ˌsɒfədʒiəl 'riːflʌks/, **gastro-oesophageal reflux disease** /ˌgæstrəʊ ɪˌsɒfədʒiəl 'riːflʌks dɪˌziːz/ *noun* the return of bitter-tasting, partly digested food from the stomach to the oesophagus

gastropexy /'gæstrəʊpeksi/ *noun* a surgical operation to attach the stomach to the wall of the abdomen

gastroplasty /'gæstrəʊplæsti/ *noun* surgery to correct a deformed stomach

gastroptosis /ˌgæstrəʊ'təʊsɪs/ *noun* a condition in which the stomach hangs down

gastrorrhoea /ˌgæstrə'rɪə/ *noun* an excessive flow of gastric juices

gastroschisis /ˌgæstrəʊ'saɪsɪs/ *noun* a split in the wall of the abdomen, with viscera passing through it

gastroscope /'gæstrəskəʊp/ *noun* an instrument formed of a tube or bundle of glass fibres with a lens attached, which a doctor can pass down into the stomach through the mouth to examine the inside of the stomach

gastroscopy /gæ'strɒskəpi/ *noun* an examination of the stomach using a gastroscope

gastrostomy /gæ'strɒstəmi/ *noun* a surgical operation to create an opening into the stomach from the wall of the abdomen, so that food can be introduced without passing through the mouth and throat

gastrotomy /gæ'strɒtəmi/ *noun* a surgical operation to open up the stomach

gastrula /gæ'struːlə/ *noun* the second stage of the development of an embryo

gathering /'gæðərɪŋ/ *noun* a swelling that is filled with pus

Gaucher's disease /'ɡəʊʃeɪz dɪˌziːz/ *noun* an enzyme disease where fatty substances accumulate in the lymph glands, spleen and liver, causing anaemia, a swollen spleen and darkening of the skin. The disease can be fatal in children. [Described 1882. After Philippe Charles Ernest Gaucher (1854–1918), French physician and dermatologist.]

gauze /ɡɔːz/ *noun* a thin light material used to make dressings

gauze dressing /ɡɔːz 'dresɪŋ/ *noun* a dressing of thin light material

gavage /gæ'vɑːʒ/ *noun* the forced feeding of someone who cannot eat or who refuses to eat

gay /ɡeɪ/ *adjective* relating to sexual activity among people of the same sex

GDC *abbr* General Dental Council

Gehrig's disease /'ɡeɪrɪgz dɪˌziːz/ *noun* same as **amyotrophic lateral sclerosis**

Geiger counter /'ɡaɪɡə ˌkaʊntə/ *noun* an instrument for the detection and measurement of radiation [Described 1908. After Hans Geiger (1882–1945), German physicist who worked with Rutherford at Manchester University, UK.]

gel /dʒel/ *noun* a suspension that sets into a jelly-like solid

gelatin /'dʒelətɪn/ *noun* a protein found in collagen which is soluble in water, used to make capsules for medicines

gelatinous /dʒə'lætɪnəs/ *adjective* referring to gelatin or something with a texture like jelly

gemellus /dʒɪ'meləs/ *noun* either of the two muscles arising from the ischium. Also called **gemellus superior muscle, gemellus inferior muscle**

gender /'dʒendə/ *noun* the fact of being of the male or female sex

gender identity disorder /ˌdʒendə aɪ'den↓tɪti dɪsˌɔːdə/ *noun* a condition in which someone experiences strong discomfort with his or her birth gender

gender reassignment surgery /ˌdʒendə riːə'saɪnmənt ˌsɜːdʒəri/ *noun* surgery to change someone's sex

gender reorientation /ˌdʒendə riːˌɔːriən'teɪʃ(ə)n/ *noun* the alteration of a person's sex through surgical and drug treatment

gene /dʒiːn/ *noun* a unit of DNA on a chromosome which governs the synthesis of a protein sequence and determines a particular characteristic

COMMENT: A gene may be dominant, in which case the characteristic it controls is always passed on to the child, or recessive, in which case the characteristic only appears if both parents have contributed the same form of the gene.

general amnesia /ˌdʒen(ə)rəl æm'niːziə/ *noun* a sudden and complete loss of memory, to the extent that a person does not even remember who he or she is

general anaesthesia /ˌdʒen(ə)rəl ˌænəs'θiːziə/ *noun* loss of feeling and loss of sensation throughout the body, after being given an anaesthetic

general anaesthetic /ˌdʒen(ə)rəl ˌænəs'θetɪk/ *noun* a substance given to make someone lose consciousness so that a major surgical operation can be carried out

General Dental Council /ˌdʒen(ə)rəl 'dent(ə)l ˌkaʊnsəl/ *noun* in the UK, the official body that registers and supervises dentists. Abbr **GDC**

general hospital /ˌdʒen(ə)rəl 'hɒspɪt(ə)l/ *noun* a hospital which does not specialise in particular types of illness or particular age groups

generalise /'dʒen(ə)rəlaɪz/, **generalize** *verb* to spread to other parts of the body

generalised /'dʒen(ə)rəlaɪzd/, **generalized** *adjective* 1. spreading throughout the body. Opposite **localised** 2. not having a specific cause

generalised anxiety disorder /ˌdʒen(ə)rəlaɪzd æŋ'zaɪəti dɪsˌɔːdə/ *noun* a state of continual anxiety for which there is no specific cause

General Medical Council /ˌdʒen(ə)rəl 'medɪk(ə)l ˌkaʊnsəl/ *noun* in the UK, the official body that licenses qualified doctors to practise medicine. Abbr **GMC**

General Optical Council /'dʒenrəl 'ɒp↓tɪk(ə)l 'kaʊnsəl/ *noun* in the UK, the official body that registers and supervises opticians

general practice /ˌdʒen(ə)rəl 'præktɪs/ *noun* a medical practice where doctors offer first-line medical care for all types of illness to people who live locally, refer them to hospital if necessary and encourage health promotion

general practitioner /ˌdʒen(ə)rəl præk'tɪʃ(ə)nə/ *noun* a doctor who provides first-line medical care for all types of illness to people who live locally, refers them to hospital if necessary and encourages health promotion. Abbr **GP**

gene replacement therapy /ˌdʒiːn rɪ'pleɪsmənt ˌθerəpi/ *noun* the replacement of missing genes or damaging gene variations in cells by the insertion of appropriate genes to treat a genetic disorder. Also called **gene therapy**

COMMENT: Gene replacement therapy has been used successfully in animals, and is in the early stages of research in humans, but may be useful in the future treatment of cystic fibrosis, thalassaemia and other genetic disorders.

generic /dʒə'nerɪk/ *adjective* 1. referring to medicine which does not have a special trademark or brand name given to it by its manufacturer **2.** referring to a genus ○ *The generic name of this type of bacterium is Staphylococcus.*

-genesis /dʒenəsɪs/ *suffix* production or origin

gene therapy /'dʒiːn ˌθerəpi/ *noun* same as **gene replacement therapy**

genetic /dʒə'netɪk/ *adjective* referring to genes

genetic code /dʒəˌnetɪk 'kəʊd/ *noun* the characteristics of the DNA of a cell which are passed on when the cell divides and so are inherited by a child from its parents

genetic counselling /dʒəˌnetɪk 'kaʊnsəlɪŋ/ *noun* advice and support given to people if they or their children might be affected by inherited genetic disorders

genetic disorder /dʒəˌnetɪk dɪs'ɔːdə/ *noun* a disorder or disease caused by a damaging gene variation that may be inherited

genetic engineering /dʒəˌnetɪk endʒɪ'nɪərɪŋ/ *noun* same as **genetic modification** (*informal*)

genetic fingerprint /dʒəˌnetɪk 'fɪŋɡəprɪnt/ *noun* the pattern of sequences of genetic material unique to an individual. Also called **DNA fingerprint**

genetic fingerprinting /dʒəˌnetɪk 'fɪŋɡəˌprɪntɪŋ/ *noun* a method of revealing an individual's genetic profile, used in paternity queries and criminal investigations. Also called **DNA fingerprinting**

geneticist /dʒə'netɪsɪst/ *noun* a person who specialises in the study of the way in which characteristics and diseases are inherited through the genes

genetic modification, **genetic manipulation** *noun* the combination of genetic material from different sources to produce organisms with altered characteristics

genetics /dʒə'netɪks/ *noun* the study of genes, and of the way characteristics and diseases are inherited through the genes

genetic screening /dʒəˌnetɪk 'skriːnɪŋ/ *noun* the process of testing large numbers of people to see if anyone has a particular genetic disorder

gene tracking /'dʒiːn ˌtrækɪŋ/ *noun* the method used to trace throughout a family the inheritance of a gene such as those causing cystic fibrosis or Huntington's Chorea, in order to diagnose and predict genetic disorders

-genic /dʒenɪk/ *suffix* referring to a product or something which produces

genicular /dʒe'nɪkjʊlə/ *adjective* referring to the knee

genital /'dʒenɪt(ə)l/ *adjective* referring to the reproductive organs ■ *plural noun* **genitals** same as **genital organs**

genitalia /ˌdʒenɪ'teɪliə/ *noun* the genital organs

genital organs /ˌdʒenɪt(ə)l 'ɔːɡənz/ *plural noun* the external organs for reproduction, i.e. the penis and testicles in males and the vulva in females. Also called **genitals**, **genitalia**

genital wart /ˌdʒenɪt(ə)l 'wɔːt/ *noun* a wart in the genital or anal area, caused by a sexually transmitted virus

genito- /dʒenɪtəʊ/ *prefix* referring to the reproductive system

genitourinary /ˌdʒenɪtəʊ'jʊərɪnəri/ *adjective* referring to both the reproductive and urinary systems. Abbr **GU**

genitourinary system /ˌdʒenɪtəʊ'jʊərɪnəri ˌsɪstəm/ *noun* the organs of reproduction and urination, including the kidneys

genome /'dʒiːnəʊm/ *noun* the set of all the genes of an individual

genotype /'dʒenətaɪp/ *noun* the genetic makeup of an individual. Compare **phenotype**

gentamicin /ˌdʒentə'maɪsɪn/ *noun* an antibiotic that is effective against a variety of different disease-causing organisms. Patients usually receive it by injection and it can cause serious side effects.

gentian violet /ˌdʒenʃən 'vaɪələt/ *noun* an antiseptic blue dye, used to paint on skin infections and also to stain specimens. Also called **crystal violet**

genu /'dʒenjuː/ *noun* the knee

genual /'dʒenjuəl/ *adjective* referring to the knee

genucubital position /ˌdʒenjuː'kjuːbɪt(ə)l pəˌzɪʃ(ə)n/ *noun* the position of someone resting on their knees and elbows

genupectoral position /ˌdʒenjuː'pektər(ə)l pəˌzɪʃ(ə)n/ *noun* the position of someone resting on their knees and upper chest

genus /'dʒiːnəs/ *noun* a category of related living organisms ○ *A genus is divided into different species.* (NOTE: The plural is **genera**.)

genu valgum /ˌdʒenjuː 'vælɡəm/ *noun* same as **knock-knee**

genu varum /ˌdʒenjuː 'veərəm/ *noun* same as **bow legs**

geri- /dʒeri/ *prefix* referring to old age

geriatric /ˌdʒeri'ætrɪk/ *adjective* **1.** referring to old people **2.** specialising in the treatment of old people ○ *geriatric unit*

geriatrician /ˌdʒeriə'trɪʃ(ə)n/ *noun* a doctor who specialises in the treatment or study of diseases of old people

geriatrics /dʒeri'ætrɪks/ *noun* the study of the diseases and disorders of old people. Compare **paediatrics**

germ /dʒɜːm/ *noun* **1.** a microorganism which causes a disease, e.g. a virus or bacterium (*informal*) ○ *Germs are not visible to the naked* *eye.* **2.** a part of an organism capable of developing into a new organism

German measles /ˌdʒɜːmən ˈmiːz(ə)lz/ *noun* same as **rubella**

germ cell /ˈdʒɜːm sel/ *noun* a cell which is capable of developing into a spermatozoon or ovum. Also called **gonocyte**

germinal /ˈdʒɜːmɪn(ə)l/ *adjective* referring to an embryo

germinal epithelium /ˌdʒɜːmɪn(ə)l epɪˈθiːliəm/ *noun* the outer layer of the ovary

germ layer /ˈdʒɜːm ˌleɪə/ *noun* one of two or three layers of cells in animal embryos which form the organs of the body

gerontologist /ˌdʒerənˈtɒlədʒɪst/ *noun* a specialist in gerontology

gerontology /ˌdʒerənˈtɒlədʒi/ *noun* the study of the process of ageing and the diseases of old people

Gerstmann's syndrome /ˈɡɜːstmænz ˌsɪndrəʊm/ *noun* a condition in which someone no longer recognises his or her body image, cannot tell the difference between left and right, cannot recognise his or her different fingers and is unable to write

Gesell's developmental chart /ɡəˌzelz dɪ ˌveləpˈment(ə)l tʃɑːt/ *noun* a chart showing the development of motor reactions and growth patterns in children

gestate /dʒeˈsteɪt/ *verb* to carry a baby in the womb from conception to birth

gestation /dʒeˈsteɪʃ(ə)n/ *noun* **1.** the process of development of a baby from conception to birth in the mother's womb **2.** same as **gestation period**

'…evaluation of fetal age and weight has proved to be of value in the clinical management of pregnancy, particularly in high-risk gestations' [*Southern Medical Journal*]

gestational age /dʒeˌsteɪʃ(ə)n(ə)l ˈeɪdʒ/ *noun* the age of a fetus, calculated from the mother's last period to the date of birth

gestational diabetes /dʒeˌsteɪʃ(ə)n(ə)l ˌdaɪəˈbiːtiːz/ *noun* a form of diabetes mellitus which develops in a pregnant woman

gestation period /dʒeˈsteɪʃ(ə)n ˌpɪəriəd/ *noun* the period, usually of 266 days, from conception to birth, during which the baby develops in the mother's womb. Also called **pregnancy**

gestodene /ˈdʒestədiːn/ *noun* an oral contraceptive

get around /ˌɡet əˈraʊnd/ *verb* to move about ○ *Since she had the accident she gets around using crutches.*

get better /ˌɡet ˈbetə/ *verb* **1.** to become healthy again after being ill ○ *He was seriously ill, but seems to be getting better.* **2.** (*of an illness*) to stop or become less severe ○ *Her cold has got better.*

get dressed /ˌɡet ˈdrest/ *verb* to put your clothes on ○ *This patient still needs helps to get dressed.*

get on with /ˌɡet ˈɒn wɪð/ *verb* to continue to do some work ○ *I must get on with the blood tests.*

get over /ˌɡet ˈəʊvə/ *verb* to become better after an illness or a shock ○ *He got over his cold.* ○ *She never got over her mother's death.*

getting on /ˌɡetɪŋ ˈɒn/ *adjective* becoming elderly ○ *Her parents are getting on.*

get up /ˌɡet ˈʌp/ *verb* **1.** to stand up ○ *Try to get up from your chair slowly and walk across the room.* **2.** to get out of bed ○ *What time did you get up this morning?*

get well /ˌɡet ˈwel/ *verb* to become healthy again after being ill ○ *We hope your mother will get well soon.*

GFR *abbr* glomerular filtration rate

GH *abbr* growth hormone

Ghon's focus /ˌɡɒnz ˈfəʊkəs/ *noun* a spot on the lung produced by the tuberculosis bacillus [Described 1912. After Anton Ghon (1866–1936), Professor of Pathological Anatomy at Prague, Czech Republic.]

GI *abbr* gastrointestinal

giant cell /ˌdʒaɪənt ˈsel/ *noun* a very large cell, e.g. an osteoclast or megakaryocyte

giant-cell arteritis /ˌdʒaɪənt sel ˌɑːtə ˈraɪtɪs/ *noun* a disease of old people, which often affects the arteries in the scalp

giant hives /ˌdʒaɪənt ˈhaɪvz/ *noun* a large flat white blister caused by an allergic reaction

Giardia /dʒiːˈɑːdiə/ *noun* a microscopic protozoan parasite which causes giardiasis

giardiasis /ˌdʒiːɑːˈdaɪəsɪs/ *noun* a disorder of the intestine caused by the parasite *Giardia lamblia,* usually with no symptoms, but in heavy infections the absorption of fat may be affected, causing diarrhoea. Also called **lambliasis**

gibbosity /ɡɪˈbɒsəti/ *noun* a sharp angle in the curvature of the spine caused by the weakening of a vertebra as a result of tuberculosis of the backbone

gibbus /ˈɡɪbəs/ *noun* same as **gibbosity**

giddiness /ˈɡɪdinəs/ *noun* a condition in which someone has difficulty in standing up and keeping their balance because of a feeling that everything is turning around ○ *He began to experience attacks of giddiness.*

giddy /ˈɡɪdi/ *adjective* feeling that everything is turning round ○ *She has had several giddy spells.*

GIFT /ɡɪft/ *noun* a procedure in which a surgeon removes eggs from a woman's ovary, mixes them with sperm and places them in one of her Fallopian tubes to help her conceive a child. Full form **gamete intrafallopian transfer**

gigantism /dʒaɪ'gæntɪz(ə)m/ *noun* a condition in which someone grows very tall, caused by excessive production of growth hormone by the pituitary gland

Gilbert's syndrome /'gɪlbəts ˌsɪndrəʊm/ *noun* an inherited disorder where the liver does not deal with bilirubin correctly

Gilles de la Tourette syndrome /ˌʒiː də læ tʊə'ret ˌsɪndrəʊm/ *noun* same as **Tourette's syndrome**

Gilliam's operation /'gɪliəmz ɒpəˌreɪʃ(ə)n/ *noun* a surgical operation to correct retroversion of the uterus [After David Tod Gilliam (1844–1923), physician, Columbus, Ohio, USA]

gingiv- /dʒɪndʒɪv/ *prefix* referring to the gums

gingiva /dʒɪn'dʒaɪvə/ *noun* same as **gum** (NOTE: The plural is **gingivae**.)

gingival /'dʒɪndʒɪv(ə)l/ *adjective* relating to the gums

gingivectomy /ˌdʒɪndʒɪ'vektəmi/ *noun* the surgical removal of excess gum tissue

gingivitis /ˌdʒɪndʒɪ'vaɪtɪs/ *noun* inflammation of the gums as a result of bacterial infection

ginglymus /'dʒɪŋglɪməs/ *noun* a joint which allows movement in two directions only, e.g. the knee or elbow. Also called **hinge joint**. Compare **ball and socket joint**

ginseng /'dʒɪnseŋ/ *noun* a plant root widely used as a tonic and a traditional Chinese herbal remedy

gippy tummy /ˌdʒɪpi 'tʌmi/ *noun* same as **diarrhoea** (*informal*)

girdle /'gɜːd(ə)l/ *noun* a set of bones making a ring or arch

Girdlestone's operation /'gɜːdəlstəʊnz ɒpəˌreɪʃ(ə)n/ *noun* a surgical operation to relieve osteoarthritis of the hip [After Gathorne Robert Girdlestone (1881–1950), Nuffield Professor of Orthopaedics at Oxford, UK]

give up /ˌgɪv 'ʌp/ *verb* not to do something any more ○ *He was advised to give up smoking.*

glabella /glə'belə/ *noun* a flat area of bone in the forehead between the eyebrows

gladiolus /ˌglædi'əʊləs/ *noun* the middle section of the sternum

gland /glænd/ *noun* an organ in the body containing cells that secrete substances such as hormones, sweat or saliva which act elsewhere

glanders /'glændəz/ *noun* a bacterial disease of horses, which can be caught by humans, with symptoms of high fever and inflammation of the lymph nodes

glandular /'glændjʊlə/ *adjective* referring to glands

glandular fever /ˌglændjʊlə 'fiːvə/ *noun* same as **infectious mononucleosis**

glans /glænz/ *noun* a rounded part at the end of the penis or clitoris. See illustration at URO-GENITAL SYSTEM (MALE) in Supplement

glare /gleə/ *noun* 1. a long stare that expresses a negative emotion such as anger 2. an uncomfortably or dazzlingly bright light 3. scattered bright light when examining something with a microscope ■ *verb* 1. to stare angrily 2. to shine uncomfortably brightly 3. to be very obvious or conspicuous

Glasgow coma scale /ˌglɑːsgəʊ 'kəʊmə ˌskeɪl/, **Glasgow scoring system** /ˌglɑːsgəʊ 'skɔːrɪŋ ˌsɪstəm/ *noun* a seven-point scale for evaluating someone's level of consciousness

glass eye /glɑːs 'aɪ/ *noun* an artificial eye made of glass

glaucoma /glɔː'kəʊmə/ *noun* a condition of the eyes, caused by unusually high pressure of fluid inside the eyeball, resulting in disturbances of vision and blindness

gleet /gliːt/ *noun* a thin discharge from the vagina, penis, a wound or an ulcer

glenohumeral /ˌgliːnəʊ'hjuːmərəl/ *adjective* referring to both the glenoid cavity and the humerus

glenohumeral joint /ˌgliːnəʊ'hjuːmərəl dʒɔɪnt/ *noun* the shoulder joint

glenoid /'gliːnɔɪd/ *adjective* shaped like a small shallow cup or socket

glenoid cavity /ˌgliːnɔɪd 'kævɪti/, **glenoid fossa** /ˌgliːnɔɪd 'fɒsə/ *noun* a socket in the shoulder joint into which the head of the humerus fits

glia /'gliːə/ *noun* connective tissue of the central nervous system, surrounding cell bodies, axons and dendrites. Also called **neuroglia**

glial cell /'gliːəl sel/ *noun* a cell in the glia

glial tissue /ˌgliːəl 'tɪʃuː/ *noun* same as **glia**

glibenclamide /glɪ'beŋkləmaɪd/ *noun* a sulphonylurea drug used to treat Type II diabetes mellitus

gliclazide /'glɪkləzaɪd/ *noun* an antibacterial drug used to treat Type II diabetes mellitus

glio- /glaɪəʊ/ *prefix* referring to brain tissue

glioblastoma /ˌglaɪəʊblæ'stəʊmə/ *noun* a rapidly developing malignant tumour of the glial tissue in the brain or spinal cord. Also called **spongioblastoma**

glioma /glaɪ'əʊmə/ *noun* any tumour of the glial tissue in the brain or spinal cord

gliomyoma /ˌglaɪəʊmaɪ'əʊmə/ *noun* a tumour of both the nerve and muscle tissue

glipizide /'glɪpɪzaɪd/ *noun* a drug used to reduce the glucose level in the blood

Glisson's capsule /ˌglɪs(ə)nz 'kæpsjuːl/ *noun* a tissue sheath in the liver containing the blood vessels [After Francis Glisson (1597–1677), philosopher, physician and anatomist at Cambridge and London, UK]

globin /'gləʊbɪn/ *noun* a protein which combines with other substances to form compounds such as haemoglobin and myoglobin

globule /'glɒbjuːl/ *noun* a round drop, especially of fat

globulin /'glɒbjʊlɪn/ *noun* a protein, present in blood, belonging to a group that includes antibodies

globulinuria /ˌglɒbjʊlɪ'njʊəriə/ *noun* the presence of globulins in the urine

globus /'gləʊbəs/ *noun* any ball-shaped part of the body

globus hystericus /ˌgləʊbəs hɪ'sterɪkəs/ *noun* a feeling of not being able to swallow, caused by worry or embarrassment

glomangioma /glə,mændʒi'əʊmə/ *noun* a tumour of the skin at the ends of the fingers and toes

glomerular /glɒ'merʊlə/ *adjective* referring to a glomerulus

glomerular capsule /glɒ,merʊlə 'kæpsjuːl/ *noun* same as **Bowman's capsule**

glomerular filtration rate /glɒ,merʊlə fɪl'treɪʃ(ə)n reɪt/ *noun* the rate at which the kidneys filter blood and remove waste matter

glomerular tuft /glɒ,merʊlə 'tʌft/ *noun* a group of blood vessels in the kidney which filter the blood

glomeruli /glɒ'merʊli/ *plural of* **glomerulus**

glomerulitis /glɒ,merʊ'laɪtɪs/ *noun* inflammation causing lesions of glomeruli in the kidney

glomerulonephritis /glɒ,merʊləʊnɪ'fraɪtɪs/ *noun* same as **Bright's disease**

glomerulus /glɒ'merʊləs/ *noun* a group of blood vessels which filter waste matter from the blood in a kidney (NOTE: The plural is **glomeruli**.)

gloss- /glɒs/ *prefix* same as **glosso-** (*used before vowels*)

glossa /'glɒsə/ *noun* same as **tongue**

glossal /'glɒs(ə)l/ *adjective* relating to the tongue

glossectomy /glɒ'sektəmi/ *noun* the surgical removal of the tongue

Glossina /glɒ'saɪnə/ *noun* a genus of African flies which cause trypanosomiasis, e.g. the tsetse fly

glossitis /glɒ'saɪtɪs/ *noun* inflammation of the surface of the tongue

glosso- /'glɒsəʊ/ *prefix* referring to the tongue

glossodynia /ˌglɒsəʊ'dɪniə/ *noun* pain in the tongue

glossopharyngeal /ˌglɒsəʊfærɪn'dʒiːəl/ *adjective* relating to the tongue and pharynx

glossopharyngeal nerve /ˌglɒsəʊfærɪn'dʒiːəl nɜːv/ *noun* the ninth cranial nerve which controls the pharynx, the salivary glands and part of the tongue

glossoplegia /ˌglɒsəʊ'pliːdʒə/ *noun* paralysis of the tongue

glossotomy /glɒ'sɒtəmi/ *noun* a surgical incision into the tongue

glottis /'glɒtɪs/ *noun* an opening in the larynx between the vocal cords, which forms the entrance to the main airway from the pharynx

gluc- /gluːk/ *prefix* referring to glucose

glucagon /'gluːkəgɒn/ *noun* a hormone secreted by the islets of Langerhans in the pancreas, which increases the level of blood sugar by stimulating the breakdown of glycogen

glucagonoma /ˌgluːkəgɒ'nəʊmə/ *noun* a tumour of the cells of the pancreas that produces glucagon

glucocorticoid /ˌgluːkəʊ'kɔːtɪkɔɪd/ *noun* any corticosteroid which breaks down carbohydrates and fats for use by the body, produced by the adrenal cortex

gluconeogenesis /ˌgluːkəʊ,niːəʊ'dʒenəsɪs/ *noun* the production of glucose in the liver from protein or fat reserves

glucose /'gluːkəʊz/ *noun* a simple sugar found in some fruit, but also broken down from white sugar or carbohydrate and absorbed into the body or secreted by the kidneys. Also called **dextrose**
    COMMENT: Combustion of glucose with oxygen to form carbon dioxide and water is the body's main source of energy.

glucose tolerance test /'gluːkəʊz ,tɒlərəns test/ *noun* a test for diabetes mellitus, in which someone eats glucose and his or her urine and blood are tested at regular intervals. Abbr **GTT**

glucosuria /ˌgluːkəʊ'sjʊəriə/ *noun* same as **glycosuria**

glucuronic acid /ˌgluːkjʊrɒnɪk 'æsɪd/ *noun* an acid formed by glucose that acts on bilirubin

glue ear /gluː 'ɪə/ *noun* a condition in which fluid forms behind the eardrum and causes deafness. Also called **secretory otitis media**

glue-sniffing /'gluː ,snɪfɪŋ/ *noun* ♦ **solvent abuse**

glutamic acid /gluː,tæmɪk 'æsɪd/ *noun* an amino acid

glutamic oxaloacetic transaminase /gluː,tæmɪk ɒksələʊə,siːtɪk træns'æmɪneɪz/ *noun* an enzyme used to test for viral hepatitis

glutamic pyruvic transaminase /gluː,tæmɪk paɪ,ruːvɪk træns'æmɪneɪz/ *noun* an enzyme produced in the liver and released into the blood if the liver is damaged

glutaminase /gluː'tæmɪneɪz/ *noun* an enzyme in the kidneys that helps to break down glutamine

glutamine /'gluːtəmiːn/ *noun* an amino acid

gluteal /'gluːtiəl/ *adjective* referring to the buttocks

gluteal artery /'gluːtiəl ˌɑːtəri/ *noun* one of the two arteries supplying the buttocks, the **inferior gluteal artery** or the **superior gluteal artery**

gluteal muscle /'gluːtiəl ˌmʌs(ə)l/ *noun* a muscle in the buttock. ◊ **gluteus**

gluteal vein /'gluːtiəl veɪn/ *noun* one of two veins draining the buttocks, the **inferior gluteal vein** and the **superior gluteal vein**

gluten /'gluːt(ə)n/ *noun* a protein found in some cereals, which makes the grains form a sticky paste when water is added

gluten enteropathy same as **gluten-induced enteropathy**

gluten-free diet /ˌgluːt(ə)n friː 'daɪət/ *noun* a diet containing only food containing no gluten

gluten-induced enteropathy /ˌgluːt(ə)n ɪnˌdjuːst ˌentə'rɒpəθi/ *noun* **1.** an allergic disease mainly affecting children, in which the lining of the intestine is sensitive to gluten, preventing the small intestine from digesting fat **2.** a condition in adults where the villi in the intestine become smaller and so reduce the surface which can absorb nutrients (NOTE: Symptoms include a swollen abdomen, pale diarrhoea, abdominal pains and anaemia.) ▶ also called **coeliac disease**

gluteus /'gluːtiəs/ *noun* one of three muscles in the buttocks, responsible for movements of the hip. The largest is the **gluteus maximus**, while the **gluteus medius** and **gluteus minimus** are smaller.

glyc- /glaɪk/ *prefix* same as **glyco-** (*used before vowels*)

glycaemia /glaɪ'siːmiə/ *noun* the level of glucose found in the blood. ◊ **hypoglycaemia, hyperglycaemia**

glycerin /'glɪsərɪn/, **glycerine**, **glycerol** /'glɪsərɒl/ *noun* a colourless viscous sweet-tasting liquid present in all fats (NOTE: Synthetic glycerin is used in various medicinal preparations and also as a lubricant in items such as toothpaste and cough medicines.)

glycine /'glaɪsiːn/ *noun* an amino acid

glyco- /glaɪkəʊ/ *prefix* referring to sugar

glycocholic acid /ˌglaɪkəʊkɒlɪk 'æsɪd/ *noun* one of the bile acids

glycogen /'glaɪkədʒən/ *noun* a type of starch, converted from glucose by the action of insulin, and stored in the liver as a source of energy

glycogenesis /ˌglaɪkəʊ'dʒenəsɪs/ *noun* the process by which glucose is converted into glycogen in the liver

glycogenolysis /ˌglaɪkəʊdʒə'nɒləsɪs/ *noun* the process by which glycogen is broken down to form glucose

glycolysis /glaɪ'kɒləsɪs/ *noun* the metabolic breakdown of glucose to release energy

glycoside /'glaɪkəʊsaɪd/ *noun* a chemical compound of a type which is formed from a simple sugar and another compound (NOTE: Many of the drugs produced from plants are glycosides.)

glycosuria /ˌglaɪkəʊ'sjʊəriə/ *noun* a high level of sugar in the urine, a symptom of diabetes mellitus

GMC *abbr* General Medical Council

gnathic /'næθɪk/ *adjective* referring to the jaw

gnathoplasty /'næθəʊˌplæsti/ *noun* surgery on the jaw

gnawing /'nɔːɪŋ/ *adjective* referring to a physical or emotional feeling that is persistent and uncomfortable ○ *a gnawing pain* ○ *gnawing anxiety*

goblet cell /'gɒblət sel/ *noun* a tube-shaped cell in the epithelium which secretes mucus

GOC *abbr* General Optical Council

go down /ˌgəʊ 'daʊn/ *verb* to become smaller ○ *The swelling has started to go down.* ○ *The blood sugar level went down.*

goitre /'gɔɪtə/ *noun* an excessive enlargement of the thyroid gland, seen as a swelling round the neck, caused by a lack of iodine (NOTE: The US spelling is **goiter**.)

goitrogen /'gɔɪtrədʒən/ *noun* a substance which causes goitre

gold /gəʊld/ *noun* a soft yellow-coloured precious metal, used as a compound in various drugs, and sometimes as a filling for teeth (NOTE: The chemical symbol is **Au**.)

golden eye ointment /ˌgəʊld(ə)n 'aɪ ˌɔɪntmənt/ *noun* a yellow ointment, made of an oxide of mercury, used to treat inflammation of the eyelids

gold injection /'gəʊld ɪnˌdʒekʃən/ *noun* an injection of a solution containing gold, used to relieve rheumatoid arthritis

golfer's elbow /ˌgɒlfəz 'elbəʊ/ *noun* inflammation of the tendons of the elbow

Golgi apparatus /'gɒldʒi æpəˌreɪtəs/ *noun* a folded membranous structure inside the cell cytoplasm which stores and transports enzymes and hormones [Described 1898. After Camillo Golgi (1843–1926), Professor of Histology and later Rector of the University of Pavia, Italy. In 1906 he shared the Nobel Prize with Santiago Ramón y Cajal for work on the nervous system.]

Golgi cell /'gɒldʒi ˌsel/ *noun* a type of nerve cell in the central nervous system, either with long axons (Golgi Type 1) or without axons (Golgi Type 2)

gomphosis /gɒm'fəʊsɪs/ *noun* a joint which cannot move, like that between a tooth and the jaw

gonad /'gəʊnæd/ *noun* a sex gland which produces gametes and also sex hormones, e.g. a testicle in males or an ovary in females

gonadotrophic hormone /ˌgəʊnədəʊˌtrɒ
fɪk ˈhɔːməʊn/ *noun* one of two hormones, the
follicle-stimulating hormone and the luteinising hormone, produced by the anterior pituitary gland which have an effect on the ovaries
in females and on the testes in males

gonadotrophin /ˌgəʊnədəʊˈtrəʊfɪn/ *noun*
any of a group of hormones produced by the
pituitary gland which stimulates the sex glands
at puberty. ◊ **human chorionic gonadotrophin**
(NOTE: The US spelling is **gonadotropin**.)

gonagra /gɒˈnægrə/ *noun* a form of gout
which occurs in the knees

goni- /gəʊni/ *prefix* same as **gonio-** (*used before a vowel*)

gonio- /gəʊniəʊ/ *prefix* referring to an angle

gonion /ˈgəʊniɒn/ *noun* the outer point at
which the lower jawbone angles upwards

goniopuncture /ˈgəʊniəʊˌpʌŋktʃə/ *noun* a
surgical operation for draining fluid from the
eyes of someone who has glaucoma

gonioscope /ˈgəʊniəskəʊp/ *noun* a lens for
measuring the angle of the front part of the eye

goniotomy /ˌgəʊniˈɒtəmi/ *noun* a surgical
operation to treat glaucoma by cutting Schlemm's canal

gonococcal /ˌgɒnəˈkɒk(ə)l/ *adjective* referring to gonococcus

gonococcus /ˌgɒnəˈkɒkəs/ *noun* a type of
bacterium, *Neisseria gonorrhoea*, which causes gonorrhoea (NOTE: The plural is **gonococci**.)

gonocyte /ˈgɒnəsaɪt/ *noun* same as **germ
cell**

gonorrhoea /ˌgɒnəˈriːə/ *noun* a sexually
transmitted disease which produces painful irritation of the mucous membrane and a watery
discharge from the vagina or penis

gonorrhoeal /ˌgɒnəˈriːəl/ *adjective* referring
to gonorrhoea

Goodpasture's syndrome /gʊdˈpɑːstʃəz
ˌsɪndrəʊm/ *noun* a rare lung disease in which
someone coughs up blood, is anaemic, and
may have kidney failure [Described 1919. After
Ernest William Goodpasture (1886–1960), US
pathologist.]

goose bumps /ˈguːs bʌmps/, **goose flesh** /
ˈguːs fleʃ/, **goose pimples** /ˈguːs ˌpɪmp(ə)lz/
noun a reaction of the skin when someone is
cold or frightened, the skin being raised into
many little bumps by the action of the arrector
pili muscles. Also called **cutis anserina**

Gordh needle /ˈgɔːd ˌniːd(ə)l/ *noun* a needle with a bag attached, so that several injections can be made one after the other

gorget /ˈgɔːdʒɪt/ *noun* a surgical instrument
used to remove stones from the bladder

gouge /gaʊdʒ/ *noun* a surgical instrument
like a chisel, used to cut bone

goundou /ˈguːnduː/ *noun* a condition caused
by yaws, in which growths form on either side
of the nose

gout /gaʊt/ *noun* a disease in which unusual
quantities of uric acid are produced and form
crystals in the cartilage round joints. Also
called **podagra**

COMMENT: Gout was formerly associated with
drinking strong wines such as port, but is now
believed to arise in three ways: excess uric
acid in the diet, overproduction of uric acid in
the body and inadequate excretion of uric acid. It is likely that both overproduction and inadequate excretion are due to inherited biochemical developments. Excess intake of alcohol can provoke an attack by interfering
with the excretion of uric acid.

gown /gaʊn/ *noun* a long robe worn over other clothes to protect them ○ *The surgeons were
wearing green gowns.* ○ *The patient was
dressed in a theatre gown, ready to go to the
operating theatre.*

GP *abbr* general practitioner

GP co-op /ˌdʒiː ˈpiː kəʊ ˌɒp/ *noun* a group of
GPs who work together to provide out-of-
hours care without making any profit

gr *symbol* grain

Graafian follicle /ˌgrɑːfiən ˈfɒlɪk(ə)l/ *noun*
same as **ovarian follicle** [After Reijnier de Graaf
(1641–73), Dutch physician]

gracilis /ˈgreɪsɪlɪs/ *noun* a thin muscle running down the inside of the leg from the top of
the leg down to the top of the tibia

graduated /ˈgrædʒueɪtɪd/ *adjective* with
marks showing various degrees or levels ○ *a
graduated measuring jar*

Graefe's knife /ˈgrefəz ˌnaɪf/ *noun* a sharp
knife used in operations on cataracts [After
Friedrich Wilhelm Ernst Albrecht von Graefe
(1828–70), Professor of Ophthalmology in Berlin, Germany]

graft /grɑːft/ *noun* **1.** the act of transplanting
an organ or tissue to replace one which is not
functioning or which is diseased ○ *a skin graft*
2. an organ or tissue which is transplanted ○
The corneal graft was successful. ○ *The patient was given drugs to prevent the graft being
rejected.* ■ *verb* to take a healthy organ or tissue and transplant it in place of diseased or
malfunctioning organ or tissue ○ *The surgeons
grafted a new section of bone at the side of the
skull.* ◆ **autograft, homograft**

graft versus host disease /ˌgrɑːft ˌvɜːsəs
ˈhəʊst dɪˌziːz/ *noun* a condition which develops when cells from the grafted tissue react
against the person's own tissue, causing skin
disorders. Abbr **GVHD**

grain /greɪn/ *noun* **1.** a very small piece of
something hard such as salt **2.** a measure of
weight equal to 0.0648 grams. Symbol **gr**

-gram /græm/ *suffix* a record in the form of a
picture

Gram-negative bacterium /græm
ˈnegətɪv bækˌtɪəriəm/ *noun* a bacterium
which takes up the red counterstain, after the
alcohol has washed out the first violet dye

Gram-positive bacterium /græm 'pɒzɪtɪv bæk,tɪəriəm/ *noun* a bacterium which retains violet dye and appears blue-black when viewed under the microscope

Gram's stain /græmz 'steɪn/ *noun* a method of staining bacteria so that they can be identified [Described 1884. After Hans Christian Joachim Gram (1853–1938), Professor of Medicine in Copenhagen, Denmark. He discovered the stain by accident as a student in Berlin, Germany.]

COMMENT: The tissue sample is first stained with a violet dye, treated with alcohol, and then counterstained with a red dye.

grand mal /,grɒn 'mæl/ *noun* a type of epilepsy, in which someone becomes unconscious and falls down, while the muscles become stiff and twitch violently

grand multiparity /,græn ,mʌlti'pærɪti/ *noun* the fact of having given birth to more than four children

granular /'grænjʊlə/ *adjective* made up of granules

granular cast /,grænjʊlə 'kɑːst/ *noun* a cast composed of cells filled with protein and fatty granules

granular leucocyte /,grænjʊlə 'luːkəsaɪt/ *noun* same as **granulocyte**

granulation /,grænjʊ'leɪʃ(ə)n/ *noun* the formation of rough red tissue on the surface of a wound or site of infection, the first stage in the healing process

granulation tissue /,grænjʊ'leɪʃ(ə)n ,tɪʃuː/ *noun* soft tissue, consisting mainly of tiny blood vessels and fibres, which forms over a wound

granule /'grænjuːl/ *noun* a very small piece of something hard

granulocyte /'grænjʊləsaɪt/ *noun* a type of leucocyte or white blood cell which contains granules, e.g. a basophil, eosinophil or neutrophil

granulocytopenia /,grænjʊləʊ,saɪtəʊ'piːniə/ *noun* a usually fatal disease caused by the lowering of the number of granulocytes in the blood due to bone marrow malfunction

granuloma /,grænjʊ'ləʊmə/ *noun* a mass of granulation tissue which forms at the site of bacterial infections (NOTE: The plural is **granulomata** or **granulomas**.)

granuloma inguinale /grænjʊ,ləʊmə ,ɪŋgwɪ'neɪli/ *noun* a sexually transmitted disease affecting the anus and genitals in which the skin becomes covered with ulcers, usually occurring in the tropics

granulomatosis /,grænjʊləʊmə'təʊsɪs/ *noun* persistent inflammation leading to the formation of nodules

granulopoiesis /,grænjuːləʊpɔɪ'iːsɪs/ *noun* the normal production of granulocytes in the bone marrow

graph /grɑːf/ *noun* a diagram which shows the relationship between quantities as a line

graph- /græf/ *prefix* writing

-graph /grɑːf/ *suffix* a machine which records something as pictures

-grapher /grəfə/ *suffix* a technician who operates a machine which records

-graphy /grəfi/ *suffix* the technique of study through pictures

grattage /græ'tɑːʒ/ *noun* a procedure that involves scraping the surface of an ulcer which is healing slowly to make it heal more rapidly

gravel /'græv(ə)l/ *noun* small stones which pass from the kidney to the urinary system, causing pain in the ureter

Graves' disease /'greɪvz dɪ,ziːz/ *noun* same as **exophthalmic goitre** [Described 1835. After Robert James Graves (1796–1853), Irish physician at the Meath Hospital, Dublin, Ireland, where he was responsible for introducing clinical ward work for medical students.]

gravid /'grævɪd/ *adjective* pregnant

gravides multiparae /,grævɪdiːz ,mʌlti'pɑːriː/ *plural noun* women who have given birth to at least four live babies

gravity /'grævɪti/ *noun* the importance or potential danger of a disease or situation

Grawitz tumour /'grɑːvɪts ,tjuːmə/ *noun* a malignant tumour in kidney cells [Described 1883. After Paul Albert Grawitz (1850–1932), Professor of Pathology at Greifswald, Germany.]

gray /greɪ/ *noun* an SI unit of measurement of absorbed radiation equal to 100 rads. Symbol **Gy.** ◊ **rad**

graze /greɪz/ *noun* a scrape on the skin surface, making some blood flow ■ *verb* to scrape the skin surface accidentally

great cerebral vein /,greɪt 'serəbrəl veɪn/ *noun* a median vein draining the choroid plexuses of the lateral and third ventricles

greater curvature /,greɪtə 'kɜːvətʃə/ *noun* a convex line of the stomach

greater vestibular glands /,greɪtə ve'stɪbjʊlə glændz/ *noun* same as **Bartholin's glands**

great toe /'greɪt təʊ/ *noun* same as **big toe**

green monkey disease /,griːn 'mʌŋki dɪ,ziːz/ *noun* same as **Marburg disease**

greenstick fracture /'griːnstɪk ,fræktʃə/ *noun* a type of fracture occurring in children, where a long bone bends, but is not completely broken

grey commissure /greɪ 'kɒmɪsjʊə/ *noun* part of the grey matter nearest to the central canal of the spinal cord, where axons cross over each other

grey matter /'greɪ ,mætə/ *noun* nerve tissue which is of a dark grey colour and forms part of the central nervous system

COMMENT: In the brain, grey matter encloses the white matter, but in the spinal cord, white matter encloses the grey matter.

grief counsellor /ˈgriːf ˌkaʊns(ə)lə/ *noun* a person who helps someone to cope with the feelings they have when someone such as a close relative dies

Griffith's types /ˈgrɪfɪθs ˌtaɪps/ *noun* various types of haemolytic streptococci, classified according to the antigens present in them

gripe water /ˈgraɪp ˌwɔːtə/ *noun* a solution of glucose and alcohol, used to relieve abdominal pains in babies

griping /ˈgraɪpɪŋ/ *adjective* referring to stomach pains that are sudden, sharp and intense

grocer's itch /ˌgrəʊsəz ˈɪtʃ/ *noun* a form of dermatitis on the hands caused by handling flour and sugar

groin /grɔɪn/ *noun* a junction at each side of the body where the lower abdomen joins the top of the thighs ○ *He had a dull pain in his groin.* (NOTE: For other terms referring to the groin, see **inguinal**.)

grommet /ˈgrɒmɪt/ *noun* a tube which can be passed from the external auditory meatus into the middle ear, usually to allow fluid to drain off, as in someone who has glue ear

gross anatomy /ˌgrəʊs əˈnætəmi/ *noun* the study of the structure of the body that can be seen without the use of a microscope

ground substance /ˌgraʊnd ˈsʌbstəns/ *noun* same as **matrix**

group /gruːp/ *noun* several people, animals or things which are all close together ○ *A group of patients were waiting in the surgery.* ■ *verb* to bring things or people together in a group, or come together in a group ○ *The drugs are grouped under the heading 'antibiotics'.*

group practice /ˌgruːp ˈpræktɪs/ *noun* a medical practice where several doctors or dentists share the same office building and support services

group therapy /ˌgruːp ˈθerəpi/ *noun* a type of psychotherapy where a group of people with the same disorder meet together with a therapist to discuss their condition and try to help each other

growing pains /ˈgrəʊɪŋ peɪnz/ *plural noun* pains associated with adolescence, which can be a form of rheumatic fever

growth /grəʊθ/ *noun* **1.** the process of increasing in size ○ *the growth in the population since 1960* ○ *The disease stunts children's growth.* **2.** a cyst or tumour ○ *The doctor found a cancerous growth on the left breast.* ○ *He had an operation to remove a small growth from his chin.*

growth factor /ˈgrəʊθ ˌfæktə/ *noun* a chemical, especially a polypeptide, produced in the body which encourages particular cells to grow ○ *a nerve growth factor*

growth hormone /ˈgrəʊθ ˌhɔːməʊn/ *noun* a hormone secreted by the pituitary gland during deep sleep, which stimulates growth of the

long bones and protein synthesis. Also called **somatropin**

grumbling appendix /ˌgrʌmblɪŋ əˈpendɪks/ *noun* a vermiform appendix that is always slightly inflamed (*informal*) ◊ **chronic appendicitis**

GTT *abbr* glucose tolerance test

GU *abbr* **1.** gastric ulcer **2.** genitourinary

guanine /ˈgwɑːniːn/ *noun* one of the four basic chemicals in DNA

guardian ad litem /ˌgɑːdiən æd ˈliːtəm/ *noun* a person who acts on behalf of a minor who is a defendant in a court case

guardian Caldicott /ˌgɑːdiən ˈkɔːldɪkɒt/ *noun* in the UK, a person appointed by a hospital or Health Trust to make sure that information about patients is kept confidential, following the Caldicott Report of 1997

gubernaculum /ˌguːbəˈnækjʊləm/ *noun* in a fetus, fibrous tissue connecting the testes (the gonads) to the groin

Guillain-Barré syndrome /ˌgiːjæn ˈbæreɪ ˌsɪndrəʊm/ *noun* a nervous disorder in which, after a non-specific infection, demyelination of the spinal roots and peripheral nerves takes place, leading to generalised weakness and sometimes respiratory paralysis. Also called **Landry's paralysis** [Described 1916. After Georges Guillain (1876–1961), Professor of Neurology in Paris, France, Jean Alexandre Barré (1880–1967), Professor of Neurology in Strasbourg, France.]

guillotine /ˈgɪlətiːn/ *noun* a surgical instrument for cutting out tonsils

guinea worm /ˈgɪni wɜːm/ *noun* same as **Dracunculus**

Gulf War syndrome /gʌlf ˈwɔː ˌsɪndrəʊm/ *noun* a collection of unexplained symptoms, including fatigue, skin disorders, and muscle pains, affecting some soldiers who fought in the Gulf War in 1991

gullet /ˈgʌlɪt/ *noun* same as **oesophagus**

gum /gʌm/ *noun* the soft tissue covering the part of the jaw which surrounds the teeth ○ *Her gums are red and inflamed.* ○ *A build-up of tartar can lead to gum disease.* Also called **gingiva** (NOTE: For other terms referring to the gums, see words beginning with **gingiv-**.)

gumboil /ˈgʌmbɔɪl/ *noun* an abscess on the gum near a tooth

gumma /ˈgʌmə/ *noun* an abscess of dead tissue and overgrown scar tissue, which develops in the later stages of syphilis

gustation /gʌˈsteɪʃ(ə)n/ *noun* the act of tasting

gustatory /ˈgʌstət(ə)ri/ *adjective* referring to the sense of taste

gut /gʌt/ *noun* **1.** the tubular organ for the digestion and absorption of food. Also called **intestine 2.** a type of thread, made from the intestines of sheep. It is used to sew up internal incisions and dissolves slowly so does not need to be removed. ◊ **catgut**

Guthrie test /ˈgʌθri test/ *noun* a test used on babies to detect the presence of phenylketonuria [After R. Guthrie (b. 1916), US paediatrician.]

gutta /ˈgʌtə/ *noun* a drop of liquid, as used in treatment of the eyes (NOTE: The plural is **guttae**.)

gutter splint /ˈgʌtə splɪnt/ *noun* a shaped container in which a broken limb can rest without being completely surrounded

GVHD *abbr* graft versus host disease

gyn- /gaɪn/ *prefix* same as **gynae-** (*used before a vowel*)

gynae- /gaɪni/ *prefix* referring to women (NOTE: In US English words beginning with **gynae-** are spelled **gyne-**.)

gynaecological /ˌgaɪnɪkəˈlɒdʒɪk(ə)l/ *adjective* referring to the treatment of diseases of women

gynaecologist /ˌgaɪnɪˈkɒlədʒɪst/ *noun* a doctor who specialises in the treatment of diseases of women

gynaecology /gaɪnɪˈkɒlədʒi/ *noun* the study of female sex organs and the treatment of diseases of women in general

gynaecomastia /ˌgaɪnɪkəˈmæstiə/ *noun* the unusual development of breasts in a male

gyne /ˈgaɪni/ same as **gynaecology, gynaecological** (*informal*) ○ *a gyne appointment*

gypsum /ˈdʒɪpsəm/ *noun* calcium sulphate, used as plaster of Paris

gyrus /ˈdʒaɪərəs/ *noun* a raised part of the cerebral cortex between the sulci

H

H2-receptor antagonist /ˌeɪt ʃ tuː rɪ 'septər ænˌtægənɪst/ *noun* a drug that inhibits its production of stomach acid and so relieves indigestion and gastric ulcers

HA *abbr* health authority

habit /'hæbɪt/ *noun* **1.** an action which is an automatic response to a stimulus **2.** a regular way of doing something ○ *He got into the habit of swimming every day before breakfast.* ○ *She's got out of the habit of taking any exercise.* □ **from force of habit** because you do it regularly ○ *I wake up at 6 o'clock from force of habit.*

habit-forming /'hæbɪt ˌfɔːmɪŋ/ *adjective* making someone addicted

habit-forming drug /'hæbɪt ˌfɔːmɪŋ drʌg/ *noun* a drug which is addictive

habitual /həˈbɪtʃuəl/ *adjective* done frequently or as a matter of habit

habitual abortion /həˌbɪtʃuəl əˈbɔːʃ(ə)n/ *noun* a condition in which a woman has abortions with successive pregnancies

habituation /həˌbɪtʃuˈeɪʃ(ə)n/ *noun* the fact of being psychologically but not physically addicted to or dependent on a drug, alcohol or other substance

habitus /'hæbɪtəs/ *noun* the general physical appearance of a person, including build and posture

hacking cough /ˌhækɪŋ 'kɒf/ *noun* a continuous short dry cough

haem /hiːm/ *noun* a molecule containing iron which binds proteins to form haemoproteins such as haemoglobin and myoglobin

haem- /hiːm/ *prefix* same as **haemo-** (*used before vowels*) (NOTE: In US English, words beginning with the prefix **haem-** are spelled **hem-**.)

haemagglutination /ˌhiːməɡluːtɪˈneɪʃ(ə)n/ *noun* the clumping of red blood cells, often used to test for the presence of antibodies

haemangioma /ˌhiːmændʒiˈəumə/ *noun* a harmless tumour which forms in blood vessels and appears on the skin as a birthmark

haemarthrosis /ˌhiːmɑːˈθrəusɪs/ *noun* pain and swelling caused by blood leaking into a joint

haematemesis /ˌhiːməˈteməsɪs/ *noun* a condition in which someone vomits blood, usually because of internal bleeding

haematic /hiːˈmætɪk/ *adjective* referring to blood

haematin /'hiːmətɪn/ *noun* a substance which forms from haemoglobin when bleeding takes place

haematinic /ˌhiːməˈtɪnɪk/ *noun* a drug which increases haemoglobin in blood, used to treat anaemia, e.g. an iron compound

haemato- /hiːmətəu/ *prefix* referring to blood

haematocoele /'hiːmətəusiːl/, **haematocele** *noun* a swelling caused by blood leaking into a cavity, especially the scrotum

haematocolpos /ˌhiːmətəuˈkɒlpəs/ *noun* a condition in which the vagina is filled with blood at menstruation because the hymen has no opening

haematocrit /'hiːmətəukrɪt/ *noun* **1.** same as **packed cell volume 2.** an instrument for measuring haematocrit

haematocyst /'hiːmətəusɪst/ *noun* a cyst which contains blood

haematogenous /ˌhiːməˈtɒdʒənəs/ *adjective* **1.** producing blood **2.** produced by blood

haematological /ˌhiːmətəuˈlɒdʒɪk(ə)l/ *adjective* referring to haematology

haematologist /ˌhiːməˈtɒlədʒɪst/ *noun* a doctor who specialises in haematology

haematology /ˌhiːməˈtɒlədʒi/ *noun* the scientific study of blood, its formation and its diseases

haematoma /ˌhiːməˈtəumə/ *noun* a mass of blood under the skin caused by a blow or by the effects of an operation

haematometra /ˌhiːməˈtɒmɪtrə/ *noun* **1.** excessive bleeding in the uterus **2.** a swollen uterus, caused by haematocolpos

haematomyelia /ˌhiːmətəumaɪˈiːliə/ *noun* a condition in which blood leaks into the spinal cord

haematopoiesis /ˌhiːmətəupɔɪˈiːsɪs/ *noun* same as **haemopoiesis**

haematoporphyrin /ˌhiːmətəʊˈpɔːfərɪn/ *noun* porphyrin produced from haemoglobin

haematosalpinx /ˌhiːmətəʊˈsælpɪŋks/ *noun* same as **haemosalpinx**

haematospermia /ˌhiːmætəʊˈspɜːmiə/ *noun* the presence of blood in the sperm

haematozoon /ˌhiːmətəʊˈzəʊɒn/ *noun* a parasite living in the blood (NOTE: The plural is **haematozoa**.)

haematuria /ˌhiːməˈtjʊəriə/ *noun* the unusual presence of blood in the urine, as a result of injury or disease of the kidney or bladder

haemin /ˈhiːmɪn/ *noun* a salt derived from haemoglobin, used in the treatment of porphyria

haemo- /hiːməʊ/ *prefix* referring to blood

haemochromatosis /ˌhiːməʊkrəʊməˈtəʊsɪs/ *noun* an inherited disease in which the body absorbs and stores too much iron, causing cirrhosis of the liver and giving the skin a dark colour. Also called **bronze diabetes**

haemoconcentration /ˌhiːməʊˌkɒnsənˈtreɪʃ(ə)n/ *noun* an increase in the percentage of red blood cells because the volume of plasma is reduced. Compare **haemodilution**

haemocytoblast /ˌhiːməʊˈsaɪtəʊblæst/ *noun* an embryonic blood cell in the bone marrow from which red and white blood cells and platelets develop

haemocytometer /ˌhiːməʊsaɪˈtɒmɪtə/ *noun* a glass jar in which a sample of blood is diluted and the blood cells counted

haemodialyse /ˌhiːməʊˈdaɪəlaɪz/ *verb* to remove waste matter from the blood using a dialyser (kidney machine)

haemodialysed patient /ˌhiːməʊ daɪəlaɪzd ˈpeɪʃ(ə)nt/ *noun* someone who has undergone haemodialysis

haemodialysis /ˌhiːməʊdaɪˈæləsɪs/ *noun* same as **kidney dialysis**

haemodilution /ˌhiːməʊdaɪˈluːʃ(ə)n/ *noun* a decrease in the percentage of red blood cells because the volume of plasma has increased. Compare **haemoconcentration**

haemoglobin /ˌhiːməʊˈɡləʊbɪn/ *noun* a red respiratory pigment formed of haem and globin in red blood cells which gives blood its red colour. It absorbs oxygen in the lungs and carries it in the blood to the tissues. Abbr **Hb**. ◊ **oxyhaemoglobin, carboxyhaemoglobin**

haemoglobinaemia /ˌhiːməʊɡləʊbɪˈniːmiə/ *noun* a condition in which haemoglobin is found in blood plasma

haemoglobinopathy /ˌhiːməʊɡləʊbɪˈnɒpəθi/ *noun* an inherited disease of a group which result from damaging variations in the production of haemoglobin, e.g. sickle-cell anaemia

haemoglobinuria /ˌhiːməʊɡləʊbɪˈnjʊəriə/ *noun* a condition in which haemoglobin is found in the urine

haemogram /ˈhiːməʊɡræm/ *noun* the printed result of a blood test

haemolysin /ˌhiːməʊˈlaɪsɪn/ *noun* a protein which destroys red blood cells

haemolysis /hiːˈmɒləsɪs/ *noun* the destruction of red blood cells

haemolytic /ˌhiːməʊˈlɪtɪk/ *adjective* destroying red blood cells ■ *noun* a substance which destroys red blood cells, e.g. snake venom

haemolytic anaemia /ˌhiːməlɪtɪk əˈniːmiə/ *noun* a condition in which the destruction of red blood cells is about six times the usual rate, and the supply of new cells from the bone marrow cannot meet the demand

haemolytic disease of the newborn /ˌhiːməʊlɪtɪk dɪˌziːz əv ðə ˈnjuːbɔːn/ *noun* a condition in which the red blood cells of the fetus are destroyed because antibodies in the mother's blood react against them

haemolytic jaundice /ˌhiːməʊlɪtɪk ˈdʒɔːndɪs/ *noun* jaundice caused by haemolysis of the red blood cells. Also called **prehepatic jaundice**

haemolytic uraemic syndrome /ˌhiːməʊlɪtɪk jʊˈriːmɪk ˌsɪndrəʊm/ *noun* a condition in which haemolytic anaemia damages the kidneys

haemopericardium /ˌhiːməʊperɪˈkɑːdiəm/ *noun* a condition in which blood is found in the pericardium

haemoperitoneum /ˌhiːməʊperɪtəˈniːəm/ *noun* a condition in which blood is found in the peritoneal cavity

haemophilia /ˌhiːməˈfɪliə/ *noun* a disorder linked to a recessive gene on the X-chromosome in which the blood clots much more slowly than usual, resulting in extensive bleeding from even minor injuries. The gene is passed by women to their male children and the disorder is seen almost exclusively in boys.

haemophilia A /ˌhiːməʊfɪliə ˈeɪ/ *noun* the most common type of haemophilia, in which the inability to synthesise Factor VIII, a protein that promotes blood clotting, means that the blood clots very slowly

haemophilia B /ˌhiːməfɪliə ˈbiː/ *noun* a less common type of haemophilia, in which the inability to synthesise Factor IX, a protein that promotes blood clotting, means that the blood clots very slowly. Also called **Christmas disease**

haemophiliac /ˌhiːməˈfɪliæk/ *noun* a person who has haemophilia

haemophilic /ˌhiːməʊˈfɪlɪk/ *adjective* referring to haemophilia

Haemophilus /hiːˈmɒfɪləs/ *noun* a genus of bacteria which needs specific factors in the blood to grow

Haemophilus influenzae /hiːˌmɒfɪləs ˌɪnↆfluˈenzə/ *noun* a bacterium which lives in healthy throats, but which can cause pneumonia if a person's resistance is lowered by a bout of flu

Haemophilus influenzae type b /ˌhiːˌmɒ fɪləs ˌɪnfluˌenzə taɪp ˈbiː/ *noun* a bacterium which causes meningitis. Abbr **Hib**

haemophthalmia /ˌhiːmɒfˈθælmiə/ *noun* a condition in which blood is found in the vitreous humour of the eye

haemopneumothorax /ˌhiːməʊˌnjuːməʊ ˈθɔːræks/ *noun* same as **pneumohaemothorax**

haemopoiesis /ˌhiːməʊpɔɪˈiːsɪs/ *noun* the continual production of blood cells and blood platelets in the bone marrow. Also called **blood formation**

haemopoietic /ˌhiːməʊpɔɪˈetɪk/ *adjective* referring to the formation of blood in the bone marrow

haemoptysis /hiːˈmɒptəsɪs/ *noun* a condition in which someone coughs blood from the lungs, caused by a serious illness such as anaemia, pneumonia, tuberculosis or cancer

haemorrhage /ˈhem(ə)rɪdʒ/ *noun* the loss of a large quantity of blood, especially from a burst blood vessel ○ *He died of a brain haemorrhage.* ■ *verb* to bleed heavily ○ *The injured man was haemorrhaging from the mouth.*

haemorrhagic /ˌheməˈrædʒɪk/ *adjective* referring to heavy bleeding

haemorrhagic disease of the newborn /ˌhemərædʒɪk dɪˌziːz əv ðə ˈnjuːbɔːn/ *noun* a disease of newly born babies, which makes them haemorrhage easily, caused by temporary lack of prothrombin

haemorrhagic disorder /ˌheməˌrædʒɪk dɪsˈɔːdə/ *noun* a disorder in which haemorrhages occur, e.g. haemophilia

haemorrhagic fever /ˌhemərædʒɪk ˈfiːvə/ *noun* a viral infection that results in profuse internal bleeding from the capillaries, e.g. dengue or Ebola

haemorrhagic stroke /ˌhemərædʒɪk ˈstrəʊk/ *noun* a stroke caused by a burst blood vessel

haemorrhoidal /ˌheməˈrɔɪdəl/ *adjective* referring to haemorrhoids

haemorrhoidectomy /ˌhemərɔɪˈdektəmi/ *noun* the surgical removal of haemorrhoids

haemorrhoids /ˈhemərɔɪdz/ *plural noun* swollen veins in the anorectal passage. Also called **piles**

haemosalpinx /hiːˈməʊˈsælpɪŋks/ *noun* the accumulation of blood in the Fallopian tubes

haemosiderosis /ˌhiːməʊsɪdəˈrəʊsɪs/ *noun* a disorder in which iron forms large deposits in the tissue, causing haemorrhaging and destruction of red blood cells

haemostasis /ˌhiːməʊˈsteɪsɪs/ *noun* the process of stopping bleeding or slowing the movement of blood

haemostat /ˈhiːməʊstæt/ *noun* a device which stops bleeding, e.g. a clamp

haemostatic /ˌhiːməʊˈstætɪk/ *adjective* stopping bleeding ■ *noun* a drug which stops bleeding

haemothorax /ˌhiːməʊˈθɔːræks/ *noun* a condition in which blood is found in the pleural cavity

Hageman factor /ˈhɑːgəmən ˌfæktə/ *noun* same as **Factor XII**

HAI *abbr* Hospital Acquired Infection

hair cell /ˈheə sel/ *noun* a receptor cell which converts fluid pressure changes into nerve impulses carried in the auditory nerve (NOTE: For other terms referring to hair, see words beginning with pilo-, trich-, tricho-.)

hair follicle /ˈheə ˌfɒlɪk(ə)l/ *noun* the cells and tissue that surround the root of a hair

hairline fracture /ˈheəlaɪn ˌfræktʃə/ *noun* a very slight crack in a bone caused by injury

hair papilla /heə pəˈpɪlə/ *noun* a part of the skin containing capillaries which feed blood to the hair

hairy cell leukaemia /ˌheəri sel luːˈkiəmiə/ *noun* a form of leukaemia in which white blood cells have fine projections

half-life /ˈhɑːf laɪf/ *noun* 1. a measurement of the period of time taken before the concentration of a drug has reached half of what it was when it was administered 2. the time taken for half the atoms in a radioactive isotope to decay

halitosis /ˌhælɪˈtəʊsɪs/ *noun* a condition in which a person has breath which smells unpleasant. Also called **bad breath**

COMMENT: Halitosis can have several causes: caries in the teeth, infection of the gums, and indigestion are the most usual. The breath can also have an unpleasant smell during menstruation, or in association with certain diseases such as diabetes mellitus and uraemia.

halluces /ˈhælusiːz/ *plural of* **hallux**

hallucinate /həˈluːsɪneɪt/ *verb* to have hallucinations ○ *The patient was hallucinating.*

hallucination /həˌluːsɪˈneɪʃ(ə)n/ *noun* an experience of seeing an imaginary scene or hearing an imaginary sound as clearly as if it were really there

hallucinatory /həˈluːsɪnət(ə)ri/ *adjective* referring to a drug which causes hallucinations

hallucinogen /ˌhæluːˈsɪnədʒən/ *noun* a drug which causes hallucinations, e.g. cannabis or LSD

hallucinogenic /həˌluːsɪnəˈdʒenɪk/ *adjective* referring to a substance which produces hallucinations ○ *a hallucinogenic fungus*

hallux /ˈhæləks/ *noun* the big toe (NOTE: The plural is **halluces**.)

hallux valgus /ˌhæləks ˈvælgəs/ *noun* a condition of the foot, where the big toe turns towards the other toes and a bunion is formed

haloperidol /ˌhæləʊˈperɪdɒl/ *noun* a tranquilliser used in the treatment of schizophrenia, mania and psychoses

halo splint /ˈheɪləʊ splɪnt/ *noun* a device used to keep the head and neck still so that they can recover from injury or an operation

halothane /ˈhæləʊθeɪn/ *noun* a general anaesthetic that is given by inhalation

hamamelis /ˌhæməˈmiːlɪs/ ♦ **witch hazel**

hamartoma /ˌhæmɑːˈtəʊmə/ *noun* a benign tumour containing tissue from any organ

hamate /ˈheɪmeɪt/, **hamate bone** /ˈheɪmeɪt bəʊn/ *noun* one of the eight small carpal bones in the wrist, shaped like a hook. Also called **unciform bone**. See illustration at HAND in Supplement

hammer /ˈhæmə/ *noun* same as **malleus**

hammer toe /ˈhæmə təʊ/ *noun* a toe which has the middle joint permanently bent downwards

hamstring /ˈhæmstrɪŋ/ *noun* one of a group of tendons behind the knee, which link the thigh muscles to the bones in the lower leg

hamstring muscles /ˈhæmstrɪŋ ˌmʌs(ə)lz/ *plural noun* a group of muscles at the back of the thigh, which flex the knee and extend the gluteus maximus

hand /hænd/ *noun* the part at the end of the arm, beyond the wrist, which is used for holding things ○ *He injured his hand with a saw.* ■ *verb* to pass something to someone

COMMENT: The hand is formed of 27 bones: 14 phalanges in the fingers, 5 metacarpals in the main part of the hand, and 8 carpals in the wrist.

hand, foot and mouth disease /ˌhænd fʊt ən ˈmaʊθ dɪˌziːz/ *noun* a mild viral infection in children, causing small blisters

handicap /ˈhændɪkæp/ *noun* a physical or mental condition which prevents someone from doing some everyday activities ■ *verb* to prevent someone from doing an everyday activity (NOTE: The word 'handicap' is now usually avoided.)

'…handicap – disadvantage for a given individual, resulting from an impairment or a disability, that limits or prevents the fulfilment of a role that is normal for that individual' [*WHO*]

handicapped /ˈhændɪkæpt/ *adjective* referring to a person who has a disability (NOTE: The word 'handicapped' is now usually avoided.)

Hand-Schüller Christian disease /ˌhænt ˌʃʊlə ˈkrɪʃən dɪˌziːz/ *noun* a disturbance of cholesterol metabolism in young children which causes disorders in membranous bone, mainly in the skull, exophthalmos, diabetes insipidus, and a yellow-brown colour of the skin [First described 1893 then 1915 by Schüller and 1920 by Christian. After Alfred Hand Jr. (1868–1949), US paediatrician; Artur Schüller (1874–1958), Austrian neurologist; Henry Asbury Christian (1876–1951), Professor of Medicine at Harvard, USA.]

hangnail /ˈhæŋneɪl/ *noun* a piece of torn skin at the side of a nail

hangover /ˈhæŋəʊvə/ *noun* a condition occurring after a person has drunk too much alcohol, with dehydration caused by inhibition of the antidiuretic hormone in the kidneys. The symptoms include headache, inability to stand noise and trembling of the hands.

Hansen's bacillus /ˌhænsənz bəˈsɪləs/ *noun* the bacterium which causes leprosy, *Mycobacterium leprae* [Discovered 1873. After Gerhard Henrik Armauer Hansen (1841–1912), Norwegian physician.]

Hansen's disease /ˈhænsənz dɪˌziːz/ *noun* same as **leprosy**

haploid /ˈhæplɔɪd/ *adjective* referring to a cell such as a gamete where each chromosome occurs only once. In humans the haploid number of chromosomes is 23.

hapt- /hæpt/ *prefix* relating to the sense of touch

hapten /ˈhæpten/ *noun* a substance which causes an allergy, probably by changing a protein so that it becomes antigenic

hardening of the arteries /ˌhɑːd(ə)nɪŋ əv ðə ˈɑːtəriz/ *noun* same as **atherosclerosis**

hard of hearing /ˌhɑːd əv ˈhɪərɪŋ/ *adjective* same as **hearing-impaired**

hard palate /ˌhɑːd ˈpælət/ *noun* the front part of the roof of the mouth between the upper teeth

harelip /ˈheəlɪp/ *noun* same as **cleft lip**

harm /hɑːm/ *noun* injury or damage as a result of something that you do ○ *Walking to work every day won't do you any harm.* □ **there's no harm in taking the tablets only for one week** there will be no side effects from taking the tablets for a week ■ *verb* to damage or hurt someone or something ○ *Walking to work every day won't harm you.*

harmful /ˈhɑːmf(ə)l/ *adjective* causing injury or damage ○ *Bright light can be harmful to your eyes.* ○ *Sudden violent exercise can be harmful.*

harmless /ˈhɑːmləs/ *adjective* causing no injury or damage ○ *These herbal remedies are quite harmless.*

Harrison's sulcus /ˌhærɪsənz ˈsʌlk(ə)s/, **Harrison's groove** /ˌhærɪs(ə)nz ˈɡruːv/ *noun* a hollow on either side of the chest which develops in children who have difficulty in breathing, seen especially in cases of rickets

Harris's operation /ˈhærɪsɪz ɒpəˌreɪʃ(ə)n/ *noun* the surgical removal of the prostate gland [After S.H. Harris (1880–1936), Australian surgeon]

Hartmann's solution /ˈhɑːtmənz səˌluːʃ(ə)n/ *noun* a chemical solution used in drips to replace body fluids lost in dehydration, particularly as a result of infantile gastroenteritis [Described 1932. After Alexis Frank

Hartmann (1898–1964), paediatrician, St Louis, Missouri, USA.]

Hartnup disease /'hɑːtnəp dɪˌziːz/ *noun* an inherited condition affecting amino acid metabolism and producing thick skin and impaired mental development [After the name of the family in which this hereditary disease was first recorded]

harvest /'hɑːvɪst/ *verb* to take something for use elsewhere, e.g. a piece of skin for a graft or eggs for IVF

Hashimoto's disease /ˌhæʃɪ'məʊtəz dɪ ˌziːz/ *noun* a type of goitre in middle-aged women, where the woman is sensitive to secretions from her own thyroid gland, and, in extreme cases, the face swells and the skin turns yellow [Described 1912. After Hakuru Hashimoto (1881–1934), Japanese surgeon.]

hashish /'hæʃɪʃ/ *noun* ♦ cannabis

haustrum /'hɔːstrəm/ *noun* a sac on the outside of the colon (NOTE: The plural is **haustra**.)

HAV *abbr* hepatitis A virus

Haversian canal /hə'vɜːʃ(ə)n kə,næl/ *noun* a fine canal which runs vertically through the Haversian systems in compact bone, containing blood vessels and lymph ducts [Described 1689. After Clopton Havers (1657–1702), English surgeon.]

Haversian system /hə'vɜːʃ(ə)n ,sɪstəm/ *noun* a unit of compact bone built around a Haversian canal, made of a series of bony layers which form a cylinder. Also called **osteon**

hayfever /'heɪˌfiːvə/ *noun* inflammation in the nasal passage and eyes caused by an allergic reaction to plant pollen. ◊ allergic rhinitis

HAZ *abbr* health action zone

Hb *abbr* haemoglobin

HBV *abbr* hepatitis B virus

hCG *abbr* human chorionic gonadotrophin

HCHS *abbr* Health and Community Health Services

HDL *abbr* high density lipoprotein

head /hed/ *noun* 1. the round top part of the body, which contains the eyes, nose, mouth, brain, etc (NOTE: For other terms referring to the head, see words beginning with **cephal-, cephalo-**.) 2. a rounded top part of a bone which fits into a socket ○ *head of humerus* ○ *head of femur*

headache /'hedeɪk/ *noun* a pain in the head, caused by changes in pressure in the blood vessels feeding the brain which act on the nerves. Also called **cephalalgia**

COMMENT: Headaches can be caused by a blow to the head, lack of sleep or food, by eye strain, sinus infections and many other causes. Mild headaches can be treated with an analgesic and rest. Severe headaches which recur may be caused by serious disorders in the head or nervous system.

head cold /hed kəʊld/ *noun* a minor illness, with inflammation of the nasal passages, excess mucus in the nose and sneezing

head louse /'hed laʊs/ *noun* a small insect of the *Pediculus* genus, which lives on the scalp and sucks blood. Also called **Pediculus capitis** (NOTE: The plural is **head lice**.)

Heaf test /'hiːf test/ *noun* a test in which tuberculin is injected into the skin to find out whether a person is immune to tuberculosis. ◊ **Mantoux test**

heal /hiːl/ *verb* 1. (*of wound*) to return to a healthy state ○ *After six weeks, her wound had still not healed.* ○ *A minor cut will heal faster if it is left without a bandage.* 2. to make someone or something get better

healing /'hiːlɪŋ/ *noun* the process of getting better ○ *a substance which will accelerate the healing process*

healing by first intention /ˌhiːlɪŋ baɪ ˌfɜːst ɪn'tenʃən/ *noun* the healing of a clean wound where the tissue reforms quickly

healing by second intention /ˌhiːlɪŋ baɪ ˌsekənd ɪn'tenʃən/ *noun* the healing of an infected wound or ulcer, which takes place slowly and may leave a permanent scar

health /helθ/ *noun* the general condition of the mind or body ○ *He's in good health.* ○ *She had suffered from bad health for some years.* ○ *The council said that fumes from the factory were a danger to public health.* ○ *All cigarette packets carry a government health warning.*

health action zone /ˌhelθ 'ækʃən zəʊn/ *noun* in the UK, an area in which the government has funded specific actions to redress health inequalities. Abbr **HAZ**

Health and Safety at Work Act /ˌhelθ ən ˌseɪfti ət 'wɜːk ækt/ *noun* in the UK, an Act of Parliament which rules how the health of workers should be protected by the companies they work for

Health and Safety Executive /ˌhelθ ən 'seɪfti ɪgˌzekjʊtɪv/ *noun* in the UK, a government organisation responsible for overseeing the health and safety of workers

health authority /helθ ɔː'θɒrəti/ *noun* ♦ **Strategic Health Authority**

healthcare /'helθkeə/, **health care** *noun* the general treatment of people with medical disorders, especially the use of measures to stop a disease from occurring

healthcare assistant /'helθkeər əˌsɪstənt/ *noun* someone who assists health professionals in looking after a sick or dependent person

healthcare delivery /'helθkeə dɪˌlɪv(ə)ri/ *noun* the provision of care and treatment by the health service

healthcare professional /'helθkeə prəˌfeʃ(ə)n(ə)l/ *noun* a qualified person who works in an occupation related to health care, e.g. a nurse

healthcare system /ˈhelθkeə ˌsɪstəm/ *noun* any organised set of health services

health centre /ˈhelθ ˌsentə/ *noun* a public building in which a group of doctors practise

health education /helθ ˌedjʊˈkeɪʃ(ə)n/ *noun* the process of teaching people, both school children and adults, to do things to improve their health, e.g. to take more exercise

Health Education Authority /ˌhelθ ˌedjʊˈkeɪʃ(ə)n ɔːˌθɒrɪti/ *noun* a government health promotion agency in England designed to help people make aware of how they can improve their health. Abbr **HEA**

health food /ˈhelθ fuːd/ *noun* food that is regarded as good for health, especially containing ingredients such as cereals, dried fruit and nuts and without additives

health inequality /helθ ˌɪnɪˈkwɒlɪti/ *noun* the differences that exist in health across the social classes, with poorer people tending to experience poorer health

health information service /ˌhelθ ˌɪnfəˈmeɪʃ(ə)n ˌsɜːvɪs/ *noun* a nation-wide information service delivered via a free telephone helpline. Abbr **HIS**

health insurance /ˈhelθ ɪnˌʃʊərəns/ *noun* insurance which pays the cost of treatment for illness

Health Ombudsman /ˈhelθ ˌɒmbʊdzmən/ *noun* same as **Health Service Commissioner**

'…the HA told the Health Ombudsman that nursing staff and students now received full training in the use of the nursing process' [*Nursing Times*]

health promotion /ˈhelθ prəˌməʊʃ(ə)n/ *noun* the act of improving the health of a particular community or of the public generally, e.g. using health education, immunisation and screening

Health Protection Agency /ˌhelθ prəˈtekʃ(ə)n ˌeɪdʒ(ə)nsi/ *noun* a national organisation for England and Wales, established in 2003, dedicated to the protection of people's health, especially by reducing the impact of infectious diseases, chemicals, poisons and radiation. It brings together existing sources of expertise in public health, communicable diseases, emergency planning, infection control, poisons and radiation hazards.

health service /ˈhelθ ˌsɜːvɪs/ *noun* an organisation which is in charge of providing health care to a particular community

Health Service Commissioner /ˌhelθ ˌsɜːvɪs kəˈmɪʃ(ə)nə/, **Health Service Ombudsman** /ˈhelθ ˌsɜːvɪs ˌɒmbʊdzmən/ *noun* in the UK, an official who investigates complaints from the public about the National Health Service

health service manager /ˌhelθ ˌsɜːvɪs ˈmænɪdʒə/ *noun* someone who is responsible for the provision of local health care, through the management of hospital, GP, and community health services

health service planning /ˌhelθ ˌsɜːvɪs ˈplænɪŋ/ *noun* the process of deciding what the health care needs of a community are, with the help of statistics, and what resources can be provided for that community

health visitor /ˈhelθ ˌvɪzɪtə/ *noun* a registered nurse with qualifications in midwifery or obstetrics and preventive medicine, who visits mothers and babies and sick people in their homes and advises on treatment

'…in the UK, the main screen is carried out by health visitors at 6–10 months' [*Lancet*]

healthy /ˈhelθi/ *adjective* **1.** in good physical condition **2.** helping you to stay in good physical condition ○ *People are healthier than they were fifty years ago.* ○ *This town is the healthiest place in England.* ○ *If you eat a healthy diet and take plenty of exercise there is no reason why you should fall ill.* (NOTE: **healthier – healthiest**)

hear /hɪə/ *verb* to sense sounds with the ears ○ *I can't hear what you're saying.* (NOTE: **hearing – heard**)

hearing /ˈhɪərɪŋ/ *noun* the ability to hear, or the function performed by the ear of sensing sounds and sending sound impulses to the brain ○ *His hearing is failing.* (NOTE: For other terms referring to hearing, see words beginning with **audi-, audio-**.)

hearing aid /ˈhɪərɪŋ eɪd/ *noun* a small electronic device fitted into or near the ear, to improve someone's hearing by making the sounds louder

hearing-impaired /ˌhɪərɪŋ ɪmˈpeəd/ *adjective* having a degree of hearing loss

hearing loss /ˈhɪərɪŋ lɒs/ *noun* partial or complete loss of the ability to hear

heart /hɑːt/ *noun* the main organ in the body, which maintains the circulation of the blood around the body by its pumping action ○ *The doctor listened to his heart.* ○ *She has heart trouble.* (NOTE: For other terms referring to the heart, see also words beginning with **cardi-, cardio-**.)

COMMENT: The heart is situated slightly to the left of the central part of the chest, between the lungs. It is divided into two parts by a vertical septum; each half is itself divided into an upper chamber (the atrium) and a lower chamber (the ventricle). The veins bring blood from the body into the right atrium; from there it passes into the right ventricle and is pumped into the pulmonary artery which takes it to the lungs. Oxygenated blood returns from the lungs to the left atrium, passes to the left ventricle and from there is pumped into the aorta for circulation round the arteries. The heart expands and contracts by the force of the heart muscle (the myocardium) under impulses from the sinoatrial node, and an average heart beats about 70 times a minute. The contracting beat as it pumps blood out (the systole) is followed by a weaker diastole, where the muscles relax to allow blood to flow back into the heart. In a heart attack, part of the myocardium is deprived of blood because of a clot in a coronary artery. This has an effect on the rhythm of the heartbeat and can be fatal. In heart block, impulses from the sinoatrial node fail to reach the ventricles properly.

heart attack /'hɑːt ə,tæk/ *noun* a condition in which the heart has a reduced blood supply because one of the arteries becomes blocked by a blood clot, causing myocardial ischaemia and myocardial infarction (*informal*)

heartbeat /'hɑːtbiːt/ *noun* the regular noise made by the heart as it pumps blood

heart block /'hɑːt blɒk/ *noun* the slowing of the action of the heart because the impulses from the sinoatrial node to the ventricles are delayed or interrupted. There are either longer impulses (first degree block) or missing impulses (second degree block) or no impulses at all (complete heart block), in which case the ventricles continue to beat slowly and independently of the sinoatrial node.

heartburn /'hɑːtbɜːn/ *noun* indigestion which causes a burning feeling in the stomach and oesophagus, and a flow of acid saliva into the mouth (*informal*)

heart bypass /,hɑːt 'baɪpɑːs/, **heart bypass operation** /,hɑːt 'baɪpɑːs ɒpə,reɪʃ(ə)n/ *noun* same as **coronary artery bypass graft**

heart disease /'hɑːt dɪ,ziːz/ *noun* any disease of the heart in general

heart failure /'hɑːt ,feɪljə/ *noun* the failure of the heart to maintain the output of blood to meet the demands of the body. It may affect the left or right sides of the heart, or both sides.
◊ **congestive heart failure**

heart-lung machine /hɑːt 'lʌŋ mə,ʃiːn/ *noun* a machine used to pump blood round the body and maintain the supply of oxygen to the blood during heart surgery

heart-lung transplant /hɑːt 'lʌŋ ,træns plɑːnt/ *noun* an operation to transplant a new heart and lungs into someone

heart massage /'hɑːt ,mæsɑːʒ/ *noun* a treatment which involves pressing on the chest to make a heart which has stopped beating start working again

heart murmur /'hɑːt ,mɜːmə/ *noun* an unusual sound made by turbulent blood flow, sometimes as a result of valve disease

heart rate /'hɑːt reɪt/ *noun* the number of times the heart beats per minute

heart sounds /'hɑːt saʊndz/ *plural noun* two different sounds made by the heart as it beats.
♦ **lubb-dupp**

heart stoppage /'hɑːt ,stɒpɪdʒ/ *noun* a situation where the heart has stopped beating

heart surgeon /'hɑːt ,sɜːdʒən/ *noun* a surgeon who specialises in operations on the heart

heart surgery /'hɑːt ,sɜːdʒəri/ *noun* a surgical operation to remedy a condition of the heart

heart tamponade /hɑːt tæmpə'neɪd/ *noun* same as **cardiac tamponade**

heart transplant /'hɑːt ,trænsplɑːnt/ *noun* a surgical operation to transplant a heart into someone

heat cramp /'hiːt kræmp/ *noun* cramp produced by loss of salt from the body in very hot conditions

heat exhaustion /'hiːt ɪg,zɔːstʃ(ə)n/ *noun* collapse caused by physical exertion in hot conditions, involving loss of salt and body fluids

heat rash /'hiːt ræʃ/ *noun* same as **miliaria**

heat spots /'hiːt spɒts/ *plural noun* little red spots which develop on the face in very hot weather

heatstroke /'hiːtstrəʊk/ *noun* a condition in which someone becomes too hot and his or her body temperature rises abnormally, leading to headaches, stomach cramps and sometimes loss of consciousness

heat therapy /'hiːt ,θerəpi/, **heat treatment** /'hiːt ,triːtmənt/ *noun* same as **thermotherapy**

heavy period /,hevi 'pɪəriəd/ *noun* a monthly period during which a woman loses an unusually large amount of blood. It is often painful and sometimes indicates possible health problems, such as fibroids or hypothyroidism.

hebephrenia /,hiːbɪ'friːniə/, **hebephrenic schizophrenia** /,hiːbɪfrenɪk skɪtsəʊ'friːniə/ *noun* a condition in which someone, usually an adolescent, has hallucinations, delusions and deterioration of personality, talks rapidly and generally acts in a strange manner

Heberden's node /,hiːbədənz 'nəʊd/ *noun* a small bony lump which develops on the end joints of fingers in osteoarthritis [Described 1802. After William Heberden (1767–1845), British physician, specialist in rheumatic diseases.]

hebetude /'hebɪtjuːd/ *noun* dullness of the senses during acute fever, which makes the person uninterested in his or her surroundings and unable to respond to stimuli

hectic /'hektɪk/ *adjective* recurring regularly

hectic fever /,hektɪk 'fiːvə/ *noun* an attack of fever which occurs each day in someone who has tuberculosis

heel /hiːl/ *noun* the back part of the foot

heel bone /'hiːl bəʊn/ *noun* the bone forming the heel, beneath the talus. Also called **calcaneus**

Hegar's sign /'heɪɡəz ,saɪn/ *noun* a way of detecting pregnancy, by inserting the fingers into the uterus and pressing with the other hand on the pelvic cavity to feel if the neck of the uterus has become soft [After Alfred Hegar (1830–1914), Professor of Obstetrics and Gynaecology at Freiburg, Germany]

Heimlich manoeuvre /'haɪmlɪk mə,nuːvə/ *noun* an emergency treatment for choking, in which a strong upward push beneath the breastbone of a patient clasped from behind forces the blockage out of the windpipe

helco- /'helkəʊ/ *prefix* relating to an ulcer

helcoplasty /'helkəʊplæsti/ *noun* a skin graft to cover an ulcer to aid healing

Helicobacter pylori /ˌhelɪkəʊbæktə paɪ 'lɔːriː/ *noun* a bacterium found in gastric secretions, strongly associated with duodenal ulcers and gastric carcinoma

helicopter-based emergency medical services /ˌhelɪkɒptə beɪst ɪˌmɜːdʒənsi 'medɪk(ə)l ˌsɜːvɪsɪz/ *plural noun* full form of **HEMS**

helio- /hiːliəʊ/ *prefix* relating to the sun

heliotherapy /ˌhiːliəʊ'θerəpi/ *noun* treatment by sunlight or sunbathing

helium /'hiːliəm/ *noun* a very light gas used in combination with oxygen, especially to relieve asthma or sickness caused by decompression (NOTE: The chemical symbol is **He**.)

helix /'hiːlɪks/ *noun* the curved outer edge of the ear

Heller's operation /'heləz ɒpəˌreɪʃ(ə)n/ *noun* same as **cardiomyotomy** [After E. Heller (1877–1964), German surgeon.]

Heller's test /'heləz test/ *noun* a test for protein in the urine [After Johann Florenz Heller (1813–71), Austrian physician]

Hellin's law /ˌhelɪnz 'lɔː/ *noun* a finding which states that twins should occur naturally once in 90 live births, triplets once in 8,100 live births, quadruplets once in 729, 000 live births, and quintuplets once in 65, 610, 000 live births (NOTE: Since the 1960s the numbers have changed due to fertility treatment. For example, twins now occur once in only 38 births.)

HELLP syndrome /'help ˌsɪndrəʊm/ *noun* a serious pre-eclamptic disorder which makes it necessary to terminate a pregnancy. Full form **haemolysis-elevated liver enzymes–low platelet count syndrome**

helminth /'helmɪnθ/ *noun* a parasitic worm, e.g. a tapeworm or fluke

helminthiasis /ˌhelmɪn'θaɪəsɪs/ *noun* infestation with parasitic worms

heloma /hɪ'ləʊmə/ *noun* same as **corn**

helper /'helpə/ *noun* a person who helps someone to do something, especially without payment

helper T-cell /ˌhelpə 'tiː sel/ *noun* a type of white blood cell that stimulates the production of cells that destroy antigens

hemeralopia /ˌhemərə'ləʊpiə/ *noun* a usually congenital condition in which someone is able to see better in bad light than in ordinary daylight. Also called **day blindness**

hemi- /hemi/ *prefix* half

hemianopia /ˌhemiə'nəʊpiə/ *noun* a state of partial blindness in which someone has only half the usual field of vision in each eye

hemiarthroplasty /ˌhemi'ɑːθrəʊplæsti/ *noun* an operation to repair a joint which replaces one of its surfaces with an artificial substance, often metal

hemiatrophy /ˌhemi'ætrəfi/ *noun* a condition in which half of the body or half of an organ or part is atrophied

hemiballismus /ˌhemibə'lɪzməs/ *noun* a sudden movement of the limbs on one side of the body, caused by a disease of the basal ganglia

hemicolectomy /ˌhemikə'lektəmi/ *noun* the surgical removal of part of the colon

hemicrania /ˌhemi'kreɪniə/ *noun* a headache in one side of the head, as in migraine

hemimelia /ˌhemi'miːliə/ *noun* a congenital condition in which someone has absent or extremely short arms or legs

hemiparesis /ˌhemipə'riːsɪs/ *noun* slight paralysis of the muscles of one side of the body

hemiplegia /ˌhemi'pliːdʒə/ *noun* severe paralysis affecting one side of the body due to damage of the central nervous system. Compare **diplegia**

hemiplegic /ˌhemi'pliːdʒɪk/ *adjective* referring to paralysis of one side of the body

hemisphere /'hemɪsfɪə/ *noun* half of a sphere

hemo- /hiːməʊ/ *prefix* US spelling of **haemo-**

HEMS /hemz/ *plural noun* a system of delivering a paramedic crew to the scene of an accident or medical emergency by helicopter and then transporting patients to the nearest major hospital or specialist unit. Full form **helicopter-based emergency medical services**

Henderson's model /'hendəs(ə)nz ˌmɒd(ə)l/ *noun* a model of nurse–patient relationships based on 14 basic principles of nursing. The main idea is that 'the nurse does for others what they would do for themselves if they had the strength, the will, and the knowledge…but that the nurse makes the patient independent of him or her as soon as possible'.

Henle's loop /ˌhenliːz 'luːp/ *noun* same as **loop of Henle** [Described 1862. After Friedrich Gustav Jakob Henle (1809–85), Professor of Anatomy at Göttingen, Germany.]

Henoch-Schönlein purpura /ˌhenək ˌʃɜːnlaɪn 'pɜːpjʊrə/, **Henoch's purpura** /ˌhenəks 'pɜːpjʊrə/ *noun* a condition in which blood vessels become inflamed and bleed into the skin, causing a rash called purpura and also pain in the stomach and the joints, vomiting and diarrhoea. It often occurs after an upper respiratory infection, mostly in children aged two to 11. [Described 1832 by Schönlein and 1865 by Henoch. Eduard Heinrich Henoch (1820–1910), Professor of Paedriatrics at Berlin, Germany; Johannes Lukas Schönlein (1793–1864), physician and pathologist at Würzburg, Zürich and Berlin.]

hep /hep/ *noun* same as **hepatitis** (*informal*)

heparin /'hepərɪn/ *noun* an anticoagulant substance found in the liver and lungs, and also produced artificially for use in the treatment of thrombosis

hepat- /hɪpæt/ *prefix* same as **hepato-** (*used before vowels*)

hepatalgia /ˌhepə'tældʒə/ *noun* pain in the liver

hepatectomy /ˌhepə'tektəmi/ *noun* the surgical removal of part of the liver

hepatic /hɪ'pætɪk/ *adjective* referring to the liver

hepatic artery /hɪ,pætɪk 'ɑːtəri/ *noun* an artery which takes the blood to the liver

hepatic cell /hɪ,pætɪk 'sel/ *noun* an epithelial cell of the liver acini

hepatic duct /hɪ,pætɪk 'dʌkt/ *noun* a duct which links the liver to the bile duct leading to the duodenum

hepatic flexure /hɪ,pætɪk 'flekʃə/ *noun* a bend in the colon, where the ascending and transverse colons join

hepaticostomy /hɪ,pætɪ'kɒstəmi/ *noun* a surgical operation to make an opening in the hepatic duct taking bile from the liver

hepatic portal system /hɪ,pætɪk 'pɔːt(ə)l ˌsɪstəm/ *noun* a group of veins linking to form the portal vein, which brings blood from the pancreas, spleen, gall bladder and the abdominal part of the alimentary canal to the liver

hepatic vein /hɪ,pætɪk 'veɪn/ *noun* a vein which takes blood from the liver to the inferior vena cava

hepatis /'hepətɪs/ ♦ **porta hepatis**

hepatitis /ˌhepə'taɪtɪs/ *noun* inflammation of the liver through disease or drugs

COMMENT: Infectious hepatitis and serum hepatitis are caused by different viruses called A and B, and having had one does not give immunity against an attack of the other. Hepatitis A is less serious than the B form, which can cause severe liver failure and death. Other hepatitis viruses have also been identified.

hepatitis A /ˌhepətaɪtɪs 'eɪ/ *noun* a relatively mild form of viral hepatitis that is transmitted through contaminated food and water

hepatitis A virus /ˌhepətaɪtɪs 'eɪ ˌvaɪrəs/ *noun* a virus which causes hepatitis A. Abbr **HAV**

hepatitis B /ˌhepətaɪtɪs 'biː/ *noun* a severe form of viral hepatitis that is transmitted by contact with infected blood or other body fluids

hepatitis B virus /ˌhepətaɪtɪs 'biː ˌvaɪrəs/ *noun* a virus which causes hepatitis B. Abbr **HBV**

hepatitis C *noun* a form of viral hepatitis that is transmitted by contact with infected blood or other body fluids but is often without symptoms (NOTE: It was formerly called non-A, non-B hepatitis.)

hepatitis C virus *noun* a virus which causes hepatitis C. Abbr **HCV**

hepatitis delta /ˌhepə,taɪtɪs 'deltə/ *noun* same as **delta hepatitis**

hepato- /hepətəʊ/ *prefix* referring to the liver

hepatoblastoma /ˌhepətəʊblæ'stəʊmə/ *noun* a malignant tumour in the liver, made up of epithelial-type cells often with areas of immature cartilage and embryonic bone

hepatocele /'hepətəʊsiːl/ *noun* a hernia of the liver through the diaphragm or the abdominal wall

hepatocellular /ˌhepətəʊ'seljʊlə/ *adjective* referring to liver cells

hepatocellular jaundice /ˌhepətəʊ ˌseljʊlə 'dʒɔːndɪs/ *noun* jaundice caused by injury to or disease of the liver cells

hepatocirrhosis /ˌhepətəʊsɪ'rəʊsɪs/ *noun* same as **cirrhosis**

hepatocolic ligament /ˌhepətəʊkɒlɪk 'lɪgəmənt/ *noun* a ligament which links the gall bladder and the right bend of the colon

hepatocyte /'hepətəʊsaɪt, hɪ'pætəsaɪt/ *noun* a liver cell which synthesises and stores substances, and produces bile

hepatogenous /ˌhepə'tɒdʒənəs/ *noun* referring to or originating in the liver ○ *hepatogenous jaundice*

hepatolenticular degeneration /ˌhepətəʊ len,tɪkjʊlə dɪ,dʒenə'reɪʃ(ə)n/ *noun* same as **Wilson's disease**

hepatoma /ˌhepə'təʊmə/ *noun* a malignant tumour of the liver formed of mature cells, especially found in people with cirrhosis

hepatomegaly /ˌhepətəʊ'megəli/ *noun* a condition in which the liver becomes very large

hepatosplenomegaly /ˌhepətəʊ,spliːnəʊ 'megəli/ *noun* enlargement of both the liver and the spleen, as occurs in leukaemia or lymphoma

hepatotoxic /ˌhepətəʊ'tɒksɪk/ *adjective* destroying the liver cells

herald patch /'herəld ˌpætʃ/ *noun* a small spot of a rash such as pityriasis rosea which appears some time before the main rash

herb /hɜːb/ *noun* a plant which can be used in preparing medicines

herbal /'hɜːb(ə)l/ *adjective* referring to plants which are used as medicines

herbalism /'hɜːbəlɪz(ə)m/ *noun* ♦ **herbal medicine**

herbalist /'hɜːbəlɪst/ *noun* a person who treats illnesses or disorders with substances extracted from plants

herbal medicine /ˌhɜːb(ə)l 'med(ə)sɪn/ *noun* a system of medical treatment involving the use of substances extracted from plants

herbal remedy /ˌhɜːb(ə)l 'remədi/ *noun* a medicine made from plants, e.g. an infusion made from dried leaves or flowers in hot water

herd immunity /'hɜːd ɪˌmjuːnɪti/ *noun* the fact of a group of people being resistant to a specific disease, because many individuals in the group are immune to or immunised against the microorganism which causes it

hereditary /hə'redɪt(ə)ri/ *adjective* passed as from parents to children through the genes

hereditary spherocytosis /həˌredɪt(ə)ri ˌsfɪərəʊsaɪ'təʊsɪs/ *noun* same as **acholuric jaundice**

heredity /hə'redɪti/ *noun* the process by which genetically controlled characteristics pass from parents to children

Hering-Breuer reflexes /ˌherɪŋ 'brɔɪə ˌriːfleksɪz/ *plural noun* the reflexes which maintain the usual rhythmic inflation and deflation of the lungs

hermaphrodite /hɜː'mæfrədaɪt/ *noun* a person with both male and female characteristics

hermaphroditism /hɜː'mæfrədaɪtɪz(ə)m/ *noun* a condition in which a person has both male and female characteristics

hernia /'hɜːniə/ *noun* a condition in which an organ bulges through a hole or weakness in the wall which surrounds it. Also called **rupture** □ **reduction of a hernia** putting a hernia back into the correct position

hernial /'hɜːniəl/ *adjective* referring to a hernia

hernial sac /ˌhɜːniəl 'sæk/ *noun* a sac formed where a membrane has pushed through a cavity in the body

herniated /'hɜːnieɪtɪd/ *adjective* referring to an organ which has developed a hernia

herniated disc /ˌhɜːnieɪtɪd 'dɪsk/ *noun* ♦ displaced intervertebral disc

herniation /ˌhɜːni'eɪʃ(ə)n/ *noun* the development of a hernia

hernio- /hɜːniəʊ/ *prefix* relating to a hernia

hernioplasty /'hɜːniəʊˌplæsti/ *noun* a surgical operation to reduce a hernia

herniorrhaphy /ˌhɜːni'ɔːrəfi/ *noun* a surgical operation to remove a hernia and repair the organ through which it protruded

herniotomy /ˌhɜːni'ɒtəmi/ *noun* a surgical operation to remove a hernial sac

heroin /'herəʊɪn/ *noun* a narcotic drug in the form of a white powder derived from morphine

herpangina /ˌhɜːpæn'dʒaɪnə/ *noun* an infectious disease of children, where the tonsils and back of the throat become inflamed and ulcerated, caused by a Coxsackie virus

herpes /'hɜːpiːz/ *noun* inflammation of the skin or mucous membrane, caused by a virus, where small blisters are formed

herpes simplex /ˌhɜːpiːz 'sɪmpleks/ *noun* **1.** (*Type I*) a virus that produces a painful blister, called a cold sore, usually on the lips **2.** (*Type II*) a sexually transmitted disease which

forms blisters in the genital region. Also called **genital herpes**

herpesvirus /'hɜːpiːzˌvaɪrəs/ *noun* one of a group of viruses which cause herpes and chickenpox (herpesvirus Type I), and genital herpes (herpesvirus Type II)

COMMENT: Because the same virus causes herpes and chickenpox, anyone who has had chickenpox as a child carries the dormant herpesvirus in his or her bloodstream and can develop shingles in later life. It is not known what triggers the development of shingles, though it is known that an adult suffering from shingles can infect a child with chickenpox.

herpes zoster /ˌhɜːpiːz 'zɒstə/ *noun* inflammation of a sensory nerve, characterised by pain along the nerve and causing a line of blisters to form on the skin, usually found mainly on the abdomen or back, or on the face. Also called **shingles, zona**

herpetic /hɜː'petɪk/ *adjective* referring to herpes

herpetiformis /hɜːˌpetɪ'fɔːmɪs/ ♦ **dermatitis herpetiformis**

hetero- /hetərəʊ/ *prefix* different

heterochromia /ˌhetərəʊ'krəʊmiə/ *noun* a condition in which the irises of the eyes are different colours

heterogametic /ˌhetərəʊgə'metɪk/ *adjective* producing gametes with different sex chromosomes, as in the human male

heterogeneous /ˌhetərəʊ'dʒiːniəs/ *adjective* having different characteristics or qualities (NOTE: Do not confuse with **heterogenous**.)

heterogenous /ˌhetə'rɒdʒɪnəs/ *adjective* coming from a different source (NOTE: Do not confuse with **heterogeneous**.)

heterograft /'hetərəʊgrɑːft/ *noun* tissue taken from one species and grafted onto an individual of another species. Compare **homograft**

heterologous /hetə'rɒləgʌs/ *adjective* of a different type

heterophoria /ˌhetərəʊ'fɔːriə/ *noun* a condition in which if an eye is covered it tends to squint

heteroplasty /'hetərəʊplæsti/ *noun* same as **heterograft**

heteropsia /ˌhetə'rɒpsiə/ *noun* a condition in which the two eyes see differently

heterosexual /ˌhetərəʊ'sekʃuəl/ *adjective* attracted to people of the opposite sex or relating to relations between males and females ■ *noun* a person who is sexually attracted to people of the opposite sex. Compare **bisexual, homosexual**

heterosexuality /ˌhetərəʊsekʃu'ælɪti/ *noun* sexual attraction towards persons of the opposite sex

heterotopia /ˌhetərəʊ'təʊpiə/ *noun* **1.** a state where an organ is placed in a different position from usual or is malformed or deformed

2. the development of tissue which is not natural to the part in which it is produced

heterotropia /ˌhetərəʊ'trəʊpiə/ *noun* same as **strabismus**

heterozygous /ˌhetərəʊ'zaɪgəs/ *adjective* having two or more different versions of a specific gene. Compare **homozygous**

hex- /heks/ *prefix* same as **hexa-** (NOTE: used before vowels)

hexa- /heksə/ *prefix* six

HFEA *abbr* Human Fertilization and Embryology Authority

hGH *abbr* human growth hormone

HGPRT *abbr* hypoxanthine guanine phosphoribosyl transferase. ✦ **HPRT**

HI *abbr* hearing-impaired

hiatus /haɪ'eɪtəs/ *noun* an opening or space

hiatus hernia /haɪˌeɪtəs 'hɜːniə/, **hiatal hernia** /haɪˌeɪt(ə)l 'hɜːniə/ *noun* a hernia where the stomach bulges through the opening in the diaphragm muscle through which the oesophagus passes

Hib /hɪb/ *abbr Haemophilus influenzae* type B

Hib vaccine /'hɪb ˌvæksiːn/ *noun* a vaccine used to inoculate against the bacterium *Haemophilius influenzae* that causes meningitis

hiccup /'hɪkʌp/, **hiccough** *noun* a spasm in the diaphragm which causes a sudden inhalation of breath followed by sudden closure of the glottis which makes a characteristic sound ○ *She had an attack of hiccups* or *had a hiccupping attack* or *got the hiccups.* Also called **singultus** ■ *verb* to make a hiccup

COMMENT: Many cures have been suggested for hiccups, but the main treatment is to try to get the patient to think about something else. A drink of water, holding the breath and counting, breathing into a paper bag, are all recommended.

Hickman catheter /ˌhɪkmən 'kæθɪtə/, **Hickman line** /ˌhɪkmən 'laɪn/ *noun* a plastic tube which is put into the large vein above the heart so that drugs can be given and blood samples can be taken easily

hidr- /haɪdr/ *prefix* referring to sweat

hidradenitis /ˌhaɪdrədə'naɪtɪs/ *noun* inflammation of the sweat glands

hidrosis /haɪ'drəʊsɪs/ *noun* sweating, especially when it is excessive

hidrotic /haɪ'drɒtɪk/ *adjective* referring to sweating ■ *noun* a substance which makes someone sweat

Higginson's syringe /'hɪgɪnsənz sɪˌrɪnʒ/ *noun* a syringe with a rubber bulb in the centre that allows flow in one direction only, used mainly to give enemas [After Alfred Higginson (1808–84), British surgeon]

high-altitude sickness /haɪ 'æltɪtjuːd ˌsɪknəs/ *noun* same as **altitude sickness**

high blood pressure /ˌhaɪ 'blʌd ˌpreʃə/ *noun* same as **hypertension**

high-calorie diet /haɪ ˌkæləri 'daɪət/ *noun* a diet containing over 4000 calories per day

high-density lipoprotein /haɪ ˌdensɪti lɪpəʊ'prəʊtɪn/ *noun* a lipoprotein with a low percentage of cholesterol. Abbr **HDL**

high-energy food /ˌhaɪ ˌenədʒi 'fuːd/ *noun* food such as fats or carbohydrates which contain a large number of calories and give a lot of energy when they are broken down in the body

high-fibre diet /haɪ ˌfaɪbə 'daɪət/ *noun* a diet which contains a high percentage of cereals, nuts, fruit and vegetables

high-protein diet /haɪ ˌprəʊtiːn 'daɪət/ *noun* a diet containing mostly foods high in protein and low in carbohydrates and saturated fat, adopted by people who are trying to lose weight

high-risk /ˌhaɪ 'rɪsk/ *adjective* referring to someone who is very likely to catch or develop a disease, develop a cancer or have an accident

high-risk patient /ˌhaɪ rɪsk 'peɪʃ(ə)nt/ *noun* a patient who has a high risk of catching an infection or developing a disease

hilar /'haɪlə/ *adjective* referring to a hilum

hilum /'haɪləm/ *noun* a hollow where blood vessels or nerve fibres enter an organ such as a kidney or lung (NOTE: The plural is **hila**.)

hindbrain /'haɪndbreɪn/ *noun* the part of brain of an embryo from which the medulla oblongata, the pons and the cerebellum eventually develop

hindgut /'haɪndgʌt/ *noun* part of an embryo which develops into the colon and rectum

hinge joint /'hɪndʒ dʒɔɪnt/ *noun* same as **ginglymus**

hip /hɪp/ *noun* a ball and socket joint where the thigh bone or femur joins the acetabulum of the hip bone

hip bone /'hɪp bəʊn/ *noun* a bone made of the ilium, the ischium and the pubis which are fused together, forming part of the pelvic girdle. Also called **innominate bone**

hip fracture /'hɪp ˌfræktʃə/ *noun* a fracture of the ball at the top of the femur

hip girdle /'hɪp ˌɡɜːd(ə)l/ *noun* same as **pelvic girdle**

hip joint /'hɪp dʒɔɪnt/ *noun* the place where the hip is joined to the upper leg. See illustration at PELVIS in Supplement

Hippel-Lindau /ˌhɪpəl 'lɪndaʊ/ ✦ **von Hippel-Lindau syndrome**

hippocampal formation /ˌhɪpəkæmp(ə)l fɔː'meɪʃ(ə)n/ *noun* curved pieces of cortex inside each part of the cerebrum

hippocampus /ˌhɪpəʊ'kæmpəs/ *noun* a long rounded elevation projecting into the lateral ventricle in the brain

Hippocratic oath /ˌhɪpəkrætɪk 'əʊθ/ *noun* an ethical code observed by doctors, by which they will treat patients equally, put patients'

welfare first and not discuss openly the details of a patient's case

hippus /'hɪpəs/ *noun* alternating rapid contraction and dilatation of the pupil of the eye

hip replacement /'hɪp rɪ,pleɪsmənt/ *noun* a surgical operation to replace the whole ball and socket joint at the hip with an artificial one

Hirschsprung's disease /'hɪəʃsprʌŋz dɪ ,ziːz/ *noun* a congenital condition where parts of the lower colon lack nerve cells, making peristalsis impossible, so that food accumulates in the upper colon which becomes swollen [Described 1888. After Harald Hirschsprung (1830–1916), Professor of Paediatrics in Copenhagen, Denmark.]

hirsute /'hɜːsjuːt/ *adjective* with a lot of hair

hirsutism /'hɜːsjuːtɪz(ə)m/ *noun* the condition of having excessive hair, especially a condition in which a woman grows hair on the body in the same way as a man

hirudin /hɪ'ruːdɪn/ *noun* an anticoagulant substance produced by leeches, which is injected into the bloodstream while the leech is feeding on a body

HIS *abbr* Health Information Service

hist- /hɪst/ same as **histo-** (NOTE: used before vowels)

histamine /'hɪstəmiːn/ *noun* a substance released in response to allergens from mast cells throughout the body. Histamines dilate blood vessels, constrict the cells of smooth muscles and cause an increase in acid secretions in the stomach.

histamine headache /'hɪstəmiːn ,hedeɪk/ *noun* ♦ Horton's syndrome

histamine receptor /'hɪstəmiːn rɪ,septə/ *noun* a cell which is stimulated by histamine. H1 receptors in blood vessels are involved in allergic reactions, H2 receptors in the stomach are involved in gastric acid secretion.

histamine test /'hɪstəmiːn test/ *noun* a test to determine the acidity of gastric juice

histaminic /,hɪstə'mɪnɪk/ *adjective* referring to histamines

histaminic headache /,hɪstəmɪnɪk 'hedeɪk/ *noun* ♦ Horton's syndrome

histidine /'hɪstədiːn/ *noun* an amino acid from which histamine is derived

histiocyte /'hɪstɪəʊsaɪt/ *noun* a macrophage of the connective tissue, involved in tissue defence

histiocytoma /,hɪstɪəʊsaɪ'təʊmə/ *noun* a tumour containing histiocytes

histiocytosis /hɪstɪəʊsaɪ'təʊsɪs/ *noun* a condition in which histiocytes are present in the blood

histiocytosis X /,hɪstɪəʊsaɪ,təʊsɪs 'eks/ *noun* any form of histiocytosis where the cause is not known, e.g. Hand-Schüller-Christian disease

histo- /hɪstəʊ/ *prefix* relating to the body's tissue ○ *histology*

histochemistry /,hɪstəʊ'kemɪstri/ *noun* the study of the chemical constituents of cells and tissues and also their function and distribution, using a light or electron microscope to evaluate the stains

histocompatibility /,hɪstəʊkəmpætə'bɪlɪ ti/ *noun* compatibility between the antigens of tissues from two individuals, important in transplants

histocompatible /,hɪstəʊkəm'pætɪb(ə)l/ *adjective* referring to tissues from two individuals which have compatible antigens

histogenesis /,hɪstəʊ'dʒenəsɪs/ *noun* the formation and development of tissue from the embryological germ layer

histogram /'hɪstəgræm/ *noun* a way of displaying frequency values as columns whose height is proportional to the corresponding frequency ○ *a histogram showing numbers of patients with the condition in each age group*

histoid /'hɪstɔɪd/ *adjective* **1.** made of or developed from a particular tissue **2.** like standard tissue

histological /,hɪstə'lɒdʒɪk(ə)l/ *adjective* referring to histology

histological grade /,hɪstəlɒdʒɪk(ə)l 'greɪd/ *noun* a system of classifying tumours according to how malignant they are

histology /hɪ'stɒlədʒi/ *noun* the study of the anatomy of tissue cells and minute cellular structure

histolysis /hɪ'stɒləsɪs/ *noun* the disintegration of tissue

histolytica /,hɪstə'lɪtɪkə/ ♦ Entamoeba histolytica

histoplasmosis /,hɪstəʊplæz'məʊsɪs/ *noun* a lung disease caused by infection with the fungus *Histoplasma*

history /'hɪst(ə)ri/ *noun* the background information on someone's illness. ◊ **case history, medical history** □ **to take a patient's history** to ask someone to tell what has happened to them in their own words on being admitted to hospital

'…these children gave a typical history of exercise-induced asthma' [*Lancet*]

'…the need for evaluation of patients with a history of severe heart disease' [*Southern Medical Journal*]

histotoxic /,hɪstəʊ'tɒksɪk/ *adjective* referring to a substance which is poisonous to tissue

HIV *abbr* human immunodeficiency virus

'HIV-associated dementia is characterized by psychomotor slowing and inattentiveness' [*British Journal of Nursing*]

COMMENT: HIV is the virus which causes AIDS. Three strains of HIV virus have been identified: HIV-1, HIV-2 and HIV-3.

hives /haɪvz/ *noun* same as **urticaria** (NOTE: Takes a singular verb.)

HIV-negative /ˌeɪt ʃ aɪ ˌviː 'negətɪv/ *adjective* referring to someone who has been tested and shown not to have HIV

HIV-positive /ˌeɪt ʃ aɪ ˌviː 'pɒzɪtɪv/ *adjective* referring to someone who has been tested and shown to have HIV

HLA *abbr* human leucocyte antigen

HLA system /ˌeɪt ʃ el 'eɪ ˌsɪstəm/ *noun* a system of HLA antigens on the surface of cells which need to be histocompatible to allow transplants to take place

COMMENT: HLA-A is the most important of the antigens responsible for rejection of transplants.

HMO *abbr US* Health Maintenance Organization

hoarse /hɔːs/ *adjective* referring to a voice which is harsh and rough

hoarseness /'hɔːsnəs/ *noun* a harsh and rough sound of the voice, often caused by laryngitis

hobnail liver /ˌhɒbneɪl 'lɪvə/ *noun* same as **atrophic cirrhosis**

Hodgkin's disease /'hɒdʒkɪnz dɪˌziːz/ *noun* a malignant disease in which the lymph glands are enlarged and there is an increase in the lymphoid tissues in the liver, spleen and bone marrow. It is frequently fatal if not treated early. [Described 1832. After Thomas Hodgkin (1798–1866), British physician.]

hoist /hɔɪst/ *noun* a device with pulleys and wires for raising a bed or a patient

hole in the heart /ˌhəʊl ɪn ðə 'hɑːt/ *noun* same as **septal defect** (*informal*)

Holger-Nielsen method /ˌhɒlgə 'nɪlsən ˌmeθəd/ *noun* a formerly used method of giving artificial respiration by pressing a person's back and raising their arms backwards

holism /'həʊlɪz(ə)m/ *noun* the theory that all of a person's physical, mental and social conditions should be considered in the treatment of his or her illness

holistic /həʊ'lɪstɪk/ *adjective* referring to a method of treatment involving all of someone's mental and family circumstances rather than just dealing with the condition from which he or she is suffering

holistic care /həʊˌlɪstɪk 'keə/ *noun* the care and treatment of a whole person rather than just of his or her medical symptoms

holo- /hɒləʊ/ *prefix* entire, complete

holocrine /'hɒləkrɪn/ *adjective* referring to a gland where the secretions are made up of disintegrated cells of the gland itself

Homans' sign /'həʊmənz saɪn/ *noun* pain in the calf when the foot is bent back, a sign of deep-vein thrombosis [Described 1941. After John Homans (1877–1954), Professor of Clinical Surgery at Harvard, USA.]

homeo- /həʊmiəʊ/ *prefix* like or similar

homeopathic /ˌhəʊmiə'pæθɪk/, **homeopathic** /həʊmiə'pæθɪk/ *adjective* **1.** referring to homeopathy ○ *a homeopathic clinic* ○ *She is having a course of homeopathic treatment.* **2.** referring to a drug which is given in very small quantities

homeopathist /ˌhəʊmi'ɒpəθɪst/, **homeopathist** /həʊmi'ɒpəθɪst/ *noun* a person who practises homeopathy

homeopathy /ˌhəʊmi'ɒpəθi/, **homoeopathy** /həʊmi'ɒpəθi/ *noun* the treatment of a condition by giving the person very small quantities of a substance which, when given to a healthy person, would cause symptoms like those of the condition being treated. Compare **allopathy**

homeostasis /ˌhəʊmiəʊ'steɪsɪs/ *noun* the process by which the functions and chemistry of a cell or internal organ are kept stable, even when external conditions vary greatly

homo- /həʊməʊ/ *prefix* the same

homoeo- /həʊmiəʊ/ *prefix* another spelling of **homeo-** (*used before vowels*)

homogenise /hə'mɒdʒənaɪz/, **homogenize** *verb* to give something a uniform nature

homograft /'hɒməɡrɑːft/ *noun* the graft of an organ or tissue from a donor to a recipient of the same species, e.g. from one person to another. Also called **allograft**. Compare **heterograft**

homolateral /ˌhɒmə'læt(ə)rəl/ *adjective* same as **ipsilateral**

homologous /hɒ'mɒləgəs/ *adjective* **1.** of the same type **2.** referring to chromosomes which form a pair

homonymous /hə'mɒnɪməs/ *adjective* affecting the two eyes in the same way

homonymous hemianopia /həˌmɒnɪməs hemiə'nəʊpiə/ *noun* a condition in which the same half of the field of vision is lost in each eye

homoplasty /'həʊməʊplæsti/ *noun* surgery to replace lost tissues by grafting similar tissues from another person

homosexual /ˌhəʊməʊ'sekʃuəl/ *adjective* referring to homosexuality ■ *noun* a person who is sexually attracted to people of the same sex. Compare **bisexual, heterosexual** (NOTE: Although **homosexual** can apply to both males and females, it is commonly used for males only, and **lesbian** is used for females.)

homosexuality /ˌhəʊməʊsekʃu'ælɪti/ *noun* sexual attraction to people of the same sex or sexual relations with people of the same sex

homozygous /ˌhəʊməʊ'zaɪgəs/ *adjective* having two identical versions of a specific gene. Compare **heterozygous**

hook /hʊk/ *noun* a surgical instrument with a bent end used for holding structures apart in operations

hookworm /'hʊkwɜːm/ *noun* a parasitic worm

hookworm disease /'hʊkwɜːm dɪˌziːz/ *noun* ♦ ancylostomiasis

hordeolum /hɔːˈdiːələm/ *noun* an infection of the gland at the base of an eyelash. Also called **stye**

horizontal /ˌhɒrɪˈzɒnt(ə)l/ *adjective* lying flat or at a right angle to the vertical

horizontal fissure /ˌhɒrɪˌzɒnt(ə)l 'fɪʃə/ *noun* ANAT a horizontal groove between the superior and middle lobes of a lung. See illustration at **LUNGS** in Supplement

horizontal plane /ˌhɒrɪzɒnt(ə)l 'pleɪn/ *adjective* same as **transverse plane**. see illustration at **ANATOMICAL TERMS** in Supplement

hormonal /hɔːˈməʊn(ə)l/ *adjective* referring to hormones

hormone /'hɔːməʊn/ *noun* a substance which is produced by one part of the body, especially the endocrine glands and is carried to another part of the body by the bloodstream where it has particular effects or functions

hormone replacement therapy /ˌhɔːməʊn rɪˈpleɪsmənt ˌθerəpi/, **hormone therapy** /'hɔːməʊn ˌθerəpi/ *noun* **1.** treatment for someone whose endocrine glands have been removed **2.** treatment to relieve the symptoms of the menopause by supplying oestrogen and reducing the risk of osteoporosis ▶ Abbr **HRT**

horn /hɔːn/ *noun* **1.** (*in humans*) tissue which grows out of an organ **2.** (*in humans*) one of the H-shaped limbs of grey matter seen in a cross-section of the spinal cord **3.** (*in humans*) an extension of the pulp chamber of a tooth towards the cusp

Horner's syndrome /'hɔːnəz ˌsɪndrəʊm/ *noun* a condition caused by paralysis of the sympathetic nerve in one side of the neck, making the eyelids hang down and the pupils contract [Described 1869. After Johann Friedrich Horner (1831–86), Professor of Ophthalmology in Zürich, Switzerland.]

horny /'hɔːni/ *adjective* referring to skin which is very hard (NOTE: For terms referring to horny tissue, see words beginning with **kerat-**, **kerato-**.)

horseshoe kidney /ˌhɔːsʃuː 'kɪdni/ *noun* a congenital condition of the kidney, where sometimes the upper but usually the lower parts of both kidneys are joined together

Horton's syndrome /'hɔːt(ə)nz ˌsɪn drəʊm/ *noun* a severe headache, often with constant pain around one eye, which starts usually within a few hours of going to sleep. It is caused by the release of histamine in the body. [After Bayard Taylor Horton (b. 1895), US physician]

hose /həʊz/ *noun* **1.** a long rubber or plastic tube **2.** ♦ support hose

hospice /'hɒspɪs/ *noun* a hospital which offers palliative care for terminally ill people

hospital /'hɒspɪt(ə)l/ *noun* a place where sick or injured people are looked after ◇ **hospital bed 1.** a special type of bed used in hospitals, usually adjustable in many ways for the comfort of the patient ○ *A hospital bed is needed if the patient has to have traction.* **2.** a place in a hospital which can be occupied by a patient ○ *There will be no reduction in the number of hospital beds.*

hospital-acquired infection /ˌhɒspɪt(ə)l ə ˌkwaɪəd ɪnˈfekʃən/ *noun* a disease caught during a stay in hospital

Hospital Activity Analysis /ˌhɒspɪt(ə)l ækˈtɪvɪti əˌnæləsɪs/ *noun* a regular detailed report on patients in hospitals, including information about treatment, length of stay and outcome

hospital care /'hɒspɪt(ə)l keə/ *noun* treatment in a hospital

hospital chaplain /ˌhɒspɪt(ə)l 'tʃæplɪn/ *noun* a religious minister attached to a hospital, who visits and comforts patients and their families and gives them the sacraments if necessary

hospital corner /ˌhɒspɪt(ə)l 'kɔːnə/ *noun* a way of folding the overlapping bedding at each corner of a bed that keeps it tight

hospital doctor /ˌhɒspɪt(ə)l 'dɒktə/ *noun* a doctor who works only in a hospital and does not receive people in his or her own surgery

hospital gangrene /ˌhɒspɪt(ə)l 'ɡæŋɡriːn/ *noun* gangrene caused by insanitary hospital conditions

hospital infection /'hɒspɪt(ə)l ɪnˌfekʃən/ *noun* an infection which someone gets during a hospital visit, or one which develops among hospital staff

COMMENT: Hospital infection is an increasingly common problem due to growing antimicrobial resistance and inappropriate antibiotic use. Strains of bacteria such as MRSA have evolved which seem to be more easily transmitted between patients and are difficult to treat.

hospitalisation /ˌhɒspɪt(ə)laɪˈzeɪʃ(ə)n/, **hospitalization** *noun* the act of sending someone to hospital ○ *The doctor recommended immediate hospitalisation.*

hospitalise /'hɒspɪt(ə)laɪz/, **hospitalize** *verb* to send someone to hospital ○ *He is so ill that he has had to be hospitalised.*

hospital orderly /ˌhɒspɪt(ə)l 'ɔːdəli/ *noun* a person who does heavy work in a hospital, such as wheeling patients into the operating theatre or moving equipment about

hospital trust /'hɒspɪt(ə)l trʌst/ *noun* same as **self-governing hospital**

host /həʊst/ *noun* a person or animal on which a parasite lives

hot /hɒt/ *adjective* very warm or having a high temperature

hot flush /ˌhɒt ˈflʌʃ/ *noun* a condition in menopausal women, in which the woman becomes hot and sweats, and which is often accompanied by redness of the skin

hotpack /ˈhɒtpæk/ *noun* a cloth bag or a pad filled with gel or grains which can be heated and applied to the skin to relieve pain or stiffness

hot wax treatment /ˌhɒt ˈwæks ˌtriːtmənt/ *noun* a treatment for arthritis in which the joints are painted with hot liquid wax

hourglass contraction /ˈaʊəɡlɑːs kən ˌtrækʃən/ *noun* a condition in which an organ such as the stomach is constricted in the centre

hourglass stomach /ˈaʊəɡlɑːs ˌstʌmək/ *noun* a condition in which the wall of the stomach is pulled in so that it is divided into two cavities, cardiac and pyloric

hourly /ˈaʊəli/ *adjective, adverb* happening every hour

houseman /ˈhaʊsmən/ *noun* same as **house officer**

house mite /haʊs maɪt/, **house dust mite** /ˈhaʊs dʌst ˌmaɪt/ *noun* a tiny insect living mainly in bedding and soft furnishings, that can cause an allergic reaction

house officer /ˈhaʊs ˌɒfɪsə/ *noun* a doctor who works in a hospital as a house surgeon or house physician during the final year of training before registration by the General Medical Council (NOTE: The US term is **intern**.)

HPRT *noun* an enzyme that is lacking in children, usually boys, who have Lesch-Nyhan disease. Full form **hypoxanthine phosphoribosyl transferase**. Also called **HGPRT** (hypoxanthine guanine phosphoribosyl transferase)

HPV *abbr* human papillomavirus

HRT *abbr* hormone replacement therapy

Huhner's test /ˈhuːnəz ˌtest/ *noun* a test carried out several hours after sexual intercourse to determine the number and motility of spermatozoa [After Max Huhner (1873–1947), US urologist]

human /ˈhjuːmən/ *adjective* referring to any man, woman or child ■ *noun* a person ○ *Most animals are afraid of humans.*

human anatomy /ˌhjuːmən əˈnætəmi/ *noun* the structure, shape and functions of the human body

human being /ˌhjuːmən ˈbiːɪŋ/ *noun* a person

human chorionic gonadotrophin /ˌhjuːmən kɔːriˌɒnɪk ˌɡəʊnədəˈtrəʊfɪn/ *noun* a hormone produced by the placenta, which suppresses the mother's usual menstrual cycle during pregnancy. It is found in the urine during pregnancy, and can be given by

injection to encourage ovulation and help a woman to become pregnant. Abbr **hCG**

human crutch /ˌhjuːmən ˈkrʌtʃ/ *noun* a method of helping an injured person to walk, where they rest one arm over the shoulders of the person helping

human immunodeficiency virus /ˌhjuːmən ˌɪmjʊnəʊdɪˈfɪʃ(ə)nsi ˌvaɪrəs/ *noun* a virus which causes AIDS. Abbr **HIV**

human leucocyte antigen /ˌhjuːmən ˈluːkəsaɪt ˌæntɪdʒ(ə)n/ *noun* any of the system of antigens on the surface of cells which need to be histocompatible to allow transplants to take place. Abbr **HLA**. ♦ **HLA system**

human nature /ˌhjuːmən ˈneɪtʃə/ *noun* the general behavioural characteristics of human beings

human papillomavirus /ˌhjuːmən pæpɪ ˈləʊmə ˌvaɪrəs/ *noun* a virus that causes genital warts in humans. Abbr **HPV**

humectant /hjuːˈmektənt/ *adjective* able to absorb or retain moisture ■ *noun* a substance that can absorb or retain moisture, e.g. a skin lotion

humeroulnar joint /ˌhjuːmərəʊˈʌlnə dʒɔɪnt/ *noun* part of the elbow joint, where the trochlea of the humerus and the trochlear notch of the ulna move next to each other

humerus /ˈhjuːmərəs/ *noun* the top bone in the arm, running from the shoulder to the elbow (NOTE: The plural is **humeri**.)

humid /ˈhjuːmɪd/ *adjective* damp, containing moisture vapour

humoral /ˈhjuːmərəl/ *adjective* relating to human body fluids, in particular blood serum

humour /ˈhjuːmə/, **humor** *noun* a fluid in the body

hunchback /ˈhʌntʃbæk/ *noun* ♦ **kyphosis**

hunger /ˈhʌŋɡə/ *noun* a need to eat

hunger pains /ˈhʌŋɡə peɪnz/ *plural noun* pains in the abdomen when a person feels hungry, sometimes a sign of a duodenal ulcer

Hunter's syndrome /ˈhʌntəz ˌsɪndrəʊm/ *noun* an inherited disorder caused by an enzyme deficiency, which leads to learning difficulties

Huntington's chorea /ˌhʌntɪŋtənz kɔː ˈriːə/ *noun* a progressive hereditary disease which affects adults, where the outer layer of the brain degenerates and the person makes involuntary jerky movements and develops progressive dementia [Described 1872. After George Sumner Huntington (1850–1916), US physician.]

Hurler's syndrome /ˈhɜːləz ˌsɪndrəʊm/ *noun* same as **gargoylism** [Described 1920. After Gertrud Hurler, German paediatrician.]

hurt /hɜːt/ *noun* 1. emotional pain 2. a painful area (*used by children*) ○ *She has a hurt on her knee.* ■ *verb* 1. to have pain ○ *He's hurt his hand.* 2. to cause someone pain ○ *His arm is* *hurting so much he can't write.* ○ *She fell down and hurt herself.* (NOTE: **hurting – hurt**) ■ *adjective* **1.** feeling physical pain ○ *He was slightly hurt in the car crash.* ○ *Two players got hurt in the football game.* **2.** feeling emotional pain ○ *Her parents' divorce hurt her deeply.*

husky /ˈhʌski/ *adjective* slightly hoarse

Hutchinson's tooth /ˈhʌtʃɪnsənz ˌtuːθ/ *noun* a narrow upper incisor tooth, with notches along the cutting edge, a symptom of congenital syphilis but also occurring naturally (NOTE: The plural is **Hutchinson's teeth**.) [After Sir Jonathan Hutchinson (1828–1913), British surgeon]

hyal- /haɪəl/ *prefix* like glass (*used before vowels*)

hyalin /ˈhaɪəlɪn/ *noun* a transparent substance produced from collagen and deposited around blood vessels and scars when some tissues degenerate

hyaline /ˈhaɪəlɪn/ *adjective* nearly transparent like glass

hyaline cartilage /ˌhaɪəlɪn ˈkɑːtɪlɪdʒ/ *noun* a type of cartilage found in the nose, larynx and joints. It forms most of the skeleton of the fetus. See illustration at CARTILAGINOUS JOINT in Supplement

hyaline membrane disease /ˌhaɪəlɪn ˈmembreɪn dɪˌziːz/ *noun* same as **respiratory distress syndrome**

hyalitis /ˌhaɪəˈlaɪtɪs/ *noun* inflammation of the vitreous humour or the hyaloid membrane in the eye. Also called **vitritis**

hyaloid membrane /ˈhaɪəlɔɪd ˌmembreɪn/ *noun* a transparent membrane round the vitreous humour in the eye

hyaluronic acid /ˌhaɪəlʊrɒnɪk ˈæsɪd/ *noun* a substance which binds connective tissue and is found in the eyes

hyaluronidase /ˌhaɪəlʊˈrɒnɪdeɪz/ *noun* an enzyme which destroys hyaluronic acid

hybrid /ˈhaɪbrɪd/ *noun* an organism that is a result of a cross between individuals that are not genetically the same as each other

HYCOSY *abbr* hysterosalpingo-contrast sonography

hydatid /ˈhaɪdətɪd/ *noun* any cyst-like structure

hydatid cyst /ˌhaɪdətɪd ˈsɪst/ *noun* the larval form of the tapeworms of the genus *Echinococcus*

hydatid disease /ˈhaɪdətɪd dɪˌziːz/, **hydatidosis** /ˌhaɪdətɪˈdəʊsɪs/ *noun* an infection, usually in the lungs or liver, caused by expanding hydatid cysts that destroy the tissues of the infected organ

hydatid mole /ˌhaɪdətɪd ˈməʊl/ *noun* an abnormal pregnancy from a pathologic ovum, resulting in a mass of cysts shaped like a bunch of grapes

hydr- /haɪdr/ *prefix* same as **hydro-** (*used before vowels*)

hydraemia /haɪˈdriːmiə/ *noun* an excess of water in the blood

hydragogue /ˈhaɪdrəgɒg/ *noun* a laxative or substance which produces watery faeces

hydralazine /haɪˈdræləziːn/ *noun* a drug that lowers blood pressure. People usually receive it in combination with other drugs that increase the output of urine.

hydramnios /haɪˈdræmnɪɒs/ *noun* an unusually large amount of amniotic fluid surrounding the fetus

hydrarthrosis /ˌhaɪdrɑːˈθrəʊsɪs/ *noun* swelling caused by excess synovial liquid at a joint

hydrate /ˈhaɪdreɪt/ *verb* to give water to someone so as to re-establish or maintain fluid balance ■ *noun* a chemical compound containing water molecules that can usually be driven off by heat without altering the compound's structure

hydro- /haɪdrəʊ/ *prefix* referring to water

hydroa /haɪˈdrəʊə/ *noun* an eruption of small itchy blisters, e.g. those caused by sunlight

hydrocalycosis /ˌhaɪdrəʊˌkælɪˈkəʊsɪs/ *noun* same as **caliectasis**

hydrocele /ˈhaɪdrəʊsiːl/ *noun* the collection of watery liquid found in a cavity such as the scrotum

hydrocephalus /ˌhaɪdrəʊˈkefələs/ *noun* an excessive quantity of cerebrospinal fluid in the brain

hydrochloric acid /haɪdrəʊˈklɒrɪk ˈæsɪd/ *noun* an acid found in the gastric juices which helps to break apart the food

hydrocolloid strip /ˌhaɪdrəʊkɒlɔɪd ˈstrɪp/ *noun* a waterproof gel dressing that seals a wound, retaining moisture and preventing access to germs and dirt

hydrocolpos /ˌhaɪdrəʊˈkɒlpəs/ *noun* a cyst in the vagina containing clear fluid

hydrocortisone /ˌhaɪdrəʊˈkɔːtɪzəʊn/ *noun* a steroid hormone secreted by the adrenal cortex or produced synthetically, used in the treatment of rheumatoid arthritis and inflammatory and allergic conditions

hydrocyanic acid /ˌhaɪdrəʊsaɪænɪk ˈæsɪd/ *noun* an acid which forms cyanide. Abbr **HCN**

hydrogen /ˈhaɪdrədʒən/ *noun* a chemical element, a gas which combines with oxygen to form water, and with other elements to form acids, and is present in all animal tissue (NOTE: The chemical symbol is **H**.)

hydrogen peroxide /ˌhaɪdrədʒən pəˈrɒksaɪd/ *noun* a solution used as a disinfectant

hydrolysis /haɪˈdrɒləsɪs/ *noun* the breaking down of a chemical compound when it reacts with water to produce two or more different compounds, as in the conversion of starch to glucose

hydroma /haɪˈdrəʊmə/ *noun* same as **hygroma**

hydrometer /haɪˈdrɒmɪtə/ *noun* an instrument which measures the density of a liquid

hydromyelia /ˌhaɪdrəʊmaɪˈiːliə/ *noun* a condition in which fluid swells the central canal of the spinal cord

hydronephrosis /ˌhaɪdrəʊneˈfrəʊsɪs/ *noun* swelling of the pelvis of a kidney caused by accumulation of water due to infection or a kidney stone blocking the ureter

hydropathy /haɪˈdrɒpəθi/ *noun* the treatment of injuries or disease by bathing in water or drinking mineral waters

hydropericarditis /ˌhaɪdrəʊˌperikɑːˈdaɪtɪs/, **hydropericardium** /ˌhaɪdrəʊˌperiˈkɑːdiəm/ *noun* an accumulation of liquid round the heart

hydroperitoneum /ˌhaɪdrəʊˌperitəˈniːəm/ *noun* a build-up of fluid in the peritoneal cavity (NOTE: The plural is **hydroperitoneums** or **hydroperitonea**.)

hydrophobia /ˌhaɪdrəˈfəʊbiə/ *noun* same as **rabies**

COMMENT: Hydrophobia affects the mental balance, and the symptoms include difficulty in breathing or swallowing and a horror of water.

hydropneumoperitoneum /ˌhaɪdrəʊˌnjuːməʊˌperitəˈniːəm/ *noun* a condition in which watery fluid and gas collect in the peritoneal cavity

hydropneumothorax /ˌhaɪdrəʊˌnjuːməʊˈθɔːræks/ *noun* a condition in which watery fluid and gas collect in the pleural cavity (NOTE: The plural is **hydropneumothoraxes** or **hydropneumothoraces**.)

hydrops /ˈhaɪdrɒps/ *noun* same as **oedema** (NOTE: The plural is **hydropses**.)

hydrorrhoea /ˌhaɪdrəʊˈriːə/ *noun* a discharge of watery fluid (NOTE: The US spelling is **hydrorrhea**.)

hydrosalpinx /ˌhaɪdrəʊˈsælpɪŋks/ *noun* an occasion when watery fluid collects in one or both of the Fallopian tubes, causing swelling (NOTE: The plural is **hydrosalpinges**.)

hydrotherapy /ˌhaɪdrəʊˈθerəpi/ *noun* a type of physiotherapy involving treatment in water, where people are put in hot baths or are encouraged to swim

hydrothorax /ˌhaɪdrəʊˈθɔːræks/ *noun* the collection of liquid in the pleural cavity

hydrotubation /ˌhaɪdrəʊtjuːˈbeɪʃ(ə)n/ *noun* an act of putting a fluid through the neck of the uterus and the Fallopian tubes under pressure to check whether the tubes are blocked

hydroureter /ˌhaɪdrəʊjuˈriːtə/ *noun* a condition in which water or urine collect in the ureter because it is blocked

hydroxide /haɪˈdrɒksaɪd/ *noun* a chemical compound containing a hydroxyl group

hydroxyproline /haɪˌdrɒksiˈprəʊliːn/ *noun* an amino acid present in some proteins, especially in collagen

hygiene /ˈhaɪdʒiːn/ *noun* **1.** the procedures and principles designed to keep things clean and to keep conditions healthy ○ *Nurses have to maintain a strict personal hygiene.* **2.** the science of health

hygienic /haɪˈdʒiːnɪk/ *adjective* **1.** clean ○ *Don't touch the food with dirty hands – it isn't hygienic.* **2.** producing healthy conditions

hygienist /ˈhaɪdʒiːnɪst/ *noun* a person who specialises in hygiene and its application

hygr- /haɪgr/ *prefix* same as **hygro-** (*used before vowels*)

hygro- /haɪgrəʊ/ *prefix* relating to moisture

hygroma /haɪˈgrəʊmə/ *noun* a kind of cyst which contains a thin fluid

hymen /ˈhaɪmen/ *noun* a membrane which partially covers the vaginal passage in a female who has never had sexual intercourse

hymenectomy /ˌhaɪməˈnektəmi/ *noun* **1.** the surgical removal of the hymen, or an operation to increase the size of the opening of the hymen **2.** the surgical removal of any membrane

hymenotomy /ˌhaɪməˈnɒtəmi/ *noun* an incision of the hymen during surgery

hyo- /haɪəʊ/ *prefix* relating to the hyoid bone

hyoglossus /ˌhaɪəʊˈglɒsəs/ *noun* a muscle which is attached to the hyoid bone and depresses the tongue

hyoid /ˈhaɪɔɪd/ *adjective* relating to the hyoid bone

hyoid bone /ˈhaɪɔɪd bəʊn/ *noun* a small U-shaped bone at the base of the tongue

hyoscine /ˈhaɪəʊsiːn/ *noun* a drug used as a sedative, in particular for treatment of motion sickness

hyp- /haɪp/ *prefix* same as **hypo-** (*used before vowels*)

hypaemia /haɪˈpiːmiə/ *noun* an insufficient amount of blood in the body

hypalgesia /ˌhaɪpælˈdʒiːziə/ *noun* low sensitivity to pain

hyper- /haɪpə/ *prefix* higher or too much. Opposite **hypo-**

hyperacidity /ˌhaɪpərəˈsɪdɪti/ *noun* the production of more acid in the stomach than is usual. Also called **acidity, acid stomach**

hyperacousia /ˌhaɪpərəˈkjuːziə/ *noun* same as **hyperacusis**

hyperactive /haɪpərˈæktɪv/ *adjective* very or unusually active

hyperactivity /haɪpərækˈtɪvəti/ *noun* a condition in which something or someone, e.g. a gland or a child, is too active

hyperacusis /ˌhaɪpərəˈkjuːsɪs/ *noun* a condition in which someone is very sensitive to sounds

hyperadrenalism /ˌhaɪpərəˈdriːn(ə)lɪz(ə)m/ noun a disorder in which too many adrenal hormones are produced, e.g. because of pituitary gland malfunction, a tumour of the adrenal gland or high doses of steroids

hyperaemia /ˌhaɪpərˈiːmiə/ noun excess blood in any part of the body

hyperaesthesia /ˌhaɪpəriːsˈθiːziə/ noun an extremely high sensitivity in the skin

hyperalgesia /ˌhaɪpərælˈdʒiːziə/ noun an increased sensitivity to pain

hyperalimentation /ˌhaɪpərˌælɪmenˈteɪʃ(ə)n/ noun the feeding of large amounts of nutrients by mouth or intravenously to someone with serious nutritional deficiency

hyperandrogenism /ˌhaɪpəræˈdrɒdʒənɪz(ə)m/ noun a condition in which a woman produces too many androgens, associated with many problems such as hirsutism, acne, infertility and polycystic ovarian disease

hyperbaric /ˌhaɪpəˈbærɪk/ adjective referring to a treatment in which someone is given oxygen at high pressure, used to treat carbon monoxide poisoning

hypercalcaemia /ˌhaɪpəkælˈsiːmiə/ noun an excess of calcium in the blood

hypercalcinuria /ˌhaɪpəkælsɪˈnjʊəriə/ noun a condition in which an unusually high amount of calcium occurs in the urine

hypercapnia /ˌhaɪpəˈkæpniə/ noun an unusually high concentration of carbon dioxide in the bloodstream

hypercatabolism /ˌhaɪpəkəˈtæbəlɪz(ə)m/ noun a condition in which the body breaks down its own tissues or a particular substance too much. It causes weight loss and wasting.

hyperchloraemia /ˌhaɪpəklɔːˈriːmiə/ noun a condition in which there is too much chloride in the blood

hyperchlorhydria /ˌhaɪpəklɔːˈhaɪdriə/ noun an excess of hydrochloric acid in the stomach

hyperdactylism /ˌhaɪpəˈdæktɪlɪz(ə)m/ noun the condition of having more than the usual number of fingers or toes. Also called **polydactylism**

hyperemesis /ˌhaɪpərˈemɪsɪs/ noun excessive vomiting (NOTE: The plural is **hyperemeses**.)

hyperemesis gravidarum /ˌhaɪpəremɪsɪs ˌɡrævɪˈdeərəm/ noun uncontrollable vomiting in pregnancy

hyperextension /ˌhaɪpərɪkˈstenʃən/ noun the act of stretching an arm or leg beyond its usual limits of movement

hyperflexion /ˌhaɪpəˈflekʃən/ noun the act of flexing a joint beyond the usual limit ○ a hyperflexion injury

hyperfunction /ˈhaɪpəˌfʌŋkʃ(ə)n/ noun excessive activity of a gland or other organ of the body

hypergalactia /ˌhaɪpəɡəˈlæktiə/, **hypergalactosis** /ˌhaɪpəˌɡæləkˈtəʊsɪs/ noun a condition in which too much milk is secreted

hyperglycaemia /ˌhaɪpəɡlaɪˈsiːmiə/ noun an excess of glucose in the blood

hyperhidrosis /ˌhaɪpəhaɪˈdrəʊsɪs/ noun a condition in which too much sweat is produced

hyperinsulinism /ˌhaɪpərˈɪnsjʊlɪnɪz(ə)m/ noun the reaction of a diabetic to an excessive dose of insulin or to hypoglycaemia

hyperkalaemia /ˌhaɪpəkæˈliːmiə/ noun a condition in which too much potassium occurs in the blood, which can result in cardiac arrest. Various possible causes include kidney failure and chemotherapy.

hyperkeratosis /ˌhaɪpəkerəˈtəʊsɪs/ noun a condition in which the outer layer of the skin becomes unusually thickened

hyperkinesia /ˌhaɪpəkɪˈniːziə/ noun a condition in which there is unusually great strength or movement

hyperkinetic syndrome /ˌhaɪpəkɪˈnetɪk ˌsɪndrəʊm/ noun a condition in which someone experiences fatigue, shortness of breath, pain under the heart and palpitation

hyperlipidaemia /ˌhaɪpəlɪpɪˈdiːmiə/ noun the pathological increase of the amount of lipids, or fat, in the blood

hypermenorrhoea /ˌhaɪpəmenəˈriːə/ noun menstruation in which the flow is excessive

hypermetropia /ˌhaɪpəmɪˈtrəʊpiə/, **hyperopia** /ˌhaɪpəˈrəʊpiə/ noun a condition in which someone sees more clearly objects which are a long way away, but cannot see objects which are close. Also called **longsightedness**, **hyperopia**

hypernatraemia /ˌhaɪpənæˈtriːmiə/ noun a serious condition occurring most often in babies or elderly people, in which too much sodium is present in the blood as a result of loss of water and electrolytes through diarrhoea, excessive sweating, not drinking enough or excessive salt intake

hypernephroma /ˌhaɪpənəˈfrəʊmə/ noun same as **Grawitz tumour**

hyperopia /ˌhaɪpəˈrəʊpiə/ noun same as **hypermetropia**

hyperostosis /haɪpərɒˈstəʊsɪs/ noun excessive overgrowth on the outside surface of a bone, especially the frontal bone

hyperparathyroidism /ˌhaɪpəˌpærəˈθaɪrɔɪdɪz(ə)m/ noun an unusually high concentration of parathyroid hormone in the body. It causes various medical problems including damage to the kidneys.

hyperphagia /ˌhaɪpəˈfeɪdʒiə/ noun long-term compulsive overeating

hyperpiesia /ˌhaɪpəpaɪˈiːziə/ noun same as **hypertension**

hyperpiesis /ˌhaɪpəpaɪˈiːsɪs/ noun unusually high pressure, especially of the blood

hyperpituitarism /ˌhaɪpəˈpɪtjuːɪtər ˌɪz(ə)m/ noun a condition in which the pituitary gland is overactive

hyperplasia /ˌhaɪpəˈpleɪziə/ noun a condition in which there is an increase in the number of cells in an organ

hyperpnoea /ˌhaɪpəˈpniːə/ noun unusually deep or fast breathing, e.g. after physical exercise

hyperpyrexia /ˌhaɪpəpaɪˈreksiə/ noun a body temperature of above 41.1°C

hypersecretion /ˌhaɪpəsɪˈkriːʃ(ə)n/ noun a condition in which too much of a substance is secreted

hypersensitive /ˌhaɪpəˈsensɪtɪv/ adjective referring to a person who reacts more strongly than usual to an antigen

hypersensitivity /ˌhaɪpəsensɪˈtɪvɪti/ noun a condition in which someone reacts very strongly to something such as an allergic substance ○ her hypersensitivity to dust ○ Anaphylactic shock shows hypersensitivity to an injection.

hypersplenism /ˌhaɪpəˈsplɪnɪz(ə)m/ noun a condition in which too many red blood cells are destroyed by the spleen, which is often enlarged

hypertelorism /ˌhaɪpəˈtelərɪz(ə)m/ noun a condition in which there is too much space between two organs or parts of the body

hypertension /ˌhaɪpəˈtenʃən/ noun arterial blood pressure that is higher than the usual range for gender and age. Also called **high blood pressure, hyperpiesia**. Compare **hypotension**

COMMENT: Hypertension is without a specific cause in more than 50% of cases (**essential hypertension**) but may be associated with other diseases. It is treated with drugs such as beta blockers, ACE inhibitors, diuretics and calcium channel blockers.

hypertensive /ˌhaɪpəˈtensɪv/ adjective referring to high blood pressure

hypertensive headache /ˌhaɪpətensɪv ˈhedeɪk/ noun a headache caused by high blood pressure

hypertensive retinopathy /ˌhaɪpətensɪv ˌretɪnˈɒpəθi/ noun changes in the retina caused by local bleeding and a restricted blood supply that threaten eyesight, as the condition indicates that the blood pressure is excessively high

hyperthermia /ˌhaɪpəˈθɜːmiə/ noun a very high body temperature

hyperthyroidism /ˌhaɪpəˈθaɪrɔɪdɪz(ə)m/ noun a condition in which the thyroid gland is too active and releases unusual amounts of thyroid hormones into the blood, giving rise to a rapid heartbeat, sweating and trembling. It

can be treated with carbimazole. Also called **thyrotoxicosis**

hypertonia /ˌhaɪpəˈtəuniə/ noun an increased rigidity and spasticity of the muscles

hypertonic /ˌhaɪpəˈtɒnɪk/ adjective **1.** referring to a solution which has a higher osmotic pressure than another specified solution **2.** referring to a muscle which is under unusually high tension

hypertrichosis /ˌhaɪpətrɪˈkəusɪs/ noun a condition in which someone has excessive growth of hair on the body or on part of the body

hypertrophic /ˌhaɪpəˈtrɒfɪk/ adjective associated with hypertrophy

hypertrophic rhinitis /ˌhaɪpətrɒfɪk raɪ ˈnaɪtɪs/ noun a condition in which the mucous membranes in the nose become thicker

hypertrophy /haɪˈpɜːtrəfi/ noun an increase in the number or size of cells in a tissue

hypertropia /ˌhaɪpəˈtrəupiə/ noun US same as **hypermetropia**

hyperventilate /ˌhaɪpəˈventɪleɪt/ verb to breathe very fast ○ We hyperventilate as an expression of fear or excitement.

hyperventilation /ˌhaɪpəventɪˈleɪʃ(ə)n/ noun very fast breathing which can be accompanied by dizziness or tetany

hypervitaminosis /ˌhaɪpəˌvɪtəmɪˈnəusɪs/ noun a condition caused by taking too many synthetic vitamins, especially Vitamins A and D

hypervolaemia /ˌhaɪpəvɒˈliːmiə/ noun a condition in which there is too much plasma in the blood

hyphaema /haɪˈfiːmiə/ noun bleeding into the front chamber of the eye

hypn- /hɪpn/ prefix referring to sleep

hypnosis /hɪpˈnəusɪs/ noun a state like sleep, but caused artificially, where a person can remember forgotten events in the past and will do whatever the hypnotist tells him or her to do

hypnotherapist /ˌhɪpnəuˈθerəpɪst/ noun a person who practises hypnotherapy

hypnotherapy /ˌhɪpnəuˈθerəpi/ noun treatment by hypnosis, used in treating some addictions

hypnotic /hɪpˈnɒtɪk/ adjective **1.** relating to hypnosis and hypnotism **2.** referring to a state which is like sleep but which is caused artificially **3.** referring to a drug which causes sleep

hypnotise /ˈhɪpnətaɪz/, **hypnotize** verb to make someone go into a state where he or she appears to be asleep, and will do whatever the hypnotist suggests ○ He hypnotises his patients, and then persuades them to reveal their hidden problems.

hypnotism /ˈhɪpnətɪz(ə)m/ noun the techniques used to induce hypnosis

hypnotist /'hɪpnətɪst/ *noun* a person who hypnotises other people ○ *The hypnotist passed his hand in front of her eyes and she went immediately to sleep.*

hypo /'haɪpəʊ/ *noun* (*informal*) **1.** same as **hypodermic syringe 2.** an attack of hypoglycaemia, experienced, e.g., by people who are diabetic

hypo- /haɪpəʊ/ *prefix* less, too little or beneath

hypoacidity /ˌhaɪpəʊə'sɪdɪti/ *noun* unusually low acidity, especially in the stomach

hypoaesthesia /ˌhaɪpəʊiːs'θiːziə/ *noun* a condition in which someone has a diminished sense of touch

hypoallergenic /ˌhaɪpəʊələ'dʒenɪk/ *adjective* not likely to cause an allergic reaction

hypocalcaemia /ˌhaɪpəʊkæl'siːmiə/ *noun* an unusually low amount of calcium in the blood, which can cause tetany

hypocapnia /ˌhaɪpəʊ'kæpniə/ *noun* a condition in which there is not enough carbon dioxide in the blood

hypochloraemia /ˌhaɪpəʊklɔː'riːmiə/ *noun* a condition in which there are not enough chlorine ions in the blood

hypochlorhydria /ˌhaɪpəʊklɔː'haɪdriə/ *noun* a condition in which there is not enough hydrochloric acid in the stomach

hypochondria /ˌhaɪpəʊ'kɒndriə/ *noun* a condition in which a person is too worried about his or her own health and believes he or she is ill

hypochondriac /ˌhaɪpəʊ'kɒndriæk/ *noun* a person who worries about his or her health too much

hypochondriac region /ˌhaɪpəʊ'kɒndriæk ˌriːdʒən/ *noun* one of two parts of the upper abdomen, on either side of the epigastrium below the floating ribs

hypochondrium /ˌhaɪpəʊ'kɒndriəm/ *noun* one of the two hypochondriac regions in the upper part of the abdomen

hypochromic /ˌhaɪpəʊ'krəʊmɪk/ *adjective* referring to blood cells or body tissue which do not have the usual amount of pigmentation ○ *hypochromic scars*

hypochromic anaemia /ˌhaɪpəʊkrəʊmɪk ə'niːmiə/ *noun* anaemia where haemoglobin is reduced in proportion to the number of red blood cells, which then appear very pale

hypodermic /ˌhaɪpə'dɜːmɪk/ *adjective* beneath the skin ■ *noun* a hypodermic syringe, needle or injection (*informal*)

hypodermic injection /ˌhaɪpədɜːmɪk ɪn'dʒekʃən/ *noun* an injection of a liquid, e.g. a painkilling drug, beneath the skin. Also called **subcutaneous injection**

hypodermic needle /ˌhaɪpədɜːmɪk 'niːd(ə)l/ *noun* a needle for injecting liquid under the skin

hypodermic syringe /ˌhaɪpədɜːmɪk sɪ'rɪndʒ/ *noun* a syringe fitted with a hypodermic needle for injecting liquid under the skin

hypofibrinogenaemia /ˌhaɪpəʊˌfɪbrɪnəʊdʒə'niːmiə/ *noun* a condition in which there is not enough fibrinogen in the blood, e.g. because of several blood transfusions or as an inherited condition

hypogammaglobulinaemia /ˌhaɪpəʊgæməˌglɒbjʊlɪn'iːmiə/ *noun* an unusually low concentration of gamma globulin in the blood that causes an immune deficiency. It may be present from birth or acquired later in life.

hypogastrium /ˌhaɪpə'gæstriəm/ *noun* the part of the abdomen beneath the stomach

hypoglossal /ˌhaɪpəʊ'glɒsəl/ *adjective* **1.** underneath or on the lower side of the tongue **2.** relating to the hypoglossal nerve

hypoglossal nerve /haɪpə'glɒs(ə)l nɜːv/ *noun* the twelfth cranial nerve which governs the muscles of the tongue

hypoglycaemia /ˌhaɪpəʊglaɪ'siːmiə/ *noun* a low concentration of glucose in the blood

COMMENT: Hypoglycaemia affects diabetics who feel weak from lack of sugar. A hypoglycaemic attack can be prevented by eating glucose or a lump of sugar when feeling faint.

hypoglycaemic /ˌhaɪpəʊglaɪ'siːmɪk/ *adjective* having hypoglycaemia

hypoglycaemic coma /ˌhaɪpəʊglaɪˌsiːmɪk 'kəʊmə/ *noun* a state of unconsciousness affecting diabetics after taking an overdose of insulin

hypohidrosis /ˌhaɪpəʊhaɪ'drəʊsɪs/, **hypoidrosis** /haɪpɔɪ'drəʊsɪs/ *noun* a condition in which someone produces too little sweat

hypoinsulinism /ˌhaɪpəʊ'ɪnsjʊlɪnɪz(ə)m/ *noun* a condition in which the body does not have enough insulin, often because of a problem with the pancreas

hypokalaemia /ˌhaɪpəʊkæ'liːmiə/ *noun* a deficiency of potassium in the blood

hypomania /ˌhaɪpəʊ'meɪniə/ *noun* a state of mild mania or overexcitement, especially when part of a manic-depressive cycle

hypomenorrhoea /ˌhaɪpəmenə'riːə/ *noun* the production of too little blood at menstruation

hypometropia /ˌhaɪpəʊmɪ'trəʊpiə/ *noun* same as **myopia**

hyponatraemia /ˌhaɪpəʊnæ'triːmiə/ *noun* a lack of sodium in the body

hypoparathyroidism /ˌhaɪpəʊˌpærə'θaɪrɔɪdɪz(ə)m/ *noun* a condition in which the parathyroid glands do not secrete enough parathyroid hormone, leading to low blood calcium and muscle spasms

hypopharynx /ˌhaɪpəʊ'færɪŋks/ *noun* the part of the pharynx between the hyoid bone and the bottom of the cricoid cartilage (NOTE: The plural is **hypopharynxes** or **hypopharynges**.)

hypophyseal /ˌhaɪpəˈfɪziəl/ *adjective* referring to the pituitary gland

hypophyseal stalk /ˌhaɪpəfɪziəl ˈstɔːk/ *noun* a funnel-shaped stem which attaches the pituitary gland to the hypothalamus

hypophysectomy /haɪˌpɒfɪˈsektəmi/ *noun* the surgical removal of the pituitary gland

hypophysis cerebri /haɪˌpɒfəsɪs ˈserəbri/ *noun* same as **pituitary gland**

hypopiesis /ˌhaɪpəʊpaɪˈiːsɪs/ *noun* a condition in which the blood pressure is too low

hypopituitarism /ˌhaɪpəʊpɪˈtjuːɪtərˌɪz(ə)m/ *noun* a condition in which the pituitary gland is underactive

hypoplasia /ˌhaɪpəʊˈpleɪziə/ *noun* a lack of development or incorrect formation of a body tissue or an organ

hypoplastic left heart /haɪpəʊˌplæstɪk left ˈhɑːt/ *noun* a serious heart disorder in which the left side of the heart does not develop properly, leading to death within six weeks of birth unless surgery is performed

hypopnoea /ˌhaɪpəʊˈpniːə/ *noun* unusually shallow and slow breathing

hypoproteinaemia /ˌhaɪpəʊprəʊtɪˈniːmiə/ *noun* a condition in which there is not enough protein in the blood

hypoprothrombinaemia /ˌhaɪpəʊprəʊˌθrɒmbɪˈniːmiə/ *noun* a condition in which there is not enough prothrombin in the blood, so that the person bleeds and bruises easily

hypopyon /ˌhaɪpəˈpaɪən/ *noun* an accumulation of pus in the aqueous humour in the front chamber of the eye

hyposensitise /ˌhaɪpəʊˈsensɪtaɪz/, **hyposensitize** *verb* to reduce someone's sensitivity to something, e.g. in the treatment of allergies

hyposensitive /ˌhaɪpəʊˈsensɪtɪv/ *adjective* being less sensitive than usual

hyposensitivity /ˌhaɪpəʊˌsensɪˈtɪvɪti/ *noun* an unusually low sensitivity to stimuli such as allergens

hypospadias /ˌhaɪpəˈspeɪdiəs/ *noun* a congenital condition of the wall of the male urethra or the vagina, so that the opening occurs on the under side of the penis or in the vagina. Compare **epispadias**

hypostasis /haɪˈpɒstəsɪs/ *noun* a condition in which fluid accumulates in part of the body because of poor circulation

hypostatic /ˌhaɪpəʊˈstætɪk/ *adjective* referring to hypostasis

hypostatic eczema /ˌhaɪpəʊstætɪk ˈeksɪmə/ *noun* same as **varicose eczema**

hypostatic pneumonia /ˌhaɪpəʊstætɪk njuːˈməʊniə/ *noun* pneumonia caused by fluid accumulating in the lungs of a bedridden person with a weak heart

hyposthenia /ˌhaɪpɒsˈθiːniə/ *noun* a condition of unusual bodily weakness

hypotension /ˌhaɪpəʊˈtenʃən/ *noun* a condition in which the pressure of the blood is unusually low. Also called **low blood pressure**. Compare **hypertension**

hypotensive /ˌhaɪpəˈtensɪv/ *adjective* having low blood pressure

hypothalamic /ˌhaɪpəʊθəˈlæmɪk/ *adjective* referring to the hypothalamus

hypothalamic hormone /ˌhaɪpəʊθəˌlæmɪk ˈhɔːməʊn/ *noun* same as **releasing hormone**

hypothalamus /ˌhaɪpəʊˈθæləməs/ *noun* the part of the brain above the pituitary gland, which controls the production of hormones by the pituitary gland and regulates important bodily functions such as hunger, thirst and sleep. See illustration at **BRAIN** in Supplement

hypothalmus /ˌhaɪpəʊˈθælməs/ *noun* same as **hypothalamus** (NOTE: The plural is **hypothalmuses** or **hypothalmi**.)

hypothenar /haɪˈpɒθɪnə/ *adjective* referring to the soft fat part of the palm beneath the little finger

hypothenar eminence /haɪˌpɒθɪnə ˈemɪnəns/ *noun* a lump on the palm beneath the little finger. Compare **thenar**

hypothermal /ˌhaɪpəʊˈθɜːm(ə)l/ *adjective* referring to hypothermia

hypothermia /ˌhaɪpəʊˈθɜːmiə/ *noun* a reduction in body temperature below normal, for medical purposes taken to be below 35°C

'…inadvertent hypothermia can readily occur in patients undergoing surgery when there is reduced heat production and a greater potential for heat loss to the environment' [*British Journal of Nursing*]

hypothermic /ˌhaɪpəˈθɜːmɪk/ *adjective* suffering from hypothermia ○ *Examination revealed that she was hypothermic, with a rectal temperature of only 29.4°C.*

hypothermic perfusion /haɪpəθɜːmɪk pə ˈfjuːʒ(ə)n/ *noun* a method of preserving a donor organ by introducing a preserving solution and storing the organ at a low temperature

hypothesis /haɪˈpɒθəsɪs/ *noun* a suggested explanation for an observation or experimental result, which is then refined or disproved by further investigation

hypothyroidism /ˌhaɪpəʊˈθaɪrɔɪdɪz(ə)m/ *noun* underactivity of the thyroid gland

hypotonia /ˌhaɪpəʊˈtəʊniə/ *noun* reduced tone of the skeletal muscles

hypotonic /ˌhaɪpəʊˈtɒnɪk/ *adjective* **1.** showing hypotonia **2.** referring to a solution with a lower osmotic pressure than plasma

hypotrichosis /ˌhaɪpəʊtrɪˈkəʊsɪs/ *noun* a condition in which less hair develops than usual. Compare **alopecia** (NOTE: The plural is **hypotrichoses**.)

hypotropia /ˌhaɪpəʊˈtrəʊpiə/ *noun* a form of squint where one eye looks downwards

hypoventilation /ˌhaɪpəʊventɪˈleɪʃ(ə)n/ *noun* very slow breathing

hypovitaminosis /ˌhaɪpəʊˌvɪtəmɪˈnəʊsɪs/ *noun* a lack of vitamins

hypoxaemia /ˌhaɪpɒkˈsiːmiə/ *noun* an inadequate supply of oxygen in the arterial blood

hypoxanthine phosphoribosyl transferase *noun* full form of **HPRT**

hypoxia /haɪˈpɒksiə/ *noun* **1.** an inadequate supply of oxygen to tissue as a result of a lack of oxygen in the arterial blood **2.** same as **hypoxaemia**

hyster- /hɪstə/ *prefix* same as **hystero-** (*used before vowels*)

hysteralgia /ˌhɪstərˈældʒə/ *noun* pain in the uterus

hysterectomy /ˌhɪstəˈrektəmi/ *noun* the surgical removal of the uterus, often either to treat cancer or because of the presence of fibroids

hysteria /hɪˈstɪəriə/ *noun* a term formerly used in psychiatry, but now informally used for a condition in which the person appears unstable, and may scream and wave their arms about, but also is repressed, and may be slow to react to outside stimuli (*dated*)

hysterical /hɪˈsterɪk(ə)l/ *adjective* referring to a reaction showing hysteria (*informal*)

hysterically /hɪˈsterɪkli/ *adverb* in a hysterical way (*informal*)

hysterical personality /hɪˌsterɪk(ə)l ˌpɜːsəˈnælɪti/ *noun* the mental condition of a person who is unstable, lacks usual feelings and is dependent on others (*dated*)

hysterics /hɪˈsterɪks/ *noun* an attack of hysteria (*dated*)

hystericus /hɪˈsterɪkəs/ ♦ **globus hystericus**

hystero- /hɪstərəʊ/ *prefix* referring to the uterus

hysterocele /ˈhɪstərəʊsiːl/ *noun* same as **uterocele**

hystero-oöphorectomy /ˌhɪstərəʊ ˌəʊəfəˈrektəmi/ *noun* the surgical removal of the uterus, the uterine tubes and the ovaries

hysteroptosis /ˌhɪstərɒpˈtəʊsɪs/ *noun* prolapse of the uterus

hysterosalpingo-contrast sonography /ˌhɪstərəʊˌsælpɪŋgəʊ ˌkɒntrɑːst sɒnˈɒgrəfi/ *noun* examination of the uterus and Fallopian tubes by ultrasound. Abbr **HYCOSY**

hysterosalpingography /ˌhɪstərəʊˌsælpɪŋˈgɒgrəfi/ *noun* an X-ray examination of the uterus and Fallopian tubes following injection of radio-opaque material. Also called **uterosalpingography**

hysterosalpingostomy /ˌhɪstərəʊˌsælpɪŋˈgɒstəmi/ *noun* an operation to remake an opening between the uterine tube and the uterus, to help with infertility problems

hysteroscope /ˈhɪstərəskəʊp/ *noun* a tube for inspecting the inside of the uterus

hysteroscopy /ˌhɪstəˈrɒskəpi/ *noun* an examination of the uterine cavity using a hysteroscope or fibrescope

hysterotomy /ˌhɪstəˈrɒtəmi/ *noun* a surgical incision into the uterus, as in caesarean section or for some types of abortion

hysterotrachelorrhaphy /ˌhɪstərəʊˌtrækiəˈlɒrəfi/ *noun* an operation to repair a tear in the cervix

I

-iasis /aɪəsɪs/ *suffix* disease caused by something ○ *amoebiasis*

iatro- /aɪætrəʊ/ *prefix* relating to medicine or doctors

iatrogenesis /aɪˌætrəʊˈdʒenəsɪs/ *noun* any condition caused by the actions of doctors or other healthcare professionals

iatrogenic /aɪˌætrəˈdʒenɪk/ *adjective* referring to a condition which is caused by a doctor's treatment for another disease or condition ○ *an iatrogenic infection*

COMMENT: An iatrogenic condition can be caused by a drug, i.e. a side effect, by infection from the doctor or simply by worry about possible treatment.

IBS *abbr* irritable bowel syndrome

ibuprofen /ˌaɪbjuːˈprəʊfən/ *noun* a nonsteroidal anti-inflammatory drug that relieves pain and swelling, especially in arthritis and rheumatism. It is also widely used as a household painkiller.

ice bag /ˈaɪs bæg/, **icebag**, **ice pack** /ˈaɪs pæk/ *noun* a cold compress made of lumps of ice wrapped in a cloth or put in a special bag and held against an injured part of the body to reduce pain or swelling

ichthamol /ɪkˈθæmɒl/ *noun* a thick dark red liquid which is a mild antiseptic and analgesic, used in the treatment of skin diseases

ichthyosis /ˌɪkθɪˈəʊsɪs/ *noun* a hereditary condition in which the skin does not form properly, resulting in a dry, non-inflammatory and scaly appearance

ICM *abbr* International Confederation of Midwives

ICN *abbr* **1.** International Council of Nurses **2.** infection control nurse

ICP *abbr* intracranial pressure

ICRC *abbr* International Committee of the Red Cross

ICSH *abbr* interstitial cell stimulating hormone

icteric /ɪkˈterɪk/ *adjective* referring to someone with jaundice

icterus /ˈɪktərəs/ *noun* same as **jaundice**

icterus gravis neonatorum /ˌɪktərəs ˌgrævɪs ˌniːəʊnəˈtɔːrəm/ *noun* jaundice associated with erythroblastosis fetalis

ictus /ˈɪktəs/ *noun* a stroke or fit

ICU *abbr* intensive care unit

id /ɪd/ *noun* (*in Freudian psychology*) the basic unconscious drives which exist in hidden forms in a person

ideation /ˌaɪdiˈeɪʃ(ə)n/ *noun* the act or process of imagining or forming thoughts and ideas

identical twins /aɪˈdentɪk(ə)l twɪnz/ *plural noun* twins who are exactly the same in appearance because they developed from the same ovum. Also called **monozygotic twins**, **uniovular twins**

identification /aɪˌdentɪfɪˈkeɪʃ(ə)n/ *noun* the act of discovering or stating who someone is or what something is □ **identification with someone** the act of associating with and unconsciously taking on the viewpoints and behaviours of one or more other people

identity bracelet /aɪˈdentɪti ˌbreɪslət/, **identity label** /aɪˈdentɪti ˌleɪb(ə)l/ *noun* a label attached to the wrist of a newborn baby or patient in hospital, so that he or she can be identified

ideo- /aɪdiəʊ/ *prefix* involving ideas

idio- /ɪdiəʊ/ *prefix* referring to one particular person

idiopathic /ˌɪdiəˈpæθɪk/ *adjective* **1.** referring to a disease with no obvious cause **2.** referring to idiopathy

idiopathic epilepsy /ˌɪdiəpæθɪk ˈepɪˌlepsi/ *noun* epilepsy not caused by a brain disorder, beginning during childhood or adolescence

idiopathy /ˌɪdiˈɒpəθi/ *noun* a condition which develops without any known cause

idiosyncrasy /ˌɪdiəʊˈsɪŋkrəsi/ *noun* a way of behaving which is particular to one person

idiot savant /ˌɪdiəʊ ˈsævɒŋ/ *noun* a person with learning difficulties who also possesses a single particular mental ability, such as the ability to play music by ear, to draw remembered objects or to do mental calculations, which is very highly developed

idioventricular /ˌɪdiəʊven'trɪkjʊlə/ *adjective* relating to the ventricles of the heart

idioventricular rhythm /ˌɪdiəʊven,trɪkjʊlə 'rɪð(ə)m/ *noun* a slow natural rhythm in the ventricles of the heart, but not in the atria

IDK *abbr* internal derangement of the knee

Ig *abbr* immunoglobulin

Ig A antiendomysial antibody /ˌaɪ dʒiː eɪ ˌæntiendəʊˌmaɪsiəl 'æntɪbɒdi/ *noun* a serological screening test for coeliac disease

IHD *abbr* ischaemic heart disease

IL-1 *abbr* interleukin-1

IL-2 *abbr* interleukin-2

ile- /ɪli/ *prefix* same as **ileo-** (*used before vowels*)

ilea /'ɪliə/ plural of **ileum**

ileac /'ɪliæk/ *adjective* **1.** relating to an ileus **2.** relating to the ileum

ileal /'ɪliəl/ *adjective* referring to the ileum

ileal bladder /ˌɪliəl 'blædə/, **ileal conduit** /ˌɪliəl 'kɒndjuɪt/ *noun* an artificial tube formed when the ureters are linked to part of the ileum, and that part is linked to an opening in the abdominal wall

ileal pouch /ˌɪliəl 'paʊtʃ/ *noun* a part of the small intestine which is made into a new rectum in a surgical operation, freeing someone from the need for an ileostomy after their colon is removed

ileectomy /ˌɪli'ektəmi/ *noun* the surgical removal of all or part of the ileum

ileitis /ˌɪli'aɪtɪs/ *noun* inflammation of the ileum

ileo- /ɪliəʊ/ *prefix* relating to the ileum

ileocaecal /ˌɪliəʊ'siːk(ə)l/ *adjective* referring to the ileum and the caecum

ileocaecal orifice /ˌɪliəʊsiːk(ə)l 'ɒrɪfɪs/ *noun* an opening where the small intestine joins the large intestine

ileocaecal valve /ˌɪli:əʊsiːk(ə)l 'vælv/ *noun* a valve at the end of the ileum, which allows food to pass from the ileum into the caecum

ileocaecocystoplasty /ˌɪliəʊˌsiːkəʊ'saɪtəʊplæsti/ *noun* an operation to reconstruct the bladder using a piece of the combined ileum and caecum

ileocolic /ˌɪliəʊ'kɒlɪk/ *adjective* referring to both the ileum and the colon

ileocolic artery /ˌɪli:əʊkɒlɪk 'ɑːtəri/ *noun* a branch of the superior mesenteric artery

ileocolitis /ˌɪliəʊkə'laɪtɪs/ *noun* inflammation of both the ileum and the colon

ileocolostomy /ˌɪliəʊkə'lɒstəmi/ *noun* a surgical operation to make a link directly between the ileum and the colon

ileoproctostomy /ˌɪliəʊprɒk'tɒstəmi/ *noun* a surgical operation to create a link between the ileum and the rectum

ileorectal /ˌɪliəʊ'rekt(ə)l/ *adjective* referring to both the ileum and the rectum

ileosigmoidostomy /ˌɪliəʊsɪgmɔɪ'dɒstəmi/ *noun* a surgical operation to create a link between the ileum and the sigmoid colon

ileostomy /ˌɪli'ɒstəmi/ *noun* a surgical operation to make an opening between the ileum and the abdominal wall to act as an artificial opening for excretion of faeces

ileostomy bag /ɪli'ɒstəmi bæg/ *noun* a bag attached to the opening made by an ileostomy, to collect faeces as they are passed out of the body

ileum /'ɪliəm/ *noun* the lower part of the small intestine, between the jejunum and the caecum. Compare **ilium**. See illustration at DIGESTIVE SYSTEM in Supplement (NOTE: The plural is **ilea**.)

COMMENT: The ileum is the longest section of the small intestine, being about 2.5 metres long.

ileus /'ɪliəs/ *noun* obstruction of the intestine, usually distension caused by loss of muscular action in the bowel. ♦ **paralytic ileus**

ili- /ɪli/ *prefix* same as **ilio-** (*used before vowels*)

ilia /'ɪliə/ plural of **ilium**

iliac /'ɪliæk/ *adjective* referring to the ilium

iliac crest /ˌɪliæk 'krest/ *noun* a curved top edge of the ilium. See illustration at PELVIS in Supplement

iliac fossa /ˌɪliæk 'fɒsə/ *noun* a depression on the inner side of the hip bone

iliac region /'ɪliæk ˌriːdʒən/ *noun* one of two regions of the lower abdomen, on either side of the hypogastrium

iliac spine /'ɪliæk spaɪn/ *noun* a projection at the posterior end of the iliac crest

iliacus /ɪli'ækəs/ *noun* a muscle in the groin which flexes the thigh

ilio- /ɪliəʊ/ *prefix* relating to the ilium

iliococcygeal /ˌɪliəʊkɒk'sɪdʒiəl/ *adjective* referring to both the ilium and the coccyx

iliolumbar /ˌɪliəʊ'lʌmbə/ *adjective* referring to the iliac and lumbar regions

iliopectineal /ˌɪliəʊpek'tɪniəl/ *adjective* referring to both the ilium and the pubis

iliopectineal eminence /ˌɪliəʊpektɪniəl 'emɪnəns/ *noun* a raised area on the inner surface of the innominate bone

iliopsoas /ˌɪliəʊ'səʊəs/ *noun* a muscle formed from the iliacus and psoas muscles

iliopubic /ˌɪliəʊ'pjuːbɪk/ *adjective* same as **iliopectineal**

iliopubic eminence /ˌɪliəʊˌpjuːbɪk 'emɪnəns/ *noun* same as **iliopectineal eminence**

iliotibial tract /ˌɪliəʊ'tɪbiəl ˌtrækt/ *noun* a thick fascia which runs from the ilium to the tibia

ilium /'ɪliəm/ *noun* the top part of each of the hip bones, which form the pelvis. Compare **ileum**. See illustration at PELVIS in Supplement (NOTE: The plural is **ilia**.)

ill /ɪl/ *adjective* not well ○ *If you feel very ill you ought to see a doctor.*

illegal abortion /ɪˌliːg(ə)l əˈbɔːʃ(ə)n/ *noun* same as **criminal abortion**

ill health /ˌɪl 'helθ/ *noun* the fact of not being well ○ *He has been in ill health for some time.* ○ *She has a history of ill health.* ○ *He had to retire early for reasons of ill health.*

illness /'ɪlnəs/ *noun* **1.** a state of not being well ○ *Most of the children stayed away from school because of illness.* **2.** a type of disease ○ *Scarlet fever is no longer considered to be a very serious illness.* ○ *He is in hospital with an infectious tropical illness.*

illusion /ɪ'luːʒ(ə)n/ *noun* a condition in which a person has a wrong perception of external objects

i.m., IM *abbr* intramuscular

image /'ɪmɪdʒ/ *noun* a sensation, e.g. a smell, sight or taste, which is remembered clearly

imagery /'ɪmɪdʒəri/ *noun* visual sensations clearly produced in the mind

imaginary /ɪ'mædʒɪn(ə)ri/ *adjective* referring to something which does not exist but is imagined

imaginary playmate /ɪˌmædʒɪnəri 'pleɪↄmeɪt/ *noun* a friend who does not exist but who is imagined by a small child to exist

imagination /ɪˌmædʒɪ'neɪʃ(ə)n/ *noun* the ability to see or invent things in your mind ○ *In her imagination she saw herself sitting on a beach in the sun.*

imagine /ɪ'mædʒɪn/ *verb* to see, hear or feel something in your mind ○ *Imagine yourself sitting on the beach in the sun.* ○ *I thought I heard someone shout, but I must have imagined it because there is no one there.* □ **to imagine things** to have delusions ○ *She keeps imagining things.* ○ *Sometimes he imagines he is swimming in the sea.*

imaging /'ɪmɪdʒɪŋ/ *noun* a technique for creating pictures of sections of the body, using scanners attached to computers

imbalance /ɪm'bæləns/ *noun* a situation in which things are unequal or in the wrong proportions to one another, e.g. in the diet

imipramine /ɪ'mɪprəmiːn/ *noun* a drug that is used as a treatment for depression

immature /ˌɪmə'tjʊə/ *adjective* not mature, lacking insight and emotional stability

immature cell /ˌɪmətjʊə 'sel/ *noun* a cell which is still developing

immaturity /ˌɪmə'tjʊərɪti/ *noun* behaviour which is lacking in maturity

immersion foot /ɪˌmɜːʃ(ə)n 'fʊt/ *noun* same as **trench foot**

immiscible /ɪ'mɪsəb(ə)l/ *adjective* (*of liquids*) not able to be mixed

immobile /ɪ'məʊbaɪl/ *adjective* not moving, which cannot move

immobilisation /ɪˌməʊbɪlaɪ'zeɪʃ(ə)n/, **immobilization** *noun* the act of preventing somebody or something from being able to move

immobilise /ɪ'məʊbɪlaɪz/, **immobilize** *verb* **1.** to keep someone from moving **2.** to attach a splint to a joint or fractured limb to prevent the bones from moving

immovable /ɪ'muːvəb(ə)l/ *adjective* referring to a joint which cannot be moved

immune /ɪ'mjuːn/ *adjective* protected against an infection or allergic disease ○ *She seems to be immune to colds.* ○ *The injection should make you immune to yellow fever.*

immune deficiency /ɪˌmjuːn dɪ'fɪʃ(ə)nsi/ *noun* a lack of immunity to a disease. ◊ **AIDS**

immune reaction /ɪˌmjuːn ri'ækʃən/, **immune response** /ɪˌmjuːn rɪ'spɒns/ *noun* a reaction of a body to an antigen

immune system /ɪ'mjuːn ˌsɪstəm/ *noun* a complex network of cells and cell products, which protects the body from disease. It includes the thymus, spleen, lymph nodes, white blood cells and antibodies.

'...the reason for this susceptibility is a profound abnormality of the immune system in children with sickle-cell disease' [*Lancet*]

'...the AIDS virus attacks a person's immune system and damages his or her ability to fight other diseases' [*Journal of the American Medical Association*]

immunisation /ˌɪmjʊnaɪ'zeɪʃ(ə)n/, **immunization** *noun* the process of making a person immune to an infection, either by injecting an antiserum, passive immunisation or by inoculation

'...vaccination is the most effective way to prevent children getting the disease. Children up to 6 years old can be vaccinated if they missed earlier immunization' [*Health Visitor*]

immunise /'ɪmjʊnaɪz/, **immunize** *verb* to give someone immunity from an infection. ◊ **vaccinate** (NOTE: You **immunise** someone **against** a disease.)

COMMENT: In the UK, infants are immunised routinely against diphtheria, pertussis, polio, tetanus, Hib, mumps, measles and rubella, unless there are contra-indications or the parents object.

immunity /ɪ'mjuːnɪti/ *noun* the ability to resist attacks of a disease because antibodies are produced ○ *The vaccine gives immunity to tuberculosis.*

immuno- /ɪmjʊnəʊ, ɪmjuːnəʊ/ *prefix* immune, immunity

immunoassay /ˌɪmjʊnəʊæ'seɪ/ *noun* a test for the presence and strength of antibodies

immunocompetence /ˌɪmjʊnəʊ'kɒmpɪtəns/ *noun* the ability to develop an immune response following exposure to an antigen

immunocompromised /ˌɪmjʊnəʊ'kɒmprəmaɪzd/ *adjective* not able to offer resistance to infection

immunodeficiency /ˌɪmjʊnəʊdɪˈfɪʃ(ə)nsi/ *noun* a lack of immunity to a disease

immunodeficiency virus /ˌɪmjʊnəʊdɪ ˈfɪʃ(ə)nsi ˌvaɪrəs/ *noun* a retrovirus which attacks the immune system

immunodeficient /ˌɪmjʊnəʊdɪˈfɪʃ(ə)nt/ *adjective* lacking immunity to a disease ○ *This form of meningitis occurs in persons who are immunodeficient.*

immunoelectrophoresis /ˌɪmjʊnəʊɪˌlektrəʊfə ˈriːsɪs/ *noun* a method of identifying antigens in a laboratory, using electrophoresis

immunogenic /ˌɪmjʊnəʊˈdʒenɪk/ *adjective* producing an immune response

immunogenicity /ˌɪmjʊnəʊdʒəˈnɪsɪti/ *noun* the property which makes a substance able to produce an immune response in an organism

immunoglobulin /ˌɪmjʊnəʊˈglɒbjʊlɪn/ *noun* an antibody, a protein produced in blood plasma as protection against infection, the commonest being gamma globulin. Abbr **Ig** (NOTE: The five main classes are called: **immunoglobulin G, A, D, E and M** or **IgG, IgA, IgD, IgE and IgM.**)

immunological /ˌɪmjʊnəˈlɒdʒɪk(ə)l/ *adjective* referring to immunology

immunological staining /ˌɪmjʊnə ˈlɒdʒɪk(ə)l ˈsteɪnɪŋ/ *noun* the process of checking if cancer is likely to return after someone has been declared free of the disease, by staining cells

immunological tolerance /ˌɪmjʊnə ˈlɒdʒɪk(ə)l ˈtɒlərəns/ *noun* tolerance of the lymphoid tissues to an antigen

immunologist /ˌɪmjʊˈnɒlədʒɪst/ *noun* a specialist in immunology

immunology /ˌɪmjʊˈnɒlədʒi/ *noun* the study of immunity and immunisation

immunosuppressant /ˌɪmjʊnəʊsə ˈpres(ə)nt/ *noun* a drug used to act against the response of the immune system to reject a transplanted organ

immunosuppression /ˌɪmjʊnəʊsə ˈpreʃ(ə)n/ *noun* the suppression of the body's natural immune system so that it will not reject a transplanted organ

immunosuppressive /ˌɪmjʊnəʊsəˈpresɪv/ *adjective* counteracting the immune system

immunotherapy /ˌɪmjʊnəʊˈθerəpi/ *noun* ▶ adoptive immunotherapy

immunotransfusion /ˌɪmjʊnəʊtræns ˈfjuːʒ(ə)n/ *noun* a transfusion of blood, serum or plasma containing immune bodies

Imodium /ɪˈməʊdiəm/ a trade name for Ioperamide hydrochloride

impacted /ɪmˈpæktɪd/ *adjective* tightly pressed or firmly lodged against something

impacted faeces /ɪmˌpæktɪd ˈfiːsiːz/ *plural noun* extremely hard dry faeces which cannot

pass through the anus and have to be surgically removed

impacted fracture /ɪmˌpæktɪd ˈfræktʃə/ *noun* a fracture where the broken parts of the bones are pushed into each other

impacted tooth /ɪmˌpæktɪd ˈtuːθ/ *noun* a tooth which is held against another tooth and so cannot grow normally

impacted ureteric calculus /ɪmˌpæktɪd ˌjʊəriterɪk ˈkælkjʊləs/ *noun* a small hard mass of mineral salts which is lodged in a ureter

impaction /ɪmˈpækʃən/ *noun* a condition in which two things are impacted

impair /ɪmˈpeə/ *verb* to harm a sense or function so that it does not work properly

impaired hearing /ɪmˌpeəd ˈhɪərɪŋ/ *noun* hearing which is not clear and sharp

impaired vision /ɪmˌpeəd ˈvɪʒ(ə)n/ *noun* eyesight which is not fully clear

impairment /ɪmˈpeəmənt/ *noun* a condition in which a sense or function is harmed so that it does not work properly ○ *His hearing impairment does not affect his work.* ○ *The impairment was progressive, but she did not notice that her eyesight was getting worse.*

'…impairment – any loss or abnormality of psychological, physical or anatomical structure or function' [WHO]

impalpable /ɪmˈpælpəb(ə)l/ *adjective* not able to be felt when touched

impediment /ɪmˈpedɪmənt/ *noun* an obstruction

imperforate /ɪmˈpɜːf(ə)rət/ *adjective* without an opening

imperforate anus /ɪmˌpɜːf(ə)rət ˈeɪnəs/ *noun* same as **proctatresia**

imperforate hymen /ɪmˌpɜːf(ə)rət ˈhaɪmen/ *noun* a membrane in the vagina which is missing the opening for the menstrual flow

impermeable /ɪmˈpɜːmiəb(ə)l/ *adjective* not allowing liquids or gases to pass through

impetigo /ˌɪmpɪˈtaɪgəʊ/ *noun* an irritating and very contagious skin disease caused by staphylococci, which spreads rapidly and is easily passed from one child to another, but can be treated with antibiotics

implant *noun* /ˈɪmplɑːnt/ something grafted or inserted into a person, e.g. tissue, a drug, inert material or a device such as a pacemaker ■ *verb* /ɪmˈplɑːnt/ **1.** to fix into something ○ *The ovum implants in the wall of the uterus.* **2.** to graft or insert tissue, a drug, inert material or a device ○ *The site was implanted with the biomaterial.*

implantation /ˌɪmplɑːnˈteɪʃ(ə)n/ *noun* **1.** the act of grafting or inserting tissue, a drug, inert material or a device into a person, or the introduction of one tissue into another surgically **2.** same as **nidation**

implant material /'ımplɑ:nt mə,tɪərɪəl/ *noun* a substance grafted or inserted into a person

implant site /'ımplɑ:nt saɪt/ *noun* a place in or on the body where the implant is positioned

impotence /'ımpət(ə)ns/ *noun* the inability in a male to have an erection or to ejaculate, and so have sexual intercourse

impotent /'ımpət(ə)nt/ *adjective* (*of a man*) unable to have sexual intercourse

impregnate /'ımpregneɪt/ *verb* **1.** to make a female pregnant **2.** to soak a cloth with a liquid ○ *a cloth impregnated with antiseptic*

impregnation /,ımpreg'neɪʃ(ə)n/ *noun* the action of impregnating

impression /ım'preʃ(ə)n/ *noun* **1.** a mould of a person's jaw by a dentist before making a denture **2.** a depression on an organ or structure into which another organ or structure fits ◇ **cardiac impression 1.** concave area near the centre of the upper surface of the liver under the heart **2.** depression on the mediastinal part of the lungs where they touch the pericardium

improve /ım'pru:v/ *verb* to get better, or make something better ○ *She was very ill, but she is improving now.*

improvement /ım'pru:vmənt/ *noun* the act of getting better ○ *The patient's condition has shown a slight improvement.* ○ *Doctors have not detected any improvement in her asthma.*

impulse /'ımpʌls/ *noun* **1.** a message transmitted by a nerve **2.** a sudden feeling of wanting to act in a specific way

impure /ım'pjʊə/ *adjective* not pure

impurity /ım'pjʊərɪti/ *noun* a substance which is not pure or clean ○ *The kidneys filter impurities out of the blood.*

in- /ın/ *prefix* **1.** in, into, towards **2.** not

inaccessible /,ınək'sesıb(ə)l/ *adjective* **1.** physically difficult or impossible to reach **2.** very technical and difficult to understand

inactive /ın'æktıv/ *adjective* **1.** not being active, not moving ○ *Patients must not be allowed to become inactive.* **2.** not working ○ *The serum makes the poison inactive.*

inactivity /,ınæk'tıvıti/ *noun* a lack of activity

inanition /,ınə'nıʃ(ə)n/ *noun* a state of exhaustion caused by starvation

inarticulate /,ınɑ:'tıkjʊlət/ *adjective* **1.** without joints or segments, as in the bones of the skull **2.** unable to speak fluently or intelligibly **3.** not understandable as speech or language

in articulo mortis /ın ɑ:,tıkjʊləʊ 'mɔ:tıs/ *adverb* a Latin phrase meaning 'at the onset of death'

inborn /ın'bɔ:n/ *adjective* congenital, which is in the body from birth ○ *A body has an inborn tendency to reject transplanted organs.*

inbreeding /'ınbri:dıŋ/ *noun* a situation where closely related males and females, or those with very similar genetic make-up, have children together, so allowing congenital conditions to be passed on

incapacitated /,ınkə'pæsıteıtıd/ *adjective* not able to act or work ○ *He was incapacitated for three weeks by his accident.*

incarcerated /ın'kɑ:səreıtıd/ *adjective* referring to a hernia which cannot be corrected by physical manipulation

incest /'ınsest/ *noun* an act of sexual intercourse or other sexual activity with so close a relative, that it is illegal or culturally not allowed

incidence /'ınsıd(ə)ns/ *noun* the number of times something happens in a specific population over a period of time ○ *the incidence of drug-related deaths* ○ *Men have a higher incidence of strokes than women.*

incidence rate /'ınsıd(ə)ns reıt/ *noun* the number of new cases of a disease during a given period, per thousand of population

incipient /ın'sıpıənt/ *adjective* just beginning or in its early stages ○ *He has an incipient appendicitis.* ○ *The tests detected incipient diabetes mellitus.*

incise /ın'saız/ *verb* to cut into something

incised wound /ın'saızd wu:nd/ *noun* a wound with clean edges, caused by a sharp knife or razor

incision /ın'sıʒ(ə)n/ *noun* a cut in a person's body made by a surgeon using a scalpel, or any cut made with a sharp knife or razor ○ *The first incision is made two millimetres below the second rib.* Compare **excision**

incisional /ın'sıʒ(ə)n(ə)l/ *adjective* referring to an incision

incisional hernia /ın,sıʒ(ə)n(ə)l 'hɜ:nıə/ *noun* a hernia which breaks through the abdominal wall at a place where a surgical incision was made during an operation

incisor /ın'saızə/, **incisor tooth** /ın'saızə tu:θ/ *noun* one of the front teeth, of which there are four each in the upper and lower jaws, which are used to cut off pieces of food. See illustration at TEETH in Supplement

inclusion /ın'klu:ʒ(ə)n/ *noun* something enclosed inside something else

inclusion bodies /ın'klu:ʒ(ə)n ,bɒdiz/ *plural noun* very small particles found in cells infected by a virus

inclusive /ın'klu:sıv/ *adjective* (*of health services*) provided whether or not someone has a disability or special needs

incoherent /,ınkəʊ'hıərənt/ *adjective* not able to speak in a way which makes sense

incompatibility /,ınkəmpætı'bılıti/ *noun* the fact of being incompatible ○ *the incompatibility of the donor's blood with that of the patient*

incompatible /ˌɪnkəm'pætɪb(ə)l/ *adjective*
1. referring to something which does not go together with something else **2.** referring to drugs which must not be used together because they undergo chemical change and the therapeutic effect is lost or changed to something undesirable **3.** referring to tissue which is genetically different from other tissue, making it impossible to transplant into that tissue

incompatible blood /ˌɪnkəmpætəb(ə)l 'blʌd/ *noun* blood from a donor that does not match the blood of the person receiving the transfusion

incompetence /ɪn'kɒmpɪt(ə)ns/ *noun* the inability to do a particular act, especially a lack of knowledge or skill which makes a person unable to do particular job

incompetent cervix /ɪn,kɒmpɪt(ə)nt 'sɜːvɪks/ *noun* a dysfunctional cervix of the uterus which is often the cause of spontaneous abortions and premature births and can be remedied by purse-string stitching

incomplete abortion /ˌɪnkəmpliːt ə'bɔːʃ(ə)n/ *noun* an abortion where part of the contents of the uterus is not expelled

incomplete fracture /ˌɪnkəmpliːt 'fræktʃə/ *noun* a fracture that does not go all the way through a bone

incontinence /ɪn'kɒntɪnəns/ *noun* the inability to control the discharge of urine or faeces (NOTE: Single incontinence is the inability to control the bladder. Double incontinence is the inability to control both the bladder and the bowels.)

incontinence pad /ɪn'kɒntɪnəns pæd/ *noun* a pad of material to absorb urine

incontinent /ɪn'kɒntɪnənt/ *adjective* unable to control the discharge of urine or faeces

incoordination /ˌɪnkəʊɔːdɪ'neɪʃ(ə)n/ *noun* a situation in which the muscles in various parts of the body do not act together, making it impossible to carry out some actions

incubation /ˌɪŋkjʊ'beɪʃ(ə)n/ *noun* **1.** the development of an infection inside the body before the symptoms of the disease appear **2.** the keeping of an ill or premature baby in a controlled environment in an incubator **3.** the process of culturing cells or microorganisms under controlled conditions

incubation period /ˌɪŋkjʊ'beɪʃ(ə)n ˌpɪəriəd/ *noun* the time during which a virus or bacterium develops in the body after contamination or infection, before the appearance of the symptoms of the disease. Also called **stadium invasioni**

incubator /'ɪŋkjʊbeɪtə/ *noun* **1.** an apparatus for growing bacterial cultures **2.** an enclosed container in which a premature baby can be kept, within which conditions such as temperature and oxygen levels can be controlled

incudes /ɪn'kjuːdiːz/ plural of **incus**

incus /'ɪŋkəs/ *noun* one of the three ossicles in the middle ear, shaped like an anvil. See illustration at EAR in Supplement

independent /ˌɪndɪ'pendənt/ *adjective* not controlled by someone or something else

independent nursing function /ˌɪndɪ pendənt 'nɜːsɪŋ ˌfʌŋkʃən/ *noun* any part of the nurse's job for which the nurse takes full responsibility

Inderal /'ɪndəræl/ a trade name for propranolol

index finger /'ɪndeks ˌfɪŋgə/ *noun* the first finger next to the thumb

indican /'ɪndɪkæn/ *noun* potassium salt

indication /ˌɪndɪ'keɪʃ(ə)n/ *noun* a situation or sign which suggests that a specific treatment should be given or that a condition has a particular cause ○ *Sulpha drugs have been replaced by antibiotics in many indications.* ◊ **contraindication**

indicator /'ɪndɪkeɪtə/ *noun* **1.** a substance which shows something, e.g. a substance secreted in body fluids which shows which blood group a person belongs to **2.** something that serves as a warning or guide

indigenous /ɪn'dɪdʒɪnəs/ *adjective* **1.** natural or inborn **2.** native to or representative of a country or region

indigestion /ˌɪndɪ'dʒestʃən/ *noun* a disturbance of the normal process of digestion, where the person experiences pain or discomfort in the stomach ○ *He is taking tablets to relieve his indigestion* or *He is taking indigestion tablets.* ◊ **dyspepsia**

indigo carmine /ˌɪndɪgəʊ 'kɑːmaɪn/ *noun* a blue dye which is injected into a person to test how well their kidneys are working

indirect contact /ˌɪndaɪrekt 'kɒntækt/ *noun* the fact of catching a disease by inhaling germs or by being in contact with a vector

indisposed /ˌɪndɪ'spəʊzd/ *adjective* slightly ill ○ *My mother is indisposed and cannot see any visitors.*

indisposition /ˌɪndɪspə'zɪʃ(ə)n/ *noun* a slight illness

individualise /ˌɪndɪ'vɪdʒuə,laɪz/, **individualize** *verb* to provide something that matches the needs of a specific person or situation ○ *individualised care*

individualised nursing care /ˌɪndɪ,vɪd juəlaɪzd 'nɜːsɪŋ keə/ *noun* care which is designed to provide exactly what one particular patient needs ○ *The home's staff are specially trained to provide individualised nursing care.*

Indocid /'ɪndəsɪd/ a trade name for indomethacin

indolent /'ɪndələnt/ *adjective* **1.** causing little pain **2.** referring to an ulcer which develops slowly and does not heal

indomethacin /ˌɪndəʊˈmeθəsɪn/ *noun* a drug that reduces pain, fever and inflammation, especially that caused by arthritis

indrawing /ɪnˈdrɔːɪŋ/ *noun* the act of pulling towards the inside

indrawn /ɪnˈdrɔːn/ *adjective* pulled inside

induce /ɪnˈdjuːs/ *verb* to make something happen □ **to induce labour** to make a woman go into labour

induced abortion /ɪnˌdjuːst əˈbɔːʃ(ə)n/ *noun* an abortion which is deliberately caused by drugs or by surgery

induction /ɪnˈdʌkʃən/ *noun* **1.** the process of starting or speeding up the birth of a baby **2.** the stimulation of an enzyme's production when the substance on which it acts increases in concentration **3.** a process by which one part of an embryo influences another part's development **4.** information and support given to new employees in an organisation

induction of labour /ɪnˌdʌkʃən əv ˈleɪbə/ *noun* the action of starting childbirth artificially

induration /ˌɪndjʊəˈreɪʃ(ə)n/ *noun* the hardening of tissue or of an artery because of pathological change

induratum /ˌɪndjʊəˈreɪtəm/ ♦ **erythema**

industrial disease /ɪnˈdʌstriəl dɪˌziːz/ *noun* a disease which is caused by the type of work done by a worker or by the conditions in which he or she works, e.g. by dust produced or chemicals used in the factory

indwelling catheter /ɪnˌdwelɪŋ ˈkæθɪtə/ *noun* a catheter left in place for a period of time after its introduction

inebriation /ɪˌniːbrɪˈeɪʃ(ə)n/ *noun* a state where a person is drunk, especially habitually drunk

inert /ɪˈnɜːt/ *adjective* **1.** (*of person*) not moving **2.** (*of chemical, etc.*) not active or not producing a chemical reaction

inertia /ɪˈnɜːʃə/ *noun* a lack of activity in the body or mind

in extremis /ɪn ɪksˈtriːmɪs/ *adverb* at the moment of death

infant /ˈɪnfənt/ *noun* a child under two years of age

infanticide /ɪnˈfæntɪsaɪd/ *noun* **1.** the act of killing an infant **2.** a person who kills an infant

infantile /ˈɪnfəntaɪl/ *adjective* **1.** referring to small children **2.** referring to a disease which affects children

infantile convulsions /ˌɪnfəntaɪl kənˈvʌlʃənz/, **infantile spasms** /ˌɪnfəntaɪl ˈspæzəmz/ *plural noun* convulsions or minor epileptic fits in small children

infantile paralysis /ˌɪnfəntaɪl pəˈræləsɪs/ *noun* a former name for poliomyelitis

infantilism /ɪnˈfæntɪlɪz(ə)m/ *noun* a condition in which a person keeps some characteristics of an infant when he or she becomes an adult

infant mortality rate /ˌɪnfənt mɔːˈtælɪti reɪt/ *noun* the number of infants who die per thousand births

infant respiratory distress syndrome /ˌɪnfənt rɪˌspɪrət(ə)ri dɪˈstres ˌsɪndrəʊm/ *noun* a condition of newborn babies in which the lungs do not function properly. Abbr **IRDS**

infarct /ˈɪnfɑːkt/ *noun* an area of tissue which is killed when the blood supply is cut off by the blockage of an artery

infarction /ɪnˈfɑːkʃ(ə)n/ *noun* a condition in which tissue is killed by the cutting off of the blood supply

'…cerebral infarction accounts for about 80% of first-ever strokes' [*British Journal of Hospital Medicine*]

infect /ɪnˈfekt/ *verb* to contaminate someone or something with microorganisms that cause disease or toxins ○ *The disease infected her liver.* ○ *The whole arm soon became infected.*

infected wound /ɪnˌfektɪd ˈwuːnd/ *noun* a wound into which bacteria have entered

infection /ɪnˈfekʃən/ *noun* **1.** the entry or introduction into the body of microorganisms, which then multiply ○ *As a carrier he was spreading infection to other people in the office.* **2.** an illness which is caused by the entry of microbes into the body ○ *She is susceptible to minor infections.*

infectious /ɪnˈfekʃəs/ *adjective* referring to a disease which is caused by microorganisms and can be transmitted to other persons by direct means ○ *This strain of flu is highly infectious.* ○ *Her measles is at the infectious stage.*

infectious disease /ɪnˌfekʃəs dɪˈziːz/ *noun* a disease caused by microorganisms such as bacteria, viruses or fungi. ◊ **communicable disease, contagious disease**

infectious hepatitis /ɪnˌfekʃəs ˌhepəˈtaɪtɪs/ *noun* hepatitis A, transmitted by a carrier through food or drink. Also called **infective hepatitis**

infectious mononucleosis /ɪnˌfekʃəs ˌmɒnəʊˌnjuːkliˈəʊsɪs/ *noun* an infectious disease where the body has an excessive number of white blood cells. Also called **glandular fever**

infectious parotitis /ɪnˌfekʃəs ˌpærəˈtaɪtɪs/ *noun* same as **mumps**

infectious virus hepatitis /ɪnˌfekʃəs ˈvaɪrəs ˌhepətaɪtɪs/ *noun* hepatitis transmitted by a carrier through food or drink

infective /ɪnˈfektɪv/ *adjective* referring to a disease caused by a microorganism, which can be caught from another person but which may not always be directly transmitted

infective enteritis /ɪnˌfektɪv ˌentəˈraɪtɪs/ *noun* enteritis caused by bacteria

infective hepatitis /ɪnˌfektɪv ˌhepəˈtaɪtɪs/ *noun* same as **infectious hepatitis**

infectivity /ˌɪnfek'tɪvɪti/ *noun* the fact of being infective ○ *The patient's infectivity can last about a week.*

inferior /ɪn'fɪəriə/ *adjective* referring to a lower part of the body. Opposite **superior**

inferior aspect /ɪnˌfɪəriər 'æspekt/ *noun* a view of the body from below

inferiority /ɪnˌfɪəri'ɒrɪti/ *noun* the fact of being lower in value or quality, substandard. Opposite **superiority**

inferiority complex /ɪnˌfɪəri'ɒrɪti ˌkɒmpleks/ *noun* a mental disorder arising from a combination of wanting to be noticed and fear of humiliation. The resulting behaviour may either be aggression or withdrawal from the external world.

inferior mesenteric artery /ɪnˌfɪəriə mesenˌterɪk 'ɑːtəri/ *noun* one of the arteries which supply the transverse colon and rectum

inferior vena cava /ɪnˌfɪəriə ˌviːnə 'kɑːvə/ *noun* the main vein carrying blood from the lower part of the body to the heart. See illustration at HEART in Supplement, KIDNEY in Supplement

infertile /ɪn'fɜːtaɪl/ *adjective* not fertile, not able to reproduce

infertility /ˌɪnfə'tɪlɪti/ *noun* the fact of not being fertile, not able to reproduce

infest /ɪn'fest/ *verb* (*of parasites*) to be present somewhere in large numbers ○ *The child's hair was infested with lice.*

infestation /ˌɪnfe'steɪʃ(ə)n/ *noun* the fact of having large numbers of parasites, or an invasion of the body by parasites ○ *The condition is caused by infestation of the hair with lice.*

infiltrate /'ɪnfɪltreɪt/ *verb* (*of liquid or waste*) to pass from one part of the body to another through a wall or membrane and be deposited in the other part ■ *noun* a substance which has infiltrated a part of the body

'…the chest roentgenogram often discloses interstitial pulmonary infiltrates, but may occasionally be normal' [*Southern Medical Journal*]

infiltration /ˌɪnfɪl'treɪʃ(ə)n/ *noun* **1.** the process where a liquid passes through the walls of one part of the body into another part **2.** a condition in which waste is brought to and deposited around cells

'…the lacrimal and salivary glands become infiltrated with lymphocytes and plasma cells. The infiltration reduces lacrimal and salivary secretions which in turn leads to dry eyes and dry mouth' [*American Journal of Nursing*]

infirm /ɪn'fɜːm/ *adjective* old and weak

infirmary /ɪn'fɜːməri/ *noun* **1.** a room in a school or workplace where people can go if they are ill **2.** a former name for a hospital (NOTE: **Infirmary** is still used in the names of some hospitals: **the Glasgow Royal Infirmary**.)

infirmity /ɪn'fɜːmɪti/ *noun* a lack of strength and energy because of illness or age (*formal*)

inflame /ɪn'fleɪm/ *verb* to make an organ or a tissue react to an infection, an irritation or a blow by becoming sore, red and swollen

inflamed /ɪn'fleɪmd/ *adjective* sore, red and swollen ○ *The skin has become inflamed around the sore.*

inflammation /ˌɪnflə'meɪʃ(ə)n/ *noun* the fact of having become sore, red and swollen as a reaction to an infection, an irritation or a blow ○ *She has an inflammation of the bladder* or *a bladder inflammation.* ○ *The body's reaction to infection took the form of an inflammation of the eyelid.*

inflammatory /ɪn'flæmət(ə)ri/ *adjective* causing an organ or a tissue to become sore, red and swollen

inflammatory bowel disease /ɪnˌflæmət(ə)ri 'bauəl dɪˌziːz/ *noun* any condition, e.g. Crohn's disease, colitis or ileitis, in which the bowel becomes inflamed

inflammatory response /ɪnˌflæmət(ə)ri rɪ 'spɒns/, **inflammatory reaction** /ɪn ˌflæmət(ə)ri rɪ'ækʃən/ *noun* any condition where an organ or a tissue reacts to an external stimulus by becoming inflamed ○ *She showed an inflammatory response to the ointment.*

inflate /ɪn'fleɪt/ *verb* to fill something with air, or be filled with air ○ *The abdomen is inflated with air before a coelioscopy.* ○ *In valvuloplasty, a balloon is introduced into the valve and inflated.*

influenza /ˌɪnflu'enzə/ *noun* an infectious disease of the upper respiratory tract with fever and muscular aches, which is transmitted by a virus and can occur in epidemics. Also called **flu**

COMMENT: The influenza virus is spread by droplets of moisture in the air, so the disease can be spread by coughing or sneezing. Influenza can be quite mild, but virulent strains occur from time to time, such as Spanish influenza or Hong Kong flu, and can weaken the person so much that he or she becomes susceptible to pneumonia and other more serious infections.

informal patient /ɪnˌfɔːm(ə)l 'peɪʃ(ə)nt/ *noun* a patient who has admitted himself or herself to a hospital, without being referred by a doctor

information /ˌɪnfə'meɪʃ(ə)n/ *noun* facts about something ○ *Have you any information about the treatment of sunburn?* ○ *The police won't give us any information about how the accident happened.* ○ *You haven't given me enough information about when your symptoms started.* ○ *That's a very useful piece* or *bit of information.* (NOTE: No plural: **some information; a piece of information**.)

informed /ɪn'fɔːmd/ *adjective* having the latest information

informed consent /ɪnˌfɔːmd kən'sent/ *noun* an agreement to allow a procedure to be carried out, given by a patient, or the guardian of a patient, who has been provided with all the necessary information

infra- /'ɪnfrə/ *prefix* below

infracostal /,ɪnfrə'kɒst(ə)l/ *adjective* lying below the ribs

infraorbital nerve /,ɪnfrɔ:'bɪt(ə)l 'nɜ:v/ *noun* a continuation of the maxillary nerve below the orbit of the eye

infraorbital vein /,ɪnfrɔ:'bɪt(ə)l 'veɪn/ *noun* a vessel draining the face through the infraorbital canal to the pterygoid plexus

infrared /,ɪnfrə'red/ *adjective* relating to infrared radiation ■ *noun* invisible electromagnetic radiation between light and radio waves

infrared radiation /,ɪnfrəred ,reɪdi'eɪʃ(ə)n/ *noun* same as **infrared rays**

infrared rays /,ɪnfrəred 'reɪz/ *plural noun* long invisible rays, below the visible red end of the colour spectrum, used to produce heat in body tissues in the treatment of traumatic and inflammatory conditions. ◊ **light therapy**

infundibulum /,ɪnfʌn'dɪbjʊləm/ *noun* any part of the body shaped like a funnel, especially the stem which attaches the pituitary gland to the hypothalamus

infuse /ɪn'fju:z/ *verb* to introduce a solution such as saline, sucrose or glucose using a drip into a vein, body cavity or the intestinal tract in order to treat or feed someone

infusion /ɪn'fju:ʒ(ə)n/ *noun* **1.** a drink made by pouring boiling water on a dry substance such as herb tea or a powdered drug **2.** the process of putting of liquid into someone's body, using a drip

ingesta /ɪn'dʒestə/ *plural noun* food or liquid that enters the body via the mouth

ingestion /ɪn'dʒestʃən/ *noun* **1.** the act of taking in food, drink or medicine by the mouth **2.** the process by which a foreign body such as a bacillus is surrounded by a cell

ingredient /ɪn'gri:diənt/ *noun* a substance which is used with others to make something

ingrowing toenail /,ɪngrəʊɪŋ 'təʊneɪl/, **ingrowing nail** /,ɪngrəʊɪŋ 'neɪl/, **ingrown toenail** /,ɪngrəʊn 'təʊneɪl/ *noun* a toenail which is growing into the skin at the side of the nail, causing pain and swelling. The toenail cuts into the tissue on either side of it, creating inflammation and sometimes sepsis and ulceration.

inguinal /'ɪŋgwɪn(ə)l/ *adjective* referring to the groin

inguinal canal /,ɪŋgwɪn(ə)l kə'næl/ *noun* a passage in the lower abdominal wall, carrying the spermatic cord in the male and the round ligament of the uterus in the female

inguinale /,ɪŋgwɪ'neɪli/ ♦ **granuloma inguinale**

inguinal hernia /,ɪŋgwɪn(ə)l 'hɜ:niə/ *noun* a hernia where the intestine bulges through the muscles in the groin

inguinal ligament /,ɪŋgwɪn(ə)l 'lɪgəmənt/ *noun* a ligament in the groin, running from the spine to the pubis. Also called **Poupart's ligament**

inguinal region /,ɪŋgwɪn(ə)l 'ri:dʒən/ *noun* the part of the body where the lower abdomen joins the top of the thigh. ◊ **groin**

INH *abbr* isoniazid

inhalant /ɪn'heɪlənt/ *noun* a medicinal substance which is breathed in

inhalation /,ɪnhə'leɪʃ(ə)n/ *noun* **1.** the act of breathing in. Opposite **exhalation 2.** the action of breathing in a medicinal substance as part of a treatment

inhale /ɪn'heɪl/ *verb* **1.** to breathe in, or breathe something in ○ *She inhaled some toxic gas fumes and was rushed to hospital.* **2.** to breathe in a medicinal substance as part of a treatment. Opposite **exhale**

inhaler /ɪn'heɪlə/ *noun* a small device for administering medicinal substances into the mouth or nose so that they can be breathed in

inherent /ɪn'hɪərənt/ *adjective* referring to a thing which is part of the essential character of a person or a permanent characteristic of an organism

inherit /ɪn'herɪt/ *verb* to receive genetically controlled characteristics from a parent ○ *She inherited her father's red hair.* ○ *Haemophilia is a condition which is inherited through the mother's genes.*

inheritance /ɪn'herɪt(ə)ns/ *noun* **1.** the process by which genetically controlled characteristics pass from parents to offspring ○ *the inheritance of chronic inflammatory bowel disease* **2.** all of the qualities and characteristics which are passed down from parents ○ *an unfortunate part of our genetic inheritance*

inherited /ɪn'herɪtɪd/ *adjective* passed on from a parent through the genes ○ *an inherited disorder of the lungs*

inhibit /ɪn'hɪbɪt/ *verb* to prevent an action happening, or stop a functional process ○ *Aspirin inhibits the clotting of blood.* □ **to have an inhibiting effect on something** to block something, to stop something happening

inhibition /,ɪnhɪ'bɪʃ(ə)n/ *noun* **1.** the action of blocking or preventing something happening, especially of preventing a muscle or organ from functioning properly **2.** (*in psychology*) the suppression of a thought which is associated with a sense of guilt **3.** (*in psychology*) the blocking of a spontaneous action by some mental influence

inhibitor /ɪn'hɪbɪtə/ *noun* a substance which inhibits

inhibitory nerve /ɪn'hɪbɪtəri ,nɜ:v/ *noun* a nerve which stops a function taking place ○ *The vagus nerve is an inhibitory nerve which slows down the action of the heart.*

inion /'ɪnɪən/ *noun* a part of the occipital bone that can be felt as a slight lump at the back of the skull just above the neck

inject /ɪn'dʒekt/ *verb* to put a liquid into someone's body under pressure, by using a hollow needle inserted into the tissues ○ *He was injected with morphine.* ○ *She injected herself with a drug.*

injected /ɪn'dʒektɪd/ *adjective* **1.** referring to a liquid or substance introduced into the body **2.** referring to surface blood vessels which are swollen

injection /ɪn'dʒekʃən/ *noun* **1.** the act of injecting a liquid into the body ○ *He had a penicillin injection.* **2.** a liquid introduced into the body

injure /'ɪndʒə/ *verb* to hurt someone or a part of the body ○ *Six people were injured in the accident.*

injured /'ɪndʒəd/ *adjective* referring to someone who has been hurt ■ *plural noun* □ **the injured** people who have been injured ○ *All the injured were taken to the nearest hospital.*

injury /'ɪndʒəri/ *noun* damage or a wound caused to a person's body ○ *His injuries required hospital treatment.* ○ *He received severe facial injuries in the accident.*

injury scoring system /,ɪndʒəri 'skɔːrɪŋ ,sɪstəm/ *noun* any system used for deciding how severe an injury is ○ *a standard lung injury scoring system* Abbr **ISS**

inlay /'ɪnleɪ/ *noun* (*in dentistry*) a type of filling for teeth

inlet /'ɪnlet/ *noun* a passage or opening through which a cavity can be entered

INN *abbr* international nonproprietary name

innards /'ɪnədz/ *plural noun* the internal organs of the body, especially the intestines

innate /ɪ'neɪt/ *adjective* inherited, which is present in a body from birth

inner /'ɪnə/ *adjective* referring to a part which is inside

inner ear /,ɪnər 'ɪə/ *noun* the part of the ear inside the head, behind the eardrum, containing the semicircular canals, the vestibule and the cochlea

inner pleura /,ɪnə 'plʊərə/ *noun* same as **visceral pleura**

innervate /'ɪnɜːveɪt/ *verb* to cause a muscle, organ or other part of the body to act

innervation /,ɪnɜː'veɪʃ(ə)n/ *noun* the nerve supply to an organ, including both motor nerves and sensory nerves

innocent /'ɪnəs(ə)nt/ *adjective* referring to a growth which is benign, not malignant

innominate /ɪ'nɒmɪnət/ *adjective* with no name

innominate artery /ɪ,nɒmɪnət 'ɑːtəri/ *noun* the largest branch of the arch of the aorta, which continues as the right common carotid and right subclavian arteries

innominate bone /ɪ,nɒmɪnət 'bəʊn/ *noun* same as **hip bone**

innominate vein /ɪ,nɒmɪnət 'veɪn/ *noun* same as **brachiocephalic vein**

inoculant /ɪ'nɒkjʊlənt/ *noun* same as **inoculum**

inoculate /ɪ'nɒkjʊleɪt/ *verb* to introduce vaccine into a person's body in order to make the body create its own antibodies, so making the person immune to the disease ○ *The baby was inoculated against diphtheria.* (NOTE: You inoculate someone **with** or **against** a disease.)

inoculation /ɪ,nɒkjʊ'leɪʃ(ə)n/ *noun* the action of inoculating someone ○ *Has the baby had a diphtheria inoculation?*

inoculum /ɪ'nɒkjʊləm/ *noun* a substance used for inoculation, e.g. a vaccine (NOTE: The plural is **inocula**.)

inoperable /ɪn'ɒpər(ə)b(ə)l/ *adjective* referring to a condition which cannot be operated on ○ *The surgeon decided that the cancer was inoperable.*

inorganic /,ɪnɔː'gænɪk/ *adjective* referring to a substance which is not made from animal or vegetable sources

inorganic acid /,ɪnɔːgænɪk 'æsɪd/ *noun* an acid which comes from minerals, used in dilute form to help indigestion

inotropic /,ɪnəʊ'trɒpɪk/ *adjective* affecting the way muscles contract, especially those of the heart

inpatient /'ɪn,peɪʃ(ə)nt/ *noun* someone who stays overnight or for some time in a hospital for treatment or observation. Compare **outpatient**

inquest /'ɪŋkwest/ *noun* an inquiry by a coroner into the cause of a death

COMMENT: An inquest has to take place where death is violent or not expected, where death could be murder or where a prisoner dies and when police are involved.

insane /ɪn'seɪn/ *adjective* mentally unwell (*dated, informal*)

insanitary /ɪn'sænɪt(ə)ri/ *adjective* not hygienic ○ *Cholera spread rapidly because of the insanitary conditions in the town.*

insect /'ɪnsekt/ *noun* a small animal with six legs and a body in three parts

insect bite /'ɪnsekt baɪt/ *noun* a sting caused by an insect which punctures the skin to suck blood, and in so doing introduces irritants

COMMENT: Most insect bites are simply irritating. Others can be more serious, as insects can carry the organisms which produce typhus, sleeping sickness, malaria, filariasis and many other diseases.

insecticide /ɪn'sektɪsaɪd/ *noun* a substance which kills insects

insemination /ɪn,semɪ'neɪʃ(ə)n/ *noun* the introduction of sperm into the vagina

insensible /ɪn'sensɪb(ə)l/ *adjective* **1.** lacking feeling or consciousness **2.** not aware of or responding to a stimulus **3.** too slight to be perceived by the senses

insert /ɪn'sɜːt/ *verb* to put something into something ○ *The catheter is inserted into the passage.*

insertion /ɪn'sɜːʃ(ə)n/ *noun* **1.** the point of attachment of a muscle to a bone **2.** the point where an organ is attached to its support **3.** a change in the structure of a chromosome, where a segment of the chromosome is introduced into another member of the complement

insides /ɪn'saɪdz/ *plural noun* internal organs, especially the stomach and intestines (*informal*) ○ *He says he has a pain in his insides.* ○ *You ought to see the doctor if you think there is something wrong with your insides.*

insidious /ɪn'sɪdiəs/ *adjective* causing harm without showing any obvious signs

insidious disease /ɪn,sɪdiəs dɪ'ziːz/ *noun* a disease which causes damage before being detected

insight /'ɪnsaɪt/ *noun* the ability of a person to realise that he or she is ill or has particular problems or characteristics

insipidus /ɪn'sɪpɪdəs/ ♦ **diabetes insipidus**

in situ /ɪn 'sɪtjuː/ *adverb* in place

insoluble /ɪn'sɒljʊb(ə)l/ *adjective* not able to be dissolved in liquid

insoluble fibre /ɪn,sɒljʊb(ə)l 'faɪbə/ *noun* the fibre in bread and cereals, which is not digested but which swells inside the intestine

insomnia /ɪn'sɒmniə/ *noun* the inability to sleep ○ *She experiences insomnia.* ○ *What does the doctor give you for your insomnia?* Also called **sleeplessness**

insomniac /ɪn'sɒmniæk/ *noun* a person who has insomnia

inspiration /,ɪnspɪ'reɪʃ(ə)n/ *noun* the act of taking air into the lungs. Opposite **expiration**
   COMMENT: Inspiration takes place when the muscles of the diaphragm contract, allowing the lungs to expand.

inspiratory /ɪn'spaɪrət(ə)ri/ *adjective* referring to breathing in

inspire /ɪn'spaɪə/ *verb* to inhale air or a gas into the lungs

inspissated /ɪn'spɪseɪtɪd/ *adjective* referring to a liquid which is thickened by removing water from it

inspissation /,ɪnspɪ'seɪʃ(ə)n/ *noun* the act of removing water from a solution to make it thicker

instep /'ɪnstep/ *noun* an arched top part of the foot

instil /ɪn'stɪl/, **instill** *verb* to put a liquid in something drop by drop ○ *Instil four drops in each nostril twice a day.*

instillation /,ɪnstɪ'leɪʃ(ə)n/ *noun* **1.** the process of putting a liquid in drop by drop **2.** a liquid put in drop by drop

instinct /'ɪnstɪŋkt/ *noun* a tendency or ability which the body has from birth and does not need to learn ○ *The body has a natural instinct to protect itself from danger.*

instinctive /ɪn'stɪŋktɪv/ *adjective* automatic or unconscious rather than planned ○ *an instinctive reaction*

institution /,ɪnstɪ'tjuːʃ(ə)n/ *noun* a place where people are cared for, e.g. a hospital or clinic, especially a psychiatric hospital or children's home

institutionalisation /,ɪnstɪ,tjuːʃ(ə)nəlaɪ'zeɪʃ(ə)n/, **institutionalization**, **institutional neurosis** /,ɪnstɪtjuːʃən(ə)l njʊ'rəʊsɪs/ *noun* a condition in which someone has become so adapted to life in an institution that it is impossible for him or her to live outside it

institutionalise /,ɪnstɪ'tjuːʃ(ə)nəlaɪz/, **institutionalize** *verb* to put someone into an institution

instructions /ɪn'strʌkʃənz/ *plural noun* spoken or written information which explains how something is used or how to do something ○ *She gave the taxi driver instructions on how to get to the hospital.* ○ *The instructions are written on the medicine bottle.* ○ *We can't use this machine because we have lost the book of instructions.*

instrument /'ɪnstrʊmənt/ *noun* a piece of equipment or a tool ○ *The doctor had a box of surgical instruments.*

instrumental /,ɪnstrʊ'ment(ə)l/ *adjective* □ **instrumental in** helping to do something ○ *She was instrumental in developing the new technique.*

instrumental delivery /,ɪnstrʊment(ə)l dɪ'lɪv(ə)ri/ *noun* childbirth where the doctor uses forceps to help the baby out of the mother's uterus

insufficiency /,ɪnsə'fɪʃ(ə)nsi/ *noun* **1.** the fact of not being strong or large enough to perform usual functions ○ *The patient is suffering from a renal insufficiency.* **2.** the incompetence of an organ

insufflate /'ɪnsəfleɪt/ *verb* to blow gas, vapour or powder into the lungs or another body cavity as a treatment

insufflation /,ɪnsə'fleɪʃ(ə)n/ *noun* the act of blowing gas, vapour or powder into the lungs or another body cavity as a treatment

insula /'ɪnsjʊlə/ *noun* part of the cerebral cortex which is covered by the folds of the sulcus

insulin /'ɪnsjʊlɪn/ *noun* a hormone produced by the islets of Langerhans in the pancreas
   COMMENT: Insulin controls the way in which the body converts sugar into energy and regulates the level of sugar in the blood. A lack of insulin caused by diabetes mellitus makes the level of glucose in the blood rise. Insulin injections are regularly used to treat diabetes mellitus, but care has to be taken not to exceed the dose as this will cause hyperinsulinism and hypoglycaemia.

insulinase /'ɪnsjʊlɪneɪz/ *noun* an enzyme which breaks down insulin

insulin dependence /,ɪnsjʊlɪn dɪ'pendəns/ *noun* the fact of being dependent on insulin injections

insulin-dependent diabetes /,ɪnsjʊlɪn dɪ,pendənt daɪə'biːtiz/ *noun* same as **Type I diabetes mellitus**

insulinoma /,ɪnsjʊlɪ'nəʊmə/ *noun* a tumour in the islets of Langerhans

insulin-resistant /,ɪnsjʊlɪn rɪ'zɪst(ə)nt/ *adjective* referring to a condition in which the muscle and other tissue cells respond inadequately to insulin, as in Type II diabetes

insulin shock /'ɪnsjʊlɪn ,ʃɒk/ *noun* a serious drop in blood sugar, caused by too much insulin accompanied by sweating, dizziness, trembling and eventually coma

insuloma /,ɪnsjʊ'ləʊmə/ *noun* same as **insulinoma**

insult /'ɪnsʌlt/ *noun* **1.** a physical injury or trauma **2.** something that causes a physical injury or trauma

intact /ɪn'tækt/ *adjective* having all body parts present and undamaged

intake /'ɪnteɪk/ *noun* **1.** the amount of a substance taken in ○ *a high intake of alcohol* ○ *She was advised to reduce her intake of sugar.* **2.** the process of taking in a substance

Intal /'ɪntæl/ a trade name for a preparation of cromolyn sodium

integrated service /,ɪntɪɡreɪtɪd 'sɜːvɪs/ *noun* a broad care service provided by health and social agencies acting together

integrative medicine /,ɪntɪɡreɪtɪv 'med(ə)s(ə)n/ *noun* the combination of mainstream therapies and those complementary or alternative therapies for which there is scientific evidence of efficacy and safety

integument /ɪn'teɡjʊmənt/ *noun* a covering layer, e.g. the skin

intellect /'ɪntɪlekt/ *noun* a person's ability to think, reason and understand

intelligence /ɪn'telɪdʒəns/ *noun* the ability to learn and understand quickly

intelligence quotient /ɪn'telɪdʒəns ,kwəʊʃ(ə)nt/ *noun* the ratio of the mental age, as given by an intelligence test, to the chronological age of the person. Abbr **IQ**

intense /ɪn'tens/ *adjective* referring to a very strong pain ○ *She is suffering from intense post herpetic neuralgia.*

intensity /ɪn'tensɪti/ *noun* the strength of e.g. pain

intensive care /ɪn,tensɪv 'keə/ *noun* **1.** the continual supervision and treatment of an extremely ill person in a special section of a hospital ○ *The patient was put in intensive care.* ◊ **residential care 2.** same as **intensive care unit**

intensive care unit /ɪn,tensɪv 'keə ,juːnɪt/ *noun* a section of a hospital equipped with life-saving and life-support equipment in which seriously ill people who need constant medical attention are cared for. Abbr **ICU**

intention /ɪn'tenʃən/ *noun* a plan to do something

intention tremor /ɪn'tenʃən ,tremə/ *noun* a trembling of the hands seen when people suffering from particular brain diseases make voluntary movements to try to touch something

inter- /ɪntə/ *prefix* between

interaction /,ɪntər'ækʃən/ *noun* an effect which two or more substances such as drugs have on each other

interatrial septum /,ɪntər'eɪtriəl ,septəm/ *noun* a membrane between the right and left atria in the heart

intercalated /ɪn'tɜːkəleɪtɪd/ *adjective* inserted between other tissues

intercalated disc /ɪn,tɜːkəleɪtɪd 'dɪsk/ *noun* closely applied cell membranes at the end of adjacent cells in cardiac muscle, seen as transverse lines

intercellular /,ɪntə'seljʊlə/ *adjective* between the cells in tissue

intercostal /,ɪntə'kɒst(ə)l/ *adjective* between the ribs ■ *noun* same as **intercostal muscle**

intercostal muscle /ɪntə,kɒst(ə)l 'mʌs(ə)l/ *noun* one of the muscles between the ribs

COMMENT: The intercostal muscles expand and contract the thorax, so changing the pressure in the thorax and making the person breathe in or out. There are three layers of intercostal muscle: external, internal and innermost or intercostalis intimis.

intercourse /'ɪntəkɔːs/ *noun* same as **sexual intercourse**

intercurrent disease /,ɪntəkʌrənt dɪ'ziːz/, **intercurrent infection** /,ɪntəkʌrənt ɪn'fekʃən/ *noun* a disease or infection which affects someone who has another disease

interdigital /,ɪntə'dɪdʒɪt(ə)l/ *adjective* referring to the space between the fingers or toes

interdisciplinary /,ɪntə,dɪsɪ'plɪnəri/ *adjective* combining two or more different areas of medical or scientific study

interferon /,ɪntə'fɪərɒn/ *noun* a protein produced by cells, usually in response to a virus, and which then reduces the spread of viruses

COMMENT: Although it is now possible to synthesise interferon outside the body, large-scale production is extremely expensive and the substance has not proved as successful at combating viruses as had been hoped, though it is used in multiple sclerosis with some success.

interior /ɪn'tɪəriə/ *noun* a part which is inside ■ *adjective* inside

interleukin /,ɪntə'luːkɪn/ *noun* a protein produced by the body's immune system

interleukin-1 /,ɪntəluːkɪn 'wʌn/ *noun* a protein which causes high temperature. Abbr **IL-1**

interleukin-2 /ˌɪntəluːkɪn 'tuː/ *noun* a protein which stimulates T-cell production, used in the treatment of cancer. Abbr **IL-2**

interlobar /ˌɪntə'ləʊbə/ *adjective* between lobes

interlobar artery /ˌɪntələʊbər 'ɑːtəri/ *noun* an artery running towards the cortex on each side of a renal pyramid

interlobular /ˌɪntə'lɒbjʊlə/ *adjective* between lobules

interlobular artery /ɪntə'lɒbjʊlə ˌɑːtəri/ *noun* one of the arteries running to the glomeruli of the kidneys

intermediate care /ˌɪntəmiːdiət 'keə/ *noun* care following surgery or illness that can be delivered in special units attached to a hospital or in the person's home by a special multidisciplinary team

intermedius /ˌɪntə'miːdiəs/ ◗ **vastus intermedius**

intermenstrual /ˌɪntə'menstruəl/ *adjective* between the menstrual periods

intermittent /ˌɪntə'mɪt(ə)nt/ *adjective* occurring at intervals

intermittent claudication /ˌɪntəmɪt(ə)nt ˌklɔːdɪ'keɪʃ(ə)n/ *noun* a condition of the arteries causing severe pain in the legs which makes the person limp after having walked a short distance (NOTE: The symptoms increase with walking, stop after a short rest and recur when the person walks again.)

intermittent fever /ˌɪntəmɪt(ə)nt 'fiːvə/ *noun* fever which rises and falls regularly, as in malaria

intermittent self-catheterisation /ˌɪntəmɪt(ə)nt self ˌkæθitəraɪ'zeɪʃ(ə)n/ *noun* a procedure in which someone puts a catheter through the urethra into their own bladder from time to time to empty out the urine. Abbr **ISC**

intern /'ɪntɜːn/ *noun US* a medical graduate who is working in a hospital before being licensed to practise medicine. ◊ **house officer**

interna /ɪn'tɜːnə/ ◗ **otitis interna**

internal /ɪn'tɜːn(ə)l/ *adjective* inside the body or a body part. Opposite **external** □ **the drug is for internal use only** it should not be used on the outside of the body

internal auditory meatus /ɪnˌtɜːn(ə)l ɔːdɪt(ə)ri mi'eɪtəs/ *noun* a channel which takes the auditory nerve through the temporal bone

internal bleeding /ɪnˌtɜːn(ə)l 'bliːdɪŋ/ *noun* loss of blood inside the body, e.g. from a wound in the intestine

internal capsule /ɪnˌtɜːn(ə)l 'kæpsjuːl/ *noun* a bundle of fibres linking the cerebral cortex and other parts of the brain

internal cardiac massage /ɪnˌtɜːn(ə)l ˌkɑːdiæk 'mæsɑːʒ/ *noun* a method of making the heart start beating again by pressing on the heart itself

internal carotid /ɪnˌtɜːn(ə)l kæ'rɒtɪd/ *noun* an artery in the neck, behind the external carotid, which gives off the ophthalmic artery and ends by dividing into the anterior and middle cerebral arteries

internal derangement of the knee /ɪnˌtɜːn(ə)l dɪ'reɪnʒmənt əv ðə 'niː/ *noun* a condition in which the knee cannot function properly because of a torn meniscus. Abbr **IDK**

internal ear /ɪnˌtɜːn(ə)l 'ɪə/ *noun* the part of the ear inside the head, behind the eardrum, containing the semicircular canals, the vestibule and the cochlea

internal haemorrhage /ɪnˌtɜːn(ə)l 'hem(ə)rɪdʒ/ *noun* a haemorrhage which takes place inside the body

internal haemorrhoids /ɪnˌtɜːn(ə)l 'hemərɔɪdz/ *plural noun* swollen veins inside the anus

internal iliac artery /ɪnˌtɜːn(ə)l 'ɪliæk ˌɑːtəri/ *noun* an artery which branches from the aorta in the abdomen and leads to the pelvis

internal injury /ɪnˌtɜːn(ə)l 'ɪndʒəri/ *noun* damage to one of the internal organs

internal jugular /ɪnˌtɜːn(ə)l 'dʒʌgjʊlə/ *noun* the largest jugular vein in the neck, leading to the brachiocephalic veins

internally /ɪn'tɜːn(ə)li/ *adverb* inside the body ○ *He was bleeding internally.*

internal medicine /ɪnˌtɜːn(ə)l 'med(ə)s(ə)n/ *noun US* the treatment of diseases of the internal organs by specialists

internal nares /ɪnˌtɜːn(ə)l 'neəriːz/ *plural noun* the two openings shaped like funnels leading from the nasal cavity to the pharynx. Also called **posterior nares**

internal oblique /ɪnˌtɜːn(ə)l ə'bliːk/ *noun* the middle layer of muscle covering the abdomen, beneath the external oblique

internal organ /ɪnˌtɜːn(ə)l 'ɔːgən/ *noun* an organ situated inside the body

internal respiration /ɪnˌtɜːn(ə)l ˌrespɪ'reɪʃ(ə)n/ *noun* the part of respiration concerned with the passage of oxygen from the blood to the tissues, and the passage of carbon dioxide from the tissues to the blood

International Committee of the Red Cross /ɪntəˌnæʃ(ə)n(ə)l kəˌmɪti əv ðə ˌred 'krɒs/ *noun* an international organisation which provides mainly emergency medical help, but also relief to victims of earthquakes, floods and other disasters, or to prisoners of war. Abbr **ICRC**

International Council of Nurses /ˌɪntənæʃ(ə)n(ə)l ˌkaʊnsəl əv 'nɜːsɪz/ *noun* an organisation founded in 1899 which now represents nurses in more than 120 countries. Its aims are to bring nurses together, to advance nursing worldwide and to influence health policies. Abbr **ICN**

international nonproprietary name /ˌɪntənæʃ(ə)nəl ˌnɒnprəpraɪət(ə)ri 'neɪm/ *noun* each of 8,000 names selected by the World Health Organization that are the legally required generic names for pharmaceutical product labelling for most countries in the world, including all EU countries. Abbr **INN**

international unit /ˌɪntənæʃ(ə)nəl 'juːnɪt/ *noun* an internationally agreed standard used in pharmacy as a measure of a substance such as a drug or hormone. Abbr **IU**

interneurone /ˌɪntə'njuːrəʊn/ *noun* a neurone with short processes which is a link between two other neurones in sensory or motor pathways

internist /'ɪntɜːnɪst/ *noun* a specialist who treats diseases of the internal organs by non-surgical means

internodal /ˌɪntə'nəʊd(ə)l/ *adjective* between two nodes

internuncial neurone /ˌɪntənʌnʃ(ə)l 'njuːrəʊn/ *noun* a neurone which links two other nerve cells

internus /ɪn'tɜːnəs/ *noun* medial rectus muscle in the orbit of the eye

interoceptor /ˌɪntərəʊ'septə/ *noun* a nerve cell which reacts to a change taking place inside the body

interosseous /ˌɪntər'ɒsiəs/ *adjective* between bones

interparietal /ˌɪntəpə'raɪət(ə)l/ *adjective* between parietal parts, especially between the parietal bones ■ *noun* same as **interparietal bone**

interparietal bone /ˌɪntəpə'raɪət(ə)l ˌbəʊn/ *noun* a triangular bone in the back of the skull, rarely present in humans

interpeduncular cistern /ˌɪntəpə'dʌŋkjʊlər ˌsɪstən/ *noun* subarachnoid space between the two cerebral hemispheres beneath the midbrain and the hypothalamus

interphalangeal joint /ˌɪntəfə'lændʒɪəl dʒɔɪnt/ *noun* a joint between the phalanges. Also called **IP joint**

interphase /'ɪntəfeɪz/ *noun* a stage of a cell between divisions

interpubic joint /ˌɪntəpjuːbɪk 'dʒɔɪnt/ *noun* a piece of cartilage which joins the two sections of the pubic bone. Also called **pubic symphysis**

interruptus /ˌɪntə'rʌptəs/ ♦ **coitus interruptus**

intersex /'ɪntəseks/ *noun* an organism that has both male and female characteristics

intersexuality /ˌɪntəsekʃu'ælɪti/ *noun* a condition in which a baby has both male and female characteristics, as in Klinefelter's syndrome and Turner's syndrome

interstice /ɪn'tɜːstɪs/ *noun* a small space between body parts or within a tissue

interstitial /ˌɪntə'stɪʃ(ə)l/ *adjective* referring to tissue located in the spaces between parts of something, especially between the active tissues in an organ

interstitial cell /ˌɪntə'stɪʃ(ə)l sel/ *noun* a testosterone-producing cell between the tubules in the testes. Also called **Leydig cell**

interstitial cell stimulating hormone /ˌɪntə,stɪʃ(ə)l sel 'stɪmjʊleɪtɪŋ ˌhɔːməʊn/ *noun* a hormone produced by the pituitary gland which stimulates the formation of corpus luteum in females and testosterone in males. Abbr **ICSH**. Also called **luteinising hormone**

interstitial cystitis /ˌɪntəstɪʃ(ə)l sɪ'staɪtɪs/ *noun* a persistent nonbacterial condition in which someone has bladder pain and wants to pass urine frequently. It is often associated with Hunner's ulcer.

intertrigo /ˌɪntə'traɪgəʊ/ *noun* an irritation which occurs when two skin surfaces rub against each other, as in the armpit or between the buttocks

intertubercular plane /ˌɪntətjuˌbɜːkjʊlə 'pleɪn/ *noun* same as **transtubercular plane**

intervention /ˌɪntə'venʃən/ *noun* a treatment

interventional radiology /ˌɪntəvenʃən(ə)l ˌreɪdi'ɒlədʒi/ *noun* the area of medicine which uses X-rays, ultrasound and computer-assisted tomography to guide small instruments into the body for procedures such as biopsies, draining fluids or widening narrow vessels

interventricular /ˌɪntəven'trɪkjʊlə/ *adjective* between ventricles in the heart or brain

interventricular foramen /ˌɪntəven,trɪkjʊlə fə'reɪmən/ *noun* an opening in the brain between the lateral ventricle and the third ventricle, through which the cerebrospinal fluid passes

interventricular septum /ˌɪntəven,trɪkjʊlə 'septəm/ *noun* a membrane between the right and left ventricles in the heart

intervertebral /ˌɪntə'vɜːtɪbr(ə)l/ *adjective* between vertebrae

intervertebral disc /ˌɪntə,vɜːtɪbrəl 'dɪsk/ *noun* a round plate of cartilage which separates two vertebrae in the spinal column. See illustration at **CARTILAGINOUS JOINT** in Supplement. Also called **vertebral disc**

intervertebral foramen /ˌɪntə,vɜːtɪbrəl fə'reɪmən/ *noun* a space between two vertebrae

intestinal /ɪn'testɪn(ə)l/ *adjective* referring to the intestine

intestinal anastomosis /ɪn,testɪn(ə)l ə,næstə'məʊsɪs/ *noun* a surgical operation to join one part of the intestine to another, after a section has been removed

intestinal flora /ɪn,testɪn(ə)l 'flɔːrə/ *plural noun* beneficial bacteria which are always present in the intestine

intestinal glands /ɪn'testɪn(ə)l glændz/ *plural noun* tubular glands found in the mucous membrane of the small and large intestine, especially those between the bases of the villi in the small intestine. Also called **Lieberkühn's glands, crypts of Lieberkühn**

intestinal infection /ɪn'testɪn(ə)l ɪn ,fekʃ(ə)n/ *noun* an infection in the intestines

intestinal juice /ɪn'testɪn(ə)l dʒuːs/ *noun* alkaline liquid secreted by the small intestine which helps to digest food

intestinal obstruction /ɪn,testɪn(ə)l əb 'strʌkʃən/ *noun* a blocking of the intestine

intestinal villi /ɪn,testɪn(ə)l 'vɪlaɪ/ *plural noun* projections on the walls of the intestine which help in the digestion of food

intestinal wall /ɪn,testɪn(ə)l 'wɔːl/ *noun* the layers of tissue which form the intestine

intestine /ɪn'testɪn/ *noun* the part of the digestive system between the stomach and the anus that digests and absorbs food. ◊ **large intestine, small intestine** (NOTE: For other terms referring to the intestines, see words beginning with **entero-**.)

intima /'ɪntɪmə/ ♦ **tunica intima**

intolerance /ɪn'tɒlərəns/ *noun* the fact of being unable to endure something such as pain or to take a medicine without an adverse reaction ○ *He developed an intolerance to penicillin.*

intoxicant /ɪn'tɒksɪkənt/ *noun* a substance which induces a state of intoxication or poisoning, e.g. an alcoholic drink

intoxicate /ɪn'tɒksɪkeɪt/ *verb* to make someone incapable of controlling his or her actions, because of the influence of alcohol on the nervous system ○ *He drank six glasses of whisky and became completely intoxicated.*

intoxication /ɪn,tɒksɪ'keɪʃ(ə)n/ *noun* a condition which results from the absorption and diffusion in the body of a substance such as alcohol ○ *She was driving in a state of intoxication.*

intra- /ɪntrə/ *prefix* inside

intra-abdominal /,ɪntrə æb'dɒmɪn(ə)l/ *adjective* inside the abdomen

intra-articular /,ɪntrə ɑː'tɪkjʊlə/ *adjective* inside a joint

intracellular /,ɪntrə'seljʊlə/ *adjective* inside a cell

intracerebral haematoma /,ɪntrə ,serəbrəl ,hiːmə'təʊmə/ *noun* a blood clot inside a cerebral hemisphere

intracranial /,ɪntrə'kreɪnɪəl/ *adjective* inside the skull

intracranial pressure /,ɪntrəkreɪnɪəl 'preʃə/ *noun* the pressure of the subarachnoi-

dal fluid, which fills the space between the skull and the brain. Abbr **ICP**

intractable /ɪn'træktəb(ə)l/ *adjective* not able to be controlled ○ *an operation to relieve intractable pain*

intracutaneous /,ɪntrəkjuː'teɪnɪəs/ *adjective* inside layers of skin tissue

intracutaneous injection /,ɪntrəkjuː ,teɪnɪəs ɪn'dʒekʃən/ *noun* an injection of a liquid between the layers of skin, as for a test for an allergy

intradermal /,ɪntrə'dɜːm(ə)l/ *adjective* within or introduced between the layers of the skin

intradermal test /ɪntrə'dɜːm(ə)l test/ *noun* a test requiring an injection into the thickness of the skin, e.g. a Mantoux test or an allergy test

intradermic /,ɪntrə'dɜːmɪk/ *adjective* same as **intradermal**

intradural /,ɪntrə'djʊərəl/ *adjective* inside the dura mater

intramedullary /,ɪntrəme'dʌləri/ *adjective* inside the bone marrow or spinal cord

intramural /,ɪntrə'mjʊərəl/ *adjective* inside the wall of an organ

intramuscular /,ɪntrə'mʌskjʊlə/ *adjective* inside a muscle

intramuscular injection /,ɪntrə,mʌskjʊlə ɪn'dʒekʃən/ *noun* an injection of liquid into a muscle, e.g. for a slow release of a drug

intranasal /,ɪntrə'neɪz(ə)l/ *adjective* inside or into the nose

intraocular /,ɪntrə'ɒkjʊlə/ *adjective* inside the eye

intraocular lens /,ɪntrə,ɒkjʊlə 'lenz/ *noun* an artificial lens implanted inside the eye. Abbr **IOL**

intraocular pressure /,ɪntrə,ɒkjʊlə 'preʃə/ *noun* the pressure inside the eyeball (NOTE: If the pressure is too high, it causes glaucoma.)

intraoperative ultrasound *noun* high-resolution imaging used in surgery. Abbr **IOUS**

intraorbital /,ɪntrə'ɔːbɪt(ə)l/ *adjective* within the orbit of the eye

intraosseous /,ɪntrə'ɒsɪəs/ *adjective* within a bone

intrathecal /,ɪntrə'θiːk(ə)l/ *adjective* inside a sheath, especially inside the intradural or subarachnoid space

intratracheal /,ɪntrətrə'kɪəl/ *adjective* within the trachea. Also called **endotracheal**

intratubercular plane /,ɪntrətjuːbɜːkjʊlə 'pleɪn/ *noun* a plane at right angles to the sagittal plane, passing through the tubercles of the iliac crests

intrauterine /,ɪntrə'juːtəraɪn/ *adjective* inside the uterus

intrauterine contraceptive device /,ɪntrə juːtəraɪn ,kɒntrə'septɪv dɪ,vaɪs/, **intrauterine device** /,ɪntrəjuːtəraɪn dɪ'vaɪs/ *noun* a plastic coil placed inside the uterus to prevent pregnancy. Abbr **IUCD, IUD**

intravascular /ˌɪntrə'væskjʊlə/ *adjective* inside the blood vessels

intravenous /ˌɪntrə'viːnəs/ *adjective* into a vein. Abbr **IV**

intravenous drip /ˌɪntrəviːnəs 'drɪp/ *noun* a thin tube that is inserted into a vein and is used to very gradually give a person fluids, either for rehydration, feeding or medication purposes

intravenous feeding /ˌɪntrəviːnəs 'fiːdɪŋ/ *noun* the procedure of giving someone liquid food by means of a tube inserted into a vein

intravenous injection /ˌɪntrəviːnəs ɪn 'dʒekʃən/ *noun* an injection of liquid into a vein, e.g. for the fast release of a drug

intravenously /ˌɪntrə'viːnəsli/ *adverb* into a vein ○ *a fluid given intravenously*

intravenous pyelogram /ˌɪntrəviːnəs 'paɪələgræm/, **intravenous urogram** /ˌɪntrə viːnəs 'jʊərəgræm/ *noun* a series of X-ray photographs of the kidneys using pyelography. Abbr **IVP**

intravenous pyelography /ˌɪntrəviːnəs ˌpaɪə'lɒgrəfi/, **intravenous urography** /ˌɪntrə viːnəs jʊ'rɒgrəfi/ *noun* an X-ray examination of the urinary tract after opaque liquid has been injected intravenously into the body and taken by the blood into the kidneys

intraventricular /ˌɪntrəven'trɪkjʊlə/ *adjective* inside or placed into a ventricle in the heart or the brain

intra vitam /ˌɪntrə 'vaɪtəm/ *adverb* during life

intrinsic /ɪn'trɪnsɪk/ *adjective* belonging to the essential nature of an organism, or entirely within an organ or part

intrinsic factor /ɪnˌtrɪnsɪk 'fæktə/ *noun* a protein produced in the gastric glands which reacts with the extrinsic factor, and which, if lacking, causes pernicious anaemia

intrinsic ligament /ɪnˌtrɪnsɪk 'lɪgəmənt/ *noun* a ligament which forms part of the capsule surrounding a joint

intrinsic muscle /ɪnˌtrɪnsɪk 'mʌs(ə)l/ *noun* a muscle lying completely inside the part or segment, especially of a limb, which it moves

intro- /ɪntrəʊ/ *prefix* inward

introduce /ˌɪntrə'djuːs/ *verb* **1.** to put something into something ○ *He used a syringe to introduce a medicinal substance into the body.* ○ *The nurse introduced the catheter into the vein.* **2.** to present two people to one another when they have never met before ○ *Can I introduce my new assistant?* **3.** to start a new way of doing something ○ *The hospital has introduced a new screening process for cervical cancer.*

introduction /ˌɪntrə'dʌkʃən/ *noun* **1.** the act of putting something inside something ○ *the*

introduction of semen into the woman's uterus ○ *the introduction of an endotracheal tube into the patient's mouth* **2.** the act of starting a new process

introitus /ɪn'trəʊɪtəs/ *noun* an opening into any hollow organ or canal

introjection /ˌɪntrəʊ'dʒekʃən/ *noun* a person's unconscious adoption of the attitudes or values of another person whom he or she wants to impress

introspection /ˌɪntrə'spekʃən/ *noun* a detailed and sometimes obsessive mental self-examination of feelings, thoughts and motives

introversion /ˌɪntrə'vɜːʃ(ə)n/ *noun* a condition in which a person is excessively interested in himself or herself and his or her own mental state. Compare **extroversion**

introvert /'ɪntrəvɜːt/ *noun* a person who thinks only about himself or herself and his or her own mental state. Compare **extrovert**

introverted /'ɪntrəʊˌvɜːtɪd/ *adjective* referring to someone who thinks only about himself or herself

intubate /'ɪntjuːbeɪt/ *verb* to insert a tube into any organ or part of the body. Also called **catheterise**

intubation /ˌɪntjuː'beɪʃ(ə)n/ *noun* the therapeutic insertion of a tube into the larynx through the glottis to allow the passage of air. Also called **catheterisation**

intumescence /ˌɪntjuː'mes(ə)ns/ *noun* the swelling of an organ

intussusception /ˌɪntəsə'sepʃən/ *noun* a condition in which part of the gastrointestinal tract becomes folded down inside the part beneath it, causing an obstruction and strangulation of the folded part

inunction /ɪn'ʌŋkʃən/ *noun* **1.** the act of rubbing an ointment into the skin so that the medicine in it is absorbed **2.** an ointment which is rubbed into the skin

in utero /ɪn 'juːtərəʊ/ *adverb, adjective* in, or while still inside, a woman's womb

invade /ɪn'veɪd/ *verb* to enter and spread gradually throughout a part of the body, e.g. the entry of a microorganism that causes disease

invagination /ɪnˌvædʒɪ'neɪʃ(ə)n/ *noun* **1.** same as **intussusception 2.** the surgical treatment of hernia, in which a sheath of tissue is made to cover the opening

invalid /'ɪnvəlɪd/ *(dated) noun* someone who has had an illness and has not fully recovered from it or who has been permanently disabled ■ *adjective* weak or disabled

invalidity /ˌɪnvə'lɪdɪti/ *noun* the condition of being disabled

invasion /ɪn'veɪʒ(ə)n/ *noun* the entry of bacteria into a body, or the first attack of a disease

invasive /ɪn'veɪsɪv/ *adjective* **1.** referring to cancer which tends to spread throughout the body **2.** referring to an inspection or treatment which involves entering the body by making an incision. ◊ **non-invasive**

inverse care law /ˌɪnvɜːs ˈkeə lɔː/ noun the idea that the people who most need care and services are least likely or able to access them

inversion /ɪnˈvɜːʃ(ə)n/ noun the fact of being turned towards the inside ○ *inversion of the foot* See illustration at **ANATOMICAL TERMS** in Supplement □ **inversion of the uterus** a condition in which the top part of the uterus touches the cervix, as if it were inside out, which may happen after childbirth

invertase /ɪnˈvɜːteɪz/ noun an enzyme in the intestine which splits sucrose

investigation /ɪnˌvestɪˈɡeɪʃ(ə)n/ noun an examination to find out the cause of something which has happened ○ *The Health Authority ordered an investigation into how the drugs were stolen.*

investigative surgery /ɪnˌvestɪɡətɪv ˈsɜːdʒəri/ noun surgery to investigate the cause of a condition

in vitro /ɪn ˈviːtrəʊ/ adjective, adverb a Latin phrase meaning 'in a glass', i.e. in a test tube or similar container used in a laboratory □ **in vitro activity**, **in vitro experiment** experiment which takes place in the laboratory

in vitro fertilisation /ɪn ˌviːtrəʊ ˌfɜːtəlaɪˈzeɪʃ(ə)n/ noun the fertilisation of an ovum in the laboratory. ◊ **test-tube baby**. Abbr **IVF**

in vivo /ɪn ˈviːvəʊ/ adjective, adverb a Latin phrase meaning 'in living tissue', i.e. referring to an experiment which takes place on the living body

in vivo experiment /ɪn ˌviːvəʊ ɪkˈsperɪmənt/ noun an experiment on a living body, e.g. that of an animal

involucrum /ˌɪnvəˈluːkrəm/ noun a covering of new bone which forms over diseased bone

involuntary /ɪnˈvɒlənt(ə)ri/ adjective done automatically, without any conscious thought or decision-making being involved ○ *Patients are advised not to eat or drink, to reduce the risk of involuntary vomiting while on the operating table.*

involuntary action /ɪnˌvɒlənt(ə)ri ˈækʃən/ noun an action which someone does without thinking or making a conscious decision

involuntary muscle /ɪnˌvɒlənt(ə)ri ˈmʌs(ə)l/ noun a muscle supplied by the autonomic nervous system, and therefore not under voluntary control, e.g. the muscle which activates a vital organ such as the heart

involution /ˌɪnvəˈluːʃ(ə)n/ noun **1.** the return of an organ to its usual size, e.g. the shrinking of the uterus after childbirth **2.** a period of decline of organs which sets in after middle age

involutional /ˌɪnvəˈluːʃ(ə)n(ə)l/ adjective referring to involution

involutional melancholia /ɪnvəˌluːʃ(ə)n(ə)l melənˈkəʊliə/ noun a depression

which occurs in people, mainly women, after middle age, probably caused by a change of endocrine secretions

iodine /ˈaɪədiːn/ noun a chemical element which is essential to the body, especially to the functioning of the thyroid gland (NOTE: Lack of iodine in the diet can cause goitre. The chemical symbol is **I**.)

IOL abbr intraocular lens

ion /ˈaɪən/ noun an atom that has an electric charge (NOTE: Ions with a positive charge are called cations and those with a negative charge are called anions.)

COMMENT: It is believed that living organisms, including human beings, react to the presence of ionised particles in the atmosphere. Hot dry winds contain a higher proportion of positive ions than usual and these winds cause headaches and other illnesses. If negative ionised air is introduced into an air-conditioning system, the incidence of headaches and nausea among people working in the building may be reduced.

ionise /ˈaɪənaɪz/, **ionize** verb to give an atom an electric charge

ioniser /ˈaɪənaɪzə/, **ionizer** noun a machine that increases the amount of negative ions in the atmosphere of a room, so counteracting the effect of positive ions

ionotherapy /aɪˌɒnəˈθerəpi/ noun treatment by ions introduced into the body via an electric current

iontophoresis /aɪˌɒntəʊfəˈriːsɪs/ noun the movement of ions through a biological material when an electric current passes through it

IOUS abbr intraoperative ultrasound

IPAV abbr intermittent positive airway ventilation. ◊ **positive pressure ventilation**

ipecacuanha /ˌɪpɪkækjuˈænə/ noun a drug made from the root of an American plant, used as a treatment for coughs, and also as an emetic (NOTE: The US term is **ipecac**.)

IP joint /ˌaɪ ˈpiː dʒɔɪnt/ noun same as **interphalangeal joint**

IPPV abbr intermittent positive pressure ventilation. ◊ **positive pressure ventilation**

ipratropium /ˌaɪprəˈtrəʊpiəm/, **ipratropium bromide** /ˌaɪprəˌtrəʊpiəm ˈbrəʊmaɪd/ noun a drug which helps to relax muscles in the airways, used in the treatment of conditions such as asthma, bronchitis and emphysema

ipsilateral /ˌɪpsɪˈlæt(ə)rəl/ adjective located on or affecting the same side of the body. Also called **homolateral**. Opposite **contralateral**

IQ abbr intelligence quotient

IRDS abbr infant respiratory distress syndrome

irid- /ˈɪrɪd/ prefix referring to the iris

iridectomy /ˌɪrɪˈdektəmi/ noun the surgical removal of part of the iris

iridencleisis /ˌɪrɪdenˈklaɪsɪs/ noun an operation to treat glaucoma, where part of the iris is used as a drainage channel through a hole in the conjunctiva

iridocyclitis /ˌɪrɪdəʊsɪˈklaɪtɪs/ *noun* inflammation of the iris and the tissues which surround it

iridodialysis /ˌɪrɪdəʊdaɪˈæləsɪs/ *noun* the separation of the iris from its insertion

iridoplegia /ˌɪrɪdəʊˈpliːdʒə/ *noun* paralysis of the iris

iridoptosis /ˌɪrɪdəʊˈtəʊsɪs/ *noun* the pushing forward of the iris through a wound in the cornea

iridotomy /ˌɪrɪˈdɒtəmi/ *noun* a surgical incision into the iris

iris /ˈaɪrɪs/ *noun* a coloured ring in the eye, with the pupil at its centre. See illustration at EYE in Supplement

COMMENT: The iris acts like the aperture in a camera shutter, opening and closing to allow more or less light through the pupil into the eye.

iritis /aɪˈraɪtɪs/ *noun* inflammation of the iris

iron /ˈaɪən/ *noun* **1.** a chemical element essential to the body, present in foods such as liver and eggs **2.** a common grey metal (NOTE: The chemical symbol is **Fe**.)

COMMENT: Iron is an essential part of the red pigment in red blood cells. Lack of iron in haemoglobin results in iron-deficiency anaemia. Storage of too much iron in the body results in haemochromatosis.

iron-deficiency anaemia /ˌaɪən dɪˈfɪʃ(ə)nsi əˌniːmiə/ *noun* anaemia caused by a lack of iron in red blood cells

iron lung /ˌaɪən ˈlʌŋ/ *noun* same as **Drinker respirator**

irradiation /ɪˌreɪdiˈeɪʃ(ə)n/ *noun* **1.** the process of spreading from a centre, as e.g., nerve impulses do **2.** the use of radiation to treat people or to kill bacteria in food

irreducible hernia /ɪrɪˌdjuːsəb(ə)l ˈhɜːniə/ *noun* a hernia where the organ cannot be returned to its usual position

irregular /ɪˈreɡjʊlə/ *adjective* not regular or normal ○ *The patient's breathing was irregular.* ○ *The nurse noted that the patient had developed an irregular pulse.* ○ *He has irregular bowel movements.*

irrigate /ˈɪrɪɡeɪt/ *verb* to wash out a cavity in the body

irrigation /ˌɪrɪˈɡeɪʃ(ə)n/ *noun* the washing out of a cavity in the body

irritability /ˌɪrɪtəˈbɪlɪti/ *noun* the state of being irritable

irritable /ˈɪrɪtəb(ə)l/ *adjective* **1.** easily able to become inflamed and painful **2.** feeling annoyed and impatient

irritable bowel syndrome /ˌɪrɪtəb(ə)l ˈbaʊəl ˌsɪndrəʊm/ *noun* ♦ **mucous colitis**. Abbr **IBS**

irritable colon /ˌɪrɪtəb(ə)l ˈkəʊlɒn/ *noun* ♦ **mucous colitis**

irritable hip /ˌɪrɪtəb(ə)l ˈhɪp/ *noun* a condition of pain in the hip which is caused by swelling of the synovium. Treatment involves bed rest, traction and anti-inflammatory drugs.

irritant /ˈɪrɪt(ə)nt/ *noun* a substance which can irritate

irritant dermatitis /ˌɪrɪt(ə)nt ˌdɜːməˈtaɪtɪs/ *noun* same as **contact dermatitis**

irritate /ˈɪrɪteɪt/ *verb* to cause a painful reaction in part of the body, especially to make it inflamed ○ *Some types of wool can irritate the skin.*

irritation /ˌɪrɪˈteɪʃ(ə)n/ *noun* a feeling of being irritated ○ *an irritation caused by the ointment*

ISC *abbr* intermittent self-catheterisation

isch- /ɪsk/ *prefix* too little

ischaemia /ɪˈskiːmiə/ *noun* a deficient blood supply to a part of the body

ischaemic /ɪˈskiːmɪk/ *adjective* lacking in blood

'…the term stroke does not refer to a single pathological entity. Stroke may be haemorrhagic or ischaemic: the latter is usually caused by thrombosis or embolism' [*British Journal of Hospital Medicine*]

ischaemic heart disease /ɪˌskiːmɪk ˈhɑːt dɪˌziːz/ *noun* a disease of the heart caused by a failure in the blood supply, as in coronary thrombosis. Abbr **IHD**

ischi- /ɪski/ *prefix* same as **ischio-** (*used before vowels*)

ischia /ˈɪskiə/ plural of **ischium**

ischial /ˈɪskiəl/ *adjective* referring to the ischium or hip joint

ischial tuberosity /ˌɪskiəl ˌtjuːbəˈrɒsɪti/ *noun* a lump of bone forming the ring of the ischium

ischio- /ɪskiəʊ/ *prefix* referring to the ischium

ischiocavernosus muscle /ˌɪskiəʊkævə ˈnəʊsəs ˌmʌs(ə)l/ *noun* a muscle along one side of the perineum

ischiorectal /ˌɪskiəʊˈrekt(ə)l/ *adjective* referring to both the ischium and the rectum

ischiorectal abscess /ˌɪskiəʊˌrekt(ə)l ˈæbses/ *noun* an abscess which forms in fat cells between the anus and the ischium

ischiorectal fossa /ˌɪskiəʊˌrekt(ə)l ˈfɒsə/ *noun* a space on either side of the lower end of the rectum and anal canal

ischium /ˈɪskiəm/ *noun* the lower part of the hip bone in the pelvis. See illustration at PELVIS in Supplement (NOTE: The plural is **ischia**.)

Ishihara colour charts /ˌɪʃɪhɑːrə ˈkʌlə ˌtʃɑːts/ *plural noun* charts used in a test for colour vision in which numbers or letters are shown in dots of primary colours with dots of other colours around them. People with normal colour vision can see them, but people who are colour-blind cannot.

Ishihara test /ˌɪʃɪhɑːrə test/ *noun* a test using **Ishihara colour charts**

islets of Langerhans /ˌaɪləts əv ˈlæŋəhæns/, **islands of Langerhans** /ˌaɪləndz əv ˈlæŋəhænz/, **islet cells** /ˈaɪlət selz/ *plural noun* groups of cells in the pancreas which secrete the hormones glucagon, insulin and gastrin [Described 1869. After Paul Langerhans (1847–88), Professor of Pathological Anatomy at Freiburg, Germany.]

iso- /aɪsəʊ/ *prefix* equal

isoantibody /ˌaɪsəʊˈæntɪbɒdi/ *noun* an antibody which forms in one person as a reaction to antigens from another person (NOTE: The plural is **isoantibodies**.)

isograft /ˈaɪsəʊɡrɑːft/ *noun* a graft of tissue from an identical twin. Also called **syngraft**

isoimmunisation /ˌaɪsəʊˌɪmjunaɪˈzeɪʃ(ə)n/, **isoimmunization** *noun* immunisation of a person with antigens derived from another person

isolate /ˈaɪsəleɪt/ *verb* **1.** to keep one person apart from others because he or she has a dangerous infectious disease **2.** to identify a single virus, bacterium or other pathogen among many ○ *Scientists have been able to isolate the virus which causes Legionnaires' disease.* ○ *Candida is easily isolated from the mouths of healthy adults.*

isolation /ˌaɪsəˈleɪʃ(ə)n/ *noun* the separation of a person, especially one with an infectious disease, from others

isolation ward /ˌaɪsəˈleɪʃ(ə)n wɔːd/ *noun* a special ward where people who have dangerous infectious diseases can be kept isolated from others

isolator /ˈaɪsəleɪtə/ *noun* **1.** a large clear plastic bag in which a person can be nursed, or operated on, in a sterile environment **2.** a room or piece of equipment which keeps people or substances separated from others which may contaminate them ○ *an isolator stretcher* ○ *an isolator cabinet*

isoleucine /aɪsəʊˈluːsiːn/ *noun* an essential amino acid

isometric /ˌaɪsəʊˈmetrɪk/ *adjective* **1.** involving equal measurement ○ *an isometric view of the system* **2.** referring to muscle contraction in which tension occurs with very little shortening of muscle fibres **3.** referring to exercises in which the muscles are put under tension but not contracted

isometrics /ˌaɪsəʊˈmetrɪks/ *plural noun* exercises to strengthen the muscles, in which the muscles contract but do not shorten

isoniazid /ˌaɪsəˈnaɪəzɪd/ *noun* a colourless crystalline compound that is used in the treatment of tuberculosis. Abbr **INH**

isoprenaline /ˌaɪsəʊˈprenəliːn/, **isoproterenol** *noun* a drug that relieves asthma by widening the bronchial tubes in the lungs

isosorbide dinitrate /ˌaɪsəʊˌsɔːbaɪd daɪˈnaɪtreɪt/ *noun* a compound which causes widening or relaxation of the blood vessels, used in the treatment of angina pectoris

isotonic /ˌaɪsəʊˈtɒnɪk/ *adjective* referring to a solution, e.g. a saline drip, which has the same osmotic pressure as blood serum and which can therefore be passed directly into the body. Compare **hypertonic**, **hypotonic**

isotonicity /ˌaɪsətɒˈnɪsɪti/ *noun* the equal osmotic pressure of two or more solutions

isotonic solution /ˌaɪsəʊtɒnɪk səˈluːʃ(ə)n/ *noun* a solution which has the same osmotic pressure as blood serum, or as another liquid it is compared with

isotope /ˈaɪsətəʊp/ *noun* a form of a chemical element which has the same chemical properties as other forms but a different atomic mass

isotretinoin /ˌaɪsəʊtreˈtɪnɔɪn/ *noun* a drug used in the treatment of severe acne and several other skin diseases

ispaghula /ˌɪspəˈɡuːlə/, **ispaghula husk** /ˌɪspəˈɡuːlə hʌsk/ *noun* a natural dietary fibre used to treat constipation, diverticulitis and irritable bowel syndrome

ISS *abbr* injury scoring system

isthmus /ˈɪsməs/ *noun* **1.** a short narrow canal or cavity **2.** a narrow band of tissue joining two larger masses of similar tissue, e.g. the section in the centre of the thyroid gland, which joins the two lobes (NOTE: The plural is **isthmi** or **isthmuses**.)

itch /ɪtʃ/ *noun* **1.** an irritated place on the skin which makes a person want to scratch **2. the itch** same as **scabies** (*informal*) ■ *verb* to produce an irritating sensation, making someone want to scratch

itching /ˈɪtʃɪŋ/ *noun* same as **pruritus**

itchy /ˈɪtʃi/ *adjective* making a person want to scratch ○ *The main symptom of the disease is an itchy red rash.*

-itis /aɪtɪs/ *suffix* inflammation

ITU *abbr* intensive therapy unit

IU *abbr* international unit

IUCD *abbr* intrauterine contraceptive device

IUD *abbr* **1.** intrauterine death **2.** intrauterine device

IUS *abbr* intrauterine system

IV *abbr* intravenous

IVF *abbr* in vitro fertilisation

IVP *abbr* intravenous pyelogram

IVU *abbr* intravenous urography

J

J /dʒeɪ/ *abbr* joule

jab /dʒæb/ *noun* an injection or inoculation (*informal*) ○ *a tetanus jab*

Jacksonian epilepsy /dʒæk,səʊnɪən 'epɪlepsi/ *noun* a form of epilepsy in which the jerking movements start in one part of the body before spreading to others [Described 1863. After John Hughlings Jackson (1835–1911), British neurologist.]

Jacquemier's sign /'dʒækəmɪəz ,saɪn/ *noun* a sign of early pregnancy in which the vaginal mucosa becomes slightly blue due to an increased amount of blood in the arteries [After Jean Marie Jacquemier (1806–79), French obstetrician]

jactitation /,dʒæktɪ'teɪʃ(ə)n/ *noun* the action of constantly moving the body around in a restless way, especially because of mental illness

jag /dʒæg/ *noun* in Scotland, an injection or inoculation (*informal*)

jargon /'dʒɑːgən/ *noun* **1.** the words used by people who have a particular area of knowledge, which are usually only understood by those people ○ *medical jargon* **2.** a stream of words that makes no sense, produced by someone with aphasia or a severe mental disorder

jaundice /'dʒɔːndɪs/ *noun* a condition in which there is an excess of bile pigment in the blood, and in which the pigment is deposited in the skin and the whites of the eyes, which have a yellow colour. Also called **icterus**
> COMMENT: Jaundice can have many causes, usually relating to the liver: the most common are blockage of the bile ducts by gallstones or by disease of the liver and Weil's disease.

jaw /dʒɔː/ *noun* the bones in the face which hold the teeth and form the mouth ○ *He fell down and broke his jaw.* ○ *The punch on his mouth broke his jaw.*
> COMMENT: The jaw has two parts, the upper (the maxillae) being fixed parts of the skull, and the lower (the mandible) being attached to the skull with a hinge so that it can move up and down.

jawbone /'dʒɔːbəʊn/ *noun* one of the bones which form the jaw, especially the lower jaw or mandible

jejun- /dʒɪdʒuːn/ *prefix* same as **jejuno-** (*used before vowels*)

jejunal /dʒɪ'dʒuːn(ə)l/ *adjective* referring to the jejunum

jejunal ulcer /dʒɪ,dʒuːn(ə)l 'ʌlsə/ *noun* an ulcer in the jejunum

jejunectomy /,dʒɪdʒuː'nektəmi/ *noun* a surgical operation to remove all or part of the jejunum (NOTE: The plural is **jejunectomies**.)

jejuno- /dʒiːdʒuːnəʊ/ *prefix* referring to the jejunum

jejunoileostomy /dʒɪ,dʒuːnəʊ,ɪli'ɒstəmi/ *noun* a surgical operation to make an artificial link between the jejunum and the ileum (NOTE: The plural is **jejunoileostomies**.)

jejunostomy /,dʒɪdʒuː'nɒstəmi/ *noun* a surgical operation to make an artificial passage to the jejunum through the wall of the abdomen (NOTE: The plural is **jejunostomies**.)

jejunotomy /,dʒɪdʒuː'nɒtəmi/ *noun* a surgical operation to cut into the jejunum (NOTE: The plural is **jejunotomies**.)

jejunum /dʒɪ'dʒuːnəm/ *noun* the part of the small intestine between the duodenum and the ileum, about 2 metres long. See illustration at DIGESTIVE SYSTEM in Supplement

jerk /dʒɜːk/ *noun* a sudden movement of part of the body which indicates that the local reflex arc is intact ■ *verb* to make sudden movements, or cause something to make sudden movements ○ *In some forms of epilepsy the limbs jerk.*

jet lag /'dʒet læg/ *noun* a condition suffered by people who travel long distances in planes, caused by rapid changes in time zones which affect sleep patterns and meal times and thus interfere with the body's metabolism ○ *We had jet lag when we flew from Australia.*

jet-lagged /'dʒet lægd/ *adjective* experiencing jet lag ○ *jet-lagged travellers* ○ *We were jet-lagged for a week.*

joint /dʒɔɪnt/ *noun* a structure at a point where two or more bones join, especially one which allows movement of the bones ○ *The elbow is a joint in the arm.* ○ *Arthritis is accompanied by stiffness in the joints.* ◊ **Charcot's**

joint (NOTE: For other terms referring to joints, see words beginning with **arthr-, arthro-**.)

joint-breaker fever /'dʒɔɪnt ˌbreɪkə ˌfiːvə/ *noun* same as **o'nyong-nyong fever**

joint capsule /'dʒɔɪnt ˌkæpsjuːl/ *noun* white fibrous tissue which surrounds and holds a joint together. See illustration at SYNO-VIAL JOINT in Supplement

joint investment plan /ˌdʒɔɪnt ɪn 'vestmənt plæn/ *noun* a plan that health and social services draw up together for specific areas of care

joint mouse /'dʒɔɪnt maʊs/ *plural noun* a loose piece of bone or cartilage in the knee joint, making the joint lock

joule /dʒuːl/ *noun* the SI unit of measurement of work or energy. 4.184 joules equals one calorie. Symbol **J**

jugular /'dʒʌgjʊlə/ *adjective* referring to the throat or neck ■ *noun* same as **jugular vein**

COMMENT: There are three jugular veins on each side: the **internal jugular** is large and leads to the brachiocephalic vein, the **external jugular** is smaller and leads to the subclavian vein and the **anterior jugular** is the smallest.

jugular nerve /'dʒʌgjʊlə nɜːv/ *noun* one of the nerves in the neck

jugular trunk /'dʒʌgjʊlə trʌŋk/ *noun* a terminal lymph vessel in the neck, draining into the subclavian vein

jugular vein /'dʒʌgjʊlə veɪn/ *noun* one of the veins which pass down either side of the neck. Also called **jugular**

juice /dʒuːs/ *noun* **1.** liquid from a fruit or vegetable ○ *a glass of orange juice* or *tomato juice* **2.** a natural fluid of the body. ♦ **gastric juice**

jumper's knee /ˌdʒʌmpəz 'niː/ *noun* a painful condition suffered by athletes and dancers in which inflammation develops in the knee joint

junction /'dʒʌŋkʃən/ *noun* a joining point

junior doctor /ˌdʒuːniə 'dɒktə/ *noun* a doctor who is completing his or her training in hospital

junk food /'dʒʌŋk fuːd/ *noun* food of little nutritional value, e.g. high-fat processed snacks, eaten between or instead of meals

juvenile /'dʒuːvənaɪl/ *adjective* relating to or affecting children or adolescents

juxta- /dʒʌkstə/ *prefix* beside or near

juxta-articular /ˌdʒʌkstə ɑː'tɪkjʊlə/ *adjective* occurring near a joint

juxtaposition /ˌdʒʌkstəpə'zɪʃ(ə)n/ *noun* the placing of two or more things side by side so as to make their similarities or differences more obvious

K

k *symbol* kilo-

Kahn test /'kɑːn test/ *noun* a test of blood serum to diagnose syphilis [Described 1922. After Reuben Leon Kahn, Lithuanian-born serologist who worked in the USA.]

kala-azar /ˌkɑːlə ə'zɑː/ *noun* an often fatal form of leishmaniasis caused by the infection of the intestines and internal organs by a parasite, *Leishmania*, spread by flies. Symptoms are fever, anaemia, general wasting of the body and swelling of the spleen and liver.

kalium /'keɪliəm/ *noun* same as **potassium**

kaolin /'keɪəlɪn/ *noun* a fine soft clay used in the making of medical preparations, especially for the treatment of diarrhoea

Kaposi's sarcoma /kəˌpəʊziz sɑː'kəʊmə/ *noun* a cancer which takes the form of many haemorrhagic nodes affecting the skin, especially on the extremities [Described 1872. After Moritz Kohn Karposi (1837–1902), Professor of Dermatology at Vienna, Austria.]

COMMENT: Formerly a relatively rare disease, found mainly in tropical countries, Kaposi's sarcoma is now more common as it is one of the diseases associated with AIDS.

Kartagener's syndrome /ˌkɑːtə'dʒiːnəz ˌsɪndrəʊm/ *noun* a hereditary condition in which all the organs in the chest and abdomen are positioned on the opposite side from the usual one, i.e. the heart and stomach are on the right

karyo- /kæriəʊ/ *prefix* relating to a cell nucleus

karyotype /'kæriəʊtaɪp/ *noun* the chromosome complement of a cell, shown as a diagram or as a set of letters and numbers

Kawasaki disease /ˌkɑːwə'sɑːkiz dɪˌziːz/ *noun* a retrovirus infection that often occurs in small children and causes a high temperature, rash, reddened eyes, peeling skin and swollen lymph nodes

Kayser-Fleischer ring /ˌkaɪzə 'flaɪʃə ˌrɪŋ/ *noun* a brown ring on the outer edge of the cornea, which is a diagnostic sign of hepatolenticular degeneration [Described 1902 by Kayser, 1903 by Fleischer. Bernard Kayser (1869–1954), German ophthalmologist; Bruno Richard Fleischer (1848–1904), German physician.]

kcal *abbr* kilocalorie

Kegel exercises /'keɪg(ə)l ˌeksəsaɪzɪz/ *plural noun* exercises which strengthen the muscles of the pelvic floor in women and help to prevent any accidental leakage of urine when they cough, sneeze or lift things

Keller's operation /'keləz ɒpəˌreɪʃ(ə)n/ *noun* a surgical operation on the big toe to remove a bunion or to correct an ankylosed joint [Described 1904. After William Lordan Keller (1874–1959), US surgeon.]

keloid /'kiːlɔɪd/ *noun* an excessive amount of scar tissue at the site of a skin injury

kerat- /kerət/ *prefix* same as **kerato-** (*used before vowels*)

keratalgia /ˌkerə'tældʒiə/ *noun* pain felt in the cornea

keratectasia /ˌkerətek'teɪziə/ *noun* a condition in which the cornea bulges

keratectomy /ˌkerə'tektəmi/ *noun* a surgical operation to remove the whole or part of the cornea (NOTE: The plural is **keratectomies**.)

keratic /kə'rætɪk/ *adjective* **1.** relating to horny tissue or to keratin **2.** relating to the cornea

keratin /'kerətɪn/ *noun* a protein found in horny tissue such as fingernails, hair or the outer surface of the skin

keratinisation /ˌkerətɪnaɪ'zeɪʃ(ə)n/, **keratinization** *noun* the appearance of horny characteristics in tissue. Also called **cornification**

keratinise /'kerətɪnaɪz, kə'rætɪnaɪz/, **keratinize** *verb* to convert something into keratin or into horny tissue (NOTE: **keratinising – keratinised**)

keratinocyte /ˌkerə'tɪnəʊsaɪt/ *noun* a cell which produces keratin

keratitis /ˌkerə'taɪtɪs/ *noun* inflammation of the cornea

kerato- /kerətəʊ/ *prefix* referring to horn, horny tissue or the cornea

keratoacanthoma /ˌkerətəʊˌækən'θəʊmə/ *noun* a type of benign skin tumour which disappears after a few months (NOTE: The plural is **keratoacanthomas** or **keratoacanthomata**.)

keratoconjunctivitis /ˌkerətəʊkən ˌdʒʌŋktɪˈvaɪtɪs/ *noun* inflammation of the cornea with conjunctivitis

keratoconus /ˌkerətəʊˈkəʊnəs/ *noun* a cone-shaped lump on the cornea

keratoglobus /ˌkerətəʊˈgləʊbəs/ *noun* swelling of the eyeball

keratoma /ˌkerəˈtəʊmə/ *noun* a hard thickened growth due to hypertrophy of the horny zone of the skin (NOTE: The plural is **keratomas** or **keratomata**.)

keratomalacia /ˌkerətəʊməˈleɪʃə/ *noun* **1.** a softening of the cornea frequently caused by Vitamin A deficiency **2.** softening of the horny layer of the skin

keratome /ˈkerətəʊm/ *noun* a surgical knife used for operations on the cornea

keratometer /ˌkerəˈtɒmɪtə/ *noun* an instrument for measuring the curvature of the cornea

keratometry /ˌkerəˈtɒmɪtri/ *noun* the process of measuring the curvature of the cornea

keratopathy /ˌkerəˈtɒpəθi/ *noun* any non-inflammatory disorder of the cornea (NOTE: The plural is **keratopathies**.)

keratoplasty /ˈkerətəplæsti/ *noun* a surgical operation to graft corneal tissue from a donor in place of diseased tissue (NOTE: The plural is **keratoplasties**.)

keratoprosthesis /ˌkerətəʊprɒsˈθiːsɪs/ *noun* **1.** a surgical operation to replace the central area of a cornea with clear plastic, when it has become opaque **2.** a piece of clear plastic put into the cornea (NOTE: The plural is **keratoprostheses**.)

keratoscope /ˈkerətəskəʊp/ *noun* an instrument for examining the cornea to see if it has an unusual curvature. Also called **Placido's disc**

keratosis /ˌkerəˈtəʊsɪs/ *noun* a lesion of the skin (NOTE: The plural is **keratoses**.)

keratotomy /ˌkerəˈtɒtəmi/ *noun* a surgical operation to make a cut in the cornea, the first step in many intraocular operations (NOTE: The plural is **keratotomies**.)

kerion /ˈkɪərɪɒn/ *noun* a painful soft mass, usually on the scalp, caused by ringworm

kernicterus /kəˈnɪktərəs/ *noun* yellow pigmentation of the basal ganglia and other nerve cells in the spinal cord and brain, found in children with icterus

Kernig's sign /ˈkɜːnɪgz saɪn/ *noun* a symptom of meningitis in which the knee cannot be straightened if the person is lying down with the thigh brought up against the abdomen [Described 1882. After Vladimir Mikhailovich Kernig (1840–1917), Russian neurologist.]

ketamine /ˈketəmiːn/ *noun* a white crystalline powder that is a general anaesthetic, used in human and veterinary medicine

ketoacidosis /ˌkiːtəʊˌæsɪˈdəʊsɪs/ *noun* an accumulation of ketone bodies in tissue in diabetes, causing acidosis

ketoconazole /ˌkiːtəʊˈkɒnəzəʊl/ *noun* a drug which is effective against a wide range of fungal infections such as cryptococcosis and thrush

ketogenesis /ˌkiːtəʊˈdʒenəsɪs/ *noun* the production of ketone bodies

ketogenic /ˌkiːtəʊˈdʒenɪk/ *adjective* forming ketone bodies

ketogenic diet /ˌkiːtəʊdʒenɪk ˈdaɪət/ *noun* a diet with a high fat content, producing ketosis

ketonaemia /ˌkiːtəʊˈniːmiə/ *noun* a morbid state in which ketone bodies exist in the blood

ketone /ˈkiːtəʊn/ *noun* a chemical compound produced when glucose is unavailable for use as energy, as in untreated diabetes, and fats are used instead, leading to ketosis

ketone bodies /ˈkiːtəʊn ˌbɒdiz/ *plural noun* ketone compounds formed from fatty acids

ketone group /ˈkiːtəʊn gruːp/ *noun* a chemical group characteristic of ketones, with carbon atoms doubly bonded to an oxygen atom and to the carbon atoms of two other organic groups

ketonuria /ˌkiːtəʊˈnjʊəriə/ *noun* a state in which ketone bodies are excreted in the urine

ketoprofen /ˌkiːtəʊˈprəʊfən/ *noun* an anti-inflammatory drug used in the treatment of rheumatoid arthritis and osteoarthritis

ketosis /kiːˈtəʊsɪs/ *noun* a state in which ketone bodies such as acetone and acetic acid accumulate in the tissues, a late complication of Type I diabetes mellitus

ketosteroid /ˌkiːtəʊˈstɪərɔɪd/ *noun* a steroid such as cortisone which contains a ketone group

keyhole surgery /ˈkiːhəʊl ˌsɜːdʒəri/ *noun* surgery carried out by inserting tiny surgical instruments through an endoscope (*informal*) Also called **laparoscopic surgery**

kg *abbr* kilogram

kidney /ˈkɪdni/ *noun* either of two organs situated in the lower part of the back on either side of the spine behind the abdomen, whose function is to maintain the usual concentrations of the main constituents of blood, passing the waste matter into the urine. See illustration at **KIDNEY** in Supplement

COMMENT: A kidney is formed of an outer cortex and an inner medulla. The nephrons which run from the cortex into the medulla filter the blood and form urine. The urine is passed through the ureters into the bladder. Sudden sharp pain in back of the abdomen, going downwards, is an indication of a kidney stone passing into the ureter.

kidney dialysis /ˈkɪdni daɪˌæləsɪs/ *noun* the process of removing waste matter from blood by passing it through a kidney machine. Also called **haemodialysis**

kidney donor /ˈkɪdni ˌdəʊnə/ *noun* a person who gives one of his or her kidneys as a transplant

kidney failure /ˈkɪdni ˌfeɪljə/ *noun* a situation in which the kidneys do not function properly

kidney machine /ˈkɪdni məˌʃiːn/ *noun* an apparatus through which blood is passed to be cleaned by dialysis if the person's kidneys have failed

kidney stone /ˈkɪdni stəʊn/ *noun* a hard mass of calcium like a little piece of stone which forms in the kidney

kidney transplant /ˈkɪdni ˌtrænsplɑːnt/ *noun* a surgical operation to give someone with a diseased or damaged kidney a kidney from another person

kill /kɪl/ *verb* to make someone or something die ○ *She was killed in a car crash.* ○ *Heart attacks kill more people every year.* ○ *Antibodies are created to kill bacteria.*

killer /ˈkɪlə/ *noun* a person or disease which kills ○ *In the winter, bronchitis is the killer of hundreds of senior citizens.* ○ *Virulent typhoid fever can be a killer disease.* ◊ **painkiller**

killer cell /ˈkɪlə sel/, **killer T cell** *noun* a type of immune cell that recognises and destroys cells that have specific antigens on their surface, e.g. virus-infected or cancerous cells

Killian's operation /ˈkɪliənz ɒpəˌreɪʃ(ə)n/ *noun* a surgical operation to clear the frontal sinus by curetting in which the incision is made in the eyebrow [After Gustav Killian (1860–1921), German laryngologist]

kilo- /kɪləʊ/ *prefix* one thousand (10³). Symbol **k**

kilogram /ˈkɪləgræm/ *noun* an SI unit of measurement of weight equal to 1 000 grams ○ *She weighs 62 kilos (62 kg).* Symbol **kg**

kilojoule /ˈkɪləʊdʒuːl/ *noun* an SI unit of measurement of energy or heat equal to 1 000 joules. Symbol **kJ**

kilopascal /ˈkɪləʊpæskəl/ *noun* an SI unit of measurement of pressure equal to 1 000 pascals. Symbol **kPa**

Kimmelstiel-Wilson disease /ˌkɪməlstiːl ˈwɪlsən dɪˌziːz/, **Kimmelstiel-Wilson syndrome** /ˌkɪməlstiːl ˈwɪlsən ˌsɪndrəʊm/ *noun* a form of nephrosclerosis found in people with diabetes [Described 1936. After Paul Kimmelstiel (1900–70), US pathologist; Clifford Wilson (1906–98), Professor of Medicine, London University, UK.]

kin /kɪn/ *noun* relatives or close members of the family

kin- /kɪn/ *prefix* same as **kine-** (*used before vowels*)

kinaesthesia /ˌkɪniːsˈθiːziə/ *noun* the fact of being aware of the movement and position of parts of the body (NOTE: The US spelling is **kinesthesia**.)

COMMENT: Kinaesthesia is the result of information from muscles and ligaments which is passed to the brain and which allows the brain to recognise movements, touch and weight.

kinanaesthesia /ˌkɪnæniːsˈθiːziə/ *noun* the fact of not being able to sense the movement and position of parts of the body (NOTE: The US spelling is **kinanesthesia**.)

kinase /ˈkaɪneɪz/ *noun* an enzyme belonging to a large family of related substances that bind to the energy-providing molecule ATP and regulate functions such as cell division and signalling between cells

kine- /kɪni/ *prefix* movement

kinematics /ˌkɪnɪˈmætɪks/ *noun* the science of movement, especially of body movements

kineplasty /ˈkɪnɪplæsti/ *noun* an amputation in which the muscles of the stump of the amputated limb are used to operate an artificial limb (NOTE: The plural is **kineplasties**.)

kinesi- /kaɪniːsi/ *prefix* movement (NOTE: used before vowels)

kinesiology /ˌkaɪniːsiˈɒlədʒi/ *noun* the study of human movements, particularly with regard to their use in treatment

kinesis *noun* the movement of a cell in response to a stimulus. Compare **taxis**

-kinesis /kɪniːsɪs/ *suffix* **1.** activity or motion **2.** a change in the movement of a cell, though not in any particular direction. Examples are a change in its speed or in its turning behaviour.

kinesitherapy /ˌkaɪniːsiˈθerəpi/ *noun* therapy involving movement of parts of the body

kinetic /kɪˈnetɪk, kaɪˈnetɪk/ *adjective* relating to movement

King's Fund /ˈkɪŋz fʌnd/ *noun* a major independent health charity in London

King's model /ˈkɪŋz ˌmɒd(ə)l/ *noun* a model of nurse–patient relationships based on ten principles: interaction, perception, communication, transaction, role, stress, growth and development, time, self and space. Through an exchange of information nurses and patients work together to help individuals and groups attain, maintain and restore health.

kinin /ˈkaɪnɪn/ *noun* a polypeptide that makes blood vessels widen and smooth muscles contract

Kirschner wire /ˌkɜːʃ(ə)nə ˈwaɪə/, **Kirschner's wire** *noun* a wire attached to a bone and tightened to provide traction to a fracture [Described 1909. After Martin Kirschner (1879–1942), Professor of Surgery at Heidelberg, Germany.]

kiss of life /ˌkɪs əv ˈlaɪf/ *noun* same as **cardiopulmonary resuscitation** (*informal*)

kJ *abbr* kilojoule

Klebsiella /ˌklebsiˈelə/ *noun* a Gram-negative bacterium, one form of which, *Klebsiella pneumoniae*, can cause pneumonia

Klebs-Loeffler bacillus /ˌklebz ˈleflə bəˌsɪləs/ *noun* the bacterium which causes diphtheria, *Corynebacterium diphtheriae* [After Theodor Albrecht Klebs (1834–1913), bacteriologist in Zürich, Switzerland, and Chicago, USA; Friedrich August Loeffler (1852–1915), bacteriologist in Berlin, Germany]

Kleihauer test /'klaɪhaʊə test/, **Kleihauer-Betke test** *noun* a test used to check whether there has been any blood loss from a fetus to the mother across the placenta. It is usually done immediately after delivery.

klepto- /kleptəʊ/ *prefix* stealing or theft

kleptomania /ˌkleptəʊ'meɪniə/ *noun* a form of mental disorder in which someone has a compulsive desire to steal things, even things of little value

kleptomaniac /ˌkleptəʊ'meɪniæk/ *noun* a person who has a compulsive desire to steal

Klinefelter's syndrome /'klaɪnfeltəz ˌsɪn drəʊm/ *noun* a genetic disorder in which a male has an extra female chromosome, making an XXY set, giving sterility and partial female characteristics [Described 1942. After Harry Fitch Klinefelter Jr. (b. 1912), Associate Professor of Medicine, John Hopkins Medical School, Baltimore, USA.]

Klumpke's paralysis /ˌkluːmpkəz pə'ræləsɪs/ *noun* a form of paralysis due to an injury during birth, affecting the forearm and hand. Also called **Déjerine-Klumpke's syndrome** [Described 1885. After Augusta Klumpke (Madame Déjerine-Klumpke) (1859–1937), French neurologist, one of the first women to qualify in Paris in 1888.]

knee /niː/ *noun* a joint in the middle of the leg, joining the femur and the tibia (NOTE: For other terms referring to the knee, see **genu**.)

kneecap /'niːkæp/ *noun* same as **patella**

knee jerk /'niː dʒɜːk/ *noun* same as **patellar reflex**

knee joint /niː dʒɔɪnt/ *noun* a joint where the femur and the tibia are joined, covered by the kneecap

knit /nɪt/ *verb* (*of broken bones*) to join together again ○ *Broken bones take longer to knit in elderly people than in children.* (NOTE: **knitting – knitted – knit**)

knock-knee /ˌnɒk 'niː/ *noun* a state in which the knees touch and the ankles are apart when a person is standing straight. Also called **genu valgum**

knock-kneed /nɒk 'niːd/ *adjective* referring to a person whose knees touch when he or she stands straight with feet slightly apart

knock out /ˌnɒk 'aʊt/ *verb* to hit someone so hard that he or she is no longer conscious ○ *He was knocked out by a blow on the head.*

knuckle /'nʌk(ə)l/ *noun* the back of each joint on a person's hand

Kocher manoeuvre /'kɒkə mə,nuːvə/ *noun* a method for realigning a dislocated shoulder in which the arm is raised and a sudden change is made between inward and outward rotation of the head of the joint

Koch's bacillus /ˌkəʊks bə'sɪləs/ *noun* the bacterium which causes tuberculosis, *Mycobacterium tuberculosis* [Described 1882. After Robert Koch (1843–1910), Professor of Hygiene in Berlin, Germany, later Director of the Institute for Infectious Diseases. (Nobel Prize 1905).]

Koch-Weeks bacillus /ˌkəʊk 'wiːks bə,sɪləs/ *noun* the bacillus which causes conjunctivitis

Köhler's disease /'kɜːləz dɪˌsiːz/ *noun* a degeneration of the navicular bone in children. Also called **scaphoiditis** [Described 1908 and 1926. After Alban Köhler (1874–1947), German radiologist.]

koilonychia /ˌkɔɪləʊ'nɪkiə/ *noun* a condition in which the fingernails are brittle and concave, caused by iron-deficiency anaemia

Koplik's spots /'kɒplɪks spɒts/ *plural noun* small white spots with a blue tinge surrounded by a red areola, found in the mouth in the early stages of measles [Described 1896. After Henry Koplik (1858–1927), US paediatrician.]

Korotkoff's method /'kɒrətkɒfs ˌmeθəd/ *noun* a method of finding a person's blood pressure by inflating a cuff around his or her upper arm to a pressure well above the systolic blood pressure and then gradually decreasing it

Korsakoff's syndrome /'kɔːsəkɒfs ˌsɪn drəʊm/ *noun* a condition, caused usually by chronic alcoholism or disorders in which there is a deficiency of vitamin B, in which a person's memory fails and he or she invents things which have not happened and is confused [Described 1887. After Sergei Sergeyevich Korsakoff (1854–1900), Russian psychiatrist.]

kraurosis penis /krɔːˌrəʊsɪs 'piːnɪs/ *noun* a condition in which the foreskin becomes dry and shrivelled

kraurosis vulvae /krɔːˌrəʊsɪs 'vʌlvə/ *noun* a condition in which the vulva becomes thin and dry due to lack of oestrogen, found usually in elderly women

Krause corpuscles /'krauzə ˌkɔːpʌs(ə)lz/ *plural noun* encapsulated nerve endings in the mucous membrane of the mouth, nose, eyes and genitals [Described 1860. After Wilhelm Johann Friedrich Krause (1833–1910), German anatomist.]

Krebs cycle /'krebz ˌsaɪk(ə)l/ *noun* same as **citric acid cycle** [Described 1937. After Sir Hans Adolf Krebs (1900–81), German biochemist who emigrated to England in 1934. Shared the Nobel prize for Medicine 1953 with F.A. Lipmann.]

Krukenberg tumour /'kruːkənbɜːg ˌtjuːmə/ *noun* a malignant tumour in the ovary secondary to a tumour in the stomach [After Friedrich Krukenberg (1871–1946), German gynaecologist]

Kuntscher nail /ˈkʌntʃə neɪl/, **Küntscher nail** *noun* a long steel nail used in operations to pin fractures of long bones, especially the femur, through the bone marrow [Described 1940. After Gerhard Küntscher (1900–72), German surgeon.]

Kupffer's cells /ˈkʊpfəz selz/, **Kupffer cells** *plural noun* large specialised liver cells which break down haemoglobin into bile [Described 1876. After Karl Wilhelm von Kupffer (1829–1902), German anatomist.]

Kveim test /ˈkvaɪm test/ *noun* a skin test to confirm the presence of sarcoidosis [After Morten Ansgar Kveim (b. 1892), Swedish physician]

kwashiorkor /ˌkwɒʃiˈɔːkɔː/ *noun* malnutrition of small children, mostly in tropical countries, causing anaemia, wasting of the body and swollen liver

kypho- /kaɪfəʊ/ *prefix* a hump

kyphoscoliosis /ˌkaɪfəʊˌskɒliˈəʊsɪs/ *noun* a condition in which someone has both backward and lateral curvature of the spine

kyphosis /kaɪˈfəʊsɪs/ *noun* an excessive backward curvature of the top part of the spine (NOTE: The plural is **kyphoses**.)

kyphotic /kaɪˈfɒtɪk/ *adjective* referring to kyphosis

L

l, L symbol **litre**

lab /læb/ *noun* same as **laboratory** (*informal*) ○ *The samples have been returned by the lab.* ○ *We'll send the specimens away for a lab test.*

lab- /leɪb/ *prefix* same as **labio-** (used before vowels)

label /'leɪb(ə)l/ *noun* a piece of paper or card attached to an object or person for identification ■ *verb* to attach a label to an object ○ *The bottle is labelled 'poison'.* (NOTE: **labelling – labelled**. The US spellings are **labeling – labeled**.)

labia /'leɪbiə/ plural of **labium**

labial /'leɪbiəl/ *adjective* referring to the lips or to labia

labia majora /ˌleɪbiə mə'dʒɔːrə/ *plural noun* two large fleshy folds at the outside edge of the vulva. See illustration at **UROGENITAL SYSTEM (FEMALE)** in Supplement

labia minora /ˌleɪbiə mɪ'nɔːrə/ *plural noun* two small fleshy folds on the inside edge of the vulva. See illustration at **UROGENITAL SYSTEM (FEMALE)** in Supplement. Also called **nymphae**

labile /'leɪbaɪl/ *adjective* referring to a drug which is unstable and likely to change if heated or cooled

lability of mood /ləˌbɪlɪti əv 'muːd/ *noun* a tendency for a person's mood to change suddenly

labio- /leɪbiəʊ/ *prefix* referring to the lips or to labia

labioplasty /'leɪbiəʊˌplæsti/ *noun* a surgical operation to repair damaged or deformed lips (NOTE: The plural is **labioplasties**.)

labium /'leɪbiəm/ *noun* **1.** any of the four fleshy folds which surround the female genital organs **2.** a structure which looks like a lip (NOTE: The plural is **labia**.)

labor /'leɪbə/ *noun* US spelling of **labour**

laboratory /lə'bɒrət(ə)ri/ *noun* a special room or place where scientists can do specialised work such as research, the testing of chemical substances or the growing of tissues in culture ○ *The samples of water from the hospital have been sent to the laboratory for testing.* ○ *The new drug has passed its laboratory tests.* (NOTE: The plural is **laboratories**.)

laboratory officer /lə'bɒrət(ə)ri ˌɒfɪsə/ *noun* a qualified person in charge of a laboratory

laboratory technician /lə,bɒrət(ə)ri tek'nɪʃ(ə)n/ *noun* a person who does practical work in a laboratory and has particular care of equipment

laboratory techniques /lə'bɒrət(ə)ri tek,niːkz/ *plural noun* the methods or skills needed to perform experiments in a laboratory

laboratory test /lə'bɒrət(ə)ri test/ *noun* a test carried out in a laboratory

labour /'leɪbə/ *noun* childbirth, especially the contractions in the uterus which take place during childbirth □ **in labour** experiencing the physical changes such as contractions in the uterus which precede the birth of a child ○ *She was in labour for 14 hours.* □ **to go into labour** to start to experience the contractions which indicate the birth of a child is imminent ○ *She went into labour at 6 o'clock.*

COMMENT: Labour usually starts about nine months, or 266 days, after conception. The cervix expands and the muscles in the uterus contract, causing the amnion to burst. The muscles continue to contract regularly, pushing the baby into, and then through, the vagina.

laboured breathing /ˌleɪbəd 'briːðɪŋ/ *noun* difficult breathing, which can be due to various causes such as asthma

labour pains /'leɪbə peɪnz/ *plural noun* the pains felt at regular intervals by a woman as the muscles of the uterus contract during childbirth

labrum /'leɪbrəm/ *noun* a ring of cartilage around the rim of a joint (NOTE: The plural is **labra**.)

labyrinth /'læbərɪnθ/ *noun* a series of interconnecting tubes, especially those in the inside of the ear

COMMENT: The labyrinth of the inner ear is in three parts: the three semicircular canals, the vestibule and the cochlea. The osseous labyrinth is filled with a fluid (perilymph) and the membranous labyrinth is a series of ducts and canals inside the osseous labyrinth. The membranous labyrinth contains a fluid (endolymph). As the endolymph moves about in the membranous labyrinth it stimulates the vestibular nerve which communicates the sense of movement of the head to the brain. If a person turns round and round and then stops, the endolymph continues to move and creates the sensation of giddiness.

labyrinthectomy /ˌlæbərɪn'θektəmi/ *noun* a surgical operation to remove the labyrinth of the inner ear (NOTE: The plural is **labyrinthectomies**.)

labyrinthitis /ˌlæbərɪn'θaɪtɪs/ *noun* same as **otitis interna**

lacerated /'læsəreɪtɪd/ *adjective* torn or with a rough edge

lacerated wound /ˌlæsəreɪtɪd 'wuːnd/ *noun* a wound where the skin is torn, as by a rough surface or barbed wire

laceration /ˌlæsə'reɪʃ(ə)n/ *noun* **1.** a wound which has been cut or torn with rough edges, and is not the result of stabbing or pricking **2.** the act of tearing tissue

lachrymal /'lækrɪm(ə)l/ *adjective* same as **lacrimal**

lacrimal /'lækrɪm(ə)l/ *adjective* referring to tears, the tear ducts or the tear glands. ◊ **nasolacrimal**

lacrimal apparatus /ˌlækrɪm(ə)l ˌæpə'reɪtəs/ *noun* the arrangement of glands and ducts which produce and drain tears. Also called **lacrimal system**

lacrimal bone /'lækrɪm(ə)l bəʊn/ *noun* one of two little bones which join with others to form the orbits

lacrimal canaliculus /ˌlækrɪm(ə)l kænə'lɪkjʊləs/ *noun* a small canal draining tears into the lacrimal sac

lacrimal caruncle /ˌlækrɪm(ə)l kə'rʌŋk(ə)l/ *noun* a small red point at the inner corner of each eye

lacrimal duct /'lækrɪm(ə)l dʌkt/ *noun* a small duct leading from the lacrimal gland. Also called **tear duct**

lacrimal gland /'lækrɪm(ə)l glænd/ *noun* a gland beneath the upper eyelid which secretes tears. Also called **tear gland**

lacrimal puncta /ˌlækrɪm(ə)l 'pʌŋktə/ *plural noun* small openings of the lacrimal canaliculus at the corners of the eyes through which tears drain into the nose

lacrimal sac /ˌlækrɪm(ə)l 'sæk/ *noun* a sac at the upper end of the nasolacrimal duct, linking it with the lacrimal canaliculus

lacrimal system /'lækrɪm(ə)l ˌsɪstəm/ *noun* same as **lacrimal apparatus**

lacrimation /ˌlækrɪ'meɪʃ(ə)n/ *noun* the production of tears

lacrimator /'lækrɪmeɪtə/ *noun* a substance which irritates the eyes and makes tears flow

lacrymal /'lækrɪml/, **lachrymal** /'lækrɪm(ə)l/ *adjective* another spelling of **lacrimal**

lact- /lækt/ *prefix* same as **lacto-** (*used before vowels*)

lactase /'lækteɪz/ *noun* an enzyme, secreted in the small intestine, which converts milk sugar into glucose and galactose

lactate /læk'teɪt/ *verb* to produce milk in the body (NOTE: **lactating – lactated**)

lactation /læk'teɪʃ(ə)n/ *noun* **1.** the production of milk in the body **2.** the period during which a mother is breastfeeding a baby

COMMENT: Lactation is stimulated by the production of the hormone prolactin by the pituitary gland. It starts about three days after childbirth, before which period the breasts secrete colostrum.

lacteal /'læktɪəl/ *adjective* referring to milk ■ *noun* a lymph vessel in a villus which helps the digestive process in the small intestine by absorbing fat

lactic /'læktɪk/ *adjective* relating to milk

lactic acid /ˌlæktɪk 'æsɪd/ *noun* a sugar which forms in cells and tissue, and also in sour milk, cheese and yoghurt

COMMENT: Lactic acid is produced as the body uses up sugar during exercise. Excessive amounts of lactic acid in the body can produce muscle cramp.

lactiferous /læk'tɪfərəs/ *adjective* producing, secreting or carrying milk

lactiferous duct /læk,tɪfərəs 'dʌkt/ *noun* a duct in the breast which carries milk

lactiferous sinus /læk,tɪfərəs 'saɪnəs/ *noun* a dilatation of the lactiferous duct at the base of the nipple

lacto- *prefix* referring to milk

Lactobacillus /ˌlæktəʊbə'sɪləs/ *noun* a genus of Gram-positive bacteria which produces lactic acid from glucose and may be found in the digestive tract and the vagina

lactogenic hormone /ˌlæktəʊ,dʒenɪk 'hɔːməʊn/ *noun* same as **prolactin**

lactose /'læktəʊs/ *noun* a type of sugar found in milk

lactose intolerance /'læktəʊs ɪn,tɒlərəns/ *noun* a condition in which a person cannot digest lactose because lactase is absent in the intestine or because of an allergy to milk, causing diarrhoea

lactosuria /ˌlæktəʊ'sjʊəriə/ *noun* the excretion of lactose in the urine

lactovegetarian /ˌlæktəʊvedʒɪ'teəriən/ *noun* a person who does not eat meat, but eats vegetables, fruit, dairy produce and eggs and sometimes fish ○ *He has been a lactovegetarian for twenty years.* Compare **vegan, vegetarian**

lactulose /'læktjʊləʊs/ *noun* an artificially produced sugar used as a laxative

lacuna /læ'kjuːnə/ *noun* a small hollow or cavity (NOTE: The plural is **lacunae**.)

lacunar /læ'kjuːnə/ *adjective* relating to hollows or cavities in tissue such as in bone or cartilage, especially ones that are unusual

Laënnec's cirrhosis /ˌleɪəneks səˈrəʊsɪs/ *noun* the commonest form of alcoholic cirrhosis of the liver [Described 1819. After René Théophile Hyacinthe Laennec (1781–1826), Professor of medicine at the Collège de France, and inventor of the stethoscope.]

laevocardia /ˌliːvəʊˈkɑːdiə/ *noun* the condition of having the heart in the usual position, with the apex towards the left side of the body. Compare **dextrocardia**

-lalia /leɪliə/ *suffix* speech or a speech disorder

lambda /ˈlæmdə/ *noun* 1. the 11th letter of the Greek alphabet 2. the point at the back of the skull where the sagittal suture and lambdoidal suture meet

lambdoid /ˈlæmdɔɪd/ *adjective* shaped like the capital Greek letter lambda, like an upside down V or y

lambdoid suture /læmˌdɔɪd ˈsuːtʃə/, **lambdoidal suture** /læmˌdɔɪd(ə)l ˈsuːtʃə/ *noun* a horizontal joint across the back of the skull between the parietal and occipital bones

lamblia /ˈlæmbliə/ *noun* same as **Giardia**

lambliasis /læmˈblaɪəsɪs/ *noun* same as **giardiasis**

lame /leɪm/ *adjective* not able to walk easily because of pain, stiffness or damage in a leg or foot (NOTE: This term is regarded as offensive.)

lamella /ləˈmelə/ *noun* 1. a thin sheet of tissue 2. a thin disc placed under the eyelid to apply a drug to the eye (NOTE: The plural is **lamellae**.)

lameness /ˈleɪmnəs/ *noun* the inability to walk normally because of pain, stiffness or damage in a leg or foot

lamina /ˈlæmɪnə/ *noun* 1. a thin membrane 2. a side part of the posterior arch in a vertebra (NOTE: The plural is **laminae**.)

lamina propria /ˌlæmɪnə ˈprəʊpriə/ *noun* the connective tissue of mucous membranes containing, e.g., blood vessels and lymphatic tissues

laminectomy /ˌlæmɪˈnektəmi/ *noun* a surgical operation to cut through the lamina of a vertebra in the spine to get to the spinal cord. Also called **rachiotomy** (NOTE: The plural is **laminectomies**.)

lamotrigine /ləˈmɒtrɪdʒiːn/ *noun* a drug that helps to control petit mal epilepsy

lance /lɑːns/ *verb* to make a cut in a boil or abscess to remove the pus

lancet /ˈlɑːnsɪt/ *noun* 1. a sharp two-edged pointed knife formerly used in surgery 2. a small pointed implement used to take a small capillary blood sample, e.g. to measure blood glucose levels

lancinate /ˈlɑːnsɪneɪt/ *verb* to lacerate or cut something (NOTE: **lancinating – lancinated**)

lancinating /ˈlɑːnsɪneɪtɪŋ/ *adjective* referring to pain which is sharp and cutting

Landry's paralysis /ˌlændrɪz pəˈræləsɪs/ *noun* same as **Guillain-Barré syndrome** (*see*)

[After Jean-Baptiste Octave Landry (1826–65), French physician]

Landsteiner's classification /ˌlændstaɪnəz ˌklæsɪfɪˈkeɪʃ(ə)n/ *noun* same as **ABO system**

Langerhans' cells /ˈlæŋəhænz selz/ *plural noun* cells on the outer layers of the skin

Langer's lines /ˈlæŋəz laɪnz/ *plural noun* the arrangement of collagen protein fibres which causes the usual skin creases. Cuts made along these lines sever fewer fibres and heal better than other cuts. Also called **cleavage lines**

Lange test /ˈlæŋə test/ *noun* a method of detecting globulin in the cerebrospinal fluid [Described 1912. After Carl Friedrich August Lange (b. 1883), German physician.]

lanolin /ˈlænəlɪn/ *noun* grease from sheep's wool which absorbs water and is used to rub on dried skin, or in the preparation of cosmetics

lanugo /ləˈnjuːgəʊ/ *noun* 1. soft hair on the body of a fetus or newborn baby 2. soft hair on the body of an adult, except on the palms of the hands, the soles of the feet and the parts where long hair grows

laparo- /læpərəʊ/ *prefix* the lower abdomen

laparoscope /ˈlæpərəskəʊp/ *noun* a surgical instrument which is inserted through a hole in the abdominal wall to allow a surgeon to examine the inside of the abdominal cavity. Also called **peritoneoscope**

laparoscopic /ˌlæpərəˈskɒpɪk/ *adjective* using a laparoscope

laparoscopic surgery /ˌlæpərəˌskɒpɪk ˈsɜːdʒəri/ *noun* same as **keyhole surgery**

laparoscopy /ˌlæpəˈrɒskəpi/ *noun* a procedure in which a laparoscope is used to examine the inside of the abdominal cavity. Also called **peritoneoscopy** (NOTE: The plural is **laparoscopies**.)

laparotomy /ˌlæpəˈrɒtəmi/ *noun* a surgical operation to cut open the abdominal cavity (NOTE: The plural is **laparotomies**.)

large intestine /lɑːdʒ ɪnˈtestɪn/ *noun* the section of the digestive system from the caecum to the rectum

Lariam /ˈlæriəm/ a trade name for mefloquine hydrochloride

larva /ˈlɑːvə/ *noun* a stage in the development of an insect or tapeworm, after the egg has hatched but before the animal becomes adult (NOTE: The plural is **larvae**.)

laryng- /lərɪndʒ/ *prefix* same as **laryngo-** (*used before vowels*)

laryngeal /ləˈrɪndʒiəl/ *adjective* referring to the larynx

laryngeal inlet /ləˌrɪndʒiəl ˈɪnlət/ *noun* the entrance from the laryngopharynx leading through the vocal cords to the trachea

laryngeal prominence /ləˌrɪndʒiəl ˈprɒmɪnəns/ *noun* same as **Adam's apple**

laryngeal reflex /lə,rɪndʒiəl 'riːfleks/ *noun* the reflex that makes a person cough

laryngectomy /,lærɪn'dʒektəmi/ *noun* a surgical operation to remove the larynx, usually as treatment for throat cancer (NOTE: The plural is **laryngectomies**.)

larynges /lə'rɪndʒiːz/ plural of **larynx**

laryngismus /,lærɪn'dʒɪzməs/, **laryngismus stridulus** /lærɪn,dʒɪzməs 'strɪdjʊləs/ *noun* a spasm of the throat muscles with a sharp intake of breath which occurs when the larynx is irritated, as in children who have croup

laryngitis /,lærɪn'dʒaɪtɪs/ *noun* inflammation of the larynx

laryngo- /lərɪŋgəʊ/ *prefix* larynx

laryngofissure /lə,rɪŋgəʊ'fɪʃə/ *noun* a surgical operation to make an opening into the larynx through the thyroid cartilage

laryngologist /,lærɪn'gɒlədʒɪst/ *noun* a doctor who specialises in diseases of the larynx, throat and vocal cords

laryngology /,lærɪn'gɒlədʒi/ *noun* the study of diseases of the larynx, throat and vocal cords

laryngomalacia /lə,rɪŋgəʊmə'leɪʃə/ *noun* a condition in which breathing is made difficult by softness of the larynx, occurring mainly in children under the age of two

laryngopharyngeal /lə,rɪŋgəʊfə'rɪndʒiəl/ *adjective* referring to both the larynx and the pharynx

laryngopharynx /lərɪŋgəʊ'færɪŋks/ *noun* the part of the pharynx below the hyoid bone

laryngoscope /lə'rɪŋgəskəʊp/ *noun* an instrument for examining the inside of the larynx using a light and mirrors

laryngoscopy /,lærɪŋ'gɒskəpi/ *noun* an examination of the larynx with a laryngoscope (NOTE: The plural is **laryngoscopies**.)

laryngospasm /lə'rɪŋgəspæzəm/ *noun* a muscular spasm which suddenly closes the larynx

laryngostenosis /lə,rɪŋgəʊstə'nəʊsɪs/ *noun* narrowing of the lumen of the larynx

laryngostomy /,lærɪŋ'gɒstəmi/ *noun* a surgical operation to make a permanent opening from the neck into the larynx (NOTE: The plural is **laryngostomies**.)

laryngotomy /,lærɪŋ'gɒtəmi/ *noun* a surgical operation to make an opening in the larynx through the membrane, especially in an emergency, when the throat is blocked (NOTE: The plural is **laryngotomies**.)

laryngotracheal /lə,rɪŋgəʊ'treɪkiəl/ *adjective* relating to both the larynx and the trachea ○ *laryngotracheal stenosis*

laryngotracheobronchitis /lə,rɪŋgəʊ,treɪkiəʊbrɒŋ'kaɪtɪs/ *noun* inflammation of the larynx, trachea and bronchi, as in croup

larynx /'lærɪŋks/ *noun* the organ in the throat which produces sounds. Also called **voice box** (NOTE: The plural is **larynges** or **larynxes**.)
COMMENT: The larynx is a hollow passage made of cartilage, containing the vocal cords, situated behind the Adam's apple. It is closed by the epiglottis when swallowing or before coughing.

laser /'leɪzə/ *noun* an instrument which produces a highly concentrated beam of light which can be used to cut or attach tissue, as in operations for a detached retina

laser laparoscopy /,leɪzə læpə'rɒskəpi/ *noun* surgery performed through a laparoscope using a laser

laser probe /'leɪzə prəʊb/ *noun* a metal probe which is inserted into the body and through which a laser beam can be passed to remove a blockage in an artery

laser surgery /'leɪzə ,sɜːdʒəri/ *noun* surgery using lasers, e.g. for the removal of tumours, sealing blood vessels, or the correction of shortsightedness

Lasix /'leɪzɪks/ a trade name for frusemide

Lassa fever /'læsə ,fiːvə/ *noun* a highly infectious and often fatal virus disease found in Central and West Africa, causing high fever, pains, and ulcers in the mouth [After a village in northern Nigeria where the fever was first reported]

Lassar's paste /'læsəz ,peɪst/ *noun* an ointment made of zinc oxide, used to treat eczema [After Oskar Lassar (1849–1907), German dermatologist]

lassitude /'læsɪtjuːd/ *noun* a state where a person does not want to do anything, sometimes because he or she is depressed

lata /'lætə/ ♦ **fascia lata**

latent /'leɪt(ə)nt/ *adjective* referring to a disease which is present in the body but does not show any signs ○ *The children were tested for latent viral infection.*

lateral /'læt(ə)rəl/ *adjective* **1.** further away from the midline of the body **2.** referring to one side of the body

lateral aspect /,læt(ə)rəl 'æspekt/ *noun* a view of the side of part of the body. Also called **lateral view**. See illustration at ANATOMICAL TERMS in Supplement

lateral epicondyle /,læt(ə)rəl ,epɪ'kɒndaɪl/, **lateral epicondyle of the humerus** /,læt(ə)rəl epɪ,kɒndaɪl əv ðə 'hjuːmərəs/ *noun* a lateral projection on the rounded end of the humerus at the elbow joint

lateral epicondylitis /,læt(ə)rəl ,epɪkɒndɪ'laɪtɪs/ *noun* same as **tennis elbow**

lateral fissure /,læt(ə)rəl 'fɪʃə/ *noun* a groove along the side of each cerebral hemisphere

laterally /'læt(ə)rəli/ *adverb* towards or on the side of the body. See illustration at ANATOMICAL TERMS in Supplement

lateral malleolus /ˌlæt(ə)rəl məˈliːələs/ *noun* the part of the end of the fibula which protrudes on the outside of the ankle

lateral view /ˌlæt(ə)rəl ˈvjuː/ *noun* same as **lateral aspect**

lateroversion /ˌlæt(ə)rəʊˈvɜːʃ(ə)n/ *noun* a condition in which an organ is turned to one side

latissimus dorsi /ləˌtɪsɪməs ˈdɔːsi/ *noun* a large flat triangular muscle covering the lumbar region and the lower part of the chest

laudanum /ˈlɔːd(ə)nəm/ *noun* a solution of opium in alcohol that was formerly in widespread use for pain relief

laughing gas /ˈlɑːfɪŋ gæs/ *noun* same as **nitrous oxide** (*informal*)

lavage /ˈlævɪdʒ, læˈvɑːʒ/ *noun* the act of washing out or irrigating an organ such as the stomach

laxative /ˈlæksətɪv/ *adjective* causing a bowel movement ■ *noun* a medicine which causes a bowel movement, e.g. bisacodyl, which stimulates intestinal motility, or lactulose which alters fluid retention in the bowel ▶ also called (all senses) **purgative**

COMMENT: Laxatives are very commonly used without prescription to treat constipation, although they should only be used as a short term solution. Change of diet and regular exercise are better ways of treating most types of constipation.

lazy eye /ˌleɪzi ˈaɪ/ *noun* an eye which does not focus properly without an obvious cause (*informal*) ◊ **amblyopia**

LD *abbr* lethal dose

LDL *abbr* low-density lipoprotein

L-dopa /el ˈdəʊpə/ *noun* same as **levodopa**

LE *abbr* lupus erythematosus

lead /led/ *noun* a very heavy soft metallic element, which is poisonous in compounds (NOTE: The chemical symbol is **Pb**.)

lead-free /ˌled ˈfriː/ *adjective* with no lead in it ○ *lead-free paint* ○ *lead-free petrol*

lead line /ˈled laɪn/ *noun* a blue line seen on the gums in cases of lead poisoning

lead poisoning /led ˈpɔɪz(ə)nɪŋ/ *noun* poisoning caused by taking in lead salts. Also called **plumbism, saturnism**

COMMENT: Lead salts are used externally to treat bruises or eczema, but if taken internally produce lead poisoning. Lead poisoning can also be caused by paint (children's toys must be painted in lead-free paint) or by lead fumes from car engines not using lead-free petrol.

learning /ˈlɜːnɪŋ/ *noun* the act of gaining knowledge of something or of how to do something

learning disability /ˈlɜːnɪŋ dɪsəˌbɪlɪti/, **learning difficulty** /ˈlɜːnɪŋ ˌdɪfɪk(ə)lti/ *noun* a condition that results in someone finding it difficult to learn skills or information at the same rate as others of similar age ○ *children with learning disabilities*

LE cells /ˌel ˈiː selz/ *plural noun* white blood cells which show that someone has lupus erythematosus

lecithin /ˈlesɪθɪn/ *noun* a chemical which is a constituent of all animal and plant cells and is involved in the transport and absorption of fats

leech /liːtʃ/ *noun* a blood-sucking parasitic worm which lives in water, occasionally used in specialist procedures

COMMENT: Leeches were formerly commonly used in medicine to remove blood from a patient. Today they are used in special cases, where it is necessary to make sure that blood does not build up in part of the body, e.g. in a severed finger which has been sewn back on.

left-handed /ˌleft ˈhændɪd/ *adjective* using the left hand in preference to the right in most everyday tasks

left-handedness /ˌleft ˈhændɪdnəs/ *noun* the fact of being left-handed

leg /leg/ *noun* a part of the body with which a person or animal walks and stands

COMMENT: The leg is formed of the thigh, with the thighbone or femur, the knee with the kneecap or patella, and the lower leg, with two bones – the tibia and fibula.

legal abortion /ˌliːg(ə)l əˈbɔːʃ(ə)n/ *noun* an abortion which is carried out legally

Legg-Calvé disease /ˌleg ˈkælveɪ dɪˌziːz/, **Legg-Calvé-Perthes disease** /ˌleg ˌkælveɪ ˈpɜːtɪz dɪˌziːz/ *noun* degeneration of the upper end of the thighbone in young boys, which prevents the bone growing properly and can result in a permanent limp [Described 1910 separately by all three workers. Arthur Thornton Legg (1874–1939), American orthopaedic surgeon; Jacques Calvé (1875–1954), French orthopaedic surgeon; Georg Clemens Perthes (1869–1927), German surgeon.]

Legionnaires' disease /ˌliːdʒəˈneəz dɪˌziːz/ *noun* a bacterial disease similar to pneumonia

COMMENT: The disease is thought to be transmitted in droplets of moisture in the air, and so the bacterium is found in central air-conditioning systems. It can be fatal to elderly or sick people, and so is especially dangerous if present in a hospital.

leio- /ˈleɪəʊ/ *prefix* smooth or smoothness

leiomyoma /ˌlaɪəʊmaɪˈəʊmə/ *noun* a tumour of smooth muscle, especially the smooth muscle coating the uterus (NOTE: The plural is **leiomyomas** or **leiomyomata**.)

leiomyosarcoma /ˌlaɪəʊˌmaɪəʊsɑːˈkəʊmə/ *noun* a sarcoma in which large bundles of smooth muscle are found (NOTE: The plural is **leiomyosarcomas** or **leiomyosarcomata**.)

Leishmania /liːʃˈmeɪniə/ *noun* a tropical parasite which is passed to humans by the bites of sandflies and causes the group of infections known as leishmaniasis

leishmaniasis /ˌliːʃməˈnaɪəsɪs/ *noun* a disease caused by the parasite *Leishmania*, one form of which causes disfiguring ulcers, while another attacks the liver and bone marrow

Lembert's suture /ˈlɑːmbeəz ˌsuːtʃə/ *noun* a suture used to close a wound in the intestine which includes all the coats of the intestine [Described 1826. After Antoine Lembert (1802–51), French surgeon.]

lens /lenz/ *noun* **1.** the part of the eye behind the iris and pupil, which focuses light coming from the cornea onto the retina. See illustration at EYE in Supplement **2.** a piece of shaped glass or plastic which forms part of a pair of spectacles or microscope **3.** same as **contact lens**

COMMENT: The lens in the eye is elastic, and can change its shape under the influence of the ciliary muscle, to allow the eye to focus on objects at different distances.

lens implant /lenz ˈɪmplɑːnt/ *noun* an artificial lens implanted in the eye when the natural lens is removed, as in the case of cataract

lenticular /lenˈtɪkjʊlə/ *adjective* referring to or like a lens

lentigo /lenˈtaɪɡəʊ/ *noun* a small brown spot on the skin often caused by exposure to sunlight. Also called **freckle** (NOTE: The plural is **lentigines**.)

leontiasis /ˌliːɒnˈtaɪəsɪs/ *noun* a rare disorder in which the skull bones become enlarged and may give the appearance of a lion's head. It occurs if Paget's disease is not treated.

lepidosis /ˌlepɪˈdəʊsɪs/ *noun* a skin eruption in which pieces of skin fall off in flakes

leproma /leˈprəʊmə/ *noun* a lesion of the skin caused by leprosy (NOTE: The plural is **lepromas** or **lepromata**.)

leprosy /ˈleprəsi/ *noun* an infectious bacterial disease of skin and peripheral nerves caused by *Mycobacterium leprae*, which destroys the tissues and causes severe disfigurement if left untreated. Also called **Hansen's disease**

COMMENT: Leprosy attacks the nerves in the skin, and finally the patient loses all feeling in a limb, and parts such as fingers or toes can drop off.

leptin /ˈleptɪn/ *noun* a hormone produced by fat cells that signals the body's level of hunger to the hypothalamus of the brain

lepto- /leptəʊ/ *prefix* thin

leptocyte /ˈleptəsaɪt/ *noun* a thin red blood cell found in anaemia

leptomeninges /ˌleptəʊmeˈnɪndʒiːz/ *plural noun* the two inner meninges, the pia mater and arachnoid

leptomeningitis /ˌleptəʊmenɪnˈdʒaɪtɪs/ *noun* inflammation of the leptomeninges

Leptospira /ˌleptəʊˈspaɪrə/ *noun* a genus of bacteria excreted continuously in the urine of rats and many domestic animals. It can infect humans, causing leptospirosis or Weil's disease.

leptospirosis /ˌleptəʊspaɪˈrəʊsɪs/ *noun* an infectious disease caused by the spirochaete *Leptospira*, transmitted to humans from rat urine, causing jaundice and kidney damage. Also called **Weil's disease**

leresis /ləˈriːsɪs/ *noun* uncoordinated speech, a sign of dementia

lesbian /ˈlezbiən/ *noun* a woman who experiences sexual attraction towards other women ■ *adjective* referring to a lesbian

lesbianism /ˈlezbiənɪz(ə)m/ *noun* sexual attraction in one woman for another. Compare **homosexuality**

Lesch-Nyhan disease /ˌleʃ ˈnaɪhən dɪˌziːz/, **Lesch-Nyhan syndrome** /ˌleʃ ˈnaɪhən ˌsɪndrəʊm/ *noun* a rare genetic disorder in boys caused by a lack of the enzyme HPRT. Symptoms include uncontrolled muscle movements and learning disabilities, and life expectancy is 20 – 25.

lesion /ˈliːʒ(ə)n/ *noun* a wound, sore or damage to the body (NOTE: Used to refer to any damage to the body, from the fracture of a bone to a cut on the skin.)

lesser /ˈlesə/ *adjective* smaller

lesser circulation /ˌlesə ˌsɜːkjʊˈleɪʃ(ə)n/ *noun* same as **pulmonary circulation**

lesser trochanter /ˌlesə trəˈkæntə/ *noun* a projection on the femur which is the insertion of the psoas major muscle

lesser vestibular gland /ˌlesə veˈstɪbjʊlə ɡlænd/ *noun* the more anterior of the vestibular glands

lethal /ˈliːθ(ə)l/ *adjective* killing or able to kill ○ *These fumes are lethal if inhaled.*

lethal dose /ˈliːθl dəʊs/ *noun* the amount of a drug or other substance which will kill the person who takes it ○ *She took a lethal dose of aspirin.* Abbr **LD**

lethal gene /ˈliːθ(ə)l ˈdʒiːn/, **lethal mutation** /ˈliːθ(ə)l mjuːˈteɪʃ(ə)n/ *noun* a gene, usually recessive, that results in the premature death of an individual who inherits it, e.g. the gene controlling sickle-cell anaemia

lethargic /lɪˈθɑːdʒɪk/ *adjective* showing lethargy

lethargic encephalitis /ləˌθɑːdʒɪk enˌkefəˈlaɪtɪs/ *noun* a common type of virus encephalitis occurring in epidemics in the 1920s. Also called **encephalitis lethargica, sleepy sickness**

lethargy /ˈleθədʒi/ *noun* a state in which someone is not mentally alert, has slow movements and is almost inactive

Letterer-Siwe disease /ˌletərə ˈsiːweɪ dɪˌziːz/ *noun* a usually fatal disease, most common in infants, caused by the overproduction of a specialised type of immune cell

leucine /ˈluːsiːn/ *noun* an essential amino acid

leuco- /ˈluːkəʊ/, **leuko-** /luːkəʊ/ *prefix* white

leucocyte /ˈluːkəsaɪt/, **leukocyte** *noun* a white blood cell which contains a nucleus but has no haemoglobin

COMMENT: In average conditions the blood contains far fewer leucocytes than erythrocytes (red blood cells), but their numbers increase rapidly when infection is present in the body. Leucocytes are either granular (with granules in the cytoplasm) or nongranular. The main types of leucocyte are: lymphocytes and monocytes which are nongranular, and neutrophils, eosinophils and basophils which are granular (granulocytes). Granular leucocytes are produced by the bone marrow, and their main function is to remove foreign particles from the blood and fight infection by forming antibodies.

leucocytolysis /ˌluːkəʊsaɪˈtɒləsɪs/, **leukocytolysis** /luːkəsaɪˈtɒləsɪs/ *noun* destruction of leucocytes

leucocytosis /ˌluːkəʊsaɪˈtəʊsɪs/, **leukocytosis** /luːkəsaɪˈtəʊsɪs/ *noun* an increase in the numbers of leucocytes in the blood above the usual upper limit, in order to fight an infection

leucodeplete /ˌluːkəʊdɪˈpliːt/, **leukodeplete** *verb* to remove white cells from the blood (NOTE: **leucodepleting – leucodepleted**)

leucoderma /ˌluːkəʊˈdɜːmə/, **leukoderma** *noun* same as **vitiligo**

leucolysin /ˌluːkəʊˈlaɪsɪn/, **leukolysin** *noun* a protein which destroys white blood cells

leucoma /luˈkəʊmə/, **leukoma** *noun* a white scar of the cornea (NOTE: The plural is **leucomas** or **leucomata**.)

leuconychia /ˌluːkəʊˈnɪkiə/, **leukonychia** *noun* a condition in which white marks appear on the fingernails

leucopenia /ˌluːkəˈpiːniə/, **leukopenia** *noun* a reduction in the number of leucocytes in the blood, usually as the result of a disease

leucoplakia /ˌluːkəʊˈplækiə/, **leukoplakia** *noun* a condition in which white patches form on mucous membranes, e.g. on the tongue or inside of the mouth

leucopoiesis /ˌluːkəʊpɔɪˈiːsɪs/, **leukopoiesis** *noun* the production of leucocytes

leucorrhoea /ˌluːkəˈriːə/, **leukorrhoea** *noun* an excessive discharge of white mucus from the vagina. Also called **whites** (NOTE: The US spelling is **leukorrhea**.)

leukaemia /luːˈkiːmiə/ *noun* any of several malignant diseases where an unusual number of leucocytes form in the blood (NOTE: The US spelling is **leukemia**.)

COMMENT: Apart from the increase in the number of leucocytes, the symptoms include swelling of the spleen and the lymph glands. There are several forms of leukaemia: the commonest is acute lymphoblastic leukaemia which is the commonest cancer occurring in children and can be treated by radiotherapy.

leuko- /luːkəʊ/ *prefix* same as **leuco-**

levator /ləˈveɪtə/ *noun* **1.** a surgical instrument for lifting pieces of fractured bone **2.** a muscle which lifts a limb or a part of the body

level of care /ˌlev(ə)l əv ˈkeə/ *noun* any of the planned divisions within the system of health care which is offered by a particular organisation ○ *Our care homes offer six different levels of care to allow the greatest independence possible.*

levodopa /ˌliːvəˈdəʊpə/ *noun* a natural chemical that stimulates the production of dopamine in the brain and is used to treat Parkinson's disease

levonorgestrel /ˌliːvəʊnɔːˈdʒestrəl/ *noun* an artificially produced female sex hormone, used mostly in birth control pills or capsules

Lewy body /ˈluːwi ˌbɒdi/ *noun* an unusual deposit of protein in neurons in the brain

Lewy body dementia /ˌluːwi ˌbɒdi dɪˈmenʃə/ *noun* a disease characterised by the presence of Lewy bodies in the brain, which affects the mental processes. It is similar to Alzheimer's disease, but people with it are more prone to hallucinations and delusions.

Leydig cells /ˈlaɪdɪg selz/ *plural noun* testosterone-producing cells between the tubules in the testes. Also called **interstitial cells** [Described 1850. After Franz von Leydig (1821–1908), Professor of Histology at Würzburg, Tübingen and then Bonn, Germany.]

Leydig tumour /ˈlaɪdɪg ˌtjuːmə/ *noun* a tumour of the Leydig cells of the testis. It often releases testosterone, which makes young boys show early signs of maturing.

l.g.v. *abbr* lymphogranuloma venereum

LH *abbr* luteinising hormone

libido /lɪˈbiːdəʊ/ *noun* **1.** the sexual urge **2.** (*in psychology*) a force which drives the unconscious mind

Librium /ˈlɪbriəm/ a trade name for chlordiazepoxide

lice /laɪs/ *plural of* **louse**

licence /ˈlaɪs(ə)ns/ *noun* an official document which allows someone to do something, e.g. one allowing a doctor to practise, a pharmacist to make and sell drugs or, in the USA, a nurse to practise ○ *He was practising as a doctor without a licence.* ○ *She is sitting her registered nurse licence examination.* (NOTE: The US spelling is **license**.)

licensure /ˈlaɪsənʃə/ *noun US* the act of licensing a nurse to practise nursing

licentiate /laɪˈsenʃiət/ *noun* a person who has been given a licence to practise as a doctor

lichen /ˈlaɪken/ *noun* a type of skin disease with thick skin and small lesions

lichenification /laɪˌkenɪfɪˈkeɪʃ(ə)n/ *noun* a thickening of the skin at the site of a lesion

lichenoid /ˈlaɪkənɔɪd/ *adjective* like lichen

lichen planus /ˌlaɪken ˈpleɪnəs/ *noun* a skin disease where itchy purple spots appear on the arms and thighs

lid /lɪd/ *noun* the top which covers a container ○ *a medicine bottle with a child-proof lid*

lidocaine /ˈlaɪdəkeɪn/ *noun* US a drug used as a local anaesthetic. Also called **lignocaine**

lie /laɪ/ *noun* same as **lie of fetus** ■ *verb* to be in a flat position ○ *The accident victim was lying on the pavement.* ○ *Make sure the patient lies still and does not move.* (NOTE: **lying – lay – lain**)

Lieberkühn's glands /ˈliːbəkuːnz glændz/ *plural noun* same as **crypts of Lieberkühn**

lien- /laɪən/ *prefix* spleen

lienal /ˈlaɪən(ə)l/ *adjective* relating to or affecting the spleen ○ *the lienal artery*

lienculus /ləˈeŋkjʊləs/ *noun* a small secondary spleen sometimes found in the body (NOTE: The plural is **lienculi**.)

lienorenal /ˌlaɪənəʊˈriːn(ə)l/ *adjective* relating to or affecting both the spleen and the kidneys

lientery /ˈlaɪəntri/, **lienteric diarrhoea** /ˌlaɪənterɪk ˌdaɪəˈriːə/ *noun* a form of diarrhoea where the food passes through the intestine rapidly without being digested

lie of fetus /ˌlaɪ əv ˈfiːtəs/ *noun* the position of the fetus in the uterus ○ *Cause of rupture: abnormal lie of fetus.*

life /laɪf/ *noun* the quality that makes a person or thing alive and not dead or inorganic ○ *The surgeons saved the patient's life.* ○ *Her life is in danger because the drugs are not available.* ○ *The victim showed no sign of life.*

life event /ˈlaɪf ɪˌvent/ *noun* a significant event which alters a person's status as regards taxation, insurance or employment benefits, e.g. the birth of a child or the onset of a disability

life expectancy /laɪf ɪkˈspektənsi/ *noun* the number of years a person of a particular age is likely to live

life-saving equipment /ˌlaɪf ˌseɪvɪŋ ɪˈkwɪpmənt/ *noun* equipment kept ready in case of an emergency, e.g. boats, stretchers or first-aid kits

life-support system /laɪf səˈpɔːt ˌsɪstəm/ *noun* a machine that takes over one or more vital functions such as breathing when someone is unable to survive unaided because of a disease or injury

life-threatening disease /laɪf ˌθret(ə)nɪŋ dɪˈziːz/ *noun* a disease which may kill

lift /lɪft/ *noun* 1. a particular way of carrying an injured or unconscious person ○ *a four-handed lift* ○ *a shoulder lift* 2. a cosmetic operation to remove signs of age or to change a body feature ○ *a face lift*

ligament /ˈlɪgəmənt/ *noun* a thick band of fibrous tissue which connects the bones at a joint and forms the joint capsule

ligate /ˈlaɪgeɪt/ *verb* to tie something with a ligature, e.g. to tie a blood vessel to stop bleeding or to tie the Fallopian tubes as a sterilisation procedure (NOTE: **ligating – ligated**)

ligation /laɪˈgeɪʃ(ə)n/ *noun* a surgical operation to tie up a blood vessel

ligature /ˈlɪgətʃə/ *noun* a thread used to tie vessels or a lumen, e.g. to tie a blood vessel to stop bleeding ■ *verb* same as **ligate** (NOTE: **ligaturing – ligatured**)

light /laɪt/ *adjective* 1. bright so that a person can see ○ *At six o'clock in the morning it was just getting light.* 2. referring to hair or skin which is very pale ○ *She has a very light complexion.* ○ *He has light-coloured hair.* 3. weighing a comparatively small amount ■ *noun* the energy that makes things bright and helps a person to see ○ *There's not enough light in here to take a photo.*

light adaptation /ˈlaɪt ædæpˌteɪʃ(ə)n/ *noun* changes in the eye to adapt to an unusually bright or dim light or to adapt to light after being in darkness

lightening /ˈlaɪtənɪŋ/ *noun* a late stage in pregnancy where the fetus goes down into the pelvic cavity

lightning pains /ˈlaɪtnɪŋ peɪnz/ *plural noun* sharp pains in the legs in someone who has tabes dorsalis

light reflex /ˈlaɪt ˌriːfleks/ *noun* same as **pupillary reaction**

light therapy /ˈlaɪt ˌθerəpi/, **light treatment** /ˈlaɪt ˌtriːtmənt/ *noun* the treatment of a disorder by exposing the person to light such as sunlight or infrared light

light wave /ˈlaɪt weɪv/ *noun* a wave travelling in all directions from a source of light which stimulates the retina and is visible

lignocaine /ˈlɪgnəkeɪn/ *noun* same as **lidocaine**

limb /lɪm/ *noun* one of the legs or arms

limbi /ˈlɪmbi/ *plural of* **limbus**

limbic system /ˈlɪmbɪk ˌsɪstəm/ *noun* a system of nerves in the brain, including the hippocampus, the amygdala and the hypothalamus, which are associated with emotions such as fear and anger

limb lead /ˈlɪm liːd/ *noun* an electrode attached to an arm or leg when taking an electrocardiogram

limb lengthening /ˈlɪm ˌleŋθənɪŋ/ *noun* a procedure in which an arm or a leg is made longer. Its bone is divided in two and new bone forms in the gap between the ends.

limbless /ˈlɪmləs/ *adjective* lacking one or more limbs

limbus /'lɪmbəs/ *noun* an edge, especially the edge of the cornea where it joins the sclera (NOTE: The plural is **limbi**.)

liminal /'lɪmɪn(ə)l/ *adjective* referring to a stimulus at the lowest level which can be sensed

limp /lɪmp/ *noun* a way of walking awkwardly because of pain, stiffness or malformation of a leg or foot ○ *She walks with a limp.* ■ *verb* to walk awkwardly because of pain, stiffness or malformation of a leg or foot ○ *He was still limping three weeks after the accident.*

linctus /'lɪŋktəs/ *noun* a sweet cough medicine

line /laɪn/ ♦ **catheter**

linea /'lɪniə/ *noun* a thin line (NOTE: The plural is **lineae**.)

linea alba /ˌlɪniə 'ælbə/ *noun* a tendon running from the breastbone to the pubic area, to which abdominal muscles are attached (NOTE: The plural is **lineae albae**.)

linea nigra /ˌlɪniə 'naɪɡrə/ *noun* a dark line on the skin from the navel to the pubis which appears during the later months of pregnancy (NOTE: The plural is **lineae nigrae**.)

linear /'lɪniə/ *adjective* **1.** long and narrow in shape **2.** able to be represented by a straight line

lingual /'lɪŋɡwəl/ *adjective* referring to the tongue

lingual artery /ˌlɪŋɡwəl 'ɑːtəri/ *noun* an artery which supplies blood to the tongue

lingual tonsil /ˌlɪŋɡwəl 'tɒns(ə)l/ *noun* a mass of lymphoid tissue on the top surface of the back of the tongue

lingual vein /ˌlɪŋɡwəl 'veɪn/ *noun* a vein which takes blood away from the tongue

lingula /'lɪŋɡjʊlə/ *noun* a long thin piece of bone or other tissue ○ *the lingula of the left lung* (NOTE: The plural is **lingulae**.)

lingular /'lɪŋɡjʊlə/ *adjective* relating to a lingula

liniment /'lɪnɪmənt/ *noun* an oily liquid rubbed on the skin to ease the pain or stiffness of a sprain or bruise by acting as a vasodilator or counterirritant. Also called **embrocation**

lining /'laɪnɪŋ/ *noun* a substance or tissue on the inside of an organ ○ *the thick lining of the aorta*

link /lɪŋk/ *verb* **1.** to join things together ○ *The ankle bone links the bones of the lower leg to the calcaneus.* **2.** to be related to or associated with something ○ *Health is linked to diet.*

linkage /'lɪŋkɪdʒ/ *noun* (*of genes*) the fact of being close together on a chromosome, and therefore likely to be inherited together

linoleic acid /ˌlɪnəʊliːɪk 'æsɪd/ *noun* one of the essential fatty acids, found in grains and seeds

linolenic acid /ˌlɪnəʊˌlenɪk 'æsɪd/ *noun* one of the essential fatty acids, found in linseed and other natural oils

lint /lɪnt/ *noun* thick flat cotton wadding, used as part of a surgical dressing

liothyronine /ˌlaɪəʊ'θaɪrəʊniːn/ *noun* a hormone produced by the thyroid gland which can be artificially synthesised for use as a rapid-acting treatment for hypothyroidism

lip /lɪp/ *noun* **1.** each of two fleshy muscular parts round the edge of the mouth ○ *Her lips were dry and cracked.* **2.** an edge of flesh round an opening **3.** same as **labium**

lipaemia /lɪ'piːmiə/ *noun* an excessive amount of fat in the blood (NOTE: The US spelling is **lipemia**.)

lipase /'lɪpeɪz/ *noun* an enzyme which breaks down fats in the intestine. Also called **lipolytic enzyme**

lipid /'lɪpɪd/ *noun* an organic compound which is insoluble in water, e.g. a fat, oil or wax

COMMENT: Lipids are not water soluble. They float in the blood and can attach themselves to the walls of arteries causing atherosclerosis.

lipid-lowering drug /'lɪpɪd ˌləʊərɪŋ ˌdrʌɡ/ *noun* a drug which lowers serum triglycerides and low-density lipoprotein cholesterol and raises high-density lipoprotein cholesterol to reduce the progression of coronary artherosclerosis. Lipid-lowering drugs are used in people with, or at high risk of developing coronary heart disease. (NOTE: Lipid-lowering drugs have names ending in **-fibrate: bezafibrate**.)

lipid metabolism /ˌlɪpɪd mə'tæbəlɪz(ə)m/ *noun* the series of chemical changes by which lipids are broken down into fatty acids

lipidosis /ˌlɪpɪ'dəʊsɪs/ *noun* a disorder of lipid metabolism in which subcutaneous fat is not present in some parts of the body

lipochondrodystrophy /ˌlɪpəʊˌkɒndrəʊ'dɪstrəfi/ *noun* a congenital disorder affecting lipid metabolism, the bones and the main organs, causing learning difficulties and physical deformity

lipodystrophy /ˌlɪpəʊ'dɪstrəfi/ *noun* a disorder of lipid metabolism

lipogenesis /ˌlɪpəʊ'dʒenəsɪs/ *noun* the production or making of deposits of fat

lipoid /'lɪpɔɪd/ *noun* a compound lipid, or a fatty substance such as cholesterol which is like a lipid ■ *adjective* like a lipid

lipoidosis /ˌlɪpɔɪ'dəʊsɪs/ *noun* a group of diseases with reticuloendothelial hyperplasia and unusual deposits of lipoids in the cells

lipolysis /lɪ'pɒlɪsɪs/ *noun* the process of breaking down fat by lipase

lipolytic enzyme /ˌlɪpəlɪtɪk 'enzaɪm/ *noun* same as **lipase**

lipoma /lɪˈpəʊmə/ *noun* a benign tumour formed of fatty tissue (NOTE: The plural is **lipomas** or **lipomata**.)

lipomatosis /ˌlɪpəʊməˈtəʊsɪs/ *noun* an excessive deposit of fat in the tissues in tumour-like masses

lipoprotein /ˌlɪpəʊˈprəʊtiːn/ *noun* a protein which combines with lipids and carries them in the bloodstream and lymph system (NOTE: Lipoproteins are classified according to the percentage of protein which they carry.)

liposarcoma /ˌlɪpəʊsɑːˈkəʊmə/ *noun* a rare malignant tumour found in fatty tissue (NOTE: The plural is **liposarcomas** or **liposarcomata**.)

liposuction /ˈlɪpəʊˌsʌkʃ(ə)n/ *noun* the surgical removal of fatty tissue for cosmetic reasons

lipotrophic /ˌlɪpəʊˈtrɒfɪk/ *adjective* referring to a substance which increases the amount of fat present in the tissues

Lippes loop /ˌlɪpəz ˈluːp/ *noun* a type of intrauterine device

lipping /ˈlɪpɪŋ/ *noun* a condition in which bone tissue grows over other bones

lip salve /ˈlɪp sælv/ *noun* an ointment, usually sold as a soft stick, used to rub on lips to prevent them cracking

lipuria /lɪˈpjʊəriə/ *noun* the presence of fat or oily emulsion in the urine

liquid diet /ˌlɪkwɪd ˈdaɪət/ *noun* a diet consisting only of liquids ○ *The clear liquid diet is a temporary diet used in preparation for surgery.*

liquid paraffin /ˌlɪkwɪd ˈpærəfɪn/ *noun* an oil used as a laxative

liquor /ˈlɪkə/ *noun* (*in pharmacy*) a solution, usually aqueous, of a pure substance

lisp /lɪsp/ *noun* a speech condition in which someone replaces 's' sounds with 'th' ■ *verb* to talk with a lisp

Listeria /lɪˈstɪəriə/ *noun* a genus of bacteria found in domestic animals and in unpasteurised milk products which can cause uterine infection or meningitis

listeriosis /lɪˌstɪəriˈəʊsɪs/ *noun* an infectious disease transmitted from animals to humans by the bacterium *Listeria*

listless /ˈlɪstləs/ *adjective* weak and tired

listlessness /ˈlɪstləsnəs/ *noun* the fact of being generally weak and tired

liter /ˈliːtə/ *noun* US spelling of **litre**

lith- /lɪθ/ *prefix* same as **litho-** (*used before vowels*)

lithaemia /lɪˈθiːmiə/ *noun* an unusual amount of uric acid in the blood. Also called **uricacidaemia** (NOTE: The US spelling is **lithemia**.)

lithagogue /ˈlɪθəɡɒɡ/ *noun* a drug which helps to remove stones from the urine

lithiasis /lɪˈθaɪəsɪs/ *noun* the formation of stones in an organ

lithium /ˈlɪθiəm/ *noun* a soft silver-white metallic element that forms compounds, used as a medical treatment for bipolar disorder

litho- *prefix* referring to a calculus

litholapaxy /lɪˈθɒləpæksi/ *noun* the evacuation of pieces of a stone in the bladder after crushing it with a lithotrite. Also called **lithotrity**

lithonephrotomy /ˌlɪθəʊnəˈfrɒtəmi/ *noun* a surgical operation to remove a stone in the kidney (NOTE: The plural is **lithonephrotomies**.)

lithotomy /lɪˈθɒtəmi/ *noun* a surgical operation to remove a stone from the bladder (NOTE: The plural is **lithotomies**.)

lithotomy position /lɪˈθɒtəmi pəˌzɪʃ(ə)n/ *noun* a position for some medical examinations in which the person lies on his or her back with the legs flexed and the thighs against the abdomen

lithotripsy /ˈlɪθətrɪpsi/ *noun* the process of breaking up kidney or gall bladder stones into small fragments that the body can eliminate them unaided

lithotrite /ˈlɪθətraɪt/ *noun* a surgical instrument which crushes a stone in the bladder

lithotrity /lɪˈθɒtrɪti/ *noun* same as **litholapaxy**

lithuresis /ˌlɪθjʊˈriːsɪs/ *noun* the passage of small stones from the bladder during urination

lithuria /lɪˈθjʊəriə/ *noun* the presence of excessive amounts of uric acid or urates in the urine

litmus /ˈlɪtməs/ *noun* a substance which turns red in acid and blue in alkali

litmus paper /ˈlɪtməs ˌpeɪpə/ *noun* a small piece of paper impregnated with litmus, used to test for acidity or alkalinity

litre /ˈliːtə/ *noun* a unit of measurement of liquids equal to 1.76 pints. Abbr **l**, **L** (NOTE: With figures, usually written **l** or **L**: *2.5l*, but it can be written in full to avoid confusion with the numeral **1**. The US spelling is **liter**.)

little finger /ˌlɪt(ə)l ˈfɪŋɡə/ *noun* the smallest finger on the hand

Little's area /ˈlɪt(ə)lz ˌeəriə/ *noun* an area of blood vessels in the nasal septum

Little's disease /ˈlɪt(ə)lz dɪˌziːz/ *noun* same as **spastic diplegia** [Described 1843. After William John Little (1810–94), physician at the London Hospital, UK.]

little toe /ˌlɪt(ə)l ˈtəʊ/ *noun* the smallest toe on the foot ○ *Her little toe was crushed by the door.*

live *adjective* /laɪv/ **1.** living, not dead ○ *graft using live tissue* ◊ **birth 2.** carrying electricity ○ *He was killed when he touched a live wire.* ■ *verb* /lɪv/ to be alive ○ *She is very ill, and the doctor doesn't think she will live much longer.* (NOTE: **living – lived**)

live birth /ˌlaɪv ˈbɜːθ/ noun the birth of a baby which is alive ○ *The number of live births has remained steady.*

livedo /lɪˈviːdəʊ/ noun discoloured spots on the skin

liver /ˈlɪvə/ noun a large gland in the upper part of the abdomen. See illustration at DIGESTIVE SYSTEM in Supplement (NOTE: For other terms referring to the liver, see words beginning with **hepat-, hepato-**.)

COMMENT: The liver is situated in the top part of the abdomen on the right side of the body next to the stomach. It is the largest gland in the body, weighing almost 2 kg. Blood carrying nutrients from the intestines enters the liver by the hepatic portal vein; the nutrients are removed and the blood returned to the heart through the hepatic vein. The liver is the major detoxicating organ in the body; it destroys harmful organisms in the blood, produces clotting agents, secretes bile, stores glycogen and metabolises proteins, carbohydrates and fats. Diseases affecting the liver include hepatitis and cirrhosis; the symptom of liver disease is often jaundice.

liver fluke /ˈlɪvə fluːk/ noun a parasitic flatworm which can infest the liver

liver spot /ˈlɪvə spɒt/ noun a little brown patch on the skin of the backs of the hands, attributed to sun damage (NOTE: Liver spots are unconnected with any liver disorder.)

liver transplant /ˈlɪvə ˌtrænsplɑːnt/ noun a surgical operation to give a person the liver of another person who has died

livid /ˈlɪvɪd/ adjective referring to skin with a blue colour because of being bruised or because of asphyxiation

living will /ˌlɪvɪŋ ˈwɪl/ noun a document signed by a person while in good health to specify the decisions he or she wishes to be taken about medical treatment if he or she becomes incapable of making or communicating them

LMC abbr local medical committee

loa loa /ˌləʊə ˈləʊə/ noun a tropical disease of the eye caused when the threadworm *Loa loa* enters the eye or the skin around the eye

Loa loa /ˌləʊə ˈləʊə/ noun a tropical threadworm which digs under the skin, especially around and into the eye, causing loa loa and loiasis

lobar /ˈləʊbə/ adjective referring to a lobe

lobar bronchi /ˌləʊbə ˈbrɒŋkiː/ plural noun air passages supplying a lobe of a lung. Also called **secondary bronchi**

lobar pneumonia /ˌləʊbə njuːˈməʊniə/ noun pneumonia which affects one or more lobes of the lung

lobe /ləʊb/ noun 1. a rounded section of an organ such as the brain, lung or liver. See illustration at LUNGS in Supplement 2. the soft fleshy part at the bottom of the ear 3. a cusp on the crown of a tooth

lobectomy /ləʊˈbektəmi/ noun a surgical operation to remove one of the lobes of an organ such as the lung ○ *The plural is lobectomies.*

lobotomy /ləʊˈbɒtəmi/ noun a surgical operation formerly used to treat mental illness by cutting into a lobe of the brain to cut the nerve fibres (NOTE: The plural is **lobotomies**.)

lobular /ˈlɒbjʊlə/ adjective relating to a lobule ○ *lobular carcinoma*

lobule /ˈlɒbjuːl/ noun a small section of a lobe in the lung, formed of acini

local /ˈləʊk(ə)l/ adjective 1. referring to a separate place 2. confined to one part ■ noun same as **local anaesthetic**

local anaesthesia /ˌləʊk(ə)l ænəsˈθiːziə/ noun loss of feeling in a single part of the body

local anaesthetic /ˌləʊk(ə)l ænəsˈθetɪk/ noun an anaesthetic such as lignocaine which removes the feeling in a single part of the body only ○ *The surgeon removed the growth under local anaesthetic.*

localise /ˈləʊkəlaɪz/, **localize** verb 1. to restrict the spread of something to a specific area 2. to find where something is 3. to transfer power from a central authority to local organisations (NOTE: **localising – localised**)

localised /ˈləʊkəlaɪzd/, **localized** adjective referring to an infection which occurs in one part of the body only. Opposite **generalised**

Local Medical Committee /ˌləʊk(ə)l ˈmedɪk(ə)l kəˌmɪti/ noun a committee responsible for monitoring the interests of providers of primary care such as GPs, dentists and pharmacists in a district. Abbr **LMC**

local supervising authority /ˌləʊk(ə)l ˈsuːpəvaɪzɪŋ ɔːˌθɒrɪti/ noun an organisation which controls midwife services within its area

lochia /ˈlɒkiə/ noun a discharge from the vagina after childbirth or abortion

lochial /ˈləʊkiəl/ adjective referring to lochia

lochiometra /ˈlɒkiəmiːtrə/ noun a condition in which lochia remains in the uterus after a baby is born, making it swollen

lock /lɒk/ verb to fix something in a position

locked-in syndrome /ˌlɒkt ˈɪn ˌsɪndrəʊm/ noun a condition in which only the eyes and eyelids can move although the person is fully alert and conscious. It results from severe damage to the brain stem.

locked knee /ˌlɒkt ˈniː/ noun a condition in which a piece of the cartilage in the knee slips out of position. The symptom is a sharp pain, and the knee remains permanently bent.

locking joint /ˌlɒkɪŋ ˈdʒɔɪnt/ noun a joint which can be locked in an extended position, e.g. the knee or elbow

lockjaw /ˈlɒkjɔː/ noun same as **tetanus** (dated informal)

locomotion /ˌləʊkə'məʊʃ(ə)n/ *noun* the fact of being able to move

locomotor /ˌləʊkə'məʊtə/ *adjective* relating to locomotion

locomotor ataxia /ˌləʊkə,məʊtər ə'tæksiə/ *noun* same as **tabes dorsalis**

loculated /'lɒkjʊleɪtɪd/ *adjective* referring to an organ or a growth which is divided into many compartments ○ *a loculated renal abscess*

locule /'lɒkjuːl/ *noun* same as **loculus**

loculus /'lɒkjʊləs/ *noun* a small space in an organ (NOTE: The plural is **loculi**.)

locum /'ləʊkəm/ *noun* a healthcare professional such as a doctor or pharmacist who takes the place of another for a time. Also called **locum tenens**

locum tenens *noun* same as **locum** (NOTE: The plural is **locum tenentes**.)

locus /'ləʊkəs/ *noun* **1.** an area or point where an infection or disease is to be found **2.** a position on a chromosome occupied by a gene (NOTE: The plural is **loci**.)

lodge /lɒdʒ/ *verb* to stay or stick somewhere, or to stick something somewhere ○ *The piece of bone lodged in her throat.* ○ *The larvae of the tapeworm lodge in the walls of the intestine.*

lofepramine /lɒ'feprəmiːn/ *noun* an antidepressant drug

log roll /'lɒg rəʊl/ *noun* a method of turning people in bed onto their side by putting them into a straight position and pulling on the sheet under them

logrolling /'lɒgrəʊlɪŋ/ *noun* the process of moving a person who is lying down into another position using the log roll method

-logy /lədʒi/ *suffix* **1.** science or study ○ *psychology* ○ *embryology* **2.** speech or expression

loiasis /ləʊ'aɪəsɪs/ *noun* a tropical disease of the eye caused when the threadworm *Loa loa* enters the eye or the skin around the eye

loin /lɔɪn/ *noun* the lower back part of the body above the buttocks

Lomotil /ləʊ'məʊtɪl/ a trade name for a preparation containing diphenoxalate

long-acting /ˌlɒŋ 'æktɪŋ/ *adjective* referring to a drug or treatment which has an effect that lasts a long time

long bone /'lɒŋ bəʊn/ *noun* any long limb bone that contains marrow and ends in a part that forms a joint with another bone

longitudinal /ˌlɒŋgɪ't juːdɪn(ə)l/ *adjective* **1.** positioned lengthwise **2.** in the direction of the long axis of the body

longitudinal arch /ˌlɒŋgɪt juːdɪn(ə)l 'ɑːt ʃ/ *noun* same as **plantar arch**

longitudinal fissure /ˌlɒŋgɪt juːdɪn(ə)l 'fɪʃə/ *noun* a groove separating the two cerebral hemispheres

longitudinal lie /ˌlɒŋgɪt juːdɪn(ə)l 'laɪ/ *noun* the usual position of a fetus, lying along the axis of the mother's body

longitudinal study /ˌlɒŋgɪt juːdɪn(ə)l 'stʌdi/ *noun* a study of individuals or groups of people and of how some aspect such as their health or education changes over a long time

longsighted /ˌlɒŋ'saɪtɪd/ *adjective* able to see clearly things which are far away but not things which are close

longsightedness /ˌlɒŋ'saɪtɪdnəs/ *noun* the condition of being longsighted. Also called **hypermetropia**

long-stay /'lɒŋ steɪ/ *adjective* referring to staying a long time in hospital ○ *patients in long-stay units*

long stay patient /ˌlɒŋ steɪ 'peɪʃ(ə)nt/ *noun* a patient who will stay in hospital for a long time

long stay ward /ˌlɒŋ 'steɪ ˌwɔːd/ *noun* a ward for patients who will stay in hospital for a long time

loo /luː/ *noun* a toilet, or a room containing a toilet (*informal*) □ **to go to the loo** to urinate or defecate

look after /ˌlʊk 'ɑːftə/ *verb* to take care of a person and attend to his or her needs ○ *The nurses looked after him very well* or *He was very well looked after in hospital.* ○ *She is off work looking after her children who have mumps.*

loop /luːp/ *noun* **1.** a curve or bend in a line, especially one of the particular curves in a fingerprint **2.** a curved piece of wire placed in the uterus to prevent contraception

loop of Henle /ˌluːp əv 'henli/ *noun* a curved tube which forms the main part of a nephron in the kidney

loperamide /ləʊ'perəmaɪd/, **loperamide hydrochloride** /ləʊ,perəmaɪd ˌhaɪdrəʊ'klɔːraɪd/ *noun* a drug that relieves severe diarrhoea by slowing down the movements of the intestine

loratidine /lɒr'ætɪdiːn/ *noun* an antihistamine drug

lorazepam /lɔː'ræzɪpæm/ *noun* a mild tranquilliser that people often receive before surgery to lessen anxiety

lordosis /lɔː'dəʊsɪs/ *noun* excessive forward curvature of the lower part of the spine. ◊ **kyphosis**

lordotic /lɔː'dɒtɪk/ *adjective* referring to lordosis

lotion /'ləʊʃ(ə)n/ *noun* a medicinal liquid used to rub on the skin ○ *a mild antiseptic lotion*

louse /laʊs/ *noun* a small insect of the *Pediculus* genus, which sucks blood and lives on the skin as a parasite on animals and humans (NOTE: The plural is **lice**.)

COMMENT: There are several forms of louse: the commonest are the body louse, the crab louse and the head louse. Some diseases can be transmitted by lice.

low /ləʊ/ *adjective* **1.** relatively little in height **2.** close to the bottom or base of something

low blood pressure /ˌləʊ ˈblʌd ˌpreʃə/ *noun* same as **hypotension**

low-calorie diet /ˌləʊ ˌkæləri ˈdaɪət/ *noun* a diet with few calories, to help a person to lose weight

low-density lipoprotein /ləʊ ˌdensɪti ˈlɪpəʊprəʊtiːn/ *noun* a lipoprotein with a large percentage of cholesterol which deposits fats in muscles and arteries. Abbr **LDL**

lower /ˈləʊə/ *adjective* in a position below another thing

lower jaw /ˌləʊə ˈdʒɔː/ *noun* same as **mandible**

lower limb /ˌləʊə ˈlɪm/ *noun* a leg

lower motor neurones /ˌləʊə ˈməʊtə ˌnjʊərəʊnz/ *plural noun* linked neurones which carry motor impulses from the spinal cord to the muscles

low-fat diet /ˌləʊ ˌfæt ˈdaɪət/ *noun* a diet with little animal fat, which can help reduce the risk of heart disease and alleviate some skin conditions

low-risk patient /ˌləʊ rɪsk ˈpeɪʃ(ə)nt/ *noun* a person not likely to catch or develop a particular disease

low-salt diet /ˌləʊ ˌsɔːlt ˈdaɪət/ *noun* a diet with little salt, which has been shown to help reduce high blood pressure

lozenge /ˈlɒzɪndʒ/ *noun* a sweet medicinal tablet ○ *She was sucking a cough lozenge.*

LPN *abbr US* licensed practical nurse

LRCP *abbr* licentiate of the Royal College of Physicians

LSA *abbr* local supervising authority

LSD *abbr* lysergic acid diethylamide

lubb-dupp /lʌbˈdʌb/ *noun* two sounds made by the heart, which represent each cardiac cycle when heard through a stethoscope

lubricant /ˈluːbrɪkənt/ *noun* a fluid which lubricates

lubricate /ˈluːbrɪkeɪt/ *verb* to cover something with a fluid to reduce friction (NOTE: **lubricating – lubricated**)

lubricating jelly /ˈluːbrɪkeɪt ˌdʒeli/ *noun* a jelly used to make a surface slippery

lucid /ˈluːsɪd/ *adjective* with a clearly working mind ○ *In spite of the pain, he was still lucid.*

lucid interval /ˌluːsɪd ˈɪntəv(ə)l/ *noun* a period of clear thinking which occurs between two periods of unconsciousness or of mental illness

Ludwig's angina /ˌluːdvɪgz ænˈdʒaɪnə/ *noun* cellulitis of the mouth and some parts of the neck which causes the neck to swell and may obstruct the airway [Described 1836. After Wilhelm Friedrich von Ludwig (1790–1865), Professor of Surgery and Midwifery at Tübingen, Germany, and Court Physician to King Frederick II.]

lues /ˈluːiːz/ *noun* a former name for syphilis or the plague

lumbago /lʌmˈbeɪgəʊ/ *noun* pain in the lower back (*informal*) ○ *She has been suffering from lumbago for years.* ○ *He has had an attack of lumbago.*

lumbar /ˈlʌmbə/ *adjective* referring to the lower part of the back

lumbar artery /ˈlʌmbə ˌɑːtəri/ *noun* one of four arteries which supply blood to the back muscles and skin

lumbar cistern /ˌlʌmbə ˈsɪstən/ *noun* a subarachnoid space in the spinal cord, where the dura mater ends, filled with cerebrospinal fluid

lumbar enlargement /ˌlʌmbə ɪn ˈlɑːdʒmənt/ *noun* the wider part of the spinal cord in the lower spine, where the nerves of the lower limbs are attached

lumbar plexus /ˌlʌmbə ˈpleksəs/ *noun* the point where several nerves which supply the thighs and abdomen join together, lying in the upper psoas muscle

lumbar puncture /ˌlʌmbə ˈpʌŋktʃə/ *noun* a surgical operation to remove a sample of cerebrospinal fluid by inserting a hollow needle into the lower part of the spinal canal. Also called **spinal puncture** (NOTE: The US term is usually **spinal tap.**)

lumbar region /ˈlʌmbə ˌriːdʒən/ *noun* the two parts of the abdomen on each side of the umbilical region

lumbar vertebra /ˌlʌmbə ˈvɜːtɪbrə/ *plural noun* each of the five vertebrae between the thoracic vertebrae and the sacrum

lumbo- /lʌmbəʊ/ *prefix* the lumbar region

lumbosacral /ˌlʌmbəʊˈseɪkrəl/ *adjective* referring to both the lumbar vertebrae and the sacrum

lumbosacral joint /ˌlʌmbəʊˈseɪkrəl dʒɔɪnt/ *noun* a joint at the bottom of the back between the lumbar vertebrae and the sacrum

lumen /ˈluːmɪn/ *noun* **1.** an SI unit of light emitted per second **2.** the inside width of a passage in the body or of an instrument such as an endoscope **3.** a hole at the end of an instrument such as an endoscope

lump /lʌmp/ *noun* a mass of hard tissue which rises on the surface or under the surface of the skin ○ *He has a lump where he hit his head on the low door.* ○ *She noticed a lump in her right breast and went to see the doctor.*

lumpectomy /lʌmˈpektəmi/ *noun* a surgical operation to remove a hard mass of tissue such as a breast tumour, leaving the surrounding tissue intact (NOTE: The plural is **lumpectomies.**)

lunate /ˈluːneɪt/, **lunate bone** /ˈluːneɪt bəʊn/ *noun* one of the eight small carpal bones in the wrist. See illustration at HAND in Supplement

Lund and Browder chart /ˌlʌnd ən ˈbraʊdə tʃɑːt/ *noun* a chart for calculating the surface area of a burn

lung /lʌŋ/ *noun* one of two organs of respiration in the body into which air is sucked when a person breathes (NOTE: For other terms referring to the lungs, see words beginning with **bronch-, broncho-, pneum-, pneumo-, pneumon-, pneumono-, pulmo-.**)

COMMENT: The two lungs are situated in the chest cavity, protected by the ribcage. The heart lies between the lungs. The right lung has three lobes, the left lung only two. Air goes down into the lungs through the trachea and bronchi. It passes to the alveoli where its oxygen is deposited in the blood in exchange for waste carbon dioxide which is exhaled (gas exchange). Lung cancer can be caused by smoking tobacco, and is commonest in people who are heavy smokers.

lung cancer /ˈlʌŋ ˌkænsə/ *noun* cancer in the lung

lunula /ˈluːnjʊlə/ *noun* a curved white mark at the base of a fingernail (NOTE: The plural is **lunulae.**)

lupus /ˈluːpəs/ *noun* a persistent skin disease, of which there are several unrelated types

lupus erythematosus /ˌluːpəs ˌerɪθiːməˈtəʊsəs/ *noun* an inflammatory disease of connective tissue of which the more serious, systemic, form affects the heart, joints and blood vessels. Abbr **LE**

lupus vulgaris /ˌluːpəs vʌlˈgeərɪs/ *noun* a form of tuberculosis of the skin in which red spots appear on the face and become infected

lutein /ˈluːtiɪn/ *noun* a yellow pigment in the corpus luteum

luteinising hormone /ˈluːtiːɪnaɪzɪŋ ˌhɔːməʊn/, **luteinizing hormone** *noun* a hormone produced by the pituitary gland, which stimulates the formation of the corpus luteum in females and of testosterone in males. Abbr **LH**. Also called **interstitial cell stimulating hormone**

luteo- /luːtiəʊ/ *prefix* **1.** yellow **2.** corpus luteum

luxation /lʌkˈseɪʃ(ə)n/ *noun* same as **dislocation**

Lyme disease /ˈlaɪm dɪˌziːz/ *noun* a viral disease caused by *Borrelia burgdorferi* transmitted by bites from deer ticks. It causes rashes, nervous pains, paralysis and, in extreme cases, death.

lymph /lɪmf/ *noun* a colourless liquid containing white blood cells which circulates in the lymph system from all body tissues, carrying waste matter away from tissues to the veins. Also called **lymph fluid**

COMMENT: Lymph drains from the tissues through capillaries into lymph vessels. It is formed of water, protein and white blood cells (lymphocytes). Waste matter such as infection in the lymph is filtered out and destroyed as it passes through the lymph nodes, which

then add further lymphocytes to the lymph before it continues in the system. It eventually drains into the brachiocephalic (innominate) veins, and joins the venous bloodstream. Lymph is not pumped round the body like blood but moves by muscle pressure on the lymph vessels and by the negative pressure of the large veins into which the vessels empty. Lymph is an essential part of the body's defence against infection.

lymph- /lɪmf/ *prefix meaning* same as **lympho-** (*used before vowels*)

lymphaden- /lɪmfædən/ *prefix* relating to the lymph nodes

lymphadenectomy /ˌlɪmfædəˈnektəmi/ *noun* the surgical removal of a lymph node (NOTE: The plural is **lymphadenectomies.**)

lymphadenitis /ˌlɪmfædəˈnaɪtɪs/ *noun* inflammation of the lymph nodes

lymphadenoma /ˌlɪmfædəˈnəʊmə/ *noun* same as **lymphoma**

lymphadenopathy /ˌlɪmfædəˈnɒpəθi/ *noun* any unusual condition of the lymph nodes (NOTE: The plural is **lymphadenopathies.**)

lymphangi- /lɪmfændʒi/ *prefix* lymphatic vessel

lymphangiectasis /ˌlɪmfændʒiˈektəsɪs/ *noun* swelling of the smaller lymph vessels as a result of obstructions in larger vessels

lymphangiography /ˌlɪmfændʒiˈɒgrəfi/ *noun* an X-ray examination of the lymph vessels following introduction of radio-opaque material (NOTE: The plural is **lymphangiographies.**)

lymphangioma /ˌlɪmfændʒiˈəumə/ *noun* a benign tumour formed of lymph tissues (NOTE: The plural is **lymphangiomas** or **lymphangiomata.**)

lymphangioplasty /lɪmfˈændʒiəplæsti/ *noun* a surgical operation to make artificial lymph channels (NOTE: The plural is **lymphangioplasties.**)

lymphangiosarcoma /lɪmfˌændʒiəʊsɑːˈkəʊmə/ *noun* a malignant tumour of the endothelial cells lining the lymph vessels (NOTE: The plural is **lymphangiosarcomas** or **lymphangiosarcomata.**)

lymphangitis /ˌlɪmfænˈdʒaɪtɪs/ *noun* inflammation of the lymph vessels

lymphatic /lɪmˈfætɪk/ *adjective* referring to lymph

lymphatic capillary /lɪmˌfætɪk kəˈpɪləri/ *plural noun* any of the capillaries which lead from tissue and join lymphatic vessels

lymphatic duct /lɪmˈfætɪk dʌkt/ *noun* the main channel for carrying lymph

lymphatic node /lɪmˈfætɪk nəʊd/ *noun* same as **lymph gland**

lymphatic nodule /lɪmˌfætɪk ˈnɒdjuːl/ *noun* a small lymph node found in clusters in tissues

lymphatic system /lɪmˈfætɪk ˌsɪstəm/ *noun* a series of vessels which transport lymph from the tissues through the lymph nodes and into the bloodstream

lymphatic vessel /lɪm'fætɪk ˌves(ə)l/ *noun* a tube which carries lymph round the body from the tissues to the veins

lymph duct /'lɪmf dʌkt/ *noun* any channel carrying lymph

lymph fluid /'lɪmf ˌfluːɪd/ *noun* same as **lymph**

lymph gland /'lɪmf glænd/, **lymph node** /'lɪmf nəʊd/ *noun* a mass of lymphoid tissue situated in various points of the lymphatic system, especially under the armpits and in the groin, through which lymph passes and in which lymphocytes are produced. Also called **lymphatic node**

lympho- /lɪmfəʊ/ *prefix meaning* lymph

lymphoblast /'lɪmfəʊblæst/ *noun* an unusual cell which forms in acute lymphoblastic leukaemia as a result of the change which takes place in a lymphocyte on contact with an antigen

lymphoblastic /ˌlɪmfəʊ'blæstɪk/ *adjective* referring to lymphoblasts, or forming lymphocytes

lymphocele /'lɪmfəsiːl/ *noun* a cyst containing lymph from injured or diseased lymph nodes or ducts

lymphocyte /'lɪmfəsaɪt/ *noun* a type of mature leucocyte or white blood cell formed by the lymph nodes and concerned with the production of antibodies

lymphocytopenia /ˌlɪmfəʊˌsaɪtəʊ'piːniə/ *noun* same as **lymphopenia**

lymphocytosis /ˌlɪmfəʊsaɪ'təʊsɪs/ *noun* an increased number of lymphocytes in the blood

lymphoedema /ˌlɪmfəʊɪ'diːmə/ *noun* a swelling caused by obstruction of the lymph vessels or unusual development of lymph vessels (NOTE: The US spelling is **lymphedema**.)

lymphogranuloma inguinale /ˌlɪmfəʊ grænjʊˌləʊmə ˌɪŋgwɪ'neɪli/ *noun* same as **lymphogranuloma venereum**

lymphogranuloma venereum /ˌlɪmfəʊ ˌgrænjʊˌləʊmə və'nɪərəm/ *noun* a sexually transmitted bacterial infection that causes swelling of the genital lymph nodes and, especially in men, a genital ulcer. Abbr **l.g.v.**

lymphography /lɪm'fɒgrəfi/ *noun* the making of images of the lymphatic system after having introduced a radio-opaque substance

lymphoid /'lɪmfɔɪd/ *adjective* referring to lymph, lymphatic tissue, or the lymphatic system

lymphoid tissue /'lɪmfɔɪd ˌtɪʃuː/ *noun* tissue in the lymph nodes, the tonsils and the spleen where masses of lymphocytes are supported by a network of reticular fibres and cells

lymphokine /'lɪmfəʊkaɪn/ *noun* a protein produced by lymphocytes that has an effect on other cells in the immune system. ◊ **cytokine**

lymphoma /lɪm'fəʊmə/ *noun* a malignant tumour arising from lymphoid tissue. Also called **lymphadenoma** (NOTE: The plural is **lymphomas** or **lymphomata**.)

lymphopenia /ˌlɪmfəʊ'piːniə/ *noun* a reduction in the number of lymphocytes in the blood. Also called **lymphocytopenia**

lymphopoiesis /ˌlɪmfəʊpɔɪ'iːsɪs/ *noun* the production of lymphocytes or lymphoid tissue

lymphorrhagia /ˌlɪmfə'reɪdʒə/, **lymphorrhoea** /ˌlɪmfə'riə/ *noun* escape of lymph from ruptured or severed lymphatic vessels

lymphosarcoma /ˌlɪmfəʊsɑː'kəʊmə/ *noun* a malignant growth arising from lymphocytes and their cells of origin in the lymph nodes (NOTE: The plural is **lymphosarcomas** or **lymphosarcomata**.)

lymphotropic /ˌlɪmfə'trɒpɪk/ *adjective* affecting the lymphatic system

lymphuria /lɪm'fjʊəriə/ *noun* the presence of lymph in the urine

lymph vessel /'lɪmf ˌves(ə)l/ *noun* one of the tubes which carry lymph round the body from the tissues to the veins

lyophilisation /laɪˌɒfɪlaɪ'zeɪʃ(ə)n/, **lyophilization** *noun* the act of preserving tissue, plasma or serum by freeze-drying it in a vacuum

lyophilise /laɪ'ɒfɪlaɪz/, **lyophilize** *verb* to preserve tissue, plasma or serum by freeze-drying in a vacuum (NOTE: **lyophilising – lyophilised**)

lysergic acid diethylamide /laɪ'sɜːdʒɪk 'æsɪd daɪ'eθɪləmaɪd/ *noun* a powerful hallucinogenic drug which can cause psychosis. Abbr **LSD**

lysin /'laɪsɪn/ *noun* **1.** a protein in the blood which destroys the cell against which it is directed **2.** a toxin which causes the lysis of cells

lysine /'laɪsiːn/ *noun* an essential amino acid

lysis /'laɪsɪs/ *noun* **1.** the destruction of a cell by a lysin, in which the membrane of the cell is destroyed **2.** a reduction in a fever or disease slowly over a period of time. Opposite **crisis**

-lysis /lɪsɪs/ *suffix* referring to processes which involve breaking up or decaying, or to objects which are doing this ○ *haemolysis*

lysol /'laɪsɒl/ *noun* a strong disinfectant, made of cresol and soap

lysosome /'laɪsəsəʊm/ *noun* a particle in a cell which contains enzymes which break down substances such as bacteria which enter the cell

lysozyme /'laɪsəzaɪm/ *noun* an enzyme found in the whites of eggs and in tears, which destroys specific bacteria

M

m *symbol* **1.** metre **2.** milli-

M *symbol* mega-

MAAG *abbr* medical audit advisory group

macerate /ˈmæsəreɪt/ *verb* to make something soft by letting it lie in a liquid for a time (NOTE: **macerating – macerated**)

maceration /ˌmæsəˈreɪʃ(ə)n/ *noun* the process of softening a solid by letting it lie in a liquid so that the soluble matter dissolves

Mackenrodt's ligaments /ˈmækənrəʊdz ˌlɪgəmənts/ *plural noun* same as **cardinal ligaments**

Macmillan nurse /məkˈmɪlən nɜːs/ *noun* a nurse who specialises in cancer care and is employed by the organisation Macmillan Cancer Relief

macro- /mækrəʊ/ *prefix* large. Opposite **micro-**

macrobiotic /ˌmækrəʊbaɪˈɒtɪk/ *adjective* referring to food which has been produced naturally without artificial additives or preservatives

COMMENT: Macrobiotic diets are usually vegetarian and are prepared in a special way. They consist of beans, coarse flour, fruit and vegetables. They may not contain enough protein or trace elements, especially to satisfy the needs of children.

macrocephaly /ˌmækrəʊˈkefli/ *noun* the condition of having an unusually large head

macrocheilia /ˌmækrəʊˈkaɪliə/ *noun* the condition of having large lips

macrocyte /ˈmækrəʊsaɪt/ *noun* an unusually large red blood cell found in people who have pernicious anaemia

macrocythaemia /ˌmækrəʊsaɪˈθiːmiə/ *noun* same as **macrocytosis**

macrocytic /ˌmækrəʊˈsɪtɪk/ *adjective* referring to macrocytes

macrocytic anaemia /ˌmækrəʊsɪtɪk əˈniːmiə/ *noun* anaemia in which someone has unusually large red blood cells

macrocytosis /ˌmækrəʊsaɪˈtəʊsɪs/ *noun* the condition of having macrocytes in the blood. Also called **macrocythaemia**

macrodactyly /ˌmækrəʊˈdæktɪli/ *noun* a condition in which a person has unusually large or long fingers or toes

macrogenitosoma /ˌmækrəʊˌdʒenɪtəˈsəʊmə/ *noun* premature development of the body with the genitals being of an unusually large size

macroglobulin /ˌmækrəʊˈglɒbjʊlɪn/ *noun* a class of immunoglobulin, a globulin protein of high molecular weight, which serves as an antibody

macroglossia /ˌmækrəʊˈglɒsiə/ *noun* the condition of having an unusually large tongue

macrognathia /ˌmækrəʊˈneɪθiə/ *noun* a condition in which the jaw is larger than usual

macrolide drug /ˈmækrəlaɪd drʌg/ *noun* a drug used in the treatment of bacterial infection, often in place of penicillin in people sensitive to penicillin (NOTE: Macrolide drugs have names ending in **-omycin: erythromycin.**)

macromastia /ˌmækrəʊˈmæstiə/ *noun* overdevelopment of the breasts

macromelia /ˌmækrəʊˈmiːliə/ *noun* a condition in which a person has unusually large limbs

macronutrient /ˈmækrəʊˌnjuːtriənt/ *noun* a substance which an organism needs in large amounts for normal growth and development, e.g. nitrogen, carbon or potassium. Compare **micronutrient**

macrophage /ˈmækrəʊfeɪdʒ/ *noun* any of several large cells which destroy inflammatory tissue, found in connective tissue, wounds, lymph nodes and other parts

macropsia /mæˈkrɒpsiə/ *noun* a condition in which a person sees objects larger than they really are, caused by an unusual development in the retina

macroscopic /ˌmækrəʊˈskɒpɪk/ *adjective* able to be seen with the naked eye

macrosomia /ˌmækrəʊˈsəʊmiə/ *noun* a condition in which the body grows too much

macrostomia /ˌmækrəʊˈstəʊmiə/ *noun* a condition in which the mouth is too wide because the bones of the upper and lower jaw have not fused, either on one or on both sides

macula /'mækjʊlə/ *noun* **1.** same as **macule 2.** a small coloured area, e.g. a macula lutea **3.** an area of hair cells inside the utricle and saccule of the ear (NOTE: The plural is **maculae.**)

macula lutea /,mækjʊlə 'luːtiə/ *noun* a yellow spot on the retina, surrounding the fovea, the part of the eye which sees most clearly. Also called **yellow spot**

macular /'mækjʊlə/ *adjective* referring to a macula

macular degeneration /,mækjʊlə dɪ,dʒenə'reɪʃ(ə)n/ *noun* an eye disorder in elderly people in which fluid leaks into the retina and destroys cones and rods, reducing central vision

macular oedema /,mækjʊlə ɪ'diːmə/ *noun* a disorder of the eye in which fluid gathers in the fovea

macule /'mækjuːl/ *noun* a small flat coloured spot on the skin. Compare **papule**

maculopapular /,mækjʊləʊ'pæpjʊlə/ *adjective* made up of both macules and papules ○ *maculopapular rash*

mad cow disease *noun* same as **bovine spongiform encephalopathy** (*informal*)

maduromycosis /mə,djʊərəʊmaɪ'kəʊsɪs/, **maduromycetoma** /mə,djʊərəʊ,maɪsə'təʊmə/, **Madura foot** /mə,djʊərə 'fʊt/ *noun* a tropical fungus infection in the feet which can destroy tissue and infect bones

Magendie's foramen /mə,dʒendɪz fə'reɪmen/ *noun* an opening in the fourth ventricle of the brain which allows cerebrospinal fluid to flow [Described 1828. After François Magendie (1783–1855), French physician and physiologist.]

magna /'mægnə/ ◆ **cisterna magna**

magnesium /mæg'niːziəm/ *noun* a chemical element found in green vegetables, which is essential especially for the correct functioning of muscles (NOTE: The chemical symbol is **Mg.**)

magnesium sulphate /mæg,niːziəm 'sʌl↓feɪt/ *noun* a magnesium salt used as a laxative. Also called **Epsom salts**

magnesium trisilicate /mæg,niːziəm traɪ'sɪlɪkət/ *noun* a magnesium compound used to treat peptic ulcers

magnetic /mæg'netɪk/ *adjective* able to attract objects, like a magnet

magnetic field /mæg,netɪk 'fiːld/ *noun* an area round an object which is under the influence of the magnetic force exerted by the object

magnetic resonance imaging /mæg,netɪk 'rezənəns ,ɪmɪdʒɪŋ/ *noun* a scanning technique which exposes the body to a strong magnetic field and uses the electromagnetic signals emitted by the body to form an image of soft tissue and cells. Abbr **MRI**

magnum /'mægnəm/ ◆ **foramen magnum**

maim /meɪm/ *verb* to incapacitate someone with a major injury

main bronchi /meɪn 'brɒŋkiː/ *plural noun* the two main air passages which branch from the trachea outside the lung. Also called **primary bronchi**

major /'meɪdʒə/ *adjective* **1.** important or serious **2.** more important or serious than others of the same type ○ *The operation was a major one.* ▶ opposite **minor**

major surgery /,meɪdʒə 'sɜːdʒəri/ *noun* surgical operations involving important organs in the body. Compare **minor surgery**

mal /mæl/ *noun* an illness or disease

mal- /mæl/ *prefix* bad or unusual

malabsorption /,mæləb'sɔːpʃən/ *noun* a situation where the intestines are unable to absorb the fluids and nutrients in food properly

malabsorption syndrome /,mæləb'sɔːpʃən ,sɪndrəʊm/ *noun* a group of symptoms and signs, including malnutrition, anaemia, oedema and dermatitis, which results from steatorrhoea and malabsorption of vitamins, protein, carbohydrates and water

malacia /mə'leɪʃə/ *noun* the pathological softening of an organ or tissue

maladjusted /,mælə'dʒʌstɪd/ *adjective* referring to a person who has difficulty fitting into society or family

maladjustment /,mælə'dʒʌstmənt/ *noun* difficulty experienced in fitting into society or family

malaise /mə'leɪz/ *noun* a feeling of discomfort

malaligned /,mælə'laɪnd/ *adjective* not in the correct position relative to other parts of the body

malalignment /,mælə'laɪnmənt/ *noun* a condition in which something is malaligned, especially in which a tooth is not in its correct position in the mouth

malar /'meɪlə/ *adjective* referring to the cheek

malar bone /'meɪlə bəʊn/ *noun* same as **cheekbone**

malaria /mə'leəriə/ *noun* a mainly tropical disease caused by a parasite *Plasmodium*, which enters the body after a bite from the female anopheles mosquito

COMMENT: Malaria is a recurrent disease. It produces headaches, shivering, vomiting, sweating and sometimes hallucinations which are caused by toxins coming from the waste of the parasite *Plasmodium* in the blood.

malarial /mə'leəriəl/ *adjective* referring to malaria

malarial parasite /mə,leəriəl 'pærəsaɪt/ *noun* a parasite transmitted into the human bloodstream by the bite of the female anopheles mosquito

malarial therapy /mə'leəriə ,θerəpi/ *noun* a treatment in which a person is given a form of malaria in the belief that the high fevers they experience can stimulate the immune system to fight off serious diseases such as syphilis and HIV

male menopause /meɪl 'menəpɔːz/ *noun* a period in middle age when a man may feel insecure and anxious about the fact that his physical powers are declining (*informal*)

male sex hormone /ˌmeɪl 'seks ˌhɔːməʊn/ *noun* same as **testosterone**

male sex organs /ˌmeɪl 'seks ˌɔːgənz/ *plural noun* the testes, epididymis, vasa deferentia, seminal vesicles, ejaculatory ducts and penis

malformation /ˌmælfɔːˈmeɪʃ(ə)n/ *noun* an unusual variation in the shape, structure or development of something

malformed /mælˈfɔːmd/ *adjective* unusual in shape, structure or development

malfunction /mælˈfʌŋkʃən/ *noun* a situation in which a particular organ does not work in the usual way ○ *Her loss of consciousness was due to a malfunction of the kidneys* or *to a kidney malfunction.* ■ *verb* to fail to work correctly ○ *During the operation his heart began to malfunction.*

malignancy /məˈlɪɡnənsi/ *noun* **1.** the state of being malignant ○ *The tests confirmed the malignancy of the growth.* **2.** a cancerous growth (NOTE: The plural is **malignancies**.)

malignant /məˈlɪɡnənt/ *adjective* likely to cause death or serious disablement if not properly treated

malignant hypertension /məˌlɪɡnənt ˌhaɪpəˈtenʃən/ *noun* dangerously high blood pressure

malignant melanoma /məˌlɪɡnənt ˌmeləˈnəʊmə/ *noun* a dark tumour which develops on the skin from a mole, caused by exposure to strong sunlight

malignant pustule /məˌlɪɡnənt 'pʌstjuːl/ *noun* a pus-filled swelling that results from infection of the skin with anthrax

malignant tumour /məˌlɪɡnənt 'tjuːmə/ *noun* a tumour which is cancerous and can grow again or spread into other parts of the body, even if removed surgically. Opposite **benign tumour**

malingerer /məˈlɪŋɡərə/ *noun* a person who pretends to be ill

malingering /məˈlɪŋɡərɪŋ/ *adjective* the act of pretending to be ill

malleolar /məˈliːələ/ *adjective* referring to a malleolus

malleolus /məˈliːələs/ *noun* one of two bony prominences at each side of the ankle (NOTE: The plural is **malleoli**.)

mallet finger /ˌmælɪt 'fɪŋɡə/ *noun* a finger which cannot be straightened because the tendon attaching the top joint has been torn

malleus /'mælɪəs/ *noun* the largest of the three ossicles in the middle ear, shaped like a hammer. See illustration at EAR in Supplement

Mallory bodies /'mæləri ˌbɒdiz/ *plural noun* large irregular masses which occur in the cytoplasm of damaged liver cells, often a sign of an alcohol-related disease

Mallory's stain /'mælərɪz steɪn/ *noun* trichrome stain, used in histology to distinguish collagen, cytoplasm and nuclei

Mallory-Weiss syndrome /ˌmæləri 'vaɪs ˌsɪndrəʊm/, **Mallory-Weiss tear** /ˌmæləri 'vaɪs ˌteə/ *noun* a condition in which there is a tearing in the mucous membrane where the stomach and oesophagus join, e.g. because of strain on them due to vomiting [Described 1929. After G. Kenneth Mallory (b. 1900), Professor of Pathology, Boston University, USA; Konrad Weiss (1898–1942) US physician.]

malnourished /mælˈnʌrɪʃt/ *adjective* not having enough to eat or having only poor-quality food, leading to ill-health

malnutrition /ˌmælnjuːˈtrɪʃ(ə)n/ *noun* **1.** a lack of food or of good-quality food, leading to ill-health **2.** the state of not having enough to eat

malocclusion /ˌmæləˈkluːʒ(ə)n/ *noun* a condition in which the teeth in the upper and lower jaws do not meet properly when the person's mouth is closed

malodorous /mælˈəʊdərəs/ *adjective* with a strong unpleasant smell

Malpighian body /mælˈpɪɡiən ˌbɒdi/, **Malpighian corpuscle** /mælˈpɪɡiən ˌkɔːpʌs(ə)l/ *noun* same as **renal corpuscle** [Described 1666. After Marcello Malpighi (1628–94), anatomist and physiologist in Rome and Bologna, Italy.]

Malpighian glomerulus /mælˌpɪɡiən glɒ'merʊləs/ *noun* same as **Bowman's capsule**

Malpighian layer /mælˈpɪɡiən ˌleiə/ *noun* the deepest layer of the epidermis

malposition /ˌmælpəˈzɪʃ(ə)n/ *noun* an unusual or unexpected position of something such as a fetus in the uterus or fractured bones

malpractice /mælˈpræktɪs/ *noun* **1.** illegal, unethical, negligent or immoral behaviour by a professional person, especially a healthcare professional ○ *The surgeon was found guilty of malpractice.* **2.** wrong treatment of a patient for which a healthcare professional may be tried in court

malpresentation /ˌmælprez(ə)nˈteɪʃ(ə)n/ *noun* an unusual position of a fetus in the uterus just before it is ready to be born

Malta fever /'mɔːltə ˌfiːvə/ *noun* same as **brucellosis**

maltase /'mɔːlteɪz/ *noun* an enzyme in the small intestine which converts maltose into glucose

maltose /'mɔːltəʊs/ *noun* a sugar formed by digesting starch or glycogen

malunion /mælˈjuːnjən/ *noun* a bad join of the pieces of a broken bone

mamilla /məˈmɪlə/ *noun* another spelling of **mammilla**

mamillary /ˈmæmɪlri/ *adjective* another spelling of **mammillary**

mamm- *prefix* same as **mammo-** (*used before vowels*)

mamma /ˈmæmə/ *noun* same as **breast** (NOTE: The plural is **mammae**.)

mammary /ˈmæməri/ *adjective* referring to the breast

mammary gland /ˈmæməri glænd/ *noun* a gland in female mammals which produces milk

mammilla /məˈmɪlə/, **mamilla** *noun* the protruding part in the centre of the breast, containing the milk ducts through which the milk flows. Also called **nipple**

mammillary /ˈmæmɪl(ə)ri/, **mamillary** *adjective* referring to the nipple

mammillary body /ˌmæmɪl(ə)ri ˈbɒdi/ *noun* one of two little projections on the base of the hypothalamus

mammo- *prefix* referring to breasts

mammogram /ˈmæməgræm/ *noun* a picture of a breast made using a special X-ray technique

mammography /mæˈmɒgrəfi/ *noun* examination of the breast using a special X-ray technique

'…mammography is the most effective technique available for the detection of occult (non-palpable) breast cancer. It has been estimated that mammography can detect a carcinoma two years before it becomes palpable.' [*Southern Medical Journal*]

mammoplasty /ˈmæməplæsti/ *noun* plastic surgery to alter the shape or size of the breasts

mammothermography /ˌmæməʊθɜːˈmɒgrəfi/ *noun* thermography of a breast

manage /ˈmænɪdʒ/ *verb* **1.** to be in charge or control of something ○ *She manages the ward very efficiently.* ○ *Bleeding can usually be managed, but sometimes an operation may be necessary.* **2.** to be able to do something, or to succeed in doing something ○ *Did you manage to phone the doctor?* ○ *Can she manage to feed herself?* (NOTE: **managing – managed**)

management /ˈmænɪdʒmənt/ *noun* **1.** the organising or running of an organisation such as a hospital, clinic or health authority **2.** the organisation of a series of different treatments for a person

manager /ˈmænɪdʒə/ *noun* a person in charge of a department in the health service or in charge of a group of hospitals

Manchester operation /ˈmæntʃɪstər ɒpə ˌreɪʃ(ə)n/ *noun* a surgical operation to correct downward movement of the uterus, involving removal of the cervix

mandible /ˈmændɪb(ə)l/ *noun* the lower bone in the jaw. Also called **lower jaw**

COMMENT: The jaw is formed of two bones, the mandible which is attached to the skull with a

hinge joint and can move up and down, and the maxillae which are fixed parts of the skull.

mandibular /mænˈdɪbjʊlə/ *adjective* referring to the lower jaw

mandibular fossae /mænˌdɪbjʊlə ˈfɒsi/ *plural noun* sockets in the skull into which the ends of the lower jaw fit

mandibular nerve /mænˈdɪbjʊlə nɜːv/ *noun* a sensory nerve which supplies the teeth in the lower jaw, the temple, the floor of the mouth and the back part of the tongue

mane /ˈmeɪni/ *adverb* (*used on prescriptions*) during the daytime. Opposite **nocte**

'…he was diagnosed as having diabetes mellitus at age 14, and was successfully controlled on insulin 15 units mane and 10 units nocte' [*British Journal of Hospital Medicine*]

manganese /ˈmæŋgəniːz/ *noun* a metallic trace element (NOTE: The chemical symbol is **Mn**.)

mania /ˈmeɪniə/ *noun* a state of bipolar disorder in which the person is excited, very sure of his or her own abilities and has increased energy

-mania /meɪniə/ *suffix* obsession with something

maniac /ˈmeɪniæk/ *noun* a person who behaves in an uncontrolled way or is considered to have an obsession (NOTE: This term is regarded as offensive.)

manic /ˈmænɪk/ *adjective* referring to mania

manic depression /ˌmænɪk dɪˈpreʃ(ə)n/ *noun* same as **bipolar disorder**

manic-depressive /ˌmænɪk dɪˈpresɪv/ *adjective* relating to bipolar disorder ■ *noun* a person with bipolar disorder

manic-depressive illness /ˌmænɪk dɪ ˈpresɪv ˌɪlnəs/, **manic-depressive psychosis** /ˌmænɪk dɪˌpresɪv saɪˈkəʊsɪs/ *noun* same as **bipolar disorder**

manifestation /ˌmænɪfeˈsteɪʃ(ə)n/ *noun* a sign, indication or symptom of a disease

'…the reason for this susceptibility is a profound abnormality of the immune system in children with sickle cell disease. The major manifestations of pneumococcal infection in SCD are septicaemia, meningitis and pneumonia.' [*Lancet*]

manikin /ˈmænɪkɪn/ *noun* an anatomical model of the human body, used in teaching anatomy

manipulate /məˈnɪpjʊˌleɪt/ *verb* to rub or move parts of the body with the hands to treat a joint, a slipped disc or a hernia (NOTE: **manipulating – manipulated**)

manipulation /məˌnɪpjʊˈleɪʃ(ə)n/ *noun* a form of treatment that involves moving or rubbing parts of the body with the hands, e.g. to treat a disorder of a joint

manner /ˈmænə/ *noun* a way of doing something or of behaving ○ *He was behaving in a strange manner.* ◊ **bedside manner**

mannitol /ˈmænɪtɒl/ *noun* a diuretic drug used in the treatment of oedema of the brain

manometer /məˈnɒmɪtə/ *noun* an instrument for comparing pressures

manometry /məˈnɒmɪtri/ *noun* the measurement of pressures within organs of the body which contain gases or liquids, e.g. the oesophagus or parts of the brain

Mantoux test /mæntuː test/ *noun* a test for tuberculosis, in which a person is given an intracutaneous injection of tuberculin. ◊ **Heaf test** [Described 1908. After Charles Mantoux (1877–1947), French physician.]

manual /ˈmænjuəl/ *adjective* done by hand

manual examination /ˌmænjuəl ɪɡˌzæmɪˈneɪʃ(ə)n/ *noun* an examination using the hands and fingers

manubrium /məˈnuːbriəm/ *noun* a handle-shaped anatomical part, e.g. part of the inner ear

manubrium sterni /məˌnuːbriəm ˈstɜːnaɪ/ *noun* the upper part of the sternum

MAO *abbr* monoamine oxidase

MAOI *abbr* monoamine oxidase inhibitor

MAO inhibitor /ˌem eɪ ˈəʊ ɪnˌhɪbɪtə/ *noun* same as **monoamine oxidase inhibitor**

maple syrup urine disease /ˌmeɪp(ə)l ˌsɪrəp ˈjʊərɪn dɪˌziːz/ *noun* an inherited condition caused by not having enough of a particular enzyme which helps the body to deal with amino acid. The urine smells like maple syrup. It can be fatal if not treated.

marasmus /məˈræzməs/ *noun* a wasting disease which affects small children who have difficulty in absorbing nutrients or who are malnourished. Also called **failure to thrive**

marble bone disease /ˌmɑːb(ə)l ˈbəʊn dɪˌziːz/ *noun* same as **osteopetrosis**

Marburg disease /ˈmɑːbɜːɡ dɪˌziːz/, **Marburg virus disease** /ˈmɑːbɜːɡ ˌvaɪrəs dɪˌziːz/ *noun* a severe viral infection causing high fever, bleeding from mucous membranes, vomiting and often death. Also called **green monkey disease**

COMMENT: The disease is transmitted to humans from green monkeys. Because the monkeys are used in laboratory experiments, the disease mainly affects laboratory workers.

march fracture /mɑːtʃ ˈfræktʃə/ *noun* a fracture of one of the metatarsal bones in the foot, caused by excessive exercise to which the body is not accustomed

Marfan's syndrome /ˈmɑːfɑːnz ˌsɪndrəʊm/, **Marfan syndrome** /ˈmɑːfɑːn ˌsɪndrəʊm/ *noun* a hereditary condition in which a person has extremely long fingers and toes, with disorders of the heart, aorta and eyes [Described 1896. After Bernard Jean Antonin Marfan (1858–1942), French paediatrician.]

marijuana /ˌmærɪˈwɑːnə/ *noun* same as **cannabis**

mark /mɑːk/ *noun* a spot or small area of a different colour ○ *There's a red mark where you hit your head.* ○ *The rash has left marks* on the chest and back. ■ *verb* to make a mark on something □ **the door is marked 'Supervisor'** the door has the word 'Supervisor' written on it

marked /mɑːkt/ *adjective* obvious or noticeable ○ *There has been a marked improvement in his condition.*

marker /ˈmɑːkə/ *noun* **1.** something which acts an indicator of something else **2.** a substance introduced into the body to make internal structures clearer to X-rays

marrow /ˈmærəʊ/ *noun* soft tissue in cancellous bone. In young animals **red marrow** is concerned with blood formation while in adults it becomes progressively replaced with fat and is known as yellow marrow. Also called **bone marrow**. See illustration at **BONE STRUCTURE** in Supplement

marsupialisation /mɑːˌsuːpiəlaɪˈzeɪʃ(ə)n/, **marsupialization** *noun* a surgical procedure in which the inside of a cyst is opened up so that the cyst can be allowed to shrink gradually, because it cannot be cut out

masculinisation /ˌmæskjʊlɪnaɪˈzeɪʃ(ə)n/, **masculinization** *noun* the development of male characteristics such as body hair and a deep voice in a woman, caused by hormone deficiency or by treatment with male hormones

mask /mɑːsk/ *noun* **1.** a metal and rubber frame that fits over the nose and mouth and is used to administer an anaesthetic **2.** a piece of gauze which fits over the mouth and nose to prevent droplet infection **3.** a cover which fits over the face of a person who has suffered facial damage in an accident

masked /mɑːskt/ *adjective* used to describe diseases that are present but not observable

Maslow's hierarchy of human needs /ˌmæzləʊz ˌhaɪrɑːki əv ˌhjuːmən ˈniːdz/ *noun* a system which explains human behaviour by organising human needs in order of priority, from basic ones such as eating to complex ones such as finding self-fulfilment, a higher level of motivation not being activated until the lesser needs have been satisfied

masochism /ˈmæsəkɪz(ə)m/ *noun* a sexual condition in which a person takes pleasure in being hurt or badly treated

masochist /ˈmæsəkɪst/ *noun* a person suffering from masochism

masochistic /ˌmæsəˈkɪstɪk/ *adjective* referring to masochism

mass /mæs/ *noun* **1.** a large quantity, e.g. a large number of people ○ *The patient's back was covered with a mass of red spots.* **2.** a body of matter with no clear shape **3.** a mixture for making pills **4.** the main solid part of bone

massage /ˈmæsɑːʒ/ *noun* a treatment for muscular conditions which involves rubbing, stroking or pressing the body with the hands ■

mattress

verb to rub, stroke or press the body with the hands

masseter /mæ'siːtə/, **masseter muscle** /mæ 'siːtə ,mʌs(ə)l/ *noun* a muscle in the cheek which clenches the lower jaw making it move up, to allow chewing

massive /'mæsɪv/ *adjective* very large ○ *He was given a massive injection of penicillin.* ○ *She had a massive heart attack.*

mass radiography /,mæs ,reɪdi'ɒgrəfi/ *noun* the practice of taking X-ray photographs of large numbers of people to check for tuberculosis

mass screening /,mæs 'skriːnɪŋ/ *noun* the practice of testing large numbers of people for the presence of a disease

mast- /mæst/ *prefix* same as **masto-** (*used before vowels*)

mastalgia /mæ'stældʒə/ *noun* pain in the mammary gland

mastatrophy /mæ'stætrəfi/ *noun* atrophy of the mammary gland

mast cell /'mæst sel/ *noun* a large cell in connective tissue, which carries histamine and reacts to allergens

mastectomy /mæ'stektəmi/ *noun* the surgical removal of a breast

masticate /'mæstɪkeɪt/ *verb* to chew food

mastication /,mæstɪ'keɪʃ(ə)n/ *noun* the act of chewing food

mastitis /mæ'staɪtɪs/ *noun* inflammation of the breast

masto- /mæstəʊ/ *prefix* referring to a breast

mastoid /'mæstɔɪd/ *adjective* 1. shaped like a nipple 2. belonging to the part of the temporal bone which protrudes at the side of the head behind the ear ■ *noun* same as **mastoid process**

mastoid air cell /,mæstɔɪd 'eə sel/, **mastoid cell** /'mæstɔɪd sel/ *noun* an air cell in the mastoid process

mastoid antrum /,mæstɔɪd 'æntrəm/ *noun* a cavity linking the air cells of the mastoid process with the middle ear

mastoid bone /'mæstɔɪd bəʊn/ *noun* same as **mastoid process**

mastoidectomy /,mæstɔɪ'dektəmi/ *noun* a surgical operation to remove part of the mastoid process, as a treatment for mastoiditis

mastoiditis /,mæstɔɪ'daɪtɪs/ *noun* inflammation of the mastoid process and air cells. The symptoms are fever and pain in the ears.

COMMENT: The mastoid process can be infected by infection from the middle ear through the mastoid antrum. Mastoiditis can cause deafness and can affect the meninges if not treated.

mastoidotomy /,mæstɔɪ'dɒtəmi/ *noun* a surgical operation to make a cut into the mastoid process to treat infection

mastoid process /,mæstɔɪd 'prəʊses/ *noun* part of the temporal bone which protrudes at the side of the head behind the ear

masturbate /'mæstəbeɪt/ *verb* to excite one's own genitals so as to produce an orgasm

masturbation /,mæstə'beɪʃ(ə)n/ *noun* stimulation of one's own genitals to produce an orgasm. Also called **onanism**

match /mætʃ/ *verb* 1. to examine two things to see if they are similar or fit together ○ *They are trying to match the donor to the recipient.* 2. to fit together in a specific way ○ *The two samples don't match.*

'…bone marrow from donors has to be carefully matched with the recipient or graft-versus-host disease will ensue' [*Hospital Update*]

mater /'meɪtə/ ♦ **dura mater**

material /mə'tɪəriəl/ *noun* 1. matter which can be used to make something 2. cloth ○ *The wound should be covered with gauze or other light material.* 3. all that is necessary in surgery

materia medica /mə,tɪəriə 'medɪkə/ *noun* the study of drugs or dosages as used in treatment (NOTE: It comes from a Latin term meaning 'medical substance'.)

maternal /mə'tɜːn(ə)l/ *adjective* referring to a mother

maternal death /mə,tɜːn(ə)l 'deθ/ *noun* the death of a mother during pregnancy, childbirth or up to twelve months after childbirth

maternal deprivation /mə,tɜːn(ə)l ,depri 'veɪʃ(ə)n/ *noun* a psychological condition caused when a child does not have a proper relationship with a mother

maternal dystocia /mə,tɜːn(ə)l dɪs'təʊsiə/ *noun* difficult childbirth caused by a physical problem in the mother

maternal instincts /mə,tɜːn(ə)l 'ɪn↓ stɪŋkts/ *plural noun* instinctive feelings in a woman to look after and protect her child

maternity /mə'tɜːnɪti/ *noun* childbirth, the fact of becoming a mother

maternity case /mə'tɜːnɪti keɪs/ *noun* a woman who is about to give birth

maternity clinic /mə'tɜːnɪti ,klɪnɪk/ *noun* same as **antenatal clinic**

maternity hospital /mə'tɜːnɪti ,hɒspɪt(ə)l/, **maternity ward** /mə'tɜːnɪti wɔːd/, **maternity unit** /mə'tɜːnɪti ,juːnɪt/ *noun* a hospital, ward or unit which deals only with women giving birth

matrix /'meɪtrɪks/ *noun* an amorphous mass of cells forming the basis of connective tissue. Also called **ground substance**

matron /'meɪtrən/ *noun* a title formerly given to a woman in charge of the nurses in a hospital. ◊ **modern matron**

matter /'mætə/ *noun* a substance

mattress /'mætrəs/ *noun* the thick soft part of a bed for lying on

mattress suture /'mætrəs ˌsuːtʃə/ *noun* a suture made with a loop on each side of the incision

maturation /ˌmætʃʊ'reɪʃ(ə)n/ *noun* the process of becoming mature or fully developed

mature /mə'tʃʊə/ *adjective* fully developed

mature follicle /məˌtʃʊə 'fɒlɪk(ə)l/ *noun* a Graafian follicle just before ovulation

maturing /mə'tʃʊərɪŋ/ *adjective* becoming mature

maturing egg /məˌtʃʊərɪŋ 'eg/, **maturing ovum** /'əʊvəm/ *noun* an ovum contained by a Graafian follicle

maturity /mə'tʃʊərɪti/ *noun* **1.** being fully developed **2.** (*in psychology*) the state of being a responsible adult

maxilla /mæk'sɪlə/, **maxilla bone** /mæk'sɪlə bəʊn/ *noun* the upper jaw bone (NOTE: The plural is **maxillae**. It is more correct to refer to the upper jaw as the **maxillae**, as it is in fact formed of two bones which are fused together.)

maxillary /mæk'sɪləri/ *adjective* referring to the maxilla

maxillary antrum /mækˌsɪləri 'æntrəm/, **maxillary air sinus** /mækˌsɪləri 'eə ˌsaɪnəs/ *noun* one of two sinuses behind the cheekbones in the upper jaw. Also called **antrum of Highmore**

maxillo-facial /mækˌsɪləʊ'feɪʃ(ə)l/ *adjective* referring to the maxillary bone and the face ○ *maxillo-facial surgery*

MB *abbr* bachelor of medicine

McBurney's point /məkˌbɜːniz 'pɔɪnt/ *noun* a point which indicates the usual position of the appendix on the right side of the abdomen, between the hip bone and the navel, which is extremely painful if pressed when the person has appendicitis [Described 1899. After Charles McBurney (1845–1913), US surgeon.]

McNaghten's Rules on Insanity at Law /məkˌnɔːtənz ˌruːlz ɒn ɪnˌsænɪti ət 'lɔː/, **McNaghten's Rules** /mək'nɔːtənz ˌruːlz/ *plural noun* a set of principles which explain how people can defend themselves in law by claiming that they committed a murder because they were mentally ill, and therefore not responsible for any of their actions. In 1957 it was adapted to include the idea of knowing that an action is wrong but being unable to stop yourself from committing it because of your mental condition.

MCP joint /ˌem si: 'pi: ˌdʒɔɪnt/ *noun* same as **metacarpophalangeal joint**

MCU, MCUG *abbr* micturating cysto(-urethro)gram

MD *abbr* doctor of medicine

ME *abbr* myalgic encephalomyelitis

meal /miːl/ *noun* food eaten at a particular time

measles /'miːz(ə)lz/ *noun* an infectious disease of children, where the body is covered with a red rash ○ *She's in bed with measles.* ○ *He's got measles.* ○ *They caught measles from their friend at school.* ○ *Have you had the measles?* Also called **morbilli, rubeola** (NOTE: Takes a singular or plural verb.)

COMMENT: Measles can be a serious disease as it weakens the body's resistance to other diseases, especially bronchitis and ear infections. It can be prevented by immunisation. If caught by an adult it can be very serious.

measure /'meʒə/ *noun* a unit of size, quantity or degree ○ *A metre is a measure of length.* ■ *verb* **1.** to find out the size of something ○ *A thermometer measures temperature.* **2.** to be a particular size ○ *The room measures 3 metres by 2 metres.*

measurement /'meʒəmənt/ *noun* the size, length, etc. of something which has been measured

meat /miːt/ *noun* animal flesh which is eaten (NOTE: No plural: *some meat*, *a piece* or *a slice of meat*; *he refuses to eat meat*.)

meat- /mieɪt/ *prefix* relating to a meatus

meatus /mi'eɪtəs/ *noun* an opening leading to an internal passage in the body, e.g. the urethra or the nasal cavity (NOTE: The plural is **meatuses** or **meatus**.)

mechanism /'mekənɪz(ə)m/ *noun* **1.** a physical or chemical change by which a function is carried out **2.** a system in the body which carries out or controls a particular function ○ *The inner ear is the body's mechanism for the sense of balance.*

mechanism of labour /ˌmekənɪz(ə)m əv 'leɪbə/ *noun* all the forces and processes which combine to push a foetus out of the uterus during its birth, together with the ones which oppose it

mechanotherapy /ˌmekənəʊ'θerəpi/ *noun* the treatment of injuries through mechanical means, such as massage and exercise machines

Meckel's diverticulum /ˌmekəlz ˌdaɪvə'tɪkjʊləm/ *noun* a congenital formation of a diverticulum in the ileum [Described 1809. After Johann Friedrich Meckel II (1781–1833), German surgeon and anatomist.]

meconism /'mekəʊnɪz(ə)m/ *noun* poisoning by opium or morphine

meconium /mɪ'kəʊniəm/ *noun* the first dark green faeces produced by a newborn baby

med. *abbr* **1.** medical **2.** medicine

media /'miːdiə/ *noun* same as **tunica media**

medial /'miːdiəl/ *adjective* nearer to the central midline of the body or to the centre of an organ. Compare **lateral**

medial arcuate ligament /ˌmiːdiəl 'ɑːkjuɪt ˌlɪgəmənt/ *noun* a fibrous arch to which the diaphragm is attached

medial epicondyle /ˌmiːdiəl ˌepɪˈkɒndaɪl/
noun a medial projection on the condyle of the
humerus

medially /ˈmiːdiəli/ *adverb* towards or on the
sagittal plane of the body. See illustration at
ANATOMICAL TERMS in Supplement

medial malleolus /ˌmiːdiəl məˈliːələs/
noun a bone at the end of the tibia which protrudes at the inside of the ankle

medial rectus /ˌmiːdiəl ˈrektəs/ *noun* a
muscle inserted into the sclera of the eyeball

median /ˈmiːdiən/ *adjective* towards the central midline of the body, or placed in the middle

median nerve /ˈmiːdiən nɜːv/ *noun* one of
the main nerves of the forearm and hand

median plane /ˈmiːdiən pleɪn/ *noun* an imaginary flat surface on the midline and at right
angles to the coronal plane, which divides the
body into right and left halves. See illustration
at ANATOMICAL TERMS in Supplement

mediastinal /miːdiəˈstaɪn(ə)l/ *adjective* referring to the mediastinum ○ *the mediastinal
surface of pleura* or *of the lungs*

mediastinitis /ˌmiːdiəstɪˈnaɪtɪs/ *noun* inflammation of the mediastinum

mediastinoscopy /ˌmiːdiəstɪˈnɒskəpi/
noun an operation in which a tube is put into
the mediastinum so that its organs can be examined

mediastinum /ˌmiːdiəˈstaɪnəm/ *noun* the
section of the chest between the lungs, where
the heart, oesophagus and phrenic and vagus
nerves are situated

medic /ˈmedɪk/ *noun* a doctor or medical student (*informal*)

medical /ˈmedɪk(ə)l/ *adjective* 1. referring to
the study of diseases ○ *a medical student* 2. referring to treatment of disease which does not
involve surgery ○ *Medical help was provided
by the Red Cross.* 3. referring to treatment giv-
en by a doctor, as opposed to a surgeon, in a
hospital or in his or her surgery ■ *noun* an official examination of a person by a doctor ○
*He wanted to join the army, but failed his med-
ical.* ○ *You will have to have a medical if you
take out an insurance policy.*

medical administration /ˌmedɪk(ə)l əd
ˌmɪnɪˈstreɪʃ(ə)n/ *noun* the running of hospitals and other health services ○ *She started her
career in medical administration.*

medical aid /ˈmedɪk(ə)l eɪd/ *noun* treatment
of someone who is ill or injured, given by a
doctor. ◊ **first aid**

medical alert bracelet /ˌmedɪk(ə)l əˈlɜːt
ˌbreɪslət/ *noun* a band or chain worn around
the wrist giving information about the wearer's
medical needs, allergies or condition

medical assistance /ˌmedɪk(ə)l ə
ˈsɪst(ə)ns/ *noun* help provided by a nurse, an
ambulanceman or a member of an association

such as the Red Cross, to a person who is ill or
injured

medical assistant /ˈmedɪk(ə)l əˌsɪst(ə)nt/
noun someone who performs routine administrative and clinical tasks to help in the offices
and clinics of doctors and other medical practitioners

medical audit /ˌmedɪk(ə)l ˈɔːdɪt/ *noun* a
systematic critical analysis of the quality of
medical care provided to a person, which examines the procedures used for diagnosis and
treatment, the use of resources and the resulting outcome and quality of life for the person

medical audit advisory group /
ˌmedɪk(ə)l ˌɔːdɪt ədˈvaɪz(ə)ri gruːp/ *noun* a
body with the responsibility of advising on
medical audit in primary care. Abbr **MAAG**

medical centre /ˈmedɪk(ə)l ˌsentə/ *noun* a
place where several different doctors and specialists practise

medical certificate /ˈmedɪk(ə)l səˌtɪfɪkət/
noun an official document signed by a doctor,
giving someone permission to be away from
work or not to do specific types of work

medical committee /ˈmedɪk(ə)l kəˌmɪti/
noun a committee of doctors in a hospital who
advise the management on medical matters

medical diathermy /ˌmedɪk(ə)l ˌdaɪə
ˈθɜːmi/ *noun* the use of heat produced by electricity for treatment of muscle and joint disorders such as rheumatism

medical doctor /ˈmedɪk(ə)l ˌdɒktə/ *noun* a
doctor who practises medicine, but is not usually a surgeon

medical ethics /ˌmedɪk(ə)l ˈeθɪks/ *plural
noun* the moral and professional principles
which govern how doctors and nurses should
work, and, in particular, what type of relationship they should have with their patients

medical examination /ˌmedɪk(ə)l ɪg
ˌzæmɪˈneɪʃ(ə)n/ *noun* an examination of a
person by a doctor

medical history /ˌmedɪk(ə)l ˈhɪst(ə)ri/
noun the details of a person's medical condition and treatment over a period of time

medical intervention /ˌmedɪk(ə)l ˌɪntə
ˈvenʃən/ *noun* the treatment of illness by
drugs

medicalisation /ˌmedɪkəlaɪˈzeɪʃ(ə)n/,
medicalization *noun* the act of looking at
something as a medical issue or problem

medical jurisprudence /ˌmedɪk(ə)l
dʒʊərɪsˈpruːd(ə)ns/ *noun* the use of the principles of law as they relate to the practice of
medicine and the relationship of doctors with
each other, their patients and society. ◊ **forensic medicine**

Medical Officer of Health /ˌmedɪk(ə)l
ˌɒfɪsər əv ˈhelθ/ *noun* formerly, a local government official in charge of the health services in an area. Abbr **MOH**

medical practitioner /ˌmedɪk(ə)l præk
'tɪʃ(ə)nə/ *noun* a person qualified in medicine,
i.e. a doctor or surgeon

medical profession /'medɪk(ə)l prə
ˌfeʃ(ə)n/ *noun* all doctors

medical records /'medɪk(ə)l ˌrekɔːdz/ *plural noun* information about a person's medical
history

Medical Register /ˌmedɪk(ə)l 'redʒɪstə/
noun a list of doctors approved by the General
Medical Council ○ *The committee ordered his
name to be struck off the Medical Register.*

Medical Research Council /ˌmedɪk(ə)l rɪ
'sɜːtʃ ˌkaυnsəl/ *noun* a government body
which organises and pays for medical research. Abbr **MRC**

medical school /'medɪk(ə)l skuːl/ *noun* a
section of a university which teaches medicine
○ *He is at medical school.*

medical secretary /ˌmedɪk(ə)l
'sekrɪt(ə)ri/ *noun* a qualified secretary who
specialises in medical documentation, either in
a hospital or in a doctor's surgery

medical social worker /ˌmedɪk(ə)l
'səυʃ(ə)l ˌwɜːkə/ *noun* someone who helps
people with family problems or problems related to their work which may have an effect
on their response to treatment

medical ward /'medɪk(ə)l wɔːd/ *noun* a
ward for people who do not have to undergo
surgical operations

Medicare /'medɪkeə/ *noun* a system of public health insurance in the US

medicated /'medɪkeɪtɪd/ *adjective* containing a medicinal drug ○ *medicated cough sweet*

medicated shampoo /ˌmedɪkeɪtɪd ʃæm
'puː/ *noun* a shampoo containing a chemical
which is supposed to prevent dandruff

medication /ˌmedɪ'keɪʃ(ə)n/ *noun* **1.** the
treatment of illnesses by giving people drugs.
◊ **premedication 2.** a drug used to treat a particular illness ○ *What sort of medication has
she been taking?* ○ *80% of elderly patients admitted to geriatric units are on medication.*

medicinal /mə'dɪs(ə)n(ə)l/ *adjective* which
has healing properties or a beneficial effect on
someone's health ○ *He has a drink of whisky
before he goes to bed for medicinal purposes.*

medicinal bath /mə,dɪs(ə)n(ə)l 'bɑːθ/ *noun*
treatment in which someone lies in a bath of
hot water containing particular chemicals, in
hot mud or in other substances

medicinal drug /mə,dɪs(ə)n(ə)l 'drʌg/
noun a drug used to treat a disease as opposed
to hallucinatory or addictive drugs

medicinal leech /mə,dɪs(ə)n(ə)l 'liːtʃ/
noun a leech which is raised specially for use
in medicine

medicinally /mə'dɪs(ə)n(ə)li/ *adverb* used as
a medicine ○ *The herb can be used medicinally.*

medicine /'med(ə)s(ə)n/ *noun* **1.** a preparation taken to treat a disease or condition, especially one in liquid form ○ *Take some cough
medicine if your cough is bad.* ○ *You should
take the medicine three times a day.* **2.** the
study of diseases and how to cure or prevent
them ○ *She is studying medicine because she
wants to be a doctor.* **3.** the study and treatment
of diseases which does not involve surgery

medicine bottle /'med(ə)s(ə)n ˌbɒt(ə)l/
noun a special bottle which contains medicine

medicine cabinet /'med(ə)s(ə)n
ˌkæbɪnət/, **medicine chest** /'med(ə)s(ə)n
tʃest/ *noun* a cupboard where medicines,
bandages, thermometers and other pieces of
medical equipment can be left locked up, but
ready for use in an emergency

medico /'medɪkəυ/ *noun* a doctor (*informal*)
○ *The medico said I was perfectly fit.*

medico- /medɪkəυ/ *prefix* referring to medicine or to doctors

medicochirurgical /ˌmedɪkəυkaɪ
'rɜːdʒɪk(ə)l/ *adjective* referring to both medicine and surgery

medicolegal /ˌmedɪkəυ'liːg(ə)l/ *adjective*
referring to both medicine and the law

medicosocial /ˌmedɪkəυ 'səυʃ(ə)l/ *adjective* involving both medical and social factors

medium /'miːdiəm/ *adjective* average, in the
middle or at the halfway point ■ *noun* a substance through which something acts

medroxyprogesterone /məˌdrɒksiprəυ
'dʒestərəυn/ *noun* a synthetic hormone used
to treat menstrual disorders, in oestrogen replacement therapy and as a contraceptive

medulla /me'dʌlə/ *noun* **1.** the soft inner part
of an organ, as opposed to the outer cortex. See
illustration at **KIDNEY** in Supplement **2.** bone
marrow **3.** any structure similar to bone marrow

medulla oblongata /me,dʌlə ˌɒblɒŋ
'geɪtə/ *noun* a continuation of the spinal cord
going through the foramen magnum into the
brain

medullary /me'dʌləri/ *adjective* **1.** similar to
marrow **2.** referring to a medulla

medullary cavity /me,dʌləri 'kævɪti/ *noun*
a hollow centre of a long bone, containing
bone marrow. See illustration at **BONE STRUC-
TURE** in Supplement

medullary cord /me'dʌləri kɔːd/ *noun* an
epithelial fibre found near the hilum of the fetal ovary

medullated nerve /'medəleɪtɪd nɜːv/ *noun*
a nerve surrounded by a myelin sheath

medulloblastoma /me,dʌləυblæ'stəυmə/
noun a tumour which develops in the medulla
oblongata and the fourth ventricle of the brain
in children

mefenamic acid /ˌmefənæmɪk 'æsɪd/ *noun*
a drug which reduces inflammation and pain,

used in the treatment of rheumatoid arthritis and menstrual problems

mefloquine /'meflǝkwiːn/, **mefloquine hydrochloride** /ˌmeflǝkwiːn ˌhaɪdrǝʊ'klɔːraɪd/ *noun* a drug used in the prevention and treatment of malaria

mega- /megǝ/ *prefix* **1.** large. Opposite **micro- 2.** one million, or 10^6

megacolon /ˌmegǝ'kǝʊlǝn/ *noun* a condition in which the lower colon is very much larger than normal, because part of the colon above is constricted, making bowel movements impossible

megajoule /'megǝdʒuːl/ *noun* a unit of measurement of energy equal to one million joules. Symbol **Mj**

megakaryocyte /ˌmegǝ'kæriǝsaɪt/ *noun* a bone marrow cell which produces blood platelets

megalo- /megǝlǝʊ/ *prefix* large

megaloblast /'megǝlǝʊblæst/ *noun* an unusually large blood cell found in the bone marrow of people who have some types of anaemia caused by Vitamin B_{12} deficiency

megaloblastic /ˌmegǝlǝʊ'blæstɪk/ *adjective* referring to megaloblasts

megaloblastic anaemia /ˌmegǝlǝʊ ˌblæstɪk ǝ'niːmiǝ/ *noun* anaemia caused by Vitamin B_{12} deficiency

megalocephaly /ˌmegǝlǝʊ'kefǝli/ *noun* the condition of having an unusually large head

megalocyte /'megǝlǝʊsaɪt/ *noun* an unusually large red blood cell, found in pernicious anaemia

megalomania /ˌmegǝlǝʊ'meɪniǝ/ *noun* a psychiatric disorder in which a person believes they are very powerful and important

megalomaniac /ˌmegǝlǝʊ'meɪniæk/ *noun* someone who has megalomania ■ *adjective* having megalomania

-megaly /megǝli/ *suffix* enlargement

megaureter /ˌmegǝjʊ'riːtǝ/ *noun* a condition in which a part of the ureter becomes very wide, above the site of a blockage

meibomian cyst /maɪˌbǝʊmiǝn 'sɪst/ *noun* the swelling of a sebaceous gland in the eyelid. Also called **chalazion**

meibomian gland /maɪ'bǝʊmiǝn ˌglænd/ *noun* a sebaceous gland on the edge of the eyelid which secretes a liquid to lubricate the eyelid. Also called **tarsal gland**

meibomianitis /maɪˌbǝʊmiǝ'naɪtɪs/ *noun* a condition in which the meibomian glands become swollen

Meigs' syndrome /'megz ˌsɪndrǝʊm/ *noun* a condition in which liquid collects in the chest and abdominal cavities. It is associated with pelvic tumours.

meiosis /maɪ'ǝʊsɪs/ *noun* the process of cell division which results in two pairs of haploid cells, i.e. cells with only one set of chromo-

somes. Compare **mitosis** (NOTE: The US spelling is **miosis**.)

Meissner's corpuscle /ˌmaɪsnǝz 'kɔːpʌs(ǝ)l/ *noun* a receptor cell in the skin which is thought to be sensitive to touch

Meissner's plexus /ˌmaɪsnǝz 'pleksǝs/ *noun* a network of nerve fibres in the wall of the alimentary canal [Described 1853. After Georg Meissner (1829–1905), German anatomist and physiologist.]

melaena /mǝ'liːnǝ/ *noun* black faeces where the colour is caused by bleeding in the intestine

melan- /melǝn/ *prefix* same as **melano-** (*used before vowels*)

melancholia /ˌmelǝn'kǝʊliǝ/ *noun* **1.** a severe depressive illness occurring usually between the ages of 45 and 65 **2.** a clinical syndrome with a tendency to delusion, fixed personality and agitated movements

melanin /'melǝnɪn/ *noun* a dark pigment which gives colour to skin and hair, also found in the choroid of the eye and in some tumours

melanism /'melǝnɪz(ǝ)m/ *noun* **1.** the unexpected depositing of dark pigment **2.** the staining of all body tissue with melanin in a form of carcinoma

melano- /melǝnǝʊ/ *prefix* black or dark

melanocyte /'melǝnǝʊsaɪt/ *noun* any cell which carries pigment

melanocyte-stimulating hormone /ˌmelǝnǝʊsaɪt 'stɪmjʊleɪtɪŋ ˌhɔːmǝʊn/ *noun* a hormone produced by the pituitary gland which causes darkening in the colour of the skin. Abbr **MSH**

melanoderma /ˌmelǝnǝʊ'dɜːmǝ/ *noun* **1.** a large amount of melanin in the skin **2.** discoloration of patches of the skin

melanoma /ˌmelǝ'nǝʊmǝ/ *noun* a tumour formed of dark pigmented cells

COMMENT: ABCD is the key to remember if you want to know if there is a risk of developing a melanoma: A = ASYMMETRY, ie. the two sides are not quite the same, and the mole does not have a perfect shape; B = BORDER, the edge becomes irregular; C = COLOUR, there may be a change in colour, with the mole becoming darker; D = DIAMETER, any change in diameter should be considered an important factor. Among other features, pain is rarely an important feature but itching could be one.

melanophore /'melǝnǝʊfɔː/ *noun* a cell which contains melanin

melanoplakia /'melǝnǝʊpleɪkiǝ/ *noun* areas of pigment in the mucous membrane inside the mouth

melanosis /ˌmelǝ'nǝʊsɪs/ *noun* same as **melanism**

melanuria /ˌmelǝ'njʊǝriǝ/ *noun* **1.** the presence of dark colouring in the urine **2.** a condition in which the urine turns black after being allowed to stand, e.g. in cases of malignant melanoma

melasma /məˈlæzmə/ *noun* the presence of little brown, yellow or black spots on the skin

melatonin /ˌmeləˈtəʊnɪn/ *noun* a hormone produced by the pineal gland during the hours of darkness, which makes animals sleep during the winter months. It is thought to control the body's rhythms.

melena /məˈliːnə/ *noun* same as **melaena**

mellitus /ˈmelɪtəs/ ♦ **diabetes mellitus**

membrane /ˈmembreɪn/ *noun* a thin layer of tissue which lines or covers an organ

membrane bone /ˈmembreɪn bəʊn/ *noun* a bone which develops from tissue and not from cartilage

membranous /ˈmembrənəs/ *adjective* referring to membranes, or like a membrane

membranous labyrinth /ˌmembrənəs ˈlæbərɪnθ/ *noun* a series of ducts and canals formed of membrane inside the osseous labyrinth

memory /ˈmem(ə)ri/ *noun* the ability to remember ○ *He has a very good memory for dates.* ○ *He said the whole list from memory.*

menarche /məˈnɑːki/ *noun* the start of menstrual periods

mend /mend/ *verb* to repair something ○ *The surgeons are trying to mend the damaged heart valves.*

Mendel's laws /ˈmendəlz lɔːz/ *plural noun* the laws of heredity, that are the basis of the science of genetics [Described 1865. After Gregor Johann Mendel (1822–84), Austrian Augustinian monk and naturalist of Brno, whose work was rediscovered by de Vries in 1900.]

Mendelson's syndrome /ˈmendəlsənz ˌsɪndrəʊm/ *noun* a sometimes fatal condition in which acid fluid from the stomach is brought up into the windpipe and passes into the lungs, occurring mainly in obstetric patients [Described 1946. After Curtis L. Mendelson (b. 1913), US obstetrician and gynaecologist.]

Ménière's disease /meniˈeəz dɪˌziːz/, **Ménière's syndrome** /ˈsɪndrəʊm/ *noun* a disease of the middle ear, in which someone becomes dizzy, hears ringing in the ears and may vomit, and becomes progressively deaf. The causes may include infections or allergies, which increase the fluid contents of the labyrinth in the middle ear. [Described 1861. After Prosper Ménière (1799–1862) and his son, Emile Antoine Ménière (1839–1905), French physicians.]

mening- /menɪndʒ/ *prefix* same as **meningo-** (used before vowels)

meningeal /meˈnɪndʒiəl/ *adjective* referring to the meninges

meningeal haemorrhage /meˌnɪndʒiəl ˈhem(ə)rɪdʒ/ *noun* a haemorrhage from a meningeal artery

meningeal sarcoma /meˌnɪndʒiəl sɑːˈkəʊmə/ *noun* a malignant tumour in the meninges

meninges /meˈnɪndʒiːz/ *plural noun* the membranes which surround the brain and spinal cord (NOTE: The singular is **meninx**.)

COMMENT: The meninges are divided into three layers: the tough outer layer (dura mater) which protects the brain and spinal cord; the middle layer (arachnoid mater) and the delicate inner layer (pia mater) which contains the blood vessels. The cerebrospinal fluid flows in the space (subarachnoid space) between the arachnoid mater and pia mater.

meningioma /ˌmenɪndʒiˈəʊmə/ *noun* a benign tumour in the meninges

meningism /meˈnɪndʒɪz(ə)m/ *noun* a condition in which there are signs of meningeal irritation suggesting meningitis, but where there is no pathological change in the cerebrospinal fluid

meningitis /ˌmenɪnˈdʒaɪtɪs/ *noun* inflammation of the meninges, causing someone to have violent headaches, fever, and stiff neck muscles, and sometimes to become delirious

COMMENT: Meningitis is a serious viral or bacterial disease which can cause brain damage and even death. The bacterial form can be treated with antibiotics. The most common forms of bacterial meningitis are Hib and meningococcal.

meningo- /məˈnɪŋgəʊ/ *prefix* referring to the meninges

meningocele /məˈnɪŋgəʊsiːl/ *noun* a condition in which the meninges protrude through the vertebral column or skull

meningococcal /məˌnɪŋgəʊˈkɒk(ə)l/ *adjective* referring to meningococci

meningococcal disease /məˌnɪŋgəʊ ˈkɒk(ə)l dɪˌziːz/ *noun* a disease caused by a meningococcus

meningococcal meningitis /məˌnɪŋgəʊ ˌkɒk(ə)l ˌmenɪnˈdʒaɪtɪs/ *noun* the commonest epidemic form of meningitis, caused by a bacterium *Neisseria meningitidis*, where the meninges become inflamed causing headaches and fever

meningococcus /məˌnɪŋgəʊˈkɒkəs/ *noun* the bacterium *Neisseria meningitidis* which causes meningococcal meningitis (NOTE: The plural is **meningococci**.)

meningoencephalitis /məˌnɪŋgəʊenˌkefəˈlaɪtɪs/ *noun* inflammation of the meninges and the brain

meningoencephalocele /məˌnɪŋgəʊen ˈkefələʊsiːl/ *noun* a condition in which part of the meninges and the brain push through a gap in the skull

meningomyelocele /məˌnɪŋgəʊˈmaɪələʊ siːl/ *noun* the pushing forward of part of the

meninges and spinal cord through a gap in the spine. Also called **myelomeningocele, myelocele**

meningovascular /mə,nɪŋgəʊˈvæskjʊlə/ *adjective* referring to the meningeal blood vessels

meninx /ˈmenɪŋks/ *noun* ♦ **meninges**

meniscectomy /,menɪˈsektəmi/ *noun* the surgical removal of a cartilage from the knee

meniscus /məˈnɪskəs/ *noun* one of two pads of cartilage, the lateral meniscus and medial meniscus, between the femur and tibia in a knee joint. Also called **semilunar cartilage** (NOTE: The plural is **menisci**.)

meno- /menəʊ/ *prefix* referring to menstruation

menopausal /,menəˈpɔːz(ə)l/ *adjective* referring to the menopause

menopause /ˈmenəpɔːz/ *noun* a period, usually between 45 and 55 years of age, when a woman stops menstruating and can no longer bear children. Also called **climacteric, change of life**

menorrhagia /,menəˈreɪdʒiə/ *noun* very heavy bleeding during menstruation. Also called **flooding**

menorrhoea /,menəˈriːə/ *noun* normal bleeding during menstruation

menses /ˈmensiːz/ *plural noun* same as **menstruation**

menstrual /ˈmenstruəl/ *adjective* referring to menstruation

menstrual cramp /,menstruəl ˈkræmp/ *noun* a cramp in the muscles round the uterus during menstruation

menstrual cycle /ˈmenstruəl ,saɪk(ə)l/ *noun* a period, usually of 28 days, during which a woman ovulates, the walls of the uterus swell and bleeding takes place if the ovum has not been fertilised

menstrual flow /ˈmenstruəl fləʊ/ *noun* the discharge of blood from the uterus during menstruation

menstruate /ˈmenstrueɪt/ *verb* to bleed from the uterus during menstruation

menstruation /,menstruˈeɪʃ(ə)n/ *noun* bleeding from the uterus which occurs in a woman each month when the lining of the uterus is shed because no fertilised egg is present

menstruum /ˈmenstruːəm/ *noun* a liquid used in the extract of active principles from an unrefined drug

mental /ˈment(ə)l/ *adjective* **1.** referring to the mind **2.** referring to the chin

mental aberration /,ment(ə)l ,æbəˈreɪʃ(ə)n/ *noun* slight forgetfulness or confusion (*often humorous*) ○ *I thought the meeting was at 11 – I must have had a mental aberration.*

mental age /,ment(ə)l ˈeɪdʒ/ *noun* a measurement based on intelligence tests that shows a person's intellectual development, usually compared to standardised data for a chronological age □ **he's nine, but he has a mental age of five** although he is nine years old, his level of intellectual development is the same as that of an average child of five

mental block /,ment(ə)l ˈblɒk/ *noun* a temporary inability to remember something, caused by the effect of nervous stress on the mental processes

mental deficiency /,ment(ə)l dɪˈfɪʃ(ə)nsi/ *noun* a former term for learning disability (NOTE: This term is regarded as offensive.)

mental development /,ment(ə)l dɪˈveləpmənt/ *noun* the development of the mind ○ *Her mental development is higher than usual for her age.*

mental disorder /,ment(ə)l dɪsˈɔːdə/ *noun* a temporary or permanent change in a person's mental state which makes them function less effectively than they would usually, or than the average person would be expected to function

mental faculties /,ment(ə)l ˈfækəltiːz/ *plural noun* abilities such as thinking and decision-making ○ *There has been no impairment of the mental faculties.*

mental handicap /,ment(ə)l ˈhændikæp/ *noun* a former term for learning disability (NOTE: This term is regarded as offensive.)

mental health /ˈment(ə)l helθ/ *noun* the condition of someone's mind

Mental Health Acts /,ment(ə)l ˈhelθ ækts/ *plural noun* laws made by a parliament which lay down rules for the care of people with mental illness

Mental Health Review Tribunal /,ment(ə)l helθ rɪˈvjuː traɪ,bjuːn(ə)l/ *noun* a committee which makes decisions about whether people who have been detained under the Mental Health Acts should be released. It consists of medical members, legal experts and lay members, who include people with experience in social services. Abbr **MHRT**

mental hospital /ˈment(ə)l ,hɒspɪt(ə)l/ *noun* a psychiatric hospital (NOTE: This term is regarded as offensive.)

mental illness /,ment(ə)l ˈɪlnəs/ *noun* any disorder which affects the mind

mental impairment /,ment(ə)l ɪm ˈpeəmənt/ *noun* a temporary or permanent condition which affects a person's mental state, making them function less effectively than they would usually, or than the average person would be expected to function

mentalis muscle /menˈteɪlɪs ,mʌs(ə)l/ *noun* a muscle attached to the front of the lower jaw and the skin of the chin

mentally /ˈment(ə)li/ *adverb* in the mind ○ *Mentally, she is very advanced for her age.*

mentally handicapped /,ment(ə)li ˈhændikæpt/ *adjective* a former term for someone with learning disability (NOTE: This term is usually regarded as offensive.)

mentally ill /ˌment(ə)li ˈɪl/ *adjective* experiencing mental illness

mental nerve /ˈment(ə)l nɜːv/ *noun* a nerve which supplies the chin

mental patient /ˈment(ə)l ˌpeɪʃ(ə)nt/ *noun* a former term of a patient who has mental illness (NOTE: This term is regarded as offensive.)

mental retardation /ˌment(ə)l ˌriːtɑːˈdeɪʃ(ə)n/ *noun* a former term for learning disability, a condition that results in someone finding it difficult to learn skills or information at the same rate as others of a similar age (NOTE: This term is regarded as offensive.)

mental subnormality /ˌment(ə)l ˌsʌbnɔːˈmælɪti/ *noun* a former term for mental impairment (NOTE: This term is usually regarded as offensive.)

menthol /ˈmenθɒl/ *noun* a strongly scented compound, produced from peppermint oil, used in cough medicines and in the treatment of neuralgia

mentholated /ˈmenθəleɪtɪd/ *adjective* impregnated with menthol

mento- /mentəʊ/ *prefix* relating to the chin

mentor /ˈmentɔː/ *noun* somebody who advises and guides a younger, less experienced person ■ *verb* to act as a mentor to somebody

mentum /ˈmentəm/ *noun* the chin

meralgia /məˈrældʒə/, **meralgia paraesthetica** /məˌrældʒə ˌpæresˈθetɪkə/ *noun* pain in the top of the thigh caused by a pinched nerve

mercurialism /məˈkjʊəriəlɪz(ə)m/ *noun* mercury poisoning

mercurochrome /məˈkjʊərəʊkrəʊm/ *noun* a red antiseptic solution

mercury /ˈmɜːkjʊri/ *noun* a poisonous liquid metal, used in thermometers (NOTE: The chemical symbol is **Hg**.)

mercury poisoning /ˈmɜːkjʊri ˌpɔɪz(ə)nɪŋ/ *noun* poisoning by drinking mercury or mercury compounds or by inhaling mercury vapour

mercy killing /ˈmɜːsi ˌkɪlɪŋ/ *noun* same as euthanasia

meridian /məˈrɪdiən/ *noun* in acupuncture and Chinese medicine, one of the pathways in the body along which its energy is believed to flow

Merkel's cells /ˈmɜːkelz selz/, **Merkel's discs** /ˈmɜːkelz dɪsks/ *plural noun* epithelial cells in the deeper part of the dermis which form touch receptors [After Friedrich Siegmund Merkel (1845–1919), German anatomist]

merocrine /ˈmerəʊkraɪn/ *adjective* same as eccrine

mes- /mes/ *prefix* same as **meso-** (*used before vowels*)

mesaortitis /ˌmeseɪɔːˈtaɪtɪs/ *noun* inflammation of the media of the aorta

mesarteritis /mesˌɑːtəˈraɪtɪs/ *noun* inflammation of the media of an artery

mesencephalon /mesenˈkefəlɒn/ *noun* same as **midbrain**

mesenteric /ˌmesenˈterɪk/ *adjective* referring to the mesentery

mesenterica /mesenˈterɪkə/ ♦ **tabes mesenterica**

mesenteric artery /ˌmesenterɪk ˈɑːtəri/ *noun* one of two arteries, the superior and inferior mesenteric arteries, which supply the small intestine or the transverse colon and rectum

mesenteric ganglion /ˌmesenterɪk ˈɡæŋɡliən/ *noun* a plexus of sympathetic nerve fibres and ganglion cells around the superior mesenteric artery

mesenteric vein /ˌmesenterɪk ˈveɪn/ *noun* a vein in the portal system running from the intestine to the portal vein

mesentery /ˈmesent(ə)ri/ *noun* a double-layer peritoneum which attaches the small intestine and other abdominal organs to the abdominal wall

mesial /ˈmiːsiəl/ *adjective* **1.** in dentistry, relating to the middle of the front of the jaw, or occurring in a place near this **2.** relating to or located in the middle part of something

meso- /mesəʊ/ *prefix* middle

mesoappendix /ˌmesəʊəˈpendɪks/ *noun* a fold of peritoneum which links the appendix and the ileum

mesocolon /ˌmesəʊˈkəʊlən/ *noun* a fold of peritoneum which supports the colon. In an adult it supports the transverse and sigmoid sections only.

mesoderm /ˈmesəʊdɜːm/ *noun* the middle layer of an embryo, which develops into muscles, bones, blood, kidneys, cartilages, urinary ducts and the cardiovascular and lymphatic systems

mesodermal /ˌmesəʊˈdɜːm(ə)l/ *adjective* referring to the mesoderm

mesometrium /ˌmesəʊˈmiːtriəm/ *noun* a muscle layer of the uterus

mesonephros /ˌmesəʊˈnefrɒs/ *noun* kidney tissue which exists in a human embryo

mesosalpinx /ˌmesəʊˈsælpɪŋks/ *noun* the upper part of the broad ligament around the Fallopian tubes

mesotendon /ˌmesəʊˈtendən/ *noun* synovial membrane connecting the lining of the fibrous sheath to that of a tendon

mesothelioma /ˌmesəʊtiːliˈəʊmə/ *noun* a tumour of the serous membrane, which can be benign or malignant

mesothelium /ˌmesəʊˈθiːliəm/ *noun* a layer of cells lining a serous membrane. Compare **epithelium, endothelium**

mesovarium /ˌmesəʊˈveəriəm/ *noun* a fold of peritoneum around the ovaries

messenger RNA /ˌmes(ə)ndʒə ˌɑːr en 'eɪ/ *noun* a type of ribonucleic acid which transmits the genetic code from the DNA to the ribosomes which form the proteins coded on the DNA. Abbr **mRNA**

mestranol /'miːstrənɒl/ *noun* a synthetically produced oestrogen used in birth control pills

meta- /metə/ *prefix* referring to change

meta analysis /'metə əˌnæləsɪs/ *noun* a statistical procedure to combine the results from many studies to give a single estimate, giving weight to large studies

metabolic /ˌmetə'bɒlɪk/ *adjective* referring to metabolism

metabolic acidosis /ˌmetəbɒlɪk ˌæsɪ'dəʊsɪs/ *noun* acidosis caused by a malfunction of the body's metabolism

metabolic alkalosis /ˌmetəbɒlɪk ælkə'ləʊsɪs/ *noun* alkalosis caused by a malfunction of the body's metabolism

metabolise /mə'tæbəlaɪz/, **metabolize** *verb* to change the nature of something by metabolism ○ *The liver metabolises proteins and carbohydrates.*

metabolism /mə'tæbəlɪz(ə)m/ *noun* the chemical processes which are continually taking place in the human body and which are essential to life, especially the processes that convert food into energy

> COMMENT: Metabolism covers all changes which take place in the body: the building of tissue (anabolism); the breaking down of tissue (catabolism); the conversion of nutrients into tissue; the elimination of waste matter and the action of hormones.

metabolite /mə'tæbəlaɪt/ *noun* a substance produced by metabolism, or a substance taken into the body in food and then metabolised

metacarpal bone /ˌmetə'kɑːp(ə)l bəʊn/, **metacarpal** /ˌmetə'kɑːp(ə)l/ *noun* one of the five bones in the metacarpus

metacarpophalangeal /ˌmetəˌkɑːpəʊfə'lændʒiəl/ *adjective* relating to the part of the hand between the wrist and the fingers

metacarpophalangeal joint /ˌmetəˌkɑːpəʊfə'lændʒiəl ˌdʒɔɪnt/ *noun* a joint between a metacarpal bone and a finger. Also called **MCP joint, MP joint**

> '…replacement of the MCP joint is usually undertaken to relieve pain, deformity and immobility due to rheumatoid arthritis' [*Nursing Times*]

metacarpus /ˌmetə'kɑːpəs/ *noun* the five bones in the hand between the fingers and the wrist. See illustration at **HAND** in Supplement

metal /'met(ə)l/ *noun* material, either an element or a compound, which can carry heat and electricity. Some metals are essential for life.

metallic /me'tælɪk/ *adjective* like a metal, referring to a metal

metallic element /meˌtælɪk 'elɪmənt/ *noun* a chemical element which is a metal

metamorphopsia /ˌmetəmɔː'fɒpsiə/ *noun* a condition in which someone sees objects in distorted form, usually due to inflammation of the choroid

metaphase /'metəfeɪz/ *noun* one of the stages in mitosis or meiosis

metaphysis /me'tæfəsɪs/ *noun* the end of the central section of a long bone, where the bone grows and where it joins the epiphysis

metaplasia /metə'pleɪziə/ *noun* a change of one tissue to another

metastasis /me'tæstəsɪs/ *noun* the spreading of a malignant disease from one part of the body to another through the bloodstream or the lymph system. Also called **secondary growth** (NOTE: The plural is **metastases**.)

> '…he suddenly developed problems with his balance and a solitary brain metastasis was diagnosed' [*British Journal of Nursing*]

metastasise /me'tæstəsaɪz/, **metastasize** *verb* to spread by metastasis

metastatic /metə'stætɪk/ *adjective* relating to, or produced by, metastasis ○ *Metastatic growths developed in the liver.*

metatarsal /ˌmetə'tɑːs(ə)l/ *noun* one of the five bones in the metatarsus ■ *adjective* relating to the metatarsus

metatarsal arch /ˌmetə'tɑːs(ə)l ɑːtʃ/ *noun* an arched part of the sole of the foot, running across the sole of the foot from side to side. Also called **transverse arch**

metatarsalgia /ˌmetətɑː'sældʒə/ *noun* pain in the heads of the metatarsal bones

metatarsophalangeal joint /metəˌtɑːsəʊfə'lændʒiəl ˌdʒɔɪnt/ *noun* a joint between a metatarsal bone and a toe

metatarsus /ˌmetə'tɑːsəs/ *noun* the five long bones in the foot between the toes and the tarsus. See illustration at **FOOT** in Supplement (NOTE: The plural is **metatarsi**.)

metatarsus adductus /ˌmetətɑːsəs ə'dʌktəs/ *noun* a condition found in newborn babies or young infants in which the front half of the foot is twisted inwards at an angle to the heel

meteorism /'miːtiərɪz(ə)m/ *noun* same as **tympanites**

meter /'miːtə/ *noun* US same as **metre**

-meter /miːtə, mɪtə/ *suffix* measuring instrument

metformin /met'fɔːmɪn/ *noun* a drug which reduces the level of the blood sugar levels, used to treat non-insulin dependent diabetes which does not respond to dietary measures

methadone /'meθədəʊn/ *noun* a synthetically produced narcotic drug, used to reduce pain and as a substitute for heroin in the treatment of addiction

methaemoglobin /metˌhiːməʊ'gləʊbɪn/ *noun* a dark brown substance formed from haemoglobin which develops during illness, following treatment with some drugs. Methaemoglobin cannot transport oxygen round the body, and so causes cyanosis.

methaemoglobinaemia /met,hi:məʊ,gləʊbɪ'ni:miə/ *noun* the presence of methaemoglobin in the blood

methane /'mi:θeɪn, 'meθeɪn/ *noun* a colourless flammable gas with no smell

methanol /'meθənɒl/ *noun* a colourless poisonous liquid, used as a solvent and a fuel. It changes easily into a gas. Also called **methyl alcohol**

methicillin /,meθɪ'sɪlɪn/ *noun* a synthetically produced antibiotic, used in the treatment of infections which are resistant to penicillin

methicillin-resistant Staphylococcus aureus /meθɪ,sɪlɪn rɪ,zɪstənt stæfɪlə,kɒkəs 'ɔ:riəs/ *noun* a bacterium resistant to almost all antibiotics and which can cause life-threatening infection in people recovering from surgery. Abbr **MRSA**

methionine /me'θaɪəni:n/ *noun* an essential amino acid

method /'meθəd/ *noun* a way of doing something

methotrexate /,meθə'trekseɪt/ *noun* a drug which helps to prevent cells reproducing, used in the treatment of cancer

methyl alcohol /,mi:θaɪl 'ælkəhɒl/ *noun* same as **methanol**

methylated spirits /,meθəleɪtɪd 'spɪrɪts/ *plural noun* almost pure alcohol, with wood alcohol and colouring added

methylene blue /,meθɪli:n 'blu:/ *noun* a blue dye, formerly used as a mild urinary antiseptic, now used to treat drug-induced methaemoglobinaemia

methylenedioxymethamphetamine /,meθɪli:n,daɪɒksɪ,meθæm'fetəmi:n/ *noun* same as **ecstasy**

methylphenidate /,mi:θaɪl'fenɪdeɪt/ *noun* a drug which stimulates the central nervous system, used in the treatment of narcolepsy and attention deficit disorder

methylprednisolone /,mi:θaɪlpred'nɪsələʊn/ *noun* a corticosteroid drug which reduces inflammation, used in the treatment of arthritis, allergies and asthma

metoclopramide /,metəʊ'kləʊprəmaɪd/ *noun* a drug used to treat nausea, vomiting and indigestion

metoprolol /mɪ'tɒprəlɒl/ *noun* a drug which controls the activity of the heart, used to treat angina and high blood pressure

metr- /metr/ *prefix* same as **metro-** (*used before vowels*)

metra /'metrə/ *noun* the uterus

metralgia /me'trældʒə/ *noun* pain in the uterus

metre /'mi:tə/ *noun* an SI unit of length ○ *The room is four metres by three.* Symbol **m** (NOTE: The US spelling is **meter.**)

metritis /me'traɪtɪs/ *noun* same as **myometritis**

metro- /metrəʊ/ *prefix* referring to the uterus

metrocolpocele /,metrə'kɒlpəʊsi:l/ *noun* a condition in which the uterus protrudes into the vagina

metronidazole /,metrə'nɪdəzəʊl/ *noun* a yellow antibiotic compound, used especially in the treatment of vaginal infections

metropathia haemorrhagica /,metrəpæθiə ,hemə'reɪdʒɪkə/ *noun* an essential uterine haemorrhage, where the lining of the uterus swells and there is heavy menstrual bleeding

metroptosis /,metrə'təʊsɪs/ *noun* a condition in which the uterus has moved downwards out of its usual position. Also called **prolapse of the uterus**

metrorrhagia /,mi:trəʊ'reɪdʒiə/ *noun* unusual bleeding from the vagina between the menstrual periods

metrostaxis /,mi:trəʊ'stæksɪs/ *noun* a continual light bleeding from the uterus

-metry /mətri/ *suffix* relating to the process of measuring, or to instruments which are used for measuring

mg *abbr* milligram

MI *abbr* **1.** mitral incompetence **2.** myocardial infarction

micelle /mɪ'sel/ *noun* a tiny particle formed by the digestion of fat in the small intestine

Michel's clips /mɪ,ʃelz 'klɪps/ *plural noun* metal clips used to suture a wound [After Gaston Michel (1874–1937), Professor of Clinical Surgery at Nancy, France]

miconazole /maɪ'kɒnəzəʊl/ *noun* a drug used to treat fungal infections of the skin and nails

micro- /maɪkrəʊ/ *prefix* **1.** very small. Opposite **macro-, mega-, megalo- 2.** one millionth (10^{-6})

microaneurysm /,maɪkrəʊ'ænjərɪz(ə)m/ *noun* a tiny swelling in the wall of a capillary in the retina

microangiopathy /,maɪkrəʊ,ændʒi'ɒpəθi/ *noun* any disease of the capillaries

microbe /'maɪkrəʊb/ *noun* a microorganism which may cause disease and which can only be seen with a microscope, e.g. a bacterium

microbial /maɪ'krəʊbiəl/ *adjective* referring to microbes

microbial disease /maɪ,krəʊbiəl dɪ'zi:z/ *noun* a disease caused by a microbe

microbiological /,maɪkrəʊ,baɪə'lɒdʒɪk(ə)l/ *adjective* referring to microbiology

microbiologist /,maɪkrəʊbaɪ'ɒlədʒɪst/ *noun* a scientist who specialises in the study of microorganisms

microbiology /,maɪkrəʊbaɪ'ɒlədʒi/ *noun* the scientific study of microorganisms

microcephalic /ˌmaɪkrəʊke'fælɪk/ *adjective* having microcephaly

microcephaly /ˌmaɪkrəʊ'kefəli/ *noun* a condition in which a person has an unusually small head, sometimes caused by the mother having had a rubella infection during pregnancy

microcheilia /ˌmaɪkrəʊ'kaɪliə/ *noun* the condition of having unusually small lips

Micrococcus /ˌmaɪkrəʊ'kɒkəs/ *noun* a genus of bacterium, some species of which cause arthritis, endocarditis and meningitis

microcyte /'maɪkrəʊsaɪt/ *noun* an unusually small red blood cell

microcythaemia /ˌmaɪkrəʊsaɪ'θiːmiə/ *noun* same as **microcytosis**

microcytic /ˌmaɪkrə'sɪtɪk/ *adjective* referring to microcytes

microcytosis /ˌmaɪkrəʊsaɪ'təʊsɪs/ *noun* the presence of excess microcytes in the blood

microdactylia /ˌmaɪkrəʊdæk'tɪliə/, **microdactyly** /ˌmaɪkrəʊ'dæktɪli/ *noun* a condition in which a person has unusually small or short fingers or toes

microdiscectomy /ˌmaɪkrəʊdɪsk'ektəmi/ *noun* a surgical operation to remove all or part of a disc in the spine which is pressing on a nerve

microdontism /ˌmaɪkrəʊ'dɒntɪz(ə)m/, **microdontia** /ˌmaɪkrəʊ'dɒntiə/ *noun* the condition of having unusually small teeth

microglia /maɪ'krɒgliə/ *noun* tissue in the central nervous system composed of tiny cells which destroy other cells

microglossia /ˌmaɪkrəʊ'glɒsiə/ *noun* a condition in which a person has an unusually small tongue

micrognathia /ˌmaɪkrəʊ'neɪθiə/ *noun* a condition in which one jaw is unusually smaller than the other

microgram /'maɪkrəgræm/ *noun* a unit of measurement of weight equal to one millionth of a gram

micromastia /ˌmaɪkrəʊ'mæstiə/ *noun* a condition in which a person has unusually small breasts

micromelia /ˌmaɪkrəʊ'miːliə/ *noun* a condition in which a person has unusually small arms or legs

micrometer /maɪ'krɒmɪtə/ *noun* **1.** an instrument for taking very small measurements, such as the width or thickness of very thin pieces of tissue **2.** *US* same as **micrometre**

micrometre /'maɪkrəʊˌmiːtə/ *noun* a unit of measurement of thickness (= one millionth of a metre) (NOTE: With figures, usually written **μm**.)

micromole /'maɪkrəʊˌməʊl/ *noun* a unit of measurement of the amount of substance equal to one millionth of a mole. Symbol **μ**

micron /'maɪkrɒn/ *noun* same as **micrometre**

micronutrient /'maɪkrəʊˌnjuːtriənt/ *noun* a substance which an organism needs for normal growth and development, but only in very small quantities, e.g. a vitamin or mineral. Compare **macronutrient**

microorganism /ˌmaɪkrəʊ'ɔːgənɪz(ə)m/ *noun* an organism which can only be seen under a microscope and which may cause disease. Viruses, bacteria and protozoa are microorganisms.

microphthalmia /ˌmaɪkrɒf'θælmiə/ *noun* a condition in which the eyes are unusually small

micropsia /maɪ'krɒpsiə/ *noun* a condition in which someone sees objects smaller than they really are, caused by an unusual development in the retina

microscope /'maɪkrəskəʊp/ *noun* a scientific instrument with lenses, which makes very small objects appear larger ○ *The tissue was examined under the microscope.* ○ *Under the microscope it was possible to see the cancer cells.*

COMMENT: In an ordinary or light microscope the image is magnified by lenses. In an electron microscope the lenses are electromagnets and a beam of electrons is used instead of light, thereby achieving much greater magnifications.

microscopic /ˌmaɪkrə'skɒpɪk/ *adjective* so small that it can only be seen through a microscope

microscopy /maɪ'krɒskəpi/ *noun* the science of the use of microscopes

microsecond /'maɪkrəʊˌsekənd/ *noun* a unit of measurement of time (= one millionth of a second) (NOTE: With figures, usually written **μs**.)

Microsporum /'maɪkrəʊspɔːrəm/ *noun* a type of fungus which causes ringworm of the hair, skin and sometimes nails

microsurgery /'maɪkrəʊˌsɜːdʒəri/ *noun* surgery using tiny instruments and a microscope. Microsurgery is used in operations on eyes and ears, and also to connect severed nerves and blood vessels.

microvillus /ˌmaɪkrəʊ'vɪləs/ *noun* a very small process found on the surface of many cells, especially the epithelial cells in the intestine (NOTE: The plural is **microvilli**.)

microwave therapy /'maɪkrəʊweɪv ˌθerəpi/ *noun* treatment using high-frequency radiation

micturate /'mɪktjʊreɪt/ *verb* same as **urinate**

micturating cystogram /ˌmɪktjʊreɪtɪŋ 'sɪstəʊgræm/, **micturating cysto-urethrogram** /ˌmɪktjʊreɪtɪŋ ˌsɪstəʊ jʊ'riːθrəgræm/ *noun* an X-ray of the bladder and urethra taken while the bladder is being filled and then emptied. Abbr **MCU, MCUG**

micturition /ˌmɪktjʊ'rɪʃ(ə)n/ *noun* same as **urination**

mid- /mɪd/ *prefix* middle

midazolam /mɪ'dæzələm/ *noun* a drug used to produce sleepiness and to reduce anxiety before surgery or other procedures

midbrain /'mɪdbreɪn/ *noun* the small middle section of the brain stem above the pons and between the cerebrum and the hindbrain. Also called **mesencephalon**

midcarpal /mɪd'kɑːp(ə)l/ *adjective* between the two rows of carpal bones

middle /'mɪd(ə)l/ *noun* **1.** the centre or central point of something **2.** the waist or stomach area (*informal*)

middle-aged /ˌmɪd(ə)l 'eɪdʒd/ *adjective* not young and not old, in the middle years of life ○ *a disease which affects middle-aged women*

middle colic /ˌmɪd(ə)l 'kɒlɪk/ *noun* an artery which leads from the superior mesenteric artery

middle ear /ˌmɪd(ə)l 'ɪə/ *noun* a section of the ear between the eardrum and the inner ear
COMMENT: The middle ear contains the three ossicles which receive vibrations from the eardrum and transmit them to the cochlea. The middle ear is connected to the throat by the Eustachian tube.

middle ear infection /ˌmɪd(ə)l 'ɪər ɪn ˌfekʃən/ *noun* same as **otitis media**

middle finger /ˌmɪd(ə)l 'fɪŋgə/ *noun* the longest of the five fingers

midgut /'mɪdgʌt/ *noun* the middle part of the gut in an embryo, which develops into the small intestine

mid-life crisis /ˌmɪd laɪf 'kraɪsɪs/ *noun* a period in early middle age when some people experience feelings of anxiety, insecurity and self-doubt

midline /'mɪdlaɪn/ *noun* an imaginary line drawn down the middle of the body from the head through the navel to the point between the feet
'…patients admitted with acute abdominal pains were referred for study. Abdominal puncture was carried out in the midline immediately above or below the umbilicus.' [*Lancet*]

midriff /'mɪdrɪf/ *noun* the diaphragm

midstream specimen /'mɪdstriːm ˌspesɪmɪn/, **midstream specimen of urine** /ˌmɪd striːm ˌspesɪmɪn əv 'jʊərɪn/ *noun* a sample of urine collected in a sterile bottle in the middle of a flow of urine, because the first part of the flow may be contaminated with bacteria from the skin. Abbr **MSU**

midtarsal /mɪd'tɑːs(ə)l/ *adjective* between the tarsal bones

midwife /'mɪdwaɪf/ *noun* a professional person who helps a woman give birth to a child, often at home
COMMENT: To become a Registered Midwife (RM), a Registered General Nurse has to take a further 18 month course, or alternatively can follow a full 3 year course.

midwifery /mɪd'wɪfəri/ *noun* **1.** the profession of a midwife **2.** the study of the practical aspects of obstetrics

midwifery course /mɪd'wɪfəri kɔːs/ *noun* a training course to teach nurses the techniques of being a midwife

migraine /'miːgreɪn, 'maɪgreɪn/, **migraine headache** /ˌmiːgreɪn 'hedeɪk/ *noun* a very severe throbbing headache which can be accompanied by nausea, vomiting, visual disturbance and vertigo. The cause is not known. Attacks may be preceded by an 'aura', where the patient sees flashing lights, or the eyesight becomes blurred. The pain is usually intense and affects one side of the head only.

migrainous /'maɪgreɪnəs/ *adjective* referring to someone who is subject to migraine attacks

mild /maɪld/ *adjective* not severe, not cold, gentle ○ *a mild throat infection*

mildly /'maɪldli/ *adverb* slightly, not strongly ○ *a mildly infectious disease* ○ *a mildly antiseptic solution*

milia /'mɪliə/ *plural of* **milium**

miliaria /ˌmɪli'eəriə/ *noun* itchy red spots which develop on the chest, under the armpits and between the thighs in hot countries, caused by blocked sweat glands. Also called **prickly heat, heat rash**

miliary /'mɪliəri/ *adjective* small in size, like a seed

miliary tuberculosis /ˌmɪliəri tjuːˌbɜːkjʊ 'ləʊsɪs/ *noun* a form of tuberculosis which occurs as little nodes in many parts of the body, including the meninges of the brain and spinal cord

milium /'mɪliəm/ *noun* **1.** a white pinhead-sized tumour on the face in adults **2.** a retention cyst in infants **3.** a cyst on the skin (NOTE: [all senses] The plural is **milia**.)

milk /mɪlk/ *noun* **1.** a white liquid produced by female mammals to feed their young. Cow's milk and other dairy products are important parts of most diets, especially children's. ○ *The patient can only drink warm milk.* (NOTE: No plural: *some milk, a bottle of milk* or *a glass of milk*.) **2.** the breast milk produced by a woman ○ *The milk will start to flow a few days after childbirth.* (NOTE: For other terms referring to milk, see words beginning with **galact-, galacto-, lact-, lacto-**.)

milk dentition /mɪlk den'tɪʃ(ə)n/ *noun* same as **deciduous dentition**

milk leg /'mɪlk leg/ *noun* acute oedema of the leg, a condition which affects women after childbirth, where a leg becomes pale and inflamed as a result of lymphatic obstruction. Also called **white leg, phlegmasia alba dolens**

milk rash /'mɪlk ræʃ/ *noun* a temporary blotchiness of the skin seen in young babies

milk sugar /mɪlk 'ʃʊɡə/ *noun* same as **lactose**

milk tooth /'mɪlk tuːθ/ *noun* same as **primary tooth**

milky /'mɪlki/ *adjective* referring to liquid which is white like milk

Miller-Abbott tube /ˌmɪlər 'æbət tjuːb/ *noun* a tube with a balloon at the end, used to clear the small intestine. The balloon is inflated after the tip of the tube reaches an obstruction.

milli- /mɪli/ *prefix* one thousandth (10⁻³). Symbol **m**

milligram /'mɪlɪɡræm/ *noun* a unit of measurement of weight equal to one thousandth of a gram. Symbol **mg**

millilitre /'mɪlɪˌliːtə/ *noun* a unit of measurement of liquid equal to one thousandth of a litre. Abbr **ml** (NOTE: The US spelling is **milliliter**.)

millimetre /'mɪlɪmiːtə/ *noun* a unit of measurement of length equal to one thousandth of a metre. Abbr **mm** (NOTE: The US spelling is **millimeter**.)

millimole /'mɪliməʊl/ *noun* a unit of measurement of the amount of a substance equal to one thousandth of a mole. Abbr **mmol**

millisievert /'mɪlisiːvət/ *noun* a unit of measurement of radiation □ **millisievert/year (mSv/year)** number of millisieverts per year

'…radiation limits for workers should be cut from 50 to 5 millisieverts, and those for members of the public from 5 to 0.25' [*Guardian*]

Milroy's disease /'mɪlrɔɪz dɪˌziːz/ *noun* a hereditary condition where the lymph vessels are blocked and the legs swell [Described 1892. After William Forsyth Milroy (1855–1942), Professor of Clinical Medicine in Nebraska, USA.]

Milwaukee brace /mɪlˌwɔːki 'breɪs/ *noun* a support for people with unusually curved spines, consisting of a leather or metal pelvic girdle with two bars at the back and one at the front, which connect into a neck ring

mimesis /mɪ'miːsɪs/ *noun* the appearance of the symptoms of a disease in someone who does not have the disease

Minamata disease /ˌmɪnə'mɑːtə dɪˌziːz/ *noun* a form of mercury poisoning from eating polluted fish, found first in Japan

mind /maɪnd/ *noun* the part of the brain which controls memory, consciousness or reasoning □ **he's got something on his mind** he's worrying about something □ **let's try to take her mind off her exams** try to stop her worrying about them

miner /'maɪnə/ *noun* a person who works in a coal mine

mineral /'mɪn(ə)rəl/ *noun* an inorganic substance

COMMENT: The most important minerals required by the body are: calcium (found in cheese, milk and green vegetables) which

helps the growth of bones and encourages blood clotting; iron (found in bread and liver) which helps produce red blood cells; phosphorus (found in bread and fish) which helps in the growth of bones and the metabolism of fats; iodine (found in fish) which is essential to the functioning of the thyroid gland.

mineral water /'mɪn(ə)rəl ˌwɔːtə/ *noun* a drinking water containing dissolved mineral salts from the ground the water is piped from. It is bottled and sold.

minim /'mɪnɪm/ *noun* a liquid measure used in pharmacy (one sixtieth of a drachm)

minimal /'mɪnɪm(ə)l/ *adjective* very small

minimally invasive surgery /ˌmɪnɪm(ə)l ɪnˌveɪsɪv 'sɜːdʒəri/ *noun* surgery which involves the least possible disturbance to the body. It often uses lasers and other high-tech devices.

mini mental state examination /ˌmɪni 'ment(ə)l ˌsteɪt ɪɡzæmɪˌneɪʃ(ə)n/ *noun* a test performed mainly by psychiatrists to determine someone's mental ability, used in the diagnosis of dementia

minimum /'mɪnɪməm/ *adjective* smallest possible ■ *noun* the smallest possible amount (NOTE: The plural is **minimums** or **minima**.)

minimum lethal dose /ˌmɪnɪməm ˌliːθ(ə)l 'dəʊs/ *noun* the smallest amount of a substance required to kill someone or something. Abbr **MLD**

ministroke /'mɪnistrəʊk/ *noun* same as **transient ischaemic attack**

minitracheostomy /ˌmɪnitreɪki'ɒstəmi/ *noun* a temporary tracheostomy

minor /'maɪnə/ *adjective* 1. not very serious or life-threatening 2. less important or serious than others of the same type ▶ opposite **major**

'…practice nurses play a major role in the care of patients with chronic disease and they undertake many preventive procedures. They also deal with a substantial amount of minor trauma' [*Nursing Times*]

minor illness /ˌmaɪnər 'ɪlnəs/ *noun* an illness which is not serious

minor injuries unit /ˌmaɪnər 'ɪndʒəriz ˌjuːnɪt/ *noun* a hospital department which treats most accidents and emergencies. Abbr **MIU**

minor surgery /ˌmaɪnə 'sɜːdʒəri/ *noun* surgery which can be undertaken even when there are no hospital facilities. Compare **major surgery**

mio- /maɪəʊ/ *prefix* less

miosis /maɪ'əʊsɪs/ *noun* 1. the contraction of the pupil of the eye, as in bright light 2. *US* same as **meiosis**

miotic /maɪ'ɒtɪk/ *noun* a drug which makes the pupil of the eye become smaller ■ *adjective* causing the pupil of the eye to become smaller

mis- /mɪs/ *prefix* wrong

miscarriage /'mɪskærɪdʒ/ *noun* a situation in which an unborn baby leaves the uterus before the end of the pregnancy, especially during the first seven months of pregnancy ○ *She had two miscarriages before having her first child.* Also called **spontaneous abortion**

miscarry /mɪsˈkæri/ *verb* to have a miscarriage ○ *The accident made her miscarry.* ○ *She miscarried after catching the infection.*

misconduct /mɪsˈkɒndʌkt/ *noun* action by a professional person such as a doctor which is considered wrong

misdiagnose /ˌmɪsˈdaɪəgˌnəʊz/ *verb* to make an incorrect diagnosis of a condition

misdiagnosis /ˌmɪsdaɪəgˈnəʊsɪs/ *noun* an incorrect diagnosis

mismatch /ˈmɪsmætʃ/ *verb* to match tissues wrongly

'…finding donors of correct histocompatible type is difficult but necessary because results using mismatched bone marrow are disappointing' [*Hospital Update*]

miso- /mɪsɒ/ *prefix* indicating hatred of something

missed case /ˌmɪst ˈkeɪs/ *noun* someone with an infection or disease which is not identified by a doctor

mist. /mɪst/, **mistura** /mɪsˈtjʊərə/ ♦ **re. mist.**

misuse *noun* /mɪsˈjuːs/ wrong use ○ *He was arrested for misuse of drugs.* ■ *verb* /mɪsˈjuːz/ to use something such as a drug wrongly

Misuse of Drugs Act 1971 /mɪsˌjuːs əv ˈdrʌgz ækt/ *noun* a law relating to all aspects of the supply and possession of dangerous drugs such as morphine, anabolic steroids, LSD and cannabis. In 2002 many new benzodiazepines were added.

mite /maɪt/ *noun* a very small parasite, which causes dermatitis

mitochondrial /ˌmaɪtəˈkɒndriəl/ *adjective* referring to mitochondria

mitochondrion /ˌmaɪtəˈkɒndriən/ *noun* a tiny rod-shaped part of a cell's cytoplasm responsible for cell respiration (NOTE: The plural is **mitochondria**.)

mitomycin C /ˌmaɪtəʊmaɪsɪn ˈsiː/ *noun* an antibiotic which helps to prevent cancer cells from growing, used especially in the chemotherapy treatment of bladder and rectal cancers

mitosis /maɪˈtəʊsɪs/ *noun* the process of cell division, where the mother cell divides into two identical daughter cells. Compare **meiosis**

mitral /ˈmaɪtrəl/ *adjective* referring to the mitral valve

mitral incompetence /ˌmaɪtrəl ɪnˈkɒmpɪt(ə)ns/ *noun* Abbr **MI**. Now called **mitral regurgitation**

mitral regurgitation /ˌmaɪtrəl rɪˌɡɜːdʒɪˈteɪʃ(ə)n/ *noun* a situation in which the mitral valve does not close completely so that blood goes back into the atrium

mitral stenosis /ˌmaɪtrəl steˈnəʊsɪs/ *noun* a condition in which the opening in the mitral valve becomes smaller because the cusps have

fused (NOTE: This condition is almost always the result of rheumatic endocarditis.)

mitral valve /ˈmaɪtrəl vælv/ *noun* a valve in the heart which allows blood to flow from the left atrium to the left ventricle but not in the opposite direction. Also called **bicuspid valve**

mitral valvotomy /ˌmaɪtrəl vælˈvɒtəmi/ *noun* a surgical operation to separate the cusps of the mitral valve in mitral stenosis

mittelschmerz /ˈmɪt(ə)lˌʃmeəts/ *noun* a pain felt by women in the lower abdomen at ovulation

MIU *abbr* minor injuries unit

mix /mɪks/ *verb* to put things together ○ *The pharmacist mixed the chemicals in a bottle.*

mixture /ˈmɪkstʃə/ *noun* chemical substances mixed together ○ *The doctor gave me an unpleasant mixture to drink.* ○ *Take one spoonful of the mixture every three hours.*

ml *abbr* millilitre

MLD *abbr* minimum lethal dose

MLSO *abbr* medical laboratory scientific officer

mm *abbr* millimetre

mmol *abbr* millimole

MMR /ˌem em ˈɑː/, **MMR vaccine** /ˌem em ˈɑː ˌvæksiːn/ *noun* a single vaccine given to small children to protect them against measles, mumps and rubella

Mn *symbol* manganese

MND *abbr* motor neurone disease

MO *abbr* medical officer

mobile /ˈməʊbaɪl/ *adjective* able to move about ○ *It is important for elderly patients to remain mobile.*

mobilisation /ˌməʊbɪlaɪˈzeɪʃ(ə)n/, **mobilization** *noun* the act of making something mobile

mobility /məʊˈbɪlɪti/ *noun* (*of patients*) the ability to move about

mobility allowance /məʊˈbɪlɪti əˌlaʊəns/ *noun* a government benefit to help disabled people pay for transport

modality /məʊˈdælɪti/ *noun* a method used in the treatment of a disorder, e.g. surgery or chemotherapy

moderate /ˈmɒd(ə)rət/ *adjective* not high or low

moderately /ˈmɒd(ə)rətli/ *adverb* not at one or other extreme ○ *The patient had a moderately comfortable night.*

modern matron /ˌmɒd(ə)n ˈmeɪtrən/ *noun* a nursing post which supports the ward sister in ensuring that basic care of patients, including cleanliness of the ward and infection control, is carried out to a high standard

modiolus /məʊˈdiːələs/ *noun* the central stalk in the cochlea

MODS *abbr* multiple organ dysfunction syndrome

MOF *abbr* **1.** male or female **2.** multi-organ failure

Mogadon /'mɒɡədɒn/ a trade name for nitrazepam

MOH *abbr* Medical Officer of Health

moist /mɔɪst/ *adjective* slightly wet or damp ○ *The compress should be kept moist.*

moisten /'mɔɪs(ə)n/ *verb* to make something damp

moist gangrene /ˌmɔɪst 'ɡæŋɡriːn/ *noun* a condition in which dead tissue decays and swells with fluid because of infection and the tissues have an unpleasant smell

moisture /'mɔɪstʃə/ *noun* water or other liquid

moisture content /'mɔɪstʃə ˌkɒntent/ *noun* the amount of water or other liquid which a substance contains

mol /məʊl/ *symbol* mole *noun* 2

molar /'məʊlə/ *adjective* **1.** referring to the large back teeth **2.** referring to the mole, the SI unit of amount of a substance ■ *noun* one of the large back teeth, used for grinding food. In milk teeth there are eight molars and in permanent teeth there are twelve. See illustration at TEETH in Supplement

molarity /məʊ'lærɪti/ *noun* the strength of a solution shown as the number of moles of a solution per litre of solution

molasses /mə'læsɪz/ *noun* a dark sweet substance made of sugar before it has been refined

mole /məʊl/ *noun* **1.** a dark raised spot on the skin ○ *She has a large mole on her chin.* ◊ **melanoma 2.** an SI unit of measurement of the amount of a substance. Symbol **mol**

molecular /mə'lekjʊlə/ *adjective* referring to a molecule

molecular biology /məˌlekjʊlə baɪ'ɒlədʒi/ *noun* the study of the molecules of living matter

molecular weight /məˌlekjʊlə 'weɪt/ *noun* the weight of one molecule of a substance

molecule /'mɒlɪkjuːl/ *noun* the smallest independent mass of a substance

molluscum /mə'lʌskəm/ *noun* a soft round skin tumour

molluscum contagiosum /məˌlʌskəm kənˌteɪdʒi'əʊsəm/ *noun* a contagious viral skin infection which gives a small soft sore

molluscum fibrosum /məˌlʌskəm ˌfaɪ'brəʊsəm/ *noun* same as **neurofibromatosis**

molluscum sebaceum /məˌlʌskəm sɪ'beɪʃəm/ *noun* a benign skin tumour which disappears after a short time

molybdenum /mɒ'lɪbdənəm/ *noun* a metallic trace element (NOTE: The chemical symbol is **Mo**.)

monaural /mɒn'ɔːrəl/ *adjective* referring to the use of one ear only

Mönckeberg's arteriosclerosis /ˌmʌnkəbeəɡz ˌɑːtiːriəʊskleˈrəʊsɪs/ *noun* a condition of elderly people, where the media of the arteries in the legs harden, causing limping [Described 1903. After Johann Georg Mönckeberg (1877–1925), German physician and pathologist.]

mongolism /'mɒŋɡəlɪz(ə)m/ *noun* a former name for Down's syndrome (NOTE: This term is regarded as offensive.)

Monilia /məʊ'nɪliə/ *noun* same as **Candida**

moniliasis /mɒni'laɪəsɪs/ *noun* same as **candidiasis**

monitor /'mɒnɪtə/ *noun* a screen on a computer ■ *verb* **1.** to check something **2.** to examine how someone is progressing

monitoring /'mɒnɪt(ə)rɪŋ/ *noun* the regular examination and recording of a person's temperature, weight, blood pressure and other essential indicators

mono- /mɒnəʊ/ *prefix* single or one

monoamine oxidase /ˌmɒnəʊˌæmiːn 'ɒkↃsɪdeɪz/ *noun* an enzyme which breaks down the catecholamines to their inactive forms. Abbr **MAO**

monoamine oxidase inhibitor /ˌmɒnəʊ ˌæmiːn ˌɒksɪdeɪz ɪn'hɪbɪtə/ *noun* a drug which inhibits monoamine oxidase and is used to treat depression, e.g. phenelzine. Its use is limited, because of the potential for drug and dietary interactions and the necessity for slow withdrawal. It can also cause high blood pressure. Abbr **MAOI**. Also called **MAO inhibitor**

monoblast /'mɒnəʊblæst/ *noun* a cell which produces a monocyte

monochromatism /ˌmɒnəʊ'krəʊmətɪz(ə)m/ *noun* colour blindness in which all colours appear to be black, grey or white. Compare **dichromatism, trichromatism**

monoclonal /ˌmɒnəʊ'kləʊn(ə)l/ *adjective* referring to cells or products of cells which are formed or derived from a single clone

monoclonal antibody /ˌmɒnəʊkləʊn(ə)l 'æntɪbɒdi/ *noun* an antibody which can be easily made in the laboratory by a single clone of cells. It may be useful in the treatment of cancer.

monocular /mɒ'nɒkjʊlə/ *adjective* referring to one eye. Compare **binocular**

monocular vision /məˌnɒkjʊlə 'vɪʒ(ə)n/ *noun* the ability to see with one eye only, so that the sense of distance is impaired

monocyte /'mɒnəʊsaɪt/ *noun* a white blood cell with a nucleus shaped like a kidney, which destroys bacterial cells

monocytosis /ˌmɒnəʊsaɪ'təʊsɪs/ *noun* a condition in which there is an unusually high number of monocytes in the blood. Symptoms include sore throat, swelling of the lymph nodes and fever. It is probably caused by the Epstein–Barr virus. Also called **glandular fever**

monodactylism /ˌmɒnəʊˈdæktɪlɪz(ə)m/ *noun* a congenital condition in which only one finger or toe is present on the hand or foot

monomania /ˌmɒnəʊˈmeɪnɪə/ *noun* a state of mental disorder in which a person concentrates attention on one idea

mononeuritis /ˌmɒnəʊnjuˈraɪtɪs/ *noun* a neuritis which affects one nerve

mononuclear /ˌmɒnəʊˈnjuːkliə/ *adjective* referring to a cell such as a monocyte which has one nucleus

mononucleosis /ˌmɒnəʊˌnjuːkliˈəʊsɪs/ *noun* same as **monocytosis**

monoplegia /ˌmɒnəʊˈpliːdʒə/ *noun* the paralysis of one part of the body only, i.e. one muscle or one limb

monorchism /ˈmɒnɔːkɪz(ə)m/ *noun* a condition in which only one testis is visible

monosaccharide /ˌmɒnəʊˈsækraɪd/ *noun* a simple sugar which cannot be broken down any further, such as glucose or fructose

monosodium glutamate /ˌmɒnəʊ ˌsəʊdiəm ˈgluːtəmeɪt/ *noun* a sodium salt of glutamic acid, often used to make food taste better. ◊ **Chinese restaurant syndrome**

monosomy /ˈmɒnəʊsəʊmi/ *noun* a condition in which a person has a chromosome missing from one or more pairs

monosynaptic /ˌmɒnəʊsɪˈnæptɪk/ *adjective* referring to a nervous pathway with only one synapse

monovalent /ˌmɒnəʊˈveɪlənt/ *adjective* having a valency of one

monoxide /məˈnɒksaɪd/ ◆ **carbon**

monozygotic twins /ˌmɒnəʊzaɪˌgɒtɪk ˈtwɪnz/ *plural noun* same as **identical twins**

mons /mɒnz/ *noun* a fleshy body part which sticks out, especially the one formed by the pad of flesh where the pubic bones join (NOTE: The plural is **montes**.)

mons pubis /ˌmɒnz ˈpjuːbɪs/ *noun* a cushion of fat covering the pubis

monster /ˈmɒnstə/ *noun* a former term for a fetus or infant with severe developmental malformations, usually not able to live

mons veneris /ˌmɒnz vəˈnɪərɪs/ *noun* same as **mons pubis**

Montezuma's revenge /ˌmɒntɪzuːməz rɪ ˈvendʒ/ *noun* a diarrhoea which affects people travelling in foreign countries, often due to eating unwashed fruit or drinking water which has not been boiled (*informal*)

Montgomery's glands /məntˈgʌməriz glændz/ *plural noun* sebaceous glands around the nipple which become more marked in pregnancy [After William Fetherstone Montgomery (1797–1859), Dublin gynaecologist]

mood /muːd/ *noun* a person's mental state at a particular time ○ *a mood of excitement* □ **in a bad mood** feeling angry or irritable □ **in a good mood** feeling happy

moon face /ˈmuːn feɪs/ *noun* a condition in which someone has a round red face, occurring in Cushing's syndrome and when there are too many steroid hormones in the body

Mooren's ulcer /ˈmɔːrənz ˌʌlsə/ *noun* a persistent ulcer of the cornea, found in elderly people [After Albert Mooren (1828–99), ophthalmologist in Düsseldorf, Germany]

morbid /ˈmɔːbɪd/ *adjective* **1.** showing symptoms of being diseased ○ *The X-ray showed a morbid condition of the kidneys.* **2.** referring to disease **3.** referring to an unhealthy mental faculty

morbid anatomy /ˌmɔːbɪd əˈnætəmi/ *noun* same as **pathology**

morbidity /mɔːˈbɪdɪti/ *noun* the condition of being diseased or sick

'...apart from death, coronary heart disease causes considerable morbidity in the form of heart attack, angina and a number of related diseases' [*Health Education Journal*]

morbidity rate /mɔːˈbɪdɪti reɪt/ *noun* the number of cases of a disease per hundred thousand of population

morbilli /mɔːˈbɪli/ *noun* same as **measles**

morbilliform /mɔːˈbɪlifɔːm/ *adjective* referring to a rash which is similar to measles

morbus /ˈmɔːbəs/ *noun* disease

moribund /ˈmɒrɪbʌnd/ *adjective* dying ■ *noun* a dying person

morning /ˈmɔːnɪŋ/ *noun* the first part of the day before 12 o'clock noon

morning-after feeling /ˌmɔːnɪŋ ˈɑːftə ˌfiːlɪŋ/ *noun* ◆ **hangover** (*informal*)

morning-after pill /ˌmɔːnɪŋ ˈɑːftə pɪl/ *noun* a contraceptive pill taken after intercourse. Also called **next-day pill**

morning sickness /ˈmɔːnɪŋ ˌsɪknəs/ *noun* nausea and vomiting experienced by women in the early stages of pregnancy when they get up in the morning

Moro reflex /ˈmɔːrəʊ ˌriːfleks/ *noun* a reflex of a newborn baby when it hears a loud noise (NOTE: The baby is laid on a table and observed to see if it raises its arms when the table is struck.) [After Ernst Moro (1874–1951), paediatrician in Heidelberg, Germany]

morphea /mɔːˈfiə/ *noun* a form of scleroderma, a disease where the skin is replaced by thick connective tissue

morphia /ˈmɔːfiə/ same as **morphine**

morphine /ˈmɔːfiːn/ *noun* an analgesic derived from opium that is used to treat severe pain and may become addictive with prolonged use

morpho- /ˈmɔːfəʊ/ *prefix* relating to form, shape or structure

morphoea /mɔːˈfiə/ *noun* same as **morphea**

morphology /mɔːˈfɒlədʒi/ *noun* the study of the structure and shape of living organisms

-morphous /ˈmɔːfəs/ *suffix* relating to form or structure of a particular type

mortality rate /mɔːˈtælɪti reɪt/ *noun* the number of deaths per year, shown per hundred thousand of population

mortification /ˌmɔːtɪfɪˈkeɪʃ(ə)n/ *noun* ♦ necrosis

mortis /ˈmɔːtɪs/ ♦ rigor

mortuary /ˈmɔːtjuəri/ *noun* a room in a hospital where dead bodies are kept until removed by an undertaker for burial

morula /ˈmɒrʊlə/ *noun* an early stage in the development of the ovum into an embryo, where the cleavage of the ovum creates a mass of cells

mosquito /mɒˈskiːtəʊ/ *noun* an insect which sucks human blood, some species of which can pass viruses or parasites into the bloodstream

COMMENT: In northern countries a mosquito bite merely produces an itchy spot. In tropical countries dengue, filariasis, malaria and yellow fever are transmitted by mosquitoes, and are major causes of morbidity and mortality. Mosquitoes breed in water and they spread rapidly in lakes or canals created by dams and other irrigation schemes as well as in containers of water stored for household use.

mother /ˈmʌðə/ *noun* a biological or adoptive female parent

mother-fixation /ˈmʌðə fɪkˌseɪʃ(ə)n/ *noun* a condition in which a person's development has been stopped at a stage where he or she remains like a child, dependent on his or her mother

motile /ˈməʊtaɪl/ *adjective* referring to a cell or microorganism which can move spontaneously ○ *Sperm cells are extremely motile.*

motility /məʊˈtɪlɪti/ *noun* **1.** (*of cells or microbes*) the fact of being able to move about **2.** (*of the gut*) the action of peristalsis

motion /ˈməʊʃ(ə)n/ *noun* **1.** movement **2.** same as **bowel movement**

motionless /ˈməʊʃ(ə)n(ə)ləs/ *adjective* not moving ○ *Catatonic patients can sit motionless for hours.*

motion sickness /ˌməʊʃ(ə)n ˈsɪknəs/ *noun* illness and nausea felt when travelling. It is caused by the movement of liquid inside the labyrinth of the middle ear and is particularly noticeable in vehicles which are closed, such as planes, coaches or hovercraft. (*informal*)

COMMENT: The movement of liquid inside the labyrinth of the middle ear causes motion sickness, which is particularly noticeable in vehicles which are closed, such as planes, coaches, hovercraft.

motor /ˈməʊtə/ *adjective* referring to movement, which produces movement

motor area /ˈməʊtər ˌeəriə/, **motor cortex** /ˌməʊtə ˈkɔːteks/ *noun* the part of the cortex in the brain which controls voluntary muscle movement by sending impulses to the motor nerves

motor disorder /ˈməʊtə dɪsˌɔːdə/ *noun* impairment of the nerves or neurons that cause muscles to contract to produce movement

motor end plate /ˌməʊtər ˈend pleɪt/ *noun* the end of a motor nerve where it joins muscle fibre

motor nerve /ˈməʊtə nɜːv/ *noun* a nerve which carries impulses from the brain and spinal cord to muscles and causes movements. Also called **efferent nerve**

motor neurone /ˌməʊtə ˈnjʊərəʊn/ *noun* a neurone which is part of a nerve pathway transmitting impulses from the brain to a muscle or gland

motor neurone disease /ˌməʊtə ˈnjʊərəʊn dɪˌziːz/ *noun* a disease of the nerve cells which control the movement of the muscles. Abbr **MND**

COMMENT: Motor neurone disease has three forms: progressive muscular atrophy (PMA), which affects movements of the hands, lateral sclerosis, and bulbar palsy, which affects the mouth and throat.

motor pathway /ˌməʊtə ˈpɑːθweɪ/ *noun* a series of motor neurones leading from the motor cortex to a muscle

mottled /ˈmɒt(ə)ld/ *adjective* with patches of different colours

mountain fever /ˈmaʊntɪn ˌfiːvə/ *noun* same as **brucellosis**

mountain sickness /ˈmaʊntɪn ˌsɪknəs/ *noun* same as **altitude sickness**

mouth /maʊθ/ *noun* an opening at the head of the alimentary canal, through which food and drink are taken in, and through which a person speaks and can breathe ○ *She was sleeping with her mouth open.* (NOTE: For other terms referring to the mouth, see **oral** and words beginning with **stomat-, stomato-**.)

mouthful /ˈmaʊθfʊl/ *noun* the amount which you can hold in your mouth

mouth-to-mouth /ˌmaʊθ tə ˈmaʊθ/, **mouth-to-mouth resuscitation** /ˌmaʊθ tə ˌmaʊθ rɪˌsʌsɪˈteɪʃ(ə)n/, **mouth-to-mouth ventilation** /ˌmaʊθ tə ˌmaʊθ ˌventɪˈleɪʃ(ə)n/ *noun* same as **cardiopulmonary resuscitation** (*informal*)

mouth ulcer /ˈmaʊθ ˌʌlsə/ *noun* a small white ulcer that appears in groups in the mouth and on the tongue

mouthwash /ˈmaʊθwɒʃ/ *noun* an antiseptic solution used to treat infection in the mouth

move /muːv/ *verb* to change from one place to another, or change something from one place to another ○ *Try to move your arm.* ○ *He found he was unable to move.*

movement /ˈmuːvmənt/ *noun* **1.** the act of changing position or the fact of not being still **2.** same as **bowel movement**

moxybustion /ˌmɒksɪˈbʌstʃ(ə)n/ *noun* a treatment used in the Far East, where dried herbs are placed on the skin and set on fire

MP joint /ˌem ˈpiː ˌdʒɔɪnt/ *noun* same as **metacarpophalangeal joint**

MPS *abbr* member of the pharmaceutical society

MRC *abbr* Medical Research Council

MRCGP *abbr* Member of the Royal College of General Practitioners

MRCP *abbr* Member of the Royal College of Physicians

MRCS *abbr* Member of the Royal College of Surgeons

MRI *abbr* magnetic resonance imaging

'...during an MRI scan, the patient lies within a strong magnetic field as selected sections of his body are stimulated with radio frequency waves. Resulting energy changes are measured and used by the MRI computer to generate images.' [*Nursing 87*]

mRNA *abbr* messenger RNA

MRSA *abbr* methicillin-resistant Staphylococcus aureus

MS *abbr* **1.** mitral stenosis **2.** multiple sclerosis

MSH *abbr* melanocyte-stimulating hormone

MSU *abbr* midstream specimen of urine

mSv *abbr* millisievert

mucin /ˈmjuːsɪn/ *noun* a compound of sugars and protein which is the main substance in mucus

muco- /mjuːkəʊ/ *prefix* referring to mucus

mucocele /ˈmjuːkəʊsiːl/ *noun* a cavity containing an accumulation of mucus

mucociliary transport /ˌmjuːkəʊˌsɪliəri ˈtrænspɔːt/ *noun* the process in which the cilia, the microscopic structures within the nose, move mucus towards the oesophagus, cleansing the nose of dust and bacteria

mucocoele /ˈmjuːkəʊsiːl/ *noun* **1.** a condition in which a cavity or organ becomes swollen because there is too much mucus in it **2.** the swelling produced by this condition

mucocutaneous /ˌmjuːkəʊkjuːˈteɪniəs/ *adjective* referring to both mucous membrane and the skin

mucocutaneous leishmaniasis /ˌmjuːkəʊkjuːˌteɪniəs ˌliːʃməˈnaɪəsɪs/ *noun* a disorder affecting the skin and mucous membrane

mucoid /ˈmjuːkɔɪd/ *adjective* similar to mucus

mucolytic /ˌmjuːkəʊˈlɪtɪk/ *noun* a substance which dissolves mucus

mucomembranous colitis /ˌmjuːkəʊ ˌmembrənəs kəˈlaɪtɪs/ *noun* same as **mucous colitis**

mucoprotein /ˌmjuːkəʊˈprəʊtiːn/ *noun* a form of protein found in blood plasma

mucopurulent /ˌmjuːkəʊˈpjʊərʊlənt/ *adjective* consisting of a mixture of mucus and pus

mucopus /ˌmjuːkəʊˈpʌs/ *noun* a mixture of mucus and pus

mucormycosis /ˌmjuːkɔːmaɪˈkəʊsɪs/ *noun* a disease of the ear and throat caused by the fungus *Mucor*

mucosa /mjuːˈkəʊzə/ *noun* same as **mucous membrane** (NOTE: The plural is **mucosae**.)

mucosal /mjuːˈkəʊz(ə)l/ *adjective* referring to a mucous membrane

mucous /ˈmjuːkəs/ *adjective* referring to mucus, covered in mucus

mucous cell /ˈmjuːkəs sel/ *noun* a cell which contains mucinogen which secretes mucin

mucous colic /ˌmjuːkəs ˈkɒlɪk/ *noun* an inflammation of the colon, with painful spasms in the muscles of the walls of the colon

mucous colitis /ˌmjuːkəs kəˈlaɪtɪs/ *noun* an inflammation of the mucous membrane in the intestine, in which the person experiences pain caused by spasms in the muscles of the walls of the colon, accompanied by constipation or diarrhoea or alternating attacks of both. Also called **irritable bowel syndrome**

mucous membrane /ˌmjuːkəs ˈmembreɪn/ *noun* a wet membrane which lines internal passages in the body, e.g. the nose, mouth, stomach and throat, and secretes mucus. Also called **mucosa**

mucous plug /ˈmjuːkəs plʌg/ *noun* a plug of mucus which blocks the cervical canal during pregnancy

mucoviscidosis /ˌmjuːkəʊvɪsɪˈdəʊsɪs/ *noun* same as **cystic fibrosis**

mucus /ˈmjuːkəs/ *noun* a slippery liquid secreted by mucous membranes inside the body, which protects those membranes (NOTE: For other terms referring to mucus, see words beginning with **blenno-**.)

muddled /ˈmʌd(ə)ld/ *adjective* referring to someone whose thought processes are confused

Müllerian duct /mʌˌlɪəriən ˈdʌkt/ *noun* same as **paramesonephric duct** [Described 1825. After Johannes Peter Müller (1801–58), Professor of Anatomy at Bonn, later Professor of Anatomy and Physiology at Berlin, Germany.]

multi- /mʌlti/ *prefix* many

multicentric /ˌmʌltiˈsentrɪk/ *adjective* in several centres

multicentric trial /ˌmʌltisentrɪk ˈtraɪəl/, **multicentric testing** /ˌmʌltisentrɪk ˈtestɪŋ/ *noun* trials carried out in several centres at the same time

multidisciplinary /ˌmʌltiˈdɪsɪplɪnəri/ *adjective* using or involving several specialised subjects or skills ○ *a multidisciplinary team*

multifactorial /ˌmʌltifækˈtɔːriəl/ *adjective* **1.** involving several different factors or elements **2.** referring to inheritance which depends on more than one gene. Height and weight are examples of characteristics determined by multifactorial inheritance.

multifocal lens /ˌmʌltiˌfəʊk(ə)l ˈlenz/ *noun* a lens in spectacles whose focus changes from top to bottom so that the person wearing the spectacles can see objects clearly at different distances

multiforme /'mʌltifɔːm/ ♦ **erythema multiforme**

multigravida /ˌmʌlti'grævidə/ *noun* a pregnant woman who has been pregnant two or more times before

multi-infarct dementia /ˌmʌlti 'ɪnfɑːkt dɪ ˌmenʃə/ *noun* dementia caused by a number of small strokes, when the dementia is not progressive as in Alzheimer's disease but increases in steps as new strokes occur

multilocular /ˌmʌlti'lɒkjulə/ *adjective* referring to a body part or growth which has a lot of separate compartments or locules

multinucleated /ˌmʌlti'njuːklieɪtɪd/ *adjective* referring to a cell with several nuclei, such as a megakaryocyte

multi-organ failure /ˌmʌlti 'ɔːgən ˌfeɪljə/ *noun* an extremely serious condition in which several of the body's organs stop functioning at the same time. The person may survive, depending on how many organs fail and the length of time that the failure lasts. Abbr **MOF**

multipara /mʌl'tɪpərə/ *noun* a woman who has given birth to two or more live children

multiple /'mʌltɪp(ə)l/ *adjective* occurring several times or in several places

multiple birth /ˌmʌltɪp(ə)l 'bɜːθ/ *noun* a birth where more than one child is born at the same time

multiple fracture /ˌmʌltɪp(ə)l 'fræktʃə/ *noun* a condition in which a bone is broken in several places

multiple myeloma /ˌmʌltɪp(ə)l ˌmaɪə 'ləʊmə/ *noun* a malignant tumour in bone marrow, most often affecting flat bones

multiple organ dysfunction syndrome /ˌmʌltɪp(ə)l ˌɔːgən dɪs'fʌŋkʃ(ə)n ˌsɪn drəʊm/ *noun* a state of continuous disturbances and abnormalities in organ systems, rather than true failure, e.g. following trauma and sepsis. It is often fatal. Abbr **MODS**

multiple pregnancy /ˌmʌltɪp(ə)l 'pregnənsi/ *noun* a pregnancy where the mother is going to give birth to more than one child

multiple sclerosis /ˌmʌltɪp(ə)l sklə 'rəʊsɪs/ *noun* a nervous disease which gets progressively worse, where patches of the fibres of the central nervous system lose their myelin, causing numbness in the limbs and progressive weakness and paralysis. Abbr **MS**. Also called **disseminated sclerosis**. ◊ **arteriosclerosis, atherosclerosis**

multipolar neurone /mʌlti,pəʊlə 'njʊərəʊn/ *noun* a neurone with several processes. See illustration at **NEURONE** in Supplement. Compare **bipolar neurone, unipolar neurone**

multiresistant /ˌmʌltiri'zɪstənt/ *adjective* resistant to several types of antibiotic

multivitamin /'mʌltiˌvɪtəmɪn/ *noun* a preparation containing several vitamins and sometimes minerals, used as a dietary supplement ■ *adjective* referring to a preparation containing several vitamins, and sometimes minerals ○ *multivitamin pills* ○ *multivitamin supplement*

mumps /mʌmps/ *noun* an infectious disease of children, with fever and swellings in the salivary glands, caused by a paramyxovirus ○ *He caught mumps from the children next door.* Also called **infectious parotitis** (NOTE: Takes a singular or a plural verb.)

COMMENT: Mumps is a relatively mild disease in children. In adult males it can have serious complications and cause inflammation of the testicles (mumps orchitis).

Münchausen's syndrome /'mʌnt ʃaʊz(ə)nz ˌsɪndrəʊm/ *noun* a mental disorder in which someone tries to get hospital treatment by claiming symptoms of an illness which he or she does not have. Many people will undergo very painful procedures which they do not need. [Described by Richard Asher in 1951, and named after Baron von Münchhausen, a 16th century traveller and inveterate liar]

Münchausen's syndrome by proxy /ˌmʌntʃaʊz(ə)nz ˌsɪndrəʊm baɪ 'prɒksi/ *noun* a mental disorder in which someone tries to get hospital treatment for someone else such as their child or an elderly relative. It is regarded as a form of child abuse, as the person may cause a child to be ill in order to receive attention.

mural thrombus /ˌmjʊərəl 'θrɒmbəs/ *noun* a thrombus which forms on the wall of a vein or artery

murder /'mɜːdə/ *noun* the crime of killing someone intentionally ■ *verb* to kill someone intentionally

murmur /'mɜːmə/ *noun* a sound, usually the sound of the heart, heard through a stethoscope

Murphy's sign /'mɜːfiz saɪn/ *noun* a sign of an inflamed gall bladder, where the person will experience pain if the abdomen is pressed while he or she inhales [Described 1912. After John Benjamin Murphy (1857–1916), US surgeon.]

muscae volitantes /ˌmʌskaɪ ˌvɒlɪ 'tænteɪz/ *plural noun* pieces of cellular or blood debris present in the vitreous of the eye, common in old age but, if a sudden event, can be a symptom of retinal haemorrhage. Also called **floaters**

muscarine /'mʌskəriːn/ *noun* a poison found in fungi

muscarinic /ˌmʌskə'rɪnɪk/ *adjective* referring to a neurone or receptor stimulated by acetylcholine and muscarine

muscle /'mʌs(ə)l/ *noun* **1.** an organ in the body, which contracts to make part of the body move ○ *If you do a lot of exercises you develop strong muscles.* ○ *The muscles in his legs were still weak after he had spent two months in bed.* ○ *She had muscle cramp after going into the cold water.* See illustration at EYE in Supplement 2. same as **muscle tissue**

COMMENT: There are two types of muscle: voluntary (striated) muscles, which are attached to bones and move parts of the body when made to do so by the brain, and involuntary (smooth) muscles which move essential organs such as the intestines and bladder automatically. The heart muscle also works automatically.

muscle coat /'mʌs(ə)l kəʊt/ *noun* one of two layers of muscle forming part of the lining of the intestine

muscle fatigue /'mʌs(ə)l fə,tiːg/, **muscular fatigue** /,mʌskjʊlə fə'tiːg/ *noun* tiredness in the muscles after strenuous exercise

muscle fibre /'mʌs(ə)l ,faɪbə/ *noun* a component fibre of muscles (NOTE: There are two types of fibre which form striated and smooth muscles.)

muscle relaxant /'mʌs(ə)l rɪ,læksənt/ *noun* a drug which reduces contractions in the muscles, e.g. baclofen

muscle spasm /'mʌs(ə)l ,spæz(ə)m/ *noun* a sudden contraction of a muscle

muscle spindle /'mʌs(ə)l ,spɪnd(ə)l/ *noun* one of the sensory receptors which lie along striated muscle fibres

muscle tissue /'mʌs(ə)l ,tɪʃuː/, **muscular tissue** /,mʌskjʊlə 'tɪʃuː/ *noun* the specialised type of tissue which forms the muscles and which can contract and expand

muscle wasting /'mʌs(ə)l ,weɪstɪŋ/ *noun* a condition in which the muscles lose weight and become thin

muscular /'mʌskjʊlə/ *adjective* referring to muscle

muscular branch /'mʌskjʊlə brɑːntʃ/ *noun* a branch of a nerve to a muscle carrying efferent impulses to produce contraction

muscular defence /,mʌskjʊlə dɪ'fens/ *noun* a rigidity of muscles associated with inflammation such as peritonitis

muscular disorder /'mʌskjʊlə dɪs,ɔːdə/ *noun* a disorder which affects the muscles, e.g. cramp or strain

muscular dystrophy /,mʌskjʊlə 'dɪstrəfi/ *noun* a type of muscle disease where some muscles become weak and are replaced with fatty tissue. ◊ **Duchenne muscular dystrophy**

muscular fatigue /,mʌskjʊlə fə'tiːg/ *noun* same as **muscle fatigue**

muscularis /,mʌskjʊ'leərɪs/ *noun* muscular layer of an internal organ

muscular relaxant /,mʌskjʊlə rɪ'læksənt/ *noun* a drug which relaxes the muscles

muscular rheumatism /,mʌskjʊlə 'ruːmə,tɪz(ə)m/ *noun* a disease giving pains in the

back or neck, usually caused by fibrositis or inflammation of the muscles

muscular system /'mʌskjʊlə ,sɪstəm/ *noun* the muscles in the body, usually applied only to striated muscles

muscular tissue /,mʌskjʊlə 'tɪʃuː/ *noun* same as **muscle tissue**

musculo- /mʌskjʊləʊ/ *prefix* relating to or affecting muscle

musculocutaneous /,mʌskjʊləʊkjuː'teɪniəs/ *adjective* referring to muscle and skin

musculocutaneous nerve /,mʌskjʊləʊ kjuː,teɪniəs 'nɜːv/ *noun* a nerve in the brachial plexus which supplies the muscles in the arm

musculoskeletal /,mʌskjʊləʊ'skelɪt(ə)l/ *adjective* referring to muscles and bone

musculotendinous /,mʌskjʊləʊ'tendɪnəs/ *adjective* referring to both muscular and tendinous tissue

mutant /'mjuːt(ə)nt/ *adjective* in which mutation has occurred ■ *noun* an organism carrying a mutant gene

mutant gene /,mjuːt(ə)nt 'dʒiːn/ *noun* a gene which has undergone mutation

mutate /mjuː'teɪt/ *verb* to undergo a genetic change ○ *Bacteria can mutate suddenly, and become increasingly able to infect.*

mutation /mjuː'teɪʃ(ə)n/ *noun* a change in DNA which changes the physiological effect of the DNA on the cell

COMMENT: A mutation in the gene for amyloid precursor protein (APP) in some families causes early-onset Alzheimer's disease, when unusual deposits of beta amyloid are formed and dementia occurs.

mute /mjuːt/ *adjective* 1. unwilling or unable to speak 2. felt or expressed without speech ■ *noun* somebody who is unable or unwilling to speak (NOTE: This term is sometimes considered offensive.)

mutism /'mjuːtɪz(ə)m/ *noun* the condition of being unable to speak. Also called **dumbness**

my- /maɪ/ *prefix* same as **myo-** (*used before vowels*)

myalgia /maɪ'ældʒə/ *noun* a muscle pain

myalgic encephalomyelitis /maɪ,ældʒɪk en,kefələʊmaɪə'laɪtɪs/ *noun* a long-term condition affecting the nervous system, in which someone feels tired and depressed and has pain and weakness in the muscles. Abbr **ME**. Also called **chronic fatigue syndrome**, **postviral fatigue syndrome**

myasthenia /,maɪəs'θiːniə/, **myasthenia gravis** /,maɪəs,θiːniə 'grɑːvɪs/ *noun* a general weakness and dysfunction of the muscles, caused by poor conduction at the motor end plates

myc- /maɪk, maɪs/ *prefix* same as **myco-** (*used before vowels*)

mycelium /maɪˈsiːliəm/ *noun* a mass of threads which forms the main part of a fungus

mycetoma /ˌmaɪsɪˈtəʊmə/ *noun* same as **maduromycosis**

myco- /maɪkəʊ/ *prefix* referring to fungus

Mycobacterium /ˌmaɪkəʊbækˈtɪəriəm/ *noun* one of a group of bacteria including those which cause leprosy and tuberculosis

mycology /maɪˈkɒlədʒi/ *noun* the study of fungi

Mycoplasma /ˈmaɪkəʊˌplæzmə/ *noun* a type of microorganism, similar to a bacterium, associated with diseases such as pneumonia and urethritis

mycosis /maɪˈkəʊsɪs/ *noun* any disease caused by a fungus, e.g. athlete's foot

mycosis fungoides /maɪˌkəʊsɪs fʌŋ ˈɡɔɪdiz/ *noun* a form of skin cancer, with irritating nodules

mydriasis /maɪˈdraɪəsɪs/ *noun* an enlargement of the pupil of the eye

mydriatic /ˌmɪdriˈætɪk/ *noun* a drug which makes the pupil of the eye become larger

myectomy /maɪˈektəmi/ *noun* the surgical removal of part or all of a muscle

myel- /maɪəl/ *prefix* same as **myelo-** (*used before vowels*)

myelin /ˈmaɪəlɪn/ *noun* the substance of the cell membrane of Schwann cells that coils into a protective covering around nerve fibres called a myelin sheath

myelinated /ˈmaɪəlɪneɪtɪd/ *adjective* referring to nerve fibre covered by a myelin sheath

myelination /ˌmaɪəlɪˈneɪʃ(ə)n/ *noun* the process by which a myelin sheath forms around nerve fibres

myelin sheath /ˈmaɪəlɪn ʃiːθ/ *noun* a layer of myelin that insulates some nerve cells and speeds the conduction of nerve impulses. See illustration at **NEURONE** in Supplement

myelitis /ˌmaɪəˈlaɪtɪs/ *noun* **1.** inflammation of the spinal cord **2.** an inflammation of bone marrow

myelo- /maɪələʊ/ *prefix* **1.** referring to bone marrow **2.** referring to the spinal cord

myeloblast /ˈmaɪələblæst/ *noun* a precursor of a granulocyte

myelocele /ˈmaɪələsiːl/ *noun* same as **meningomyelocele**

myelocyte /ˈmaɪələsaɪt/ *noun* a cell in bone marrow which develops into a granulocyte

myelofibrosis /ˌmaɪələfaɪˈbrəʊsɪs/ *noun* fibrosis of bone marrow, associated with anaemia

myelogram /ˈmaɪələɡræm/ *noun* a record of the spinal cord taken by myelography

myelography /ˌmaɪəˈlɒɡrəfi/ *noun* an X-ray examination of the spinal cord and subarachnoid space after a radio-opaque substance has been injected

myeloid /ˈmaɪəlɔɪd/ *adjective* **1.** referring to bone marrow, or produced by bone marrow **2.** referring to the spinal cord

myeloid leukaemia /ˌmaɪəlɔɪd luːˈkiːmiə/ *noun* an acute form of leukaemia in adults

myeloid tissue /ˈmaɪəlɔɪd ˌtɪʃuː/ *noun* red bone marrow

myeloma /ˌmaɪəˈləʊmə/ *noun* a malignant tumour in bone marrow, at the ends of long bones or in the jaw

myelomalacia /ˌmaɪələʊməˈleɪʃə/ *noun* softening of tissue in the spinal cord

myelomatosis /ˌmaɪələʊməˈtəʊsɪs/ *noun* a disease where malignant tumours infiltrate the bone marrow

myelomeningocele /ˌmaɪələʊməˈnɪŋɡəʊ siːl/ *noun* same as **meningomyelocele**

myelopathy /ˌmaɪəˈlɒpəθi/ *noun* any disorder of the spinal cord or bone marrow

myelosuppression /ˌmaɪələʊsəˈpreʃ(ə)n/ *noun* a condition in which the bone marrow does not produce enough blood cells, often occurring after chemotherapy

myenteron /maɪˈentərɒn/ *noun* a layer of muscles in the small intestine, which produces peristalsis

myiasis /ˈmaɪəsɪs/ *noun* an infestation by larvae of flies

mylohyoid /ˌmaɪləˈhaɪɔɪd/ *noun, adjective* referring to the molar teeth in the lower jaw and the hyoid bone

mylohyoid line /ˌmaɪləˈhaɪɔɪd ˌlaɪn/ *noun* a line running along the outside of the lower jawbone, dividing the upper part of the bone which forms part of the mouth from the lower part which is part of the neck

myo- /maɪəʊ/ *prefix* referring to muscle

myoblast /ˈmaɪəblæst/ *noun* an embryonic cell which develops into muscle

myoblastic /ˌmaɪəʊˈblæstɪk/ *adjective* referring to myoblast

myocardial /ˌmaɪəʊˈkɑːdiəl/ *adjective* referring to the myocardium

myocardial infarction /ˌmaɪəʊˌkɑːdiəl ɪn ˈfɑːkʃən/ *noun* the death of part of the heart muscle after coronary thrombosis. Abbr **MI**

myocarditis /ˌmaɪəʊkɑːˈdaɪtɪs/ *noun* inflammation of the heart muscle

myocardium /ˌmaɪəʊˈkɑːdiəm/ *noun* the middle layer of the wall of the heart, formed of heart muscle. See illustration at **HEART** in Supplement

myocele /ˈmaɪəsiːl/ *noun* a condition in which a muscle pushes through a gap in the surrounding membrane

myoclonic /ˌmaɪəʊˈklɒnɪk/ *adjective* referring to myoclonus

myoclonic epilepsy /ˌmaɪəʊklɒnɪk ˈepɪ lepsi/ *noun* a form of epilepsy where the limbs jerk frequently

myoclonus /maɪ'ɒklənəs/ *noun* a muscle spasm which makes a limb give an involuntary jerk

myocyte /'maɪəʊsaɪt/ *noun* a muscle cell

myodynia /ˌmaɪəʊ'dɪniə/ *noun* a pain in the muscles

myofibril /ˌmaɪəʊ'faɪbrɪl/ *noun* a long thread of striated muscle fibre

myofibrosis /ˌmaɪəʊfaɪ'brəʊsɪs/ *noun* a condition in which muscle tissue is replaced by fibrous tissue

myogenic /ˌmaɪəʊ'dʒenɪk/ *adjective* referring to movement which comes from an involuntary muscle

myoglobin /ˌmaɪəʊ'ɡləʊbɪn/ *noun* a muscle haemoglobin, which takes oxygen from blood and passes it to the muscle

myoglobinuria /ˌmaɪəʊˌɡləʊbɪ'njʊəriə/ *noun* the presence of myoglobin in the urine

myogram /'maɪəʊɡræm/ *noun* a record showing how a muscle is functioning

myograph /'maɪəʊɡrɑːf/ *noun* an instrument which records the degree and strength of a muscle contraction

myography /maɪ'ɒɡrəfi/ *noun* the process of recording the degree and strength of a muscle contraction with a myograph

myokymia /ˌmaɪəʊ'kɪmiə/ *noun* twitching of a particular muscle

myology /maɪ'ɒlədʒi/ *noun* the study of muscles and associated structures and diseases

myoma /maɪ'əʊmə/ *noun* a benign tumour in a smooth muscle

myomectomy /ˌmaɪəʊ'mektəmi/ *noun* **1.** the surgical removal of a benign growth from a muscle, especially removal of a fibroid from the uterus **2.** same as **myectomy**

myometritis /ˌmaɪəʊmə'traɪtɪs/ *noun* inflammation of the myometrium. Also called **metritis**

myometrium /ˌmaɪəʊ'miːtriəm/ *noun* the muscular tissue in the uterus

myoneural /ˌmaɪəʊ'njʊərəl/ *adjective* relating to or involving both the muscles and the nerves

myoneural junction /ˌmaɪəʊnjʊər(ə)l 'dʒʌŋkʃ(ə)n/ *noun* same as **neuromuscular junction**

myopathy /maɪ'ɒpəθi/ *noun* a disease of a muscle, especially one in which the muscle wastes away

myopia /maɪ'əʊpiə/ *noun* a condition in which someone can see clearly objects which are close, but not ones which are further away. Also called **shortsightedness**. Opposite **longsightedness**

myopic /maɪ'ɒpɪk/ *adjective* able to see close objects clearly, but not objects which are further away. Also called **shortsighted**

myoplasm /'maɪəʊplæz(ə)m/ *noun* same as **sarcoplasm**

myoplasty /'maɪəʊplæsti/ *noun* a form of plastic surgery to repair a muscle

myosarcoma /ˌmaɪəʊsɑː'kəʊmə/ *noun* **1.** a malignant tumour containing unstriated muscle **2.** combined myoma and sarcoma

myosis /maɪ'əʊsɪs/ *noun* another spelling of **miosis 1**

myositis /ˌmaɪəʊ'saɪtɪs/ *noun* inflammation and degeneration of a muscle

myotatic /ˌmaɪəʊ'tætɪk/ *adjective* referring to the sense of touch in a muscle

myotatic reflex /ˌmaɪəʊtætɪk 'riːfleks/ *noun* a reflex action in a muscle which contracts after being stretched

myotic /maɪ'ɒtɪk/ *noun* a drug which causes the pupil of the eye to contract

myotomy /maɪ'ɒtəmi/ *noun* a surgical operation to cut a muscle

myotonia /ˌmaɪəʊ'təʊniə/ *noun* difficulty in relaxing a muscle after exercise

myotonic /ˌmaɪəʊ'tɒnɪk/ *adjective* referring to tone in a muscle

myotonic dystrophy /ˌmaɪəʊtɒnɪk 'dɪstrəfi/ *noun* a hereditary disease with muscle stiffness leading to atrophy of the muscles of the face and neck

myotonus /maɪ'ɒtənəs/ *noun* a muscle tone

myringa /mɪ'rɪŋɡə/ *noun* same as **eardrum**

myringitis /ˌmɪrɪn'dʒaɪtɪs/ *noun* inflammation of the eardrum

myringoplasty /mɪ'rɪŋɡəʊplæsti/ *noun* the surgical repair of a perforated eardrum. Also called **tympanoplasty**

myringotome /mɪ'rɪŋɡəʊtəʊm/ *noun* a sharp knife used in myringotomy

myringotomy /ˌmɪrɪŋ'ɡɒtəmi/ *noun* a surgical operation to make an opening in the eardrum to allow fluid to escape

myx- /mɪks/, **myxo-** /mɪksəʊ/ *prefix* referring to mucus

myxoedema /ˌmɪksə'diːmə/ *noun* a condition caused when the thyroid gland does not produce enough thyroid hormone. The person, often a middle-aged woman, becomes overweight, moves slowly and develops coarse skin. It can be treated with thyroxine. (NOTE: The US spelling is **myxedema**.)

myxoedematous /ˌmɪksə'demətəs/ *adjective* referring to myxoedema

myxoid cyst /ˌmɪksɔɪd 'sɪst/ *noun* a cyst which develops at the base of a fingernail or toenail

myxoma /mɪk'səʊmə/ *noun* a benign tumour of mucous tissue, usually found in subcutaneous tissue of the limbs and neck

myxosarcoma /ˌmɪksəʊsɑː'kəʊmə/ *noun* a malignant tumour of mucous tissue

myxovirus /ˌmɪksəʊ'vaɪrəs/ *noun* any virus which has an affinity for the mucoprotein receptors in red blood cells. One of these viruses causes influenza.

N

n *symbol* nano-

nabothian cyst /nə,bəʊθiən 'sɪst/, **nabothian follicle** /nə,bəʊθiən 'fɒlɪk(ə)l/, **nabothian
gland** /nə,bəʊθiən 'glænd/ *noun* a cyst which
forms in the cervix of the uterus when the
ducts in the cervical glands are blocked

Naegele rule /'neɪɡələ ruːl/ *noun* a method
used to determine when a pregnant woman is
likely to go into labour, in which nine months
and seven days are added to the date on which
her last period started. If the woman does not
have a 28-day menstrual cycle, an adjustment
is made: e.g., if she has a 26-day cycle you
would subtract 2 days from the Naegele's estimated due date.

naevus /'niːvəs/ *noun* same as **birthmark**
(NOTE: The plural is **naevi**.)

Naga sore /'nɑːɡə sɔː/ *noun* same as **tropical
ulcer**

nagging pain /,næɡɪŋ 'peɪn/ *noun* a dull,
continuous throbbing pain

NAI *abbr* non-accidental injury

nail /neɪl/ *noun* a hard growth, made of keratin, which forms on the top surface at the end
of each finger and toe. Also called **unguis**
(NOTE: For terms referring to nail, see words beginning with **onych-, onycho-**.)

nail avulsion /'neɪl ə,vʌlʃən/ *noun* the act of
pulling away an ingrowing toenail

nail bed /'neɪl bed/ *noun* the part of the finger
which is just under the nail and on which the
nail rests

nail biting /'neɪl ,baɪtɪŋ/ *noun* the obsessive
chewing of the fingernails, usually a sign of
stress

nail matrix /neɪl 'meɪtrɪks/ *noun* the internal
structure of the nail, the part of the finger from
which the nail grows

naloxone /nə'lɒksəʊn/ *noun* a drug resembling morphine, used in the diagnosis of narcotics addiction and to reverse the effects of
narcotics poisoning

named nurse /,neɪmd 'nɜːs/ *noun* a nurse,
midwife or health visitor who is responsible
for communicating with a particular person
and ensuring that his or her needs for care and
information are met

nandrolone /'nændrələʊn/ *noun* an anabolic
steroid which builds muscle. Its use is banned
by the International Amateur Athletics Feder-
ation.

nano- /nænəʊ/ *prefix* one thousand millionth
(10^{-9}). Symbol **n**

nanometre /'nænəʊmitə/ *noun* a unit of
measurement of length equal to one thousand
millionth of a metre. Symbol **nm**

nanomole /'nænəʊməʊl/ *noun* a unit of
measurement of the amount of a substance
equal to one thousand millionth of a mole.
Symbol **nmol**

nanosecond /'nænəʊ,sekənd/ *noun* a unit
of measurement of time equal to one thousand
millionth of a second. Symbol **ns**

nape /neɪp/ *noun* the back of the neck. Also
called **nucha**

napkin /'næpkɪn/ *noun* a soft cloth, used for
wiping or absorbing

nappy /'næpi/ *noun* a cloth used to wrap
round a baby's bottom and groin, to keep
clothing clean and dry (NOTE: The US term is
diaper.)

nappy rash /'næpi ræʃ/ *noun* sore red skin
on a baby's buttocks and groin, caused by long
contact with ammonia in a wet nappy (NOTE:
The US term is **diaper rash**.)

naproxen /næ'prɒksen/ *noun* a drug which
reduces inflammation and pain, used in the
treatment of arthritis

narcissism /'nɑːsɪsɪz(ə)m/ *noun* in psychiatry, a personality disorder in which someone
has a very confident opinion about their own
appearance and abilities, and a great need to be
admired by other people. It sometimes involves sexual interest in their own body.

narco- /nɑːkəʊ/ *prefix* referring to sleep or
stupor

narcoanalysis /,nɑːkəʊə'næləsɪs/ *noun* the
use of narcotics to induce a comatose state in
someone about to undergo psychoanalysis
which may be emotionally disturbing

narcolepsy /'nɑːkəlepsi/ *noun* a condition
in which someone has an uncontrollable tendency to fall asleep at any time

narcoleptic /ˌnɑːkəˈleptɪk/ *adjective* **1.** causing narcolepsy **2.** having narcolepsy ■ *noun* **1.** a substance which causes narcolepsy **2.** someone who has narcolepsy

narcosis /nɑːˈkəʊsɪs/ *noun* a state of lowered consciousness induced by a drug

narcotic /nɑːˈkɒtɪk/ *noun* a pain-relieving drug which makes someone sleep or become unconscious ○ *The doctor put her to sleep with a powerful narcotic.* ■ *adjective* causing sleep or unconsciousness ○ *the narcotic side-effects of an antihistamine*

COMMENT: Although narcotics are used medicinally as painkillers, they are highly addictive. The main narcotics are barbiturates, cocaine and opium, and drugs derived from opium, such as morphine, codeine and heroin. Addictive narcotics are widely used for the relief of pain in terminally ill patients.

nares /ˈneəriːz/ *plural noun* the nostrils (NOTE: The singular is **naris**.)

narrow /ˈnærəʊ/ *adjective* not wide ○ *The blood vessel is a narrow channel which takes blood to the tissues.* ○ *The surgeon inserted a narrow tube into the vein.* ■ *verb* to make something narrow, or become narrow ○ *The bronchial tubes are narrowed causing asthma.*

nasal /ˈneɪz(ə)l/ *adjective* referring to the nose

nasal apertures /ˌneɪz(ə)l ˈæpətʃəs/ *plural noun* the two openings shaped like funnels leading from the nasal cavity to the pharynx. ◊ **choana**

nasal bone /ˈneɪz(ə)l bəʊn/ *noun* one of two small bones which form the bridge at the top of the nose

nasal cartilage /ˈneɪz(ə)l ˌkɑːtəlɪdʒ/ *noun* one of two cartilages in the nose. The upper is attached to the nasal bone and the front of the maxilla. The lower is thinner and curls round each nostril to the septum.

nasal cavity /ˌneɪz(ə)l ˈkævɪti/ *noun* the cavity behind the nose between the cribriform plates above and the hard palate below, divided in two by the nasal septum and leading to the nasopharynx

nasal conchae /ˌneɪz(ə)l ˈkɒŋkiː/ *plural noun* the three ridges of bone, called the superior, middle and inferior conchae, which project into the nasal cavity from the side walls. Also called **turbinate bones**

nasal congestion /ˌneɪz(ə)l kənˈdʒestʃ(ə)n/ *noun* the blocking of the nose by inflammation as a response to a cold or other infection

nasal drops /ˈneɪz(ə)l drɒps/ *plural noun* drops of liquid inserted into the nose

nasal septum /ˌneɪz(ə)l ˈseptəm/ *noun* a wall of cartilage between the two nostrils and the two parts of the nasal cavity

nasal spray /ˈneɪz(ə)l spreɪ/ *noun* a spray of liquid into the nose

nascent /ˈnæs(ə)nt, ˈneɪs(ə)nt/ *adjective* **1.** in the process of coming into existence and starting to develop **2.** referring to a substance, especially hydrogen, in the process of being created. At this stage it is often in a highly active form.

Naseptin /næˈseptɪn/ a trade name for a mixture containing chlorhexidine and neomycin, used to treat nasal infection by organisms such as staphylococci

nasion /ˈneɪziən/ *noun* the place at which the bridge of the nose meets the forehead

naso- /neɪzəʊ/ *prefix* referring to the nose

nasogastric /ˌneɪzəʊˈgæstrɪk/ *adjective* referring to the nose and stomach

nasogastrically /ˌneɪzəʊˈgæstrɪkli/ *adverb* referring to a method of feeding someone via a tube passed through the nose into the stomach

'…all patients requiring nutrition are fed enterally, whether nasogastrically or directly into the small intestine' [*British Journal of Nursing*]

nasogastric tube /ˌneɪzəʊˌgæstrɪk ˈtjuːb/ *noun* a tube passed through the nose into the stomach

nasolacrimal /ˌneɪzəʊˈlækrɪm(ə)l/ *adjective* referring to the nose and the tear glands

nasolacrimal duct /ˌneɪzəʊˌlækrɪm(ə)l ˈdʌkt/ *noun* a duct which drains tears from the lacrimal sac into the nose

nasopharyngeal /ˌneɪzəʊˌfærɪnˈdʒiːəl/ *adjective* referring to the nasopharynx

nasopharyngitis /ˌneɪzəʊˌfærɪnˈdʒaɪtɪs/ *noun* inflammation of the mucous membrane of the nasal part of the pharynx

nasopharynx /ˌneɪzəʊˈfærɪŋks/ *noun* the top part of the pharynx which connects with the nose

nasosinusitis /ˌneɪzəʊˌsaɪnəˈsaɪtɪs/ *noun* a condition in which the nose and sinuses swell up

nasty /ˈnɑːsti/ *adjective* unpleasant ○ *This medicine has a nasty taste.* ○ *This new drug has some nasty side-effects.* (NOTE: **nastier** – **nastiest**)

nates /ˈneɪtiːz/ *noun* same as **buttock**

National Boards /ˌnæʃ(ə)nəl ˈbɔːdz/ *plural noun* the National Boards for Nursing, Midwifery, and Health Visiting, which were formerly responsible for the education of professionals in these fields in England, Wales, Scotland and Northern Ireland

National Council for Vocational Qualifications /ˌnæʃ(ə)nəl ˌkaʊns(ə)l fə vəʊˌkeɪʃ(ə)nəl ˌkwɒlɪfɪˈkeɪʃ(ə)nz/ *noun* full form of **NCVQ**

National Health Service /ˌnæʃ(ə)nəl ˈhelθ ˌsɜːvɪs/ *noun* a government service in the UK which provides medical services free of charge at the point of delivery, or at reduced cost, to the whole population. The service is paid for out of tax revenue. Abbr **NHS** □ **on the NHS** paid for by the NHS ○ *He had his operation on* *the NHS.* ○ *She went to see a specialist on the NHS.* Compare **privately**

'...figures reveal that 5% more employees in the professional and technical category were working in the NHS compared with three years before' [*Nursing Times*]

National Institute for Clinical Excellence /ˌnæʃ(ə)n(ə)l ˌɪnstɪtjuːt fə ˌklɪnɪk(ə)l 'eksələns/ *noun* an organisation in the UK which produces recommendations for treatments based on clinical evidence and cost-effectiveness. Abbr **NICE**

National Insurance /ˌnæʃ(ə)nəl ɪn'ʃʊərəns/ *noun* a weekly payment from a person's wages, with a supplement from the employer, which pays for state assistance and medical treatment, in the UK

natriuretic /ˌneɪtrɪjʊ'retɪk/ *noun* something which helps sodium to be excreted in the urine

natural /'nætʃ(ə)rəl/ *adjective* **1.** usual or expected in particular conditions ○ *It's natural for people to be anxious before an operation.* **2.** referring to something which comes from nature and is not made by humans ○ *natural products* **3.** relaxed and not consciously changed ○ *His behaviour seemed quite natural.*

natural childbirth /ˌnætʃ(ə)rəl 'tʃaɪldbɜːθ/ *noun* childbirth where the mother is not given any pain-killing drugs or anaesthetic but is encouraged to give birth after having prepared herself through relaxation and breathing exercises and a new psychological outlook

natural immunity /ˌnætʃ(ə)rəl ɪ'mjuːnɪti/ *noun* the immunity from disease which a newborn baby has from birth and which is inherited or acquired in the uterus or from the mother's milk

natural killer cell /ˌnætʃ(ə)rəl 'kɪlə sel/ *noun* a white blood cell which can recognise microorganisms and tumour cells as foreign without any previous exposure to them, and destroy them

natural mother /ˌnætʃ(ə)rəl 'mʌðə/, **natural parent** /ˌnætʃ(ə)rəl 'peərənt/ *noun* same as **birth mother, birth parent**

nature /'neɪtʃə/ *noun* **1.** the essential quality of something **2.** kind or sort **3.** the genetic make-up which affects personality, behaviour or risk of disease. ◊ **nurture 4.** plants and animals

nature nurture debate /ˌneɪtʃə 'nɜːtʃə dɪ ˌbeɪt/ *noun* the arguments put forward about whether human beings behave in the way they do because of their genetic make-up and instincts or because of the way they are educated and the influences they are exposed to when they are young

naturopathy /ˌneɪtʃə'rɒpəθi/ *noun* a method of treatment of diseases and disorders which does not use medical or surgical means, but

natural forces such as light, heat, massage, eating natural foods and using herbal remedies

nausea /'nɔːziə/ *noun* a feeling that you want to vomit ○ *She suffered from nausea in the morning.* ○ *He felt slight nausea after getting onto the boat.*

COMMENT: Nausea can be caused by eating habits, such as eating too much rich food or drinking too much alcohol. It can also be caused by sensations such as unpleasant smells or motion sickness. Other causes include stomach disorders, such as gastritis, ulcers and liver infections. Nausea is commonly experienced by women in the early stages of pregnancy, and is called morning sickness.

nauseated /'nɔːzieɪtɪd/ *adjective* feeling as if you are about to vomit ○ *The casualty may feel nauseated.* (NOTE: The US term is **nauseous**.)

nauseous /'nɔːziəs/ *adjective* having the feeling in the stomach that precedes the urge to vomit

navel /'neɪv(ə)l/ *noun* the scar with a depression in the middle of the abdomen where the umbilical cord was detached after birth. Also called **umbilicus** (NOTE: For other terms referring to the navel, see words beginning with **omphal-, omphalo-**.)

navicular /nə'vɪkjʊlə/ *adjective* relating to a navicular bone ■ *noun* same as **navicular bone**

navicular bone /nə'vɪkjʊlə bəʊn/ *noun* one of the tarsal bones in the foot. See illustration at FOOT in Supplement

NCVQ *noun* a government body in the UK responsible for setting standards of qualification for specific jobs. Full form **National Council for Vocational Qualifications**

NDU *abbr* Nursing Development Unit

nearsighted /nɪə'saɪtɪd/ *adjective* same as **myopic**

nearsightedness /ˌnɪə'saɪtɪdnəs/ *noun* same as **myopia**

nebula /'nebjʊlə/ *noun* **1.** a slightly cloudy spot on the cornea **2.** a spray of medicinal solution, applied to the nose or throat using a nebuliser

nebuliser /'nebjʊlaɪzə/, **nebulizer** *noun* same as **atomiser**

Necator /ne'keɪtə/ *noun* a genus of hookworm which infests the small intestine

necatoriasis /neˌkeɪtə'raɪəsɪs/ *noun* infestation of the small intestine by the parasite Necator

neck /nek/ *noun* **1.** the part of the body which joins the head to the body ○ *He is suffering from pains in the neck.* ○ *The front of the neck is swollen with goitre.* ○ *The jugular veins run down the side of the neck.* **2.** a narrow part of a bone or organ □ **neck of the femur, femoral neck** the narrow part between the head and the diaphysis of the femur □ **neck of a tooth** point where a tooth narrows slightly, between the crown and the root

COMMENT: The neck is formed of the seven cervical vertebrae, and is held vertical by strong muscles. Many organs pass through the neck, including the oesophagus, the larynx and the arteries and veins which connect the brain to the bloodstream. The front of the neck is usually referred to as the throat.

neck collar /ˈnek ˌkɒlə/ *noun* a strong high collar to support the head of a person with neck injuries or a condition such as cervical spondylosis

necro- /nekrəʊ/ *prefix* referring to death

necrobiosis /ˌnekrəʊbaɪˈəʊsɪs/ *noun* **1.** the death of cells surrounded by living tissue **2.** the gradual localised death of a part or tissue

necrology /neˈkrɒlədʒi/ *noun* the scientific study of mortality statistics

necrophilia /ˌnekrəʊˈfɪliə/, **necrophilism** /neˈkrɒfɪlɪz(ə)m/ *noun* **1.** unusual pleasure in corpses **2.** sexual attraction to dead bodies

necropsy /ˈnekrɒpsi/ *noun* same as **post mortem**

necrosed /ˈnekrəʊsd/ *adjective* referring to dead tissue or bone

necrosis /neˈkrəʊsɪs/ *noun* the death of a part of the body such as a bone, tissue or an organ as a result of disease or injury ○ *Gangrene is a form of necrosis.*

necrospermia /ˌnekrəʊˈspɜːmiə/ *noun* a condition in which dead sperm exist in the semen

necrotic /neˈkrɒtɪk/ *adjective* referring to, or affected with, necrosis ○ *necrotic tissue*

necrotising enterocolitis /ˌnekrətaɪzɪŋ ˌentərəʊkəˈlaɪtɪs/ *noun* a disorder in which patches of dead tissue are found in the small or large intestine as a result of severe bacterial infection. It occurs in babies, especially premature ones.

necrotising fasciitis /ˌnekrətaɪzɪŋ ˌfæʃi ˈaɪtɪs/ *noun* a severe bacterial infection that causes cell tissue to decay rapidly (NOTE: It is sometimes referred to in the media as the 'flesh-eating bug'.)

necrotomy /neˈkrɒtəmi/ *noun* the dissection of a dead body (NOTE: The plural is **necrotomies**.)

needle /ˈniːd(ə)l/ *noun* **1.** a thin metal instrument with a sharp point at one end and a hole at the other for attaching a thread, used for sewing up surgical incisions **2.** the hollow pointed end of a hypodermic syringe, or the syringe itself

needle myopathy /ˌniːd(ə)l maɪˈɒpəθi/ *noun* destruction of muscle tissue caused by using a large needle for intramuscular injections

needlestick /ˈniːd(ə)lstɪk/ *noun* an accidental pricking of your own skin by a needle, as by a nurse picking up a used syringe

needlestick injury /ˈniːd(ə)lstɪk ˌɪndʒəri/ *noun* the real or potential harm resulting from

a prick with a needle previously used to take blood or give an injection. The main concern is the risk of HIV or hepatitis B infection.

needling /ˈniːdlɪŋ/ *noun* the puncture of a cataract with a needle

needs assessment /ˈniːdz əˌsesmənt/ *noun* the investigation of what a particular group of people need in terms of health and social care, so that services can be matched to their needs

needs deprivation /ˈniːdz deprɪˌveɪʃ(ə)n/ *noun* a state in which someone does not have the opportunity or capacity to fulfil his or her basic needs

negative /ˈnegətɪv/ *adjective* **1.** meaning or showing 'no' □ **the answer is in the negative** the answer is 'no' **2.** indicating that something being tested for is not present ○ *The test results were negative.* Opposite **positive**

negative feedback /ˌnegətɪv ˈfiːdbæk/ *noun* a situation in which the result of a process represses the process which caused it

negativism /ˈnegətɪvɪz(ə)m/ *noun* the attitude of a person who opposes advice or instructions

COMMENT: There are two types of negativism: active, where someone does the opposite of what a doctor tells him or her, and passive, where someone does not do what he or she has been asked to do.

negligence /ˈneglɪdʒəns/ *noun* the act of causing injury or harm to another person or to property as the result of doing something wrongly or failing to provide a proper level of care

Negri body /ˈneɪgri ˌbɒdi/ *noun* a round or oval inclusion in the cytoplasm of nerve cells of people or animals who have rabies [Described 1903. After Adelchi Negri (1876–1912), Professor of Bacteriology at Pavia, Italy.]

Neil Robertson stretcher /ˌniːl ˈrɒbətsən ˌstretʃə/ *noun* a stretcher to which a person can be strapped and moved about in an upright position

Neisseria /naɪˈsɪəriə/ *noun* a genus of bacteria which includes gonococcus, which causes gonorrhoea, and meningococcus, which causes meningitis

nematode /ˈnemətəʊd/ *noun* a type of parasitic roundworm, e.g. a hookworm, pinworm or roundworm

neo- /niːəʊ/ *prefix* new

neoadjuvant chemotherapy /ˌniːəʊ ˌædʒʊvənt ˌkiːməʊˈθerəpi/ *noun* chemotherapy given to people with tumours instead of immediate surgery or radiotherapy, in the hope of reducing the need for these later

neocerebellum /ˌniːəʊserəˈbeləm/ *noun* the middle part of the cerebellum (NOTE: The plural is **neocerebellums** or **neocerebella**.)

neomycin /ˌniːəʊˈmaɪsɪn/ *noun* a drug used externally to treat bacterial infections

neonatal /ˌniːəʊˈneɪt(ə)l/ *adjective* referring to the first few weeks after birth

'...one of the most common routes of neonatal poisoning is percutaneous absorption following topical administration' [*Southern Medical Journal*]

neonatal death rate /ˌniːəʊneɪt(ə)l ˈdeθ ˌreɪt/ *noun* the number of babies who die soon after birth, shown per thousand babies born

neonatal maceration /ˌniːəʊneɪt(ə)l ˌmæsəˈreɪʃ(ə)n/ *noun* softening or rotting of fetal tissue after the fetus has died in the uterus and has remained in the amniotic fluid

neonatal screening /ˌniːəʊˌneɪt(ə)l ˈskriːnɪŋ/ *noun* a set of tests performed on babies soon after birth so that any problems can be treated immediately (NOTE: Tests for certain diseases such as hypothyroidism and phenylketonuria are a legal duty.)

neonate /ˈniːəʊneɪt/ *noun* a baby which is less than four weeks old

neonatologist /ˌniːənəˈtɒlədʒɪst/ *noun* a specialist who looks after babies during the first few weeks of life, or premature babies and babies with some congenital disorders

neonatology /ˌniːəʊnəˈtɒlədʒi/ *noun* the branch of medicine dealing with babies in the first few weeks of life

neonatorum /ˌniːəʊneɪˈtɔːrəm/ ♦ **asphyxia neonatorum**

neoplasia /ˌniːəʊˈpleɪziə/ *noun* the formation of tumours

neoplasm /ˈniːəʊplæz(ə)m/ *noun* any new and morbid formation of tissue

'...testicular cancer comprises only 1% of all malignant neoplasms in the male, but it is one of the most frequently occurring types of tumours in late adolescence' [*Journal of American College Health*]

neoplastic /ˌniːəʊˈplæstɪk/ *adjective* referring to neoplasms, neoplasty or neoplasia

neoplasty *noun* the surgical repair or replacement of damaged tissue

neostigmine /ˌniːəʊˈstɪgmiːn/ *noun* a white crystalline compound used in the treatment of muscle fatigue myasthenia and to reverse the effects of muscle relaxant drugs

nephr- /nefr/ *prefix* kidney

nephralgia /neˈfrældʒə/ *noun* pain in the kidney

nephralgic /neˈfrældʒɪk/ *adjective* relating to pain in the kidney

nephrectomy /neˈfrektɒmi/ *noun* a surgical operation to remove the whole kidney (NOTE: The plural is **nephrectomies**.)

nephric /ˈnefrɪk/, **nephritic** /neˈfrɪtɪk/ *adjective* referring to the kidneys

nephritis /neˈfraɪtɪs/ *noun* inflammation of the kidney

COMMENT: Acute nephritis can be caused by a streptococcal infection. Symptoms can include headaches, swollen ankles, and fever.

nephroblastoma /ˌnefrəʊblæˈstəʊmə/ *noun* a malignant tumour in the kidneys in young children, usually under the age of 10, leading to swelling of the abdomen. It is treated by removal of the affected kidney. Also called **Wilms' tumour** (NOTE: The plural is **nephroblastomas** or **nephrobrastomata**.)

nephrocalcinosis /ˌnefrəʊˌkælsɪˈnəʊsɪs/ *noun* a condition in which calcium deposits are found in the kidney

nephrocapsulectomy /ˌnefrəʊˌkæpsjʊˈlektəmi/ *noun* a surgical operation to remove the capsule round a kidney (NOTE: The plural is **nephrocapsulectomies**.)

nephrogram /ˈnefrəgræm/ *noun* a radiographic examination of the kidney

nephrolith /ˈnefrəlɪθ/ *noun* a stone in the kidney

nephrolithiasis /ˌnefrəʊlɪˈθaɪəsɪs/ *noun* a condition in which stones form in the kidney

nephrolithotomy /ˌnefrəʊlɪˈθɒtəmi/ *noun* a surgical operation to remove a stone in the kidney (NOTE: The plural is **nephrolithotomies**.)

nephrologist /neˈfrɒlədʒɪst/ *noun* a doctor who specialises in the study of the kidney and its diseases

nephrology /neˈfrɒlədʒi/ *noun* the study of the kidney and its diseases

nephroma /neˈfrəʊmə/ *noun* a tumour in the kidney, or a tumour derived from renal substances (NOTE: The plural is **nephromas** or **nephromata**.)

nephron /ˈnefrɒn/ *noun* a tiny structure in the kidney through which fluid is filtered

COMMENT: A nephron is formed of a series of tubules, the loop of Henle, Bowman's capsule and a glomerulus. Blood enters the nephron from the renal artery, and waste materials are filtered out by the Bowman's capsule. Some substances return to the bloodstream by reabsorption in the tubules. Urine is collected in the ducts leading from the tubules to the ureters.

nephropathy /neˈfrɒpəθi/ *noun* a disease or medical disorder of the kidney (NOTE: The plural is **nephropathies**.)

nephropexy /ˈnefrəʊpeksi/ *noun* a surgical operation to attach a mobile kidney (NOTE: The plural is **nephropexies**.)

nephroptosis /ˌnefrɒpˈtəʊsɪs/ *noun* a condition in which a kidney is mobile. Also called **floating kidney**

nephrosclerosis /ˌnefrəʊskləˈrəʊsɪs/ *noun* a kidney disease due to vascular change

nephroscope /ˈnefrəskəʊp/ *noun* a type of endoscope used to examine the kidneys

nephrosis /neˈfrəʊsɪs/ *noun* degeneration of the tissue of a kidney

nephrostomy /neˈfrɒstəmi/ *noun* a surgical operation to make a permanent opening into the pelvis of the kidney from the surface (NOTE: The plural is **nephrostomies**.)

nephrotic /neˈfrɒtɪk/ *adjective* relating to or caused by nephrosis

nephrotic syndrome /ne̩frɒtɪk 'sɪn drəʊm/ *noun* increasing oedema, albuminuria and raised blood pressure resulting from nephrosis

nephrotomy /ne'frɒtəmi/ *noun* a surgical operation to cut into a kidney (NOTE: The plural is **nephrotomies.**)

nephrotoxic /ˌnefrəʊ'tɒksɪk/ *adjective* poisonous or damaging to kidney cells

nephroureterectomy /ˌnefrəʊˌjʊərɪtə 'rektəmi/ *noun* a surgical operation to remove all or part of a kidney and the ureter attached to it. Also called **ureteronephrectomy** (NOTE: The plural is **nephroureterectomies.**)

nerve /nɜːv/ *noun* **1.** a bundle of fibres that can transmit electrochemical impulses and that forms part of the network that connects the brain and spinal cord to the body's organs **2.** the sensitive tissue in the root of a tooth (NOTE: For other terms referring to nerves, see words beginning with **neur-, neuro-**.)

COMMENT: Nerves are the fibres along which impulses are carried. Motor nerves or efferent nerves take messages between the central nervous system and muscles, making the muscles move. Sensory nerves or afferent nerves transmit impulses such as sight or pain from the sense organs to the brain.

nerve block /'nɜːv blɒk/ *noun* the act of stopping the function of a nerve by injecting an anaesthetic

nerve centre /'nɜːv ˌsentə/ *noun* the point at which nerves come together

nerve ending /nɜːv 'endɪŋ/ *noun* same as **sensory receptor**

nerve entrapment syndrome /ˌnɜːv ɪn 'træpmənt ˌsɪndrəʊm/ *noun* pain caused by pressure on a nerve, especially where nerves occur in narrow passages such as the wrist (NOTE: The most common nerve entrapment syndrome in the body is carpal tunnel syndrome.)

nerve fibre /'nɜːv ˌfaɪbə/ *noun* a thin structure leading from a nerve cell and carrying nerve impulses, e.g. an axon

nerve gas /'nɜːv gæs/ *noun* a gas which attacks the nervous system

nerve impulse /nɜːv 'ɪmpʌls/ *noun* an electrochemical impulse which is transmitted by nerve cells

nerve regeneration /ˌnɜːv rɪdʒenə'reɪʃ(ə)n/ *noun* the growth of new nerve tissue after damage has occurred

nerve root /'nɜːv ruːt/ *noun* the first part of a nerve as it leaves or joins the spinal column (NOTE: The dorsal nerve root is the entry for a sensory nerve, and the ventral nerve root is the exit for a motor nerve.)

nerve tissue /'nɜːv ˌtɪʃuː/ *noun* tissue which forms nerves, and which is able to transmit the nerve impulses

nervosa /nə'vəʊsə/ ♦ **anorexia nervosa**

nervous /'nɜːvəs/ *adjective* **1.** referring to nerves **2.** very easily worried ○ *Don't be nervous – the operation is a very simple one.*

nervous breakdown /ˌnɜːvəs 'breɪkdaʊn/ *noun* any sudden mental illness (*informal*)

nervous complaint /ˌnɜːvəs kəm'pleɪnt/, **nervous disorder** *noun* an emotional or mental illness (*informal*)

nervousness /'nɜːvəsnəs/ *noun* the state of being nervous

nervous system /'nɜːvəs ˌsɪstəm/ *noun* the nervous tissues of the body, including the peripheral nerves, spinal cord, ganglia and nerve centres

nervy /'nɜːvi/ *adjective* worried and nervous (*informal*)

nether parts /'neðə pɑːts/, **nether regions** /ˌneðə 'riːdʒ(ə)ns/ *plural noun* the lower part of the body, especially the buttocks or genital area (*informal*)

nettle rash /'net(ə)l ræʃ/ *noun* same as **urticaria**

network /'netwɜːk/ *noun* an interconnecting system of lines and spaces, like a net ○ *a network of fine blood vessels*

Neuman's model /'nɔɪmənz ˌmɒd(ə)l/ *noun* a modern model for nursing in which prevention is the primary nursing aim (NOTE: Prevention focuses on keeping both the things which cause stress and the patient's response to stress from having a damaging effect on the body.)

neur- /njʊər/ *prefix* same as **neuro-** (*used before vowels*)

neural /'njʊərəl/ *adjective* referring to a nerve or the nervous system

neural arch /ˌnjʊərəl 'ɑːtʃ/ *noun* a curved part of a vertebra, which forms the space through which the spinal cord passes

neural crest /'njʊərəl krest/ *noun* the ridge of cells in an embryo which forms nerve cells of the sensory and autonomic ganglia

neuralgia /njʊ'rældʒə/ *noun* a spasm of pain which runs along a nerve

neural groove /'njʊərəl gruːv/ *noun* a groove on the back of an embryo formed as the neural plate closes to form the neural tube

neural plate /'njʊərəl pleɪt/ *noun* a thickening of an embryonic disc which folds over to form the neural tube

neural tube /'njʊərəl tjuːb/ *noun* a tube lined with ectodermal cells running the length of an embryo, which develops into the brain and spinal cord

neural tube defect /ˌnjʊərəl 'tjuːb dɪ ˌfekt/ *noun* a congenital anomaly which occurs when the edges of the neural tube do not close up properly while the fetus develops in the uterus, e.g. spina bifida (NOTE: There is less risk of a neural tube defect if the mother takes folic acid during her pregnancy.)

neurapraxia /ˌnjʊərəˈpræksiə/ *noun* a lesion of a nerve which leads to paralysis for a very short time, giving a tingling feeling and loss of function

neurasthenia /ˌnjʊərəsˈθiːniə/ *noun* a type of neurosis in which a person is mentally and physically irritable and extremely fatigued

neurasthenic /ˌnjʊərəsˈθenɪk/ *noun* a person affected by neurasthenia

neurectasis /njʊˈrektəsɪs/ *noun* a surgical operation to stretch a peripheral nerve (NOTE: The plural is **neurectases**.)

neurectomy /njʊˈrektəmi/ *noun* a surgical operation to remove all or part of a nerve (NOTE: The plural is **neurectomies**.)

neurilemma /ˌnjʊərɪˈlemə/ *noun* the outer sheath, formed of Schwann cells, which covers the myelin sheath around a nerve fibre. Also called **neurolemma**. See illustration at NEURONE in Supplement

neurilemmoma /ˌnjʊərileˈməʊmə/, **neurinoma** /njʊəriˈnəʊmə/ *noun* a benign tumour of a nerve, formed from the neurilemma (NOTE: The plurals are **neurilemmomas** or **neurolemmomata** and **neurinomas** or **neurinomata**.)

neuritis /njʊˈraɪtɪs/ *noun* inflammation of a nerve, giving a constant pain

neuro- /njʊərəʊ/ *prefix* nerve or nervous system

neuroanatomy /ˌnjʊərəʊəˈnætəmi/ *noun* the scientific study of the structure of the nervous system

neuroblast /ˈnjʊərəʊblæst/ *noun* a cell in the embryonic spinal cord which forms a nerve cell

neuroblastoma /ˌnjʊərəʊblæˈstəʊmə/ *noun* a malignant tumour formed from the neural crest, found mainly in young children (NOTE: The plural is **neuroblastomas** or **neuroblastomata**.)

neurocranium /ˌnjʊərəʊˈkreɪniəm/ *noun* a part of the skull which encloses and protects the brain (NOTE: The plural is **neurocraniums** or **neurocrania**.)

neurodegenerative /ˌnjʊərəʊdɪˈdʒenərətɪv/ *adjective* referring to a disorder such as Alzheimer's disease or Parkinson's disease that causes damage to the nerves

neurodermatitis /ˌnjʊərəʊdɜːməˈtaɪtɪs/ *noun* inflammation of the skin caused by psychological factors

neurodermatosis /ˌnjʊərəʊdɜːməˈtəʊsɪs/ *noun* a nervous condition involving the skin

neuroendocrine system /ˌnjʊərəʊˈendəkrɪn ˌsɪstəm/ *noun* a system in which the central nervous system and hormonal systems interact to control the function of organs and tissues

neuroepithelial /ˌnjʊərəʊepɪˈθiːliəl/ *adjective* referring to the neuroepithelium

neuroepithelioma /ˌnjʊərəʊepiθiːliˈəʊmə/ *noun* a malignant tumour in the retina (NOTE: The plural is **neuroepitheliomas** or **neuroepitheliomata**.)

neuroepithelium /ˌnjʊərəʊepɪˈθiːliəm/ *noun* the layer of epithelial cells forming part of the lining of the mucous membrane of the nose or the labyrinth of the middle ear

neurofibril /ˌnjʊərəʊˈfaɪbrɪl/ *noun* a fine thread in the cytoplasm of a neurone

neurofibrilla /ˌnjʊərəʊˈfɪbrɪlə/ *noun* same as **neurofibril**. see illustration at NEURONE in Supplement (NOTE: The plural is **neurofibrillae**.)

neurofibroma /ˌnjʊərəʊfaɪˈbrəʊmə/ *noun* a benign tumour of a nerve, formed from the neurilemma (NOTE: The plural is **neurofibromas** or **neurofibromata**.)

neurofibromatosis /ˌnjʊərəʊˌfaɪbrəʊməˈtəʊsɪs/ *noun* a hereditary condition in which a person has neurofibromata on the nerve trunks, limb plexuses or spinal roots, and pale brown spots appear on the skin. Abbr **NF**. Also called **molluscum fibrosum, von Recklinghausen's disease**

neurogenesis /ˌnjʊərəʊˈdʒenəsɪs/ *noun* the development and growth of nerves and nervous tissue

neurogenic /ˌnjʊərəʊˈdʒenɪk/ *adjective* **1.** coming from the nervous system **2.** referring to neurogenesis

neurogenic bladder /ˌnjʊərəʊdʒenɪk ˈblædə/ *noun* a disturbance of the bladder function caused by lesions in the nerve supply to the bladder

neurogenic shock /ˌnjʊərəʊˌdʒenɪk ˈʃɒk/ *noun* a state of shock caused by bad news or an unpleasant surprise

neuroglandular junction /ˌnjʊərəʊˌglændjʊlə ˈdʒʌŋkʃən/ *noun* the point where a nerve joins the gland which it controls

neuroglia /njʊˈrɒgliə/ *noun* same as **glia**

neurohormone /ˌnjʊərəʊˈhɔːməʊn/ *noun* a hormone produced in some nerve cells and secreted from the nerve endings

neurohypophysis /ˌnjʊərəʊhaɪˈpɒfəsɪs/ *noun* the lobe at the back of the pituitary gland, which secretes oxytocin and vasopressin (NOTE: The plural is **neurohypophyses**.)

neurolemma /ˌnjʊərəʊˈlemə/ *noun* same as **neurilemma**

neuroleptic /ˌnjʊərəʊˈleptɪk/ *noun* an antipsychotic drug which calms a person and stops him or her from worrying, e.g. chlorpromazine hydrochloride

neurological /ˌnjʊərəˈlɒdʒɪk(ə)l/ *adjective* referring to neurology

neurological assessment /ˌnjʊərəlɒdʒɪk(ə)l əˈsesmənt/ *noun* an evaluation of the health of a person with a disorder of the nervous system, using interviews, a physical examination, and specific diagnostic tests, sometimes with the help of a family member or close friend

neurologist /njʊˈrɒlədʒɪst/ *noun* a doctor who specialises in the study of the nervous system and the treatment of its diseases

neurology /njʊˈrɒlədʒi/ *noun* the scientific study of the nervous system and its diseases

neuroma /njʊˈrəʊmə/ *noun* a benign tumour formed of nerve cells and nerve fibres (NOTE: The plural is **neuromas** or **neuromata**.)

neuromuscular /ˌnjʊərəʊˈmʌskjʊlə/ *adjective* referring to both nerves and muscles

neuromuscular junction /ˌnjʊərəʊmʌskjʊlə ˈdʒʌŋkʃən/ *noun* the point where a motor nerve joins muscle fibre. Also called **myoneural junction**

neuromyelitis optica /ˌnjʊərəʊmaɪəlaɪtɪs ˈɒptɪkə/ *noun* a condition, similar to multiple sclerosis, in which a person has acute myelitis and the optic nerve is also affected. Also called **Devic's disease**

neuron /ˈnjʊərɒn/, **neurone** /ˈnjʊərɒn/ *noun* a cell in the nervous system which transmits nerve impulses. Also called **nerve cell**

neuropathic bladder /ˌnjʊərəʊpæθɪk ˈblædə/ *noun* a condition in which the bladder does not function properly because its nerve supply is damaged, e.g. due to an injury to the spinal cord

neuropathology /ˌnjʊərəʊpəˈθɒlədʒi/ *noun* the study of diseases of the nervous system

neuropathy /njʊəˈrɒpəθi/ *noun* a disease involving destruction of the tissues of the nervous system (NOTE: The plural is **neuropathies**.)

neurophysiology /ˌnjʊərəʊfɪziˈɒlədʒi/ *noun* the study of the physiology of nerves

neuroplasty /ˈnjʊərəʊplæsti/ *noun* surgery to repair damaged nerves

neuropsychiatric /ˌnjʊərəʊsaɪkiˈætrɪk/ *adjective* referring to neuropsychiatry

neuropsychiatrist /ˌnjʊərəʊsaɪˈkaɪətrɪst/ *noun* a doctor who specialises in the study and treatment of mental and nervous disorders

neuropsychiatry /ˌnjʊərəʊsaɪˈkaɪətri/ *noun* the study of mental and nervous disorders

neurorrhaphy /njʊˈrɔːrəfi/ *noun* a surgical operation to join by suture a nerve which has been cut (NOTE: The plural is **neurorraphies**.)

neurosarcoma /ˌnjʊərəʊsɑːˈkəʊmə/ *noun* a malignant neuroma (NOTE: The plural is **neurosarcomas** or **neurosarcomata**.)

neurosecretion /ˌnjʊərəʊsɪˈkriːʃ(ə)n/ *noun* **1.** a substance secreted by a nerve cell **2.** the process of secretion of an active substance by nerve cells

neurosis /njʊˈrəʊsɪs/ *noun* a disorder of the personality in which a person experiences obsessive negative emotions towards someone or something, e.g. fear of empty spaces or jealousy of a sibling. ◊ **psychoneurosis** (NOTE: The plural is **neuroses**.)

neurosurgeon /ˈnjʊərəʊˌsɜːdʒən/ *noun* a surgeon who operates on the nervous system, including the brain and spinal cord

neurosurgery /ˈnjʊərəʊˌsɜːdʒəri/ *noun* surgery on the nervous system, including the brain and spinal cord

neurosyphilis /ˌnjʊərəʊˈsɪfəlɪs/ *noun* syphilis which attacks the nervous system

neurotic /njʊˈrɒtɪk/ *adjective* relating to or having neurosis ■ *noun* a person who is worried about or obsessed with something (*informal*)

neurotically /njʊˈrɒtɪkli/ *adverb* in a neurotic way ○ *She is neurotically obsessed with keeping herself clean.*

neurotmesis /ˌnjʊərɒtˈmiːsɪs/ *noun* an act of cutting a nerve completely (NOTE: The plural is **neurotmeses**.)

neurotomy /njʊˈrɒtəmi/ *noun* a surgical operation to cut a nerve (NOTE: The plural is **neurotomies**.)

neurotoxic /ˌnjʊərəʊˈtɒksɪk/ *adjective* harmful or poisonous to nerve cells

neurotransmitter /ˌnjʊərəʊtrænsˈmɪtə/ *noun* a chemical substance which transmits nerve impulses from one neurone to another

COMMENT: The main neurotransmitters are the catecholamines (adrenaline, noradrenaline and 5-hydroxytryptamine) and acetylcholine. Other neurotransmitters such as gamma aminobutyric acid, glutamine and substance P are less common.

neurotripsy /ˈnjʊərəʊtrɪpsi/ *noun* surgical bruising or crushing of a nerve

neurotrophic /ˌnjʊərəʊˈtrəʊfɪk/ *adjective* relating to the nutrition and maintenance of tissue of the nervous system

neurotropic /ˌnjʊərəʊˈtrɒpɪk/ *adjective* referring to a bacterium which is attracted to and attacks nerves

neuter /ˈnjuːtə/ *adjective* neither male nor female

neutral /ˈnjuːtrəl/ *adjective* neither acid nor alkali ○ *A pH factor of 7 is neutral.*

neutralise /ˈnjuːtrəlaɪz/, **neutralize** *verb* **1.** to counteract the effect of something ○ *Alkali poisoning can be neutralised by applying acid solution.* (NOTE: **neutralising – neutralised**) **2.** to form a salt from an acid

neutropenia /ˌnjuːtrəˈpiːniə/ *noun* a condition in which there are fewer neutrophils than usual in the blood

neutrophil /ˈnjuːtrəfɪl/ *noun* a type of white blood cell with an irregular nucleus, which can attack and destroy bacteria. Also called **polymorph**

newborn /ˈnjuːbɔːn/ *adjective* born recently. ◊ **neonatal** ■ *noun* a recently born baby. ◊ **neonate**

newton /'nju:t(ə)n/ *noun* an SI unit of measurement of force. Symbol **N**

COMMENT: One newton is the force required to move one kilogram at the speed of one metre per second

new variant CJD /nju: ˌveəriənt ˌsi:dʒeɪ 'di:/ *noun* ♦ **variant CJD**

next-day pill /ˌnekst deɪ 'pɪl/ *noun* same as **morning-after pill**

next of kin /ˌnekst əv 'kɪn/ *noun* the person or persons who are most closely related to someone ○ *The hospital has notified the next of kin of the death of the accident victim.* (NOTE: Takes a singular or plural verb.)

nexus /'neksəs/ *noun* **1.** a link (NOTE: The plural is **nexus** or **nexuses**.) **2.** a point where two organs or tissues join

NF *abbr* neurofibromatosis

NHS *abbr* National Health Service

NHS Direct /ˌen eɪt ʃ es dɪ'rekt/ *noun* in the UK, a national telephone helpline run by nurses to provide information about health and health services for the public

niacin /'naɪəsɪn/ *noun* a vitamin of the vitamin B complex found in milk, meat, liver, kidney, yeast, beans, peas and bread, lack of which can cause mental disorders and pellagra. Also called **nicotinic acid**

nicardipine /nɪ'kɑ:dɪpi:n/ *noun* a drug which slows down the movement of calcium ions into smooth muscle cells, used especially to treat angina

NICE /naɪs/ *abbr* National Institute for Clinical Excellence

nick /nɪk/ *noun* a little cut ○ *She had a nick in her ear lobe which bled.* ■ *verb* to make a little cut in something ○ *He nicked his chin while shaving.*

niclosamide /nɪ'kləʊsəmaɪd/ *noun* a drug used for removing tapeworms

nicotine /'nɪkəti:n/ *noun* the main alkaloid substance found in tobacco

nicotine addiction /'nɪkəti:n əˌdɪkʃən/ *noun* an addiction to nicotine, derived from smoking tobacco

nicotine patch /'nɪkəti:n pætʃ/ *noun* a patch containing nicotine which is released slowly into the bloodstream, applied to the skin as a method of curing nicotine addiction

nicotine poisoning /'nɪkəti:n ˌpɔɪz(ə)nɪŋ/ *noun* poisoning of the autonomic nervous system with large quantities of nicotine. Also called **nicotinism**

nicotine receptor /'nɪkəti:n rɪˌseptə/ *noun* a cholinergic receptor found at the neuromuscular junction on skeletal muscle and in the autonomic ganglia, which responds to nicotine and nicotine-like drugs. Also called **nicotinic receptor**

nicotine replacement /'nɪkəti:n rɪˌpleɪsmənt/ *noun* the use of nicotine patches or other products to help during an attempt to give up smoking

nicotinic acid /ˌnɪkətɪnɪk 'æsɪd/ same as **niacin**

nicotinic receptor /nɪkəˌtɪnɪk rɪ'septə/ *noun* same as **nicotine receptor**

nicotinism /'nɪkətiːnɪz(ə)m/ *noun* same as **nicotine poisoning**

nictation /nɪk'teɪʃ(ə)n/, **nictitation** /nɪktɪ'teɪʃ(ə)n/ *noun* the act of winking

nidation /naɪ'deɪʃ(ə)n/ *noun* **1.** the process of building the endometrial layers of the uterus between menstrual periods **2.** the point in the development of an embryo at which the fertilised ovum reaches the uterus and implants in the wall of the uterus. Also called **implantation**

nidus /'naɪdəs/ *noun* a site where bacteria can settle and breed, which becomes a centre of infection (NOTE: The plural is **niduses** or **nidi**.)

Niemann-Pick disease /ˌni:mən 'pɪk dɪ ˌzi:z/ *noun* a rare inherited disease of a group which affect metabolism. Signs in babies include feeding difficulties, a large abdomen within 3 to 6 months, and progressive loss of early motor skills.

nifedipine /nɪ'fedɪpi:n/ *noun* a drug which stops the heart muscles from taking up calcium, used in the treatment of high blood pressure and angina pectoris

night duty /'naɪt ˌdju:ti/ *noun* the situation of working at night ○ *Nurse Smith is on night duty this week.*

Nightingale ward *noun* an old-fashioned type of long ward with a row of beds along each wall and a centrally placed point for the nurse in charge to work from

nightmare /'naɪtmeə/ *noun* a dream which frightens the dreamer ○ *The child had a nightmare and woke up screaming.*

night nurse /'naɪt nɜ:s/ *noun* a nurse who is on duty at night

night sweat /'naɪt swet/ *noun* heavy sweating when a person is asleep at night

night terror /naɪt 'terə/ *noun* a period of disturbed sleep, which a child does not remember afterwards

nigra /'naɪgrə/ ♦ **linea nigra**

nihilism /'naɪhɪlɪz(ə)m/ *noun* the rejection of all the usual social conventions and beliefs, especially of morality and religion

nihilistic /ˌnaɪhɪ'lɪstɪk/ *adjective* relating to or showing a belief in nihilism

ninety-nine /ˌnaɪnti 'naɪn/ *number* a number which a doctor asks a person to say so that he or she can inspect the back of the throat ○ *The doctor told him to open his mouth wide and say ninety-nine.*

nipple /'nɪp(ə)l/ *noun* **1.** same as **mammilla 2.** *US* a rubber teat on a baby's feeding bottle

Nissl granule /ˈnɪs(ə)l ˌgrænjuːl/, **Nissl body** /ˈnɪs(ə)l ˌbɒdi/ *noun* one of the coarse granules surrounding the nucleus in the cytoplasm of nerve cells. See illustration at NEU-RONE in Supplement [Described 1894. After Franz Nissl (1860–1919), German psychiatrist.]

nit /nɪt/ *noun* an egg or larva of a louse

nitrate /ˈnaɪtreɪt/ *noun* 1. a salt or an ester of nitric acid 2. a drug such as glyceryl trinitrate which dilates the vessels leading to the heart muscle and lowers cardiac work by reducing venous return to the heart, for rapid relief of angina and in heart failure (NOTE: Patients can develop tolerance to these drugs.)

-nitrate /naɪtreɪt/ *suffix* used in names of nitrate drugs

nitrazepam /naɪˈtræzɪpæm/ *noun* a tranquilliser used in some sleeping pills

nitrofurantoin /ˌnaɪtrəʊfjʊˈræntəʊɪn/ *noun* a drug which helps to prevent the growth of bacteria, used in the treatment of urinary infections

nitrogen /ˈnaɪtrədʒən/ *noun* a chemical element, which is a gas that is the main component of air and is an essential part of protein (NOTE: The chemical symbol is **N**.)

COMMENT: Nitrogen is taken into the body by digesting protein-rich foods; excess nitrogen is excreted in urine. When the intake of nitrogen and the excretion rate are equal, the body is in nitrogen balance or protein balance.

nitrogen narcosis /ˌnaɪtrədʒ(ə)n nɑːˈkəʊsɪs/ *noun* loss of consciousness due to the formation of nitrogen in the tissues, caused by pressure change

nitroglycerin /ˌnaɪtrəʊˈglɪsərɪn/ *noun* a drug which helps the veins and coronary arteries to become wider

nitrous oxide /ˌnaɪtrəs ˈɒksaɪd/ *noun* a colourless gas with a sweet smell, used in combination with other gases as an anaesthetic in dentistry and surgery. Also called **laughing gas**

nm *abbr* nanometre

NMC *abbr* Nursing and Midwifery Council

nmol *abbr* nanomole

NMR *abbr* nuclear magnetic resonance

Nocardia /nəʊˈkɑːdiə/ *noun* a genus of bacteria found in soil, some species of which cause nocardiosis and maduramycosis

nocardiosis /nəʊˌkɑːdiˈəʊsɪs/, **nocardiasis** /ˌnəʊkɑːˈdaɪəsɪs/ *noun* a lung infection which may metastasise to other tissue, caused by *Nocardia*

noci- /nəʊsi/ *prefix* pain or injury

nociassociation /ˌnəʊsiəsəʊsiˈeɪʃ(ə)n/ *noun* an unconscious release of nervous energy, e.g. as a result of shock

nociceptive /ˌnəʊsiˈseptɪv/ *adjective* referring to nerves which carry pain to the brain

nociceptor /ˈnəʊsiˌseptə/ *noun* a sensory nerve which carries pain to the brain

noct- /nɒkt/ *prefix* night

noctambulation /ˌnɒktæmbjuleɪʃ(ə)n/ *noun* same as **somnambulism**

nocte /ˈnɒkti/ *adverb* at night. Opposite **mane** (NOTE: used on prescriptions)

nocturia /nɒkˈtjʊəriə/ *noun* the fact of passing an unusually large quantity of urine during the night

nocturnal /nɒkˈtɜːn(ə)l/ *adjective* referring to or taking place at night

nocturnal emission /nɒkˌtɜːn(ə)l ɪˈmɪʃ(ə)n/ *noun* the production of semen from the penis while a man is asleep

nocturnal enuresis /nɒkˌtɜːn(ə)l enjʊˈriːsɪs/ *noun* the act of passing urine when asleep in bed at night. Also called **bedwetting**

nodal /ˈnəʊd(ə)l/ *adjective* referring to nodes

nodal tachycardia /ˌnəʊd(ə)l tækiˈkɑːdiə/ *noun* a sudden attack of rapid heartbeats. Also called **paroxysmal tachycardia**

node /nəʊd/ *noun* 1. a small mass of tissue 2. a group of nerve cells

node of Ranvier /ˌnəʊd əv ˈrænviə/ *noun* one of a series of gaps in the myelin sheath surrounding a nerve fibre. See illustration at NEU-RONE in Supplement

nod off *verb* to fall asleep (*informal*)

nodosum /nəʊˈdəʊsəm/ ♦ **erythema nodosum**

nodular /ˈnɒdjʊlə/ *adjective* formed of nodules

nodule /ˈnɒdjuːl/ *noun* 1. a small node or group of cells. ◊ **Bohn's nodules** 2. the anterior part of the inferior vermis

noma /ˈnəʊmə/ *noun* same as **cancrum oris**

nomen proprium /ˌnəʊmən ˈprəʊpriəm/ *noun* full form of **n.p.**

non- /nɒn/ *prefix* not

non-A, non-B hepatitis *noun* now called **hepatitis C**

non-absorbable suture /ˌnɒn əbˌzɔːbəb(ə)l ˈsuːtʃə/ *noun* a suture made of a substance which cannot be absorbed into the body and which eventually has to be removed

non-accidental injury /ˌnɒn æksɪˌdent(ə)l ˈɪndʒəri/ *noun* an injury which is not caused accidentally

non-allergenic /ˌnɒn æləˈdʒenɪk/ *adjective* not aggravating an allergy

non-cancerous /ˌnɒn ˈkænsərəs/ *adjective* not malignant

non-clinical /ˌnɒn ˈklɪnɪk(ə)l/ *adjective* referring to the wider non-medical aspects of patient care ○ *non-clinical services such as administration and catering* ○ *non-clinical guidelines including confidentiality protocols*

non-compliance /ˌnɒn kəmˈplaɪəns/ *noun* the failure to take drugs at the correct times and in the dosages prescribed, or to take them at all

non compos mentis /ˌnɒn ˌkɒmpəs ˈmentɪs/ *adjective* referring to a person who is mentally incapable of managing his or her own affairs (NOTE: From a Latin phrase meaning 'not of sound mind'.)

non-contagious /ˌnɒn kənˈteɪdʒəs/ *adjective* not contagious

non-drowsy /ˌnɒn ˈdraʊzi/ *adjective* not causing drowsiness

non-emergency surgery /ˌnɒn ɪˌmɜːdʒənsi ˈsɜːdʒəri/ *noun* a surgical operation which does not need to be performed immediately because it is for a condition which is not life-threatening, e.g. joint replacement. Also called **non-urgent surgery**

non-granular leucocyte /ˌnɒn ˌɡrænjʊlə ˈluːkəʊsaɪt/ *noun* a leucocyte which has no granules, e.g. a lymphocyte or monocyte

non-Hodgkins lymphoma /ˌnɒn ˌhɒdʒkɪnz lɪmˈfəʊmə/ *noun* a cancer of the lymph nodes which differs from Hodgkin's disease by the absence of a particular type of cell with double nuclei

non-insulin-dependent diabetes /ˌnɒn ˌɪnsjʊlɪn dɪˌpendənt ˌdaɪəˈbiːtiːz/ *noun* same as **Type II diabetes mellitus**

non-invasive /ˌnɒn ɪnˈveɪzɪv/ *adjective* referring to treatment which does not involve entering the body by making an incision

non-maleficence /nɒn məˈlefɪs(ə)ns/ *noun* the concept that professionals in the health service have a duty to protect the patient from harm (NOTE: Under this principle, professionals' obligations include keeping their knowledge and skills current, realising their own limitations and knowing when to refer a case to a specialist or other professional.)

non-malignant /ˌnɒn məˈlɪɡnənt/ *adjective* not cancerous, or not life-threatening ○ *a non-malignant growth*

non-medical /ˌnɒn ˈmedɪk(ə)l/ *adjective* **1.** not relating to medicine ○ *non-medical genetics* **2.** not according to medical practice, or not as directed by a doctor ○ *non-medical use of stimulant drugs* **3.** not used in specialised medical speech ○ *'Nervous breakdown' is a non-medical term for a type of sudden mental illness.*

non-nucleated /ˌnɒn ˈnjuːklieɪtɪd/ *adjective* referring to a cell with no nucleus

non-official drug /ˌnɒn əˌfɪʃ(ə)l ˈdrʌɡ/ *noun* a drug that is not listed in the national pharmacopoeia

non-palpable /nɒn ˈpælpəb(ə)l/ *adjective* not able to be felt when touched

non-paralytic poliomyelitis /nɒn ˌpærəlɪtɪk ˌpəʊliəʊˌmaɪəˈlaɪtɪs/ *noun* a form of poliomyelitis similar to abortive poliomyelitis but which also affects the muscles to some degree

non-secretor /ˌnɒn sɪˈkriːtə/ *noun* a person who does not secrete substances indicating ABO blood group into mucous fluids such as semen or saliva

non-smoker /nɒn ˈsməʊkə/ *noun* a person who does not smoke

non-specific /ˌnɒn spəˈsɪfɪk/ *adjective* not caused by any single identifiable cause

non-specific urethritis /ˌnɒn spəˌsɪfɪk ˌjʊərɪˈθraɪtɪs/ *noun* any sexually transmitted inflammation of the urethra not caused by gonorrhoea (*dated*) Abbr **NSU**

non-sterile /ˌnɒn ˈsteraɪl/ *adjective* not sterile or sterilised

non-steroidal /ˌnɒn steˈrɔɪd(ə)l/ *adjective* not containing steroids

non-steroidal anti-inflammatory drug /ˌnɒnsteˌrɔɪd(ə)l ˌænti ɪnˈflæmət(ə)ri drʌɡ/ *noun* a drug used in the treatment of pain associated with inflammation, including rheumatic disease, post-operative analgesia and dysmenorrhoea, by inhibiting the release of prostaglandins. Abbr **NSAID** (NOTE: Non-steroidal anti-inflammatory drugs have names ending in **-fen: ibuprofen**.)

COMMENT: Serious gastro-intestinal side effects can occur, especially in the elderly. Asthma can worsen.

non-union /nɒn ˈjuːnjən/ *noun* a condition in which the two parts of a fractured bone do not join together and do not heal

non-urgent surgery /ˌnɒn ˌɜːdʒənt ˈsɜːdʒəri/ same as **non-emergency surgery**

noradrenaline /ˌnɔːrəˈdrenəlɪn/ *noun* a hormone secreted by the medulla of the adrenal glands which acts as a vasoconstrictor and is used to maintain blood pressure in shock, haemorrhage or hypotension (NOTE: The US term is **norepinephrine**.)

norma /ˈnɔːmə/ *noun* a view of the skull as seen from a particular angle (NOTE: The plural is **normae**.)

normal /ˈnɔːm(ə)l/ *adjective* usual, ordinary or conforming to a standard ○ *After he took the tablets, his blood pressure went back to normal.* ○ *Her temperature is two degrees above normal.* ○ *He had an above-normal pulse rate.* ○ *Is it normal for a person with myopia to suffer from headaches?*

normally /ˈnɔːm(ə)li/ *adverb* in an ordinary way, on most occasions or in most circumstances ○ *The patients are normally worried before the operation.* ○ *He was breathing normally.*

normo- /nɔːməʊ/ *prefix* normal, usual or expected

normoblast /ˈnɔːməʊblæst/ *noun* an early form of a red blood cell, usually found only in bone marrow but occurring in the blood in some types of leukaemia and anaemia

normocyte /ˈnɔːməʊsaɪt/ *noun* a red blood cell

normocytic /ˌnɔːməʊˈsaɪtɪk/ *adjective* referring to a normocyte

normocytosis /ˌnɔːməʊsaɪˈtəʊsɪs/ *noun* the condition of having the standard number of red blood cells in the peripheral blood

normotension /ˌnɔːməʊˈtenʃən/ *noun* blood pressure at the usual level

normotensive /ˌnɔːməʊˈtensɪv/ *adjective* referring to blood pressure at the usual level

Norton score /ˈnɔːt(ə)n skɔː/ *noun* a scale for deciding how likely it is that pressure sores will develop, used mostly in assessing elderly patients

nortriptyline /nɔːˈtrɪptəliːn/ *noun* a drug used to reduce pain and as an antidepressant and tranquilliser

nose /nəʊz/ *noun* an organ through which a person breathes and smells □ **her nose is running** liquid mucus is dripping from her nose □ **he blew his nose** he blew air through his nose into a handkerchief to get rid of mucus in his nose □ **to speak through your nose** to speak as if your nose is blocked, so that you say 'b' instead of 'm' and 'd' instead of 'n'

COMMENT: The nose is formed of cartilage and small bones making the bridge at the top. It leads into two passages, the nostrils, which in turn lead to the nasal cavity, divided in two by the septum. The nasal passages connect with the sinuses, with the ears through the Eustachian tubes, and with the pharynx. The receptors which detect smell are in the top of the nasal passage.

nosebleed /ˈnəʊzbliːd/ *noun* an incident of bleeding from the nose, usually caused by a blow or by sneezing, by blowing the nose hard or by high blood pressure (*informal*) ○ *She had a headache, followed by a violent nosebleed.* Also called **epistaxis**

noso- /nɒsəʊ/ *prefix* disease

nosocomial /ˌnɒsəʊˈkəʊmiəl/ *adjective* referring to hospitals

nosocomial infection /ˌnɒsəʊˌkəʊmiəl ɪnˈfekʃən/ *noun* an infection which is passed on to a person being treated in a hospital

nosology /nɒˈsɒlədʒi/ *noun* the classification of diseases

nostril /ˈnɒstrɪl/ *noun* one of the two passages in the nose through which air is breathed in or out ○ *His right nostril is blocked.* (NOTE: The nostrils are also referred to as the **nares**.)

notch /nɒtʃ/ *noun* a depression on a surface, usually on a bone, but sometimes on an organ. ◊ **cardiac notch, occipital notch**

notice /ˈnəʊtɪs/ *noun* **1.** a piece of writing giving information, usually put in a place where everyone can see it **2.** a warning ○ *They had to leave with ten minutes' notice.* **3.** attention □ **to take notice (of something *or* someone)** to give attention (to something or someone) ○ *We need to take notice of this feedback.* ■ *verb* to see or be aware of something ○ *Nobody noticed that she was sweating.* ○ *Did you notice the development of any new symptoms?* (NOTE: **noticing – noticed**)

noticeable /ˈnəʊtɪsəb(ə)l/ *adjective* able to be noticed ○ *The disease has no easily noticeable symptoms.*

noticeboard /ˈnəʊtɪsbɔːd/ *noun* a flat piece of wood, or board fixed on a wall, on which notices can be pinned

notifiable disease /ˌnəʊtɪfaɪəb(ə)l dɪˈziːz/ *noun* a serious infectious disease which, in the UK, has to be reported by a doctor to the Department of Health so that steps can be taken to stop it spreading

COMMENT: The following are notifiable diseases: cholera, diphtheria, dysentery, encephalitis, food poisoning, jaundice, malaria, measles, meningitis, ophthalmia neonatorum, paratyphoid, plague, poliomyelitis, relapsing fever, scarlet fever, smallpox, tuberculosis, typhoid, typhus, whooping cough and yellow fever.

notify /ˈnəʊtɪfaɪ/ *verb* to inform a person or authority officially ○ *The local doctor notified the Health Service of the case of cholera.* (NOTE: **notifies – notifying – notified**. You notify a person **of** something.)

nourish /ˈnʌrɪʃ/ *verb* to give food or nutrients to a person

nourishment /ˈnʌrɪʃmənt/ *noun* **1.** the act of supplying nutrients to a person **2.** food and the nutrients in it, e.g. proteins, fats or vitamins

noxious /ˈnɒkʃəs/ *adjective* harmful ○ *a noxious gas*

n.p. *noun* the name of the drug written on the label of its container. Full form **nomen proprium**

NPO *abbreviation* used to refer to patients being kept without food ○ *The patient should be kept NPO for five hours before the operation.* Full form **ne per oris**

NSAID *abbr* non-steroidal anti-inflammatory drug

NSU *abbr* non-specific urethritis

nucha /ˈnjuːkə/ *noun* same as **nape** (NOTE: The plural is **nuchae**.)

nuchal /ˈnjuːk(ə)l/ *adjective* referring to the back of the neck

nucle- /njuːkli/ *prefix* same as **nucleo-** (*used before vowels*)

nuclear /ˈnjuːkliə/ *adjective* referring to nuclei, e.g. of a cell or an atom

nuclear magnetic resonance /ˌnjuːkliə mæɡˌnetɪk ˈrezənəns/ *noun* a scanning technique using magnetic fields and radio waves which reveals abnormalities in soft tissue and body fluids. ◊ **magnetic resonance imaging**. Abbr **NMR**

nuclear medicine /ˌnjuːkliə ˈmed(ə)s(ə)n/ *noun* the use of radioactive substances for detecting and treating disorders

nuclease /ˈnjuːklieɪz/ *noun* an enzyme which breaks down nucleic acids

nucleic acid /njuːˌkliːɪk ˈæsɪd/ *noun* an organic acid of a type found in all living cells, which consists of complex nucleotide chains which pass on genetic information, e.g. DNA or RNA

nucleo- /njuːkliəʊ/ *prefix* referring to a cell or atomic nucleus

nucleolus /njuːkliːələs/ *noun* a structure inside a cell nucleus, containing RNA (NOTE: The plural is **nucleoli**.)

nucleoprotein /ˌnjuːkliəʊˈprəʊtiːn/ *noun* a compound of protein and nucleic acid, e.g. a chromosome or ribosome

nucleus /ˈnjuːkliəs/ *noun* **1.** a central part which has others grouped or built around it **2.** the central body in a cell, which contains DNA and RNA and controls the function and characteristics of the cell. See illustration at NEURONE in Supplement **3.** a group of nerve cells in the brain or spinal cord (NOTE: The plural is **nuclei**.)

nucleus pulposus /ˌnjuːkliəs pʊlˈpəʊsəs/ *noun* a soft central part of an intervertebral disc which disappears in old age (NOTE: The plural is **nuclei pulposi**)

nullipara /nʌˈlɪpərə/ *noun* a woman who has never had a child (NOTE: The plural is **nulliparas** or **nulliparae**.) ■ *adjective* referring to a woman who has never had a child

numb /nʌm/ *adjective* **1.** referring to a part of the body which has no feeling **2.** unable to feel emotion

numbness /ˈnʌmnəs/ *noun* a loss of feeling

nurse /nɜːs/ *noun* a person who looks after sick people in a hospital or helps a doctor in a local surgery. Some nurses may be trained to diagnose and treat patients. ○ *She works as a nurse in the local hospital.* ○ *He's training to be a nurse.* ◊ **nurse practitioner** ■ *verb* **1.** to look after a sick person, or to be employed as a nurse ○ *When he was ill his mother nursed him until he was better.* **2.** to behave so as not to aggravate a condition ○ *nursing a sprained ankle* (NOTE: **nurses – nursing – nursed**)

nurse executive director /nɜːs ɪɡˌzekjʊtɪv daɪˈrektə/ *noun* in the UK, a senior nurse who sits on the Board of an NHS Trust and has corporate as well as professional responsibilities in the organisation for nursing and sometimes other aspects such as quality or human resources

nurse manager /ˌnɜːs ˈmænɪdʒə/ *noun* a nurse who has administrative duties in a hospital or a health service

nurse practitioner /ˌnɜːs prækˈtɪʃ(ə)nə/ *noun* a nurse with additional clinical training at degree level who often works independently, assessing, diagnosing and treating patients, particularly in primary care

nurse station /ˈnɜːs ˌsteɪʃ(ə)n/, **nurses' station** /ˈnɜːsɪz ˌsteɪʃ(ə)n/ *noun* an area in or near a ward from which nurses work, keep records and control the activities of the ward

nurse tutor /ˌnɜːs ˈtjuːtə/ *noun* an experienced nurse who teaches student nurses

nursing /ˈnɜːsɪŋ/ *noun* **1.** the work or profession of being a nurse ○ *He has chosen nursing as his career.* **2.** care for sick people provided by a nurse ■ *adjective* providing care as a nurse

'…few would now dispute the need for clear, concise nursing plans to guide nursing practice, provide educational tools and give an accurate legal record' [*Nursing Times*]

'…all relevant sections of the nurses' care plan and nursing process records had been left blank' [*Nursing Times*]

Nursing and Midwifery Council /ˌnɜːsɪŋ ən ˌmɪdˈwɪfəri ˌkaʊnsəl/ *noun* in the UK, an organisation that sets standards for the education, practice and conduct of nurses, midwives and health visitors. Abbr **NMC**

nursing audit /ˈnɜːsɪŋ ˌɔːdɪt/ *noun* a formal detailed review of records or observation of nursing actions so that judgments can be made about the quality of nursing care being provided (NOTE: The documented evidence is compared with accepted standards and criteria.)

nursing development unit /ˌnɜːsɪŋ dɪ ˈveləpmənt/ *noun* a nurse-led ward or unit that sets out to demonstrate by example innovative high-quality care, to reflect on practice and draw lessons from this experience, and to provide learning opportunities for other nurses. Abbr **NDU**

nursing home /ˈnɜːsɪŋ həʊm/ *noun* a house where convalescents or dependent elderly people can live under medical supervision by a qualified nurse

nursing intervention /ˌnɜːsɪŋ ɪntə ˈvenʃən/ *noun* the treatment of illness by nursing care, without surgery

nursing model /ˈnɜːsɪŋ ˌmɒd(ə)l/ *noun* a set of stated principles about nursing which gives professionals a way of formulating a plan of care, assessing its success and addressing any problems which arise from it

nursing mother /ˌnɜːsɪŋ ˈmʌðə/ *noun* a mother who breast-feeds her baby

Nursing Officer /ˈnɜːsɪŋ ˌɒfɪsə/ *noun* in the UK, a nurse employed by the Department of Health to assist the Chief Nursing Officer in providing professional advice to Ministers and policy-makers

nursing practice /ˈnɜːsɪŋ ˌpræktɪs/ *noun* treatment given by nurses

nursing process /ˌnɜːsɪŋ ˈprəʊses/ *noun* a standard method of treatment and documentation of treatment carried out by nurses

nursing sister /ˌnɜːsɪŋ ˈsɪstə/ *noun* a hospital sister who has administrative duties

nursing standard /ˈnɜːsɪŋ ˌstændəd/ *noun* an accepted level of achievement by which nursing care can be assessed or compared

nurture /'nɜːtʃə/ *noun* care given to a child while it is developing ■ *verb* to bring up and care for children (NOTE: **nurturing – nurtured**)

nutans /'njuːt(ə)ns/ ♦ **spasmus nutans**

nutation /njuːˈteɪʃ(ə)n/ *noun* involuntary nodding of the head

nutrient /'njuːtriənt/ *noun* a substance in food which is necessary to provide energy or to help the body grow, e.g. protein, fat or a vitamin

nutrition /njuːˈtrɪʃ(ə)ⁿn/ *noun* 1. the study of the supply of nutrients to the body from digesting food 2. nourishment or food

nutritional /njuːˈtrɪʃ(ə)n(ə)l/ *adjective* referring to nutrition

nutritional anaemia /njuːˌtrɪʃ(ə)n(ə)l ə ˈniːmiə/ *noun* anaemia caused by an imbalance in the diet

nutritional disorder /njuˈtrɪʃ(ə)n(ə)l dɪsˌɔːdə/ *noun* a disorder related to food and nutrients, e.g. obesity

nutritionist /njuːˈtrɪʃ(ə)nɪst/ *noun* a person who specialises in the study of nutrition and advises on diets. ◊ **dietitian**

nyct- /nɪkt/ *prefix* night or darkness

nyctalopia /ˌnɪktəˈləʊpiə/ *noun* the condition of being unable to see in bad light. Also called **night blindness**

nyctophobia /ˌnɪktəˈfəʊbiə/ *noun* fear of the dark

nymphae /'nɪmfiː/ *plural noun* same as **labia minora**

nympho- /nɪmfəʊ/ *prefix* 1. female sexuality 2. nymphae

nymphomania /ˌnɪmfəˈmeɪniə/ *noun* an obsessive sexual urge in a woman (NOTE: A similar condition in a man is called **satyriasis**.)

nymphomaniac /ˌnɪmfəˈmeɪniæk/ *noun* a woman who has an unusually obsessive sexual urge (NOTE: This term is regarded as offensive.)

nystagmus /nɪˈstægməs/ *noun* a rapid, involuntary movement of the eyes up and down or from side to side

COMMENT: Nystagmus can be horizontal, vertical, torsional or rotary; it can be congenital, but is also a symptom of multiple sclerosis and Ménière's disease.

nystatin /naɪˈstætɪn/ *noun* an anti-microbial drug used in the treatment of fungal infections, especially thrush

O

oat cell carcinoma /ˈəʊt sel kɑːsɪˌnəʊmə/ *noun* a type of cancer of the bronchi, with distinctive small cells

OB *abbr* obstetrics

obese /əʊˈbiːs/ *adjective* so overweight as to be at risk of several serious illnesses, including diabetes and heart disease

obesity /əʊˈbiːsɪti/ *noun* the condition of being seriously overweight

COMMENT: Obesity is caused by excess fat accumulating under the skin and around organs in the body. It is sometimes due to glandular disorders, but it is usually caused by eating or drinking too much. A tendency to obesity can be hereditary.

obey /əˈbeɪ/ *verb* to do what a person, authority or rule says you should do ○ *You ought to obey the doctor's instructions and go to bed.*

objective /əbˈdʒektɪv/ *noun* an aim or goal ■ *adjective* **1.** existing independently of any individual person's mind **2.** not influenced by any bias or prejudice caused by personal feelings **3.** referring to symptoms of illness which can be observed by somebody other than the person who is ill. Compare **subjective**

obligate /ˈɒblɪɡeɪt/ *adjective* referring to an organism which exists and develops in only one way, e.g. a virus which is a parasite only inside cells

oblique /əˈbliːk/ *adjective* lying at an angle ■ *noun* also called **oblique muscle**

'…there are four recti muscles and two oblique muscles in each eye, which coordinate the movement of the eyes and enable them to work as a pair' [*Nursing Times*]

oblique fissure /əˌbliːk ˈfɪʃə/ *noun* a groove between the superior and inferior lobes of a lung. See illustration at LUNGS in Supplement

oblique fracture /əˌbliːk ˈfræktʃə/ *noun* a fracture in which the bone is broken diagonally

oblique muscle /əˌbliːk ˈmʌs(ə)l/ *noun* **1.** each of two muscles in the wall of the abdomen **2.** each of two muscles which control the movement of the eyeball

obliterate /əˈblɪtəreɪt/ *verb* **1.** to destroy something completely **2.** to block a cavity completely (NOTE: **obliterating – obliterated**)

obliteration /əˌblɪtəˈreɪʃ(ə)n/ *noun* **1.** the complete destruction of something **2.** the complete blocking of something such as a cavity

oblongata /ˌɒblɒŋˈɡeɪtə/ ◆ **medulla oblongata**

observable /əbˈzɜːvəb(ə)l/ *noun* which can be seen or measured

observation /ˌɒbzəˈveɪʃ(ə)n/ *noun* the process of watching and examining a person or thing over a period of time ○ *She was admitted to hospital for observation.*

observation register /ˌɒbzəˈveɪʃ(ə)n ˌredʒɪstə/ *noun* a record of children who have had problems at birth, or soon after their birth, and so need particular follow-up care from a health visitor, general practitioner or social worker

observe /əbˈzɜːv/ *verb* **1.** to see something ○ *The nurses observed signs of improvement in the patient's condition.* ○ *The girl's mother observed symptoms of anorexia.* **2.** to watch a person or thing carefully in order to discover something ○ *Observe the way in which the patient is lying.* **3.** to take something into account ○ *You're expected to observe the rules of conduct.*

obsessed /əbˈsest/ *adjective* having an obsession ○ *He is obsessed with the idea that someone is trying to kill him.*

obsession /əbˈseʃ(ə)n/ *noun* a mental disorder in which a person has a fixed idea or emotion which he or she cannot get rid of, even if he or she knows it is wrong or unpleasant ○ *She has an obsession about cats.*

obsessional /əbˈseʃ(ə)n(ə)l/ *adjective* referring to or having an obsession ○ *He is suffering from an obsessional disorder.*

obsessive /əbˈsesɪv/ *adjective* having or showing an obsession ○ *He has an obsessive desire to steal little objects.*

obsessive action /əbˌsesɪv ˈækʃən/ *noun* an action such as washing which is repeated over and over again and indicates a mental disorder

obsessive–compulsive disorder /əbˌsel↓sɪv kəmˈpʌlsɪv dɪsˌɔːdə/ *noun* a mental disorder characterised by the need to perform repeated ritual acts such as checking or cleaning, which can be treated with psychotherapy and antidepressants. Abbr **OCD**

obstetric /əb'stetrɪk(ə)l/, **obstetrical** /əb 'stetrɪkəl/ adjective referring to obstetrics

obstetrical forceps /əb,stetrɪk(ə)l 'fɔːseps/ plural noun a type of large forceps used to hold a baby's head during childbirth

obstetrician /,ɒbstə'trɪʃ(ə)n/ noun a doctor who specialises in obstetrics

obstetric patient /əb'stetrɪk ,peɪʃ(ə)nt/ noun a woman who is being treated by an obstetrician

obstetrics /əb'stetrɪks/ noun a branch of medicine and surgery dealing with pregnancy, childbirth and the period immediately after childbirth. Abbr **OB**

obstipation /,ɒbstɪ'peɪʃ(ə)n/ noun severe constipation, often caused by a blockage in the intestines

obstruct /əb'strʌkt/ verb to block something ○ The artery was obstructed by a blood clot.

obstruction /əb'strʌkʃən/ noun **1.** something which blocks a passage or a blood vessel **2.** the blocking of a passage or blood vessel

obstructive /əb'strʌktɪv/ adjective caused by an obstruction

obstructive jaundice /əb,strʌktɪv 'dʒɔːndɪs/ noun jaundice caused by an obstruction of the bile ducts. Also called **posthepatic jaundice**. ◊ **acholuric jaundice, icterus gravis neonatorum**

obstructive lung disease /əb,strʌktɪv 'lʌŋ dɪ,ziːz/ noun bronchitis and emphysema

obstructive sleep apnoea /əb,strʌktɪv 'sliːp ,æpnɪə/ noun the stopping of breathing, or difficulty in breathing, during sleep, resulting in loud snoring

obtain /əb'teɪn/ verb to get something ○ Some amino acids are obtained from food. ○ Where did he obtain the drugs?

obtrusive /əb'truːsɪv/ adjective **1.** forcing your presence on others **2.** referring to a scar which is very noticeable

obturation /,ɒbtjʊ'reɪʃ(ə)n/ noun the act of obstructing a body passage, or the state of a body passage when it is obstructed, e.g. by hard faeces

obturator /'ɒbtjʊreɪtə/ noun **1.** one of two muscles in the pelvis which govern the movement of the hip and thigh **2.** a device which closes an opening, e.g. a dental prosthesis which covers a cleft palate **3.** a metal bulb which fits into a bronchoscope or sigmoidoscope

obturator foramen /,ɒbtjʊreɪtə fə'reɪmən/ noun an opening in the hip bone near the acetabulum. See illustration at **PELVIS** in Supplement (NOTE: The plural is **obturator foramina**.)

obtusion /əb'tjuːʒ(ə)n/ noun a condition in which perception and feelings become dulled

OC abbr oral contraceptive

occipita /ɒk'sɪpɪtə/ plural of **occiput**

occipital /ɒk'sɪpɪt(ə)l/ adjective referring to the back of the head ■ noun same as **occipital bone**

occipital bone /ɒk'sɪpɪt(ə)l bəʊn/ noun the bone at the back of the head. Also called **occipital**

occipital condyle /ɒk,sɪpɪt(ə)l 'kɒndaɪl/ noun a round part of the occipital bone which joins it to the atlas

occipital lobe /ɒk'sɪpɪt(ə)l ləʊb/ noun the lobe at the back of each cerebral hemisphere

occipital notch /ɒk'sɪpɪt(ə)l nɒtʃ/ noun a point on the lower edge of the cerebral hemisphere where the surface has a notch

occipito-anterior /ɒk,sɪpɪtəʊ æn'tɪərɪə/ adjective referring to a position of a baby during birth, in which the baby faces the mother's back

occipito-posterior /ɒk,sɪpɪtəʊ pɒ'stɪərɪə/ adjective referring to a position of a baby during birth in which the baby faces the front

occiput /'ɒksɪpʌt/ noun the lower part of the back of the head or skull (NOTE: The plural is **occiputs** or **occipita**.)

occluded /ə'kluːdɪd/ adjective closed or blocked

occlusion /ə'kluːʒ(ə)n/ noun **1.** a thing which blocks a passage or which closes an opening **2.** the way in which the teeth in the upper and lower jaws fit together when the jaws are closed (NOTE: A bad fit between the teeth is a **malocclusion**.)

occlusive /ə'kluːsɪv/ adjective referring to occlusion or blocking

occlusive stroke /ə,kluːsɪv 'strəʊk/ noun a stroke caused by a blood clot

occlusive therapy /ə,kluːsɪv 'θerəpi/ noun a treatment for a squint in which the good eye is covered up in order to encourage the squinting eye to become straight

occult /ə'kʌlt/ adjective **1.** not easy to see with the naked eye. Opposite **overt 2.** referring to a symptom or sign which is hidden

occult blood /ə,kʌlt 'blʌd/ noun very small quantities of blood in the faeces, which can only be detected by tests

occupancy rate /'ɒkjʊpənsi reɪt/ noun the number of beds occupied in a hospital, shown as a percentage of all the beds

occupation /,ɒkjʊ'peɪʃ(ə)n/ noun **1.** a job or work ○ What is his occupation? ○ People in sedentary occupations are liable to digestive disorders. **2.** the state or fact of occupying something or of being occupied

occupational /,ɒkjʊ'peɪʃ(ə)nəl/ adjective referring to work

occupational asthma /ˌɒkjupeɪʃ(ə)n(ə)l ˈæsmə/ *noun* asthma caused by materials with which people come into contact at work

occupational dermatitis /ˌɒkjupeɪʃ(ə)n(ə)l ˌdɜːməˈtaɪtɪs/ *noun* dermatitis caused by materials touched at work

occupational disease /ɒkjuˈpeɪʃ(ə)nəl dɪ ˌziːz/ *noun* a disease which is caused by the type of work a person does or the conditions in which a person works, e.g. a disease caused by dust or chemicals in a factory

occupational hazard /ˌɒkjupeɪʃ(ə)n(ə)l ˈhæzəd/ *noun* a dangerous situation related to the working environment

occupational health nurse /ˌɒkju peɪʃ(ə)n(ə)l ˈhelθ nɜːs/ *noun* a nurse who deals with health problems of people at work. Abbr **OH nurse**

occupational medicine /ˌɒkju peɪʃ(ə)n(ə)l ˈmed(ə)sɪn/ *noun* the branch of medicine concerned with accidents and diseases connected with work

occupational therapist /ˌɒkjupeɪʃ(ə)n(ə)l ˈθerəpɪst/ *noun* a qualified health professional who offers patients occupational therapy

occupational therapy /ˌɒkjupeɪʃ(ə)n(ə)l ˈθerəpi/ *noun* light work or hobbies used as a means of treatment, especially for physically challenged or mentally ill people, to promote independence during the recovery period after an illness or operation

occur /əˈkɜː/ *verb* **1.** to take place ○ *one of the most frequently occurring types of tumour* ○ *Thrombosis occurred in the artery.* ○ *a form of glaucoma which occurs in infants.* **2.** to come into a person's mind ○ *It occurred to her that she might be pregnant.* (NOTE: **occurring – occurred**)

occurrence /əˈkʌrəns/ *noun* something that takes place ○ *Neuralgia is a common occurrence after shingles.*

OCD *abbr* obsessive-compulsive disorder

ochronosis /ˌɒkrəʊˈnəʊsɪs/ *noun* a condition in which cartilage, ligaments and other fibrous tissue become dark as a result of a metabolic disorder, and in which the urine turns black on exposure to air

ocular /ˈɒkjulə/ *adjective* referring to the eye ○ *Opticians are trained to detect all kinds of ocular imbalance.*

ocular dominance /ˌɒkjulə ˈdɒmɪnəns/ *noun* a condition in which a person uses one eye more than the other

ocular prosthesis /ˌɒkjulə prɒsˈθiːsɪs/ *noun* a false eye

oculi /ˈɒkjulaɪ/ ♦ **orbicularis oculi**

oculist /ˈɒkjulɪst/ *noun* a qualified physician or surgeon who specialises in the treatment of eye disorders

oculo- /ˈɒkjuləʊ/ *prefix* eye

oculogyric /ˌɒkjuləʊˈdʒaɪrɪk/ *adjective* causing eye movements

oculomotor /ˌɒkjuləʊˈməʊtə/ *adjective* referring to movements of the eyeball

oculomotor nerve /ˌɒkjuləʊˈməʊtə nɜːv/ *noun* the third cranial nerve which controls the eyeballs and eyelids

oculonasal /ˌɒkjuləʊˈneɪz(ə)l/ *adjective* referring to both the eye and the nose

oculoplethysmography /ˌɒkjuləʊˌpleθɪz ˈmɒgrəfi/ *noun* measurement of the pressure inside the eyeball

OD *abbr* overdose

o.d. *adverb* (*written on a prescription*) every day. Full form **omni die**

ODA *abbr* operating department assistant

odont- /ɒdɒnt/ *prefix* same as **odonto-** (*used before vowels*)

odontalgia /ˌɒdɒnˈtældʒə/ *noun* same as **toothache**

odontitis /ˌɒdɒnˈtaɪtɪs/ *noun* inflammation of the pulpy interior of a tooth

odonto- /ɒdɒntəʊ/ *prefix* tooth

odontoid /ɒˈdɒntɔɪd/ *adjective* similar to a tooth, especially in shape

odontoid process /ɒˌdɒntɔɪd ˈprəʊses/ *noun* a projecting part of a vertebra, shaped like a tooth

odontology /ˌɒdɒnˈtɒlədʒi/ *noun* the study of teeth and associated structures, and their disorders

odontoma /ˌɒdɒnˈtəʊmə/, **odontome** /ˈɒdɒntəʊm/ *noun* **1.** a structure like a tooth which has an unusual arrangement of its component tissues **2.** a solid or cystic tumour derived from cells concerned with the development of a tooth (NOTE: The plural is **odontomas** or **odontomata**.)

odourless /ˈəʊdələs/ *adjective* with no smell

odyn- /ɒdɪn/ *prefix* same as **odyno-** (*used before vowels*)

-odynia /ədɪniə/ *suffix* pain

odyno- /ɒdɪnəʊ/ *prefix* pain

odynophagia /ɒˌdɪnəˈfeɪdʒə/ *noun* a condition in which pain occurs when food is swallowed

oedema /ɪˈdiːmə/ *noun* the swelling of part of the body caused by accumulation of fluid in the intercellular tissue spaces ○ *Her main problem is oedema of the feet.* Also called **dropsy.** ◊ **tumescence** (NOTE: The US spelling is **edema**.)

oedematous /ɪˈdemətəs/ *adjective* referring to oedema (NOTE: The US spelling is **edematous**.)

Oedipus complex /ˈiːdɪpəs ˌkɒmpleks/ *noun* (*in Freudian psychology*) a condition in which a boy feels sexually attracted to his mother and sees his father as an obstacle

oesophag- /iːsɒfədʒ/ *prefix* same as **oesophago-** (*used before vowels*)

oesophageal /iːˌsɒfəˈdʒiːəl/ *adjective* referring to the oesophagus (NOTE: The US spelling is **esophageal**.)

oesophageal hiatus /iːˌsɒfəˌdʒiːəl haɪ'eɪtəs/ *noun* the opening in the diaphragm through which the oesophagus passes

oesophageal varices /iːˌsɒfəˌdʒiːəl 'værɪsiːz/ *plural noun* varicose veins in the oesophagus

oesophagectomy /iːˌsɒfəˈdʒektəmi/ *noun* a surgical operation to remove part of the oesophagus (NOTE: The plural is **oesophagectomies**.)

oesophagi /iːˈsɒfəgi/ *plural of* **oesophagus**

oesophagitis /iːˌsɒfəˈdʒaɪtɪs/ *noun* inflammation of the oesophagus, caused by acid juices from the stomach or by infection

oesophago- /iːˈsɒfəgəʊ/ *prefix* oesophagus (NOTE: The US spelling is **esophago-**.)

oesophagocele /iːˈsɒfəgəʊsiːl/ *noun* a condition in which the mucous membrane lining the oesophagus protrudes through the wall

oesophagogastroduodenoscopy /iːˌsɒfəgəʊˌgæstrəʊˌdjuːəʊdəˈnɒskəpi/ *noun* a surgical operation in which a tube is put down into the oesophagus so that the doctor can examine it, the stomach and the duodenum. Abbr **OGD** (NOTE: The plural is **oesophagogastroduodenoscopies**.)

oesophagojejunostomy /iːˌsɒfəgəʊdʒiˌdʒuːˈnɒstəmi/ *noun* a surgical operation to create a junction between the jejunum and the oesophagus after the stomach has been removed (NOTE: The plural is **oesophagojejunostomies**.)

oesophagoscope /iːˈsɒfəgəʊskəʊp/ *noun* a thin tube with a light at the end, which is passed down the oesophagus to examine it

oesophagoscopy /iːˌsɒfəˈgɒskəpi/ *noun* an examination of the oesophagus with an oesophagoscope (NOTE: The plural is **oesophagoscopies**.)

oesophagostomy /iːˌsɒfəˈgɒstəmi/ *noun* a surgical operation to make an opening in the oesophagus to allow the person to be fed, usually after an operation on the pharynx (NOTE: The plural is **oesophagostomies**.)

oesophagotomy /iːˌsɒfəˈgɒtəmi/ *noun* a surgical operation to make an opening in the oesophagus to remove something which is blocking it (NOTE: The plural is **oesophagotomies**.)

oesophagus /iːˈsɒfəgəs/ *noun* a tube down which food passes from the pharynx to the stomach (NOTE: The plural is **oesophagi**. The US spellings are **esophagus** and **esophagi**.)

oestradiol /ˌiːstrəˈdaɪɒl/ *noun* a type of oestrogen secreted by an ovarian follicle, which stimulates the development of secondary sexual characteristics in females at puberty (NOTE: A synthetic form of oestradiol is given as treatment for oestrogen deficiency. The US spelling is **estradiol**.)

oestriol /ˈiːstrɪɒl/ *noun* a placental hormone with oestrogenic properties, found in the urine of pregnant women (NOTE: The US spelling is **estriol**.)

oestrogen /ˈiːstrədʒən/ *noun* any steroid hormone which stimulates the development of secondary sexual characteristics in females at puberty (NOTE: The US spelling is **estrogen**.)

COMMENT: Synthetic oestrogens form most oral contraceptives, and are also used in the treatment of menstrual and menopausal disorders.

oestrogenic hormone /ˌiːstrədʒenɪk 'hɔːməʊn/ *noun* synthetic oestrogen used to treat conditions which develop during menopause (NOTE: The US spelling is **estrogenic hormone**.)

oestrone /ˈiːstrəʊn/ *noun* a type of oestrogen produced in the ovaries (NOTE: The US spelling is **estrone**.)

official /əˈfɪʃ(ə)l/ *adjective* **1.** accepted or permitted by an authority ○ *We need to undertake a review of the official procedures.* **2.** constituting an authority

official drug /əˌfɪʃ(ə)l 'drʌg/ *noun* any drug listed in the national pharmacopoeia

officially /əˈfɪʃ(ə)li/ *adverb* in a way that is approved by an authority ○ *officially listed as a dangerous drug*

OGD *abbr* oesophagogastroduodenoscopy

OH nurse /əʊ 'eɪtʃ nɜːs/ *abbr* occupational health nurse

-oid /ɔɪd/ *suffix* like or related to

oil /ɔɪl/ *noun* a liquid which cannot be mixed with water (NOTE: There are three types of oil: fixed vegetable or animal oils, volatile oils and mineral oils.)

oily /ˈɔɪli/ *adjective* containing or resembling oil

ointment /ˈɔɪntmənt/ *noun* a smooth oily medicinal preparation which can be spread on the skin to soothe or to protect

old age /əʊld 'eɪdʒ/ *noun* a period in a person's life, usually taken to be after the age of sixty-five

oleaginous /ˌəʊliˈædʒɪnəs/ *adjective* same as **oily**

olecranon /əʊˈlekrənɒn/, **olecranon process** /əʊˈlekrənɒn ˌprəʊsəs/ *noun* a curved projecting part at the end of the ulna at the elbow, which gives rise to a painful tingling sensation if hit by accident. Also called **funny bone**

oleic /əʊˈliːɪk/ *adjective* referring to oil

oleic acid /əʊˌliːɪk 'æsɪd/ *noun* a fatty acid which is present in most oils

oleo- /ˈəʊliəʊ/ *prefix* oil

oleum /ˈəʊliəm/ *noun* oil (*used in pharmacy*)

olfaction /ɒlˈfækʃən/ noun **1.** the sense of smell **2.** the way in which a person's sensory organs detect smells

olfactory /ɒlˈfækt(ə)ri/ adjective referring to the sense of smell

olfactory area /ɒlˌfækt(ə)ri ˈeəriə/ noun the part of the brain that registers smell

olfactory bulb /ɒlˈfækt(ə)ri bʌlb/ noun the end of the olfactory tract, where the processes of the sensory cells in the nose are linked to the fibres of the olfactory nerve

olfactory cortex /ɒlˌfækt(ə)ri ˈkɔːteks/ noun the parts of the cerebral cortex which receive information about smell

olfactory nerve /ɒlˈfækt(ə)ri nɜːv/ noun the first cranial nerve which controls the sense of smell

olfactory tract /ɒlˈfækt(ə)ri trækt/ noun a nerve tract which takes the olfactory nerve from the nose to the brain

olig- /ɒlɪg/ prefix same as **oligo-** (used before vowels)

oligaemia /ˌɒlɪˈgiːmiə/ noun a condition in which a person has too little blood in his or her circulatory system (NOTE: The US spelling is **oligemia**.)

oligo- /ɒlɪgəʊ/ prefix few or little

oligodactylism /ˌɒlɪgəʊˈdæktɪlɪz(ə)m/ noun a congenital condition in which a baby is born without some fingers or toes

oligodipsia /ˌɒlɪgəʊˈdɪpsiə/ noun a condition in which a person does not want to drink

oligodontia /ˌɒlɪgəʊˈdɒnʃə/ noun a state in which most of the teeth are lacking

oligohydramnios /ˌɒlɪgəʊhaɪˈdræmniəs/ noun a condition in which the amnion surrounding the fetus contains too little amniotic fluid

oligomenorrhoea /ˌɒlɪgəʊmenəˈriːə/ noun a condition in which a person menstruates infrequently (NOTE: The US spelling is **oligomenorrhea**.)

oligo-ovulation /ˌɒlɪgəʊ ˌɒvjʊˈleɪʃ(ə)n/ noun ovulation which does not occur as often as is usual

oligospermia /ˌɒlɪgəʊˈspɜːmiə/ noun a condition in which there are too few spermatozoa in the semen

oliguria /ˌɒlɪˈgjʊəriə/ noun a condition in which a person does not produce enough urine

olive /ˈɒlɪv/ noun **1.** the fruit of a tree, which gives an edible oil **2.** a swelling containing grey matter, on the side of the pyramid of the medulla oblongata

-ology /ɒlədʒi/ suffix area of study

-olol /əlɒl/ suffix beta blocker ○ atenolol ○ propranolol hydrochloride

o.m. adverb (written on a prescription) every morning. Full form **omni mane**

-oma /əʊmə/ suffix tumour

Ombudsman /ˈɒmbʊdzmən/ ♦ **Health Service Commissioner**

oment- /əʊment/ prefix omentum

omenta /əʊˈmentə/ plural of **omentum**

omental /əʊˈment(ə)l/ adjective referring to the omentum

omentectomy /ˌəʊmenˈtektəmi/ noun a surgical operation to remove part of the omentum (NOTE: The plural is **omentectomies**.)

omentopexy /əʊˈmentəpeksi/ noun a surgical operation to attach the omentum to the abdominal wall (NOTE: The plural is **omentopexies**.)

omentum /əʊˈmentəm/ noun a double fold of peritoneum hanging down over the intestines. Also called **epiploon** (NOTE: The plural is **omenta**. For other terms referring to the omentum see words beginning with **epiplo-**.)

COMMENT: The omentum is in two sections: the **greater omentum** which covers the intestines, and the **lesser omentum** which hangs between the liver and the stomach and the liver and the duodenum.

omeprazole /əʊˈmeprəzəʊl/ noun a drug which reduces the amount of acid released in the stomach, used in the treatment of ulcers and heartburn

omphal- /ɒmfəl/ prefix same as **omphalo-** (used before vowels)

omphali /ˈɒmfəli/ plural of **omphalus**

omphalitis /ˌɒmfəˈlaɪtɪs/ noun inflammation of the navel

omphalo- /ɒmfələʊ/ prefix navel

omphalocele /ˈɒmfələsiːl/ noun a hernia in which part of the intestine protrudes through the abdominal wall near the navel

omphalus /ˈɒmfələs/ noun a scar with a depression in the middle of the abdomen where the umbilical cord was detached after birth. Also called **navel, umbilicus** (NOTE: The plural is **omphali**.)

-omycin /əʊmaɪsɪn/ suffix macrolide drug ○ erythromycin

o.n. adverb (written on a prescription) every night. Full form **omni nocte**

onanism /ˈəʊnənɪz(ə)m/ noun same as **masturbation**

Onchocerca /ˌɒŋkəʊˈsɜːkə/ noun a genus of tropical parasitic threadworms

onchocerciasis /ˌɒŋkəʊsɜːˈkaɪəsɪs/ noun infestation with Onchocerca in which the larvae can move into the eye, causing river blindness

onco- /ɒŋkəʊ/ prefix tumour

oncogene /ˈɒŋkədʒiːn/ noun a part of the genetic system which causes malignant tumours to develop

'…all cancers may be reduced to fundamental mechanisms based on cancer risk genes or oncogenes within ourselves. An oncogene is a gene that encodes a protein that contributes to the malignant phenotype of the cell' [British Medical Journal]

oncogenesis /ˌɒŋkə'dʒenəsɪs/ *noun* the origin and development of a tumour

oncogenic /ˌɒŋkə'dʒenɪk/ *adjective* causing tumours to develop ○ *an oncogenic virus*

oncologist /ɒŋ'kɒlədʒɪst/ *noun* a doctor who specialises in oncology, especially cancer

oncology /ɒŋ'kɒlədʒi/ *noun* the scientific study of new growths, especially cancers

oncolysis /ɒŋ'kɒləsɪs/ *noun* the destruction of a tumour or of tumour cells

oncometer /ɒŋ'kɒmɪtə/ *noun* **1.** an instrument for measuring swelling in an arm or leg using changes in their blood pressure **2.** an instrument for measuring the variations in size of the kidney and other organs of the body

oncotic /ɒŋ'kɒtɪk/ *adjective* referring to a tumour

ondansetron /ɒn'dænsɪtrɒn/ *noun* a drug which helps to prevent the production of serotonin, used to control nausea and vomiting caused by drug treatment and radiotherapy for cancer

onset /'ɒnset/ *noun* the beginning of something ○ *The onset of the illness is marked by sudden high temperature.*

ontogeny /ɒn'tɒdʒəni/ *noun* the origin and development of an individual organism

onych- /ɒnɪk/ *prefix* same as **onycho-** (*used before vowels*)

onychauxis /ˌɒnɪ'kɔːksɪs/ *noun* excessive growth of the nails of the fingers or toes

onychia /ɒ'nɪkiə/ *noun* an irregularity of the nails caused by inflammation of the matrix

onycho- /ɒnɪkəʊ/ *prefix* nails

onychogryphosis /ˌɒnɪkəʊgrɪ'fəʊsɪs/ *noun* a condition in which the nails are bent or curved over the ends of the fingers or toes

onycholysis /ˌɒnɪ'kɒləsɪs/ *noun* a condition in which a nail becomes separated from its bed, without falling out

onychomadesis /ˌɒnɪkəʊmə'diːsɪs/ *noun* a condition in which the nails fall out

onychomycosis /ˌɒnɪkəʊmaɪ'kəʊsɪs/ *noun* an infection of a nail with a fungus

onychosis /ˌɒnɪ'kəʊsɪs/ *noun* any disease of the nails (NOTE: The plural is **onychoses**.)

o'nyong-nyong fever /ˌəʊ 'njɒŋ ˌnjɒŋ ˌfiːvə/ *noun* an infectious virus disease prevalent in East Africa, spread by mosquitoes. The symptoms are high fever, inflammation of the lymph nodes and excruciating pains in the joints. Also called **joint-breaker fever**

oo- /əʊə/ *prefix* ovum or embryo

oocyesis /ˌəʊəsaɪ'iːsɪs/ *noun* a pregnancy which develops in the ovary (NOTE: The plural is **oocyeses**.)

oocyte /'əʊəsaɪt/ *noun* a cell which forms from an oogonium and becomes an ovum by meiosis

oocyte donation /ˌəʊəsaɪt dəʊ'neɪʃ(ə)n/ *noun* the transfer of oocytes from one woman to another who cannot produce her own, so that she can have a baby. The oocytes are removed in a laparoscopy and fertilised in vitro.

oogenesis /ˌəʊə'dʒenəsɪs/ *noun* the formation and development of ova

COMMENT: In oogenesis, an oogonium produces an oocyte, which develops through several stages to produce a mature ovum. Polar bodies are also formed which do not develop into ova.

oogenetic /ˌəʊədʒə'netɪk/ *adjective* referring to oogenesis

oogonium /ˌəʊə'gəʊniəm/ *noun* a cell produced at the beginning of the development of an ovum (NOTE: The plural is **oogonia**.)

oophor- /əʊəfɔʊr/ *prefix* same as **oophoro-** (*used before vowels*)

oophoralgia /ˌəʊəfə'rældʒə/ *noun* pain in the ovaries

oophore /'əʊəfɔː/ *noun* same as **ovary**

oophorectomy /ˌəʊəfə'rektəmi/ *noun* a surgical operation to remove an ovary. Also called **ovariectomy** (NOTE: The plural is **oophorectomies**.)

oophoritis /ˌəʊəfə'raɪtɪs/ *noun* inflammation in an ovary, which can be caused by mumps. Also called **ovaritis**

oophoro- /əʊɒfərəʊ/ *prefix* ovary

oophorocystectomy /əʊˌɒfərəʊsɪ'stektəmi/ *noun* a surgical operation to remove an ovarian cyst (NOTE: The plural is **oophorocystectomies**.)

oophorocystosis /əʊˌɒfərəʊsɪ'stəʊsɪs/ *noun* the development of one or more ovarian cysts

oophoroma /ˌəʊəfə'rəʊmə/ *noun* a rare ovarian tumour, occurring in middle age (NOTE: The plural is **oophoromas** or **oophoromata**.)

oophoron /əʊ'ɒfərɒn/ *noun* same as **ovary** (*technical*) (NOTE: The plural is **oophora**.)

oophoropexy /əʊ'ɒfərəpeksi/ *noun* a surgical operation to attach an ovary (NOTE: The plural is **oophoropexies**.)

oophorosalpingectomy /əʊˌɒfərəˌsælpɪn'dʒektəmi/ *noun* a surgical operation to remove an ovary and the Fallopian tube attached to it (NOTE: The plural is **oophorosalpingectomies**.)

ooze /uːz/ *verb* **1.** (*of pus, blood or other liquid*) to flow slowly **2.** to leak a substance such as pus or blood (NOTE: **oozing – oozed**)

op /ɒp/ *noun* an operation (*informal*)

OP *abbr* outpatient

opacification /əʊpæsɪfɪ'keɪʃ(ə)n/ *noun* the fact of becoming opaque, as the lens does in a case of cataract

opacity /əʊ'pæsɪti/ *noun* **1.** the fact of not allowing light to pass through **2.** an area in the eye which is not clear (NOTE: The plural is **opacities**.)

opaque /əʊ'peɪk/ *adjective* not allowing light to pass through. Opposite **transparent**

open /ˈəʊpən/ *adjective* not closed

open-angle glaucoma /ˌəʊpən ˌæŋg(ə)l glɔːˈkəʊmə/ *noun* an unusually high pressure of fluid inside the eyeball caused by a blockage in the channel through which the aqueous humour drains. Also called **chronic glaucoma**

open fracture /ˌəʊpən ˈfræktʃə/ *noun* same as **compound fracture**

open-heart surgery /ˌəʊpən ˈhɑːt ˌsɜːdʒəri/ *noun* surgery to repair part of the heart or one of the coronary arteries performed while the heart has been bypassed and the blood is circulated by a pump

opening /ˈəʊp(ə)nɪŋ/ *noun* a place where something opens

open visiting /ˌəʊpən ˈvɪzɪtɪŋ/ *noun* an arrangement in a hospital by which visitors can enter the wards at any time

operable /ˈɒp(ə)rəb(ə)l/ *adjective* referring to a condition which can be treated by a surgical operation ○ *The cancer is still operable.*

operant conditioning /ˈɒpərənt kənˌdɪʃ(ə)nɪŋ/ *noun* a form of learning which takes place when a piece of spontaneous behaviour is either reinforced by a reward or discouraged by punishment

operate /ˈɒpəreɪt/ *verb* **1.** to function or work, or to make something function or work **2.** to treat a person for a condition by cutting open the body and removing a part which is diseased or repairing a part which is not functioning correctly ○ *The patient was operated on yesterday.* ○ *The surgeons decided to operate as the only way of saving the baby's life.* (NOTE: **operating – operated**)

operating department *noun* a hospital department specialising in surgical operations

operating department assistant /ˌɒpəreɪtɪŋ dɪˌpɑːtmənt əˈsɪstənt/ *noun* a person who works in an operating department. Abbr **ODA**

operating microscope /ˈɒpəreɪtɪŋ ˌmaɪkrəskəʊp/ *noun* a special microscope with two eyepieces and a light, used in very delicate surgery

operating room *US* same as **operating theatre**. Abbr **OR**

operating table /ˈɒpəreɪtɪŋ ˌteɪb(ə)l/ *noun* a special table on which the patient is placed to undergo a surgical operation

operating theatre /ˈɒpəreɪtɪŋ ˌθɪətə/ *noun* a special room in a hospital, where surgical operations are carried out (NOTE: The US term is **operating room**.)

operation /ˌɒpəˈreɪʃ(ə)n/ *noun* **1.** the way in which something operates **2.** a surgical procedure carried out to repair or remove a damaged body part ○ *She's had an operation on her foot.* ○ *The operation to remove the cataract was successful.* ○ *A team of surgeons performed the operation.* ○ *Heart operations are always difficult.* (NOTE: A surgeon **performs** or

carries out an operation **on** a patient.) **3.** the way in which a drug acts

operative /ˈɒp(ə)rətɪv/ *adjective* taking place during a surgical operation. ◊ **peroperative, postoperative, preoperative**

operator /ˈɒpəreɪtə/ *noun* **1.** someone whose job is to operate a machine or piece of equipment **2.** a surgeon who operates on people

operculum /əˈpɜːkjʊləm/ *noun* **1.** a part of the cerebral hemisphere which overlaps the insula **2.** a plug of mucus which can block the cervical canal during pregnancy (NOTE: The plural is **opercula** or **operculums**.)

ophth- /ɒfθ, ɒpθ/ *prefix* eye

ophthalm- /ɒfθælm, ɒpθælm/ *prefix* same as **ophthalmo-** (*used before vowels*)

ophthalmectomy /ˌɒfθælˈmektəmi/ *noun* a surgical operation to remove an eye (NOTE: The plural is **ophthalmectomies**.)

ophthalmia /ɒfˈθælmiə/ *noun* inflammation of the eye

ophthalmia neonatorum /ɒfˌθælmiə niːˌəʊneɪˈtɔːrəm/ *noun* conjunctivitis of a newborn baby, beginning 21 days after birth, caused by infection in the birth canal

ophthalmic /ɒfˈθælmɪk/ *adjective* referring to the eye

ophthalmic nerve /ɒfˈθælmɪk nɜːv/ *noun* a branch of the trigeminal nerve, supplying the eyeball, the upper eyelid, the brow and one side of the scalp

ophthalmic optician /ɒfˌθælmɪk ɒpˈtɪʃ(ə)n/, **ophthalmic practitioner** *noun* same as **optician**

ophthalmic surgeon /ɒfˌθælmɪk ˈsɜːdʒən/ *noun* a surgeon who specialises in surgery to treat eye disorders

ophthalmitis /ˌɒfθælˈmaɪtɪs/ *noun* inflammation of the eye

ophthalmo- /ɒfθælməʊ, ɒpθælməʊ/ *prefix* eye or eyeball

ophthalmological /ɒfˌθælməˈlɒdʒɪk(ə)l/ *adjective* referring to ophthalmology

ophthalmologist /ˌɒfθælˈmɒlədʒɪst/ *noun* a doctor who specialises in the study of the eye and its diseases. Also called **eye specialist**

ophthalmology /ˌɒfθælˈmɒlədʒi/ *noun* the study of the eye and its diseases

ophthalmoplegia /ˌɒfθælməˈpliːdʒə/ *noun* paralysis of the muscles of the eye

ophthalmoscope /ɒfˈθælməskəʊp/ *noun* an instrument containing a bright light and small lenses, used by a doctor to examine the inside of an eye

ophthalmoscopy /ˌɒfθælˈmɒskəpi/ *noun* an examination of the inside of an eye using an ophthalmoscope (NOTE: The plural is **ophthalmoscopies**.)

ophthalmotomy /ˌɒfθælˈmɒtəmi/ *noun* a surgical operation to make a cut in the eyeball (NOTE: The plural is **ophthalmotomies**.)

ophthalmotonometer /ˌɒfθælmətə
'nɒmɪtə/ *noun* an instrument which measures
pressure inside the eye

-opia /əʊpiə/ *suffix* eye condition

opiate /'əʊpiət/ *noun* a sedative which is prepared from opium, e.g. morphine or codeine

opinion /ə'pɪnjən/ *noun* what a person thinks
about something ○ *What's the surgeon's opinion of the case?* ○ *The doctor asked the consultant for his opinion as to the best method of
treatment.*

opioid /'əʊpiɔɪd/ *adjective* based on opium ○
Codeine is an opioid analgesic.

opistho- /ɒpɪsθəʊ/ *prefix* backbone

opisthotonos /ˌɒpɪs'θɒtənəs/ *noun* a spasm
of the body in which the spine is arched backwards, occurring, e.g., in people with tetanus

opium /'əʊpiəm/ *noun* a substance made
from poppies which is used in the preparation
of codeine and heroin

opponens /ə'pəʊnənz/ *noun* one of a group
of muscles which control the movements of
the fingers, especially one which allows the
thumb and little finger to come together

opportunist /ˌɒpə'tjuːnɪst/, **opportunistic** /
ˌɒpətjuːˈnɪstɪk/ *adjective* referring to a parasite or microorganism which takes advantage
of the host's weakened state to cause infection

opposition /ˌɒpə'zɪʃ(ə)n/ *noun* **1.** hostility
towards something **2.** a movement of the hand
muscles in which the tip of the thumb is made
to touch the tip of another finger so as to hold
something

opsonic index /ɒpˌsɒnɪk 'ɪndeks/ *noun* a
number which gives the strength of a person's
serum reaction to bacteria

opsonin /'ɒpsənɪn/ *noun* a substance, usually an antibody, in blood which sticks to the surface of bacteria and helps to destroy them

optic /'ɒptɪk/ *adjective* referring to the eye or
to sight

optical /'ɒptɪk(ə)l/ *adjective* **1.** same as **optic**
2. relating to the visible light spectrum

optical fibre /ˌɒptɪk(ə)l 'faɪbə/ *noun* an artificial fibre which can carry light or images

optical illusion /ˌɒptɪk(ə)l ɪ'luːʒ(ə)n/ *noun*
something which is seen wrongly so that it appears to be something else

optic chiasma /ˌɒptɪk kaɪ'æzmə/ *noun* a
structure where some of the optic nerves from
each eye partially cross each other in the hypothalamus

optic disc /'ɒptɪk dɪsk/ *noun* the point on the
retina where the optic nerve starts. Also called
optic papilla

optic fundus /ˌɒptɪk 'fʌndəs/ *noun* the back
part of the inside of the eye, opposite the lens

optician /ɒp'tɪʃ(ə)n/ *noun* a qualified person
who specialises in making glasses and in testing eyes and prescribing lenses. Also called
ophthalmic optician (NOTE: In US English, an

optician is a technician who makes lenses and
fits glasses, but cannot test patient's eyesight.)

COMMENT: In the UK qualified opticians must
be registered by the General Optical Council
before they can practise.

optic nerve /'ɒptɪk nɜːv/ *noun* the second
cranial nerve which transmits the sensation of
sight from the eye to the brain. See illustration
at EYE in Supplement

optic neuritis /ˌɒptɪk njʊ'raɪtɪs/ *noun* same
as **retrobulbar neuritis**

optic papilla /ˌɒptɪk pə'pɪlə/ *noun* same as
optic disc

optic radiation /ˌɒptɪk ˌreɪdi'eɪʃ(ə)n/ *noun*
a nerve tract which takes the optic impulses
from the optic tract to the visual cortex

optics /'ɒptɪks/ *noun* the study of the visible
light spectrum and sight

optic tract /ˌɒptɪk 'trækt/ *noun* a nerve tract
which takes the optic nerve from the optic chiasma to the optic radiation

opto- /ɒptəʊ/ *prefix* sight

optometer /ɒp'tɒmɪtə/ *noun* same as **refractometer**

optometrist /ɒp'tɒmətrɪst/ *noun mainly US*
a person who specialises in testing eyes and
prescribing lenses

optometry /ɒp'tɒmətri/ *noun* the testing of
eyes and prescribing of lenses to correct sight

-oquine /əkwɪn/ *suffix* antimalarial drug ○
chloroquine

OR *abbr US* operating room

ora /'ɔːrə/ *plural noun* plural of **os** *noun* 2

oral /'ɔːrəl/ *adjective* **1.** referring to the mouth
2. referring to medication that is swallowed ○
an oral contraceptive Compare **enteral,
parenteral**

oral cavity /ˌɔːrəl 'kævɪti/ *noun* the mouth

oral contraceptive /ˌɔːrəl ˌkɒntrə'septɪv/
noun a contraceptive pill which is swallowed

oral hygiene /ˌɔːrəl 'haɪdʒiːn/ *noun* the
practice of keeping the mouth clean by gar-
gling and mouthwashes

orally /'ɔːrəli/ *adverb* by swallowing ○ *not to
be taken orally*

oral medication /ˌɔːrəl ˌmedɪ'keɪʃ(ə)n/
noun medication which is taken by swallowing

oral rehydration solution /ˌɔːrəl ˌriːhaɪ
'dreɪʃ(ə)n səˌluːʃ(ə)n/ *noun* a liquid given as
a drink to correct the water, mineral and nutritional deficiencies in a person who is affected
by dehydration

oral rehydration therapy /ˌɔːrəl ˌriːhaɪ
'dreɪʃ(ə)n ˌθerəpi/ *noun* the administration of
a simple glucose and electrolyte solution to
treat acute diarrhoea, particularly in children,
which has greatly reduced the number of
deaths from dehydration. Abbr **ORT**

oral thermometer /ˌɔːrəl θə'mɒmɪtə/ *noun*
a thermometer which is put into the mouth to
take someone's temperature

orbicularis /ɔːˌbɪkjʊˈleərɪs/ *noun* a circular muscle in the face

orbicularis oculi /ɔːˌbɪkjʊˌleərɪs ˈɒkjʊlaɪ/ *noun* a muscle which opens and closes the eye

orbicularis oris /ɔːˌbɪkjʊˌleərɪs ˈɔːrɪs/ *noun* a muscle which closes the lips tight

orbit /ˈɔːbɪt/ *noun* the hollow bony depression in the front of the skull in which each eye and lacrimal gland are situated. Also called **eye socket**

orbital /ˈɔːbɪt(ə)l/ *adjective* referring to the orbit

orchi- /ɔːkɪ/ *prefix* testis

orchidalgia /ˌɔːkɪˈdældʒə/ *noun* a neuralgic-type pain in a testis

orchidectomy /ˌɔːkɪˈdektəmi/ *noun* a surgical operation to remove a testis (NOTE: The plural is **orchidectomies**.)

orchidopexy /ˈɔːkɪdəʊˌpeksi/ *noun* a surgical operation to place an undescended testis in the scrotum. Also called **orchiopexy** (NOTE: The plural is **orchidopexies**.)

orchidotomy /ˌɔːkɪˈdɒtəmi/ *noun* a surgical operation to make a cut into a testis (NOTE: The plural is **orchidotomies**.)

orchiepididymitis /ˌɔːkiˌepɪdɪdɪˈmaɪtɪs/ *noun* a condition in which a testicle and its epididymis become swollen

orchiopexy /ˈɔːkiəʊˌpeksi/ *noun* same as **orchidopexy** (NOTE: The plural is **orchiopexies**.)

orchis /ˈɔːkɪs/ *noun* a testis

orchitis /ɔːˈkaɪtɪs/ *noun* inflammation of the testes, characterised by hypertrophy, pain and a sensation of weight

orderly /ˈɔːdəli/ *noun* a person who does general work in a hospital (NOTE: The plural is **orderlies**.)

Orem's model /ˈɔːrəmz ˌmɒd(ə)l/ *noun* a modern model for nursing which focuses on a person's ability to perform self-care, defined as activities which individuals initiate and perform on their own behalf to maintain life, health and well-being

organ /ˈɔːgən/ *noun* a part of the body which is distinct from other parts and has a particular function, e.g. the liver, an eye or ovaries

organic /ɔːˈgænɪk/ *adjective* 1. referring to organs in the body 2. coming from an animal, plant or other organism 3. referring to food which has been cultivated naturally, without certain fertilisers or pesticides

organically /ɔːˈgænɪkli/ *adverb* in a natural or apparently natural way

organic disease /ɔːˌgænɪk dɪˈziːz/, **organic disorder** /ɔːˌgænɪk dɪsˈɔːdə/ *noun* a disease or disorder associated with physical changes in one or more organs of the body

organisation /ˌɔːgənaɪˈzeɪʃ(ə)n/, **organization** *noun* 1. a group of people set up for a particular purpose 2. the planning or arranging of something ○ *the organisation of the rota* 3. the

way in which the component parts of something are arranged

organism /ˈɔːgənɪz(ə)m/ *noun* any single plant, animal, bacterium, fungus or other living thing

organo- /ɔːgənəʊ, ɔːgænəʊ/ *prefix* organ

organ of Corti /ˌɔːgən əv ˈkɔːti/ *noun* a membrane in the cochlea which takes sounds and converts them into impulses sent to the brain along the auditory nerve. Also called **spiral organ** [Described 1851. After Marquis Alfonso Corti (1822–88), Italian anatomist and histologist.]

organotherapy /ˌɔːgənəʊˈθerəpi/ *noun* the treatment of a disease by using an extract from the organ of an animal, e.g. using liver extract to treat anaemia

organ transplant /ˈɔːgən ˌtrænsplɑːnt/ *noun* a surgical operation to transplant an organ from one person to another

orgasm /ˈɔːgæz(ə)m/ *noun* the climax of the sexual act, when a person experiences a moment of great excitement

oriental sore /ˌɔːrient(ə)l ˈsɔː/ *noun* a skin disease of tropical countries caused by the parasite *Leishmania.* ◊ **leishmaniasis**

orifice /ˈɒrɪfɪs/ *noun* an opening in the body, e.g. the mouth or anus

origin /ˈɒrɪdʒɪn/ *noun* 1. the source or beginning of something 2. a place where a muscle is attached, or where the branch of a nerve or blood vessel begins

original /əˈrɪdʒən(ə)l/ *adjective* as before a change was made ○ *The surgeon was able to move the organ back to its original position.*

originate /əˈrɪdʒɪneɪt/ *verb* to start in a place, or make something start ○ *drugs which originated in the tropics* ○ *The treatment originated in China.* (NOTE: **originating – originated**)

oris /ˈɔːrɪs/ ♦ **cancrum oris, orbicularis oris**

ornithine /ˈɔːnɪθaɪn/ *noun* an amino acid produced by the liver

ornithosis /ˌɔːnɪˈθəʊsɪs/ *noun* a disease of birds which can be passed to humans as a form of pneumonia

oro- /ɔːrəʊ/ *prefix* mouth

orogenital /ˌɔːrəʊˈdʒenɪt(ə)l/ *adjective* relating to both the mouth and the genitals

oropharynx /ˌɔːrəʊˈfærɪŋks/ *noun* a part of the pharynx below the soft palate at the back of the mouth (NOTE: The plural is **oropharynxes** or **oropharynges**.)

ORT *abbr* oral rehydration therapy

ortho- /ɔːθəʊ/ *prefix* correct or straight

orthodiagraph /ˌɔːθəʊˈdaɪəgrɑːf/ *noun* an X-ray photograph of an organ taken using only a thin stream of X-rays which allows accurate measurements of the organ to be made

orthodontia /ˌɔːθəˈdɒnʃə/ *noun US* same as **orthodontics**

orthodontic /ˌɔːθəʊˈdɒntɪk/ *adjective* correcting badly formed or placed teeth ○ *He had to undergo a course of orthodontic treatment.*

orthodontics /ˌɔːθəʊˈdɒntɪks/ *noun* a branch of dentistry which deals with correcting badly placed teeth (NOTE: The US term is **orthodontia**.)

orthodontist /ˌɔːθəʊˈdɒntɪst/ *noun* a dental surgeon who specialises in correcting badly placed teeth

orthopaedic /ˌɔːθəˈpiːdɪk/ *adjective* **1.** referring to treatment which corrects badly formed bones or joints **2.** referring to or used in orthopaedics (NOTE: The US spelling is **orthopedic**.)

orthopaedic collar /ˌɔːθəˌpiːdɪk ˈkɒlə/ *noun* a special strong collar to support the head of a person with neck injuries or a condition such as cervical spondylosis

orthopaedic hospital /ˌɔːθəpiːdɪk ˈhɒspɪt(ə)l/ *noun* a hospital which specialises in operations to correct badly formed joints or bones

orthopaedics /ˌɔːθəˈpiːdɪks/ *noun* a branch of surgery dealing with irregularities, diseases and injuries of the locomotor system (NOTE: The US spelling is **orthopedics**.)

orthopaedic surgeon /ˌɔːθəpiːdɪk ˈsɜːdʒən/ *noun* a surgeon who specialises in orthopaedics

orthopaedist /ˌɔːθəˈpiːdɪst/ *noun* a surgeon who specialises in orthopaedics (NOTE: The US spelling is **orthopedist**.)

orthopnoea /ˌɔːθəpˈniːə/ *noun* a condition in which a person has great difficulty in breathing while lying down. ◊ **dyspnoea** (NOTE: The US spelling is **orthopnea**.)

orthopnoeic /ˌɔːθəpˈniːɪk/ *adjective* referring to orthopnoea (NOTE: The US spelling is **orthopneic**.)

orthopsychiatry /ˌɔːθəʊsaɪˈkaɪətri/ *noun* the science and treatment of behavioural and personality disorders

orthoptics /ɔːˈθɒptɪks/ *noun* the study of methods used to treat squints

orthoptist /ɔːˈθɒptɪst/ *noun* an eye specialist, working in an eye hospital, who treats squints and other disorders of eye movement

orthoptoscope /ɔːˈθɒptəskəʊp/ *noun* same as **amblyoscope**

orthosis /ɔːˈθəʊsɪs/ *noun* a device which is fitted to the outside of the body to support a weakness or correct a malformation, e.g. a surgical collar or leg brace (NOTE: The plural is **orthoses**.)

orthostatic /ˌɔːθəˈstætɪk/ *adjective* referring to the position of the body when standing up straight

orthostatic hypotension /ˌɔːθəstætɪk haɪpəʊˈtenʃən/ *noun* a common condition where the blood pressure drops when a person stands up suddenly, causing dizziness

orthotics /ɔːˈθɒtɪks/ *plural noun* the branch of medical engineering which deals with the design and fitting of devices such as braces in the treatment of orthopaedic disorders

orthotist /ˈɔːθətɪst/ *noun* a qualified person who fits orthoses

Ortolani's sign /ˌɔːtəˈlɑːniz saɪn/, **Ortolani manoeuvre** /ˌɔːtəˈlɑːni mə,nuːvə/, **Ortolani's test** /ˌɔːtəˈlɑːniz test/ *noun* a test for congenital dislocation of the hip in babies aged 6–12, in which the hip makes sharp sounds if the joint is rotated [Described 1937. After Marius Ortolani, Italian orthopaedic surgeon.]

os /ɒs/ *noun* (*technical*) **1.** a bone (NOTE: The plural is **ossa**.) **2.** the mouth (NOTE: The plural is **ora**.)

OSA *abbr* obstructive sleep apnoea

oscillation /ˌɒsɪˈleɪʃ(ə)n/ *noun* **1.** the action of moving backwards and forwards between two points at a regular speed **2.** a single movement between two points

oscilloscope /ɒˈsɪləskəʊp/ *noun* a device which produces a visual record of an electrical current on a screen using a cathode ray tube. It is used in the testing of electronic equipment and in measuring electrical impulses of the heart or the brain.

osculum /ˈɒskjʊləm/ *noun* a small opening or pore (NOTE: The plural is **oscula**.)

-osis /əʊsɪs/ *suffix* disease

Osler's nodes /ˈɒsləz nəʊdz/ *plural noun* tender swellings at the ends of fingers and toes in people who have subacute bacterial endocarditis [Described 1885. After Sir William Osler (1849–1919), Professor of Medicine in Montreal, Philadelphia, Baltimore and then Oxford.]

osm- /ɒzm/ *prefix* **1.** smell **2.** osmosis

osmoreceptor /ˌɒzməʊrɪˈseptə/ *noun* a cell in the hypothalamus which checks the level of osmotic pressure in the blood by altering the secretion of ADH and regulates the amount of water in the blood

osmosis /ɒzˈməʊsɪs/ *noun* the movement of a solvent from one part of the body through a semipermeable membrane to another part where there is a higher concentration of molecules

osmotic pressure /ɒzˌmɒtɪk ˈpreʃə/ *noun* the pressure required to stop the flow of a solvent through a membrane

ossa /ˈɒsə/ *plural of* **os** *noun* 1

osseous /ˈɒsɪəs/ *adjective* referring to or resembling bone

osseous labyrinth /ˌɒsɪəs ˈlæbərɪnθ/ *noun* same as **bony labyrinth**

ossicle /ˈɒsɪk(ə)l/ *noun* a small bone

COMMENT: The auditory ossicles pick up the vibrations from the eardrum and transmit them through the oval window to the cochlea in the inner ear. The three bones are articulated together; the stapes is attached to the membrane of the oval window, the malleus to the eardrum, and the incus lies between the other two.

ossification /ˌɒsɪfɪˈkeɪʃ(ə)n/ *noun* the formation of bone. Also called **osteogenesis**

ossium /ˈɒsiəm/ ♦ **fragilitas ossium**

ost- /ɒst/ *prefix* same as **osteo-** (*used before vowels*)

ostectomy /ɒˈstektəmi/ *noun* a surgical operation in which a bone, or a piece of bone, is removed (NOTE: The plural is **ostectomies**.)

osteitis /ˌɒstiˈaɪtɪs/ *noun* inflammation of a bone due to injury or infection

osteitis deformans /ˌɒstiˌaɪtɪs diː ˈfɔːmənz/ *noun* a disease which gradually softens bones in the spine, legs and skull, so that they become curved. Also called **Paget's disease**

osteitis fibrosis cystica /ˌɒstiaɪtɪs faɪ ˌbrəʊsɪs ˈsɪstɪkə/ *noun* a generalised weakness of bones, caused by excessive activity of the thyroid gland and associated with formation of cysts, in which bone tissue is replaced by fibrous tissue. Also called **von Recklinghausen's disease** (NOTE: The localised form is **osteitis fibrosis localista**.)

osteo- /ɒstiəʊ/ *prefix* bone

osteoarthritis /ˌɒstiəʊɑːˈθraɪtɪs/ *noun* a degenerative disease of middle-aged and elderly people characterised by inflamed joints which become stiff and painful. Also called **osteoarthrosis**

osteoarthropathy /ˌɒstiəʊɑːˈθrɒpəθi/ *noun* a disease of the bone and cartilage at a joint, particularly the ankles, knees or wrists, associated with carcinoma of the bronchi

osteoarthrosis /ˌɒstiəʊɑːˈθrəʊsɪs/ *noun* same as **osteoarthritis**

osteoarthrotomy /ˌɒstiəʊɑːˈθrɒtəmi/ *noun* a surgical operation to remove the articular end of a bone (NOTE: The plural is **osteoarthrotomies**.)

osteoblast /ˈɒstiəʊblæst/ *noun* a cell in an embryo which forms bone

osteochondritis /ˌɒstiəʊkənˈdraɪtɪs/ *noun* degeneration of the epiphyses

osteochondritis dissecans /ˌɒstiəʊkɒn ˌdraɪtɪs ˈdɪsəkænz/ *noun* a painful condition where pieces of articular cartilage become detached from the joint surface

osteochondroma /ˌɒstiəʊkənˈdrəʊmə/ *noun* a tumour containing both bony and cartilaginous cells (NOTE: The plural is **osteochondromas** or **osteochondromata**.)

osteochondrosis /ˌɒstiəʊkɒnˈdrəʊsɪs/ *noun* a disorder of cartilage and bone formation which affects the joints in children, causing pain and a limp, probably due to circulation disturbances to that part of the bone

osteoclasia /ˌɒstiəʊˈkleɪziə/, **osteoclasis** /ˌɒstiˈɒkləsɪs/ *noun* **1.** destruction of bone tissue by osteoclasts **2.** a surgical operation to

fracture or refracture bone to correct a deformity

osteoclast /ˈɒstiəʊklæst/ *noun* **1.** a cell which destroys bone **2.** a surgical instrument for breaking bones

osteoclastoma /ˌɒstiəʊklæˈstəʊmə/ *noun* a usually benign tumour occurring at the ends of long bones (NOTE: The plural is **osteoclastomas** or **osteoclastomata**.)

osteocyte /ˈɒstiəʊsaɪt/ *noun* a bone cell

osteodystrophia /ˌɒstiəʊdɪˈstrəʊfiə/, **osteodystrophy** /ˌɒstiəʊˈdɪstrəfi/ *noun* a bone disease, especially one caused by disorder of the metabolism

osteogenesis /ˌɒstiəʊˈdʒenəsɪs/ *noun* same as **ossification**

osteogenesis imperfecta /ˌɒstiəʊ ˌdʒenəsɪs ɪmpəˈfektə/ *noun* a congenital condition in which bones are brittle and break easily due to unusual bone formation. Also called **brittle bone disease**

osteogenic /ˌɒstiəʊˈdʒenɪk/ *adjective* made of or originating in bone tissue

osteology /ˌɒstiˈɒlədʒi/ *noun* the study of bones and their structure

osteolysis /ˌɒstiˈɒləsɪs/ *noun* **1.** destruction of bone tissue by osteoclasts **2.** loss of bone calcium

osteolytic /ˌɒstiəʊˈlɪtɪk/ *adjective* referring to osteolysis

osteoma /ˌɒstiˈəʊmə/ *noun* a benign tumour in a bone (NOTE: The plural is **osteomas** or **osteomata**.)

osteomalacia /ˌɒstiəʊməˈleɪʃə/ *noun* a condition in adults in which the bones become soft because of lack of calcium and Vitamin D, or limited exposure to sunlight

osteomyelitis /ˌɒstiəʊmaɪəˈlaɪtɪs/ *noun* inflammation of the interior of bone, especially the marrow spaces

osteon /ˈɒstiɒn/ *noun* same as **Haversian system**

osteopath /ˈɒstiəʊˌpæθ/ *noun* a person who practises osteopathy

osteopathy /ˌɒstiˈɒpəθi/ *noun* **1.** the treatment of disorders by massage and manipulation of joints **2.** any disease of bone (NOTE: The plural is **osteopathies**.)

osteopetrosis /ˌɒstiəʊpəˈtrəʊsɪs/ *noun* a disease of a group in which bones increase in density. Also called **marble bone disease**

osteophony /ˌɒstiˈɒfəni/ *noun* the conduction of sound by bone, as occurs in the ear. Also called **bone conduction**

osteophyte /ˈɒstiəʊfaɪt/ *noun* a bony growth

osteoplastic necrotomy /ˌɒstiəʊplæstɪk nekˈrɒtəmi/ *noun* a surgical operation to remove a piece of dead bone tissue

osteoplasty /ˈɒstiəʊplæsti/ *noun* plastic surgery on bones

osteoporosis /ˌɒstiəʊpɔːˈrəʊsɪs/ *noun* a condition in which the bones become thin, porous and brittle, due to low levels of oestrogen, lack of calcium and lack of physical exercise. Also called **brittle bone disease**

COMMENT: Osteoporosis mainly affects postmenopausal women, increasing the risk of fractures. Hormone replacement therapy is the most effective method of preventing osteoporosis though there are other risks to health from long-term use.

osteosarcoma /ˌɒstiəʊsɑːˈkəʊmə/ *noun* a malignant tumour of bone cells (NOTE: The plural is **osteosarcomas** or **osteosarcomata**.)

osteosclerosis /ˌɒstiəʊskləˈrəʊsɪs/ *noun* a condition in which the bony spaces become hardened as a result of persistent inflammation

osteotome /ˈɒstiəʊtəʊm/ *noun* a type of chisel used by surgeons to cut bone

osteotomy /ˌɒstiˈɒtəmi/ *noun* a surgical operation to cut a bone, especially to relieve pain in a joint (NOTE: The plural is **osteotomies**.)

ostia /ˈɒstiə/ plural of **ostium**

ostium /ˈɒstiəm/ *noun* an opening into a passage (NOTE: The plural is **ostia**.)

ostomy /ˈɒstəmi/ *noun* a colostomy or ileostomy (*informal*) (NOTE: The plural is **ostomies**.)

-ostomy /ɒstəmi/ *suffix* operation to make an opening

OT *abbr* occupational therapist

ot- /əʊt/ *prefix* same as **oto-** (*used before vowels*)

otalgia /əʊˈtældʒə/ *noun* same as **earache**

OTC *abbreviation* referring to medication which can be bought freely at a chemist's shop, and does not need a prescription. Full form **over the counter**

OTC drug /ˌəʊ tiː ˈsiː drʌg/ *noun* same as **over-the-counter drug**

otic /ˈəʊtɪk/ *adjective* referring to the ear

otic ganglion /ˌəʊtɪk ˈgæŋgliən/ *noun* a ganglion associated with the mandibular nerve where it leaves the skull

otitis /əʊˈtaɪtɪs/ *noun* inflammation of the ear

otitis externa /əʊˌtaɪtɪs ɪkˈstɜːnə/ *noun* inflammation of the external auditory meatus to the eardrum

otitis interna /əʊˌtaɪtɪs ɪnˈtɜːnə/ *noun* inflammation of the inner ear. Also called **labyrinthitis**

otitis media /əʊˌtaɪtɪs ˈmiːdiə/ *noun* an infection of the middle ear, usually accompanied by headaches and fever. Also called **middle ear infection, tympanitis**

oto- /əʊtəʊ/ *prefix* ear

otolaryngologist /ˌəʊtəʊlærɪŋˈgɒlədʒɪst/ *noun* a doctor who specialises in treatment of diseases of the ear and throat

otolaryngology /ˌəʊtəʊlærɪŋˈgɒlədʒi/ *noun* the study of diseases of the ear and throat

otolith /ˈəʊtəlɪθ/ *noun* a tiny piece of calcium carbonate attached to the hair cells in the saccule and utricle of the inner ear

otolith organ /ˌəʊtəlɪθ ˈɔːgən/ *noun* one of two pairs of sensory organs in the inner ear, the saccule and the utricle, which pass information to the brain about the position of the head

otologist /əʊˈtɒlədʒɪst/ *noun* a doctor who specialises in the study of the ear

otology /əʊˈtɒlədʒi/ *noun* the scientific study of the ear and its diseases

-otomy /ɒtəmi/ *suffix* an act of cutting into an organ or part of the body in a surgical operation

otomycosis /ˌəʊtəmaɪˈkəʊsɪs/ *noun* an infection of the external auditory meatus by a fungus

otoplasty /ˈəʊtəplæsti/ *noun* plastic surgery of the external ear to repair damage or deformity

otorhinolaryngologist /ˌəʊtəʊˌraɪnəʊˌlærɪŋˈgɒlədʒɪst/ *noun* a doctor who specialises in the study of the ear, nose and throat

otorhinolaryngology /ˌəʊtəʊˌraɪnəʊˌlærɪŋˈgɒlədʒi/ *noun* the study of the ear, nose and throat. Also called **ENT**

otorrhagia /ˌəʊtəˈreɪdʒə/ *noun* bleeding from the external ear

otorrhoea /ˌəʊtəˈriːə/ *noun* the discharge of pus from the ear (NOTE: The US spelling is **otorrhea**.)

otosclerosis /ˌəʊtəʊskləˈrəʊsɪs/ *noun* a condition in which the ossicles in the middle ear become thicker and the stapes becomes fixed to the oval window leading to deafness

otoscope /ˈəʊtəskəʊp/ *noun* same as **auriscope**

otospongiosis /ˌəʊtəˌspʌndʒiˈəʊsɪs/ *noun* the formation of spongy bone in the labyrinth of the ear which occurs in otosclerosis

Otosporin /ˈəʊtəspɒrɪn/ a trade name for ear drops containing hydrocortisone, neomycin and polymyxin

ototoxic /ˌəʊtəˈtɒksɪk/ *adjective* referring to a drug or an effect which is damaging to organs or nerves involved in hearing or balance

outbreak /ˈaʊtbreɪk/ *noun* a series of cases of a disease which starts suddenly ○ *There was an outbreak of typhoid fever* or *a typhoid outbreak.*

outcome /ˈaʊtkʌm/ *noun* 1. what happens as the result of something 2. a measure of the result of an intervention or treatment, e.g. the mortality rate following different methods of surgery ○ *medical outcomes*

outer /ˈaʊtə/ *adjective* outside or external

outer ear /ˌaʊtər ˈɪə/ *noun* the part of the ear which is on the outside of the head, together with the passage leading to the eardrum. Also called **external ear**

outer pleura /ˌaʊtə ˈplʊərə/ *noun* same as **parietal pleura**

outlet /ˈaʊtlet/ *noun* an opening or channel through which something can go out

out-of-body experience /ˌaʊt əv ˈbɒdi ɪk ˌspɪərɪəns/ *noun* an occasion when a person feels as though they have left their body and, often, travelled along a tunnel towards a bright light (NOTE: It may happen after anaesthesia, perhaps caused by the brain not having enough oxygen.)

outpatient /ˈaʊtpeɪʃ(ə)nt/ *noun* someone who comes to a hospital for treatment but does not stay overnight ○ *She goes for treatment as an outpatient.* Abbr **OP**. Compare **inpatient**

outpatient department /ˈaʊtpeɪʃ(ə)nt dɪ ˌpɑːtmənt/, **outpatients' department** /ˈaʊt peɪʃ(ə)nts dɪˌpɑːtmənt/, **outpatients' clinic** / ˈaʊtpeɪʃ(ə)nts ˌklɪnɪk/ *noun* a department of a hospital which deals with outpatients

outreach /ˈaʊtriːtʃ/ *noun* services provided for patients or the public in general, outside a hospital or clinic

ova /ˈəʊvə/ plural of **ovum**

oval window /ˈəʊv(ə)l ˌwɪndəʊ/ *noun* an oval opening between the middle ear and the inner ear. Also called **fenestra ovalis**. See illustration at EAR in Supplement

ovar- /əʊvər/ *prefix* same as **ovari-** (*used before vowels*)

ovaralgia /ˌəʊvəˈrældʒə/ *noun* pain in the ovaries. Also called **ovarialgia**

ovari- /əʊvəri/ *prefix* ovaries

ovarialgia /ˌəʊveəriˈældʒə/ *noun* same as **ovaralgia**

ovarian /əʊˈveəriən/ *adjective* referring to the ovaries

ovarian cancer /əʊˌveəriən ˈkænsə/ *noun* a malignant tumour of the ovary, which occurs especially after the menopause

ovarian cycle /əʊˌveəriən ˈsaɪk(ə)l/ *noun* the regular changes in the ovary during a woman's reproductive life

ovarian cyst /əʊˌveəriən ˈsɪst/ *noun* a cyst which develops in the ovaries

ovarian follicle /əʊˌveəriən ˈfɒlɪk(ə)l/ *noun* a cell which contains an ovum. Also called **Graafian follicle**

ovariectomy /ˌəʊvəriˈektəmi/ *noun* same as **oophorectomy** (NOTE: The plural is **ovariectomies**.)

ovariocele /əʊˈveəriəʊsiːl/ *noun* a hernia of an ovary

ovariotomy /ˌəʊvəriˈɒtəmi/ *noun* a surgical operation to remove an ovary or a tumour in an ovary (NOTE: The plural is **ovariotomies**.)

ovaritis /ˌəʊvəˈraɪtɪs/ *noun* same as **oophoritis**

ovary /ˈəʊv(ə)ri/ *noun* one of two organs in a woman which produce ova or egg cells and secrete the female hormone oestrogen. Also

called **oophoron**. See illustration at UROGENITAL SYSTEM (FEMALE) in Supplement (NOTE: The plural is **ovaries**. For other terms referring to ovaries, see words beginning with **oophor-**, **oophoro-**.)

over- /əʊvə/ *prefix* too much

overbite /ˈəʊvəbaɪt/ *noun* the usual formation of the teeth, in which the top incisors come down over and in front of the bottom incisors when the jaws are closed

overcome /ˌəʊvəˈkʌm/ *verb* **1.** to fight something and win **2.** to make a person lose consciousness ○ *Two people were overcome by smoke in the fire.* (NOTE: **overcoming – overcame – overcome**)

overcompensate /ˌəʊvəˈkɒmpənseɪt/ *verb* to try too hard to cover the effects of a condition or quality (NOTE: **overompensating – overcompensated**)

overcompensation /ˌəʊvəkɒmpən ˈseɪʃ(ə)n/ *noun* an attempt by a person to remove the bad effects of a mistake or a fault in their character in which they make too much effort, and so cause some other problem

overdo /ˌəʊvəˈduː/ *verb* □ **to overdo it** *or* **to overdo things** to work too hard or to do too much exercise (*informal*) ○ *She overdid it, working until 9 o'clock every evening.* ○ *He has been overdoing things and has to rest.*

overdose /ˈəʊvədəʊs/ *noun* a dose of a drug which is larger than the recommended or usual dose

overeating /ˌəʊvərˈiːtɪŋ/ *noun* eating too much food

overexertion /ˌəʊvərɪɡˈzɜːʃ(ə)n/ *noun* doing too much physical work or taking too much exercise

overflow incontinence /ˌəʊvəfləʊ ɪnˈkɒn tɪnəns/ *noun* a leakage of urine because the bladder is too full

overgrow /ˌəʊvəˈɡrəʊ/ *verb* (*of a tissue*) to grow over another tissue (NOTE: **overgrew – overgrown**)

overgrowth /ˈəʊvəɡrəʊθ/ *noun* a growth of tissue over another tissue

overjet /ˈəʊvədʒet/ *noun* a space which separates the top incisors from the bottom incisors when the jaws are closed

overlap /ˌəʊvəˈlæp/ *verb* (*of bandages, etc.*) to lie partly on top of another (NOTE: **overlapping – overlapped**)

overprescribe /əʊvəprɪˈskraɪb/ *verb* to issue too many prescriptions for something ○ *Some doctors seriously overprescribe tranquillisers.* (NOTE: **overprescribing – overprescribed**)

overproduction /ˌəʊvəprəˈdʌkʃən/ *noun* the act of producing too much of something ○ *The condition is caused by overproduction of thyroxine by the thyroid gland.*

oversew /ˈəʊvəsəʊ/ *verb* to sew a patch of tissue over a perforation (NOTE: **oversewing – oversewed – oversewn**)

overt /əʊˈvɜːt/ *adjective* easily seen with the naked eye. Opposite **occult**

over-the-counter drug /ˌəʊvə ðə ˈkaʊntə drʌg/ *noun* a drug which you can buy from a pharmacy without a doctor's prescription. Also called **OTC drug**

overweight /ˌəʊvəˈweɪt/ *adjective* fatter and heavier than is medically advisable ○ *He is several kilos overweight for his age and height.*

overwork /ˌəʊvəˈwɜːk/ *noun* too much work ○ *He collapsed from overwork.* ■ *verb* to work too much, or make something work too much ○ *He has been overworking his heart.*

overwrought /ˌəʊvəˈrɔːt/ *adjective* very tense and nervous

ovi- /əʊvi/ *prefix* eggs or ova

oviduct /ˈəʊvidʌkt/ *noun* same as **Fallopian tube**

ovulate /ˈɒvjʊleɪt/ *verb* to release a mature ovum into a Fallopian tube (NOTE: **ovulating – ovulated**)

ovulation /ˌɒvjʊˈleɪʃ(ə)n/ *noun* the release of an ovum from the mature ovarian follicle into the Fallopian tube

ovum /ˈəʊvəm/ *noun* a female egg cell which, when fertilised by a spermatozoon, begins to develop into an embryo (NOTE: The plural is **ova**. For other terms referring to ova, see words beginning with **oo-**.)

-oxacin /ɒksəsɪn/ *suffix* quinolone drug ○ *ciprofloxacin*

oxidase /ˈɒksɪdeɪz/ *noun* an enzyme which encourages oxidation by removing hydrogen. ◊ **monoamine oxidase**

oxidation /ˌɒksɪˈdeɪʃ(ə)n/ *noun* the action of making oxides by combining with oxygen or removing hydrogen

COMMENT: Carbon compounds form oxides when metabolised with oxygen in the body, producing carbon dioxide.

oxide /ˈɒksaɪd/ *noun* a compound formed with oxygen

oximeter /ɒkˈsɪmɪtə/ *noun* an instrument which measures the amount of oxygen in something, especially in blood

oxybutynin /ˌɒksiˈbjuːtənɪn/, **oxybutinin** *noun* a drug which reduces the need to pass urine

oxycephalic /ˌɒksɪkəˈfælɪk/ *adjective* referring to oxycephaly

oxycephaly /ˌɒksɪˈkefəli/ *noun* a condition in which the skull is shaped into a point, with exophthalmos and poor sight. Also called **turricephaly**

oxygen /ˈɒksɪdʒən/ *noun* a chemical element that is a common colourless gas which is

present in the air and essential to human life (NOTE: The chemical symbol is **O**.)

COMMENT: Oxygen is absorbed into the bloodstream through the lungs and is carried to the tissues along the arteries. It is essential to healthy metabolism and given to patients with breathing difficulties.

oxygenate /ˈɒksɪdʒəneɪt/ *verb* to combine blood with oxygen (NOTE: **oxygenating – oxygenated**)

oxygenated blood /ˌɒksɪdʒəneɪtɪd ˈblʌd/ *noun* blood which has received oxygen in the lungs and is being carried to the tissues along the arteries. Also called **arterial blood**. Compare **deoxygenated blood** (NOTE: Oxygenated blood is brighter red than venous deoxygenated blood.)

oxygenation /ˌɒksɪdʒəˈneɪʃ(ə)n/ *noun* the fact of becoming combined or filled with oxygen ○ *Blood is carried along the pulmonary artery to the lungs for oxygenation.*

oxygenator /ˈɒksɪdʒəˌneɪtə/ *noun* a machine which puts oxygen into the blood, used as an artificial lung in surgery

oxygen cylinder /ˈɒksɪdʒən ˌsɪlɪndə/ *noun* a heavy metal tube which contains oxygen and is connected to a patient's oxygen mask

oxygen mask /ˈɒksɪdʒən mɑːsk/ *noun* a mask connected to a supply of oxygen, which can be put over the face to help someone with breathing difficulties

oxygen tent /ˈɒksɪdʒən tent/ *noun* a type of cover put over a person so that he or she can breathe in oxygen

oxygen therapy /ˈɒksɪdʒən θerəpi/ *noun* any treatment involving the administering of oxygen, e.g. in an oxygen tent or in emergency treatment for heart failure

oxyhaemoglobin /ˌɒksi,hiːməˈgləʊbɪn/ *noun* a compound of haemoglobin and oxygen, which is the way oxygen is carried in arterial blood from the lungs to the tissues. ◊ **haemoglobin** (NOTE: The US spelling is **oxyhemoglobin**.)

oxyntic /ɒkˈsɪntɪk/ *adjective* referring to glands and cells in the stomach which produce acid

oxyntic cell /ɒkˈsɪntɪk sel/ *noun* a cell in the gastric gland which secretes hydrochloric acid. Also called **parietal cell**

oxytetracycline /ˌɒksi,tetrəˈsaɪkliːn/ *noun* an antibiotic which is effective against a wide range of organisms

oxytocic /ˌɒksiˈtəʊsɪk/ *noun* a drug which helps to start the process of childbirth, or speeds it up ■ *adjective* starting or speeding up childbirth by causing contractions in the muscles of the uterus

oxytocin /ˌɒksiˈtəʊsɪn/ *noun* a hormone secreted by the posterior pituitary gland, which controls the contractions of the uterus and encourages the flow of milk

COMMENT: An extract of oxytocin is used as an injection to start contractions of the uterus and to assist in the third stage of labour.

oxyuriasis /ˌɒksɪjʊˈraɪəsɪs/ *noun* same as **enterobiasis**

Oxyuris /ˌɒksɪˈjʊərɪs/ *noun* same as **Enterobius**

ozaena /əʊˈziːnə/ *noun* **1.** a disease of the nose in which the nasal passage is blocked and mucus forms, giving off an unpleasant smell **2.** any unpleasant discharge from the nose (NOTE: The US spelling is **ozena**.)

ozone /ˈəʊzəʊn/ *noun* a gas present in the atmosphere in small quantities, which is harmful at high levels of concentration

COMMENT: The maximum amount of ozone which is considered safe for humans to breathe is 80 parts per billion. Even in lower concentrations it irritates the throat, makes people cough and gives headaches and asthma attacks similar to hay fever. The ozone layer in the stratosphere acts as a protection against the harmful effects of the sun's radiation, and the destruction or reduction of the layer has the effect of allowing more radiation to pass through the atmosphere with harmful effects such as skin cancer on humans.

ozone sickness /ˈəʊzəʊn ˌsɪknəs/ *noun* a condition experienced by jet travellers, due to levels of ozone in aircraft

P

P ◆ substance P

Pa *abbr* pascal

pacemaker /'peɪsmeɪkə/ *noun* **1.** a node in the heart which regulates the heartbeat. Also called **sinoatrial node, SA node 2.** ◊ **cardiac pacemaker, epicardial pacemaker**

COMMENT: An electrode is usually attached to the epicardium and linked to the device which can be implanted in various positions in the chest.

pachy- /pæki/ *prefix* thickening

pachydactyly /ˌpæki'dæktɪli/ *noun* a condition in which the fingers and toes become thicker than usual

pachydermia /ˌpæki'dɜːmiə/, **pachyderma** /ˌpæki'dɜːmə/ *noun* a condition in which the skin becomes thicker than normal

pachymeningitis /ˌpæki,menɪn'dʒaɪtɪs/ *noun* inflammation of the dura mater

pachymeninx /ˌpæki'miːnɪŋks/ *noun* same as **dura mater**

pachyonychia /ˌpækiə'nɪkiə/ *noun* unusual thickness of the nails

pachysomia /ˌpæki'səʊmiə/ *noun* a condition in which soft tissues of the body become unusually thick

pacifier /'pæsɪfaɪə/ *noun* US a child's dummy

pacing /'peɪsɪŋ/ *noun* a surgical operation to implant or attach a cardiac pacemaker

Pacinian corpuscle /pə,sɪniən 'kɔːpʌs(ə)l/ *noun* a sensory nerve ending in the skin which is sensitive to touch and vibrations

pack /pæk/ *noun* **1.** a tampon of gauze or cotton wool, used to fill an orifice such as the nose or vagina **2.** a piece of wet material folded tightly, used to press on the body **3.** a treatment in which a blanket or sheet is used to wrap round the body **4.** a box or bag of goods for sale ○ *a pack of sticking plaster* ○ *The cough tablets are sold in packs of fifty.* ■ *verb* **1.** to fill an orifice with a tampon ○ *The ear was packed with cotton wool to absorb the discharge.* **2.** to put things in cases or boxes ○ *The transplant organ arrived at the hospital packed in ice.*

packed cell volume /ˌpækt 'sel ˌvɒljuːm/ *noun* the volume of red blood cells in a person's blood shown against the total volume of blood. Also called **haematocrit**

packing /'pækɪŋ/ *noun* absorbent material put into a wound or part of the body to absorb fluids

pack up /ˌpæk 'ʌp/ *verb* to stop working (*informal*) ○ *His heart simply packed up under the strain.*

PACT *abbr* prescribing analyses and cost

pad /pæd/ *noun* **1.** a piece or mass of soft absorbent material, placed on part of the body to protect it ○ *She wrapped a pad of soft cotton wool round the sore.* **2.** a thickening of part of the skin

paed- /piːd/ *prefix* same as **paedo-** (*used before vowels*) (NOTE: The US spelling is **ped-**.)

paediatric /ˌpiːdi'ætrɪk/ *adjective* referring to the treatment of the diseases of children ○ *A new paediatric hospital has been opened.* ○ *Parents can visit children in the paediatric wards at any time.*

'Paediatric day surgery minimizes the length of hospital stay and therefore is less traumatic for both child and parents' [*British Journal of Nursing*]

paediatrician /ˌpiːdiə'trɪʃ(ə)n/ *noun* a doctor who specialises in the treatment of diseases of children

paediatrics /ˌpiːdi'ætrɪks/ *noun* the study of children, their development and diseases. Compare **geriatrics**

paedo- /piːdəʊ/ *prefix* referring to children

paedodontia *noun* another spelling of **pedodontia**

Paget's disease /'pædʒəts dɪ,ziːz/ *noun* **1.** same as **osteitis deformans 2.** a form of breast cancer which starts as an itchy rash round the nipple [Described 1877. After Sir James Paget (1814–99), British surgeon.]

pain /peɪn/ *noun* the feeling of severe discomfort which a person has when hurt ○ *The doctor gave him an injection to relieve the pain.* ○ *She is suffering from back pain.* (NOTE: Pain can be used in the plural to show that it recurs: **She has pains in her left leg.**) □ **to be in great**

pain to have very sharp pains which are difficult to bear

COMMENT: Pain is carried by the sensory nerves to the central nervous system. From the site it travels up the spinal column to the medulla and through a series of neurones which use Substance P as the neurotransmitter to the sensory cortex. Pain is the method by which a person knows that part of the body is damaged or infected, though the pain is not always felt in the affected part. See synalgia.

pain clinic /'peɪn ˌklɪnɪk/ *noun* a centre which looks after people with severe persistent pain and whose staff include professionals from many specialist areas of medicine

painful /'peɪnf(ə)l/ *adjective* causing pain ○ She has a painful skin disease. ○ His foot is so painful he can hardly walk. ○ Your eye looks very red – is it very painful?

painkiller /'peɪnkɪlə/ *noun* a drug that reduces pain

painless /'peɪnləs/ *adjective* not causing pain ○ a painless method of removing warts

pain pathway /'peɪn ˌpɑːθweɪ/ *noun* a series of linking nerve fibres and neurones which carry impulses of pain from the site to the sensory cortex

pain receptor /'peɪn rɪˌseptə/ *noun* a nerve ending which is sensitive to pain

pain relief /'peɪn rɪˌliːf/ *noun* the act of easing pain by using analgesics

paint /peɪnt/ *noun* a coloured antiseptic, analgesic or astringent liquid which is put on the surface of the body ■ *verb* to cover a wound with an antiseptic, analgesic or astringent liquid or lotion ○ She painted the rash with calamine.

painter's colic /ˌpeɪntəz 'kɒlɪk/ *noun* a form of lead poisoning caused, especially formerly, by working with paint

pain threshold /'peɪn ˌθreʃhəʊld/ *noun* the point at which a person finds it impossible to bear pain without crying

palatal /'pælət(ə)l/ *adjective* referring to the palate

palate /'pælət/ *noun* the roof of the mouth and floor of the nasal cavity, formed of the hard and soft palates

palate bone /'pælət bəʊn/ *noun* one of two bones which form part of the hard palate, the orbits of the eyes and the cavity behind the nose. Also called **palatine bone**

palatine /'pælətaɪn/ *adjective* referring to the palate

palatine arch /'pælətaɪn ɑːtʃ/ *noun* a fold of tissue between the soft palate and the pharynx

palatine bone /'pælətaɪn bəʊn/ *noun* same as **palate bone**

palatine tonsil /ˌpælətaɪn 'tɒns(ə)l/ *noun* same as **tonsil**

palato- /pælətəʊ/ *prefix* the palate

palatoglossal arch /ˌpælətəʊˌglɒs(ə)l 'ɑːtʃ/ *noun* a fold between the soft palate and the tongue, anterior to the tonsil

palatopharyngeal arch /ˌpælətəʊfærɪnˌdʒɪəl 'ɑːtʃ/ *noun* a fold between the soft palate and the pharynx, posterior to the tonsil

palatoplasty /'pælətəplæsti/ *noun* plastic surgery of the roof of the mouth, e.g. to repair a cleft palate

palatoplegia /ˌpælətə'pliːdʒə/ *noun* paralysis of the soft palate

palatorrhaphy /ˌpælə'tɔːrəfi/ *noun* a surgical operation to suture and close a cleft palate. Also called **staphylorrhaphy, uraniscorrhaphy**

pale /peɪl/ *adjective* light coloured or white ○ After her illness she looked pale and tired. □ **to turn pale** to become white in the face, because the flow of blood is reduced ○ Some people turn pale at the sight of blood.

paleness /'peɪlnəs/ *noun* the fact of being pale

pali- /pælɪ/ *prefix* same as **palin-**

palilalia /ˌpælɪ'leɪliə/ *noun* a speech disorder in which the person repeats words

palin- /'pælɪn/ *prefix* repeating

palindromic /ˌpælɪn'drəʊmɪk/ *adjective* recurring ○ a palindromic disease

palliative /'pælɪətɪv/ *noun* a treatment or drug which relieves symptoms but does nothing to cure the disease which causes the symptoms. For example, a painkiller can reduce the pain in a tooth, but will not cure the caries which causes the pain. ■ *adjective* providing relief

'...coronary artery bypass grafting is a palliative procedure aimed at the relief of persistent angina pectoris' [*British Journal of Hospital Medicine*]

palliative care /'pælɪətɪv 'keə/, **palliative treatment** /ˌpælɪətɪv 'triːtmənt/ *noun* treatment which helps to reduce the symptoms of a disease, especially a terminal or chronic condition, but does not cure it

COMMENT: Palliative care may involve giving antibiotics, transfusions, pain-killing drugs, low-dose chemotherapy and psychological and social support to help the person and their family adjust to the illness. The treatment is often provided in a hospice.

pallidotomy /ˌpælɪ'dɒtəmi/ *noun* an operation on the brain which can reduce many of the symptoms of Parkinson's disease, such as tremor, bradykinesia and bent posture

pallium /'pælɪəm/ *noun* the layer of grey matter on the surface of the cerebral cortex

pallor /'pælə/ *noun* the condition of being pale

palm /pɑːm/ *noun* the inner surface of the hand, extending from the bases of the fingers to the wrist

palmar /'pælmə/ *adjective* referring to the palm of the hand

palmar arch /'pælmər ɑːtʃ/ *noun* one of two arches or joins within the palm formed by two arteries which link together

palmar fascia /ˌpælmə 'feɪʃə/ *noun* the tendons in the palm of the hand

palmar interosseus /ˌpælmər ˌɪntər 'ɒsɪəs/ *noun* a deep muscle between the bones in the hand

palmar region /'pælmə ˌriːdʒ(ə)n/ *noun* an area of skin around the palm

palpable /'pælpəb(ə)l/ *adjective* **1.** able to be felt when touched **2.** able to be examined with the hand

'…mammography is the most effective technique available for the detection of occult (non-palpable) breast cancer. It has been estimated that mammography can detect a carcinoma two years before it becomes palpable' [*Southern Medical Journal*]

palpate /pæl'peɪt/ *verb* to examine part of the body by feeling it with the hand

palpation /pæl'peɪʃ(ə)n/ *noun* an examination of part of the body by feeling it with the hand

palpebra /'pælpɪbrə/ *noun* same as **eyelid** (NOTE: The plural is **palpebrae**.)

palpebral /'pælpɪbrəl/ *adjective* referring to the eyelids

palpitate /'pælpɪteɪt/ *verb* to beat rapidly or irregularly

palpitation /pælpɪ'teɪʃ(ə)n/ *noun* awareness that the heart is beating rapidly or irregularly, possibly caused by stress or by a disease

pan- /pæn/ *prefix* referring to everything

panacea /ˌpænə'siːə/ *noun* a medicine which is supposed to cure everything

Panadol /'pænədɒl/ a trade name for paracetamol

panarthritis /ˌpænɑː'θraɪtɪs/ *noun* inflammation of all the tissues of a joint or of all the joints in the body

pancarditis /ˌpænkɑː'daɪtɪs/ *noun* inflammation of all the tissues in the heart, i.e. the heart muscle, the endocardium and the pericardium

pancreas /'pæŋkrɪəs/ *noun* a gland which lies across the back of the body between the kidneys. See illustration at **DIGESTIVE SYSTEM** in Supplement

COMMENT: The pancreas has two functions: the first is to secrete the pancreatic juice which goes into the duodenum and digests proteins and carbohydrates; the second function is to produce the hormone insulin which regulates the use of sugar by the body. This hormone is secreted into the bloodstream by the islets of Langerhans which are in the pancreas.

pancreatectomy /ˌpæŋkrɪə'tektəmi/ *noun* the surgical removal of all or part of the pancreas

pancreatic /ˌpæŋkri'ætɪk/ *adjective* referring to the pancreas

pancreatic duct /ˌpæŋkri'ætɪk dʌkt/ *noun* a duct leading through the pancreas to the duodenum

pancreatic juice /ˌpæŋkri'ætɪk dʒuːs/, **pancreatic secretion** /ˌpæŋkri,ætɪk sɪ 'kriːʃ(ə)n/ *noun* a digestive juice, formed of enzymes produced by the pancreas, which digests fats and carbohydrates

pancreatin /'pæŋkrɪətɪn/ *noun* a substance made from enzymes secreted by the pancreas, used to treat someone whose pancreas does not produce pancreatic enzymes

pancreatitis /ˌpæŋkrɪə'taɪtɪs/ *noun* inflammation of the pancreas

pancreatomy /ˌpæŋkri'ætəmi/, **pancreatotomy** /ˌpæŋkrɪə'tɒtəmi/ *noun* a surgical operation to open the pancreatic duct

pancytopenia /ˌpænsaɪtə'piːnɪə/ *noun* a condition in which there are too few red and white blood cells and blood platelets

pandemic /pæn'demɪk/ *noun* an epidemic disease which affects many parts of the world. Compare **endemic, epidemic** ■ *adjective* widespread

pang /pæŋ/ *noun* a sudden sharp pain, especially in the intestine ○ *After not eating for a day, she suffered pangs of hunger.*

panhysterectomy /ˌpænhɪstə'rektmi/ *noun* the surgical removal of all the uterus and the cervix

panic /'pænɪk/ *noun* a feeling of great fear which cannot be stopped and which sometimes results in irrational behaviour ○ *He was in a panic as he sat in the consultant's waiting room.* ■ *verb* to be suddenly afraid ○ *She panicked when the surgeon told her she might need to have an operation.*

panic attack /'pænɪk ə,tæk/ *noun* a sudden onset of panic

panic disorder /'pænɪk dɪs,ɔːdə/ *noun* a condition in which somebody has frequent panic attacks

panniculitis /pə,nɪkjʊ'laɪtɪs/ *noun* inflammation of the panniculus adiposus, producing tender swellings on the thighs and breasts

panniculus /pə'nɪkjʊləs/ *noun* a layer of membranous tissue

panniculus adiposus /pə,nɪkjʊləs ,ædɪ'pəʊsəs/ *noun* a layer of fat underneath the skin

pannus /'pænəs/ *noun* a growth on the cornea containing tiny blood vessels

panophthalmia /ˌpænɒf'θælmɪə/, **panophthalmitis** /ˌpænɒfθæl'maɪtɪs/ *noun* inflammation of the whole of the eye

panosteitis /ˌpænɒsti'aɪtɪs/, **panostitis** /pænɒ'staɪtɪs/ *noun* inflammation of the whole of a bone

panotitis /ˌpænəʊ'taɪtɪs/ *noun* inflammation affecting all of the ear, but especially the middle ear

panproctocolectomy /ˌpænprɒktəkəˈleↄktəmi/ *noun* the surgical removal of the whole of the rectum and the colon

pant /pænt/ *verb* to take short breaths because of too much exercise, to gasp for breath ○ *He was panting when he reached the top of the stairs.*

pant- /pænt/ *prefix* same as **pan-**

panto- /pæntəʊ/ *prefix* same as **pan-**

pantothenic acid /ˌpæntəˌθenɪk ˈæsɪd/ *noun* a vitamin of the vitamin B complex, found in liver, yeast and eggs

pantotropic /ˌpæntəˈtrɒpɪk/, **pantropic** /pænˈtrɒpɪk/ *adjective* referring to a virus which attacks many different parts of the body

Papanicolaou test /ˌpæpənɪkəˈleɪu: test/ *noun* a method of staining samples from various body secretions to test for malignancy, e.g. testing a cervical smear sample to see if cancer is present. Also called **Pap test** [Described 1933. After George Nicholas Papanicolaou (1883–1962), Greek anatomist and physician who worked in the USA.]

papaveretum /pəˌpævəˈri:təm/ *noun* a preparation of opium used to reduce pain

papilla /pəˈpɪlə/ *noun* a small swelling which sticks up above the usual surface level ○ *The upper surface of the tongue is covered with papillae.* (NOTE: The plural is **papillae**.)

papillary /pəˈpɪləri/ *adjective* referring to papillae

papillitis /ˌpæpɪˈlaɪtɪs/ *noun* inflammation of the optic disc at the back of the eye

papilloedema /ˌpæpɪləʊˈdi:mə/ *noun* an accumulation of fluid in the optic disc at the back of the eye

papilloma /ˌpæpɪˈləʊmə/ *noun* a benign tumour on the skin or mucous membrane (NOTE: The plural is **papillomas** or **papillomata**.)

papillomatosis /ˌpæpɪləʊməˈtəʊsɪs/ *noun* **1.** being affected with papillomata **2.** the formation of papillomata

papillotomy /ˌpæpɪˈlɒtəmi/ *noun* the operation of cutting into the body at the point where the common bile duct and pancreatic duct meet to go into the duodenum, in order to improve bile drainage and allow any stones to pass out

papovavirus /pəˈpəʊvəvaɪrəs/ *noun* a family of viruses which start tumours, some of which are malignant, and some of which, such as warts, are benign

Pap test /ˈpæp test/, **Pap smear** /ˈpæp smɪə/ *noun* same as **Papanicolaou test**

papular /ˈpæpjʊlə/ *adjective* referring to a papule

papule /ˈpæpju:l/ *noun* a small coloured spot raised above the surface of the skin as part of a rash (NOTE: A flat spot is a **macule**.)

papulo- /pæpjʊləʊ/ *prefix* relating to a papule

papulopustular /ˌpæpjʊləʊˈpʌstjʊlə/ *adjective* referring to a rash with both papules and pustules

papulosquamous /ˌpæpjʊləʊˈskweɪməs/ *adjective* referring to a rash with papules and a scaly skin

para- /pærə/ *prefix* **1.** similar to or near **2.** changed or beyond

parabiosis /ˌpærəbaɪˈəʊsɪs/ *noun* a condition in which two individuals are joined, e.g. conjoined twins

paracentesis /ˌpærəsenˈti:sɪs/ *noun* the procedure of draining fluid from a cavity inside the body using a hollow needle, either for diagnostic purposes or because the fluid is harmful. Also called **tapping**

paracetamol /ˌpærəˈsi:təmɒl/ *noun* a common drug used to relieve mild to moderate pain and reduce fever (NOTE: The US name is **acetaminophen**.)

paracolpitis /ˌpærəkɒlˈpaɪtɪs/ same as **pericolpitis**

paracusis /ˌpærəˈkju:sɪs/, **paracousia** /ˌpærəˈku:siə/ *noun* a disorder of hearing

paradoxical breathing /ˌpærədɒksɪk(ə)l ˈbri:ðɪŋ/, **paradoxical respiration** /ˌpærədɒksɪk(ə)l ˌrespɪˈreɪʃ(ə)n/ *noun* a condition affecting someone with broken ribs, where the chest appears to move in when he or she breathes in, and appears to move out when he or she breathes out

paradoxical sleep /ˌpærədɒksɪk(ə)l ˈsli:p/ *noun* same as **REM sleep**

paradoxus /ˌpærəˈdɒksəs/ ⊳ **pulsus paradoxus**

paraesthesia /ˌpæri:sˈθi:ziə/ *noun* an unexplained tingling sensation. ◊ **pins and needles** (NOTE: The plural is **paraesthesiae**.)

'…the sensory symptoms are paraesthesiae which may spread up the arm over the course of about 20 minutes' [*British Journal of Hospital Medicine*]

paraffin /ˈpærəfɪn/ *noun* an oil produced from petroleum, forming the base of some ointments, and also used for heating and light

paraffin gauze /ˈpærəfɪn gɔ:z/ *noun* gauze covered with solid paraffin, used as a dressing

parageusia /ˌpærəˈgju:siə/ *noun* **1.** a disorder of the sense of taste **2.** an unpleasant taste in the mouth

paragonimiasis /ˌpærəgɒnɪˈmaɪəsɪs/ *noun* a tropical disease in which the lungs are infested with the fluke of the genus Paragonimus and the person has bronchitis and coughs up blood. Also called **endemic haemoptysis**

paragraphia /ˌpærəˈgræfiə/ *noun* the writing of different words or letters from the ones intended, as a result of a stroke or disease

paraguard stretcher /ˈpærəgɑ:d ˌstretʃə/ *noun* a type of strong stretcher to which the injured person is attached securely, so that he or she can be carried upright. It is used for rescuing people from mountains or from tall buildings.

para-influenza virus /ˌpærə ˌɪnfluˈenzə ˌvaɪrəs/ *noun* a virus which causes upper respiratory tract infection. In its structure it is identical to paramyxoviruses and the measles virus.

paralyse /ˈpærəlaɪz/ *verb* to make a part of the body unable to carry out voluntary movements by weakening or damaging muscles or nerves so that they cannot function, or by using a drug ○ *His arm was paralysed after the stroke.* ○ *She is paralysed from the waist down.* (NOTE: The US spelling is **paralyze**.)

paralysis /pəˈræləsɪs/ *noun* a condition in which part of the body cannot be moved because the motor nerves have been damaged or the muscles have been weakened ○ *The condition causes paralysis of the lower limbs.* ○ *He suffered temporary paralysis of the right arm.*
   COMMENT: Paralysis can have many causes: the commonest are injuries to or diseases of the brain or the spinal column.

paralysis agitans /pəˌræləsɪs ˈædʒɪtəns/ *noun* same as **Parkinsonism**

paralytic /ˌpærəˈlɪtɪk/ *adjective* **1.** referring to paralysis **2.** referring to a person who is paralysed

paralytica /pærəˈlɪtɪkə/ ♦ **dementia paralytica**

paralytic ileus /ˌpærəlɪtɪk ˈɪliəs/ *noun* an obstruction in the ileum caused by paralysis of the muscles of the intestine. Also called **adynamic ileus**

paralytic poliomyelitis /ˌpærəlɪtɪk ˌpəʊliəʊˌmaɪəˈlaɪtɪs/ *noun* poliomyelitis which affects the muscles

paramedian /ˌpærəˈmiːdiən/ *adjective* near the midline of the body

paramedian plane /ˌpærəˈmiːdiən pleɪn/ *noun* a plane near the midline of the body, parallel to the sagittal plane and at right angles to the coronal plane. See illustration at ANATOMICAL TERMS in Supplement

paramedic /ˌpærəˈmedɪk/ *noun* a person whose work involves the restoration of health and normal functioning (NOTE: **Paramedic** is used to refer to all types of services and staff, from therapists and hygienists, to ambulance drivers and radiographers, but does not include doctors, nurses or midwives.)

paramedical /ˌpærəˈmedɪk(ə)l/ *adjective* referring to services linked to those given by nurses, doctors and surgeons

paramesonephric duct /ˌpærəmesəˈnefrɪk ˌdʌkt/ *noun* one of the two ducts in an embryo which develop into the uterus and Fallopian tubes. Also called **Müllerian duct**

parameter /pəˈræmɪtə/ *noun* a measurement of something such as blood pressure which may be an important consideration in treating the condition which the person has

parametritis /ˌpærəmɪˈtraɪtɪs/ *noun* inflammation of the parametrium

parametrium /ˌpærəˈmiːtriəm/ *noun* the connective tissue around the uterus

paramnesia /ˌpærəmˈniːziə/ *noun* a disorder of the memory in which someone remembers events which have not happened

paramyxovirus /ˌpærəmɪksəʊˈvaɪrəs/ *noun* one of a group of viruses, which cause mumps, measles and other infectious diseases

paranasal /ˌpærəˈneɪz(ə)l/ *adjective* by the side of the nose

paranasal sinus /ˌpærəneɪz(ə)l ˈsaɪnəs/, **paranasal air sinus** /ˌpærəneɪz(ə)l ˈeə ˌsaɪnəs/ *noun* one of the four pairs of sinuses in the skull near the nose, which open into the nasal cavity and are lined with sticky mucus (NOTE: They are the frontal, maxillary, ethmoidal and sphenoidal sinuses.)

paranoia /ˌpærəˈnɔɪə/ *noun* a behaviour characterised by mistaken ideas or delusions of persecution or self-importance

paranoiac /ˌpærəˈnɔɪæk/ *noun* a person affected by paranoia

paranoid /ˈpærənɔɪd/ *adjective* having a fixed delusion

paranoid disorder /ˌpærənɔɪd dɪsˈɔːdə/ *noun* a mental disorder which causes someone experiencing it to believe strongly that something is not right with them, with someone else or with the world generally and to maintain the belief even when given evidence against it (NOTE: The preferred term is delusional disorder.)

paranoid schizophrenia /ˌpærənɔɪd ˌskɪtsəʊˈfriːniə/ *noun* a form of schizophrenia in which the person believes he or she is being persecuted

paraparesis /ˌpærəpəˈriːsɪs/ *noun* incomplete paralysis of the legs

paraphasia /ˌpærəˈfeɪziə/ *noun* a speech disorder in which the person uses a wrong sound in the place of the correct word or phrase

paraphimosis /ˌpærəfaɪˈməʊsɪs/ *noun* a condition in which the foreskin around the penis is tight and may have to be removed by circumcision

paraphrenia /ˌpærəˈfriːniə/ *noun* a dated term for a mental disorder involving delusions without severe personality deterioration

paraplegia /ˌpærəˈpliːdʒə/ *noun* paralysis which affects the lower part of the body and the legs, usually caused by an injury to the spinal cord

paraplegic /ˌpærəˈpliːdʒɪk/ *noun* someone who has paraplegia ■ *adjective* paralysed in the lower part of the body and legs

paraprofessional /ˌpærəprəˈfeʃ(ə)n(ə)l/ *noun* somebody with training who acts as an assistant to a professional person

parapsoriasis /ˌpærəsəˈraɪəsɪs/ *noun* a group of skin diseases with scales, similar to psoriasis

parapsychology /ˌpærəsaɪˈkɒlədʒi/ *noun* the study of effects of the mind which appear not to be explained by known psychological or scientific principles, e.g. extrasensory perception and telepathy

Paraquat /ˈpærəkwɒt/ a trade name for dimethyl dupyridilium used as a weedkiller

parasagittal /ˌpærəˈsædʒɪt(ə)l/ *adjective* near the midline of the body

parasagittal plane /ˌpærəˈsædʒɪt(ə)l pleɪn/ *noun* a plane near the midline of the body, parallel to the sagittal plane and at right angles to the coronal plane. Also called **paramedian plane**. See illustration at ANATOMICAL TERMS in Supplement

parasitaemia /ˌpærəsɪˈtiːmiə/ *noun* the presence of parasites in the blood

parasite /ˈpærəsaɪt/ *noun* a plant or animal which lives on or inside another organism and draws nourishment from that organism

COMMENT: The commonest parasites affecting humans are lice on the skin, and various types of worms in the intestines. Many diseases such as malaria and amoebic dysentery are caused by infestation with parasites.

parasitic /ˌpærəˈsɪtɪk/ *adjective* referring to parasites

parasitic cyst /ˌpærəsɪtɪk ˈsɪst/ *noun* a cyst caused by the growing larvae of a parasite in the body

parasiticide /ˌpærəˈsaɪtɪsaɪd/ *noun* a substance which kills parasites ■ *adjective* killing parasites

parasitology /ˌpærəsaɪˈtɒlədʒi/ *noun* the scientific study of parasites

parasuicide /ˌpærəˈsuːɪsaɪd/ *noun* an act where someone tries to kill himself or herself, but without really intending to do so, rather as a way of drawing attention to his or her psychological condition

parasympathetic /ˌpærəsɪmpəˈθetɪk/ *adjective* referring to the parasympathetic nervous system

parasympathetic nervous system /ˌpærəsɪmpəˌθetɪk ˈnɜːvəs ˌsɪstəm/, **parasympathetic system** /ˌpærəsɪmpəˈθetɪk ˌsɪstəm/ *noun* one of two parts of the autonomic nervous system. Its messages reach the organs of the body through the cranial and sacral nerves to the eyes, the gastrointestinal system and other organs. ◊ **sympathetic nervous system**

COMMENT: The parasympathetic nervous system acts in opposition to the sympathetic nervous system, slowing down the action of the heart, reducing blood pressure and increasing the rate of digestion.

parasympatholytic /ˌpærəsɪmˌpæθəˈlɪtɪk/ *noun* a drug which reduces the effects of the parasympathetic nervous system by relaxing smooth muscle, reducing the amount of sweat and saliva produced and widening the pupil of the eye. An example is atropine. ■ *adjective* relating to a parasympatholytic drug

parasympathomimetic /ˌpærəsɪmˌpæθəʊmɪˈmetɪk/ *noun* a drug which stimulates the parasympathetic nervous system by making smooth muscle more tense, widening the blood vessels, slowing the heart rate, increasing the amount of sweat and saliva produced and contracting the pupil of the eye ■ *adjective* producing effects similar to those of a parasympathomimetic drug

parathormone /ˌpærəˈθɔːməʊn/ *noun* the hormone secreted by the parathyroid glands which regulates the level of calcium in blood plasma. Also called **parathyroid hormone**

parathyroid /ˌpærəˈθaɪrɔɪd/ *noun* same as **parathyroid gland** ■ *adjective* **1.** relating to a parathyroid gland **2.** located close to the thyroid gland

parathyroidectomy /ˌpærəˌθaɪrɔɪˈdektəmi/ *noun* the surgical removal of a parathyroid gland

parathyroid gland /ˌpærəˈθaɪrɔɪd glænd/ *noun* one of four small glands which are situated in or near the wall of the thyroid gland and secrete a hormone which controls the way in which calcium and phosphorus are deposited in bones

parathyroid hormone /ˌpærəˈθaɪrɔɪd ˌhɔːməʊn/ *noun* same as **parathormone**

paratyphoid /ˌpærəˈtaɪfɔɪd/, **paratyphoid fever** /ˌpærəˈtaɪfɔɪd ˌfiːvə/ *noun* an infectious disease which has similar symptoms to typhoid and is caused by bacteria transmitted by humans or animals

COMMENT: There are three forms of paratyphoid fever, known by the letters A, B, and C, caused by three types of bacterium, *Salmonella paratyphi* A, B, and C. TAB injections give immunity against paratyphoid A and B, but not against C.

paravertebral /ˌpærəˈvɜːtɪbrəl/ *adjective* near the vertebrae, beside the spinal column

paravertebral injection /ˌpærəˌvɜːtɪbrəl ɪnˈdʒekʃən/ *noun* an injection of local anaesthetic into the back near the vertebrae

parenchyma /pəˈreŋkɪmə/ *noun* tissues which contain the working cells of an organ

parenchymal /pəˈreŋkɪməl/ *adjective* relating to parenchyma

parent /ˈpeərənt/ *noun* a biological or adoptive mother or father ■ *verb* to carry out the role of a parent

'…in most paediatric wards today open visiting is the norm, with parent care much in evidence. Parents who are resident in the hospital also need time spent with them' [*Nursing Times*]

parent cell /ˈpeərənt sel/ *noun* an original cell which divides into daughter cells by mitosis

parenteral /pæ'rentərəl/ *adjective* referring to medication which is not given by mouth but in the form of injections or suppositories. Compare **enteral, oral**

parenteral nutrition /pæ,rentərəl nju:'trɪʃ(ə)n/, **parenteral feeding** /pæ,rentərəl 'fi:dɪŋ/ *noun* the process of feeding someone by means other than the digestive tract, especially by giving injections of glucose to someone critically ill

parenthood /'peərənthʊd/ *noun* the state of being a parent

parenting /'peərəntɪŋ/ *noun* the activities involved in bringing up children □ **parenting skills** the abilities and experience that make someone a good parent

paresis /pə'ri:sɪs/ *noun* partial paralysis

paresthesia /,pæri:s'θi:ziə/ *noun US* same as **paraesthesia**

paries /'peəri:z/ *noun* **1.** a superficial part of a structure of an organ **2.** the wall of a cavity (NOTE: [all senses] The plural is **parietes**.)

parietal /pə'raɪət(ə)l/ *adjective* referring to the wall of a cavity or any organ

parietal bone /pə'raɪət(ə)l bəʊn/, **parietal** /pə'raɪət(ə)l/ *noun* one of two bones which form the sides of the skull

parietal cell /pə'raɪət(ə)l sel/ *noun* same as **oxyntic cell**

parietal lobe /pə'raɪət(ə)l ləʊb/ *noun* the middle lobe of the cerebral hemisphere, which is associated with language and other mental processes, and also contains the postcentral gyrus

parietal pericardium /pə,raɪət(ə)l ,peri'kɑ:diəm/ *noun* the outer layer of the serous pericardium, not in direct contact with the heart muscle, which lies inside and is attached to the fibrous pericardium

parietal peritoneum /pə,raɪət(ə)l ,peritə'ni:əm/ *noun* part of the peritoneum which lines the abdominal cavity and covers the abdominal viscera

parietal pleura /pə,raɪət(ə)l 'plʊərə/ *noun* a membrane attached to the diaphragm and covering the chest cavity. Also called **outer pleura**. See illustration at LUNGS in Supplement

-parin /pərɪn/ *suffix* used for anticoagulants ○ *heparin*

Paris /'pærɪs/ ♦ **plaster of Paris**

parity /'pærɪti/ *noun* **1.** equality of status or position, especially in terms of pay or rank **2.** the number of children that a woman has given birth to

parkinsonian /,pɑːkɪn'səʊniən/ *adjective* referring to Parkinson's disease ○ *parkinsonian tremor*

Parkinsonism /'pɑːkɪnsənɪz(ə)m/ *noun* a progressive nervous disorder, which may be an effect of some drugs, repeated head injuries or brain tumours. The main symptoms are trem-

bling hands and a slow shuffling walk. Also called **paralysis agitans**

Parkinson's disease /'pɑːkɪnsənz dɪ,zi:z/ *noun* a progressive nervous disorder without a known cause which is a type of Parkinsonism, the main symptoms of which are trembling hands, a slow shuffling walk and difficulty in speaking [Described 1817. After James Parkinson (1755–1824), English physician.]

COMMENT: Parkinson's disease affects the basal ganglia of the brain which control movement, due to the destruction of dopaminergic neurones. Some cases can be improved by treatment with levodopa, which is the precursor of the missing neurotransmitter dopamine, or by drugs which inhibit the breakdown of dopamine.

paronychia /,pærə'nɪkiə/ *noun* inflammation near the nail which forms pus, caused by an infection in the fleshy part of the tip of a finger. ◊ **whitlow**

parosmia /pə'rɒzmiə/ *noun* a disorder of the sense of smell

parotid /pə'rɒtɪd/ *adjective* near the ear

parotid gland /pə'rɒtɪd glænd/, **parotid** /pə'rɒtɪd/ *noun* one of the glands which produces saliva, situated in the neck behind the joint of the jaw and ear

parotitis /,pærə'taɪtɪs/ *noun* inflammation of the parotid glands

COMMENT: Mumps is the commonest form of parotitis, where the parotid gland becomes swollen and the sides of the face appear fat.

parous /'peərəs/ *adjective* referring to a woman who has given birth to one or more children

paroxetine /pə'rɒksɪti:n/ *noun* an antidepressant drug which prolongs the effects of serotonin in the brain

paroxysm /'pærəksɪz(ə)m/ *noun* **1.** a sudden movement of the muscles ○ *She suffered paroxysms of coughing during the night.* **2.** the sudden re-appearance of symptoms of the disease **3.** a sudden attack of coughing or sneezing

paroxysmal /,pærək'sɪzm(ə)l/ *adjective* referring to a paroxysm, or similar to a paroxysm

paroxysmal dyspnoea /pærək,sɪzm(ə)l dɪsp'ni:ə/ *noun* an attack of breathlessness at night, usually caused by congestive heart failure

paroxysmal tachycardia /pærək,sɪzm(ə)l tæki'kɑːdiə/ *noun* same as **nodal tachycardia**

parrot disease /'pærət dɪ,zi:z/ *noun* same as **psittacosis**

pars /pɑːz/ *noun* the Latin word for part

part /pɑːt/ *noun* a piece, one of the sections which make up a whole organ or body

partial /'pɑːʃ(ə)l/ *adjective* not complete, affecting only part of something ○ *He only made a partial recovery.*

partial amnesia /ˌpɑːʃ(ə)l æmˈniːziə/ *noun* an inability to remember specific facts, such as names of people

partial deafness /ˌpɑːʃ(ə)l ˈdefnəs/ *noun* the condition of being able to hear some sounds but not all

partial denture /ˌpɑːʃ(ə)l ˈdentʃə/ *noun* part of a set of false teeth, replacing only a few teeth

partial gastrectomy /ˌpɑːʃ(ə)l gæ ˈstrektəmi/ *noun* an operation to remove part of the stomach

partially /ˈpɑːʃ(ə)li/ *adverb* not completely ○ *He is partially paralysed in his right side.* □ **partially deaf** able to hear some sounds but not all □ **partially sighted** having only partial vision ○ *Large print books are available for people who are partially sighted.*

partially sighted register /ˌpɑːʃ(ə)li ˈsaɪtɪd ˌredʒɪstə/ *noun* a list of people who have poor sight but are not blind, and may require some special services

partial mastectomy /ˌpɑːʃ(ə)l mæ ˈstektəmi/ *noun* an operation to remove part of a breast

partial pancreatectomy /ˌpɑːʃ(ə)l ˌpæŋkriəˈtektəmi/ *noun* an operation to remove part of the pancreas

partial thickness burn /ˌpɑːʃ(ə)l ˈθɪknəs bɜːn/ *noun* a burn which leaves enough tissue for the skin to grow again. Also called **superficial thickness burn**

partial vision /ˌpɑːʃ(ə)l ˈvɪʒ(ə)n/ *noun* the ability to see only a part of the total field of vision, or not being able to see anything very clearly

particle /ˈpɑːtɪk(ə)l/ *noun* a very small piece of matter

particulate /pɑːˈtɪkjʊlət/ *adjective* **1.** referring to or composed of particles **2.** made up of separate particles

particulate matter /pɑːˈtɪkjʊlət ˌmætə/ *noun* particles of less than a specified size, usually of carbon, which are used as a measure of air pollution and can affect asthma

partly /ˈpɑːtli/ *adverb* not completely ○ *She is partly paralysed.*

parturient /pɑːˈtjʊəriənt/ *adjective* referring to childbirth ■ *noun* a woman who is in labour

parturifacient /ˌpɑːtjʊəriˈfeɪʃənt/ *adjective* starting off birth or making it easier to give birth ■ *noun* a drug that starts off birth or makes it easier to give birth

parturition /ˌpɑːtjʊˈrɪʃ(ə)n/ *noun* same as **childbirth**

parulis /pəˈruːlɪs/ same as **gumboil**

Paschen bodies /ˈpæʃ(ə)n ˌbɒdiz/ *plural noun* particles which occur in the skin lesions of people who have smallpox [After Enrique Paschen (1860–1936), German pathologist]

pass /pɑːs/ *verb* to allow faeces, urine or any other body product to come out of the body ○ *Have you passed anything this morning?* ○ *He passed a small stone in his urine.* □ **to pass blood** to produce faeces or urine that contain blood □ **to pass water** to urinate (*informal*)

passage /ˈpæsɪdʒ/ *noun* **1.** a long narrow channel inside the body **2.** the process of moving from one place to another **3.** evacuation of the bowels **4.** the introduction of an instrument into a cavity □ **air passage** a tube which takes air to the lungs

pass away /ˌpɑːs əˈweɪ/ *verb* used to avoid saying 'die' (*informal*) ○ *Mother passed away during the night.*

passive /ˈpæsɪv/ *adjective* receiving rather than initiating an action

passive immunity /ˌpæsɪv ɪˈmjuːnɪti/ *noun* immunity which is acquired by a baby in the uterus or by a person through an injection with an antitoxin

passive movement /ˌpæsɪv ˈmuːvmənt/ *noun* movement of a limb or other body part by a doctor or therapist, not by the person

passive smoking /ˌpæsɪv ˈsməʊkɪŋ/ *noun* the act of breathing in smoke from other people's cigarettes when you do not smoke yourself

pass on /ˌpɑːs ˈɒn/ *verb* **1.** to give a disease to someone ○ *Haemophilia is passed on by a woman to her sons.* ○ *The disease was quickly passed on by carriers to the rest of the population.* **2.** used to avoid saying 'die' ○ *My father passed on two years ago.*

pass out /ˌpɑːs ˈaʊt/ *verb* to faint (*informal*) ○ *When we told her that her father was ill, she passed out.*

past /pɑːst/ *adjective* referring to time which has passed

paste /peɪst/ *noun* a medicinal ointment which is very thick and is spread or rubbed onto the skin

Pasteurella /ˌpæstəˈrelə/ *noun* a genus of parasitic bacteria, one of which causes the plague

pasteurisation /ˌpɑːstʃəraɪˈzeɪʃ(ə)n/, **pasteurization** *noun* the process of heating food or food products to destroy bacteria [After Louis Pasteur (1822–95), French chemist and bacteriologist]

COMMENT: Pasteurisation is carried out by heating food for a short time at a lower temperature than that used for sterilisation: the two methods used are heating to 72°C for fifteen seconds (the high-temperature short-time method) or to 65°C for half an hour, and then cooling rapidly. This will kill tuberculosis bacteria that may be present in milk, for example.

pasteurise /ˈpɑːstʃəraɪz/, **pasteurize** *verb* to kill bacteria in food by heating it ○ *The government is telling people to drink only pasteurised milk.*

past history /ˌpɑːst ˈhɪst(ə)ri/ *noun* records of earlier illnesses ○ *He has no past history of renal disease.*

pastille /ˈpæst(ə)l/ *noun* **1.** a sweet jelly with medication in it, which can be sucked to relieve a sore throat **2.** a small paper disc covered with barium platinocyanide, which changes colour when exposed to radiation

pat /pæt/ *verb* to hit someone or something lightly and gently with the palm of the hand or some other flat surface ○ *She patted the baby on the back to make it burp.*

patch /pætʃ/ *noun* a piece of sticking plaster with a substance on it, which is stuck to the skin to allow the substance to be gradually absorbed into the system through the skin, e.g. in HRT

COMMENT: Patches are available on prescription for various treatments, especially for administering hormone replacement therapy. They are also used for treating nicotine addiction and can be bought without a prescription.

patch test /ˈpætʃ test/ *noun* a test for allergies or tuberculosis, where a piece of sticking plaster containing an allergic substance or tuberculin is stuck to the skin to see if there is a reaction

patella /pəˈtelə/ *noun* the small bone in front of the knee joint. Also called **kneecap**

patellar /pəˈtelə/ *adjective* referring to the kneecap

patellar reflex /pəˌtelə ˈriːfleks/ *noun* the jerk made as a reflex action by the knee, when the legs are crossed and the patellar tendon is tapped sharply. Also called **knee jerk**

patellar tendon /pəˌtelə ˈtendən/ *noun* a tendon just below the kneecap

patellectomy /ˌpætəˈlektəmi/ *noun* a surgical operation to remove the kneecap

patency /ˈpeɪtənsi/ *noun* the condition of being wide open ○ *A salpingostomy was performed to restore the patency of the Fallopian tube.*

patent /ˈpeɪtənt, ˈpætənt/ *adjective* open, exposed ○ *The presence of a pulse shows that the main blood vessels from the heart to the site of the pulse are patent.*

patent ductus arteriosus /ˌpeɪtənt ˌdʌktəs ɑːˌtɪəriˈəʊsəs/ *noun* a congenital condition in which the ductus arteriosus does not close, allowing blood into the circulation without having passed through the lungs

patent medicine /ˌpeɪtənt ˈmed(ə)sɪn/ *noun* a medicinal preparation which is made and sold under a trade name and is protected by law from being copied or sold by other manufacturers for a certain length of time after its invention. ◊ **proprietary medicine**

paternity /pəˈtɜːnɪti/ *noun* **1.** the fact of being or becoming a father ○ *paternity leave* Compare **maternity 2.** the identity of a father

paternity test /pəˈtɜːnɪti test/ *noun* a test such as blood grouping which makes it possible to determine the identity of the father of a child

COMMENT: DNA fingerprinting may be required in order to identify a man who might be the father according to his blood group and that of the child, but is not in fact the father.

path- /pæθ/, **patho-** /ˈpæθəʊ/ *prefix* referring to disease

pathogen /ˈpæθədʒən/ *noun* a microorganism which causes a disease

pathogenesis /ˌpæθəˈdʒenəsɪs/ *noun* the origin, production and development of a morbid or diseased condition

pathogenetic /ˌpæθədʒəˈnetɪk/ *adjective* referring to pathogenesis

pathogenic /ˌpæθəˈdʒenɪk/ *adjective* causing or producing a disease

pathogenicity /ˌpæθədʒəˈnɪsɪti/ *noun* the ability of a pathogen to cause a disease

pathognomonic /ˌpæθəgnəʊˈmɒnɪk/ *adjective* referring to a symptom which is typical and characteristic, and which indicates that someone has a particular disease

pathological /ˌpæθəˈlɒdʒɪk(ə)l/, **pathologic** /ˌpæθəˈlɒdʒɪk/ *adjective* **1.** referring to a disease, or caused by a disease **2.** indicating a disease

pathological depression /ˌpæθə ˌlɒdʒɪk(ə)l dɪˈpreʃ(ə)n/ *noun* an unusually severe state of depression, possibly leading to suicide

pathological dislocation /ˌpæθəlɒdʒɪk(ə)l ˌdɪsləˈkeɪʃ(ə)n/ *noun* the dislocation of a diseased joint

pathological fracture /ˌpæθəˌlɒdʒɪk(ə)l ˈfræktʃə/ *noun* a fracture of a diseased bone

pathologist /pəˈθɒlədʒɪst/ *noun* **1.** a doctor who specialises in the study of diseases and the changes in the body caused by disease, examining tissue specimens from patients and reporting on the presence or absence of disease in them **2.** a doctor who examines dead bodies in order to find out the cause of death

pathology /pəˈθɒlədʒi/ *noun* the study of diseases and the changes in structure and function which diseases cause in the body. Also called **morbid anatomy**

pathology report /pəˈθɒlədʒi rɪˌpɔːt/ *noun* a report on tests carried out to find the cause of a disease

pathophysiology /ˌpæθəʊfɪziˈɒlədʒi/ *noun* the study of unusual or diseased organs

pathway /ˈpɑːθweɪ/ *noun* a series of linked neurones along which nerve impulses travel

-pathy /pəθi/ *suffix* **1.** disease **2.** treatment of a disease

patient /ˈpeɪʃ(ə)nt/ *adjective* being able to wait a long time without becoming annoyed ○ *You will have to be patient if you are waiting for treatment – the doctor is late with his ap-*

pointments. ■ *noun* a person who is in hospital or who is being treated by a doctor ○ *The patients are all asleep in their beds.* ○ *The doctor is taking the patient's temperature.*

patient allocation /ˌpeɪʃ(ə)nt ˌælə'keɪʃ(ə)n/ *noun* a system of assigning each patient to a particular nurse for all their care needs

patient identifier /ˌpeɪʃ(ə)nt aɪ'dentɪfaɪə/ *noun* a code of letters and numbers attached to the patient's medical records by which all information concerning the patient can be tracked, e.g. cause of death

patulous /'pætjʊləs/ *adjective* stretched open, patent

Paul–Bunnell reaction /ˌpɔːl 'bʌn(ə)l rɪˌækʃən/, **Paul–Bunnell test** /ˌpɔːl 'bʌn(ə)l ˌtest/ *noun* a blood test to see if someone has glandular fever, where the person's blood is tested against a solution containing glandular fever bacilli [Described 1932. After John Rodman Paul (b. 1893), US physician; Walls Willard Bunnell (1902–66), US physician.]

Paul's tube /'pɔːlz tjuːb/ *noun* a glass tube used to remove the contents of the bowel after an opening has been made between the intestine and the abdominal wall [Described 1891. After Frank Thomas Paul (1851–1941), British surgeon.]

pavement epithelium /'peɪvmənt epɪˌθiːliəm/ *noun* same as **squamous epithelium**

Pavlov's method /'pævlɒvz ˌmeθəd/ *noun* a set of procedures for the study or production of conditioned reflexes

PBI test /ˌpiː biː 'aɪ test/ *noun* same as **protein-bound iodine test**

p.c. /ˌpiː 'siː/ *adverb* (*used on prescriptions*) after food. Full form **post cibum**

PCC *abbr* Professional Conduct Committee

PCG *abbr* primary care group

PCOD *abbr* polycystic ovary disease

PCOS *abbr* polycystic ovary syndrome

PCP *abbr* pneumocystis carinii pneumonia

PCR *abbr* polymerase chain reaction

PCT *abbr* primary care trust

p.d.[1] *adverb* (*used on prescriptions*) per day. Full form **per diem**

p.d.[2] *abbr* per diem

PE *abbr* pulmonary embolism

peak /piːk/ *noun* the highest point

peak expiratory flow rate /ˌpiːk ɪkˌspaɪərət(ə)ri 'fləʊ ˌreɪt/ *noun* the rate at which someone can expel air from their lungs when they are full and with no time limit. Abbr **PEFR**

peak period /'piːk ˌpɪəriəd/ *noun* the time of the day, days of the month or months of the year, during which something such as a fever, tiredness, infectious disease or cold reaches its highest point or occurs most frequently in a population

peaky /'piːki/ *adjective* thin, pale, and sickly in appearance (*informal*)

pearl /pɜːl/ ♦ **Bohn's nodules**

Pearson bed /'pɪəs(ə)n bed/ *noun* a type of bed with a Balkan frame, a rectangular frame attached to and overhanging the bed, used mainly for people with splints

peau d'orange /ˌpəʊ dɒ'rɑːnʒ/ *noun* thickened skin with many little depressions caused by lymphoedema which forms over a breast tumour or in elephantiasis (NOTE: From the French phrase meaning 'orange peel'.)

pecten /'pektən/ *noun* **1.** the middle section of the wall of the anal passage **2.** a hard ridge on the pubis

pectineal /pek'tɪniəl/ *adjective* **1.** referring to the pecten of the pubis **2.** referring to a structure with ridges like a comb

pectoral /'pekt(ə)rəl/ *noun* **1.** a therapeutic substance which has a good effect on respiratory disease **2.** same as **pectoral muscle** ■ *adjective* referring to the chest

pectoral girdle /ˌpekt(ə)rəl 'ɡɜːd(ə)l/ *noun* the shoulder bones, the scapulae and clavicles, to which the upper arm bones are attached. Also called **shoulder girdle**

pectoralis /ˌpektə'reɪlɪs/ *noun* a chest muscle

pectoralis major /pektəˌreɪlɪs 'meɪdʒə/ *noun* a large chest muscle which pulls the arm forward or rotates it

pectoralis minor /pektəˌreɪlɪs 'maɪnə/ *noun* a small chest muscle which allows the shoulder to be depressed

pectoral muscle /'pekt(ə)rəl ˌmʌs(ə)l/ *noun* one of two muscles which lie across the chest and control movements of the shoulder and arm. Also called **chest muscle**

pectus /'pektəs/ *noun* the anterior part of the chest

pectus carinatum /ˌpektəs ˌkærɪ'nɑːtəm/ *noun* a condition in which the sternum is unusually prominent. Also called **pigeon breast**

pectus excavatum /ˌpektəs ˌekskə'veɪtəm/ *noun* a congenital condition, in which the chest is depressed in the centre because the lower part of the breastbone is curved backwards. Also called **funnel chest**

pedes /'piːdiz/ *plural of* **pes**

pediatrics /ˌpiːdi'ætrɪks/ *noun* US same as **paediatrics**

pedicle /'pedɪk(ə)l/ *noun* **1.** a long thin piece of skin which attaches a skin graft to the place where it was growing originally **2.** a piece of tissue which connects a tumour to healthy tissue **3.** a bridge which connects the lamina of a vertebra to the body

pediculicide /pɪ'dɪkjʊlɪsaɪd/ *noun* a chemical substance that kills lice

pediculosis /pɪˌdɪkjʊ'ləʊsɪs/ *noun* a skin disease caused by being infested with lice

Pediculus /pɪ'dɪkjʊləs/ *noun* same as **louse** (NOTE: The plural is **Pediculi**.)

Pediculus capitis /pɪˌdɪkjʊləs kə'paɪtɪs/ *noun* same as **head louse**

pedo- /piːd/ *prefix* same as **paedo-**

pedodontia /ˌpiːdə'dɒnʃə/ *noun* the study of children's teeth

pedodontist /ˌpiːdə'dɒntɪst/ *noun* a dentist who specialises in the treatment of children's teeth

peduncle /pɪ'dʌŋkəl/ *noun* a stem or stalk

pedunculate /pɪ'dʌŋkjuleɪt/ *adjective* having a stem or stalk. Opposite **sessile**

pee /piː/ *verb* same as **urinate** (*informal*)

peel /piːl/ *verb* 1. to take the skin off a fruit or vegetable 2. (*of skin*) to come off in pieces ○ *After getting sunburnt, his skin began to peel.*

PEEP *abbr* positive end-expiratory pressure

peer review /'pɪə rɪˌvjuː/ *noun* an assessment of a piece of someone's work by people who are experts on the subject

PEFR *abbr* peak expiratory flow rate

Pel–Ebstein fever /ˌpel 'ebstaɪn ˌfiːvə/ *noun* a fever associated with Hodgkin's disease which recurs regularly [Described 1885. After Pieter Klaases Pel (1852–1919), Professor of Medicine in Amsterdam, Netherlands; Wilhelm Ebstein (1836–1912), Professor of Medicine at Göttingen, Germany.]

pellagra /pə'læɡrə/ *noun* a disease caused by a deficiency of nicotinic acid, riboflavine and pyridoxine from the vitamin B complex, where patches of skin become inflamed, and the person has anorexia, nausea and diarrhoea

COMMENT: In some cases of pellagra the patient's mental faculties can be affected, with depression, headaches and numbness of the extremities. Treatment is by improving the patient's diet.

Pellegrini–Stieda's disease /peləˌɡriːni 'stiːdəz dɪˌziːz/ *noun* a disease where an injury to the knee causes the ligament to become calcified [Described 1905. After Augusto Pellegrini, surgeon in Florence, Italy; Alfred Stieda (1869–1945), Professor of Surgery at Königsberg, Germany.]

pellet /'pelɪt/ *noun* 1. a small rod- or oval-shaped pill of steroid hormone, usually either oestrogen or testosterone, that is implanted under the skin for slow absorption 2. solid sediment at the base of a container after centrifuging

pellicle /'pelɪk(ə)l/ *noun* a thin layer of skin tissue

pellucida /pɪ'luːsɪdə/ ♦ **zona pellucida**

pelves /'pelviːz/ *plural of* **pelvis**

pelvic /'pelvɪk/ *adjective* referring to the pelvis

pelvic brim /ˌpelvɪk 'brɪm/ *noun* a line on the ilium which separates the false pelvis from the true pelvis

pelvic cavity /ˌpelvɪk 'kævɪti/ *noun* a space below the abdominal cavity, above the pelvis

pelvic colon /ˌpelvɪk 'kəʊlɒn/ *noun* same as **sigmoid colon**

pelvic diaphragm /ˌpelvɪk 'daɪəfræm/ *noun* a sheet of muscle between the pelvic cavity and the peritoneum

pelvic floor /ˌpelvɪk 'flɔː/ *noun* the lower part of the space beneath the pelvic girdle, formed of muscle

pelvic fracture /ˌpelvɪk 'fræktʃə/ *noun* a fracture of the pelvis

pelvic girdle /ˌpelvɪk 'ɡɜːd(ə)l/ *noun* the ring formed by the two hip bones to which the thigh bones are attached. Also called **hip girdle**

pelvic inflammatory disease /ˌpelvɪk ɪn'flæmət(ə)ri dɪˌziːz/ *noun* an inflammation of a woman's reproductive organs in the pelvic area, which can cause infertility

pelvic outlet /ˌpelvɪk 'aʊtlet/ *noun* an opening at the base of the pelvis

pelvic version /ˌpelvɪk 'vɜːʃ(ə)n/ *noun* turning a fetus around in the uterus by moving the buttocks of the fetus

pelvimeter /pel'vɪmɪtə/ *noun* an instrument to measure the diameter and capacity of the pelvis

pelvimetry /pel'vɪmɪtri/ *noun* the act of measuring the pelvis, especially to see if the internal ring is wide enough for a baby to pass through in childbirth

pelvis /'pelvɪs/ *noun* 1. the strong basin-shaped ring of bone near the bottom of the spine, formed of the hip bones at the front and sides and the sacrum and coccyx at the back 2. the internal space inside the pelvic girdle (NOTE: [all senses] The plural is **pelvises** or **pelves**.)

COMMENT: The hip bones are each in three sections: the ilium, the ischium and the pubis and are linked in front by the pubic symphysis. The pelvic girdle is shaped in a different way in men and women, the internal space being wider in women. The top part of the pelvis, which does not form a complete ring, is called the 'false pelvis'; the lower part is the 'true pelvis'.

pelvis of the kidney /ˌpelvɪs əv ðə 'kɪdni/ *noun* same as **renal pelvis**. See illustration at KIDNEY in Supplement (NOTE: For other terms referring to the pelvis of the kidney, see words beginning with **pyel-, pyelo-**.)

pemphigoid /'pemfɪɡɔɪd/ *noun* a skin disease which is similar to pemphigus ■ *adjective* referring to a skin disease similar to pemphigus

pemphigus /'pemfɪɡəs/ *noun* a rare disease where large blisters form inside the skin

pendulous /'pendjʊləs/ *adjective* referring to an object or body part which hangs loosely or swings freely

penes /'piːniz/ *plural of* **penis**

penetrate /'penɪtreɪt/ verb to go through or into something ○ The end of the broken bone has penetrated the liver. ○ The ulcer burst, penetrating the wall of the duodenum.

penetration /ˌpenɪ'treɪʃ(ə)n/ noun the act of penetrating ○ the penetration of the vagina by the penis ○ penetration of an ovum by a spermatozoon

-penia /piːniə/ suffix meaning a deficiency or not enough of something

penicillamine /ˌpenɪ'sɪləmiːn/ noun a chelating agent which is used to help the body get rid of toxic metals

penicillin /ˌpenɪ'sɪlɪn/ noun a common antibiotic originally produced from a fungus (NOTE: Penicillin drugs have names ending in -cillin: amoxicillin.)

COMMENT: Penicillin is effective against many microbial diseases, but some people can be allergic to it, and this fact should be noted on medical record cards.

penicillinase /ˌpenɪ'sɪlɪneɪz/ noun an enzyme produced by some bacteria that inactivates penicillin, used to treat adverse reactions to penicillin

penicillin resistance /ˌpenɪsɪlɪn rɪ'zɪstəns/ noun the ability of bacteria to resist penicillin

Penicillium /ˌpenɪ'sɪliəm/ noun the fungus from which penicillin is derived

penile /'piːnaɪl/ adjective referring to the penis

penile urethra /ˌpiːnaɪl jʊ'riːθrə/ noun a tube in the penis through which urine and semen pass

penis /'piːnɪs/ noun the male genital organ, which also passes urine. See illustration at UROGENITAL SYSTEM (MALE) in Supplement. ◊ kraurosis penis

COMMENT: The penis is a mass of tissue containing the urethra. When stimulated the tissue of the penis fills with blood and becomes erect.

pentamidine /pen'tæmɪdiːn/ noun an antibiotic used in the treatment of African sleeping sickness and of pneumonia in people with AIDS

pentazocine /pen'tæzəsiːn/ noun an artificially produced narcotic drug used to reduce pain

pentose /'pentəʊz/ noun a sugar containing five carbon atoms

pentosuria /ˌpentə'sjʊəriə/ noun a condition in which pentose is present in the urine

Pentothal /'pentəθæl/ a trade name for thiopentone

Peplau's model /'peplaʊ ˌmɒd(ə)l/ noun a model for nursing which describes the individual as a system with physiological, psychological and social components. The nurse and patient work together to define the patient's problems and to understand their reactions to

one another, and the nurse takes on different roles in each phase of the relationship, such as a teacher, counsellor, leader, and technical expert, until the patient no longer needs their care.

pepsin /'pepsɪn/ noun an enzyme in the stomach which breaks down the proteins in food into peptones

pepsinogen /pep'sɪnədʒən/ noun a secretion from the gastric gland which is the inactive form of pepsin

peptic /'peptɪk/ adjective referring to digestion or to the digestive system

peptic ulcer /ˌpeptɪk 'ʌlsə/ noun a benign ulcer in the duodenum or in the stomach

peptidase /'peptɪdeɪz/ noun an enzyme which breaks down proteins in the intestine into amino acids

peptide /'peptaɪd/ noun a compound formed of two or more amino acids

peptone /'peptəʊn/ noun a substance produced by the action of pepsins on proteins in food

peptonuria /ˌpeptə'njʊəriə/ noun a condition in which peptones are present in the urine

per /pɜː, pə/ preposition 1. out of each ○ ten per thousand 2. by or through ○ per rectum

per cent /pə 'sent/ noun, adjective, adverb in or for every hundred ○ Fifty per cent (50%) of the tests were positive. ○ Seventy-five per cent (75%) of hospital cases remain in hospital for less than four days. □ there has been a five per cent increase in applications the number of applications has gone up by five in every hundred □ new cases have decreased twenty per cent this year the number of new cases has gone down by twenty in every hundred

percentage /pə'sentɪdʒ/ noun the proportion rate in every hundred or for every hundred ○ What is the percentage of long-stay patients in the hospital?

perception /pə'sepʃən/ noun an impression formed in the brain as a result of information about the outside world which is passed back by the senses

perceptive deafness /peˌseptɪv 'defnəs/ noun same as sensorineural deafness

percussion /pə'kʌʃ(ə)n/ noun a test, usually on the heart and lungs, in which the doctor taps part of the person's body and listens to the sound produced

percutaneous /ˌpɜːkjuː'teɪniəs/ adjective through the skin

percutaneous absorption /ˌpɜːkjuːˌteɪniəs əb'zɔːpʃən/ noun the process of absorbing a substance through the skin

percutaneous angioplasty /ˌpɜːkjuːˌteɪniəs 'ændʒiəplæsti/ noun the repair of a narrowed artery by passing a balloon into the artery through a catheter and then inflating it. Also called **balloon angioplasty**

percutaneous epididymal sperm aspiration /ˌpɜːkjuːteɪniəs ˌepɪdɪdɪm(ə)l 'spɜːm ˌæspɪreɪʃ(ə)n/ *noun* the removal of sperm from the epididymis by withdrawing it through the skin, usually as part of fertility treatment. Abbr **PESA**

per diem /pɜː 'diːem/ *adverb* (*written on prescriptions*) per day

perennial /pə'reniəl/ *adjective* which continues all the time, for a period of years ○ *She has perennial bronchial asthma.*

perforate /'pɜːfəreɪt/ *verb* to make a hole through something ○ *The ulcer perforated the duodenum.*

perforated eardrum /ˌpɜːfəreɪtɪd 'ɪədrʌm/ *noun* an eardrum with a hole in it

perforated ulcer /ˌpɜːfəreɪtɪd 'ʌlsə/ *noun* an ulcer which has made a hole in the wall of the intestine

perforation /ˌpɜːfə'reɪʃ(ə)n/ *noun* a hole through the whole thickness of a tissue or membrane such as the intestine or eardrum

perform /pə'fɔːm/ *verb* **1.** to do an operation ○ *A team of three surgeons performed the heart transplant operation.* **2.** to work ○ *The new heart has performed very well.* ○ *The kidneys are not performing as well as they should.*

performance /pə'fɔːməns/ *noun* a way in which something works ○ *The doctors are not satisfied with the performance of the transplanted heart.*

performance indicators /pə'fɔːməns ˌɪndɪkeɪtəz/ *plural noun* statistical information needed for analysis of how effectively health organisations are meeting their objectives, produced by health authorities and sent to the government. Abbr **PIs**

perfuse /pə'fjuːz/ *verb* to introduce a liquid into tissue or an organ, especially by circulating it through blood vessels

perfusion /pə'fjuːʒ(ə)n/ *noun* the process of passing a liquid through vessels, an organ or tissue, e.g. the flow of blood into lung tissue

perfusion scan /pə'fjuːʒ(ə)n skæn/ *noun* a procedure in which radioactive or radiopaque substances are introduced into the body so that the blood supply of an organ can be traced

peri- /peri/ *prefix* near, around or enclosing

periadenitis /ˌperiədɪ'naɪtɪs/ *noun* inflammation of tissue around a gland

perianal /ˌperi'eɪn(ə)l/ *adjective* around the anus

perianal haematoma /ˌperieɪn(ə)l ˌhiːmə'təʊmə/ *noun* a small painful swelling outside the anus caused by forcing a bowel movement

periarteritis /ˌperiɑːtə'raɪtɪs/ *noun* inflammation of the outer coat of an artery and the tissue round it

periarteritis nodosa /ˌperiɑːtəˌraɪtɪs nəʊ'dəʊsə/ *noun* same as **polyarteritis nodosa**

periarthritis /ˌperiɑː'θraɪtɪs/ *noun* inflammation of the tissue round a joint

pericard- /perikɑːd/ *prefix* referring to the pericardium

pericardectomy /ˌperikɑː'dektəmi/ *noun* the surgical removal of the pericardium

pericardial /ˌperi'kɑːdiəl/ *adjective* referring to the pericardium

pericardial effusion /ˌperikɑːdiəl ɪ'fjuːʒ(ə)n/ *noun* an excess of fluid which forms in the pericardial sac

pericardial friction /ˌperikɑːdiəl 'frɪkʃ(ə)n/ *noun* the rubbing together of the two parts of the pericardium in pericarditis

pericardial sac /ˌperikɑːdiəl 'sæk/ *noun* the inner part of the pericardium forming a bag-like structure or sac which contains fluid to prevent the two parts of the pericardium rubbing together

pericardiectomy /perikɑːdi'ektəmi/ *noun* same as **pericardectomy**

pericardiocentesis /ˌperiˌkɑːdiəʊsen'tiːsɪs/ *noun* the puncture of the pericardium to remove fluid

pericardiorrhaphy /ˌperikɑːdi'ɔːrəfi/ *noun* a surgical operation to repair a wound in the pericardium

pericardiostomy /ˌperikɑːdi'ɒstəmi/ *noun* a surgical operation to open the pericardium through the thoracic wall to drain off fluid

pericardiotomy /ˌperikɑːdi'ɒtəmi/ *noun* same as **pericardotomy**

pericarditis /ˌperikɑː'daɪtɪs/ *noun* inflammation of the pericardium □ **acute pericarditis** a sudden attack of fever and pains in the chest, caused by the two parts of the pericardium rubbing together

pericardium /ˌperi'kɑːdiəm/ *noun* a membrane which surrounds and supports the heart

pericardotomy /ˌperikɑː'dɒtəmi/ *noun* a surgical operation to open the pericardium

perichondritis /ˌperikɒn'draɪtɪs/ *noun* inflammation of cartilage, especially in the outer ear

perichondrium /ˌperi'kɒndriəm/ *noun* the fibrous connective tissue which covers cartilage

pericolpitis /ˌperikɒl'paɪtɪs/ *noun* inflammation of the connective tissue round the vagina. Also called **paracolpitis**

pericranium /ˌperi'kreɪniəm/ *noun* connective tissue which covers the surface of the skull

pericystitis /ˌperisi'staɪtɪs/ *noun* inflammation of the structures round the bladder, usually caused by infection in the uterus

perifolliculitis /ˌperiˌfɒlɪkju'laɪtɪs/ *noun* inflammation of the skin round hair follicles

perihepatitis /ˌperihepə'taɪtɪs/ *noun* inflammation of the membrane round the liver

perilymph /'perilɪmf/ *noun* a fluid found in the labyrinth of the inner ear

perimenopause /ˌperiˈmenəpɔːz/ *noun* the few years before the menopause, in which oestrogen levels start to fall

perimeter /pəˈrɪmɪtə/ *noun* **1.** an instrument to measure the field of vision **2.** the length of the outside line around an enclosed area

perimetritis /ˌperiməˈtraɪtɪs/ *noun* inflammation of the perimetrium

perimetrium /ˌperiˈmiːtriəm/ *noun* a membrane round the uterus

perimetry /pəˈrɪmɪtri/ *noun* a measurement of the field of vision

perimysium /ˌperiˈmaɪsiəm/ *noun* a sheath which surrounds a bundle of muscle fibres

perinatal /ˌperiˈneɪt(ə)l/ *adjective* referring to the period just before and after childbirth

perinatal mortality rate /ˌperineɪt(ə)l mɔː ˈtælɪti reɪt/ *noun* the number of babies born dead or who die during the period immediately after childbirth, shown per thousand babies born

perinatal period /ˌperiˈneɪt(ə)l ˌpɪəriəd/ *noun* the period of time before and after childbirth, from the 28th week after conception to the first week after delivery

perinatologist /ˌperinəˈtɒlədʒɪst/ *noun* an obstetrician who is a specialist in perinatology

perinatology /ˌperinəˈtɒlədʒi/ *noun* a branch of medicine which studies and treats physiological and pathological conditions affecting the mother and/or infant just before and just after the birth of a baby

perineal /ˌperɪˈniːəl/ *adjective* referring to the perineum

perineal body /ˌperiniːəl ˈbɒdi/ *noun* the mass of muscle and fibres between the anus and the vagina or prostate

perineal muscle /ˌperiniːəl ˈmʌs(ə)l/ *noun* one of the muscles which lie in the perineum

perineoplasty /ˌperiˈniːəplæsti/ *noun* a surgical operation to repair the perineum by grafting tissue

perineorrhaphy /ˌperiniˈɔːrəfi/ *noun* a surgical operation to stitch up a perineum which has torn during childbirth

perinephric /ˌperiˈnefrɪk/ *adjective* around the kidney

perinephritis /ˌperinɪˈfraɪtɪs/ *noun* inflammation of tissue round the kidney, which spreads from an infected kidney

perinephrium /ˌperiˈnefriəm/ *noun* the fatty tissue that is around a kidney

perineum /ˌperɪˈniːəm/ *noun* the skin and tissue between the opening of the urethra and the anus

perineurium /ˌperiˈnjʊəriəm/ *noun* connective tissue which surrounds bundles of nerve fibres

periocular /ˌperiˈɒkjʊlə/ *adjective* around the eyeball

period /ˈpɪəriəd/ *noun* **1.** a length of time ○ *The patient regained consciousness after a short period of time.* ○ *She is allowed out of bed for two periods each day.* **2.** menstruation or the menses, bleeding from the uterus which occurs in a woman each month when the lining of the uterus is shed because no fertilised egg is present ○ *She always has heavy periods.* ○ *Some women experience abdominal pain during their periods.* ○ *She has bleeding between periods.*

periodic /ˌpɪəriˈɒdɪk/ *adjective* occurring from time to time ○ *He has periodic attacks of migraine.* ○ *She has to go to the clinic for periodic checkups.*

periodic fever /ˌpɪəriɒdɪk ˈfiːvə/ *noun* a disease of the kidneys, common in Mediterranean countries

periodicity /ˌpɪəriəˈdɪsɪti/ *noun* the timing of recurrent attacks of a disease

periodic paralysis /ˌpɪəriɒdɪk pəˈræləsɪs/ *noun* recurrent attacks of weakness where the level of potassium in the blood is low

periodontal /ˌperiəʊˈdɒnt(ə)l/, **periodontic** /ˌperiəʊˈdɒntɪk/ *adjective* referring to the area around the teeth

periodontal membrane /ˌperiəʊˌdɒnt(ə)l ˈmembreɪn/, **periodontal ligament** /ˌperiəʊ ˌdɒnt(ə)l ˈlɪgəmənt/ *noun* a ligament which attaches a tooth to the bone of the jaw

periodontics /ˌperiəʊˈdɒntɪks/, **periodontia** /ˌperiəʊˈdɒnʃə/ *noun* the study of diseases of the periodontal membrane

periodontist /ˌperiəʊˈdɒntɪst/ *noun* a dentist who specialises in the treatment of gum diseases

periodontitis /ˌperiəʊdɒnˈtaɪtɪs/ *noun* an infection of the periodontal membrane leading to pyorrhoea, and resulting in the teeth falling out if untreated

periodontium /ˌperiəʊˈdɒnʃiəm/ *noun* **1.** the gums, bone and periodontal membrane around a tooth **2.** same as **periodontal membrane**

perionychia /ˌperiəʊˈnɪkiə/, **perionyxis** /ˌperiəʊˈnɪksɪs/ *noun* a painful swelling round a fingernail

perionychium /ˌperiəʊˈnɪkiəm/ *noun* the skin that is round a fingernail or toenail

perioperative /ˌperiˈɒp(ə)rətɪv/ *adjective* before and after a surgical operation

'During the perioperative period little attention is given to thermoregulation.' [*British Journal of Nursing*]

periorbital /ˌperiəʊˈɔːbɪt(ə)l/ *adjective* around the eye socket

periosteal /ˌperiˈɒstiəl/ *adjective* referring to, or attached to, the periosteum

periosteotome /periˈɒstiəʊtəʊm/ *noun* a surgical instrument used to cut the periosteum

periosteum /ˌperiˈɒstiəm/ *noun* a dense layer of connective tissue around a bone. See illustration at BONE STRUCTURE in Supplement

periosteum elevator /ˌperiˌɒstiəm ˈeləveɪtə/ *noun* a surgical instrument used to remove the periosteum from a bone

periostitis /ˌperiəˈstaɪtɪs/ *noun* inflammation of the periosteum

periotic /ˌperiˈɒtɪk/ *adjective* referring to the area around the ear, especially the bones around the inner ear

peripheral /pəˈrɪf(ə)rəl/ *adjective* at the edge

peripheral nerves /pəˈrɪf(ə)rəl nɜːvz/ *plural noun* the parts of motor and sensory nerves which branch from the brain and spinal cord

peripheral nervous system /pəˌrɪf(ə)rəl ˈnɜːvəs ˌsɪstəm/ *noun* all the nerves in different parts of the body which are linked and governed by the central nervous system. Abbr **PNS**

peripheral resistance /pəˌrɪf(ə)rəl rɪˈzɪstəns/ *noun* the ability of the peripheral blood vessels to slow down the flow of blood inside them

peripheral vascular disease /pəˌrɪf(ə)rəl ˈvæskjʊlə dɪˌziːz/ *noun* a disease affecting the blood vessels which supply the arms and legs

peripheral vasodilator /pəˌrɪf(ə)rəl ˌveɪzəʊdaɪˈleɪtə/ *noun* a chemical substance which acts to widen the blood vessels in the arms and legs and so improves bad circulation

periphery /pəˈrɪf(ə)ri/ *noun* **1.** the regions of the body where the nerves end, such as the sense organs or the muscles **2.** the surface of something

periphlebitis /ˌperɪfləˈbaɪtɪs/ *noun* **1.** inflammation of the outer coat of a vein **2.** an inflammation of the connective tissue round a vein

periproctitis /ˌperiprɒkˈtaɪtɪs/ *noun* swelling of the tissues around the rectum

perisalpingitis /ˌperisælpɪnˈdʒaɪtɪs/ *noun* inflammation of the peritoneum and other parts round a Fallopian tube

perisplenitis /ˌperispləˈnaɪtɪs/ *noun* inflammation of the peritoneum and other parts round the spleen

peristalsis /ˌperiˈstælsɪs/ *noun* the movement, like waves ,produced by alternate contraction and relaxation of muscles along an organ such as the intestine or oesophagus, which pushes the contents of the organ along it. Compare **antiperistalsis**

peristaltic /ˌperiˈstæltɪk/ *adjective* occurring in waves, as in peristalsis

peritendinitis /peritendiˈnaɪtɪs/ *noun* same as **tenosynovitis**

peritomy /pəˈrɪtəmi/ *noun* **1.** a surgical operation on the eye, where the conjunctiva is cut in a circle round the cornea **2.** circumcision

peritoneal /ˌperitəˈniːəl/ *adjective* referring to, or belonging to, the peritoneum

peritoneal cavity /ˌperitəˌniːəl ˈkæviti/ *noun* a space between the layers of the peritoneum, containing the major organs of the abdomen

peritoneal dialysis /ˌperitəˌniːəl daɪ ˈæləsɪs/ *noun* removing waste matter from someone's blood by introducing fluid into the peritoneum which then acts as a filter, as opposed to haemodialysis

peritoneoscope /ˌperiˈtəʊniəskəʊp/ *noun* same as **laparoscope**

peritoneoscopy /ˌperitəʊniˈɒskəpi/ *noun* same as **laparoscopy**

peritoneum /ˌperitəˈniːəm/ *noun* a membrane which lines the abdominal cavity and covers the organs in it

peritonitis /ˌperitəˈnaɪtɪs/ *noun* inflammation of the peritoneum as a result of bacterial infection

COMMENT: Peritonitis is a serious condition and can have many causes. One of its effects is to stop the peristalsis of the intestine so making it impossible for a person to eat and digest.

peritonsillar /ˌperiˈtɒnsɪlə/ *adjective* around the tonsils

peritonsillar abscess /ˌperiˌtɒnsɪlə ˈæbses/ *noun* same as **quinsy**

peritrichous /pəˈrɪtrɪkəs/ *adjective* referring to bacteria where the surface of the cell is covered with flagella

perityphlitis /ˌperitɪˈflaɪtɪs/ *noun* swelling of the tissues around the caecum

periumbilical /ˌperiʌmˈbɪlɪk(ə)l/ *adjective* around the navel

periureteritis /ˌperijʊəritəˈraɪtɪs/ *noun* inflammation of the tissue round a ureter, usually caused by inflammation of the ureter itself

periurethral /ˌperijʊəˈriːθrəl/ *adjective* around the urethra

PERLA *abbreviation* Pupils Equal and Reactive to Light and Accommodation

perle /pɜːl/ *noun* a soft capsule of medicine

perleche /pɜːˈleʃ/ *noun* **1.** inflammation, with small cracks, at the corners of the mouth, caused by infection, poor diet, or producing too much saliva **2.** candidiasis

permanent /ˈpɜːmənənt/ *adjective* always existing ○ *The accident left him with a permanent disability.*

permanently /ˈpɜːmənəntli/ *adverb* always, forever ○ *He was permanently disabled by the accident.*

permanent teeth /ˈpɜːmənənt tiːθ/ *noun* the teeth in an adult, which replace the child's milk teeth during childhood

COMMENT: The permanent teeth consist of eight incisors, four canines, eight premolars and twelve molars, the last four molars (one on each side of the upper and lower jaw) being called the wisdom teeth.

permeability /ˌpɜːmɪəˈbɪlɪti/ *noun* (*of a membrane*) the ability to allow some substances to pass through

permeable membrane /ˌpɜːmɪəb(ə)l ˈmembreɪn/ *noun* a membrane which allows some substances to pass through it

pernicious /pəˈnɪʃəs/ *adjective* harmful or dangerous, or unusually severe and likely to end in death

pernicious anaemia /pəˌnɪʃəs əˈniːmɪə/ *noun* a disease where an inability to absorb vitamin B$_{12}$ prevents the production of red blood cells and damages the spinal cord. Also called **Addison's anaemia**

perniosis /ˌpɜːniˈəʊsɪs/ *noun* any condition caused by cold which affects blood vessels in the skin

pero- /perəʊ/ *prefix* malformed or impaired

peromelia /ˌperəʊˈmiːlɪə/ *noun* a congenital condition in which the limbs have developed unusually

peroneal /ˌperəʊˈniːəl/ *adjective* referring to the outside of the leg

peroneal muscle /ˌperəʊˈniːəl ˌmʌs(ə)l/, **peroneus** /ˌperəʊˈniːəs/ *noun* one of three muscles, the peroneus brevis, longus and tertius, on the outside of the lower leg which make the leg turn outwards

peroperative /pəˈrɒp(ə)rətɪv/ *adjective* taking place during a surgical operation

peroral /pəˈrɔːrəl/ *adjective* through the mouth

per os /pər ˈɒs/ *adverb* referring to a drug or other substance to be taken through the mouth

persecute /ˈpɜːsɪkjuːt/ *verb* to make someone suffer all the time ○ *In paranoia, the patient feels he is being persecuted.*

persecution /ˌpɜːsɪˈkjuːʃ(ə)n/ *noun* the act of being made to suffer

perseveration /ˌpɜːsevəˈreɪʃ(ə)n/ *noun* the act of repeating actions or words without any stimulus

persist /pəˈsɪst/ *verb* to continue for some time ○ *The weakness in the right arm persisted for two weeks.*

persistent /pəˈsɪstənt/ *adjective* continuing for some time ○ *treatment aimed at the relief of persistent angina* ○ *She had a persistent cough.*

persistent vegetative state /pəˌsɪstənt ˈvedʒɪtətɪv steɪt/ *noun* a condition in which someone is alive and breathes, but shows no brain activity, and will never recover consciousness. Abbr **PVS**

person /ˈpɜːs(ə)n/ *noun* a man or woman

personal /ˈpɜːs(ə)n(ə)l/ *adjective* referring or belonging to a person ○ *Only certain senior members of staff can consult the personal records of the patients.*

personal care /ˈpɜːs(ə)nəl keə/ *noun* the act of washing, toileting and dressing someone who cannot do these things for themselves

personal hygiene /ˌpɜːs(ə)n(ə)l ˈhaɪdʒiːn/ *noun* the standards someone has of looking after parts of their body such as hair, skin, teeth and breath, hands and nails, and keeping them clean

personality /ˌpɜːsəˈnælɪti/ *noun* all the characteristics which are typical of one particular person and the way he or she thinks and behaves, and which make him or her different from other people

'Alzheimer's disease is a progressive disorder which sees a gradual decline in intellectual functioning and deterioration of personality and physical coordination and activity' [*Nursing Times*]

personality disorder /ˌpɜːsəˈnælɪti dɪsˌɔːdə/ *noun* a disorder which affects the way a person behaves, especially in relation to other people

personnel /ˌpɜːsəˈnel/ *noun* members of staff ○ *All hospital personnel must be immunised against hepatitis.* ○ *Only senior personnel can inspect the patients' medical records.* (NOTE: **Personnel** is singular.)

perspiration /ˌpɜːspəˈreɪʃ(ə)n/ *noun* sweat or the action of sweating ○ *Perspiration broke out on her forehead.*

COMMENT: Perspiration is formed in the sweat glands under the epidermis and cools the body as the moisture evaporates from the skin. Sweat contains salt, and in hot countries it may be necessary to take salt tablets to replace the salt lost through perspiration.

perspire /pəˈspaɪə/ *verb* to produce moisture through the sweat glands

Perthes' disease /ˈpɜːtiːz dɪˌziːz/, **Perthes' hip** /ˌpɜːtiːz ˈhɪp/ *noun* a disease found in young boys, in which the upper end of the femur degenerates and does not develop as expected, sometimes resulting in a permanent limp

pertussis /pəˈtʌsɪs/ *noun* same as **whooping cough**

perversion /pəˈvɜːʃ(ə)n/ *noun* a form of behaviour which is thought to be unnatural, dangerous or disgusting ○ *He is suffering from a form of sexual perversion.*

pes /pes/ *noun* a foot

PESA *abbr* percutaneous epididymal sperm aspiration

pes cavus /pes ˈkeɪvəs/ *noun* same as **claw foot**

pes planus /pes ˈpleɪnəs/ *noun* same as **flat foot**

pessary /ˈpesəri/ *noun* **1.** a drug in soluble material which is pushed into the vagina and absorbed into the blood there. Also called **vaginal suppository 2.** a contraceptive device worn inside the vagina to prevent spermatozoa entering **3.** a device like a ring, which is put into the vagina as treatment for prolapse of the uterus

pest /pest/ *noun* an animal which carries disease, attacks plants and animals and harms or kills them ○ *a spray to remove insect pests*

pesticide /'pestɪsaɪd/ *noun* a substance which kills pests

PET *abbr* positron-emission tomography

petechia /pe'tiːkiə/ *noun* a small red spot which does not go white when pressed, caused by bleeding under the skin (NOTE: The plural is **petechiae**.)

pethidine /'peθɪdiːn/ *noun* a synthetically produced narcotic drug, used to reduce pain and as a sedative

petit mal /,peti 'mæl/ *noun* a less severe form of epilepsy, where loss of consciousness attacks last only a few seconds and the person appears simply to be thinking deeply. Compare **grand mal**

Petri dish /'piːtri dɪʃ/ *noun* a small glass or plastic dish with a lid, in which a culture is grown

petrissage /,petrɪ'sɑːʒ/ *noun* an action used in massaging the muscles

petrosal /pə'trəʊs(ə)l/ *adjective* referring to the petrous part of the temporal bone

petrositis /,petrəʊ'saɪtɪs/ *noun* inflammation of the petrous part of the temporal bone

petrous /'petrəs/ *adjective* **1.** like stone **2.** petrosal

petrous bone /'petrəs bəʊn/ *noun* the part of the temporal bone which forms the base of the skull and the inner and middle ears

PET scan /'pet skæn/ *noun* an image of a cross-section, usually of the brain, that shows metabolic processes

-pexy /peksi/ *suffix* referring to fixation of an organ by surgery

Peyer's patches /,paɪəz 'pætʃɪz/ *plural noun* patches of lymphoid tissue on the mucous membrane of the small intestine [Described 1677. After Johann Conrad Peyer (1653–1712), Swiss anatomist.]

Peyronie's disease /'perəniːz dɪ,ziːz/ *noun* a condition associated with Dupuytren's contracture in which hard fibre develops in the penis which becomes painful when erect [Described 1743. After François de la Peyronie (1678–1747), Surgeon to Louis XV in Paris, France.]

PGEA *abbr* postgraduate education allowance

pH /,piː 'eɪtʃ/ *noun* the concentration of hydrogen ions in a solution, which determines its acidity

COMMENT: The pH factor is shown as a number: pH 7 is neutral, pH 8 and above show that the solution is alkaline and pH 6 and below show that the solution is acid.

phaco- /fækəʊ/ *prefix* referring to the lens of the eye

phacoemulsification /,fækəʊɪ,mʌlsɪfɪ'keɪʃ(ə)n/ *noun* an ultrasonic technique which turns a cataract in the eye into liquid. It is then removed by suction and a plastic lens is put into the eye.

phaeochromocytoma /,fiːəʊ,krəʊməʊsaɪ'təʊmə/ *noun* a tumour of the adrenal glands which affects the secretion of hormones such as adrenaline, which in turn results in hypertension and hyperglycaemia

phag- /fæg/ *prefix* same as **phago-** (used before vowels)

phage /feɪdʒ/ *noun* same as **bacteriophage**

-phage /feɪdʒ/ *suffix* referring to something which eats

phagedaena /,fædʒə'diːnə/ *noun* an ulcer that spreads rapidly

-phagia /feɪdʒə/ *suffix* referring to eating

phago- /fægəʊ/ *prefix* referring to eating

phagocyte /'fægəʊ,saɪt/ *noun* a cell, especially a white blood cell, which can surround and destroy other cells such as bacteria cells

phagocytic /,fægə'sɪtɪk/ *adjective* **1.** referring to phagocytes ○ *Monocytes become phagocytic during infection.* **2.** destroying cells

phagocytosis /,fægəʊsaɪ'təʊsɪs/ *noun* destruction of bacteria cells and foreign bodies by phagocytes

phakic /'fækɪk/ *adjective* referring to an eye which has its natural lens

phako- /fækəʊ/ *prefix* same as **phaco-**

phalangeal /fə'lændʒiəl/ *adjective* referring to the phalanges

phalanges /fə'lændʒiːz/ plural of **phalanx**

phalangitis /,fælən'dʒaɪtɪs/ *noun* inflammation of the fingers or toes caused by infection of tissue

phalanx /'fælæŋks/ *noun* a bone in a finger or toe. See illustration at HAND in Supplement, FOOT in Supplement

COMMENT: The fingers and toes have three phalanges each, except the thumb and big toe, which have only two.

phalloplasty /'fæləʊplæsti/ *noun* a surgical operation to repair a damaged or deformed penis

phantom /'fæntəm/ *noun* **1.** a model of the whole body or part of the body, used to practise or demonstrate surgical operations **2.** an image not brought about by actual stimuli, something which is not there but seems to be there

phantom limb /,fæntəm 'lɪm/ *noun* a condition in which someone seems to feel sensations in a limb which has been amputated

phantom pregnancy /,fæntəm 'pregnənsi/ *noun* same as **pseudocyesis**

phantom tumour /,fæntəm 'tjuːmə/ *noun* a condition in which a swelling occurs which imitates a swelling caused by a tumour

Pharm. *abbr* **1.** pharmacopoeia **2.** pharmacy **3.** pharmaceutical

pharmaceutical /ˌfɑːməˈsjuːtɪk(ə)l/ *adjective* referring to pharmacy or drugs

pharmaceutical products /ˌfɑːmə ˌsjuːtɪk(ə)l ˈprɒdʌkts/ *plural noun* medicines, pills, lozenges or creams which are sold in chemists' shops

pharmaceuticals /ˌfɑːməˈsjuːtɪk(ə)lz/ *plural noun* drugs prescribed as medicines

Pharmaceutical Society /ˌfɑːmə ˈsjuːtɪk(ə)l səˌsaɪəti/ *noun* a professional association for pharmacists

pharmaceutics /ˌfɑːməˈsjuːtɪks/ *noun* the science of the preparation and dispensing of prescribed drugs ■ *plural noun* drugs prescribed as medicines

pharmacist /ˈfɑːməsɪst/ *noun* a trained person who is qualified to prepare medicines according to the instructions on a doctor's prescription

COMMENT: In the UK, qualified pharmacists must be registered by the Royal Pharmaceutical Society of Great Britain before they can practise.

pharmaco- /fɑːməkəʊ/ *prefix* referring to drugs

pharmacodynamic /ˌfɑːməkəʊdaɪ ˈnæmɪk/ *adjective* referring to a property of a drug which affects the part where it is applied

pharmacodynamics /ˌfɑːməkəʊdaɪ ˈnæmɪks/ *plural noun* the study of the effects of drugs on living organisms, and especially of how much the body's response changes when you increase the dose of a drug. Compare **pharmacokinetics** (NOTE: Takes a singular verb.)

pharmacogenomics /ˌfɑːməkəʊdʒi ˈnɒmɪks/ *plural noun* the study of the relationship between a person's genetic makeup and response to drug treatments (NOTE: Takes a singular verb.)

pharmacokinetic /ˌfɑːməkəʊkaɪˈnetɪk/ *adjective* referring to a property of a drug which has an effect over a period of time

pharmacokinetics /ˌfɑːməkəʊkaɪˈnetɪks/ *plural noun* **1.** the study of how the body reacts to drugs over a period of time. Compare **pharmacodynamics** (NOTE: Takes a singular verb.) **2.** the way in which a drug interacts with the body

pharmacological /ˌfɑːməkəˈlɒdʒɪk(ə)l/ *adjective* referring to pharmacology

pharmacologist /ˌfɑːməˈkɒlədʒɪst/ *noun* a scientist who specialises in the study of drugs

pharmacology /ˌfɑːməˈkɒlədʒi/ *noun* the study of drugs or medicines, and their actions, properties and characteristics

pharmacopoeia /ˌfɑːməkəˈpiːə/ *noun* an official list of drugs, their methods of preparation, dosages and the ways in which they should be used

COMMENT: The British Pharmocopoeia is the official list of drugs used in the UK The drugs listed in it have the letters BP after their name. In the US the official list is the United States Pharmacopeia or USP.

pharmacotherapy /ˌfɑːməkəʊˈθerəpi/ *noun* the use of drugs to treat conditions, especially psychiatric disorders

pharmacy /ˈfɑːməsi/ *noun* **1.** the study of the making and dispensing of drugs ○ *He has a qualification in pharmacy.* **2.** a shop or department in a hospital where drugs are prepared

Pharmacy Act /ˈfɑːməsi ækt/ *noun* in the UK, one of several Acts of Parliament which regulate the making, prescribing and selling of drugs, e.g. the Pharmacy and Poisons Act 1933, the Misuse of Drugs Act 1971 and the Poisons Act 1972

pharyng- /færɪndʒ/ *prefix* same as **pharyngo-** (*used before vowels*)

pharyngeal /ˌfærɪnˈdʒiːəl/ *adjective* referring to the pharynx

pharyngeal pouch /ˌfærɪndʒiːəl ˈpaʊtʃ/ *noun* one of the pouches on each side of the throat of an embryo. Also called **visceral pouch**

pharyngeal tonsils /ˌfærɪndʒiːəl ˈtɒns(ə)lz/ *plural noun* same as **adenoids**

pharyngectomy /ˌfærɪnˈdʒektəmi/ *noun* the surgical removal of part of the pharynx, especially in cases of cancer of the pharynx

pharynges /fəˈrɪndʒiːz/ *plural of* **pharynx**

pharyngismus /ˌfærɪnˈdʒɪzməs/, **pharyngism** /ˈfærɪndʒɪz(ə)m/ *noun* a spasm which contracts the muscles of the pharynx

pharyngitis /ˌfærɪnˈdʒaɪtɪs/ *noun* inflammation of the pharynx

pharyngo- /fərɪŋgəʊ/ *prefix* referring to the pharynx

pharyngocele /fəˈrɪŋgəʊsiːl/ *noun* **1.** a cyst which opens off the pharynx **2.** a hernia of part of the pharynx

pharyngolaryngeal /fəˌrɪŋgəʊləˈrɪndʒiəl/ *adjective* referring to the pharynx and the larynx

pharyngology /ˌfærɪnˈgɒlədʒi/ *noun* the specialty in medicine that deals with the throat, its diseases and their treatment

pharyngoscope /fəˈrɪŋgəʊskəʊp/ *noun* an instrument with a light attached, used by a doctor to examine the pharynx

pharyngotympanic tube /fəˌrɪŋgəʊtɪm ˌpænɪk ˈtjuːb/ *noun* one of two tubes which connect the back of the throat to the middle ear. Also called **Eustachian tube**

pharynx /ˈfærɪŋks/ *noun* a muscular passage leading from the back of the mouth to the oesophagus (NOTE: The plural is **pharynges** or **pharynxes**.)

COMMENT: The nasal cavity (or nasopharynx) leads to the back of the mouth (or oropharynx) and then into the pharynx itself, which in turn becomes the oesophagus when it reaches the sixth cervical vertebra. The pharynx is the channel both for air and food; the trachea (or windpipe) leads off it before it joins the oesophagus. The upper part of the pharynx (the nasopharynx) connects with the middle ear through the Eustachian tubes. When air pressure in the middle ear is not equal to that outside, as when going up or down in an aeroplane, the tube becomes blocked and pressure can be reduced by swallowing.

phase /feɪz/ *noun* a stage or period of development ○ *If the cancer is diagnosed in its early phase, the chances of complete cure are much greater.*

phenazopyridine /fə,næzəʊ'pɪrɪdiːn/ *noun* a drug used to reduce pain in conditions of the urinary tract, such as cystitis

phenobarbitone /,fiːnəʊ'bɑːbɪtəʊn/ *noun* a barbiturate drug which is used as a sedative, a hypnotic and an anticonvulsant

phenol /'fiːnɒl/ *noun* a strong disinfectant used for external use. Also called **carbolic acid**

phenomenon /fə'nɒmɪnən/ *noun* **1.** a fact or situation which can be observed **2.** someone or something that is considered to be extraordinary and marvellous

phenotype /'fiːnəʊtaɪp/ *noun* the particular characteristics of an organism. Compare **genotype**

'…all cancers may be reduced to fundamental mechanisms based on cancer risk genes or oncogenes within ourselves. An oncogene is a gene that encodes a protein that contributes to the malignant phenotype of the cell.' [*British Medical Journal*]

phenylalanine /,fiːnaɪl'æləniːn/ *noun* an essential amino acid

phenylketonuria /,fiːnaɪl,kiːtəʊ'njʊəriə/ *noun* a hereditary condition which affects the way in which the body breaks down phenylalanine, which in turn concentrates toxic metabolites in the nervous system causing brain damage

COMMENT: To have phenylketonuria, a child has to inherit the gene from both parents. The condition can be treated by giving the child a special diet but early diagnosis is essential to avoid brain damage.

phenytoin /'fenɪtɔɪn/ *noun* a drug which helps to prevent convulsions, used in the treatment of epilepsy

pH factor /,piː 'eɪtʃ ,fæktə/ *noun* a factor which indicates acidity or alkalinity

phial /'faɪəl/ *noun* a small medicine bottle

-philia /fɪliə/ *suffix* attraction to or liking for something

philtrum /'fɪltrəm/ *noun* **1.** a groove in the centre of the top lip **2.** a drug believed to stimulate sexual desire

phimosis /faɪ'məʊsɪs/ *noun* a condition in which the foreskin is tight and has to be removed by circumcision

phleb- /fleb/ *prefix* same as **phlebo-** (*used before vowels*)

phlebectomy /flɪ'bektəmi/ *noun* the surgical removal of a vein or part of a vein

phlebitis /flɪ'baɪtɪs/ *noun* inflammation of a vein

phlebo- /flebəʊ/ *prefix* referring to a vein

phlebogram /'flebəgræm/ *noun* an X-ray picture of a vein or system of veins. Also called **venogram**

phlebography /flɪ'bɒɡrəfi/ *noun* an X-ray examination of a vein using a radio-opaque dye so that the vein will show up on the film. Also called **venography**

phlebolith /'flebəlɪθ/ *noun* a stone which forms in a vein as a result of an old thrombus becoming calcified

phlebothrombosis /,flebəʊθrɒm'bəʊsɪs/ *noun* a blood clot in a deep vein in the legs or pelvis, which can easily detach and form an embolus in a lung

phlebotomise /flɪ'bɒtəmaɪz/, **phlebotomize** *verb* to make a cut in a person's vein to take blood for testing

phlebotomy /flɪ'bɒtəmi/ *noun* an operation where a vein or an artery is cut so that blood can be removed, as when taking blood from a donor

phlegm /flem/ *noun* same as **sputum** ○ *She was coughing up phlegm into her handkerchief.*

phlegmasia alba dolens /fleg,meɪziə ,ælbə 'dəʊləns/ *noun* same as **milk leg**

phlyctena /flɪk'tiːnə/, **phlycten** /'flɪktən/ *noun* **1.** a small blister caused by a burn **2.** a small vesicle on the conjunctiva

phlyctenule /flɪk'tenjuːl/ *noun* **1.** a tiny blister on the cornea or conjunctiva **2.** any small blister

phobia /'fəʊbiə/ *noun* an unusually strong and irrational fear ○ *She has a phobia about* or *of dogs.* ○ *Fear of snakes is one of the commonest phobias.*

-phobia /fəʊbiə/ *suffix* neurotic fear of something ○ *agoraphobia* ○ *claustrophobia*

phobic /'fəʊbɪk/ *adjective* referring to a phobia

-phobic /fəʊbɪk/ *suffix* a person who has a phobia of something

phobic anxiety /,fəʊbɪk æŋ'zaɪəti/ *noun* state of worry caused by a phobia

phocomelia /,fəʊkə'miːliə/, **phocomely** /fəʊ'kɒməli/ *noun* **1.** a congenital condition in which the upper parts of the limbs are missing or poorly developed, leaving the hands or feet directly attached to the body **2.** a congenital condition in which the legs develop as usual, but the arms are absent or underdeveloped

phon- /fəʊn/ *prefix* same as **phono-** (*used before vowels*)

phonation /fəʊ'neɪʃ(ə)n/ *noun* the production of vocal sounds, especially speech

phoniatrics /ˌfəʊni'ætrɪks/ *noun* the study of speech and disorders related to it

phono- /fəʊnəʊ/ *prefix* referring to sound or voice

phonocardiogram /ˌfəʊnəʊ'kɑːdiəgræm/ *noun* a chart of the sounds made by the heart

phonocardiograph /ˌfəʊnəʊ'kɑːdiəgræf/ *noun* an instrument that amplifies heart sounds and converts them into a visual display

phonocardiography /ˌfəʊnəʊˌkɑːdi'ɒgrəfi/ *noun* the process of recording the sounds made by the heart

phonology /fə'nɒlədʒi/ *noun* the study of the system of speech sounds used in a particular language or in human speech generally

phonosurgery /'fəʊnəʊˌsɜːdʒəri/ *noun* surgery performed to alter the quality of the voice

phosphataemia /ˌfɒsfə'tiːmiə/ *noun* the presence of excess phosphates in the blood

phosphatase /'fɒsfəteɪz/ *noun* a group of enzymes which are important in the cycle of muscle contraction and in the calcification of bones

phosphate /'fɒsfeɪt/ *noun* a salt of phosphoric acid

phosphaturia /ˌfɒsfə'tjʊəriə/ *noun* the presence of excess phosphates in the urine

COMMENT: In phosphaturia the urine becomes cloudy, which can indicate stones in the bladder or kidney.

phospholipid /ˌfɒsfəʊ'lɪpɪd/ *noun* a compound with fatty acids, which is one of the main components of membranous tissue

phosphonecrosis /ˌfɒsfəʊne'krəʊsɪs/ *noun* a necrotic condition affecting the kidneys, liver and bones, usually seen in people who work with phosphorus

phosphorescent /ˌfɒsfə'res(ə)nt/ *adjective* shining without producing heat

phosphoric acid /fɒsˌfɒrɪk 'æsɪd/ *noun* an acid which is very soluble in water and gives rise to acid, neutral and alkali salts

phosphorus /'fɒsf(ə)rəs/ *noun* a toxic chemical element which is present in very small quantities in bones and nerve tissue. It causes burns if it touches the skin, and can poison if swallowed. (NOTE: The chemical symbol is **P**.)

phosphorylase /fɒs'fɒrɪleɪz/ *noun* an enzyme that aids the process of carbohydrate metabolism

phossy jaw /ˌfɒsi 'dʒɔː/ *noun* a type of phosphonecrosis, caused by inhaling phosphorus fumes, which results in disintegration of the bones of the lower jaw. The disease was once common among workers in match factories.

phot- /fɒt, fəʊt/ *prefix* same as **photo-** (*used before vowels*)

photalgia /fəʊ'tældʒə/ *noun* **1.** pain in the eye caused by bright light **2.** severe photophobia

photo- /fəʊtəʊ/ *prefix* referring to light

photoablation /ˌfəʊtəʊə'bleɪʃ(ə)n/ *noun* the removal of tissue using lasers

photocoagulation /ˌfəʊtəʊkəʊæɡjʊ'leɪʃ(ə)n/ *noun* the process in which tissue coagulates from the heat caused by light, used to treat a detached retina

photodermatosis /ˌfəʊtəʊˌdɜːmə'təʊsɪs/ *noun* a lesion of the skin after exposure to bright light

photogenic /ˌfəʊtə'dʒenɪk/ *adjective* **1.** produced by the action of light **2.** producing light

photograph /'fəʊtəɡrɑːf/ *noun* a picture taken with a camera, which uses the chemical action of light on sensitive film ■ *verb* to take a picture of something with a camera

photography /fə'tɒɡrəfi/ *noun* the act of taking pictures with a camera ○ *The development of X-ray photography has meant that internal disorders can be more easily diagnosed.*

photophobia /ˌfəʊtəʊ'fəʊbiə/ *noun* **1.** a condition in which the eyes become sensitive to light and conjunctivitis may be caused (NOTE: It can be associated with measles and some other infectious diseases.) **2.** a morbid fear of light

photophobic /ˌfəʊtəʊ'fəʊbɪk/ *adjective* having an unusual fear of light

photophthalmia /ˌfəʊtɒf'θælmiə/ *noun* inflammation of the eye caused by bright light, as in snow blindness

photopic vision /fəʊˌtɒpɪk 'vɪʒ(ə)n/ *noun* vision which is adapted to bright light such as daylight, using the cones in the retina instead of the rods, which are used in scotopic vision. ◊ **light adaptation**

photopsia /fəʊ'tɒpsiə/ *noun* a condition of the eye in which someone sees flashes of light

photoreceptor neurone /ˌfəʊtəʊriˌseptə 'njʊərəʊn/ *noun* a rod or cone in the retina, which is sensitive to light or colour

photoretinitis /ˌfəʊtəʊretɪ'naɪtɪs/ *noun* damage to a retina caused by looking directly at the sun. Also called **sun blindness**

photosensitive /ˌfəʊtəʊ'sensɪtɪv/ *adjective* sensitive to light, or stimulated by light

photosensitivity /ˌfəʊtəʊsensə'tɪvəti/ *noun* the fact of being sensitive to light

phototherapy /fəʊtəʊ'θerəpi/ *noun* a treatment for jaundice and vitamin D deficiency, which involves exposing the person to ultraviolet rays

phototoxic /ˌfəʊtəʊ'tɒksɪk/ *adjective* making the skin unusually sensitive to damage by light, as in sunburn

phototoxicity /ˌfəʊtəʊtɒk'sɪsɪti/ *noun* a cause of damage to the retina of the eye due to exposure to too much ultraviolet light or radiation ○ *Children's retinas are more likely to experience damage as a result of phototoxicity from excess ultraviolet light than those of adults.* ◊ **retinopathy**

photuria /fəʊˈtjʊəriə/ *noun* phosphorescent urine

phren- /fren/ *prefix* same as **phreno-** (*used before vowels*)

phrenemphraxis /ˌfrenemˈfræksɪs/ *noun* a surgical operation to crush the phrenic nerve in order to paralyse the diaphragm

-phrenia /friːniə/ *suffix* disorder of the mind

phrenic /ˈfrenɪk/ *adjective* 1. referring to the diaphragm 2. referring to the mind or intellect

phrenic avulsion /ˌfrenɪk əˈvʌlʃ(ə)n/ *noun* the surgical removal of part of the phrenic nerve in order to paralyse the diaphragm

phrenicectomy /ˌfrenɪˈsektəmi/ *noun* the surgical removal of all or part of the phrenic nerve

phreniclasia /ˌfrenɪˈkleɪziə/ *noun* an operation to clamp the phrenic nerve

phrenic nerve /ˈfrenɪk nɜːv/ *noun* a pair of nerves which controls the muscles in the diaphragm

phrenicotomy /ˌfrenɪˈkɒtəmi/ *noun* an operation to divide the phrenic nerve

phreno- /frenəʊ/ *prefix* 1. referring to the brain 2. referring to the phrenic nerve

pH test /ˌpiː ˈeɪtʃ test/ *noun* a test to see how acid or alkaline a solution is

phthiriasis /θɪˈraɪəsɪs/ *noun* infestation with the crab louse

Phthirius pubis /ˌθaɪəriəs ˈpjuːbɪs/ *noun* a louse which infests the pubic region. Also called **pubic louse, crab**

phthisis /ˈθaɪsɪs/ *noun* an old term for tuberculosis

phycomycosis /ˌfaɪkəʊmaɪˈkəʊsɪs/ *noun* an acute infection of the lungs, central nervous system and other organs by a fungus

physi- /fɪzi/ *prefix* same as **physio-** (*used before vowels*)

physical /ˈfɪzɪk(ə)l/ *adjective* referring to the body, as opposed to the mind ■ *noun* a physical examination ○ *He has to pass a physical before being accepted by the police force.*

physical dependence /ˌfɪzɪk(ə)l dɪ ˈpendəns/, **physical drug dependence** /ˌfɪzɪk(ə)l ˈdrʌg dɪˌpendəns/ *noun* a state where a person is addicted to a drug such as heroin and suffers physical effects if he or she stops taking the drug

physical education /ˌfɪzɪk(ə)l ˌedjʊ ˈkeɪʃ(ə)n/ *noun* the teaching of sports and exercises in school

physical examination /ˌfɪzɪk(ə)l ɪgˌzæmɪ ˈneɪʃ(ə)n/ *noun* an examination of someone's body to see if he or she is healthy

physical genetic trait /ˌfɪzɪk(ə)l dʒəˈnetɪk treɪt/ *noun* a characteristic of the body of a person, e.g. red hair or big feet, which is inherited

physically /ˈfɪzɪkli/ *adverb* referring to the body ○ *Physically he is very weak, but his mind is still alert.*

physically challenged /ˌfɪzɪkli ˈtʃælɪndʒd/ *adjective* describing someone whose condition makes it difficult to perform some or all of the basic activities of daily life

physical medicine /ˌfɪzɪk(ə)l ˈmed(ə)sɪn/ *noun* a branch of medicine which deals with physical disabilities or with treatment of disorders after they have been diagnosed

physical sign /ˌfɪzɪk(ə)l ˈsaɪn/ *noun* a symptom which can be seen on someone's body or which can be produced by percussion and palpitation

physical therapy /ˌfɪzɪk(ə)l ˈθerəpi/ *noun* the treatment of disorders by heat, by massage, by exercise and other physical means

physician /fɪˈzɪʃ(ə)n/ *noun* a registered doctor who is not a surgeon (NOTE: In British English, physician refers to a specialist doctor, though not usually a surgeon, while in US English it is used for any qualified doctor.)

physio /ˈfɪziəʊ/ *noun* (*informal*) 1. a session of physiotherapy treatment 2. a physiotherapist

physio- /fɪziəʊ/ *prefix* 1. referring to physiology 2. physical

physiological /ˌfɪziəˈlɒdʒɪk(ə)l/ *adjective* referring to physiology and the regular functions of the body

physiological saline /ˌfɪziəlɒdʒɪk(ə)l ˈseɪlaɪn/, **physiological solution** /ˌfɪziəlɒdʒɪk(ə)l səˈluːʃ(ə)n/ *noun* any solution used to keep cells or tissue alive

physiological tremor /ˌfɪziəˌlɒdʒɪk(ə)l ˈtremə/ *noun* a small movement of the limbs which takes place when a person tries to remain still

physiologist /ˌfɪziˈɒlədʒɪst/ *noun* a scientist who specialises in the study of the functions of living organisms

physiology /ˌfɪziˈɒlədʒi/ *noun* the study of regular body functions

physiotherapist /ˌfɪziəʊˈθerəpɪst/ *noun* a trained specialist who gives physiotherapy

physiotherapy /ˌfɪziəʊˈθerəpi/ *noun* the treatment of a disorder or condition by exercise, massage, heat treatment, infrared lamps or other external means, e.g. to restore strength or function after a disease or injury

physiotherapy clinic /ˌfɪziəʊˈθerəpi ˌklɪnɪk/ *noun* a clinic where people can have physiotherapy

physique /fɪˈziːk/ *noun* the shape and size of a person's body

physo- /faɪsəʊ/ *prefix* 1. tending to swell 2. relating to air or gas

physostigmine /ˌfaɪsəʊˈstɪgmiːn/ *noun* an extract of the dried leaves of the vine that produces Calabar bean, which is toxic but may be used in the treatment of glaucoma and to counter the effects of anticholinergic drugs on the central nervous system

phyt- /faɪt/, **phyto-** /faɪtəʊ/ *prefix* referring to plants or coming from plants

phytooestrogen /ˌfaɪtəʊˈiːstrədʒən/ *noun* a substance obtained from cereals, legumes and seeds which has a similar effect on the body as oestrogen, used increasingly as an alternative to hormone replacement therapy

phyto-photo dermatitis /ˌfaɪtəʊ ˌfəʊtəʊ ˌdɜːməˈtaɪtɪs/ *noun* an acute skin reaction due to the combination of plant irritation and sunlight

PI *abbr* pressure index

pia /ˈpaɪə/, **pia mater** /ˌpaɪə ˈmeɪtə/ *noun* the delicate innermost membrane of the three which cover the brain. ◊ **arachnoid, dura mater**

pian /piːˈɑːn/ *noun* same as **yaws**

pica /ˈpaɪkə/ *noun* a desire to eat things which are not food, e.g. wood or paper, often found in pregnant women and small children

pick /pɪk/ *verb* to take away small pieces of something with the fingers or with a tool ○ *She picked the pieces of glass out of the wound with tweezers.*

Pick's disease /ˈpɪks dɪˌziːz/ *noun* a rare form of presenile dementia, in which a disorder of the lipoid metabolism causes mental impairment, anaemia, loss of weight and swelling of the spleen and liver

pick up /ˌpɪk ˈʌp/ *verb* (*informal*) **1.** to catch a disease ○ *She must have picked up the disease when she was travelling in Africa.* **2.** to get stronger or better ○ *He was ill for months, but he's picking up now.*

pico- /piːkəʊ/ *prefix* one million millionth (10⁻¹²). Symbol **p**

picomole /ˈpiːkəʊməʊl/ *noun* a unit of measurement of the amount of substance equal to one million millionth of a mole. Symbol **pmol**

picornavirus /piːˈkɔːnəˌvaɪrəs/ *noun* a virus containing RNA, e.g. enteroa viruses and rhinoa viruses

PID *abbr* prolapsed intervertebral disc

PIDS *abbr* primary immune deficiency syndrome

Pierre Robin syndrome /ˌpjeə rɒˈbæn ˌsɪndrəʊm/ *noun* a combination of facial features including a small lower jaw and a cleft palate that exist at birth, causing breathing and feeding problems early in a child's life

pigeon breast /ˈpɪdʒɪn brest/, **pigeon chest** /ˈpɪdʒɪn tʃest/ *noun* same as **pectus carinatum**

pigeon toes /ˈpɪdʒɪn təʊz/ *plural noun* a condition in which the feet turn towards the inside when a person is standing upright

pigment /ˈpɪɡmənt/ *noun* **1.** a substance which gives colour to part of the body such as blood, the skin or hair **2.** (*in pharmacy*) a paint

COMMENT: The body contains several substances which control colour: melanin gives dark colour to the skin and hair; bilirubin gives yellow colour to bile and urine; haemoglobin in the blood gives the skin a pink colour; carotene can give a reddish-yellow colour to the skin if the patient eats too many tomatoes or carrots. Some pigment cells can carry oxygen and are called 'respiratory pigments'.

pigmentation /ˌpɪɡmenˈteɪʃ(ə)n/ *noun* the colouring of the body, especially that produced by deposits of pigment

pigmented /pɪɡˈmentɪd/ *adjective* **1.** coloured **2.** showing an unusual colour

pigmented epithelium /ˌpɪɡməntɪd ˌepiˈθiːliəm/, **pigmented layer** /ˌpɪɡməntɪd ˈleɪə/ *noun* coloured tissue at the back of the retina

PIH *abbr* pregnancy-induced hypertension

Pilates /pɪˈlɑːtiz/ *noun* a holistic form of exercise and postural therapy that develops the deep abdominal muscles to control body movement and protect the back

piles /paɪlz/ *plural noun* same as **haemorrhoids**

pili /ˈpaɪlaɪ/ ◆ **arrector pili**

pill /pɪl/ *noun* a small hard round ball of medication that is taken by swallowing ○ *He has to take the pills twice a day.* □ **the pill** an oral contraceptive. ◊ **morning-after pill** □ **on the pill** taking a regular course of contraceptive pills

pillar /ˈpɪlə/ *noun* a part that is long and thin

pillow /ˈpɪləʊ/ *noun* a soft cushion on a bed which the head lies on when the person is lying down ○ *The nurse gave her an extra pillow to keep her head raised.*

pill-rolling /ˈpɪl ˌrəʊlɪŋ/ *noun* nervous action of the fingers, in which the person seems to be rolling a very small object, associated with Parkinson's disease

pilo- /paɪləʊ/ *prefix* referring to hair

pilocarpine /ˌpaɪləʊˈkɑːpiːn/ *noun* an organic compound of plant origin which is used in eye drops to treat glaucoma

pilomotor /ˌpaɪləʊˈməʊtə/ *adjective* referring to something that moves the hairs of the skin

pilomotor nerve /ˌpaɪləʊˈməʊtə nɜːv/ *noun* a nerve which supplies the arrector pili muscles attached to hair follicles

pilomotor reflex /ˌpaɪləʊˈməʊtə ˌriːfleks/ *noun* a reaction of the dermal papillae of the skin to cold and fear which causes the hairs on the skin to become erect

pilonidal /ˌpaɪləˈnaɪd(ə)l/ *adjective* relating to a cyst or cavity which has a growth of hair

pilonidal cyst /ˌpaɪləˌnaɪd(ə)l ˈsɪst/ *noun* a cyst containing hair, usually found at the bottom of the spine near the buttocks

pilonidal sinus /ˌpaɪləˌnaɪd(ə)l 'saɪnəs/ *noun* a small depression with hairs at the base of the spine

pilosebaceous /ˌpaɪləʊsə'beɪʃəs/ *adjective* referring to the hair follicles and the glands attached to them

pilosis /paɪ'ləʊsɪs/, **pilosism** /'paɪləsɪz(ə)m/ *noun* a condition in which someone has an unusual amount of hair or where hair is present in an unusual place

pilot study /'paɪlət ˌstʌdi/ *noun* a small version of a project which is carried out first, in order to discover how well it works and to solve any problems, before going ahead with the full version

pilus /'paɪləs/ *noun* **1.** one hair (NOTE: The plural is **pili**.) **2.** hair-like process on the surface of a bacterium

pimple /'pɪmpəl/ *noun* a small swelling on the skin, containing pus ○ *He had pimples on his neck.*

pimply /'pɪmpli/ *adjective* covered with pimples

pin /pɪn/ *noun* **1.** a small sharp piece of metal for attaching things together ○ *The nurse fastened the bandage with a pin.* **2.** a metal nail used to attach broken bones ○ *He has had a pin inserted in his hip.* ■ *verb* to attach something with a pin ○ *She pinned the bandages carefully to stop them slipping.* ○ *The bone had fractured in several places and needed pinning.*

pinch /pɪntʃ/ *noun* **1.** an act of squeezing the thumb and first finger together **2.** a quantity of something which can be held between the thumb and first finger ○ *She put a pinch of salt into the water.* ■ *verb* **1.** to squeeze something tightly between the thumb and first finger **2.** to squeeze something ○ *She developed a sore on her ankle where her shoe pinched.*

pineal /'pɪniəl/ *adjective* relating to or released by the pineal gland

pineal body /'pɪniəl ˌbɒdi/, **pineal gland** /'pɪniəl glænd/ *noun* a small cone-shaped gland situated below the corpus callosum in the brain, which produces melatonin and is believed to be associated with the circadian rhythm. See illustration at **BRAIN** in Supplement

pinguecula /pɪŋ'gwekjʊlə/, **pinguicula** /pɪŋ'gwɪkjʊlə/ *noun* a condition affecting elderly people, in which the conjunctiva in the eyes has small yellow growths near the edge of the cornea, usually on the nasal side

pink disease /'pɪŋk dɪˌziːz/ *noun* same as **acrodynia**

pinna /'pɪnə/ *noun* the outer ear, the part of the ear which is outside the head, connected by a passage to the eardrum. See illustration at **EAR** in Supplement

pinnaplasty /'pɪnəplæsti/ *noun* a cosmetic surgical procedure to correct the shape of the ear

pinocytosis /ˌpiːnəʊsaɪ'təʊsɪs/ *noun* the process by which a cell surrounds and takes in fluid

pins and needles /ˌpɪnz ən 'niːd(ə)lz/ *noun* an unpleasant tingling sensation, usually occurring after a temporarily restricted blood supply returns to an arm or leg (*informal*) ◊ **paraesthesia**

pint /paɪnt/ *noun* a unit of measurement of liquids (= about 0.56 of a litre) ○ *He lost two pints of blood during the operation.*

pinta /'pɪntə/ *noun* a skin disease of the tropical regions of America, in which the skin on the hands and feet swells and loses colour, caused by a spirochaete *Treponema*

pinworm /'pɪnwɜːm/ *noun* US same as **threadworm**

PIP *abbr* proximal interphalangeal joint

pipette /pɪ'pet/ *noun* a thin glass tube used in the laboratory for taking or measuring samples of liquid

piriform fossae /ˌpɪrifɔːm 'fɒsiː/ *plural noun* the two hollows at the sides of the upper end of the larynx

Piriton /'pɪrɪtɒn/ a trade name for chlorpheniramine

piroxicam /pɪ'rɒksɪkæm/ *noun* a non-steroidal anti-inflammatory drug used in the treatment of rheumatoid arthritis and osteoarthritis

PIs *abbr* performance indicators

pisiform /'pɪsifɔːm/, **pisiform bone** /'pɪsifɔːm bəʊn/ *noun* one of the eight small carpal bones in the wrist. See illustration at **HAND** in Supplement

pit /pɪt/ *noun* a hollow place on a surface □ **the pit of the stomach** the epigastrium, the part of the upper abdomen between the ribcage above the navel. ◊ **armpit**

pithiatism /pɪ'θaɪətɪz(ə)m/ *noun* a way of influencing someone's mind by persuading him or her of something, as when a doctor treats a condition by telling the person that he or she is in fact well

pitted /'pɪtɪd/ *adjective* covered with small hollows ○ *His skin was pitted by acne.*

pitting /'pɪtɪŋ/ *noun* the formation of hollows in the skin

pituitary /pɪ'tjuːɪt(ə)ri/ *adjective* **1.** relating to or produced by the pituitary gland **2.** caused by a disturbance of the pituitary gland ■ *noun* same as **pituitary gland**

pituitary body /pɪ'tjuːɪt(ə)ri ˌbɒdi/ *noun* same as **pituitary gland**

pituitary fossa /pɪˌtjuːɪt(ə)ri 'fɒsə/ *noun* same as **sella turcica**

pituitary gland /pɪ'tjuːɪt(ə)ri ˌglænd/ *noun* the main endocrine gland in the body which secretes hormones that stimulate other glands.

Also called **pituitary body, hypophysis cerebri**. See illustration at BRAIN in Supplement

COMMENT: The pituitary gland is about the size of a pea and hangs down from the base of the brain, inside the sphenoid bone, on a stalk which attaches it to the hypothalamus. The front lobe of the gland (the adenohypophysis) secretes several hormones (TSH, ACTH) which stimulate the adrenal and thyroid glands, or which stimulate the production of sex hormones, melanin and milk. The posterior lobe of the pituitary gland (the neurohypophysis) secretes the antidiuretic hormone (ADH) and oxytocin.

pituitrin /pɪˈtjuːɪtrɪn/ *noun* a hormone secreted by the pituitary gland

pityriasis /ˌpɪtɪˈraɪəsɪs/ *noun* any skin disease in which the skin develops thin scales

pityriasis alba /ˌpɪtɪˌraɪəsɪs ˈælbə/ *noun* a disease affecting children which results in flat white patches on the cheeks that usually heal naturally

pityriasis capitis /ˌpɪtɪˌraɪəsɪs kəˈpaɪtɪs/ *noun* ♦ **dandruff**

pityriasis rosea /ˌpɪtɪˌraɪəsɪs ˈrəʊzɪə/ *noun* a mild irritating rash affecting young people, which appears especially in the early part of the year and has no known cause

pityriasis rubra /ˌpɪtɪˌraɪəsɪs ˈruːbrə/ *noun* a serious, sometimes fatal, skin disease, a type of exfoliative dermatitis in which the skin turns dark red and is covered with white scales

pivot /ˈpɪvət/ *noun* a stem used to attach an artificial crown to the root of a tooth ■ *verb* to rest and turn on a point ○ *The atlas bone pivots on the second vertebra.*

pivot joint /ˈpɪvət dʒɔɪnt/ *noun* same as **trochoid joint**

PKD *abbr* polycystic kidney disease

PKU *abbr* phenylketonuria

placebo /pləˈsiːbəʊ/ *noun* a tablet which appears to be a drug, but has no medicinal substance in it

COMMENT: Placebos may be given to patients who have imaginary illnesses. Placebos can also help in treating real disorders by stimulating the patient's psychological will to be cured. Placebos are also used on control groups in tests of new drugs (a placebo-controlled study).

placebo effect /pləˈsiːbəʊ ɪˌfekt/ *noun* the apparently beneficial effect of telling someone that he or she is having a treatment, even if this is not true, caused by the hope that the treatment will be effective

placenta /pləˈsentə/ *noun* the tissue which grows inside the uterus during pregnancy and links the baby to the mother

COMMENT: The vascular system of the fetus is not directly connected to that of the mother. The placenta allows an exchange of oxygen and nutrients to be passed from the mother to the fetus to which she is linked by the umbilical cord. It stops functioning when the baby

breathes for the first time and is then passed out of the uterus as the afterbirth.

placental /pləˈsent(ə)l/ *adjective* referring to the placenta

placental barrier /pləˌsent(ə)l ˈbærɪə/ *noun* a barrier which prevents the blood of a fetus and that of the mother from mixing, but allows water, oxygen and hormones to pass from mother to fetus

placental insufficiency /pləˌsent(ə)l ˌɪnsəˈfɪʃ(ə)nsi/ *noun* a condition in which the placenta does not provide the fetus with the necessary oxygen and nutrients

placenta praevia /pləˌsentə ˈpriːvɪə/ *noun* a condition in which the fertilised egg becomes implanted in the lower part of the uterus, which means that the placenta lies across the cervix and may become detached during childbirth and cause brain damage to the baby

placentography /ˌplæsənˈtɒɡrəfi/ *noun* an X-ray examination of the placenta of a pregnant woman after a radiopaque dye has been injected

Placido's disc /pləˈsaɪdəʊz dɪsk/ *noun* same as **keratoscope** [After A. Placido, Portuguese oculist.]

plagiocephaly /ˌpleɪdʒɪəˈkefəli/ *noun* a condition in which a person has a distorted head shape, from irregular closure of the cranial sutures

plague /pleɪɡ/ *noun* an infectious disease which occurs in epidemics where many people are killed

COMMENT: Bubonic plague was the Black Death of the Middle Ages; its symptoms are fever, delirium, prostration, rigor and swellings on the lymph nodes.

plan /plæn/ *noun* arrangement of how something should be done ■ *verb* to arrange how something is going to be done □ **they are planning to have a family** they expect to have children and so are not taking contraceptives

'…one issue has arisen – the amount of time and effort which nurses need to put into the writing of detailed care plans. Few would now dispute the need for clear, concise nursing plans to guide nursing practice, provide educational tools and give an accurate legal record' [*Nursing Times*]

plane /pleɪn/ *noun* a flat surface, especially that of the body seen from a specific angle

planned parenthood /ˌplænd ˈpeərənthʊd/ *noun* a situation in which two people plan to have a specific number of children, and take contraceptives to control the number of children in the family

planning /ˈplænɪŋ/ *noun* the work of deciding and arranging how something should be done

planta /ˈplæntə/ *noun* the sole of the foot

plantar /ˈplæntə/ *adjective* referring to the sole of the foot

plantar arch /ˌplæntər ˈɑːtʃ/ *noun* the curved part of the sole of the foot running along the length of the foot. Also called **longitudinal arch**

plantar flexion /ˌplæntə ˈflekʃən/ *noun* the bending of the toes downwards

plantar reflex /ˌplæntə ˈriːfleks/, **plantar response** /ˌplæntə rɪˈspɒns/ *noun* the usual downward movement of the toes when the sole of the foot is stroked in the Babinski test

plantar region /ˈplæntə ˌriːdʒən/ *noun* the sole of the foot

plantar surface /ˈplæntə ˌsɜːfɪs/ *noun* the skin of the sole of the foot

plantar wart /ˈplæntə wɔːt/ *noun* a wart on the sole of the foot

planus /ˈpleɪnəs/, ♦ **lichen planus**

plaque /plæk, plɑːk/ *noun* 1. a flat area 2. a film of saliva, mucus, bacteria and food residues that builds up on the surface of teeth and can cause gum damage

-plasia /pleɪziə/ *suffix* referring to something which develops or grows

plasm- /plæz(ə)m/ *prefix* same as **plasmo-** (*used before vowels*)

plasma /ˈplæzmə/ *noun* 1. a yellow watery liquid which makes up the main part of blood 2. lymph with no corpuscles 3. cytoplasm

COMMENT: If blood does not clot it separates into blood corpuscles and plasma, which is formed of water and proteins, including the clotting agent fibrinogen. If blood clots, the corpuscles separate from serum, which is a watery liquid similar to plasma, but not containing fibrinogen. Dried plasma can be kept for a long time, and is used, after water has been added, for transfusions.

plasma cell /ˈplæzmə sel/ *noun* a lymphocyte which produces a particular type of antibody

plasmacytoma /ˌplæzməsaɪˈtəʊmə/ *noun* a malignant tumour of plasma cells, usually found in lymph nodes or bone marrow

plasmapheresis /ˌplæzməfəˈriːsɪs/ *noun* an operation to take blood from someone, then to separate the red blood cells from the plasma, and to return the red blood cells suspended in a saline solution to the patient through a transfusion

plasma protein /ˈplæzmə ˌprəʊtiːn/ *noun* a protein in plasma, e.g. albumin, gamma globulin or fibrinogen

plasmin /ˈplæzmɪn/ *noun* same as **fibrinolysin**

plasminogen /plæzˈmɪnədʒən/ *noun* a substance in blood plasma which becomes activated and forms plasmin

plasmo- /plæzməʊ/ *prefix* referring to blood plasma

Plasmodium /plæzˈməʊdiəm/ *noun* a type of parasite which infests red blood cells and causes malaria

plasmolysis /plæzˈmɒlɪsɪs/ *noun* the contraction of a cell protoplasm by dehydration, where the surrounding cell wall becomes smaller

plaster /ˈplɑːstə/ *noun* a white powder which is mixed with water and used to make a solid support to cover a broken limb ○ *After his accident he had his leg in plaster for two months.*

plaster cast /ˈplɑːstə kɑːst/ *noun* a hard support made of bandage soaked in liquid plaster of Paris, which is allowed to harden after being wrapped round a broken limb and which prevents the limb moving while the bone heals

plaster of Paris /ˌplɑːstər əv ˈpærɪs/ *noun* a fine white plaster used to make plaster casts

plastic /ˈplæstɪk/ *noun* an artificial material made from petroleum, and used to make many objects, including replacement organs ■ *adjective* able to change shape or develop in different shapes

plastic lymph /ˈplæstɪk lɪmf/ *noun* a yellow liquid produced by an inflamed wound which helps the healing process

plastic surgeon /ˌplæstɪk ˈsɜːdʒən/ *noun* a surgeon who specialises in plastic surgery

plastic surgery /ˌplæstɪk ˈsɜːdʒəri/ *noun* surgery to repair damaged or malformed parts of the body (*informal*) ◊ **reconstructive surgery**

COMMENT: Plastic surgery is especially important in treating accident victims or people who have suffered burns. It is also used to correct congenital disorders such as a cleft palate. When the aim is simply to improve the patient's appearance, it is usually referred to as 'cosmetic surgery'.

plastin /ˈplæstɪn/ *noun* same as **fibrinolysin**

-plasty /plæsti/ *suffix* referring to plastic surgery

plate /pleɪt/ *noun* 1. a flat sheet of metal or bone ○ *The surgeon inserted a plate in her skull.* 2. a flat piece of metal attached to a fractured bone to hold the broken parts together

platelet /ˈpleɪtlət/ *noun* a small blood cell which releases thromboplastin and which multiplies rapidly after an injury, encouraging the coagulation of blood. Also called **thrombocyte**

platelet count /ˈpleɪt(ə)lət kaʊnt/ *noun* a test to count the number of platelets in a specific quantity of blood

platy- /plæti/ *prefix* flat

platysma /pləˈtɪzmə/ *noun* a flat muscle running from the collarbone to the lower jaw

pledget /ˈpledʒɪt/ *noun* a small piece of gauze or cotton wool used to protect or apply medication to a small enclosed space, such as the ear passage

-plegia /pliːdʒə/ *suffix* paralysis

pleio- /plaɪəʊ/ *prefix* same as **pleo-**

pleo- /pliːəʊ/ *prefix* too many

pleocytosis /ˌpliːəʊsaɪˈtəʊsɪs/ *noun* a condition in which there are an unusual number of leucocytes in the cerebrospinal fluid

pleoptics /pliːˈɒptɪks/ *noun* treatment to help the partially sighted

plessor /ˈplesə/ *noun* a little hammer with a rubber tip, used by doctors to tap tendons to test for reflexes or for percussion of the chest. Also called **plexor**

plethora /ˈpleθərə/ *noun* too much blood in a part of the body

plethoric /pleˈθɒrɪk/ *adjective* referring to an appearance that is due to dilatation of superficial blood vessels, e.g. a red complexion

plethysmography /ˌpleθɪzˈmɒɡrəfi/ *noun* a method of recording the changes in the volume of organs, mainly used to measure blood flow in the limbs

pleur- /plʊər/ *prefix* same as **pleuro-** (*used before vowels*)

pleura /ˈplʊərə/ *noun* one of two membranes lining the chest cavity and covering each lung (NOTE: The plural is **pleuras** or **pleurae**.)

pleuracentesis /ˌplʊərəsenˈtiːsɪs/ *noun* same as **pleurocentesis**

pleural /ˈplʊərəl/ *adjective* referring to the pleura

pleural cavity /ˌplʊərəl ˈkæviti/ *noun* a space between the inner and outer pleura of the chest. See illustration at LUNGS in Supplement

pleural effusion /ˌplʊərəl ɪˈfjuːʒ(ə)n/ *noun* an excess of fluid formed in the pleural sac

pleural fluid /ˌplʊərəl ˈfluːɪd/ *noun* a fluid which forms between the layers of the pleura in pleurisy

pleural membrane /ˌplʊərəl ˈmembreɪn/ *noun* same as **pleura**

pleural mesothelioma /ˌplʊərəl ˌmesəʊθeliˈəʊmə/ *noun* a tumour of the pleura, caused by inhaling asbestos dust

pleurectomy /plʊəˈrektəmi/ *noun* the surgical removal of part of the pleura which has been thickened or made stiff by chronic empyema

pleurisy /ˈplʊərɪsi/ *noun* inflammation of the pleura, usually caused by pneumonia

COMMENT: The symptoms of pleurisy are coughing, fever, and sharp pains when breathing, caused by the two layers of pleura rubbing together.

pleuritis /plʊəˈraɪtɪs/ *noun* same as **pleurisy**

pleuro- /plʊərəʊ/ *prefix* referring to the pleura

pleurocele /ˈplʊərəʊsiːl/ *noun* 1. a condition in which part of the lung or pleura is herniated 2. fluid in the pleural cavity

pleurocentesis /ˌplʊərəʊsenˈtiːsɪs/ *noun* an operation in which a hollow needle is put into the pleura to drain liquid. Also called **pleuracentesis**

pleurodesis /ˌplʊərəʊˈdiːsɪs/ *noun* treatment for a collapsed lung, in which the inner and outer pleura are stuck together

pleurodynia /ˌplʊərəʊˈdɪniə/ *noun* pain in the muscles between the ribs, due to rheumatic inflammation

pleuron /ˈplʊərɒn/ *noun* a membrane that encases the lung

pleuropneumonia /ˌplʊərəʊnjʊˈməʊniə/ *noun* acute lobar pneumonia, the classic type of pneumonia

plexor /ˈpleksə/ *noun* same as **plessor**

plexus /ˈpleksəs/ *noun* a network of nerves, blood vessels or lymphatics

pliable /ˈplaɪəb(ə)l/ *adjective* able to be bent easily

plica /ˈplaɪkə/ *noun* a fold

plicate /ˈplaɪkeɪt/ *adjective* folded

plication /plaɪˈkeɪʃ(ə)n/ *noun* 1. a surgical operation to reduce the size of a muscle or a hollow organ by making folds in its walls and attaching them 2. the action of folding 3. a fold

ploidy /ˈplɔɪdi/ *noun* the number of sets of chromosomes within a cell

plombage /plɒmˈbɑːʒ/ *noun* 1. the act of packing bone cavities with antiseptic material 2. the act of packing of the lung or pleural cavities with inert material

PLSS *abbr* portable life-support system

plumbing /ˈplʌmɪŋ/ *noun* any system of tubes or vessels in the body, but especially the urinary system (*informal humorous*)

plumbism /ˈplʌmbɪz(ə)m/ *noun* same as **lead poisoning**

Plummer–Vinson syndrome /ˌplʌmə ˈvɪnsən ˌsɪndrəʊm/ *noun* a type of iron-deficiency anaemia, in which the tongue and mouth become inflamed and the person cannot swallow [Described 1912 by Plummer, 1919 by Vinson (also described in 1919 by Patterson and Brown Kelly, whose names are frequently associated with the syndrome). Henry Stanley Plummer (1874–1937), US physician; Porter Paisley Vinson (1890–1959), physician at the Mayo Clinic, Minnesota, USA.]

plunger /ˈplʌndʒə/ *noun* the part of a hypodermic syringe which slides up and down inside the tube, either sucking liquid into the syringe or forcing the contents out

pluri- /plʊəri/ *prefix* indicating more than one of something

PM *abbr* 1. particulate matter 2. post mortem

PMA *abbr* progressive muscular atrophy

pmol *symbol* picomole

PMR *abbr* polymyalgia rheumatica

PMS *abbr* premenstrual syndrome

PMT *abbr* premenstrual tension

-pnea /pniːə/ *suffix* same as **-pnoea**

pneo- /niːəʊ/ *prefix* relating to breathing

pneum- /njuːm/ *prefix* same as **pneumo-** (used before vowels)

pneumat- /njuːmət/ *prefix* same as **pneumato-** (used before vowels)

pneumato- /njuːmətəʊ/ *prefix* relating to air, gas or breath

pneumatocele /njuːˈmætəʊsiːl/ *noun* 1. a sac or tumour filled with gas 2. herniation of the lung

pneumatonometer /ˌnjuːmətəˈnɒmɪtə/ *noun* an instrument which measures the air pressure in the eye, used in testing for glaucoma. It blows a puff of air onto the cornea.

pneumatosis /ˌnjuːməˈtəʊsɪs/ *noun* the occurrence of gas in an unusual place in the body

pneumaturia /ˌnjuːməˈtjʊəriə/ *noun* the act of passing air or gas in the urine

pneumo- /njuːməʊ/ *prefix* referring to air, to the lungs or to breathing

pneumocephalus /ˌnjuːməʊˈkefələs/ *noun* the presence of air or gas in the brain

pneumococcal /ˌnjuːməʊˈkɒk(ə)l/ *adjective* referring to pneumococci

pneumococcus /ˌnjuːməʊˈkɒkəs/ *noun* a bacterium which causes respiratory tract infections including pneumonia (NOTE: The plural is **pneumococci**.)

pneumoconiosis /ˌnjuːməʊkəʊniˈəʊsɪs/ *noun* a lung disease in which fibrous tissue forms in the lungs because the person has inhaled particles of stone or dust over a long period of time

pneumocystis carinii pneumonia /ˌnjuːməʊsɪstɪs kəˌriːniːi njuːˈməʊniə/ *noun* a form of pneumonia found in people with impaired immune systems after radiotherapy or with AIDS. Abbr **PCP**

pneumocyte /ˈnjuːməʊsaɪt/ *noun* a cell of the walls between the air sacs in the lung

pneumoencephalography /ˌnjuːməʊenˌkefəˈlɒgrəfi/ *noun* same as **encephalogram**

pneumogastric /ˌnjuːməʊˈgæstrɪk/ *adjective* referring to the lungs and the stomach

pneumograph /ˈnjuːməgrɑːf/ *noun* an instrument which records chest movements during breathing

pneumohaemothorax /ˌnjuːməʊˌhiːməʊˈθɔːræks/ *noun* blood or air in the pleural cavity. Also called **haemopneumothorax**

pneumomycosis /ˌnjuːməʊmaɪˈkəʊsɪs/ *noun* an infection of the lungs caused by a fungus

pneumon- /njuːmən/ *prefix* same as **pneumono-** (used before vowels)

pneumonectomy /ˌnjuːməˈnektəmi/ *noun* the surgical removal of all or part of a lung. Also called **pulmonectomy**

pneumonia /njuːˈməʊniə/ *noun* inflammation of a lung, where the tiny alveoli of the lung become filled with fluid ○ He developed pneumonia and had to be hospitalised. ○ She died of pneumonia.

COMMENT: The symptoms of pneumonia are shivering, pains in the chest, high temperature and sputum brought up by coughing.

pneumonic /njuːˈmɒnɪk/ *adjective* 1. referring to the lungs 2. referring to pneumonia

pneumonic plague /njuːˌmɒnɪk ˈpleɪg/ *noun* a form of bubonic plague which mainly affects the lungs

pneumonitis /ˌnjuːməʊˈnaɪtɪs/ *noun* inflammation of the lungs

pneumono- /njuːmənəʊ/ *prefix* referring to the lungs

pneumoperitoneum /ˌnjuːməʊperɪtəˈniːəm/ *noun* air in the peritoneal cavity

pneumoradiography /ˌnjuːməʊˌreɪdiˈɒgrəfi/ *noun* an X-ray examination of part of the body after air or a gas has been inserted to make the organs show more clearly

pneumothorax /ˌnjuːməʊˈθɔːræks/ *noun* a condition in which air or gas is in the thorax. Also called **collapsed lung**

-pnoea /pniːə/ *suffix* referring to breathing

PNS *abbr* peripheral nervous system

pock /pɒk/ *noun* a localised lesion on the skin, due to smallpox or chickenpox

pocket /ˈpɒkɪt/ *noun* a cavity in the body □ **pocket of infection** place where an infection remains

pockmark /ˈpɒkmɑːk/ *noun* a scar left by a pustule, as in smallpox

pockmarked /ˈpɒkmɑːkt/ *adjective* referring to a face with scars from smallpox

pod- /pɒd/ *prefix* referring to the foot

podagra /pɒˈdægrə/ same as **gout**

podalic /pəʊˈdælɪk/ *adjective* relating to the feet

podalic version /pəʊˌdælɪk ˈvɜːʃ(ə)n/ *noun* the procedure of turning a fetus in the uterus by its feet

podarthritis /ˌpəʊdɑːˈθraɪtɪs/ *noun* the swelling of one or more joints of the foot

podiatrist /pəʊˈdaɪətrɪst/ *noun* US a person who specialises in the care of the foot and its diseases

podiatry /pəʊˈdaɪətri/ *noun* US the study of minor diseases and disorders of the feet

-poiesis /pɔɪˈiːsɪs/ *suffix* referring to something which forms

poikilo- /pɔɪkɪləʊ/ *prefix* irregular or varied

poikilocyte /ˈpɔɪkɪləʊsaɪt/ *noun* an unusually large red blood cell with an irregular shape

poikilocytosis /ˌpɔɪkɪləʊsaɪˈtəʊsɪs/ *noun* a condition in which poikilocytes exist in the blood

point /pɔɪnt/ *noun* 1. a sharp end ○ Surgical needles have to have very sharp points. 2. the dot used to show the division between whole numbers and parts of numbers (NOTE: **3.256:** say 'three point two five six'; **his temperature**

was 38.7: say 'thirty-eight point seven'.) **3.** a mark in a series of numbers ○ *the freezing point of water*

pointed /ˈpɔɪntɪd/ *adjective* with a sharp point

poison /ˈpɔɪz(ə)n/ *noun* a substance which can kill or harm body tissues if eaten or drunk ■ *verb* to harm or kill someone with a poison
COMMENT: The commonest poisons, of which even a small amount can kill, are arsenic, cyanide and strychnine. Many common foods and drugs can be poisonous if taken in large doses. Common household materials such as bleach, glue and insecticides can also be poisonous. Some types of poisoning, such as Salmonella, can be passed to other people through lack of hygienic conditions.

poisoning /ˈpɔɪz(ə)nɪŋ/ *noun* a condition in which a person is made ill or is killed by a poisonous substance

poison ivy /ˌpɔɪz(ə)n ˈaɪvi/, **poison oak** /ˌpɔɪz(ə)n ˈəʊk/ *noun* American plants whose leaves can cause a painful rash if touched

poisonous /ˈpɔɪz(ə)nəs/ *adjective* referring to a substance which is full of poison or which can kill or harm

poisonous gas /ˌpɔɪz(ə)nəs ˈɡæs/ *noun* a gas which can kill or can make someone ill

Poisons Act /ˈpɔɪz(ə)nz ækt/ *noun* in the UK, one of several Acts of Parliament which regulate the making, prescribing and selling of drugs, e.g. the Pharmacy and Poisons Act 1933, Misuse of Drugs Act 1971, or Poisons Act 1972

polar /ˈpəʊlə/ *adjective* with a pole

polar body /ˌpəʊlə ˈbɒdi/ *noun* a small cell which is produced from an oocyte but does not develop into an ovum

pole /pəʊl/ *noun* **1.** the end of an axis **2.** the end of a rounded organ, e.g. the end of a lobe in the cerebral hemisphere

pole and canvas stretcher /ˌpəʊl ən ˈkænvəs ˌstretʃə/ *noun* a simple stretcher made of a piece of canvas and two poles which slide into tubes at the side of the canvas

poli- /ˈpɒli/ *prefix* same as **polio-** (*used before vowels*)

polio /ˈpəʊliəʊ/ *noun* same as **poliomyelitis** (*informal*)

polio- /ˈpəʊliəʊ/ *prefix* grey matter in the nervous system

polioencephalitis /ˌpəʊliəʊenˌkefəˈlaɪtɪs/ *noun* a type of viral encephalitis, an inflammation of the grey matter in the brain caused by the same virus as poliomyelitis

polioencephalomyelitis /ˌpəʊliəʊenˌkefələʊˌmaɪəˈlaɪtɪs/ *noun* polioencephalitis which also affects the spinal cord

poliomyelitis /ˌpəʊliəʊˌmaɪəˈlaɪtɪs/ *noun* an infection of the anterior horn cells of the spinal cord caused by a virus which attacks the motor neurones and can lead to paralysis. Also called **polio, infantile paralysis**
COMMENT: Symptoms of poliomyelitis are paralysis of the limbs, fever and stiffness in the neck. The bulbar form may start with difficulty in swallowing. Poliomyelitis can be prevented by immunisation and two vaccines are used: Sabin vaccine is formed of live polio virus and is taken orally on a piece of sugar; Salk vaccine is given as an injection of dead virus.

poliovirus /ˈpəʊliəʊˌvaɪrəs/ *noun* a virus which causes poliomyelitis

Politzer bag /ˈpɒlɪtsə bæɡ/ *noun* a rubber bag which is used to blow air into the middle ear to unblock a Eustachian tube [Described 1863. After Adam Politzer (1835–1920), Professor of Otology in Vienna, Austria.]

pollen /ˈpɒlən/ *noun* a powdery substance consisting of male gametes from plants, produced by the flower stamens, which floats in the air in spring and summer, and which causes hay fever

pollen count /ˈpɒlən kaʊnt/ *noun* a figure which shows the amount of pollen in a sample of air

pollex /ˈpɒleks/ *noun* the thumb (*technical*) (NOTE: The plural is **pollices**.)

pollutant /pəˈluːt(ə)nt/ *noun* a substance which causes pollution

pollute /pəˈluːt/ *verb* to make e.g. the air, a river or the sea dirty, especially with industrial waste (NOTE: **polluting – polluted**)

pollution /pəˈluːʃ(ə)n/ *noun* the act of making dirty, or substances which make e.g. air or water impure

poly- /ˈpɒli/ *prefix* **1.** many or much **2.** touching many organs

polyarteritis /ˌpɒliɑːtəˈraɪtɪs/ *noun* a condition in which a lot of arteries swell up at the same time

polyarteritis nodosa /ˌpɒliɑːtəˌraɪtɪs nəˈdəʊsə/ *noun* a collagen disease in which the walls of the arteries in various parts of the body become inflamed, leading to asthma, high blood pressure and kidney failure. Also called **periarteritis nodosa**

polyarthritis /ˌpɒliɑːˈθraɪtɪs/ *noun* inflammation of several joints, as in rheumatoid arthritis

polycystic /ˌpɒliˈsɪstɪk/ *adjective* referring to an organ which has developed more than one cyst, or to a disease caused by the development of cysts

polycystic kidney disease /ˌpɒlisɪstɪk ˈkɪdni dɪˌziːz/ *noun* a condition in which there are multiple cysts on each kidney which grow and multiply over time. Abbr **PKD**
COMMENT: The diseased kidney finally shuts down in over 60% of cases, and dialysis and transplantation are the only forms of treatment.

polycystic ovary disease /ˌpɒlisɪstɪk ˈəʊvəri dɪˌziːz/ *noun* same as **polycystic ovary syndrome**. Abbr **PCOD**

polycystic ovary syndrome /ˌpɒlisɪstɪk ˈəʊvəri ˌsɪndrəʊm/, **polycystic ovarian syndrome** /ˌpɒlisɪstɪk əʊˈveəriən ˌsɪndrəʊm/ *noun* a hormonal disorder in which a woman's ovaries are enlarged and contain many small painless cysts, hair growth is excessive, acne develops and infertility may occur. Also called **Stein Leventhal syndrome**. Abbr **PCOS**

polycystitis /ˌpɒlisɪˈstaɪtɪs/ *noun* a congenital disease in which several cysts form in the kidney at the same time

polycythaemia /ˌpɒlisaɪˈθiːmiə/ *noun* a condition in which the number of red blood cells increases (NOTE: The US spelling is **polycythemia**.)

polycythaemia vera /ˌpɒlisaɪθiːmiə ˈvɪərə/ *noun* a blood disease in which the number of red blood cells increases, together with an increase in the number of white blood cells, making the blood thicker and slowing its flow. Also called **erythraemia, Vaquez-Osler disease**

polydactyl /ˌpɒliˈdæktɪl/ *adjective* having more than the usual number of fingers or toes

polydactylism /ˌpɒliˈdæktɪlɪz(ə)m/ *noun* same as **hyperdactylism**

polydipsia /ˌpɒliˈdɪpsiə/ *noun* a condition, often caused by diabetes insipidus, in which a person is unusually thirsty

polygraph /ˈpɒligrɑːf/ *noun* an instrument which records the pulse in several parts of the body at the same time

polymenorrhoea /ˌpɒlimenəˈriːə/ *noun* unusually frequent menstruations (NOTE: The US spelling is **polymenorrhea**.)

polymerase chain reaction /ˌpɒliməreɪz ˌtʃeɪn riˈækʃ(ə)n/ *noun* the technique used to amplify genetic material in order to analyse it for genetic disorders, e.g. material from a single cell in an embryo. Abbr **PCR**

polymorph /ˈpɒlimɔːf/ *noun* same as **neutrophil**

polymyalgia rheumatica /ˌpɒlimaɪˌældʒə ruːˈmætɪkə/ *noun* a disease of elderly people characterised by pain and stiffness in the shoulder and hip muscles making them weak and sensitive

polymyositis /ˌpɒlimaɪəʊˈsaɪtɪs/ *noun* a condition in which a lot of muscles swell up at the same time, especially the ones in the trunk of the body, causing weakness. It is treated with steroid drugs or immunosuppressants, and also exercise.

polyneuritis /ˌpɒlinjʊˈraɪtɪs/ *noun* inflammation of many nerves

polyneuropathy /ˌpɒlinjʊˈrɒpəθi/ *noun* any disease which affects several nerves (NOTE: The plural is **polyneuropathies**.)

polyopia /ˌpɒliˈəʊpiə/, **polyopsia** /ˌpɒliˈɒpsiə/, **polyopy** /ˈpɒliəʊpi/ *noun* a condition in which a person sees several images of one object at the same time. Compare **diplopia**

polyp /ˈpɒlɪp/ *noun* a tumour growing on a stalk in mucous membrane, which can be cauterised. Polyps are often found in the nose, mouth or throat. Also called **polypus**

polypectomy /ˌpɒliˈpektəmi/ *noun* a surgical operation to remove a polyp (NOTE: The plural is **polypectomies**.)

polypeptide /ˌpɒliˈpeptaɪd/ *noun* a type of protein formed of linked amino acids

polyphagia /ˌpɒliˈfeɪdʒə/ *noun* **1.** a condition in which a person eats too much **2.** a compulsive desire for every kind of food

polypharmacy /ˌpɒliˈfɑːməsi/ *noun* the practice of prescribing several drugs to be taken at the same time

polyploid /ˈpɒliplɔɪd/ *adjective* referring to a cell where there are more than two copies of each chromosome, which is not viable in humans

polypoid /ˈpɒlipɔɪd/ *adjective* looking like a polyp

polyposis /ˌpɒliˈpəʊsɪs/ *noun* a condition in which many polyps form in the mucous membrane of the colon. ◊ **familial adenomatous polyposis**

polypus /ˈpɒlipəs/ *noun* same as **polyp** (NOTE: The plural is **polypi**.)

polyradiculitis /ˌpɒliræˌdɪkjuˈlaɪtɪs/ *noun* a disease of the nervous system which affects the roots of the nerves

polysaccharide /ˌpɒliˈsækəraɪd/ *noun* a type of carbohydrate made up of a lot of monosaccharides joined together in chains. They include starch and cellulose, are insoluble in water and do not form crystals.

polyserositis /ˌpɒlisɪərəʊˈsaɪtɪs/ *noun* inflammation of the membranes lining the abdomen, chest and joints and exudation of serous fluid

polysomnograph /ˌpɒliˈsɒmnəgrɑːf/ *noun* a record of bodily activity during sleep to identify possible causes of sleep disorders

polyspermia /ˌpɒliˈspɜːmiə/, **polyspermism** /ˌpɒliˈspɜːmɪz(ə)m/, **polyspermy** /ˌpɒli ˈspɜːmi/ *noun* **1.** excessive seminal secretion **2.** fertilisation of one ovum by several spermatozoa

polyunsaturated fat /ˌpɒliʌnsætʃəreɪtɪd ˈfæt/ *noun* a fatty acid capable of absorbing more hydrogen than most others, typical of vegetable and fish oils

polyuria /ˌpɒliˈjʊəriə/ *noun* a condition in which a person passes a large quantity of urine, usually as a result of diabetes insipidus

polyvalent /ˌpɒliˈveɪlənt/ *adjective* having more than one valency

POM *abbr* prescription-only medicine

pompholyx /'pɒmfɒliks/ *noun* **1.** a type of eczema with many irritating little blisters on the hands and feet **2.** a skin condition with bulbous swellings

pons /pɒnz/ *noun* a bridge of tissue joining parts of an organ. See illustration at BRAIN in Supplement (NOTE: The plural is **pontes**.)

pons Varolii /ˌpɒnz vəˈrəʊliaɪ/ *noun* part of the hindbrain, formed of fibres which continue the medulla oblongata. See illustration at BRAIN in Supplement (NOTE: The plural is **pontes Varolii**.) [After Constanzo Varolius (1543–75), Italian physician and anatomist, doctor to Pope Gregory XIII]

pontes /'pɒntiz/ *plural of* **pons**

pontine /'pɒntaɪn/ *adjective* referring to a pons

pontine cistern /ˌpɒntaɪn 'sɪstən/ *noun* a subarachnoid space in front of the pons, containing the basilar artery

poor /pɔː/ *adjective* not very good ○ *He's in poor health.* ○ *She's always had poor circulation.*

poorly /'pɔːli/ *adjective* not very well (*informal*) ○ *Her mother has been quite poorly recently.* ○ *He felt poorly and stayed in bed.*

POP *abbr* progesterone only pill

popeyes /'pɒpaɪz/ *plural noun US* protruding eyes

popliteal /ˌpɒplɪˈtiːəl/ *adjective* referring to the back of the knee

popliteal artery /ˌpɒplɪtiːəl 'ɑːtəri/ *noun* an artery which branches from the femoral artery behind the knee and leads into the tibial arteries

popliteal fossa /ˌpɒplɪtiːəl 'fɒsə/ *noun* a space behind the knee between the hamstring and the calf muscle. Also called **popliteal space**

popliteal muscle /ˌpɒplɪˈtiːəl ˌmʌs(ə)l/ *noun* same as **popliteus**

popliteal space /ˌpɒplɪtiːəl 'speɪs/ *noun* same as **popliteal fossa**

popliteus /pɒˈplɪtiəs/ *noun* a muscle at the back of the knee. Also called **popliteal muscle**

population /ˌpɒpjʊˈleɪʃ(ə)n/ *noun* **1.** the number of people living in a country or town ○ *Population statistics show that the birth rate is slowing down.* ○ *The government has decided to screen the whole population of the area.* **2.** the number of patients in hospital ○ *The hospital population in the area has fallen below 10,000.*

pore /pɔː/ *noun* **1.** a tiny hole in the skin through which the sweat passes **2.** a small communicating passage between cavities

porencephaly /ˌpɔːrenˈkefəli/, **porencephalia** /ˌpɔːrenkəˈfeɪliə/, **porencephalus** /ˌpɔːrenˈkefələs/ *noun* a condition in which there are cysts in the cerebral cortex, as a result of unusual development

porous /'pɔːrəs/ *adjective* **1.** containing pores ○ *Porous bone surrounds the Eustachian tubes.* **2.** referring to tissue which allows fluid to pass through it

porphyria /pɔːˈfɪriə/ *noun* a hereditary disease affecting the metabolism of porphyrin pigments

COMMENT: Porphyria causes abdominal pains and attacks of mental confusion. The skin becomes sensitive to light and the urine becomes coloured and turns dark brown when exposed to the light.

porphyrin /'pɔːfərɪn/ *noun* a member of a family of metal-containing biological pigments, the commonest of which is protoporphyrin IX

porphyrinuria /ˌpɔːfɪrɪˈnjʊəriə/ *noun* the presence of excess porphyrins in the urine, a sign of porphyria or of metal poisoning

porta /'pɔːtə/ *noun* an opening which allows blood vessels to pass into an organ (NOTE: The plural is **portae**.)

portable /'pɔːtəb(ə)l/ *adjective* referring to something which can be carried ○ *He keeps a portable first aid kit in his car.* ○ *The ambulance team carried a portable blood testing unit.*

Portacath /'pɔːtəkæθ/ *noun* a type of catheter put in place under a person's skin to make it easier to have chemotherapy, transfusions and blood tests. It is accessed by the use of a special needle and flushed regularly with sterile saline.

portacaval /ˌpɔːtəˈkeɪv(ə)l/ *adjective* another spelling of **portocaval**

portae /'pɔːti/ *plural of* **porta**

porta hepatis /ˌpɔːtə 'hepətɪs/ *noun* an opening in the liver through which the hepatic artery, hepatic duct and portal vein pass (NOTE: The plural is **portae hepatitis**.)

portal /'pɔːt(ə)l/ *adjective* referring to a porta, especially the portal system or the portal vein

portal hypertension /ˌpɔːt(ə)l ˌhaɪpə'tenʃən/ *noun* high pressure in the portal vein, caused by cirrhosis of the liver or a clot in the vein and causing internal bleeding

portal pyaemia /ˌpɔːt(ə)l paɪˈiːmiə/ *noun* an infection of the portal vein in the liver, giving abscesses

portal system /'pɔːt(ə)l ˌsɪstəm/ *noun* a group of veins which have capillaries at both ends and do not go to the heart

portal vein /'pɔːt(ə)l veɪn/ *noun* a vein which takes blood from the stomach, pancreas, gall bladder, intestines and spleen to the liver (NOTE: For other terms referring to the portal vein, see words beginning with **pyl-**, **pyle-**.)

porter /'pɔːtə/ *noun* a hospital worker who does general work such as wheeling a patient's trolley into the operating theatre or moving heavy equipment

portocaval /ˌpɔːtəʊˈkeɪv(ə)l/ *adjective* linking the portal vein to the inferior vena cava

portocaval anastomosis /pɔːtəʊˌkeɪv(ə)l ənæstəˈməʊsɪs/ *noun* a surgical operation to join the portal vein to the inferior vena cava and divert blood past the liver

portocaval shunt /ˌpɔːtəʊˌkeɪv(ə)l ˈʃʌnt/ *noun* an artificial passage made between the portal vein and the inferior vena cava to relieve portal hypertension

porto-systemic encephalopathy /ˌpɔːtəʊ sɪsˌtiːmɪk ˌenkefəˈlɒpəθi/ *noun* a mental disorder and coma caused by liver disorder due to portal hypertension

port wine stain /pɔːt ˈwaɪn steɪn/ *noun* a purple birthmark

position /pəˈzɪʃ(ə)n/ *noun* 1. the place where something is ○ *The exact position of the tumour is located by an X-ray.* 2. the way a person's body is arranged ○ *in a sitting position* ○ *The accident victim had been placed in the recovery position.* ■ *verb* to place something in a particular position ○ *The fetus is correctly positioned in the uterus.*

positive /ˈpɒzɪtɪv/ *adjective* 1. indicating the answer 'yes' 2. indicating the presence of something being tested for ○ *Her cervical smear was positive.* Opposite **negative**

positive end-expiratory pressure /ˌpɒzɪtɪv ˌend ɪkˌspɪrət(ə)ri ˈpreʃə/ *noun* the procedure of forcing a person to breathe through a mask in cases where fluid has collected in the lungs. Abbr **PEEP**

positive feedback /ˌpɒzɪtɪv ˈfiːdbæk/ *noun* a situation in which the result of a process stimulates the process which caused it

positively /ˈpɒzɪtɪvli/ *adverb* in a positive way ○ *She reacted positively to the test.*

positive pressure respirator /ˌpɒzɪtɪv ˈpreʃə ˌrespɪreɪtə/ *noun* a machine which forces air into the lungs through a tube inserted in the mouth

positive pressure ventilation /ˌpɒzɪtɪv ˈpreʃə ventɪˌleɪʃ(ə)n/ *noun* the act of forcing air into the lungs to encourage the lungs to expand. Abbr **PPV**

positron-emission tomography /ˌpɒzɪtrɒn ɪˈmɪʃ(ə)n təˌmɒgrəfi/ *noun* a method of scanning the tissues of the brain, chest and abdomen for unusual metabolic activity after injecting a radioactive substance into the body. Abbr **PET**

posology /pəˈsɒlədʒi/ *noun* the study of doses of medicine

posseting /ˈpɒsɪtɪŋ/ *noun* (*in babies*) the act of bringing up small quantities of curdled milk into the mouth after feeding

Possum /ˈpɒsəm/ *noun* a device using electronic switches which helps a person who is severely paralysed to work a machine such as a telephone (NOTE: The name is derived from the first letters of **patient-operated selector mechanism**.)

post- /pəʊst/ *prefix* after or later

postcentral gyrus /pəʊstˌsentr(ə)l ˈdʒaɪrəs/ *noun* a sensory area of the cerebral cortex which receives impulses from receptor cells and registers sensations such as pain, heat and touch

post-cibal /pəʊst ˈsaɪb(ə)l/ *adjective* after having eaten food

post cibum *adverb* full form of **p.c.**

post-coital /pəʊst ˈkɔɪt(ə)l/ *adjective* taking place after sexual intercourse

postconcussional syndrome /ˌpəʊstkən ˈkʌʃ(ə)n(ə)l ˌsɪndrəʊm/ *noun* a set of symptoms which sometimes follow a head injury in which a person lost consciousness, including headache, loss of concentration, memory loss, depression and irritability

post-epileptic /ˌpəʊst epɪˈleptɪk/ *adjective* taking place after an epileptic fit

posterior /pɒˈstɪəriə/ *adjective* at the back. Opposite **anterior** □ **posterior to** behind ○ *The cerebellum is posterior to the medulla oblongata.* ■ *noun* same as **buttock** (*informal*)

posterior approach /pɒˈstɪəriər əˌprəʊtʃ/ *noun* an operation carried out from the back

posterior aspect /pɒˈstɪəriər ˌæspekt/ *noun* a view of the back of the body, or of the back of part of the body. See illustration at ANATOMICAL TERMS in Supplement

posterior chamber /pɒˌstɪəriə ˈtʃeɪmbə/ *noun* a part of the aqueous chamber which is behind the iris. Compare **anterior chamber**

posterior fontanelle /pɒˌstɪəriə fɒntəˈnel/ *noun* a cartilage at the back of the head where the parietal bones join the occipital. ◊ **bregma**

posterior lobe *noun* same as **caudate lobe**

posteriorly /pɒˈstɪəriəli/ *adverb* in or from a position behind ○ *An artery leads to a posteriorly placed organ.* ○ *Rectal biopsy specimens are best taken posteriorly.*

posterior nares /pɒˌstɪəriə ˈneəriːz/ *plural noun* same as **internal nares**

posterior synechia /pɒˌstɪəriə sɪˈnekiə/ *noun* a condition of the eye in which the iris sticks to the anterior surface of the lens

postero- /ˈpɒstərəʊ/ *prefix* back or behind

posteroanterior /ˌpɒstərəʊænˈtɪəriə/ *adjective* lying from the back to the front

post-exposure prophylaxis /ˌpəʊst ɪk ˌspəʊʒə ˌprɒfəˈlæksɪs/ *noun* a treatment given to a person who has been exposed to a harmful agent, in an effort to prevent or reduce injury or infection

postganglionic /ˌpəʊstgæŋliˈɒnɪk/ *adjective* placed after a ganglion

postganglionic fibre /ˌpəʊstgæŋliˌɒnɪk ˈfaɪbə/ *noun* an axon of a nerve cell which starts in a ganglion and extends beyond the ganglion

COMMENT: Postganglionic fibres go to the nose, palate, pharynx and lacrimal glands.

postganglionic neurone /ˌpəʊstgæŋgli ˌɒnɪk 'njʊərəʊn/ noun a neurone which starts in a ganglion and ends in a gland or unstriated muscle

postgastrectomy syndrome /ˌpəʊst gæ 'strektəmi ˌsɪndrəʊm/ noun a group of symptoms which can occur after eating in people who have had stomach operations. It is caused by a lot of food passing into the small intestine too fast and can cause dizziness, nausea, sweating and weakness. Also called **dumping syndrome**

postgraduate education allowance / 'pəʊst'grædjʊət edjʊ'keɪʃ(ə)n ə'laʊəns/ noun a payment made to GPs to reward continued education. Abbr **PGEA**

posthepatic /ˌpəʊsthɪ'pætɪk/ adjective positioned behind or coming into effect after the liver

posthepatic bilirubin /ˌpəʊsthɪˌpætɪk ˌbili 'ruːbɪn/ noun bilirubin which enters the plasma after being treated by the liver

posthepatic jaundice /ˌpəʊsthɪˌpætɪk 'dʒɔːndɪs/ noun same as **obstructive jaundice**

post herpetic neuralgia /ˌpəʊst hə,petɪk njʊ'rældʒə/ noun pains felt after an attack of shingles

posthitis /pɒs'θaɪtɪs/ noun inflammation of the foreskin

posthumous /'pɒstjʊməs/ adjective occurring after death ◇ **posthumous birth 1.** the birth of a baby after the death of the father **2.** the birth of a baby by caesarean section after the mother has died

post-irradiation /ˌpəʊst ɪˌreɪdi'eɪʃ(ə)n/ adjective referring to pain or disorder caused by X-rays

post-irradiation enteritis /ˌpəʊst ɪˌreɪdi eɪʃ(ə)n ˌentə'raɪtɪs/ noun enteritis caused by X-rays

postmature /ˌpəʊstmə't ʃʊə/ adjective referring to a baby born after the usual gestation period of 42 weeks

postmaturity /ˌpəʊstmə'tʃʊərɪti/ noun a pregnancy which lasts longer than the usual gestation period of 42 weeks

postmenopausal /ˌpəʊstmenəʊ'pɔːz(ə)l/ adjective happening or existing after the menopause ◇ She experienced some postmenopausal bleeding.

post mortem /ˌpəʊst 'mɔːtəm/, **post mortem examination** /ˌpəʊst 'mɔːtəm ɪgzæmɪ ˌneɪʃ(ə)n/ noun an examination of a dead body by a pathologist to find out the cause of death ◇ The post mortem showed that he had been poisoned. Abbr **PM**. Also called **autopsy**

postnasal /pəʊst'neɪz(ə)l/ adjective situated or happening behind the nose

postnasal drip /ˌpəʊstˌneɪz(ə)l 'drɪp/ noun a condition in which mucus from the nose runs down into the throat and is swallowed

postnatal /ˌpəʊst'neɪt(ə)l/ adjective referring to the period after the birth of a child

postnatal care /ˌpəʊstˌneɪt(ə)l 'keə/ noun the care given to a woman after the birth of her child

postnatal depression /ˌpəʊstˌneɪt(ə)l dɪ 'preʃ(ə)n/ noun depression which sometimes affects a woman after childbirth

postnecrotic cirrhosis /ˌpəʊstnekrɒtɪk sɪ 'rəʊsɪs/ noun cirrhosis of the liver caused by viral hepatitis

post-op /ˌpəʊst 'ɒp/ (informal) adjective same as **postoperative** ■ adverb same as **postoperatively**

postoperative /ˌpəʊst'ɒp(ə)rətɪv/ adjective referring to the period after a surgical operation ◇ The patient has suffered postoperative nausea and vomiting. ◇ Occlusion may appear as postoperative angina pectoris.

'...the nurse will help ensure that the parent is physically fit to cope with the postoperative child' [British Journal of Nursing]

postoperatively /ˌpəʊst'ɒp(ə)rətɪvli/ adverb after a surgical operation

postoperative pain /ˌpəʊstˌɒp(ə)rətɪv 'peɪn/ noun pain felt after a surgical operation

postorbital /ˌpəʊst'ɔːbɪt(ə)l/ adjective situated behind the eye or the eye socket

postpartum /ˌpəʊst'pɑːtəm/ adjective referring to the period after the birth of a child

postpartum fever /ˌpəʊstˌpɑːtəm 'fiːvə/ noun same as **puerperal infection**

postpartum haemorrhage /ˌpəʊstˌpɑːtəm 'hem(ə)rɪdʒ/ noun heavy bleeding after childbirth. Abbr **PPH**

post-primary tuberculosis /ˌpəʊst ˌpraɪməri tjuːˌbɜːkjʊ'ləʊsɪs/ noun the reappearance of tuberculosis in a person who has been infected with it before

post-registration education and practice /ˌpəʊst redʒɪˌstreɪʃ(ə)n edjʊˌkeɪʃ(ə)n ənd 'præktɪs/ noun in the UK, the requirement for all registered nurses and midwives to undertake educational activities and keep up with contemporary practice, and also for their employers to address the learning needs of staff. It was started by the UKCC in 1993. Abbr **PREP**

postsynaptic /ˌpəʊstsɪ'næptɪk/ adjective situated behind a synapse

postsynaptic axon /ˌpəʊstsɪnæptɪk 'æksɒn/ noun an axon of the nerves on either side of a synapse

post-traumatic /ˌpəʊst trɔː'mætɪk/ adjective appearing after a trauma, e.g. after an accident, rape or fire

post-traumatic amnesia /ˌpəʊst trɔː ˌmætɪk æm'niːziə/ noun amnesia which follows a trauma

post-traumatic stress disorder /ˌpəʊst trɔːˌmætɪk ˈstres dɪsˌɔːdə/ *noun* a psychological condition affecting people who have suffered severe emotional trauma, e.g. occasioned by war or natural disaster. Its symptoms include chest pain, dizziness, sleep disturbances, flashbacks, anxiety, tiredness, and depression. Abbr **PTSD**

postural /ˈpɒstʃərəl/ *adjective* referring to posture ○ *a study of postural disorders*

postural drainage /ˌpɒstʃərəl ˈdreɪnɪdʒ/ *noun* a procedure for removing matter from infected lungs by making the person lie down with the head lower than the feet, so that he or she can cough more easily

postural hypotension /ˌpɒstʃərəl haɪpəʊ ˈtenʃən/ *noun* low blood pressure when standing up suddenly, causing dizziness

posture /ˈpɒstʃə/ *noun* the position in which a body is arranged, or the way a person usually holds his or her body when standing ○ *Bad posture can cause pain in the back.* ○ *She has to do exercises to correct her bad posture.*

postviral /pəʊstˈvaɪrəl/ *adjective* occurring after a viral infection

postviral fatigue syndrome /pəʊstˌvaɪrəl fəˈtiːg ˌsɪndrəʊm/ *noun* same as **myalgic encephalomyelitis**

potassium /pəˈtæsiəm/ *noun* a metallic element (NOTE: The chemical symbol is **K**.)

potassium permanganate /pəˌtæsiəm pə ˈmæŋgənət/ *noun* a purple-coloured poisonous salt, used as a disinfectant

potentiate /pəˈtenʃieɪt/ *verb* to improve the effectiveness of a drug or treatment, especially by adding another drug or agent (NOTE: **potentiating – potentiated**)

Pott's disease /ˈpɒts dɪˌziːz/, **Pott's caries** /ˈpɒts ˌkeəriːz/ *noun* tuberculosis of the spine, causing paralysis [Described 1779. After Sir Percivall Pott (1714–88), London surgeon.]

Pott's fracture /ˈpɒts ˌfræktʃə/ *noun* a fracture of the lower end of the fibula together with displacement of the ankle and foot outwards [Described 1765. After Sir Percivall Pott (1714–88), London surgeon.]

pouch /paʊtʃ/ *noun* a small sac or pocket attached to an organ

poultice /ˈpəʊltɪs/ *noun* a compress made of hot water and flour paste or other substances which is pressed onto an infected part to draw out pus, to relieve pain or to encourage the circulation. Also called **fomentation**

pound /paʊnd/ *noun* a measure of weight equal to about 450 grams ○ *The baby weighed only four pounds at birth.* Abbr **lb** (NOTE: With figures, usually written **lb: The baby weighs 6lb**.)

Poupart's ligament /ˈpuːpɑːts ˌlɪgəmənt/ *noun* same as **inguinal ligament** [Described

1705. After François Poupart (1616–1708), French surgeon and anatomist.]

powder /ˈpaʊdə/ *noun* a medicine in the form of a fine dry dust made from particles of drugs ○ *He took a powder to help his indigestion* or *He took an indigestion powder.*

powdered /ˈpaʊdəd/ *adjective* crushed so that it forms a fine dry dust ○ *The medicine is available in tablets or in powdered form.*

pox /pɒks/ *noun* **1.** a disease with eruption of vesicles or pustules **2.** same as **syphilis** (*old*)

poxvirus /ˈpɒksˌvaɪrəs/ *noun* any of a group of viruses which cause cowpox, smallpox and related diseases

'Molluscum contagiosum is a harmless skin infection caused by a poxvirus that affects mainly children and young adults' [*British Medical Journal*]

p.p. *abbreviation* after a meal. Full form **post prandium**. Compare **a.p.**

PPD *abbr* purified protein derivative

PPH *abbr* postpartum haemorrhage

PPV *abbr* positive pressure ventilation

PQRST complex *noun* the set of deflections on an electrocardiogram, labelled P to T, which show ventricular contraction

p.r. *adverb* (*of an examination*) by the rectum. Full form **per rectum**

practice /ˈpræktɪs/ *noun* **1.** the business, or the premises occupied by, a doctor, dentist, or a group of doctors or dentists working together ○ *After qualifying she joined her father's practice.* □ **in practice** doing the work of a doctor or dentist ○ *He has been in practice for six years.* **2.** the fact of doing something, as opposed to thinking or talking about it ○ *theory and practice* **3.** a usual way of doing something ○ *Such practices are now regarded as unsafe.*

practice nurse /ˈpræktɪs nɜːs/ *noun* a nurse employed by a GP or primary care trust to work in a GP's practice providing treatment, health promotion, screening and other services to patients of the practice

'…practice nurses play a major role in the care of patients with chronic disease and they undertake many preventive procedures' [*Nursing Times*]

practise /ˈpræktɪs/ *verb* **1.** to work as a doctor ○ *He practises in North London.* ○ *She practises homeopathy.* **2.** to work in a particular branch of medicine (NOTE: **practising – practised**. The US spelling is **practice**.)

practitioner /prækˈtɪʃ(ə)nə/ *noun* a qualified person who works in the medical profession ◇ **nurse practitioner** *US* **1.** a nurse employed by a clinic or doctor's practice who can give advice to patients **2.** a trained nurse who has not been licensed

praecox /ˈpriːkɒks/ *noun* ♦ **ejaculatio praecox**

praevia /ˈpriːviə/ *noun* ♦ **placenta praevia**

pravastatin /ˌprævə'stætɪn/ noun a drug used to reduce unusually high levels of blood cholesterol

prazosin /'præzəsɪn/ noun a drug which relaxes or widens the blood vessels, used to treat hypertension

pre- /priː/ prefix before or in front of

preadmission information /ˌpriːəd'mɪʃ(ə)n ɪnfəˌmeɪʃ(ə)n/ noun information given to a person before he or she is admitted to hospital

pre-anaesthetic round /ˌpriːænəs'θetɪk raʊnd/ noun an examination of patients by the surgeon before they are anaesthetised

precancer /priː'kænsə/ noun a growth or cell which is not malignant but which may become cancerous

precancerous /priː'kænsərəs/ adjective referring to a growth which is not malignant now, but which can become cancerous later

precaution /prɪ'kɔːʃ(ə)n/ noun an action taken before something happens ○ She took the tablets as a precaution against seasickness.

precede /prɪ'siːd/ verb to happen before or earlier than something ○ The attack was preceded by a sudden rise in body temperature. (NOTE: **preceding – preceded**)

precentral gyrus /prɪˌsentr(ə)l 'dʒaɪrəs/ noun a motor area of the cerebral cortex

preceptor /prɪ'septə/ noun a specialist who gives practical training to a student

preceptorship /prɪ'septəʃɪp/ noun a period of time during which a recently trained nurse, midwife or health visitor can gain practical experience working with a specialist who advises and guides them

precipitate /prɪ'sɪpɪtət/ noun a substance which is precipitated during a chemical reaction ■ verb **1.** to make a substance separate from a chemical compound and fall to the bottom of a liquid during a chemical reaction ○ Casein is precipitated when milk comes into contact with an acid. **2.** to make something start suddenly (NOTE: [all verb senses] **precipitating – precipitated**)

'…it has been established that myocardial infarction and sudden coronary death are precipitated in the majority of patients by thrombus formation in the coronary arteries' [*British Journal of Hospital Medicine*]

precipitate labour /prɪˌsɪpɪtət 'leɪbə/ noun unusually fast labour, lasting two hours or less. It can be dangerous both to the mother and to the child.

precipitation /prɪˌsɪpɪ'teɪʃ(ə)n/ noun the action of forming a precipitate

precipitin /prɪ'sɪpɪtɪn/ noun an antibody which reacts to an antigen and forms a precipitate, used in many diagnostic tests

precise /prɪ'saɪs/ adjective very exact or correct ○ The instrument can give precise measurements of changes in heartbeat.

preclinical /priː'klɪnɪk(ə)l/ adjective **1.** taking place before diagnosis ○ the preclinical stage of an infection **2.** referring to the first part of a medical course, before the students are allowed to examine real patients

precocious /prɪ'kəʊʃəs/ adjective more physically or mentally developed than is usual for a specific age

precocious puberty /prɪˌkəʊʃəs 'pjuːbəti/ noun the development of signs of puberty in girls before the age of seven, and in boys before the age of nine. If untreated, affected boys typically grow no taller than 1.6 metres and girls rarely reach 1.5 metres.

precocity /prɪ'kɒsɪti/ noun the state or fact of being precocious

precordia /priː'kɔːdiə/ plural noun plural of **precordium**

precordial /priː'kɔːdiəl/ adjective referring to the precordium

precordium /priː'kɔːdiəm/ noun the part of the thorax over the heart (NOTE: The plural is **precordia**.)

precursor /prɪ'kɜːsə/ noun a substance or cell from which another substance or cell is developed, e.g. dopa, the precursor for dopamine, which is converted to dopamine by the enzyme dopa decarboxylase

predict /prɪ'dɪkt/ verb to say what will happen in the future ○ Doctors are predicting a rise in cases of whooping cough.

prediction /prɪ'dɪkʃən/ noun an act of saying what you expect will happen in the future, or what is said ○ the Health Ministry's prediction of a rise in cases of hepatitis B

predictive /prɪ'dɪktɪv/ adjective referring to prediction ○ The predictive value of the test is high.

predigest /ˌpriːdaɪ'dʒest/ verb to treat food with chemicals or enzymes so that it is more easily digested by people with digestion problems

predigested food /ˌpriːdaɪdʒestɪd 'fuːd/ noun food which has undergone predigestion

predigestion /ˌpriːdaɪ'dʒestʃ(ə)n/ noun the artificial starting of the digestive process before food is eaten

predisposed to /ˌpriːdɪ'spəʊzd tʊ/ adjective having a tendency or susceptibility to a condition ○ All the members of the family are predisposed to vascular diseases.

predisposing factor /ˌpriːdɪspəʊzɪŋ 'fæktə/ noun a factor which will increase the risk of disease

predisposition /ˌpriːdɪspə'zɪʃ(ə)n/ noun a tendency or susceptibility ○ She has a predisposition to obesity.

prednisolone /predˈnɪsələʊn/ *noun* a synthetically produced steroid hormone, similar to cortisone, used especially to control inflammatory diseases such as rheumatoid arthritis

prednisone /ˈprednɪsəʊn/ *noun* a synthetically produced steroid hormone produced from cortisone, used to treat allergies and rheumatoid arthritis

predominant /prɪˈdɒmɪnənt/ *adjective* more powerful than others

pre-eclampsia /ˌpriː ɪˈklæmpsiə/ *noun* a condition in pregnant women towards the end of the pregnancy which may lead to eclampsia. Symptoms are high blood pressure, oedema and protein in the urine. Also called **pregnancy-induced hypertension**

preemie /ˈpriːmi/ *noun US* a premature baby (*informal*)

prefrontal /priːˈfrʌnt(ə)l/ *adjective* situated in or affecting the front part of the frontal lobe

prefrontal leucotomy /priːˌfrʌnt(ə)l luːˈkɒtəmi/ *noun* a surgical operation to divide some of the white matter in the prefrontal lobe, formerly used as a treatment for schizophrenia

prefrontal lobe /priːˈfrʌnt(ə)l ləʊb/ *noun* an area of the brain in the front part of each hemisphere, in front of the frontal lobe, which is concerned with memory and learning

preganglionic /ˌpriːgæŋɡliˈɒnɪk/ *adjective* near to and in front of a ganglion

preganglionic fibre /ˌpriːgæŋɡliɒnɪk ˈfaɪbə/ *noun* a nerve fibre which ends in a ganglion where it is linked in a synapse to a postganglionic fibre

preganglionic neurone /ˌpriːgæŋɡliˌɒnɪk ˈnjʊərəʊn/ *noun* a neurone which ends in a ganglion

pregnancy /ˈpregnənsi/ *noun* **1.** same as **gestation period 2.** the condition of being pregnant. Also called **cyesis**

pregnancy-associated hypertension /ˌpregnənsi əˌsəʊsieɪtɪd ˌhaɪpəˈtenʃən/ *noun* high blood pressure which is associated with pregnancy

pregnancy-induced hypertension /ˌpregnənsi ɪnˈdjuːsd ˌhaɪpəˈtenʃən/ *noun* Abbr **PIH**. same as **pre-eclampsia**

pregnancy test /ˈpregnənsi test/ *noun* a test to see if a woman is pregnant or not

pregnant /ˈpregnənt/ *adjective* with an unborn child in the uterus ○ *She is six months pregnant.*

prehepatic /ˌpriːhɪˈpætɪk/ *adjective* in front of or before the liver

prehepatic bilirubin /ˌpriːhɪˌpætɪk bɪliˈruːbɪn/ *noun* bilirubin in plasma before it passes through the liver

prehepatic jaundice /ˌpriːhɪˌpætɪk ˈdʒɔːndɪs/ *noun* same as **haemolytic jaundice**

prem /prem/ (*informal*) *adjective* same as **premature** ■ *noun* a premature baby

premature /ˈpremətʃə/ *adjective* before the expected or desirable time ○ *The baby was five weeks premature.*

COMMENT: Babies can survive even if born several weeks premature. Even babies weighing less than one kilo at birth can survive in an incubator, and develop healthily.

premature baby /ˌpremətʃə ˈbeɪbi/ *noun* a baby born earlier than 37 weeks from conception, or weighing less than 2.5kg, but capable of independent life

premature birth /ˌpremətʃə ˈbɜːθ/ *noun* the birth of a baby earlier than 37 weeks from conception

premature ejaculation /ˌpremətʃə ɪˌdʒækjʊˈleɪʃ(ə)n/ *noun* a situation in which a man ejaculates too early during sexual intercourse

premature labour /ˌpremətʃə ˈleɪbə/ *noun* the condition of starting to give birth earlier than 37 weeks from conception ○ *After the accident she went into premature labour.*

prematurely /ˈpremətʃʊəli/ *adverb* before the expected or desirable time ○ *The baby was born two weeks prematurely.* ○ *A large number of people die prematurely from ischaemic heart disease.*

prematurity /ˌpreməˈtʃʊərɪti/ *noun* a situation in which something occurs before the expected or desirable time

premed /ˈpriːmed/ *noun* a stage of being given en premedication (*informal*) ○ *The patient is in premed.*

premedical /priːˈmedɪk(ə)l/ *adjective* referring to the studies that a person must complete before entering medical school

premedication /ˌpriːmedɪˈkeɪʃ(ə)n/, **premedicant drug** /priːˌmedɪkənt ˈdrʌg/ *noun* a drug given before an operation in order to block the parasympathetic nervous system and prevent vomiting during the operation, e.g. a sedative

premenopausal /ˌpriːmenəˈpɔːz(ə)l/ *adjective* referring to the stage in a woman's life just before the start of the menopause

premenstrual /priːˈmenstruəl/ *adjective* happening before menstruation

premenstrual syndrome /priːˌmenstruəl ˈsɪndrəʊm/, **premenstrual tension** /priːˌmenstruəl ˈtenʃən/ *noun* nervous stress experienced by a woman for one or two weeks before a menstrual period starts. Abbr **PMS, PMT**

premolar /priːˈməʊlə/ *noun* a tooth with two points, situated between the canines and the first proper molar. See illustration at TEETH in Supplement

prenatal /priːˈneɪt(ə)l/ *adjective* during the period between conception and childbirth

prenatal diagnosis /priːˌneɪt(ə)l ˌdaɪəgˈnəʊsɪs/ *noun* same as **antenatal diagnosis**

pre-op /priː ˈɒp/ *adjective* same as **preoperative** (*informal*)

preoperative /priː'ɒp(ə)rətɪv/ *adjective* during the period before a surgical operation

preoperatively /priː'ɒp(ə)rətɪvli/ *adverb* before a surgical operation

preoperative medication /priː,ɒp(ə)rətɪv ,medɪ'keɪʃən/ *noun* a drug given before an operation, e.g. a sedative

preovulatory /priː'ɒvjələt(ə)ri/ *adjective* referring to the 6 to 13 days in the menstrual cycle between menstruation and ovulation

prep /prep/ (*informal*) *noun* same as **preparation** ○ *The prep is finished, so the patient can be taken to the operating theatre.* ■ *verb* same as **prepare** ○ *Has the patient been prepped?* (NOTE: **prepping – prepped**)

PREP *abbr* post-registration education and practice

preparation /,prepə'reɪʃ(ə)n/ *noun* **1.** the act of getting a person ready for a surgical operation. Also called **prep 2.** a medicine or liquid containing a drug ○ *He was given a preparation containing an antihistamine.*

prepare /prɪ'peə/ *verb* **1.** to get something or someone ready ○ *Six rooms in the hospital were prepared for the accident victims.* ○ *The nurses were preparing him for the operation.* **2.** to make something ○ *He prepared a soothing linctus.*

prepatellar bursitis /,priːpə,telə bɜː'saɪtɪs/ *noun* a condition in which the fluid sac at the knee becomes inflamed, caused by kneeling on hard surfaces. Also called **housemaid's knee**

prepubertal /priː'pjuːbət(ə)l/ *adjective* referring to the period before puberty

prepuberty /priː'pjuːbəti/ *noun* the period before puberty

prepubescent /,priːpjuː'besənt/ *adjective* referring to a person at the stage of life just before puberty

prepuce /'priːpjuːs/ *noun* same as **foreskin**

presby- /prezbi/ *prefix* same as **presbyo-** (*used before vowels*)

presbyacusis /,prezbi'kuːsɪs/ *noun* a condition in which an elderly person's hearing fails gradually, through to degeneration of the internal ear

presbyo- /prezbiəʊ/ *prefix* referring to the last stages of the natural life span

presbyopia /,prezbi'əʊpiə/ *noun* a condition in which an elderly person's sight fails gradually, through hardening of the lens

prescribe /prɪ'skraɪb/ *verb* to give instructions for a person to get a specific dosage of a drug or a specific form of therapeutic treatment ○ *The doctor prescribed a course of antibiotics.* (NOTE: **prescribing – prescribed**)

prescribed disease /prɪ,skraɪbd dɪ'ziːz/ *noun* an illness caused by the type of work a person does which is on an annually reviewed official list, entitling the person to claim bene-

fit. Examples are deafness, pneumoconiosis and RSI.

prescribed illness /prɪ,skraɪbd 'ɪlnəs/ *noun* an illness developing in the workplace from exposure to chemicals, e.g. mercury poisoning, or to dangerous activities, e.g. decompression sickness

prescribing analyses and cost /prɪ ,skraɪbɪŋ ə,næləsiːz ənd 'kɒst/ *plural noun* data on the prescribing of drugs in primary care. Abbr **PACT**

prescription /prɪ'skrɪpʃən/ *noun* an order written by a doctor to a pharmacist asking for a drug to be prepared and given or sold to a person

prescription drug /prɪ'skrɪpʃən drʌg/ *noun* a drug which can only be obtained by having a legally valid prescription

presence /'prez(ə)ns/ *noun* the act or fact of being there ○ *Tests showed the presence of sugar in the urine.*

presenile /priː'siːnaɪl/ *adjective* **1.** prematurely showing the effects of advanced age **2.** referring to a condition which affects people of early or middle age but has characteristics of a more advanced age

presenile dementia /priː,siːnaɪl dɪ'menʃə/ *noun* mental degeneration affecting adults of around 40–60 years of age (*dated*)

COMMENT: Patients used to be diagnosed with presenile dementia if they showed symptoms of dementia and were under the age of 65, and senile dementia if over 65. However, the terms are no longer often used and instead the type of dementia is used for diagnostic purposes, e.g. Alzheimer's disease, multi-infarct or vascular

presenility /,priːsə'nɪlɪti/ *noun* the ageing of the body or brain before the expected time, with a person showing symptoms which are usually associated with people of very advanced years

present *verb* /prɪ'zent/ **1.** (*of a patient*) to show particular symptoms ○ *The patient presented with severe chest pains.* **2.** (*of a symptom*) to be present ○ *The doctors' first task is to relieve the presenting symptoms.* ○ *The condition may also present in a baby.* **3.** (*of a baby*) to appear in the vaginal channel ■ *adjective* / 'prez(ə)nt/ currently existing in a place ○ *All the symptoms of the disease are present.*

'…chlamydia in the male commonly presents a urethritis characterized by dysuria' [*Journal of American College Health*]

'26 patients were selected from the outpatient department on grounds of disabling breathlessness present for at least five years' [*Lancet*]

'…sickle cell chest syndrome is a common complication of sickle cell disease, presenting with chest pain, fever and leucocytosis' [*British Medical Journal*]

'…a 24 year-old woman presents with an influenza-like illness of five days' duration' [*British Journal of Hospital Medicine*]

'...the presenting symptoms of Crohn's disease may be extremely variable' [*New Zealand Medical Journal*]

presentation /ˌprez(ə)n'teɪʃ(ə)n/ *noun* the way in which a baby will be born, in respect of the part of the baby's body which will appear first in the vaginal channel

presenting part /prɪ'zentɪŋ pɑːt/ *noun* the part of a baby which appears first during birth

preservation /ˌprezə'veɪʃ(ə)n/ *noun* the keeping of a tissue sample or donor organ in good condition

preserve /prɪ'zɜːv/ *verb* to keep something from rotting (NOTE: **preserving – preserved**)

press /pres/ *verb* to push or squeeze something ○ *The tumour is pressing against a nerve.*

pressor /'presə/ *adjective* 1. referring to a nerve which increases the action of part of the body 2. raising blood pressure

pressure /'preʃə/ *noun* 1. the action of squeezing or forcing something 2. the force of something on its surroundings 3. mental or physical stress caused by external events

pressure area /'preʃər ˌeəriə/ *noun* an area of the body where a bone is near the surface of the skin, so that if the skin is pressed the circulation will be cut off

pressure bandage /'preʃə ˌbændɪdʒ/ *noun* a bandage which presses on a part of the body

pressure index /'preʃər ˌɪndeks/ *noun* a method for determining the extent of obstruction to the artery in the leg by measuring the blood pressure in the arms and legs and then dividing the systolic pressure in the leg by that in the arm. Abbr **PI**

pressure point /'preʃə pɔɪnt/ *noun* a place where an artery crosses over a bone, so that the blood can be cut off by pressing with the finger

presynaptic /ˌpriːsɪ'næptɪk/ *adjective* situated in front of a synapse

presynaptic axon /ˌprisɪnæptɪk 'nɜːv/ *noun* a nerve leading to one side of a synapse

presystole /priː'sɪstəli/ *noun* the period before systole in the cycle of heartbeats

preterm birth /ˌpriː'tɜːm bɜːθ/ *noun* the birth of a baby before 37 completed weeks of pregnancy, which presents a greater risk of serious health problems (NOTE: About 12 per cent of births in the UK are preterm births.)

prevalence /'prevələns/ *noun* the number of cases of a disease in a specific place at a specific time ○ *the prevalence of malaria in some tropical countries* ○ *the prevalence of cases of malnutrition in large towns* ○ *a high prevalence of renal disease*

prevalent /'prevələnt/ *adjective* common in comparison to something else ○ *The disease is prevalent in some African countries.* ○ *The condition is more prevalent in the cold winter months.*

prevent /prɪ'vent/ *verb* to stop something from happening, or a person from doing something ○ *The treatment is given to prevent the patient's condition from getting worse.* ○ *Doctors are trying to prevent the spread of the outbreak of Legionnaires' disease.*

preventative /prɪ'ventətɪv/ *adjective* same as **preventive**

prevention /prɪ'venʃən/ *noun* action to stop something happening

preventive /prɪ'ventɪv/ *adjective* referring to an action taken to stop something happening, especially to stop a disease or infection from spreading ○ *preventive treatment* ○ *preventive action*

preventive measure /prɪˌventɪv 'meʒə/ *noun* an action taken to prevent a disease from occurring or spreading

COMMENT: Preventive measures include immunisation, vaccination, sterilisation, quarantine and improving standards of housing and sanitation. Health education also has an important role to play in the prevention of disease.

preventive medicine /prɪˌventɪv 'med(ə)s(ə)n/ *noun* action carried out to stop disease from occurring, e.g. by education in health-related issues, immunisation and screening for known diseases

prevertebral /priː'vɜːtɪbr(ə)l/ *adjective* situated in front of the spinal column or a vertebra

Priadel /'praɪədel/ a trade name for lithium

priapism /'praɪəpɪz(ə)m/ *noun* an erection of the penis without sexual stimulus, caused by a blood clot in the tissue of the penis, injury to the spinal cord or stone in the urinary bladder

prick /prɪk/ *verb* to make a small hole in something with a sharp point ○ *The nurse pricked the patient's finger to take a blood sample.*

prickle cell /'prɪk(ə)l sel/ *noun* a cell with many processes connecting it to other cells, found in the inner layer of the epidermis

prickly heat /'prɪkli hiːt/ *noun* same as **miliaria**

-pril /prɪl/ *suffix* used for ACE inhibitors ○ *Captopril*

prilocaine /'praɪləkeɪn/ *noun* a local anaesthetic used especially in dentistry

primaquine /'praɪməkwiːn/ *noun* a synthetically produced drug used in the treatment of malaria

primary /'praɪməri/ *adjective* 1. happening first, and leading to something else 2. most important 3. referring to a condition which comes first and is followed by another. Compare **secondary**

primary amenorrhoea /ˌpraɪməri ˌeɪmenə'riːə/ *noun* a condition in which a woman has never had menstrual periods

primary biliary cirrhosis /ˌpraɪməri ˌbɪliəri sɪˈrəʊsɪs/ *noun* cirrhosis of the liver caused by autoimmune disease

primary bronchi /ˌpraɪməri ˈbrɒŋkiː/ *plural noun* same as **main bronchi**

primary care /ˌpraɪməri ˈkeə/ *noun* in the UK, health services offered directly to individuals by GPs, dentists, opticians and other health professionals who may also refer a patient on to specialists for further treatment. Also called **primary health care, primary medical care**. Compare **secondary care, tertiary care**

'…primary care is largely concerned with clinical management of individual patients, while community medicine tends to view the whole population as its patient' [*Journal of the Royal College of General Practitioners*]

primary care group /ˌpraɪməri ˈkeə gruːp/ *noun* an organisation responsible for overseeing the provision of primary healthcare and the commissioning of secondary care in a district. Key members include GPs, community nurses, social services and lay members. Abbr **PCG**

primary care team /ˌpraɪməri ˈkeə tiːm/ *noun* same as **primary health care team**

primary care trust /ˌpraɪməri ˈkeə trʌst/ *noun* in the UK, the top level of the primary care group with extra responsibilities such as direct employment of community staff. Abbr **PCT**

primary cartilaginous joint /ˌpraɪməri ˌkɑːtəˈlædʒɪnəs dʒɔɪnt/ *noun* a temporary joint where the intervening cartilage is converted into adult bone

primary complex /ˌpraɪməri ˈkɒmpleks/ *noun* the first lymph node to be infected by tuberculosis

primary dysmenorrhoea /ˌpraɪməri ˌdɪsmenəˈriːə/ *noun* dysmenorrhoea which occurs at the first menstrual period. Also called **essential dysmenorrhoea**

primary haemorrhage /ˌpraɪməri ˈhem(ə)rɪdʒ/ *noun* bleeding which occurs immediately after an injury has taken place

primary health care /ˌpraɪməri ˈhelθ keə/ *noun* same as **primary care**

'…among primary health care services, 1.5% of all GP consultations are due to coronary heart disease' [*Health Services Journal*]

primary health care team /ˌpraɪməri ˈhelθ keə ˌtiːm/ *noun* a group of professional medical workers who have first contact with someone needing medical attention and are responsible for delivering a range of health care services. Abbr **PHCT**

primary medical care /ˌpraɪməri ˈmedɪk(ə)l keə/ *noun* same as **primary care**

primary nurse /ˌpraɪməri ˈnɜːs/ *noun* a nurse who is responsible for planning a person's nursing care in consultation with that person and his or her family. In the absence of the primary nurse, associate nurses provide care based on the plan designed by the primary nurse.

primary nursing /ˌpraɪməri ˈnɜːsɪŋ/ *noun* a model of nursing that involves the delivery of comprehensive, continuous, co-ordinated and individualised patient care through a primary nurse, who has autonomy, accountability and authority in relation to his or her patient's care

primary peritonitis /ˌpraɪməri ˌperɪtəˈnaɪtɪs/ *noun* peritonitis caused by direct infection from the blood or the lymph

primary tooth /ˈpraɪməri tuːθ/ *noun* any one of the first twenty teeth which develop in children between about six months and two-and-a-half years of age, and are replaced by the permanent teeth at around the age of six. Also called **milk tooth, deciduous tooth**

primary tubercle /ˌpraɪməri ˈtjuːbək(ə)l/ *noun* the first infected spot where tuberculosis starts to infect a lung

primary tuberculosis /ˌpraɪməri tjuːˌbɜːkjʊˈləʊsɪs/ *noun* a person's first infection with tuberculosis

primary tumour /ˌpraɪməri ˈtjuːmə/ *noun* a site of the original malignant growth from which cancer spreads

prime /praɪm/ *adjective* 1. of the greatest importance or the highest rank 2. of the highest quality ◼ *noun* the best state or period of something, especially the most active and enjoyable period in adult life ◼ *verb* to make something ready for use, or to become ready for use (NOTE: **priming – primed**)

prime mover /praɪm ˈmuːvə/ *noun* 1. same as **agonist** 2. somebody or something which has the most influence over the starting of a process or activity

primigravida /ˌpraɪmɪˈɡrævɪdə/, **primigravid patient** /ˌpraɪmɪˈɡrævɪd ˈpeɪʃ(ə)nt/ *noun* a woman who is pregnant for the first time (NOTE: The plural is **primigravidas** or **primigravidae**.)

primipara /praɪˈmɪpərə/ *noun* a woman who has given birth to one child. Also called **unipara** (NOTE: The plural is **primiparas** or **primiparae**.)

primordial /praɪˈmɔːdiəl/ *adjective* in the very first stage of development

primordial follicle /praɪˌmɔːdiəl ˈfɒlɪk(ə)l/ *noun* the first stage of development of an ovarian follicle

principle /ˈprɪnsɪp(ə)l/ *noun* 1. a rule or theory 2. a standard of ethical behaviour

P-R interval /ˌpiː ˈɑːr ˌɪntəv(ə)l/ *noun* the time recorded on an electrocardiogram between the start of atrial activity and ventricular activity

prion /ˈpriːɒn/ *noun* a particle of protein which contains no nucleic acid, does not trigger an immune response and is not destroyed by extreme heat or cold. Prions are considered to be the agents responsible for scrapie, BSE, and Creutzfeldt-Jakob disease.

priority despatch /praɪˈɒrəti dɪˌspætʃ/ noun the process of talking to people who need medical help on the telephone in order to make sure that ambulances are sent to the most urgent cases first

priority matrix /praɪˈɒrəti ˌmeɪtrɪks/ noun a way of trying to make sure that each community has a fair number of services for its particular health needs

private /ˈpraɪvət/ adjective not supported by government or paid for by the National Health Service ○ He runs a private clinic for alcoholics.

private hospital /ˌpraɪvət ˈhɒspɪt(ə)l/ noun a hospital which takes only paying patients

privately /ˈpraɪvətli/ adverb by a private practitioner or company, not by the National Health Service ○ She decided to have the operation done privately.

private parts /ˈpraɪvət pɑːts/ plural noun the genital area (informal) Also called **privates**

private patient /ˌpraɪvət ˈpeɪʃ(ə)nt/ noun a patient who is paying for treatment and who is not being treated under the National Health Service

private practice /ˌpraɪvət ˈpræktɪs/ noun the services of a doctor, surgeon or dentist which are paid for by the patients themselves or by a medical insurance company, but not by the National Health Service

privates /ˈpraɪvəts/ plural noun same as **private parts** (informal)

p.r.n. adverb (written on a prescription) as and when required. Full form **pro re nata**

pro- /prəʊ/ prefix before or in front of

probang /ˈprəʊbæŋ/ noun a surgical instrument like a long rod with a brush at one end, formerly used to test and find strictures in the oesophagus and to push foreign bodies into the stomach

probe /prəʊb/ noun 1. an instrument used to explore inside a cavity or wound 2. a device inserted into a medium to obtain information ■ verb to investigate the inside of something ○ The surgeon probed the wound with a scalpel. (NOTE: **probing – probed**)

problem /ˈprɒbləm/ noun 1. something which is difficult to find an answer to ○ Scientists are trying to find a solution to the problem of drug-related disease. 2. a medical disorder ○ heart problems 3. an addiction to something ○ has a drug problem

problem child /ˈprɒbləm tʃaɪld/ noun a child who is difficult to control

problem drinking /ˌprɒbləm ˈdrɪŋkɪŋ/ noun alcoholism or heavy drinking which has a bad effect on a person's behaviour or work

problem-oriented record /ˌprɒbləm ˌɔːriəntɪd ˈrekɔːd/ noun a record of patient care which links patients' clinical data with their problems, so that all aspects of the care process are focused on resolving those problems

problem-solving approach /ˈprɒbləm ˌsɒlvɪŋ əˌprəʊtʃ/ noun the provision of nursing care based on assessment, problem identification (nursing diagnosis), planning implementation (nursing intervention) and evaluation

procedure /prəˈsiːdʒə/ noun 1. a standard way of doing something 2. a type of treatment ○ The hospital has developed some new procedures for treating Parkinson's disease. 3. a treatment given at one time ○ We are hoping to increase the number of procedures carried out per day.

'…disposable items now available for medical and nursing procedures range from cheap syringes to expensive cardiac pacemakers' [Nursing Times]

'…the electromyograms and CT scans were done as outpatient procedures' [Southern Medical Journal]

process /ˈprəʊses/ noun 1. a technical or scientific action ○ A new process for testing serum samples has been developed in the research laboratory. 2. a projecting part of the body ■ verb 1. to deal with a person or thing according to a standard procedure 2. to examine or test samples ○ The blood samples are being processed by the laboratory.

'…the nursing process serves to divide overall patient care into that part performed by nurses and that performed by the other professions' [Nursing Times]

prochlorperazine /ˌprəʊklɔːˈperəziːn/ noun a drug used to control nausea and vomiting, and to reduce the symptoms of Ménière's disease, migraine and anxiety

procidentia /ˌprəʊsɪˈdenʃə/ noun movement of an organ downwards

proct- /prɒkt/ prefix same as **procto-** (used before vowels)

proctalgia /prɒkˈtældʒə/ noun pain in the lower rectum or anus, caused by neuralgia

proctalgia fugax /prɒkˌtældʒə ˈfjuːgæks/ noun a condition in which a person has sudden pains in the rectum during the night, usually relieved by eating or drinking

proctatresia /ˌprɒktəˈtriːziə/ noun a condition in which the anus does not have an opening. Also called **imperforate anus**

proctectasia /prɒktekˈteɪziə/ noun a condition in which the rectum or anus is dilated because of continued constipation

proctectomy /prɒkˈtektəmi/ noun a surgical operation to remove the rectum (NOTE: The plural is **proctectomies**.)

proctitis /prɒkˈtaɪtɪs/ noun inflammation of the rectum

procto- /prɒktəʊ/ prefix the anus or rectum

proctocele /ˈprɒktəsiːl/ noun same as **rectocele**

proctoclysis /prɒk'tɒkləsɪs/ *noun* the introduction of a lot of fluid into the rectum slowly

proctocolectomy /ˌprɒktəʊkɒ'lektəmi/ *noun* a surgical operation to remove the rectum and the colon (NOTE: The plural is **proctocolectomies.**)

proctocolitis /ˌprɒktəkə'laɪtɪs/ *noun* inflammation of the rectum and part of the colon

proctodynia /ˌprɒktə'dɪniə/ *noun* a sensation of pain in the anus

proctogram /'prɒktəgræm/ *noun* an X-ray photograph of the rectum taken after a contrast agent is introduced

proctologist /prɒk'tɒlədʒɪst/ *noun* a specialist in proctology

proctology /prɒk'tɒlədʒi/ *noun* the scientific study of the rectum and anus and their associated diseases

proctorrhaphy /prɒk'tɔːrəfi/ *noun* a surgical operation to stitch up a tear in the rectum or anus (NOTE: The plural is **proctorrhaphies.**)

proctoscope /'prɒktəskəʊp/ *noun* a surgical instrument consisting of a long tube with a light in the end, used to examine the rectum

proctoscopy /prɒk'tɒskəpi/ *noun* an examination of the rectum using a proctoscope (NOTE: The plural is **proctoscopies.**)

proctosigmoiditis /ˌprɒktəʊˌsɪgmɔɪ'daɪtɪs/ *noun* inflammation of the rectum and the sigmoid colon

proctotomy /prɒk'tɒtəmi/ *noun* 1. a surgical operation to divide a structure of the rectum or anus 2. an opening of an imperforate anus (NOTE: [all senses] The plural is **proctotomies.**)

prodromal /prəʊ'drəʊml/ *adjective* occurring between the appearance of the first symptoms of a disease and the major effect, e.g. a fever or rash

prodromal rash /prəʊˌdrəʊm(ə)l 'ræʃ/ *noun* a rash which appears as a symptom of a disease before the major rash

prodrome /'prəʊdrəʊm/, **prodroma** /prəʊ'drəʊmə/ *noun* an early symptom of an attack of a disease

'…in classic migraine a prodrome is followed by an aura, then a headache, and finally a recovery phase. The prodrome may not be recognised' [*British Journal of Hospital Medicine*]

produce /prə'djuːs/ *verb* to make or cause something ○ *The drug produces a sensation of dizziness.* ○ *Doctors are worried by the side-effects produced by the new painkiller.* (NOTE: **producing – produced**)

product /'prɒdʌkt/ *noun* 1. something which is produced 2. a result or effect of a process

productive cough /prəˌdʌktɪv 'kɒf/ *noun* a cough where phlegm is produced

proenzyme /prəʊ'enzaɪm/ *noun* the first mature form of an enzyme, before it develops into an active enzyme. Also called **zymogen**

profession /prə'feʃ(ə)n/ *noun* 1. a type of job for which special training is needed 2. all

people working in a specialised type of employment for which they have been trained ○ *They are both doctors by profession.*

professional /prə'feʃ(ə)n(ə)l/ *adjective* referring to a profession

professional body /prəˌfeʃ(ə)n(ə)l 'bɒdi/ *noun* an organisation which acts for all the members of a profession

Professional Conduct Committee /prəˌfeʃ(ə)n(ə)l 'kɒndʌkt kəˌmɪti/ *noun* a committee of the General Medical Council which decides on cases of professional misconduct. Abbr **PCC**

professional misconduct /prəˌfeʃ(ə)n(ə)l mɪs'kɒndʌkt/ *noun* actions which are considered to be wrong by the body which regulates a profession, e.g. an action by a doctor which is considered wrong by the Professional Conduct Committee of the General Medical Council

profile /'prəʊfaɪl/ *noun* 1. a brief description of the characteristics of a person or thing 2. a set of data, usually in graph or table form, which indicates to what extent something has the same characteristics as a group tested or considered standard 3. the amount that other people notice somebody or something ■ *verb* to give a short description or assessment of somebody or something (NOTE: **profiling – profiled**)

profound /prə'faʊnd/ *adjective* very great or serious ○ *a profound impairment of the immune system*

profunda /prə'fʌndə/ *adjective* referring to blood vessels which lie deep in tissues

profundaplasty /prə'fʌndəplæsti/ *noun* a surgical operation to widen a junction of the femoral artery, in order to relieve narrowing by atherosclerosis (NOTE: The plural is **profundaplasties.**)

profuse /prə'fjuːs/ *adjective* existing in very large quantities ○ *fever accompanied by profuse sweating* ○ *pains with profuse internal bleeding*

progeny /'prɒdʒəni/ *noun* a person's child or children (NOTE: Takes a singular or plural verb.)

progeria /prəʊ'dʒɪəriə/ *noun* a condition of premature ageing. Also called **Hutchinson-Gilford syndrome**

progestational /prəʊˌdʒes'teɪʃ(ə)nəl/ *adjective* referring to the stage of the menstrual cycle after ovulation when progesterone is produced

progesterone /prəʊ'dʒestərəʊn/ *noun* a hormone which is produced in the second part of the menstrual cycle by the corpus luteum and which stimulates the formation of the placenta if an ovum is fertilised (NOTE: Progesterone is also produced by the placenta itself.)

progestogen /prə'dʒestədʒən/ *noun* any substance which has the same effect as progesterone

COMMENT: Because natural progesterones prevent ovulation during pregnancy, synthetically produced progestogens are used to make contraceptive pills.

prognathic jaw /prɒɡˌnæθɪk 'dʒɔː/ *noun* a jaw which protrudes further than the other

prognathism /'prɒɡnəθɪz(ə)m/ *noun* a condition in which one jaw, especially the lower jaw, or both jaws protrude

prognosis /prɒɡ'nəʊsɪs/ *noun* an opinion of how a disease or disorder will develop ○ *This cancer has a prognosis of about two years.* ○ *The prognosis is not good.* (NOTE: The plural is **prognoses**.)

prognostic /prɒɡ'nɒstɪk/ *adjective* referring to a prognosis

prognostic test /prɒɡˌnɒstɪk 'test/ *noun* a test to suggest how a disease will develop or how long a person will survive after an operation

programme /'prəʊɡræm/ *noun* a series of medical treatments given in a set way at set times ○ *The doctor prescribed a programme of injections.* ○ *She took a programme of steroid treatment.* (NOTE: The US spelling is **program**.)

progress *noun* /'prəʊɡres/ **1.** development and improvement ○ *Progress has been made in cutting waiting times.* **2.** the way in which a person is becoming well ○ *The doctors seem pleased that she has made such good progress since her operation.* ■ *verb* /prəʊ'ɡres/ **1.** to develop and improve, or to continue to do well ○ *The patient is progressing well.* **2.** to move to a more advanced stage ○ *As the disease progressed, he spent more and more time sleeping.*

progression /prəʊ'ɡreʃ(ə)n/ *noun* development ○ *The progression of the disease was swift.*

progressive /prə'ɡresɪv/ *adjective* developing all the time ○ *Alzheimer's disease is a progressive disorder which sees a gradual decline in intellectual functioning.*

progressive deafness /prəˌɡresɪv 'de↓fnəs/ *noun* a condition, common in people as they get older, in which a person gradually becomes more and more deaf

progressively /prəʊ'ɡresɪvli/ *adverb* more and more ○ *He became progressively more disabled.*

progressive muscular atrophy /prəˌɡresɪv ˌmʌskjʊlə 'ætrəfi/ *noun* muscular dystrophy, with progressive weakening of the muscles, particularly in the pelvic and shoulder girdles

proguanil /prəʊ'ɡwænɪl/ *noun* a drug used in the prevention and treatment of malaria

proinsulin /prəʊ'ɪnsʊlɪn/ *noun* a substance produced by the pancreas, then converted to insulin

project /prə'dʒekt/ *verb* to protrude or stick out

projection /prə'dʒekʃən/ *noun* **1.** a part of the body which sticks out or stands out. Also called **prominence**. Compare **promontory 2.** (*in psychology*) mental action in which a person blames another person for his or her own faults

projection tract /prə'dʒekʃ(ə)n trækt/ *noun* fibres connecting the cerebral cortex with the lower parts of the brain and spinal cord

prolactin /prəʊ'læktɪn/ *noun* a hormone secreted by the pituitary gland which stimulates the production of milk. Also called **lactogenic hormone**

prolapse /'prəʊlæps/ *noun* a condition in which an organ has moved downwards out of its usual position ■ *verb* to move downwards out of the usual position (NOTE: **prolapsing – prolapsed**)

prolapsed intervertebral disc /prəʊ ˌlæpsd ˌɪntəˌvɜːtəbrəl 'dɪsk/ *noun* a condition in which an intervertebral disc becomes displaced or where the soft centre of a disc passes through the hard cartilage of the exterior and presses onto a nerve. Abbr **PID**. Also called **slipped disc**

prolapse of the rectum /ˌprəʊlæps əv ðə 'rektəm/ *noun* a condition in which mucous membrane of the rectum moves downwards and passes through the anus

prolapse of the uterus /ˌprəʊlæps əv ðə 'juːtərəs/, **prolapse of the womb** /ˌprəʊlæps əv ðə 'wuːm/ *noun* a movement of the uterus downwards due to weakening of the structures of the pelvic floor, e.g. because of age or a difficult childbirth. Also called **metroptosis, prolapsed uterus, uterine prolapse**

proliferate /prə'lɪfəreɪt/ *verb* to produce many similar cells or parts, and so grow (NOTE: **proliferating – proliferated**)

proliferation /prəˌlɪfə'reɪʃ(ə)n/ *noun* the process of proliferating

proliferative /prə'lɪfərətɪv/ *adjective* multiplying

proliferative phase /prə'lɪfərətɪv feɪz/ *noun* a period when a disease is spreading fast

proline /'prəʊlɪn/ *noun* an amino acid found in proteins, especially in collagen

prolong /prə'lɒŋ/ *verb* to make something last longer ○ *The treatment prolonged her life by three years.*

prolonged /prə'lɒŋd/ *adjective* very long ○ *She had to undergo a prolonged course of radiation treatment.*

promethazine /prəʊ'meθəziːn/ *noun* an antihistamine drug used in the treatment of allergies and motion sickness

prominence /'prɒmɪnəns/ *noun* a part of the body which sticks out or stands out. Also called **projection**. Compare **promontory**

prominent /'prɒmɪnənt/ *adjective* standing out, very visible ○ *She had a prominent scar* *on her neck which she wanted to have removed.*

promontory /ˈprɒmənt(ə)ri/ *noun* a section of an organ, especially the middle ear and sacrum which stands out above the rest. Compare **projection, prominence**

promote /prəˈməʊt/ *verb* **1.** to help something to take place ○ *The drug is used to promote blood clotting.* **2.** to raise a person to a more senior job or a higher position (NOTE: **promoting – promoted**)

pronate /ˈprəʊneɪt/ *verb* **1.** to lie face downwards **2.** to turn the hand so that palm faces downwards (NOTE: **pronating – pronated**)

pronation /prəʊˈneɪʃ(ə)n/ *noun* the act of turning the hand round so that the palm faces downwards. Opposite **supination**. See illustration at ANATOMICAL TERMS in Supplement

pronator /prəʊˈneɪtə/ *noun* a muscle which makes the hand turn face downwards

prone /prəʊn/ *adjective* **1.** lying face downwards. Opposite **supine 2.** referring to the arm with the palm facing downwards

pronounced /prəˈnaʊnst/ *adjective* very obvious or marked ○ *She has a pronounced limp.*

propagate /ˈprɒpəɡeɪt/ *verb* to multiply something, or cause something to multiply (NOTE: **propagating – propagated**)

propagation /ˌprɒpəˈɡeɪʃ(ə)n/ *noun* an act of causing something to spread or multiply

properdin /ˈprəʊpədɪn/ *noun* protein in blood plasma which can destroy Gram-negative bacteria and neutralise viruses when acting together with magnesium

prophase /ˈprəʊfeɪz/ *noun* the first stage of mitosis when the chromosomes are visible as long thin double threads

prophylactic /ˌprɒfəˈlæktɪk/ *noun* a substance which helps to prevent the development of a disease ■ *adjective* preventive

prophylaxis /ˌprɒfəˈlæksɪs/ *noun* **1.** the prevention of disease **2.** a preventive treatment (NOTE: [all senses] The plural is **prophylaxes.**)

proportion /prəˈpɔːʃ(ə)n/ *noun* a quantity of something, especially as compared to the whole ○ *A high proportion of cancers can be treated by surgery.* ○ *The proportion of outpatients to inpatients is increasing.*

'...the target cells for adult myeloid leukaemia are located in the bone marrow, and there is now evidence that a substantial proportion of childhood leukaemias also arise in the bone marrow' [*British Medical Journal*]

propranolol /prəʊˈpænəlɒl/ *noun* a drug that slows heart rate and heart output, used in the treatment of angina pectoris, irregular heart rhythms, migraine and high blood pressure

proprietary /prəˈpraɪət(ə)ri/ *adjective* belonging to a commercial company

proprietary medicine /prəˌpraɪət(ə)ri ˈmed(ə)s(ə)n/, **proprietary drug** /prə-

,praɪət(ə)ri ˈdrʌɡ/ *noun* a drug which is sold under a trade name. ◊ **patent medicine**

proprietary name /prəˌpraɪət(ə)ri ˈneɪm/ *noun* a trade name for a drug

proprioception /ˌprəʊpriəˈsepʃən/ *noun* the reaction of nerves to body movements and the relaying of information about movements to the brain

proprioceptive /ˌprəʊpriəˈseptɪv/ *adjective* referring to sensory impulses from the joints, muscles and tendons, which relay information about body movements to the brain

proprioceptor /ˌprəʊpriəˈseptə/ *noun* the end of a sensory nerve which reacts to stimuli from muscles and tendons as they move

proptosis /prɒpˈtəʊsɪs/ *noun* forward displacement of the eyeball

prop up /ˌprɒp ˈʌp/ *verb* to support a person, e.g. with pillows (NOTE: **propping up – propped up**)

prospective /prəˈspektɪv/ *adjective* **1.** applying to the future. ◊ **retrospective 2.** following what happens to selected patients

prostaglandin /ˌprɒstəˈɡlændɪn/ *noun* any of a class of unsaturated fatty acids found in all mammals which control smooth muscle contraction, inflammation and body temperature, are associated with the sensation of pain and have an effect on the nervous system, blood pressure and in particular the uterus at menstruation

prostate /ˈprɒsteɪt/ *noun* same as **prostate gland** (NOTE: Do not confuse with **prostrate**.) □ **prostate trouble** inflammation or enlargement of the prostate gland (*informal*)

prostate cancer /ˈprɒsteɪt ˌkænsə/ *noun* a malignant tumour of the prostate gland, found especially in men over 55

prostatectomy /ˌprɒstəˈtektəmi/ *noun* a surgical operation to remove all or part of the prostate gland (NOTE: The plural is **prostatectomies.**)

prostate gland /ˈprɒˌsteɪt ɡlænd/ *noun* an O-shaped gland in males which surrounds the urethra below the bladder and secretes a fluid containing enzymes into the sperm. See illustration at UROGENITAL SYSTEM (MALE) in Supplement. Also called **prostate**

COMMENT: As a man grows older, the prostate gland tends to enlarge and constrict the point at which the urethra leaves the bladder, making it difficult to pass urine.

prostatic /prɒˈstætɪk/ *adjective* referring to or belonging to the prostate gland

prostatic hypertrophy /prɒˌstætɪk haɪˈpɜːtrəfi/ *noun* an enlargement of the prostate gland

prostatic massage /prɒˌstætɪk ˈmæsɑːʒ/ *noun* the removal of fluid from the prostate gland through the rectum

prostatic urethra /prɒˌstætɪk jʊˈriːθrə/ *noun* a section of the urethra which passes through the prostate gland

prostatic utricle /prɒˌstætɪk ˈjuːtrɪk(ə)l/ *noun* a sac branching off the urethra as it passes through the prostate gland

prostatism /ˈprɒsteɪtɪz(ə)m/ *noun* a disorder of the prostate gland, especially enlargement that blocks or inhibits urine flow

prostatitis /ˌprɒstəˈtaɪtɪs/ *noun* inflammation of the prostate gland

prostatocystitis /ˌprɒstætəʊsɪˈstaɪtɪs/ *noun* inflammation of the prostatic urethra and the bladder

prostatorrhoea /ˌprɒstətəˈriːə/ *noun* discharge of fluid from the prostate gland (NOTE: The US spelling is **prostatorrhea**.)

prosthesis /prɒsˈθiːsɪs/ *noun* a device which is attached to the body to take the place of a part which is missing, e.g. an artificial leg or glass eye (NOTE: The plural is **prostheses**.)
'The average life span of a joint prosthesis is 10–15 years' [*British Journal of Nursing*]

prosthetic /prɒsˈθetɪk/ *adjective* replacing a part of the body which has been amputated or removed ○ *He was fitted with a prosthetic hand.*

prosthetic dentistry /prɒsˌθetɪk ˈdentɪstri/ *noun* the branch of dentistry which deals with replacing missing teeth parts of the jaw, and fitting dentures, bridges and crowns. Also called **prosthodontics**

prosthetics /prɒsˈθetɪks/ *noun* the study and making of prostheses

prosthetist /ˈprɒsθətɪst/ *noun* a qualified person who fits prostheses

prosthodontics /ˌprɒsθəˈdɒntɪks/ *noun* same as **prosthetic dentistry** (NOTE: Takes a singular verb.)

prostrate /ˈprɒstreɪt/ *adjective* lying face down (NOTE: Do not confuse with **prostate**.)

prostration /prɒˈstreɪʃ(ə)n/ *noun* extreme tiredness of body or mind

protamine /ˈprəʊtəmiːn/ *noun* a simple protein found in fish, used with insulin to slow down the insulin absorption rate

protanopia /ˌprəʊtəˈnəʊpiə/ *noun* same as **Daltonism**

protease /ˈprəʊtieɪz/ *noun* a digestive enzyme which breaks down protein in food by splitting the peptide link. Also called **proteolytic enzyme**

protect /prəˈtekt/ *verb* to keep a person or thing safe from harm ○ *The population must be protected against the spread of the virus.*

protection /prəˈtekʃən/ *noun* **1.** the act of keeping a person or thing safe from harm **2.** something which protects ○ *Children are vaccinated as a protection against disease.*

Protection of Children Act 1999 /prəˌtekʃən əv ˈtʃɪldrən ækt/ *noun* in the UK, an Act of Parliament to protect children by restricting the employment of certain nurses, teachers or other workers whose jobs bring them into contact with children, on grounds such as misconduct or health

protective /prəˈtektɪv/ *adjective* providing protection

protective isolation /prəˌtektɪv ˌaɪsəˈleɪʃ(ə)n/ *noun* a set of procedures used to protect people who have impaired resistance to infectious disease, e.g. those with leukaemia and lymphoma, Aids and graft patients. Also called **reverse isolation**

protein /ˈprəʊtiːn/ *noun* a nitrogen compound which is present in and is an essential part of all living cells in the body, formed by the linking of amino acids
COMMENT: Proteins are necessary for growth and repair of the body's tissue. They are mainly formed of carbon, nitrogen and oxygen in various combinations as amino acids. Foods such as beans, meat, eggs, fish and milk are rich in protein.

protein balance /ˈprəʊtiːn ˌbæləns/ *noun* a situation when the nitrogen intake in protein is equal to the excretion rate in the urine

protein-bound iodine /ˌprəʊtiːn baʊnd ˈaɪədiːn/ *noun* a compound of thyroxine and iodine

protein-bound iodine test /ˌprəʊtiːn baʊnd ˈaɪədiːn test/ *noun* a test to measure if the thyroid gland is producing adequate quantities of thyroxine. Abbr **PBI test**

protein deficiency /ˈprəʊtiːn dɪˌfɪʃ(ə)nsi/ *noun* a lack of enough proteins in the diet

proteinuria /ˌprəʊtiˈnjʊəriə/ *noun* a condition in which there are proteins in the urine

proteolysis /ˌprəʊtiˈɒləsɪs/ *noun* the breaking down of proteins in food into amino acids by enzymes

proteolytic /ˌprəʊtiəʊˈlɪtɪk/ *adjective* referring to proteolysis

proteolytic enzyme /ˌprəʊtiəʊlɪtɪk ˈenzaɪm/ *noun* same as **protease**

proteose /ˈprəʊtiəʊs/ *noun* a water-soluble compound formed during hydrolytic processes such as digestion

Proteus /ˈprəʊtiəs/ *noun* a genus of bacteria commonly found in the intestines

prothrombin /prəʊˈθrɒmbɪn/ *noun* a protein in blood which helps blood to coagulate and which needs Vitamin K to be effective. Also called **Factor II**

prothrombin time /prəʊˈθrɒmbɪn taɪm/ *noun* the time taken in Quick test for clotting to take place

proto- /prəʊtəʊ/ *prefix* first or at the beginning

protocol /ˈprəʊtəkɒl/ *noun* the set of instructions for the clinical management of a particular condition, including tests, surgery and drug treatments

proton pump /ˈprəʊtɒn pʌmp/ *noun* an enzyme system within the gastric mucosa that secretes gastric acids ○ *The drug acts on the proton pump mechanism.*

proton-pump inhibitor /ˈprəʊtɒn pʌmp ɪnˌhɪbɪtə/ *noun* a drug which suppresses the final stage of gastric acid secretion by the proton pump in the gastric mucosa

protopathic /ˌprəʊtəʊˈpæθɪk/ *adjective* **1.** referring to nerves which are able to sense only strong sensations **2.** referring to a first symptom or lesion **3.** referring to the first sign of partially restored function in an injured nerve ▶ compare **epicritic**

protoplasm /ˈprəʊtəʊˌplæz(ə)m/ *noun* a substance like a jelly which makes up the largest part of each cell

protoplasmic /ˌprəʊtəʊˈplæzmɪk/ *adjective* referring to protoplasm

protoporphyrin IX /ˌprəʊtəʊˌpɔːfərɪn ˈnaɪn/ *noun* the commonest form of porphyrin, found in haemoglobin and chlorophyll

protozoa /ˌprəʊtəˈzəʊə/ plural of **protozoon**

protozoan /ˌprəʊtəˈzəʊən/ *adjective* referring to protozoa

protozoon *noun* a tiny simple organism with a single cell (NOTE: The plural is **protozoa** or **protozoons**.)

COMMENT: Parasitic protozoa can cause several diseases, including amoebiasis, malaria and other tropical diseases.

protract /prəʊˈtrækt/ *verb* **1.** to make something last a long time **2.** to extend or lengthen a body part

protractor /prəˈtræktə/ *noun* a muscle with the function of extending a body part

protrude /prəˈtruːd/ *verb* to stick out ○ *She wears a brace to correct her protruding teeth.* ○ *Protruding eyes are associated with some forms of goitre.* (NOTE: **protruding – protruded**)

protuberance /prəˈtjuːb(ə)rəns/ *noun* a rounded part of the body which projects above the rest

proud flesh /ˌpraʊd ˈfleʃ/ *noun* new vessels and young fibrous tissue which form when a wound, incision or lesion is healing

provide /prəˈvaɪd/ *verb* to supply something ○ *A balanced diet should provide the necessary proteins required by the body.* ○ *The hospital provides an ambulance service to the whole area.* (NOTE: **providing – provided**)

provider /prəˈvaɪdə/ *noun* a hospital which provides secondary care which is paid for by another body such as a PCG or social services. ◊ **purchaser**

provision /prəˈvɪʒ(ə)n/ *noun* **1.** the act of providing something ○ *the provision of aftercare facilities for patients recently discharged from hospital* **2.** something provided

provisional /prəˈvɪʒ(ə)n(ə)l/ *adjective* temporary and which may be changed ○ *The hospital has given me a provisional date for the operation.* ○ *The paramedical team attached sticks to the broken leg to act as provisional splints.*

provisionally /prəˈvɪʒ(ə)nəli/ *adverb* in a temporary way, not certainly ○ *She has provisionally accepted the offer of a bed in the hospital.*

provitamin /prəʊˈvɪtəmɪn/ *noun* a chemical compound which is converted to a vitamin during usual biochemical processes, e.g. the amino acid tryptophan, which is converted to niacin, and beta carotene, which is converted into vitamin A

provoke /prəˈvəʊk/ *verb* **1.** to make a person angry **2.** to make something happen ○ *The medication provoked a sudden rise in body temperature.* ○ *The fit was provoked by the shock of the accident.* **3.** to make something be felt ○ *His lack of visitors provoked the nurses' sympathy.* (NOTE: **provokes – provoking – provoked**)

proximal /ˈprɒksɪm(ə)l/ *adjective* near the midline, the central part of the body

proximal convoluted tubule /ˌprɒksɪm(ə)l ˌkɒnvəluːtɪd ˈtjuːbjuːl/ *noun* a part of the kidney filtering system between the loop of Henle and the glomerulus

proximal interphalangeal joint /ˌprɒksɪm(ə)l ɪntəfəˈlændʒiəl dʒɔɪnt/ *noun* a joint nearest the point of attachment of a finger or toe. Abbr **PIP**

proximally /ˈprɒksɪmli/ *adverb* further towards the centre or point of attachment. Opposite **distally**. See illustration at ANATOMICAL TERMS in Supplement

Prozac /ˈprəʊzæk/ a trade name for fluoxetine

prurigo /pruːˈraɪgəʊ/ *noun* an itchy eruption of papules

pruritus /pruːˈraɪtəs/ *noun* an irritation of the skin which makes a person want to scratch. Also called **itching**

pruritus ani /pruːˌraɪtɪs ˈeɪnaɪ/ *noun* itching round the anal orifice

pruritus vulvae /pruːˌraɪtɪs ˈvʌlviː/ *noun* itching round the vulva

prussic acid /ˌprʌsɪk ˈæsɪd/ *noun* same as **cyanide**

PSA test /ˌpiː es ˈeɪ test/ *noun* a blood test for prostate cancer which detects a protein produced by prostate cells. Full form **prostatic specific antigen test**

pseud- /sjuːd/ *prefix* same as **pseudo-** (*used before vowels*)

pseudarthrosis /ˌsjuːdɑːˈθrəʊsɪs/ *noun* a false joint, as when the two broken ends of a fractured bone do not bind together but heal separately (NOTE: The plural is **pseudarthroses**.)

pseudo- /ˈsjuːdəʊ/ *prefix* similar to something but not the same

pseudoangina /ˌsjuːdəʊænˈdʒaɪnə/ *noun* pain in the chest, caused by worry but not indicating heart disease

pseudocoxalgia /ˌsjuːdəʊkɒkˈsældʒə/ *noun* the degeneration of the upper end of the femur in young boys which prevents the femur from growing properly and can result in a permanent limp. Also called **Legg-Calvé-Perthes disease**

pseudocrisis /ˈsjuːdəʊˌkraɪsɪs/ *noun* a sudden fall in the temperature of a person with fever which does not mark the end of the fever

pseudocroup /ˌsjuːdəʊˈkruːp/ *noun* **1.** same as **laryngismus 2.** a form of asthma in which contractions take place in the larynx

pseudocyesis /ˌsjuːdəʊsaɪˈiːsɪs/ *noun* a condition in which a woman has the physical symptoms of pregnancy but is not pregnant. Also called **phantom pregnancy, pseudopregnancy**

pseudocyst /ˈsjuːdəʊsɪst/ *noun* a space which fills with fluid in an organ but without the walls which would form a cyst, as a result of softening or necrosis of the tissue

pseudodementia /ˌsjuːdəʊdɪˈmenʃə/ *noun* a condition of extreme apathy found in hysterical people in which their behaviour corresponds to what they imagine to be insanity, though they show no signs of true dementia

pseudogynaecomastia /ˌsjuːdəʊˌgaɪnɪkəʊˈmæstiə/ *noun* enlargement of the male breast because of extra fatty tissue (NOTE: The US spelling is **pseudogynecomastia**.)

pseudohermaphroditism /ˌsjuːdəʊhɜːˈmæfrədaɪtɪz(ə)m/ *noun* a condition in which a person has either ovaries or testes but external genitalia that are not clearly of either sex

pseudohypertrophic muscular dystrophy /ˌsjuːdəʊhaɪpəˌtrɒfɪk ˌmʌskjʊlə ˈdɪstrəfi/ *noun* a hereditary disease affecting the muscles, which swell and become weak, beginning in early childhood. Also called **Duchenne muscular dystrophy**

pseudohypertrophy /ˌsjuːdəʊhaɪˈpɜːtrəfi/ *noun* an overgrowth of fatty or fibrous tissue in a part or organ, which results in the part or organ being enlarged

pseudomonad /ˌsjuːdəʊˈməʊnəd/ *noun* a rod-shaped bacterium which lives in soil or decomposing organic material and can cause disease in plants and sometimes in humans

pseudomyxoma /ˌsjuːdəʊmɪkˈsəʊmə/ *noun* a tumour rich in mucus (NOTE: The plural is **pseudomyxomas** or **pseudomyxomata**.)

pseudo-obstruction /ˌsjuːdəʊ əbˈstrʌkʃən/ *noun* a condition in which symptoms such as stomach cramps, nausea and bloating indicate a blockage in the intestines although no blockage exists

pseudoplegia /ˌsjuːdəʊˈpliːdʒə/, **pseudoparalysis** /ˌsjuːdəʊpəˈræləsɪs/ *noun* **1.** loss of muscular power in the limbs without true paralysis **2.** paralysis caused by hysteria

pseudopolyposis /ˌsjuːdəʊpɒliˈpəʊsɪs/ *noun* a condition in which polyps are found in many places in the intestine, usually resulting from an earlier infection

pseudopregnancy /ˌsjuːdəʊˈpregnənsi/ *noun* also called **pseudocyesis**

psilosis /saɪˈləʊsɪs/ *noun* a disease of the small intestine which prevents a person from absorbing food properly. Also called **sprue**

> COMMENT: The condition is often found in the tropics, and results in diarrhoea and loss of weight.

psittacosis /ˌsɪtəˈkəʊsɪs/ *noun* a disease of parrots which can be transmitted to humans. It is similar to typhoid fever, but atypical pneumonia is present. Symptoms include fever, diarrhoea and distension of the abdomen. Also called **parrot disease**

psoas /ˈsəʊəs/ *noun* either of two pairs of muscles in the groin, psoas major and psoas minor, which help to move the hip joint

psoas major /ˌsəʊæs ˈmeɪdʒə/ *noun* a muscle in the groin which flexes the hip

psoas minor /ˌsəʊæs ˈmaɪnə/ *noun* a small muscle similar to the psoas major but not always present

psoriasis /səˈraɪəsɪs/ *noun* a common inflammatory skin disease where red patches of skin are covered with white scales

psoriatic /ˌsɔːriˈætɪk/ *adjective* referring to psoriasis

psoriatic arthritis /ˌsɔːriætɪk ɑːˈθraɪtɪs/ *noun* a form of psoriasis which is associated with arthritis

psych- /saɪk/ *prefix* same as **psycho-** (*used before vowels*)

psychasthenia /ˌsaɪkæsˈθiːniə/ *noun* **1.** any psychoneurosis other than hysteria **2.** psychoneurosis characterised by fears and phobias

psyche /ˈsaɪki/ *noun* the mind

psychedelic /ˌsaɪkəˈdelɪk/ *adjective* referring to drugs such as LSD which expand a person's consciousness

psychiatric /ˌsaɪkiˈætrɪk/ *adjective* referring to psychiatry ○ *He is undergoing psychiatric treatment.*

psychiatric hospital /ˌsaɪkiˈætrɪk ˌhɒspɪt(ə)l/ *noun* a hospital which specialises in the treatment of patients with mental disorders

psychiatrist /saɪˈkaɪətrɪst/ *noun* a doctor who specialises in the diagnosis and treatment of mental and behavioural disorders

psychiatry /saɪˈkaɪətri/ *noun* a branch of medicine concerned with the diagnosis and treatment of mental and behavioural disorders

psychic /'saɪkɪk/, **psychical** /'saɪkɪk(ə)l/ *adjective* **1.** referring to a person who is supposedly able to guess thoughts which people have not expressed, or to foresee the future **2.** relating to or originating in the human mind

psycho- /saɪkəʊ/ *prefix* referring to the mind

psychoanalysis /ˌsaɪkəʊə'næləsɪs/ *noun* a form of treatment for mental disorders in which a specialist and patient talk and together analyse the patient's condition and past events which may have contributed to it

psychoanalyst /ˌsaɪkəʊ'æn(ə)lɪst/ *noun* a person who is trained in psychoanalysis

psychodrama /'saɪkəʊ,drɑːmə/ *noun* a type of psychotherapy in which patients act out roles in dramas illustrating their emotional problems, in front of other patients

psychodynamics /ˌsaɪkəʊdaɪ'næmɪks/ *noun* the study of how the forces which affect human behaviour and mental states work, especially on a subconscious level

psychogenic /ˌsaɪkə'dʒenɪk/, **psychogenetic** /ˌsaɪkəʊdʒə'netɪk/, **psychogenous** /saɪ'kɒdʒənəs/ *adjective* referring to an illness which starts in the mind, rather than in a physical state

psychogeriatrics /ˌsaɪkəʊdʒeri'ætrɪks/ *noun* the study of the mental disorders of the late stages of the natural life span

psychological /ˌsaɪkə'lɒdʒɪk(ə)l/ *adjective* referring to psychology, or caused by a mental state

psychological dependence /ˌsaɪkə,lɒdʒɪk(ə)l dɪ'pendəns/, **psychological drug dependence** /ˌsaɪkə,lɒdʒɪk(ə)l 'drʌg dɪ,pendəns/ *noun* a state in which a person is addicted to a drug such as cannabis or alcohol but does not suffer physical effects if he or she stops taking it

psychologically /ˌsaɪkə'lɒdʒɪkli/ *adverb* in a way which is caused by a mental state ○ *He is psychologically addicted to tobacco.*

psychologist /saɪ'kɒlədʒɪst/ *noun* a person who specialises in the study of the mind and mental processes

psychology /saɪ'kɒlədʒi/ *noun* the study of the mind and mental processes

psychometrics /ˌsaɪkə'metrɪks/ *noun* a way of measuring intelligence and personality in which the result is shown as a number on a scale

psychomotor /ˌsaɪkə'məʊtə/ *adjective* referring to muscle movements caused by mental activity

psychomotor disturbance /ˌsaɪkəməʊtə dɪ'stɜːbəns/ *noun* muscle movements caused by a mental disorder, e.g. twitching

psychomotor epilepsy /ˌsaɪkəməʊtə 'epɪlepsi/ *noun* epilepsy in which fits are characterised by blurring of consciousness and accompanied by coordinated but wrong movements

psychomotor retardation /ˌsaɪkəməʊtə ˌriːtɑː'deɪʃ(ə)n/ *noun* the slowing of movement and speech, caused by depression

psychoneuroimmunology /ˌsaɪkəʊ ˌnjʊərəʊ,ɪmjʊ'nɒlədʒi/ *noun* a branch of medicine which deals with how emotions affect the immune system

psychoneurosis /ˌsaɪkəʊnjʊ'rəʊsɪs/ *noun* any of a group of mental disorders in which a person has a faulty response to the stresses of life. ◊ **neurosis** (NOTE: The plural is **psychoneuroses.**)

psychopath /'saɪkəpæθ/ *noun* a person with a long-term mental disorder characterised by antisocial and often violent behaviour

psychopathic /ˌsaɪkə'pæθɪk/ *adjective* referring to psychopaths or psychopathy

psychopathological /ˌsaɪkəʊpæθə'lɒdʒɪk(ə)l/ *adjective* referring to psychopathology

psychopathology /ˌsaɪkəpə'θɒlədʒi/ *noun* a branch of medicine concerned with the pathology of mental disorders and diseases

psychopathy /saɪ'kɒpəθi/ *noun* any disease of the mind (NOTE: The plural is **psychopathies.**)

psychopharmacology /ˌsaɪkəʊ,fɑːmə'kɒlədʒi/ *noun* the study of the actions and applications of drugs which have a powerful effect on the mind and behaviour

psychophysiological /ˌsaɪkəʊ,fɪziə'lɒdʒɪk(ə)l/ *adjective* referring to psychophysiology

psychophysiology /ˌsaɪkəʊ,fɪzi'ɒlədʒi/ *noun* the physiology of the mind and its functions

psychoses /saɪ'kəʊsiːz/ plural of **psychosis**

psychosexual /ˌsaɪkəʊ'sekʃʊəl/ *adjective* relating to the mental and emotional aspects of sexuality and sexual development

psychosexual development /ˌsaɪkəʊ ˌsekʃʊəl dɪ'veləpmənt/ *noun* the development of human personality in stages based upon the ability to experience sexual pleasure, and the way in which sexuality plays a role in a person's life

psychosis /saɪ'kəʊsɪs/ *noun* any serious mental disorder in which a person has a distorted perception of reality (NOTE: The plural is **psychoses.**)

psychosocial /ˌsaɪkəʊ'səʊʃ(ə)l/ *adjective* relating to the interaction of psychological and social factors

'...recent efforts to redefine nursing have moved away from the traditional medically dominated approach towards psychosocial care and forming relationships with patients' [*British Journal of Nursing*]

psychosomatic /ˌsaɪkəʊsəˈmætɪk/ *adjective* referring to the relationship between body and mind

COMMENT: Many physical disorders, including duodenal ulcers and high blood pressure, can be caused by mental conditions like worry or stress, and are then termed psychosomatic in order to distinguish them from the same conditions having physical or hereditary causes.

psychosurgery /ˌsaɪkəʊˈsɜːdʒəri/ *noun* brain surgery, used as a treatment for psychological disorders

psychosurgical /ˌsaɪkəʊˈsɜːdʒɪk(ə)l/ *adjective* referring to psychosurgery

psychotherapeutic /ˌsaɪkəʊθerəˈpjuːtɪk/ *adjective* referring to psychotherapy

psychotherapist /ˌsaɪkəʊˈθerəpɪst/ *noun* a person trained to give psychotherapy

psychotherapy /ˌsaɪkəʊˈθerəpi/ *noun* the treatment of mental disorders by psychological methods, as when a psychotherapist encourages a person to talk about his or her problems. ◊ **therapy**

psychotic /saɪˈkɒtɪk/ *adjective* **1.** referring to psychosis **2.** characterised by mental disorder

psychotropic /ˌsaɪkəˈtrɒpɪk/ *adjective* referring to a drug such as a stimulant or sedative which affects a person's mood

pt *abbr* pint

pterion /ˈtɪəriɒn/ *noun* the point on the side of the skull where the frontal, temporal parietal and sphenoid bones meet

pteroylglutamic acid /ˌterəʊaɪlglu-ˌtæmɪk ˈæsɪd/ *noun* same as **folic acid**

pterygium /təˈrɪdʒiəm/ *noun* a degenerative condition in which a triangular growth of conjunctiva covers part of the cornea, with its apex towards the pupil

pterygo- /terɪɡəʊ/ *suffix* the pterygoid process

pterygoid plate /ˌterɪɡɔɪd ˈpleɪt/ *noun* a small flat bony projection on the pterygoid process

pterygoid plexus /ˌterɪɡɔɪd ˈpleksəs/ *noun* a group of veins and sinuses which join together behind the cheek

pterygoid process /ˈterɪɡɔɪd ˌprəʊses/ *noun* one of two projecting parts on the sphenoid bone

pterygomandibular /ˌterɪɡəʊmænˈdɪbjʊlə/ *adjective* referring to the pterygoid process and the mandible

pterygopalatine fossa /ˌterɪɡəʊpælətaɪn ˈfɒsə/ *noun* the space between the pterygoid process and the upper jaw

pterygopalatine ganglion /ˌterɪɡəʊ-pælətaɪn ˈɡæŋɡliən/ *noun* a ganglion in the pterygopalatine fossa associated with the maxillary nerve. Also called **sphenopalatine ganglion**

ptomaine /ˈtəʊmeɪn/ *noun* a group of nitrogenous substances produced in rotting food, which gives the food a special smell (NOTE: **Ptomaine poisoning** was the term formerly used to refer to any form of food poisoning.)

ptosis /ˈtəʊsɪs/ *noun* **1.** prolapse of an organ **2.** drooping of the upper eyelid, which makes the eye stay half closed

-ptosis /ˈtəʊsɪs/ *suffix* prolapse

PTSD *abbr* post-traumatic stress disorder

ptyal- /taɪəl/ *prefix* same as **ptyalo-** (*used before vowels*)

ptyalin /ˈtaɪəlɪn/ *noun* an enzyme in saliva which cleanses the mouth and converts starch into sugar

ptyalism /ˈtaɪəlɪz(ə)m/ *noun* the production of an excessive amount of saliva

ptyalith /ˈtaɪəlɪθ/ *noun* same as **sialolith**

ptyalo- /taɪələʊ/ *prefix* referring to saliva

ptyalography /ˌtaɪəˈlɒɡrəfi/ *noun* same as **sialography**

pubertal /ˈpjuːbət(ə)l/, **puberal** /ˈpjuːbərəl/ *adjective* referring to puberty

puberty /ˈpjuːbəti/ *noun* **1.** the physical and psychological changes which take place when childhood ends and adolescence and sexual maturity begin and the sex glands become active **2.** the time when these changes take place

COMMENT: Puberty starts at about the age of 10 in girls, and slightly later in boys.

pubes¹ /ˈpjuːbiːz/ *noun* the part of the body just above the groin, where the pubic bones are found

pubes² /ˈpjuːbiːz/ plural of **pubis**

pubescent /pjuːˈbesənt/ *adjective* reaching or having reached puberty

pubic /ˈpjuːbɪk/ *adjective* referring to the area near the genitals

pubic bone /ˌpjuːbɪk ˈbəʊn/ *noun* the bone in front of the pelvis. Also called **pubis**. See illustration at UROGENITAL SYSTEM (MALE) in Supplement

pubic hair /ˌpjuːbɪk ˈheə/ *noun* tough hair growing in the genital region

pubic louse /ˌpjuːbɪk ˈlaʊs/ *noun* also called **Pediculus pubis**

pubic symphysis /ˌpjuːbɪk ˈsɪmfəsɪs/ *noun* a piece of cartilage which joins the two sections of the pubic bone. Also called **symphysis pubis**

COMMENT: In a pregnant woman, the pubic symphysis stretches to allow the pelvic girdle to expand so that there is room for the baby to pass through.

pubiotomy /ˌpjuːbiˈɒtəmi/ *noun* a surgical operation to divide the pubic bone during labour, in order to make the pelvis wide enough for the child to be born safely (NOTE: The plural is **pubiotomies**.)

pubis /ˈpjuːbɪs/ *noun* a bone forming the front part of the pelvis. See illustration at PELVIS in Supplement (NOTE: The plural is **pubes**.)

public health /ˌpʌblɪk 'helθ/ *noun* the study of illness, health and disease in the community

public health laboratory service /ˌpʌblɪk ˌhelθ ləˈbɒrət(ə)ri ˌsɜːvɪs/ *noun* in the UK, a former service of the NHS which detected, diagnosed and monitored suspected cases of infectious disease in a countrywide network of laboratories. Abbr **PHLS**

public health medicine /ˌpʌblɪk ˌhelθ 'med(ə)s(ə)n/ *noun* the branch of medicine concerned with health and disease in populations, with the responsibilities of monitoring health, identification of health needs, development of policies which promote health and evaluation of health services

public health nurse /ˌpʌblɪk ˌhelθ 'nɜːs/ *noun* a nurse such as a school nurse, health visitor or other community nurse who monitors health and works to prevent illness in community situations

public health physician /ˌpʌblɪk ˌhelθ fɪ 'zɪʃ(ə)n/ *noun* a consultant who has special training in public health medicine

pudenda /pjuːˈdendə/ plural of **pudendum**

pudendal /pjuːˈdend(ə)l/ *adjective* referring to the pudendum

pudendal block /pjuːˌdend(ə)l 'blɒk/ *noun* an operation to anaesthetise the pudendum during childbirth

pudendum /pjuːˈdendəm/ *noun* an external genital organ of a woman (NOTE: The plural is **pudenda**.)

puerpera /pjuːˈɜːp(ə)rə/ *noun* a woman who has recently given birth, or is giving birth, and whose uterus is still distended (NOTE: The plural is **puerperae**.)

puerperal /pjuːˈɜːp(ə)rəl/ *adjective* **1.** referring to the puerperium **2.** referring to childbirth **3.** occurring after childbirth

puerperal infection /pjuːˌɜːp(ə)rəl ɪnˈfekʃən/, **puerperal fever** /pjuːˌɜːp(ə)rəl 'fiːvə/ *noun* an infection of the uterus and genital tract after the birth of a baby, which is more common in women who have had a caesarean section. It causes a high fever, and occasionally sepsis, which can be fatal and was commonly so in the past. Also called **postpartum fever**

puerperalism /pjuːˈɜːp(ə)rəlɪz(ə)m/ *noun* an illness of a baby or its mother resulting from or associated with childbirth

puerperal psychosis /pjuːˌɜːp(ə)rəl saɪ 'kəʊsɪs/ *noun* a psychiatric disorder that some women may experience in the first two weeks after giving birth

puerperal sepsis /pjuːˌɜːp(ə)rəl 'sepsɪs/ *noun* blood poisoning following childbirth, caused by infection of the placental site

puerperium /ˌpjuːɪəˈpɪəriəm/ *noun* a period of about six weeks which follows immediately after the birth of a child, during which the mother's sexual organs recover from childbirth

puerperous /pjuːˈɜːprəs/ *adjective* same as **puerperal**

puke /pjuːk/ *verb* same as **vomit** (*informal*)

Pulex /'pjuːleks/ *noun* a genus of human fleas

pull /pʊl/ *verb* to make a muscle move in a wrong direction ○ *He pulled a muscle in his back.* □ **to pull the plug** to switch off life support (*informal*) ■ □ **to pull yourself together** to become calmer ○ *Although he was very angry he soon pulled himself together.*

pulley /'pʊli/ *noun* a device with rings through which wires or cords pass, used in traction to make wires tense

pull through /ˌpʊl 'θruː/ *verb* to recover from a serious illness (*informal*) ○ *The doctor says she is strong and should pull through.*

pulmo- /'pʌlməʊ/, **pulmon-** /'pʌlmən/ *prefix* referring to the lungs

pulmonale /ˌpʌlməˈneɪli/ ♦ **cor pulmonale**

pulmonary /'pʌlmən(ə)ri/ *adjective* referring to the lungs

pulmonary artery /ˌpʌlmən(ə)ri 'ɑːtəri/ *noun* one of the two arteries which take deoxygenated blood from the heart to the lungs for oxygenation. See illustration at HEART in Supplement

pulmonary circulation /ˌpʌlmən(ə)ri ˌsɜːkjʊ'leɪʃ(ə)n/ *noun* the circulation of blood from the heart through the pulmonary arteries to the lungs for oxygenation and back to the heart through the pulmonary veins. Also called **lesser circulation**

pulmonary embolism /ˌpʌlmən(ə)ri 'embəliz(ə)m/ *noun* a blockage of a pulmonary artery by a blood clot. Abbr **PE**

pulmonary hypertension /ˌpʌlmən(ə)ri ˌhaɪpə'tenʃən/ *noun* high blood pressure in the blood vessels supplying blood to the lungs

pulmonary insufficiency /ˌpʌlmən(ə)ri ˌɪnsə'fɪʃ(ə)nsi/, **pulmonary incompetence** /ˌpʌlmən(ə)ri ɪn'kɒmpɪt(ə)ns/ *noun* a condition characterised by dilatation of the main pulmonary artery and stretching of the valve ring, due to pulmonary hypertension

pulmonary oedema /ˌpʌlmən(ə)ri ɪ 'diːmə/ *noun* the collection of fluid in the lungs, as occurs in left-sided heart failure

pulmonary stenosis /ˌpʌlmən(ə)ri ste 'nəʊsɪs/ *noun* a condition in which the opening to the pulmonary artery in the right ventricle becomes narrow

pulmonary tuberculosis /ˌpʌlmən(ə)ri tjuːˌbɜːkjʊ'ləʊsɪs/ *noun* tuberculosis in the lungs, which makes the person lose weight, cough blood and have a fever

pulmonary valve /'pʌlmən(ə)ri vælv/ *noun* a valve at the opening of the pulmonary artery

pulmonary vein /'pʌlmən(ə)ri veɪn/ *noun* one of the four veins which carry oxygenated blood from the lungs back to the left atrium of the heart. See illustration at HEART in Supplement (NOTE: The pulmonary veins are the only veins which carry oxygenated blood.)

pulmonectomy /ˌpʌlmə'nektəmi/ *noun* same as **pneumonectomy** (NOTE: The plural is **pulmonectomies**.)

pulmonology /ˌpʌlmən'ɒlədʒi/ *noun* the branch of medicine that deals with the structure, physiology and diseases of the lungs

pulp /pʌlp/ *noun* soft tissue, especially when surrounded by hard tissue as in the inside of a tooth

pulp cavity /'pʌlp ˌkævɪti/ *noun* the central part of a tooth containing soft tissue

pulpy /'pʌlpi/ *adjective* made of pulp ○ *the pulpy tissue inside a tooth*

pulsate /pʌl'seɪt/ *verb* to expand and contract with a strong regular beat (NOTE: **pulsating – pulsated**)

pulsation /pʌl'seɪʃ(ə)n/ *noun* the action of beating regularly, e.g. the visible pulse which can be seen under the skin in some parts of the body

pulse /pʌls/ *noun* the regular expansion and contraction of an artery caused by the heart pumping blood through the body, which can be felt with the fingers especially where an artery is near the surface of the body, as in the wrist or neck ○ *Her pulse is very irregular.* □ **to take** *or* **feel a person's pulse** to measure a person's pulse rate by pressing on the skin above an artery with the fingers ○ *Has the patient's pulse been taken?*

COMMENT: The standard adult pulse is about 72 beats per minute, but it is higher in children. The pulse is usually taken by placing the fingers on the patient's wrist, at the point where the radial artery passes through the depression just below the thumb.

pulseless /'pʌlsləs/ *adjective* referring to a person who has no pulse because the heart is beating very weakly

pulse oximetry /ˌpʌls ɒk'sɪmətri/ *noun* a method of measuring the oxygen content of arterial blood

pulse point /'pʌls pɔɪnt/ *noun* a place on the body where the pulse can be taken

pulse pressure /'pʌls ˌpreʃə/ *noun* the difference between the diastolic and systolic pressure. ◊ **Corrigan's pulse**

pulse rate /'pʌls reɪt/ *noun* the number of times the pulse beats per minute

pulsus /'pʌlsəs/ *noun* same as **pulse**

pulsus alternans /ˌpʌlsəs 'ɔːltənænz/ *noun* a pulse with a beat which is alternately strong and weak

pulsus bigeminus /ˌpʌlsəs baɪ'gemɪnəs/ *noun* a double pulse, with an extra ectopic beat

pulsus paradoxus /ˌpʌlsəs pærə'dɒksəs/ *noun* a condition in which there is a sharp fall in the pulse when the person breathes in

pulvis /'pʌlvɪs/ *noun* powder

pump /pʌmp/ *noun* a machine which forces liquids or air into or out of something ■ *verb* to force liquid or air along a tube ○ *The heart pumps blood round the body.* ○ *The nurses tried to pump the poison out of the stomach.*

pumping chamber /'pʌmpɪŋ ˌtʃeɪmbə/ *noun* one of the sections of the heart where blood is pumped

punch drunk syndrome /ˌpʌntʃ 'drʌŋk ˌsɪndrəʊm/ *noun* a condition affecting a person, usually a boxer, who has been hit on the head many times and develops impaired mental faculties, trembling limbs and speech disorders

puncta /'pʌŋktə/ plural of **punctum**

puncta lacrimalia /ˌpʌŋktə lækrɪ'meɪliə/ *plural noun* small openings at the corners of the eyes through which tears drain into the nose

punctate /'pʌŋkteɪt/ *adjective* referring to tissue or a surface which has tiny spots, holes or dents in it

punctum /'pʌŋktəm/ *noun* a point (NOTE: The plural is **puncta**.)

puncture /'pʌŋktʃə/ *noun* **1.** a neat hole made by a sharp instrument **2.** the making of a hole in an organ or swelling to take a sample of the contents or to remove fluid ■ *verb* to make a hole in tissue with a sharp instrument (NOTE: **puncturing – punctured**)

puncture wound /'pʌŋktʃə wuːnd/ *noun* a wound made by a sharp instrument which makes a hole in the tissue

pupil /'pjuːp(ə)l/ *noun* the central opening in the iris of the eye, through which light enters the eye. See illustration at EYE in Supplement

pupillary /'pjuːpɪləri/ *adjective* referring to the pupil

pupillary reaction /ˌpjuːpɪləri ri'ækʃən/ *noun* a reflex of the pupil of the eye which contracts when exposed to bright light. Also called **light reflex**

purchaser /'pɜːtʃɪsə/ *noun* a body, usually a PCG, which commissions health care and manages the budget to pay for the service. ◊ **provider**

pure /pjʊə/ *adjective* **1.** not mixed with other substances **2.** very clean

pure alcohol /ˌpjʊə 'ælkəhɒl/ *noun* alcohol BP, alcohol with 5% water

purgation /pɜː'geɪʃ(ə)n/ *noun* the use of a drug to cause a bowel movement

purgative /'pɜːgətɪv/ *noun* a drug used to empty the bowels. ◊ **laxative**

purge /pɜːdʒ/ *verb* to induce evacuation of the bowels (NOTE: **purging – purged**)

purified protein derivative /ˌpjʊərɪfaɪd 'prəʊtiːn dɪˌrɪvətɪv/ *noun* a pure form of tuberculin, used in tuberculin tests. Abbr **PPD**

purify /'pjʊərɪfaɪ/ *verb* to make something pure (NOTE: **purifies – purifying – purified**)

purine /'pjʊəriːn/ *noun* **1.** a nitrogen-containing substance derived from uric acid which is the parent compound of several biologically important substances **2.** a derivative of purine, especially either of the bases adenine and guanine, which are found in RNA and DNA

Purkinje cells /pə'kɪndʒi selz/ *plural noun* neurones in the cerebellar cortex [Described 1837. After Johannes Evangelista Purkinje (1787–1869), Professor of Physiology at Breslau, now in Poland, and then Prague, Czech Republic.]

Purkinje fibres /pə'kɪndʒi ,faɪbəz/ *plural noun* a bundle of fibres which form the atrioventricular bundle and pass from the atrioventricular node to the septum [Described 1839. After Johannes Evangelista Purkinje (1787–1869), Professor of Physiology at Breslau, now in Poland, and then Prague, Czech Republic.]

Purkinje shift /pə'kɪndʒi ʃɪft/ *noun* the change in colour sensitivity which takes place in the eye in low light when the eye starts using the rods in the retina because the light is too weak to stimulate the cones

purpura /'pɜːpjʊrə/ *noun* a purple colouring on the skin, similar to a bruise, caused by blood disease and not by trauma

pursestring operation /,pɜːsstrɪŋ ,ɒpə'reɪʃ(ə)n/ *same as* **Shirodkar's operation**

pursestring stitch /'pɜːsstrɪŋ stɪtʃ/ *noun* *same as* **Shirodkar suture**

purulent /'pjʊərʊlənt/ *adjective* containing or producing pus

pus /pʌs/ *noun* a yellow liquid composed of blood serum, pieces of dead tissue, white blood cells and the remains of bacteria, formed by the body in reaction to infection (NOTE: For other terms referring to pus, see words beginning with **py-** or **pyo-**.)

pustular /'pʌstjʊlə/ *adjective* **1.** covered with or composed of pustules **2.** referring to pustules

pustulate /'pʌstjʊleɪt/ *verb* to become covered with pustules, or cause pustules to appear on the skin (NOTE: **pustulating – pustulated**) ■ *adjective* covered with pustules

pustule /'pʌstjuːl/ *noun* a small pimple filled with pus

putrefaction /,pjuːtrɪ'fækʃən/ *noun* the decomposition of organic substances by bacteria, making an unpleasant smell

putrefy /'pjuːtrɪfaɪ/ *verb* to rot or decompose (NOTE: **putrefies – putrefying – putrefied**)

put up /,pʊt 'ʌp/ *verb* to arrange something such as a drip (NOTE: **putting up – put up**)

p.v. *adverb* by way of the vagina. Full form **per vaginam**

PVS *abbr* persistent vegetative state

PWA /,piː dʌbljuː 'eɪ/ *noun* a person with Aids

py- /paɪ/, **pyo-** /paɪəʊ/ *prefix* same as **pyo-** (used before vowels)

pyaemia /paɪ'iːmiə/ *noun* invasion of blood with bacteria which then multiply and form many little abscesses in various parts of the body (NOTE: The US spelling is **pyemia**.)

pyarthrosis /,paɪɑː'θrəʊsɪs/ *noun* a condition in which a joint becomes infected with pyogenic organisms and fills with pus. Also called **acute suppurative arthritis**

pyel- /paɪəl/ *prefix* same as **pyelo-** (used before vowels)

pyelitis /,paɪə'laɪtɪs/ *noun* inflammation of the central part of the kidney

pyelo- /paɪələʊ/ *prefix* referring to the pelvis of the kidney

pyelocystitis /,paɪələʊsɪ'staɪtɪs/ *noun* inflammation of the pelvis of the kidney and the urinary bladder

pyelogram /'paɪələgræm/ *noun* an X-ray photograph of a kidney and the urinary tract

pyelography /,paɪə'lɒgrəfi/ *noun* X-ray examination of a kidney after introduction of a contrast medium

pyelolithotomy /,paɪələʊlɪ'θɒtəmi/ *noun* a surgical operation to remove a stone from the pelvis of the kidney (NOTE: The plural is **pyelolithotomies**.)

pyelonephritis /,paɪələʊnɪ'fraɪtɪs/ *noun* inflammation of the kidney and the pelvis of the kidney

pyeloplasty /'paɪələplæsti/ *noun* any surgical operation on the pelvis of the kidney (NOTE: The plural is **pyeloplasties**.)

pyelotomy /,paɪə'lɒtəmi/ *noun* a surgical operation to make an opening in the pelvis of the kidney (NOTE: The plural is **pyelotomies**.)

pyemia /paɪ'iːmiə/ *noun US* same as **pyaemia**

pykno- /pɪknəʊ/ *prefix* indicating thickness or density

pyknolepsy /'pɪknə,lepsi/ *noun* a former name for a type of frequent attack of petit mal epilepsy affecting children

pyl- /paɪl/, **pyle-** /'paɪli/ *prefix* referring to the portal vein

pylephlebitis /,paɪliflə'baɪtɪs/ *noun* thrombosis of the portal vein

pylethrombosis /,paɪliθrɒm'bəʊsɪs/ *noun* a condition in which blood clots are present in the portal vein or any of its branches

pylor- /paɪ'lɔːr/ *prefix* same as **pyloro-** (used before vowels)

pylorectomy /,paɪlə'rektəmi/ *noun* a surgical operation to remove the pylorus and the antrum of the stomach (NOTE: The plural is **pylorectomies**.)

pylori /paɪ'lɔːri/ *plural of* **pylorus**

pyloric /paɪ'lɒrɪk/ *adjective* referring to the pylorus

pyloric antrum /paɪˌlɒrɪk 'æntrəm/ *noun* a space at the bottom of the stomach, before the pyloric sphincter

pyloric orifice /paɪˌlɒrɪk 'ɒrɪfɪs/ *noun* an opening where the stomach joins the duodenum

pyloric sphincter /paɪˌlɒrɪk 'sfɪŋktə/ *noun* a muscle which surrounds the pylorus, makes it contract and separates it from the duodenum

pyloric stenosis /paɪˌlɒrɪk ste'nəʊsɪs/ *noun* a blockage of the pylorus, which prevents food from passing from the stomach into the duodenum

pyloro- /paɪ'lɔːrəʊ/ *prefix* the pylorus

pyloroplasty /paɪ'lɔːrəplæsti/ *noun* a surgical operation to make the pylorus larger, sometimes combined with treatment for peptic ulcers (NOTE: The plural is **pyloroplasties**.)

pylorospasm /paɪ'lɔːrəspæz(ə)m/ *noun* a muscle spasm which closes the pylorus so that food cannot pass through into the duodenum

pylorotomy /ˌpaɪlə'rɒtəmi/ *noun* a surgical operation to cut into the muscle surrounding the pylorus to relieve pyloric stenosis. Also called **Ramstedt's operation** (NOTE: The plural is **pylorotomies**.)

pylorus /paɪ'lɔːrəs/ *noun* an opening at the bottom of the stomach leading into the duodenum (NOTE: The plural is **pylori**.)

pyo- /paɪəʊ/ *prefix* referring to pus

pyocele /'paɪəsiːl/ *noun* an enlargement of a tube or cavity due to accumulation of pus

pyocolpos /ˌpaɪə'kɒlpəs/ *noun* an accumulation of pus in the vagina

pyoderma /ˌpaɪə'dɜːmə/ *noun* an eruption of pus in the skin

pyoderma gangrenosum /ˌpaɪədɜːmə ˌgæŋgrɪ'nəʊsəm/ *noun* a serious ulcerating disease of the skin, especially the legs, usually treated with steroid drugs

pyogenesis /ˌpaɪə'dʒenɪsɪs/ *noun* the production or formation of pus

pyogenic /ˌpaɪə'dʒenɪk/ *adjective* producing or forming pus

pyometra /ˌpaɪə'miːtrə/ *noun* an accumulation of pus in the uterus

pyomyositis /ˌpaɪəʊmaɪə'saɪtɪs/ *noun* inflammation of a muscle caused by staphylococci or streptococci

pyonephrosis /ˌpaɪəʊnɪ'frəʊsɪs/ *noun* the distension of the kidney with pus

pyopericarditis /ˌpaɪəʊperɪkɑː'daɪtɪs/ *noun* an inflammation of the pericardium due to infection with staphylococci, streptococci or pneumococci

pyopneumothorax /ˌpaɪəʊˌnjuːməʊ'θɔːræks/ *noun* an accumulation of pus and gas or air in the pleural cavity

pyorrhoea /ˌpaɪə'rɪə/ *noun* discharge of pus (NOTE: The US spelling is **pyorrhea**.)

pyorrhoea alveolaris /ˌpaɪərɪə ˌælvɪəʊ'lɑːrɪs/ *noun* suppuration from the supporting tissues round the teeth

pyosalpinx /ˌpaɪə'sælpɪŋks/ *noun* inflammation and formation of pus in a Fallopian tube

pyothorax /ˌpaɪə'θɔːræks/ *noun* same as **empyema**

pyr- /paɪr/ *prefix* same as **pyro-** (used before vowels)

pyramid /'pɪrəmɪd/ *noun* a cone-shaped part of the body, especially a cone-shaped projection on the surface of the medulla oblongata or in the medulla of the kidney. See illustration at KIDNEY in Supplement

pyramidal /pɪ'ræmɪd(ə)l/ *adjective* referring to a pyramid

pyramidal cell /pɪ'ræmɪd(ə)l sel/ *noun* a cone-shaped cell in the cerebral cortex

pyramidal system /pɪ'ræmɪd(ə)l 'sɪstəm/, **pyramidal tract** /pɪ'ræmɪd(ə)l trækt/ *noun* a group of nerve fibres within the pyramid of the medulla oblongata in the brain. It is thought to be vital in controlling movement and speech.

pyretic /paɪ'retɪk/ *adjective* referring to fever ■ *noun* an agent that causes fever

pyrexia /paɪ'reksɪə/ *noun* same as **fever**

pyrexic /paɪ'reksɪk/ *adjective* having fever

pyridostigmine /ˌpɪrɪdəʊ'stɪgmiːn/ *noun* a drug which stops or delays the action of the enzyme cholinesterase, used to treat myasthenia gravis

pyridoxine /ˌpɪrɪ'dɒksɪn/ *noun* same as **Vitamin B$_6$**

pyrimidine /pɪ'rɪmɪdiːn/ *noun* 1. a strong-smelling nitrogenous based compound with a six-sided ring structure that is the parent compound of several biologically important substances 2. a derivative of pyrimidine, especially any of the bases cytosine, thymine, and uracil which are found in RNA and DNA

pyro- /paɪrəʊ/ *prefix* burning or fever

pyrogen /'paɪrədʒen/ *noun* a substance which causes a fever

pyrogenic /ˌpaɪrə'dʒenɪk/ *adjective* causing a fever

pyromania /ˌpaɪrəʊ'meɪnɪə/ *noun* an uncontrollable desire to start fires

pyrophobia /ˌpaɪrəʊ'fəʊbɪə/ *noun* an unusual fear of fire

pyruvic acid /paɪˌruːvɪk 'æsɪd/ *noun* a substance formed from glycogen in the muscles when it is broken down to release energy

pyuria /paɪ'jʊərɪə/ *noun* pus in the urine

Q

q.d.s. *adverb (written on prescriptions)* to be taken four times a day. Full form **quater in die sumendus**

Q fever /ˈkjuː ˌfiːvə/ *noun* an infectious rickettsial disease of sheep and cows caused by *Coxiella burnetti* transmitted to humans

COMMENT: Q fever mainly affects farm workers and workers in the meat industry. The symptoms are fever, cough and headaches.

q.i.d. *adverb (written on prescriptions)* four times a day. Full form **quater in die**

q.l. *adverb (written on prescriptions)* as much as you like. Full form **quantum libet**

q.m. *adverb (written on prescriptions)* every morning. Full form **quaque mane**

q.n. *adverb (written on prescriptions)* every night. Full form **quaque nocte**

QRS complex /ˌkjuː ɑːr ˈes ˌkɒmpleks/ *noun* the deflections on an electrocardiogram, labelled Q, R, and S, which show ventricular contraction. ◊ **PQRST complex**

q.s. *adverb (written on prescriptions)* as much as necessary. Full form **quantum sufficiat**

Q-T interval /ˌkjuː ˈtiː ˌɪntəv(ə)l/, **Q-S2 interval** /ˌkjuː es ˈtuː ˌɪntəv(ə)l/ *noun* the length of the QRS complex in an electrocardiogram. ◊ **PQRST complex**

quad /kwɒd/ *noun* same as **quadruplet** *(informal)*

quadrant /ˈkwɒdrənt/ *noun* one of four sectors of the body thought of as being divided by the sagittal plane and the intertubercular plane ○ *tenderness in the right lower quadrant*

quadrantanopia /ˌkwɒdræntəˈnəʊpiə/ *noun* blindness in a quarter of the field of vision

quadrate lobe /ˈkwɒdreɪt ləʊb/ *noun* a lobe on the lower side of the liver

quadratus /kwɒˈdreɪtəs/ *noun* any muscle with four sides

quadratus femoris /kwɒˌdreɪtəs ˈfemərɪs/ *noun* a muscle at the top of the femur which rotates the thigh

quadri- /kwɒdri/ *prefix* four

quadriceps /ˈkwɒdrɪseps/, **quadriceps femoris** /ˌkwɒdrɪseps ˈfemərɪs/ *noun* a large muscle in the front of the thigh, which extends to the leg

COMMENT: The quadriceps femoris is divided into four parts: the rectus femoris, vastus lateralis, vastus medialis and vastus intermedius. It is the sensory receptors in the quadriceps which react to give a knee jerk when the patellar tendon is tapped.

quadriplegia /ˌkwɒdrɪˈpliːdʒə/ *noun* paralysis of all four limbs, both arms and both legs

quadriplegic /ˌkwɒdrɪˈpliːdʒɪk/ *adjective* paralysed in both arms and both legs ■ *noun* a person paralysed in both arms and both legs

quadruple /ˈkwɒdrʊp(ə)l/ *adjective* 1. consisting of four times as much 2. having four parts

quadruplet /ˈkwɒdrʊplət/ *noun* one of four babies born to a mother at the same time. Also called **quad**

quadruple vaccine /ˌkwɒdrʊp(ə)l ˈvæksiːn/ *noun* a vaccine which immunises against four diseases, diphtheria, whooping cough, poliomyelitis and tetanus

quadrupod /ˈkwɒdrʊpɒd/ *noun* a walking stick which ends in four little legs

qualification /ˌkwɒlɪfɪˈkeɪʃ(ə)n/ *noun* 1. a quality which makes a person suitable to do something 2. an official recognition of a standard of achievement, e.g. a degree or diploma ○ *She has a qualification in pharmacy.* ○ *Are his qualifications recognised in Great Britain?*

qualify /ˈkwɒlɪfaɪ/ *verb* 1. to make a person suitable to do something 2. to pass a course of study and be accepted as being able to practise ○ *He qualified as a doctor two years ago.* (NOTE: [all senses] **qualifies – qualifying – qualified**)

qualitative /ˈkwɒlɪtətɪv/ *adjective* referring to a study in which descriptive information is collected. Compare **quantitative**

quality /ˈkwɒlɪti/ *noun* 1. a characteristic of somebody or something 2. the general standard or grade of something 3. the highest or finest standard

quality assurance /ˈkwɒlɪti əˌʃʊərəns/ *noun* a set of criteria which are designed to check that people in an organisation maintain a high standard in the products or services they supply

quality circle /ˈkwɒləti ˌsɜːk(ə)l/ *noun* a group of employees from different levels of an organisation who meet regularly to discuss ways of improving the quality of its products or services

Qualpacs /ˈkwɒlpæks/, **Quality Patient Care Scale** /ˌkwɒliti ˌpeɪʃ(ə)nt ˈkeə skeɪl/ *noun* a method which guides nurses to evaluate their activity in terms of efficiency of cost, time, use of skill level and workload

quantitative /ˈkwɒntɪtətɪv/ *adjective* referring to a study in which numerical information is collected. Compare **qualitative**

quantitative digital radiography /ˌkwɒn tɪtətɪv ˌdɪdʒɪt(ə)l reɪdiˈɒgrəfi/ *noun* the use of digital X-ray scans to find out whether a person has a bone disease such as osteoporosis. The levels of calcium in the bones are measured, usually in the spine and hip.

quarantine /ˈkwɒrəntiːn/ *noun* **1.** the situation in which a person, animal or ship just arrived in a country is kept isolated in case it carries a serious disease, to allow the disease time to develop and be detected **2.** the period of such isolation to prevent the spread of disease ○ *six months' quarantine* ■ *verb* to put a person or animal in quarantine (NOTE: **quarantining – quarantined**)

COMMENT: People who are suspected of having an infectious disease can be kept in quarantine for a period which varies according to the incubation period of the disease. The main diseases concerned are cholera, yellow fever and typhus.

quartan /ˈkwɔːt(ə)n/ *adjective* referring to a fever which occurs every fourth day, e.g. in some types of malaria

quartan fever /ˈkwɔːt(ə)n ˌfiːvə/ *noun* a form of malaria caused by *Plasmodium malariae* in which the fever returns every four days. ◊ **tertian fever**

queasiness /ˈkwiːzɪnəs/ *noun* the feeling of being about to vomit

queasy /ˈkwiːzi/ *adjective* feeling as though about to vomit

Queckenstedt test /ˈkwekənstedt test/ *noun* a test done during a lumbar puncture in which pressure is applied to the jugular veins to see if the cerebrospinal fluid is flowing correctly [Described 1916. After Hans Heinrich George Queckenstedt (1876–1918), German physician.]

quickening /ˈkwɪknɪŋ/ *noun* the first sign of life in an unborn baby, usually after about four months of pregnancy, when the mother can feel it moving in her uterus

Quick test /ˈkwɪk test/, **Quick's test** *noun* a test to identify the clotting factors in a blood sample [Described 1932. After Armand James Quick (1894–1978), Professor of Biochemistry, Marquette University, USA.]

quiescent /kwiˈes(ə)nt/ *adjective* referring to a disease with symptoms reduced either by treatment or in the usual course of the disease

quin /kwɪn/ *noun* same as **quintuplet** (*informal*) (NOTE: The US term is **quint**.)

quinine /kwɪˈniːn/ *noun* an alkaloid drug made from the bark of cinchona, a South American tree

COMMENT: Quinine was formerly used to treat the fever symptoms of malaria, but is not often used now because of its side-effects. Small amounts of quinine have a tonic effect and are used in tonic water.

quinine poisoning /kwɪˈniːn ˌpɔɪz(ə)nɪŋ/, **quininism** /ˈkwɪniːnɪz(ə)m/, **quinism** /ˈkwɪnɪz(ə)m/ *noun* an illness caused by taking too much quinine, leading to dizziness and noises in the head

quinolone /kwɪnəˈləʊn/ *noun* a drug used to treat Gram-negative and Gram-positive bacterial infections of the respiratory and urinary tracts and of the gastro-intestinal system (NOTE: Quinolone drugs have names ending in -**oxacin: ciprofloxacin**)

COMMENT: Contraindications include use in pregnancy, renal disease and for use in children.

quinsy /ˈkwɪnzi/ *noun* acute throat inflammation with an abscess round a tonsil. Also called **peritonsillar abscess**

quint /kwɪnt/ *noun* US same as **quintuplet**

quintan /ˈkwɪntən/ *adjective* referring to a fever that occurs every fifth day

quintuplet /ˈkwɪntjʊplət/ *noun* one of five babies born to a mother at the same time. Also called **quin, quint**

quotidian /kwəʊˈtɪdiən/ *adjective* recurring daily

quotidian fever /kwəʊˌtɪdiən ˈfiːvə/ *noun* a violent form of malaria in which the fever returns at daily or even shorter intervals

quotient /ˈkwəʊʃ(ə)nt/ *noun* the result when one number is divided by another

Q wave /ˈkjuː weɪv/ *noun* a negative deflection at the start of the QRS complex on an electrocardiogram, going downwards

R

R *symbol* roentgen

R/ *abbreviation* prescription. Full form **recipe**

rabbit fever /ˈræbɪt ˌfiːvə/ *noun* same as **tularaemia**

rabid /ˈræbɪd/ *adjective* referring to rabies, or affected by rabies ○ *She was bitten by a rabid dog.*

rabid encephalitis /ˌræbɪd enˌkefəˈlaɪtɪs/ *noun* a fatal form of encephalitis resulting from the bite of a rabid animal

rabies /ˈreɪbiːz/ *noun* a frequently fatal viral disease transmitted to humans by infected animals ○ *The hospital ordered a batch of rabies vaccine.* Also called **hydrophobia**

COMMENT: Rabies affects the mental balance, and the symptoms include difficulty in breathing or swallowing and an intense fear of water (hydrophobia) to the point of causing convulsions at the sight of water.

racemose /ˈræsɪməʊs/ *adjective* referring to glands which look like a bunch of grapes

rachi- /reɪki/ *prefix* same as **rachio-** (*used before vowels*)

rachianaesthesia /ˌreɪkiænəsˈθiːziə/ same as **spinal anaesthesia** (NOTE: The US spelling is **rachianesthesia**.)

rachio- /reɪkiəʊ/ *prefix* referring to the spine

rachiotomy /ˌreɪkiˈɒtəmi/ *noun* same as **laminectomy** (NOTE: The plural is **rachiotomies**.)

rachis /ˈreɪkɪs/ *noun* same as **backbone** (NOTE: The plural is **rachises** or **rachides**.)

rachischisis /reɪˈkɪskɪsɪs/ *noun* same as **spina bifida**

rachitic /rəˈkɪtɪk/ *adjective* referring to rickets

rachitis /rəˈkaɪtɪs/ *noun* same as **rickets**

rad /ræd/ *noun* a unit of measurement of absorbed radiation dose. ◊ **becquerel, gray** (NOTE: **Gray** is now used to mean one hundred rads.)

radial /ˈreɪdiəl/ *adjective* **1.** referring to something which branches **2.** referring to the radius bone in the arm

radial artery /ˈreɪdiəl ɑːtəri/ *noun* an artery which branches from the brachial artery, running near the radius, from the elbow to the palm of the hand

radial nerve /ˈreɪdiəl nɜːv/ *noun* the main motor nerve in the arm, running down the back of the upper arm and the outer side of the forearm

radial pulse /ˈreɪdiəl pʌls/ *noun* the main pulse in the wrist, taken near the outer edge of the forearm just above the wrist

radial recurrent /ˌreɪdiəl rɪˈkʌrənt/ *noun* an artery in the arm which forms a loop beside the brachial artery

radial reflex /ˌreɪdiəl ˈriːfleks/ *noun* a jerk made by the forearm when the insertion in the radius of one of the muscles, the brachioradialis, is hit

radiate /ˈreɪdieɪt/ *verb* **1.** to spread out in all directions from a central point ○ *The pain radiates from the site of the infection.* **2.** to send out rays ○ *Heat radiates from the body.* (NOTE: **radiating – radiated**)

radiation /ˌreɪdiˈeɪʃ(ə)n/ *noun* waves of energy which are given off by some substances, especially radioactive substances

COMMENT: Prolonged exposure to many types of radiation can be harmful. Nuclear radiation is the most obvious, but exposure to X-rays, either as a patient being treated or as a radiographer, can cause radiation sickness. First symptoms of the sickness are diarrhoea and vomiting, but radiation exposure can also be followed by skin burns and loss of hair. Massive exposure to radiation can kill quickly, and any person exposed to radiation is more likely to develop certain types of cancer than other members of the population.

radiation burn /ˌreɪdiˈeɪʃ(ə)n bɜːn/ *noun* a burn on the skin caused by exposure to large amounts of radiation

radiation enteritis /ˌreɪdieɪʃ(ə)n ˌentəˈraɪtɪs/ *noun* enteritis caused by X-rays

radiation sickness /ˌreɪdiˈeɪʃ(ə)n ˌsɪknəs/ *noun* an illness caused by exposure to radiation from radioactive substances

radiation treatment /ˌreɪdiˈeɪʃ(ə)n ˌtriːtmənt/ *noun* same as **radiotherapy**

radical /ˈrædɪk(ə)l/ *adjective* **1.** aiming to deal with the root of a problem, taking thorough action to remove the source of a disease rather than treat its symptoms **2.** referring to an operation which removes the whole of a part or of an organ, together with its lymph system and other tissue

radical mastectomy /ˌrædɪk(ə)l mæ 'stektəmi/ *noun* a surgical operation to remove a breast and the lymph nodes and muscles associated with it

radical mastoidectomy /ˌrædɪk(ə)l mæstɔɪ'dektəmi/ *noun* a surgical operation to remove all of the mastoid process

radical treatment /ˌrædɪk(ə)l 'triːtmənt/ *noun* treatment which aims at complete eradication of a disease

radicle /'rædɪk(ə)l/ *noun* **1.** a small root or vein **2.** a tiny fibre which forms the root of a nerve

radicular /rə'dɪkjʊlə/ *adjective* referring to a radicle

radiculitis /rəˌdɪkjʊ'laɪtɪs/ *noun* inflammation of a radicle of a cranial or spinal nerve

radio- /reɪdiəʊ/ *prefix* **1.** referring to radiation **2.** referring to radioactive substances **3.** referring to the radius in the arm

radioactive /ˌreɪdiəʊ'æktɪv/ *adjective* with a nucleus which disintegrates and gives off energy in the form of radiation which can pass through other substances

COMMENT: The commonest naturally radioactive substances are radium and uranium. Other substances can be made radioactive for medical purposes by making their nuclei unstable, so forming radioactive isotopes. Radioactive iodine is used to treat conditions such as thyrotoxicosis. Radioactive isotopes of various chemicals are used to check the functioning of, or disease in, internal organs.

radioactive isotope /ˌreɪdiəʊæktɪv 'aɪsətəʊp/ *noun* an isotope which sends out radiation, used in radiotherapy and scanning

radioactivity /ˌreɪdiəʊæk'tɪvɪti/ *noun* energy in the form of radiation emitted by a radioactive substance

radiobiologist /ˌreɪdiəʊbaɪ'ɒlədʒɪst/ *noun* a doctor who specialises in radiobiology

radiobiology /ˌreɪdiəʊbaɪ'ɒlədʒi/ *noun* the scientific study of radiation and its effects on living things

radiocarpal joint /reɪdiəʊ'kɑːp(ə)l dʒɔɪnt/ *noun* the joint where the radius articulates with the scaphoid, one of the carpal bones. Also called **wrist joint**

radiodermatitis /ˌreɪdiəʊˌdɜːmə'taɪtɪs/ *noun* inflammation of the skin caused by exposure to radiation

radiodiagnosis /ˌreɪdiəʊdaɪəg'nəʊsɪs/ *noun* an X-ray diagnosis

radiograph /'reɪdiəgrɑːf/ *noun* an image produced on film or another sensitive surface when radiation such as X-rays or gamma rays passes through an object ■ *verb* to make a radiograph of something, especially a part of the body

radiographer /ˌreɪdi'ɒɡrəfə/ *noun* **1.** a person specially trained to operate a machine to take X-ray photographs or radiographs. Also called **diagnostic radiographer 2.** a person specially trained to use X-rays or radioactive isotopes in the treatment of patients. Also called **therapeutic radiographer**

radiography /ˌreɪdi'ɒɡrəfi/ *noun* the work of examining the internal parts of the body by taking X-ray photographs

radioimmunoassay /ˌreɪdiəʊˌɪmjʊnəʊ 'æseɪ/ *noun* the use of radioactive tracers to investigate the presence of antibodies in blood samples, in order to measure the antibodies themselves or the amount of particular substances, such as hormones, in the blood

radioisotope /ˌreɪdiəʊ'aɪsətəʊp/ *noun* an isotope of a chemical element which is radioactive

COMMENT: Radioisotopes are used in medicine to provide radiation for radiation treatment. Radioactive isotopes of various chemicals are used to check the way organs function or if they are diseased: for example, radioisotopes of iodine are used to investigate thyroid activity.

radiologist /ˌreɪdi'ɒlədʒɪst/ *noun* a doctor who specialises in radiology

radiology /ˌreɪdi'ɒlədʒi/ *noun* the use of radiation to diagnose disorders, e.g. through the use of X-rays or radioactive tracers, or to treat diseases such as cancer

radiomimetic /ˌreɪdiəʊmɪ'metɪk/ *adjective* referring to a drug or chemical which produces similar effects to those of radiation, e.g. the nitrogen mustard group of chemicals used in chemotherapy

radionuclide /ˌreɪdiəʊ'njuːklaɪd/ *noun* an element which gives off radiation

radionuclide scan /ˌreɪdiəʊ'njuːklaɪd ˌskæn/ *noun* a scan, especially of the brain, where radionuclides are put in compounds which are concentrated in particular parts of the body

radio-opaque /ˌreɪdiəʊ əʊ'peɪk/ *adjective* absorbing and blocking radiant energy, e.g. X-rays

COMMENT: Radio-opaque substances appear light or white on X-rays and are used to make it easier to have clear radiographs of certain organs.

radio-opaque dye /ˌreɪdiəʊ əʊˌpeɪk 'daɪ/ *noun* a liquid which appears on an X-ray, and which is introduced into soft organs such as the kidney so that they show up clearly on an X-ray photograph

radiopaque /ˌreɪdiəʊ'peɪk/ *adjective* same as **radio-opaque**

radiopharmaceutical /ˌreɪdiəʊˌfɑːmə 'suːtɪk(ə)l/ *noun* a radioisotope used in medical diagnosis or treatment

radio pill /'reɪdiəʊ pɪl/ *noun* a tablet with a tiny radio transmitter

COMMENT: The person swallows the pill and as it passes through the body it gives off information about the digestive system.

radioscopy /ˌreɪdi'ɒskəpi/ *noun* an examination of an X-ray photograph on a fluorescent screen

radiosensitive /ˌreɪdiəu'sensɪtɪv/ *adjective* referring to a cancer cell which is sensitive to radiation and can be treated by radiotherapy

radiosensitivity /ˌreɪdiəusensə'tɪvɪti/ *noun* sensitivity of a cell to radiation

radiotherapist /ˌreɪdiəu'θerəpɪst/ *noun* a doctor who specialises in radiotherapy

radiotherapy /ˌreɪdiəu'θerəpi/ *noun* the treatment of diseases by exposing the affected part to radioactive rays such as X-rays or gamma rays

COMMENT: Many forms of cancer can be treated by directing radiation at the diseased part of the body.

radium /'reɪdiəm/ *noun* a radioactive metallic element (NOTE: The chemical symbol is **Ra**.)

radius /'reɪdiəs/ *noun* the shorter and outer of the two bones in the forearm between the elbow and the wrist. See illustration at **HAND** in Supplement (NOTE: The plural is **radii**. The other bone in the forearm is the **ulna**.)

radix /'reɪdɪks/ *noun* same as **root** (NOTE: The plural is **radices** or **radixes**.)

radon /'reɪdɒn/ *noun* a radioactive gas, formed from the radioactive decay of radium, and used in capsules called radon seeds to treat cancers inside the body (NOTE: The chemical symbol is **Rn**.)

COMMENT: Radon occurs naturally in soil, in construction materials and even in ground water. It can seep into houses and causes radiation sickness.

raise /reɪz/ *verb* **1.** to lift something ○ *Lie with your legs raised above the level of your head.* **2.** to increase something ○ *Anaemia causes a raised level of white blood cells in the body.*

rale /rɑːl/ *noun* same as **crepitation**

rally /'ræli/ *verb* to recover after a period of illness ■ *noun* a sudden recovery after a period of illness

Ramstedt's operation /'rɑːmstets ɒpə-ˌreɪʃ(ə)n/ *noun* same as **pylorotomy** [Described 1912. After Wilhelm Conrad Ramstedt (1867–1963), German surgeon.]

ramus /'reɪməs/ *noun* **1.** a branch of a nerve, artery or vein **2.** the ascending part on each side of the mandible (NOTE: The plural is **rami**.)

R & D /ˌɑːr ən 'diː/ *abbr* research and development

randomised /'rændəmaɪzd/, **randomized** *adjective* involving subjects which have been selected without a prearranged plan and in no particular pattern or order

range /reɪndʒ/ *noun* **1.** a series of different but similar things ○ *The drug offers protection against a wide range of diseases.* ○ *Doctors*

have a range of drugs which can be used to treat arthritis. **2.** the difference between lowest and highest values in a series of data

ranitidine /ræ'nɪtɪdiːn/ *noun* a drug which reduces the amount of acid released by the stomach. It is used to treat peptic ulcers and gastritis.

ranula /'rænjʊlə/ *noun* a small cyst under the tongue, on the floor of the mouth, which forms when a salivary duct is blocked

Ranvier /'rɑːnvɪˌeɪ/ ♦ **node of Ranvier**

rape /reɪp/ *noun* the crime of forcing somebody to have sexual intercourse ■ *verb* to force somebody to have sexual intercourse

raphe /'reɪfi/ *noun* a long thin fold which looks like a seam, along a midline such as on the dorsal face of the tongue

rapid /'ræpɪd/ *adjective* fast

rapid-acting /ˌræpɪd 'æktɪŋ/ *adjective* referring to a drug or treatment which has an effect very quickly

rapid eye movement sleep /ˌræpɪd aɪ 'muːvmənt sliːp/ *noun* same as **REM sleep**

rapport /ræ'pɔː/ *noun* an emotional bond or friendly relationship between people ○ *a psychiatrist who quickly establishes a rapport with his patients*

rare /reə/ *adjective* referring to something such as a disease of which there are very few cases ○ *He is suffering from a rare blood disorder.*

rarefaction /ˌreərɪ'fækʃən/ *noun* a condition in which bone tissue becomes more porous and less dense because of a lack of calcium

rarefy /'reərɪfaɪ/ *verb* **1.** (*of bones*) to become less dense **2.** to make something less dense

rash /ræʃ/ *noun* a mass of small spots which stays on the skin for a period of time, and then disappears □ **to break out in a rash** to have a rash which starts suddenly ○ *She had a high temperature and then broke out in a rash.*

COMMENT: Many common diseases such as chickenpox and measles have a characteristic rash as their main symptom. Rashes can be very irritating, but the itching can be relieved by applying calamine lotion.

raspatory /'ræspət(ə)ri/ *noun* a surgical instrument like a file, which is used to scrape the surface of a bone

ratbite fever /'rætbaɪt ˌfiːvə/, **ratbite disease** /'rætbaɪt dɪˌziːz/ *noun* fever caused by either of two bacteria *Spirillum minor* or *Streptobacillus moniliformis* and transmitted to humans by rats

rate /reɪt/ *noun* **1.** the amount or proportion of something compared with something else **2.** the number of times something happens in a set time ○ *The heart was beating at a rate of only 59 per minute.*

ratio /'reɪʃiəu/ *noun* a number which shows a proportion or which is the result of one number divided by another ○ *An IQ is the ratio* *of the person's mental age to his or her chronological age.*

rattle /'ræt(ə)l/ *noun* a harsh noise made in the throat, caused by a blockage to breathing and heard especially near death

Rauwolfia /rɔː'wʊlfiə/ *noun* a tranquillising drug extracted from the plant *Rauwolfia serpentine*, sometimes used to treat high blood pressure

raw /rɔː/ *adjective* **1.** not cooked **2.** sensitive ○ *The scab came off leaving the raw wound exposed to the air.* **3.** referring to skin scraped or partly removed

ray /reɪ/ *noun* a line of light, radiation or heat

Raynaud's disease /'reɪnəʊz dɪ,ziːz/, **Raynaud's phenomenon** /'reɪnəʊz fɪ,nɒmɪnən/ *noun* a condition with various possible causes in which the blood supply to the fingers and toes is restricted and they become cold, white and numb. Also called **dead man's fingers**, **vasospasm** [Described 1862. After Maurice Raynaud (1834–81), French physician.]

RBC *abbr* red blood cell

RCGP *abbr* Royal College of General Practitioners

RCN *abbr* Royal College of Nursing

RCOG *abbr* Royal College of Obstetricians and Gynaecologists

RCP *abbr* Royal College of Physicians

RCPsych /ˌɑː siː 'saɪk/ *abbr* Royal College of Psychiatrists

RCS *abbr* Royal College of Surgeons

RCT *abbr* randomised controlled trial

reabsorb /ˌriːəb'zɔːb/ *verb* to absorb or take up something again ○ *Glucose is reabsorbed by the tubules in the kidney.*

reabsorption /ˌriːəb'zɔːpʃ(ə)n/ *noun* the process of being reabsorbed ○ *Some substances which are filtered into the tubules of the kidney, then pass into the bloodstream by tubular reabsorption.*

reach /riːtʃ/ *noun* **1.** the distance which one can stretch to get hold of or touch something ○ *Medicines should be kept out of the reach of children.* **2.** the distance which one can travel easily ○ *The hospital is in easy reach of the railway station.* ■ *verb* to arrive at a point ○ *The infection has reached the lungs.*

react /ri'ækt/ *verb* **1.** □ **to react to something** to act because of something else, to act in response to something ○ *The tissues reacted to the cortisone injection.* ○ *The patient reacted badly to the penicillin.* ○ *She reacted positively to the Widal test.* **2.** □ **to react with something** (*of a chemical substance*) to change because of the presence of another substance

reaction /ri'ækʃən/ *noun* **1.** an action which takes place as a direct result of something which has happened earlier ○ *A rash appeared as a reaction to the penicillin injection.* **2.** an effect produced by a stimulus ○ *The patient*

experienced an allergic reaction to oranges. **3.** the particular response of someone to a test

reactionary /ri'ækʃən(ə)ri/ *adjective* same as **reactive**

reactionary haemorrhage /ri,ækʃən(ə)ri 'hem(ə)rɪdʒ/ *noun* bleeding which follows an operation

reactivate /ri'æktɪveɪt/ *verb* to make something active again ○ *His general physical weakness has reactivated the dormant virus.*

reactive /ri'æktɪv/ *adjective* taking place as a reaction to something else

reactive arthritis /ri,æktɪv ɑː'θraɪtɪs/ *noun* arthritis caused by a reaction to something

reactive hyperaemia /ri,æktɪv ,haɪpər 'iːmiə/ *noun* congestion of blood vessels after an occlusion has been removed

reading /'riːdɪŋ/ *noun* a note taken of figures, especially of degrees on a scale ○ *The sphygmomanometer gave a diastolic reading of 70.*

reagent /ri'eɪdʒənt/ *noun* a chemical substance which reacts with another substance, especially one which is used to detect the presence of the second substance

reagin /'riːədʒɪn/ *noun* an antibody which reacts against an allergen

real-time imaging /ˌriːəl taɪm 'ɪmɪdʒɪŋ/ *noun* the use of ultrasound information to produce a series of images of a process or changing object almost instantly

reappear /ˌriːə'pɪə/ *verb* to appear again

rear /rɪə/, **rear end** /rɪə end/ *noun* same as **buttock** (*informal*)

reason /'riːz(ə)n/ *noun* **1.** something which explains why something happens ○ *What was the reason for the sudden drop in the patient's pulse rate?* **2.** the fact of being mentally stable ○ *Her reason was beginning to fail.*

reassurance /ˌriːə'ʃʊərəns/ *noun* an act of reassuring

reassure /ˌriːə'ʃʊə/ *verb* to calm someone who is worried and give them hope ○ *The doctor reassured her that the drug had no unpleasant side-effects.* ○ *He reassured the old lady that she should be able to walk again in a few weeks.*

Reaven's Syndrome /'riːvənz ,sɪndrəʊm/ *noun* a clinical syndrome characterised by Type 2 diabetes, abdominal obesity, hypertension and dyslipidaemia. Insulin resistance may be a key factor. [Described 1988. After Gerald Reaven, US physician.]

rebore /'riːbɔː/ *noun* same as **endarterectomy** (*informal*)

rebuild /riː'bɪld/ *verb* to make good again a damaged structure or part of the body ○ *After the accident, she had several operations to rebuild her pelvis.*

recalcitrant /rɪ'kælsɪtrənt/ *adjective* not responding to treatment ○ *a recalcitrant condition*

recall /rɪ'kɔːl/ *noun* the act of remembering something from the past ■ *verb* to remember something which happened in the past

recanalisation /riːˌkænəlaɪ'zeɪʃ(ə)n/, **recanalization** *noun* surgery to unblock a vessel within the body or reconnect a tube or duct

receive /rɪ'siːv/ *verb* to get something, especially a transplanted organ ○ *She received six pints of blood in a transfusion.* ○ *He received a new kidney from his brother.*

receptaculum /riːsep'tækjʊləm/ *noun* part of a tube which is expanded to form a sac

receptor /rɪ'septə/, **receptor cell** /rɪ'septə sel/ *noun* a nerve ending or cell which senses a change such as cold or heat in the surrounding environment or in the body and reacts to it by sending an impulse to the central nervous system

recess /rɪ'ses/ *noun* a hollow part in an organ

recessive /rɪ'sesɪv/ *adjective* (*of an allele*) having the characteristic that leads to the trait which it controls being suppressed by the presence of the corresponding dominant allele. Compare **dominant**

COMMENT: Since each physical characteristic is governed by two genes, if one is dominant and the other recessive, the resulting trait will be that of the dominant gene. Traits governed by recessive genes will appear if both genes are recessive.

recipient /rɪ'sɪpiənt/ *noun* a person who receives something such as a transplant or a blood transfusion from a donor

'...bone marrow from donors has to be carefully matched with the recipient or graft-versus-host disease will ensue' [*Hospital Update*]

recognise /'rekəgnaɪz/, **recognize** *verb* **1.** to see or sense something or someone and remember it from an earlier occasion ○ *She did not recognise her mother.* **2.** to approve of something officially ○ *The diploma is recognised by the Department of Health.*

recombinant DNA /rɪˌkɒmbɪnənt diː en 'eɪ/ *noun* DNA extracted from two or more different sources and joined together to form a single molecule or fragment. This technology is used to produce molecules and organisms with new properties.

recommend /ˌrekə'mend/ *verb* to suggest that it would be a good thing if someone did something ○ *The doctor recommended that she should stay in bed.* ○ *I would recommend following a diet to try to lose some weight.*

reconstruct /ˌriːkən'strʌkt/ *verb* to repair and rebuild a damaged part of the body

reconstruction /ˌriːkən'strʌkʃən/ *noun* the process of repairing and rebuilding a damaged part of the body

reconstructive surgery /ˌriːkənstrʌktɪv 'sɜːdʒəri/ *noun* surgery which rebuilds a damaged part of the body. ◊ **plastic surgery**

record /'rekɔːd/ *verb* /rɪ'kɔːd/ to note information ○ *The chart records the variations in the patient's blood pressure.* ○ *You must take the patient's temperature every hour and record it in this book.* ■ *noun* a piece of information about something

COMMENT: Patients now have a legal right to have access to their medical records.

recover /rɪ'kʌvə/ *verb* **1.** to get better after an illness, operation or accident ○ *She recovered from her concussion in a few days.* ○ *It will take him weeks to recover from the accident.* (NOTE: You recover **from** an illness.) **2.** to get back something which has been lost ○ *Will he ever recover the use of his legs?* ○ *She recovered her eyesight even though the doctors had thought she would be permanently blind.*

recovery /rɪ'kʌv(ə)ri/ *noun* the process of returning to health after being ill or injured □ **he is well on the way to recovery** he is getting better □ **she made only a partial recovery** she is better, but is not completely well □ **she has made a complete** *or* **splendid recovery** she is completely well

recovery position /rɪ'kʌvəri pəˌzɪʃ(ə)n/ *noun* a position in which someone is lying face downwards, with one knee and one arm bent forwards and the face turned to one side

COMMENT: It is called the recovery position because it is recommended for accident victims or for people who are suddenly ill, while waiting for an ambulance to arrive. The position prevents the person from swallowing and choking on blood or vomit.

recovery room /rɪ'kʌv(ə)ri ruːm/ *noun* a room in a hospital where patients are cared for after they have had a surgical operation and are recovering from the effects of the anaesthetic. Abbr **RR**

recreational drug /ˌrekri'eɪʃ(ə)n(ə)l drʌg/ *noun* a drug that is taken for pleasure rather than because of medical need

recrudescence /ˌriːkruː'des(ə)ns/ *noun* the reappearance of symptoms of a disease which seemed to have got better

recrudescent /ˌriːkruː'des(ə)nt/ *adjective* referring to a symptom which has reappeared

recruit /rɪ'kruːt/ *verb* to get people to join the staff or a group ○ *We are trying to recruit more nursing staff.*

'...patients presenting with symptoms of urinary tract infection were recruited in a general practice surgery' [*Journal of the Royal College of General Practitioners*]

rect- /rekt/ *prefix* same as **recto-** (*used before vowels*)

recta /'rektə/ plural of **rectum**

rectal /'rekt(ə)l/ *adjective* referring to the rectum

rectal fissure /ˌrekt(ə)l 'fɪʃə/ *noun* a crack in the wall of the anal canal

rectally /'rekt(ə)li/ *adverb* through the rectum ○ *The temperature was taken rectally.*

rectal prolapse /ˌrekt(ə)l ˈprəʊlæps/ *noun* a condition in which part of the rectum moves downwards and passes through the anus

rectal temperature /ˌrekt(ə)l ˈtemprɪtʃə/ *noun* the temperature in the rectum, taken with a rectal thermometer

rectal thermometer /ˌrekt(ə)l θəˈmɒmɪtə/ *noun* a thermometer which is inserted into the rectum to take the person's temperature

rectal triangle /ˌrekt(ə)l ˈtraɪæŋg(ə)l/ *noun* same as **anal triangle**

recti /ˈrekti/ plural of **rectus**

recto- /rektəʊ/ *prefix* referring to the rectum

rectocele /ˈrektəʊsiːl/ *noun* a condition associated with prolapse of the uterus, in which the rectum protrudes into the vagina. Also called **proctocele**

rectopexy /ˈrektəʊpeksi/ *noun* a surgical operation to attach a rectum which has prolapsed

rectoscope /ˈrektəskəʊp/ *noun* an instrument for looking into the rectum

rectosigmoid /ˌrektəʊˈsɪgmɔɪd/ *noun* the part of the large intestine where the sigmoid colon joins the rectum

rectosigmoidectomy /ˌrektəʊˌsɪgmɔɪˈdektəmi/ *noun* the surgical removal of the sigmoid colon and the rectum

rectovaginal /ˌrektəʊvəˈdʒaɪn(ə)l/ *adjective* relating to both the rectum and the vagina

rectovaginal examination /ˌrektəʊvəˌdʒaɪn(ə)l ɪgˌzæmɪˈneɪʃ(ə)n/ *noun* an examination of the rectum and vagina

rectovesical /ˌrektəʊˈvesɪk(ə)l/ *adjective* referring to the rectum and the bladder

rectum /ˈrektəm/ *noun* the end part of the large intestine leading from the sigmoid colon to the anus. See illustration at DIGESTIVE SYSTEM in Supplement, UROGENITAL SYSTEM (MALE) in Supplement (NOTE: For other terms referring to the rectum, see words beginning with **proct-, procto-**.)

rectus /ˈrektəs/ *noun* a straight muscle (NOTE: The plural is **recti**.)

'…there are four recti muscles and two oblique muscles in each eye, which coordinate the movement of the eyes and enable them to work as a pair' [*Nursing Times*]

rectus abdominis /ˌrektəs æbˈdɒmɪnɪs/ *noun* a long straight muscle which runs down the front of the abdomen

rectus femoris /ˌrektəs ˈfemərɪs/ *noun* a flexor muscle in the front of the thigh, one of the four parts of the quadriceps femoris. ◊ **medial**

recumbent /rɪˈkʌmbənt/ *adjective* lying down

recuperate /rɪˈkuːpəreɪt/ *verb* to recover, to get better after an illness or accident ○ *He is recuperating after an attack of flu.* ○ *She is going to stay with her mother while she recuperates.*

recuperation /rɪˌkuːpəˈreɪʃ(ə)n/ *noun* the process of getting better after an illness ○ *His recuperation will take several months.*

recur /rɪˈkɜː/ *verb* to return ○ *The headaches recurred frequently, but usually after the patient had eaten chocolate.*

recurrence /rɪˈkʌrəns/ *noun* an act of returning ○ *He had a recurrence of a fever which he had caught in the tropics.*

recurrent /rɪˈkʌrənt/ *adjective* **1.** occurring in the same way many times **2.** referring to a vein, artery or nerve which forms a loop

recurrent abortion /rɪˌkʌrənt əˈbɔːʃ(ə)n/ *noun* a condition in which a woman has abortions with one pregnancy after another

recurrent fever /rɪˌkʌrənt ˈfiːvə/ *noun* a fever like malaria which returns at regular intervals

red /red/ *adjective* **1.** of a similar colour to blood ○ *Blood in an artery is bright red, but venous blood is darker.* **2.** (of an area of skin) with an increased blood flow because of heat or infection ■ *noun* a colour similar to that of blood

red blood cell /red blʌd sel/ *noun* a blood cell which contains haemoglobin and carries oxygen to the tissues and takes carbon dioxide from them. Abbr RBC. Also called **erythrocyte**

red corpuscle /ˌred ˈkɔːpʌs(ə)l/ *noun* same as **red blood cell**

Red Crescent /red ˈkrez(ə)nt/ *noun* in Islamic countries, an international organisation dedicated to the medical care of the sick and wounded in wars and natural disasters (NOTE: It is known as the Red Cross elsewhere.)

Red Cross /red ˈkrɒs/ *noun* an international organisation dedicated to the medical care of the sick and wounded in wars and natural disasters (NOTE: It is known as the Red Crescent in Islamic countries.)

red–green colourblindness /ˌred griːn ˈkʌləˌblaɪndnəs/ *noun* same as **deuteranopia**

Redivac drain /ˈredɪvæk dreɪn/, **Redivac drainage tube** /ˌredɪvæk ˈdreɪnɪdʒ tjuːb/ *trademark* a tube which drains fluid away from the inside of a wound into a bottle, used mainly after operations on the abdomen

red marrow /ˌred ˈmærəʊ/ *noun* the type of bone marrow where red blood cells and some white blood cells are formed

redness /ˈrednəs/ *noun* **1.** an area of skin to which the blood flow is increased because of heat or infection ○ *The redness showed where the skin had reacted to the injection.* **2.** a red colour

reduce /rɪˈdjuːs/ *verb* **1.** to make something smaller or lower ○ *They used ice packs to try to reduce the patient's temperature.* **2.** to put something such as a dislocated or fractured bone, a displaced organ or part or a hernia back into its proper position so that it can heal

'...blood pressure control reduces the incidence of first stroke and aspirin appears to reduce the risk of stroke after transient ischaemic attacks by some 15%' [*British Journal of Hospital Medicine*]

reducible /rɪ'djuːsɪb(ə)l/ *adjective* capable of being reduced

reducible hernia /rɪ,djuːsɪb(ə)l 'hɜːniə/ *noun* a hernia where the organ can be pushed back into place without an operation

reduction /rɪ'dʌkʃən/ *noun* **1.** the lessening of something, the process of becoming less ○ *They noted a reduction in body temperature.* **2.** the action of putting a hernia, a dislocated joint or a broken bone back into the correct position

reduction division /rɪ'dʌkʃən dɪ,vɪʒ(ə)n/ *noun* same as **meiosis**

re-emerge /,riː ɪ'mɜːdʒ/ *verb* to come out again

re-emergence /,riː ɪ'mɜːdʒəns/ *noun* an act of coming out again

refer /rɪ'fɜː/ *verb* **1.** to mention or to talk about something ○ *The doctor referred to the patient's history of sinus problems.* **2.** to suggest that someone should consult something ○ *For method of use, please refer to the manufacturer's instructions.* ○ *The user is referred to the page giving the results of the tests.* **3.** to pass on information about a patient to someone else ○ *They referred her case to a gynaecologist.* **4.** to send someone to another doctor, usually a specialist, for advice or treatment ○ *She was referred to a cardiologist.* □ **the GP referred the patient to a consultant** he or she passed details about the patient's case to the consultant so that the consultant could examine them

'27 adult patients admitted to hospital with acute abdominal pains were referred for study because their attending clinicians were uncertain whether to advise an urgent laparotomy' [*Lancet*]

'...many patients from outside districts were referred to London hospitals by their GPs' [*Nursing Times*]

referral /rɪ'fɜːrəl/ *noun* the act of sending someone to a specialist ○ *She asked for a referral to a gynaecologist.*

'...he subsequently developed colicky abdominal pain and tenderness which caused his referral' [*British Journal of Hospital Medicine*]

referred pain /rɪ,fɜːd 'peɪn/ *noun* same as **synalgia**

reflection /rɪ'flekʃən/ *noun* **1.** the image of somebody or something which is seen in a mirror or still water **2.** the process of reflecting something, especially light, sound or heat **3.** careful thought **4.** a situation in which an anatomical structure bends back upon itself

reflective practice /rɪ,flektɪv 'præktɪs/ *noun* the process of improving professional skills by monitoring your own actions while they are being carried out, and by then later evaluating them by talking or writing about

them and asking other professionals to give their assessments of you

reflex /'riːfleks/, **reflex action** /'riːfleks ,ækʃən/ *noun* a physiological reaction without any conscious thought involved, e.g. a knee jerk or a sneeze, which happens in response to a particular stimulus □ **light reflex**, **pupillary reflex to light** reaction of the pupil of the eye which changes size according to the amount of light going into the eye

reflex arc /'riːfleks ,ɑːk/ *noun* the basic system of a reflex action, where a receptor is linked to a motor neurone which in turn is linked to an effector muscle

reflexologist /,riːflək'sɒlədʒɪst/ *noun* a person specialising in reflexology

reflexology /,riːflek'sɒlədʒi/ *noun* a treatment to relieve tension by massaging the soles of the feet and thereby stimulating the nerves and increasing the blood supply

reflux /'riːflʌks/ *noun* a situation where a fluid flows in the opposite direction to its usual flow ○ *The valves in the veins prevent blood reflux.* ◊ **vesicoureteric reflux**

reflux oesophagitis /,riːflʌks iː,sɒfə'dʒaɪtɪs/ *noun* inflammation of the oesophagus caused by regurgitation of acid juices from the stomach

refract /rɪ'frækt/ *verb* to make light rays change direction as they go from one medium such as air to another such as water at an angle ○ *The refracting media in the eye are the cornea, the aqueous humour, the vitreous humour and the lens.*

refraction /rɪ'frækʃən/ *noun* **1.** a change of direction of light rays as they enter a medium such as the eye **2.** the measurement of the angle at which the light rays bend, as a test to see if someone needs to wear glasses

refractive /rɪ'fræktɪv/ *adjective* referring to refraction

refractometer /,riːfræk'tɒmɪtə/ *noun* an instrument which measures the refraction of the eye. Also called **optometer**

refractory /rɪ'frækt(ə)ri/ *adjective* difficult or impossible to treat, or not responding to treatment

refractory period /rɪ,frækt(ə)ri 'pɪəriəd/ *noun* a short space of time after the ventricles of the heart have contracted, when they cannot contract again

refrigerate /rɪ'frɪdʒəreɪt/ *verb* to make something cold ○ *The serum should be kept refrigerated.*

refrigeration /rɪ,frɪdʒə'reɪʃ(ə)n/ *noun* **1.** the process of making something cold **2.** the process of making part of the body very cold, to give the effect of an anaesthetic

refrigerator /rɪ'frɪdʒəreɪtə/ *noun* a machine which cools and keeps things cold

regain /rɪˈɡeɪn/ *verb* to get back something which was lost ○ *He has regained the use of his left arm.* ○ *She went into a coma and never regained consciousness.*

regenerate /rɪˈdʒenəreɪt/ *verb* to grow again, or grow something again

regeneration /rɪˌdʒenəˈreɪʃ(ə)n/ *noun* the process where tissue that has been destroyed grows again

regenerative medicine /rɪˌdʒenərətɪv ˈmed(ə)s(ə)n/ *noun* the branch of medicine that deals with the repair or replacement of tissues and organs by using advanced materials and methods such as cloning

regimen /ˈredʒɪmən/ *noun* a fixed course of treatment, e.g. a course of drugs or a special diet

region /ˈriːdʒən/ *noun* an area or part which is around something ○ *She experienced itching in the anal region.* ○ *The rash started in the region of the upper thigh.* ○ *The plantar region is very sensitive.*

regional /ˈriːdʒ(ə)nəl/ *adjective* in a particular region, referring to a particular region

regional enteritis /ˌriːdʒ(ə)nəl ˌentəˈraɪtɪs/ *noun* same as **Crohn's disease**

Regional Health Authority /ˌriːdʒ(ə)nəl ˈhelθ ɔːˌθɒrɪti/ *noun* an administrative unit in the National Health Service which is responsible for planning the health service in a region. Abbr **RHA**

regional ileitis /ˌriːdʒ(ə)nəl ˌɪliˈaɪtɪs/ *noun* compare **ulcerative colitis**. same as **Crohn's disease**

register /ˈredʒɪstə/ *noun* an official list ■ *verb* to write a name on an official list, especially the official list of patients treated by a GP or dentist, or the list of people with a particular disease ○ *He is a registered heroin addict.* ○ *They went to register the birth with the Registrar of Births, Marriages and Deaths.* □ **to register with someone** to put your name on someone's official list, especially the list of patients treated by a GP or dentist ○ *Before registering with the GP, she asked if she could visit him.* ○ *All practising doctors are registered with the General Medical Council.*

registered midwife /ˌredʒɪstəd ˈmɪdwaɪf/ *noun* a qualified midwife who is registered to practise

Registered Nurse /ˈredʒɪstəd ˈnɜːs/, **Registered General Nurse** /ˌredʒɪstəd ˈdʒen(ə)rəl nɜːs/, **Registered Theatre Nurse** /ˌredʒɪstəd ˈθɪətə nɜːs/ *noun* a nurse who has been registered by the UKCC. Abbr **RN, RGN, RTN**

registrar /ˌredʒɪˈstrɑː/ *noun* **1.** a qualified doctor or surgeon in a hospital who supervises house officers **2.** a person who registers something officially

Registrar of Births, Marriages and Deaths /ˌredʒɪstrɑː əv ˌbɜːθs ˌmærɪdʒɪz ən ˈdeθs/ *noun* an official who keeps the records of people who have been born, married or who have died in a particular area

registration /ˌredʒɪˈstreɪʃ(ə)n/ *noun* the act of registering ○ *A doctor cannot practise without registration by the General Medical Council.*

regress /rɪˈɡres/ *verb* to return to an earlier stage or condition

regression /rɪˈɡreʃ(ə)n/ *noun* **1.** a stage where symptoms of a disease are disappearing and the person is getting better **2.** (*in psychiatry*) the process of returning to a mental state which existed when the person was younger

regular /ˈreɡjʊlə/ *adjective* **1.** taking place again and again after the same period of time ○ *He was advised to make regular visits to the dentist.* ○ *She had her regular six-monthly checkup.* **2.** happening at the same time each day

regularly /ˈreɡjʊləli/ *adverb* happening repeatedly after the same period of time ○ *The tablets must be taken regularly every evening.* ○ *You should go to the dentist regularly.*

regulate /ˈreɡjʊˌleɪt/ *verb* to make something work in a regular way ○ *The heartbeat is regulated by the sinoatrial node.*

regulation /ˌreɡjʊˈleɪʃ(ə)n/ *noun* the act of regulating ○ *the regulation of the body's temperature*

regurgitate /rɪˈɡɜːdʒɪteɪt/ *verb* to bring into the mouth food which has been partly digested in the stomach

regurgitation /rɪˌɡɜːdʒɪˈteɪʃ(ə)n/ *noun* the process of flowing back in the opposite direction to the usual flow, especially of bringing up partly digested food from the stomach into the mouth

rehabilitate /ˌriːəˈbɪlɪteɪt/ *verb* to make someone fit to work or to lead their usual life

rehabilitation /ˌriːəbɪlɪˈteɪʃ(ə)n/ *noun* the process of making someone fit to work or to lead an ordinary life again

rehydrate /ˌriːhaɪˈdreɪt/ *verb* to restore body fluids to a healthy level, or cause this to occur

rehydration /ˌriːhaɪˈdreɪʃ(ə)n/ *noun* the act of giving water or liquid to someone who has dehydration

reinfect /ˌriːɪnˈfekt/ *verb* to infect someone or something again

reinfection /ˌriːɪnˈfekʃ(ə)n/ *noun* infection of an area for another time after recovery, especially with the same microorganism

Reiter's syndrome /ˈraɪtəz ˌsɪndrəʊm/, **Reiter's disease** /ˈraɪtəz dɪˈziːz/ *noun* an illness which may be sexually transmitted and affects mainly men, causing arthritis, urethritis and conjunctivitis at the same time [Described 1916. After Hans Conrad Reiter (1881–1969), German bacteriologist and hygienist.]

reject /rɪ'dʒekt/ *verb* **1.** to refuse to accept something **2.** to be unable to tolerate tissue or an organ transplanted from another body because it is immunologically incompatible ○ *The new heart was rejected by the body.* ○ *They gave the patient drugs to prevent the transplant being rejected.* **3.** to be unable to keep food down and vomit it up again

rejection /rɪ'dʒekʃən/ *noun* the act of rejecting tissue ○ *The patient was given drugs to reduce the possibility of tissue rejection.*

relapse /'riːlæps/ *noun* a situation in which someone gets worse after seeming to be getting better, or where a disease appears again after seeming to be cured ■ *verb* to return to an earlier and worse state, especially to get ill again after getting better ○ *She relapsed into a coma.*

relapsing fever /rɪ'læpsɪŋ ˌfiːvə/ *noun* a disease caused by a bacterium, where attacks of fever recur from time to time

relapsing pancreatitis /rɪˌlæpsɪŋ ˌpæŋkriə'taɪtɪs/ *noun* a form of pancreatitis where the symptoms recur, but in a less painful form

relate /rɪ'leɪt/ *verb* to connect something to something else ○ *The disease is related to the weakness of the heart muscles.*

-related /rɪleɪtɪd/ *suffix* connected to ○ *drug-related diseases*

relationship /rɪ'leɪʃ(ə)nʃɪp/ *noun* a way in which someone or something is connected to another ○ *The incidence of the disease has a close relationship to the environment.* ○ *He became withdrawn and broke off all relationships with his family.*

relative density /ˌrelətɪv 'densɪti/ *noun* the ratio of the density of a substance to the density of a standard substance at the same temperature and pressure. For liquids and solids the standard substance is usually water, and for gases, it is air.

relative risk /ˌrelətɪv 'rɪsk/ *noun* a measure of the likelihood of developing a disease for people who are exposed to a particular risk, relative to people who are not exposed to the same risk. For example, the relative risk of myocardial infarction for oral contraceptive users is 1.6 times that of non-users. Abbr **RR**

relax /rɪ'læks/ *verb* to become less tense, or cause someone or something to become less tense ○ *He was given a drug to relax the muscles.* ○ *The muscle should be fully relaxed.*

relaxant /rɪ'læksənt/ *noun* a substance which relieves strain ■ *adjective* relieving strain

relaxation /ˌriːlæk'seɪʃ(ə)n/ *noun* **1.** the process of reducing strain in a muscle **2.** the reduction of stress in a person

relaxation therapy /ˌriːlæk'seɪʃ(ə)n ˌθerəpi/ *noun* a treatment in which people are encouraged to relax their muscles to reduce stress

relaxative /rɪ'læksətɪv/ *noun* US a drug which reduces stress

relaxin /rɪ'læksɪn/ *noun* a hormone which is secreted by the placenta to make the cervix relax and open fully in the final stages of pregnancy before childbirth

release /rɪ'liːs/ *noun* the process of allowing something to go out ○ *the slow release of the drug into the bloodstream* ■ *verb* to let something out ○ *Hormones are released into the body by glands.*

releasing factor /rɪ'liːsɪŋ ˌfæktə/ *noun* a substance produced in the hypothalamus which encourages the release of hormones

releasing hormone /rɪ'liːsɪŋ ˌhɔːməʊn/ *noun* a hormone secreted by the hypothalamus which makes the pituitary gland release particular hormones. Also called **hypothalamic hormone**

relief /rɪ'liːf/ *noun* the process of making something better or easier ○ *The drug provides rapid relief for patients with bronchial spasms.*

'...complete relief of angina is experienced by 85% of patients subjected to coronary artery bypass surgery' [*British Journal of Hospital Medicine*]

relieve /rɪ'liːv/ *verb* to make something better or easier ○ *Nasal congestion can be relieved by antihistamines.* ○ *The patient was given an injection of morphine to relieve the pain.* ○ *The condition is relieved by applying cold compresses.*

'...replacement of the metacarpophalangeal joint is mainly undertaken to relieve pain, deformity and immobility due to rheumatoid arthritis' [*Nursing Times*]

rem /rem/ *noun* a unit for measuring amounts of radiation, equal to the effect that one roentgen of X-rays or gamma-rays would produce in a human being. It is used in radiation protection and monitoring.

REM /rem/ *abbr* rapid eye movement. ♦ **REM sleep**

remedial /rɪ'miːdiəl/ *adjective* acting as a cure

remedy /'remədi/ *noun* a cure, a drug which will cure ○ *Honey and glycerine is an old remedy for sore throats.*

remember /rɪ'membə/ *verb* to bring back into the mind something which has been seen or heard before ○ *He remembers nothing* or *he can't remember anything about the accident.*

remission /rɪ'mɪʃ(ə)n/ *noun* a period when an illness or fever is less severe

re. mist. /ˌriː 'mɪst/ *adverb* (*on a prescription*) repeat the same mixture. Full form **repetatur mistura**

remittent /rɪ'mɪtənt/ *adjective* lessening and then intensifying again at intervals

remittent fever /rɪˌmɪtənt 'fiːvə/ *noun* fever which goes down for a period each day, like typhoid fever

removal /rɪ'muːv(ə)l/ *noun* the action of removing something ○ *An appendicectomy is the surgical removal of an appendix.*

remove /rɪ'muːv/ *verb* to take something away ○ *He will have an operation to remove an ingrowing toenail.*

REM sleep /'rem sliːp/ *noun* a stage of sleep which happens several times each night and is characterised by dreaming, rapid eye movement and increased pulse rate and brain activity. Also called **rapid eye movement sleep**

COMMENT: During REM sleep, a person dreams, breathes lightly and has a raised blood pressure and an increased rate of heartbeat. The eyes may be half-open, and the sleeper may make facial movements.

ren- /riːn/ *prefix* same as **reno-** (*used before vowels*)

renal /'riːn(ə)l/ *adjective* referring to the kidneys

renal artery /ˌriːn(ə)l 'ɑːtəri/ *noun* one of two arteries running from the abdominal aorta to the kidneys

renal calculus /ˌriːn(ə)l 'kælkjʊləs/ *noun* a small hard mineral mass called a stone in the kidney

renal capsule /ˌriːn(ə)l 'kæpsjuːl/ *noun* same as **fibrous capsule**

renal clearance /'riːn(ə)l ˌklɪərəns/ *noun* the measurement of the rate at which kidneys filter impurities from blood

renal colic /ˌriːn(ə)l 'kɒlɪk/ *noun* a sudden pain caused by a kidney stone or stones in the ureter

renal corpuscle /ˌriːn(ə)l 'kɔːpʌs(ə)l/ *noun* part of a nephron in the cortex of a kidney. Also called **Malpighian body**

renal cortex /ˌriːn(ə)l 'kɔːteks/ *noun* the outer covering of the kidney, immediately beneath the capsule. See illustration at KIDNEY in Supplement

renal dialysis /ˌriːn(ə)l daɪ'æləsɪs/ *noun* a method of artificially maintaining the chemical balance of the blood when the kidneys have failed, or the process of using this method. Also called **dialysis**

renal hypertension /ˌriːn(ə)l ˌhaɪpə'tenʃən/ *noun* high blood pressure linked to kidney disease

renal medulla /ˌriːn(ə)l me'dʌlə/ *noun* the inner part of a kidney containing no glomeruli. See illustration at KIDNEY in Supplement

renal pelvis /ˌriːn(ə)l 'pelvɪs/ *noun* the upper and wider part of the ureter leading from the kidney where urine is collected before passing down the ureter into the bladder. Also called **pelvis of the kidney**. See illustration at KIDNEY in Supplement

renal rickets /ˌriːn(ə)l 'rɪkɪts/ *noun* a form of rickets caused by kidneys which do not function properly

renal sinus /ˌriːn(ə)l 'saɪnəs/ *noun* a cavity in which the renal pelvis and other tubes leading into the kidney fit

renal transplant /ˌriːn(ə)l 'trænsplɑːnt/ *noun* a kidney transplant

renal tubule /ˌriːn(ə)l 'tjuːbjuːl/ *noun* a tiny tube which is part of a nephron. Also called **uriniferous tubule**

renew /rɪ'njuː/ *verb* □ **to renew a prescription** to get a new prescription for the same drug as before

reni- /riːni/ *prefix* referring to the kidneys

renin /'riːnɪn/ *noun* an enzyme secreted by the kidney to prevent loss of sodium, and which also affects blood pressure

rennin /'renɪn/ *noun* an enzyme which makes milk coagulate in the stomach, so as to slow down the passage of the milk through the digestive system

reno- /riːnəʊ/ *prefix* referring to the kidneys

renogram /'riːnəʊɡræm/ *noun* **1.** an X-ray image of a kidney **2.** a visual record of kidney function that shows how quickly a radioactive substance introduced into the bloodstream is removed by the kidneys

renography /riː'nɒɡrəfi/ *noun* an examination of a kidney after injection of a radioactive substance, using a gamma camera

renovascular /ˌriːnəʊ'væskjʊlə/ *adjective* relating to the blood vessels of the kidneys

renovascular system /ˌriːnəʊ'væskjʊlə ˌsɪstəm/ *noun* the blood vessels associated with the kidney

reorganisation /riːˌɔːɡənaɪ'zeɪʃ(ə)n/, **reorganization** *noun* **1.** a change in the way something is organised or done **2.** the process of changing the way something is organised or done **3.** an occasion when a business or organisation is given a completely new structure

reovirus /'riːəʊˌvaɪrəs/ *noun* a virus which affects both the intestine and the respiratory system, but does not cause serious illness. Compare **echovirus**

rep /rep/ *adverb* (*written on a prescription*) repeat. Full form **repetatur**

repair /rɪ'peə/ *verb* to make something that is damaged good again ○ *Surgeons operated to repair a hernia.*

repeat /rɪ'piːt/ *verb* to say or do something again ○ *The course of treatment was repeated after two months.*

repeat prescription /rɪˌpiːt prɪ'skrɪpʃən/ *noun* a prescription which is exactly the same as the previous one, and is often given without examination of the person by the doctor and may sometimes be requested by telephone

repel /rɪ'pel/ *verb* to make something go away ○ *If you spread this cream on your skin it will repel insects.*

repetitive strain injury /rɪˌpetɪtɪv 'streɪn ˌɪndʒəri/, **repetitive stress injury** /rɪˌpetɪtɪv 'stres ˌɪndʒəri/ *noun* pain, usually in a limb, felt by someone who performs the same movement many times over a period, e.g. when operating a computer terminal or playing a musical instrument. Abbr **RSI**

replace /rɪ'pleɪs/ *verb* **1.** to put something back ○ *an operation to replace a prolapsed uterus* **2.** to exchange one part for another ○ *The surgeons replaced the diseased hip with a metal one.*

replacement /rɪ'pleɪsmənt/ *noun* an operation to replace part of the body with an artificial part

replacement transfusion /rɪˌpleɪsmənt ˌtræns'fjuːʒ(ə)n/ *noun* an exchange transfusion, a treatment for leukaemia or erythroblastosis where almost all the unhealthy blood is removed from the body and replaced by healthy blood

replant /riː'plɑːnt/ *verb* to reattach or reinsert a body part such as a limb or tooth that has become detached

replantation /ˌriːplɑːn'teɪʃ(ə)n/ *noun* a surgical technique which reattaches parts of the body which have been accidentally cut or torn off

replicate /'replɪkeɪt/ *verb* (*of a cell*) to make a copy of itself

replication /ˌreplɪ'keɪʃ(ə)n/ *noun* the process in the division of a cell, where the DNA makes copies of itself

repolarisation /riːˌpəʊləraɪ'zeɪʃ(ə)n/, **repolarization** *noun* the restoration of the usual electrical polarity of a nerve or muscle cell membrane after reversal of its polarity while a nerve impulse or muscle contraction travelled along it

report /rɪ'pɔːt/ *noun* an official note stating what action has been taken, what treatment given or what results have come from a test ○ *The patient's report card has to be filled in by the nurse.* ○ *The inspector's report on the hospital kitchens is good.* ■ *verb* to make an official report about something ○ *The patient reported her doctor for misconduct.* ○ *Occupational diseases* or *serious accidents at work must be reported to the local officials.*

reportable diseases /rɪˌpɔːtəb(ə)l dɪ'ziːzɪz/ *plural noun* diseases such as asbestosis, hepatitis or anthrax which may be caused by working conditions or may infect other workers and must be reported to the District Health Authority

repositor /rɪ'pɒzɪtə/ *noun* a surgical instrument used to push a prolapsed organ back into its usual position

repress /rɪ'pres/ *verb* to decide to ignore or forget feelings or thoughts which may be unpleasant or painful

repression /rɪ'preʃ(ə)n/ *noun* (*in psychiatry*) the act of ignoring or forgetting feelings or thoughts which might be unpleasant

reproduce /ˌriːprə'djuːs/ *verb* **1.** to produce children **2.** (*of microorganisms*) to produce new cells **3.** to do a test again in exactly the same way

reproduction /ˌriːprə'dʌkʃən/ *noun* the process of making new living beings by existing ones, e.g. producing children or derived other descendants

reproductive /ˌriːprə'dʌktɪv/ *adjective* referring to reproduction

reproductive organs /ˌriːprə'dʌktɪv ˌɔːgənz/ *plural noun* parts of the bodies of men and women which are involved in the conception and development of a fetus

reproductive system /ˌriːprə'dʌktɪv ˌsɪstəm/ *noun* the arrangement of organs and ducts in the bodies of men and women which produce spermatozoa or ova

COMMENT: In the human male, the testes produce the spermatozoa which pass through the vasa efferentia and the vasa deferentia where they receive liquid from the seminal vesicles, then out of the body through the urethra and penis on ejaculation. In the female, an ovum, produced by one of the two ovaries, passes through the Fallopian tube where it is fertilised by a spermatozoon from the male. The fertilised ovum moves down into the uterus where it develops into an embryo.

reproductive tract /ˌriːprə'dʌktɪv trækt/ *noun* the series of tubes and ducts which carry spermatozoa or ova from one part of the body to another

require /rɪ'kwaɪə/ *verb* to need something ○ *His condition may require surgery.* ○ *Is it a condition which requires immediate treatment?* □ **required effect** effect which a drug is expected to have ○ *If the drug does not produce the required effect, the dose should be increased.*

requirement /rɪ'kwaɪəmənt/ *noun* something which is necessary ○ *One of the requirements of the position is a qualification in pharmacy.*

RES *abbr* reticuloendothelial system

research /rɪ'sɜːtʃ/ *noun* a scientific study which investigates something new ○ *He is the director of a medical research unit.* ○ *She is doing research into finding a cure for leprosy.* ○ *Research workers* or *Research teams are trying to find a vaccine against AIDS.* ■ *verb* to carry out scientific study ○ *He is researching the origins of cancer.*

research and development /rɪˌsɜːtʃ ən dɪ'veləpmənt/ *noun* the process by which pharmaceutical companies find new drugs and test their suitability. Abbr **R & D**

resect /rɪ'sekt/ *verb* to remove any part of the body by surgery

resection /rɪ'sekʃən/ *noun* the surgical removal of any part of the body

resection of the prostate /rɪˌsekʃən əv ðə ˈprɒsteɪt/ *noun* same as **transurethral prostatectomy**

resectoscope /rɪˈsektəskəʊp/ *noun* a surgical instrument used to carry out a transurethral resection

reservoir /ˈrezəvwɑː/ *noun* 1. a cavity in an organ or group of tissues in which fluids collect and are stored 2. an organism in which a parasite lives and develops without damaging it, but from which the parasite then passes to another species which is damaged by it 3. a part of a machine or piece of equipment where liquid is stored for it to use

reset /riːˈset/ *verb* to break a badly set bone and set it again correctly ○ *His arm had to be reset.*

residency /ˈrezɪd(ə)nsi/ *noun US* a period when a doctor is receiving specialist training in a hospital

resident /ˈrezɪd(ə)nt/ *noun* 1. someone who lives in a place ○ *All the residents of the old people's home were tested for food poisoning.* 2. *US* a qualified doctor who is employed by a hospital and sometimes lives in the hospital. Compare **intern** ■ *adjective* living in a place

resident doctor /ˌrezɪd(ə)nt ˈdɒktə/ *noun* a doctor who lives in a building such as an old people's home

residential /ˌrezɪˈdenʃəl/ *adjective* 1. living in a hospital 2. living at home

residential care /ˌrezɪˈdenʃəl keə/ *noun* the care of patients either in a hospital or at home, but not as outpatients

residual /rɪˈzɪdjuəl/ *adjective* remaining, which is left behind

residual air /rɪˌzɪdjuəl ˈeə/, **residual volume** /rɪˌzɪdjuəl ˈvɒljuːm/ *noun* air left in the lungs after a person has breathed out as much air as possible

residual urine /rɪˌzɪdjuəl ˈjʊərɪn/ *noun* urine left in the bladder after a person has passed as much urine as possible

resin /ˈrezɪn/ *noun* a sticky sap or liquid which comes from some types of tree

resist /rɪˈzɪst/ *verb* to be strong enough to avoid being killed or attacked by a disease ○ *A healthy body can resist some infections.*

resistance /rɪˈzɪstəns/ *noun* 1. the ability of a person not to get a disease 2. the ability of bacteria or a virus to remain unaffected by a drug ○ *The bacteria have developed a resistance to certain antibiotics.* 3. opposition to a force

resistant /rɪˈzɪst(ə)nt/ *adjective* able not to be affected by something ○ *The bacteria are resistant to some antibiotics.*

resistant strain /rɪˌzɪst(ə)nt ˈstreɪn/ *noun* a strain of bacterium which is not affected by antibiotics

resolution /ˌrezəˈluːʃ(ə)n/ *noun* 1. the amount of detail which can be seen in a microscope or on a computer monitor 2. a point in the development of a disease where the inflammation begins to disappear

resolve /rɪˈzɒlv/ *verb* (*of inflammation*) to begin to disappear

'…valve fluttering disappears as the pneumothorax resolves. Always confirm resolution with a physical examination and X-ray' [*American Journal of Nursing*]

resolvent /rɪˈzɒlvənt/ *adjective* able to reduce inflammation or swelling

resonance /ˈrez(ə)nəns/ *noun* a sound made by a hollow part of the body when hit. ◊ **magnetic**

resorption /rɪˈsɔːpʃən/ *noun* the process of absorbing a substance produced by the body back into the body

respiration /ˌrespəˈreɪʃ(ə)n/ *noun* the act of taking air into the lungs and blowing it out again through the mouth or nose. Also called **breathing**

COMMENT: Respiration includes two stages: breathing in (inhalation) and breathing out (exhalation). Air is taken into the respiratory system through the nose or mouth, and goes down into the lungs through the pharynx, larynx and windpipe. In the lungs, the bronchi take the air to the alveoli (air sacs) where oxygen in the air is passed to the bloodstream in exchange for waste carbon dioxide which is then breathed out.

respiration rate /ˌrespəˈreɪʃ(ə)n reɪt/ *noun* the number of times a person breathes per minute

respirator /ˈrespəreɪtə/ *noun* 1. same as **ventilator** □ **the patient was put on a respirator** the patient was attached to a machine which forced him to breathe 2. a mask worn to prevent someone breathing harmful gas or fumes

respiratory /rɪˈspɪrət(ə)ri/ *adjective* referring to breathing

respiratory allergy /rɪˌspɪrət(ə)ri ˈælədʒi/ *noun* an allergy caused by a substance which is inhaled. ◊ **alveolitis, food allergy**

respiratory bronchiole /rɪˌspɪrət(ə)ri ˈbrɒŋkiəʊl/ *noun* the end part of a bronchiole in the lung, which joins the alveoli

respiratory centre /rɪˌspɪrət(ə)ri ˈsentə/ *noun* a nerve centre in the brain which regulates the breathing

respiratory distress syndrome /rɪˌspɪrət(ə)ri dɪˈstres ˌsɪndrəʊm/ *noun* a condition of newborn babies, and especially common in premature babies, in which the lungs do not expand properly, due to lack of surfactant. Also called **hyaline membrane disease**

respiratory failure /rɪˌspɪrət(ə)ri ˈfeɪljə/ *noun* failure of the lungs to oxygenate the blood correctly

respiratory illness /rɪˌspɪrət(ə)ri ˈɪlnəs/ *noun* an illness which affects someone's breathing

respiratory pigment /rɪˌspɪrət(ə)ri ˈpɪgmənt/ *noun* blood pigment which can carry oxygen collected in the lungs and release it in tissues

respiratory quotient /rɪˌspɪrət(ə)ri ˈkwəʊʃ(ə)nt/ *noun* the ratio of the amount of carbon dioxide taken into the alveoli of the lungs from the blood to the amount of oxygen which the alveoli take from the air. Abbr **RQ**

respiratory syncytial virus /rɪˌspɪrət(ə)ri sɪnˈsɪtiəl ˌvaɪrəs/ *noun* a virus which causes infections of the nose and throat in adults, but serious bronchiolitis in children. Abbr **RSV**

respiratory system /rɪˈspɪrət(ə)ri ˈsɪstəm/, **respiratory tract** /rɪˈspɪrət(ə)ri trækt/ *noun* the series of organs and passages which take air into the lungs, and exchange oxygen for carbon dioxide

respite care /ˈrespaɪt keə/ *noun* temporary care provided to people with disabilities, serious conditions or terminal illness, so that their families can have a rest from the daily routine

respond /rɪˈspɒnd/ *verb* **1.** to react to something ○ *The cancer is not responding to drugs.* **2.** to begin to get better because of a treatment ○ *She is responding to treatment.*

'…many severely confused patients, particularly those in advanced stages of Alzheimer's disease, do not respond to verbal communication' [*Nursing Times*]

response /rɪˈspɒns/ *noun* a reaction by an organ, tissue or a person to an external stimulus ◇ **immune response 1.** reaction of a body to an antigen **2.** reaction of a body which rejects a transplant

'…anaemia may be due to insufficient erythrocyte production, in which case the reticulocyte count will be low, or to haemolysis or haemorrhage, in which cases there should be a reticulocyte response' [*Southern Medical Journal*]

responsibility /rɪˌspɒnsɪˈbɪlɪti/ *noun* **1.** somebody or something which a person or organisation has a duty to take care of ○ *Checking the drip is your responsibility.* **2.** the blame for something bad which has happened ○ *She has taken full responsibility for the mix-up.* **3.** the position of having to explain to somebody why something was done ○ *Whose responsibility is it to talk to the family?*

responsible /rɪˈspɒnsɪb(ə)l/ *adjective* referring to something which is the cause of something else ○ *the allergen which is responsible for the patient's reaction* ○ *This is one of several factors which can be responsible for high blood pressure.*

responsive /rɪˈspɒnsɪv/ *adjective* reacting positively to medical treatment

responsiveness /rɪˈspɒnsɪvnəs/ *noun* the ability to respond to other people or to sensations

rest /rest/ *noun* a period of time spent relaxing or sleeping ○ *What you need is a good night's rest.* ■ *verb* **1.** to spend time relaxing or sleeping **2.** to use a body part less for a period of time ○ *Rest your arm for a week.*

restenosis /ˌriːstəˈnəʊsɪs/ *noun* an occasion when something becomes narrow again, e.g. a coronary artery which has previously been widened by balloon angioplasty (NOTE: The plural is **restenoses**.)

restless /ˈrestləs/ *adjective* not able to relax or be still ○ *restless sleep* ○ *She had a restless night.*

restless leg syndrome /ˌrestləs ˈleg ˌsɪndrəʊm/ *noun* painful discomfort in the legs when not active that can lead to interrupted sleep and fatigue

restore /rɪˈstɔː/ *verb* to give something back ○ *She needs vitamins to restore her strength.* ○ *The physiotherapy should restore the strength of the muscles.* ○ *A salpingostomy was performed to restore the patency of the Fallopian tube.*

restrict /rɪˈstrɪkt/ *verb* **1.** to make something less or smaller ○ *The blood supply is restricted by the tight bandage.* **2.** to set limits to something ○ *The doctor suggested she should restrict her intake of alcohol.*

restrictive /rɪˈstrɪktɪv/ *adjective* restricting, making something smaller

result /rɪˈzʌlt/ *noun* figures at the end of a calculation, at the end of a test ○ *What was the result of the test?* ○ *The doctor told the patient the result of the pregnancy test.* ○ *The result of the operation will not be known for some weeks.*

resuscitate /rɪˈsʌsɪteɪt/ *verb* to make someone who appears to be dead start breathing again, and to restart the circulation of blood

resuscitation /rɪˌsʌsɪˈteɪʃ(ə)n/ *noun* the act of reviving someone who seems to be dead, by making him or her breathe again and restarting the heart

COMMENT: The commonest methods of resuscitation are artificial respiration and cardiac massage.

retain /rɪˈteɪn/ *verb* to keep or hold something ○ *He was incontinent and unable to retain urine in his bladder.* ◇ **retention**

retard /rɪˈtɑːd/ *verb* to make something slower, e.g. to slow down the action of a drug ○ *The drug will retard the onset of the fever.* ○ *The injections retard the effect of the anaesthetic.*

retardation /ˌriːtɑːˈdeɪʃ(ə)n/ *noun* the process of making something slower

retch /retʃ/ *verb* to try to vomit without bringing any food up from the stomach

retching /ˈretʃɪŋ/ *noun* the fact of attempting to vomit without being able to do so

rete /ˈriːtiː/ *noun* a network of veins, arteries or nerve fibres in the body. ◇ **reticular** (NOTE: The plural is **retia**.)

retention /rɪˈtenʃən/ noun the act of not letting out something, especially a fluid, which is usually released from the body, e.g. holding back urine in the bladder

retention cyst /rɪˈtenʃən sɪst/ noun a cyst which is formed when a duct from a gland is blocked

retention of urine /rɪˌtenʃən əv ˈjʊərɪn/ noun a condition in which passing urine is difficult or impossible because the urethra is blocked or because the prostate gland is enlarged

rete testis /ˌriːtiː ˈtestɪs/ noun a network of channels in the testis which take the sperm to the epididymis. ◊ **reticular**

retia /ˈriːʃiə/ plural of **rete**

reticular /rɪˈtɪkjʊlə/ adjective relating to or in the form of a network

reticular fibres /rɪˌtɪkjʊlə ˈfaɪbəs/ plural noun fibres in connective tissue which support, e.g., organs or blood vessels

reticular tissue /rɪˌtɪkjʊlə ˈtɪʃuː/ noun same as **reticular fibres**

reticulin /rɪˈtɪkjʊliːn/ noun a fibrous protein which is one of the most important components of reticular fibres

reticulocyte /rɪˈtɪkjʊləʊsaɪt/ noun a red blood cell which has not yet fully developed

reticulocytosis /rɪˌtɪkjʊləʊsaɪˈtəʊsɪs/ noun a condition in which the number of reticulocytes in the blood increases unusually

reticuloendothelial cell /rɪˌtɪkjʊləʊˌendəʊˈθiːliəl sel/ noun a phagocytic cell in the reticuloendolethial system

reticuloendothelial system /rɪˌtɪkjʊləʊˌendəʊˈθiːliəl ˌsɪstəm/ noun a series of phagocytic cells in the body, found especially in bone marrow, lymph nodes, liver and spleen, which attack and destroy bacteria and form antibodies. Abbr **RES**

reticuloendotheliosis /rɪˌtɪkjʊləʊˌendəʊθiːliˈəʊsɪs/ noun a condition in which cells in the RES grow large and form swellings in bone marrow or destroy bones

reticulosis /rɪˌtɪkjʊˈləʊsɪs/ noun any of several conditions where cells in the reticuloendothelial system grow large and form usually malignant tumours

reticulum /rɪˈtɪkjʊləm/ noun a series of small fibres or tubes forming a network

retin- /retɪn/ prefix same as **retino-** (used before vowels)

retina /ˈretɪnə/ noun the inside layer of the eye which is sensitive to light. ◊ **detached retina**. See illustration at EYE in Supplement (NOTE: The plural is **retinae**.)

COMMENT: Light enters the eye through the pupil and strikes the retina. Light-sensitive cells in the retina (cones and rods) convert the light to nervous impulses. The optic nerve sends these impulses to the brain which interprets them as images. The point where the optic nerve joins the retina has no light-sensitive cells, and is known as the blind spot.

retinaculum /ˌretɪˈnækjʊləm/ noun a band of tissue which holds a structure in place, as found in the wrist and ankle over the flexor tendons

retinae /ˈretɪni/ plural of **retina**

retinal /ˈretɪn(ə)l/ adjective referring to the retina

retinal artery /ˈretɪn(ə)l ˌɑːtəri/ noun the only artery of the retina, which accompanies the optic nerve

retinal detachment /ˌretɪn(ə)l dɪˈtætʃmənt/ noun a condition in which the retina is partly detached from the choroid

retinitis /ˌretɪˈnaɪtɪs/ noun inflammation of the retina

retinitis pigmentosa /ˌretɪˌnaɪtɪs ˌpɪgmenˈtəʊsə/ noun a hereditary condition in which inflammation of the retina can result in blindness

retino- /retɪnəʊ/ prefix referring to the retina

retinoblastoma /ˌretɪnəʊblæˈstəʊmə/ noun a rare tumour in the retina, affecting infants

retinol /ˈretɪnɒl/ noun a vitamin found in liver, vegetables, eggs and cod liver oil which is essential for good vision. Also called **Vitamin A**

retinopathy /ˌretɪˈnɒpəθi/ noun any disease of the retina

retinoscope /ˈretɪnəskəʊp/ noun an instrument with various lenses, used to measure the refraction of the eye

retinoscopy /ˌretɪˈnɒskəpi/ noun a method of measuring refractive errors in the eye using a retinoscope

retire /rɪˈtaɪə/ verb to stop work at a particular age ○ Most men retire at 65, but women only go on working until they are 60. ○ Although she has retired, she still does voluntary work at the clinic.

retirement /rɪˈtaɪəmənt/ noun **1.** the act of retiring ○ The retirement age for men is 65. **2.** the act of being retired

retraction /rɪˈtrækʃən/ noun the fact of moving backwards or becoming shorter ○ There is retraction of the overlying skin.

retraction ring /rɪˈtrækʃən rɪŋ/ noun a groove round the uterus, separating its upper and lower parts, which, in obstructed labour, prevents the baby from moving forward as expected into the cervical canal. Also called **Bandl's ring**

retractor /rɪˈtræktə/ noun a surgical instrument which pulls and holds back the edge of the incision in an operation

retro- /retrəʊ/ prefix at the back, behind

retrobulbar /ˌretrəʊˈbʌlbə/ adjective behind the eyeball

retrobulbar neuritis /ˌretrəʊˌbʌlbə njuːˈraɪtɪs/ noun inflammation of the optic nerve which makes objects appear blurred. Also called **optic neuritis**

retroflexion /ˌretrəʊˈflekʃ(ə)n/ *noun* the fact of being bent backwards □ **retroflexion of the uterus** a condition in which the uterus bends backwards away from its usual position

retrograde /ˈretrəʊɡreɪd/ *adjective* going backwards or deteriorating, getting worse

retrograde pyelography /ˌretrəʊɡreɪd ˌpaɪəˈlɒɡrəfi/ *noun* an X-ray examination of the kidney where a catheter is passed into the kidney and an opaque liquid is injected directly into it

retrogression /ˌretrəʊˈɡreʃ(ə)n/ *noun* returning to an earlier state

retrolental fibroplasia /ˌretrəʊˌlent(ə)l ˌfaɪbrəʊˈpleɪziə/ *noun* a condition in which fibrous tissue develops behind the lens of the eye, resulting in blindness

COMMENT: Retrolental fibroplasia can occur in premature babies if they are treated with large amounts of oxygen immediately after birth.

retro-ocular /ˌretrəʊ ˈɒkjʊlə/ *adjective* at the back of the eye

retroperitoneal /ˌretrəʊˌperɪtəˈniːəl/ *adjective* at the back of the peritoneum

retroperitoneal space /ˌretrəʊˌperɪtəʊniːəl ˈspeɪs/ *noun* the area between the posterior parietal peritoneum and the posterior abdominal wall, containing the kidneys, adrenal glands, duodenum, ureters and pancreas

retropharyngeal /ˌretrəʊˌfærɪnˈdʒiːəl/ *adjective* at the back of the pharynx

retropubic /ˌretrəʊˈpjuːbɪk/ *adjective* at the back of the pubis

retropubic prostatectomy /ˌretrəʊpjuːbɪk ˌprɒstəˈtektəmi/ *noun* removal of the prostate gland which is carried out through a suprapubic incision and by cutting the membrane which surrounds the gland

retrospection /ˌretrəˈspekʃən/ *noun* the act of recalling what happened in the past

retrospective /ˌretrəˈspektɪv/ *adjective* applying to the past, tracing what has happened already to selected people

retroversion /ˌretrəʊˈvɜːʃ(ə)n/ *noun* the fact of sloping backwards □ **retroversion of the uterus** Same as **retroverted uterus**

retroverted uterus /ˌretrəʊvɜːtɪd ˈjuːtərəs/ *noun* a condition in which the uterus slopes backwards away from its usual position. Also called **retroversion of the uterus, tipped womb**

retrovirus /ˈretrəʊvaɪrəs/ *noun* a virus whose genetic material contains RNA from which DNA is synthesised (NOTE: The AIDS virus and many carcinogenic viruses are retroviruses.)

revascularisation /riːˌvæskjʊləraɪˈzeɪʃ(ə)n/, **revascularization** *noun* 1. the act of restoring an adequate blood supply to an organ or tissue, especially in a surgical operation using a blood vessel graft 2. the condition of having an adequate blood supply restored

reveal /rɪˈviːl/ *verb* to show something ○ *Digital palpation revealed a growth in the breast.*

reversal /rɪˈvɜːs(ə)l/ *noun* the procedure to change something back ○ *reversal of sterilisation*

reverse isolation /rɪˌvɜːs ˌaɪsəˈleɪʃ(ə)n/ *noun* same as **protective isolation**

revision /rɪˈvɪʒ(ə)n/ *noun* an examination of a surgical operation after it has been carried out ○ *a revision of a radical mastoidectomy*

revive /rɪˈvaɪv/ *verb* to bring someone back to life or to consciousness ○ *They tried to revive him with artificial respiration.* ○ *She collapsed on the floor and had to be revived by the nurse.*

Reye's syndrome /ˈraɪz ˌsɪndrəʊm/ *noun* a form of brain disease affecting young children, which is possibly due to viral infection and has a suspected link with aspirin

RGN *abbr* Registered General Nurse

Rh *abbr* rhesus

RHA *abbr* Regional Health Authority

rhabdomyosarcoma /ˌræbdəʊˌmaɪəʊsɑːˈkəʊmə/ *noun* a malignant tumour of striated muscle tissue. It occurs mostly in children.

rhabdovirus /ˈræbdəʊvaɪrəs/ *noun* any of a group of viruses containing RNA, one of which causes rabies

rhachio- /ˈreɪkiəʊ/ *prefix* referring to the spine

rhagades /ˈræɡədiːz/ *plural noun* long thin scars in the skin round the nose, mouth or anus, seen in syphilis. ◊ **fissure**

Rh disease /ɑːr ˈeɪtʃ dɪˌziːz/ *noun* same as **rhesus factor disease**

rheo- /ˈriːəʊ/ *prefix* 1. relating to the flow of liquids 2. relating to the flow of electrical current

rheometer /riˈɒmɪtə/ *noun* a device that measures the flow of thick liquids such as blood

rhesus baby /ˈriːsəs ˌbeɪbi/ *noun* a baby with erythroblastosis fetalis

rhesus factor /ˈriːsəs ˌfæktə/ *noun* an antigen in red blood cells, which is an element in blood grouping. Also called **Rh factor**

COMMENT: The rhesus factor is important in blood grouping, because, although most people are Rh-positive, an Rh-negative patient should not receive an Rh-positive blood transfusion as this will cause the formation of permanent antibodies. If an Rh-negative mother has a child by an Rh-positive father, the baby will inherit Rh-positive blood, which may then pass into the mother's circulation at childbirth and cause antibodies to form. This can be prevented by an injection of anti D immunoglobulin immediately after the birth of the first Rh-positive child and any subsequent Rh-positive children. If an Rh-negative mother has formed antibodies to Rh-positive blood in the past, these antibodies will affect the blood of the fetus and may cause erythroblastosis fetalis.

rhesus factor disease /'ri:səs ˌfæktə dɪ ˌziːz/ *noun* a disease which occurs when the blood of a fetus has a different rhesus factor from that of the mother. Also called **Rh disease**

rheumatic /ruː'mætɪk/ *adjective* referring to rheumatism

rheumatic fever /ruːˌmætɪk 'fiːvə/ *noun* a collagen disease of young people and children, caused by haemolytic streptococci, where the joints and also the valves and lining of the heart become inflamed. Also called **acute rheumatism**

COMMENT: Rheumatic fever often follows another streptococcal infection such as a strep throat or tonsillitis. Symptoms are high fever, pains in the joints, which become red, formation of nodules on the ends of bones and difficulty in breathing. Although recovery can be complete, rheumatic fever can recur and damage the heart permanently.

rheumatism /'ruːmətɪz(ə)m/ *noun* pains and stiffness in the joints and muscles (*informal*) ○ *She has rheumatism in her hips.* ○ *He complained of rheumatism in the knees.*

rheumatoid /'ruːmətɔɪd/ *adjective* relating to rheumatism

rheumatoid arthritis /ˌruːmətɔɪd ɑː'θraɪtɪs/ *noun* a general painful disabling collagen disease affecting any joint, but especially the hands, feet and hips, making them swollen and inflamed. ◊ **osteoarthritis**

'...rheumatoid arthritis is a chronic inflammatory disease which can affect many systems of the body, but mainly the joints. 70% of sufferers develop the condition in the metacarpophalangeal joints' [*Nursing Times*]

rheumatoid erosion /ˌruːmətɔɪd ɪ'rəʊʒ(ə)n/ *noun* erosion of bone and cartilage in the joints caused by rheumatoid arthritis

rheumatoid factor /'ruːmətɔɪd ˌfæktə/ *noun* an antibody found in the blood serum of many people who have rheumatoid arthritis

rheumatologist /ˌruːmə'tɒlədʒɪst/ *noun* a doctor who specialises in rheumatology

rheumatology /ˌruːmə'tɒlədʒi/ *noun* a branch of medicine dealing with rheumatic disease of muscles and joints

Rh factor /ˌɑːr 'eɪtʃ ˌfæktə/ *noun* same as **rhesus factor**

rhin- /raɪn/ *prefix* same as **rhino-** (*used before vowels*)

rhinal /'raɪn(ə)l/ *adjective* referring to the nose

rhinencephalon /ˌraɪnen'kefəlɒn/ *noun* the area of the forebrain that controls the sense of smell

rhinitis /raɪ'naɪtɪs/ *noun* inflammation of the mucous membrane in the nose, which makes the nose run, caused, e.g., by a virus infection or an allergic reaction to dust or flowers

rhino- /raɪnəʊ/ *prefix* referring to the nose

rhinology /raɪ'nɒlədʒi/ *noun* a branch of medicine dealing with diseases of the nose and the nasal passages

rhinomycosis /ˌraɪnəʊmaɪ'kəʊsɪs/ *noun* an infection of the nasal passages by a fungus

rhinopharyngitis /ˌraɪnəʊfærɪn'dʒaɪtɪs/ *noun* inflammation of the mucous membranes in the nose and pharynx

rhinophyma /ˌraɪnəʊ'faɪmə/ *noun* a condition caused by rosacea, in which the nose becomes permanently red and swollen

rhinoplasty /'raɪnəʊplæsti/ *noun* plastic surgery to correct the appearance of the nose

rhinorrhoea /ˌraɪnəʊ'rɪə/ *noun* a watery discharge from the nose

rhinoscope /'raɪnəskəʊp/ *noun* an instrument for examining the inside of the nose

rhinoscopy /raɪ'nɒskəpi/ *noun* an examination of the inside of the nose

rhinosinusitis /ˌraɪnəʊˌsaɪnə'saɪtɪs/ *noun* swelling of the lining of the nose and paranasal sinuses, as a result of either a viral infection or allergic rhinitis. It is usually treated with antibiotics, antihistamines or steroids.

rhinosporidiosis /ˌraɪnəʊˌspɒrɪdi'əʊsɪs/ *noun* an infection of the nose, eyes, larynx and genital organs by the fungus *Rhinosporidium seeberi*

rhinovirus /'raɪnəʊˌvaɪrəs/ *noun* a group of viruses containing RNA, which cause infection of the nose and include the virus which causes the common cold

rhiz- /raɪz/, **rhizo-** /'raɪzəʊ/ *prefix* referring to a root

rhizotomy /raɪ'zɒtəmi/ *noun* a surgical operation to cut or divide the roots of a nerve to relieve severe pain

Rh-negative /ˌɑː eɪtʃ 'negətɪv/ *adjective* who does not have the rhesus factor in his or her blood

rhodopsin /rəʊ'dɒpsɪn/ *noun* a light-sensitive purple pigment in the rods of the retina, which makes it possible to see in dim light. Also called **visual purple**

rhombencephalon /ˌrɒmben'kefəlɒn/ *noun* the hindbrain, the part of the brain which contains the cerebellum, the medulla oblongata and the pons

rhomboid /'rɒmbɔɪd/ *noun* one of two muscles in the top part of the back which move the shoulder blades

rhonchus /'rɒŋkəs/ *noun* an unusual sound in the chest, heard through a stethoscope, caused by a partial blockage in the bronchi (NOTE: The plural is **rhonchi**.)

Rh-positive /ˌɑː eɪtʃ 'pɒzɪtɪv/ *adjective* who has the rhesus factor in his or her blood

rhythm /'rɪð(ə)m/ *noun* a regular movement or beat

rhythmic /'rɪðmɪk/ *adjective* regular, with a repeated rhythm

rhythm method /'rɪð(ə)m ˌmeθəd/ *noun* a method of birth control where sexual intercourse should take place only during the safe periods when conception is least likely to occur, i.e. at the beginning and at the end of the menstrual cycle

COMMENT: This method is not as safe or reliable as other methods of contraception because the time when ovulation takes place cannot be accurately calculated if a woman does not have regular periods.

rib /rɪb/ *noun* one of twenty-four curved bones which protect the chest (NOTE: For other terms referring to the ribs, see words beginning with **cost-**, **costo-**.)

ribavirin /'raɪbəˌvaɪrɪn/ *noun* a synthetic drug which helps to prevent the synthesis of viral DNA and RNA, used in the treatment of viral diseases

rib cage /'rɪb keɪdʒ/ *noun* the ribs and the space enclosed by them

COMMENT: The rib cage is formed of twelve pairs of curved bones. The top seven pairs, the true ribs, are joined to the breastbone in front by costal cartilage. The other five pairs of ribs, the false ribs, are not attached to the breastbone, though the 8th, 9th and 10th pairs are each attached to the rib above. The bottom two pairs, which are not attached to the breastbone at all, are called the floating ribs.

riboflavine /ˌraɪbəʊ'fleɪvɪn/ same as **Vitamin B₂** (NOTE: The US spelling is **riboflavin**.)

ribonuclease /ˌraɪbəʊ'njuːklieɪz/ *noun* an enzyme which breaks down RNA

ribonucleic acid /ˌraɪbəʊnjuːˌkliːɪk 'æsɪd/ *noun* one of the nucleic acids in the nucleus of all living cells, which takes coded information from DNA and translates it into specific enzymes and proteins. ◊ **DNA**. Abbr **RNA**

ribose /'raɪbəʊs/ *noun* a type of sugar found in RNA

ribosomal /ˌraɪbə'səʊm(ə)l/ *adjective* referring to ribosomes

ribosome /'raɪbəsəʊm/ *noun* a tiny particle in a cell, containing RNA and protein, where protein is synthesised

ricewater stools /'raɪswɔːtə stuːlz/ *plural noun* watery faeces that are typically passed by people who have cholera

rich /rɪtʃ/ *adjective* **1.** well supplied **2.** referring to food which has a high calorific value

'...the sublingual region has a rich blood supply derived from the carotid artery' [*Nursing Times*]

ricin /'raɪsɪn/ *noun* a highly toxic albumin found in the seeds of the castor oil plant

rick /rɪk/ *noun* a slight injury to a joint caused by wrenching or spraining it ■ *verb* to wrench or sprain a joint of the body slightly

rickets /'rɪkɪts/ *noun* a disease of children, where the bones are soft and do not develop

properly due to lack of Vitamin D. Also called **rachitis**

COMMENT: Initial treatment for rickets in children is a vitamin-rich diet, together with exposure to sunshine which causes vitamin D to form in the skin.

Rickettsia /rɪ'ketsɪə/ *noun* a genus of microorganisms which causes several diseases including Q fever and typhus

rickettsial /rɪ'ketsɪəl/ *adjective* referring to Rickettsia

rickettsial pox /rɪ'ketsɪəl pɒks/ *noun* a disease found in North America, caused by *Rickettsia akari* passed to humans by bites from mites which live on mice

rid /rɪd/ *verb* □ **to get rid of something** to make something go away ○ *He can't get rid of his cold – he's had it for weeks.* □ **to be rid of something** not to have something unpleasant any more ○ *I'm very glad to be rid of my flu.*

ridge /rɪdʒ/ *noun* a long raised part on the surface of a bone or organ

rifampicin /rɪf'æmpɪsɪn/ *noun* an antibiotic which works by interfering with RNA synthesis in the infecting bacteria, used in the treatment of tuberculosis, leprosy and other bacterial infections

right /raɪt/ *noun* the fact of being legally entitled to do or to have something ○ *You always have the right to ask for a second opinion.*

right colic /ˌraɪt 'kɒlɪk/ *noun* an artery which leads from the superior mesenteric artery

right-handed /ˌraɪt 'hændɪd/ *adjective* using the right hand more often than the left ○ *He's right-handed.* ○ *Most people are right-handed.*

right-left shunt /ˌraɪt left 'ʃʌnt/ *noun* a malformation in the heart, allowing blood to flow from the pulmonary artery to the aorta

right lymphatic duct /ˌraɪt lɪmˌfætɪk 'dʌkt/ *noun* one of the main terminal channels for carrying lymph, draining the right side of the head and neck and entering the junction of the right subclavian and internal jugular veins. It is the smaller of the two main discharge points of the lymphatic system into the venous system, the larger being the thoracic duct.

rigid /'rɪdʒɪd/ *adjective* stiff, not moving

rigidity /rɪ'dʒɪdɪti/ *noun* the fact of being rigid, bent or not able to be moved. ◊ **spasticity**

rigor /'rɪgə/ *noun* an attack of shivering, often with fever

rigor mortis /ˌrɪgə 'mɔːtɪs/ *noun* a condition in which the muscles of a dead body become stiff after death and then become relaxed again

COMMENT: Rigor mortis starts about eight hours after death, and begins to disappear several hours later. Environment and temperature play a large part in the timing.

rima /'raɪmə/ *noun* a narrow crack or cleft

rima glottidis /ˌriːmə 'glɒtɪdɪs/ *noun* a space between the vocal cords

ring /rɪŋ/ *noun* a circle of tissue, or tissue or muscle shaped like a circle

ring block /'rɪŋ blɒk/ *noun* the process of inserting local anaesthetic all the way round a digit, e.g. a finger, in order to perform a procedure distal to the block.

Ringer's solution /'rɪŋəz sə,lu:ʃ(ə)n/ *noun* a solution of inorganic salts which is used both to treat burns and cuts and to keep cells, tissues or organs alive outside the body

ring finger /'rɪŋ ,fɪŋgə/ *noun* the third finger, the finger between the little finger and the middle finger

ringing in the ear /,rɪŋɪŋ ɪn ði 'ɪə/ ♦ **tinnitus**

ringworm /'rɪŋwɜːm/ *noun* any of various infections of the skin by a fungus, in which the infection spreads out in a circle from a central point. It is very contagious and difficult to get rid of. Also called **tinea**

Rinne's test /'rɪniz test/ *noun* a hearing test in which a tuning fork is hit and its handle placed near the ear, to test for air conduction, and then on the mastoid process, to test for bone conduction. It is then possible to determine the type of lesion which exists by finding if the sound is heard for a longer period by air or by bone conduction. [Described 1855. After Friedrich Heinrich Rinne (1819–68), otologist at Göttingen, Germany.]

rinse out /,rɪns 'aʊt/ *verb* to lightly wash the inside of something to make it clean, e.g. to get rid of soap ○ *She rinsed out the measuring jar.* ○ *Rinse your mouth out with mouthwash.*

ripple bed /'rɪp(ə)l bed/ *noun* a type of bed with an air-filled mattress divided into sections, in which the pressure is continuously being changed so that the body can be massaged and bedsores can be avoided

rise /raɪz/ *verb* to go up ○ *His temperature rose sharply.* (NOTE: **rising – rose – risen**)

risk /rɪsk/ *noun* the possibility of something harmful happening ○ *There is a risk of a cholera epidemic.* ○ *There is no risk of the disease spreading to other members of the family.* □ **at risk** in danger of being harmed ○ *Businessmen are particularly at risk of having a heart attack.* □ **children at risk** children who are more likely to be harmed or to catch a disease ■ *verb* to do something which may possibly cause harm or have bad results ○ *If the patient is not moved to an isolation ward, all the patients and staff in the hospital risk catching the disease.*

'…adenomatous polyps are a risk factor for carcinoma of the stomach' [*Nursing Times*]

'…three quarters of patients aged 35–64 on GPs' lists have at least one major risk factor: high cholesterol, high blood pressure or addiction to tobacco' [*Health Services Journal*]

risk factor /'rɪsk ,fæktə/ *noun* a characteristic that increases a person's likelihood of getting a particular disease ○ *Smoking is a risk*

factor for lung cancer. ○ *Obesity is a risk factor for diabetes.*

risus sardonicus /,raɪsəs sɑː'dɒnɪkəs/ *noun* a twisted smile which is a symptom of tetanus

rite of passage /,raɪt əv 'pæsɪdʒ/ *noun* a ceremony which shows that somebody is moving from one stage of their life to another, e.g. from childhood to puberty or from unmarried to married life

river blindness /'rɪvə ,blaɪndnəs/ *noun* blindness caused by larvae getting into the eye in cases of onchocerciasis

RM *abbr* Registered Midwife

RMN *abbr* Registered Mental Nurse

RN *abbr* Registered Nurse

RNA *abbr* ribonucleic acid

RNMH *abbr* Registered Nurse for the Mentally Handicapped

Rocky Mountain spotted fever /,rɒki ,maʊntɪn ,spɒtɪd 'fiːvə/ *noun* a type of typhus caused by *Rickettsia rickettsii*, transmitted to humans by ticks

rod /rɒd/ *noun* **1.** a stick shape with rounded ends ○ *Some bacteria are shaped like rods or are rod-shaped.* **2.** one of two types of light-sensitive cell in the retina of the eye. Rods are sensitive to dim light, but not to colour. ◊ **cone**

COMMENT: Rod cells in the eye are sensitive to poor light. They contain rhodopsin or visual purple, which produces the nervous impulse which the rod transmits to the optic nerve.

rodent ulcer /,rəʊd(ə)nt 'ʌlsə/ *noun* a malignant tumour on the face

COMMENT: Rodent ulcers are different from some other types of cancer in that they do not spread to other parts of the body and do not metastasise, but remain on the face, usually near the mouth or eyes. Rodent ulcer is rare before middle age.

roentgen /'rɒntgən/ *noun* a unit of radiation used to measure the exposure of someone or something to X-rays or gamma rays. Symbol **R** [After Wilhelm Konrad von Röntgen (1845–1923), physicist at Strasbourg, Geissen, Würzburg and Munich, and then Director of the physics laboratory at Würzburg where he discovered X-rays in 1895. Nobel prize for Physics 1901.]

roentgenogram /'rɒntgenəgræm/ *noun* an X-ray photograph

roentgenology /,rɒntgə'nɒlədʒi/ *noun* the study of X-rays and their use in medicine

roentgen ray /'rɒntgən reɪ/ *noun* an X-ray or gamma ray which can pass through tissue and leave an image on a photographic film

role /rəʊl/ *noun* **1.** the usual or expected function of somebody or something in a particular process or event ○ *the role of haemoglobin in blood clotting* **2.** the characteristic or expected pattern of behaviour of a particular member of a social group ○ *the eldest child's role in the family*

role playing /ˈrəʊl ˌpleɪɪŋ/ *noun* the act of pretending to be somebody else in a situation, so that you have to imagine how that person feels and thinks. It usually involves several people. It is used in many training exercises and psychiatric evaluations.

rolled bandage /ˌrəʊld ˈbændɪdʒ/, **roller bandage** /ˌrəʊlə ˈbændɪdʒ/ *noun* a bandage in the form of a long strip of cloth which is rolled up from one or both ends

Romberg's sign /ˈrɒmbɜːgz saɪn/ *noun* a swaying of the body or falling when standing with the feet close together and the eyes closed, the result of loss of the joint position sense [Described 1846. After Moritz Heinrich Romberg (1795–1873), German physician and pioneer neurologist.]

COMMENT: If a patient cannot stand upright when his or her eyes are closed, this shows that nerves in the lower limbs which transmit joint position sense to the brain are damaged.

rongeur /rɒŋˈɡɜː/ *noun* a strong surgical instrument like a pair of pliers, used for cutting bone

roof /ruːf/ *noun* the top part of a cavity □ **roof of the mouth** Same as **palate**

root /ruːt/ *noun* **1.** a point from which a part of the body grows ○ *root of hair* or *hair root* ○ *root of nerve* or *nerve root* **2.** part of a tooth which is connected to a socket in the jaw ▸ also called **radix**

root canal /ˈruːt kəˌnæl/ *noun* a canal in the root of a tooth through which the nerves and blood vessels pass

rooting reflex /ˈruːtɪŋ ˌriːfleks/ *noun* the instinct in new babies to turn their heads towards a touch on the cheek or mouth, which is important for breastfeeding

Roper, Logan and Tierney model /ˌrəʊpə ˌləʊɡən ən ˈtɪəni ˌmɒd(ə)l/ *noun* an important model of nursing developed in the UK in 1980. Various factors such as necessary daily tasks, lifespan and health status are used to assess the relative independence of an individual, which the nurse will help them to increase.

Rorschach test /ˈrɔːʃɑːk test/ *noun* the ink blot test, used in psychological diagnosis, where someone is shown a series of blots of ink on paper and is asked to say what each blot reminds him or her of. The answers give information about the person's psychological state. [Described 1921. After Hermann Rorschach (1884–1922), German-born psychiatrist who worked in Bern, Switzerland.]

rosacea /rəʊˈzeɪʃə/ *noun* a common skin disease seen from middle age affecting the face, and especially the nose, which becomes red because of enlarged blood vessels. The cause is not known. Also called **acne rosacea** (NOTE: Despite its alternative name, rosacea is not a type of acne.)

rosea /ˈrəʊzɪə/ ♦ **pityriasis**

roseola infantum /rəʊˌziːələ ɪnˈfæntəm/ *noun* a sudden infection of small children, with fever, swelling of the lymph glands and a rash. It is caused by herpesvirus 6. Also called **exanthem subitum**

rostral /ˈrɒstr(ə)l/ *adjective* like the beak of a bird

rostrum /ˈrɒstrəm/ *noun* a projecting part of a bone or structure shaped like a beak (NOTE: The plural is **rostra**.)

rot /rɒt/ *verb* to decay, to become putrefied ○ *The flesh was rotting round the wound as gangrene set in.* ○ *The fingers can rot away in leprosy.*

rotate /rəʊˈteɪt/ *verb* to move in a circle, or make something move in a circle

rotation /rəʊˈteɪʃ(ə)n/ *noun* the act of moving in a circle. See illustration at ANATOMICAL TERMS in Supplement □ **lateral and medial rotation** turning part of the body to the side, towards the midline

rotator /rəʊˈteɪtə/ *noun* a muscle which makes a limb rotate

rotavirus /ˈrəʊtəvaɪrəs/ *noun* any of a group of viruses associated with gastroenteritis in children

'…rotavirus is now widely accepted as an important cause of childhood diarrhoea in many different parts of the world' [*East African Medical Journal*]

Rothera's test /ˈrɒðərəz test/ *noun* a test to see if acetone is present in urine, a sign of ketosis which is a complication of diabetes mellitus [After Arthur Cecil Hamel Rothera (1880–1915), biochemist in Melbourne, Australia]

Roth spot /ˈrəʊt spɒt/ *noun* a pale spot which sometimes occurs on the retina of a person who has leukaemia or some other diseases [After Moritz Roth (1839–1915), Swiss pathologist and physician]

rotunda /rəʊˈtʌndə/ ♦ **fenestra**

rough /rʌf/ *adjective* not smooth ○ *rough skin*

roughage /ˈrʌfɪdʒ/ *noun* same as **dietary fibre**

COMMENT: Roughage is found in cereals, nuts, fruit and vegetables. It is believed to be necessary to help digestion and avoid developing constipation and obesity.

rouleau /ruːˈləʊ/ *noun* a roll of red blood cells which have stuck together like a column of coins (NOTE: The plural is **rouleaux**.)

round /raʊnd/ *adjective* shaped like a circle ■ *noun* a regular visit □ **to do the rounds of the wards** to visit various wards in a hospital and talk to the nurses and check on patients' progress or condition □ **a health visitor's rounds** regular series of visits made by a health visitor

round ligament /raʊnd ˈlɪɡəmənt/ *noun* a band of muscle which stretches from the uterus to the labia

round window /raʊnd ˈwɪndəʊ/ *noun* a round opening between the middle ear and the cochlea, and closed by a membrane. Also called **fenestra rotunda**. See illustration at EAR in Supplement

roundworm /ˈraʊndwɜːm/ *noun* any of several common types of parasitic worms with round bodies, such as hookworms. Compare **flatworm**

Rovsing's sign /ˈrɒvsɪŋz saɪn/ *noun* pain in the right iliac fossa when the left iliac fossa is pressed, which is a sign of acute appendicitis [Described 1907. After Nils Thorkild Rovsing (1862–1927), Professor of Surgery at Copenhagen, Denmark.]

Royal College of General Practitioners /ˌrɔɪəl ˌkɒlɪdʒ əv ˈdʒen(ə)rəl/ *noun* a professional association which represents family doctors. Abbr **RCGP**

Royal College of Nursing /ˌrɔɪəl ˌkɒlɪdʒ əv ˈnɜːsɪŋ/ *noun* a professional association which represents nurses. Abbr **RCN**

Roy's model /ˈrɔɪz ˌmɒd(ə)l/ *noun* a model for nursing developed in the US in the 1970s. It describes a person's health as being a state of successful positive adaptation to all those stimuli from the environment which could interfere with their basic need satisfaction. Illness results from an inability to adapt to such stimuli, so nurses should help patients to overcome this.

RQ *abbr* respiratory quotient

RR *abbr* **1.** recovery room **2.** relative risk

-rrhage /rɪdʒ/, **-rrhagia** /ˈreɪdʒə/ *suffix* referring to an unusual flow or discharge of blood

-rrhaphy /rəfi/ *suffix* referring to surgical sewing or suturing

-rrhexis /reksɪs/ *suffix* referring to splitting or rupture

-rrhoea /rɪə/ *suffix* referring to an unusual flow or discharge of fluid from an organ

RSCN *abbr* Registered Sick Children's Nurse

RSI *abbr* repetitive strain injury

RSV *abbr* respiratory syncytial virus

RTN *abbr* Registered Theatre Nurse

rub /rʌb/ *noun* a lotion used to rub on the skin ○ *The ointment is used as a rub.* ■ *verb* **1.** to move something, especially the hands, backwards and forwards over a surface ○ *She rubbed her leg after she knocked it against the table.* ○ *He rubbed his hands to make the circulation return.* **2.** □ **to rub into** to make an ointment go into the skin by rubbing ○ *Rub the liniment gently into the skin.*

rubber /ˈrʌbə/ *noun* **1.** a material which can be stretched and compressed, made from the thick white liquid called latex, from a tropical tree **2.** a condom (*informal*)

rubber sheet /ˌrʌbə ˈʃiːt/ *noun* a waterproof sheet put on hospital beds or on the bed of a child who is prone to bedwetting, to protect the mattress

rubbing alcohol /ˈrʌbɪŋ ˌælkəhɒl/ *noun US* same as **surgical spirit**

rubefacient /ˌruːbɪˈfeɪʃ(ə)nt/ *noun* a substance which makes the skin warm, and pink or red ■ *adjective* causing the skin to become red

rubella /ruːˈbelə/ *noun* a common infectious viral disease of children with mild fever, swollen lymph nodes and rash. Also called **German measles**

COMMENT: Rubella can cause stillbirth or malformation of an unborn baby if the mother catches the disease while pregnant. One component of the MMR vaccine immunises against rubella.

rubeola /ruːˈbiːələ/ *noun* same as **measles**

Rubin's test /ˈruːbɪnz test/ *noun* a test to see if the Fallopian tubes are free from obstruction [After Isador Clinton Rubin (b. 1883), US gynaecologist]

rubor /ˈruːbə/ *noun* redness of the skin or tissue

rudimentary /ˌruːdɪˈment(ə)ri/ *adjective* existing in a small form, or not developed fully ○ *The child was born with rudimentary arms.*

Ruffini corpuscles /ruːˈfiːni ˌkɔːpʌs(ə)lz/, **Ruffini nerve endings** /ruːˌfiːni ˈnɜːv ˌendɪŋz/ *plural noun* branching nerve endings in the skin, which are thought to be sensitive to heat

ruga /ˈruːgə/ *noun* a fold or ridge, especially in a mucous membrane such as the lining of the stomach (NOTE: The plural is **rugae**.)

rule out /ˌruːl ˈaʊt/ *verb* to state that someone does not have a specific disease ○ *We can rule out shingles.*

rumbling /ˈrʌmblɪŋ/ *noun* borborygmus, noise in the abdomen, caused by gas in the intestine

rumination /ˌruːmɪˈneɪʃ(ə)n/ *noun* **1.** a condition in which someone has constant irrational thoughts which they cannot control **2.** the regurgitation of food from the stomach which is then swallowed again

run /rʌn/ *verb* (*of the nose*) to drip with liquid secreted from the mucous membrane in the nasal passage ○ *His nose is running.* ○ *If your nose is running, blow it on a handkerchief.* ○ *One of the symptoms of a cold is a running nose.*

run-down /ˌrʌn ˈdaʊn/ *adjective* exhausted and unwell

running /ˈrʌnɪŋ/ *adjective* from which liquid is flowing ○ *running eyes*

running sore /ˌrʌnɪŋ ˈsɔː/ *noun* a sore which is discharging pus

runny nose /ˌrʌni ˈnəʊz/ *noun* a nose which is dripping with liquid from the mucous membrane

runs /rʌnz/ *noun* **the runs** same as **diarrhoea** (*informal*) ○ *I've got the runs again.* (NOTE: Takes a singular or plural verb.)

rupture /ˈrʌptʃə/ *noun* **1.** the breaking or tearing of an organ such as the appendix **2.** same as **hernia** ■ *verb* to break or tear something

ruptured spleen /ˌrʌptʃəd ˈspliːn/ *noun* a spleen which has been torn by piercing or by a blow

Russell traction /ˈrʌs(ə)l ˌtrækʃ(ə)n/ *noun* a type of traction with weights and slings used to straighten a femur which has been fractured

[Described 1924. After R. Hamilton Russell (1860–1933), Australian surgeon.]

Ryle's tube /ˈraɪlz ˌtjuːb/ *noun* a thin tube which is passed into the stomach through either the nose or mouth, used to pump out the contents of the stomach or to introduce a barium meal in the stomach [Described 1921. After John Alfred Ryle (1882–1950), physician at London, Cambridge and Oxford, UK.]

S

Sabin vaccine /ˈseɪbɪn ˌvæksiːn/ *noun* an oral vaccine against poliomyelitis, consisting of weak live polio virus. Compare **Salk vaccine** (NOTE: This is the vaccine used in the UK) [Developed 1955. After Albert Bruce Sabin (1906–93), Russian-born New York bacteriologist.]

sac /sæk/ *noun* a part of the body shaped like a bag

saccades /sæˈkeɪdz/ *plural noun* controlled rapid movements of the eyes made when a person is changing the direction in which they are focusing, e.g. when they are reading

sacchar- /sækə/ *prefix* same as **saccharo-** (*used before vowels*)

saccharide /ˈsækəraɪd/ *noun* a form of carbohydrate

saccharin /ˈsækərɪn/ *noun* a white crystalline substance, used in place of sugar because, although it is nearly 500 times sweeter than sugar, it contains no carbohydrates

saccharine /ˈsækəraɪn/ *adjective* relating to, resembling or containing sugar

saccharo- /sækərəʊ/ *prefix* referring to sugar

saccule /ˈsækjuːl/, **sacculus** /ˈsækjʊləs/ *noun* the smaller of two sacs in the vestibule of the inner ear which is part of the mechanism which relates information about the position of the head in space

sacra /ˈseɪkrə/ *plural of* **sacrum**

sacral /ˈseɪkrəl/ *adjective* referring to the sacrum

sacral foramen /ˌseɪkrəl fəˈreɪmən/ *noun* one of the openings in the sacrum through which the sacral nerves pass. See illustration at PELVIS in Supplement (NOTE: The plural is **sacral foramina**.)

sacralisation /ˌsækrəlaɪˈzeɪʃ(ə)n/, **sacralization** *noun* a condition in which the lowest lumbar vertebra fuses with the sacrum

sacral nerve /ˈsækrəl ˌnɜːv/ *noun* one of the nerves which branch from the spinal cord in the sacrum and govern the legs, the arms and the genital area

sacral plexus /ˌseɪkrəl ˈpleksəs/ *noun* a group of nerves inside the pelvis near the sacrum which lead to nerves in the buttocks, back of the thigh and lower leg and foot

sacral vertebrae /ˌseɪkrəl ˈvɜːtɪbriː/ *plural noun* the five vertebrae in the lower part of the spine which are fused together to form the sacrum

sacro- /seɪkrəʊ/ *prefix* referring to the sacrum

sacrococcygeal /ˌseɪkrəʊkɒkˈsiːdʒiəl/ *adjective* referring to the sacrum and the coccyx

sacroiliac /ˌseɪkrəʊˈɪliæk/ *adjective* referring to the sacrum and the ilium

sacroiliac joint /ˌseɪkrəʊˈɪliæk dʒɔɪnt/ *noun* a joint where the sacrum joins the ilium

sacroiliitis /ˌseɪkrəʊɪliˈaɪtɪs/ *noun* inflammation of the sacroiliac joint

sacrotuberous ligament /ˌseɪkrəʊ ˌtjuːbərəs ˈlɪɡəmənt/ *noun* the large ligament between the iliac spine, the sacrum, the coccyx and the ischial tuberosity

sacro-uterine ligament /ˌseɪkrəʊ ˌjuːtəraɪn ˈlɪɡəmənt/ *noun* a ligament which goes from the neck of the uterus to the sacrum, passing on each side of the rectum

sacrum /ˈseɪkrəm/ *noun* a flat triangular bone, formed of five sacral vertebrae fused together, located between the lumbar vertebrae and the coccyx. It articulates with the coccyx and also with the hip bones. See illustration at PELVIS in Supplement (NOTE: The plural is **sacra**.)

SAD *abbr* seasonal affective disorder

saddle joint /ˈsæd(ə)l dʒɔɪnt/ *noun* a synovial joint where one element is concave and the other convex, like the joint between the thumb and the wrist

saddle-nose /ˈsæd(ə)l nəʊz/ *noun* a deep bridge of the nose, usually a sign of injury but sometimes a sign of tertiary syphilis

sadism /ˈseɪdɪz(ə)m/ *noun* a sexual condition in which a person finds sexual pleasure in hurting others

sadist /ˈseɪdɪst/ *noun* a person whose sexual urge is linked to sadism

sadistic /səˈdɪstɪk/ *adjective* referring to sadism. Compare **masochism**

SADS *abbr* seasonal affective disorder syndrome

safe /seɪf/ *adjective* **1.** not likely to cause harm ○ *Is it safe to use this drug on someone who is diabetic?* **2.** in a protected place or situation and not likely to be harmed or lost ○ *Keep the drugs in a safe place.* ○ *He's safe in hospital being looked after by the doctors and nurses.* (NOTE: **safer – safest**)

'…a good collateral blood supply makes occlusion of a single branch of the coeliac axis safe' [*British Medical Journal*]

safe dose /seɪf 'dəʊs/ *noun* the amount of a drug which can be given without being harmful

safely /'seɪfli/ *adverb* without danger, without being hurt ○ *You can safely take six tablets a day without any risk of side-effects.*

safe period /'seɪf ˌpɪəriəd/ *noun* the time during the menstrual cycle, when conception is not likely to occur, and sexual intercourse can take place, used as a method of contraception. ◊ **rhythm method**

safe sex /seɪf 'seks/ *noun* the use of measures such as a contraceptive sheath and having only one sexual partner to reduce the possibility of catching a sexually transmitted disease

safety /'seɪfti/ *noun* the fact of being safe □ **to take safety precautions** to do things which make your actions or condition safe

safety pin /'seɪfti pɪn/ *noun* a special type of bent pin with a guard which protects the point, used for attaching nappies or bandages

sagittal /'sædʒɪt(ə)l/ *adjective* going from the front of the body to the back, dividing it into right and left

sagittal plane /ˌsædʒɪt(ə)l 'pleɪn/ *noun* the division of the body along the midline, at right angles to the coronal plane, dividing the body into right and left parts. Also called **median plane**. See illustration at ANATOMICAL TERMS in Supplement

sagittal section /ˌsædʒɪt(ə)l 'sekʃən/ *noun* any section or cut through the body, going from the front to the back along the length of the body

sagittal suture /ˌsædʒɪt(ə)l 'suːtʃə/ *noun* a joint along the top of the head where the two parietal bones are fused

StHA *abbr* Strategic Health Authority

St John Ambulance Association and Brigade /sənt ˌdʒɒn 'æmbjʊləns əˌsəʊsɪeɪʃ(ə)n ən brɪ'geɪd/ *noun* a voluntary organisation which gives training in first aid and whose members provide first aid at public events such as football matches and demonstrations

St Louis encephalitis /seɪnt ˌluːɪs en,kefə 'laɪtɪs/ *noun* a sometimes fatal form of encephalitis, transmitted by the ordinary house mosquito, *Culex pipiens* [After St Louis, Missouri, USA, where it was first diagnosed]

St Vitus's dance /sənt 'vaɪtəsɪz dɑːns/ *noun* a former name for Sydenham's chorea

salbutamol /sæl'bjuːtəmɒl/ *noun* a drug which relaxes and dilates the bronchi, used in the relief of asthma, emphysema and chronic bronchitis

salicylate /sə'lɪsɪleɪt/ *noun* one of various pain-killing substances derived from salicylic acid, e.g. aspirin

salicylic acid /ˌsælɪˌsɪlɪk 'æsɪd/ *noun* a white antiseptic substance which destroys bacteria and fungi and which is used in ointments to treat corns, warts and other skin disorders

salicylism /'sælɪsɪlɪz(ə)m/ *noun* the effects of poisoning due to too much salicylic acid. Symptoms include headache, tinnitus, faintness and vomiting.

saline /'seɪlaɪn/ *adjective* referring to or containing salt ○ *The patient was given a saline transfusion.* ■ *noun* same as saline solution

saline drip /ˌseɪlaɪn 'drɪp/ *noun* a drip containing a saline solution

saline solution /'seɪlaɪn səˌluːʃ(ə)n/ *noun* a solution made of distilled water and sodium chloride, which is introduced into the body intravenously through a drip

saliva /sə'laɪvə/ *noun* a fluid in the mouth, secreted by the salivary glands, which starts the process of digesting food (NOTE: For terms referring to saliva, see words beginning with **ptyal-**, **ptyalo-** or **sial-, sialo-**.)

COMMENT: Saliva is a mixture of a large quantity of water and a small amount of mucus, secreted by the salivary glands. Saliva acts to keep the mouth and throat moist, allowing food to be swallowed easily. It also contains the enzyme ptyalin, which begins the digestive process of converting starch into sugar while food is still in the mouth. Because of this association with food, the salivary glands produce saliva automatically when food is seen, smelt or even simply talked about.

salivary /sə'laɪv(ə)ri/ *adjective* referring to saliva

salivary calculus /səˌlaɪv(ə)ri 'kælkjʊləs/ *noun* a stone which forms in a salivary gland

salivary gland /sə'laɪv(ə)ri glænd/ *noun* a gland which secretes saliva, situated under the tongue (the **sublingual gland**), beneath the lower jaw (the **submandibular gland**) and in the neck at the back of the lower jaw joint (the **parotid gland**)

salivate /'sælɪveɪt/ *verb* to produce saliva

salivation /ˌsælɪ'veɪʃ(ə)n/ *noun* the production of saliva

Salk vaccine /'sɔːk ˌvæksiːn/ *noun* an injected vaccine against poliomyelitis, consisting of inactivated polio virus. Compare **Sabin vaccine** [Developed 1954. After Jonas Edward Salk (1914–95), virologist in Pittsburgh, USA.]

salmeterol /sæl'metərɒl/ *noun* a drug which relaxes and widens the airways, used to treat severe asthma

Salmonella /ˌsælməˈnelə/ *noun* a genus of pathogenic bacteria which live in the intestines and are usually acquired by eating contaminated food, responsible for many cases of gastroenteritis and for typhoid or paratyphoid fever (NOTE: The plural is **Salmonellae.**)

Salmonella poisoning /ˌsælməˈnelə ˌpɔɪz(ə)nɪŋ/ *noun* poisoning caused by Salmonellae which develop in the intestines ○ *Five people were taken to hospital with Salmonella poisoning.*

salmonellosis /ˌsælmənəˈləʊsɪs/ *noun* food poisoning caused by *Salmonella* in the digestive system

salping- /sælpɪndʒ/ *prefix* same as **salpingo-** (used before vowels)

salpingectomy /ˌsælpɪnˈdʒektəmi/ *noun* a surgical operation to remove or cut a Fallopian tube, used as a method of contraception

salpingitis /ˌsælpɪnˈdʒaɪtɪs/ *noun* inflammation, usually of a Fallopian tube

salpingo- /sælpɪŋgəʊ/ *prefix* 1. referring to the Fallopian tubes 2. referring to the auditory meatus

salpingography /ˌsælpɪŋˈgɒgrəfi/ *noun* an X-ray examination of the Fallopian tubes

salpingolysis /ˌsælpɪŋˈgɒlɪsɪs/ *noun* a surgical operation to open up blocked Fallopian tubes by removing any adhesions near the ovaries

salpingo-oophorectomy /sælˌpɪŋgəʊ ˌəʊəfəˈrektəmi/ *noun* a surgical operation to remove a Fallopian tube and ovary

salpingo-oophoritis /sælˌpɪŋgəʊ ˌəʊəfəˈraɪtɪs/, **salpingo-oothecitis** /sælˌpɪŋgəʊ ˌəʊəθɪˈsaɪtɪs/ *noun* inflammation of a Fallopian tube and the ovary connected to it

salpingo-oophorocele /sælˌpɪŋgəʊ əʊˈpfərəʊsiːl/, **salpingo-oothecocele** /sælˌpɪŋgəʊ əʊəˈθiːkəʊsiːl/ *noun* a hernia where a Fallopian tube and its ovary pass through a weak point in the surrounding tissue

salpingostomy /ˌsælpɪŋˈgɒstəmi/ *noun* a surgical operation to open up a blocked Fallopian tube

salpinx /ˈsælpɪŋks/ *noun* same as **Fallopian tube** (NOTE: The plural is **salpinges.**)

salt /sɔːlt/ *noun* 1. small white crystals mainly of sodium chloride used to flavour and preserve food 2. a crystalline compound, usually containing a metal, formed when an acid is neutralised by an alkali

COMMENT: Salt forms a necessary part of diet, as it replaces salt lost in sweating and helps to control the water balance in the body. It also improves the working of the muscles and nerves. Most diets contain more salt than each person actually needs, and although it has not been proved to be harmful, it is generally wise to cut down on salt consumption. Salt is one of the four tastes, the others being sweet, sour and bitter.

salt depletion /ˈsɔːlt dɪˌpliːʃ(ə)n/ *noun* loss of salt from the body, by sweating or vomiting, which causes cramp

salt-free diet /ˌsɔːlt friː ˈdaɪət/ *noun* a diet in which no salt is allowed

salve /sælv/ *noun* an ointment

sample /ˈsɑːmpəl/ *noun* a small quantity of something used for testing ○ *Blood samples were taken from all the staff in the hospital.* ○ *The doctor asked her to provide a urine sample.*

sanatorium /ˌsænəˈtɔːriəm/ *noun* an institution, similar to a hospital, which treats particular types of disorder such as tuberculosis, or offers special treatment such as hot baths or massage (NOTE: The plural is **sanatoria** or **sanatoriums.**)

sandflea /ˈsændfliː/ *noun* the jigger, a tropical insect which enters the skin between the toes and digs under the skin, causing intense irritation

sandfly fever /ˈsændflaɪ ˌfiːvə/ *noun* a virus infection like influenza, which is transmitted by the bite of the sandfly *Phlebotomus papatasii* and is common in the Middle East

sandwich therapy /ˈsænwɪdʃ ˌθerəpi/ *noun* a system in which one type of treatment is used between exposures to a different treatment, e.g., chemotherapy given before and after radiation, or radiation given before and after surgery

sangui- /sæŋgwɪ/ *prefix* relating to blood

sanguineous /sæŋˈgwɪniəs/ *adjective* referring to blood, containing blood

sanies /ˈseɪniːz/ *noun* a discharge from a sore or wound which has an unpleasant smell

sanitary /ˈsænɪt(ə)ri/ *adjective* 1. clean 2. referring to hygiene or to health

sanitary towel /ˈsænɪt(ə)ri ˌtaʊəl/ *noun* a disposable pad of absorbent material worn by women to absorb the blood flow during menstruation

sanitation /ˌsænɪˈteɪʃ(ə)n/ *noun* the practice of being hygienic, especially referring to public hygiene ○ *Poor sanitation in crowded conditions can result in the spread of disease.*

SA node /ˌes ˈeɪ nəʊd/, **S-A node** *noun* same as **sinoatrial node**

saphena /səˈfiːnə/ *noun* same as **saphenous vein** (NOTE: The plural is **saphenae.**)

saphenous /səˈfiːnəs/ *adjective* relating to the saphenous veins

saphenous nerve /səˈfiːnəs nɜːv/ *noun* a branch of the femoral nerve which connects with the sensory nerves in the skin of the lower leg

saphenous opening /səˌfiːnəs ˈəʊp(ə)nɪŋ/ *noun* a hole in the fascia of the thigh through which the saphenous vein passes

saphenous vein /sə'fiːnəs veɪn/ *noun* one of two veins which take blood from the foot up the leg. Also called **saphena**

COMMENT: The long (internal) saphenous vein, the longest vein in the body, runs from the foot up the inside of the leg and joins the femoral vein. The short (posterior) saphenous vein runs up the back of the lower leg and joins the popliteal vein.

sapphism /'sæfɪz(ə)m/ *noun* same as **lesbianism**

sapraemia /sæ'priːmiə/ *noun* blood poisoning by saprophytes

saprophyte /'sæprəfaɪt/ *noun* a microorganism which lives on dead or decaying tissue

saprophytic /sæprəʊ'fɪtɪk/ *adjective* referring to an organism which lives on dead or decaying tissue

sarc- /sɑːk/, **sarco-** /sɑːkəʊ/ *prefix* **1.** referring to flesh **2.** referring to muscle

sarcoid /'sɑːkɔɪd/ *noun* a tumour which is like a sarcoma ■ *adjective* like a sarcoma

sarcoidosis /ˌsɑːkɔɪ'dəʊsɪs/ *noun* a disease causing enlargement of the lymph nodes, where small nodules or granulomas form in certain tissues, especially in the lungs or liver and other parts of the body. Also called **Boeck's disease, Boeck's sarcoid** (NOTE: The Kveim test confirms the presence of sarcoidosis.)

sarcolemma /ˌsɑːkəʊ'lemə/ *noun* a membrane surrounding a muscle fibre

sarcoma /sɑː'kəʊmə/ *noun* a cancer of connective tissue such as bone, muscle or cartilage

sarcomatosis /sɑːˌkəʊmə'təʊsɪs/ *noun* a condition in which a sarcoma has spread through the bloodstream to many parts of the body

sarcomatous /sɑː'kɒmətəs/ *adjective* referring to a sarcoma

sarcomere /'sɑːkəmɪə/ *noun* a filament in myofibril

sarcoplasm /'sɑːkəplæz(ə)m/ *noun* semi-liquid cytoplasm in muscle membrane. Also called **myoplasm**

sarcoplasmic /ˌsɑːkəʊ'plæzmɪk/ *adjective* referring to sarcoplasm

sarcoplasmic reticulum /ˌsɑːkəʊ plæzmɪk rɪ'tɪkjʊləm/ *noun* a network in the cytoplasm of striated muscle fibres

sarcoptes /sɑː'kɒptiːz/ *noun* a type of mite which causes scabies

sardonicus /sɑː'dɒnɪkəs/ ▶ **risus sardonicus**

SARS /sɑːz/ *noun* a serious, sometimes fatal, infection affecting the respiratory system, first seen in China. Suspected cases of SARS must be isolated with full barrier nursing precautions. Full form **severe acute respiratory syndrome**

sartorius /sɑː'tɔːriəs/ *noun* a very long muscle, the longest muscle in the body, which runs

from the anterior iliac spine, across the thigh down to the tibia

saturated fat /ˌsætʃəreɪtɪd 'fæt/ *noun* a fat which has the largest amount of hydrogen possible

COMMENT: Animal fats such as butter and fat meat are saturated fatty acids. It is thought that increasing the amount of unsaturated and polyunsaturated fats, mainly vegetable fats and oils, and fish oil, and reducing saturated fats in the food intake helps reduce the level of cholesterol in the blood, and so lessens the risk of atherosclerosis.

saturnism /'sætənɪz(ə)m/ *noun* lead poisoning

satyriasis /ˌsætə'raɪəsɪs/ *noun* an obsessive sexual urge in a man (NOTE: A similar condition in a woman is called **nymphomania**.)

saucerisation /ˌsɔːsəraɪ'zeɪʃ(ə)n/, **saucerization** *noun* **1.** a surgical operation in which tissue is cut out in the form of a saucer-like depression, usually in order to help material drain away from infected areas of bone **2.** the shallow saucer-like appearance of the upper surface of a vertebra after a compression fracture

save /seɪv/ *verb* **1.** to stop someone from being hurt or killed ○ *The doctors saved the little boy from dying of cancer.* □ **the surgeons saved her life** they stopped the patient from dying **2.** to stop something from being damaged ○ *The surgeons were unable to save the sight of their patient.*

saw /sɔː/ *noun* a tool with a long metal blade with teeth along its edge, used for cutting ■ *verb* to cut something with a saw (NOTE: **sawing – sawed – sawn**)

Sayre's jacket /'seɪəz ˌdʒækɪt/ *noun* a plaster cast which supports the spine when vertebrae have been deformed by tuberculosis or spinal disease [After Lewis Albert Sayre (1820–1901), US surgeon]

s.c. *abbr* subcutaneous

scab /skæb/ *noun* a crust of dry blood which forms over a wound and protects it

scabicide /'skeɪbəsaɪd/ *noun* a solution which kills mites ■ *adjective* killing mites

scabies /'skeɪbiːz/ *noun* a very irritating infection of the skin caused by a mite which lives under the skin

scala /'skɑːlə/ *noun* a spiral canal in the cochlea

COMMENT: The cochlea is formed of three spiral canals: the **scala vestibuli** which is filled with perilymph and connects with the oval window; the **scala media** which is filled with endolymph and transmits vibrations from the scala vestibuli through the basilar membrane to the **scala tympani**, which in turn transmits the sound vibrations to the round window.

scald /skɔːld/ *noun* an injury to the skin caused by touching a very hot liquid or steam. Also called **wet burn** ■ *verb* to injure the skin with a very hot liquid or steam

scalding /'skɔːldɪŋ/ *adjective* **1.** referring to a liquid which is very hot **2.** referring to urine which gives a burning sensation when passed

scale /skeɪl/ *noun* **1.** a thin flat piece of something such as dead skin **2.** same as **tartar 3.** a system of measurement or valuation based on a series of marks or levels with regular intervals between them ○ *a pay scale* **4.** same as **scales** ■ *verb* to remove the calcium deposits from teeth

scalenus /skeɪ'liːnəs/, **scalene** /'skeɪliːn/ *noun* one of a group of muscles in the neck which bend the neck forwards and sideways, and also help expand the lungs in deep breathing

scalenus syndrome /skeɪ'liːnəs ˌsɪnˈdrəʊm/ *noun* a pain in an arm, caused by the scalenus anterior muscle pressing the subclavian artery and the brachial plexus against the vertebrae. Also called **thoracic outlet syndrome**

scale off /ˌskeɪl 'ɒf/ *verb* to fall off in scales

scaler /'skeɪlə/ *noun* a surgical instrument for scaling teeth

scales /skeɪlz/ *noun* a machine for weighing ○ *The nurses weighed the baby on the scales.*

scalp /skælp/ *noun* the thick skin and muscle, with the hair, which covers the skull

scalpel /'skælpəl/ *noun* a small sharp-pointed knife used in surgery

scaly /'skeɪli/ *adjective* covered in scales ○ *The pustules harden and become scaly.*

scan /skæn/ *noun* **1.** an examination of part of the body using computer-interpreted X-rays to create a picture of the part on a screen **2.** a picture of part of the body created on a screen using computer-interpreted X-rays ■ *verb* to examine part of the body using computer-interpreted X-rays to create a picture of the part on a screen

scanner /'skænə/ *noun* **1.** a machine which scans a part of the body **2.** a person who examines a test slide **3.** a person who operates a scanning machine

scanning /'skænɪŋ/ *noun* **1.** the act of examining an area with the eyes **2.** the act of examining internal organs of the body with a piece of electronic equipment

scanning speech /'skænɪŋ spiːtʃ/ *noun* a disorder in speaking, where each sound is spoken separately and given equal stress

scaphocephalic /ˌskæfəʊsə'fælɪk/ *adjective* having a long narrow skull

scaphocephaly /ˌskæfəʊ'kefəli, ˌskæfəʊ'sefəli/ *noun* a condition in which the skull is unusually long and narrow

scaphoid /'skæfɔɪd/, **scaphoid bone** /'skæfɔɪd bəʊn/ *noun* one of the carpal bones in the wrist. See illustration at HAND in Supplement

scapula /'skæpjʊlə/ *noun* one of two large flat bones covering the top part of the back. Also called **shoulder blade** (NOTE: The plural is **scapulae**.)

scapular /'skæpjʊlə/ *adjective* referring to the shoulder blade

scapulo- /skæpjʊləʊ/ *prefix* relating to the scapula

scapulohumeral /ˌskæpjʊləʊ'hjuːmərəl/ *adjective* referring to the scapula and humerus

scar /skɑː/ *noun* the mark left on the skin after a wound or surgical incision has healed ○ *He still has the scar of his appendicectomy.* Also called **cicatrix** ■ *verb* to leave a scar on the skin ○ *The burns have scarred him for life.* ○ *Plastic surgeons have tried to repair the scarred arm.* ○ *Patients were given special clothes to reduce hypertrophic scarring.*

scarification /ˌskærɪfɪ'keɪʃ(ə)n/ *noun* scratching, making minute cuts on the surface of the skin, e.g. for a smallpox vaccination

scarificator /'skærɪfəkeɪtə/ *noun* an instrument used for scarification

scarlatina /ˌskɑːlə'tiːnə/, **scarlet fever** /ˌskɑːlət 'fiːvə/ *noun* an infectious disease with a fever, sore throat and a red rash. It is caused by a haemolytic streptococcus and can sometimes have serious complications if the kidneys are infected.

Scarpa's triangle /ˌskɑːpɑːz 'traɪæŋgəl/ *noun* same as **femoral triangle** [After Antonio Scarpa (1747–1832), Italian anatomist and surgeon]

scar tissue /'skɑː ˌtɪʃuː/ *noun* fibrous tissue which forms a scar

scat- /skæt/, **scato-** /'skætəʊ/ *prefix* referring to the faeces

scatole /'skætəʊl/ *noun* a substance in faeces, formed in the intestine, which causes a strong smell (NOTE: Also spelled **skatole**.)

SCC *abbr* squamous cell carcinoma

scent /sent/ *noun* **1.** a pleasant smell ○ *The scent of flowers makes me sneeze.* **2.** a cosmetic substance which has a pleasant smell **3.** a smell given off by a substance which stimulates the sense of smell

scented /'sentɪd/ *adjective* with a strong pleasant smell ○ *He is allergic to scented soap.*

schema /'skiːmə/ *noun* same as **body image**

Scheuermann's disease /'ʃɔɪəmənz dɪˌziːz/ *noun* inflammation of the bones and cartilage in the spine, usually affecting adolescents [Described 1920. After Holger Werfel Scheuermann (1877–1960), Danish orthopaedic surgeon and radiologist.]

Schick test /'ʃɪk test/ *noun* a test to see if a person is immune to diphtheria [Described 1908. After Bela Schick (1877–1967), paediatrician in Vienna, Austria, and New York, USA.]

COMMENT: In the Schick test, a small amount of diphtheria toxin is injected, and if the point of injection becomes inflamed it shows the person is not immune to the disease (a positive reaction).

Schilling test /'ʃɪlɪŋ test/ *noun* a test to see if someone can absorb Vitamin B$_{12}$ through the intestines, to determine cases of pernicious anaemia [After Robert Frederick Schilling (b. 1919), US physician]

-schisis /skaɪsɪs/ *suffix* referring to a fissure or split

schisto- /ʃɪstəʊ/ *prefix* referring to something which is split

Schistosoma /ˌʃɪstə'səʊmə/, **schistosome** /'ʃɪstəsəʊm/ same as **bilharzia**

schistosomiasis /ˌʃɪstəsəʊ'maɪəsɪs/ *noun* same as **bilharziasis**

schiz- /skɪts/, **schizo-** /skɪtsəʊ/ *prefix* referring to something which is split

schizoid /'skɪtsɔɪd/ *adjective* referring to schizophrenia ■ *noun* a person who has a less severe form of schizophrenia

schizoid personality /ˌskɪtsɔɪd ˌpɜːsə'nælɪti/ *noun* a disorder in which someone is cold towards other people, thinks mainly about himself or herself and behaves in an odd way. Also called **split personality**

schizophrenia /ˌskɪtsəʊ'friːniə/ *noun* a mental disorder in which someone withdraws from contact with other people, has delusions and seems to lose contact with the real world

schizophrenic /ˌskɪtsəʊ'frenɪk/ *noun* someone who has schizophrenia ■ *adjective* having schizophrenia

schizotypal personality disorder /ˌskɪtsəʊtaɪpəl ˌpɜːsə'nælɪti dɪsˌɔːdə/ *noun* a schizoid personality type disorder

Schlatter's disease /'ʃlætəz dɪˌziːz/ *noun* inflammation in the bones and cartilage at the top of the tibia [Described 1903. After Carl Schlatter (1864–1934), Professor of Surgery at Zürich, Switzerland.]

Schlemm's canal /'ʃlemz kəˌnæl/ *noun* a circular canal in the sclera of the eye, which drains the aqueous humour [Described 1830. After Friedrich Schlemm (1795–1858), Professor of Anatomy in Berlin, Germany.]

Schönlein–Henoch purpura /ˌʃɜːnlaɪn 'henɒk ˌpɜːpjʊərə/, **Schönlein's purpura** /'ʃɜːnlaɪnz ˌpɜːpjʊərə/ *noun* a blood disorder of children, in which the skin becomes purple on the buttocks and lower legs, the joints are swollen and painful and there are gastrointestinal problems

school /skuːl/ *noun* **1.** a place where children are taught **2.** a specialised section of a university

school health service /skuːl 'helθ ˌsɜːvɪs/ *noun* a special service, part of the local health authority, which looks after the health of children in school

school nurse /skuːl 'nɜːs/ *noun* a nurse who works in a school, treating health problems and promoting health and safety

Schwann cells /'ʃvɒn selz/ *plural noun* the cells which form the myelin sheath around a nerve fibre. See illustration at **NEURONE** in Supplement [Described 1839. After Friedrich Theodor Schwann (1810–82), German anatomist.]

schwannoma /ʃvɒ'nəʊmə/ *noun* a neurofibroma, a benign tumour of a peripheral nerve

Schwartze's operation /'ʃvɔːtsɪz ˌɒpəreɪʃ(ə)n/ *noun* the original surgical operation to drain fluid and remove infected tissue from the mastoid process [After Hermann Schwartze (1837–1910), German otologist]

sciatic /saɪ'ætɪk/ *adjective* **1.** referring to the hip **2.** referring to the sciatic nerve

sciatica /saɪ'ætɪkə/ *noun* pain along the sciatic nerve, usually at the back of the thighs and legs

COMMENT: Sciatica can be caused by a slipped disc which presses on a spinal nerve, or can simply be caused by straining a muscle in the back.

sciatic nerve /saɪ'ætɪk nɜːv/ *noun* one of two main nerves which run from the sacral plexus into each of the thighs, dividing into a series of nerves in the lower legs and feet. They are the largest nerves in the body.

SCID *abbr* severe combined immunodeficiency

science /'saɪəns/ *noun* a study based on looking at and recording facts, especially facts arranged into a system

scientific /ˌsaɪən'tɪfɪk/ *adjective* referring to science ○ *He carried out scientific experiments.*

scientist /'saɪəntɪst/ *noun* a person who specialises in scientific studies

scintigram /'sɪntɪgræm/ *noun* an image recording radiation from radioactive isotopes injected into the body

scintillascope /sɪn'tɪləskəʊp/ *noun* an instrument which produces a scintigram

scintillator /'sɪntɪleɪtə/ *noun* a substance which produces a flash of light when struck by radiation

scintiscan /'sɪntɪskæn/ *noun* a scintigram which shows the variations in radiation from one part of the body to another

scirrhous /'sɪrəs/ *adjective* hard ○ *a scirrhous tumour*

scirrhus /'sɪrəs/ *noun* a hard malignant tumour, especially in the breast

scissor leg /'sɪzə leg/ *noun* a condition in which someone walks with one leg crossing over the other, usually as a result of spasticity of the leg's adductor muscles

scissor legs /'sɪzə legz/ *plural noun* malformed legs, where one leg is permanently crossed over in front of the other

scissors /'sɪzəz/ *plural noun* an instrument for cutting, made of two blades and two handles fastened together

scissura /'sɪʃʊrə/ *noun* an opening in something or a splitting of something

scler- /sklɪə/ *prefix* same as **sclero-** (*used before vowels*)

sclera /'sklɪərə/ *noun* the hard white outer covering of the eyeball. See illustration at EYE in Supplement. Also called **sclerotic, sclerotic coat, albuginea oculi**

COMMENT: The front part of the sclera is the transparent cornea, through which the light enters the eye. The conjunctiva, or inner skin of the eyelids, connects with the sclera and covers the front of the eyeball.

scleral /'sklɪərəl/ *adjective* referring to the sclera

scleral lens /'sklɪərəl lenz/ *noun* a large contact lens which covers most of the front of the eye

scleritis /sklə'raɪtɪs/ *noun* inflammation of the sclera

sclero- /sklɪərəʊ/ *prefix* **1.** hard, thick **2.** referring to the sclera

scleroderma /ˌsklɪərə'dɜːmə/ *noun* a collagen disease which thickens connective tissue and produces a hard thick skin

scleroma /sklə'rəʊmə/ *noun* a patch of hard skin or hard mucous membrane

scleromalacia /ˌsklɪərəʊmə‚leɪʃiə pə 'fɔːrəns/, **scleromalacia perforans** /ˌsklɪərəʊmə 'leɪʃiə/ *noun* a condition of the sclera in which holes appear in it

sclerosant agent /sklə'rəʊs(ə)nt ‚eɪdʒənt/ *noun* an irritating liquid injected into tissue to harden it

sclerosing /sklə'rəʊsɪŋ/ *adjective* becoming hard, or making tissue hard

sclerosing agent /sklə'rəʊsɪŋ ‚eɪdʒ(ə)nt/, **sclerosing solution** /sklə'rəʊsɪŋ sə‚luːʃ(ə)n/ *noun* same as **sclerosant agent**

sclerosis /sklə'rəʊsɪs/ *noun* a condition in which tissue becomes hard

sclerotherapy /ˌsklɪərəʊ'θerəpi/ *noun* the treatment of a varicose vein by injecting a sclerosant agent into the vein, and so encouraging the blood in the vein to clot

sclerotic /sklə'rɒtɪk/ *adjective* referring to sclerosis, or having sclerosis ■ *noun* same as **sclera**

sclerotic coat /sklə‚rɒtɪk 'kəʊt/ *noun* same as **sclera**

sclerotome /'sklɪərətəʊm/ *noun* a sharp knife used in sclerotomy

sclerotomy /sklə'rɒtəmi/ *noun* a surgical operation to cut into the sclera

scolex /'skəʊleks/ *noun* the head of a tapeworm, with hooks which attach it to the wall of the intestine (NOTE: The plural is **scolices** or **scolexes**.)

scoliosis /ˌskəʊli'əʊsɪs/ *noun* a condition in which the spine curves sideways

scoliotic /ˌskəʊli'ɒtɪk/ *adjective* referring to a spine which curves sideways

scoop stretcher /'skuːp ‚stretʃə/ *noun* a type of stretcher formed of two jointed sections which can slide under someone and lock together

-scope /skəʊp/ *suffix* referring to an instrument for examining by sight

scopolamine /skə'pɒləmiːn/ *noun* a colourless thick liquid poisonous alkaloid found in some plants of the nightshade family. It is used especially to prevent motion sickness and as a sedative.

scorbutic /skɔː'bjuːtɪk/ *adjective* referring to scurvy

scorbutus /skɔː'bjuːtəs/ *noun* same as **scurvy**

scoto- /skəʊtə/ *prefix* dark

scotoma /skɒ'təʊmə/ *noun* a small area in the field of vision where someone cannot see

scotometer /skəʊ'tɒmɪtə/ *noun* an instrument used to measure areas of impaired vision

scotopia /skəʊ'təʊpiə/ *noun* the power of the eye to adapt to poor lighting conditions and darkness

scotopic /skəʊ'tɒpɪk/ *adjective* referring to scotopia

scotopic vision /skəʊ‚tɒpɪk 'vɪʒ(ə)n/ *noun* vision in the dark and in dim light, where the rods of the retina are used instead of the cones, which are used for photopic vision. ♦ **dark adaptation**

scrape /skreɪp/ *verb* to remove the surface of something by moving a sharp knife across it

scratch /skrætʃ/ *noun* a slight wound on the skin made when a sharp point is pulled across it ○ *She had scratches on her legs and arms.* ○ *Wash the dirt out of that scratch in case it gets infected.* ■ *verb* to harm the skin by moving a sharp point across it ○ *The cat scratched the girl's face.* ○ *Be careful not to scratch yourself on the wire.*

scratch test /'skrætʃ test/ *noun* a test for allergy, in which a small amount of a substance is placed on a lightly scratched area of skin to see if a reaction occurs

scream /skriːm/ *noun* a loud sharp cry ■ *verb* to make a loud sharp cry

screen /skriːn/ *noun* **1.** a light wall, sometimes with a curtain, which can be moved about and put round a bed to shield a person **2.** same as **screening** ■ *verb* to examine large numbers of people to test them for a disease ○ *The population of the village was screened for meningitis.*

'…in the UK the main screen is carried out by health visitors at 6–10 months. With adequately staffed and trained community services, this method of screening can be extremely effective' [*Lancet*]

screening /'skri:nɪŋ/ *noun* the process of testing large numbers of people to see if any of them have a particular type of disease. ◊ **genetic screening**

'GPs are increasingly requesting blood screening for patients concerned about HIV' [*Journal of the Royal College of General Practitioners*]

screening test /'skri:nɪŋ test/ *noun* a test for a particular disease which is given to people who have no symptoms in order to identify how many of them have that disease or are showing early signs of it

scrip /skrɪp/ *noun* a doctor's prescription (*informal*)

scrofula /'skrɒfjʊlə/ *noun* a form of tuberculosis in the lymph nodes in the neck, formerly caused by unpasteurised milk but now rare

scrofuloderma /ˌskrɒfjʊləʊ'dɜːmə/ *noun* a form of tuberculosis of the skin, forming ulcers, and secondary to tuberculous infection of an underlying lymph gland or structure

scrota /'skrəʊtə/ *plural of* **scrotum**

scrotal /'skrəʊt(ə)l/ *adjective* referring to the scrotum

scrototomy /skrəʊ'tɒtəmi/ *noun* a surgical operation to open up and examine the scrotum (NOTE: The plural is **scrototomies**.)

scrotum /'skrəʊtəm/ *noun* a bag of skin hanging from behind the penis, containing the testes, epididymides and part of the spermatic cord. See illustration at UROGENITAL SYSTEM (MALE) in Supplement (NOTE: The plural is **scrotums** or **scrota**.)

scrub nurse /'skrʌb ˌnɜːs/ *noun* a nurse who cleans the operation site on someone's body before an operation

scrub typhus /'skrʌb ˌtaɪfəs/ *noun* same as **tsutsugamushi disease**

scrub up /ˌskrʌb 'ʌp/ *verb* (*of a surgeon or theatre nurse*) to clean the hands and arms thoroughly before performing surgery (NOTE: **scrubbing up – scrubbed up**)

scrumpox /'skrʌmpɒks/ *noun* a form of herpes simplex found especially in male sports players, passed on easily due to the presence of small cuts in the skin combined with the abrasive effects of facial stubble

scurf /skɜːf/ *noun* same as **dandruff**

scurvy /'skɜːvi/ *noun* a disease caused by lack of vitamin C or ascorbic acid which is found in fruit and vegetables. Also called **scorbutus**

COMMENT: Scurvy causes general weakness and anaemia, with bleeding from the gums and joints, and under the skin. In severe cases, the teeth drop out. Treatment consists of vitamin C tablets and a change of diet to include more fruit and vegetables.

scybalum /'sɪbələm/ *noun* very hard faeces

seasick /'si:sɪk/ *adjective* feeling sick because of the movement of a ship ○ *As soon as the ferry started to move she felt seasick.*

seasickness /'si:sɪknəs/ *noun* illness, with nausea, vomiting and sometimes headache, caused by the movement of a ship ○ *Take some seasickness tablets if you are going on a long journey.*

seasonal affective disorder /ˌsi:z(ə)n(ə)l ə'fektɪv dɪsˌɔːdə/, **seasonal affective disorder syndrome** /ˌsi:z(ə)n(ə)l ə'fektɪv dɪs ˌɔːdə ˌsɪndrəʊm/ *noun* a condition in which a person becomes depressed and anxious during the winter when there are fewer hours of daylight. Its precise cause is not known, but it is thought that the shortage of daylight may provoke a reaction between various hormones and neurotransmitters in the brain. Abbr **SAD**, **SADS**

seat-belt syndrome /'si:t belt ˌsɪndrəʊm/ *noun* a group of injuries between the neck and the abdomen which occur in a car accident when a person is using either a lap belt or a shoulder belt incorrectly, not over the strongest part of the chest

sebaceous /sə'beɪʃəs/ *adjective* **1.** referring to sebum **2.** producing oil

sebaceous cyst /sə,beɪʃəs 'sɪst/ *noun* a cyst which forms when a sebaceous gland is blocked. ◊ **steatoma**

sebaceous gland /sə,beɪʃəs 'glænd/ *noun* a gland in the skin which secretes sebum at the base of each hair follicle

seborrhoea /ˌsebə'ri:ə/ *noun* an excessive secretion of sebum by the sebaceous glands, common in young people at puberty, and sometimes linked to seborrhoeic dermatitis (NOTE: The US spelling is **seborrhea**.)

seborrhoeic /ˌsebə'ri:ɪk/ *adjective* **1.** caused by seborrhoea **2.** having an oily secretion (NOTE: [all senses] The US spelling is **seborrheic**.)

seborrhoeic dermatitis /ˌsebəri:ɪk ˌdɜːmə 'taɪtɪs/, **seborrhoeic eczema** /ˌsebəri:ɪk 'ek↓sɪmə/ *noun* a type of eczema where scales form on the skin

seborrhoeic rash /ˌsebəri:ɪk 'ræʃ/ *noun* ♦ **seborrhoeic dermatitis**

sebum /'si:bəm/ *noun* an oily substance secreted by a sebaceous gland, which makes the skin smooth. It also protects the skin against bacteria and the body against rapid evaporation of water.

second /'sekənd/ *noun* a unit of time equal to 1/60 of a minute ■ *adjective* coming after the first

secondary /'sekənd(ə)ri/ *adjective* **1.** occurring after the first stage **2.** less important than something else **3.** referring to a condition which develops from another condition ■ *noun* a malignant tumour which has developed and spread from another malignant tumour. ◊ **primary** (NOTE: The plural is **secondaries**.)

secondary amenorrhoea /ˌsekənd(ə)ri eɪmenə'ri:ə/ *noun* a situation in which a premenopausal woman's menstrual periods have stopped

secondary biliary cirrhosis /ˌsekənd(ə)ri ˌbɪliəri səˈrəʊsɪs/ *noun* cirrhosis of the liver caused by an obstruction of the bile ducts

secondary bronchi /ˌsekənd(ə)ri ˈbrɒŋkiː/ *plural noun* same as **lobar bronchi**

secondary care /ˌsekənd(ə)ri ˈkeə/ *noun* treatment provided by the professional team in a hospital, rather than by a GP or other primary care provider and the primary health care team. Compare **primary care, tertiary care.** Also called **secondary health care**

secondary cartilaginous joint /ˌsekənd(ə)ri kɑːtəˈlædʒɪnəs ˌdʒɔɪnt/ *noun* a joint where the surfaces of the two bones are connected by a piece of cartilage so that they cannot move, e.g. the pubic symphysis

secondary dysmenorrhoea /ˌsekənd(ə)ri dɪsˌmenəˈriːə/ *noun* dysmenorrhoea which starts at some time after the first menstruation

secondary growth /ˌsekənd(ə)ri ˈɡrəʊθ/ *noun* same as **metastasis**

secondary haemorrhage /ˌsekənd(ə)ri ˈhem(ə)rɪdʒ/ *noun* a haemorrhage which occurs some time after an injury, usually due to infection of the wound

secondary health care /ˌsekənd(ə)ri ˈhelθ keə/ *noun* same as secondary care

secondary infection /ˌsekənd(ə)ri ɪnˈfekʃən/ *noun* an infection which affects a person while he or she is weakened through having another infection

secondary medical care /ˌsekənd(ə)ri ˈmedɪk(ə)l keə/ *noun* specialised treatment provided by a hospital

secondary peritonitis /ˌsekənd(ə)ri ˌperɪtəˈnaɪtɪs/ *noun* peritonitis caused by infection from an adjoining tissue, e.g. from the rupturing of the appendix

secondary prevention /ˌsekənd(ə)ri prɪˈvenʃən/ *noun* the use of methods such as screening tests which avoid a serious disease by detecting it early

secondary sexual characteristic /ˌsekənd(ə)ri ˌsekʃuəl kærɪktəˈrɪstɪk/ *noun* a sexual characteristic which develops after puberty, e.g. pubic hair or breasts

second-degree burn /ˌsekənd dɪˌɡriː ˈbɜːn/ *noun* a burn where the skin becomes very red and blisters

second-degree haemorrhoids /ˌsekənd dɪˌɡriː ˈhemərɔɪdz/ *plural noun* haemorrhoids which protrude into the anus but return into the rectum automatically

second intention /ˌsekənd ɪnˈtenʃ(ə)n/ *noun* healing of an infected wound or ulcer, which takes place slowly and leaves a prominent scar

second-level nurse /ˌsekənd ˌlev(ə)l ˈnɜːs/, **second-level registered nurse** /ˌsekənd ˌlev(ə)l ˌredʒɪstəd ˈnɜːs/ *noun* a trained person who delivers nursing care under the direction and supervision of a first-level nurse. Compare **first-level nurse**

second molar /ˌsekənd ˈməʊlə/ *noun* any of the molars at the back of the jaw, before the wisdom teeth, erupting at about 12 years of age

second opinion /ˌsekənd əˈpɪnjən/ *noun* a diagnosis or opinion on treatment from a second doctor, often a hospital specialist

secrete /sɪˈkriːt/ *verb* (*of a gland*) to produce a substance such as hormone, oil or enzyme (NOTE: **secreting – secreted**)

secretin /sɪˈkriːtɪn/ *noun* a hormone secreted by the duodenum which encourages the production of pancreatic juice

secretion /sɪˈkriːʃ(ə)n/ *noun* **1.** the process by which a substance is produced by a gland ○ *The pituitary gland stimulates the secretion of hormones by the adrenal gland.* **2.** a substance produced by a gland ○ *Sex hormones are bodily secretions.*

secretor /sɪˈkriːtə/ *noun* a person who secretes substances indicating ABO blood group into mucous fluids such as semen or saliva

secretory /sɪˈkriːtəri/ *adjective* referring to, accompanied by or producing a secretion

secretory otitis media /sɪˌkriːtəri əʊ ˌtaɪtɪs ˈmiːdiə/ *noun* same as **glue ear**

section /ˈsekʃən/ *noun* **1.** a part of something ○ *the middle section of the aorta* **2.** the action of cutting tissue **3.** a cut made in tissue **4.** a slice of tissue cut for examination under a microscope **5.** a part of a document such as an Act of Parliament ○ *She was admitted under section 5 of the Mental Health Act.*

Section 47 /ˌsekʃən fɔːti ˈsev(ə)n/ *noun* a UK law under which a local authority has the power to seek an order from a magistrate's court authorising the removal of a person at severe risk from their home. The authority must have a doctor's certificate that the person is either suffering from a grave and chronic disease or is unable to look after himself or herself and is not receiving proper care and attention from other people.

security blanket /sɪˈkjʊərəti ˌblæŋkɪt/ *noun* a familiar blanket, toy or other object which a child carries around because it makes him or her feel safe

sedate /sɪˈdeɪt/ *verb* to calm a person by giving them a drug which acts on the nervous system and relieves stress or pain, and in larger doses makes the person sleep ○ *Elderly or confused patients may need to be sedated to prevent them wandering.* (NOTE: **sedating – sedated**)

sedation /sɪˈdeɪʃ(ə)n/ *noun* the act of calming someone using a sedative □ **under sedation** having been given a sedative ○ *He was* *still under sedation, and could not be seen by the police.*

sedative /'sedətiv/ *noun* an anxiolytic or hypnotic drug such as benzodiazepine, which acts on the nervous system to help a person sleep or to relieve stress (*dated*) ○ *She was prescribed sedatives by the doctor.* ■ *adjective* acting to help a person sleep or to relieve stress

sedentary /'sed(ə)nt(ə)ri/ *adjective* involving a lot of sitting and little exercise

'…changes in lifestyle factors have been related to the decline in mortality from ischaemic heart disease. In many studies a sedentary lifestyle has been reported as a risk factor for ischaemic heart disease' [*Journal of the American Medical Association*]

sedentary occupation /,sed(ə)nt(ə)ri ,ɒkjʊ'peɪʃ(ə)n/ *noun* a job where the workers sit down for most of the time

sediment /'sedɪmənt/ *noun* solid particles, usually insoluble, which fall to the bottom of a liquid

sedimentation /,sedɪmen'teɪʃ(ə)n/ *noun* the action of solid particles falling to the bottom of a liquid

sedimentation rate /,sedɪmen'teɪʃ(ə)n reɪt/ *noun* the rate at which solid particles are deposited from a solution, measured especially in a centrifuge

segment /'segmənt/ *noun* a part of an organ or piece of tissue which is clearly separate from other parts

segmental /seg'ment(ə)l/ *adjective* formed of segments

segmental ablation /seg,ment(ə)l æ'bleɪʃ(ə)n/ *noun* a surgical operation to remove part of a nail, e.g. treatment for an ingrowing toenail

segmental bronchi /seg,ment(ə)l 'brɒŋkiː/ *plural noun* air passages supplying a segment of a lung. Also called **tertiary bronchi**

segmentation /,segmən'teɪʃ(ə)n/ *noun* the movement of separate segments of the wall of the intestine to mix digestive juice with the food before it is passed along by the action of peristalsis

segmented /'segməntɪd/ *adjective* formed of segments

segregation /,segrɪ'geɪʃ(ə)n/ *noun* **1.** the act of separating one person, group or thing from others, or of dividing people or things into separate groups which are kept apart from each other **2.** the separation of the alleles of each gene and their distribution to separate sex cells during the formation of these cells in organisms with paired chromosomes

seizure /'siːʒə/ *noun* a fit, convulsion or sudden contraction of the muscles, especially in a heart attack, stroke or epileptic fit

select /sɪ'lekt/ *verb* to choose one person, thing or group, but not others ○ *She was selected to go on a midwifery course*

selection /sɪ'lekʃən/ *noun* an act of choosing one person, thing or group, but not others ○ *the selection of a suitable donor for a bone marrow transplant* ○ *The candidates for the post have to go through a selection process.*

selective /sɪ'lektɪv/ *adjective* choosing only one person, thing or group, and not others

selective oestrogen receptor modulator /sɪ,lektɪv 'iːstrədʒ(ə)n rɪ,septə ,mɒdjʊ leɪtə/, **selective estrogen receptor modulator** *noun* a drug which acts on specific oestrogen receptors to prevent bone loss without affecting other oestrogen receptors, e.g. raloxifene hydrochloride. Abbr **SERM**

selective serotonin re-uptake inhibitor /sɪ,lektɪv serə,təʊnɪn riː'ʌpteɪk ɪn,hɪbɪtə/ *noun* a drug which causes a selective accumulation of serotonin in the central nervous system, and is used in the treatment of depression, e.g. fluoxetine. Abbr **SSRI**

COMMENT: The drug should not be started immediately after stopping an MAOI and should be withdrawn slowly.

selenium /sə'liːniəm/ *noun* a non-metallic trace element (NOTE: The chemical symbol is **Se**.)

self- /self/ *prefix* yourself

self-abuse /,self ə'bjuːs/ *noun* same as **self-harm**

self-actualisation /self ,æktjuəlaɪ'zeɪʃ(ə)n/, **self-actualization** *noun* the successful development and use of personal talents and abilities

self-admitted /,self əd'mɪtɪd/ *adjective* referring to a patient who has admitted himself or herself to hospital without being sent by a doctor

self-care /self 'keə/ *noun* the act of looking after yourself properly, so that you remain healthy

self-catheterisation /self ,kæθɪtəraɪ 'zeɪʃ(ə)n/, **self-catheterization** *noun* a procedure in which a person puts a catheter through the urethra into his or her own bladder to empty out the urine

self-defence /,self dɪ'fens/ *noun* the act of defending yourself when someone is attacking you

self-examination /,self ɪg,zæmɪ'neɪʃ(ə)n/ *noun* the regular examination of parts of your own body for signs of disease

self-governing hospital /self ,gʌvənɪŋ 'hɒspɪt(ə)l/ *noun* in the UK, a hospital which earns its revenue from services provided to the District Health Authorities and family doctors. Also called **hospital trust**

self-harm /,self 'hɑːm/ *noun* a deliberate act by which someone injures part of their body as the result of a personal trauma. Cutting and burning are two of the most common forms of self-harm. Also called **self-abuse, self-injury, self-mutilation, self-wounding**

self-image /self 'ɪmɪdʒ/ *noun* the opinion which a person has about how worthwhile, attractive, or intelligent he or she is

self-injury /ˌself 'ɪndʒəri/, **self-mutilation** /ˌself ˌmjuːtɪ'leɪʃ(ə)n/ *noun* same as **self-harm**

self-retaining catheter /self rɪˌteɪnɪŋ 'kæθɪtə/ *noun* a catheter which remains in place until it is deliberately removed

self-wounding *noun* same as **self-harm**

sella turcica /ˌselə 'tɜːsɪkə/ *noun* a hollow in the upper surface of the sphenoid bone in which the pituitary gland sits. Also called **pituitary fossa**

semeiology /ˌsiːmaɪ'ɒlədʒi/ *noun* same as **symptomatology**

semen /'siːmən/ *noun* a thick pale fluid containing spermatozoa, produced by the testes and seminal vesicles and ejaculated from the penis

semi- /semi/ *prefix* half

semicircular /ˌsemi'sɜːkjʊlə/ *adjective* shaped like half a circle

semicircular canal /ˌsemisɜːkjʊlə kə'næl/ *noun* any one of three tubes in the inner ear which are partly filled with fluid and help to maintain balance. See illustration at **EAR** in Supplement

COMMENT: The three semicircular canals are on different planes. When a person's head moves, as when he or she bends down, the fluid in the canals moves and this movement is communicated to the brain through the vestibular section of the auditory nerve.

semicircular duct /ˌsemisɜːkjʊlə 'dʌkt/ *noun* a duct in the semicircular canals in the ear

semicomatose /ˌsemi'kəʊmətəʊs/ *adjective* almost unconscious or half asleep, but capable of being woken up

semi-conscious /ˌsemi 'kɒnʃəs/ *adjective* half conscious, only partly aware of what is going on ○ *She was semi-conscious for most of the operation.*

semi-liquid /ˌsemi 'lɪkwɪd/ *adjective* half liquid and half solid

semilunar /ˌsemi'luːnə/ *adjective* shaped like half a moon

semilunar cartilage /ˌsemiˌluːnə 'kɑːtəlɪdʒ/ *noun* same as **meniscus**

semilunar valve /ˌsemiˌluːnə 'vælv/ *noun* either of two valves in the heart, the pulmonary valve and the aortic valve, through which blood flows out of the ventricles

seminal /'semɪn(ə)l/ *adjective* referring to semen

seminal fluid /'semɪn(ə)l ˌfluːɪd/ *noun* the fluid part of semen, formed in the epididymis and seminal vesicles

seminal vesicle /ˌsemɪn(ə)l 'vesɪk(ə)l/ *noun* one of two glands at the end of the vas deferens which secrete the fluid part of semen.

See illustration at **urogenital system (male)** in Supplement

seminiferous tubule /semiˌnɪfərəs 'tjuːbjuːl/ *noun* a tubule in the testis which carries semen

seminoma /ˌsemi'nəʊmə/ *noun* a malignant tumour in the testis (NOTE: The plural is **seminomas** or **seminomata**.)

semipermeable /ˌsemi'pɜːmiəb(ə)l/ *adjective* allowing some types of particle to pass through but not others

semipermeable membrane /ˌsemi ˌpɜːmiəb(ə)l 'membreɪn/ *noun* a membrane which allows some substances in liquid solution to pass through but not others

semiprone /semi'prəʊn/ *adjective* referring to a position in which someone lies face downwards, with one knee and one arm bent forwards and the face turned to one side

semi-solid /ˌsemi 'sɒlɪd/ *adjective* half solid and half liquid

SEN *abbr* State Enrolled Nurse

senescence /sɪ'nesəns/ *noun* the ageing process

senescent /sɪ'nesənt/ *adjective* approaching the last stages of the natural life span

Sengstaken tube /'seŋzteɪkən tjuːb/ *noun* a tube with a balloon, which is passed through the mouth into the oesophagus to stop oesophageal bleeding [After Robert William Sengstaken (b. 1923), US surgeon]

senile /'siːnaɪl/ *adjective* **1.** referring to the last stages of the natural life span or to the medical conditions associated with it **2.** referring to someone whose mental faculties have become weak because of age

senile cataract /ˌsiːnaɪl 'kætərækt/ *noun* a cataract which occurs in an elderly person

senile dementia /ˌsiːnaɪl dɪ'menʃə/ *noun* mental degeneration affecting elderly people (*dated*)

senile plaque /'siːnaɪl plæk/ *noun* a spherical deposit of beta amyloid in brain areas in Alzheimer's disease

senilis /sə'naɪlɪs/ ♦ **arcus senilis**

senility /sə'nɪləti/ *noun* the deterioration of mental activity associated with the last stages of the natural life span

senior /'siːniə/ *adjective* **1.** older than another person or other people **2.** holding a more important position than others ○ *He is the senior anaesthetist in the hospital.* ○ *Senior members of staff are allowed to consult the staff records.* ■ *noun* a senior person

senna /'senə/ *noun* a laxative made from the dried fruit and leaves of a tropical tree

sensation /sen'seɪʃ(ə)n/ *noun* a feeling or information about something which has been sensed by a sensory nerve and is passed to the brain

sense /sens/ *noun* **1.** one of the five faculties by which a person notices things in the outside world: sight, hearing, smell, taste and touch ○ *When she had a cold, she lost her sense of smell.* **2.** the ability to discern or judge something ■ *verb* to notice something by means other than sight ○ *Teeth can sense changes in temperature.*

sense of balance /,sens əv 'bæləns/ *noun* a feeling that keeps a person upright, governed by the fluid in the inner ear balance mechanism

sense organ /sens 'ɔːgən/ *noun* an organ in which there are various sensory nerves which can detect environmental stimuli such as scent, heat or pain, and transmit information about them to the central nervous system, e.g. the nose or the skin

sensibility /,sensɪ'bɪlɪti/ *noun* the ability to detect and interpret sensations

sensible /'sensɪb(ə)l/ *adjective* **1.** showing common sense or good judgment **2.** able to be detected by the senses

sensible perspiration /,sensəb(ə)l ,pɜːspə'reɪʃ(ə)n/ *noun* drops of sweat which can be seen on the skin, secreted by the sweat glands

sensitisation /,sensɪtaɪ'zeɪʃ(ə)n/, **sensitization** *noun* **1.** the process of making a person sensitive to something **2.** an unexpected reaction to an allergen or to a drug, caused by the presence of antibodies which were created when the person was exposed to the drug or allergen in the past

sensitise /'sensɪtaɪz/, **sensitize** *verb* to make someone sensitive to a drug or allergen (NOTE: **sensitising – sensitised**)

sensitised person /,sensɪtaɪzd 'pɜːs(ə)n/, **sensitized person** *noun* a person who is allergic to a drug

sensitising agent /'sensɪtaɪzɪŋ ,eɪdʒənt/, **sensitizing agent** *noun* a substance which, by acting as an antigen, makes the body form antibodies

sensitive /'sensɪtɪv/ *adjective* **1.** able to detect and respond to an outside stimulus **2.** having an unexpected reaction to an allergen or to a drug, caused by the presence of antibodies which were created when the person was exposed to the drug or allergen in the past

sensitivity /,sensɪ'tɪvɪti/ *noun* **1.** the fact of being able to detect and respond to an outside stimulus **2.** the rate of positive responses in a test from persons with a specific disease. A high rate of sensitivity means a low rate of people being incorrectly classed as negative. Compare **specificity**

sensorineural deafness /,sensəri,njʊərəl 'defnəs/, **sensorineural hearing loss** /,sensəri,njʊərəl 'hɪərɪŋ lɒs/ *noun* deafness caused by a disorder in the auditory nerves or the brain centres which receive impulses from the nerves. Also called **perceptive deafness**

sensory /'sensəri/ *adjective* referring to the detection of sensations by nerve cells

sensory cortex /,sensəri 'kɔːteks/ *noun* the area of the cerebral cortex which receives information from nerves in all parts of the body (dated)

sensory deprivation /,sensəri ,deprɪ'veɪʃ(ə)n/ *noun* a condition in which a person becomes confused because they lack sensations

sensory nerve /'sensəri nɜːv/ *noun* a nerve which registers a sensation such as heat, taste or smell and carries impulses to the brain and spinal cord. Also called **afferent nerve**

sensory neurone /,sensəri 'njʊərəʊn/ *noun* a nerve cell which transmits impulses relating to sensations from the receptor to the central nervous system

sensory receptor /,sensəri rɪ'septə/ *noun* a cell which senses a change in the surrounding environment, e.g. cold or pressure, and reacts to it by sending out an impulse through the nervous system. Also called **nerve ending**

separate *verb* /'sepəreɪt/ to move two or more people or things apart ○ *The surgeons believe it may be possible to separate the conjoined twins.* ○ *The retina has become separated from the back of the eye.* (NOTE: **separating – separated**) ■ *adjective* /'sep(ə)rət/ **1.** not touching, together or in the same place **2.** distinct and not related or the same

separation /,sepə'reɪʃ(ə)n/ *noun* the act of separating or dividing two or more people or things, or the state of being separated

separation anxiety /,sepə'reɪʃ(ə)n æŋ,zaɪəti/ *noun* a state of anxiety caused in someone, especially a young child, by the thought or fact of being separated from his or her mother or primary caregiver

sepsis /'sepsɪs/ *noun* the presence of bacteria and their toxins in the body, which kill tissue and produce pus, usually following the infection of a wound

sept- /sept/ *prefix* same as **septi-** (used before vowels)

septa /'septə/ plural of **septum**

septal /'sept(ə)l/ *adjective* referring to a septum

septal defect /,sept(ə)l 'diːfekt/ *noun* a congenital condition in which a hole exists in the wall between the left and right sides of the heart allowing an excessive amount of blood to flow through the lungs, leading in severe cases to pulmonary hypertension and sometimes heart failure

septate /'septeɪt/ *adjective* divided by a septum

septi- /septɪ/ *prefix* referring to sepsis

septic /'septɪk/ *adjective* referring to or produced by sepsis

septicaemia /ˌseptɪ'siːmiə/ *noun* a condition in which bacteria or their toxins are present in the blood, multiply rapidly and destroy tissue. ◊ **blood poisoning** (NOTE: The US spelling is **septicemia**.)

septicaemic /ˌseptɪ'siːmɪk/ *adjective* caused by septicaemia, associated with septicaemia (NOTE: The US spelling is **septicemic**.)

septicaemic plague /ˌseptɪsiːmɪk 'pleɪg/ *noun* a form of bubonic plague in which the symptoms are generalised throughout the body

septic shock /ˌseptɪk 'ʃɒk/ *noun* shock caused by bacterial toxins in the blood as a result of infection. There is a dramatic drop in blood pressure, preventing the delivery of blood to the organs. Toxic shock syndrome is one type of septic shock.

septo- /septəʊ/ *prefix* referring to a septum

septoplasty /'septəʊplæsti/ *noun* a surgical operation to straighten the cartilage in the septum (NOTE: The plural is **septoplasties**.)

Septrin /'septrɪn/ *a trade name for co-trimoxazole*

septum /'septəm/ *noun* a wall between two parts of an organ, e.g. between two parts of the heart or between the two nostrils in the nose. See illustration at HEART in Supplement (NOTE: The plural is **septa**.)

septum defect /'septəm ˌdiːfekt/ *noun* a condition in which a hole exists in a septum, usually the septum of the heart

sequela /sɪ'kwiːlə/ *noun* a disease or disorder that is caused by a disease or injury which the person had previously ○ *a case of osteomyelitis as a sequela of multiple fractures of the mandible* ○ *biochemical and hormonal sequelae of the eating disorders* ○ *Kaposi's sarcoma can be a sequela of Aids.* (NOTE: The plural is **sequelae**.)

sequence /'siːkwəns/ *noun* a series of things, numbers etc., which follow each other in order ■ *verb* 1. to put things in order 2. to show how amino acids are linked together in chains to form protein (NOTE: **sequences – sequencing – sequenced**)

sequestra /sɪ'kwestrə/ plural of **sequestrum**

sequestration /ˌsiːkwe'streɪʃ(ə)n/ *noun* 1. the act of putting someone in an isolated place 2. the loss of blood into spaces in the body, reducing the circulating volume. It can occur naturally or can be produced artificially by applying tourniquets. ○ *pulmonary sequestration* ○ *A dry hacking cough can cause sequestration of the peritoneum in the upper abdomen.* 3. the formation of a sequestrum

sequestrectomy /ˌsiːkwɪ'strektəmi/ *noun* a surgical operation to remove a sequestrum (NOTE: The plural is **sequestrectomies**.)

sequestrum /sɪ'kwestrəm/ *noun* a piece of dead bone which is separated from whole bone (NOTE: The plural is **sequestra**.)

ser- /sɪər/ *prefix* same as **sero-** (used before vowels)

sera /'sɪərə/ *plural noun* plural of **serum**

serine /'serɪn/ *noun* an amino acid produced in the hydrolysis of protein

serious /'sɪəriəs/ *adjective* 1. having very bad consequences ○ *He's had a serious illness.* ○ *There was a serious accident on the motorway.* ○ *There is a serious shortage of plasma.* 2. thoughtful and not superficial or humorous ○ *a serious discussion on the appropriateness of the treatment* ○ *serious about becoming a GP*

seriously /'sɪəriəsli/ *adverb* in a serious way ○ *She is seriously ill.*

SERM *abbr* selective (o)estrogen receptor modulator

sero- /sɪərəʊ/ *prefix* 1. referring to blood serum 2. referring to the serous membrane

seroconvert /ˌsɪərəʊkən'vɜːt/ *verb* to produce specific antibodies in response to the presence of an antigen such as a bacterium or virus

serological /ˌsɪərə'lɒdʒɪk(ə)l/ *adjective* referring to serology

serological diagnosis /ˌsɪərəʊlɒdʒɪk(ə)l ˌdaɪəg'nəʊsɪs/ *noun* a diagnosis which comes from testing serum

serological type /ˌsɪərəlɒdʒɪk(ə)l 'taɪp/ *noun* same as **serotype**

serology /sɪə'rɒlədʒi/ *noun* the scientific study of serum and the antibodies contained in it

seronegative /ˌsɪərəʊ'negətɪv/ *adjective* referring to someone who gives a negative reaction to a serological test

seropositive /ˌsɪərəʊ'pɒzɪtɪv/ *adjective* referring to someone who gives a positive reaction to a serological test

seropus /'sɪərəʊ,pʌs/ *noun* a mixture of serum and pus

serosa /sɪ'rəʊsə/ *noun* same as **serous membrane** (NOTE: The plural is **serosas** or **serosae**.)

serositis /ˌsɪərəʊ'saɪtɪs/ *noun* inflammation of a serous membrane

serotherapy /ˌsɪərəʊ'θerəpi/ *noun* treatment of a disease using serum from immune people or immunised animals

serotonin /ˌsɪərə'təʊnɪn/ *noun* a compound which is a neurotransmitter and exists mainly in blood platelets. It is released after tissue is injured and is important in sleep, mood and vasoconstriction.

serotype /'sɪərəʊtaɪp/ *noun* 1. a category of microorganisms or bacteria which have some antigens in common 2. a series of common antigens which exists in microorganisms and bacteria ▶ also called **serological type** ■ *verb* to group microorganisms and bacteria according to their antigens (NOTE: **serotyping – serotyped**)

serous /'sɪərəs/ *adjective* referring to, producing, or like serum

serous membrane /ˌsɪərəs 'membreɪn/ *noun* a membrane which both lines an internal cavity and covers the organs in the cavity, e.g. the peritoneum lining the abdominal cavity or pleura lining the chest cavity. Also called **serosa**

serous pericardium /ˌsɪərəs ˌperɪ'kɑːdiəm/ *noun* the inner part of the pericardium, forming a double sac which contains fluid to prevent the two parts of the pericardium from rubbing together

serpens /'sɜːpenz/ ✦ **erythema serpens**

serpiginous /sə'pɪdʒɪnəs/ *adjective* **1.** referring to an ulcer or eruption which creeps across the skin **2.** referring to a wound or ulcer with a wavy edge

serrated /sə'reɪtɪd/ *adjective* with a zigzag or saw-like edge

serration /sə'reɪʃ(ə)n/ *noun* one of the points in a zigzag or serrated edge

Sertoli cells /sə'təʊli selz/ *plural noun* cells which support the seminiferous tubules in the testis [Described 1865. After Enrico Sertoli (1842–1910), Italian histologist, Professor of Experimental Physiology at Milan, Italy.]

sertraline /'sɜːtrəliːn/ *noun* an antidepressant drug which extends the action of the neurotransmitter serotonin. It is also used in the treatment of obsessive-compulsive disorder and post-traumatic stress disorder.

serum /'sɪərəm/ *noun* **1.** a fluid which separates from clotted blood and is similar to plasma except that it has no clotting agents. Also called **blood serum 2.** blood serum taken from an animal which has developed antibodies to bacteria, used to give humans temporary immunity to a disease. Also called **antiserum 3.** any clear watery body fluid, especially a fluid that comes from a serous membrane (NOTE: The plural is **serums** or **sera**.)

COMMENT: Blood serum is plasma without the clotting agents. It contains salt and small quantities of albumin, globulin, amino acids, fats and sugars; its main component is water.

serum albumin /ˌsɪərəm 'ælbjʊmɪn/ *noun* a major protein in blood plasma

serum bilirubin /ˌsɪərəm bɪlɪ'ruːbɪn/ *noun* bilirubin in serum, converted from haemoglobin as red blood cells are destroyed

serum globulin /ˌsɪərəm 'glɒbjʊlɪn/ *noun* a major protein in blood serum that is an antibody

serum glutamic–oxalacetic transaminase /ˌsɪərəm gluːˌtæmɪk ˌɒksælɒsiːtɪk trænsˈæmɪneɪz/ *noun* an enzyme excreted by damaged heart muscle, which appears in the blood of people who have had a heart attack. Abbr **SGOT**

serum glutamic–pyruvic transaminase /ˌsɪərəm gluːˌtæmɪk paɪˌruːvɪk trænsˈæmɪneɪz/ *noun* an enzyme secreted by the parenchymal cells of the liver, occurring in increased amounts in the blood of people with infectious hepatitis. Abbr **SGPT**

serum hepatitis /ˌsɪərəm ˌhepə'taɪtɪs/ *noun* a serious form of hepatitis transmitted by infected blood, unsterilised surgical instruments, shared needles or sexual intercourse. Also called **hepatitis B, viral hepatitis**

serum sickness /'sɪərəm ˌsɪknəs/ *noun* an allergic reaction to serum therapy which was formerly used as a way of boosting passive immunity

serum therapy *noun* the administration of treated serum, often from horses, formerly used as a way of boosting passive immunity

serve *verb* **1.** to give a person food or drink ○ *Lunch is served in the ward at 12:30.* **2.** to be useful or helpful to a person or group ○ *The clinic serves the local community well.* **3.** to have a particular effect or result ○ *The letter serves to remind you of your outpatients' appointment.* (NOTE: [all senses] **serves – serving – served**)

service /'sɜːvɪs/ *noun* **1.** the act or fact of serving a person or group **2.** a group of people working together

sesamoid /'sesəmɔɪd/, **sesamoid bone** /'sesəmɔɪd bəʊn/ *noun* any small bony nodule in a tendon, the largest being the kneecap

sessile /'sesaɪl/ *adjective* referring to something, especially a tumour, which has no stem. Opposite **pedunculate**

session /'seʃ(ə)n/ *noun* a visit to a therapist for treatment ○ *She has two sessions a week of physiotherapy.* ○ *The evening session had to be cancelled because the therapist was ill.*

set /set/ *verb* **1.** to put the parts of a broken bone back into their proper places and keep the bone fixed until it has mended ○ *The doctor set the man's broken arm.* **2.** (of a broken bone) to mend, to form a solid bone again ○ *His arm has set very quickly.* ○ *Her broken wrist is setting very well.* ◊ **reset** (NOTE: **setting – set**)

settle /'set(ə)l/ *verb* **1.** to begin to feel comfortable or at ease, or to make a person feel comfortable or at ease (NOTE: **settles – settling – settled**) **2.** (of a sediment) to fall to the bottom of a liquid **3.** (of a parasite) to attach itself, to stay in a part of the body ○ *The fluke settles in the liver.* (NOTE: **settles – settling – settled**)

sever /'sevə/ *verb* to cut something off ○ *His hand was severed at the wrist.* ○ *Surgeons tried to sew the severed finger back onto the patient's hand.*

severe /sɪ'vɪə/ *adjective* very bad or dangerous ○ *The patient experienced severe bleeding* ○ *A severe outbreak of whooping cough occurred during the winter.*

severe acute respiratory disorder /sɪ
ˌvɪə ə‚kjuːt rɪˈspɪrət(ə)ri dɪs‚ɔːdə/ *noun* full
form of **SARS**

severely /sɪˈvɪəli/ *adverb* very badly or dangerously ○ *Her breathing was severely affected.*

'…many severely confused patients, particularly
those in advanced stages of Alzheimer's disease, do
not respond to verbal communication' [*Nursing
Times*]

severity /sɪˈverɪti/ *noun* the degree to which
something is bad or dangerous ○ *Treatment
depends on the severity of the attack.*

sex /seks/ *noun* **1.** one of two groups, male
and female, into which animals and plants can
be divided ○ *The sex of a baby can be identified before birth.* **2.** same as **sexual intercourse**

sex act /ˈseks ækt/ *noun* an act of sexual intercourse

sexarche /ˈseksɑːki/ *noun* the age when a
person first has sexual intercourse

sex change /ˈseks tʃeɪndʒ/ *noun* a surgical
operation accompanied by hormone treatment
to change someone's physical sex-linked characteristics from female to male or from male to
female

sex chromosome /ˈseks ‚krəʊməsəʊm/
noun a chromosome which determines if a person is male or female

COMMENT: Out of the twenty-three pairs of
chromosomes in each human cell, two are
sex chromosomes, which are known as X and
Y. Females have a pair of X chromosomes
and males have a pair consisting of one X and
one Y chromosome. The sex of a baby is determined by the father's sperm. While the
mother's ovum only carries X chromosomes,
the father's sperm can carry either an X or a Y
chromosome. If the ovum is fertilised by a
sperm carrying an X chromosome, the embryo will contain the XX pair and so be female.
Disordered chromosomes affect sexual development: a person with an XO chromosome
pair (i.e. one X chromosome alone) has Turner's syndrome; a person with an extra X chromosome (making an XXY set) has Klinefelter's syndrome. Haemophilia is a disorder
linked to the X chromosome.

sex determination /ˈseks dɪtɜːmɪ
‚neɪʃ(ə)n/ *noun* the way in which the sex of an
individual organism is fixed by the number of
chromosomes which make up its cell structure

sex hormone /seks ˈhɔːməʊn/ *noun* an oestrogen or androgen which promotes the growth
of secondary sexual characteristics

sex-linkage /ˈseks ‚lɪŋkɪdʒ/ *noun* the existence of characteristics which are transmitted
through the X chromosomes

sex-linked /ˈseks ‚lɪŋkt/ *adjective* **1.** referring to genes which are linked to X chromosomes **2.** referring to characteristics such as
colour-blindness which are transmitted
through the X chromosomes

sexology /sekˈsɒlədʒi/ *noun* the study of sex
and sexual behaviour

sex organ /ˈseks ‚ɔːgən/ *noun* an organ
which is associated with reproduction and sexual intercourse, e.g. the testes and penis in
men, and the ovaries, Fallopian tubes, vagina
and vulva in women

sex selection /ˈseks sɪ‚lekʃ(ə)n/ *noun* the
determination of a baby's sex before conception by separating the spermatozoa carrying Y
chromosomes from those carrying X chromosomes

sextuplet /ˈsekstjʊplət/ *noun* one of six babies born to a mother at the same time

sexual /ˈsekʃuəl/ *adjective* referring to sex

sexual act /ˈsekʃuəl ækt/ *noun* an act of sexual intercourse

sexual attraction /‚sekʃuəl əˈtrækʃ(ə)n/
noun a feeling of wanting to have sexual intercourse with someone

sexual deviation /‚sekʃuəl diːviˈeɪʃ(ə)n/
noun any sexual behaviour which is not accepted as usual in the society in which you
live. Examples in Western society are sadism
and voyeurism.

sexual intercourse /‚sekʃuəl ˈɪntəkɔːs/
noun physical contact between people which
involves stimulation of the genitals, especially
the insertion of a man's erect penis into a
woman's vagina with release of spermatozoa
from the penis by ejaculation, which may fertilise ova from the woman's ovaries. Also
called **sex, coitus, copulation**

sexually transmitted disease /‚sekʃuəli
træns‚mɪtɪd dɪˈziːz/, **sexually transmitted
infection** /‚sekʃuəli træns‚mɪtɪd ɪn
ˈfekʃ(ə)n/ *noun* a disease or infection transmitted from an infected person to another person during sexual intercourse. Abbr **STD, STI**

COMMENT: Among the commonest STDs are
non-specific urethritis, genital herpes, hepatitis B and gonorrhoea; AIDS is also a sexually
transmitted disease. The spread of sexually
transmitted diseases can be limited by use of
condoms. Other forms of contraceptive offer
no protection against the spread of disease.

sexual reproduction /‚sekʃuəl ‚riːprə
ˈdʌkʃən/ *noun* reproduction in which gametes
from two individuals fuse together

SFD *abbr* small for dates

SGOT *abbr* serum glutamic-oxalacetic
transaminase

SGPT *abbr* serum glutamic-pyruvic transaminase

shaft /ʃɑːft/ *noun* **1.** the long central section
of a long bone **2.** main central section of the
erect penis

shake /ʃeɪk/ *verb* to move, or make something move, with short quick movements
(NOTE: **shaking – shook – shaken**)

shaken baby syndrome /‚ʃeɪkən ˈbeɪbi
‚sɪndrəʊm/, **shaken infant syndrome** /

ˌʃeɪkən 'ɪnfənt ˌsɪndrəʊm/ *noun* a series of internal head injuries in a very young child, caused by being shaken violently. It can result in brain damage leading to speech and learning disabilities, paralysis, seizures and hearing loss, and may be life-threatening.

shaky /'ʃeɪki/ *adjective* feeling weak and unsteady

share /ʃeə/ *verb* **1.** to use or do something together with others **2.** to divide something and give parts of it to different people or groups (NOTE: [all verb senses] **shares – sharing – shared**) ■ *noun* a single part of something divided among different people or groups

shared care /ˌʃeəd 'keə/ *noun* antenatal care given jointly by an obstetrician in a hospital together with a general practitioner or a midwife working in the community

sharp /ʃɑːp/ *adjective* **1.** able to cut easily ○ *A surgeon's knife has to be kept sharp.* **2.** hurting in a sudden and intense way ○ *She felt a sharp pain in her shoulder.*

sharply /'ʃɑːpli/ *adverb* suddenly and to a significant extent ○ *His condition deteriorated sharply during the night.*

sharps /ʃɑːps/ *plural noun* objects with points, e.g. syringes (*informal*)

shave /ʃeɪv/ *noun* the removal of hair by cutting it off at skin level with a razor ■ *verb* to remove hair with a razor (NOTE: **shaving – shaved**)

sheath /ʃiːθ/ *noun* **1.** a layer of tissue which surrounds a muscle or a bundle of nerve fibres **2.** same as **condom**

shed /ʃed/ *verb* to lose blood or tissue ○ *The lining of the uterus is shed at each menstrual period.* ○ *He was given a transfusion because he had shed a lot of blood.* (NOTE: **shedding – shed**)

sheet /ʃiːt/ *noun* a large piece of cloth which is put on a bed ○ *The sheets must be changed each day.* ○ *The soiled sheets were sent to the hospital laundry.* ◊ **draw-sheet**

shelf operation /'ʃelf ˌɒpəreɪʃ(ə)n/ *noun* a surgical operation to treat congenital dislocation of the hip in children, in which bone tissue is grafted onto the acetabulum

sheltered accommodation /ˌʃeltəd ə ˌkɒmə'deɪʃ(ə)n/, **sheltered housing** /ˌʃeltəd 'haʊzɪŋ/ *noun* rooms or small flats provided for elderly people, with a resident supervisor or nurse

shiatsu /ʃiˈætsuː/ *noun* a form of healing massage in which the hands are used to apply pressure at acupuncture points on the body in order to stimulate and redistribute energy

shift /ʃɪft/ *noun* **1.** a way of working in which one group of workers work for a period and are then replaced by another group ○ *She is working on the night shift.* ○ *The day shift comes on duty at 6.30 in the morning.* **2.** the period of time worked by a group of workers **3.** a movement

Shigella /ʃɪ'gelə/ *noun* a genus of bacteria which causes dysentery

shigellosis /ˌʃɪge'ləʊsɪs/ *noun* infestation of the digestive tract with *Shigella,* causing bacillary dysentery

shin /ʃɪn/ *noun* the front part of the lower leg

shinbone /'ʃɪnbəʊn/ *noun* same as **tibia**

shiner /'ʃaɪnə/ *noun* same as **black eye** (*informal*)

shingles /'ʃɪŋgəlz/ *noun* same as **herpes zoster**

shin splints /'ʃɪn splɪnts/ *plural noun* extremely sharp pains in the front of the lower leg, felt by athletes

Shirodkar's operation /ʃɪ'rɒdkɑːz ɒpəˌreɪʃ(ə)n/, **Shirodkar pursestring** /ʃɪˌrɒdkɑː 'pɜːsstrɪŋ/ *noun* a surgical operation to narrow the cervix of the uterus in a woman who experiences habitual abortion in order to prevent another miscarriage, the suture being removed before labour starts. Also called **purestring operation** [After N. V. Shirodkar (1900–71), Indian obstetrician.]

Shirodkar suture /ʃɪ'rɒdkɑː ˌsuːtʃə/ *noun* a type of suture which is placed around a cervix to tighten it during pregnancy and prevent miscarriage. Also called **pursestring stitch**

shiver /'ʃɪvə/ *verb* to tremble or shake all over the body because of cold or a fever, caused by the involuntary rapid contraction and relaxation of the muscles

shivering /'ʃɪvərɪŋ/ *noun* the condition of trembling or shaking all over the body because of cold or a fever, caused by the involuntary rapid contraction and relaxation of the muscles

shivery /'ʃɪvəri/ *adjective* trembling from cold, fear or a medical condition

shock /ʃɒk/ *noun* a state of weakness caused by illness or injury that suddenly reduces the blood pressure ○ *The patient went into shock.* ○ *Several of the passengers were treated for shock.* □ **traumatic shock** a state of shock caused by an injury which leads to loss of blood ■ *verb* to give someone an unpleasant surprise, and so put him or her in a state of shock ○ *She was still shocked several hours after the accident.* (NOTE: You say that someone is **in shock**, **in a state of shock** or that they **went into shock**.)

shock lung /ʃɒk 'lʌŋ/ *noun* a serious condition in which a person's lungs fail to work following a trauma

shock syndrome /'ʃɒk ˌsɪndrəʊm/ *noun* a group of symptoms, a pale face, cold skin, low blood pressure and rapid and irregular pulse, which show that someone is in a state of shock. ◊ **anaphylactic shock**

shock therapy /'ʃɒk ˌθerəpi/, **shock treatment** /'ʃɒk ˌtriːtmənt/ *noun* a method of treat-

ing some mental disorders by giving an anaesthetised patient an electric shock to induce an
epileptic convulsion

shoot /ʃuːt/ *verb* (*of pain*) to seem to move
suddenly through the body with a piercing
feeling ○ *The pain shot down his arm.*

shooting /ˈʃuːtɪŋ/ *adjective* (*of pain*) sudden
and intense

short /ʃɔːt/ *adjective* **1.** not having enough of
something **2.** not very tall or long

short-acting /ˌʃɔːt ˈæktɪŋ/ *adjective* effective only for a short period

shortness of breath /ˌʃɔːtnəs əv ˈbreθ/
noun the inability to breathe quickly enough to
supply the oxygen needed

short of breath /ˌʃɔːt əv ˈbreθ/ *adjective* unable to breathe quickly enough to supply the
oxygen needed ○ *After running up the stairs
he was short of breath.*

shortsighted /ʃɔːtˈsaɪtɪd/ *adjective* same as
myopic

shortsightedness /ˌʃɔːtˈsaɪtɪdnəs/ *noun*
same as **myopia**

shot /ʃɒt/ *noun* same as **injection** (*informal*) ○
The doctor gave her a tetanus shot. ○ *He needed a shot of morphine to relieve the pain.*

shoulder /ˈʃəʊldə/ *noun* a joint where the top
of the arm joins the main part of the body ○ *He
dislocated his shoulder.* ○ *She was complain-
ing of pains in her shoulder* or *of shoulder
pains.*

shoulder blade /ˈʃəʊldə bleɪd/ *noun* same
as **scapula**

shoulder girdle /ˈʃəʊldə ˌɡɜːd(ə)l/ *noun*
same as **pectoral girdle**

shoulder joint /ˈʃəʊldə dʒɔɪnt/ *noun* a ball
and socket joint which allows the arm to rotate
and move in any direction

shoulder lift /ˈʃəʊldə lɪft/ *noun* a way of carrying a heavy person, in which the upper part
of his or her body rests on the shoulders of two
carriers

shoulder presentation /ˈʃəʊldə ˌprez(ə)n
ˌteɪʃ(ə)n/ *noun* a position of a baby in the uterus, in which the shoulder will first appear

show /ʃəʊ/ *noun* the first discharge of blood at
the beginning of childbirth ■ *verb* **1.** to cause
or allow something to be visible **2.** to provide
convincing evidence of something

shrivel /ˈʃrɪv(ə)l/ *verb* to become dry and
wrinkled (NOTE: **shrivelling – shrivelled**. The
US spellings are **shriveling – shriveled**.)

shuffling walk /ˌʃʌf(ə)lɪŋ ˈwɔːk/, **shuffling
gait** /ˌʃʌf(ə)lɪŋ ˈɡeɪt/ *noun* a way of walking
in which the feet are not lifted off the ground,
e.g. in Parkinson's disease

shunt /ʃʌnt/ *noun* **1.** the passing of fluid
through a channel which is not the usual one **2.**
a channel which links two different blood vessels and carries blood from one to the other ■
verb (*of blood*) to pass through a channel which

is not the usual one ○ *As much as 5% of venous
blood can be shunted unoxygenated back to
the arteries.*

shunting /ˈʃʌntɪŋ/ *noun* a condition in which
some of the deoxygenated blood in the lungs
does not come into contact with air, and full
gas exchange does not take place

SI *abbreviation* the international system of
metric measurements. Full form **Système International**

sial- /saɪəl/ *prefix* same as **sialo-** (*used before
vowels*)

sialadenitis /ˌsaɪəlˌædɪˈnaɪtɪs/ *noun* inflammation of a salivary gland. Also called
sialoadenitis, sialitis

sialagogue /saɪˈæləɡɒɡ/ *noun* a substance
which increases the production of saliva

sialitis /ˌsaɪəlˈaɪtɪs/ *noun* same as **sialadenitis**

sialo- /saɪələʊ/ *prefix* **1.** referring to saliva **2.**
referring to a salivary gland

sialoadenitis /ˌsaɪələʊˌædɪˈnaɪtɪs/ *noun*
same as **sialadenitis**

sialogogue /saɪˈæləɡɒɡ/ *noun* same as **sialagogue**

sialography /ˌsaɪəˈlɒɡrəfi/ *noun* X-ray examination of a salivary gland. Also called **ptyalography**

sialolith /saɪˈæləʊlɪθ/ *noun* a stone in a salivary gland. Also called **ptyalith**

sialorrhoea /ˌsaɪələʊˈriːə/ *noun* the production of an excessive amount of saliva (NOTE:
The US spelling is **sialorrhea**.)

Siamese twins /ˌsaɪəmiːz ˈtwɪnz/ *plural
noun* same as **conjoined twins**

sib /sɪb/ *noun* same as **sibling** (*informal*)

sibilant /ˈsɪbɪlənt/ *adjective* referring to a
sound which whistles

sibling /ˈsɪblɪŋ/ *noun* a brother or sister

Sichuan flu /ˌsɪtʃwɑːn ˈfluː/ *noun* a virulent
type of flu which has the same symptoms as
those of ordinary flu (e.g. fever, sore throat and
aching muscles) but they are more pronounced
(*informal*) (NOTE: The virus was first discovered
in 1987 in Sichuan, a southwestern province of
China.)

sick /sɪk/ *adjective* **1.** having an illness ○ *He
was sick for two weeks.* □ **to report** *or* **call in
sick** to say officially that you are unwell and
cannot work **2.** about to vomit ○ *The patient
got up this morning and felt sick.* □ **to be sick**
to vomit ○ *The child was sick all over the floor.*
□ **to make someone sick** to cause someone to
vomit ○ *He was given something to make him
sick.*

sickbay /ˈsɪkbeɪ/ *noun* a room in a factory or
on a ship where people can visit a doctor for
treatment

sickbed /ˈsɪkbed/ *noun* a bed where a person
is lying sick ○ *She sat for hours beside her
daughter's sickbed.*

sick building syndrome /ˌsɪk ˈbɪldɪŋ ˌsɪn droʊm/ *noun* a condition in which many people working in a building feel ill or have headaches, caused by blocked air-conditioning ducts in which stale air is recycled round the building, often carrying allergenic substances or bacteria (*informal*)

sicken for /ˈsɪkən fɔː/ *verb* to feel the first symptoms of an illness (*informal*) ○ *She's looking pale – she must be sickening for something.*

sickle cell /ˈsɪk(ə)l sel/ *noun* a red blood cell shaped like a sickle, formed as a result of the presence of an unusual form of haemoglobin. Also called **drepanocyte**

sickle-cell anaemia /ˈsɪk(ə)l sel əˌniːmiə/ *noun* an inherited condition in which someone develops sickle cells which block the circulation, causing anaemia and pains in the joints and abdomen. Also called **drepanocytosis, sickle cell disease**

'…children with sickle-cell anaemia are susceptible to severe bacterial infection. Even children with the milder forms of sickle-cell disease have an increased frequency of pneumococcal infection' [*Lancet*]

COMMENT: Sickle-cell anaemia is a hereditary condition which is mainly found in people from Africa and the West Indies.

sickle-cell chest syndrome /ˌsɪk(ə)l sel ˈtʃest ˌsɪndroʊm/ *noun* a common complication of sickle-cell disease, with chest pain, fever and leucocytosis

sickle-cell disease /ˈsɪk(ə)l sel dɪˌziːz/ *noun* same as **sickle-cell anaemia**. Abbr **SCD**.

sickle-cell trait /ˈsɪk(ə)l sel ˌtreɪt/ *noun* a hereditary condition of the blood in which some red cells become sickle-shaped, but there are not enough affected cells to cause anaemia

sicklist /ˈsɪklɪst/ *noun* a list of people who are sick, e.g. children in a school or workers in a factory ○ *We have five members of staff on the sicklist.*

sickly /ˈsɪkli/ *adjective* (*usually of children*) subject to frequent sickness ○ *He was a sickly child, but now is a strong and healthy man.*

sickness /ˈsɪknəs/ *noun* **1.** a state of having an illness ○ *There is a lot of sickness in the winter months.* ○ *Many children are staying away from school because of sickness.* ◊ **seasickness, motion sickness 2.** a feeling of wanting to vomit

sickroom /ˈsɪkruːm/ *noun* a room where someone is ill ○ *Visitors are not allowed into the sickroom.*

side /saɪd/ *noun* **1.** the part of the body between the hips and the shoulder ○ *She was lying on her side.* **2.** the part of an object which is not the front, back, top or bottom ○ *The nurse wheeled the trolley to the side of the bed.*

side-effect /ˈsaɪd ɪˌfekt/ *noun* an effect produced by a drug or treatment which is not the main effect intended ○ *One of the side-effects of chemotherapy is that the patient's hair falls out.*

'…the treatment is not without possible side-effects, some of which can be particularly serious. The side-effects may include middle ear discomfort, claustrophobia, increased risk of epilepsy' [*New Zealand Medical Journal*]

side rail /ˈsaɪd ˌreɪl/ *noun* a rail at the side of a bed which can be lifted to prevent the person falling out

sidero- /saɪdərəʊ/ *prefix* referring to iron

sideropenia /ˌsaɪdərəʊˈpiːniə/ *noun* a lack of iron in the blood usually caused by insufficient iron in the diet

siderophilin /saɪdəˈrɒfəlɪn/ *noun* same as **transferrin**

siderosis /ˌsaɪdəˈrəʊsɪs/ *noun* **1.** a condition in which iron deposits form in tissue **2.** inflammation of the lungs caused by inhaling dust containing iron

SIDS *abbr* sudden infant death syndrome

sight /saɪt/ *noun* one of the five senses, the ability to see ○ *His sight is beginning to fail.* □ **to lose your sight** to become blind

sighted /ˈsaɪtɪd/ *adjective* able to see, as opposed to visually impaired

sigmoid /ˈsɪɡmɔɪd/ *adjective* **1.** shaped like the letter S **2.** referring to the sigmoid colon ■ *noun* same as **sigmoid colon**

sigmoid colon /ˌsɪɡmɔɪd ˈkəʊlɒn/ *noun* the fourth section of the colon which continues as the rectum. See illustration at DIGESTIVE SYSTEM in Supplement. Also called **pelvic colon, sigmoid, sigmoid flexure**

sigmoidectomy /ˌsɪɡmɔɪˈdektəmi/ *noun* a surgical operation to remove the sigmoid colon (NOTE: The plural is **sigmoidectomies**.)

sigmoid flexure *noun* same as **sigmoid colon**

sigmoidoscope /sɪɡˈmɔɪdəskəʊp/ *noun* a surgical instrument with a light at the end which can be passed into the rectum so that the sigmoid colon can be examined

sigmoidoscopy /ˌsɪɡmɔɪˈdɒskəpi/ *noun* a procedure in which the rectum and sigmoid colon are examined with a sigmoidoscope

sigmoidostomy /ˌsɪɡmɔɪˈdɒstəmi/ *noun* a surgical operation to bring the sigmoid colon out through a hole in the abdominal wall (NOTE: The plural is **sigmoidostomies**.)

sign /saɪn/ *noun* a movement, mark, colouring or change which has a meaning and can be recognised by a doctor as indicating a condition (NOTE: A change in function which is also noticed by the patient is a **symptom**.) ■ *verb* to write your name on a document such as a form or cheque, or at the end of a letter ○ *The doctor signed the death certificate.*

significant /sɪɡˈnɪfɪkənt/ *adjective* important or worth noting ○ *No significant inflammatory responses were observed.*

significantly /sɪɡˈnɪfɪkəntli/ *adverb* in an important or noteworthy manner ○ *He was not significantly better on the following day.*

sign language /'saɪn ˌlæŋgwɪdʒ/ *noun* a set of agreed signs made with the fingers and hands, used to indicate words by or for people who cannot hear or speak

sildenafil citrate /ˌsɪldənəfɪl 'saɪtreɪt/ *noun* an enzyme-inhibiting drug used in the treatment of male impotence

silent /'saɪlənt/ *adjective* **1.** not making any noise or talking **2.** not visible or showing no symptoms ○ *Genital herpes may be silent in women.* ○ *Graft occlusion is often silent with 80% of patients.*

silica /'sɪlɪkə/ *noun* a compound of silicon, the mineral which forms quartz and sand. Also called **silicon dioxide**

silicon /'sɪlɪkən/ *noun* a non-metallic chemical element (NOTE: The chemical symbol is **Si**.)

silicon dioxide /ˌsɪlɪkən daɪ'ɒksaɪd/ same as **silica**

silicosis /ˌsɪlɪ'kəʊsɪs/ *noun* a disease of the lungs caused by inhaling silica dust from mining or stone-crushing operations

COMMENT: This is a serious disease which makes breathing difficult and can lead to emphysema and bronchitis.

silver /'sɪlvə/ *noun* a white-coloured metallic element (NOTE: The chemical symbol is **Ag**.)

silver nitrate /ˌsɪlvə 'naɪtreɪt/ *noun* a salt of silver that is mixed with a cream or solution and used, e.g., to disinfect burns or to kill warts

Silvester method /sɪl'vestə ˌmeθəd/ *noun* a method of giving artificial respiration. The person lies on his or her back, then the first-aider brings the person's hands together on the chest and moves them above the person's head. ◊ **Holger-Nielsen method**

Simmonds' disease /'sɪməndz dɪˌziːz/ *noun* a condition of women due to postpartum haemorrhage, in which there is lack of activity in the pituitary gland, resulting in wasting of tissue, brittle bones and premature senility [Described 1914. After Morris Simmonds (1855–1925), German physician and pathologist.]

simple /'sɪmpəl/ *adjective* **1.** ordinary **2.** not very complicated

simple epithelium /ˌsɪmpəl ˌepɪ'θiːliəm/ *noun* an epithelium formed of a single layer of cells

simple fracture /ˌsɪmpəl 'fræktʃə/ *noun* a fracture where the skin surface around the damaged bone has not been broken and the broken ends of the bone are close together. Also called **closed fracture**

simple tachycardia /ˌsɪmpəl tæki'kɑːdiə/ *noun* same as **sinus tachycardia**

simplex /'sɪmpleks/ ♦ **herpes simplex**

Sims' position /'sɪmz pəˌzɪʃ(ə)n/ *noun* a position of the body in which the person lies on his or her left side with their left arm behind their back and their right knee and thigh flexed. It is used to allow the anal or vaginal area to be examined easily.

simvastatin /sɪm'væstɪn/ *noun* a drug which lowers lipid levels in the blood, used in the treatment of high cholesterol

sinciput /'sɪnsɪpʌt/ *noun* the part of the skull that includes the forehead and the area above it

sinew /'sɪnjuː/ *noun* same as **tendon**

singer's nodule /ˌsɪŋəz 'nɒdjuːl/ *noun* a small white polyp which can develop in the larynx of people who use their voice too much or too loudly

single parent family /ˌsɪŋg(ə)l ˌpeərənt 'fæm(ə)li/ *noun* a family which consists of a child or children and only one parent, e.g. because of death, divorce or separation

single photon emission computed tomography /ˌsɪŋg(ə)l ˌfəʊtɒn ɪˌmɪʃ(ə)n kəmˌpjuːtɪd təˈmɒgrəfi/ *noun* a scan to study brain blood flow in conditions such as Alzheimer's disease

singultus /sɪŋ'gʌltəs/ *noun* same as **hiccup**

sinistral /'sɪnɪstrəl/ *adjective* relating to or located on the left side, especially the left side of the body

sino- /saɪnəʊ/ *prefix* referring to a sinus

sinoatrial /ˌsaɪnəʊ'eɪtriəl/ *adjective* relating to the sinus venosus and the right atrium of the heart

sinoatrial node /ˌsaɪnəʊ'eɪtriəl nəʊd/ *noun* a node in the heart at the junction of the superior vena cava and the right atrium, which regulates the heartbeat. Also called **SA node, sinus node**

sinogram /'saɪnəʊgræm/ *noun* an X-ray photograph of a sinus

sinography /saɪ'nɒgrəfi/ *noun* examination of a sinus by taking an X-ray photograph

sinu- /saɪnə/ *prefix* same as **sino-**

sinuatrial *adjective* same as **sinoatrial**

sinus /'saɪnəs/ *noun* **1.** a cavity inside the body, including the cavities inside the head behind the cheekbone, forehead and nose ○ *The doctor diagnosed a sinus infection.* **2.** a tract or passage which develops between an infected place where pus has gathered and the surface of the skin **3.** a wide venous blood space

sinusitis /ˌsaɪnə'saɪtɪs/ *noun* inflammation of the mucous membrane in the sinuses, especially the maxillary sinuses

sinus nerve /'saɪnəs nɜːv/ *noun* a nerve which branches from the glossopharyngeal nerve

sinus node /'saɪnəs nəʊd/ *noun* same as **sinoatrial node**

sinusoid /'saɪnəsɔɪd/ *noun* a specially shaped small blood vessel in the liver, adrenal glands and other organs

sinus tachycardia /ˌsaɪnəs tæki'kɑːdiə/ *noun* rapid beating of the heart caused by stimulation of the sinoatrial node. Also called **simple tachycardia**

sinus venosus /ˌsaɪnəs vəˈnəʊsɪs/ *noun* a cavity in the heart of an embryo, part of which develops into the coronary sinus and part of which is absorbed into the right atrium

siphonage /ˈsaɪfənɪdʒ/ *noun* the removal of liquid from one place to another with a tube, as used to empty the stomach of its contents

Sippy diet /ˈsɪpi ˌdaɪət/ *noun US* an alkaline diet of milk and dry biscuits as a treatment for peptic ulcers [After Bertram Welton Sippy (1866–1924), physician in Chicago, USA]

sister /ˈsɪstə/ *noun* **1.** a female who has the same father and mother as someone ○ *He has three sisters.* ○ *Her sister works in a children's clinic.* **2.** a senior nurse □ **sister in charge** a senior nurse in charge of a hospital ward

sit /sɪt/ *verb* **1.** to rest with your weight largely supported by the buttocks **2.** to cause a person to sit somewhere (NOTE: [all senses] **sitting – sat**)

site /saɪt/ *noun* **1.** the position of something ○ *The X-ray showed the site of the infection.* **2.** the place where something happened **3.** the place where an incision is to be made in a surgical operation ■ *verb* to put something in a particular place, or be in a particular place ○ *The infection is sited in the right lung.* (NOTE: **siting – sited**)

'…arterial thrombi have a characteristic structure: platelets adhere at sites of endothelial damage and attract other platelets to form a dense aggregate' [*British Journal of Hospital Medicine*]

'…the sublingual site is probably the most acceptable and convenient for taking temperature' [*Nursing Times*]

'…with the anaesthetist's permission, the scrub nurse and surgeon began the process of cleaning up the skin round the operation site' [*NATNews*]

situated /ˈsɪtʃueɪtɪd/ *adjective* in a particular place ○ *The tumour is situated in the bowel.* ○ *The atlas bone is situated above the axis.*

sit up /ˌsɪt ˈʌp/ *verb* **1.** to sit with your back straight ○ *The patient is sitting up in bed.* **2.** to move from a lying to a sitting position (NOTE: **sitting up – sat up**)

situs /ˈsaɪtəs/ *noun* the position of an organ or part of the body, especially the usual position (NOTE: The plural is **situs**.)

situs inversus /ˌsaɪtəs ɪnˈvɜːsəs/, **situs inversus viscerum** /ˌsaɪtəs ɪnˌvɜːsəs ˈvɪsərəm/ *noun* a congenital condition, in which the organs are not on the usual side of the body, i.e. where the heart is on the right side and not the left

sitz bath /ˈsɪts bɑːθ/ *noun* a small low bath where someone can sit, but not lie down

SI units /ˌes ˈaɪ ˌjuːnɪts/ *plural noun* the units used in an international system of units for measuring physical properties such as weight, speed and light

Sjögren's syndrome /ˈʃɜːgrenz ˌsɪn drəʊm/ *noun* a chronic autoimmune disease in which the lacrimal and salivary glands become infiltrated with lymphocytes and plasma cells, and the mouth and eyes become dry

skatole /ˈskætəʊl/ *noun* another spelling of **scatole**

skeletal /ˈskelɪt(ə)l/ *adjective* referring to the skeleton

skeletal muscle /ˈskelɪt(ə)l ˌmʌs(ə)l/ *noun* a muscle attached to a bone, which makes a limb move

skeleton /ˈskelɪt(ə)n/ *noun* all the bones which make up a body

Skene's glands /ˈskiːnz glændz/ *noun* small mucous glands in the urethra in women [Described 1880. After Alexander Johnston Chalmers Skene (1838–1900), Scottish-born New York gynaecologist.]

skia- /skaɪə/ *prefix* referring to shadow

skiagram /ˈskaɪəgræm/ *noun* an old term for X-ray photograph

skier's thumb /ˌskiːəz ˈθʌm/ *noun* an injury to the thumb caused by falling directly onto it when it is outstretched, resulting in tearing or stretching of the ligaments of the main thumb joint

skill /skɪl/ *noun* an ability to do difficult work, which is acquired by training ○ *You need special skills to become a doctor.*

skilled /skɪld/ *adjective* having acquired a particular skill by training ○ *He's a skilled plastic surgeon.*

skill mix /ˈskɪl mɪks/ *noun* the range of different skills possessed by the members of a group or required for a particular job

skin /skɪn/ *noun* the tissue which forms the outside surface of the body ○ *His skin turned brown in the sun.* ○ *Skin problems in adolescents may be caused by diet.* (NOTE: For other terms referring to skin, see words beginning with **cut-, derm-, derma-, dermato-, dermo-**.)

COMMENT: The skin is the largest organ in the human body. It is formed of two layers: the epidermis is the outer layer, and includes the top layer of particles of dead skin which are continuously flaking off. Beneath the epidermis is the dermis, which is the main layer of living skin. Hairs and nails are produced by the skin, and pores in the skin secrete sweat from the sweat glands underneath the dermis. The skin is sensitive to touch and heat and cold, which are sensed by the nerve endings in the skin. The skin is a major source of vitamin D which it produces when exposed to sunlight.

skin graft /ˈskɪn grɑːft/ *noun* a layer of skin transplanted from one part of the body to cover an area where the skin has been destroyed ○ *After the operation she had to have a skin graft.*

skinny /ˈskɪni/ *adjective* very thin (*informal*)

skin test /ˈskɪn test/ *noun* a test for allergy, in which a substance is applied to the skin to see if a reaction occurs

skull /skʌl/ *noun* the eight bones which are fused or connected together to form the head, along with the fourteen bones which form the face. Also called **cranium** □ **skull fracture** a condition in which one of the bones in the skull has been fractured

slash /slæʃ/ *noun* a long cut with a knife ○ *He had bruises on his face and slashes on his hands.* ○ *The slash on her leg needs three stitches.* ■ *verb* **1.** to cut something with a knife or sharp edge □ **to slash your wrists** to try to kill yourself by cutting the blood vessels in the wrists **2.** to cut costs or spending sharply (*informal*)

SLE *abbr* systemic lupus erythematosus

sleep /sliːp/ *noun* the state or a period of resting, usually at night, when the eyes are closed and you are not conscious of what is happening ○ *You need to get a good night's sleep if you have a lot of work to do tomorrow.* ○ *He had a short sleep in the middle of the afternoon.* □ **to get to sleep** *or* **go to sleep** to start sleeping ■ *verb* to be in a state of sleep (NOTE: **sleeping – slept**)

COMMENT: Sleep is a period when the body rests and rebuilds tissue, especially protein. Most adults need eight hours' sleep each night. Children require more (ten to twelve hours) but older people need less, possibly only four to six hours. Sleep forms a regular pattern of stages: during the first stage the person is still conscious of his or her surroundings, and will wake on hearing a noise; afterwards the sleeper goes into very deep sleep (slow-wave sleep), where the eyes are tightly closed, the pulse is regular and the sleeper breathes deeply. During this stage the pituitary gland produces the growth hormone somatotrophin. It is difficult to wake someone from deep sleep. This stage is followed by rapid eye movement sleep (REM sleep), in which the sleeper's eyes are half open and move about, he or she makes facial movements, the blood pressure rises and he or she has dreams. After this stage the sleeper relapses into the first sleep stage again.

sleep apnoea /sliːp æp,niːə/ *noun* a condition related to heavy snoring, with prolonged respiratory pauses leading to cerebral hypoxia and subsequent daytime drowsiness

sleeping pill /'sliːpɪŋ pɪl/ *noun* a pill containing a drug, usually a barbiturate, which makes a person sleep ○ *She died of an overdose of sleeping pills.*

sleeping sickness /'sliːpɪŋ ,sɪknəs/ *noun* an African disease, spread by the tsetse fly, where trypanosomes infest the blood. Also called **African trypanosomiasis**

COMMENT: Symptoms are headaches, lethargy and long periods of sleep. The disease is fatal if not treated.

sleeping tablet *noun* a tablet containing a drug, usually a barbiturate, which makes a person sleep

sleeplessness /'sliːpləsnəs/ *noun* ♦ **insomnia**

sleep off /,sliːp 'ɒf/ *verb* to recover from a mild illness or hangover by sleeping (NOTE: **sleeping off – slept off**)

sleep terror disorder /,sliːp 'terə dɪs,ɔːdə/ *noun* a condition in which a person regularly wakes from sleep in a state of terror and confusion but remembers nothing about it in the morning

sleepwalker /'sliːpwɔːkə/ *noun* same as **somnambulist**

sleepwalking /'sliːpwɔːkɪŋ/ *noun* same as **somnambulism**

sleepy /'sliːpi/ *adjective* feeling ready to go to sleep (NOTE: **sleepier – sleepiest**)

sleepy sickness /'sliːpi ,sɪknəs/ *noun* same as **lethargic encephalitis**

slice /slaɪs/ *noun* a thin flat piece of tissue which has been cut off ○ *He examined the slice of brain tissue under the microscope.*

slide /slaɪd/ *noun* a piece of glass, on which a tissue sample is placed, to be examined under a microscope ■ *verb* to move along smoothly ○ *The plunger slides up and down the syringe.* (NOTE: **sliding – slid**)

sliding traction /,slaɪdɪŋ 'trækʃ(ə)n/ *noun* traction for a fracture of a femur, in which weights are attached to pull the leg

slight /slaɪt/ *adjective* not very serious ○ *He has a slight fever.* ○ *She had a slight accident.*

slim /slɪm/ *adjective* pleasantly thin ○ *She has become slim again after being pregnant.* ■ *verb* to try to become thinner or weigh less ○ *She is trying to slim before she goes on holiday.* (NOTE: **slimming – slimmed**)

slimming /'slɪmɪŋ/ *noun* the use of a special diet or special food which is low in calories and which is supposed to stop a person getting fat

sling /slɪŋ/ *noun* a triangular bandage attached round the neck, used to support an injured arm and prevent it from moving ○ *She had her left arm in a sling.*

slipped disc /,slɪpt 'dɪsk/ *noun* same as **displaced intervertebral disc, prolapsed intervertebral disc**

slit lamp /'slɪt læmp/ *noun* a piece of equipment which provides a narrow beam of light and is connected to a special microscope, used to examine the eye

slough /slaʊ/ *noun* dead tissue, especially dead skin, which has separated from healthy tissue ■ *verb* to lose dead skin which falls off

slow-release vitamin tablet /sləʊ rɪ,liːs 'vɪtəmɪn ,tæblət/ *noun* a vitamin tablet which will dissolve slowly in the body and give a longer and more constant effect

slow-wave sleep /,sləʊ ,weɪv 'sliːp/ *noun* a period of sleep during which the sleeper sleeps deeply and the eyes do not move

COMMENT: During slow-wave sleep, the pituitary gland secretes the hormone somatotrophin.

small /smɔːl/ *adjective* **1.** not large ○ *His chest was covered with small red spots.* ○ *She has a small cyst in the colon.* **2.** young ○ *He had chickenpox when he was small.*

small children /ˌsmɔːl ˈtʃɪldrən/ *noun* young children, between about 1 and 10 years of age

small for dates /ˌsmɔːl fə ˈdeɪts/ *adjective* referring to an unborn baby which is small in comparison to the average size for that number of weeks. Abbr **SFD**

small intestine /ˌsmɔːl ɪnˈtestɪn/ *noun* a section of the intestine from the stomach to the caecum, consisting of the duodenum, the jejunum and the ileum

small of the back /ˌsmɔːl əv ðə ˈbæk/ *noun* the middle part of the back between and below the shoulder blades

smallpox /ˈsmɔːlpɒks/ *noun* a very serious, usually fatal, contagious disease caused by the pox virus, with a severe rash, leaving masses of small scars on the skin. Also called **variola**

COMMENT: It is more than 200 years since the first smallpox vaccine experiments and vaccination has proved effective in eradicating smallpox.

small stomach /ˌsmɔːl ˈstʌmək/ *noun* a stomach which is reduced in size after an operation, making the person unable to eat large meals

smear /smɪə/ *noun* a sample of soft tissue, e.g. blood or mucus, taken from a person and spread over a glass slide to be examined under a microscope

smear test /ˈsmɪə test/ *noun* same as **Papanicolaou test**

smegma /ˈsmegmə/ *noun* an oily secretion with an unpleasant smell which collects on and under the foreskin of the penis

smell /smel/ *noun* one of the five senses, the sense which is experienced through the nose ■ *verb* **1.** to notice the smell of something through the nose ○ *I can smell smoke.* ○ *He can't smell anything because he's got a cold.* **2.** to produce a smell ○ *The room smells of disinfectant.* (NOTE: **smelling – smelled** *or* **smelt**)

COMMENT: The senses of smell and taste are closely connected, and together give the real taste of food. Smells are sensed by receptors in the nasal cavity which transmit impulses to the brain. When food is eaten, the smell is sensed at the same time as the taste is sensed by the taste buds, and most of what we think of as taste is in fact smell, which explains why food loses its taste when someone has a cold and a blocked nose.

smelling salts /ˈsmelɪŋ ˌsɔːlts/ *noun* crystals of an ammonia compound which give off a strong smell and can revive someone who has fainted

Smith-Petersen nail /ˌsmɪθ ˈpiːtəs(ə)n neɪl/ *noun* a metal nail used to attach the fractured neck of a femur [Described 1931. After Marius Nygaard Smith-Petersen (1886–1953), Norwegian-born Boston orthopaedic surgeon.]

Smith's fracture /ˈsmɪθs ˌfræktʃə/ *noun* a fracture of the radius just above the wrist

smog /smɒg/ *noun* pollution of the atmosphere in towns, caused by warm damp air combining with smoke and exhaust fumes from cars

smoke /sməʊk/ *noun* a white, grey or black product made of small particles, given off by something which is burning ■ *verb* to breathe in smoke from a cigarette, cigar or pipe which is held in the lips ○ *Doctors are trying to persuade people to stop smoking.* (NOTE: **smoking – smoked**)

COMMENT: The connection between smoking tobacco, especially cigarettes, and lung cancer has been proved to the satisfaction of the British government, which prints a health warning on all packets of cigarettes. Smoke from burning tobacco contains nicotine and other substances which stick in the lungs, and can in the long run cause cancer and heart disease.

smoke inhalation /ˈsməʊk ɪnhəˌleɪʃ(ə)n/ *noun* the breathing in of smoke, as in a fire

smoker /ˈsməʊkə/ *noun* a person who smokes cigarettes

smoker's cough /ˌsməʊkəz ˈkɒf/ *noun* a dry asthmatic cough, often found in people who smoke large numbers of cigarettes

smoking /ˈsməʊkɪŋ/ *noun* the action of smoking a cigarette, pipe or cigar ○ *Smoking can injure your health.*

'…three quarters of patients aged 35–64 on GPs' lists have at least one major risk factor: high cholesterol, high blood pressure or addiction to tobacco. Of the three risk factors, smoking causes a quarter of heart disease deaths' [*Health Services Journal*]

smooth /smuːð/ *adjective* flat, not rough ■ *verb* to make something smooth ○ *She smoothed down the sheets on the bed.*

smooth muscle /smuːð ˈmʌs(ə)l/ *noun* a type of muscle found in involuntary muscles. Also called **unstriated muscle**

SMR *abbr* submucous resection

snare /sneə/ *noun* a surgical instrument made of a loop of wire, used to remove growths without the need of an incision

sneeze /sniːz/ *noun* a reflex action to blow air suddenly out of the nose and mouth because of irritation in the nasal passages ○ *She gave a loud sneeze.* ■ *verb* to blow air suddenly out of the nose and mouth because of irritation in the nasal passages ○ *The smell of flowers makes her sneeze.* ○ *He was coughing and sneezing and decided to stay in bed.* (NOTE: **sneezing – sneezed**)

COMMENT: A sneeze sends out a spray of droplets of liquid, which, if infectious, can then infect anyone who happens to inhale them.

sneezing fit /ˈsniːzɪŋ fɪt/ *noun* a sudden attack when someone sneezes many times

Snellen chart /'snelən tʃɑːt/ *noun* a chart commonly used by opticians to test eyesight [Described 1862. After Hermann Snellen (1834–1908), Dutch ophthalmologist.]

COMMENT: The Snellen chart has rows of letters, the top row being very large, and the bottom very small, with the result that the more rows a person can read, the better his or her eyesight.

Snellen type /'snelən taɪp/ *noun* different type sizes used on a Snellen chart

sniff /snɪf/ *noun* an act of breathing in air or smelling through the nose ○ *They gave her a sniff of smelling salts to revive her.* ■ *verb* to breathe in air or to smell through the nose ○ *He was sniffing because he had a cold.* ○ *She sniffed and said that she could smell smoke.*

sniffle /'snɪf(ə)l/ *verb* to keep on sniffing because you have a cold or are crying (NOTE: **sniffling – sniffled**)

sniffles /'snɪf(ə)lz/ *plural noun* a slight head cold, or an allergy that causes a running nose (*informal; used to children*) ○ *Don't go out into the cold when you have the sniffles.*

snore /snɔː/ *noun* a loud noise produced in the nose and throat when a person is asleep ■ *verb* to make a loud noise in the nose and throat when asleep (NOTE: **snoring – snored**)

COMMENT: A snore is produced by the vibration of the soft palate at the back of the mouth, and occurs when a sleeping person breathes through both mouth and nose.

snoring /'snɔːrɪŋ/ *noun* noisy breathing while asleep

snot /snɒt/ *noun* mucus in the nose (*informal*)

snow blindness /'snəʊ ˌblaɪndnəs/ *noun* temporary painful blindness caused by bright sunlight shining on snow

snuffles /'snʌf(ə)lz/ *plural noun* the condition of breathing noisily through a nose which is blocked with mucus, which is usually a symptom of the common cold, but can sometimes be a sign of congenital syphilis (*informal; used to children*)

soak /səʊk/ *verb* to put something in liquid so that it absorbs some of it ○ *Use a compress made of cloth soaked in warm water.*

social /'səʊʃ(ə)l/ *adjective* referring to society or to groups of people

social disease /ˌsəʊʃ(ə)l dɪˈziːz/ *noun US* sexually transmitted disease

socialisation /ˌsəʊʃ(ə)laɪˈzeɪʃ(ə)n/, **socialization** *noun* the process involved when young children are becoming aware of society and learning how they are expected to behave

social medicine /ˌsəʊʃ(ə)l ˈmed(ə)s(ə)n/ *noun* medicine as applied to treatment of diseases which occur in particular social groups

social services /ˌsəʊʃ(ə)l ˈsɜːvɪsɪz/ *plural noun* the special facilities which the government or local authorities provide to people in the community who need help, such as the eld-

erly, children whose parents have died or the unemployed

social worker /'səʊʃ(ə)l ˌwɜːkə/ *noun* a government employee who works to provide social services to people in need and improve their living standards

society /səˈsaɪəti/ *noun* **1.** the community of people who live in a particular country and share its institutions and customs **2.** an organisation of people who have a shared interest

sociopath /'səʊsiəpæθ/ *noun* same as **psychopath**

socket /'sɒkɪt/ *noun* a hollow part in a bone, into which another bone or organ fits ○ *The tip of the femur fits into a socket in the pelvis.*

sodium /'səʊdiəm/ *noun* a chemical element which is the basic substance in salt (NOTE: The chemical symbol is **Na**.)

COMMENT: Sodium is an essential mineral and exists in the extracellular fluid of the body. Sweat and tears also contain a high proportion of sodium chloride.

sodium balance /'səʊdiəm ˌbæləns/ *noun* the balance maintained in the body between salt lost in sweat and urine and salt taken in from food. The balance is regulated by aldosterone.

sodium bicarbonate /ˌsəʊdiəm baɪˈkɑːbənət/ *noun* sodium salt used in cooking, and also as a relief for indigestion and acidity. Also called **bicarbonate of soda**

sodium chloride /ˌsəʊdiəm ˈklɔːraɪd/ *noun* common salt

sodium fusidate /ˌsəʊdiəm ˈfjuːsɪdeɪt/ *noun* an antibiotic used mainly to treat penicillin-resistant staphylococcal infections

sodium pump /'səʊdiəm pʌmp/ *noun* a cellular process in which sodium is immediately excreted from any cell which it enters and potassium is brought in

sodium valproate /ˌsəʊdiəm vælˈprəʊeɪt/ *noun* an anticonvulsant drug used especially to treat migraines, seizures and epilepsy

sodokosis /ˌsəʊdəʊˈkəʊsɪs/, **sodoku** /'səʊdəʊkuː/ *noun* a form of rat-bite fever, in which swellings in the jaws do not occur

sodomy /'sɒdəmi/ *noun* anal sexual intercourse between men

soft /sɒft/ *adjective* not hard or not resistant to pressure

soft chancre /sɒft ˈʃæŋkə/ *noun* same as **soft sore**

soften /'sɒf(ə)n/ *verb* to make something soft, or become soft

soft palate /sɒft ˈpælət/ *noun* the back part of the palate leading to the uvula. ◊ **cleft palate**

soft sore /sɒft ˈsɔː/ *noun* a venereal sore with a soft base, situated in the groin or on the genitals and caused by the bacterium *Haemophilus ducreyi*. Also called **chancroid, soft chancre**

soft tissue /ˌsɒft ˈtɪʃuː/ *noun* skin, muscles, ligaments or tendons

soil /sɔɪl/ *noun* the earth in which plants grow ■ *verb* to make something dirty ○ *He soiled his sheets.* ○ *Soiled bedclothes are sent to the hospital laundry.*

solar plexus /ˌsəʊlə ˈpleksəs/ *noun* a nerve network situated at the back of the abdomen between the adrenal glands

solar retinopathy /ˌsəʊlə retɪˈnɒpəθi/ *noun* irreparable damage to the most sensitive part of the retina, the macula, caused by looking at the sun with no protection or inadequate protection, as when looking at an eclipse of the sun

sole /səʊl/ *noun* the part under the foot ○ *The soles of the feet are very sensitive.*

soleus /ˈsəʊliəs/ *noun* a flat muscle which goes down the calf of the leg (NOTE: The plural is **solei**.)

solid /ˈsɒlɪd/ *adjective* 1. not soft or yielding 2. hard and not liquid ○ *Water turns solid when it freezes.*

solid food /ˈsɒlɪd fuːd/ *noun* food which is chewed and eaten, not drunk ○ *She is allowed some solid food.* or *She is allowed to eat solids.*

COMMENT: Solid foods are introduced gradually to babies and to patients who have had intestinal operations.

solidify /səˈlɪdɪfaɪ/ *verb* to become solid, or cause something to become solid ○ *Carbon dioxide solidifies at low temperatures.*

solids *noun* solid food

soluble /ˈsɒljʊb(ə)l/ *adjective* able to dissolve ○ *a tablet of soluble aspirin*

soluble fibre /ˌsɒljʊb(ə)l ˈfaɪbə/ *noun* a fibre in vegetables, fruit and pulses and porridge oats which is partly digested in the intestine and reduces the absorption of fats and sugar into the body, so lowering the level of cholesterol

solute /ˈsɒljuːt/ *noun* a solid substance which is dissolved in a solvent to make a solution

solution /səˈluːʃ(ə)n/ *noun* a mixture of a solid substance dissolved in a liquid

solvent /ˈsɒlv(ə)nt/ *noun* a liquid in which a solid substance can be dissolved

solvent abuse /ˈsɒlvənt əˌbjuːs/, **solvent inhalation** /ˌsɒlvənt ˌɪnhəˈleɪʃ(ə)n/ *noun* a type of drug abuse in which someone inhales the toxic fumes given off by particular types of volatile chemical. Also called **glue-sniffing**

'…deaths among teenagers caused by solvent abuse have reached record levels' [*Health Visitor*]

soma /ˈsəʊmə/ *noun* the body, as opposed to the mind (NOTE: The plural is **somata** or **somas**.)

somat- /ˈsəʊmət/ *prefix* same as **somato-** (used before vowels)

somata /ˈsəʊmətə/ plural of **soma**

somatic /səʊˈmætɪk/ *adjective* referring to the body, either as opposed to the mind, or as opposed to the intestines and inner organs. Compare **psychosomatic**

somatic nerve /səʊˈmætɪk nɜːv/ *noun* any of the sensory and motor nerves which control skeletal muscles

somatic nervous system /səʊˌmætɪk ˈnɜːvəs ˌsɪstəm/ *noun* the part of the nervous system that serves the sense organs and muscles of the body wall and limbs, and brings about activity in the voluntary muscles

somato- /ˈsəʊmətəʊ/ *prefix* 1. referring to the body 2. somatic

somatology /ˌsəʊməˈtɒlədʒi/ *noun* the study of both the physiology and anatomy of the body

somatostatin /ˌsəʊmətəʊˈstætɪn/ *noun* a hormone produced in the hypothalamus which helps to prevent the release of the growth hormone

somatotrophic hormone /ˌsəʊmətəˌtrɒfɪk ˈhɔːməʊn/, **somatotrophin** /ˌsəʊmətəˈtrəʊfɪn/ *noun* a growth hormone, secreted by the pituitary gland, which stimulates the growth of long bones (NOTE: The US term for somatotrophin is **somatotropin**.)

somatropin /ˌsəʊmətəʊˈtrəʊfɪn/ *noun* same as **growth hormone**

-some /səʊm/ *suffix* tiny cell bodies

somnambulism /sɒmˈnæmbjʊlɪz(ə)m/ *noun* a condition especially affecting children where the person gets up and walks about while still asleep. Also called **sleepwalking**

somnambulist /sɒmˈnæmbjʊlɪst/ *noun* a person who walks in his or her sleep. Also called **sleepwalker**

somnambulistic /sɒmˌæmbjʊˈlɪstɪk/ *adjective* referring to somnambulism

somnolent /ˈsɒmnələnt/ *adjective* sleepy

somnolism /ˈsɒmnəlɪz(ə)m/ *noun* a trance which is induced by hypnotism

Somogyi effect /ˈʃɒmɒdʒi ɪˌfekt/, **Somogyi phenomenon** /ˈʃɒmɒdʒi fɪˌnɒmənən/ *noun* in diabetes mellitus, a swing to a high level of glucose in the blood from an extremely low level, usually occurring after an untreated insulin reaction during the night. It is caused by the release of stress hormones to counter low glucose levels.

-somy /ˈsəʊmi/ *suffix* the presence of chromosomes

son /sʌn/ *noun* a male child of a parent ○ *They have two sons and one daughter.*

Sonne dysentery /ˈsɒnə ˌdɪsəntri/ *noun* a common form of mild dysentery in the UK, caused by *Shigella sonnei* [Described 1915. After Carl Olaf Sonne (1882–1948), Danish bacteriologist and physician.]

sonogram /ˈsəʊnəɡræm/ *noun* a chart produced using ultrasound waves to find where something is situated in the body

sonography /səˈnɒɡrəfi/ *noun* same as **ultrasonography**

sonoplacentography /ˌsəʊnəplæsənˈtɒɡrəfi/ *noun* the use of ultrasound waves to find how the placenta is placed in a pregnant woman

sonotopography /ˌsəʊnətəˈpɒɡrəfi/ *noun* the use of ultrasound waves to produce a sonogram

soothe /suːð/ *verb* to relieve pain or irritation or make a person less tense ○ *The calamine lotion will soothe the rash.* (NOTE: **soothing – soothed**)

soothing /ˈsuːðɪŋ/ *adjective* relieving pain or irritation or making someone less tense ○ *They played soothing music in the dentist's waiting room.*

sopor /ˈsəʊpə/ *noun* deep sleep or unconsciousness

soporific /ˌsɒpəˈrɪfɪk/ *noun* a drug which makes a person go to sleep ■ *adjective* causing sleep

sorbitol /ˈsɔːbɪtɒl/ *noun* a white crystalline sweet alcohol which is used as a sweetener and a moisturiser, and in the manufacture of Vitamin C

sordes /ˈsɔːdiːz/ *plural noun* dry deposits round the lips of someone who has a fever

sore /sɔː/ *noun* a small wound on any part of the skin, usually with a discharge of pus ■ *adjective* **1.** rough and inflamed ○ *a sore patch on the skin* **2.** painful ○ *My ankle still feels very sore.*

sore throat /sɔː ˈθrəʊt/ *noun* a condition in which the mucous membrane in the throat is inflamed, sometimes because the person has been talking too much, but usually because of an infection (*informal*)

s.o.s. *adverb* (*on prescriptions*) if necessary. Full form **si opus sit** (NOTE: It means that the dose should be taken once.)

sotalol /ˈsɒtəlɒl/ *noun* a drug used to treat an irregular heartbeat and high blood pressure

souffle /ˈsuːf(ə)l/ *noun* a soft breathing sound, heard through a stethoscope

sound /saʊnd/ *noun* **1.** something which can be heard ○ *The doctor listened to the sounds of the patient's lungs.* ○ *His breathing made a whistling sound.* **2.** a long rod, used to examine or to dilate the inside of a cavity in the body ■ *adjective* strong and healthy ○ *He has a sound constitution.* ○ *Her heart is sound, but her lungs are congested.* ■ *verb* **1.** to make a particular noise ○ *Her lungs sounded as if she had pneumonia.* **2.** to examine the inside of a cavity using a rod

sour /ˈsaʊə/ *adjective* not bitter, salt or sweet (NOTE: It is one of the basic tastes.)

source /sɔːs/ *noun* **1.** the substance which produces something ○ *Sugar is a source of energy.* ○ *Vegetables are important sources of vitamins.* **2.** the place where something comes from ○ *The source of the allergy has been identified.* ○ *The medical team has isolated the source of the infection.*

space /speɪs/ *noun* a place, empty area between things ○ *An abscess formed in the space between the bone and the cartilage.*

spansule /ˈspænsjuːl/ *noun* a drug in the form of a capsule which is specially designed to release its contents slowly in the stomach

spare /speə/ *adjective* extra or only used in emergencies ○ *We have no spare beds in the hospital at the moment.* ○ *The doctor carries a spare set of instruments in her car.* ■ *verb* to be able to give or spend something ○ *Can you spare the time to see the next patient?* ○ *We have only one bed to spare at the moment.* (NOTE: **sparing – spared**)

spare part surgery /ˌspeə ˈpɑːt ˌsɜːdʒəri/ *noun* surgery in which parts of the body such as bones or joints are replaced by artificial pieces

sparganosis /ˌspɑːɡəˈnəʊsɪs/ *noun* a condition caused by the larvae of the worm Sparganum under the skin. It is widespread in East Asia.

spasm /ˈspæz(ə)m/ *noun* a sudden, usually painful, involuntary contraction of a muscle, as in cramp ○ *The muscles in his leg went into spasm.* ○ *She had painful spasms in her stomach.*

spasmo- /spæzməʊ/ *prefix* referring to a spasm

spasmodic /spæzˈmɒdɪk/ *adjective* **1.** occurring in spasms **2.** happening from time to time

spasmolytic /ˌspæzməˈlɪtɪk/ *noun* a drug which relieves muscle spasms

spasmus nutans /ˌspæzməs ˈnjuːtənz/ *noun* a condition in which someone nods his or her head and at the same time has spasms in the neck muscles and rapid movements of the eyes

spastic /ˈspæstɪk/ *adjective* with spasms or sudden contractions of muscles ■ *noun* a person affected with cerebral palsy (NOTE: The noun sense is now considered to be offensive.)

spastic colon /ˌspæstɪk ˈkəʊlɒn/ *noun* same as **mucous colitis**

spastic diplegia /ˌspæstɪk daɪˈpliːdʒə/ *noun* a congenital form of cerebral palsy which affects mainly the legs. Also called **Little's disease**

spastic gait /ˌspæstɪk ˈɡeɪt/ *noun* a way of walking where the legs are stiff and the feet not lifted off the ground

spasticity /spæˈstɪsti/ *noun* a condition in which a limb resists passive movement. ◊ **rigidity**

spastic paralysis /ˌspæstɪk pəˈræləsɪs/ *noun* same as **cerebral palsy**

spastic paraplegia /ˌspæstɪk ˌpærə-ˈpliːdʒə/ *noun* paralysis of one side of the body after a stroke

spatula /ˈspætjʊlə/ *noun* **1.** a flat flexible tool with a handle, used to scoop, lift, spread or mix things **2.** a flat wooden stick used to press the tongue down when the mouth or throat is being examined

speak /spiːk/ *verb* to say words or articulate sounds with the voice ○ *He is learning to speak again after a laryngectomy.* (NOTE: **speaking – spoke – spoken**)

speak up /ˌspiːk ˈʌp/ *verb* to speak more loudly ○ *Speak up, please – I can't hear you!*

special /ˈspeʃ(ə)l/ *adjective* not ordinary, or for a specific purpose ○ *He has been given a special diet to cure his allergy.* ○ *She wore special shoes to correct a problem in her ankles.*

special care baby unit /ˌspeʃ(ə)l keə ˈbeɪbi ˌjuːnɪt/ *noun* a unit in a hospital which deals with premature babies or babies with serious disorders

special health authority /ˌspeʃ(ə)l ˈhelθ ɔːˌθɒrɪti/ *noun* a health authority which has unique national functions, or covers various regions. An example is UK Transplant, which manages the National Transplant Database and provides a 24-hour service for the matching and allocation of donor organs.

special hospital /ˌspeʃ(ə)l ˈhɒspɪt(ə)l/ *noun* a hospital for people whose mental condition makes them a potential danger to themselves and/or others

specialisation /ˌspeʃəlaɪˈzeɪʃ(ə)n/, **specialization** *noun* **1.** the act of specialising in a particular branch of medicine **2.** a particular branch of medicine which a doctor specialises in

specialise /ˈspeʃəlaɪz/, **specialize** *verb* **1.** to concentrate on a specific subject or activity **2.** to be an expert in a specific subject or area of knowledge (NOTE: **specialising – specialised**)

specialised /ˈspeʃəlaɪzd/, **specialized** *adjective* **1.** designed for a particular purpose **2.** concentrating on a particular activity or subject ○ *specialised skills*

specialise in /ˈspeʃəlaɪz ɪn/, **specialize in** *verb* to study or to treat one particular disease or one particular type of patient ○ *He specialises in children with breathing problems.* ○ *She decided to specialise in haematology.*

specialism /ˈspeʃəlɪz(ə)m/ *noun* same as **speciality**

specialist /ˈspeʃəlɪst/ *noun* a doctor who specialises in a particular branch of medicine ○ *He is a heart specialist.* ○ *She was referred to an ENT specialist.*

specialist registrar /ˌspeʃ(ə)lɪst ˈredʒɪˌstrɑː/ *noun* a junior doctor in a hospital who is doing further specialist training

speciality /ˌspeʃiˈæləti/ *noun* a particular activity or type of work which someone is specially trained for or very interested in. Also called **specialism, specialty**

special school /ˈspeʃ(ə)l skuːl/ *noun* a school for children with disabilities

specialty /ˈspeʃ(ə)lti/ *noun US* same as **speciality**

species /ˈspiːʃiːz/ *noun* a group of living things with the same characteristics and which can interbreed (NOTE: The plural is **species**.)

specific /spəˈsɪfɪk/ *adjective* referring to a disease caused by one type of microorganism only. Opposite **non-specific** ■ *noun* a drug which is only used to treat one disease

specific gravity /spəˌsɪfɪk ˈɡrævəti/ *noun* same as **relative density**

specificity /ˌspesɪˈfɪsəti/ *noun* the rate of negative responses in a test from persons free from a disease. A high specificity means a low rate of false positives. Compare **sensitivity**

specific urethritis /spəˌsɪfɪk jʊərɪˈθraɪtɪs/ *noun* inflammation of the urethra caused by gonorrhoea

specimen /ˈspesɪmɪn/ *noun* **1.** a small quantity of something given for testing ○ *He was asked to bring a urine specimen.* **2.** one item out of a group ○ *We keep specimens of diseased organs for students to examine.*

spectacles /ˈspektək(ə)lz/ *plural noun* glasses which are worn in front of the eyes to help correct problems in vision

COMMENT: Spectacles can correct problems in the focusing of the eye, such as shortsightedness, longsightedness and astigmatism. Where different lenses are required for reading, an optician may prescribe two pairs of spectacles, one for standard use and the other for reading. Otherwise, spectacles can be fitted with a divided lens (bifocals or varifocals).

spectra /ˈspektrə/ *plural of* **spectrum**

spectrography /spekˈtrɒɡrəfi/ *noun* the recording of a spectrum on photographic film

spectroscope /ˈspektrəskəʊp/ *noun* an instrument used to analyse a spectrum

spectrum /ˈspektrəm/ *noun* **1.** the range of colours, from red to violet, into which white light can be split when it is passed through something (NOTE: Different substances in solution have different spectra.) **2.** the range of organisms that an antibiotic or chemical can kill (NOTE: The plural is **spectra** or **spectrums**.)

specula /ˈspekjʊlə/ *plural of* **speculum**

specular /ˈspekjʊlə/ *adjective* carried out using a speculum

speculum /ˈspekjʊləm/ *noun* a surgical instrument which is inserted into an opening in the body such as a nostril or the vagina to keep it open in order to allow a doctor to examine the inside (NOTE: The plural is **specula** or **speculums**.)

speech /spiːtʃ/ *noun* 1. the ability to make intelligible sounds with the vocal cords 2. a talk given to an audience

speech block /ˈspiːtʃ blɒk/ *noun* a temporary inability to speak, caused by the effect of nervous stress on the mental processes

speech impediment /ˈspiːtʃ ɪmˌpedɪmənt/ *noun* an inability to speak easily or in the usual way because of the physical structure of the mouth or other disorders

speech therapist /ˈspiːtʃ ˌθerəpɪst/ *noun* a qualified person who practises speech therapy

speech therapy /ˈspiːtʃ ˌθerəpi/ *noun* treatment for a speech disorder such as stammering or one which results from a stroke or physical malformation

spell /spel/ *noun* a short period ○ *She has been having dizzy spells.* ○ *He had two spells in hospital during the winter.*

sperm /spɜːm/ *noun* same as **spermatozoon** (NOTE: The plural is **sperm.**)

spermat- /spɜːmət/ *prefix* same as **spermato-** (*used before vowels*)

spermatic /spɜːˈmætɪk/ *adjective* referring to sperm

spermatic artery /spɜːˌmætɪk ˈɑːtəri/ *noun* an artery which leads into the testes. Also called **testicular artery**

spermatic cord /spɜːˌmætɪk ˈkɔːd/ *noun* a cord running from the testis to the abdomen carrying the vas deferens, the blood vessels, nerves and lymphatics of the testis

spermatid /ˈspɜːmətɪd/ *noun* an immature male sex cell that develops into a spermatozoon

spermato- /spɜːmətəʊ/ *prefix* 1. referring to sperm 2. referring to the male reproductive system

spermatocele /ˈspɜːmətəsiːl/ *noun* a cyst which forms in the scrotum

spermatocyte /ˈspɜːmətəsaɪt/ *noun* an early stage in the development of a spermatozoon

spermatogenesis /ˌspɜːmətəˈdʒenəsɪs/ *noun* the formation and development of spermatozoa in the testes

spermatogonium /ˌspɜːmətəˈɡəʊniəm/ *noun* a cell which forms a spermatocyte (NOTE: The plural is **spermatogonia.**)

spermatorrhoea /ˌspɜːmətəˈrɪə/ *noun* the discharge of a large amount of semen frequently and without an orgasm (NOTE: The US spelling is **spermatorrhea.**)

spermatozoon /ˌspɜːmətəˈzəʊɒn/ *noun* a mature male sex cell, which is ejaculated from the penis and is capable of fertilising an ovum.

Also called **sperm** (NOTE: The plural is **spermatozoa.**)

COMMENT: A human spermatozoon is very small and is formed of a head, neck and very long tail. A spermatozoon can swim by moving its tail from side to side. The sperm are formed in the testes and ejaculated through the penis. Each ejaculation may contain millions of sperm. Once a sperm has entered the female uterus, it remains viable for about three days.

spermaturia /ˌspɜːməˈtjʊəriə/ *noun* sperm in the urine

sperm bank /ˈspɜːm bæŋk/ *noun* a place where sperm can be stored for use in artificial insemination

sperm count /ˈspɜːm kaʊnt/ *noun* a calculation of the number of sperm in a quantity of semen

sperm donor /ˈspɜːm ˌdəʊnə/ *noun* a male who gives sperm, for a fee, to allow a childless woman to bear a child

spermi- /spɜːmi/ *prefix* referring to sperm and semen

spermicidal /ˌspɜːmɪˈsaɪd(ə)l/ *adjective* killing or able to kill sperm

spermicidal jelly /ˌspɜːmɪˌsaɪd(ə)l ˈdʒeli/ *noun* a jelly-like product which acts as a contraceptive

spermicide /ˈspɜːmɪsaɪd/ *noun* a substance which kills sperm

spermio- /spɜːmiəʊ/ *prefix* same as **spermi-**

spermiogenesis /ˌspɜːmiəʊˈdʒenəsɪs/ *noun* the stage of spermatogenesis during which a spermatid changes into a spermatozoon

spheno- /sfiːnəʊ/ *prefix* referring to the sphenoid bone

sphenoid /ˈsfiːnɔɪd/ *adjective* 1. relating to the sphenoid bone 2. shaped like a wedge ■ *noun* same as **sphenoid bone**

sphenoid bone /ˈsfiːnɔɪd bəʊn/ *noun* one of two bones in the skull which form the side of the socket of the eye. Also called **sphenoid**

sphenoid sinus /ˌsfiːnɔɪd ˈsaɪnəs/ *noun* one of the sinuses in the skull behind the nasal passage

sphenopalatine ganglion /ˌsfiːnəʊ ˌpælətaɪn ˈɡæŋliɒn/ *noun* same as **pterygopalatine ganglion**

spherocyte /ˈsfɪərəʊsaɪt/ *noun* a red blood cell that is round rather than the usual disc shape

spherocytosis /ˌsfɪərəʊsaɪˈtəʊsɪs/ *noun* a condition in which someone has spherocytes in the blood, causing anaemia, enlarged spleen and gallstones, as in acholuric jaundice

sphincter /ˈsfɪŋktə/, **sphincter muscle** /ˈsfɪŋktə ˌmʌs(ə)l/ *noun* a circular band of muscle which surrounds an opening or passage in the body, especially the anus, and can narrow or close the opening or passage by contracting

sphincterectomy /ˌsfɪŋktəˈrektəmi/ *noun* **1.** a surgical operation to remove a sphincter **2.** a surgical operation to remove part of the edge of the iris in the eye (NOTE: The plural is **sphincterectomies**.)

sphincteroplasty /ˈsfɪŋktərəˌplæsti/ *noun* a surgical operation to relieve a tightened sphincter (NOTE: The plural is **sphincteroplasties**.)

sphincterotomy /ˌsfɪŋktəˈrɒtəmi/ *noun* a surgical operation to make an incision into a sphincter (NOTE: The plural is **sphincterotomies**.)

sphincter pupillae muscle /ˌsfɪŋktə ˈpjuːpɪlaɪ ˌmʌs(ə)l/ *noun* an annular muscle in the iris which constricts the pupil

sphyg /sfɪg/ *noun* same as **sphygmomanometer** (*informal*)

sphygmic /ˈsfɪgmɪk/ *adjective* referring to the pulse of an artery

sphygmo- /sfɪgməʊ/ *prefix* referring to the pulse

sphygmocardiograph /ˌsfɪgməʊˈkɑːdiəʊɡrɑːf/ *noun* a device which records heartbeats and pulse rate

sphygmograph /ˈsfɪgməɡrɑːf/ *noun* a device which records the pulse

sphygmomanometer /ˌsfɪgməʊməˈnɒmɪtə/ *noun* an instrument which measures blood pressure in the arteries

COMMENT: The sphygmomanometer is a rubber sleeve connected to a scale with a column of mercury, allowing the nurse to take a reading. The rubber sleeve is usually wrapped round the arm and inflated until the blood flow is stopped. The blood pressure is determined by listening to the pulse with a stethoscope placed over an artery as the pressure in the rubber sleeve is slowly reduced, and by the reading on the scale.

spica /ˈspaɪkə/ *noun* a way of bandaging a joint where the bandage crosses over itself like the figure 8 on the inside of the bend of the joint (NOTE: The plural is **spicae** or **spicas**.)

spicule /ˈspɪkjuːl/ *noun* a small splinter of bone

spigot /ˈspɪɡət/ *noun* the end of a pipe which is joined by insertion into the enlarged end of another pipe

spina /ˈspaɪnə/ *noun* **1.** a thin sharp piece of bone **2.** the vertebral column

spina bifida /ˌspaɪnə ˈbɪfɪdə/ *noun* a serious condition in which part of the spinal cord protrudes through the spinal column. Also called **rachischisis**

COMMENT: Spina bifida takes two forms: a mild form, spina bifida occulta, where only the bone is affected, and there are no visible signs of the condition; and the serious spina bifida cystica where part of the meninges or spinal cord passes through the gap; it may result in paralysis of the legs, and mental impair-

ment is often present where the condition is associated with hydrocephalus.

spinal /ˈspaɪn(ə)l/ *adjective* referring to the spine ○ *She suffered spinal injuries in the crash.*

spinal accessory nerve /ˌspaɪn(ə)l ək ˈsesəri nɜːv/ *noun* the eleventh cranial nerve which supplies the muscles in the neck and shoulders

spinal anaesthesia /ˌspaɪn(ə)l ˌænəsˈθiːziə/ *noun* local anaesthesia in which an anaesthetic is injected into the cerebrospinal fluid

spinal anaesthetic /ˌspaɪn(ə)l ˌænəsˈθetɪk/ *noun* an anaesthetic given by injection into the spine, which results in large parts of the body losing the sense of feeling

spinal block /ˌspaɪn(ə)l ˈblɒk/ *noun* analgesia produced by injecting the spinal cord with an anaesthetic

spinal canal /ˌspaɪn(ə)l kəˈnæl/ *noun* the hollow channel running down the back of the vertebrae, containing the spinal cord. Also called **vertebral canal**

spinal column /ˈspaɪn(ə)l ˌkɒləm/ *noun* same as **spine**

spinal cord /ˈspaɪn(ə)l kɔːd/ *noun* part of the central nervous system, running from the medulla oblongata to the filum terminale, in the vertebral canal of the spine (NOTE: For other terms referring to the spinal cord, see words beginning with **myel-**, **myelo-**.)

spinal curvature /ˌspaɪn(ə)l ˈkɜːvətʃə/ *noun* unusual bending of the spinal column

spinal fusion /ˌspaɪn(ə)l ˈfjuːʒ(ə)n/ *noun* a surgical operation to join two vertebrae together to make the spine more rigid. Also called **spondylosyndesis**

spinal ganglion /ˌspaɪn(ə)l ˈɡæŋɡliən/ *noun* a cone-shaped mass of cells on the posterior root, the main axons of which form the posterior root of the spinal nerve

spinal meningitis /ˌspaɪn(ə)l ˌmenɪnˈdʒaɪtɪs/ *noun* inflammation of the membranes around the spinal cord, which particularly affects young children

spinal nerve /ˈspaɪn(ə)l nɜːv/ *noun* one of the 31 pairs of nerves which lead from the spinal cord and govern mainly the trunk and limbs

spinal puncture /ˌspaɪn(ə)l ˈpʌŋktʃə/ *noun* same as **lumbar puncture** (NOTE: The US term is **spinal tap**.)

spinal shock /ˈspaɪn(ə)l ˈʃɒk/ *noun* a loss of feeling in the lower part of the body below a point at which the spine has been injured

spindle /ˈspɪnd(ə)l/ *noun* **1.** a long thin structure **2.** a structure formed in cells during division to which the chromosomes are attached by their centromeres

spine /spaɪn/ *noun* **1.** the series of bones, the vertebrae, linked together to form a flexible supporting column running from the pelvis to the skull ○ *She injured her spine in the crash.* Also called **backbone, spinal column, vertebral column 2.** any sharp projecting part of a bone

COMMENT: The spine is made up of twenty-four ring-shaped vertebrae, with the sacrum and coccyx, separated by discs of cartilage. The hollow canal of the spine (the spinal canal) contains the spinal cord. See also note at vertebra.

Spinhaler /spɪn'heɪlə/ a trade name for a device from which a person with breathing problems can inhale a preset dose of a drug

spinnbarkeit /'spɪnbɑːkaɪt/ *noun* a thread of mucus formed in the cervix which is used in determining the time of ovulation. At this time it can be drawn out on a glass slide to its maximum length.

spino- /spaɪnəʊ/ *prefix* **1.** referring to the spine **2.** referring to the spinal cord

spinocerebellar tract /ˌspaɪnəʊserə,belə'trækt/ *noun* a nerve fibre in the spinal cord, taking impulses to the cerebellum

spinous process /ˌspaɪnəs 'prəʊses/ *noun* a projection on a vertebra or a bone which looks like a spine

spiral /'spaɪrəl/ *adjective* running in a continuous circle upwards

spiral bandage /ˌspaɪrəl 'bændɪdʒ/ *noun* a bandage which is wrapped round a limb, each turn overlapping the one before

spiral ganglion /ˌspaɪrəl 'gæŋɡliən/ *noun* a ganglion in the eighth cranial nerve which supplies the organ of Corti

spiral organ /ˌspaɪrəl 'ɔːɡən/ *noun* same as **organ of Corti**

Spirillum /spɪ'rɪləm/ *noun* one of the bacteria which cause rat-bite fever

spiro- /spaɪrəʊ/ *prefix* **1.** referring to a spiral **2.** referring to respiration

spirochaetaemia /ˌspaɪrəʊkiː'tiːmiə/ *noun* the presence of spirochaetes in the blood (NOTE: The US spelling is **spirochetemia**.)

spirochaete /'spaɪrəʊkiːt/ *noun* a bacterium with a spiral shape, e.g. the one which causes syphilis (NOTE: The US spelling is **spirochete**.)

spirogram /'spaɪrəʊɡræm/ *noun* a record of someone's breathing made by a spirograph

spirograph /'spaɪrəʊɡrɑːf/ *noun* a device which records depth and rapidity of breathing

spirography /spaɪ'rɒɡrəfi/ *noun* the recording of a someone's breathing by use of a spirograph

spirometer /spaɪ'rɒmɪtə/ *noun* an instrument which measures the amount of air a person inhales or exhales

spirometry /spaɪ'rɒmətri/ *noun* a measurement of the vital capacity of the lungs by use of a spirometer

spironolactone /ˌspaɪrənə'læktəʊn/ *noun* a steroid which helps the body produce urine,

used in the treatment of oedema and hypertension

spit /spɪt/ *noun* saliva which is sent out of the mouth ■ *verb* to send liquid out of the mouth ○ *Rinse your mouth out and spit into the cup provided.* ○ *He spat out the medicine.* (NOTE: **spitting – spat**)

Spitz-Holter valve /ˌspɪts 'hɒltə vælv/ *noun* a valve with a one-way system, surgically placed in the skull and used to drain excess fluid from the brain in hydrocephalus

splanchnic /'splæŋknɪk/ *adjective* referring to viscera

splanchnic nerve /'splæŋknɪk nɜːv/ *noun* any sympathetic nerve which supplies organs in the abdomen

splanchnology /splæŋk'nɒlədʒi/ *noun* the study of the organs in the abdominal cavity

spleen /spliːn/ *noun* an organ in the top part of the abdominal cavity behind the stomach and below the diaphragm, which helps to destroy old red blood cells, form lymphocytes and store blood. See illustration at DIGESTIVE SYSTEM in Supplement

COMMENT: The spleen, which is the largest endocrine (ductless) gland, appears to act to remove dead blood cells and fight infection, but its functions are not fully understood and an adult can live healthily after his or her spleen has been removed.

splen- /splen/ *prefix* same as **spleno-** (*used before vowels*)

splenectomy /sple'nektəmi/ *noun* a surgical operation to remove the spleen (NOTE: The plural is **splenectomies**.)

splenic /'splenɪk/ *adjective* referring to the spleen

splenic anaemia /ˌsplenɪk ə'niːmiə/ *noun* a type of anaemia, caused by cirrhosis of the liver, in which the person has portal hypertension, an enlarged spleen and haemorrhages. Also called **Banti's syndrome**

splenic flexure /ˌsplenɪk 'flekʃə/ *noun* a bend in the colon where the transverse colon joins the descending colon

splenii /'spliːniː/ *plural noun* plural of **splenius**

splenitis /splə'naɪtɪs/ *noun* inflammation of the spleen

splenius /'spliːniəs/ *noun* either of two muscles on each side of the neck that reach from the base of the skull to the upper back and rotate and extend the head and neck (NOTE: The plural is **splenii**.)

spleno- /spliːnəʊ/ *prefix* referring to the spleen

splenomegaly /ˌspliːnəʊ'meɡəli/ *noun* a condition in which the spleen is unusually large, associated with several disorders including malaria and some cancers

splenorenal /ˌspliːnəʊ'riːn(ə)l/ *adjective* relating to both the spleen and the kidneys

splenorenal anastomosis /ˌspliːnəʊˌriːn(ə)l əˌnæstəˈməʊsɪs/ *noun* a surgical operation to join the splenic vein to a renal vein, as a treatment for portal hypertension

splenovenography /ˌspliːnəʊvəˈnɒɡrəfi/ *noun* X-ray examination of the spleen and the veins which are connected to it

splint /splɪnt/ *noun* a stiff support attached to a limb to prevent a broken bone from moving ○ *He had to keep his arm in a splint for several weeks.* ◊ **shin splints**

splinter /ˈsplɪntə/ *noun* a tiny thin piece of wood or metal which gets under the skin and can be irritating and cause infection

splinter haemorrhage /ˈsplɪntə ˌhem(ə)rɪdʒ/ *noun* a tiny line of haemorrhaging under the nails or in the eyeball

split /splɪt/ *verb* to divide something, or become divided (NOTE: **splitting – split**)

split personality /splɪt ˌpɜːsəˈnælɪti/ *noun* same as **schizoid personality**

split-skin graft /ˌsplɪt ˌskɪn ˈɡrɑːft/ *noun* a type of skin graft in which thin layers of skin are grafted over a wound. Also called **Thiersch graft**

spondyl /ˈspɒndɪl/ *noun* same as **vertebra**

spondyl- /ˈspɒndɪl/ *prefix* same as **spondylo-** (*used before vowels*)

spondylitis /ˌspɒndɪˈlaɪtɪs/ *noun* inflammation of the vertebrae

spondylo- /ˈspɒndɪləʊ/ *prefix* referring to the vertebrae

spondylolisthesis /ˌspɒndɪləʊˈlɪsθəsɪs/ *noun* a condition in which one of the lumbar vertebrae moves forwards over the one beneath

spondylosis /ˌspɒndɪˈləʊsɪs/ *noun* stiffness in the spine and degenerative changes in the intervertebral discs, with osteoarthritis. This condition is common in older people.

spondylosyndesis /ˌspɒndɪləʊsɪnˈdiːsɪs/ *noun* same as **spinal fusion**

sponge /spʌndʒ/ *noun* a piece of light absorbent material, either natural or synthetic, used in bathing and cleaning

sponge bath /ˈspʌnʒ bɑːθ/ *noun* the act of washing someone in bed, using a sponge or damp cloth ○ *The nurse gave the elderly lady a sponge bath.*

spongiform encephalopathy /ˌspʌnʒifɔːm enˌkefəˈlɒpəθi/ *noun* a brain disease in humans and animals in which areas of the brain slowly develop holes in their cells and begin to look like a sponge

spongioblastoma /ˌspʌnʒiəʊblæˈstəʊmə/ *noun* same as **glioblastoma** (NOTE: The plural is **spongioblastomas** or **spongioblastomata**.)

spongiosum /ˌspʌnʒiˈəʊsəm/ ♦ **corpus spongiosum**

spongy /ˈspʌnʒi/ *adjective* soft and full of holes like a sponge

spongy bone /ˈspʌnʒi bəʊn/ *noun* cancellous bone, light bone tissue which forms the inner core of a bone and also the ends of long bones. See illustration at **BONE STRUCTURE** in Supplement

spontaneous /spɒnˈteɪniəs/ *adjective* happening without any particular outside cause

spontaneous abortion /spɒnˌteɪniəs əˈbɔːʃ(ə)n/ *noun* same as **miscarriage**

spontaneous delivery /spɒnˌteɪniəs dɪˈlɪv(ə)ri/ *noun* a delivery of a baby which takes places naturally, without any medical or surgical help

spontaneous pneumothorax /spɒnˌteɪniəs njuːməʊˈθɔːræks/ *noun* a condition occurring when an opening is created on the surface of the lung allowing air to leak into the pleural cavity

spontaneous version /spɒnˌteɪniəs ˈvɜːʃ(ə)n/ *noun* a movement of a fetus to take up another position in the uterus, caused by the contractions of the uterus during childbirth or by the movements of the baby itself before birth

spoon /spuːn/ *noun* an instrument with a long handle at one end and a small bowl at the other, used for taking liquid medicine ○ *a 5 ml spoon*

spoonful /ˈspuːnfʊl/ *noun* the quantity which a spoon can hold ○ *Take two 5 ml spoonfuls of the medicine twice a day.*

sporadic /spəˈrædɪk/ *adjective* referring to outbreaks of disease that occur as separate cases, not in epidemics

spore /spɔː/ *noun* a reproductive body of particular bacteria and fungi which can survive in extremely hot or cold conditions for a long time

sporicidal /ˌspɔːrɪˈsaɪd(ə)l/ *adjective* killing spores

sporicide /ˈspɔːrɪsaɪd/ *noun* a substance which kills bacterial spores

sporotrichosis /ˌspɔːrəʊtraɪˈkəʊsɪs/ *noun* a fungus infection of the skin which causes abscesses

Sporozoa /ˌspɔːrəˈzəʊə/ *noun* a type of parasitic Protozoa which includes Plasmodium, the cause of malaria

sport /spɔːt/ *noun* **1.** the playing of competitive physical games **2.** a competitive physical game

sports injury /ˈspɔːts ˌɪndʒəri/ *noun* an injury caused by playing a sport, e.g. a sprained ankle or tennis elbow

sports medicine /ˈspɔːts ˌmed(ə)sɪn/ *noun* the study of the treatment of sports injuries

spot /spɒt/ *noun* a small round mark or pimple ○ *The disease is marked by red spots on the chest.* □ **to break out in spots** *or* **to come out in spots** to have a sudden rash

spotted fever /ˌspɒtɪd ˈfiːvə/ *noun* same as **meningococcal meningitis**

spotty /'spɒti/ *adjective* covered with pimples

sprain /spreɪn/ *noun* a condition in which the ligaments in a joint are stretched or torn because of a sudden movement ■ *verb* to tear the ligaments in a joint with a sudden movement ○ *She sprained her wrist when she fell.*

spray /spreɪ/ *noun* 1. a mass of tiny drops ○ *An aerosol sends out a liquid in a fine spray.* 2. a special liquid for applying to an infection in a mass of tiny drops ○ *throat spray* or *nasal spray* ■ *verb* 1. to send out a liquid in a mass of tiny drops ○ *They sprayed disinfectant everywhere.* 2. to spray an area with liquid ○ *They sprayed the room with disinfectant.*

spread /spred/ *verb* to go out over a large area, or to cause something to do this ○ *The infection spread right through the adult population.* ○ *Sneezing in a crowded bus can spread infection.* (NOTE: **spreading – spread**)

'...spreading infection may give rise to cellulitis of the abdominal wall and abscess formation' [*Nursing Times*]

Sprengel's deformity /'sprengəlz dɪ,fɔːmɪti/, **Sprengel's shoulder** /,sprengəlz 'ʃəʊldə/ *noun* a congenitally malformed shoulder, in which one scapula is smaller and higher than the other [Described 1891. After Otto Gerhard Karl Sprengel (1852–1915), German surgeon.]

sprue /spruː/ *noun* same as **psilosis**

spud /spʌd/ *noun* a needle used to get a piece of dust or other foreign body out of the eye

spur /spɜː/ *noun* a sharp projecting part of a bone

sputum /'spjuːtəm/ *noun* mucus which is formed in the inflamed nose, throat or lungs and is coughed up ○ *She was coughing up bloodstained sputum.* Also called **phlegm**

squama /'skweɪmə/ *noun* a thin piece of hard tissue, e.g. a thin flake of bone or scale on the skin (NOTE: The plural is **squamae**.)

squamo- /skweɪməʊ/ *prefix* 1. relating to the squamous part of the temporal bone 2. scaly

squamous /'skweɪməs/ *adjective* thin and hard like a scale

squamous bone /'skweɪməs bəʊn/ *noun* a part of the temporal bone which forms the side of the skull

squamous cell carcinoma /,skweɪməs sel kɑːsɪ'nəʊmə/ *noun* a common type of cancer which usually develops in the outer layer of the skin, on the lips, or inside the mouth or oesophagus. Abbr **SCC**

squamous epithelium /,skweɪməs epɪ'θiːliəm/ *noun* epithelium with flat cells like scales, which forms the lining of the pericardium, the peritoneum and the pleura. Also called **pavement epithelium**

squint /skwɪnt/ *noun* a condition in which the eyes focus on different points. Also called **strabismus** ■ *verb* to have one eye or both eyes looking towards the nose ○ *Babies often appear to squint, but it is corrected as they grow older.*

SRN *abbr* State Registered Nurse

SSRI *abbr* selective serotonin re-uptake inhibitor

stab /stæb/ *noun* a sudden burst of pain ○ *She had a stab of pain above her right eye.* ■ *verb* to cut by pushing the point of a knife into the flesh ○ *He was stabbed in the chest.* (NOTE: **stabbing – stabbed**)

stabbing pain /'stæbɪŋ peɪn/ *noun* pain which comes in a series of short sharp bursts ○ *He had stabbing pains in his chest.*

stabilise /'steɪbəlaɪz/, **stabilize** *verb* to make a condition stable ○ *We have succeeded in stabilising his blood sugar level.* (NOTE: **stabilising – stabilised**)

stable /'steɪb(ə)l/ *adjective* not changing ○ *Her condition is stable.*

stable angina /,steɪb(ə)l æn'dʒaɪnə/ *noun* angina which has not changed for a long time

stab wound /'stæb wuːnd/ *noun* a deep wound made by the point of a knife

staccato speech /stə,kɑːtəʊ 'spiːtʃ/ *noun* an unusual way of speaking with short pauses between each word

Stacke's operation /'stækiz ɒpə,reɪʃ(ə)n/ *noun* a surgical operation to remove the posterior and superior wall of the auditory meatus [After Ludwig Stacke (1859–1918), German otologist]

stadium /'steɪdiəm/ *noun* a particular stage of a disease (NOTE: The plural is **stadia**.)

stadium invasioni /,steɪdiəm ɪn,veɪʃi'əʊni/ *noun* same as **incubation period**

staff /stɑːf/ *noun* people who work in an organisation such as a hospital, clinic or doctor's surgery ○ *We have 25 full-time medical staff.* ○ *The hospital is trying to recruit more nursing staff.* ○ *The clinic has a staff of 100.*

staff midwife /stɑːf 'mɪd,waɪf/ *noun* a midwife who is on the permanent staff of a hospital

staff nurse /'stɑːf nɜːs/ *noun* a nurse who is on the permanent staff of a hospital

stage /steɪdʒ/ *noun* a point in the development of a disease at which a decision should be taken about the treatment which should be given or at which distinctive developments take place ○ *The disease has reached a critical stage.* ○ *This is a symptom of the second stage of syphilis.*

'...memory changes are associated with early stages of the disease; in later stages, the patient is frequently incontinent, immobile and unable to communicate' [*Nursing Times*]

stagger /'stægə/ *verb* to move unsteadily from side to side while walking

staging /'steɪdʒɪŋ/ *noun* the process of performing tests to learn the extent of a disease within the body, in order to decide the best treatment for someone

stagnant loop syndrome /ˌstægnənt 'luːp ˌsɪndrəʊm/ *noun* a condition which occurs in cases of diverticulosis or of Crohn's disease, with steatorrhoea, abdominal pain and megaloblastic anaemia

stain /steɪn/ *noun* a substance used to give colour to tissues which are going to be examined under the microscope ■ *verb* to treat a piece of tissue with a dye to increase contrast before it is examined under the microscope

COMMENT: Some stains are designed to have an affinity only with those chemical, cellular or bacterial elements in a specimen that are of interest to a microbiologist; thus the concentration or uptake of a stain, as well as the overall picture, can be diagnostic.

staining /'steɪnɪŋ/ *noun* the process of colouring tissue, bacterial samples or other materials to make it possible to examine them and to identify them under the microscope

stalk /stɔːk/ *noun* a piece of tissue which attaches a growth to the main tissue

Stamey procedure /'steɪmi prəˌsiːdʒə/ *noun* a surgical operation to cure stress incontinence in women. A minor abdominal incision is made as well as a vaginal incision, and the neck of the bladder is stitched to the abdominal wall.

stammer /'stæmə/ *noun* a speech difficulty in which someone repeats parts of a word or the whole word several times or stops to try to pronounce a word ○ *He has a bad stammer.* ■ *verb* to speak with a stammer

stammerer /'stæmərə/ *noun* a person who stammers

stammering /'stæmərɪŋ/ *noun* difficulty in speaking, in which the person repeats parts of a word or the whole word several times or stops to try to pronounce a word. Also called **dysphemia**

stamp out /ˌstæmp 'aʊt/ *verb* to remove something completely ○ *International organisations have succeeded in stamping out smallpox.* ○ *The government is trying to stamp out waste in the hospital service.*

stand /stænd/ *verb* **1.** to be in an upright position with your bodyweight resting on your feet, or to put a person in this position **2.** to get to your feet from a sitting position (NOTE: **stood**)

standard /'stændəd/ *adjective* usual, recommended or established ○ *It is standard practice to take the patient's temperature twice a day.* ■ *noun* **1.** something which has been agreed upon and is used to measure other things by **2.** a level of quality achieved by someone or something ○ *The standard of care in hospitals has increased over the last years.* ○ *The report criticised the standards of hygiene in the clinic.*

standardise /'stændədaɪz/, **standardize** *verb* to make all things of the same type follow the same standard

Standard Precautions /ˌstændəd prɪ 'kɔːʃ(ə)nz/ *plural noun* the most recent set of guidelines for health care workers on dealing with blood, all body fluids, secretions and excretions (except sweat), non-intact skin and mucous membranes. They are designed to reduce the risk of transmission of microorganisms. The Standard Precautions are implemented automatically for everyone, as all patients are presumed to be potentially infectious.

stand up /ˌstænd 'ʌp/ *verb* **1.** to get up from being on a seat ○ *He tried to stand up, but did not have the strength.* **2.** to hold yourself upright ○ *She still stands up straight at the age of ninety-two.* (NOTE: **standing up – stood up**)

stapedectomy /ˌsteɪpɪ'dektəmi/ *noun* a surgical operation to remove the stapes (NOTE: The plural is **stapedectomies**.)

stapedial mobilisation /stəˌpiːdiəl ˌməʊbɪlaɪ'zeɪʃ(ə)n/, **stapediolysis** /stəˌpiːdɪ 'ɒləsɪs/ *noun* a surgical operation to relieve deafness by detaching the stapes from the fenestra ovalis (NOTE: The plural of **stapediolysis** is **stapediolyses**.)

stapes /'steɪpiːz/ *noun* one of the three ossicles in the middle ear, shaped like a stirrup. See illustration at **EAR** in Supplement

COMMENT: The stapes fills the fenestra ovalis, and is articulated with the incus, which in turn articulates with the malleus.

staph /stæf/ *abbr* Staphylococcus

staphylectomy /ˌstæfɪ'lektəmi/ *noun* a surgical operation to remove the uvula (NOTE: The plural is **staphylectomies**.)

staphylococcal /ˌstæfɪlə'kɒk(ə)l/ *adjective* referring to Staphylococci

staphylococcal poisoning /ˌstæfɪləʊ ˌkɒk(ə)l 'pɔɪz(ə)nɪŋ/ *noun* poisoning by Staphylococci in food

Staphylococcus /ˌstæfɪlə'kɒkəs/ *noun* a bacterium which grows in a bunch like a bunch of grapes, and causes boils and food poisoning (NOTE: The plural is **Staphylococci**.)

staphyloma /ˌstæfɪ'ləʊmə/ *noun* a swelling of the cornea or the white of the eye (NOTE: The plural is **staphylomas** or **staphylomata**.)

staphylorrhaphy /ˌstæfɪ'lɔːrəfi/ *noun* same as **palatorrhaphy** (NOTE: The plural is **staphylorrhaphies**.)

staple /'steɪp(ə)l/ *noun* a small piece of bent metal, used to attach tissues together ■ *verb* to attach tissues with staples

stapler /'steɪplə/ *noun* a device used in surgery to attach tissues with staples, instead of suturing

starch /stɑːtʃ/ *noun* the usual form in which carbohydrates exist in food, especially in bread, rice and potatoes. It is broken down by the digestive process into forms of sugar.

starchy /'stɑːtʃi/ *adjective* referring to food which contains a lot of starch ○ *He eats too much starchy food.*

Starling's Law /'stɑːlɪŋz lɔː/ *noun* a law that the contraction of the ventricles is in proportion to the length of the ventricular muscle fibres at the end of diastole

startle reflex /'stɑːt(ə)l ˌriːfleks/ *noun* the usual response of a young baby to a sudden loud noise or a sudden fall through the air, by contracting the limb and neck muscles

starvation /stɑːˈveɪʃ(ə)n/ *noun* the fact of having had very little or no food

starvation diet /stɑːˌveɪʃ(ə)n 'daɪət/ *noun* a diet which contains little nourishment, and is not enough to keep a person healthy

starve /stɑːv/ *verb* to have little or no food or nourishment ○ *The parents let the baby starve to death.*

stasis /'steɪsɪs/ *noun* a stoppage or slowing in the flow of a liquid, such as blood in veins, or food in the intestine

'A decreased blood flow in the extremities has been associated with venous stasis which may precipitate vascular complications' [*British Journal of Nursing*]

-stasis /steɪsɪs/ *suffix* referring to stoppage in the flow of a liquid

stat. /stæt/ *adverb* (written on prescriptions) immediately. Full form **statim**

state /steɪt/ *noun* the condition of something or of a person ○ *His state of health is getting worse.* ○ *The disease is in an advanced state.*

State Enrolled Nurse /ˌsteɪt ɪnˌrəʊld 'nɜːs/ *noun* Abbr **SEN**. Now called **second-level nurse**

state of mind /ˌsteɪt əv 'maɪnd/ *noun* a general feeling ○ *He's in a very miserable state of mind.*

State Registered Nurse /ˌsteɪt ˌredʒɪstəd 'nɜːs/ *noun* Abbr **SRN**. Now called **first-level nurse**

statin /'stætɪn/ *noun* a lipid-lowering drug which inhibits an enzyme in cholesterol synthesis, used to treat people with, or at high risk of developing, coronary heart disease

-statin /stætɪn/ *suffix* used in generic names of lipid-lowering drugs ○ *pravastatin*

statistics /stəˈtɪstɪks/ *plural noun* official figures which show facts ○ *Population statistics show that the birth rate is slowing down.*

status /'steɪtəs/ *noun* a state or condition

'…the main indications being inadequate fluid and volume status and need for evaluation of patients with a history of severe heart disease' [*Southern Medical Journal*]

'…the standard pulmonary artery catheters have four lumens from which to obtain information about the patient's haemodynamic status' [*RN Magazine*]

status asthmaticus /ˌsteɪtəs æsˈmætɪkəs/ *noun* an attack of bronchial asthma which lasts for a long time and results in exhaustion and collapse

status epilepticus /ˌsteɪtəs epɪˈleptɪkəs/ *noun* repeated and prolonged epileptic seizures without recovery of consciousness between them

status lymphaticus /ˌsteɪtəs lɪmˈfætɪkəs/ *noun* a condition in which the glands in the lymphatic system are enlarged

statutory bodies /ˌstætjʊt(ə)ri 'bɒdiz/ *plural noun* organisations set up by Acts of Parliament to carry out specific functions, e.g. the Nursing and Midwifery Council, set up to regulate the nursing and midwifery professions

stay /steɪ/ *noun* the time which someone spends in a place ○ *The patient is only in hospital for a short stay.* ■ *verb* to stop in a place for some time ○ *She stayed in hospital for two weeks.* ○ *He's ill with flu and has to stay in bed.*

STD *abbr* sexually transmitted disease

steam inhalation /ˌstiːm ɪnhəˈleɪʃ(ə)n/ *noun* a treatment for respiratory disease in which someone breathes in steam with medicinal substances in it

steapsin /stiˈæpsɪn/ *noun* an enzyme produced by the pancreas, which breaks down fats in the intestine

stearic acid /stiˌærɪk 'æsɪd/ *noun* one of the fatty acids

steat- /'stiːət/, **steato-** /'stiːətəʊ/ *prefix* referring to fat

steatoma /ˌstiːəˈtəʊmə/ *noun* a cyst in a blocked sebaceous gland. ◊ **sebaceous cyst** (NOTE: The plural is **steatomata**.)

steatopygia /ˌstiːətəˈpɪdʒiə/ *noun* excessive fat on the buttocks

steatorrhoea /ˌstiːətəˈrɪə/ *noun* a condition in which fat is passed in the faeces

Stein-Leventhal syndrome /ˌstaɪn 'levəntɑːl ˌsɪndrəʊm/ *noun* ♦ **polycystic ovary syndrome** [Described 1935. After Irving F. Stein (b. 1887), US gynaecologist; Michael Leo Leventhal (1901–71), US obstetrician and gynaecologist.]

Steinmann's pin /ˌstaɪnmænz 'pɪn/ *noun* a pin for attaching traction wires to a fractured bone [Described 1907. After Fritz Steinmann (1872–1932), Swiss surgeon.]

stellate /'steleɪt/ *adjective* shaped like a star

stellate fracture /ˌsteleɪt 'fræktʃə/ *noun* a fracture of the kneecap shaped like a star

stellate ganglion /ˌsteleɪt 'gæŋgliən/ *noun* a group of nerve cells in the neck, shaped like a star

Stellwag's sign /'stelvɑːgz saɪn/ *noun* a symptom of exophthalmic goitre, where someone does not blink often, because the eyeball is protruding [After Carl Stellwag von Carion (1823–1904), ophthalmologist in Vienna, Austria]

stem /stem/ *noun* a thin piece of tissue which attaches an organ or growth to the main tissue

steno- /ˈstenəʊ/ *prefix* narrow or constricted

stenose /steˈnəʊs/ *verb* to make something narrow

stenosed valve /steˌnəʊst ˈvælv/ *noun* a valve which has become narrow or constricted

stenosing condition /steˌnəʊs kənˈdɪʃ(ə)n/ *noun* a condition which makes a passage narrow

stenosis /steˈnəʊsɪs/ *noun* a condition in which a passage becomes narrow

stenostomia /ˌstenəʊˈstəʊmiə/, **stenostomy** /steˈnɒstəmi/ *noun* the narrowing of an opening

Stensen's duct /ˌstensənz ˈdʌkt/ *noun* a duct which carries saliva from the parotid glands [Described 1661. After Niels Stensen (1638–86), Danish physician and priest, anatomist, physiologist and theologian.]

stent /stent/ *noun* a support of artificial material often inserted in a tube or vessel which has been sutured

step /step/ *noun* a movement of the foot and the leg as in walking ○ *He took two steps forward.* ○ *The baby is taking her first steps.*

step up /ˌstep ˈʌp/ *verb* to increase something (*informal*) ○ *The doctor has stepped up the dosage.*

sterco- /ˈstɜːkəʊ/ *prefix* referring to faeces

stercobilin /ˌstɜːkəˈbaɪlɪn/ *noun* a brown pigment which colours the faeces

stercobilinogen /ˌstɜːkəbaɪˈlɪnədʒen/ *noun* a substance which is broken down from bilirubin and produces stercobilin

stercolith /ˈstɜːkəlɪθ/ *noun* a hard ball of dried faeces in the bowel

stercoraceous /ˌstɜːkəˈreɪʃəs/ *adjective* **1.** made of or containing faeces **2.** similar to faeces

stereognosis /ˌsterɪɒgˈnəʊsɪs/ *noun* the ability to tell the shape of an object in three dimensions by means of touch

stereoscopic vision /ˌsterɪəskɒpɪk ˈvɪʒ(ə)n/ *noun* the ability to judge the distance and depth of an object by binocular vision

stereotactic /ˌsterɪəʊˈtæktɪk/ *adjective* referring to procedures which use coordinates put into a computer or scanner in order to locate and operate upon tumours precisely. Examples are biopsies, surgery or radiation therapy.

stereotaxy /ˌsterɪəʊˈtæksi/, **stereotaxic surgery** /ˌsterɪəʊˌtæksɪk ˈsɜːdʒəri/ *noun* a surgical procedure to identify a point in the interior of the brain, before an operation can begin, to locate exactly the area to be operated on

stereotypy /ˈsterɪəʊtaɪpi/ *noun* the repetition of the same action or word again and again

Sterets /ˈsterəts/ a trademark for a type of swab used for cleaning the skin before an injection

sterile /ˈsteraɪl/ *adjective* **1.** with no harmful microorganisms present ○ *a sterile environment* **2.** not able to produce children

sterile dressing /ˌsteraɪl ˈdresɪŋ/ *noun* a dressing which is sold in a sterile pack, ready for use

sterilisation /ˌsterɪlaɪˈzeɪʃ(ə)n/, **sterilization** *noun* **1.** the action of making instruments or areas completely free from microorganisms which might cause infection **2.** a procedure that makes someone unable to have children

COMMENT: Sterilisation of a woman can be done by removing the ovaries or cutting the Fallopian tubes. Sterilisation of a man is carried out by cutting the vas deferens (vasectomy).

sterilise /ˈsterɪlaɪz/, **sterilize** *verb* **1.** to make something completely free from microorganisms which might cause infection **2.** to make someone unable to have children

steriliser /ˈsterəlaɪzə/, **sterilizer** *noun* a machine for sterilising surgical instruments by steam or boiling water

sterilising /ˈsterɪlaɪzɪŋ/ *adjective* able to kill microorganisms ○ *Wipe the surface with sterilising fluid.*

sterility /stəˈrɪlɪti/ *noun* **1.** the state of being free from microorganisms **2.** the state of being unable to have children

Steri-Strips /ˈsteri strɪps/ a trademark for thin paper strips which are placed over an incision in the skin. They help its edges to come together and form a scar.

sternal /ˈstɜːn(ə)l/ *adjective* referring to the breastbone

sternal angle /ˌstɜːn(ə)l ˈæŋg(ə)l/ *noun* the ridge of bone where the manubrium articulates with the body of the sternum

sternal puncture /ˌstɜːn(ə)l ˈpʌŋktʃə/ *noun* a surgical operation to remove a sample of bone marrow from the breastbone for testing

sterno- /ˈstɜːnəʊ/ *prefix* relating to the breastbone

sternoclavicular /ˌstɜːnəʊkləˈvɪkjʊlə/ *adjective* referring to the sternum and the clavicle

sternoclavicular angle /ˌstɜːnəʊkləˌvɪkjʊlə ˈæŋgəl/ *noun* the angle between the sternum and the clavicle

sternocleidomastoid muscle /ˌstɜːnəʊˌklaɪdəʊˈmæstɔɪd ˌmʌs(ə)l/ *noun* a muscle in the neck, running from the breastbone to the mastoid process

sternocostal /ˌstɜːnəʊˈkɒst(ə)l/ *adjective* referring to the sternum and ribs

sternocostal joint /ˌstɜːnəʊˈkɒst(ə)l dʒɔɪnt/ *noun* a joint where the breastbone joins a rib

sternohyoid /ˌstɜːnəʊˈhaɪɔɪd/ *adjective* relating to the sternum and the hyoid bone

sternohyoid muscle /ˌstɜːnəʊˈhaɪɔɪd ˌmʌs(ə)l/ *noun* a muscle in the neck which runs from the breastbone into the hyoid bone

sternomastoid /ˌstɜːnəʊˈmæstɔɪd/ *adjective* referring to the breastbone and the mastoid

sternomastoid tumour /ˌstɜːnəʊ ˌmæstɔɪd ˈtjuːmə/ *noun* a benign tumour which appears in the sternomastoid muscle in newborn babies

sternotomy /stɜːˈnɒtəmi/ *noun* a surgical operation to cut through the breastbone, so as to be able to operate on the heart

sternum /ˈstɜːnəm/ *noun* same as **breastbone**

COMMENT: The sternum runs from the neck to the bottom of the diaphragm. It is formed of the manubrium (the top section), the body of the sternum and the xiphoid process. The upper seven pairs of ribs are attached to the sternum.

sternutatory /stɜːˈnjuːtətəri/ *noun* a substance which makes someone sneeze

steroid /ˈstɪərɔɪd/ *noun* any of several chemical compounds, including the sex hormones, which have characteristic ring systems and which affect the body and its functions

COMMENT: The word steroid is usually used to refer to corticosteroids. Synthetic steroids are used in steroid therapy, to treat arthritis, asthma and some blood disorders. They are also used by some athletes to improve their physical strength, but these are banned by athletic organisations and can have serious side-effects.

steroidal /stɪˈrɔɪdəl/ *adjective* containing steroids. Opposite **non-steroidal**

sterol /ˈstɪərɒl/ *noun* an insoluble substance which belongs to the steroid alcohols, e.g. cholesterol

stertor /ˈstɜːtə/ *noun* noisy breathing sounds in someone unconscious

stertorous /ˈstɜːt(ə)rəs/ *adjective* characterised by heavy snoring

steth- /steθ/, **stetho-** /steθə/ *prefix* referring to the chest

stethograph /ˈsteθəɡrɑːf/ *noun* an instrument which records breathing movements of the chest

stethography /steˈθɒɡrəfi/ *noun* the process of recording movements of the chest

stethometer /steˈθɒmɪtə/ *noun* an instrument which records how far the chest expands when a person breathes in

stethoscope /ˈsteθəskəʊp/ *noun* a surgical instrument with two earpieces connected to a tube and a metal disc, used by doctors to listen to sounds made inside the body, e.g. the sounds of the heart or lungs

Stevens-Johnson syndrome /ˌstiːvənz ˈdʒɒnsən ˌsɪndrəʊm/ *noun* a severe form of erythema multiforme affecting the face and genitals, caused by an allergic reaction to drugs [Described 1922. After Albert Mason Stevens (1884–1945); Frank Chambliss Johnson (1894–1934), physicians in New York, USA.]

sthenia /ˈsθiːniə/ *noun* a condition of great strength or vitality

STI *abbr* sexually transmitted infection

stick /stɪk/ *verb* to attach something, to fix things together, e.g. with glue ○ *In bad cases of conjunctivitis the eyelids can stick together.*

sticking plaster /ˈstɪkɪŋ ˌplɑːstə/ *noun* an adhesive plaster or tape used to cover a small wound or to attach a pad of dressing to the skin

sticky /ˈstɪki/ *adjective* able to become easily attached like glue

sticky eye /ˈstɪki aɪ/ *noun* a condition in babies in which the eyes remain closed because of conjunctivitis

stiff /stɪf/ *adjective* not able to be bent or moved easily ○ *My knee is stiff after playing football.*

stiffly /ˈstɪfli/ *adverb* in a stiff way ○ *He is walking stiffly because of the pain in his hip.*

stiff neck /stɪf ˈnek/ *noun* a condition in which moving the neck is painful, usually caused by a strained muscle or by sitting in a cold wind

stiffness /ˈstɪfnəs/ *noun* the fact of being stiff ○ *arthritis accompanied by stiffness in the joints*

stigma /ˈstɪɡmə/ *noun* a visible symptom which shows that someone has a particular disease (NOTE: The plural is **stigmas** or **stigmata**)

stilet /staɪˈlet/ *noun* 1. a fine wire used as a probe in surgery 2. a wire inserted in a catheter to give it rigidity

stillbirth /ˈstɪlbɜːθ/ *noun* the birth of a dead fetus, more than 28 weeks after conception (*informal*)

stillborn /ˈstɪlbɔːn/ *adjective* referring to a baby born dead ○ *Her first child was stillborn.*

Still's disease /ˈstɪlz dɪˌziːz/ *noun* arthritis affecting children, similar to rheumatoid arthritis in adults [Described 1896. After Sir George Frederic Still (1868–1941), British paediatrician and physician to the king.]

stimulant /ˈstɪmjʊlənt/ *noun* a substance which makes part of the body function faster ○ *Caffeine is a stimulant.* ■ *adjective* increasing body function

COMMENT: Natural stimulants include some hormones, and drugs such as digitalis which encourage a weak heart. Drinks such as tea and coffee contain stimulants.

stimulate /ˈstɪmjʊleɪt/ *verb* to make a person or organ react, respond or function ○ *The therapy should stimulate the patient into attempting to walk unaided.* ○ *The drug stimulates the heart.*

stimulation /ˌstɪmjʊˈleɪʃ(ə)n/ *noun* the action of stimulating something

stimulus /ˈstɪmjʊləs/ *noun* something which has an effect on a person or a part of the body and makes them react (NOTE: The plural is **stim-uli**.)

sting /stɪŋ/ *noun* the piercing of the skin by an insect which passes a toxic substance into the bloodstream ■ *verb* (*of an insect*) to make a hole in the skin and pass a toxic substance into the blood ○ *He was stung by a wasp.*

COMMENT: Stings by some insects such as tsetse flies can transmit a bacterial infection to a person. Other insects such as bees pass toxic substances into the bloodstream of the affected person, causing irritating swellings. Some people are strongly allergic to insect stings.

stinging /ˈstɪŋɪŋ/ *adjective* referring to a sharp unpleasant feeling of pricking or burning ○ *a sudden stinging sensation in the back of her leg*

stirrup /ˈstɪrəp/ *noun* same as **stapes**

stirrup bone /ˈstɪrəp bəʊn/ *noun* same as **stapes**

stitch /stɪtʃ/ *noun* **1.** same as **suture 2** ○ *He had three stitches in his head.* ○ *The doctor told her to come back in ten days' time to have the stitches taken out.* **2.** pain caused by cramp in the side of the body after running ○ *He had to stop running because he developed a stitch.* ■ *verb* same as **suture** ○ *They tried to stitch back the finger which had been cut off in an accident.*

stitch abscess /ˈstɪtʃ ˌæbses/ *noun* an abscess which forms at the site of a stitch or suture

stock culture /ˌstɒk ˈkʌltʃə/ *noun* the basic culture of bacteria, from which other cultures can be taken

stocking /ˈstɒkɪŋ/ *noun* a close-fitting piece of clothing to cover the leg

Stokes–Adams syndrome /ˌstəʊks ˈædəmz ˌsɪndrəʊm/ *noun* a loss of consciousness due to the stopping of the action of the heart because of asystole or fibrillation [After William Stokes (1804–78), Irish physician; Robert Adams (1791–1875), Irish surgeon]

stoma /ˈstəʊmə/ *noun* **1.** any opening into a cavity in the body **2.** the mouth **3.** a colostomy (*informal*) (NOTE: [all senses] The plural is **stomata**.)

stomach /ˈstʌmək/ *noun* **1.** the part of the body shaped like a bag, into which food passes after being swallowed and where the process of digestion continues ○ *She complained of pains in the stomach* or *of stomach pains.* ○ *He has had stomach trouble for some time.* See illustration at **DIGESTIVE SYSTEM** in Supplement **2.** the abdomen (*informal*) ○ *He had been kicked in the stomach.* (NOTE: For other terms referring to the stomach, see words beginning with **gastr-, gastro-**.)

COMMENT: The stomach is situated in the top of the abdomen, and on the left side of the body between the oesophagus and the duodenum. Food is partly broken down by hydro-chloric acid and other gastric juices secreted by the walls of the stomach and is mixed and squeezed by the action of the muscles of the stomach, before being passed on into the duodenum. The stomach continues the digestive process started in the mouth, but few substances, except alcohol and honey, are actually absorbed into the bloodstream in the stomach.

stomach ache /ˈstʌmək eɪk/ *noun* pain in the abdomen or stomach, caused by eating too much food or by an infection

stomach cramp /ˈstʌmək kræmp/ *noun* a sharp spasm of the stomach muscles

stomach hernia *noun* same as **gastrocele**

stomach pump /ˈstʌmək pʌmp/ *noun* an instrument for sucking out the contents of the stomach, e.g. to extract a poison that has been swallowed

stomach tube /ˈstʌmək tjuːb/ *noun* a tube passed into the stomach to wash it out or to take samples of the contents

stomach upset /ˈstʌmək ˌʌpset/ *noun* a slight infection of the stomach ○ *She is in bed with a stomach upset.* Also called **upset stomach**

stomach washout /ˌstʌmək ˈwɒʃaʊt/ *noun* same as **gastric lavage**

stomal /ˈstəʊm(ə)l/ *adjective* referring to a stoma

stomal ulcer /ˌstəʊm(ə)l ˈʌlsə/ *noun* an ulcer in the region of the jejunum

stomat- /stəʊmət/ *prefix* same as **stomato-** (*used before vowels*)

stomatitis /ˌstəʊməˈtaɪtɪs/ *noun* inflammation of the inside of the mouth

stomato- /stəʊmətə/ *prefix* referring to the mouth

stomatology /ˌstəʊməˈtɒlədʒi/ *noun* a branch of medicine which studies diseases of the mouth

-stomy /stəmi/ *suffix* meaning an operation to make an opening

stone /stəʊn/ *noun* **1.** same as **calculus** (*informal*) (NOTE: For other terms referring to stones, see words beginning with **lith-, litho-**, or ending with **-lith**.) **2.** a measure of weight equal to 14 pounds or 6.35 kilograms ○ *He tried to lose weight and lost three stone.* ○ *She weighs eight stone ten (i.e. 8 stone 10 pounds).*

stone-deaf /ˌstəʊn ˈdef/ *adjective* totally deaf

stool /stuːl/ *noun* **1.** an act of emptying the bowels **2.** a piece of solid waste matter which is passed out of the bowels ○ *an abnormal stool* ○ *loose stools* ○ *a stool test* (NOTE: Often used in the plural.) ■ *verb* to pass a piece of solid matter out of the bowels

stoop /stuːp/ *noun* a position where especially the top of your back is bent forward ○ *He walks with a stoop.* ■ *verb* to have a stoop ○ *He is seventy-five and stoops.*

stop needle /'stɒp ˌniːd(ə)l/ *noun* a needle with a ring round it, so that it can only be pushed a specific distance into the body

stoppage /'stɒpɪdʒ/ *noun* an act of stopping the function of an organ

storage disease /'stɔːrɪdʒ dɪˌziːz/ *noun* a disease in which unusual amounts of a substance accumulate in a part of the body

stove-in chest /ˌstəʊv ɪn 'tʃest/ *noun* an injury resulting from an accident, where several ribs are broken and pushed towards the inside

strabismal /strə'bɪzm(ə)l/ *adjective* with the eyes focusing on different points

strabismus /strə'bɪzməs/ *noun* a condition in which the eyes focus on different points. Also called **squint, heterotropia**

strabotomy /strə'bɒtəmi/ *noun* a surgical operation to divide the muscles of the eye in order to correct a squint

straight /streɪt/ *adjective* with no irregularities such as bends, curves or angles

straighten /'streɪt(ə)n/ *verb* to make something straight, or become straight ○ *Her arthritis is so bad that she cannot straighten her knees.*

strain /streɪn/ *noun* **1.** a condition in which a muscle has been stretched or torn by a strong or sudden movement **2.** a group of microorganisms which are different from others of the same type ○ *a new strain of influenza virus* **3.** nervous tension and stress ○ *Her work is causing her a lot of strain.* ○ *He is suffering from nervous strain and needs to relax.* ■ *verb* to stretch a muscle too far ○ *He strained his back lifting the table.* ○ *She had to leave the game with a strained calf muscle.* ○ *The effort of running upstairs strained his heart.*

strand /strænd/ *noun* a thread

strangle /'stræŋɡəl/ *verb* to kill someone by squeezing the throat so that he or she cannot breathe or swallow

strangulated /'stræŋɡjʊleɪtɪd/ *adjective* referring to part of the body which is caught in an opening in such a way that the circulation of blood is stopped

strangulated hernia /ˌstræŋɡjʊleɪtɪd 'hɜːniə/ *noun* a condition in which part of the intestine is squeezed in a hernia and the supply of blood to it is cut off

strangulation /ˌstræŋɡjʊ'leɪʃ(ə)n/ *noun* the act of squeezing a passage in the body

strangury /'stræŋɡjʊri/ *noun* a condition in which very little urine is passed, although the person wants to urinate, caused by a bladder disorder or by a stone in the urethra

strap /stræp/ *verb* □ **to strap (up)** to wrap a bandage round a limb tightly, to attach tightly ○ *The nurses strapped up his stomach wound.* ○ *The patient was strapped to the stretcher.*

strapping /'stræpɪŋ/ *noun* wide strong bandages or adhesive plaster used to bandage a large part of the body

Strategic Health Authority /strəˌtiːdʒɪk 'helθ ɔːˌθɒrɪti/ *noun* in the UK, an organisation, accountable to government, that assesses the health needs of local people and ensures that local health services are commissioned and provided to meet those needs. Abbr **StHA**

stratified /'strætɪfaɪd/ *adjective* made of several layers

stratified epithelium /ˌstrætɪfaɪd epi'θiːliəm/ *noun* epithelium formed of several layers of cells

stratum /'strɑːtəm/ *noun* a layer of tissue forming the epidermis (NOTE: The plural is **strata**.)

COMMENT: The main layers of the epidermis are: the **stratum germinativum** or **stratum basale:** this layer produces the cells that are pushed up to form the other layers; the **stratum granulosum,** a layer with granular cells under the **stratum lucidum,** a thin clear layer of dead and dying cells, and the surface layer, or **stratum corneum,** a layer of dead keratinised cells which progressively fall off.

strawberry mark /'strɔːb(ə)ri mɑːk/ *noun* a red birthmark in children, which will often disappear in later life

streak /striːk/ *noun* a long thin line of a different colour

strength /streŋθ/ *noun* the fact of being strong ○ *After her illness she had no strength in her limbs.*

strengthen /'streŋθ(ə)n/ *verb* to make something strong

strenuous /'strenjuəs/ *adjective* referring to exercise which involves using a lot of force ○ *Avoid doing any strenuous exercise for some time while the wound heals.*

strep throat /ˌstrep 'θrəʊt/ *noun* an infection of the throat by a streptococcus (*informal*)

strepto- /streptə/ *prefix* referring to organisms which grow in chains

streptobacillus /ˌstreptəbə'sɪləs/ *noun* a type of bacterium which forms a chain

streptococcal /ˌstreptə'kɒk(ə)l/ *adjective* caused by a streptococcus

streptococcus /ˌstreptə'kɒkəs/ *noun* a genus of bacteria which grows in long chains, and causes fevers such as scarlet fever, tonsillitis and rheumatic fever (NOTE: The plural is **streptococci.**)

streptodornase /ˌstreptə'dɔːneɪs/ *noun* an enzyme formed by streptococci which can make pus liquid

streptokinase /ˌstreptə'kaɪneɪz/ *noun* an enzyme formed by streptococci which can break down blood clots and is therefore used in the treatment of myocardial infarction

streptolysin /strep'tɒləsɪn/ *noun* a toxin produced by streptococci in rheumatic fever, which acts to destroy red blood cells

Streptomyces /ˌstreptə'maɪsiːz/ *noun* a genus of bacteria used to produce antibiotics

streptomycin /ˌstreptə'maɪsɪn/ *noun* an antibacterial drug used mainly for the treatment of tuberculosis

stress /stres/ *noun* **1.** physical pressure on an object or part of the body **2.** a factor or combination of factors in a person's life which make him or her feel tired and anxious **3.** a condition in which an outside influence such as overwork or a mental or emotional state such as anxiety changes the working of the body and can affect the hormone balance

stress disorder /'stres dɪsˌɔːdə/ *noun* a disorder caused by stress

stress fracture /'stres ˌfræktʃə/ *noun* a fracture of a bone caused by excessive force, as in some types of sport. Also called **fatigue fracture**

stress incontinence /'stres ɪnˌkɒntɪnəns/ *noun* a condition in women in which the muscles in the floor of the pelvis become incapable of retaining urine when the intra-abdominal pressure is raised by coughing or laughing

stress reaction /'stres riˌækʃən/ *noun* a response to an outside stimulus which disturbs the usual physiological balance of the body

stress-related illness /ˌstres rɪˌleɪtɪd 'ɪlnəs/ *noun* an illness which is due in part or completely to stress

stretch /stretʃ/ *verb* to pull something out, or make something longer

stretcher /'stretʃə/ *noun* a folding bed, with handles, on which an injured person can be carried by two people ○ *She was carried out of the restaurant on a stretcher.* ○ *Some of the accident victims could walk to the ambulances, but there were several stretcher cases.*

stretcher bearer /'stretʃə ˌbeərə/ *noun* a person who helps to carry a stretcher

stretcher case /'stretʃə keɪs/ *noun* a person who is so ill that he or she has to be carried on a stretcher

stretcher party /'stretʃə ˌpɑːti/ *noun* a group of people who carry a stretcher and look after the person on it

stretch mark /'stretʃ mɑːk/ *noun* a mark on the skin of the abdomen of a pregnant woman or of a woman who has recently given birth. ◊ **striae gravidarum**

stretch reflex /'stretʃ ˌriːfleks/ *noun* a reflex reaction of a muscle which contracts after being stretched

stria /'straɪə/ *noun* a pale line on skin which is stretched, as in obese people (NOTE: The plural is **striae**.)

striae gravidarum /ˌstraɪiː ˌgrævɪ'deərəm/ *plural noun* the lines on the skin of

the abdomen of a pregnant woman or of a woman who has recently given birth

striated /straɪ'eɪtɪd/ *adjective* marked with pale lines

striated muscle /straɪ'eɪtɪd ˌmʌs(ə)l/ *noun* a type of muscle found in skeletal muscles whose movements are controlled by the central nervous system. Also called **striped muscle**

strict /strɪkt/ *adjective* severe, which must not be changed ○ *She has to follow a strict diet.* ○ *The doctor was strict with the patients who wanted to drink alcohol in the hospital.*

stricture /'strɪktʃə/ *noun* the narrowing of a passage in the body

stricturoplasty /'strɪktʃərəʊˌplæsti/ *noun* a surgical operation in which a part of the intestine is widened

stridor /'straɪdɔː/, **stridulus** /'straɪdjʊləs/ *noun* a sharp high sound made when air passes an obstruction in the larynx. ◊ **laryngismus**

strike-through /'straɪk θruː/ *noun* blood absorbed right through a dressing so as to be visible on the outside

'If strike-through occurs, the wound dressing should be repadded, not removed' [*British Journal of Nursing*]

string sign /'strɪŋ saɪn/ *noun* a thin line which appears on the ileum, a sign of regional ileitis or Crohn's disease

strip /strɪp/ *noun* a long thin piece of material or tissue ○ *The nurse bandaged the wound with strips of gauze.* ○ *He grafted a strip of skin over the burn.* ■ *verb* to take off something, especially clothes ○ *The patients had to strip for the medical examination.* □ **to strip to the waist** to take off the clothes on the top part of the body

striped muscle /'straɪpt ˌmʌs(ə)l/ *noun* same as **striated muscle**

stripper /'strɪpə/ *noun* an instrument in the form of a flexible wire with an olive-shaped end used for stripping varicose veins

stripping /'strɪpɪŋ/ *noun* a surgical operation to remove varicose veins

stroke /strəʊk/ *noun* same as **cerebrovascular accident** ○ *He had a stroke and died.* ○ *She was paralysed after a stroke.* ■ *verb* to touch something or someone softly with the fingers

'…stroke is the third most frequent cause of death in developed countries after ischaemic heart disease and cancer' [*British Journal of Hospital Medicine*]

'…raised blood pressure may account for as many as 70% of all strokes. The risk of stroke rises with both systolic and diastolic blood pressure' [*British Journal of Hospital Medicine*]

COMMENT: There are two causes of stroke: cerebral haemorrhage (haemorrhagic stroke), when an artery bursts and blood leaks into the brain, and cerebral thrombosis (occlusive stroke), where a blood clot blocks an artery.

stroke patient /'strəʊk ˌpeɪʃ(ə)nt/ *noun* a person who has had a stroke

stroke volume /'strəʊk ˌvɒljuːm/ *noun* the amount of blood pumped out of the ventricle at each heartbeat

stroma /'strəʊmə/ *noun* tissue which supports an organ, as opposed to the parenchyma or functioning tissues in the organ

Strongyloides /ˌstrɒndʒi'lɔɪdiːz/ *noun* a parasitic worm which infests the intestines

strongyloidiasis /ˌstrɒndʒɪlɔɪ'daɪəsɪs/ *noun* the fact of being infested with *Strongyloides* which enters the skin and then travels to the lungs and the intestines

strontium /'strɒntiəm/ *noun* a metallic element (NOTE: The chemical symbol is **Sr.**)

strontium-90 /ˌstrɒntiəm 'naɪntɪ/ *noun* an isotope of strontium which is formed in nuclear reactions and, because it is part of the fallout of nuclear explosions, can enter the food chain, attacking in particular the bones of humans and animals

structure /'strʌktʃə/ *noun* the way in which an organ or muscle is formed

struma /'struːmə/ *noun* a goitre

strychnine /'strɪkniːn/ *noun* a poisonous alkaloid drug, made from the seeds of a tropical tree, and formerly used in small doses as a tonic

Stryker frame /'straɪkə freɪm/ *noun* a special piece of equipment on which a patient can easily be rotated by a nurse, used for patients with spinal injuries

ST segment /ˌes 'tiː ˌsegmənt/, **S-T segment** *noun* the part of an electrocardiogram, between the points labelled S and T, immediately before the last phase of the cardiac cycle.
◊ PQRST complex

student /'stjuːd(ə)nt/ *noun* a person who is studying at a college or university ○ *All the medical students have to spend some time in the hospital.*

student nurse /'stjuːd(ə)nt nɜːs/ *noun* a person who is studying to become a nurse

study /'stʌdi/ *noun* the act of examining something to learn about it ○ *She's making a study of diseases of small children.* ○ *They have finished their study of the effects of the drug on pregnant women.* ■ *verb* to examine something to learn about it ○ *He's studying pharmacy.* ○ *Doctors are studying the results of the screening programme.*

stuffy /'stʌfi/, **stuffed up** /ˌstʌft 'ʌp/ *adjective* referring to a nose which is blocked with inflamed mucous membrane and mucus (*informal*)

stump /stʌmp/ *noun* a short piece of a limb which is left after the rest has been amputated

stun /stʌn/ *verb* to knock someone out by a blow to the head

stunt /stʌnt/ *verb* to stop something growing ○ *The children's development was stunted by disease.*

stupe /stjuːp/ *noun* a wet medicated dressing used as a compress

stupor /'stjuːpə/ *noun* a state of being semiconscious ○ *After the party several people were found lying on the floor in a stupor.*

Sturge-Weber syndrome /ˌstɜːdʒ 'webə ˌsɪndrəʊm/ *noun* a dark red mark on the skin above the eye, together with similar marks inside the brain, possibly causing epileptic fits

stutter /'stʌtə/ *noun* a speech problem where someone repeats the sound at the beginning of a word several times ○ *He is taking therapy to try to cure his stutter.* ■ *verb* to speak with a stutter

stuttering /'stʌtərɪŋ/ *noun* same as **stammering**

stye /staɪ/ *noun* same as **hordeolum**

stylet /'staɪlət/ *noun* **1.** a very thin piece of wire which is put into a catheter or hollow needle so that it will not become blocked when it is not being used **2.** any long thin pointed instrument

stylo- /staɪləʊ/ *prefix* referring to the styloid process

styloglossus /ˌstaɪləʊ'glɒsəs/ *noun* a muscle which links the tongue to the styloid process

styloid /'staɪlɔɪd/ *adjective* pointed

styloid process /'staɪlɔɪd ˌprəʊses/ *noun* a piece of bone which projects from the bottom of the temporal bone

stylus /'staɪləs/ *noun* a long thin instrument used for applying antiseptics or ointments to the skin

styptic /'stɪptɪk/ *noun* a substance which stops bleeding ■ *adjective* used to stop bleeding

styptic pencil /ˌstɪptɪk 'pens(ə)l/ *noun* a stick of alum, used to stop bleeding from small cuts

sub- /sʌb/ *prefix* underneath or below

subabdominal /ˌsʌbəb'dɒmɪn(ə)l/ *adjective* beneath the abdomen

subacute /ˌsʌbə'kjuːt/ *adjective* referring to a condition which is not acute but may become chronic

subacute bacterial endocarditis /ˌsʌbəkjuːt bæk,tɪəriəl ˌendəʊkɑː'daɪtɪs/, **subacute infective endocarditis** /ˌsʌbəkjuːt ɪn,fektɪv ˌendəʊkɑː'daɪtɪs/ *noun* an infection of the membrane covering the inner surfaces of the heart caused by bacteria

subacute combined degeneration of the spinal cord /ˌsʌbəkjuːt kəm,baɪnd dɪ ˌdʒenəreɪʃ(ə)n əv ðə 'spaɪn(ə)l kɔːd/ *noun* a condition, caused by Vitamin B_{12} deficiency, in which the sensory and motor nerves in the spinal cord become damaged and the person has difficulty in moving

subacute sclerosing panencephalitis /sʌbəˌkjuːt sklə,rəʊsɪŋ ˌpænenkefə'laɪtɪs/

noun a rare inflammatory disease of the brain, mostly affecting children. It is linked to having measles at a very young age, and is usually fatal.

subarachnoid /ˌsʌbəˈræknɔɪd/ *adjective* beneath the arachnoid membrane

subarachnoid haemorrhage /ˌsʌbə ˌræknɔɪd ˈhem(ə)rɪdʒ/ *noun* bleeding into the cerebrospinal fluid of the subarachnoid space

subarachnoid space /ˌsʌbəˌræknɔɪd ˈspeɪs/ *noun* a space between the arachnoid membrane and the pia mater in the brain, containing cerebrospinal fluid

subaxillary /ˌsʌbækˈsɪləri/ *adjective* beneath the armpit

subcartilaginous /ˌsʌbkɑːtɪˈlædʒɪnəs/ *adjective* 1. beneath cartilage or a body part composed of cartilage 2. made partly of cartilage

subclavian /sʌbˈkleɪviən/ *adjective* underneath the clavicle

subclavian artery /sʌbˌkleɪviən ˈɑːtəri/ *noun* one of two arteries branching from the aorta on the left and from the innominate artery on the right, continuing into the brachial arteries and supplying blood to each arm

subclavian vein /sʌbˌkleɪviən ˈveɪn/ *noun* one of the veins which continue the axillary veins into the brachiocephalic vein

subclinical /sʌbˈklɪnɪk(ə)l/ *adjective* referring to a disease which is present in the body, but which has not yet developed any symptoms

subconscious /sʌbˈkɒnʃəs/ *noun* the part of a person's mental processes which he or she is not aware of most of the time, but which can affect his or her actions ■ *adjective* present in the mind although a person is not aware of it

subcortex /sʌbˈkɔːteks/ *noun* the parts of the brain immediately beneath the cerebral cortex

subcortical /sʌbˈkɔːtɪk(ə)l/ *adjective* beneath a cortex

subcostal /sʌbˈkɒst(ə)l/ *adjective* below the ribs

subcostal plane /sʌbˌkɒst(ə)l ˈpleɪn/ *noun* an imaginary horizontal line drawn across the front of the abdomen below the ribs

subcranial /sʌbˈkreɪniəl/ *adjective* beneath the dome of the skull

subculture /ˈsʌbkʌltʃə/ *noun* a culture of bacteria which is taken from a stock culture

subculturing /sʌbˈkʌltʃərɪŋ/ *noun* the act of taking a culture of bacteria from a stock culture

subcutaneous /ˌsʌbkjuːˈteɪniəs/ *adjective* under the skin. Abbr **s.c.**

subcutaneous injection /ˌsʌbkjuːˌteɪniəs ɪnˈdʒekʃən/ *noun* same as **hypodermic injection**

subcutaneous oedema /ˌsʌbkjuːˌteɪniəs ɪˈdiːmə/ *noun* a fluid collecting under the skin, usually at the ankles

subcutaneous tissue /ˌsʌbkjuːˌteɪniəs ˈtɪʃuː/ *noun* fatty tissue under the skin

subdural /sʌbˈdjʊərəl/ *adjective* between the dura mater and the arachnoid

subdural haematoma /sʌbˌdjʊərəl hiːmə ˈtəʊmə/ *noun* a haematoma between the dura mater and the arachnoid which displaces the brain, caused by a blow on the head

subglottis /sʌbˈglɒtɪs/ *noun* the lowest part of the laryngeal cavity, below the vocal folds

subinvolution /ˌsʌbɪnvəˈluːʃ(ə)n/ *noun* a condition in which a part of the body does not go back to its former size and shape after having swollen or stretched, as in the case of the uterus after childbirth

subject /ˈsʌbdʒɪkt/ *noun* 1. a patient, a person who has a particular disease ○ *The hospital has developed a new treatment for arthritic subjects.* 2. something which is being studied or written about ○ *The subject of the article is 'Rh-negative babies'.*

subjective /səbˈdʒektɪv/ *adjective* representing the views or feelings of the person concerned and not impartial ○ *The psychiatrist gave a subjective opinion on the patient's problem.* Compare **objective**

subject to /ˈsʌbdʒekt tʊ/ *adverb* likely to experience ○ *The patient is subject to fits.* ○ *After returning from the tropics she was subject to attacks of malaria.*

sublimate /ˈsʌblɪmeɪt/ *noun* a deposit left when a vapour condenses ■ *verb* to convert violent emotion into action which is not antisocial

sublimation /ˌsʌblɪˈmeɪʃ(ə)n/ *noun* a psychological process in which violent emotions which would otherwise be expressed in antisocial behaviour are directed into actions which are socially acceptable

subliminal /sʌbˈlɪmɪn(ə)l/ *adjective* too slight to be noticed by the senses

sublingual /sʌbˈlɪŋgwəl/ *adjective* under the tongue

'…the sublingual region has a rich blood supply derived from the carotid artery and indicates changes in central body temperature more rapidly than the rectum' [*Nursing Times*]

sublingual gland /sʌbˈlɪŋgwəl glænd/ *noun* a salivary gland under the tongue

subluxation /ˌsʌblʌkˈseɪʃ(ə)n/ *noun* a condition in which a joint is partially dislocated

submandibular /ˌsʌbmænˈdɪbjʊlə/ *adjective* under the lower jaw

submandibular ganglion /sʌbmænˌdɪbjʊlə ˈgæŋgliən/ *noun* a ganglion associated with the lingual nerve, relaying impulses to the submandibular and sublingual salivary glands

submandibular gland /ˌsʌbmænˈdɪbjʊlə ˌglænd/, **submaxillary gland** /sʌbˈmæksɪləri

‚glænd/ *noun* a salivary gland on each side of the lower jaw

submental /sʌb'ment(ə)l/ *adjective* under the chin

submucosa /ˌsʌbmjuː'kəʊsə/ *noun* tissue under a mucous membrane

submucous /sʌb'mjuːkəs/ *adjective* under a mucous membrane

submucous resection /sʌbˌmjuːkəs rɪ'sekʃən/ *noun* the removal of a bent cartilage from the septum in the nose. Abbr **SMR**

subnormal /sʌb'nɔːm(ə)l/ *adjective* with a mind which has not developed fully (NOTE: This term is regarded as offensive.)

subnormality /ˌsʌbnɔː'mælɪti/ *noun* a condition in which someone's mind has not developed fully (NOTE: This term is regarded as offensive.)

suboccipital /ˌsʌbɒk'sɪpɪt(ə)l/ *adjective* beneath the back of the head

suborbital /sʌb'ɔːbɪt(ə)l/ *adjective* beneath the eye socket

subperiosteal /ˌsʌbperi'ɒstɪəl/ *adjective* immediately beneath the connective tissue around bones

subphrenic /sʌb'frenɪk/ *adjective* under the diaphragm

subphrenic abscess /sʌbˌfrenɪk 'æbses/ *noun* an abscess which forms between the diaphragm and the liver

subside /səb'saɪd/ *verb* to go down or become less violent ○ *After being given the antibiotics, her fever subsided.*

substance /'sʌbstəns/ *noun* a chemical material, e.g. a drug ○ *toxic substances released into the bloodstream* ○ *He became addicted to certain substances.*

substance abuse /'sʌbstəns əˌbjuːs/, **substance misuse** /'sʌbstəns mɪsˌjuːz/ *noun* the misuse or excessive use of drugs, alcohol or other substances for pleasure or to satisfy addiction, which often causes health, emotional or social problems for the user

substance P /ˌsʌbstəns 'piː/ *noun* a neurotransmitter involved in pain pathways

substitution /ˌsʌbstɪ'tjuːʃ(ə)n/ *noun* the act of replacing one thing with another

substitution therapy /ˌsʌbstɪ'tjuːʃ(ə)n ˌθerəpi/ *noun* a way of treating a condition by using a different drug from the one used before

substrate /'sʌbstreɪt/ *noun* a substance which is acted on by an enzyme

'…insulin is a protein hormone and the body's major anabolic hormone, regulating the metabolism of all body fuels and substrates' [*Nursing 87*]

subsultus /sʌb'sʌltəs/ *noun* a twitching of the muscles and tendons, caused by fever

subtertian fever /sʌbˌtɜː'ʃ(ə)n 'fiːvə/ *noun* a type of malaria, where the fever is present most of the time

subthreshold /'sʌbθreʃhəʊld/ *adjective* describing a stimulus that is not strong enough to have an effect

subtotal /sʌb'təʊt(ə)l/ *adjective* referring to an operation to remove most of an organ

subtotal gastrectomy /ˌsʌbtəʊt(ə)l gæ'strektəmi/ *noun* the surgical removal of all but the top part of the stomach in contact with the diaphragm

subtotal hysterectomy /ˌsʌbtəʊt(ə)l ˌhɪstə'rektəmi/ *noun* the surgical removal of the uterus, but not the cervix

subtotal pancreatectomy /ˌsʌbtəʊt(ə)l ˌpæŋkriə'tektəmi/ *noun* the surgical removal of most of the pancreas

subtotal thyroidectomy /ˌsʌbtəʊt(ə)l ˌθaɪrɔɪ'dektəmi/ *noun* the surgical removal of most of the thyroid gland

subungual /sʌb'ʌŋgwəl/ *adjective* under a nail

succeed /sək'siːd/ *verb* to do well at what one was trying to do ○ *Scientists have succeeded in identifying the new influenza virus.* ○ *They succeeded in stopping the flow of blood.*

success /sək'ses/ *noun* **1.** the fact of doing something well, doing what one was trying to do ○ *They tried to isolate the virus but without success.* **2.** something which goes well ○ *The operation was a complete success.*

successful /sək'sesf(ə)l/ *adjective* working well ○ *The operation was completely successful.*

succession /sək'seʃ(ə)n/ *noun* a line of happenings, one after the other ○ *She had a succession of miscarriages.*

successive /sək'sesɪv/ *adjective* following one after the other ○ *She had a miscarriage with each successive pregnancy.*

succus /'sʌkəs/ *noun* juice secreted by an organ

succus entericus /ˌsʌkəs en'terɪkəs/ *noun* juice formed of enzymes, produced in the intestine to help the digestive process

succussion /sə'kʌʃ(ə)n/ *noun* a splashing sound made when there is a large amount of liquid inside a cavity in the body, e.g. the stomach

suck /sʌk/ *verb* to pull liquid or air into the mouth or into a tube

sucrase /'suːkreɪz/ *noun* an enzyme in the intestine which breaks down sucrose into glucose and fructose

sucrose /'suːkrəʊs/ *noun* a sugar, formed of glucose and fructose, found in plants, especially in sugar cane, beet and maple syrup

suction /'sʌkʃən/ *noun* a force created by the action of sucking ○ *The dentist hooked a suction tube into the patient's mouth.*

sudamen /suˈdeɪmən/ *noun* a little blister caused by sweat (NOTE: The plural is **sudamina.**)

sudden /ˈsʌd(ə)n/ *adjective* happening quickly

sudden death /ˌsʌd(ə)n ˈdeθ/ *noun* death without any identifiable cause, not preceded by an illness

sudden infant death syndrome /ˌsʌd(ə)n ˌɪnfənt ˈdeθ ˌsɪndrəʊm/ *noun* the sudden death of a baby under the age of about twelve months in bed, without any identifiable cause. Abbr **SIDS**. Also called **cot death**

Sudeck's atrophy /ˈsuːdeks ˌætrəfi/ *noun* osteoporosis in the hand or foot [Described 1900. After Paul Hermann Martin Sudeck (1866–1938), German surgeon.]

sudor /ˈsuːdɔː/ *noun* sweat

sudoriferous /ˌsuːdəˈrɪfərəs/ *adjective* producing sweat

sudorific /ˌsuːdəˈrɪfɪk/ *noun* a drug which makes someone sweat

suffer /ˈsʌfə/ *verb* **1.** to have an illness for a long period of time ○ *I suffer from headaches.* **2.** to feel pain ○ *I didn't suffer much.* **3.** to receive an injury ○ *He suffered multiple injuries in the accident.*

sufferer /ˈsʌfərə/ *noun* a person who has a particular disease ○ *a drug to help asthma sufferers* or *sufferers from asthma*

suffering /ˈsʌf(ə)rɪŋ/ *noun* the experiencing of pain over a long period of time

suffocate /ˈsʌfəkeɪt/ *verb* to make someone stop breathing by cutting off the supply of air to his or her nose and mouth

suffocation /ˌsʌfəˈkeɪʃ(ə)n/ *noun* the act of making someone become unconscious by cutting off his or her supply of air

suffuse /səˈfjuːz/ *verb* to spread over or through something

suffusion /səˈfjuːʒ(ə)n/ *noun* the spreading of a red flush over the skin

sugar /ˈʃʊɡə/ *noun* any of several sweet carbohydrates (NOTE: For other terms referring to sugar, see words beginning with **glyc-, glyco-**.)

COMMENT: There are several natural forms of sugar: sucrose (in plants), lactose (in milk), fructose (in fruit), glucose and dextrose (in fruit and in body tissue). Edible sugar used in the home is a form of refined sucrose. All sugars are useful sources of energy, though excessive amounts of sugar can increase weight and cause tooth decay. Diabetes mellitus is a condition in which the body is incapable of absorbing sugar from food.

sugar intolerance /ˈʃʊɡər ɪnˌtɒlərəns/ *noun* diarrhoea caused by sugar which has not been absorbed

suggest /səˈdʒest/ *verb* to mention an idea ○ *The doctor suggested that she should stop smoking.*

suggested daily intake /səˌdʒestɪd ˌdeɪli ˈɪnteɪk/ *noun* the amount of a substance which it is recommended a person should take in each day

suggestibility /səˌdʒestɪˈbɪlɪti/ *noun* a mental state in which somebody just accepts other people's ideas, attitudes or instructions, without questioning them. It is usually increased under hypnosis.

suggestible /səˈdʒestɪb(ə)l/ *adjective* easily influenced by other people

suggestion /səˈdʒestʃən/ *noun* **1.** an idea which has been mentioned ○ *The doctor didn't agree with the suggestion that the disease had been caught in the hospital.* **2.** (*in psychiatry*) the process of making a person's ideas change, by suggesting different ideas which the person can accept, such as that he or she is in fact cured

suicidal /ˌsuːɪˈsaɪd(ə)l/ *adjective* referring to someone who wants to kill himself ○ *He has suicidal tendencies.*

suicide /ˈsuːɪsaɪd/ *noun* the act of killing oneself □ **to commit suicide** to kill yourself ○ *After his wife died he committed suicide.*

sulcus /ˈsʌlkəs/ *noun* a groove or fold, especially between the gyri in the brain □ **lateral sulcus and central sulcus** two grooves which divide a cerebral hemisphere into lobes

sulfa drug /ˈsʌlfə drʌɡ/, **sulfa compound** /ˈsʌlfə ˌkɒmpaʊnd/ *noun* same as **sulfonamide**

sulfasalazine /ˌsʌlfəˈsæləziːn/ *noun* a drug belonging to the sulfonamide group of antibacterial drugs. It is used in the treatment of ulcerative colitis and Crohn's disease, and also of severe rheumatoid arthritis.

sulfate /ˈsʌlfeɪt/ *noun* same as **sulphate**

sulfonamide /sʌlˈfɒnəmaɪd/ *noun* a bacteriostatic drug, e.g. trimethoprim, used to treat bacterial infection, especially in the intestine and urinary system, but now less important due to increasing bacterial resistance

sulfonylurea /ˌsʌlfənaɪljʊˈriːə/ *noun* any of a group of drugs which lower blood sugar, used in the treatment of diabetes

sulfur /ˈsʌlfə/ *noun* another spelling of **sulphur**

sulphate /ˈsʌlfeɪt/ *noun* a salt of sulphuric acid

sulphur /ˈsʌlfə/ *noun* a yellow non-metallic chemical element which is contained in some amino acids and is used in creams to treat some skin disorders (NOTE: The chemical symbol is **S**. Note also that words beginning **sulph-** are spelt **sulf-** in US English.)

sulphuric acid /sʌlˌfjʊərɪk ˈæsɪd/ *noun* a strong colourless oily corrosive acid which has many uses

sumatriptan /ˌsuːməˈtrɪptæn/ *noun* a drug which helps to narrow the blood vessels, used in the treatment of acute migraine

sun /sʌn/ *noun* the very hot and large star around which the earth travels and which gives light and heat

sunbathing /'sʌnbeɪðɪŋ/ *noun* the practice of lying in the sun to absorb sunlight

sun blindness /'sʌn ˌblaɪndnəs/ *noun* same as **photoretinitis**

sunburn /'sʌnbɜːn/ *noun* damage to the skin by excessive exposure to sunlight

sunburnt /'sʌnbɜːnt/ *adjective* referring to skin made brown or red by exposure to sunlight

sunlight /'sʌnlaɪt/ *noun* the light from the sun ○ *He is allergic to strong sunlight.*

COMMENT: Sunlight is essential to give the body Vitamin D, but excessive exposure to sunlight will not simply turn the skin brown, but also may burn the surface of the skin so badly that it dies and pus forms beneath. Constant exposure to the sun can cause cancer of the skin.

sunscreen /'sʌnskriːn/ *noun* a cream for rubbing into the skin that acts as a block against the harmful rays of the sun, used to reduce the risk of sunburn

sunstroke /'sʌnstrəʊk/ *noun* a serious condition caused by excessive exposure to the sun or to hot conditions, in which the person becomes dizzy and has a high body temperature but does not perspire

super- /suːpə/ *prefix* **1.** above **2.** extremely

superciliary /ˌsuːpə'sɪliəri/ *adjective* referring to the eyebrows

superego /ˌsuːpər'iːgəʊ/ *noun* (*in psychology*) the part of the mind which is a person's conscience, which is concerned with right and wrong

superfecundation /ˌsuːpəfiːkən'deɪʃ(ə)n/ *noun* a condition in which two or more ova produced at the same time are fertilised by different males

superfetation /ˌsuːpəfiː'teɪʃ(ə)n/ *noun* a condition in which an ovum is fertilised in a woman who is already pregnant

superficial /ˌsuːpə'fɪʃ(ə)l/ *adjective* on the surface, close to the surface or on the skin □ **superficial burn** burn on the skin surface

superficial fascia /ˌsuːpəfɪʃ(ə)l 'feɪʃə/ *plural noun* membranous layers of connective tissue found just under the skin

superficial thickness burn /ˌsuːpəfɪʃ(ə)l 'θɪknəs bɜːn/ *noun* same as **partial thickness burn**

superficial vein /ˌsuːpəfɪʃ(ə)l 'veɪn/ *noun* a vein which is near the surface of the skin

superinfection /'suːpərɪnˌfekʃən/ *noun* a second infection which affects the treatment of the first infection, because it is resistant to the drug used to treat the first

superior /suː'pɪəriə/ *adjective* (*of part of the body*) higher up than another part

superior aspect /suːˌpɪəriə 'æspekt/ *noun* a view of the body from above

superior ganglion /suːˌpɪəriə 'gæŋgliən/ *noun* a small collection of cells in the jugular foramen

superiority /suːˌpɪəri'ɒriti/ *noun* the fact of being better than something or someone else

superiority complex /suːˌpɪəri'ɒriti ˌkɒm↓pleks/ *noun* a condition in which a person feels he or she is better and more important than others and pays little attention to them

superior mesenteric artery /suːˌpɪəriə mes(e)nˌterɪk 'ɑːtəri/ *noun* one of the arteries which supply the small intestine

superior vena cava /suːˌpɪəriə ˌviːnə 'keɪvə/ *noun* a branch of the large vein into the heart, carrying blood from the head and the top part of the body. See illustration at **HEART** in Supplement

supernumerary /ˌsuːpə'njuːmərəri/ *adjective* extra, more than the usual number

'…allocation of supernumerary students to clinical areas is for their educational needs and not for service requirements' [*Nursing Times*]

superovulation /ˌsuːpərˌɒvjʊ'leɪʃ(ə)n/ *noun* an increased frequency of ovulation, or production of a large number of ova at one time. It is often caused by giving a woman with infertility problems gonadotrophin hormones to stimulate ovulation

supervise /'suːpəvaɪz/ *verb* to manage or organise something ○ *The administration of drugs has to be supervised by a qualified person.* ○ *She has been appointed to supervise the transfer of patients to the new ward.*

supervision /ˌsuːpə'vɪʒ(ə)n/ *noun* management or organisation ○ *Elderly patients need constant supervision.* ○ *The sheltered housing is under the supervision of a full-time nurse.*

supervisor /'suːpəvaɪzə/ *noun* a person who supervises ○ *the supervisor of hospital catering services*

supinate /'suːpɪneɪt/ *verb* to turn the hand so that the palm faces upwards

supination /ˌsuːpɪ'neɪʃ(ə)n/ *noun* the act of turning the hand so that the palm faces upwards. Opposite **pronation**. See illustration at ANATOMICAL TERMS in Supplement

supinator /'suːpɪneɪtə/ *noun* a muscle which turns the hand so that the palm faces upwards

supine /'suːpaɪn/ *adjective* **1.** lying on the back. Opposite **prone 2.** with the palm of the hand facing upwards

'…the patient was to remain in the supine position, therefore a pad was placed under the Achilles tendon to raise the legs' [*NATNews*]

supplement /'sʌplɪmənt/ *noun* **1.** any extra nutrients that are taken to help a specific condition when someone is not getting all they need from their food ○ *vitamin and folic acid supplements* **2.** a pill or product regarded as helpful in improving health that can be bought without a prescription. Supplements are not tested in the same way as prescription drugs. ○ *dietary or food supplements* ■ *verb* to add on or increase above what is taken usually ○ *She supplemented her diet with folic acid when she was planning a pregnancy.*

supply /səˈplaɪ/ *noun* something which is provided ○ *The arteries provide a continuous supply of oxygenated blood to the tissues.* ○ *The hospital service needs a constant supply of blood for transfusion.* ○ *The government sent medical supplies to the disaster area.* ■ *verb* to provide or give something which is needed ○ *A balanced diet will supply the body with all the vitamins and trace elements it needs.* ○ *The brachial artery supplies the arm and hand.*

support /səˈpɔːt/ *noun* **1.** help to keep something in place ○ *The bandage provides some support for the knee.* ○ *He was so weak that he had to hold onto a chair for support.* **2.** a handle, a metal rail which a person can hold ○ *There are supports at the side of the bed.* ○ *The bath is provided with metal supports.* ■ *verb* **1.** to hold something ○ *He wore a truss to support a hernia.* **2.** to keep something in place

support hose /səˈpɔːt həʊz/ *plural noun* stockings that fit tightly to the legs, worn to help the flow of blood

supportive /səˈpɔːtɪv/ *adjective* helping or comforting someone in trouble ○ *Her family was very supportive when she was in hospital.* ○ *The local health authority has been very supportive of the hospital management.*

support stocking /səˈpɔːt ˌstɒkɪŋ/ *noun* a stocking worn to prevent postural hypotension and peripheral oedema

support worker /səˈpɔːt ˌwɜːkə/ *noun* someone who assists registered health service professionals as part of a team, e.g. as a nursing auxiliary or assistant, or in specialist areas such as mental health, speech therapy or physiotherapy

suppository /səˈpɒzɪt(ə)ri/ *noun* a piece of a soluble material such as glycerine jelly containing a drug, which is placed in the rectum to act as lubricant, or in the vagina, to treat disorders such as vaginitis, and is dissolved by the body's fluids

suppress /səˈpres/ *verb* to reduce the action of something completely, e.g. to remove a symptom or to stop the release of a hormone ○ *a course of treatment which suppresses the painful irritation* ○ *The drug suppresses the body's natural instinct to reject the transplanted tissue.* ○ *The release of adrenaline from the adrenal cortex is suppressed.*

suppression /səˈpreʃ(ə)n/ *noun* the act of suppressing something ○ *the suppression of allergic responses* ○ *the suppression of a hormone*

suppressor T-cell /sə.presə ˈtiː sel/ *noun* a T-cell which stops or reduces the immune response to an antigen of B-cells and other T-cells

suppurate /ˈsʌpjʊreɪt/ *verb* to form and discharge pus

suppurating /ˈsʌpjʊreɪtɪŋ/ *adjective* purulent, containing or discharging pus

suppuration /ˌsʌpjʊˈreɪʃ(ə)n/ *noun* the formation and discharge of pus

supra- /suːprə/ *prefix* above or over

supraglottis /ˌsuːprəˈglɒtɪs/ *noun* the part of the larynx above the vocal folds, including the epiglottis

supraoptic nucleus /ˌsuːprəɒptɪk ˈnjuːkliəs/ *noun* a nucleus in the hypothalamus from which nerve fibres run to the posterior pituitary gland

supraorbital /ˌsuːprəˈɔːbɪt(ə)l/ *adjective* above the orbit of the eye

supraorbital ridge /ˌsuːprəɔːbɪt(ə)l ˈrɪdʒ/ *noun* the ridge of bone above the eye, covered by the eyebrow

suprapubic /ˌsuːprəˈpjuːbɪk/ *adjective* above the pubic bone or pubic area

suprarenal /ˌsuːprəˈriːn(ə)l/ *adjective* above the kidneys ■ *noun* same as **suprarenal gland**

suprarenal area /ˌsuːprəriːn(ə)l ˈeəriə/ *noun* the area of the body above the kidneys

suprarenal cortical hormone /ˌsuːprəriːn(ə)l ˌkɔːtɪk(ə)l ˈhɔːməʊn/ *noun* a hormone secreted by the cortex of the adrenal glands, e.g. cortisone

suprarenal gland /ˌsuːprəˈriːn(ə)l glænd/, **suprarenal** /ˌsuːprəˈriːn(ə)l/ *noun* one of two endocrine glands at the top of the kidneys, which secrete adrenaline and other hormones

suprarenal medulla /ˌsuːprəriːn(ə)l meˈdʌlə/ *noun* same as **adrenal medulla**

suprasternal /ˌsuːprəˈstɜːn(ə)l/ *adjective* above the sternum

supraventricular tachycardia /ˌsʌpven.trɪkjʊlə ˌtækiˈkɑːdiə/ *noun* tachycardia coming from the upper chambers of the heart

surface /ˈsɜːfɪs/ *noun* the top layer of something ○ *The surfaces of the two membranes may rub together.*

surfactant /sɜːˈfæktənt/ *noun* a substance in the alveoli of the lungs which keeps the surfaces of the lungs wet and prevents lung collapse

surgeon /ˈsɜːdʒən/ *noun* a doctor who specialises in surgery (NOTE: Although surgeons are doctors, in the UK they are traditionally called 'Mr' and not 'Dr', so 'Dr Smith' may be a GP, but 'Mr Smith' is a surgeon.)

surgeon general /ˌsɜːdʒən ˈdʒen(ə)rəl/ *noun US* a government official responsible for all aspects of public health

surgery /ˈsɜːdʒəri/ *noun* **1.** the treatment of diseases or disorders by procedures which require an operation to cut into, to remove or to manipulate tissue, organs or parts ○ *The patient will need plastic surgery to remove the scars he received in the accident.* ○ *The surgical ward is for patients waiting for surgery.* ○ *Two of our patients had to have surgery.* ○ *She will have to undergo surgery.* **2.** a room where a doctor or dentist sees and examines patients ○ *There are ten patients waiting in the surgery.* ○ *Surgery hours are from 8.30 in the morning to 6.00 at night.*

surgical /'sɜːdʒɪk(ə)l/ *adjective* **1.** referring to surgery ○ *All surgical instruments must be sterilised.* **2.** referring to a disease which can be treated by surgery ○ *We manage to carry out six surgical operations in an hour.*

surgical belt /,sɜːdʒɪk(ə)l 'belt/ *noun* a fitted covering, worn to support part of the back, chest or abdomen

surgical boot /,sɜːdʒɪk(ə)l 'buːt/ *noun* a specially made boot for a person who has an unusually shaped foot, to support or correct it

surgical care /'sɜːdʒɪk(ə)l keə/ *noun* looking after patients who have had surgery

surgical diathermy /,sɜːdʒɪk(ə)l daɪə'θɜːmi/ *noun* a procedure which uses a knife or electrode which is heated by a strong electric current until it coagulates tissue

surgical emphysema /,sɜːdʒɪk(ə)l ,emfɪ'siːmə/ *noun* air bubbles in tissue, not in the lungs

surgical fixation /,sɜːdʒɪk(ə)l fɪk'seɪʃ(ə)n/ *noun* a method of immobilising something such as a bone either externally by the use of a splint or internally by a metal plate and screws

surgical gloves /'sɜːdʒɪk(ə)l glʌvz/ *plural noun* thin plastic gloves worn by surgeons

surgical hose *noun* a strong elastic stocking worn to support a weak joint in a knee or to relieve varicose veins. Also called **elastic hose, surgical stocking**

surgical intervention /,sɜːdʒɪk(ə)l ,ɪntə'venʃən/ *noun* the treatment of disease or other condition by surgery

surgically /'sɜːdʒɪkli/ *adverb* using surgery ○ *The growth can be treated surgically.*

surgical neck /,sɜːdʒɪk(ə)l 'nek/ *noun* the narrow part at the top of the humerus, where the arm can easily be broken

surgical needle /,sɜːdʒɪk(ə)l 'niːd(ə)l/ *noun* a needle for sewing up surgical incisions

surgical procedure /,sɜːdʒɪk(ə)l prə'siːdʒə/ *noun* a surgical operation

surgical shoe /,sɜːdʒɪk(ə)l 'ʃuː/ *noun* a specially made boot for a person who has an unusually shaped foot, to support or correct it

surgical spirit /,sɜːdʒɪk(ə)l 'spɪrɪt/ *noun* ethyl alcohol with an additive giving it an unpleasant taste, used as a disinfectant or for cleansing the skin. Also called **rubbing alcohol**

surgical stocking /,sɜːdʒɪk(ə)l 'stɒkɪŋ/ *noun* same as **surgical hose**

surgical ward /'sɜːdʒɪk(ə)l wɔːd/ *noun* a ward for patients who have undergone surgery

surgical wound /'sɜːdʒɪk(ə)l wuːnd/ *noun* an incision made during a surgical operation

surrogate /'sʌrəgət/ *adjective* taking the place of ■ *noun* someone or something that takes the place of another person or thing ◇ **surrogate mother 1.** a woman who has a child by artificial insemination for a woman who cannot become pregnant, with the intention of handing the child over to her when it is born **2.** a person who takes the place of a natural mother for someone

surround /sə'raʊnd/ *verb* to be all around something ○ *The wound is several millimetres deep and the surrounding flesh is inflamed.*

survival /sə'vaɪv(ə)l/ *noun* the act of continuing to live ○ *The survival rate of newborn babies has begun to fall.*

survive /sə'vaɪv/ *verb* to continue to live ○ *He survived two attacks of pneumonia.* ○ *The baby only survived for two hours.*

survivor /sə'vaɪvə/ *noun* a person who survives

susceptibility /sə,septɪ'bɪlɪti/ *noun* lack of resistance to a disease

'…low birthweight has been associated with increased susceptibility to infection' [*East African Medical Journal*]

'…even children with the milder forms of sickle-cell disease have an increased frequency of pneumococcal infection. The reason for this susceptibility is a profound abnormality of the immune system' [*Lancet*]

susceptible /sə'septɪb(ə)l/ *adjective* likely to catch a disease ○ *She is susceptible to colds* or *to throat infections.*

suspect *noun* /'sʌspekt/ a person who doctors believe may have a disease ○ *They are screening all typhoid suspects.* ■ *verb* /sə'spekt/ to think that someone may have a disease ○ *He is a suspected diphtheria carrier.* ○ *Several cases of suspected meningitis have been reported.*

'…those affected are being nursed in five isolation wards and about forty suspected sufferers are being barrier nursed in other wards' [*Nursing Times*]

suspension /sə'spenʃən/ *noun* a liquid with solid particles in it

suspensory /sə'spensəri/ *adjective* hanging down

suspensory bandage /sə,spensəri 'bændɪdʒ/ *noun* a bandage to hold a part of the body which hangs

suspensory ligament /sə,spensəri 'lɪgəmənt/ *noun* a ligament which holds a part of the body in position. See illustration at EYE in Supplement

sustain /sə'steɪn/ *verb* **1.** to keep, to support, to maintain something ○ *These bones can sustain quite heavy weights.* ○ *He is not eating* *enough to sustain life.* **2.** to experience an injury ○ *He sustained a severe head injury.*

sustentacular /ˌsʌstənˈtækjʊlə/ *adjective* referring to a sustentaculum

sustentaculum /ˌsʌstənˈtækjʊləm/ *noun* a part of the body which supports another part

suture /ˈsuːtʃə/ *noun* **1.** a fixed joint where two bones are fused together, especially the bones in the skull **2.** a procedure for attaching the sides of an incision or wound with thread, so that healing can take place. Also called **stitch 3.** a thread used for attaching the sides of a wound so that they can heal ■ *verb* to attach the sides of a wound or incision together with thread so that healing can take place. Also called **stitch**

COMMENT: Wounds are usually stitched using thread or catgut which is removed after a week or so. Sutures are either absorbable, made of a substance which is eventually absorbed into the body, or non-absorbable, in which case they need to be removed after a certain time.

suxamethonium /ˌsʌksəmiˈθəʊniəm/ *noun* a drug similar to acetylcholine in structure, used as a muscle relaxant during surgery

swab /swɒb/ *noun* **1.** a cotton wool pad, often attached to a small stick, used, e.g., to clean a wound, to apply ointment or to take a specimen **2.** a specimen taken with a swab ○ *a cervical swab*

swallow /ˈswɒləʊ/ *verb* to make liquid, food and sometimes air go down from the mouth to the stomach ○ *Patients suffering from nosebleeds should try not to swallow the blood.*

swallowing /ˈswɒləʊɪŋ/ *noun* same as **deglutition**

Swan-Ganz catheter /ˌswɒn ˈgæntz ˌkæθɪə/ *noun* a special catheter which can be floated through the right chamber of the heart into the pulmonary artery. The balloon at its tip is then inflated to measure arterial pressure.

sweat /swet/ *noun* a salty liquid produced by the sweat glands to cool the body as the liquid evaporates from the skin ○ *Sweat was running off the end of his nose.* ○ *Her hands were covered with sweat.* Also called **perspiration** ■ *verb* to produce moisture through the sweat glands and onto the skin ○ *After working in the fields she was sweating.*

sweat duct /ˈswet dʌkt/ *noun* a thin tube connecting the sweat gland with the surface of the skin

sweat gland /ˈswet glænd/ *noun* a gland which produces sweat, situated beneath the dermis and connected to the skin surface by a sweat duct

sweat pore /ˈswet pɔː/ *noun* a hole in the skin through which the sweat comes out

sweet /swiːt/ *adjective* one of the basic tastes, not bitter, sour or salt ○ *Sugar is sweet, lemons are sour.*

swell /swel/ *verb* to become larger, or cause something to become larger ○ *The disease affects the lymph glands, making them swell.* ○ *The doctor noticed that the patient had swollen glands in his neck.* ○ *She finds her swollen ankles painful.* (NOTE: **swelling – swelled – swollen**)

swelling /ˈswelɪŋ/ *noun* a condition in which fluid accumulates in tissue, making the tissue become large ○ *They applied a cold compress to try to reduce the swelling.*

swimmer's cramp /ˌswɪməz ˈkræmp/ *noun* spasms in arteries and muscles caused by cold water, or by swimming soon after a meal

sycosis /saɪˈkəʊsɪs/ *noun* a bacterial infection of hair follicles

sycosis barbae /saɪˌkəʊsɪs ˈbɑːbiː/ *noun* an infection of hair follicles on the sides of the face and chin. Also called **barber's itch, barber's rash**

Sydenham's chorea /ˌsɪdnəmz kɒˈriːə/ *noun* temporary chorea affecting children, frequently associated with endocarditis and rheumatism [Described 1686. After Thomas Sydenham (1624–89), English physician.]

symbiosis /ˌsɪmbaɪˈəʊsɪs/ *noun* a condition in which two organisms exist together and help each other to survive

symblepharon /sɪmˈblefərɒn/ *noun* a condition in which the eyelid sticks to the eyeball

symbol /ˈsɪmbəl/ *noun* a sign or letter which means something

Syme's amputation /ˌsaɪmz æmpjʊˈteɪʃ(ə)n/ *noun* a surgical operation to amputate the foot above the ankle [Described 1842. After James Syme (1799–1870), Edinburgh surgeon and teacher; one of the first to adopt antisepsis (Joseph Lister was his son-in-law), and also among the early users of anaesthesia.]

symmetry /ˈsɪmətri/ *noun* the regularity of structure and distribution of parts of the body, each side of the body being structurally similar to the other

sympathectomy /ˌsɪmpəˈθektəmi/ *noun* a surgical operation to cut part of the sympathetic nervous system, as a treatment of high blood pressure

sympathetic /ˌsɪmpəˈθetɪk/ *adjective* **1.** feeling or showing shared feelings, pity or compassion **2.** relating to or belonging to the sympathetic nervous system, or to one of its parts

sympathetic nervous system /ˌsɪmpəθetɪk ˈnɜːvəs ˌsɪstəm/, **sympathetic system** /ˌsɪmpəˈθetɪk ˈsɪstəm/ *noun* part of the autonomic nervous system, which leaves the spinal cord from the thoracic and lumbar regions to go to various important organs such as the heart, the lungs and the sweat glands, and which prepares the body for emergencies and vigorous muscular activity. ◊ **parasympathetic nervous system**

sympatholytic /ˌsɪmpəθəʊˈlɪtɪk/ *noun* a drug which stops the sympathetic nervous system working

sympathomimetic /ˌsɪmpəθəʊmɪˈmetɪk/ *adjective* referring to a drug such as dopamine hydrochloride which stimulates the activity of the sympathetic nervous system and is used in cardiac shock following myocardial infarction and in cardiac surgery

sympathy /ˈsɪmpəθi/ *noun* **1.** the feeling or expression of pity or sorrow for the pain or distress of somebody else **2.** the relationship between people which causes one of them to provoke a similar condition to their own in the other one. For example, when the first person yawns, the second feels an urge to yawn too. **3.** the influence produced on any part of the body by disease or change in another part

symphysiectomy /ˌsɪmfɪziˈektəmi/ *noun* a surgical operation to remove part of the pubic symphysis to make childbirth easier

symphysiotomy /ˌsɪmfɪziˈɒtəmi/ *noun* a surgical operation to make an incision in the pubic symphysis to make the passage for a fetus wider

symphysis /ˈsɪmfəsɪs/ *noun* the point where two bones are joined by cartilage which makes the joint rigid

symphysis menti /ˌsɪmfəsɪs ˈmenti/ *noun* a point in the front of the lower jaw where the two halves of the jaw are fused to form the chin

symphysis pubis /ˌsɪmfəsɪs ˈpjuːbɪs/ *noun* same as **pubic symphysis**

symptom /ˈsɪmptəm/ *noun* a change in the way the body works or a change in the body's appearance, which shows that a disease or disorder is present and which the person is aware of ○ *The symptoms of hay fever are a running nose and eyes.* ○ *A doctor must study the symptoms before making his diagnosis.* ○ *The patient presented all the symptoms of rheumatic fever.* (NOTE: If a symptom is noticed only by the doctor, it is a **sign**.)

symptomatic /ˌsɪmptəˈmætɪk/ *adjective* being a symptom of something ○ *The rash is symptomatic of measles.*

symptomatology /ˌsɪmptəməˈtɒlədʒi/ *noun* a branch of medicine concerned with the study of symptoms. Also called **semeiology**

syn- /sɪn/ *prefix* joint, or fused

synalgia /sɪˈnældʒə/ *noun* a pain which is felt in one part of the body, but is caused by a condition in another part, e.g. pain in the groin which can be a symptom of a kidney stone or pain in the right shoulder which can indicate gall bladder infection. Also called **referred pain**

synapse /ˈsaɪnæps/ *noun* a point in the nervous system where the axons of neurones are in contact with the dendrites of other neurones ■ *verb* to link something with a neurone

synaptic /sɪnˈæptɪk/ *adjective* referring to a synapse

synaptic connection /sɪnˌæptɪk kəˈnekʃ(ə)n/ *noun* a link between the dendrites of one neurone with another neurone

synarthrosis /ˌsɪnɑːˈθrəʊsɪs/ *noun* a joint, e.g. in the skull, where the bones have fused together

synchondrosis /ˌsɪnkɒnˈdrəʊsɪs/ *noun* a joint, as in children, where the bones are linked by cartilage, before the cartilage has changed to bone

synchysis /ˈsɪŋkɪsɪs/ *noun* a condition in which the vitreous humour in the eye becomes soft

syncope /ˈsɪŋkəpi/ *noun* a condition in which someone becomes unconscious for a short time because of reduced flow of blood to the brain. Also called **fainting fit**

syncytium /sɪnˈsɪʃiəm/ *noun* a continuous length of tissue in muscle fibres

syndactyl /sɪnˈdæktɪl/ *adjective* having two or more fingers or toes joined together when born

syndactyly /sɪnˈdæktɪli/, **syndactylism** /sɪnˈdæktɪlɪz(ə)m/ *noun* a condition in which two toes or fingers are joined together with tissue

syndesm- /sɪndesm/, **syndesmo-** /sɪndesməʊ/ *prefix* referring to ligaments

syndesmology /ˌsɪndesˈmɒlədʒi/ *noun* a branch of medicine which studies joints

syndesmosis /ˌsɪndesˈməʊsɪs/ *noun* a joint where the bones are tightly linked by ligaments

syndrome /ˈsɪndrəʊm/ *noun* a group of symptoms and other changes in the body's functions which, when taken together, show that a particular disease is present. ◊ **complex**

synechia /sɪˈnekiə/ *noun* a condition in which the iris sticks to another part of the eye

syneresis /sɪˈnɪərəsɪs/ *noun* the releasing of fluid as in a blood clot when it becomes harder

synergism /ˈsɪnədʒɪz(ə)m/ *noun* a situation where two or more things are acting together in such a way that both are more effective. Also called **synergy**

synergist /ˈsɪnədʒɪst/ *noun* a muscle or drug which acts with another and increases the effectiveness of both

synergy /ˈsɪnədʒi/ *noun* same as **synergism**

syngeneic /ˌsɪndʒəˈniːɪk/ *adjective* referring to individuals or tissues that have an identical or closely similar genetic make-up, especially one that will allow the transplanting of tissue without provoking an immune response

syngraft /ˈsɪngrɑːft/ *noun* same as **isograft**

synoptophore /sɪˈnɒptəfɔː/ *noun* an instrument used to correct a squint

synostosed /ˈsɪnɒstəʊzd/ *adjective* (*of bones*) fused together with new bone tissue

synostosis /ˌsɪnɒˈstəʊsɪs/ *noun* the fusing of two bones together by the formation of new bone tissue

synovectomy /ˌsɪnəʊˈvektəmi/ *noun* a surgical operation to remove the synovial membrane of a joint

synovia /saɪˈnəʊviə/ *noun* same as **synovial fluid**

synovial /saɪˈnəʊviəl/ *adjective* referring to the synovium

synovial cavity /saɪˌnəʊviəl ˈkævɪti/ *noun* a space inside a synovial joint. See illustration at SYNOVIAL JOINT in Supplement

synovial fluid /saɪˌnəʊviəl ˈfluːɪd/ *noun* a fluid secreted by a synovial membrane to lubricate a joint. See illustration at SYNOVIAL JOINT in Supplement

synovial joint /saɪˌnəʊviəl ˈdʒɔɪnt/ *noun* a joint where the two bones are separated by a space filled with synovial fluid which nourishes and lubricates the surfaces of the bones. Also called **diarthrosis**

synovial membrane /saɪˌnəʊviəl ˈmembreɪn/, **synovium** *noun* a smooth membrane which forms the inner lining of the capsule covering a joint and secretes the fluid which lubricates the joint. See illustration at SYNOVIAL JOINT in Supplement

synovioma /ˌsɪnəʊviˈəʊmə/ *noun* a tumour in a synovial membrane

synovitis /ˌsaɪnəˈvaɪtɪs/ *noun* inflammation of the synovial membrane

synovium /sɪˈnəʊviəm/ same as **synovial membrane**

'70% of rheumatoid arthritis sufferers develop the condition in the metacarpophalangeal joints. The synovium produces an excess of synovial fluid which is abnormal and becomes thickened' [*Nursing Times*]

synthesis /ˈsɪnθəsɪs/ *noun* **1.** the process of combining different ideas or objects into a new whole **2.** a new unified whole resulting from the combination of different ideas or objects **3.** the formation of compounds through chemical reactions involving simpler compounds or elements **4.** in psychiatry, the fusing together of all the various elements of the personality (NOTE: The plural is **syntheses**.)

synthesise /ˈsɪnθəsaɪz/, **synthesize** *verb* to make a chemical compound from its separate components ○ *Essential amino acids cannot be synthesised.* ○ *The body cannot synthesise essential fatty acids and has to absorb them from food.*

synthetic /sɪnˈθetɪk/ *adjective* made by humans, made artificially

synthetically /sɪnˈθetɪkli/ *adverb* made artificially ○ *Synthetically produced hormones are used in hormone therapy.*

syphilide /ˈsɪfɪlaɪd/ *noun* a rash or open sore which is a symptom of the second stage of syphilis

syphilis /ˈsɪfəlɪs/ *noun* a sexually transmitted disease caused by a spirochaete *Treponema pallidum*

COMMENT: Syphilis is a serious sexually transmitted disease, but it is curable with penicillin injections if the treatment is started early. Syphilis has three stages: in the first, or primary, stage, a hard sore (chancre) appears on the genitals or sometimes on the mouth; in the second, or secondary, stage about two or three months later, a rash appears, with sores round the mouth and genitals. It is at this stage that the disease is particularly infectious. After this stage, symptoms disappear for a long time, sometimes many years. The disease reappears in the third, or tertiary, stage in many different forms: blindness, brain disorders, ruptured aorta or general paralysis leading to mental disorder and death. The tests for syphilis are the Wassermann test and the less reliable Kahn test.

syring- /sɪrɪndʒ/ *prefix* same as **syringo-** (*used before vowels*)

syringe /sɪˈrɪndʒ/ *noun* a medical instrument made of a tube with a plunger which either slides down inside the tube, forcing the contents out through a needle as in an injection, or slides up the tube, allowing a liquid to be sucked into it ■ *verb* to wash out the ears using a syringe

syringo- /sɪrɪŋgəʊ/ *prefix* referring to tubes, especially the central canal of the spinal cord

syringobulbia /sɪˌrɪŋgəʊˈbʌlbiə/ *noun* syringomyelia in the brain stem

syringocystadenoma /sɪˌrɪŋgəʊsɪstədɪˈnəʊmə/, **syringoma** /ˌsɪrɪŋˈgəʊmə/ *noun* a benign tumour in sweat glands and ducts

syringomyelia /sɪˌrɪŋgəʊmaɪˈiːliə/ *noun* a disease which forms cavities in the neck section of the spinal cord, affecting the nerves so that the person loses the sense of touch and pain

syringomyelitis /sɪˌrɪŋgəʊmaɪəˈlaɪtɪs/ *noun* a swelling of the spinal cord, which results in the formation of cavities in it

syringomyelocele /sɪˌrɪŋgəʊˈmaɪələʊsiːl/ *noun* a severe form of spina bifida where the spinal cord pushes through a hole in the spine

systaltic /sɪsˈtæltɪk/ *adjective* describing an organ such as the heart that contracts and relaxes alternately

system /ˈsɪstəm/ *noun* **1.** the body as a whole ○ *Amputation of a limb gives a serious shock to the system.* **2.** the arrangement of particular parts of the body so that they work together ○ *the lymphatic system*

systematic desensitisation /ˌsɪstəmætɪk diːˌsensɪtaɪˈzeɪʃ(ə)n/ *noun* a therapy for phobias and other anxiety disorders in which patients are gradually given longer and longer exposures to the object of their fears

Système International d'Unités /sɪˌstem ˌæntəˈnæsjənɑːl ˈduːnɪteɪ/ *noun* the International System of units. ◊ **SI**

systemic /sɪˈstiːmɪk/ *adjective* referring to or affecting the whole body ○ *Septicaemia is a systemic infection.*

systemic circulation /sɪˌstiːmɪk ˌsɜːkjʊˈleɪʃ(ə)n/ *noun* the circulation of blood around the whole body, except the lungs, starting with the aorta and returning through the venae cavae

systemic lupus erythematosus /sɪˌstiːmɪk ˌluːpəs ˌerɪθiːməˈtəʊsəs/ *noun* one of several collagen diseases which are forms of lupus, where red patches form on the skin and spread throughout the body. Abbr **SLE**

systole /ˈsɪstəli/ *noun* a phase in the beating of the heart when it contracts as it pumps blood out. Opposite **diastole** □ **the heart is in systole** the heart is contracting and pumping

systolic /sɪˈstɒlɪk/ *adjective* referring to the systole

systolic murmur /sɪˌstɒlɪk ˈmɜːmə/ *noun* a sound produced during systole which indicates an unusual condition of a heart valve

systolic pressure /sɪˌstɒlɪk ˈpreʃə/ *noun* the high point of blood pressure which occurs during the systole. Systolic pressure is always higher than diastolic pressure.

T

T *symbol* tera-

TAB *abbr* typhoid-paratyphoid A and B ○ *He was given a TAB injection.* ○ *TAB injections give only temporary immunity against paratyphoid.* ♦ **TAB vaccine**

tabes /ˈteɪbiːz/ *noun* a condition in which someone is wasting away

tabes dorsalis /ˌteɪbiːz dɔːˈseɪlɪs/ *noun* a disease of the nervous system, caused by advanced syphilis, in which the person loses the sense of feeling, control of the bladder and the ability to coordinate movements of the legs, and has severe pains. Also called **locomotor ataxia**

tabes mesenterica /ˌteɪbiːz ˌmesen ˈterɪkə/ *noun* the wasting of glands in the abdomen

tabetic /təˈbetɪk/ *adjective* wasting away or affected by tabes dorsalis

tablet /ˈtæblət/ *noun* **1.** a small flat round object containing medicine that is taken by swallowing ○ *a bottle of aspirin tablets* ○ *Take two tablets three times a day.* **2.** any tablet, pill or capsule taken by swallowing (*informal*)

taboparesis /ˌteɪbəʊpəˈriːsɪs/ *noun* the final stage of syphilis in which the person has locomotor ataxia, general paralysis and mental deterioration

TAB vaccine /ˌtiː eɪ ˈbiː ˌvæksiːn/ *noun* a vaccine which immunises against typhoid fever and paratyphoid A and B

tachy- /tæki/ *prefix* fast

tachyarrhythmia /ˌtækiəˈrɪðmiə/ *noun* a fast irregular heartbeat

tachycardia /ˌtækiˈkɑːdiə/ *noun* a rapid beating of the heart

tachyphrasia /ˌtækiˈfreɪziə/, **tachyphasia** /ˌtækiˈfeɪziə/ *noun* a particularly rapid way of speaking, as occurs with some people with mental disorders

tachyphyl(l)axis /ˌtækifəˈlæksɪs/ *noun* an effect of a drug or neurotransmitter which becomes less with repeated doses

tachypnoea /ˌtækɪpˈniːə/ *noun* very fast breathing

tacrolimus /ˌtækrəˈliːməs/ *noun* a powerful immunosuppressant drug used to reduce the risk of organ transplant rejection

tactile /ˈtæktaɪl/ *adjective* able to be sensed by touch

tactile anaesthesia /ˌtæktaɪl ˌænəsˈθiːziə/ *noun* the loss of the sensation of touch

taenia /ˈtiːniə/ *noun* **1.** a long ribbon-like part of the body **2.** a large tapeworm of the genus *Taenia*

COMMENT: The various species of *Taenia* which affect humans are taken into the body from eating meat which has not been properly cooked. The most obvious symptom of tapeworm infestation is a sharply increased appetite, together with a loss of weight. The most common infestations are with *Taenia solium*, found in pork, where the larvae develop in the body and can form hydatid cysts, and *Taenia saginata*, the adult form of which grows to between four and eight metres long in the human intestine.

taeniacide /ˈtiːniəsaɪd/ *noun* a substance which kills tapeworms

taenia coli /ˌtiːniə ˈkəʊlaɪ/ *noun* the outer band of muscle running along the large intestine

taeniafuge /ˈtiːniəfjuːdʒ/ *noun* a substance which makes tapeworms leave the body

taeniasis /tiːˈnaɪəsɪs/ *noun* infestation of the intestines with tapeworms

Tagamet /ˈtægəmet/ a trade name for a preparation of cimetidine

tai chi /ˌtaɪ ˈtʃiː/, **t'ai chi** *noun* an ancient Chinese system of exercises designed for health, self-defence and spiritual development

take /teɪk/ *verb* **1.** to swallow a medicine ○ *She has to take her tablets three times a day.* ○ *The medicine should be taken in a glass of water.* **2.** to do particular actions ○ *The dentist took an X-ray of his teeth.* ○ *The patient has been allowed to take a bath.* **3.** (*of graft*) to be accepted by the body ○ *The skin graft hasn't taken.* ○ *The kidney transplant took easily.* (NOTE: **taking – took – taken**)

take after /ˈteɪk ˌɑːftə/ *verb* to be like one or other parent ○ *He takes after his father.*

take care of /ˌteɪk 'keə əv/ *verb* to look after someone ○ *The nurses will take care of the accident victims.*

take off /ˌteɪk 'ɒf/ *verb* to remove something, especially clothes ○ *The doctor asked him to take his shirt off* or *to take off his shirt.*

talc /tælk/ *noun* a soft white powder used to dust on irritated skin

talcum powder /'tælkəm ˌpaʊdə/ *noun* scented talc

tali /'teɪli/ plural of **talus**

talipes /'tælɪpiːz/ *noun* a foot with a shape that does not allow usual walking, a congenital condition. Also called **cleft foot, club foot**

COMMENT: The most usual form of talipes (**talipes equinovarus**) is where the person walks on the toes because the foot is permanently bent forward. In other forms, the foot either turns towards the inside (**talipes varus**), towards the outside (**talipes valgus**) or upwards at the ankle (**talipes calcaneus**) so that the person cannot walk on the sole of the foot.

tall /tɔːl/ *adjective* high, usually higher than other people ○ *He's the tallest in the family – he's taller than all his brothers.* ○ *How tall is he?* ○ *He's 5 foot 7 inches (5'7") tall* or *1.25 metres tall.*

talo- /teɪləʊ/ *prefix* referring to the ankle bone

talus /'teɪləs/ *noun* the top bone in the tarsus which articulates with the tibia and fibula in the leg, and with the calcaneus in the heel. Also called **anklebone**. See illustration at FOOT in Supplement (NOTE: The plural is **tali**.)

tamoxifen /tə'mɒksɪfen/ *noun* a drug which helps to prevent the actions of oestrogen, used especially in the treatment of breast cancer and some types of infertility

tampon /'tæmpɒn/ *noun* **1.** a wad of absorbent material put into a wound to soak up blood during an operation **2.** a cylindrical plug of soft material put into the vagina to absorb blood during menstruation

tamponade /ˌtæmpə'neɪd/ *noun* **1.** the action of putting a tampon into a wound **2.** abnormal pressure on part of the body

tan /tæn/ *verb* (*of skin*) to become brown in sunlight ○ *He tans easily.* ○ *She is using a tanning lotion.*

tannin /'tænɪn/, **tannic acid** /'tænɪk 'æsɪd/ *noun* a substance found in the bark of trees and in tea and other liquids, which stains brown

tantalum /'tæntələm/ *noun* a rare metal, used to repair damaged bones (NOTE: The chemical symbol is **Ta**.)

tantalum mesh /'tæntələm meʃ/ *noun* a type of net made of tantalum wire, used to repair cranial conditions

tantrum /'tæntrəm/ *noun* a sudden episode of bad behaviour, usually in a child, where the child throws things or lies on the floor and screams

tap /tæp/ *noun* **1.** a surgical procedure to drain off body fluid with a hollow needle or a tube **2.** a pipe with a closing valve and a handle which can be turned to make a liquid or gas come out of a container ■ *verb* **1.** to remove or drain liquid from part of the body. ◊ **spinal 2.** to hit someone or something lightly ○ *The doctor tapped his chest with his finger.*

tape /teɪp/ *noun* a long thin flat piece of material

tapeworm /'teɪpwɜːm/ *noun* a parasitic worm with a small head and long body like a ribbon. Tapeworms enter the intestine when a person eats raw meat or fish. The worms attach themselves with hooks to the side of the intestine and grow longer by adding sections to their bodies.

tapotement /tə'pəʊtmənt/ *noun* a type of massage where the therapist taps the person with his or her hands

tapping /'tæpɪŋ/ *noun* same as **paracentesis**

target /'tɑːgɪt/ *noun* a place which is to be hit by something ◊ **target cell, target organ 1.** cell or organ which is affected by a drug, by a hormone or by a disease **2.** large red blood cell which shows a red spot in the middle when stained

'…the target cells for adult myeloid leukaemia are located in the bone marrow' [*British Medical Journal*]

tarry stool /ˌtɑːri 'stuːl/ *noun* dark and sticky solid matter which is passed out of the bowels

tars- /tɑːs/ *prefix* same as **tarso-** (*used before vowels*)

tarsal /'tɑːs(ə)l/ *adjective* referring to the tarsus ■ *noun* same as **tarsal bone**

tarsal bone /'tɑːs(ə)l bəʊn/ *noun* one of seven small bones in the ankle, including the talus and calcaneus. Also called **tarsal**

tarsalgia /tɑː'sældʒə/ *noun* a pain in the ankle

tarsal gland /'tɑːs(ə)l glænd/ *noun* same as **meibomian gland**

tarsectomy /tɑː'sektəmi/ *noun* **1.** a surgical operation to remove one of the tarsal bones in the ankle **2.** a surgical operation to remove the tarsus of the eyelid

tarsitis /tɑː'saɪtɪs/ *noun* an inflammation of the edge of the eyelid

tarso- /tɑːsəʊ/ *prefix* **1.** relating to the ankle **2.** relating to the edge of the eyelid

tarsorrhaphy /tɑː'sɒrəfi/ *noun* an operation to join the two eyelids together to protect the eye after an operation

tarsotomy /tɑː'sɒtəmi/ *noun* an incision of the tarsus of the eyelid

tarsus /'tɑːsəs/ *noun* **1.** the seven small bones of the ankle. See illustration at FOOT in Supplement **2.** a connective tissue which supports an eyelid (NOTE: The plural is **tarsi**.)

COMMENT: The seven bones of the tarsus are: calcaneus, cuboid, the three cuneiforms, navicular and talus.

tartar /'tɑːtə/ noun a hard deposit of calcium which forms on teeth, and has to be removed by scaling. Also called **scale**

tartrazine /'tɑːtrəziːn/ noun a yellow substance (E102) added to food to give it an attractive colour. Although widely used, tartrazine provokes reactions in hypersensitive people and is banned in some countries.

task allocation /'tɑːsk ælə,keɪʃ(ə)n/ noun a system in which patient care is divided into tasks which are given to different nurses with specific skills

taste /teɪst/ noun one of the five senses, where food or substances in the mouth are noticed through the tongue ○ She doesn't like the taste of onions. ○ He has a cold, so food seems to have lost all taste or seems to have no taste. ■ verb 1. to notice the taste of something with the tongue ○ I have a cold so I can't taste anything ○ You can taste the salt in this butter. 2. to have a taste ○ The tablets taste of peppermint.

taste bud /'teɪst bʌd/ noun a tiny sensory receptor in the vallate and fungiform papillae of the tongue and in part of the back of the mouth

COMMENT: The taste buds can tell the difference between salt, sour, bitter and sweet tastes. The buds on the tip of the tongue identify salt and sweet tastes, those on the sides of the tongue identify sour, and those at the back of the mouth the bitter tastes. Note that most of what we think of as taste is in fact smell, and this is why when someone has a cold and a blocked nose, food seems to lose its taste. The impulses from the taste buds are received by the taste cortex in the temporal lobe of the cerebral hemisphere.

taurine /'tɔːriːn/ noun an amino acid which forms bile salts

taxis /'tæksɪs/ noun the procedure of pushing or massaging dislocated bones or hernias to make them return to their usual position

-taxis /tæksɪs/ suffix manipulation

taxonomy /tæk'sɒnəmi/ noun 1. the practice or principles of classification generally ○ Any diagnostic task can be aided by a taxonomy of symptoms and a taxonomy of causes together with connections between them. 2. the science of classifying plants, animals and microorganisms into increasingly broader categories based on shared features. Traditionally, organisms were grouped by physical resemblances, but recently other criteria such as genetic matching have also been used.

Tay-Sachs disease /,teɪ 'sæks dɪ,ziːz/ noun an inherited condition affecting the metabolism, characterised by progressive paralysis of the legs, blindness and learning disabilities [Described 1881. After Warren Tay (1843–1927), British ophthalmologist; Bernard Sachs (1858–1944), US neurologist.]

TB abbr tuberculosis ○ He is suffering from TB. ○ She has been admitted to a TB sanatorium.

T bandage /'tiː ,bændɪdʒ/ noun a bandage shaped like the letter T, used for bandaging the area between the legs

TBI abbreviation total body irradiation

T-cell /'tiː sel/ noun same as **T-lymphocyte**

TCP a trade name for various mild antiseptic liquids

t.d.s., TDS adverb (written on prescriptions) three times a day. Full form **ter in diem sumendus**

tea /tiː/ noun 1. the dried leaves of a plant used to make a hot drink 2. a hot drink made by pouring boiling water onto the dried leaves of a plant

teach /tiːtʃ/ verb 1. to give lessons in something ○ Professor Smith teaches neurosurgery. 2. to show someone how to do something ○ She was taught first aid by her mother. (NOTE: **teaching – taught**)

teaching hospital /'tiːtʃɪŋ ,hɒspɪt(ə)l/ noun a hospital attached to a medical school where student doctors work and study as part of their training

team /tiːm/ noun a group of people who work together ○ The heart-lung transplant was carried out by a team of surgeons.

team nursing /'tiːm ,nɜːsɪŋ/ noun a system in which the care of a group of patients is assigned to a team of four or five health workers, led by a professional nurse who assigns them various tasks. They meet at the beginning and end of each shift to exchange information.

tear /tɪə/ noun 1. a drop of the salty fluid which forms in the lacrimal gland. The fluid keeps the eyeball moist and clean and is produced in large quantities when a person cries. ○ Tears ran down her face. (NOTE: For other terms referring to tears, see words beginning with **dacryo-** or **lacrimal**.) □ **she burst into tears** she suddenly started to cry 2. /teə/ a hole or a split in a tissue often due to over-stretching ○ An episiotomy was needed to avoid a tear in the perineal tissue. ■ verb to make a hole or a split in a tissue by pulling or stretching it too much ○ He tore a ligament in his ankle. ○ They carried out an operation to repair a torn ligament. (NOTE: **tearing – tore – torn**)

tear duct /'tɪə dʌkt/ noun same as **lacrimal duct**

tear gland /'tɪə glænd/ noun same as **lacrimal gland**

teat /tiːt/ noun a rubber nipple on the end of a baby's feeding bottle

technician /tek'nɪʃ(ə)n/ noun a qualified person who does practical work in a laboratory or scientific institution ○ He is a laboratory technician in a laboratory attached to a teaching hospital.

technique /tek'niːk/ *noun* a way of doing scientific or medical work ○ *a new technique for treating osteoarthritis* ○ *She is trying out a new laboratory technique.*

'…few parts of the body are inaccessible to modern catheter techniques, which are all performed under local anaesthesia' [*British Medical Journal*]

'…the technique used to treat aortic stenosis is similar to that for any cardiac catheterization' [*Journal of the American Medical Association*]

'…cardiac resuscitation techniques used by over half the nurses in a recent study were described as 'completely ineffective'' [*Nursing Times*]

tectorial membrane /tek,tɔːriəl 'memˌbreɪn/ *noun* a membrane in the inner ear which contains the hair cells which transmit impulses to the auditory nerve

tectospinal tract /,tektəʊ,spaɪn(ə)l 'trækt/ *noun* a tract which takes nerve impulses from the mesencephalon to the spinal cord

TED *abbr* thrombo-embolic deterrent stocking

teeth /tiːθ/ plural of **tooth**

teething /'tiːðɪŋ/ *noun* the period when a baby's milk teeth are starting to erupt, and the baby is irritable ○ *He is awake at night because he is teething.* ○ *She has teething trouble and won't eat.*

Teflon /'teflɒn/ *trademark* a synthetic polymer injected into the joints of the larynx to increase movement and help hoarseness of voice

tegmen /'tegmən/ *noun* the covering for an organ (NOTE: The plural is **tegmina**.)

tegument /'tegjʊmənt/ *noun* a covering, especially the protective outer covering of an organism

tel- /tel/ *prefix* same as **tele-** (*used before vowels*)

tela /'tiːlə/ *noun* a delicate part or tissue in the body with a fine or intricate pattern like a web

telangiectasia /te,lændʒiek'teɪsiə/ *noun* a condition in which the small blood vessels, especially in the face and thighs, are permanently dilated producing dark red blotches

telangiectasis /te,lændʒi'ektəsɪs/, **telangiectasia** /te,lændʒiek'teɪsiə/ *noun* small dark red spots on the skin, formed by swollen capillaries

telangioma /te,lændʒi'əʊmə/ *noun* a tumour or haematoma of the blood capillaries

tele- /teli/ *prefix* referring to distance

teleceptor /'telɪseptə/ *noun* a sensory receptor which receives sensations from a distance. These occur in the eyes, ears and nose. Also called **telereceptor**

telemedicine /'telimed(ə)sɪn/ *noun* the provision of diagnosis and health care from a distance using media such as interactive computer programs or off-site advisers

telencephalon /,telen'kefəlɒn/ *noun* same as **cerebrum**

telepathy /tə'lepəθi/ *noun* the apparent communication directly from one person's mind to another person's, without the use of speech, writing or other signs or symbols

teleradiography /,telɪreɪdi'ɒɡrəfi/ *noun* a type of radiography where the source of the X-rays is at a distance from the person being X-rayed

teleradiology /,telɪreɪdi'ɒlədʒi/ *noun* the process of transmitting scans and other images electronically so that they can be viewed by surgeons or other health care workers in different locations at the same time

teleradiotherapy /telɪreɪdiəʊ'θerəpi/ *noun* a type of radiotherapy, where the person being treated is some way away from the source of radiation

telereceptor /'telɪrɪseptə/ *noun* same as **teleceptor**

telo- /teləʊ/ *prefix* referring to an end

telophase /'teləʊfeɪz/ *noun* the final stage of mitosis, the stage in cell division after anaphase

temazepam /tə'mæzɪpæm/ *noun* a hypnotic drug used in the short-term treatment of insomnia

temperature /'temprɪtʃə/ *noun* **1.** the heat of the body or of the surrounding air, measured in degrees ○ *The doctor asked the nurse what the patient's temperature was.* ○ *His temperature was slightly above normal.* ○ *The thermometer showed a temperature of 99°F.* □ **to take a patient's temperature** to insert a thermometer in someone's body to see what his or her body temperature is ○ *They took his temperature every four hours.* ○ *When her temperature was taken this morning, it was normal.* **2.** illness when your body is hotter than normal ○ *He's in bed with a temperature.* ○ *Her mother says she's got a temperature, and can't come to work.*

COMMENT: The average body temperature is about 37° Celsius or 98° Fahrenheit. This temperature may vary during the day, and can rise if a person has taken a hot bath or had a hot drink. If the environmental temperature is high, the body has to sweat to reduce the heat gained from the air around it. If the outside temperature is low, the body shivers, because rapid movement of the muscles generates heat. A fever will cause the body temperature to rise sharply, to 40°C (103°F) or more. Hypothermia exists when the body temperature falls below about 35°C (95°F).

temperature chart /'temprɪtʃə tʃɑːt/ *noun* a chart showing changes in a person's temperature over a period of time

temperature graph /'temprɪtʃə ɡrɑːf/ *noun* a graph showing how a person's temperature rises and falls over a period of time

temper tantrum /'tempə ,tæntrəm/ *noun* ♦ **tantrum**

temple /'tempəl/ *noun* the flat part of the side of the head between the top of the ear and the eye

temporal /'temp(ə)rəl/ *adjective* referring to the temple

temporal arteritis /,temp(ə)rəl ɑːtə'raɪtɪs/ *noun* a headache caused by inflammation of the region over the temporal artery, usually occurring in older people

temporal bone /'tempərəl bəʊn/ *noun* one of the bones which form the sides and base of the cranium. See illustration at EAR in Supplement

COMMENT: The temporal bone is in two parts: the petrous part forms the base of the skull and the inner and middle ears, while the squamous part forms the side of the skull. The lower back part of the temporal bone is the mastoid process, while the part between the ear and the cheek is the zygomatic arch.

temporal fossa /,temp(ə)rəl 'fɒsə/ *noun* a depression in the side of the head, in the temporal bone above the zygomatic arch

temporalis /,tempə'reɪlɪs/, **temporalis muscle** /,tempə'reɪlɪs ,mʌs(ə)l/ *noun* a flat muscle running down the side of the head from the temporal bone to the coronoid process, which makes the jaw move up

temporal lobe /'temp(ə)rəl ləʊb/ *noun* the lobe above the ear in each cerebral hemisphere

temporal lobe epilepsy /,temp(ə)rəl ləʊb 'epɪlepsi/ *noun* epilepsy due to a disorder of the temporal lobe and causing impaired memory, hallucinations and automatism

temporary /'temp(ə)rəri/ *adjective* not permanent ○ *The dentist gave him a temporary filling.* ○ *The accident team put a temporary bandage on the wound.*

temporo- /tempərəʊ/ *prefix* **1.** referring to the temple **2.** referring to the temporal lobe

temporomandibular /,tempərəʊmæn'dɪbjʊlə/ *adjective* relating to the temporal bone and the mandible

temporomandibular joint /,tempərəʊ mæn'dɪbjʊlə ,dʒɔɪnt/ *noun* a joint between the jaw and the skull, in front of the ear

temporomandibular syndrome /,tempərəʊmæn'dɪbjʊlə ,sɪndrəʊm/ *noun* a painful condition affecting the temporomandibular joint and the muscles used for chewing, usually associated with a faulty meeting of the teeth in biting and sometimes causing clicking sounds

tenacious /tɪ'neɪʃəs/ *adjective* sticking or clinging to something else, especially a surface

tenaculum /tə'nækjʊləm/ *noun* a surgical instrument shaped like a hook, used to pick up small pieces of tissue during an operation

tend /tend/ *verb* **1.** □ **to tend to do something** to be inclined to do something as a normal process ○ *The prostate tends to enlarge as a man grows older.* **2.** to care for or attend to someone or something

tendency /'tendənsi/ *noun* the fact of being likely to do something □ **to have a tendency to something** to be likely to have something ○ *There is a tendency to obesity in her family.* ○ *The children of the area show a tendency to vitamin-deficiency diseases.*

'…premature babies have been shown to have a higher tendency to develop a squint during childhood' [*Nursing Times*]

tender /'tendə/ *adjective* referring to skin or a body part which is painful when touched ○ *The bruise is still tender.* ○ *Her shoulders are still tender where she got sunburnt.* ○ *A tender spot on the abdomen indicates that an organ is inflamed.*

tenderness /'tendənəs/ *noun* a feel of pain when touched ○ *Tenderness when pressure is applied is a sign of inflammation.*

tendinitis /,tendɪ'naɪtɪs/ *noun* an inflammation of a tendon, especially after playing sport, and often associated with tenosynovitis

tendinous /'tendɪnəs/ *adjective* referring to a tendon

tendo calcaneus /,tendəʊ kæl'keɪniəs/ *noun* the Achilles tendon, the tendon at the back of the ankle which connects the calf muscles to the heel and which acts to pull up the heel when the calf muscle is contracted

tendon /'tendən/ *noun* a strip of connective tissue which attaches a muscle to a bone. Also called **sinew** (NOTE: For other terms referring to a tendon, see words beginning with **teno-**.)

tendonitis /,tendə'naɪtɪs/ *noun* same as **tendinitis**

tendon sheath /'tendən ʃiːθ/ *noun* a tube of membrane which covers and protects a tendon

tendovaginitis /,tendəʊvædʒɪ'naɪtɪs/ *noun* an inflammation of a tendon sheath, especially in the thumb

tenesmus /tə'nezməs/ *noun* a condition in which someone feels the need to pass faeces, or sometimes urine, but is unable to do so and experiences pain

tennis elbow /,tenɪs 'elbəʊ/ *noun* an inflammation of the tendons of the extensor muscles in the hand which are attached to the bone near the elbow. Also called **lateral epicondylitis**

teno- /tenəʊ/ *prefix* referring to a tendon

tenonitis /,tenəʊ'naɪtɪs/ *noun* the inflammation of a tendon

Tenon's capsule /'tiːnɒns ,kæpsjuːl/ *noun* a tissue which lines the orbit of the eye [After Jacques René Tenon (1724–1816), French surgeon]

tenoplasty /'tenəplæsti/ *noun* a surgical operation to repair a torn tendon

tenorrhaphy /te'nɒrəfi/ *noun* a surgical operation to stitch pieces of a torn tendon together

tenosynovitis /,tenəʊ,saɪnə'vaɪtɪs/ *noun* a painful inflammation of the tendon sheath and the tendon inside. Also called **peritendinitis**

tenotomy /təˈnɒtəmi/ *noun* a surgical operation to cut through a tendon

tenovaginitis /ˌtenəʊˌvædʒɪˈnaɪtɪs/ *noun* inflammation of the tendon sheath, especially in the thumb

TENS /tens/ *abbreviation* a method of treating pain by applying electrodes to the skin. Small electric currents are passed through sensory nerves and the spinal cord. This suppresses the transmission of pain signals. ○ *a TENS unit or machine* Full form **transcutaneous electrical nerve stimulation**

tense /tens/ *adjective* **1.** (*of a muscle*) contracted **2.** nervous and worried ○ *The patient was very tense while she waited for the report from the laboratory.*

tension /ˈtenʃən/ *noun* **1.** the act of stretching or the state of being stretched **2.** an emotional strain or stress

tension headache /ˈtenʃən ˌhedeɪk/ *noun* a headache all over the head, caused by worry and stress

tension pneumothorax /ˈtenʃən njuːməʊ ˌθɔːræks/ *noun* a condition of the pneumothorax in which rupture of the pleura forms an opening like a valve, through which air is forced during coughing but cannot escape

tensor /ˈtensə/ *noun* a muscle which makes a joint stretch out

tent /tent/ *noun* a small shelter put over and around someone's bed so that gas or vapour can be passed inside

tentorium cerebelli /tenˌtɔːriəm ˌserəˈbeli/ *noun* a part of the dura mater which separates the cerebellum from the cerebral hemispheres

tera- /terə/ *prefix* 10^{12}. Symbol **T**

terat- /ˈterət/, **terato-** /ˈterətəʊ/ *prefix* congenitally unusual

teratocarcinoma /ˌterətəʊkɑːsɪˈnəʊmə/ *noun* a malignant teratoma, usually in the testes

teratogen /təˈrætədʒen/ *noun* a substance which causes the usual development of an embryo or fetus to be disrupted, e.g. the German measles virus

teratogenesis /ˌterətəˈdʒenəsɪs/ *noun* an unusual pattern of development in an embryo and fetus

teratogenic /ˌterətəˈdʒenɪk/ *adjective* **1.** having the tendency to produce physical disorders in an embryo or fetus **2.** relating to the production of physical disorders in an embryo or fetus

teratology /ˌterəˈtɒlədʒi/ *noun* the study of the unhealthy development of embryos and fetuses

teratoma /ˌterəˈtəʊmə/ *noun* a tumour, especially in an ovary or testis, which is formed of tissue not usually found in that part of the body

terbutaline /tɜːˈbjuːtəliːn/ *noun* a drug which relaxes muscles, used in the treatment

of respiratory disorders and to control premature labour

teres /ˈtɪəriːz/ *noun* one of two shoulder muscles running from the shoulder blade to the top of the humerus. The larger of the two muscles, the teres major, makes the arm turn towards the inside, and the smaller, the teres minor, makes it turn towards the outside.

terfenadine /tɜːˈfenədiːn/ *noun* an antihistamine used in the treatment of hay fever and urticaria

term /tɜːm/ *noun* **1.** a limited period of time, especially the period from conception to childbirth, or a point in time determined for an event □ **she was coming near to term** she was near the time when she would give birth **2.** part of a college or school year ○ *The anatomy exams are at the beginning of the third term.* **3.** a name or word for a particular thing

terminal /ˈtɜːmɪn(ə)l/ *adjective* **1.** referring to the last stage of a fatal illness ○ *The disease is in its terminal stages.* **2.** referring to the end, being at the end of something ○ *He is suffering from terminal cancer.* ■ *noun* an ending, a part at the end of an electrode or nerve

terminal branch /ˈtɜːmɪn(ə)l brɑːntʃ/ *noun* the end part of a neurone which is linked to a muscle. See illustration at NEURONE in Supplement

terminale /ˌtɜːmɪˈneɪli/ ♦ **filum terminale**

terminal illness /ˌtɜːmɪn(ə)l ˈɪlnəs/ *noun* an illness from which someone will soon die

terminally ill /ˌtɜːmɪnəli ˈɪl/ *adjective* very ill and about to die ○ *She was admitted to a hospice for terminally ill patients* or *for the terminally ill.*

termination /ˌtɜːmɪˈneɪʃ(ə)n/ *noun* the act of ending something □ **termination (of pregnancy)** abortion

-terol /terɒl/ *suffix* used in names of bronchodilators

tertian /ˈtɜːʃ(ə)n/ *adjective* referring to a fever with symptoms which appear every other day ■ *noun* a tertian fever or set of symptoms

tertian fever /ˈtɜːʃ(ə)n ˌfiːvə/ *noun* a type of malaria where the fever returns every two days. ◊ **quartan fever**

tertiary /ˈtɜːʃəri/ *adjective* third, coming after secondary and primary

tertiary bronchi /ˌtɜːʃəri ˈbrɒŋkiː/ *plural noun* ◊ **syphilis.** Same as **segmental bronchi**

tertiary care /ˌtɜːʃəri ˈkeə/, **tertiary health care** /ˌtɜːʃəri ˈhelθ keə/ *noun* highly specialised treatment given in a health care centre, often using very advanced technology. Compare **primary care, secondary care**

test /test/ *noun* a short examination to see if a sample is healthy or if part of the body is working well ○ *He had an eye test this morning.* ○ *Laboratory tests showed that she was a meningitis carrier.* ○ *Tests are being carried out on* *swabs taken from the operating theatre.* □ **the urine test was positive** the examination of the urine sample showed the presence of an infection or a diagnostic substance ■ *verb* to examine a sample of tissue to see if it is healthy or an organ to see if it is working well ○ *They sent the urine sample away for testing.* ○ *I must have my eyes tested.*

testes /'testiːz/ plural of **testis**

testicle /'testɪk(ə)l/ *noun* same as **testis**

testicular /te'stɪkjʊlə/ *adjective* referring to the testes ○ *Testicular cancer comprises only 1% of all malignant neoplasms in the male.*

testicular artery /te,stɪkjʊlə 'ɑːtəri/ *noun* same as **spermatic artery**

testicular hormone /te,stɪkjʊlə 'hɔːməʊn/ *noun* testosterone

testis /'testɪs/ *noun* one of two male sex glands in the scrotum. See illustration at URO-GENITAL SYSTEM (MALE) in Supplement. Also called **testicle** (NOTE: The plural is **testes**. For other terms referring to the testes, see words beginning with **orchi-**.)

COMMENT: The testes produce both spermatozoa and the sex hormone, testosterone. Spermatozoa are formed in the testes, and passed into the epididymis to be stored. From the epididymis they pass along the vas deferens through the prostate gland which secretes the seminal fluid, and are ejaculated through the penis.

test meal /'test miːl/ *noun* a test to check the secretion of gastric juices, no longer much used

testosterone /te'stɒstərəʊn/ *noun* a male sex hormone, secreted by the Leydig cells in the testes, which causes physical changes, e.g. the development of body hair and a deep voice, to take place in males as they become sexually mature

test tube /'test tjuːb/ *noun* a small glass tube with a rounded bottom, used in laboratories to hold samples of liquids

test-tube baby /'test tjuːb ,beɪbi/ *noun* a baby conceived through in vitro fertilisation in which the mother's ova are removed from the ovaries, fertilised with a man's spermatozoa in a laboratory, and returned to the mother's uterus to continue developing in the usual way

tetanic /te'tænɪk/ *adjective* referring to tetanus

tetano- /tetənəʊ/ *prefix* **1.** relating to tetanus **2.** relating to tetany

tetanus /'tet(ə)nəs/ *noun* **1.** the continuous contraction of a muscle, under repeated stimuli from a motor nerve **2.** an infection caused by *Clostridium tetani* in the soil, which affects the spinal cord and causes spasms in the muscles which occur first in the jaw. Also called **lockjaw**

COMMENT: People who are liable to infection with tetanus, such as farm workers, should be immunised against it, and booster injections are needed from time to time.

tetany /'tetəni/ *noun* spasms of the muscles in the feet and hands, caused by a reduction in the level of calcium in the blood or by lack of carbon dioxide

tetra- /tetrə/ *prefix* four

tetracycline /,tetrə'saɪkliːn/ *noun* an antibiotic of a group used to treat a wide range of bacterial diseases such as chlamydia. However, they are deposited in bones and teeth and cause a permanent yellow stain in teeth if given to children.

COMMENT: Because of its side-effects tetracycline should not be given to children. Many bacteria are now resistant to tetracycline.

tetradactyly /,tetrə'dæktɪli/ *noun* a congenital condition in which a child has only four fingers or toes

tetralogy of Fallot /te,trælədʒi əv 'fæləʊ/ *noun* a disorder of the heart which makes a child's skin blue. Also called **Fallot's tetralogy.** ◊ **Blalock's operation, Waterston's operation**

COMMENT: The condition is formed of four conditions occurring together: the artery leading to the lungs is narrow, the right ventricle is enlarged, there is a disorder in the membrane between the ventricles and the aorta is not correctly placed.

tetraplegia /,tetrə'pliːdʒə/ same as **quadriplegia**

textbook /'tekstbʊk/ *noun* a book which is used by students ○ *a haematology textbook* or *a textbook on haematology*

textbook case /'tekstbʊk keɪs/ *noun* a case which shows symptoms which are exactly like those described in a textbook, a very typical case

thalam- /θæləm/ *prefix* same as **thalamo-** (*used before vowels*)

thalamencephalon /,θæləmen'kefəlɒn/ *noun* a group of structures in the brain linked to the brain stem, formed of the epithalamus, hypothalamus and thalamus

thalamic syndrome /θə'læmɪk ,sɪndrəʊm/ *noun* a condition in which someone is extremely sensitive to pain, caused by a disorder of the thalamus

thalamo- /θæləməʊ/ *prefix* referring to the thalamus

thalamocortical tract /,θæləməʊ ,kɔːtɪk(ə)l 'trækt/ *noun* a tract containing nerve fibres, running from the thalamus to the sensory cortex

thalamotomy /,θælə'mɒtəmi/ *noun* a surgical operation to make an incision into the thalamus to treat intractable pain

thalamus /'θæləməs/ *noun* one of two masses of grey matter situated beneath the cerebrum where impulses from the sensory neurones are transmitted to the cerebral cortex.

See illustration at BRAIN in Supplement (NOTE: The plural is **thalami.**)

thalassaemia /ˌθælæˈsiːmiə/ noun a hereditary disorder of which there are several forms caused by an anomalies in the protein component of the haemoglobin, leading to severe anaemia. It is found especially in people from Mediterranean countries, the Middle East and East Asia. Also called **Cooley's anaemia**

thalidomide /θəˈlɪdəmaɪd/ noun a synthetic drug given to pregnant women for morning sickness in the 1960s which caused babies to be born with stunted limbs. It is now used in the treatment of leprosy.

thallium scan /ˈθæliəm skæn/ noun a method of finding out about the blood supply to the heart muscle by scanning to see how the radioactive element thallium moves when injected into the bloodstream and where it attaches itself to the heart wall

thanatology /ˌθænəˈtɒlədʒi/ noun the study of the medical, psychological and sociological aspects of death and the ways in which people deal with it

thaw /θɔː/ verb to bring something which is frozen back to usual temperature

theatre /ˈθɪətə/ noun ♦ **operating theatre**
'While waiting to go to theatre, parents should be encouraged to participate in play with their children' [British Journal of Nursing]

theatre gown /ˈθɪətə ɡaʊn/ noun **1.** a loose piece of clothing worn by a person having an operation **2.** a long green robe worn over other clothes by a surgeon or nurse in an operating theatre

theatre nurse /ˈθɪətə nɜːs/ noun a nurse who is specially trained to assist a surgeon during an operation

theca /ˈθiːkə/ noun tissue shaped like a sheath

thelarche /ˈθelɑːki/ noun the beginning of the process of breast development in young women

thenar /ˈθiːnə/ adjective referring to the palm of the hand ■ noun the palm of the hand. Compare **hypothenar**

thenar eminence /ˌθiːnər ˈemɪnəns/ noun the ball of the thumb, the lump of flesh in the palm of the hand below the thumb

theophylline /θiˈɒfɪliːn/ noun a compound made synthetically or extracted from tea leaves which helps to widen blood vessels and airways, and to stimulate the central nervous system and heart. It is used in the treatment of breathing disorders.

theory /ˈθɪəri/ noun an argument which explains a scientific fact

therapeutic /ˌθerəˈpjuːtɪk/ adjective given in order to cure a disorder or disease

therapeutic abortion /ˌθerəpjuːtɪk əˈbɔːʃ(ə)n/ noun an abortion which is carried out because the health of the mother is in danger

therapeutic index /ˌθerəpjuːtɪk ˈɪndeks/ noun the ratio of the dose of a drug which causes cell damage to the dose of that drug which is typically needed to effect a cure, by which the safety of the drug is decided

therapeutic radiographer /ˌθerəˌpjuːtɪk ˌreɪdiˈɒɡrəfə/ noun someone specially trained to use X-rays or radioactive isotopes in the treatment of patients

therapeutics /ˌθerəˈpjuːtɪks/ noun the study of various types of treatment and their effect on patients

therapist /ˈθerəpɪst/ noun a person specially trained to give therapy ○ an occupational therapist ◊ **psychotherapist**

therapy /ˈθerəpi/ noun the treatment of a person to help cure a disease or disorder

therm /θɜːm/ noun a unit of heat equal to 100,000 British thermal units or 1.055×10^8 joules

thermal /ˈθɜːm(ə)l/ adjective referring to heat

thermal anaesthesia /ˌθɜːm(ə)l ˌænəsˈθiːziə/ noun the loss of the feeling of heat

thermo- /θɜːməʊ/ prefix referring to heat or temperature

thermoanaesthesia /ˌθɜːməʊˌænəsˈθiːziə/ noun a condition in which someone cannot tell the difference between hot and cold

thermocautery /ˌθɜːməʊˈkɔːtəri/ noun the procedure of removing dead tissue by heat

thermocoagulation /ˌθɜːməʊkəʊˌæɡjuˈleɪʃ(ə)n/ noun the procedure of removing tissue and coagulating blood by heat

thermogram /ˈθɜːməɡræm/ noun an infrared photograph of part of the body

thermograph /ˈθɜːməʊɡrɑːf/ noun a device that shows patterns of heat radiated from a body, used in diagnosis

thermography /θɜːˈmɒɡrəfi/ noun a technique, used especially in screening for breast cancer, where part of the body is photographed using infrared rays which record the heat given off by the skin and show variations in the blood circulating beneath the skin

thermolysis /θɜːˈmɒləsɪs/ noun a loss of body temperature, e.g. by sweating

thermometer /θəˈmɒmɪtə/ noun an instrument for measuring temperature

thermophilic /ˌθɜːməʊˈfɪlɪk/ adjective referring to an organism which needs a high temperature to grow

thermoreceptor /ˌθɜːməʊrɪˈseptə/ noun a sensory nerve which registers heat

thermotaxis /ˌθɜːməʊˈtæksɪs/ noun an automatic regulation of the body's temperature

thermotherapy /ˌθɜːməʊˈθerəpi/ noun treatment using heat, e.g. from hot water or infrared lamps, to treat conditions such as arthritis and bad circulation. Also called **heat therapy**

thiamine /ˈθaɪəmiːn/, **thiamin** /ˈθaɪəmɪn/ noun same as **Vitamin B₁**

thicken /'θɪkən/ *verb* **1.** to become wider or larger, or cause something to become wider or larger ○ *The walls of the arteries thicken under deposits of fat.* **2.** (*of liquid*) to become more dense and viscid and flow less easily ○ *The liquid thickens as its cools.*

Thiersch graft /'tɪəʃ grɑːft/, **Thiersch's graft** /'tɪəʃɪz grɑːft/ same as **split-skin graft**

thigh /θaɪ/ *noun* the top part of the leg from the knee to the groin

thighbone /'θaɪbəʊn/ *noun* the femur, the bone in the top part of the leg, which joins the acetabulum at the hip and the tibia at the knee (NOTE: For other terms referring to the thigh, see **femoral**.)

thin /θɪn/ *adjective* **1.** not fat ○ *His arms are very thin.* ○ *She's getting too thin – she should eat more.* ○ *He became quite thin after his illness.* **2.** not thick ○ *They cut a thin slice of tissue for examination under the microscope.* **3.** referring to blood which is watery (NOTE: **thinner – thinnest**)

thiopental sodium /,θaɪəʊpent(ə)l 'səʊdiəm/ *noun* a barbiturate drug used as a rapid-acting intravenous general anaesthetic. Also called **thiopentone**

thiopentone /,θaɪəʊ'pentəʊn/, **thiopentone sodium** /,θaɪəʊpentəʊn 'səʊdiəm/ *noun* same as **thiopental sodium** (NOTE: Its chemical formula is $C_{11}H_{17}N_2O2SNa$.)

thioridazine /,θaɪəʊ'rɪdəziːn/ *noun* a synthetic compound used as a tranquilliser for people who are suffering from a psychosis

third-degree burn /,θɜːd dɪ,griː 'bɜːn/ *noun* a burn in which the skin and the tissues beneath it are severely damaged

third-degree haemorrhoids /θɜːd dɪ'griː/ *plural noun* haemorrhoids which protrude into the anus permanently

third molar /θɜːd 'məʊlə/ *noun* one of the four molars at the back of the jaw, which only appears at about the age of 20 and sometimes does not appear at all. Same as **wisdom tooth**

thirst /θɜːst/ *noun* a feeling of wanting to drink ○ *He had a fever and a violent thirst.*

thirsty /'θɜːsti/ *adjective* wanting to drink ○ *If the patient is thirsty, give her a glass of water.* (NOTE: **thirstier – thirstiest**)

Thomas's splint /'tɒməsɪz splɪnt/, **Thomas splint** /'tɒməs splɪnt/ *noun* a metal splint used to keep a fractured leg still. It has a padded ring at the hip attached to rods to which bandages are bound and a bar under the foot at the lower end. [Described 1875. After Hugh Owen Thomas (1834–91), British surgeon and bonesetter.]

thorac- /θɔːrəs/ *prefix* same as **thoraco-** (*used before vowels*)

thoracectomy /,θɔːrə'sektəmi/ *noun* a surgical operation to remove one or more ribs

thoracentesis /,θɔːrəsen'tiːsɪs/ *noun* same as **thoracocentesis**

thoraces /'θɔːrəsiːz/ plural of **thorax**

thoracic /θɔː'ræsɪk/ *adjective* referring to the chest or thorax

thoracic aorta /θɔː,ræsɪk eɪ'ɔːtə/ *noun* part of the aorta which crosses the thorax

thoracic cavity /θɔː,ræsɪk 'kævɪti/ *noun* the chest cavity, containing the diaphragm, heart and lungs

thoracic duct /θɔː'ræsɪk dʌkt/ *noun* one of the main terminal ducts carrying lymph, on the left side of the neck

thoracic inlet /θɔː,ræsɪk 'ɪnlət/ *noun* a small opening at the top of the thorax

thoracic outlet /θɔː,ræsɪk 'aʊtlet/ *noun* a large opening at the bottom of the thorax

thoracic outlet syndrome /θɔː,ræsɪk 'aʊtlet ,sɪndrəʊm/ *noun* same as **scalenus syndrome**

thoracic vertebrae /θɔː,ræsɪk 'vɜːtɪbriː/ *plural noun* the twelve vertebrae in the spine behind the chest, to which the ribs are attached

thoraco- /θɔːrəkəʊ/ *prefix* relating to the thorax

thoracocentesis /,θɔːrəkəʊsen'tiːsɪs/ *noun* an operation in which a hollow needle is inserted into the pleura to drain fluid

thoracolumbar /,θɔːrəkəʊ'lʌmbə/ *adjective* referring to the thoracic and lumbar areas of the body

thoracoplasty /'θɔːrəkəʊplæsti/ *noun* a surgical operation to cut through the ribs to allow the lungs to collapse, formerly a treatment for pulmonary tuberculosis

thoracoscope /'θɔːrəkəskəʊp/ *noun* a surgical instrument, like a tube with a light at the end, used to examine the inside of the chest

thoracoscopy /,θɔːrə'kɒskəpi/ *noun* an examination of the inside of the chest, using a thoracoscope

thoracotomy /,θɔːrə'kɒtəmi/ *noun* a surgical operation to make a hole in the wall of the chest

thorax /'θɔːræks/ *noun* the cavity in the top part of the front of the body above the abdomen, containing the diaphragm, heart and lungs, and surrounded by the ribcage

thread /θred/ *noun* a thin piece of cotton, suture, etc. ○ *The surgeon used strong thread to make the suture.* ■ *verb* to insert a thin piece of cotton, suture, etc. through the eye of a needle

thread vein /'θred veɪn/ *noun* a fine vein that is visible through the skin

threadworm /'θredwɜːm/ *noun* a thin parasitic worm, *Enterobius vernicularis*, which infests the large intestine and causes itching round the anus. ♦ **Enterobius**. Also called **pinworm**

thready /'θredi/ *adjective* referring to a pulse which is very weak and can hardly be felt

thready pulse /ˌθredi ˈpʌls/ *noun* a very weak pulse which is hard to detect

threatened abortion /ˌθret(ə)nd ə ˈbɔːʃ(ə)n/ *noun* a possible abortion in the early stages of pregnancy, indicated by bleeding

threonine /ˈθriːəniːn/ *noun* an essential amino acid

threshold /ˈθreʃhəʊld/ *noun* **1.** the point at which something starts, e.g. where something can be perceived by the body or where a drug starts to have an effect ○ *She has a low hearing threshold.* **2.** the point at which a sensation is strong enough to be sensed by the sensory nerves

'...if intracranial pressure rises above the treatment threshold, it is imperative first to validate the reading and then to eliminate any factors exacerbating the rise in pressure' [*British Journal of Hospital Medicine*]

thrill /θrɪl/ *noun* a vibration which can be felt with the hands

thrive /θraɪv/ *verb* to do well, to live and grow strongly

-thrix /θrɪks/ *suffix* relating to a hair

throat /θrəʊt/ *noun* **1.** the top part of the tube which goes down from the mouth to the stomach **2.** the front part of the neck below the chin □ **to clear the throat** to give a little cough

COMMENT: The throat carries both food from the mouth and air from the nose and mouth. It divides into the oesophagus, which takes food to the stomach, and the trachea, which takes air into the lungs.

throb /θrɒb/ *verb* **1.** (*of the heart*) to beat harder and faster than usual, especially from exertion or fear **2.** (*of a painful part of the body*) to experience pain which comes and goes regularly ○ *Once the local anaesthetic wore off his thumb began to throb.*

throbbing /ˈθrɒbɪŋ/ *adjective* referring to pain which comes again and again like a heart beat ○ *She has a throbbing pain in her finger.* ○ *He has a throbbing headache.*

throbbing pain /ˌθrɒbɪŋ ˈpeɪn/ *noun* pain which continues in repeated short attacks

thrombectomy /θrɒmˈbektəmi/ *noun* a surgical operation to remove a blood clot

thrombin /ˈθrɒmbɪn/ *noun* a substance which converts fibrinogen to fibrin and so coagulates blood

thrombo- /θrɒmbəʊ/ *prefix* **1.** referring to a blood clot **2.** referring to thrombosis

thromboangiitis /ˌθrɒmbəʊˌændʒiˈaɪtɪs/ *noun* a condition in which the blood vessels swell and develop blood clots along their walls

thromboangiitis obliterans /ˌθrɒmbəʊændʒiˌaɪtɪs əbˈlɪtərənz/ *noun* a disease of the arteries in which the blood vessels in a limb, usually the leg, become narrow, causing gangrene. Also called **Buerger's disease**

thromboarteritis /ˌθrɒmbəʊˌɑːtəˈraɪtɪs/ *noun* inflammation of an artery caused by thrombosis

thrombocyte /ˈθrɒmbəʊsaɪt/ *noun* same as **platelet**

thrombocythaemia /ˌθrɒmbəʊsaɪˈθiːmiə/ *noun* a disease in which someone has an unusually high number of platelets in the blood

thrombocytopenia /ˌθrɒmbəʊˌsaɪtəʊˈpiːniə/ *noun* a condition in which someone has an unusually low number of platelets in the blood

thrombocytopenic /ˌθrɒmbəʊˌsaɪtəʊˈpenɪk/ *adjective* referring to thrombocytopenia

thrombocytosis /ˌθrɒmbəʊsaɪˈtəʊsɪs/ *noun* an increase in the number of platelets in someone's blood

thrombo-embolic deterrent stocking /ˌθrɒmbəʊ emˌbɒlɪk dɪˈterənt ˌstɒkɪŋ/ *noun* a support stocking to prevent thrombus formation following surgery. Abbr **TED**

thromboembolism /ˌθrɒmbəʊˈembəlɪz(ə)m/ *noun* a condition in which a blood clot forms in one part of the body and moves through the blood vessels to block another, usually smaller, part

thromboendarterectomy /ˌθrɒmbəʊˌendɑːtəˈrektəmi/ *noun* a surgical operation to open an artery to remove a blood clot which is blocking it

thromboendarteritis /ˌθrɒmbəʊˌendɑːtəˈraɪtɪs/ *noun* inflammation of the inside of an artery, caused by thrombosis

thrombokinase /ˌθrɒmbəʊˈkaɪneɪz/ *noun* an enzyme which converts prothrombin into thrombin, so starting the sequence for coagulation of blood. Also called **thromboplastin**

thrombolysis /θrɒmˈbɒləsɪs/ *noun* same as **fibrinolysis**

thrombolytic /ˌθrɒmbəʊˈlɪtɪk/ *adjective* same as **fibrinolytic**

thrombophlebitis /ˌθrɒmbəʊflɪˈbaɪtɪs/ *noun* the blocking of a vein by a blood clot, sometimes causing inflammation

thromboplastic /ˌθrɒmbəʊˈplæstɪk/ *adjective* causing or increasing the formation of blood clots

thromboplastin /ˌθrɒmbəʊˈplæstɪn/ *noun* same as **thrombokinase**

thrombopoiesis /ˌθrɒmbəʊpɔɪˈiːsɪs/ *noun* the process by which blood platelets are formed

thrombose /θrɒmˈbəʊz/ *verb* to cause thrombosis in a blood vessel, or be affected by thrombosis

thrombosis /θrɒmˈbəʊsɪs/ *noun* the blocking of an artery or vein by a mass of coagulated blood

thrombus /ˈθrɒmbəs/ *noun* same as **blood clot**

throw up /ˌθrəʊ ˈʌp/ *verb* same as **vomit** (*informal*)

thrush /θrʌʃ/ *noun* an infection of the mouth or the vagina with the bacterium *Candida albicans*

thumb /θʌm/ *noun* the short thick finger, with only two bones, which is separated from the other four fingers on the hand

thumb-sucking /ˈθʌm ˌsʌkɪŋ/ *noun* the action of sucking a thumb ○ *Thumb-sucking tends to push the teeth forward.*

thym- /θaɪm/ *prefix* referring to the thymus gland

thymectomy /θaɪˈmektəmi/ *noun* a surgical operation to remove the thymus gland

-thymia /θaɪmiə/ *suffix* referring to a state of mind

thymic /ˈθaɪmɪk/ *adjective* referring to the thymus gland

thymine /ˈθaɪmiːn/ *noun* one of the four basic chemicals in DNA

thymitis /θaɪˈmaɪtɪs/ *noun* inflammation of the thymus gland

thymocyte /ˈθaɪməʊsaɪt/ *noun* a lymphocyte formed in the thymus gland

thymol /ˈθaɪmɒl/ *noun* a colourless compound which is made synthetically or extracted from thyme oil, used as an antiseptic

thymoma /θaɪˈməʊmə/ *noun* a tumour in the thymus gland

thymus /ˈθaɪməs/, **thymus gland** /ˈθaɪməs glænd/ *noun* an endocrine gland in the front part of the top of the thorax, behind the breastbone

COMMENT: The thymus gland produces lymphocytes and is responsible for developing the system of natural immunity in children. It grows less active as the person becomes an adult. Lymphocytes produced by the thymus are known as T-lymphocytes or T-cells.

thyro- /θaɪrəʊ/ *prefix* referring to the thyroid gland

thyrocalcitonin /ˌθaɪrəʊkælsiˈtəʊnɪn/ *noun* same as **calcitonin**

thyrocele /ˈθaɪrəʊsiːl/ *noun* swelling of the thyroid gland

thyroglobulin /ˌθaɪrəʊˈɡlɒbjʊlɪn/ *noun* protein stored in the thyroid gland which is broken down into thyroxine

thyroglossal /ˌθaɪrəʊˈɡlɒsəl/ *adjective* referring to the thyroid gland and the throat

thyroglossal cyst /ˌθaɪrəʊɡlɒsəl ˈsɪst/ *noun* a cyst in the front of the neck

thyroid /ˈθaɪrɔɪd/, **thyroid gland** *noun* /ˈθaɪrɔɪd glænd/ an endocrine gland in the neck, which is activated by the pituitary gland and secretes a hormone which regulates the body's metabolism ■ *adjective* referring to the thyroid gland

COMMENT: The thyroid gland needs a supply of iodine in order to produce thyroxine. If the thyroid gland malfunctions, it can result in hyperthyroidism (producing too much thyroxine) leading to goitre, or in hypothyroidism (producing too little thyroxine). Hyperthyroidism can be treated with carbimazole.

thyroid cartilage /ˌθaɪrɔɪd ˈkɑːtɪlɪdʒ/ *noun* a large cartilage in the larynx, part of which forms the Adam's apple. See illustration at LUNGS in Supplement

thyroid depressant /ˈθaɪrɔɪd dɪˌpres(ə)nt/ *noun* a drug which reduces the activity of the thyroid gland

thyroid dysfunction /ˈθaɪrɔɪd dɪsˌfʌŋkʃ(ə)n/ *noun* malfunction of the thyroid gland

thyroidectomy /ˌθaɪrɔɪˈdektəmi/ *noun* a surgical operation to remove all or part of the thyroid gland

thyroid extract /ˈθaɪrɔɪd ˌekstrækt/ *noun* a substance extracted from thyroid glands of animals and used to treat hypothyroidism

thyroid gland /ˈθaɪrɔɪd glænd/ *noun* same as **thyroid**

thyroid hormone /ˈθaɪrɔɪd ˌhɔːməʊn/ *noun* a hormone produced by the thyroid gland

thyroiditis /ˌθaɪrɔɪˈdaɪtɪs/ *noun* inflammation of the thyroid gland

thyroid-stimulating hormone /ˈθaɪrɔɪd ˌstɪmjʊleɪtɪŋ ˌhɔːməʊn/ *noun* a hormone secreted by the pituitary gland which stimulates the thyroid gland. Abbr **TSH**. Also called **thyrotrophin**

thyroparathyroidectomy /ˌθaɪrəʊˌpærəˌθaɪrɔɪˈdektəmi/ *noun* a surgical operation to remove the thyroid and parathyroid glands

thyroplasty /ˈθaɪrəʊplæsti/ *noun* a surgical procedure performed on the cartilages of the larynx to improve the quality of the voice

thyrotomy /θaɪˈrɒtəmi/ *noun* a surgical opening made in the thyroid cartilage or the thyroid gland

thyrotoxic /ˌθaɪrəʊˈtɒksɪk/ *adjective* referring to severe hyperthyroidism

thyrotoxic crisis /ˌθaɪrəʊˌtɒksɪk ˈkraɪsɪs/ *noun* a sudden illness caused by hyperthyroidism

thyrotoxic goitre /ˌθaɪrəʊˌtɒksɪk ˈɡɔɪtə/ *noun* overactivity of the thyroid gland, as in hyperthyroidism

thyrotoxicosis /ˌθaɪrəʊtɒksɪˈkəʊsɪs/ *noun* same as **hyperthyroidism**

thyrotrophin /ˌθaɪrəʊˈtrəʊfɪn/ *noun* same as **thyroid-stimulating hormone** (NOTE: The US term is **thyrotropin**.)

thyrotrophin-releasing hormone /ˌθaɪrəʊˌtrəʊfɪn rɪˈliːsɪŋ ˌhɔːməʊn/ *noun* a hormone secreted by the hypothalamus, which makes the pituitary gland release thyrotrophin, which in turn stimulates the thyroid gland. Abbr **TRH**

thyroxine /θaɪˈrɒksiːn/ *noun* a hormone produced by the thyroid gland which regulates the body's metabolism and the conversion of food into heat, used in treatment of hypothyroidism

TIA *abbr* transient ischaemic attack

'...blood pressure control reduces the incidence of first stroke and aspirin appears to reduce the risk of stroke after TIAs by some 15%' [*British Journal of Hospital Medicine*]

tibia /'tɪbɪə/ *noun* the larger of the two long bones in the lower leg between the knee and the ankle. Also called **shinbone**. Compare **fibula**

tibial /'tɪbɪəl/ *adjective* referring to the tibia

tibial artery /'tɪbɪəl ˌɑːtəri/ *noun* one of two arteries which run down the front and back of the lower leg

tibialis /ˌtɪbɪ'eɪlɪs/ *noun* one of two muscles in the lower leg running from the tibia to the foot

tibial torsion /ˌtɪbɪəl 'tɔːʃ(ə)n/ *noun* a persistent slight twist in the tibia, caused by a cramped position in the uterus. It makes the feet of young children point inwards for up to a year after they begin to walk on their own, but it corrects itself as the leg grows.

tibio- /tɪbɪəʊ/ *prefix* referring to the tibia

tibiofibular /ˌtɪbɪəʊ'fɪbjʊlə/ *adjective* referring to both the tibia and the fibula

tic /tɪk/ *noun* an involuntary twitch of the muscles usually in the face (*informal*)

tic douloureux /tɪk duːlə'ruː/ *noun* same as **trigeminal neuralgia**

tick /tɪk/ *noun* a tiny parasite which sucks blood from the skin

tick fever /'tɪk ˌfiːvə/ *noun* an infectious disease transmitted by bites from ticks

t.i.d., TID *adverb* (*used on prescriptions*) three times a day. Full form **ter in die**

tidal air /'taɪd(ə)l ˌeə/, **tidal volume** /ˌtaɪd(ə)l 'vɒljuːm/ *noun* the amount of air that passes in and out of the body in breathing

-tidine /tɪdiːn/ *suffix* used for antihistamine drugs

tie /taɪ/ *verb* to attach a thread with a knot ○ *The surgeon quickly tied up the stitches.* ○ *The nurse had tied the bandage too tight.* (NOTE: **tying – tied**)

timolol /'tɪmələl/ *noun* a beta-blocker used in the treatment of migraine, high blood pressure and glaucoma

tinct. *abbr* tincture

tincture /'tɪŋktʃə/ *noun* a medicinal substance dissolved in alcohol

tincture of iodine /ˌtɪŋktʃər əv 'aɪədiːn/ *noun* a weak solution of iodine in alcohol, used as an antiseptic

tinea /'tɪnɪə/ *noun* ♦ ringworm

tinea barbae /ˌtɪnɪə 'bɑːbiː/ *noun* a fungal infection in the beard

tinea capitis /ˌtɪnɪə kə'paɪtɪs/ *noun* a fungal infection on the scalp

tinea cruris /ˌtɪnɪə 'kruːrɪs/ *noun* a fungal infection of the groin area, especially in hot climates

tinea pedis /ˌtɪnɪə 'pedɪs/ *noun* same as **athlete's foot**

tingle /'tɪŋɡəl/ *verb* to have a pricking or stinging sensation in a body part

tingling /'tɪŋɡlɪŋ/ *noun* a feeling of pricking or stinging in a body part ○ *an unpleasant tingling down her arm* ■ *adjective* pricking or stinging ○ *a tingling sensation*

tinnitus /'tɪnɪtəs/ *noun* a condition in which someone hears a ringing sound in the ears

COMMENT: Tinnitus can sound like bells, or buzzing, or a loud roaring sound. In some cases it is caused by wax blocking the auditory canal, but it is also associated with Ménière's disease, infections of the middle ear and acoustic nerve conditions.

tipped womb /ˌtɪpt 'wuːm/ *noun* US same as **retroverted uterus**

tired /'taɪəd/ *adjective* feeling a need to rest

tiredness /'taɪədnəs/ *noun* the condition of being tired

tired out /ˌtaɪəd 'aʊt/ *adjective* feeling extremely tired ○ *She is tired out after the physiotherapy.*

tissue /'tɪʃuː/ *noun* a group of cells that carries out a specific function (NOTE: For other terms referring to tissue, see words beginning with **hist-, histo-**.)

COMMENT: Most of the body is made up of soft tissue, with the exception of the bones and cartilage. The main types of body tissue are connective, epithelial, muscular and nerve tissue.

tissue culture /'tɪʃuː ˌkʌltʃə/ *noun* tissue grown in a culture medium in a laboratory

tissue plasminogen activator /ˌtɪʃuː plæz'mɪnədʒən ˌæktɪveɪtə/ *noun* an agent given to cause fibrinolysis in blood clots. Abbr **TPA**

tissue type /'tɪʃuː taɪp/ *noun* the immunological characteristics of a tissue that determine whether or not it can be successfully transplanted into another person

tissue typing /'tɪʃuː ˌtaɪpɪŋ/ *noun* the process of identifying various elements in tissue from a donor and comparing them to those of the recipient to see if a transplant is likely to be rejected

titanium /taɪ'teɪnɪəm/ *noun* a light metallic element which does not corrode (NOTE: The chemical symbol is **Ti**.)

titration /taɪ'treɪʃ(ə)n/ *noun* the process of measuring the strength of a solution

titre /'tiːtə/ *noun* a measurement of the quantity of antibodies in a serum

T-lymphocyte /'tiː ˌlɪmfəsaɪt/ *noun* a lymphocyte formed in the thymus gland. Also called **T-cell**

TNM classification /ˌtiː en 'em klæsɪfɪˌkeɪʃ(ə)n/ *noun* an internationally agreed standard which is the most widely used means for classifying the extent of cancer. T refers to the size of the tumour, N to the lymph node involvement and M to the presence or absence of metastasis.

toco- /təʊkəʊ/ *prefix* referring to childbirth

tocography /tɒˈkɒɡrəfi/ *noun* the process of recording the contractions of the uterus during childbirth

tocopherol /tɒˈkɒfərɒl/ *noun* one of a group of fat-soluble compounds which make up vitamin E, found in vegetable oils and leafy green vegetables

toddler's diarrhoea /ˌtɒdləz daɪəˈriːə/ *noun* a condition in which recurrent loose stools are produced, often containing partially digested food. It usually occurs in children between the ages of one and three years.

Todd's paralysis /ˈtɒdz pəˌræləsɪs/, **Todd's palsy** /ˈtɒdz ˌpɔːlzi/ *noun* a temporary paralysis of part of the body which has been the starting point of focal epilepsy

toe /təʊ/ *noun* one of the five separate parts at the end of the foot. Each toe is formed of three bones or phalanges, except the big toe, which only has two.

toenail /ˈtəʊneɪl/ *noun* a thin hard growth covering the end of a toe

toileting /ˈtɔɪlətɪŋ/ *noun* the act of helping someone to perform the actions of urinating or opening their bowels, including helping them to do so if they are unable to get out of bed or are incontinent

toilet training /ˈtɔɪlət ˌtreɪnɪŋ/ *noun* the process of teaching a small child to pass urine or faeces in a toilet, so that he or she no longer requires nappies

tolbutamide /tɒlˈbjuːtəmaɪd/ *noun* a drug which lowers blood-glucose levels by stimulating the pancreas to produce more insulin. It is used in the treatment of Type II diabetes.

tolerance /ˈtɒlərəns/ *noun* the ability of the body to tolerate a substance or an action ○ *He has been taking the drug for so long that he has developed a tolerance to it.*

'26 patients were selected from the outpatient department on grounds of disabling breathlessness, severely limiting exercise tolerance and the performance of activities of normal daily living' [*Lancet*]

tolerate /ˈtɒləreɪt/ *verb* **1.** not to be affected by the unpleasant effects of something, especially not to experience bad effects from being exposed to something harmful **2.** not to react to a drug through having developed a resistance to it

-tome /təʊm/ *suffix* **1.** a cutting instrument **2.** a segment ○ *a dermatome*

tomo- /təʊməʊ/ *prefix* referring to cutting or a section

tomogram /ˈtəʊməɡræm/ *noun* a picture of part of the body taken by tomography

tomography /təˈmɒɡrəfi/ *noun* the scanning of a particular part of the body using X-rays or ultrasound

-tomy /təmi/ *suffix* referring to a surgical operation

tone /təʊn/ *noun* the slightly tense state of a healthy muscle when it is not fully relaxed. Also called **tonicity, tonus**

tongue /tʌŋ/ *noun* the long muscular organ inside the mouth which can move and is used for tasting, swallowing and speaking. The top surface is covered with papillae, some of which contain taste buds. ○ *The doctor told him to stick out his tongue and say 'Ah'.* Also called **glossa** (NOTE: For other terms referring to the tongue, see **lingual** and words beginning with **gloss-, glosso-**.)

tongue depressor /ˈtʌŋ dɪˌpresə/ *noun* an instrument, usually a thin piece of wood, used by a doctor to hold someone's tongue down while the throat is being examined

tongue-tie /ˈtʌŋ taɪ/ *noun* the condition of being unable to move your tongue with the usual amount of freedom, because the small membrane which attaches the tongue to the floor of the mouth is unusually short

tonic /ˈtɒnɪk/ *adjective* referring to a muscle which is contracted ■ *noun* a substance which improves the someone's general health or which makes a tired person more energetic ○ *He is taking a course of iron tonic tablets.* ○ *She asked the doctor to prescribe a tonic for her anaemia.*

tonicity /təʊˈnɪsɪti/ *noun* same as tone

tono- /təʊnəʊ/ *prefix* referring to pressure

tonography /təʊˈnɒɡrəfi/ *noun* a measurement of the pressure inside an eyeball

tonometer /təʊˈnɒmɪtə/ *noun* an instrument which measures the pressure inside an organ, especially the eye

tonometry /təʊˈnɒmətri/ *noun* a measurement of pressure inside an organ, especially the eye

tonsil /ˈtɒns(ə)l/ *noun* an area of lymphoid tissue at the back of the throat in which lymph circulates and protects the body against germs entering through the mouth. Also called **palatine tonsil**

COMMENT: The tonsils are larger in children than in adults, and are more liable to infection. When infected, the tonsils become enlarged and can interfere with breathing.

tonsillar /ˈtɒnsɪlə/ *adjective* referring to the tonsils

tonsillectomy /ˌtɒnsɪˈlektəmi/ *noun* a surgical operation to remove the tonsils

tonsillitis /ˌtɒnsɪˈlaɪtɪs/ *noun* inflammation of the tonsils

tonsillotome /tɒnˈsɪlətəʊm/ *noun* a surgical instrument used in cutting into or removing the tonsils

tonsillotomy /ˌtɒnsɪ'lɒtəmi/ *noun* a surgical operation to make a cut into the tonsils

tonus /'təʊnəs/ *noun* same as tone

tooth /tuːθ/ *noun* one of a set of bones in the mouth which are used to chew food (NOTE: The plural is **teeth**. For other terms relating to the teeth, see words beginning with **dent-**.)

COMMENT: A tooth is formed of a soft core of pulp, covered with a layer of hard dentine. The top part of the tooth, the crown, which can be seen above the gum, is covered with hard shiny enamel which is very hard-wearing. The lower part of the tooth, the root, which attaches the tooth to the jaw, is covered with cement, also a hard substance, but which is slightly rough and holds the periodontal membrane which links the tooth to the jaw. The milk teeth in a child appear over the first two years of childhood and consist of incisors, canines and molars. The permanent teeth which replace them are formed of eight incisors, four canines, eight premolars and twelve molars. The last four molars (the third molars or wisdom teeth), are not always present, and do not appear much before the age of twenty. Permanent teeth start to appear about the age of five to six. The order of eruption of the permanent teeth is: first molars, incisors, premolars, canines, second molars, wisdom teeth.

toothache /'tuːθeɪk/ *noun* a pain in a tooth. Also called **odontalgia**

topagnosis /ˌtəʊpə'gnəʊsɪs/ *noun* an inability to tell which part of your body has been touched, caused by a disorder of the brain

tophus /'təʊfəs/ *noun* a deposit of solid crystals in the skin or in the joints, especially in someone with gout (NOTE: The plural is **tophi**.)

topical /'tɒpɪk(ə)l/ *adjective* referring to a specific area of the external surface of the body ○ *suitable for topical application*

'…one of the most common routes of neonatal poisoning is percutaneous absorption following topical administration' [*Southern Medical Journal*]

topical drug /'tɒpɪk(ə)l drʌg/ *noun* a drug which is applied to a specific external part of the body only

topically /'tɒpɪkli/ *adverb* by putting on a specific external part of the body only ○ *The cream is applied topically.*

topo- /tɒpə/ *prefix* a place or region

topographical /ˌtɒpə'græfɪk(ə)l/ *adjective* referring to topography

topography /tə'pɒgrəfi/ *noun* the description of each particular part of the body

tormina /'tɔːmɪnə/ *noun* same as **colic**

torpid /'tɔːpɪd/ *adjective* describing a part of the body that has lost the ability to move or feel

torpor /'tɔːpə/ *noun* a condition in which someone seems sleepy or slow to react

torsion /'tɔːʃ(ə)n/ *noun* **1.** the twisting of something, or a twisted state **2.** the stress placed on an object which has been twisted

torso /'tɔːsəʊ/ *noun* the main part of the body, not including the arms, legs and head. Also called **trunk**

torticollis /ˌtɔːtɪ'kɒlɪs/ *noun* a condition of the neck, where the head is twisted to one side by contraction of the sternocleidomastoid muscle. Also called **wry neck**

total /'təʊt(ə)l/ *adjective* **1.** complete ○ *He has total paralysis of the lower part of the body.* **2.** throughout the whole body

total body irradiation /ˌtəʊt(ə)l ˌbɒdi ɪˌreɪdi'eɪʃ(ə)n/ *noun* treating the whole body with radiation

total deafness /ˌtəʊt(ə)l 'defnəs/ *noun* being unable to hear any sound at all. ◊ **hearing loss**

total hip arthroplasty /ˌtəʊt(ə)l 'hɪp ˌɑːθrəʊplæsti/, **total hip replacement** /ˌtəʊt(ə)l 'hɪp rɪˌpleɪsmənt/ *noun* the replacement of both the head of the femur and the acetabulum with an artificial joint

total hysterectomy /ˌtəʊt(ə)l ˌhɪstə'rektəmi/ *noun* the surgical removal of the whole uterus

total pancreatectomy /ˌtəʊt(ə)l ˌpæŋkriə'tektəmi/ *noun* the surgical removal of the whole pancreas together with part of the duodenum. Also called **Whipple's operation**

total recall /ˌtəʊt(ə)l rɪ'kɔːl/ *noun* the fact of being able to remember something in complete detail

touch /tʌtʃ/ *noun* one of the five senses, where sensations are felt by part of the skin, especially by the fingers and lips

COMMENT: Touch is sensed by receptors in the skin which send impulses back to the brain. The touch receptors can tell the difference between hot and cold, hard and soft, wet and dry, and rough and smooth.

tough /tʌf/ *adjective* unable to break or tear easily ○ *The meninges are covered by a layer of tough tissue, the dura mater.*

Tourette's syndrome /tuː'rets ˌsɪndrəʊm/, **Tourette syndrome** /tuː'ret ˌsɪndrəʊm/ *noun* a condition which includes involuntary movements, tics, use of foul language and respiratory disorders. Also called **Gilles de la Tourette Syndrome**

tourniquet /'tɔːnɪkeɪ/ *noun* an instrument or tight bandage wrapped round a limb to constrict an artery, so reducing the flow of blood and stopping bleeding from a wound

tox- /tɒks/ *prefix* same as **toxo-** (*used before vowels*)

toxaemia /tɒk'siːmiə/ *noun* the presence of poisonous substances in the blood. ◊ **blood poisoning** (NOTE: The US spelling is **toxemia**.)

toxaemia of pregnancy /tɒkˌsiːmiə əv 'pregnənsi/ *noun* a condition which can affect women towards the end of pregnancy, in which they develop high blood pressure and pass protein in the urine

toxic /'tɒksɪk/ *adjective* poisonous

toxic goitre /,tɒksɪk 'ɡɔɪtə/ *noun* a type of goitre due to hyperthyroidism in which the limbs tremble and the eyes protrude

toxicity /tɒk'sɪsɪti/ *noun* **1.** the degree to which a substance is poisonous or harmful **2.** the amount of poisonous or harmful material in a substance

toxico- /tɒksɪkəʊ/ *prefix* referring to poison

toxicogenic /,tɒksɪkəʊ'dʒenɪk/ *adjective* same as **toxigenic**

toxicologist /,tɒksɪ'kɒlədʒɪst/ *noun* a scientist who specialises in the study of poisons

toxicology /,tɒksɪ'kɒlədʒi/ *noun* the scientific study of poisons and their effects on the human body

toxicosis /,tɒksɪ'kəʊsɪs/ *noun* poisoning

toxic shock syndrome /,tɒksɪk 'ʃɒk ,sɪn↓drəʊm/ *noun* a serious condition caused by a staphylococcus infection of the skin or soft tissue. Its symptoms include vomiting, high fever, faintness, muscle aches, a rash and confusion. Abbr **TSS**

toxigenic /,tɒksɪ'dʒenɪk/ *adjective* caused or produced by a toxin. Also called **toxicogenic**

toxin /'tɒksɪn/ *noun* a poisonous substance produced in the body by microorganisms, and which, if injected into an animal, stimulates the production of antitoxins

toxo- /tɒksəʊ/ *prefix* referring to poison

toxocariasis /,tɒksəkə'raɪəsɪs/ *noun* the infestation of the intestine with worms from a dog or cat. Also called **visceral larva migrans**

toxoid /'tɒksɔɪd/ *noun* a toxin which has been treated and is no longer poisonous, but which can still provoke the formation of antibodies. Toxoids are used as vaccines, and are injected into a patient to give immunity against specific diseases.

toxoid-antitoxin /,tɒksɔɪd ,æntɪ'tɒksɪn/ *noun* a mixture of a toxoid and an antitoxin, used as a vaccine

toxoplasmosis /,tɒksəʊplæz'məʊsɪs/ *noun* a disease caused by the parasite *Toxoplasma* which is carried by animals. Toxoplasmosis can cause encephalitis or hydrocephalus and can be fatal.

TPA *abbr* tissue plasminogen activator

trabecula /trə'bekjʊlə/ *noun* a thin strip of stiff tissue which divides an organ or bone tissue into sections (NOTE: The plural is **trabeculae**.)

trabeculectomy /trə,bekjʊ'lektəmi/ *noun* a surgical operation to treat glaucoma by cutting a channel through trabeculae to link with Schlemm's canal

trace /treɪs/ *noun* a very small amount ○ *There are traces of the drug in the blood sample.* ○ *The doctor found traces of alcohol in the patient's urine.* ■ *verb* to find someone or something that you are looking for

trace element /'treɪs ,elɪmənt/ *noun* a substance which is essential to the human body, but only in very small quantities

COMMENT: The trace elements are cobalt, chromium, copper, magnesium, manganese, molybdenum, selenium and zinc.

tracer /'treɪsə/ *noun* a substance, often a radioactive one, injected into a substance in the body, so that doctors can follow its passage round the body

trache- /treɪki/ *prefix* same as **tracheo-** (NOTE: used before vowels)

trachea /trə'kiːə/ *noun* the main air passage which runs from the larynx to the lungs, where it divides into the two main bronchi. It is about 10 cm long, and is formed of rings of cartilage and connective tissue. See illustration at LUNGS in Supplement. Also called **windpipe**

tracheal /trə'kiːəl/ *adjective* referring to the trachea

tracheal tugging /trə,kiːəl 'tʌɡɪŋ/ *noun* the feeling that something is pulling on the windpipe when the person breathes in, a symptom of aneurysm

tracheitis /,treɪki'aɪtɪs/ *noun* inflammation of the trachea due to an infection

trachelorrhaphy /,treɪki'lɒrəfi/ *noun* a surgical operation to repair tears in the cervix of the uterus

tracheo- /treɪkiəʊ/ *prefix* relating to the trachea

tracheobronchial /,treɪkiəʊ'brɒŋkiəl/ *adjective* referring to both the trachea and the bronchi

tracheobronchitis /,treɪkiəʊbrɒŋ'kaɪtɪs/ *noun* inflammation of both the trachea and the bronchi

tracheo-oesophogeal /,treɪkiəʊ iː,sɒfə'dʒiːəl/ *adjective* referring to both the trachea and the oesophagus

tracheostomy /,træki'ɒstəmi/, **tracheotomy** /,træki'ɒtəmi/ *noun* a surgical operation to make a hole through the throat into the windpipe, so as to allow air to get to the lungs in cases where the trachea is blocked, as in pneumonia, poliomyelitis or diphtheria

COMMENT: After the operation, a tube is inserted into the hole to keep it open. The tube may be permanent if it is to bypass an obstruction, but can be removed if the condition improves.

trachoma /trə'kəʊmə/ *noun* a contagious viral inflammation of the eyelids, common in tropical countries, which can cause blindness if the conjunctiva becomes scarred

tract /trækt/ *noun* **1.** a series of organs or tubes which allow something to pass from one part of the body to another **2.** a series or bundle of nerve fibres connecting two areas of the nervous system and transmitting nervous impulses in one or in both directions

'GI fistulae are frequently associated with infection because the effluent contains bowel organisms which initially contaminate the fistula tract' [*Nursing Times*]

traction /'trækʃən/ *noun* a procedure that consists of using a pulling force to straighten a broken or deformed limb ○ *The patient was in traction for two weeks.*

COMMENT: A system of weights and pulleys is fixed over the patient's bed so that the limb can be pulled hard enough to counteract the tendency of the muscles to contract and pull it back to its original position. Traction can also be used for slipped discs and other dislocations. Other forms of traction include frames attached to the body.

tractotomy /træk'tɒtəmi/ *noun* a surgical operation to cut the nerve pathway taking sensations of pain to the brain, as a treatment for severe pain that is hard to control

tragus /'treigəs/ *noun* a piece of cartilage in the outer ear which projects forward over the entrance to the auditory canal

training /'treiniŋ/ *noun* the process of educating by giving instruction and the opportunity to practise

trait /treit/ *noun* 1. a typical characteristic of someone 2. a genetically controlled characteristic

trance /trɑːns/ *noun* a condition in which a person is in a dream, but not asleep, and seems not to be aware of what is happening round him or her ○ *a hypnotic trance*

tranexamic acid /,trænek,sæmɪk 'æsɪd/ *noun* a drug used to control severe bleeding

tranquilliser /'træŋkwɪlaɪzə/, **tranquillizer, tranquillising drug** /'træŋkwɪlaɪzɪŋ drʌg/ *noun* an antipsychotic, anxiolytic or hypnotic drug which relieves someone's anxiety and calms him or her down (*informal*) ○ *She's taking tranquillisers to calm her nerves.* ○ *He's been on tranquillisers ever since he started his new job.*

trans- /træns/ *prefix* through or across

transaminase /træn'sæmɪneɪz/ *noun* an enzyme involved in the transamination of amino acids

transamination /træns,æmɪ'neɪʃ(ə)n/ *noun* the process by which amino acids are metabolised in the liver

transcendental meditation /,trænsen,dent(ə)l ,medɪ'teɪʃ(ə)n/ *noun* a type of meditation in which the same words or sounds are repeated silently

transcription /træn'skrɪpʃən/ *noun* 1. the act of copying something written, or of putting something spoken into written form 2. the first step in carrying out genetic instructions in living cells, in which the genetic code is transferred from DNA to molecules of messenger RNA, which then direct protein manufacture

transcutaneous electrical nerve stimulation /,trænskjuː,teɪniəs ɪ,lektrɪk(ə)l 'nɜːv stɪmjʊ,leɪʃ(ə)n/ *noun* full form of **TENS**

transdermal /trænz'dɜːm(ə)l/ *adjective* referring to a drug which is released through the skin

transdermal patch /trænz,dɜːm(ə)l 'pætʃ/ *noun* a patch containing medication applied to the skin and releasing its contents into the body over a period of time

transdiaphragmatic approach /trænz,daɪəfræg,mætɪk ə'prəʊtʃ/ *noun* an operation carried out through the diaphragm

transection /træn'sekʃ(ə)n/ *noun* 1. the act of cutting across part of the body 2. a sample of tissue which has been taken by cutting across a part of the body

transfer /træns'fɜː/ *verb* to pass from one place to another, or cause someone or something to pass from one place to another ○ *The hospital records have been transferred to the computer.* ○ *The patient was transferred to a special burns unit.*

transference /'trænsf(ə)rəns/ *noun* (*in psychiatry*) a condition in which someone transfers to the psychoanalyst the characteristics belonging to a strong character from his or her past such as a parent, and reacts as if the analyst were that person

transferrin /træns'ferɪn/ *noun* a substance found in the blood, which carries iron in the bloodstream. Also called **siderophilin**

transfer RNA /,trænsfɜː ,ɑːr en 'eɪ/ *noun* RNA which attaches amino acids to protein chains being made at ribosomes

transfix /træns'fɪks/ *verb* to cut through a part of the body completely, e.g. when amputating a limb

transfusion /træns'fjuːʒ(ə)n/ *noun* the procedure of transferring blood or saline fluids from a container into a someone's bloodstream

transient /'trænziənt/ *adjective* not lasting long

transient ischaemic attack /,trænziənt ɪ'skiːmɪk ə,tæk/ *noun* a mild stroke caused by a brief stoppage of blood supply to the brain. Abbr **TIA**

transillumination /,trænsɪ,luːmɪ'neɪʃ(ə)n/ *noun* an examination of an organ by shining a bright light through it

transitional /træn'zɪʃ(ə)nəl/ *adjective* in the process of developing into something

transitional epithelium /træn,zɪʃ(ə)nəl epɪ'θiːliəm/ *noun* a type of epithelium found in the urethra

translation /træns'leɪʃ(ə)n/ *noun* 1. the act of putting something written or spoken in one language into words of a different language 2. the process by which information in messenger RNA controls the sequence of amino acids assembled by a ribosome during protein synthesis

translocation /,trænsləʊ'keɪʃ(ə)n/ *noun* the movement of part of a chromosome to another part of the same chromosome or to a different chromosome pair, leading to genetic disorders

translucent /træns'lu:s(ə)nt/ *adjective* allowing light to pass through, but not enough to allow objects on the other side to be clearly distinguished

translumbar /træns'lʌmbə/ *adjective* through the lumbar region

transmigration /ˌtrænzmaɪ'greɪʃ(ə)n/ *noun* the movement of a cell through a membrane

transmission-based precautions /træns ˌmɪʃ(ə)n beɪst prɪ'kɔːʃ(ə)nz/ *plural noun* the most recent set of guidelines for health care workers on dealing with highly infectious diseases, to be used in addition to the Standard Precautions. There are three categories: Airborne Precautions, Droplet Precautions and Contact Precautions, sometimes used in combination for diseases which can be transmitted in various ways.

transmit /trænz'mɪt/ *verb* to pass something such as a message or a disease ○ *Impulses are transmitted along the neural pathways.* ○ *The disease is transmitted by lice.*

transparent /træns'pærənt/ *adjective* able to be seen through ○ *The cornea is a transparent tissue on the front of the eye.*

transplacental /ˌtrænsplə'sent(ə)l/ *adjective* through the placenta

transplant *noun* /'trænsplɑ:nt/ **1.** a procedure which involves taking an organ such as the heart or kidney, or tissue such as skin, and grafting it into someone to replace an organ or tissue which is diseased or not functioning properly ○ *She had a heart-lung transplant.* **2.** the organ or tissue which is grafted ○ *The kidney transplant was rejected.* ■ *verb* /træns 'plɑ:nt/ to graft an organ or tissue onto or into someone to replace an organ or tissue which is diseased or not functioning correctly

transplantation /ˌtrænsplɑ:n'teɪʃ(ə)n/ *noun* the act of transplanting something

'...bone marrow transplantation has the added complication of graft-versus-host disease' [*Hospital Update*]

transport /træns'pɔ:t/ *verb* to carry someone or something to another place ○ *Arterial blood transports oxygen to the tissues.*

transposition /ˌtrænspə'zɪʃ(ə)n/ *noun* a congenital condition where the aorta and pulmonary artery are placed on the opposite side of the body to their usual position

transpyloric plane /ˌtrænspaɪˌlɒrɪk 'pleɪn/ *noun* a plane at right angles to the sagittal plane, passing midway between the suprasternal notch and the symphysis pubis. See illustration at ANATOMICAL TERMS in Supplement

transrectal /træns'rekt(ə)l/ *adjective* through the rectum

transsexual /trænz'sekʃuəl/ *adjective* feeling uncomfortable with the birth gender ■ *noun* a person, especially a man, who feels uncomfortable with their birth gender

transsexualism /trænz'sekʃuəlɪz(ə)m/ *noun* a condition in which a person, especially a man, feels uncomfortable with their birth gender

transtubercular plane /ˌtrænstjʊ ˌbɜːkjʊlə 'pleɪn/ *noun* an imaginary horizontal line drawn across the lower abdomen at the level of the projecting parts of the iliac bones. See illustration at ANATOMICAL TERMS in Supplement. Also called **intertubercular plane**

transudate /'trænsjuːdeɪt/ *noun* a fluid which passes through the pores of a membrane. It contains less protein or solid material than an exudate.

transudation /ˌtrænsjuː'deɪʃ(ə)n/ *noun* the process of passing a fluid from the body's cells through the pores of a membrane

transuretero-ureterostomy /træns ˌjʊərɪtərəʊ ˌjʊərɪtə'rɒstəmi/ *noun* a surgical operation in which both ureters are brought to the same side in the abdomen, because one is damaged or obstructed

transurethral /ˌtrænsjʊ'riːθrəl/ *adjective* through the urethra

transurethral prostatectomy /ˌtrænsjʊ ˌriːθrəl prɒstə'tektəmi/, **transurethral resection** /ˌtrænsjʊˌriːθrəl rɪ'sekʃən/ *noun* a surgical operation to remove the prostate gland, where the operation is carried out through the urethra. Abbr **TUR**. Also called **resection of the prostate**

transvaginal /ˌtrænsvə'dʒaɪn(ə)l/ *adjective* across or through the vagina

transverse /trænz'vɜːs/ *adjective* across, at right angles to an organ

transverse arch /ˌtrænz'vɜːs ɑːtʃ/ *noun* same as **metatarsal arch**

transverse colon /ˌtrænzvɜːs 'kəʊlɒn/ *noun* the second section of the colon which crosses the body below the stomach. See illustration at DIGESTIVE SYSTEM in Supplement

transverse fracture /ˌtrænzvɜːs 'fræktʃə/ *noun* a fracture where the bone is broken straight across

transverse lie /ˌtrænzvɜːs 'laɪ/ *noun* the position of a fetus across the body of the mother

transverse plane /ˌtrænzvɜːs 'pleɪn/ *noun* a plane at right angles to the sagittal plane, running horizontally across the body. See illustration at ANATOMICAL TERMS in Supplement

transverse presentation /ˌtrænzvɜːs ˌprez(ə)n'teɪʃ(ə)n/ *noun* a position of the baby in the uterus, where the baby's side will appear first, usually requiring urgent manipulation or caesarean section to prevent complications

transverse process /ˌtrænzvɜːs ˈprəʊses/ *noun* the part of a vertebra which protrudes at the side

transvesical prostatectomy /træns ˌvesɪk(ə)l prɒstəˈtektəmi/ *noun* an operation to remove the prostate gland, carried out through the bladder

transvestism /trænzˈvestɪz(ə)m/ *noun* the condition of liking to dress and behave as a member of the opposite sex

transvestite /trænzˈvestaɪt/ *noun* a person who dresses and behaves as a member of the opposite sex

trapezium /trəˈpiːziəm/ *noun* one of the eight small carpal bones in the wrist, below the thumb. See illustration at **HAND** in Supplement (NOTE: The plural is **trapeziums** or **trapezia**.)

trapezius /trəˈpiːziəs/ *noun* a triangular muscle in the upper part of the back and the neck, which moves the shoulder blade and pulls the head back

trapezoid /ˈtræpɪzɔɪd/, **trapezoid bone** /ˈtræpɪzɔɪd bəʊn/ *noun* one of the eight small carpal bones in the wrist, below the first finger. See illustration at **HAND** in Supplement

trauma /ˈtrɔːmə/ *noun* **1.** a wound or injury **2.** a very frightening or distressing experience which gives a person a severe emotional shock

trauma centre /ˈtrɔːmə ˌsentə/ *noun* a hospital or a department in a hospital that treats people who have complex, life-threatening injuries

traumatic /trɔːˈmætɪk/ *adjective* **1.** caused by an injury **2.** extremely frightening, distressing or shocking

traumatic fever /trɔːˌmætɪk ˈfiːvə/ *noun* a fever caused by an injury

traumatic pneumothorax /trɔːˌmætɪk njuːməʊˈθɔːræks/ *noun* pneumothorax which results from damage to the lung surface or to the wall of the chest, allowing air to leak into the space between the pleurae

traumatology /ˌtrɔːməˈtɒlədʒi/ *noun* a branch of surgery which deals with injuries received in accidents

traveller's diarrhoea /ˌtræv(ə)ləz daɪəˈriːə/ *noun* diarrhoea that affects people who travel to foreign countries and which is due to contact with a different type of *E. coli* from the one they are used to. (*informal*)

travel sickness /ˈtræv(ə)l ˌsɪknəs/ *noun* same as **motion sickness**

trazodone /ˈtræzədəʊn/ *noun* an antidepressant drug which has a strong sedative effect, used in the treatment of depressive disorders accompanied by insomnia

Treacher Collins syndrome /ˌtriːtʃə ˈkɒlɪnz ˌsɪndrəʊm/ *noun* a hereditary disorder in which the lower jaw, the cheek bones, and the ear are not fully developed

treat /triːt/ *verb* to use medical methods to cure a disease or help a sick or injured person to recover ○ *She has been treated with a new antibiotic.* ○ *She's being treated by a specialist for heart disease.*

treatment /ˈtriːtmənt/ *noun* **1.** actions taken to look after sick or injured people or to cure disease ○ *He is receiving treatment for a slipped disc.* **2.** a particular way of looking after a sick or injured person or trying to cure a disease ○ *cortisone treatment* ○ *This is a new treatment for heart disease.*

trematode /ˈtremətəʊd/ *noun* a parasitic flatworm

tremble /ˈtrembəl/ *verb* to shake or shiver slightly

trembling /ˈtremblɪŋ/ *noun* rapid small movements of a limb or muscles ○ *Trembling of the hands is a symptom of Parkinson's disease.*

tremens /ˈtriːmenz/ ♦ **delirium tremens**

tremor /ˈtremə/ *noun* slight involuntary movements of a limb or muscle

trench fever /ˈtrenʃ ˌfiːvə/ *noun* a fever caused by Rickettsia bacteria, similar to typhus but recurring every five days

trench foot /ˌtrentʃ ˈfʊt/ *noun* a condition, caused by exposure to cold and damp, in which the skin of the foot becomes red and blistered and in severe cases turns black when gangrene sets in. Also called **immersion foot** (NOTE: Trench foot was common among soldiers serving in the trenches during the First World War.)

trench mouth /ˌtrentʃ ˈmaʊθ/ *noun* ♦ **gingivitis**

Trendelenburg's operation /tren ˈdelənbɜːgz ɒpəˌreɪʃ(ə)n/ *noun* an operation to tie a saphenous vein in the groin before removing varicose veins [After Friedrich Trendelburg (1844–1924), German surgeon]

Trendelenburg's position /tren ˈdelənbɜːg pəˌzɪʃ(ə)n/, **Trendelenburg position** /tren'delənbɜːg pəˌzɪʃ(ə)n/ *noun* a position in which someone lies on a sloping bed, with the head lower than the feet, and the knees bent. It is used in surgical operations to the pelvis and for people who have shock.

Trendelenburg's sign /tren'delənbɜːgz saɪn/ *noun* a symptom of congenital dislocation of the hip, where the person's pelvis is lower on the opposite side to the dislocation

trephination /ˌtrɪfɪˈneɪʃ(ə)n/ *noun* a surgical operation which consists of removing a small part of the skull with a trephine in order to perform surgery on the brain

trephine /trɪˈfiːn/ *noun* a surgical instrument for making a round hole in the skull or for removing a round piece of tissue

Treponema /ˌtrepəˈniːmə/ *noun* a genus of bacteria which cause diseases such as syphilis or yaws

treponematosis /ˌtrepənɪməˈtəʊsɪs/ *noun* an infection by the bacterium *Treponema pertenue*. ◊ **yaws**

TRH *abbr* thyrotrophin-releasing hormone

triad /ˈtraɪæd/ *noun* three organs or three symptoms which are linked together in a group

triage /ˈtriːɑːʒ/ *noun* the system in which a doctor or nurse sees patients briefly in order to decide who should be treated first

trial /ˈtraɪəl/ *noun* a process of testing something such as a drug or treatment to see how effective it is, especially before allowing it to be used generally ○ *clinical trials* ○ *a six-month trial period* ○ *We're supplying it on a trial basis.* ■ *verb* to test something as part of a trial

triamcinolone /ˌtraɪæmˈsɪnələʊn/ *noun* a synthetic corticosteroid drug used in the treatment of skin, mouth and joint inflammations

triangle /ˈtraɪæŋgəl/ *noun* **1.** a flat shape which has three sides **2.** part of the body with three sides

triangular /traɪˈæŋgjʊlə/ *adjective* with three sides

triangular bandage /traɪˌæŋgjʊlə ˈbændɪdʒ/ *noun* a bandage made of a triangle of cloth, used to make a sling for the arm

triceps /ˈtraɪseps/ *noun* a muscle formed of three parts, which are joined to form one tendon

triceps brachii /ˌtraɪseps ˈbreɪkiːiː/ *noun* a muscle in the back part of the upper arm which makes the forearm stretch out

trich- /trɪk/ *prefix* same as **tricho-** (*used before vowels*)

trichiasis /trɪˈkaɪəsɪs/ *noun* a painful condition in which the eyelashes grow in towards the eye and scratch the eyeball

trichinosis /ˌtrɪkɪˈnəʊsɪs/, **trichiniasis** /ˌtrɪkɪˈnaɪəsɪs/ *noun* a disease caused by infestation of the intestine by larvae of roundworms or nematodes, which pass round the body in the bloodstream and settle in muscles
COMMENT: The larvae enter the body in meat, especially pork, which has not been properly cooked.

tricho- /trɪkəʊ/ *prefix* **1.** referring to hair **2.** like hair

Trichocephalus /ˌtrɪkəˈsefələs/ *noun* same as **Trichuris**

trichology /trɪˈkɒlədʒi/ *noun* the study of hair and the diseases which affect it

Trichomonas /ˌtrɪkəˈməʊnəs/ *noun* a species of long thin parasite which infests the intestines

Trichomonas vaginalis /trɪkəˌməʊnəs vædʒɪˈneɪlɪs/ *noun* a parasite which infests the vagina and causes an irritating discharge

trichomoniasis /ˌtrɪkəʊməˈnaɪəsɪs/ *noun* infestation of the intestine or vagina with Trichomonas

trichomycosis /ˌtrɪkəʊmaɪˈkəʊsɪs/ *noun* a disease of the hair caused by a corynebacterium

Trichophyton /traɪˈkɒfɪtɒn/ *noun* a fungus which affects the skin, hair and nails

trichophytosis /ˌtrɪkəʊfaɪˈtəʊsɪs/ *noun* an infection caused by Trichophyton

trichosis /traɪˈkəʊsɪs/ *noun* any unusual condition of the hair

trichotillomania /ˌtrɪkəʊtɪləʊˈmeɪniə/ *noun* a condition in which a person pulls his or her hair out compulsively

trichromatism /traɪˈkrəʊmətɪz(ə)m/ *noun* vision which allows the difference between the three primary colours to be seen. Compare **dichromatism, monochromatism**

trichrome stain /ˈtraɪkrəʊm ˌsteɪn/ *noun* a stain in three colours used in histology

trichuriasis /ˌtrɪkjʊˈraɪəsɪs/ *noun* an infestation of the intestine with whipworms

Trichuris /trɪˈkjʊərɪs/ *noun* a thin round parasitic worm which infests the caecum. Also called **whipworm**

tricuspid /traɪˈkʌspɪd/ *noun* something which has three cusps, e.g. a tooth or leaf ■ *adjective* **1.** having three cusps or points **2.** referring to a tricuspid valve or tooth

tricuspid valve /traɪˈkʌspɪd vælv/ *noun* an inlet valve with three cusps between the right atrium and the right ventricle in the heart. See illustration at HEART in Supplement

tricyclic antidepressant /traɪˌsaɪklɪk ˌæntidɪˈpres(ə)nt/, **tricyclic antidepressant drug** /traɪˌsaɪklɪk ˌæntidɪˈpres(ə)nt drʌg/ *noun* a drug used to treat depression and panic disorder, e.g. amitriptyline and nortriptyline
COMMENT: Antimuscarinic and cardiac side-effects can occur; rapid withdrawal should be avoided.

tridactyly /traɪˈdæktɪli/ *noun* the condition of having only three fingers or toes

trifocal lenses /traɪˌfəʊk(ə)l ˈlenzɪz/, **trifocal glasses** /traɪˌfəʊk(ə)l ˈglɑːsɪz/, **trifocals** /traɪˈfəʊk(ə)lz/ *plural noun* spectacles which have three lenses combined in one piece of glass to give clear vision over different distances. ◊ **bifocal**

trigeminal /traɪˈdʒemɪn(ə)l/ *adjective* in three parts

trigeminal ganglion /traɪˌdʒemɪn(ə)l ˈgæŋgliən/ *noun* a sensory ganglion containing the cells of origin of the sensory fibres in the fifth cranial nerve. Also called **Gasserian ganglion**

trigeminal nerve /traɪˈdʒemɪn(ə)l nɜːv/ *noun* the fifth cranial nerve, formed of the ophthalmic nerve, the maxillary nerve and the mandibular nerve, which controls the sensory nerves in the forehead, face and chin, and the muscles in the jaw

trigeminal neuralgia /traɪˌdʒemɪn(ə)l njʊ'rældʒə/ *noun* a disorder of the trigeminal nerve, which sends intense pains shooting across the face. Also called **tic douloureux**

trigeminy /traɪ'dʒemɪni/ *noun* an irregular heartbeat, where a regular beat is followed by two ectopic beats

trigger /'trɪgə/ *verb* to start something happening ○ *It is not known what triggers the development of shingles.*

trigger finger /'trɪgə ˌfɪŋgə/ *noun* a condition in which a finger can bend but is difficult to straighten, probably because of a nodule on the flexor tendon

triglyceride /traɪ'glɪsəraɪd/ *noun* a substance such as fat which contains three fatty acids

trigone /'traɪgəʊn/ *noun* a triangular piece of the wall of the bladder, between the openings for the urethra and the two ureters

trigonitis /ˌtrɪgə'naɪtɪs/ *noun* inflammation of the bottom part of the wall of the bladder

trigonocephalic /traɪˌɡɒnəkə'fælɪk/ *adjective* referring to a skull which shows signs of trigonocephaly

trigonocephaly /traɪˌɡɒnə'kef(ə)li/ *noun* a condition in which the skull is in the shape of a triangle, with points on either side of the face in front of the ears

triiodothyronine /traɪˌaɪədəʊ'θaɪrəni:n/ *noun* a hormone synthesised in the body from thyroxine secreted by the thyroid gland

trimeprazine /traɪ'meprəzi:n/ *noun* an antihistamine used to relieve the itching caused by eczema and various skin rashes, including allergic skin rashes caused by poison ivy

trimester /traɪ'mestə/ *noun* one of the three 3-month periods of a pregnancy

trimethoprim /traɪ'mi:θəprɪm/ *noun* a synthetic drug used in the treatment of malaria

triphosphate /traɪ'fɒsfeɪt/ ♦ **adenosine triphosphate**

triple marker test /ˌtrɪp(ə)l 'mɑːkə test/ *noun* a blood test performed on pregnant women which can detect Down's syndrome in a fetus by analysing the relative levels of substances produced by the mother's placenta and the fetus itself

triplet /'trɪplət/ *noun* one of three babies born to a mother at the same time

triple vaccine /ˌtrɪp(ə)l 'væksiːn/ *noun* a vaccine which induces protection against three diseases e.g. diphtheria, tetanus and whooping cough

triploid /'trɪplɔɪd/ *adjective* referring to a cell where each chromosome, except the sex chromosome, occurs three times, which is not viable in humans

triquetrum /traɪ'kwetrəm/, **triquetral** /traɪ'kwetr(ə)l/, **triquetral bone** /traɪ'kwetr(ə)l bəʊn/ *noun* one of the eight small carpal bones in the wrist. See illustration at HAND in Supplement

trismus /'trɪzməs/ *noun* a spasm in the lower jaw, which makes it difficult to open the mouth, a symptom of tetanus

trisomic /traɪ'səʊmɪk/ *adjective* referring to Down's syndrome

trisomy /'traɪsəʊmi/ *noun* a condition in which someone has three chromosomes instead of a pair

trisomy 21 /ˌtraɪsəʊmi ˌtwenti 'wʌn/ *noun* same as **Down's syndrome**

tritanopia /ˌtraɪtə'nəʊpiə/ *noun* a rare form of colour blindness, in which someone cannot see blue. Compare **Daltonism, deuteranopia**

trocar /'trəʊkɑː/ *noun* a surgical instrument or pointed rod which slides inside a cannula to make a hole in tissue to drain off fluid

trochanter /trə'kæntə/ *noun* two bony lumps on either side of the top end of the femur where muscles are attached

COMMENT: The lump on the outer side is the greater trochanter, and that on the inner side is the lesser trochanter.

trochlea /'trɒkliə/ *noun* any part of the body shaped like a pulley, especially part of the lower end of the humerus, which articulates with the ulna, or a curved bone in the frontal bone through which one of the eye muscles passes (NOTE: The plural is **trochleae**.)

trochlear /'trɒkliə/ *adjective* referring to a ring in a bone

trochlear nerve /'trɒkliə nɜːv/ *noun* the fourth cranial nerve which controls the muscles of the eyeball

trochoid joint /'trəʊkɔɪd dʒɔɪnt/ *noun* a joint where a bone can rotate freely about a central axis as in the neck, where the atlas articulates with the axis. Also called **pivot joint**

trolley /'trɒli/ *noun* a wheeled table for transporting patients ○ *The patient was placed on a trolley to be taken to the operating theatre.*

troph- /trɒf/ *prefix* same as **tropho-** (*used before vowels*)

trophic /'trɒfɪk/ *adjective* relating to food and nutrition

trophic ulcer /ˌtrɒfɪk 'ʌlsə/ *noun* an ulcer caused by lack of blood, e.g. a bedsore

tropho- /'trɒfəʊ/ *prefix* referring to food or nutrition

trophoblast /'trɒfəʊblæst/ *noun* tissue which forms the wall of a blastocyst

-trophy /trəfi/ *suffix* **1.** nourishment **2.** referring to the development of an organ

tropia /'trəʊpiə/ *noun* same as **squint**

-tropic /trɒpɪk/ *suffix* **1.** turning towards **2.** referring to something which influences

tropical /'trɒpɪk(ə)l/ *adjective* located in or coming from areas around the equator where the climate is generally very hot and humid

tropical disease /,trɒpɪk(ə)l dɪ'zi:z/ *noun* a disease which is found in tropical countries, e.g. malaria, dengue or Lassa fever

tropical medicine /,trɒpɪk(ə)l 'med(ə)sɪn/ *noun* a branch of medicine which deals with tropical diseases

tropical ulcer /,trɒpɪk(ə)l 'ʌlsə/ *noun* a large area of infection which forms around a wound, found especially in tropical countries. Also called **Naga sore**

trots /trɒts/ □ **the trots** an attack of diarrhoea (*informal*)

trouble /'trʌb(ə)l/ *noun* a disorder or condition (*informal*) ○ *stomach trouble* ○ *treatment for back trouble*

Trousseau's sign /'tru:səʊz saɪn/ *noun* a spasm in the muscles in the forearm when a tourniquet is applied to the upper arm, which causes the index and middle fingers to extend. It is a sign of latent tetany, showing that the blood contains too little calcium. [After Armand Trousseau (1801–67), French physician]

true rib /,tru: 'rɪb/ *noun* one of the top seven pairs of ribs which are attached to the breastbone. Compare **false rib**

true vocal cords /,tru: 'vəʊk(ə)l ,kɔ:dz/ *plural noun* the cords in the larynx which can be brought together to make sounds as air passes between them

truncus /'trʌŋkəs/ *noun* the main blood vessel in a fetus, which develops into the aorta and pulmonary artery

trunk /trʌŋk/ *noun* same as **torso**

truss /trʌs/ *noun* a belt worn round the waist, with pads, to hold a hernia in place

trypanocide /'trɪpənəʊsaɪd/ *noun* a drug which kills trypanosomes

Trypanosoma /,trɪpənəʊ'səʊmə/, **trypanosome** /'trɪpənəʊsəʊm/ *noun* a microscopic organism which lives as a parasite in human blood. It is transmitted by the bite of insects such as the tsetse fly and causes sleeping sickness and other serious illnesses.

trypanosomiasis /,trɪpənəʊsəʊ'maɪəsɪs/ *noun* a disease, spread by insect bites, where trypanosomes infest the blood. Symptoms are pains in the head, general lethargy and long periods of sleep.

COMMENT: In Africa, sleeping sickness, and in South America, Chagas' disease, are both caused by trypanosomes.

trypsin /'trɪpsɪn/ *noun* an enzyme converted from trypsinogen by the duodenum and secreted into the digestive system where it absorbs protein

trypsinogen /trɪp'sɪnədʒən/ *noun* an enzyme secreted by the pancreas into the duodenum

tryptophan /'trɪptəfæn/ *noun* an essential amino acid

tsetse fly /'tetsi flaɪ, 'setsi flaɪ/ *noun* an African insect which passes trypanosomes into the human bloodstream, causing sleeping sickness

TSH *abbr* thyroid-stimulating hormone

TSS *abbr* toxic shock syndrome

tsutsugamushi disease /,tsu:tsəgə 'mu:ʃi dɪ,zi:z/ *noun* a form of typhus caused by the Rickettsia bacteria, passed to humans by mites found in South East Asia. Also called **scrub typhus**

tubal /'tju:b(ə)l/ *adjective* referring to a tube

tubal ligation /,tju:b(ə)l laɪ'geɪʃ(ə)n/ *noun* a surgical operation to tie up the Fallopian tubes as a sterilisation procedure

tubal occlusion /,tju:b(ə)l ə'klu:ʒ(ə)n/ *noun* a condition in which the Fallopian tubes are blocked, either as a result of disease or surgery

tubal pregnancy /,tju:b(ə)l 'pregnənsi/ *noun* the most common form of ectopic pregnancy, in which the fetus develops in a Fallopian tube instead of the uterus

tube /tju:b/ *noun* **1.** a long hollow passage in the body **2.** a soft flexible pipe for carrying liquid or gas **3.** a soft plastic or metal pipe, sealed at one end and with a lid at the other, used to dispense a paste or gel

tube feeding /'tju:b ,fi:dɪŋ/ *noun* the process of giving someone nutrients through a tube directly into their stomach or small intestine

tuber /'tju:bə/ *noun* a swollen or raised area

tuber cinereum /,tju:bə ,sɪnə'rɪəm/ *noun* the part of the brain to which the stalk of the pituitary gland is connected

tubercle /'tju:bək(ə)l/ *noun* **1.** a small bony projection, e.g. on a rib **2.** a small infected lump characteristic of tuberculosis, where tissue is destroyed and pus forms

tubercular /tjʊ'bɜ:kjʊlə/ *adjective* **1.** causing or referring to tuberculosis **2.** referring to someone who has tuberculosis **3.** with small lumps, though not always due to tuberculosis

tuberculid /tjʊ'bɜ:kjʊlɪd/, **tuberculide** *noun* a skin wound caused by tuberculosis

tuberculin /tjʊ'bɜ:kjʊlɪn/ *noun* a substance which is derived from the culture of the tuberculosis bacillus and is used to test people for the presence of tuberculosis

tuberculin test /tjʊ'bɜ:kjʊlɪn test/ *noun* a test to see if someone has tuberculosis, in which someone is exposed to tuberculin and the reaction of the skin is noted

tuberculosis /tjʊ,bɜ:kjʊ'ləʊsɪs/ *noun* an infectious disease caused by the tuberculosis bacillus, where infected lumps form in the tissue. Abbr **TB**

COMMENT: Tuberculosis can take many forms: the commonest form is infection of the lungs (pulmonary tuberculosis), but it can also attack the bones (Pott's disease), the skin (lupus), or the lymph nodes (scrofula). Tuberculosis is caught by breathing in bacillus or by eating contaminated food, especially unpasteurised milk. It can be passed from one person to another, and the carrier sometimes shows no signs of the disease. Tuberculosis can be cured by treatment with antibiotics, and can be prevented by inoculation with BCG vaccine. The tests for the presence of TB are the Mantoux test, the Heaf test and the patch test; it can also be detected by X-ray screening.

tuberculous /tjʊˈbɜːkjʊləs/ *adjective* referring to tuberculosis

tuberose /ˈtjuːbərəʊz/ *adjective* with lumps or nodules

tuberose sclerosis /ˌtjuːbərəʊs skləˈrəʊsɪs/ *noun* same as **epiloia**

tuberosity /ˌtjuːbəˈrɒsɪti/ *noun* a large lump on a bone

tuberous /ˈtjuːbərəs/ *adjective* with lumps or nodules

tubo- /tjuːbəʊ/ *prefix* referring to a Fallopian tube or to the internal or external auditory meatus

tuboabdominal /ˌtjuːbəʊæbˈdɒmɪn(ə)l/ *adjective* referring to a Fallopian tube and the abdomen

tubocurarine /ˌtjuːbəʊˈkjʊərəriːn/ *noun* a toxic alkaloid which is the active constituent of curare, used as a muscle relaxant

tubo-ovarian /ˌtjuːbəʊ əʊˈveəriən/ *adjective* referring to a Fallopian tube and an ovary

tubotympanal /ˌtjuːbəʊˈtɪmpən(ə)l/ *adjective* referring to the Eustachian tube and the tympanum

tubular /ˈtjuːbjʊlə/ *adjective* **1.** shaped like a tube **2.** referring to a tubule

tubular bandage /ˌtjuːbjʊlə ˈbændɪdʒ/ *noun* a bandage made of a tube of elastic cloth

tubular reabsorption /ˌtjuːbjʊlə riːəbˈsɔːpʃən/ *noun* the process by which some of the substances filtered into the kidney are absorbed back into the bloodstream by the tubules

tubular secretion /ˌtjuːbjʊlə sɪˈkriːʃ(ə)n/ *noun* the secretion of some substances into the urine by the tubules of the kidney

tubule /ˈtjuːbjuːl/ *noun* a small tube in the body. ◊ **renal tubule**

tuft /tʌft/ *noun* **1.** a small group of hairs **2.** a group of blood vessels. ◊ **glomerular tuft**

tugging /ˈtʌɡɪŋ/ ♦ **tracheal tugging**

tularaemia /ˌtuːləˈriːmiə/ *noun* a disease of rabbits, caused by the bacterium *Pasteurella* or *Brucella tularensis,* which can be passed to humans. In humans, the symptoms are headaches, fever and swollen lymph nodes. Also called **rabbit fever** (NOTE: The US spelling is **tularemia.**)

tulle gras /ˈtjuːl ɡrɑː/ *noun* a dressing made of open gauze covered with soft paraffin wax which prevents sticking

tumefaction /ˌtjuːmɪˈfækʃən/ *noun* swelling within body tissue, usually caused a build-up of blood or water

tumescence /tjuːˈmes(ə)ns/ *noun* swollen tissue where liquid has accumulated underneath. ◊ **oedema**

tumescent /tjuːˈmesənt/ *adjective* swollen or showing signs of swelling, usually as a result of a build-up of blood or water within body tissues

tumid /ˈtjuːmɪd/ *adjective* swollen

tummy /ˈtʌmi/ *noun* stomach or abdomen (*informal*)

tummy ache /ˈtʌmi eɪk/ *noun* stomach pain (*informal*)

tumoral /ˈtjuːmərəl/, **tumorous** /ˈtjuːmərəs/ *adjective* referring to a tumour

tumour /ˈtjuːmə/ *noun* an unusual swelling or growth of new cells ○ *The X-ray showed a tumour in the breast.* ○ *a brain tumour.* (NOTE: For other terms referring to tumours, see words beginning with **onco-**. The US spelling is **tumor.**)

tunable dye laser /ˌtjuːnəb(ə)l daɪ ˈleɪzə/ *noun* a laser which coagulates fine blood vessels, used to blanch port wine stains

tunica /ˈtjuːnɪkə/ *noun* a layer of tissue which covers an organ

tunica adventitia /ˌtjuːnɪkə ˌædvenˈtɪʃə/ *noun* an outer layer of the wall of an artery or vein. Also called **adventitia**

tunica albuginea testis /ˌtjuːnɪkə ælbjʊˌdʒɪniə ˈtestɪs/ *noun* a white fibrous membrane covering the testes and the ovaries

tunica intima /ˌtjuːnɪkə ˈɪntɪmə/ *noun* the inner layer of the wall of an artery or vein. Also called **intima**

tunica media /ˌtjuːnɪkə ˈmiːdiə/ *noun* the middle layer of the wall of an artery or vein. Also called **media**

tunica vaginalis /ˌtjuːnɪkə vædʒɪˈneɪlɪs/ *noun* a membrane covering the testes and epididymis

tuning fork /ˈtjuːnɪŋ fɔːk/ *noun* a metal fork which, if hit, gives out a perfect note, used in hearing tests such as Rinne's test

tunnel vision /ˌtʌn(ə)l ˈvɪʒ(ə)n/ *noun* vision which is restricted to the area directly in front of the eye

turbinate /ˈtɜːbɪnət/ *adjective* **1.** having a shape like a spiral or an inverted cone **2.** referring to any of the three bones found on the walls of the nasal passages of mammals

turbinate bone /ˈtɜːbɪnət bəʊn/ *noun* ♦ **nasal conchae**

turbinectomy /ˌtɜːbɪˈnektəmi/ *noun* a surgical operation to remove a turbinate bone

turbulent flow /ˌtɜːbjʊlənt 'fləʊ/ *noun* rushing or uneven flow of blood in a vessel, usually caused by a partial obstruction

turcica /'tɜːsɪkə/ ♦ **sella turcica**

turgescence /tɜː'dʒes(ə)ns/ *noun* a swelling in body tissue caused by the accumulation of fluid

turgid /'tɜːdʒɪd/ *adjective* swollen with blood

turgor /'tɜːgə/ *noun* the condition of being swollen

turn /tɜːn/ *noun* a slight illness or attack of dizziness (*informal*) ■ *verb* **1.** to move the head or body to face in another direction **2.** to change into something different ○ *The solution is turned blue by the reagent.*

Turner's syndrome /'tɜːnəz ˌsɪndrəʊm/ *noun* a congenital condition in females, caused by the absence of one of the pair of X chromosomes, in which sexual development is retarded and no ovaries develop [Described 1938. After Henry Hubert Turner (b. 1892), US endocrinologist, Clinical professor of Medicine, Oklahoma University, USA.]

turricephaly /ˌtʌrɪ'sefəli/ same as **oxycephaly**

tussis /'tʌsɪs/ *noun* coughing

tutor /'tjuːtə/ *noun* a teacher, a person who teaches small groups of students

tweezers /'twiːzəz/ *plural noun* an instrument shaped like small scissors, with ends which pinch and do not cut, used to pull out or pick up small objects

twenty-four hour flu /ˌtwenti ˌfɔː aʊə 'fluː/ *noun* any minor illness similar to flu which lasts for a short period (*informal*)

twenty-twenty vision /ˌtwenti ˌtwenti 'vɪʒ(ə)n/ *noun* perfect vision

twice /twaɪs/ *adverb* two times □ **twice daily** two times a day

twilight myopia /ˌtwaɪlaɪt maɪ'əʊpiə/ *noun* a condition of the eyes, in which someone has difficulty in seeing in dim light

twilight sleep /'twaɪlaɪt ˌsliːp/ *noun* a type of anaesthetic sleep, in which the patient is semi-conscious but cannot feel any pain

twilight state /'twaɪlaɪt steɪt/ *noun* a condition of epileptics and alcoholics in which the person can do some automatic actions, but is not conscious of what he or she is doing

COMMENT: Twilight state is induced at childbirth, by introducing anaesthetics into the rectum.

twin /twɪn/ *noun* one of two babies born to a mother at the same time

COMMENT: Twins occur at a rate of about one birth in 38. They are often found in the same family, where the tendency to have twins is passed through females.

twinge /twɪndʒ/ *noun* a sudden sharp pain ○ *He sometimes has a twinge in his right shoulder.*

twist /twɪst/ *verb* to hurt a joint by turning or bending it too much or the wrong way ○ *He twisted his ankle.*

twitch /twɪtʃ/ *noun* a small movement of a muscle in the face or hands ■ *verb* to make small movements of the muscles

twitching /'twɪtʃɪŋ/ *noun* small movements of the muscles in the face or hands

tylosis /taɪ'ləʊsɪs/ *noun* the development of a callus

tympan- /tɪmpən/ *prefix* same as **tympano-** (NOTE: used before vowels)

tympanectomy /ˌtɪmpə'nektəmi/ *noun* a surgical operation to remove the tympanic membrane

tympanic /tɪm'pænɪk/ *adjective* referring to the eardrum

tympanic bone /tɪm'pænɪk bəʊn/ *noun* the part of the temporal bone that supports and partly surrounds the auditory canal

tympanic cavity /tɪmˌpænɪk 'kævɪti/ *noun* the section of the ear between the eardrum and the inner ear, containing the three ossicles. Also called **middle ear, tympanum**

tympanic membrane /tɪmˌpænɪk 'membreɪn/ *noun* the membrane at the inner end of the external auditory meatus leading from the outer ear, which vibrates with sound and passes the vibrations on to the ossicles in the middle ear. Also called **tympanum, eardrum**. See illustration at EAR in Supplement

tympanites /ˌtɪmpə'naɪtiːz/ *noun* the expansion of the stomach with gas. Also called **meteorism**

tympanitis /ˌtɪmpə'naɪtɪs/ *noun* same as **otitis media**

tympano- /tɪmpənəʊ/ *prefix* referring to the eardrum

tympanoplasty /'tɪmpənəʊplæsti/ *noun* same as **myringoplasty**

tympanosclerosis /ˌtɪmpənəʊsklə'rəʊsɪs/ *noun* irreversible damage to the tympanic membrane and middle ear, starting with the replacement of tissues or fibrin by collagen and hyalin. Then calcification occurs, leading to deafness.

tympanotomy /ˌtɪmpə'nɒtəmi/ *noun* same as **myringotomy**

tympanum /'tɪmpənəm/ *noun* **1.** same as **tympanic membrane 2.** same as **tympanic cavity**

type A behaviour /ˌtaɪp 'eɪ bɪˌheɪvjə/ *noun* a behaviour pattern which may contribute to coronary heart disease, in which an individual is aggressive and over-competitive, and usually lives at a stressful pace. Compare **type B behaviour**

type B behaviour /ˌtaɪp 'biː bɪˌheɪvjə/ *noun* a behaviour pattern which is unlikely to contribute to coronary heart disease, in which an individual is patient, tolerant, not very competitive and lives at a more relaxed pace. Compare **type A behaviour**

Type I diabetes mellitus /taɪp ˌwʌn daɪə ˌbiːtiːz məˈlaɪtəs/ *noun* the type of diabetes mellitus in which the beta cells of the pancreas produce little or no insulin, and the person is completely dependent on injections of insulin for survival. It is more likely to develop in people under 30. Symptoms are usually severe and occur suddenly. Also called **insulin-dependent diabetes**

Type II diabetes mellitus /taɪp ˌtuː daɪə ˌbiːtiːz məˈlaɪtəs/ *noun* the type of diabetes mellitus in which cells throughout the body lose some or most of their ability to use insulin. It is more likely to develop in people who are over 40, who are overweight or obese, and who do not exercise regularly. It can be controlled in some cases with diet and exercise, but more severe cases may need oral medication which reduces glucose concentrations in the blood, or insulin injections, so that even cells with a poor uptake will capture enough insulin. Also called **non-insulin-dependent diabetes**

typhlitis /tɪˈflaɪtɪs/ *noun* inflammation of the caecum (large intestine)

typho- /taɪfəʊ/ *prefix* **1.** relating to typhoid fever **2.** relating to typhus

typhoid /ˈtaɪfɔɪd/, **typhoid fever** /ˌtaɪfɔɪd ˈfiːvə/ *noun* an infection of the intestine caused by *Salmonella typhi* in food and water

COMMENT: Typhoid fever gives a fever and diarrhoea and the person may pass blood in the faeces. It can be fatal if not treated. People who have had the disease may become carriers, and the Widal test is used to detect the presence of typhoid fever in the blood.

typhus /ˈtaɪfəs/ *noun* one of several fevers caused by the Rickettsia bacterium, transmitted by fleas and lice, producing a fever, extreme weakness and a dark rash on the skin. The test for typhus is the Weil-Felix reaction.

typical /ˈtɪpɪk(ə)l/ *adjective* showing the usual symptoms of a condition ○ *His gait was typical of a patient suffering from Parkinson's disease.*

typically /ˈtɪpɪkli/ *adverb* in a typical way

tyramine /ˈtaɪrəmiːn/ *noun* an enzyme found in cheese, beans, tinned fish, red wine and yeast extract, which can cause high blood pressure if found in excessive quantities in the brain. ◊ **monoamine oxidase**

tyrosine /ˈtaɪrəsiːn/ *noun* an amino acid in protein which is a component of thyroxine, and is a precursor to the catecholamines dopamine, noradrenaline and adrenaline

tyrosinosis /ˌtaɪrəʊsɪˈnəʊsɪs/ *noun* a condition in which there is irregular metabolism of tyrosine

U

UKCC *abbr* United Kingdom Central Council for Nursing, Midwifery and Health Visiting

ulcer /ˈʌlsə/ *noun* an open sore in the skin or in a mucous membrane, which is inflamed and difficult to heal ○ *stomach ulcer*

ulcerated /ˈʌlsəreɪtɪd/ *adjective* covered with ulcers

ulcerating /ˈʌlsereɪtɪŋ/ *adjective* developing into an ulcer

ulceration /ˌʌlsəˈreɪʃ(ə)n/ *noun* the development of an ulcer

ulcerative /ˈʌls(ə)rətɪv/ *adjective* referring to ulcers, or characterised by ulcers

ulcerative colitis /ˌʌls(ə)rətɪv kəˈlaɪtɪs/ *noun* severe pain in the colon, with diarrhoea and ulcers in the rectum, often with a psychosomatic cause

ulceromembranous gingivitis /ˌʌlsərəʊ ˌmembrənəs ˌdʒɪndʒɪˈvaɪtɪs/ *noun* inflammation of the gums, which can also affect the mucous membrane in the mouth

ulcerous /ˈʌlsərəs/ *adjective* **1.** referring to an ulcer **2.** like an ulcer

ulitis /juˈlaɪtɪs/ *noun* inflammation of the gums

ulna /ˈʌlnə/ *noun* the longer and inner of the two bones in the forearm between the elbow and the wrist. See illustration at HAND in Supplement. Compare **radius**

ulnar /ˈʌlnə/ *adjective* referring to the ulna

'…the whole joint becomes disorganised, causing ulnar deviation of the fingers resulting in the typical deformity of the rheumatoid arthritic hand' [*Nursing Times*]

ulnar artery /ˈʌlnər ˌɑːtəri/ *noun* an artery which branches from the brachial artery at the elbow and runs down the inside of the forearm to join the radial artery in the palm of the hand

ulnar nerve /ˈʌlnə nɜːv/ *noun* a nerve which runs from the neck to the elbow and controls the muscles in the forearm and some of the fingers

COMMENT: The ulnar nerve passes near the surface of the skin at the elbow, where it can easily be hit, giving the effect of the 'funny bone'.

ulnar pulse /ˈʌlnə pʌls/ *noun* a secondary pulse in the wrist, taken near the inner edge of the forearm

ultra- /ʌltrə/ *prefix* **1.** further than **2.** extremely

ultrafiltration /ˌʌltrəfɪlˈtreɪʃ(ə)n/ *noun* the process of filtering the blood to remove tiny particles, e.g. when the blood is filtered by the kidney

ultramicroscopic /ʌltrəˌmaɪkrəˈskɒpɪk/ *adjective* referring to something so small that it cannot be seen using a standard microscope

ultrasonic /ˌʌltrəˈsɒnɪk/ *adjective* referring to ultrasound

ultrasonic probe /ˌʌltrəsɒnɪk ˈprəʊb/ *noun* an instrument which locates organs or tissues inside the body using ultrasound

ultrasonics /ˌʌltrəˈsɒnɪks/ *noun* the study of ultrasound and its use in medical treatments

ultrasonic waves /ˌʌltrəsɒnɪk ˈweɪvz/ *plural noun* same as **ultrasound**

ultrasonogram /ˌʌltrəˈsɒnəgræm/ *noun* a picture made with ultrasound for the purpose of medical examination or diagnosis

ultrasonograph /ˌʌltrəˈsɒnəgrɑːf/ *noun* a machine which takes pictures of internal organs, using ultrasound

ultrasonography /ˌʌltrəsəˈnɒgrəfi/ *noun* the procedure of passing ultrasound waves through the body and recording echoes which show details of internal organs. Also called **echography**

ultrasonotomography /ʌltrəˌsɒnətəˈmɒgrəfi/ *noun* the procedure of making images using ultrasound of organs which are placed at different depths inside the body

ultrasound /ˈʌltrəsaʊnd/ *noun* very high frequency sound waves which can be reflected off internal body parts or off a fetus in the womb to create images for medical examination (NOTE: No plural for **ultrasound**.)

COMMENT: The very high frequency waves of ultrasound can be used to detect and record organs or growths inside the body, in a similar way to the use of X-rays, by recording the differences in echoes sent back from different tissues. Ultrasound is used routinely to monitor the development of a fetus in the womb, and to treat some conditions such as internal bruising. It can also destroy bacteria and calculi.

ultrasound marker /ˈʌltrəsaʊnd ˌmɑːkə/ *noun* an unusual physical characteristic seen in an ultrasound examination of a fetus which is an indication of the existence of a genetic or developmental disorder

ultrasound probe /ˈʌltrəsaʊnd prəʊb/ *noun* same as **ultrasonic probe**

ultrasound scan /ˈʌltrəsaʊnd skæn/ *noun* the examination of internal parts of the body, especially a fetus in the womb, using ultrasound technology

ultrasound scanning /ˈʌltrəsaʊnd ˌskænɪŋ/, **ultrasound screening** /ˈʌltrəsaʊnd ˌskriːnɪŋ/ *noun* a method of gathering information about the body by taking images using high-frequency sound waves

ultrasound treatment /ˈʌltrəsaʊnd ˌtriːtmənt/ *noun* the treatment of soft tissue inflammation using ultrasound waves

ultraviolet *adjective* referring to the short invisible rays beyond the violet end of the spectrum, which form the element in sunlight which tans the skin, helps the skin produce Vitamin D and kills bacteria. Abbr **UV**

ultraviolet lamp /ˌʌltrəˌvaɪələt ˈlæmp/ *noun* a lamp which gives off ultraviolet rays

ultraviolet radiation /ˌʌltrəˌvaɪələt reɪdiˈeɪʃ(ə)n/, **ultraviolet rays** /ˌʌltrəˈvaɪələt reɪs/ *noun* short invisible rays of ultraviolet light. Abbr **UVR**

umbilical /ʌmˈbɪlɪk(ə)l/ *adjective* referring to the navel

umbilical circulation /ʌmˌbɪlɪk(ə)l ˌsɜːkjʊˈleɪʃ(ə)n/ *noun* the circulation of blood from the mother's bloodstream through the umbilical cord into the fetus

umbilical cord /ʌmˈbɪlɪk(ə)l kɔːd/ *noun* a cord containing two arteries and one vein which links the fetus inside the uterus to the placenta

COMMENT: The arteries carry the blood and nutrients from the placenta to the fetus and the vein carries the waste from the fetus back to the placenta. When the baby is born, the umbilical cord is cut and the end tied in a knot. After a few days, this drops off, leaving the navel marking the place where the cord was originally attached.

umbilical hernia /ʌmˌbɪlɪk(ə)l ˈhɜːniə/ *noun* a hernia which bulges at the navel, usually in young children. Also called **exomphalos**

umbilical region /ʌmˈbɪlɪk(ə)l ˌriːdʒ(ə)n/ *noun* the central part of the abdomen, below the epigastrium

umbilicated /ʌmˈbɪlɪkeɪtɪd/ *adjective* with a small depression, like a navel, in the centre

umbilicus /ʌmˈbɪlɪkəs/ *noun* same as **navel**

umbo /ˈʌmbəʊ/ *noun* a projecting part in the middle of the outer side of the eardrum

un- /ʌn/ *prefix* not

unaided /ʌnˈeɪdɪd/ *adjective* without any help ○ *Two days after the operation, he was able to walk unaided.*

unblock /ʌnˈblɒk/ *verb* to remove something which is blocking ○ *An operation to unblock an artery.*

unciform bone /ˈʌnsɪfɔːm bəʊn/ *noun* one of the eight small carpal bones in the wrist, shaped like a hook. Also called **hamate bone**

uncinate /ˈʌnsɪnət/ *adjective* shaped like a hook

uncinate epilepsy /ˌʌnsɪnət ˈepɪlepsi/ *noun* a type of temporal lobe epilepsy, in which the person has hallucinations of smell and taste

unconditioned response /ˌʌnkən ˌdɪʃ(ə)nd rɪˈspɒns/ *noun* a response to a stimulus which occurs automatically, by instinct, and has not been learned

unconscious /ʌnˈkɒnʃəs/ *adjective* not aware of what is happening ○ *She was unconscious for two days after the accident.* ■ *noun* □ **the unconscious** (*in psychology*) the part of the mind which stores feelings, memories or desires that someone cannot consciously call up. ◊ **subconscious**

unconsciousness /ʌnˈkɒnʃəsnəs/ *noun* the state of being unconscious, e.g. as a result of lack of oxygen or from some other external cause such as a blow on the head

uncontrollable /ˌʌnkənˈtrəʊləb(ə)l/ *adjective* not able to be controlled ○ *The uncontrollable spread of the disease through the population.*

uncoordinated /ˌʌnkəʊˈɔːdɪneɪtɪd/ *adjective* not working together ○ *His finger movements are completely uncoordinated.*

uncus /ˈʌŋkəs/ *noun* a projecting part of the cerebral hemisphere, shaped like a hook

undecenoic acid /ʌnˌdesɪnəʊɪk ˈæsɪd/, **undecylenic acid** /ʌnˌdɪsɪlenɪk ˈæsɪd/ *noun* a substance made from castor bean oil, used in the treatment of fungal infections such as thrush

under- /ʌndə/ *prefix* less than usual, too little

undergo /ˌʌndəˈgəʊ/ *verb* to experience something such as a procedure or operation ○ *He underwent an appendicectomy.* ○ *There are six patients undergoing physiotherapy.*

underhydration /ˌʌndəhaɪˈdreɪʃ(ə)n/ *noun* the condition of having too little water in the body

undernourished /ˌʌndəˈnʌrɪʃt/ *adjective* having too little food

underproduction /ˌʌndəprəˈdʌkʃ(ə)n/ *noun* the act of producing less than normal

undertake /ˌʌndəˈteɪk/ *verb* to carry out a procedure such as a surgical operation ○ *Replacement of the joint is mainly undertaken to relieve pain.*

underweight /ˌʌndə'weɪt/ *adjective* weighing less than is medically advisable ○ *He is several pounds underweight for his age.*

undescended testis /ˌʌndɪˌsendɪd 'testɪs/ *noun* a condition in which a testis has not descended into the scrotum

undiagnosed /ˌʌnˌdaɪəg'nəʊzd/ *adjective* not identified as a specific disease or disorder

undigested /ˌʌndaɪ'dʒestɪd/ *adjective* referring to food which is not digested in the body

undine /'ʌndiːn/ *noun* a glass container for a solution to bathe the eyes

undress /ʌn'dres/ *verb* to remove clothes

undulant fever /'ʌndjʊlənt ˌfiːvə/ same as **brucellosis**

unfit /ʌn'fɪt/ *adjective* not physically healthy

ungual /'ʌŋgwəl/ *adjective* referring to the fingernails or toenails

unguent /'ʌŋgwənt/ *noun* a smooth oily medicinal substance which can be spread on the skin to soothe irritations

unguentum /ʌŋ'gwentəm/ *noun* (*in pharmacy*) an ointment

unguis /'ʌŋgwɪs/ same as **nail**

unhealthy /ʌn'helθɪ/ *adjective* **1.** not in good physical condition **2.** not helping someone to be healthy ○ *The children have a very unhealthy diet.*

unhygienic /ˌʌnhaɪ'dʒiːnɪk/ *adjective* not clean or good for health ○ *The conditions in the hospital laundry have been criticised as unhygienic.*

uni- /juːni/ *prefix* one

unicellular /ˌjuːni'seljʊlə/ *adjective* referring to an organism formed of one cell

uniform /'juːnɪfɔːm/ *noun* the set of official clothes worn by a group of people such as the nurses in a hospital to identify them ■ *adjective* the same or similar ○ *Healthy red blood cells are of a uniform shape and size.*

unigravida /ˌjuːni'grævɪdə/ same as **primigravida**

unilateral /ˌjuːni'læt(ə)rəl/ *adjective* affecting one side of the body only

unilateral oophorectomy /ˌjuːni ˌlæt(ə)rəl ˌəʊəfə'rektəmi/ *noun* the surgical removal of one ovary

union /'juːnjən/ *noun* the joining together of two parts of a fractured bone. Opposite **non-union.** ◊ **malunion**

uniovular /ˌjuːni'ɒvjʊlə/ *noun* consisting of, or coming from, one ovum

uniovular twins /ˌjuːniˌɒvjʊlə 'twɪnz/ *plural noun* same as **identical twins**

unipara /juː'nɪpərə/ same as **primipara**

unipolar /ˌjuːni'pəʊlə/ *adjective* referring to a neurone with a single process. Compare **bipolar.** See illustration at NEURONE in Supplement

unipolar lead /ˌjuːnipəʊlə 'liːd/ *noun* an electric lead to a single electrode

unipolar neurone /juːniˌpəʊlə 'njʊərəʊn/ *noun* a neurone with a single process. Compare **multipolar neurone, bipolar neurone**. See illustration at NEURONE in Supplement

unit /'juːnɪt/ *noun* **1.** a single part of a larger whole **2.** a part of a hospital that has a specialised function ○ *a burns unit* **3.** a named and agreed standard amount used for measuring something ○ *A gram is an SI unit of weight.* **4.** a quantity of a drug, enzyme, hormone or of blood, taken as a standard for measurement and producing a given effect ○ *three units of blood* ○ *a unit of insulin* **5.** a machine or device ○ *a waste-disposal unit*

    '…the blood loss caused his haemoglobin to drop dangerously low, necessitating two units of RBCs and one unit of fresh frozen plasma' [*RN Magazine*]

United Kingdom Central Council for Nursing, Midwifery, and Health Visiting /juːˌnaɪtɪd ˌkɪŋdəm ˌsentrəl ˌkaʊnsəl fə ˌnɜːsɪŋ mɪdˌwɪfəri ənd 'helθ ˌvɪzɪtɪŋ/ *noun* in the UK from 1979 until April 2002, an organisation which regulated nurses, midwives, and health visitors. The UKCC and the four National Boards have now been replaced by the Nursing and Midwifery Council. Abbr **UKCC**

univalent /ˌjuːni'veɪlənt/ *adjective* same as **monovalent**

universal donor /ˌjuːnɪvɜːs(ə)l 'dəʊnə/ *noun* a person with blood group O, whose blood may be given to anyone

Universal Precautions /ˌjuːnɪvɜːs(ə)l prɪ 'kɔːʃ(ə)nz/ *abbr* UP. ◊ **Standard Precautions**

universal recipient /ˌjuːnɪvɜːs(ə)l rɪ 'sɪpiənt/ *noun* a person with blood group AB who can receive blood from all the other blood groups

unmedicated dressing /ʌnˌmedɪkeɪtɪd 'dresɪŋ/ *noun* a sterile dressing with no antiseptic or other medication on it

unprofessional conduct /ˌʌnprəˌfeʃən(ə)l 'kɒndʌkt/ *noun* action by a professional person such as a doctor or nurse which is considered wrong by the body which regulates the profession

    '…refusing to care for someone with HIV-related disease may well result in disciplinary procedure for unprofessional conduct' [*Nursing Times*]

unqualified /ʌn'kwɒlɪfaɪd/ *adjective* referring to someone who has no qualifications or no licence to practise

unsaturated fat /ʌnˌsætʃəreɪtɪd 'fæt/ *noun* fat which does not have a large amount of hydrogen, and so can be broken down more easily

unstable /ʌn'steɪb(ə)l/ *adjective* referring to something which may change easily ○ *an unstable mental condition.*

unstable angina /ʌnˌsteɪb(ə)l æn'dʒaɪnə/ *noun* angina which has suddenly become worse

unsteady /ʌnˈstedi/ *adjective* likely to fall down when walking ○ *She is still very unsteady on her legs.*

unstriated muscle /ˌʌnstraɪˌeɪtɪd ˈmʌs(ə)l/ *noun* same as **smooth muscle**

unviable /ʌnˈvaɪəb(ə)l/ *adjective* referring to a fetus that cannot live if born

unwanted pregnancy /ʌnˌwɒntɪd ˈpregnənsi/ *noun* a condition in which a woman becomes pregnant without wanting to have a child

unwell /ʌnˈwel/ *adjective* ill ○ *She felt unwell and had to go home.* (NOTE: Not used before a noun: **a sick woman** but **the woman was unwell**.)

upper /ˈʌpə/ *adjective* at the top, higher

upper arm /ˌʌpə ˈɑːm/ *noun* the part of the arm from the shoulder to the elbow

upper limb /ˌʌpə ˈlɪm/ *noun* an arm ○ *There was damage to the upper limbs only.*

upper motor neurone /ˌʌpə ˈməʊtə ˌnjʊərəʊn/ *noun* a neurone which takes impulses from the cerebral cortex

upper respiratory infection /ˌʌpə rɪ ˈspɪrət(ə)ri ɪnˌfekʃən/ *noun* an infection in the upper part of the respiratory system

UPPP *abbr* uvulopalatopharyngoplasty

upset *noun* /ˈʌpset/ a slight illness ■ *adjective* /ʌpˈset/ slightly ill

upside down /ˌʌpsaɪd ˈdaʊn/ *adverb* with the top turned to the bottom

upside-down stomach /ˌʌpsaɪd daʊn ˈstʌmək/ *adverb* US ♦ **diaphragmatic hernia**

uracil /ˈjʊərəsɪl/ *noun* a pyrimidine base, one of the four bases in RNA in which it pairs with thymine

uraemia /jʊˈriːmiə/ *noun* a disorder caused by kidney failure, where urea is retained in the blood, and the person develops nausea, convulsions and in severe cases goes into a coma (NOTE: The US spelling is **uremia**.)

uraemic /jʊˈriːmɪk/ *adjective* referring to uraemia, or having uraemia (NOTE: The US spelling is **uremic**.)

uran- /jʊərən/ *prefix* referring to the palate

uraniscorrhaphy /ˌjʊərənɪˈskɒrəfi/ *noun* same as **palatorrhaphy**

urataemia /ˌjʊərəˈtiːmiə/ *noun* a condition in which urates are present in the blood, e.g. in gout

urate /ˈjʊəreɪt/ *noun* a salt of uric acid found in urine

uraturia /ˌjʊərəˈtjʊəriə/ *noun* the presence of excessive amounts of urates in the urine, e.g. in gout

urea /jʊˈriːə/ *noun* a substance produced in the liver from excess amino acids, and excreted by the kidneys into the urine

urease /ˈjʊərieɪz/ *noun* an enzyme which converts urea into ammonia and carbon dioxide

urecchysis /jʊˈrekɪsɪs/ *noun* a condition in which uric acid leaves the blood and enters connective tissue

uresis /jʊˈriːsɪs/ *noun* the act of passing urine

ureter /jʊˈriːtə, ˈjʊərɪtə/ *noun* one of the two tubes which take urine from the kidneys to the urinary bladder. See illustration at **KIDNEY** in Supplement. Also called **urinary duct**

ureter- /jʊriːtə/ *prefix* same as **uretero-** (*used before vowels*)

ureteral /jʊˈriːtərəl/ *adjective* referring to the ureters

ureterectomy /ˌjʊərɪtəˈrektəmi/ *noun* the surgical removal of a ureter

ureteric /ˌjʊərɪˈterɪk/ *adjective* same as **ureteral**

ureteric calculus /ˌjʊərɪterɪk ˈkælkjʊləs/ *noun* a kidney stone in the ureter

ureteric catheter /ˌjʊərɪterɪk ˈkæθɪtə/ *noun* a catheter passed through the ureter to the kidney, to inject an opaque solution into the kidney before taking an X-ray

ureteritis /ˌjʊərɪtəˈraɪtɪs/ *noun* inflammation of a ureter

uretero- /jʊriːtərəʊ/ *prefix* referring to the ureter

ureterocele /jʊˈriːtərəʊsiːl/ *noun* swelling in a ureter caused by narrowing of the opening where the ureter enters the bladder

ureterocolostomy /jʊˌriːtərəʊkɒˈlɒstəmi/ *noun* a surgical operation to implant the ureter into the sigmoid colon, so as to bypass the bladder

ureteroenterostomy /jʊˌriːtərəʊˌentə ˈrɒstəmi/ *noun* an artificially formed passage between the ureter and the intestine

ureterolith /jʊˈriːtərəʊlɪθ/ *noun* a stone in a ureter

ureterolithotomy /jʊˌriːtərəʊlɪˈθɒtəmi/ *noun* the surgical removal of a stone from the ureter

ureterolysis /ˌjʊərɪtəˈrɒləsɪs/ *noun* a surgical operation to free one or both ureters from adhesions or surrounding tissue

ureteroneocystostomy /jʊˌriːtərəʊ ˌniːəʊsaɪˈstɒstəmi/ *noun* a surgical operation to transplant a ureter to a different location in the bladder

ureteronephrectomy /jʊˌriːtərəʊnɪ ˈfrektəmi/ *noun* same as **nephroureterectomy**

ureteroplasty /jʊˈriːtərəʊplæsti/ *noun* a surgical operation to repair a ureter

ureteropyelonephritis /jʊˌriːtərəʊ ˌpaɪələʊnɪˈfraɪtɪs/ *noun* inflammation of the ureter and the pelvis of the kidney to which it is attached

ureteroscope /jʊˈriːtərəʊskəʊp/ *noun* an instrument which is passed into the ureter and up into the kidneys, usually used to locate or remove a stone

ureteroscopy /ˌjʊərɪtəˈrɒskəpi/ *noun* an examination of the ureter with a ureteroscope

ureterosigmoidostomy /jʊˌriːtərəʊsɪgↆmɔːɪˈdɒstəmi/ same as **ureterocolostomy**

ureterostomy /ˌjʊərɪtəˈrɒstəmi/ *noun* a surgical operation to make an artificial opening for the ureter into the abdominal wall, so that urine can be passed directly out of the body

ureterotomy /ˌjʊərɪtəˈrɒtəmi/ *noun* a surgical operation to make an incision into the ureter, mainly to remove a stone

ureterovaginal /jʊˌriːtərəʊvəˈdʒaɪn(ə)l/ *adjective* referring to the ureter and the vagina

urethr- /jʊəriːθr/ *prefix* same as **urethro-** (*used before vowels*)

urethra /juˈriːθrə/ *noun* a tube which takes urine from the bladder to be passed out of the body. See illustration at **UROGENITAL SYSTEM** in Supplement

COMMENT: In males, the urethra serves two purposes: the discharge of both urine and semen. The male urethra is about 20cm long; in women it is shorter, about 3cm and this relative shortness is one of the reasons for the predominance of bladder infection and inflammation (cystitis) in women. The urethra has sphincter muscles at either end which help control the flow of urine.

urethral /juˈriːθr(ə)l/ *adjective* referring to the urethra

urethral catheter /juˌriːθr(ə)l ˈkæθɪtə/ *noun* a catheter passed up the urethra to allow urine to flow out of the bladder, used to empty the bladder before an abdominal operation. Also called **urinary catheter**

urethral stricture /juˌriːθrəl ˈstrɪktʃə/ *noun* a condition in which the urethra is narrowed or blocked by a growth. Also called **urethrostenosis**

urethritis /ˌjʊərəˈθraɪtɪs/ *noun* inflammation of the urethra

urethro- /juriːθrəʊ/ *prefix* referring to the urethra

urethrocele /juˈriːθrəsiːl/ *noun* 1. a swelling formed in a weak part of the wall of the urethra 2. prolapse of the urethra in a woman

urethrogram /juˈriːθrəgræm/ *noun* an X-ray photograph of the urethra

urethrography /jʊərɪˈθrɒgrəfi/ *noun* X-ray examination of the urethra

urethroplasty /juˈriːθrəplæsti/ *noun* a surgical operation to repair a urethra

urethrorrhaphy /jʊərɪˈθrɒrəfi/ *noun* a surgical operation to repair a torn urethra

urethrorrhoea /juˌriːθrəˈriːə/ *noun* the discharge of fluid from the urethra, usually associated with urethritis

urethroscope /jʊˈriːθrəskəʊp/ *noun* a surgical instrument, used to examine the interior of a man's urethra

urethroscopy /ˌjʊərɪˈθrɒskəpi/ *noun* an examination of the inside of a man's urethra with a urethroscope

urethrostenosis /jʊˌriːθrəʊstəˈnəʊsɪs/ *noun* same as **urethral stricture**

urethrostomy /ˌjʊərɪˈθrɒstəmi/ *noun* a surgical operation to make an opening for a man's urethra between the scrotum and the anus

urethrotomy /ˌjʊərɪˈθrɒtəmi/ *noun* a surgical operation to open a blocked or narrowed urethra. Also called **Wheelhouse's operation**

uretic /juˈriːtɪk/ *adjective* referring to the passing of urine

urge /ɜːdʒ/ *noun* a strong need to do something

urge incontinence /ˈɜːdʒ ɪnˌkɒntɪnəns/ *noun* a condition in which someone feels a very strong need to urinate and cannot retain their urine

urgent /ˈɜːdʒənt/ *adjective* needing to be done quickly ○ *She had an urgent operation for strangulated hernia.*

urgently /ˈɜːdʒəntli/ *adverb* immediately ○ *The relief team urgently requires more medical supplies.*

-uria /jʊəriə/ *suffix* 1. a condition of the urine 2. a disease characterised by a condition of the urine

uric acid /ˌjʊərɪk ˈæsɪd/ *noun* a chemical compound which is formed from nitrogen in waste products from the body and which also forms crystals in the joints of people who have gout

uricacidaemia /ˌjʊərɪkæsɪˈdiːmiə/ *noun* same as **lithaemia**

uricosuric /ˌjʊərɪkəˈsjʊərɪk/ *noun* a drug which increases the amount of uric acid excreted in the urine

uridrosis /ˌjʊərɪˈdrəʊsɪs/ *noun* a condition in which excessive urea forms in the sweat

urin- /jʊərɪn/ *prefix* same as **urino-** (*used before vowels*)

urinalysis /ˌjʊərɪˈnæləsɪs/ *noun* the analysis of urine, to detect diseases such as diabetes mellitus

urinary /ˈjʊərɪn(ə)ri/ *adjective* referring to urine

urinary bladder /ˌjʊərɪn(ə)ri ˈblædə/ *noun* a sac where the urine collects after passing from the kidneys through the ureters, before being passed out of the body through the urethra. See illustration at **KIDNEY, UROGENITAL SYSTEM (MALE)** in Supplement

urinary catheter /ˌjʊərɪn(ə)ri ˈkæθɪtə/ *noun* same as **urethral catheter**

urinary duct /ˈjʊərɪn(ə)ri dʌkt/ *noun* same as **ureter**

urinary incontinence /ˌjʊərɪn(ə)ri ɪnˈkɒnↆtɪnəns/ *noun* the involuntary emission of urine

urinary obstruction /ˌjʊərɪn(ə)ri əb'strʌkʃən/ *noun* a blockage of the urethra, which prevents urine being passed

urinary retention /ˌjʊərɪn(ə)ri rɪ'tenʃən/ *noun* the inability to pass urine, usually because the urethra is blocked or because the prostate gland is enlarged. Also called **urine retention**

urinary system /ˌjʊərɪn(ə)ri 'sɪstəm/ *noun* a system of organs and ducts which separate waste liquids from the blood and excrete them as urine, including the kidneys, bladder, ureters and urethra

urinary tract /'jʊərɪn(ə)ri trækt/ *noun* the set of tubes down which the urine passes from the kidneys to the bladder and from the bladder out of the body

urinary tract infection /'jʊərɪn(ə)ri trækt ɪnˌfekʃən/ *noun* a bacterial infection of any part of the urinary system. Symptoms are usually a need to urinate frequently and pain on urination. Abbr **UTI**

urinate /'jʊərɪneɪt/ *verb* to pass urine from the body

urination /ˌjʊərɪ'neɪʃ(ə)n/ *noun* the passing of urine out of the body. Also called **micturition**

urine /'jʊərɪn/ *noun* a yellowish liquid, containing water and waste products, mainly salt and urea, which is excreted by the kidneys and passed out of the body through the ureters, bladder and urethra

urine retention /'jʊərɪn rɪˌtenʃ(ə)n/ *noun* same as **urinary retention**

uriniferous /ˌjʊərɪ'nɪfərəs/ *adjective* carrying urine

uriniferous tubule /ˌjʊərɪˌnɪf(ə)rəs 'tjuːbjuːl/ *noun* same as **renal tubule**

urino- /jʊərɪnəʊ/ *prefix* referring to urine

urinogenital /ˌjʊərɪnəʊ'dʒenɪt(ə)l/ *adjective* same as **urogenital**

urinometer /ˌjʊərɪ'nɒmɪtə/ *noun* an instrument which measures the specific gravity of urine

urobilin /ˌjʊərəʊ'baɪlɪn/ *noun* a yellow pigment formed when urobilinogen comes into contact with air

urobilinogen /ˌjʊərəʊbaɪ'lɪnədʒən/ *noun* a colourless pigment formed when bilirubin is reduced to stercobilinogen in the intestines

urocele /'jʊərəsiːl/ *noun* a swelling in the scrotum which contains urine

urochesia /ˌjʊərə'kiːziə/ *noun* the passing of urine through the rectum, due to injury of the urinary system (NOTE: The US spelling is **urochezia**.)

urochrome /'jʊərəkrəʊm/ *noun* the pigment which colours the urine yellow

urodynamics /ˌjʊərəʊdaɪ'næmɪks/ *plural noun* the active changes which occur during

the function of the bladder, urethral sphincter and pelvic floor muscles

urogenital /ˌjʊərəʊ'dʒenɪt(ə)l/ *adjective* referring to the urinary and genital systems. Also called **urinogenital**

urogenital diaphragm /ˌjʊərəˌdʒenɪt(ə)l ˌdaɪə'fræm/ *noun* a fibrous layer beneath the prostate gland through which the urethra passes

urogenital system /ˌjʊərəʊ'dʒenɪt(ə)l ˌsɪstəm/ *noun* the whole of the urinary tract and reproductive system

urogram /'jʊərəgræm/ *noun* an X-ray picture of the urinary tract, or of a part of it

urography /jʊ'rɒɡrəfi/ *noun* an X-ray examination of part of the urinary system after injection of radio-opaque dye

urokinase /ˌjʊərəʊ'kaɪneɪz/ *noun* an enzyme formed in the kidneys, which begins the process of breaking down blood clots

urolith /'jʊərəlɪθ/ *noun* a stone in the urinary system

urological /ˌjʊərə'lɒdʒɪk(ə)l/ *adjective* referring to urology

urologist /jʊ'rɒlədʒɪst/ *noun* a doctor who specialises in urology

urology /jʊ'rɒlədʒi/ *noun* the scientific study of the urinary system and its diseases

urostomy /jʊ'rɒstəmi/ *noun* the surgical creation of an artificial urethra

urticaria /ˌɜːtɪ'keəriə/ *noun* an allergic reaction to injections, particular foods or plants where the skin forms irritating reddish patches. Also called **hives, nettle rash**

USP *abbr* United States Pharmacopeia. ♦ **pharmacopoeia**

usual /'juːʒʊəl/ *adjective* expected or typical

uter- /juːtə/ *prefix* same as **utero-** (*used before vowels*)

uteri /'juːt(ə)ri/ *plural of* **uterus**

uterine /'juːtəraɪn/ *adjective* referring to the uterus

uterine cavity /ˌjuːtəraɪn 'kævɪti/ *noun* the inside of the uterus

uterine fibroid /ˌjuːtəraɪn 'faɪbrɔɪd/, **uterine fibroma** /ˌjuːtəraɪn faɪ'brəʊmə/ *noun* same as **fibroid tumour**

uterine procidentia /ˌjuːtəraɪn prəʊsɪ'denʃə/, **uterine prolapse** /ˌjuːtəˌraɪn 'prəʊlæps/ *noun* a condition in which part of the uterus has passed through the vagina, usually after childbirth

COMMENT: Uterine procidentia has three stages of severity: in the first the cervix descends into the vagina, in the second the cervix is outside the vagina, but part of the uterus is still inside, and in the third stage, the whole uterus passes outside the vagina.

uterine retroflexion /ˌjuːtəraɪn ˌretrəʊ'flekʃ(ə)n/ *noun* a condition in which the uterus bends backwards away from its usual position

uterine retroversion /ˌjuːtəraɪn retrəʊ
'vɜːʃ(ə)n/ *noun* a condition in which the uterus slopes backwards away from its usual position

uterine subinvolution /ˌjuːtəraɪn ˌsʌb
ɪnvə'luːʃ(ə)n/ *noun* a condition in which the uterus does not go back to its previous size after childbirth

uterine tube /'juːtəraɪn tjuːb/ *noun* same as **Fallopian tube**

utero- /juːtərəʊ/ *prefix* referring to the uterus

uterocele /'juːtərəsiːl/ *noun* a hernia of the uterus. Also called **hysterocele**

uterogestation /ˌjuːtərədʒe'steɪʃ(ə)n/ *noun* a standard pregnancy, where the fetus develops in the uterus

uterography /ˌjuːtə'rɒgrəfi/ *noun* an X-ray examination of the uterus

utero-ovarian /ˌjuːtərəʊ əʊ'veəriən/ *adjective* referring to the uterus and the ovaries

uterosalpingography /ˌjuːtərəʊsælpɪŋ
'gɒgrəfi/ same as **hysterosalpingography**

uterovesical /ˌjuːtərəʊ'vesɪk(ə)l/ *adjective* referring to the uterus and the bladder

uterus /'juːt(ə)rəs/ *noun* the hollow organ in a woman's pelvic cavity, behind the bladder and in front of the rectum in which the embryo develops before birth. Also called **womb**. See illustration at **UROGENITAL SYSTEM (FEMALE)** in Supplement (NOTE: For other terms referring to the uterus, see words beginning with **hyster-, hystero-, metr-, metro-**.)

COMMENT: The top of the uterus is joined to the Fallopian tubes which link it to the ovaries, and the lower end (cervix uteri) opens into the vagina. When an ovum is fertilised it becomes implanted in the wall of the uterus and develops into an embryo inside it. If fertilisation and pregnancy do not take place, the lining of the uterus (endometrium) is shed during menstruation. At childbirth, strong contractions of the wall of the uterus (myometrium) help push the baby out through the vagina.

uterus didelphys /ˌjuːt(ə)rəs daɪ'delfɪs/ *noun* same as **double uterus**

UTI *abbr* urinary tract infection

utricle /'juːtrɪk(ə)l/, **utriculus** /jʊ'trɪkjʊləs/ *noun* a large sac inside the vestibule of the ear, which relates information about the upright position of the head to the brain

UV *abbreviation* ultraviolet

UV-absorbing lens /juː ˌviː əb,zɔːbɪŋ
'lenz/ *noun* a lens devised to absorb UVR in order to protect the eyes against the sun

uvea /'juːviə/ *noun* a layer of organs in the eye beneath the sclera, formed of the iris, the ciliary body and the choroid. Also called **uveal tract**

uveal /'juːviəl/ *adjective* referring to the uvea

uveal tract /'juːviəl trækt/ *noun* same as **uvea**

uveitis /ˌjuːvi'aɪtɪs/ *noun* inflammation of any part of the uvea

uveoparotid fever /ˌjuːviə'pærətɪd ˌfiːvə/, **uveoparotid syndrome** /ˌjuːviə'pærətɪd ˌsɪndrəʊm/ *noun* inflammation of the uvea and of the parotid gland

UVR *abbr* ultraviolet radiation

uvula /'juːvjʊlə/ *noun* a piece of soft tissue which hangs down from the back of the soft palate

uvular /'juːvjʊlə/ *adjective* referring to the uvula

uvulectomy /ˌjuːvjʊ'lektəmi/ *noun* the surgical removal of the uvula

uvulitis /ˌjuːvjʊ'laɪtɪs/ *noun* inflammation of the uvula

uvulopalatopharyngoplasty /ˌjuːvjʊləʊ
ˌpælətəʊfə'rɪŋgəʊplæsti/ *noun* a surgical operation to remove the uvula and other soft tissue in the palate, in order to widen the airways and treat the problem of snoring. Abbr **UPPP**

V

vaccinate /'væksɪneɪt/ *verb* to introduce vaccine into a person's body in order to make the body create its own antibodies, so making the person immune to the disease (NOTE: You vaccinate someone **against** a disease.)

vaccination /ˌvæksɪ'neɪʃ(ə)n/ *noun* the action of vaccinating someone

COMMENT: Originally the words **vaccination** and **vaccine** applied only to smallpox immunisation, but they are now used for immunisation against any disease. Vaccination is mainly given against cholera, diphtheria, rabies, smallpox, tuberculosis, and typhoid.

vaccine /'væksiːn/ *noun* a substance which contains antigens to a disease or a weak form of a disease, used to protect people against it

vaccinotherapy /ˌvæksɪnəʊ'θerəpi/ *noun* the treatment of a disease with a vaccine

vacuole /'vækjuəʊl/ *noun* a space in a fold of a cell membrane

vacuum /'vækjuəm/ *noun* a space which is completely empty of all matter, including air

vacuum extraction /'vækjuəm ɪk ˌstrækʃən/ *noun* the procedure of pulling on the head of the baby with a suction instrument to aid birth

vacuum extractor /'vækjuəm ɪkˌstræktə/ *noun* a surgical instrument formed of a rubber suction cup which is used in vacuum extraction during childbirth

vacuum suction /'vækjuəm ˌsʌkʃən/ *noun* a method used to achieve an abortion, after dilatation of the cervix. Also called **aspiration**

vagal /'veɪɡ(ə)l/ *adjective* referring to the vagus nerve

vagal tone /ˌveɪɡ(ə)l 'təʊn/ *noun* the action of the vagus nerve to slow the beat of the sinoatrial node

vagin- /vədʒaɪn/ *prefix* referring to the vagina

vagina /və'dʒaɪnə/ *noun* a passage in a woman's reproductive tract between the entrance to the uterus, the cervix, and the vulva, able to stretch enough to allow a baby to pass through during childbirth. See illustration at UROGENITAL SYSTEM (FEMALE) in Supplement (NOTE: For other terms referring to the vagina, see words beginning with **colp-, colpo-**.)

vaginal /və'dʒaɪn(ə)l/ *adjective* referring to the vagina

vaginal bleeding /vəˌdʒaɪn(ə)l 'bliːdɪŋ/ *noun* bleeding from the vagina

vaginal delivery /vəˌdʒaɪn(ə)l dɪ'lɪv(ə)ri/ *noun* the birth of a baby through the mother's vagina, without surgical intervention

vaginal diaphragm /vəˌdʒaɪn(ə)l 'daɪəfræm/ *noun* a circular contraceptive device for women, which is inserted into the vagina and placed over the neck of the uterus before sexual intercourse

vaginal discharge /vəˌdʒaɪn(ə)l 'dɪstʃɑːdʒ/ *noun* the flow of liquid from the vagina

vaginal douche /vəˌdʒaɪn(ə)l 'duːʃ/ *noun* **1.** the process of washing out the vagina **2.** a device or liquid for washing out the vagina

vaginal examination /vəˌdʒaɪn(ə)l ɪɡ ˌzæmɪ'neɪʃ(ə)n/ *noun* the act of checking the vagina for signs of disease or growth

vaginalis /ˌvædʒɪ'neɪlɪs/ *noun* **1.** same as **Trichomonas vaginalis 2.** same as **tunica vaginalis**

vaginal orifice /vəˌdʒaɪn(ə)l 'ɒrɪfɪs/ *noun* an opening leading from the vulva to the uterus

vaginal proctocele /vəˌdʒaɪn(ə)l 'prɒktəsiːl/ *noun* a condition associated with prolapse of the uterus, where the rectum protrudes into the vagina

vaginal suppository *noun* same as **pessary 1**

vaginectomy /ˌvædʒɪ'nektəmi/ *noun* a surgical operation to remove the vagina or part of it

vaginismus /ˌvædʒɪ'nɪzməs/ *noun* a painful contraction of the vagina which prevents sexual intercourse

vaginitis /ˌvædʒɪ'naɪtɪs/ *noun* inflammation of the vagina which is mainly caused by the bacterium *Trichomonas vaginalis* or by a fungus *Candida albicans*

vaginography /ˌvædʒɪ'nɒɡrəfi/ *noun* an X-ray examination of the vagina

vaginoplasty /və'dʒaɪnəplæsti/ *noun* a surgical operation to graft tissue on to the vagina

vaginoscope /'vædʒɪnəʊskəʊp/ *noun* same as **colposcope**

vago- /veɪɡɒ/ *prefix* referring to the vagus nerve

vagotomy /veɪ'ɡɒtəmi/ *noun* a surgical operation to cut through the vagus nerve which controls the nerves in the stomach, as a treatment for peptic ulcers

vagus /'veɪɡəs/, **vagus nerve** /'veɪɡəs nɜːv/ *noun* either of the tenth pair of cranial nerves which carry sensory and motor neurons serving the heart, lungs, stomach, and various other organs and control swallowing. Also called **pneumogastric nerve**

valgus /'vælɡəs/, **valgum** /'vælɡəm/, **valga** /'vælɡə/ *adjective* turning outwards. ◊ **hallux valgus**. Compare **varus**

validity /və'lɪdɪti/ *noun* (*of a study*) the fact of being based on sound research and methods which exclude alternative explanations of a result

valine /'veɪliːn/ *noun* an essential amino acid

Valium /'væliəm/ a trade name for diazepam

vallate papillae /ˌvæleɪt pə'pɪliː/ *plural noun* large papillae which form a line towards the back of the tongue and contain taste buds

vallecula /və'lekjʊlə/ *noun* a natural depression or fissure in an organ as between the hemispheres of the brain (NOTE: The plural is **valleculae**.)

Valsalva's manoeuvre /væl'sælvəz mə,nuːvə/ *noun* the process of breathing out while holding the nostrils closed and keeping the mouth shut, used in order to test the functioning of the Eustachian tubes or to adjust the pressure in the middle ear

value /'væljuː/ *noun* **1.** the degree to which something is useful or necessary ○ *food with low nutritional value* **2.** a number or amount that is unknown and is shown as a symbol ■ *plural noun* **values** the views someone has about the appropriate way to behave ○ *respect for different cultural values*

valve /vælv/ *noun* a flap which opens and closes to allow liquid to pass in one direction only, e.g. in the heart, blood vessels or lymphatic vessels

valvotomy /væl'vɒtəmi/ *noun* a surgical operation to cut into a valve to make it open wider

valvula /'vælvjʊlə/ *noun* a small valve (NOTE: The plural is **valvulae**.)

valvular /'vælvjʊlə/ *adjective* referring to a valve

valvular disease of the heart /ˌvælvjʊlə dɪ,ziːz əv ði: 'hɑːt/ *noun* an inflammation of the membrane which lines the valves of the heart. Abbr **VDH**

valvulitis /ˌvælvjʊ'laɪtɪs/ *noun* inflammation of a valve in the heart

valvuloplasty /'vælvjʊləʊplæsti/ *noun* surgery to repair valves in the heart without opening the heart

'…in percutaneous balloon valvuloplasty a catheter introduced through the femoral vein is placed across the aortic valve and into the left ventricle; the catheter is removed and a valve-dilating catheter bearing a 15mm balloon is placed across the valve'
[*Journal of the American Medical Association*]

valvulotomy /ˌvælvjʊ'lɒtəmi/ *noun* same as **valvotomy**

vancomycin /ˌvænkəʊ'maɪsɪn/ *noun* an antibiotic which is effective against some bacteria which are resistant to other antibiotics. Strains of bacteria resistant to vancomycin have now developed.

van den Bergh test /ˌvæn den 'bɜːɡ ,test/ *noun* a test of blood serum to see if a case of jaundice is caused by an obstruction in the liver or by haemolysis of red blood cells [After A.A. Hijmans van den Bergh (1869–1943), Dutch physician]

vaporise /'veɪpəraɪz/, **vaporize** *verb* to turn a liquid into a vapour

vaporiser /'veɪpəraɪzə/, **vaporizer** *noun* a device which warms a liquid to which medicinal oil has been added, so that it provides a vapour which someone can inhale

vapour /'veɪpə/ *noun* **1.** a substance in the form of a gas **2.** steam from a mixture of liquid and a medicinal oil (NOTE: The US spelling is **vapor**.)

Vaquez-Osler disease /væ,keɪz 'ɒslə dɪ,ziːz/ *noun* same as **polycythaemia vera** [After Henri Vaquez (1860–1936), French physician, Sir William Osler (1849–1919), Professor of Medicine in Montreal, Philadelphia, Baltimore and then Oxford]

vara /'veərə/ *adjective* same as **varus**

variant CJD /ˌveəriənt ,siːdʒeɪ 'diː/ *noun* a form of Creutzfeldt-Jakob disease which was observed first in the 1980s, especially affecting younger people. Abbr **vCJD**

variation /ˌveəri'eɪʃ(ə)n/ *noun* a change from one level to another ○ *There is a noticeable variation in his pulse rate.* ○ *The chart shows the variations in the patient's temperature over a twenty-four hour period.*

varicectomy /ˌværi'sektəmi/ *noun* a surgical operation to remove a vein or part of a vein

varicella /ˌværi'selə/ *noun* same as **chickenpox**

varicella-zoster virus /ˌværiselə 'zɒstə ,vaɪrəs/ *noun* a herpes virus that causes chickenpox and shingles

varices /'værisiːz/ *plural of* **varix**

varicocele /'værikəʊsiːl/ *noun* swelling of a vein in the spermatic cord which can be corrected by surgery

varicose /'værikəʊs/ *adjective* **1.** affected with or having varicose veins **2.** designed for the treatment of varicose veins **3.** relating to or producing swelling

varicose eczema /ˌværɪkəʊs 'eksɪmə/ *noun* eczema which develops on the legs, caused by bad circulation. Also called **hypostatic eczema**

varicose ulcer /ˌværɪkəʊs 'ʌlsə/ *noun* an ulcer in the leg as a result of bad circulation and varicose veins

varicose vein /ˌværɪkəʊs 'veɪn/ *noun* a vein, usually in the legs, which becomes twisted and swollen

varicosity /ˌværɪ'kɒsɪti/ *noun* (*of veins*) the condition of being swollen and twisted

varicotomy /ˌværɪ'kɒtəmi/ *noun* a surgical operation to make a cut into a varicose vein

varifocals /'veərɪˌfəʊk(ə)lz/ *plural noun* spectacles with lenses which have varying focal lengths from top to bottom, for looking at things at different distances from the wearer

variola /və'raɪələ/ *noun* same as **smallpox**

varioloid /'veərɪəlɔɪd/ *noun* a type of mild smallpox which affects people who have already had smallpox or have been vaccinated against it

varix /'veərɪks/ *noun* a swollen blood vessel, especially a swollen vein in the leg (NOTE: The plural is **varices**.)

Varolii /və'rəʊli:/ ◆ **pons Varolii**

varus /'veərəs/, **varum** /'veərəm/, **vara** /'veərə/ *adjective* turning inwards. ◊ **coxa vara**. Compare **valgus**

vary /'veəri/ *verb* **1.** to change ○ *The dosage varies according to the age of the patient.* **2.** to try different actions ○ *The patient was recommended to vary her diet.*

vas /væs/ *noun* a tube in the body (NOTE: The plural is **vasa**.)

vas- /væs/ *prefix* same as **vaso-**

vasa efferentia /ˌveɪsə efə'rentɪə/ *plural noun* the group of small tubes which sperm travel down from the testis to the epididymis

vasa vasorum /ˌveɪsə veɪ'sɔːrəm/ *plural noun* tiny blood vessels in the walls of larger blood vessels

vascular /'væskjʊlə/ *adjective* referring to blood vessels

vascular dementia /ˌvæskjʊlə dɪ'menʃə/ *noun* a form of mental degeneration due to disease of the blood vessels in the brain

vascularisation /ˌvæskjʊləraɪ'zeɪʃ(ə)n/, **vascularization** *noun* the development of new blood vessels

vascular lesion /ˌvæskjʊlə 'li:ʒ(ə)n/ *noun* damage to a blood vessel

vascular system /'væskjʊlə ˌsɪstəm/ *noun* the series of vessels such as veins, arteries and capillaries, carrying blood around the body

vasculitis /ˌvæskjʊ'laɪtɪs/ *noun* inflammation of a blood vessel

vas deferens /ˌvæs 'defərenz/ *noun* see illustration at UROGENITAL SYSTEM (MALE) in Supplement. also called **ductus deferens, sperm duct** (NOTE: The plural is **vasa deferentia**.)

vasectomy /və'sektəmi/ *noun* a surgical operation to cut a vas deferens, in order to prevent sperm travelling from the epididymis up the duct. ◊ **bilateral vasectomy**

vas efferens /ˌvæs 'efərenz/ *noun* one of many tiny tubes which take the spermatozoa from the testis to the epididymis (NOTE: The plural is **vasa efferentia**.)

vaso- /veɪzəʊ/ *prefix* **1.** referring to a blood vessel **2.** referring to the vas deferens

vasoactive /ˌveɪzəʊ'æktɪv/ *adjective* having an effect on the blood vessels, especially constricting the arteries

vasoconstriction /ˌveɪzəʊkən'strɪkʃən/ *noun* a contraction of blood vessels which makes them narrower

vasoconstrictor /ˌveɪzəʊkən'strɪktə/ *noun* a chemical substance which makes blood vessels become narrower, so that blood pressure rises, e.g. ephedrine hydrochloride

vasodilatation /ˌveɪzəʊˌdaɪlə'teɪʃ(ə)n/, **vasodilation** /ˌveɪzəʊdaɪ'leɪʃ(ə)n/ *noun* the relaxation of blood vessels, especially the arteries, making them wider and leading to increased blood flow or reduced blood pressure

vasodilator /ˌveɪzəʊdaɪ'leɪtə/ *noun* a chemical substance which makes blood vessels become wider, so that blood flows more easily and blood pressure falls, e.g. hydralazine hydrochloride

'Volatile anaesthetic agents are potent vasodilators and facilitate blood flow to the skin.' [*British Journal of Nursing*]

vaso-epididymostomy /ˌveɪzəʊ ˌepɪdɪdɪ'mɒstəmi/ *noun* a surgical operation to reverse a vasectomy in which the cut end of the vas deferens is joined to a tubule within the epididymis above a blockage in it

vasoinhibitor /ˌveɪzəʊɪn'hɪbɪtə/ *noun* a chemical substance that reduces or stops the activity of the nerves that control the widening or narrowing of the blood vessels

vasoligation /ˌveɪzəlaɪ'geɪʃ(ə)n/ *noun* a surgical operation to tie the vasa deferentia to prevent infection entering the epididymis from the urinary system

vasomotion /ˌveɪzə'məʊʃ(ə)n/ *noun* the control of the diameter of blood vessels and thus of blood flow. ◊ **vasoconstriction, vasodilatation**

vasomotor /ˌveɪzəʊ'məʊtə/ *adjective* referring to the control of the diameter of blood vessels

vasomotor centre /ˌveɪzə'məʊtə sentə/ *noun* a nerve centre in the brain which changes the rate of heartbeat and the diameter of blood vessels and so regulates blood pressure

vasomotor nerve /ˌveɪzəʊ'məʊtə nɜːv/ *noun* a nerve in the wall of a blood vessel which affects the diameter of the vessel

vasopressin /ˌveɪzəʊ'presɪn/ *noun* same as **antidiuretic hormone**

vasopressor /ˌveɪzəʊ'presə/ *noun* a substance which increases blood pressure by narrowing the blood vessels

vasospasm /'veɪzəʊspæzm/ *noun* a muscle spasm causing the fingers to become cold, white and numb. ◊ **Raynaud's disease**

vasovagal /ˌveɪzəʊ'veɪg(ə)l/ *adjective* referring to the vagus nerve and its effect on the heartbeat and blood circulation

vasovagal attack /ˌveɪzəʊ'veɪg(ə)l ə,tæk/ *noun* a fainting fit as a result of a slowing down of the heartbeats caused by excessive activity of the vagus nerve

vasovasostomy /ˌveɪzəʊvə'spstəmi/ *noun* a surgical operation to reverse a vasectomy

vasovesiculitis /ˌveɪzəʊvesɪkju'laɪtɪs/ *noun* inflammation of the seminal vesicles and a vas deferens

vastus intermedius /ˌvæstəs ˌɪntə'miːdiəs/, **vastus medialis** /ˌvæstəs ˌmiːdi'eɪlɪs/, **vastus lateralis** /ˌvæstəs ˌlætə'reɪlɪs/ *noun* three of the four parts of the quadriceps femoris, the muscle of the thigh (NOTE: The fourth is the rectus femoris.)

vault /vɔːlt/ *noun* □ **vault of the skull** part of the skull which includes the frontal bone, the temporal bones and the occipital bone

VBAC *abbr* vaginal birth after Caesarean section

vCJD *abbr* variant CJD

VD *abbr* venereal disease

VD clinic /ˌviː 'diː ˌklɪnɪk/ *noun* a clinic specialising in the diagnosis and treatment of venereal diseases

VDH *abbr* valvular disease of the heart

vectis /'vektɪs/ *noun* a curved surgical instrument used in childbirth

vector /'vektə/ *noun* an insect or animal which carries a disease and can pass it to humans ○ *The tsetse fly is a vector of sleeping sickness.*

vegan /'viːgən/ *noun* someone who does not eat meat, dairy produce, eggs or fish and eats only vegetables and fruit ■ *adjective* involving a diet of only vegetables and fruit

vegetarian /ˌvedʒɪ'teəriən/ *noun* someone who does not eat meat, but eats mainly vegetables and fruit and sometimes dairy produce, eggs or fish ■ *adjective* involving a diet without meat

vegetation /ˌvedʒɪ'teɪʃ(ə)n/ *noun* a growth on a membrane, e.g. on the cusps of valves in the heart

vegetative /'vedʒɪtətɪv/ *adjective* **1.** referring to growth of tissue or organs **2.** referring

to a state after brain damage, where a person is alive and breathing but shows no responses

vehicle /'viːɪk(ə)l/ *noun* a liquid in which a dose of a drug is put

vein /veɪn/ *noun* a blood vessel which takes deoxygenated blood containing waste carbon dioxide from the tissues back to the heart (NOTE: For other terms referring to veins see words beginning **phleb-**, **phlebo-** or **vene-**, **veno-**.)

vena cava /ˌviːnə 'keɪvə/ *noun* one of two large veins which take deoxygenated blood from all the other veins into the right atrium of the heart. See illustration at HEART in Supplement, KIDNEY in Supplement (NOTE: The plural is **venae cavae**.)

> COMMENT: The superior vena cava brings blood from the head and the top part of the body, while the inferior vena cava brings blood from the abdomen and legs.

vene- /veni/ *prefix* referring to veins

venene /və'niːn/ *noun* a mixture of different venoms, used to produce antivenene

venepuncture /'venɪpʌŋktʃə/ *noun* the act of puncturing a vein either to inject a drug or to take a blood sample

venereal /və'nɪəriəl/ *adjective* **1.** relating to sex acts or sexual desire **2.** relating to the genitals **3.** referring to an infection or disease which is transmitted through sexual intercourse ○ *venereal warts*

venereal disease /vɪ'nɪəriəl dɪ,ziːz/ *noun* a disease which is passed from one person to another during sexual intercourse. Abbr **VD** (NOTE: Now usually called a **sexually transmitted disease (STD)**.)

venereal wart /və,nɪəriəl 'wɔːt/ *noun* a wart on the genitals or in the urogenital area

venereologist /və,nɪəri'plədʒɪst/ *noun* a doctor who specialises in the study of venereal diseases

venereology /və,nɪəri'plədʒi/ *noun* the scientific study of venereal diseases

venereum /və'nɪəriəm/ ♦ **lymphogranuloma venereum**

veneris /'venərɪs/ ♦ **mons**

venesection /ˌvenɪ'sekʃən/ *noun* an operation where a vein is cut so that blood can be removed, e.g. when taking blood from a donor

venipuncture /'venɪpʌŋktʃə/ *noun* same as **venepuncture**

veno- /viːnəʊ/ *prefix* referring to veins

venoclysis /və'npkləsɪs/ *noun* the procedure of slowly introducing a saline or other solution into a vein

venogram /'viːnəgræm/ *noun* same as **phlebogram**

venography /vɪ'npgrəfi/ *noun* same as **phlebography**

venom /'venəm/ *noun* a poison in the bite of a snake or insect

COMMENT: Depending on the source of the bite, venom can have a wide range of effects, from a sore spot after a bee sting, to death from a scorpion. Antivenene will counteract the effects of venom, but is only effective if the animal which gave the bite can be correctly identified.

venomous /'venəməs/ *adjective* referring to an animal which has poison in its bite ○ *The cobra is a venomous snake.* ○ *He was bitten by a venomous spider.*

venosus /vɪ'nəʊsəs/ ♦ ductus venosus

venous /'viːnəs/ *adjective* referring to the veins

'…venous air embolism is a potentially fatal complication of percutaneous venous catheterization' [*Southern Medical Journal*]

'…a pad was placed under the Achilles tendon to raise the legs, thus aiding venous return and preventing deep vein thrombosis' [*NATNews*]

venous bleeding /ˌviːnəs 'bliːdɪŋ/ *noun* bleeding from a vein

venous blood /'viːnəs blʌd/ *noun* same as deoxygenated blood

venous haemorrhage /ˌviːnəs 'hem(ə)rɪdʒ/ *noun* the escape of blood from a vein

venous system /'viːnəs ˌsɪstəm/ *noun* a system of veins which brings blood back to the heart from the tissues

venous thrombosis /ˌviːnəs θrɒm'bəʊsɪs/ *noun* the blocking of a vein by a blood clot

venous ulcer /ˌviːnəs 'ʌlsə/ *noun* an ulcer in the leg, caused by varicose veins or by a blood clot

ventilation /ˌventɪ'leɪʃ(ə)n/ *noun* the act of breathing air in or out of the lungs, so removing waste products from the blood in exchange for oxygen. ◊ dead space

ventilator /'ventɪleɪtə/ *noun* a machine which pumps air into and out of the lungs of someone who has difficulty in breathing ○ *The newborn baby was put on a ventilator.* Also called **respirator**

ventilatory failure /'ventɪleɪtri ˌfeɪljə/ *noun* a failure of the lungs to oxygenate the blood correctly

Ventimask /'ventɪmɑːsk/ a trademark for a type of oxygen mask

Ventolin /'ventəlɪn/ a trade name for salbutamol

ventouse /'ventuːs/ *noun* a cup-like vacuum device attached to the top of an unborn baby's head in the process of delivery, used to enable a distressed baby to be born quickly

ventral /'ventr(ə)l/ *adjective* 1. referring to the abdomen 2. referring to the front of the body. Opposite **dorsal**

ventricle /'ventrɪk(ə)l/ *noun* a cavity in an organ, especially in the heart or brain. See illustration at HEART in Supplement

COMMENT: There are two ventricles in the heart: the left ventricle takes oxygenated blood from the pulmonary vein through the left atrium, and pumps it into the aorta to circulate round the body; the right ventricle takes blood from the veins through the right atrium, and pumps it into the pulmonary artery to be passed to the lungs to be oxygenated. There are four ventricles in the brain, each containing cerebrospinal fluid. The two lateral ventricles in the cerebral hemispheres contain the choroid processes which produce cerebrospinal fluid. The third ventricle lies in the midline between the two thalami. The fourth ventricle is part of the central canal of the hindbrain.

ventricul- /ventrɪkjʊl/ *prefix* referring to a ventricle in the brain or heart

ventricular /ven'trɪkjʊlə/ *adjective* referring to the ventricles

ventricular fibrillation /venˌtrɪkjʊlə ˌfaɪbrɪ'leɪʃ(ə)n/ *noun* a serious heart condition where the ventricular muscles flutter and the heart no longer beats. Abbr **VF**

ventricular folds /ven'trɪkjʊlə fəʊldz/ *plural noun* same as **vocal cords**

ventricular septal defect /venˌtrɪkjʊlə 'sept(ə)l dɪˌfekt/ *noun* a condition in which blood can flow between the two ventricles of the heart, because the intraventricular septum has not developed properly. Abbr **VSD**. Compare **atrial septal defect**

ventriculitis /ˌventrɪkjʊ'laɪtɪs/ *noun* inflammation of the brain ventricles

ventriculoatriostomy /venˌtrɪkjʊləʊˌeɪtri'ɒstəmi/ *noun* an operation to relieve pressure caused by excessive quantities of cerebrospinal fluid in the brain ventricles

ventriculogram /ven'trɪkjʊləgræm/ *noun* an X-ray picture of the ventricles of the brain

ventriculography /ˌventrɪkjʊ'lɒgrəfi/ *noun* a method of taking X-ray pictures of the ventricles of the brain after air has been introduced to replace the cerebrospinal fluid

ventriculo-peritoneal shunt /venˌtrɪkjʊləʊ ˌperɪtəˌniːəl 'ʃʌnt/ *noun* an artificial drain used in hydrocephalus to drain cerebrospinal fluid from the ventricles

ventriculoscopy /venˌtrɪkjʊ'lɒskəpi/ *noun* an examination of the brain using an endoscope

ventriculostomy /venˌtrɪkjʊ'lɒstəmi/ *noun* a surgical operation to pass a hollow needle into a ventricle of the brain so as to reduce pressure, take a sample of fluid or enlarge the ventricular opening to prevent the need for a shunt

ventro- /ventrəʊ/ *prefix* 1. ventral 2. referring to the abdomen

ventrofixation /ˌventrəʊfɪk'seɪʃ(ə)n/ *noun* a surgical operation to treat retroversion of the uterus by attaching the uterus to the wall of the abdomen

ventrosuspension /ˌventrəʊsə'spenʃən/ *noun* a surgical operation to treat retroversion of the uterus

Venturi mask /ven'tjʊəri mɑːsk/ *noun* a type of disposable mask which gives the person a controlled mixture of oxygen and air

Venturi nebuliser /ven'tjʊəri ˌnebjʊlaɪzə/ *noun* a type of nebuliser which is used in aerosol therapy

venule /'venjuːl/ *noun* a small vein or vessel leading from tissue to a larger vein

verapamil /vəˈræpəmɪl/ *noun* a synthetic compound which helps to prevent the movement of calcium ions across membranes. It is used in the treatment of angina pectoris, hypertension and irregular heartbeat.

verbigeration /ˌvɜːbɪdʒəˈreɪʃ(ə)n/ *noun* a condition seen in people with mental disorders, in which they keep saying the same words over and over again

vermicide /'vɜːmɪsaɪd/ *noun* a substance which kills worms in the intestine

vermiform /'vɜːmɪfɔːm/ *adjective* shaped like a worm

vermiform appendix /ˌvɜːmɪfɔːm ə'pendɪks/ *noun* same as **appendix 1**

vermifuge /'vɜːmɪfjuːdʒ/ *noun* a substance which removes worms from the intestine

vermillion border /vəˌmɪliən 'bɔːdə/ *noun* the external red parts of the lips

vermis /'vɜːmɪs/ *noun* the central part of the cerebellum, which forms the top of the fourth ventricle

vermix /'vɜːmɪks/ *noun* a vermiform appendix

vernix caseosa /ˌvɜːnɪks keɪsi'əʊsə/ *noun* an oily substance which covers a baby's skin at birth

verruca /vəˈruːkə/ *noun* a small hard harmless growth on the sole of the foot, caused by a virus (NOTE: Verrucas are a type of wart. The plural is **verrucas** or **verrucae**.)

version /'vɜːʃ(ə)n/ *noun* the procedure of turning a fetus in a uterus so as to put it in a better position for birth

vertebra /'vɜːtɪbrə/ *noun* one of twenty-four ring-shaped bones which link together to form the backbone. See illustration at CARTILAGINOUS JOINT in Supplement (NOTE: The plural is **vertebrae**.)

COMMENT: The top vertebra (the atlas) supports the skull; the first seven vertebrae in the neck are the cervical vertebrae; then follow the twelve thoracic or dorsal vertebrae which are behind the chest and five lumbar vertebrae in the lower part of the back. The sacrum and coccyx are formed of five sacral vertebrae and four coccygeal vertebrae which have fused together.

vertebral /'vɜːtɪbrəl/ *adjective* referring to the vertebrae

vertebral artery /ˌvɜːtɪbrəl 'ɑːtəri/ *noun* one of two arteries which go up the back of the neck into the brain

vertebral canal /ˌvɜːtɪbrəl kə'næl/ *noun* same as **spinal canal**

vertebral column /'vɜːtɪbrəl ˌkɒləm/ *noun* the series of bones and discs linked together to form a flexible column running from the base of the skull to the pelvis. Also called **backbone, spinal column**. See illustration at PELVIS in Supplement

vertebral disc /ˌvɜːtɪbrəl 'dɪsk/ *noun* same as **intervertebral disc**

vertebral foramen /ˌvɜːtɪbrəl fə'reɪmən/ *noun* a hole in the centre of a vertebra which links with others to form the vertebral canal through which the spinal cord passes

vertebral ganglion /ˌvɜːtəbrəl 'gæŋgliən/ *noun* a ganglion in front of the origin of the vertebral artery

vertebro-basilar insufficiency /ˌvɜːtɪbrəʊ ˌbæzɪlə ˌɪnsə'fɪʃənsi/ *noun* a brainstem ischaemia due to temporary occlusion of the arteries

vertex /'vɜːteks/ *noun* the top of the skull

vertex delivery /'vɜːteks dɪˌlɪv(ə)ri/ *noun* a normal birth, where the baby's head appears first

vertigo /'vɜːtɪgəʊ/ *noun* **1.** feelings of dizziness or giddiness caused by a malfunction of the sense of balance **2.** a fear of heights, as a result of a sensation of dizziness which is felt when high up, especially on a tall building ○ *She won't sit near the window – she suffers from vertigo.*

very low density lipoprotein /ˌveri ləʊ ˌdensəti ˌlɪpəʊ'prəʊtiːn/ *noun* a fat produced by the liver after food has been absorbed and before it becomes low density lipoprotein. Abbr **VLDL**

vesical /'vesɪk(ə)l/ *adjective* referring to the bladder

vesicant /'vesɪkənt/ *noun* a substance which makes the skin blister. Also called **epispastic**

vesicle /'vesɪk(ə)l/ *noun* **1.** a small blister on the skin, e.g. caused by eczema **2.** a sac which contains liquid

vesico- /vesɪkəʊ/ *prefix* referring to the urinary bladder

vesicofixation /ˌvesɪkəʊfɪk'seɪʃ(ə)n/ *noun* same as **cystopexy**

vesicostomy /vesɪ'kɒstəmi/, **vesicotomy** /ˌvesɪ'kɒtəmi/ *noun* same as **cystostomy**

vesicoureteric reflux /ˌvesɪkəʊjʊəri ˌterɪk 'riːflʌks/ *noun* the flowing of urine back from the bladder up the ureters during urination, which may carry infection from the bladder to the kidneys. Also called **vesicoureteric reflux**

vesicouretic /ˌvesɪkəʊjʊ'retɪk/ *adjective* relating to the urinary bladder and the ureters

vesicouretic reflux /ˌvesɪkəʊjʊˌretɪk 'riːflʌks/ *noun* same as **vesicoureteric reflux**

vesicovaginal /ˌvesɪkəʊvə'dʒaɪn(ə)l/ *adjective* referring to the bladder and the vagina

vesicovaginal fistula /ˌvesɪkəʊvəˌdʒaɪn(ə)l ˈfɪstjʊlə/ *noun* an unusual opening between the bladder and the vagina

vesicular /vəˈsɪkjʊlə/ *adjective* referring to a vesicle

vesicular breathing /vəˌsɪkjʊlə ˈbriːðɪŋ/, **vesicular breath sound** /vəˌsɪkjʊlə ˈbreθ saʊnd/ *plural noun* the sound made during the normal breathing process

vesiculation /vəˌsɪkjʊˈleɪʃ(ə)n/ *noun* the formation of blisters on the skin

vesiculectomy /ˌvesɪkjʊˈlektəmi/ *noun* a surgical operation to remove a seminal vesicle

vesiculitis /vəˌsɪkjʊˈlaɪtɪs/ *noun* inflammation of the seminal vesicles

vesiculography /vəˌsɪkjʊˈlɒgrəfi/ *noun* an X-ray examination of the seminal vesicles

vesiculopapular /vəˌsɪkjʊləʊˈpæpjʊlə/ *adjective* referring to a skin disorder which has both blisters and papules

vesiculopustular /vəˌsɪkjʊləʊˈpʌstjʊlə/ *adjective* referring to a skin disorder which has both blisters and pustules

vessel /ˈves(ə)l/ *noun* **1.** a tube in the body along which liquid flows, especially a blood vessel **2.** a container for fluids

vestibular /veˈstɪbjʊlə/ *adjective* referring to a vestibule, especially the vestibule of the inner ear

vestibular folds /veˈstɪbjʊlə fəʊldz/ *plural noun* folds in the larynx above the vocal folds, which are not used for speech. Also called **false vocal cords**

vestibular glands /veˈstɪbjʊlə glændz/ *plural noun* the glands at the point where the vagina and vulva join, which secrete a lubricating substance

vestibular nerve /veˈstɪbjʊlə nɜːv/ *noun* the part of the auditory nerve which carries information about balance to the brain

vestibule /ˈvestɪbjuːl/ *noun* a cavity in the body at the entrance to an organ, especially the first cavity in the inner ear or the space in the larynx above the vocal cords or a nostril. See illustration at EAR in Supplement

vestibulocochlear nerve /vesˌtɪbjʊləʊ ˈkɒkliə ˌnɜːv/ *noun* the eighth cranial nerve which governs hearing and balance. Also called **acoustic nerve, auditory nerve**

vestigial /vesˈtɪdʒiəl/ *adjective* existing in a rudimentary form ○ *The coccyx is a vestigial tail.*

VF *abbr* ventricular fibrillation □ **in VF** referring to someone whose heart is no longer able to beat

viability /ˌvaɪəˈbɪlɪti/ *noun* the fact of being viable ○ *The viability of the fetus before the 22nd week is doubtful.*

viable /ˈvaɪəb(ə)l/ *adjective* referring to a fetus which can survive if born ○ *A fetus is viable by about the 28th week of pregnancy.*

Viagra /vaɪˈægrə/ a trade name for sildenafil citrate

vial /ˈvaɪəl/ *noun* same as **phial**

Vibramycin /ˌvaɪbrəˈmaɪsɪn/ a trade name for doxycycline

vibrate /vaɪˈbreɪt/ *verb* to move rapidly and continuously

vibration /vaɪˈbreɪʃ(ə)n/ *noun* rapid and continuous movement ○ *Speech is formed by the vibrations of the vocal cords.*

vibration white finger /vaɪˌbreɪʃ(ə)n ˈwaɪt ˌfɪŋgə/ *noun* a condition caused by long-term use of a chain saw or pneumatic drill, which affects the circulation in the fingers

vibrator /vaɪˈbreɪtə/ *noun* a device to produce vibrations, which may be used for massages

Vibrio /ˈvɪbriəʊ/ *noun* a genus of Gram-negative bacteria which are found in water and cause cholera

vibrissae /vaɪˈbrɪsiː/ *plural noun* hairs in the nostrils or ears

vicarious /vɪˈkeəriəs/ *adjective* done by one organ or agent in place of another

vicarious menstruation /vɪˌkeəriəs ˌmenstruˈeɪʃ(ə)n/ *noun* the discharge of blood other than by the vagina during menstrual periods

victim /ˈvɪktɪm/ *noun* a person who is injured in an accident or who has caught a disease ○ *The victims of the rail crash were taken to the local hospital.* □ **to fall victim to something** to become a victim of or to experience bad effects from something ○ *Half the people eating at the restaurant fell victim to salmonella poisoning.*

vigour /ˈvɪgə/ *noun* a combination of positive attributes expressed in rapid growth, large size, high fertility and long life in an organism (NOTE: The US spelling is **vigor**.)

villous /ˈvɪləs/ *adjective* shaped like a villus, or formed of villi

villus /ˈvɪləs/ *noun* a tiny projection like a finger on the surface of a mucous membrane (NOTE: The plural is **villi**.)

vinblastine /vɪnˈblæstiːn/ *noun* an alkaloid drug used in the treatment of cancer

vincristine /vɪnˈkrɪstiːn/ *noun* an alkaloid drug similar to vinblastine, also used in the treatment of cancer. It works by blocking cell division and is highly toxic.

vinculum /ˈvɪŋkjʊləm/ *noun* a thin connecting band of tissue (NOTE: The plural is **vincula**.)

violent /ˈvaɪələnt/ *adjective* very strong, very severe ○ *He had a violent headache.* ○ *Her reaction to the injection was violent.*

violently /ˈvaɪələntli/ *adverb* in a strong way ○ *He reacted violently to the antihistamine.*

violet /ˈvaɪələt/ *noun* a dark, purplish blue colour at the end of the visible spectrum

viraemia /vaɪˈriːmiə/ *noun* a virus in the blood (NOTE: The US spelling is **viremia**.)

viral /'vaɪrəl/ *adjective* caused by a virus, or referring to a virus

viral hepatitis *noun* same as **serum hepatitis**

viral infection /'vaɪrəl ɪn,fekʃən/ *noun* an infection caused by a virus

viral pneumonia /,vaɪrəl nju:'məʊniə/ *noun* a type of inflammation of the lungs caused by a virus. Also called **virus pneumonia**

virgin /'vɜ:dʒɪn/ *noun* a female who has not experienced sexual intercourse

virginity /və'dʒɪnɪti/ *noun* the condition of a female who has not experienced sexual intercourse

virile /'vɪraɪl/ *adjective* like a man, with strong male characteristics

virilisation /,vɪrɪlaɪ'zeɪʃ(ə)n/, **virilization** *noun* the development of male characteristics in a woman, caused by a hormone imbalance or therapy

virilism /'vɪrɪlɪz(ə)m/ *noun* male characteristics such as body hair and a deep voice in a woman

virology /vaɪ'rɒlədʒi/ *noun* the scientific study of viruses

virulence /'vɪrʊləns/ *noun* **1.** the ability of a microorganism to cause a disease **2.** the degree of effect of a disease

virulent /'vɪrʊlənt/ *adjective* **1.** referring to the ability of a microorganism to cause a disease ○ *an unusually virulent strain of the virus* **2.** referring to a disease which develops rapidly and has strong effects

virus /'vaɪrəs/ *noun* a parasite consisting of a nucleic acid surrounded by a protein coat that can only develop in other cells. Viruses cause many diseases including the common cold, AIDS, herpes and polio. (NOTE: Antibiotics have no effect on viruses, but effective vaccines have been developed for some viral diseases.)

virus pneumonia *noun* same as **viral pneumonia**

viscera /'vɪsərə/ *plural noun* the internal organs, e.g. the heart, lungs, stomach and intestines

visceral /'vɪsərəl/ *adjective* referring to the internal organs

visceral larva migrans /,vɪsərəl ,lɑ:və 'maɪgrænz/ *noun* same as **toxocariasis**

visceral muscle /'vɪsərəl ,mʌs(ə)l/ *noun* a smooth muscle in the wall of the intestine which makes the intestine contract

visceral pericardium /,vɪsərəl ,peri 'kɑ:diəm/ *noun* the inner layer of serous pericardium, attached to the wall of the heart

visceral peritoneum /,vɪsərəl ,perɪtəʊ 'ni:əm/ *noun* part of the peritoneum which covers the organs in the abdominal cavity

visceral pleura /,vɪsərəl 'plʊərə/ *noun* a membrane attached to the surface of a lung. See illustration at LUNGS in Supplement

visceral pouch /'vɪsərəl paʊtʃ/ *noun* same as **pharyngeal pouch**

viscero- /vɪsərəʊ/ *prefix* relating to the viscera

visceromotor /,vɪsərə'məʊtə/ *adjective* controlling the movement of viscera

visceroptosis /,vɪsərə'təʊsɪs/ *noun* a movement of an internal organ downwards from its usual position

visceroreceptor /,vɪsərəʊrɪ'septə/ *noun* a receptor cell which reacts to stimuli from organs such as the stomach, heart and lungs

viscid /'vɪsɪd/ *adjective* referring to a liquid which is sticky and slow-moving

viscosity /vɪ'skɒsɪti/ *noun* the state of a liquid which moves slowly

viscous /'vɪskəs/ *adjective* referring to a liquid which is thick and slow-moving

viscus /'vɪskəs/ **♦ viscera**

visible /'vɪzɪb(ə)l/ *adjective* able to be seen ○ *There were no visible symptoms of the disease.*

vision /'vɪʒ(ə)n/ *noun* the ability to see, eyesight ○ *After the age of 50, many people's vision begins to fail.*

vision centre /'vɪʒ(ə)n ,sentə/ *noun* the point in the brain where the nerves relating to the eye come together

visit /'vɪzɪt/ *noun* **1.** a short stay with someone, especially to comfort a patient ○ *The patient is too weak to have any visits.* ○ *He is allowed visits of ten minutes only.* **2.** a short stay with a professional person ○ *They had a visit from the district nurse.* ○ *She paid a visit to the chiropodist.* ○ *On the patient's last visit to the physiotherapy unit, nurses noticed a great improvement in her walking.* ■ *verb* to stay a short time with someone ○ *I am going to visit my brother in hospital.* ○ *She was visited by the health visitor.*

visiting times /'vɪzɪtɪŋ taɪmz/ *plural noun* the times of day when friends are allowed into a hospital to visit patients

visitor /'vɪzɪtə/ *noun* a person who visits ○ *Visitors are allowed into the hospital on Sunday afternoons.* ○ *How many visitors did you have this week?*

visual /'vɪʒʊəl/ *adjective* referring to sight or vision

visual acuity /,vɪʒʊəl ə'kju:ɪti/ *noun* the ability to see objects clearly

visual area /,vɪʒʊəl 'eəriə/ *noun* the part of the cerebral cortex which is concerned with sight

visual axis /,vɪʒʊəl 'æksɪs/ *noun* the line between the object on which the eye focuses, and the fovea

visual cortex /,vɪʒʊəl 'kɔ:teks/ *noun* the part of the cerebral cortex which receives information about sight

visual field /ˈvɪʒʊəl fiːlⁿd/ *noun* the area which can be seen without moving the eye. Also called **field of vision**

visualisation /ˌvɪʒʊəlaɪˈzeɪʃ(ə)n/, **visualization** *noun* **1.** a technique in which an image of an internal organ or other part of the body is produced by using X-rays or other means such as magnetic resonance imaging **2.** a technique in which someone creates a strongly positive mental picture of something such as the way in which they would like to solve a problem, in order to help them cope with it

visually impaired /ˌvɪʒʊəli ɪmˈpeəd/ *adjective* having difficulty in seeing because of an eye condition

visually impaired person /ˌvɪʒʊəli ɪm ˌpeəd ˈpɜːs(ə)n/ *noun* a person whose eyesight is not clear

visual purple /ˌvɪʒʊəl ˈpɜːp(ə)l/ *noun* same as **rhodopsin**

vitae /ˈvaɪtiː/ ♦ **arbor vitae**

vital /ˈvaɪt(ə)l/ *adjective* very important or necessary for life ○ *If circulation is stopped, vital nerve cells begin to die in a few minutes.* ○ *Oxygen is vital to the human system.*

vital capacity /ˌvaɪt(ə)l kəˈpæsɪti/ *noun* the largest amount of air which a person can exhale at one time

vital centre /ˌvaɪt(ə)l ˈsentə/ *noun* a group of nerve cells in the brain which govern a particular function of the body such as the five senses

vital organs /ˌvaɪt(ə)l ˈɔːgənz/ *plural noun* the most important organs in the body, without which a human being cannot live, e.g. the heart, lungs and brain

vital signs /ˌvaɪt(ə)l ˈsaɪnz/ *plural noun* measurements of pulse, breathing and temperature

vital statistics /ˌvaɪt(ə)l stəˈtɪstɪks/ *plural noun* a set of official statistics relating to the population of a place, such as the percentage of live births per thousand, the incidence of particular diseases and the numbers of births and deaths

vitamin /ˈvɪtəmɪn/ *noun* an essential substance not synthesised in the body, but found in most foods, and needed for good health

Vitamin A /ˌvɪtəmɪn ˈeɪ/ *noun* a vitamin which is soluble in fat and can be formed in the body from precursors but is mainly found in food such as liver, vegetables, eggs and cod liver oil. Also called **retinol**

COMMENT: Lack of Vitamin A affects the body's growth and resistance to disease and can cause night blindness or xerophthalmia. Carotene (the yellow substance in carrots) is a precursor of Vitamin A, which accounts for the saying that eating carrots helps you to see in the dark.

Vitamin B₁ /ˌvɪtəmɪn biː ˈwʌn/ *noun* a vitamin found in yeast, liver, cereals and pork. Also called **thiamine**

Vitamin B₂ /ˌvɪtəmɪn biː ˈtuː/ *noun* a vitamin found in eggs, liver, green vegetables, milk and yeast. Also called **riboflavine**

Vitamin B₆ /ˌvɪtəmɪn biː ˈsɪks/ *noun* a vitamin found in meat, cereals and molasses. Also called **pyridoxine**

Vitamin B₁₂ /ˌvɪtəmɪn biː ˈtwelv/ *noun* a vitamin found in liver and kidney, but not present in vegetables. Also called **cyanocobalamin**

Vitamin B complex /ˌvɪtəmɪn biː ˈkɒmpleks/ *noun* a group of vitamins such as folic acid, riboflavine and thiamine

Vitamin C /ˌvɪtəmɪn ˈsiː/ *noun* a vitamin which is soluble in water and is found in fresh fruit, especially oranges and lemons, raw vegetables and liver. Also called **ascorbic acid**

Vitamin D /ˌvɪtəmɪn ˈdiː/ *noun* a vitamin which is soluble in fat and is found in butter, eggs and fish. It is also produced by the skin when exposed to sunlight. It helps in the formation of bones, and lack of it causes rickets in children.

vitamin deficiency /ˈvɪtəmɪn dɪˌfɪʃ(ə)nsi/ *noun* a lack of necessary vitamins ○ *He is suffering from Vitamin A deficiency.* ○ *Vitamin C deficiency causes scurvy.*

Vitamin E /ˌvɪtəmɪn ˈiː/ *noun* a vitamin found in vegetables, vegetable oils, eggs and wholemeal bread

Vitamin K /ˌvɪtəmɪn ˈkeɪ/ *noun* a vitamin found in green vegetables such as spinach and cabbage, and which helps the clotting of blood and is needed to activate prothrombin

vitelline sac /vɪˈtelaɪn sæk/ *noun* a sac attached to an embryo, where the blood cells first form

vitellus /vɪˈteləs/ *noun* the yolk of an egg (ovum)

vitiligo /ˌvɪtiˈlaɪɡəʊ/ *noun* a condition in which white patches appear on the skin. Also called **leucoderma**

vitrectomy /vɪˈtrektəmi/ *noun* a surgical operation to remove some or all of the vitreous humour of the eye

vitreous /ˈvɪtriəs/ *adjective* **1.** having the characteristics of glass **2.** relating to the vitreous humour of the eye

vitreous body /ˈvɪtriəs ˌbɒdi/ *noun* same as **vitreous humour**

vitreous detachment /ˌvɪtriəs dɪ ˈtætʃmənt/ *noun* the separation of the vitreous humour from the retina, often due to natural ageing when the vitreous humour thins, but also occurring in other conditions such as diabetes

vitreous humour /ˌvɪtriəs ˈhjuːmə/ *noun* a transparent jelly which fills the main cavity behind the lens in the eye. See illustration at EYE in Supplement

vitritis /vɪˈtraɪtɪs/ *noun* same as **hyalitis**

vitro /ˈviːtriəʊ/ ♦ **in vitro**

Vitus /ˈvaɪtəs/ ♦ **St Vitus's dance**

viviparous /vɪˈvɪpərəs/ *adjective* referring to animals which bear live young, such as humans, as opposed to birds and reptiles which lay eggs

vivisection /ˌvɪvɪˈsekʃən/ *noun* the act of dissecting a living animal as an experiment

vocal /ˈvəʊk(ə)l/ *adjective* referring to the voice

vocal cords /ˈvəʊk(ə)l kɔːdz/ *plural noun* a pair of fibrous sheets of tissue which span the cavity of the voice box (**larynx**) and produce sounds by vibrating. Also called **ventricular folds**

vocal folds /ˈvəʊk(ə)l fəʊldz/ *plural noun* same as **vocal cords**

vocal folds abducted /ˌvəʊk(ə)l fəʊldz əbˈdʌktɪd/ *noun* the usual condition of the vocal cords in quiet breathing

vocal folds adducted /ˌvəʊk(ə)l fəʊldz əˈdʌktɪd/ *noun* the position of the vocal cords for speaking

vocal fremitus /ˌvəʊk(ə)l ˈfremɪtəs/ *noun* a vibration of the chest when a person speaks or coughs

vocal ligament /ˈvəʊk(ə)l ˌlɪgəmənt/ *noun* a ligament in the centre of the vocal cords

vocal resonance /ˌvəʊk(ə)l ˈrezənəns/ *noun* a sound heard by a doctor when he or she listens through a stethoscope to the chest while a person is speaking

voice /vɔɪs/ *noun* the sound made when a person speaks or sings □ **to lose one's voice** not to be able to speak because of a throat infection □ **his voice has broken** his voice has become deeper and adult, with the onset of puberty

voice box /ˈvɔɪs bɒks/ *noun* the larynx, a hollow organ containing the vocal cords at the back of the throat, which produces sounds

volar /ˈvəʊlə/ *adjective* referring to the palm of the hand or sole of the foot

volatile /ˈvɒlətaɪl/ *adjective* referring to a liquid which turns into gas at room temperature

volatile oils /ˌvɒlətaɪl ˈɔɪlz/ *plural noun* concentrated oils from plants used in cosmetics and as antiseptics

volitantes /vɒlɪˈtæntiːz/ ♦ **muscae volitantes**

volition /vəˈlɪʃ(ə)n/ *noun* the ability to use the will

Volkmann's canal /ˈfɒlkmɑːnz kəˌnæl/ *noun* a canal running horizontally through compact bone, carrying blood to the Haversian systems [After Richard von Volkmann (1830–89), German surgeon]

Volkmann's contracture /ˈfɒlkmɑːnz kənˌtræktʃə/ *noun* a fibrosis and tightening of the muscles of the forearm because blood supply has been restricted, leading to contraction of the fingers

volsella /vɒlˈselə/ *noun* a type of surgical forceps with claw-like hooks at the end of each arm. Also called **vulsella**

volume /ˈvɒljuːm/ *noun* an amount of a substance

voluntary /ˈvɒlənt(ə)ri/ *adjective* done because one wishes to do it

voluntary admission /ˌvɒlənt(ə)ri əd ˈmɪʃ(ə)n/ *noun* the process of taking someone into a psychiatric hospital with the person's consent

voluntary movement /ˌvɒlənt(ə)ri ˈmuːvmənt/ *noun* a movement directed by the person's willpower, using voluntary muscles, e.g. walking or speaking

voluntary muscle /ˈvɒlənt(ə)ri ˌmʌs(ə)l/ *noun* a muscle which is consciously controlled. It is usually made up of striated fibres.

COMMENT: Voluntary muscles work in pairs, where one contracts and pulls, while the other relaxes to allow the bone to move.

volunteer /ˌvɒlənˈtɪə/ *noun* a person who offers to do something for free, without being paid ○ *The hospital relies on volunteers to help with sports for disabled children.* ○ *They are asking for volunteers to test the new cold cure.* ■ *verb* to offer to do something for free ○ *The research team volunteered to test the new drug on themselves.*

volvulus /ˈvɒlvjʊləs/ *noun* a condition in which a loop of intestine is twisted and blocked, so cutting off its blood supply

vomer /ˈvəʊmə/ *noun* a thin flat vertical bone in the septum of the nose

vomica /ˈvɒmɪkə/ *noun* **1.** a cavity in the lungs containing pus **2.** the act of vomiting pus from the throat or lungs

vomit /ˈvɒmɪt/ *noun* partly digested food which has been brought up from the stomach into the mouth ○ *His bed was covered with vomit.* ○ *She died after choking on her own vomit.* Also called **vomitus** ■ *verb* to bring up partly digested food from the stomach into the mouth ○ *He had a fever, and then started to vomit.* ○ *She vomited her breakfast.*

vomiting /ˈvɒmɪtɪŋ/ *noun* the act of bringing up vomit into the mouth. Also called **emesis**

vomitus /ˈvɒmɪtəs/ *noun* same as **vomit**

von Hippel-Lindau syndrome /vɒn ˌhɪp(ə)l ˈlɪndaʊ ˌsɪndrəʊm/ *noun* a disease in which angiomas of the brain are related to angiomas and cysts in other parts of the body

von Recklinghausen's disease /ˌvɒn ˈreklɪŋhaʊz(ə)nz dɪˌziːz/ *noun* **1.** same as **neurofibromatosis 2.** same as **osteitis fibrosis cystica** [Described 1882. After Friedrich Daniel von Recklinghausen (1833–1910), Professor of Pathology at Strasbourg, France.]

von Willebrand's disease /ˌvɒn ˈvɪlɪ
brændz dɪˌziːz/ *noun* a hereditary blood disease, occurring in both sexes, in which the mucous membrane starts to bleed without any apparent reason. It is caused by a deficiency of a
clotting factor in the blood, called von Willebrand's factor. [Described 1926. After E. A. von
Willebrand (1870–1949), Finnish physician.]

von Willebrand's factor /ˌvɒn ˈvɪlɪ
brændz ˌfæktə/ *noun* a protein substance in
plasma involved in platelet aggregation

voyeurism /ˈvwaɪɜːrɪz(ə)m/ *noun* a condition in which a person experiences sexual
pleasure by watching others having intercourse

VSD *abbr* ventricular septal defect

vu /vuː/ ◆ déjà vu

vulgaris /vʌlˈgeərɪs/ ◆ lupus vulgaris

vulnerable /ˈvʌln(ə)rəb(ə)l/ *adjective* likely
to catch a disease because of being in a weakened state ○ *Premature babies are especially
vulnerable to infection.*

vulsella /vʌlˈselə/, **vulsellum** /vʌlˈseləm/
noun same as **volsella**

vulv- /vʌlv/ *prefix* referring to the vulva (*used
before vowels*)

vulva /ˈvʌlvə/ *noun* a woman's external sexual organs, at the opening leading to the vagina.
◊ **kraurosis vulvae** (NOTE: For other terms referring to the vulva, see words beginning with **epi-
si-**.)

COMMENT: The vulva is formed of folds (the labia), surrounding the clitoris and the entrance
to the vagina.

vulvectomy /vʌlˈvektəmi/ *noun* a surgical
operation to remove the vulva

vulvitis /vʌlˈvaɪtɪs/ *noun* inflammation of
the vulva, causing intense irritation

vulvovaginitis /ˌvʌlvəʊvædʒɪˈnaɪtɪs/ *noun*
inflammation of the vulva and vagina

W

wad /wɒd/ *noun* a pad of material used to put on a wound ○ *The nurse put a wad of absorbent cotton over the sore.*

wadding /'wɒdɪŋ/ *noun* material used to make a wad ○ *Put a layer of cotton wadding over the eye.*

waist /weɪst/ *noun* the narrow part of the body below the chest and above the buttocks

wait /weɪt/ *verb* to stay somewhere until something happens or someone arrives ○ *He has been waiting for his operation for six months.* ○ *There are ten patients waiting to see Dr Smith.*

waiting list /'weɪtɪŋ lɪst/ *noun* a list of people waiting for admission to hospital usually for treatment of non-urgent disorders ○ *The length of waiting lists for non-emergency surgery varies enormously from one region to another.* ○ *It is hoped that hospital waiting lists will get shorter.*

waiting room /'weɪtɪŋ ruːm/ *noun* a room at a doctor's or dentist's surgery where people wait ○ *Please sit in the waiting room – the doctor will see you in ten minutes.*

waiting time /'weɪtɪŋ taɪm/ *noun* the period between the time when someone's name has been put on the waiting list and his or her admission into hospital

wake /weɪk/ *verb* **1.** to interrupt someone's sleep ○ *The nurse woke the patient.* or *The patient was woken by the nurse.* **2.** to stop sleeping ○ *The patient had to be woken to have his injection.* (NOTE: **waking – woke – woken**)

wakeful /'weɪkf(ə)l/ *adjective* wide awake, not wanting to sleep

wakefulness /'weɪkfʊlnəs/ *noun* the condition of being wide awake

wake up /ˌweɪk 'ʌp/ *verb* to stop sleeping, or stop someone sleeping ○ *The old man woke up in the middle of the night and started calling for the nurse.*

Waldeyer's ring /ˌvɑːldaɪəz 'rɪŋ/ *noun* a ring of lymphoid tissue made by the tonsils and adenoid [Described 1884. After Heinrich Wilhelm Gottfried Waldeyer-Hartz (1836–1921), German anatomist.]

walk /wɔːk/ *verb* to go on foot ○ *The baby is learning to walk.* ○ *He walked when he was only eleven months old.* ○ *She can walk a few steps with a Zimmer frame.*

walking distance /'wɔːkɪŋ ˌdɪstəns/ *noun* the distance which someone can walk before they experience pain in their muscles, which shows the effectiveness of the blood supply to their legs

walking frame /'wɔːkɪŋ freɪm/ *noun* a metal frame used by people who have difficulty in walking. ◊ **Zimmer frame**

wall /wɔːl/ *noun* the side part of an organ or a passage in the body ○ *An ulcer formed in the wall of the duodenum.* ○ *The doctor made an incision in the abdominal wall.* ○ *They removed a fibroma from the wall of the uterus or from the uterine wall.*

wall eye /'wɔːl aɪ/, **walleye** *noun* an eye which is very pale or which is squinting so strongly that only the white sclera is visible

Wangensteen tube /'wæŋgənstiːn tjuːb/ *noun* a tube which is passed into the stomach to remove the stomach's contents by suction [Described 1832. After Owen Harding Wangensteen (1898–1980), US surgeon.]

ward /wɔːd/ *noun* a room or set of rooms in a hospital, with beds for the patients ○ *He is in Ward 8B.* ○ *The children's ward is at the end of the corridor.*

ward manager /'wɔːd ˌmænɪdʒə/ *noun* a nurse in charge of a ward

ward nurse /'wɔːd nɜːs/ *noun* a nurse who works in a hospital ward

ward sister /'wɔːd ˌsɪstə/ *noun* a senior nurse in charge of a ward

warfarin /'wɔːf(ə)rɪn/ *noun* a colourless crystalline compound used to help prevent the blood clotting

warm /wɔːm/ *adjective* quite hot, pleasantly hot ○ *The patients need to be kept warm in cold weather.*

warn /wɔːn/ *verb* to tell someone that a danger is possible ○ *The children were warned about the dangers of solvent abuse.* ○ *The doctors warned her that her husband would not live more than a few weeks.*

warning /'wɔːnɪŋ/ *noun* written or spoken information about a danger ○ *There's a warning on the bottle of medicine, saying that it should be kept away from children.* ○ *Each packet of cigarettes has a government health warning printed on it.* ○ *The health department has given out warnings about the danger of hypothermia.*

wart /wɔːt/ *noun* a small hard harmless growth on the skin, usually on the hands, feet or face, caused by a virus (NOTE: Warts on the feet are called **verrucas**.)

washbasin /'wɒʃbeɪs(ə)n/ *noun* a bowl in a kitchen or bathroom where you can wash your hands

washout /'wɒʃaʊt/ *noun* a thorough cleaning with a liquid, especially water

Wassermann reaction /'wɒsəmæn rɪˌækʃ(ə)n/, **Wassermann test** /'wɒsəmæn test/ *noun* a blood serum test to see if someone has syphilis. Abbr **WR** [Described 1906. After August Paul von Wassermann (1866–1925), German bacteriologist.]

waste /weɪst/ *adjective* referring to material or matter which is useless ○ *The veins take blood containing waste carbon dioxide back into the lungs.* ○ *Waste matter is excreted in the faeces or urine.* ■ *verb* to use more of something than is needed ○ *The hospital kitchens try not to waste a lot of food.*

waste away /ˌweɪst ə'weɪ/ *verb* to become thinner ○ *When he caught the disease he simply wasted away.*

waste product /ˌweɪst 'prɒdʌkt/ *noun* a substance which is not needed in the body and is excreted in urine or faeces

wasting /'weɪstɪŋ/ *noun* a condition in which a person or a limb loses weight and becomes thin

wasting disease /'weɪstɪŋ dɪˌziːz/ *noun* a disease which causes severe loss of weight or reduction in size of an organ

water /'wɔːtə/ *noun* **1.** the liquid essential to life which makes up a large part of the body ○ *Can I have a glass of water please?* ○ *They suffered dehydration from lack of water.* □ **water on the knee** fluid in the knee joint under the kneecap, caused by a blow on the knee **2.** urine (*informal*) ○ *He passed a lot of water during the night.* ○ *She noticed blood streaks in her water.* ○ *The nurse asked him to give a sample of his water.* ■ *plural noun* **waters** the fluid in the amnion in which a fetus floats (*informal*) Also called **amniotic fluid** ■ *verb* (*of the eyes*) to fill with tears or saliva (NOTE: For other terms referring to water, see words beginning with **hydr-, hydro-**.)

COMMENT: Since the body is formed of about 50% water, the average adult needs to drink about 2.5 litres (5 pints) of fluid each day. Water taken into the body is passed out again as urine or sweat.

water balance /'wɔːtə ˌbæləns/ *noun* a state where the water lost by the body, e.g. in urine or sweat, is made up by water absorbed from food and drink

water bed /'wɔːtə bed/ *noun* a mattress made of a large heavy plastic bag filled with water, used to prevent bedsores

waterbrash /'wɔːtəbræʃ/ *noun* a condition caused by dyspepsia, in which there is a burning feeling in the stomach and the mouth suddenly fills with acid saliva

water-hammer pulse /'wɔːtə ˌhæmə pʌls/ *noun* same as **Corrigan's pulse**

Waterhouse-Friderichsen syndrome /ˌwɔːtəhaʊs ˈfrɪdərɪksən ˌsɪndrəʊm/ *noun* a condition caused by blood poisoning with meningococci, in which the tissues of the adrenal glands die and haemorrhage [Described 1911 by Rupert Waterhouse (1873–1958), physician at Bath, UK; described 1918 by Carl Friderichsen (b. 1886), Danish physician]

watering eye /ˌwɔːtərɪŋ 'aɪ/ *noun* an eye which fills with tears because of an irritation

waterproof /'wɔːtəpruːf/ *adjective* not allowing water through ○ *Put a waterproof sheet on the baby's bed.*

water sac /'wɔːtə sæk/ *noun* ♦ **amnion**

Waterston's operation /'wɔːtəstənz ˌɒpəreɪʃ(ə)n/ *noun* a surgical operation to treat Fallot's tetralogy, in which the right pulmonary artery is joined to the ascending aorta [After David James Waterston (1910–85), paediatric surgeon in London, UK]

waterworks /'wɔːtəwɜːks/ *plural noun* same as **urinary system** (*informal*)

watery /'wɔːt(ə)ri/ *adjective* liquid, like water ○ *He passed some watery stools.*

Watson-Crick helix /ˌwɒts(ə)n 'krɪk ˌhiːlɪks/ *noun* a molecular model for DNA in which the organic base pairs are linked by hydrogen bonds which form the rungs of a ladder spiralling in the form of a helix

Watson knife /ˌwɒtsən 'naɪf/ *noun* a type of very sharp surgical knife for skin transplants

wax /wæks/ *noun* a soft yellow substance produced by bees or made from petroleum

WBC *abbr* white blood cell

weak /wiːk/ *adjective* not strong ○ *After his illness he was very weak.* ○ *She is too weak to dress herself.* ○ *He is allowed to drink weak tea or coffee.*

weaken /'wiːkən/ *verb* to make something or someone weak, or become weak ○ *He was weakened by the disease and could not resist further infection.* ○ *The swelling is caused by a weakening of the wall of the artery.*

weakness /'wiːknəs/ *noun* the fact of lacking strength ○ *The doctor noticed the weakness of the patient's pulse.*

weak pulse /ˌwiːk 'pʌls/ *noun* a pulse which is not strong, which is not easy to feel

weal /wiːl/ *noun* a small area of skin which swells because of a sharp blow or an insect bite

wean /wiːn/ *verb* to make a baby stop breast-feeding and take other liquid or solid food, or to make a baby start to eat solid food after having only had liquids to drink ○ *The baby was breastfed for two months and then was gradually weaned onto the bottle.*

wear /weə/ *verb* to become damaged through being used ○ *The cartilage of the knee was worn from too much exercise.* (NOTE: **wearing – wore – worn**)

wear and tear /ˌweər ən ˈteə/ *noun* the normal use which affects an organ ○ *A heart has to stand a lot of wear and tear.* ○ *The wear and tear of a strenuous job has begun to affect his heart.*

wear off /ˌweər ˈɒf/ *verb* to disappear gradually ○ *The effect of the painkiller will wear off after a few hours.* ○ *He started to open his eyes, as the anaesthetic wore off.*

webbing /ˈwebɪŋ/ *noun* the condition of having an extra membrane of skin joining two structures in the body together

Weber-Christian disease /ˌweɪbə ˈkrɪstʃən dɪˌziːz/ *noun* a type of panniculitis where the liver and spleen become enlarged [After Frederick Parkes Weber (1863–1962), British physician; Henry Asbury Christian (1876–1951), US physician]

Weber's test /ˈweɪbəz test/ *noun* a test to see if both ears hear correctly, where a tuning fork is struck and the end placed on the head [After Friedrich Eugen Weber-Liel (1832–91), German otologist]

web space /ˈweb speɪs/ *noun* the soft tissue between the bases of the fingers and toes

Wechsler scales /ˈvekslə skeɪlz/ *plural noun* a set of standardised scales for measuring someone's IQ. There are three separate versions developed for different age groups.

wee /wiː/ *verb* same as **urinate** (*informal*)

weep /wiːp/ *verb* **1.** to cry **2.** (*of a wound*) to ooze fluid

Wegener's granulomatosis /ˌveɡənəz ˌɡrænjʊləʊməˈtəʊsɪs/ *noun* a disease of connective tissue, where the nasal passages, lungs and kidneys are inflamed and ulcerated, with formation of granulomas. It is usually fatal.

weigh /weɪ/ *verb* **1.** to measure how heavy something is ○ *The nurse weighed the baby on the scales.* **2.** to have a particular weight ○ *She weighed seven pounds (3.5 kilos) at birth.* ○ *A woman weighs less than a man of similar height.* ○ *The doctor asked him how much he weighed.* ○ *I weigh 120 pounds* or *I weigh 54 kilos.*

weight /weɪt/ *noun* **1.** how heavy someone or something is ○ *What's the patient's weight?* □ **her weight is only 105 pounds** she weighs only 105 pounds □ **to lose weight** to get thinner ○ *She's trying to lose weight before she*

goes on holiday. □ **to put on weight** to become fatter ○ *He's put on a lot of weight in the last few months.* □ **to gain in weight** to become fatter or heavier **2.** something which is heavy ○ *Don't lift heavy weights, you may hurt your back.*

weight gain /ˈweɪt ˌɡeɪn/ *noun* the fact of becoming fatter or heavier

weight loss /ˈweɪt ˌlɒs/ *noun* the fact of losing weight or of becoming thinner ○ *Weight loss can be a symptom of certain types of cancer.*

Weil-Felix reaction /ˌvaɪl ˈfeɪlɪks rɪˌækʃən/, **Weil-Felix test** /ˌvaɪl ˈfeɪlɪks test/ *noun* a test to see if someone has typhus, in which the person's serum is tested for antibodies against *Proteus vulgaris* [Described 1916. After Edmund Weil (1880–1922) Austrian physician and bacteriologist; Arthur Felix (1887–1956), British bacteriologist.]

Weil's disease /ˈvaɪlz dɪˈziːz/ *noun* same as **leptospirosis** [Described 1886. After Adolf Weil (1848–1916), physician in Estonia who also practised in Wiesbaden, Germany.]

welder's flash /ˌweldəz ˈflæʃ/ *noun* a condition in which the eye is badly damaged by very bright light

welfare /ˈwelfeə/ *noun* **1.** good health, good living conditions ○ *They look after the welfare of the old people in the town.* **2.** money paid by the government to people who need it ○ *He exists on welfare payments.*

well /wel/ *adjective* healthy ○ *He's not a well man.* ○ *You're looking very well after your holiday.* ○ *He's quite well again after his flu.* ○ *She's not very well, and has had to stay in bed.*

well-baby clinic /ˌwel ˈbeɪbi ˌklɪnɪk/ *noun* a clinic where parents can ask a doctor or nurse any questions they have about their child's growth and development. Their babies can be weighed and measured and their development monitored.

wellbeing /ˈwel ˌbiːɪŋ/ *noun* the state of being in good health and having good living conditions ○ *She is responsible for the wellbeing of the patients under her care.*

well-man clinic /ˌwel ˈmæn ˌklɪnɪk/ *noun* a clinic just for men where they can get check-ups, advice and health information

well-woman clinic /ˌwel ˈwʊmən ˌklɪnɪk/ *noun* a clinic which specialises in preventive medicine for women, e.g. breast screening and cervical smear tests, and gives advice on pregnancy, contraception and the menopause

wen /wen/ *noun* a cyst which forms in a sebaceous gland

Werdnig-Hoffmann disease /ˌvɜːdnɪɡ ˈhɒfmən dɪˌziːz/ *noun* a disease in which the spinal muscles atrophy, making the muscles of the shoulders, arms and legs weak. In its most severe form, infants are born floppy, have feeding and breathing problems and rarely live more than two or three years.

Werner's syndrome /'wɜːnəz ˌsɪndrəʊm/ *noun* an inherited disorder involving premature ageing, persistent hardening of the skin, underdevelopment of the sex organs and cataracts

Wernicke-Korsakoff syndrome /ˌvɜːnɪkə 'kɔːsəkɒf ˌsɪndrəʊm/ *noun* a form of brain damage caused by severe nutritional deficiencies in people with long-term alcoholism

Wernicke's encephalopathy /ˌvɜːnɪkəz enˌkefə'lɒpəθi/ *noun* a condition caused by lack of Vitamin B, which often affects alcoholics and in which the person is delirious, moves the eyes about rapidly, walks unsteadily and is subject to constant vomiting [Described 1875. After Karl Wernicke (1848–1905), Breslau psychiatrist and neurologist.]

Wertheim's operation /'vɜːthaɪmz ɒpəˌreɪʃ(ə)n/ *noun* a surgical operation to remove the uterus, the lymph nodes which are next to it and most of the vagina, the ovaries and the Fallopian tubes, as treatment for cancer of the uterus [Described 1900. After Ernst Wertheim (1864–1920), Austrian gynaecologist.]

West Nile fever /ˌwest 'naɪl ˌfiːvə/ *noun* a mosquito-borne viral infection which causes fever, pains, enlarged lymph nodes and sometimes inflammation of the brain

wet /wet/ *adjective* not dry, covered in liquid ○ *He got wet waiting for the bus in the rain and caught a cold.* ○ *The baby has nappy rash from wearing a wet nappy.* ■ *verb* to make the bed wet by urinating while asleep ○ *He is eight years old and he still wets his bed every night.*

wet beriberi /ˌwet ˌberi'beri/ *noun* beriberi in which the body swells with oedema

wet burn /wet 'bɜːn/ *noun* same as **scald**

wet dream /wet driːm/ *noun* same as **nocturnal emission**

wet dressing /ˌwet 'dresɪŋ/ *noun* ♦ **compress**

Wharton's duct /ˌwɔːt(ə)nz 'dʌkt/ *noun* a duct which takes saliva into the mouth from the salivary glands under the lower jaw [After Thomas Wharton (1614–73), English physician and anatomist at St Thomas's Hospital, London, UK]

Wharton's jelly /ˌwɔːt(ə)nz 'dʒeli/ *noun* a jelly-like tissue in the umbilical cord

wheal /wiːl/ same as **weal**

Wheelhouse's operation /'wiːlhaʊsɪz ɒpəreɪʃ(ə)n/ *noun* same as **urethrotomy** [After Claudius Galen Wheelhouse (1826–1909), British surgeon]

wheeze /wiːz/ *noun* a whistling noise in the bronchi ○ *The doctor listened to his wheezes.* ■ *verb* to make a whistling sound when breathing ○ *When she has an attack of asthma, she wheezes and has difficulty in breathing.*

wheezing /'wiːzɪŋ/ *noun* whistling noises in the bronchi when breathing. Wheezing is often found in people with asthma and is also associated with bronchitis and heart disease.

wheezy /'wiːzi/ *adjective* making a whistling sound when breathing ○ *She was quite wheezy when she stopped running.*

whiplash injury /'wɪplæʃ ˌɪndʒəri/ *noun* an injury to the vertebrae in the neck, caused when the head jerks backwards, often occurring in a car that is struck from behind

whiplash shake syndrome /ˌwɪplæʃ 'ʃeɪk ˌsɪndrəʊm/ *noun* in young babies, a series of internal head injuries caused by being shaken violently. They can result in brain damage leading to speech and learning disabilities, paralysis, seizures, blindness and hearing loss. They are often life-threatening.

Whipple's disease /'wɪp(ə)lz dɪˌziːz/ *noun* a disease in which someone has difficulty in absorbing nutrients and passes fat in the faeces, the joints are inflamed and the lymph glands enlarged [Described 1907. After George Hoyt Whipple (1878–1976), US pathologist. Nobel prize for Pathology and Medicine 1934.]

Whipple's operation /'wɪp(ə)lz ɒpəˌreↄʃ(ə)n/ *noun* same as **pancreatectomy**

whipworm /'wɪpwɜːm/ *noun* same as **Trichuris**

white /waɪt/ *adjective* of a colour like snow or milk ○ *White patches developed on his skin.* ○ *Her hair has turned quite white.* (NOTE: **whiter – whitest**) ■ *noun* the main part of the eye which is white ○ *The whites of his eyes turned yellow when he developed jaundice.*

white blood cell /ˌwaɪt 'blʌd ˌsel/ *noun* a colourless blood cell which contains a nucleus but has no haemoglobin, is formed in bone marrow and creates antibodies. Abbr **WBC**. Also called **leucocyte**

white commissure /ˌwaɪt 'kɒmɪsjʊə/ *noun* part of the white matter in the spinal cord near the central canal

white corpuscle /ˌwaɪt 'kɔːpʌs(ə)l/ *noun* same as **white blood cell**

white finger /waɪt 'fɪŋgə/ *noun* a condition in which a finger has a mottled discoloured appearance because its blood vessels are damaged. The thumb is usually not affected. Very severe cases can result in finger loss. It occurs most commonly in Raynaud's disease.

whitehead /'waɪthed/ *noun* a small white swelling formed when a sebaceous gland becomes blocked

white leg /waɪt 'leg/ *noun* a condition which affects women after childbirth, in which a leg becomes pale and inflamed as a result of lymphatic obstruction. Also called **milk leg, phlegmasia alba dolens**

white matter /'waɪt ˌmætə/ *noun* nerve tissue in the central nervous system which contains more myelin than grey matter

white noise instrument /ˌwaɪt ˈnɔɪz ˌɪnstrʊmənt/ *noun* a small electronic device worn in the ear. It combines sounds of many different frequencies. It is used to mask internal noise in the ear due to tinnitus.

whites /waɪts/ *plural noun* same as **leucorrhoea** (*informal*)

whitlow /ˈwɪtləʊ/ *noun* an inflammation caused by infection near the nail in the fleshy part of the tip of a finger. Also called **felon**

WHO *abbr* World Health Organization

whoop /wuːp, huːp/ *noun* a loud noise made when inhaling by a person who has whooping cough

whooping cough /ˈhuːpɪŋ kɒf/ *noun* an infectious disease caused by *Bordetella pertussis* affecting the bronchial tubes, common in children, and sometimes very serious. Also called **pertussis**

> COMMENT: A person with whooping cough coughs very badly and makes a characteristic 'whoop' when he or she breathes in after a coughing fit. Whooping cough can lead to pneumonia, and is treated with antibiotics. Vaccination against whooping cough is given to infants.

Widal reaction /viːˈdɑːl rɪˌækʃən/, **Widal test** /viːˈdɑːl test/ *noun* a test to detect typhoid fever. A sample of the person's blood is put into a solution containing typhoid bacilli, or anti-typhoid serum is added to a sample of bacilli from the person's faeces. If the bacilli agglutinate, i.e. form into groups, this indicates that the person has typhoid fever. [Described 1896. After Georges Fernand Isidore Widal (1862–1929), French physician and teacher.]

Willis /ˈwɪlɪs/ ♦ **circle of Willis**

willpower /ˈwɪlˌpaʊə/ *noun* the fact of having a strong will ○ *The patient showed the willpower to start walking again unaided.*

Wilms' tumour /ˈvɪlmz ˌtjuːmə/ *noun* same as **nephroblastoma** [Described 1899. After Max Wilms (1867–1918), Professor of Surgery at Leipzig, Basle and Heidelberg.]

Wilson's disease /ˈwɪlsənz dɪˌziːz/ *noun* a hereditary disease where copper deposits accumulate in the liver and the brain, causing cirrhosis. Also called **hepatolenticular degeneration** [Described 1912. After Samuel Alexander Kinnier Wilson (1878–1937), British neurologist.]

wind /wɪnd/ *noun* **1.** gas which forms in the digestive system and escapes through the anus ○ *The baby is suffering from wind.* Also called **flatus 2.** an uncomfortable feeling caused by the accumulation of gas in the upper digestive system ○ *He has pains in the stomach caused by wind.* Also called **flatulence** □ **to break wind** to bring up gas from the stomach, or to let gas escape from the anus

windburn /ˈwɪndbɜːn/ *noun* redness and inflammation of the skin caused by exposure to harsh wind

window /ˈwɪndəʊ/ *noun* a small opening in the ear

windpipe /ˈwɪndpaɪp/ *noun* same as **trachea**

wiring /ˈwaɪərɪŋ/ *noun* **1.** a network of wires **2.** a neurological or physiological structure or process which controls a function in the body **3.** the act of fixing a piece of bone in place using wires

wisdom tooth /ˈwɪzdəm tuːθ/ *noun* one of the four teeth in the back of the jaw which only appear at about the age of 20 and sometimes do not appear at all. Also called **third molar**

witch hazel /ˈwɪtʃ ˌheɪz(ə)l/ *noun* a lotion made from the bark of a tree, used to check bleeding and harden inflamed tissue and bruises. Also called **hamamelis**

withdrawal /wɪðˈdrɔːəl/ *noun* **1.** a loss of interest in having contact with other people, which leads to a person becoming isolated **2.** a period during which a person who has been addicted to a drug stops taking it and experiences unpleasant symptoms

> '…she was in the early stages of physical withdrawal from heroin and showed classic symptoms: sweating, fever, sleeplessness and anxiety' [*Nursing Times*]

withdrawal symptom /wɪðˈdrɔːəl ˌsɪmptəm/ *noun* an unpleasant physical condition, e.g. vomiting, headaches or fever, which occurs when someone stops taking an addictive drug

Wolff-Parkinson-White syndrome /wʊlf ˌpɑːkɪns(ə)n ˈwaɪt ˌsɪndrəʊm/ *noun* a condition within the heart's conducting tissue which makes the heart beat dangerously fast. It can be fatal.

womb /wuːm/ *noun* same as **uterus** (NOTE: For other terms referring to the womb, see words beginning with **hyster-, hystero-, metr-, metro-, uter-, utero-**.)

women's ward /ˈwɪmɪnz wɔːd/, **women's hospital** /ˈwɪmɪnz ˌhɒspɪt(ə)l/ *noun* a ward or hospital for female patients. ♦ **well-woman clinic**

Wood's lamp /ˈwʊdz læmp/ *noun* an ultraviolet lamp which allows a doctor to see fluorescence, e.g. in the hair of someone who has a fungal infection [After Robert Williams Wood (1868–1955), US physicist]

woolsorter's disease /ˈwʊlsɔːtəz dɪˌziːz/ *noun* a form of anthrax which affects the lungs

word blindness /ˈwɜːd ˌblaɪndnəs/ *noun* same as **alexia**

work-related upper limb disorder /ˌwɜːk rɪˌleɪtɪd ˌʌpə ˈlɪm dɪsˌɔːdə/ same as **repetitive strain injury**. Abbr **WRULD**

World Health Organization /ˌwɜːld ˈhelθ ɔːɡənaɪˌzeɪʃ(ə)n/ *noun* an organisation, part of the United Nations, which aims to improve health in the world. Abbr **WHO**

worm /wɜːm/ *noun* a long thin animal with no legs or backbone, which can infest the human body, especially the intestines

wound /wuːnd/ *noun* damage to external tissue which allows blood to escape ○ *He had a knife wound in his leg.* ○ *The doctors sutured the wound in his chest.* □ **gunshot wound** wound caused by a pellet or bullet from a gun ■ *verb* to harm someone by making a hole in the tissue of the body ○ *She was wounded three times in the head.*

wound dehiscence /wuːnd diːˈhɪs(ə)ns/ *noun* the splitting open of a surgical incision

wound healing /ˈwuːnd ˌhiːlɪŋ/ *noun* the replacement of dead tissue with new tissue

WR *abbr* Wassermann reaction

wrench /rentʃ/ *verb* to injure part of the body by twisting it suddenly and forcibly

wrinkle /ˈrɪŋkəl/ *noun* a fold in the skin

wrinkled /ˈrɪŋkəld/ *adjective* covered with wrinkles

wrist /rɪst/ *noun* a joint between the hand and forearm ○ *He sprained his wrist and can't play tennis tomorrow.* See illustration at **HAND** in Supplement (NOTE: For other terms referring to the wrist, see words beginning with **carp-, carpo-**.)

COMMENT: The wrist is formed of eight small bones in the hand which articulate with the bones in the forearm. The joint allows the hand to rotate and move downwards and sideways. The joint is easily fractured or sprained.

wrist drop /ˈrɪst drɒp/ *noun* paralysis of the wrist muscles, caused by damage to the radial nerve in the upper arm, which causes the hand to hang limp

wrist joint /ˈrɪst dʒɔɪnt/ *noun* a place where the wrist joins the arm

writer's cramp /ˌraɪtəz ˈkræmp/ *noun* a painful spasm of the muscles in the forearm and hand which comes from writing too much

writhe /raɪð/ *verb* □ **to writhe in pain** to twist and turn because the pain is very severe

WRULD *abbr* work-related upper limb disorder

wry neck /ˈraɪ nek/, **wryneck** *noun* same as torticollis

Wuchereria /ˌvʊkəˈrɪəriə/ *noun* a type of tiny nematode worm which infests the lymph system, causing elephantiasis

X

xanth- /zænθ/ *prefix* same as **xantho-** (*used before vowels*)

xanthaemia /zænˈθiːmiə/ *noun* same as **carotenaemia** (NOTE: The US spelling is **xanthemia**.)

xanthelasma /ˌzænθəˈlæzmə/ *noun* the formation of little yellow fatty tumours on the eyelids

xanthine /ˈzænθiːn/ *noun* **1.** an intermediate product in the breakdown of nucleic acids to uric acid, found in blood, body tissue and urine **2.** a derivative of xanthine, e.g. caffeine or theophylline

xantho- /zænθəʊ/ *prefix* yellow

xanthochromia /ˌzænθəˈkrəʊmiə/ *noun* yellow colour of the skin as in jaundice

xanthoma /zænˈθəʊmə/ *noun* a yellow fatty mass, often on the eyelids and hands, found in people with a high level of cholesterol in the blood (NOTE: The plural is **xanthomata**.)

xanthomatosis /ˌzænθəməˈtəʊsɪs/ *noun* a condition in which several small masses of yellow fatty substance appear in the skin or some internal organs, caused by an excess of fat in the body

xanthopsia /zænˈθɒpsiə/ *noun* a disorder of the eyes, making everything appear yellow

xanthosis /zænˈθəʊsɪs/ *noun* yellow colouring of the skin, caused by eating too much food containing carotene

X chromosome /ˈeks ˌkrəʊməsəʊm/ *noun* a chromosome that determines sex. Compare **Y chromosome**. ◊ **sex chromosome**

xeno- /zenəʊ/ *prefix* different

xenograft /ˈzenəɡrɑːft/ *noun* tissue taken from an individual of one species and grafted on an individual of another species. Also called **heterograft**. Opposite **homograft**

xenotransplantation /ˌzenəʊtrænsplɑːnˈteɪʃ(ə)n/ *noun* the process of transplanting organs from one species to another, especially from animals to humans

xero- /zɪərəʊ/ *prefix* dry

xeroderma /ˌzɪərəˈdɜːmə/ *noun* a skin disorder where dry scales form on the skin

xerophthalmia /ˌzɪərɒfˈθælmiə/ *noun* a condition of the eye, in which the cornea and conjunctiva become dry because of a lack of Vitamin A

xeroradiography /ˌzɪərəʊˌreɪdiˈɒɡrəfi/ *noun* an X-ray technique used in producing mammograms on selenium plates

xerosis /zɪˈrəʊsɪs/ *noun* extreme dryness of skin or mucous membrane

xerostomia /ˌzɪərəˈstəʊmiə/ *noun* dryness of the mouth, caused by lack of a saliva

xiphi- /zɪfɪ/ *prefix* relating to the xiphoid process

xiphisternal plane /ˌzɪfɪˌstɜːn(ə)l ˈpleɪn/ *noun* an imaginary horizontal line across the middle of the chest at the point where the xiphoid process starts

xiphisternum /ˌzɪfɪˈstɜːnəm/ *noun* same as **xiphoid process**

xiphoid process /ˈzɪfɔɪd ˌprəʊses/, **xiphoid cartilage** /ˈzɪfɔɪd ˌkɑːtɪlɪdʒ/ *noun* the bottom part of the breastbone which is cartilage in young people but becomes bone by middle age. Also called **ensiform cartilage, xiphisternum**

X-linked /ˈeks ˌlɪŋkt/ *adjective* relating to the genes situated on the X chromosome

X-linked disease /ˈeks ˌlɪŋkt dɪˌziːz/ *noun* a genetic disorder caused by a mutation on the X chromosome which only appears in males, e.g. one form of haemophilia

X-ray /ˈeks reɪ/, **x-ray** *noun* **1.** a ray with a very short wavelength, which is invisible, but can go through soft tissue and register as a photograph on a film. X-rays are used in diagnosis in radiography, and in treating disease by radiotherapy. ○ *The X-ray examination showed the presence of a tumour in the colon.* **2.** a photograph taken using X-rays ○ *The dentist took some X-rays of the patient's teeth.* ○ *He pinned the X-rays to the light screen.* **3.** an examination in which X-ray photographs are taken ○ *All the staff had to have chest X-rays.* ■ *verb* to take an X-ray photograph of a patient ○ *There are six patients waiting to be X-rayed.*

COMMENT: Because X-rays go through soft tissue, it is sometimes necessary to make internal organs opaque so that they will show up on the film. In the case of stomach X-rays, people take a barium meal before being photographed (contrast radiography); in other cases, such as kidney X-rays, radioactive substances are injected into the bloodstream or into the organ itself. X-rays are used not only in radiography for diagnosis but as a treatment in radiotherapy as rapidly dividing cells such as cancer cells are most affected. Excessive exposure to X-rays, either as a person being treated, or as a radiographer, can cause radiation sickness.

X-ray imaging /'eks reɪ ˌɪmɪdʒɪŋ/ *noun* the process of showing X-ray pictures of the inside of part of the body on a screen

X-ray photograph /ˌeks reɪ 'fəʊtəɡrɑːf/ *noun* a picture produced by exposing sensitive film to X-rays ○ *He was examining the X-ray photographs of the patient's chest.*

X-ray screening /'eks reɪ ˌskriːnɪŋ/ *noun* a method of gathering information about the body by taking images using X-rays. It is carried out by a radiographer or radiologist.

Xylocaine /'zaɪləkeɪn/ a trade name for a preparation of lignocaine

xylometazoline hydrochloride /ˌzaɪləʊ məˌtæzəliːn ˌhaɪdrə'klɔːraɪd/, **xylometazoline** /ˌzaɪləʊmə'tæzəliːn/ *noun* a drug which helps to narrow blood vessels, used in the treatment of colds and sinusitis

xylose /'zaɪləʊz/ *noun* pentose which has not been metabolised

XYY syndrome /ˌeks waɪ 'waɪ ˌsɪndrəʊm/ *noun* an extremely rare condition in males in which they have two Y chromosomes instead of one. They grow faster than normal, and their final height is approximately 7cm above average. Many experience severe acne during adolescence.

Y

yawn /jɔːn/ *noun* a reflex action when tired or sleepy, in which the mouth is opened wide and after a deep intake of air, the breath exhaled slowly ○ *His yawns made everyone feel sleepy.* ■ *verb* to open the mouth wide and breathe in deeply and then breathe out slowly

yawning /ˈjɔːnɪŋ/ *noun* the act of opening the mouth wide without conscious control and slowly releasing a deep breath, usually a sign of tiredness or boredom

yaws /jɔːz/ *noun* a tropical disease caused by the spirochaete *Treponema pertenue.* Symptoms include fever with raspberry-like swellings on the skin, followed in later stages by bone malformation. Also called **framboesia, pian.** ◊ **treponematosis**

Y chromosome /ˈwaɪ ˌkrəʊməsəʊm/ *noun* a chromosome that determines sex, it is carried by males and is shorter than an X chromosome. Compare **X chromosome**. ◊ **sex chromosome**

yeast /jiːst/ *noun* a fungus which is used in the fermentation of alcohol and in making bread. It is a good source of Vitamin B.

yellow /ˈjeləʊ/ *adjective* of a colour like that of the sun or of gold ○ *His skin turned yellow when he had hepatitis.* ○ *The whites of the eyes become yellow as a symptom of jaundice.* ■ *noun* a colour like that of the sun or of gold

yellow atrophy /ˌjeləʊ ˈætrəfi/ *noun* an old name for severe damage to the liver

yellow elastic fibrocartilage /ˌjeləʊ ɪˌlæstɪk ˌfaɪbrəʊˈkɑːtɪlɪdʒ/ *noun* flexible cartilage, e.g. in the ear and epiglottis

yellow fever /ˈjeləʊ ˌfiːvə/ *noun* an infectious disease, occurring especially in Africa and South America, caused by an arbovirus carried by the mosquito *Aedes aegypti.* It affects the liver and causes jaundice. There is no known cure and it can be fatal, but vaccination can prevent it.

yellow fibre /ˌjeləʊ ˈfaɪbə/ *noun* same as **elastic fibre**

yellow marrow *noun* ◆ **marrow**

yellow spot /ˈjeləʊ spɒt/ *noun* same as **macula lutea**

Yersinia pestis /jɜːˌsɪniə ˈpestɪs/ *noun* a bacterium which causes plague

yin and yang /ˌjɪn ənd ˈjæŋ/ *noun* the two opposite and complementary principles of Chinese philosophy which are thought to exist in varying proportions in all things. They are sometimes thought of as femininity and masculinity.

yoga /ˈjəʊɡə/ *noun* **1.** a Hindu discipline which promotes spiritual unity with a Supreme Being through a system of postures and rituals **2.** any one of dozens of systems and methods derived from or based on Hindu yoga. Many include breathing exercises and postures which are thought to aid health.

yolk sac /ˈjəʊk sæk/ *noun* same as **vitelline sac**

yuppie flu /ˌjʌpi ˈfluː/ *noun* ◆ **myalgic encephalomyelitis** (*informal*)

Z

Zadik's operation /ˈzeɪdɪks ɒpəˌreɪʃ(ə)n/ *noun* a surgical operation to remove the whole of an ingrowing toenail

Zantac /ˈzæntæk/ a trade name for ranitidine

zidovudine /zɪˈdəʊvjʊdiːn/ *noun* azidothymidine or AZT, a drug used in the treatment of AIDS, which helps to slow the progress of the disease

Zimmer frame /ˈzɪmə freɪm/ a trademark for a metal frame used by people who have difficulty in walking ○ *She managed to walk some steps with a Zimmer frame.* ◊ **walking frame**

zinc /zɪŋk/ *noun* a white metallic trace element (NOTE: The chemical symbol is **Zn**.)

zinc ointment /zɪŋk ˈɔɪntmənt/ *noun* a soothing ointment made of zinc oxide and oil

zinc oxide /zɪŋk ˈɒksaɪd/ *noun* a compound of zinc and oxygen, which forms a soft white soothing powder used in creams and lotions (NOTE: Its chemical formula is ZnO.)

Zollinger-Ellison syndrome /ˌzɒlɪndʒər ˈelɪs(ə)n ˌsɪndrəʊm/ *noun* a condition in which tumours are formed in the islet cells of the pancreas together with peptic ulcers [Described 1955. After Robert Milton Zollinger (b. 1903), Professor of Surgery at Ohio State University, USA; Edwin H. Ellison (1918–70), Associate Professor of Surgery at Ohio State University, USA.]

zona /ˈzəʊnə/ *noun* **1.** same as **herpes zoster 2.** a zone or area

zona pellucida /ˌzəʊnə pɪˈluːsɪdə/ *noun* a membrane which forms around an ovum

zone /zəʊn/ *noun* an area of the body

zonula /ˈzɒnjʊlə/, **zonule** /ˈzɒnjuːl/ *noun* a small area of the body

zonule of Zinn /ˌzɒnjuːl əv ˈzɪn/ *noun* a suspensory ligament of the lens of the eye

zonulolysis /ˌzɒnjuˈlɒləsɪs/ *noun* the removal of a zonule by dissolving it

zoo- /zəʊ/ *prefix* relating to animals

zoonosis /ˌzəʊɒˈnəʊsɪs/ *noun* a disease which a human can catch from an animal (NOTE: The plural is **zoonoses**.)

zoster /ˈzɒstə/ ◆ **herpes zoster**

Z-plasty /ˈzed ˌplæsti/ *noun* a technique used in plastic surgery. A deep Z-shaped incision is made to relieve tension in the area of a scar, or to change the direction of a scar.

zygoma /zaɪˈgəʊmə/ *noun* same as **zygomatic arch** (NOTE: The plural is **zygomata**.)

zygomatic /ˌzaɪgəˈmætɪk/ *adjective* referring to the zygomatic arch

zygomatic arch /ˌzaɪgəmætɪk ˈɑːtʃ/ *noun* the ridge of bone across the temporal bone, running between the ear and the bottom of the eye socket. Also called **zygoma**

zygomatic bone /ˌzaɪgəmætɪk ˈbəʊn/ *noun* a bone which forms the prominent part of the cheek and the lower part of the eye socket. Also called **cheekbone, malar bone**

zygomatic process /ˌzaɪgəmætɪk ˈprəʊsəs/ *noun* one of the bony projections which form the zygomatic arch

zygomycosis /ˌzaɪgəmaɪˈkəʊsɪs/ *noun* a disease caused by a fungus which infests the blood vessels in the lungs

zygote /ˈzaɪgəʊt/ *noun* a fertilised ovum, the first stage of development of an embryo

zym- /zaɪm/ *prefix* (*used before vowels*) **1.** enzymes **2.** fermentation

zymogen /ˈzaɪmədʒen/ *noun* same as **proenzyme**

zymosis /zaɪˈməʊsɪs/ *noun* same as **fermentation**

zymotic /zaɪˈmɒtɪk/ *adjective* referring to zymosis

SUPPLEMENT

Anatomical Terms

The body is always described as if standing upright with the palms of the hands facing forward. There is only one central vertical plane, termed the *median* or *sagittal* plane, and this passes through the body from front to back. Planes parallel to this on either side are *parasagittal* or *paramedian* planes. Vertical planes at right angles to the median are called *coronal* planes. The term *horizontal* (or *transverse*) plane speaks for itself. Two specific horizontal planes are (a) the *transpyloric,* midway between the suprasternal notch and the symphysis pubis, and (b) the *transtubercular* or *intertubercular* plane, which passes through the tubercles of the iliac crests. Many other planes are named from the structures they pass through.

Views of the body from some different points are shown on the diagram; a view of the body from above is called the *superior aspect,* and that from below is the *inferior aspect.*

Cephalic means toward the head; *caudal* refers to positions (or in a direction) towards the tail. *Proximal* and *distal* refer to positions respectively closer to and further from the centre of the body in any direction, while *lateral* and *medial* relate more specifically to relative sideways positions, and also refer to movements. *Ventral* refers to the abdomen, front or anterior, while *dorsal* relates to the back of a part or organ. The hand has a *dorsal* and a *palmar* surface, and the foot a *dorsal* and a *plantar* surface.

Note that *flexion of the thigh* moves it forward while *flexion of the leg* moves it backwards; the movements of *extension* are similarly reversed. Movement and rotation of limbs can be *medial,* which is with the front moving towards the centre line, or *lateral,* which is in the opposite direction. Specific terms for limb movements are *adduction,* towards the centre line, and *abduction,* which is away from the centre line. Other specific terms are *supination* and *pronation* for the hand, and *inversion* and *eversion* for the foot.

HEART

1. superior vena cava
2. inferior vena cava
3. right atrium
4. left atrium
5. right ventricle

6. left ventricle
7. aorta
8. tricuspid valve
9. bicuspid valve
10. pulmonary artery

11. pulmonary veins
12. epicardium
13. myocardium
14. endocardium
15. septum

LUNGS

1. thyroid cartilage
2. cricoid cartilage
3. trachea
4. main bronchus
5. superior lobe bronchus
6. middle lobe bronchus
7. inferior lobe bronchus

8. superior lobe
9. middle lobe
10. inferior lobe
11. oblique fissure
12. horizontal fissure
13. cardiac notch

14. visceral pleura
15. parietal pleura
16. pleural cavity
17. alveolus
18. alveolar duct
19. bronchiole

DIGESTIVE SYSTEM

1. liver
2. pancreas
3. spleen
4. gall bladder
5. stomach
6. duodenum

7. jejunum
8. ileum
9. ascending colon
10. transverse colon
11. descending colon

12. sigmoid colon
13. caecum
14. appendix
15. rectum
16. anus

KIDNEY

1. kidney
2. calyx
3. pyramid
4. renal cortex

5. renal medulla
6. renal pelvis
7. adrenal gland
8. abdominal aorta

9. inferior vena cava
10. ureter
11. urinary bladder

NEURON

(a) multipolar   (b) bipolar   (c) unipolar

1. nucleus   5. axon   8. node of Ranvier
2. Nissl granules   6. myelin sheath   9. neurilemma
3. neurofibrilla   7. Schwann cell nucleus   10. terminal branch
4. dendrite

BRAIN

1. corpus callosum   5. pituitary gland   9. cerebral peduncle
2. thalamus   6. superior colliculi   10. fornix cerebri
3. hypothalamus   7. inferior colliculi   11. pons
4. pineal body   8. cerebellum

EYE

7. aqueous humour
8. lens
9. iris
10. cornea
11. ciliary body

1. optic nerve
2. vitreous humour
3. sclera
4. choroid
5. retina
6. conjunctiva

12. suspensory ligament
13. fovea
14. muscle
15. ciliary muscle
16. pupil

EAR

1. pinna
2. temporal bone
3. external auditory meatus
4. ceruminous glands
5. semicircular canals

6. cochlea
7. Eustachian tube
8. malleus
9. incus
10. stapes

11. tympanic membrane (eardrum)
12. round window
13. auditory nerve
14. vestibule
15. oval window

UROGENITAL SYSTEM (male)

1. penis
2. scrotum
3. testis
4. epididymis
5. ductus deferens
6. seminal vesicle
7. ejaculatory duct
8. prostate gland
9. glans
10. urinary bladder
11. urethra
12. rectum
13. anus
14. corpus cavernosum
15. corpus songiosum
16. pubic bone

UROGENITAL SYSTEM (female)

1. pubic bone
2. labia majora
3. labia minora
4. urethra
5. urinary bladder
6. vagina
7. uterus
8. Fallopian tube
9. ovary
10. clitoris
11. rectum
12. anus

FOOT

1. tarsus
2. metatarsus
3. phalanges

4. cuneiforms
5. navicular
6. cuboid

7. calcaneus
8. talus

HAND

1. carpus
2. metacarpus
3. phalanges
4. scaphoid
5. lunate

6. triquetrum
7. pisiform
8. trapezium
9. trapezoid
10. capitate

11. hamate
12. ulna
13. radius
14. wrist

TEETH

1. incisors
2. canines
3. premolars
4. molars

PELVIS

1. iliac crest
2. ilium
3. ischium
4. pubis

5. sacrum
6. vertebral column
7. femur

8. hip joint
9. sacral foramen
10. obturator foramen

SYNOVIAL JOINT

1. bone
2. articular cartilage
3. synovial membrane
4. synovial cavity and fluid
5. joint capsule (ligament)

CARTILAGINOUS JOINT

1. intervertebral disc
2. vertebra
3. hyaline cartilage

BONE STRUCTURE

1. periosteum
2. compact bone
3. cancellous (spongy) bone (red marrow)
4. medullary cavity (yellow marrow)
5. articular cartilage
6. epiphysis
7. diaphysis